Y0-CFT-038

COST ACCOUNTING
A Managerial Approach
Second Edition

COST ACCOUNTING

A Managerial Approach

Second Edition

J. Owen Cherrington
Brigham Young University

E. Dee Hubbard
Brigham Young University

David H. Luthy
Utah State University

West Publishing Company
Saint Paul   New York   Los Angeles   San Francisco

Cover Art: A painting by Guy John Cavalli, Albany, California; Courtesy of the William Sawyer Gallery, San Francisco. Title "Walking" 1984 55″ × 67″
Composition: The Clarinda Company.

A study guide consisting of chapter overviews, objectives, key concepts, glossaries, review questions and exercises, and solutions to the questions and exercises is available for additional practice in tandem with this text. If you cannot locate a copy of the study guide in your bookstore, please ask the bookstore's manager to order a copy of the *Study Guide to Accompany Cost Accounting: A Managerial Approach,* Second Edition, by Ray Clanton Jr., C. Dewayne Dotson, and John W. Hardy.

COPYRIGHT © 1985 By W. C. Brown Publishers
COPYRIGHT © 1988 By WEST PUBLISHING COMPANY
50 W. Kellogg Boulevard
P.O. Box 64526
St. Paul, MN 55164-1003

All rights reserved

Printed in the United States of America

Library of Congress Cataloging-in-Publication Data

Cherrington, J. Owen.
  Cost accounting.

  Rev. ed. of: Cost and managerial accounting. c1985.
  Includes bibliographies and index.
  1. Cost accounting. 2. Managerial accounting.
I. Hubbard, E. Dee. II. Luthy, David H.
III. Cherrington, J. Owen. Cost and managerial
accounting. IV. Title.
HF5686.C8C475   1988   657′.42   87-37240
ISBN 0-314-64832-1

Contents in Brief

Preface

Part One Overview of Cost and Managerial Accounting 1

Chapter 1
Introduction to Managerial and Cost Accounting 3

Chapter 2
Basic Cost Concepts 17

Chapter 3
Cost Behavior 53

Chapter 4
Contribution Analysis: Alternative Cost Groupings and Relevant Cost Analysis for Decision Making 93

Part Two Planning Business Activities 137

Chapter 5
Budgeting 139

Chapter 6
Flexible Budgeting and Responsibility Reporting 187

Chapter 7
Cost-Volume-Profit Analysis 229

Part Three Cost Determination 267

Chapter 8
Job-Order Cost Systems 269

Chapter 9
Process Costing: Basic Procedures 313

Chapter 10
Process Costing: Additional Features 347

Chapter 11
Joint Products and By-Products: Cost Allocations and Decisions 381

Chapter 12
Materials and Labor: Costing and Control 411

Chapter 13
Factory Overhead: Costing and Control I 457

Chapter 14
Factory Overhead: Costing and Control II 491

Part Four Cost Control 533

Chapter 15
Standard Costs for Materials and Labor 535

Chapter 16
Standard Costs for Factory Overhead 573

Chapter 17
Mix, Yield, and Variance Investigation 611

Chapter 18
Accounting Systems for Management Planning and Control 639

Chapter 19
Variable Costing and Contribution Margin Analysis 689

Chapter 20
Segment Performance 729

Part Five Decision Analysis 771

Chapter 21
Decision Analysis: Specialized Applications 773

Chapter 22
Transfer and Product Pricing 799

Chapter 23
Capital Budgeting: Part I 843

Chapter 24
Capital Budgeting: Part II 907

Chapter 25
Cost Accounting in an Information Age 961

Chapter 26
The Management Accounting Profession 997

Glossary 1019

Index 1027

Contents

Preface

Part One
OVERVIEW OF COST AND MANAGERIAL ACCOUNTING 1

Chapter 1
Introduction to Managerial and Cost Accounting 3

Outline 3
Specialized Areas of Accounting 4
   Financial Accounting 4
   Managerial/Cost Accounting 5
Authoritative Support for Accounting Concepts and Procedures 6
   Generally Accepted Accounting Principles 6
   Cost Accounting Standards 7
The Management Process 9
The Controller's Role 11
   Functions of the Finance Division 11
   Controller Responsibility Versus Treasurer Responsibility 13
Summary 14
Suggested Readings 15
Discussion Questions 15

Chapter 2
Basic Cost Concepts 17

Outline 17
Basic Cost Concepts 18
   Definition of Cost 18
   Cost Objectives 18
   Cost Objectives and Cost Objects 19
   Expired Versus Unexpired Costs 19
Cost Classifications 20
   Time Period for Which the Cost is Computed 20
   Management Function 21
   Generally Accepted Accounting Treatment 21
   Traceability to Products 22
   Cost Behavior 23
   Decision Significance 23
   Managerial Influence 23
   Commitment to Cost Expenditure 24

Other Cost Classifications 24
Illustration of Cost Classifications 25
Basic Financial Statements for a Manufacturing Company 26
Product Costs 28
Flow of Product Costs 29
Illustration of Financial Statements 32
Summary 35
Self-Study Problem 35
Suggested Readings 37
Discussion Questions 37
Exercises 38
Problems 44

Chapter 3
Cost Behavior 53

Outline 53
Relevant Terminology for Manufacturing Cost Behavior Analysis 54
Importance of Behavior Patterns to Management Decisions 54
Total and Unit Manufacturing Costs 55
Cost Patterns 56
Fixed Cost 56
Variable Cost 56
Semivariable Cost 57
Step-variable Cost 58
Nonlinear Costs 58
Total Manufacturing Costs 59
Product Cost Patterns 59
Total Cost Curve 61
Relevant Range of Production 61
Analysis of Cost Behavior 62
Industrial-Engineering Approach 62
Historical Cost Approach 63
Quantifying Cost Behavior 64
Mathematical Properties of a Straight Line 64
Methods for Developing an Equation 66
Application of Cost Patterns 73
Summary 73
Appendix 3.1: Alternative Approach to Least-Squares Regression
    Analysis 74
Self-Study Problem 75
Suggested Readings 78
Discussion Questions 78
Exercises 79
Problems 84

Chapter 4
Contribution Analysis: Alternative Cost Groupings and Relevant Cost Analysis for Decision Making 93

Outline 93
Relevant Cost Objectives and Terminology for Contribution Reporting 94
Data Bank Concept 94
Relevant Cost Objectives 95
Cost Groupings for Contribution Reporting 96

The Contribution Margin Concept 96
   Definition of Contribution Margin 97
   Contribution Margin Ratio 97
   Contribution Margin Versus Gross Margin 97
   An Example of Contribution Reporting 98
   Segment Margin Analysis 99
The Role of Cost Information in Decisions 101
   Fallacy of Full Costs 102
Relevant Costs in Decision Problems 102
   Expected Future Costs 103
   Costs that Differ Among Decision Alternatives 103
Analysis of Cost Information for Nonroutine Decisions 103
   Total Cost Approach 105
   Contribution Approach 106
Some Examples of Nonroutine Decisions 108
   Make or buy 108
   Special Orders 109
   Product Line Decisions 112
Other Considerations in Nonroutine Decisions 114
   Short-run Versus Long-run Considerations 115
   Taxes and the Time Value of Money 115
   The Role of Qualitative Factors 116
Summary 116
Self-Study Problems 118
Suggested Readings 120
Discussion Questions 121
Exercises 121
Problems 126

Part Two
PLANNING BUSINESS ACTIVITIES 137

Chapter 5
Budgeting 139

Outline 139
Budgeting in General 140
   The Purpose of a Budget 140
   Budgeting Relative to Time 141
   Relationship of Budgets to Standards 142
   Master Budgets 143
Developing a Master Budget 144
   Budget Committee 144
   Process of Developing a Budget 145
Master Budget Example 146
   Sales Forecast 147
   Ending Inventory Levels 148
   Production Budget 148
   Raw Materials Purchases Budget 151
   Cost-of-Goods-Sold Budget 151
   Selling-Expense Budget 152
   Administrative-Expense Budget 152
   Cash Forecast of Receipts and Disbursements 152
   Budgeted Income Statement 156
   Budgeted Balance Sheet 157
   Analysis of the Budget 157
Budgeting in the Not-for-Profit Sector 158
   Differences Between Profit and Not-for-Profit Budgets 158
   Budget Elements 159

Behavioral Considerations of Budgeting 163
Summary 165
Self-Study Problem (AICPA Adapted) 165
Suggested Readings 167
Discussion Questions 167
Exercises 168
Problems 174
Case 184

Chapter 6
Flexible Budgeting and Responsibility Reporting 187

Outline 187
Flexible Budgeting 188
   Flexible Budgeting Defined 189
   Flexible Budget Example 189
   Flexible Budget Formula 191
Developing the Flexible Budget Formula 192
   Analyzing Cost Behavior in a Production Process 192
   Direct Costs: Materials and Labor 193
   Factory Overhead 194
   Flexible Budgeting for Selling and Administrative Costs 199
Responsibility Accounting 200
   Responsibility Accounting Defined 200
   Relationship to Segmented Reporting 200
   Form and Content of Reports 200
   Analysis of Budget Variances: Management by Exception 202
   Controllable versus Uncontrollable Costs 204
Behavioral Considerations in Reporting 205
Summary 206
Appendix 6.1: Alternate Computations for Coefficient of Correlation and
    Coefficient of Determination 207
Self-Study Problem 209
Suggested Readings 211
Discussion Questions 211
Exercises 212
Problems 220

Chapter 7
Cost-Volume-Profit Analysis 229

Outline 229
Breakeven Analysis 230
   Breakeven Analysis in Units 231
   Breakeven Analysis in Sales Dollars 233
   Breakeven Analysis for Multiple Products 235
Assumptions Underlying Cost-Volume-Profit Analysis 239
   Basic Assumptions 239
   Economic Analysis 239
   Sources of Data 240
Applications of Cost-Volume-Profit Analysis 241
   Level of Volume Required to Achieve a Specified Profit 241
   Margin of Safety 242
   Sensitivity Analysis 243

Summary 249
Self-Study Problem 250
Suggested Readings 252
Discussion Questions 252
Exercises 253
Problems 259

Part Three
COST DETERMINATION 267

Chapter 8
Job-Order Cost Systems 269

Outline 269
Manufacturing Accounting Systems 270
   Chart of Accounts 271
   Flow of Costs Through the Manufacturing Accounts 274
   Financial Statements 277
Job-Order Versus Process Cost Systems 277
Job-Order Cost Systems—Manufacturing Firms 279
   Job-Order Cost Sheet 279
   Flow of Costs in Job-Order Cost System 279
Job-Order Cost Systems—Service Organizations 284
Complications to the Manufacturing Accounting System 285
   Multiple Work in Process Accounts 285
   Multiple Departments 285
   Departmental Overhead Accounts and Rates 286
   Overhead Applied Account 287
   Split Ledger System 287
   Reporting for Partially Completed Jobs 289
   Revenue Recognition for Partially Completed Jobs 290
Summary 291
Self-Study Problem 292
Suggested Readings 293
Discussion Questions 294
Exercises 294
Problems 301
Case 310

Chapter 9
Process Costing: Basic Procedures 313

Outline 313
Characteristics of Process Costing 314
Procedures for Process Costing 317
   Weighted Average Method 318
   First-in, First-Out Method 325
   Modified Methods 329
Summary 332
Self-Study Problem 333
Suggested Readings 334
Discussion Questions 335
Exercises 335
Problems 341

Chapter 10
Process Costing: Additional Features 347

Outline 347
Addition of Materials in Processes Subsequent to the First Process 348
   No Change in Units 348
   Increase in Units 349
Accounting for Lost Units 351
Cost Flows and Process-Costing Procedures 353
   FIFO Method 358
   Other Considerations 362
Summary 365
Self-Study Problem 368
Suggested Readings 368
Discussion Questions 368
Exercises 368
Problems 374

Chapter 11
Joint Products and By-Products: Cost Allocations and Decisions 381

Outline 381
The Joint Product Environment 382
Joint Product Cost Allocation Methods 384
   Physical Measures 385
   Market Measures 386
Alternatives to Making Joint Product Cost Allocations 390
Accounting for By-Products 390
   Assigning a Cost to By-Products at the Time of Production 391
   Recognizing the Cost of By-Products at the Time of Sale 393
   Comparison of the Two Methods 393
Joint Costs and Management Decisions 394
Summary 397
Self-Study Problem 397
Suggested Readings 399
Discussion Questions 399
Exercises 400
Problems 404
Case 409

Chapter 12
Materials and Labor: Costing and Control 411

Outline 411
Materials Costing 412
   Materials Received 412
   Materials Issued 416
   Spoilage and Quality 417
Materials Control 422
   Materials Control—General 423
   Two-Bin System 423
   ABC Method 424
   Economic Order Quantity (EOQ) 424

*Material Requirements Planning (MRP) and Manufacturing Resource
    Planning (MRP II)* 428
  Just-In-Time (JIT) 430
Labor Costing 432
Labor Control and Learning Curves 435
  Learning Curves 435
Summary 437
Appendix 12.1: Materials Control Procedures 438
  Purchasing Materials 438
  Maintaining and Issuing Materials 440
Appendix 12.2: Labor Control Procedures 440
Appendix 12.3: The Mathematics of the Economic Order Quantity and
    Learning Curve 441
  Economic Order Quantity 441
  Learning Curve 442
Self-Study Problems 442
Suggested Readings 444
Discussion Questions 444
Exercises 445
Problems 449

Chapter 13
Factory Overhead: Costing and Control I 457

Outline 457
Factory Overhead Cost Concepts 458
  Factory Overhead Costs 458
  Variable, Fixed, and Mixed Overhead Costs 459
Overhead Application for Product Costing 459
  Overhead Application 460
  Concepts Underlying the Overhead Application Process 462
General Ledger Accounting 466
  The Accounting Process 466
  Analysis of Budgeted Versus Actual Overhead 467
  Disposition of Under-or Overapplied Overhead 468
Management Reporting of Overhead for Planning and Control 470
  Variable Overhead Reporting 470
  Fixed Overhead Reporting 471
Summary 473
Self-Study Problem 474
Suggested Readings 476
Discussion Questions 477
Exercises 477
Problems 482

Chapter 14
Factory Overhead: Costing and Control II 491

Outline 491
Departmentalization of Overhead Costs 492
  Production and Service Departments 492
  Service Department Cost Allocation 493
  Accumulating Overhead Costs by Department 495
  Selection of an Allocation Base 496
  Allocation Methods 498

Advantages of Departmentalization 503
The Number and Configuration of Departments 503
   Homogeneity of Costs 504
   Production Departments 505
   Service Departments 505
Allocation of Costs by Behavior 506
   Variable Costs 506
   Fixed Costs 506
Summary 506
Appendix 14.1: Applicable Standards of the Cost Accounting Standards Board 507
   Standard 402: Consistency in Allocating Costs Incurred for the Same Purpose 508
   Standard 403: Allocation of Home Office Expenses to Segments 508
   Standard 410: Allocation of Business Unit General and Administrative Expenses to Final Cost Objectives 509
   Standard 418: Allocation of Indirect Cost Pools 510
Appendix 14.2: Reciprocal Allocations Using Matrix Algebra 511
Self-Study Problem 514
Suggested Readings 517
Discussion Questions 517
Exercises 518
Problems 524

Part Four
COST CONTROL 533

Chapter 15
Standard Costs for Materials and Labor 535

Outline 535
Cost Control Systems 536
Standard Costs Defined 537
   Materials Standards 537
   Labor Standards 538
Standards as Budgetary Goals and Performance Benchmarks 538
Materials and Labor Variances 540
Responsibility for Variances 542
   Materials 543
   Labor 544
Recording Materials and Related Variances 544
   Recognizing Price Variance at Time of Purchase 544
   Recognizing Price Variance at Time of Issue 545
Recording Labor and Related Variances 546
Disposition of Variances 546
Investigation of Variances 547
Development of Standards 548
   Standard-Setting Philosophies 548
   Physical Standards 549
Summary 550
Appendix 15.1: A Hybrid Method for Recognizing Materials Price Variances 551
Self-Study Problem 552
Suggested Readings 555
Discussion Questions 556
Exercises 557
Problems 561

Chapter 16
Standard Costs for Factory Overhead 573

Outline 573
Standard Costs for Factory Overhead 574
The Overhead Budget 575
Overhead Application and General Ledger Accounting 576
Special Considerations in Fixed Overhead Accounting 578
Analysis of Overhead Variances 580
   Framework for Overhead Variance Analysis 580
   Two-Way Analysis 581
   Three-Way Analysis 583
   Four-Way Analysis 583
   Reporting Variances 585
Disposition of Standard Cost Variances 585
   Treated as Period Expenses 587
   Treated as Inventoriable Costs 590
Summary 592
Appendix 16.1: Process Costing and Standard Costs 593
Self-Study Problem 595
Suggested Readings 598
Discussion Questions 598
Exercises 599
Problems 602

Chapter 17
Mix, Yield, and Variance Investigation 611

Outline 611
Production Mix and Yield 612
   Direct-Materials Mix and Yield Variances 613
   Direct-Labor Mix and Yield Variances 616
Variance Reports 618
Investigation of Variances 620
   Why Variances Occur 620
   Techniques for Deciding When to Investigate Variances 622
   Cost-Benefit Evaluation of Investigation 624
Behavioral Considerations 625
Summary 626
Self-Study Problems 626
Suggested Readings 628
Discussion Questions 628
Exercises 629
Problems 633

Chapter 18
Accounting Systems for Management Planning and Control 639

Outline 639
The Common Body of Knowledge for Management Accountants 640
   Management Decision Process 641
   Cost Accounting as a Subsystem of the Management Information System 641
   Fully Integrated Management Information System 642

How Much Information? 645
   Required Information 645
   Cost Benefit Analysis of Additional Information 646
Developing a Cost Accounting System 649
   Master Plan 650
   Systems Analysis and Design Life Cycle 652
   Behavioral Considerations 656
Data Versus Information 657
   Report Preparation 658
   Types of Reports 659
   Designing Output Reports 661
Cost Accounting System Internal Controls 661
   Administrative Controls 662
   Input Controls 665
   Processing Controls 666
   Output Controls 667
Summary 668
Self-Study Problem (CMA) 668
Suggested Readings 670
Discussion Questions 670
Exercises 671
Problems 680

Chapter 19
Variable Costing and Contribution Margin Analysis 689

Outline 689
Variable Costing 690
   Comparison of Variable Costing and Absorption Costing 690
   Variable Costing as a Management Tool 695
   External Reporting Considerations 696
Contribution Margin Analysis 698
   Isolating the Components of Variance 698
   Calculating the Variances 699
   Gross Margin Analysis 703
Summary 706
Self-Study Problems 707
Suggested Readings 710
Discussion Questions 711
Exercises 712
Problems 717
Case 727

Chapter 20
Segment Performance 729

Outline 729
Centralization and Decentralization 730
Responsibility Centers 731
Approaches for Evaluating Performance 732
   Return on Investment 733
   Residual Income 735
   Segment Margin Analysis 738

CONTENTS

Considerations for Implementation 740
  The Role of Budgets 740
  The Investment Base 741
Summary 745
Appendix 20.1: Compound Interest Method of Depreciation 746
Self-Study Problem 747
Suggested Readings 748
Discussion Questions 749
Exercises 750
Problems 757
Cases 765

Part Five
DECISION ANALYSIS 771

Chapter 21
Decision Analysis: Specialized Applications 773

Outline 773
Uncertainty and Risk 774
Decisions Under Uncertain Conditions 774
Probability Analysis 775
  Illustration of Probability Analysis 775
  Expected Values and Standard Deviation 777
  Expected Value of Perfect Information 779
Linear Programming 781
  Computer Solution and Sensitivity Analysis 784
Summary 786
Suggested Readings 786
Discussion Questions 786
Exercises 787
Problems 789
Cases 794

Chapter 22
Transfer and Product Pricing 799

Outline 799
Definition and Comparison of Transfer and Product Pricing 800
Pricing for Intracompany Transfers 800
  Alternative Approaches to Establishing Transfer Prices 803
  Accounting Entries for Intracompany Transfers 812
  Other Objectives to Transfer Pricing 813
Pricing for Product Sales 814
  Alternative Cost-Based Approaches to Product Pricing 814
  Considerations for Modification of Cost-Based Prices 819
Summary 820
Self-Study Problems 820
Suggested Readings 824
Discussion Questions 824
Exercises 825
Problems 830
Cases 838

Chapter 23
Capital Budgeting: Part I 843

Outline 843
Introduction to Capital Budgeting 844
   Cash flow Orientation 844
   Charting Cash Inflows and Outflows 846
Capital Budgeting Techniques 848
   Net Present Value 849
   Internal Rate of Return 855
   Payback 859
   Accounting Rate of Return 866
   Disinvestment Decisions 870
Selecting the Evaluation Technique 871
   Selection Criteria 871
   Planning and Control Over Capital Expenditures 874
   Complications to Capital Budgeting 875
Summary 816
Appendix 23.1: Time Value of Money 876
Self-Study Problem 883
Suggested Readings 885
Discussion Questions 885
Exercises 886
Problems 893
Case 899

Chapter 24
Capital Budgeting: Part II 907

Outline 907
Income Tax Effects on Capital Budgeting 908
   Income Tax Effect on Normal Cash Flows 908
   Accelerated Cost Recovery System—Depreciation 910
   The Impact of Accelerated Cost Recovery on Capital Investment 913
   Salvage Value 914
   Comprehensive Illustration 915
Cost of Capital 918
   Cost of Capital Defined 918
   Marginal Cost of Capital (MCC) 919
   Cost of Debt 921
   Cost of Preferred Stock 922
   Cost of Common Stock and Retained Earnings 922
   Comprehensive Illustration 924
Sensitivity Analysis in Capital Budgeting 925
   Selecting a Minimum Desired Rate of Return 926
   Errors in Estimating the Component Cost of Capital Stock 926
   Rate Adjustment for Nonproductive Projects 927
   Variable Rate Among Projects 928
   Predicting and Evaluating Cash Flows 929
Summary 930
Appendix 24.1: Investment Tax Credit (ITC) 931
Self-Study Problem 933
Suggested Readings 934
Discussion Questions 935
Exercises 935
Problems 942
Cases 950

Chapter 25
Cost Accounting in an Information Age 961

Outline 961
Computer Software 962
   Operating System 963
   Program Language Translators 963
   Utility Routines 964
   Application Programs 964
   Special-Purpose Programs 964
Decision Support Systems 964
   Decision Support Systems (DSS) Defined 965
   Decision Support Software 965
Application Programs for Transaction Processing 966
Data-Base Management Systems 967
   Data-Base 967
   Data-Base Administrator 968
   Data-Base Management System 969
   How a Data-Base Management System Works 969
Spreadsheets 973
   Spreadsheets As Decision Support Systems 973
Modeling Software 975
   Entering the Model 977
   Compiling the Model 978
   Viewing the Base Model 978
   Analyzing the Model: ("What If . . ." Analysis) 979
   Comparing Spreadsheets and Modeling Software 980
Expert Systems 982
   General Concepts 982
   Applications 983
Software Evaluation 984
Self-Study Problem 984
Suggested Readings 988
Discussion Questions 988
Cases 988

Chapter 26
The Management Accounting Profession 997

Outline 997
Definition and Objectives of Management Accounting 998
Characteristics of a Profession 999
Professional Examinations 1002
   Certificate in Management Accounting 1002
   Certified Public Accountant 1005
Code of Ethics 1009
   On-the-Job Experience 1011
   Continuing Education 1011
Summary 1011
Suggested Readings 1012
Discussion Questions 1012
Cases 1013

Glossary 1019

Index 1027

Preface

Cost and managerial accounting is a specialized area of accounting that attempts to satisfy the information needs of management. Management at all levels within an organization has the responsibility of planning, coordinating, executing, and controlling business operations. A large part of the information required to do these jobs effectively is accounting-oriented, and it is the job of the cost accountant to accumulate, prepare, and interpret this information.

Cost accounting is the process of accumulating the costs of a manufacturing process and identifying them with the units produced. It is a unique subfield of management accounting that interfaces with both managerial and financial accounting. Data prepared by the cost accountant is used in financial reporting to value ending inventories and the cost of goods sold. The same data is broken down by manufacturing component, by department, or by individual worker within a department in management reports to assist management in operating the business.

The study of cost and managerial accounting usually takes one of three focuses:

1. Managerial focus. Heavy emphasis is placed on how management interprets, applies, and implements cost accounting information in the decision process of the organization.
2. Cost finding or cost determination focus. The primary emphasis is on determining the cost per unit to manufacture a finished product. A considerable amount of time is spent in learning the procedures to be followed and the journal entries to be made to allocate and accumulate manufacturing costs.
3. Quantitative orientation. Heavy emphasis is placed on the many quantitative tools and operations research methods that are useful in analyzing and interpreting cost data.

In writing this textbook we have tried to balance the emphasis on each of these three areas. As each topic is discussed we cover the relevant cost finding techniques and provide examples of the journal entries required to record the data. We also identify the relevant quantitative techniques that can be used to analyze the data, to identify what the data means, and how management should use it in the decision-making processes. The behavioral implications associated with the use of the data are also considered with each topic. We believe that the balance provided in this textbook is the most efficient way to study cost and managerial accounting.

CHANGES IN THE SECOND EDITION

The first edition of the book received high praise for its accessible writing style, clear explanations of difficult concepts, and the correlation between chapter content and chapter-ending exercise and problem materials. Users also liked the integration of quantitative aspects and behavioral considerations with individual cost accounting topics. These features have been retained.

The second edition, in order to keep pace with changes in the field, includes the following:

1. A new chapter (17) has been added on Mix, Yield, and Variance Investigation. It discusses production mix and yield, direct material and direct labor, mix and yield variances, investigation of variances, and behavioral considerations.
2. The two chapters in the first edition on contribution reporting and relevant costs for decision-making (chapters 4 and 20) have been consolidated into one chapter. Chapter 4, Contribution Analysis: Alternative Cost Groupings and Relevant Cost Analysis for Decision-Making, has three objectives: Students will learn how to establish the contribution reporting format and organize information into a meaningful format for internal management's use; establish criteria for identifying relevant costs in decision situations; and apply relevant cost analysis to deal with typical decision problems.
3. A new computer-tools chapter (25) is highlighted in Cost Accounting in an Information Age. Concepts and tools included are computer software, decision support systems, applications programs for transaction processing, database management systems, spreadsheets, modeling software, expert systems and software evaluations.
4. The first edition's chapter on professional examinations has been expanded. Chapter 26: The Management Accounting Profession includes a discussion on professional examinations and covers codes of ethical conduct and resolving ethical dilemmas in a cost-accounting environment. Exercise, problem and case material in this chapter deals with ethical dilemmas.
5. Spreadsheet templates are used to solve selected end-of-chapter exercises, problems and cases, which are identified in the text with a computer logo. The spreadsheet materials begin with chapter 3 and continue throughout the text. Using Lotus 1-2-3, students solve problems by completing worksheets of varying degrees of difficulty. Computer literacy and knowledge of Lotus 1-2-3 is assumed on behalf of the students. Some worksheets are completely worked and students type in information and run the program; others are partially worked and students are required to work more extensively to solve the problems; a third type of worksheet is blank and students must work them from the beginning to the end of the problems. Student worksheet templates for use with Lotus 1-2-3 are available free and copyable to adopters. Also available free to adopters are disks with complete answers to the students' computer problems.
6. The number and range of difficulty in the questions, exercises and problems, which are placed at the end of chapters, has been expanded. The gradation of problems ranging from elementary to complex has been enhanced, and more difficult problems have been added.
7. Case materials (some of which are worked with the student software template in tandem with Lotus 1-2-3) have been added to approximately half of the chapters. The cases, which require students to apply and integrate material from several sources within the text, add a new dimension to the rigor of the second edition.

ORGANIZATION AND FEATURES OF THE SECOND EDITION

Cost Accounting: A Managerial Approach covers the cost accounting topics generally required of a cost accountant at an entry-level position. It is specifically designed for a cost or managerial accounting class in the curriculum of an accounting major. However, it may also be used as the textbook for a cost or managerial accounting course in an MBA program. The twenty-six chapters in the text provide an abundance of material for a two-semester or three-quarter cost or managerial series. Financial accounting is the only prerequisite for use of this textbook.

The reorganized presentation of topics in the second edition is conceptually sound. The overview in Part One provides the general framework used throughout the text for cost and managerial accounting. It provides a basis for planning business activities, which is the topic of Part Two. Implementation of these activities requires the cost accountant to record, classify and summarize costs. These activities are part of cost determination, which is the subject of Part Three. Finally, this cost data is used to control business activities and assist in management decisions, which are the topics discussed in Parts Four and Five, respectively.

Each chapter includes the following:

1. *Chapter outline:* A list of all headings and major subheadings provides students with an overview of each chapter's content.
2. *Learning objectives:* These identify what the chapter contains and what students should be able to do upon completing each chapter's questions, exercises, and problems.
3. *Chapter content:* Each chapter proceeds from basic concepts to complex topics in a logical manner. Current terminology and up-to-date accounting procedures are used throughout the text. Numerous examples and illustrations appear as they would in an actual business setting.
4. *Key terms:* Throughout the chapters important terms are set in bold type. Each term is defined in the glossary.
5. *Summary:* A brief synopsis of each chapter helps students organize and review key concepts.
6. *Self-study problems:* One or two sample problems with suggested solutions enable students to test their knowledge of chapter material and obtain immediate feedback regarding their answers.
7. *Suggested readings:* A list of references provides additional reading on chapter-related material.
8. *Problem material:* End-of-chapter problem material includes discussion questions, exercises, problems and cases. Discussion questions provide a quick check of students' understanding of basic concepts covered in each chapter. Exercises generally require some computations but take less time to complete than the problems. Problems cover more than one concept and are designed to help students integrate various concepts within a chapter and between chapters. Cases are generally longer, have less structure, and require creativity in developing solutions.
9. All key terms are integrated at the end of the book in a comprehensive glossary that serves as a valuable reference tool.
10. Several topics are covered in appendices to chapters. These include review topics, such as the time value of money, that are taught in other courses but are integral to this text's chapter material. Advanced topics, such as matrix algebra, also are discussed.

SUPPORT MATERIALS

The text's support materials are:

1. *Instructor's Manual:* Assists instructors in preparing lectures, answering students' questions, and preparing examinations. It contains lecture outlines that highlight important concepts, examples for class discussion, and test material with solutions. The test material is true/false, multiple choice and short problems; answers are provided for all the material. The quantity of questions and problems enables instructors to be selective and vary the content of examinations each term.
2. *Solutions Manual:* Provides solutions to all discussion questions, exercises, problems in the text, and cases including all material on the software templates.
3. *Transparency Acetates:* Important topics and concepts presented in the Solutions Manual have been made into acetates.
4. *Student Study Guide:* Assists students to review each chapter's content, check their progress in understanding concepts, and prepare for examinations. Each chapter contains an overview of its material, objectives, summary of key concepts and study guide, glossary, self-study questions, exercises, and problems with solutions.
5. *Software for use with Lotus 1-2-3:* Contains complete and partially completed templates that relate to selected exercises, problems, and cases in the textbook. Template assignments are identified in the text with a computer logo; (🖥); they range from introductory to difficult. The software enables students to learn how to work cost-accounting problems using commerical-grade software. Answers to all of the computer exercises are provided to instructors on separate disks and in the Solutions Manual.
6. *Transparency Masters:* Transparency masters of key figures within text are also available.

CONTRIBUTIONS OF OTHERS

We wish to express our thanks to the staff of West Educational Publishing who have contributed so much to the development and production of this text. Particularly, we wish to acknowledge the efforts and encouragement of its editorial staff for helping us to start and complete this project. They are Clyde H. Perlee, Jr., publisher and editor-in-chief; Denise Simon, executive editor; John Orr, senior production editor; and Melody A. Rotman, editorial assistant. Their efforts have been critical to the success of the second edition.

We also wish to acknowledge the helpful criticism and valuable suggestions of professors who reviewed the second edition:

James F. Brown, Jr.
University of Nebraska—Lincoln

R. W. Clanton, Jr.
Central State University, Oklahoma

Carl Dennler, Jr.
Florida Atlantic University

Robert E. Hansen
University of Detroit

Anita V. Hope
Tarrant County Junior College, Texas

Philip Jagolinzer
University of Southern Maine

Yow-Min R. Lee
California State University—Northridge

Roland A. Minch
SUNY, Albany

William K. Parmley
Southwest Missouri State University

M. H. Sarhan
University of Akron, Ohio

Larry G. Singleton
George Washington University, Washington, D.C.

Finally, we wish to express gratitude to our families for their endless patience and timely encouragement. We dedicate this book to them for their support.

Part One

OVERVIEW OF COST AND MANAGERIAL ACCOUNTING

Chapters 1 through 4 provide an overview of cost and managerial accounting. We will first consider the relationship between cost and managerial accounting and how they differ from financial accounting and other more specialized areas of accounting.

Basic to the study of cost accounting is a clear understanding of
(a) terminology used to describe various cost classifications,
(b) behavioral patterns most commonly exhibited by each cost, and
(c) procedures used to quantify cost behavior. Costs may also be grouped in a variety of ways to provide meaningful information for statement users. The traditional statement presentation will be reviewed and alternative reporting formats will be introduced.

Chapter 1

Introduction to Managerial and Cost Accounting

Outline

SPECIALIZED AREAS OF ACCOUNTING
Financial Accounting
Managerial/Cost Accounting
AUTHORITATIVE SUPPORT FOR ACCOUNTING CONCEPTS AND PROCEDURES
Generally Accepted Accounting Principles
Cost Accounting Standards
THE MANAGEMENT PROCESS
THE CONTROLLER'S ROLE
Functions of the Finance Division
  Setting Financial Goals
  Evaluating Alternatives
  Acquiring Capital
  Establishing Financial Controls
Controller Responsibility Versus Treasurer Responsibility
  Controller
  Treasurer
SUMMARY
SUGGESTED READINGS
DISCUSSION QUESTIONS

Managerial accounting is an internal accounting process designed to provide management with the information necessary to operate the business successfully. Cost accounting is a specialized area that involves accumulating the costs of a manufacturing or other functional process and identifying them with the units produced or some other object. This information is used for both financial and managerial reporting purposes. This chapter introduces the concept of cost accounting and discusses its relationship to financial and managerial accounting. After completing this chapter, you should be able to:

1. Identify what cost accounting is and explain how it relates to financial and managerial accounting.
2. Identify professional organizations that have a role in the development of cost accounting procedures and practices.
3. Describe and compare the functions of a controller within an organization with the functions performed by a treasurer.

SPECIALIZED AREAS OF ACCOUNTING

Accounting is the process of recording, classifying, summarizing, and reporting the economic activities of an organization. It is a service activity intended to provide information to users of financial reports to assist them in their decision making. The users and uses of accounting reports have significant effects on the accounting process and the type of information that is reported.

Users of accounting information can be broadly classified into two types—external users and internal users. Each group encounters a different set of problems with different informational needs. Accounting has responded by developing subfields, or area of specialization. These include financial accounting and managerial/cost accounting.

Financial Accounting

The field of **financial accounting** specializes in providing information for the needs of external users such as stockholders, potential investors, creditors, and agencies of federal, state, and local governments. To meet the needs of each of these users, financial accounting can be further subdivided into financial reporting, auditing, income tax reporting, and SEC reporting.

Stockholders and potential investors make decisions concerning the buying, holding, or selling of an ownership interest in a business organization. Creditors make decisions concerning the lending of money and the amount of interest to charge. Information on the profitability of the company, its current financial position, and its utilization of cash resources are relevant to these kinds of decisions. Also, status and progress reports are essential, because financial resources are scarce and the various parties who have their resources at risk can legitimately expect them to be used productively. *Financial reporting* provides this information in the traditional balance sheet, income statement, statement of cash flows, and statement of changes in owners' equity.

Auditing is an area within financial accounting that deals with the concepts and procedures of attesting to the fairness of external reports. The previously mentioned financial reports are prepared by management and its staff of internal accountants. Stockholders, potential investors, and creditors typically do not have access to the company's accounting records to verify their accuracy. Auditors, therefore, are employed as a third party to provide an independent review. They review the accounting system, sample transactions to see if they have been accounted for properly, and render an opinion concerning the accuracy and adequacy of the financial statements. This does not, however, guarantee that the accounting and reporting process is perfect and that no errors have been made during the period.

Governmental agencies associated with accounting are concerned primarily with raising money to finance government operations and with insuring that adequate disclosures are made by companies selling securities to the general public. Government revenue is obtained through taxation. *Income tax accounting* is a specialized field of financial accounting that deals with tax planning and compliance with federal, state, and local tax laws.

Securities and exchange commissions *(SEC)* have been established on the federal and state level to identify minimum disclosure requirements and to monitor the activities of companies selling their stock to the general public. *SEC reporting* is a specialized field of financial accounting that deals with meeting the reporting requirements of the securities and exchange commissions.

Managerial/Cost Accounting

Satisfying the information needs of internal users is the concern of **managerial accounting.** Internal users include both line and staff personnel at top, middle, and lower levels of management. Because management has the responsibility for preparing financial statements for external reporting, management accounting also includes the preparation of external reports, as illustrated in the following definition of management accounting.

> Management accounting is the process of identification, measurement, accumulation, analysis, preparation, interpretation, and communication of financial information used by management to plan, evaluate, and control within an organization and to assure appropriate use of and accountability for its resources. Management accounting also comprises the preparation of financial reports for non-management groups such as shareholders, creditors, regulatory agencies, and tax authorities.[1]

In business organizations, management is responsible for using available resources as effectively and as efficiently as possible to accomplish organizational objectives. To fulfill these responsibilities, management must make decisions concerning desirable organizational objectives, resource utilization, and personnel effectiveness. The type of information that is useful for making these decisions is entirely different than most information provided to external users. Managerial accounting provides information to managers to assist them in operating the business successfully.

Cost accounting is the process of accumulating the costs of manufacturing and other functional processes and identifying these costs with units produced or some other object. It is a unique subfield of managerial accounting that interfaces with both managerial and financial accounting. Cost accounting is applied primarily to manufacturing organizations that combine and process raw materials into finished products.

Manufacturing firms encounter cost considerations in production, marketing, and other activities. Service organizations also experience many cost accounting challenges. In financial reporting, a cost per unit for the finished product must be determined for use in valuing ending inventory and in determining the cost of goods sold. An organization's

---

1. Management Accounting Practices Statement Promulgation Subcommittee. "Statements on Management Accounting," (New York: National Association of Accountants, 1981), p. 4.

management needs similar cost data to control the manufacturing process. However, it needs these data broken down for each manufacturing operation and for each component that makes up the finished product. Cost data may be broken down by product, by department, and sometimes even by individual worker within the department. For example, it is not enough to know that the cost to produce a finished product is too high; management must be able to identify where and why it is costing too much and what can be done to reduce costs.

Some companies consider the information systems area, which involves the analysis and design of accounting and management information systems, to be a subfield within managerial accounting. However, most large organizations have a separate information systems division that designs and operates the computer-based information processing system. Regardless of where the function is located, managerial accounting personnel are relied on to identify the type of system that should be developed and the content of the reports.

This text is primarily concerned with managerial and cost accounting in manufacturing organizations. Where it is appropriate, we discuss the relationship of managerial/cost accounting to the various areas of financial reporting, including income taxes, and to systems analysis and design.

AUTHORITATIVE SUPPORT FOR ACCOUNTING CONCEPTS AND PROCEDURES

All fields of accounting have identified acceptable standards, concepts, procedures, and practices. The extent to which these concepts and procedures have been codified and systematized into a standard set of rules and procedures, however, varies among the various subfields. In this section we will identify the authoritative groups involved in the standard-setting process in each area of accounting and discuss the reasons for a lack of more extensive codification in the managerial/cost accounting area.

Generally Accepted Accounting Principles

Financial accounting is most advanced in codifying generally accepted principles and practices because of the nature of the work being performed and the uses of the financial reports. Users of financial accounting data are generally outside the organization, have no access to organizational records, and make decisions that involve the comparison of one company against another. Companies that appear to be the strongest and that have the greatest earning potential are those in which investors buy stock and to which creditors lend money. They are also the companies from which the government tries to collect the most income taxes. For there to be accurate comparisons and fair taxation, all companies must use the same set of accounting principles.

Various professional organizations, governmental agencies, and special interest groups that were created through the efforts of concerned professionals have developed extensive codification in financial accounting. Congress and the Internal Revenue Service have created a large tax code to be followed in filing income taxes. The Financial Accounting Standards Board (FASB) and the American Institute of Certified Public Accountants (AICPA) have developed an extensive set of generally accepted accounting principles (GAAP) to be followed in financial reporting. The Securities and Exchange Commission

(SEC) has also had a significant influence on the development of GAAP. In addition, the commission has identified a set of minimum disclosure requirements that must be satisfied in filings with them. The Government Accounting Standards Board (GASB) promulgates accounting and reporting standards for governmental units.

Cost Accounting Standards

Managerial/cost accounting is not as well codified as financial accounting, but the nature and objectives of the work are also very different. The primary objective of managerial/cost accounting is to help management operate the business successfully. Every business has different products, different objectives, and different management styles. What is relevant to one organization may not be relevant to another, and a procedure that works well with one style of management may not work well with another style. Therefore, managerial/cost accounting must be flexible to meet the differing needs of each organization.

There are some rules that must be followed in developing the data to be used in external reports. These rules govern the valuation of raw materials, goods that are still in the manufacturing process, and ending inventories. The other concepts and procedures that are included in cost accounting have been found to be useful in a variety of organizations and applicable to a variety of decisions. It is important to be able to distinguish the practices that are directed by GAAP from those that are not and to understand the concepts so that adjustments can be made for the differing needs of an organization.

Managerial accounting derives relevant concepts and procedures from a broad spectrum of disciplines. Various concepts come from the fields of economics, banking, finance, engineering, operations research, quantitative analysis, statistics, and several of the behavioral sciences.

The major organization responsible for the development of cost accounting procedures in the National Association of Accountants (NAA). Another organization that has had some input is the Financial Executives Institute (FEI). The NAA has a Management Accounting Practices Committee, which is charged with developing guidelines on managerial accounting concepts, policies, and practices. A separate subcommittee on statement promulgation identifies the subject areas to be explored and oversees progress on each project from initiation to completion. The results of the efforts of these committees are published in Statements on Management Accounting.[2]

The NAA issued Statement on Management Accounting (SMA) 1B in June 1982, which sets forth the two main objectives of management accounting as (1) providing information and (2) participating in the management process. SMA 1B further outlines the major responsibilities, principal activities, and processes involved in management accounting. Reference to SMA 1B and to chapter 26 in this text will provide more detail on these provisions.

The Common Body of Knowledge for Management Accountants was delineated by the NAA in SMA 1D in June 1986. This statement is categorized into three areas, as presented in the following outline.

I. Information and Decision Processes
    A. Management Decision Processes
        1. Repetitive
        2. Nonprogrammed
        3. Strategic

---

2. Ibid.

B. Internal Reporting
 1. Generating Data
 2. Organizing and Analyzing Information
 3. Presenting and Communicating Information
C. Financial Planning and Performance Evaluation
 1. Forecasting and Budgeting
 2. Analysis and Evaluation

II. Accounting Principles and Functions
 A. Organization Structure and Management
  1. Structure and Management of the Accounting Function
  2. Internal Control
  3. Internal Audit
 B. Accounting Concepts and Principles
  1. Nature and Objectives of Accounting
  2. Accounting Practices

III. Entity Operations
 A. Principal Entity Operations
  1. Finance and Investment
  2. Engineering and Research and Development
  3. Production and Operations
  4. Sales and Marketing
  5. Human Resources
 B. Operating Environment
  1. Legal Environment
  2. Economic Environment
  3. Ethical and Social Environment
 C. Taxation
  1. Taxation Policies
  2. Structure and Types of Taxes
  3. Tax Planning
 D. External Reporting
  1. Reporting Standards
  2. Information Needs of User Groups
 E. Information Systems
  1. Systems Analysis and Design
  2. Data-base Management
  3. Software Applications
  4. Technological Literacy
  5. Systems Evaluation

The outline of the Common Body of Knowledge indicates the broad base of knowledge needed by an effective management accounting professional.

The various pronouncements of the NAA and other professional organizations should be carefully studied. Although the statements may not represent mandatory accounting and reporting standards, they do provide guidance for the performance of cost and management accountants.

The Cost Accounting Standards Board (CASB) also had some influence in the development of cost accounting procedures. This unique organization was created by Congress through legislation (PL 91–379) passed August 15, 1970. The CASB was charged with formulating standards to ensure the systematic and uniform treatment of various costs in-

CHAPTER 1: INTRODUCTION TO MANAGERIAL AND COST ACCOUNTING 9

FIGURE 1.1

The CASB's Cost Accounting Standards

Number	Title	Effective Date
400	Definitions	9/01/72
401	Consistency in Estimating, Accumulating, and Reporting Costs	7/01/72
402	Consistency in Allocating Costs Incurred for the Same Purpose	7/01/72
403	Allocation of Home Office Expenses to Segments	9/30/73
404	Capitalization of Tangible Assets	7/01/73
405	Accounting for Unallowable Costs	4/01/74
406	Cost Accounting Period	7/01/74
407	Use of Standard Costs for Direct Material and Direct Labor	10/01/74
408	Accounting for Costs for Compensated Personal Absence	7/01/75
409	Depreciation of Tangible Capital Assets	7/01/75
410	Allocation of Business Unit General and Administrative Expenses to Final Cost Objectives	10/01/76
411	Accounting for Acquisition Costs of Material	1/01/76
412	Composition and Measurement of Pension Cost	1/01/76
413	Adjustment and Allocation of Pension Cost	3/10/78
414	Cost of Money as an Element of the Cost of Facilities Capital	10/01/76
415	Accounting for the Cost of Deferred Compensation	7/10/77
416	Accounting for Insurance Costs	7/10/79
417	Cost of Money as an Element of the Cost of Capital Assets Under Consideration	12/15/80
418	Allocation of Direct and Indirect Costs	9/20/80
420	Accounting for Independent Research and Development Costs and Bid and Proposal Costs	3/15/80

curred by firms entering into federal defense contracts. Having completed this charge, the CASB is no longer an active institution like the SEC or the FASB.

The CASB issued twenty standards during its existence. These cost accounting standards are listed in figure 1.1.

In the early years, all negotiated defense contracts in excess of $100,000 were subject to the provisions of cost accounting standards. In 1972, coverage of the standards was extended to virtually all government contracts (not defense only) exceeding $100,000. In 1974, firms that had never had a contract for more than $500,000 were excluded from compliance. A further exclusion from the standards was made for large firms for which government contracts amounted to less than 10 percent of their sales. Also, large firms with such contracts that totaled less than $10 million were subject to compliance with Standards 401 and 402 only.

Various standards from the list of twenty that relate to cost accounting topics will be referred to as appropriate in subsequent chapters.

THE MANAGEMENT PROCESS

The management process summarizes the major activities performed by management in leading an organization. A manager's work generally involves a cycle: (a) setting organizational objectives, (b) formulating an operating plan, (c) implementing the plan and monitoring the activities on a day-to-day basis, (d) measuring results, and (e) evaluating the results to see if the plan was properly implemented and the objectives of the organization are being accomplished. Figure 1.2 illustrates the management cycle.

FIGURE 1.2

The Management Cycle

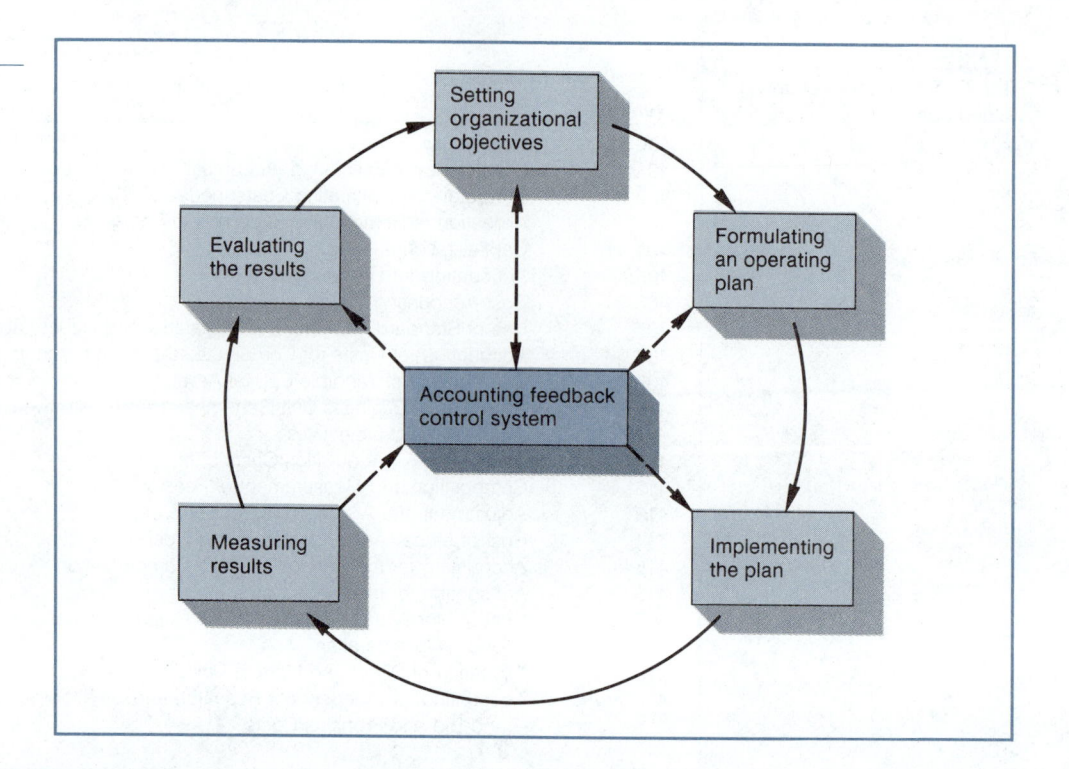

Organizational objectives are rather broad and general but they provide direction to all other activities. For example, a shoe manufacturer may have the following organizational objectives:

1. Manufacture a top-of-the-line variety of women's shoes.
2. Have an annual growth rate of 10 percent and increase market share from 15 percent to 25 percent during the next five years.
3. Maintain a 20 percent rate of return on owners' equity.

Organizational objectives are not changed frequently, although slight modifications may be made annually to keep them current and at a realistic level of aspiration.

The *operating plan* is formulated for a specified time period, such as one year, and is prepared in detail. This plan is essential for directing the organization toward achieving its long-term objectives. Without a detailed plan, the organization may not be successful.

Central to each of the planning activities is the accounting system. Financial resources available to the business, as indicated in accounting reports, are frequently a limiting factor in the development of organizational objectives. Results of operations in the previous year are generally the starting point in developing a plan for the current year. Accountants' responsibilities for various aspects of the planning process may also include the performance of market studies, analysis of product potential, analysis of major equipment purchases, and development of manufacturing cost estimates for individual products.

The planning process results in a budget representing the formal plan of operations for the coming year. Individual budgets may be prepared for personnel, plant and equipment, production, finance, and marketing. The budget not only directs organizational activities but also provides a base to which actual results can be compared.

In figure 1.2, the lines and the direction of the arrows to and from the accounting feedback control system in the center of the management cycle indicate the flow of information. For example, the line and arrow from the "accounting feedback control system" box to the "formulating an operating plan" box indicate the flow of information on prior results, organizational objectives, and constraints. The arrow back to the center box indicates the flow of budget information into the accounting system for use in evaluating the plan's implementation.

Implementating the plan involves the day-to-day activities of operating the business. Decisions about personnel, production, products, markets, equipment, and financing must be made frequently through the day, month, and year. Each decision must be made so that the organization can move toward achievement of its annual operating plan and long-term objectives.

The accounting function *measures the results* of operations and compares them with the planned level of operations. Differences between the actual results and planned results help management to *evaluate* each area of the business and to identify areas in which corrective action is required. This is the function of the accounting feedback control system at the center of the management cycle (see fig. 1.2). This feedback control process helps management answer such questions as: (a) Is the firm on target in achieving its objectives? (b) Which areas of the business are doing well and which are doing poorly? and (c) What type of minor or major adjustments are required to reach the goals set previously?

The process of operating the business on a day-to-day basis to implement the plan or budget, measuring the results of operations, evaluating the results, and taking corrective action occurs over and over again throughout the weeks and months of the year. At the end of the year the financial results are tabulated and compared to the annual budget to evaluate the success of the organization. These results and the evaluation are then used in the planning process for the next period.

Notice from the preceding discussion that accounting information is the basis for each management activity. It is the basis for identifying organizational objectives and developing an annual budget. The accounting process measures the results of operations and compares them to the budget. The differences between the two help management to identify areas of the business where corrective action is required. The final results for the year are similarly developed and used as a basis for planning the next period.

THE CONTROLLER'S ROLE

Functions of the Finance Division

Responsibility for financial planning, management, and reporting belong to a chief financial officer. The title given to that officer may vary from company to company, but we will call that person the *financial vice president*. In larger organizations the financial vice president is assisted by two other individuals called the *treasurer* and the *controller*. Organization charts differ from organization to organization because of differences in their sizes, types of products or services, and management style. The organization chart shown in figure 1.3 illustrates the position of the controller and the treasurer both in relation to each other and to other officers of the company.

Regardless of the size or type of business, accounting and finance are basic to all business activities. Engineering design, product manufacturing, sales, and all other business activities have an economic impact. Money must be made available to carry out these activities; their results affect the profits of the company.

Major activities that are assigned to the organization's accounting and finance department include setting financial goals, evaluating alternatives, acquiring capital, managing cash, and establishing financial controls.

FIGURE 1.3 Typical Organization Chart

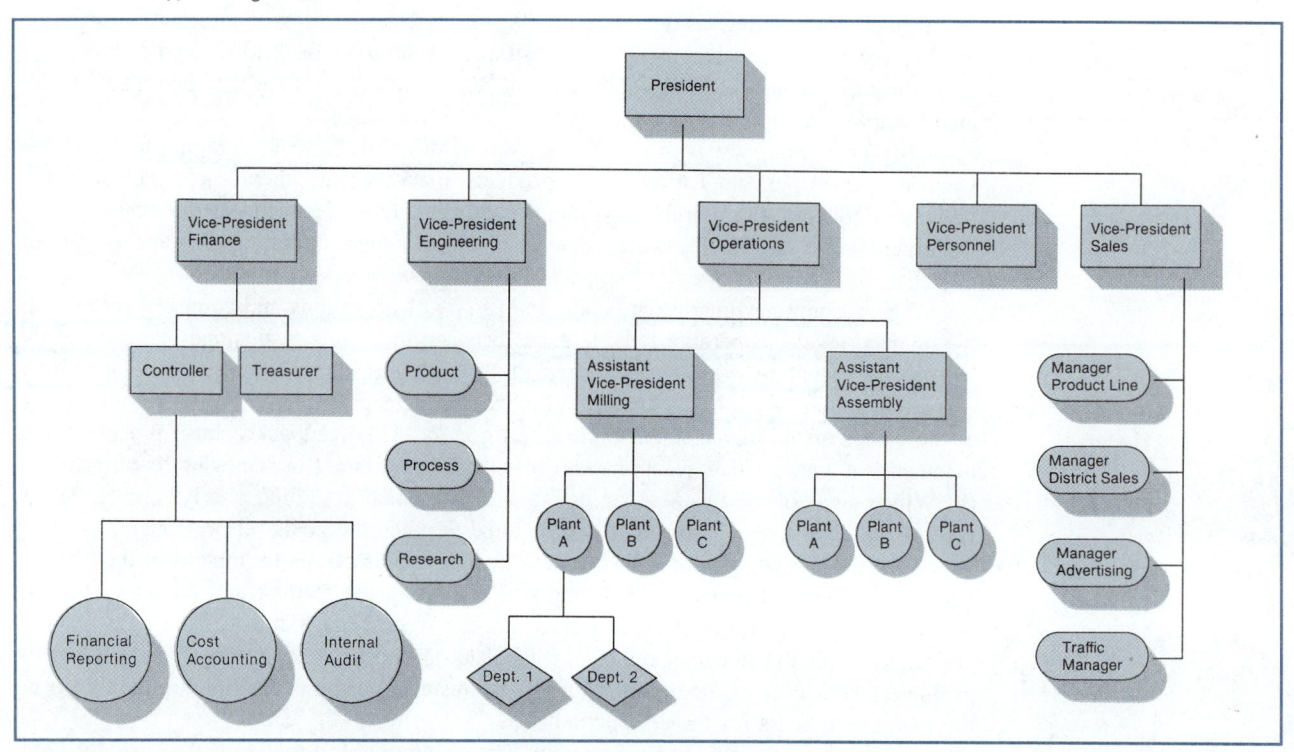

Setting Financial Goals The company's financial goals are part of the organizational objectives. Financial goals are generally a function of past performance in light of current operating conditions and future expectations. The financial officers analyze sales trends, production costs, earnings, and capital outlays and interpret these trends in light of their probable effect on company opertions. Part of this analysis includes forecasting the general economy, industry trends, and governmental policies and programs. Other factors considered include labor conditions, material costs, competitive forces, and technological advances. As a result of these analyses a recommendation is made to top management that eventually becomes part of long-term objectives and the annual operating budget.

Evaluating Alternatives Many investment proposals come from throughout the organization. These may include proposals to buy new equipment, construct a new warehouse, or manufacture a part rather than acquire it externally. The organization wants to invest in the alternatives that offer the greatest return on investment. It is the responsibility of the accounting and finance division to translate the proposals into dollars, which can be used as a common basis for the evaluation.

Acquiring Capital Before any proposal can be implemented, management must make sure it has access to the necessary capital. Once again, the accounting and finance division provides the answer. If there is not sufficient capital available, the accounting and finance division assists in obtaining the required amounts. It helps decide whether capital can be generated internally through normal operations, savings in operating expenses, and the liquidation of company-held assets, or whether it must be acquired from an outside source. Alternative outside sources include short- or long-term borrowing or increased equity capital by the sale of common or preferred stock.

CHAPTER 1: INTRODUCTION TO MANAGERIAL AND COST ACCOUNTING

Establishing Financial Controls Once the firm invests in the proposal, the accounting and finance division monitors its activities to see if they are in line with expectations. The accounting and finance division provides control when it questions waste or inefficiency or when it suggests an improved production method. The main purpose of the control is to increase rate of return on the existing investment.

Controller Responsibility versus Treasurer Responsibility

In small organizations the entire accounting and finance division will be under one individual. As the organization grows, the functions of the controller and treasurer are separated, and each may have an assistant or many people working under him or her. Let's assume we are working with a larger organization; we will identify the resonsibilities and major duties included within each of these areas.

Controller The title of controller is somewhat misleading. Strictly speaking, only line managers control. The controller is a staff person and, except in the role of manager of the controller's office, provides no direct control of the organization's operations. The term controller has evolved from "comptroller," based on the French noun "compte," which means "to account." Thus the title controller historically relates to accounting, not to controlling. Generally, the **controller** is responsible for all accounting activities within the organization.

The responsibilities of the controller combine several areas of accounting:

1. *General accounting.* Maintain the company's accounting books, accounting records, and forms. This includes:
   a. Preparing balance sheets, income statements, and other statements and reports.
   b. Giving the president interim reports on operations for the recent quarter and fiscal year to date.
   c. Supervising the preparation and filing of reports to the SEC.
2. *Budgeting.* Prepare a budget outlining the company's future operations and cash requirements.
3. *Cost accounting.* Determine the cost to manufacture a product and prepare internal reports to management of the processing divisions. This includes:
   a. Developing standard costs.
   b. Accumulating actual cost data.
   c. Preparing reports that compare standard costs to actual costs and highlight differences.
4. *Performance reporting.* Identify individuals in the organization who control activities, and prepare reports to show how well or how poorly they perform.
5. *Data processing.* Assist in the analysis and design of a computer-based information system. Frequently the data processing department is under the controller and the controller is involved in managing that department as well as other communications equipment.
6. *Other duties.* Other duties may be assigned to the controller by the president or by corporate bylaws. Some of these include:
   a. Tax planning and reporting.
   b. Service departments, such as mailing, telephone, maintenance, and filing.
   c. Forecasting.
   d. Corporate social relations and obligations.

As can be seen from this list, the controller has a wide variety of areas to account for and must be familiar with details in all facets of the business. Other than the chief executive officers, the controller probably has the best knowledge or products, services, manufacturing facilities, pricing, and competitive conditions. He or she has a unique position with the company and can observe and influence both the magnitude and direction of profits.

Treasurer The **treasurer** is the financial executive responsible for all functions classified under money management. This individual has the following major areas of responsibility:

1. *Provision of capital.* Identify the capital needs of the organization and organize a plan to provide the money required. This includes:
   a. Preparing statements on the company's financial condition.
   b. Advising the company on financial matters.
2. *Investor relations.* Establish and maintain a market for company securities. This includes:
   a. Reporting at the annual stockholders' meeting.
   b. Signing stock certificates.
   c. Negotiating the sale of securities.
   d. Maintaining the stock book and preparing dividend payments.
3. *Short-term financing.* Maintain banking arrangements for receiving, holding, and disbursing company monies. This includes:
   a. Receipting money into the company.
   b. Signing all checks.
   c. Maintaining records to account for money received and paid by the company.
4. *Credit and collection.* Establish procedures for granting credit and follow up on the collection of accounts.

SUMMARY

Managerial accounting is an internal accounting function designed to provide management with the information necessary to operate the business successfully. Cost accounting involves accumulating the costs of a manufacturing or functional process and identifying the costs with the units produced or some other object. Unit cost data are used in financial reporting to value ending inventories and cost of goods sold. They are also used by management to evaluate the manufacturing process and identify areas that need attention.

There are several professional organizations that develop managerial/cost accounting standards, concepts, and practices. These include the Financial Executives Institute (FEI), Cost Accounting Standards Board (CASB), and National Association of Accountants (NAA). The NAA has been the most active and has formed a Management Accounting Practices Committee that publishes Statements on Management Accounting.

The controller is the financial executive who is responsible for accounting, budgeting, cost accounting, performance reporting, data processing, and a variety of other activities. The controller assists management by accounting for the company's activities, comparing them to the plan or budget, and identifying areas that need management's attention. Both the controller and the treasurer are within the accounting and finance division of the company, but the treasurer is primarily responsible for money management, which includes identifying capital needs, and handling short-term financing, investments, investor relations, banking, and credit and collections.

SUGGESTED READINGS

Cost Accounting Standards Board. *Standards, Rules and Regulations as of June 30, 1975*. Washington, D.C.: Cost Accounting Standards Board, 1975.

Goodman, Sam R., and Reece, James S. *Controller's Handbook*. Homewood, Ill.: Dow-Jones Irwin, 1978.

Howell, Robert, and Soucy, Stephen R. *The New Manufacturing Environment: Major Trends for Management Accountants*. Management Accounting (July, 1987): 21.

Jayson, Susan. *Cost Accounting for the '90s*. Management Accounting (July, 1986): 58.

Johnson, H. Thomas, and Kaplan, Robert S. *The Rise and Fall of Management Accounting*. Management Accounting (January, 1987): 22.

National Association of Accountants. *Definition of Management Accounting*. Statements of Management Accounting #1A. New York: National Association of Accountants, 1981.

DISCUSSION QUESTIONS

Q1-1. What is accounting?

Q1-2. What is financial accounting?

Q1-3. Identify and briefly describe the subdivisions of financial accounting.

Q1-4. What is managerial accounting? How does it differ from financial accounting?

Q1-5. What is cost accounting? How does cost accounting relate to both financial and managerial accounting?

Q1-6. Define and briefly describe *generally accepted accounting principles* (GAAP).

Q1-7. How are generally accepted accounting principles formulated?

Q1-8. Identify the primary aspects of cost accounting that come under the provisions of GAAP.

Q1-9. Identify and briefly describe the organizations that formulate policies and practices covering financial and managerial/cost accounting.

Q1-10. Describe and briefly discuss the purpose of the Cost Accounting Standards Board.

Q1-11. Identify and briefly discuss the steps in the management process.

Q1-12. What is the role of managerial/cost accounting in the planning process and in the control (feedback) process?

Q1-13. Describe the controller's function. What does the controller control? Is the controller a part of the management team? Explain.

Q1-14. How do the roles of the treasurer and controller differ?

Q1-15. Are manufacturing firms the only types of firms with cost accounting concerns? Explain.

Chapter 2

Basic Cost Concepts

Outline

BASIC COST CONCEPTS
Definition of Cost
Cost Objectives
Cost Objectives and Cost Objects
Expired Versus Unexpired Costs
COST CLASSIFICATIONS
Time Period for Which the Cost is Computed
Management Function
Generally Accepted Accounting Treatment
Traceability to Products
Cost Behavior
Decision Significance
Managerial Influence
Commitment to Cost Expenditure
Other Cost Classifications
Illustration of Cost Classifications

BASIC FINANCIAL STATEMENTS FOR A MANUFACTURING COMPANY
Product Costs
   Direct Material
   Director Labor
   Indirect Manufacturing Costs
Flow of Product Costs
   Direct Material and Direct Labor
   Factory Overhead
   Work in Process and Finished Goods
Illustration of Financial Statements
SUMMARY
SELF-STUDY PROBLEM
SUGGESTED READINGS
DISCUSSION QUESTIONS
EXERCISES
PROBLEMS

In chapter 1 we described cost accounting as the process of collecting costs for use in financial statements and for management purposes. People are often confused by the various terms used to describe a cost. To prepare cost data so that they can be used effectively, you must understand what a cost is, what is meant by a cost object, how costs can be classified, and how a cost differs from an expense. You also need to know about the typical financial statements used by manufacturing organizations.

This chapter describes the basic cost concepts and terminology that will be used repeatedly throughout the text. After completing this chapter, you should be able to:

1. define *cost* and explain a cost object.
2. distinguish between a cost and an expense.
3. explain each of the following cost classifications:
   a. time period for which the cost is computed.
   b. management function.
   c. generally accepted accounting treatment.
   d. traceability to products.
   e. cost behavior.
   f. decision significance.
   g. managerial influence.
   h. commitment to cost expenditure.
4. prepare basic financial statements used by a manufacturing company, including a cost-of-goods-manufactured statement and a cost-of-goods-sold statement.

BASIC COST CONCEPTS

Definition of Cost

As used in accounting, **cost** refers to an outlay or expenditure of money to acquire goods and services that assist in performing business operations. Occasionally an item will be acquired by giving up an asset other than cash, such as trading marketable securities for inventory. In these cases, cost is a measurement, in monetary terms, of the amount of resources (market securities) used to acquire the goods (inventory) or services.

Goods and services that are acquired by manufacturing organizations include raw materials, production labor, production supplies, land, buildings, and equipment. These and similar costs are incurred when combining raw materials and processing them into a finished product.

Cost Objectives

A **cost objective** is the purpose for which a cost is measured, assigned, or classified. Cost objectives fall into two major areas—financial statement preparation for external users and special report preparation to assist internal management in the successful operation of the business. Terms frequently used to describe these two activities are *cost finding* and *cost analysis*, respectively. Cost analysis includes activities such as preparation of the budget, performance analysis, and pricing decisions.

Within these two major areas, cost has many objectives. This can be illustrated by comparing the word *cost* with a word like *clothing*. Clothing describes a variety of articles that may be used to cover the body. There are many different types of clothing, and clothing can be worn for several different purposes or to accomplish different ends. For example, the same pair of jeans may be worn to class, to a disco, to the beach, or perhaps even to work. The only difference in the jeans is in the way they are prepared through washing and pressing.

As with clothing, costs can serve a variety of purposes and can be used to accomplish different objectives. Some of the common cost classifications are based on (a) time (historical as opposed to future); (b) benefit (an asset as opposed to an expense); and (c) function within an organization (production as opposed to selling and administration).

The same cost can be included in several objects or objectives and can be used as a basis for making a variety of decisions. For example, consider the actual cost of producing a product that has been sold. It would be classified as a historical production cost whose benefit has expired and would be reported in the income statement as cost of goods sold. Management can use the cost data to (a) evaluate a product's profitability, (b) evaluate management's effectiveness in producing the product, or (c) determine how to adjust the product or process to improve future profitability. The same cost data are used, but they might need to be organized and presented differently in each case so that they can be most useful.

Therefore, when we talk about cost objectives, we are talking about the different ways that costs can be classified or grouped. The type of classification or grouping is contingent on the decision at hand and the type of information that is most useful for making the decision.

Cost Objectives and Cost Objects

The terms *cost objective* and *cost object* are sometimes used interchangeably. There is a difference, however, and care should be taken to use the terms correctly.

As stated previously, a cost objective is the purpose for which a cost is measured, assigned, or classified. Since a decision needs to be made, the cost information is identified that will assist in the decision-making process. This provides the objective to be used in measuring, classifying, and assigning various costs.

A **cost object** is generally some visible or tangible product or substance. A computer manufactured by IBM or an automobile manufactured by General Motors are examples of cost objects. The objective is to determine the cost to manufacture a finished product. The object is the finished product itself.

Expired versus Unexpired Costs

A cost is incurred when goods and services are acquired on account or by paying cash immediately. The journal entry to record the purchase is a debit to the resource acquired and a credit to cash or accounts payable. It is important that the resource debited be properly classified and correctly identified as an asset or an expense. If the acquired resource will provide future benefits, the debit should be recorded as an *asset*. This asset is referred to as a **capitalized cost** or **unexpired cost.** If, however, the usefulness or benefit of the asset is received immediately, the debit should be recorded as an *expense* or **expired cost.**

Periodically a firm may incur a cost that produces neither immediate or future benefit. This kind of cost is recognized as a *loss* and singled out as such on the income statement. A massive snow storm that causes the roof on part of the materials storeroom to collapse, destroying both the roof and some inventory, is an example of a loss.

The following are examples of both expired and unexpired costs.

Unexpired Costs	*Expired Costs*
Cost of unsold inventory	Cost of inventory sold
Prepaid rent	Rent for the current period
Unused supplies	Salespeople's salaries
Buildings	Depreciation on buildings

Assets are carried forward on the balance sheet as unexpired costs to be expensed in a future period. When they are written off, they become an expired cost. The name we use for this expiration process differs among assets—for tangible fixed assets it is called *depreciation,* for intangible assets it is called *amortization,* and for natural resources it is called *depletion.* Manufacturing deals primarily with the manufacture of a finished product. The manufactured product and all costs associated with it are classified as unexpired costs because of the future benefit expected when it is sold. At the time of sale the product's cost becomes an expired cost called *cost of goods sold,* and it is matched against sales revenue.

The **matching concept** is the criterion used to determine when a cost (asset) becomes an expense. Income determination is based on the concepts of *revenue recognition* and *matching of expenses.* The revenue recognition concept identifies a point in the earning process when revenue is considered earned. For most merchandising and manufacturing firms, the point of sale is considered to be the most critical event—the point at which the earning process is essentially complete and at which revenue would be recognized in the income statement.

The matching concept requires costs incurred in operating the enterprise to be associated with the revenues they generate on the income statement. The revenues that have been earned during the period are first identified, and the expenditures or costs incurred in generating those revenues are matched with them in the same fiscal time period.

The timing of the receipt of benefit from an acquired resource determines whether it is classified as an asset or an expense. If the benefit is received immediately, it is called an expired cost and is expensed immediately. If the resource contains benefits to be received in the future, it is called an unexpired cost and is capitalized in the accounting records as an asset.

COST CLASSIFICATIONS

Cost objectives were defined earlier as the different ways costs may be classified and grouped or the different purposes for which costs are measured. There are several standard cost classifications, and each classification has its own unique terminology. We will provide a rather comprehensive list of ways costs may be grouped, the concepts underlying each, and the terminology commonly used. Remember that the same cost may be included in several or in all of the following classifications.

Time Period for Which the Cost Is Computed

Time can be broadly classified into *past* and *future.* Costs can also be classified according to these time periods (see fig. 2.1). **Historical costs** are those that were incurred in a past period. Future costs, generally called **budgeted costs,** are those that are expected to be incurred in a future period.

EXAMPLE

The $10,000 cost of a delivery truck acquired in 19X3 is a historical cost in the financial statements of 19X4. The $15,000 cost to acquire a new delivery truck in 19X5 to replace the existing truck is a budgeted cost. Notice that the budgeted cost is an estimate. The actual invoice price on the new truck may be higher or lower than the budgeted amount.

CHAPTER 2: BASIC COST CONCEPTS

FIGURE 2.1

Time Period Classifications

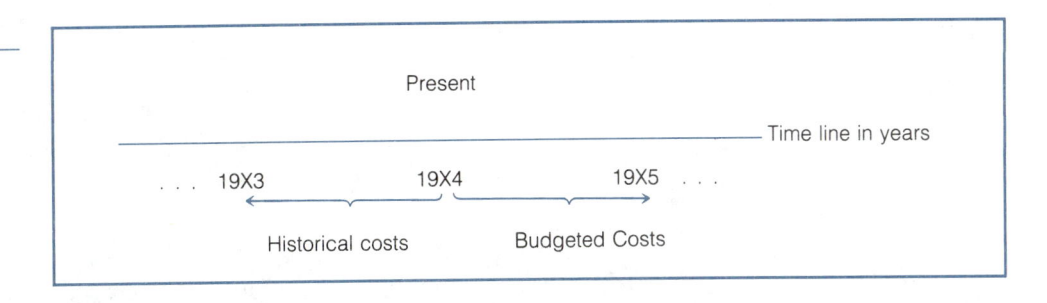

```
                              Present
    ─────────────────────────────┼──────────────────────── Time line in years
        ... 19X3          19X4           19X5 ...
                 ←────────┤ ├──────────→
                 Historical costs    Budgeted Costs
```

Generally no adjustment is made in accounting for the change in the purchasing power of the dollar when comparing historical costs with budgeted costs. High rates of inflation in recent years have created some problems in the comparability of these numbers, but as yet there has not been any comprehensive adjustment. Several methods to adjust for inflation are currently being considered, but the accepted method simply hasn't been decided on.

Management Function

An organization may be separated into functional areas. A manufacturing company's functional areas generally include *manufacturing, marketing,* and *general administration.* One individual, such as a vice president of manufacturing or a vice president of marketing, has primary responsibility for a specific functional area. To evaluate the effectiveness of the functional area and the individual in charge of it, costs also must be grouped by functional area.

Manufacturing costs include costs, from the acquisition of raw materials through production, until the product can be turned over to the marketing division to be sold. Manufacturing costs include the cost of the raw materials, payroll costs for people working on the product, and incidental costs such as taxes, power, depreciation, and repairs associated with the manufacturing equipment.

Selling costs are all costs associated with marketing and selling a product. They include all costs incurred by the marketing division from the time the manufacturing process is complete until the product is delivered to the customer. These costs include advertising, promotional offers, freight to deliver the product, and warehouse costs while the product is waiting to be sold.

Administrative costs are all costs associated with the management of the company and include expenditures for accounting, legal, and administrative activities. Interest costs are also included among administrative costs.

Generally Accepted Accounting Treatment

The alternatives in accounting for a cost are to expense it or to capitalize it. Figure 2.2 illustrates the thought process used in determining how to account for a given cost. Costs that are expensed in the period in which they are incurred are called **period costs.** Period costs possess no future benefits and are generally associated with a nonmanufacturing area of the business. Examples of period costs include advertising, interest, president's salary, and sales commissions.

Product costs consist of all costs associated with the manufacturing function of the business. They include materials, labor, and other factory costs associated with assembling and processing the units. Because the company still holds the product and its usefulness has not yet expired, it is not appropriate to expense these costs. They are capitalized as inventory and held as unexpired costs until they are sold.

FIGURE 2.2

Accounting Treatment Classification

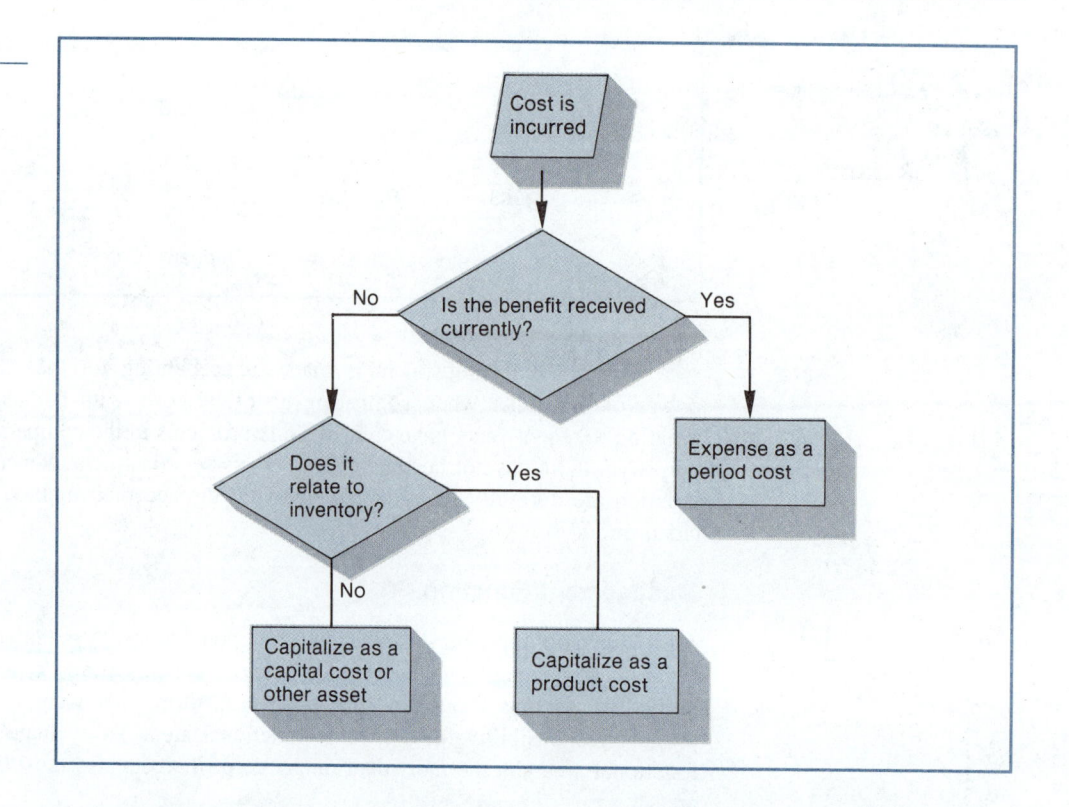

[Flowchart: Cost is incurred → Is the benefit received currently? If Yes → Expense as a period cost. If No → Does it relate to inventory? If Yes → Capitalize as a product cost. If No → Capitalize as a capital cost or other asset.]

Capital costs are similar to product costs in that they are also capitalized as assets. However, *capital cost* is the term used to describe the acquisition of plant and equipment. These items are capitalized as tangible fixed assets and are depreciated over their useful lives. Product costs are reserved for inventoriable costs associated with the manufacturing process.

Traceability to Products

A **direct cost** is one that can be economically traced to a single cost object. In manufacturing, the cost object is a unit of finished product. An **indirect cost** is one that is not directly traceable to the manufactured product, is associated with the manufacture of two or more units of finished product, or is an immaterial cost that cannot be economically traced to a single unit of finished product.

A comparison of the labor cost of an assembly worker and a repairperson in a cabinet shop will illustrate the difference between a direct and an indirect cost. The assembly worker's salary is typically classified as a direct cost because it is a significant portion of the cabinet's total cost and because it is easy to trace the assemblyworker's efforts to a particular set of cabinets.

The machine repairperson's salary would probably be classified as an indirect cost because it is difficult or impossible to trace that individual's efforts to a unit of output. The repairperson is responsible for keeping all machines running properly. Since he or she works on several machines and the machines work on several different cabinets each day, we cannot trace this person's salary to a particular set of cabinets. The lack of traceability requires that it be classified as an indirect cost.

The economics of tracing a cost to a particular unit of finished product is an important distinction between direct costs and indirect costs. Take a consumer product that requires a few screws and a little glue to complete the assembly. Both of these items can be traced to a particular unit of finished product and would, therefore, qualify as direct costs. However, these items are usually classified as indirect costs if their dollar amounts are immaterial when compared to the other materials going into the product. Also, the cost involved in tracing and recording the items as direct costs would be much greater than the benefit of having that information.

Cost Behavior

Cost behavior describes how a cost changes with time or with changes in volume. **Variable costs** are costs that vary proportionately in total as the volume of production or sales changes. For example, if it takes $10 of lumber to make one unit of finished product and if five units are produced, the total cost of the lumber is $50. The total variable cost increases proportionately with the number of units produced, but the cost of each unit remains the same.

Fixed costs remain constant in dollar amount as volume of production or sales changes. Straight-line depreciation on a piece of equipment is an example of a fixed cost. The amount of depreciation is the same regardless of the number of units produced.

Decision Significance

A decision involves making choices among alternative courses of action. The decision maker generally collects cost information to assist in making the decision. **Relevant costs** are future costs that differ with the various decision alternatives. They are costs that make a difference in a decision-making process. **Irrelevant costs** either do not relate to any of the decision alternatives, are historical in nature, or are the same under all decision alternatives. Irrelevant costs are generally excluded from the cost analysis.

EXAMPLE

Suppose it is Friday night and your best friend wants you to go out on the town. As you discuss the situation, you decide that you will have to take a taxi into town at a cost of $10 and that the alternatives for the evening are a dinner for $40 or a show for $50. You also notice in the paper that the price of a haircut has just gone to $12. The cost of a show the last time you went to town was only $30. You are very cost conscious and want to select the alternative that minimizes your cost. What are the relevant costs?

There are only two relevant costs—the dinner at $40 and the show at $50. The cost of the taxi is the same for both alternatives and the price of a haircut does not relate to either alternative. The $30 cost to go to the show on your last trip to town is historical and also is irrelevant to the current decision.

Managerial Influence

Managerial influence refers to the ability of a manager to control a particular cost. Remember that all costs are controlled by someone at some level in the organization if the time period is long enough. However, when we focus on a particular manager at a particular level in the organization and for a short period of time, there are some costs that can be influenced and some that cannot.

Controllable costs are subject to significant influence by a particular manager within the time period under consideration. *Uncontrollable costs* are those costs over which a given manager does not have a significant influence.

EXAMPLE

Suppose we are evaluating the performance of Sandra, who is the manager of Department D in a pajama factory. Department D has twenty employees. They determine how the pajama pieces are to be cut from the bolts of cloth and cut out the pieces. The amount of cloth used and the amount wasted are items that Sandra can influence. The costs associated with these are controllable costs.

Department D was recently moved from the old section of the factory into the new wing. The depreciation on the section it occupies has more than doubled with the move. Depreciation expense to Sandra is an uncontrollable cost. It results from a decision to build a new wing on the factory and to move Department D into it. Sandra had no input into these decisions. The cost of the building and depreciation on it is controlled by someone at a higher level of management.

Commitment to Cost Expenditure

Commitment to a cost expenditure focuses on fixed costs as opposed to variable costs and on budgeted costs as opposed to historical costs. Budgeted fixed costs can be broadly classified as committed costs and discretionary costs.

A **committed cost** is one that is an inevitable consequence of a previous commitment. Property tax budgeted for the coming year is an example of a committed cost. Suppose top management made the decision two years ago to construct a new warehouse. After it was completed, the tax commission placed an assessed value on it, and a property tax notice is now received annually according to the tax laws. The property taxes must be paid or the warehouse will be seized by the tax authority and sold to cover the unpaid taxes. Property tax is a committed cost that resulted from the decision to construct the warehouse.

A **discretionary cost,** also called a **programmed cost** or a **managed cost,** is one for which the amount or the time of incurrence is a matter of choice. There are some nonrecurring costs for which a final commitment has not yet been made and that can be postponed until a future period or cancelled entirely. Replacing the carpet in the administrative offices and repainting the walls of the factory are examples of discretionary costs where the right *timing* is a matter of judgment. Even though the carpet is beginning to show some wear, it could continue to be used for several months without any interruption to normal operations.

Another type of discretionary cost is one that is part of normal recurring operations and fills a function that is necessary for the operation and maintenance of facilities, but it can be changed in amount by management decision. Advertising, employee training, or outside consulting services are examples of discretionary costs where the right *amount* is a matter of judgment. Employee training is both normal and necessary for efficient operations. However, the amount of training and the related cost of the training programs may vary at management's discretion.

Other Cost Classifications

Several other cost classifications are frequently used in discussing cost accounting and management decisions but generally are excluded from the record-keeping process. Their primary usefulness is in helping to place in correct perspective the potential benefit of a possible course of action. These classifications include marginal costs, out-of-pocket costs, sunk costs, and opportunity costs.

Marginal costs, also called **incremental costs,** are the costs associated with the next unit or the next project. The term **marginal cost** is widely used in economics to refer to the added cost associated with the production of an additional unit of output. The accounting use is an adaptation of the economic concept. It refers to the incremental cost associated with an additional project, as opposed to the next discrete unit.

Out-of-pocket costs are costs that must be met with a current expenditure. Generally, an out-of-pocket cost is a cash expenditure associated with a particular decision alternative. For example, if you decide to drive your boss to lunch and pick up the tab for $15, your out-of-pocket cost for the luncheon decision is $15. The total cost associated with your decision would have to include gas, oil, and wear and tear on your automobile. However, these costs are either historical or have not yet been incurred and are not considered to be out-of-pocket costs of the luncheon.

Sunk costs are defined as past costs that have already been incurred. Because sunk costs are historical costs, they are generally irrelevant to decisions affecting the current or future use of the asset. Let's continue with the previous example and suppose that your automobile was purchased two years ago for $7,000. The $7,000 cost is referred to as a sunk cost and is not relevant to decisions relating to the automobile's current and future use. The fact that you paid $7,000 as opposed to $5,000 does not affect your decision to use it to drive to lunch. It will continue to depreciate in the parking lot the same as while driving it to the restaurant.

Opportunity cost is defined as the cost or value of an opportunity forgone when one course of action is chosen over another. Opportunity cost is not an out-of-pocket cost, or even a future cost associated with the selected alternative, but represents the lost opportunity associated with each of the alternatives that are rejected.

EXAMPLE

Suppose you work in a warehouse and your employer comes to you at lunch and indicates that a large shipment of merchandise is scheduled to arrive at 5:00 P.M. He inquires about the possibility of working two overtime hours at $15 per hour ($15 × 2 = $30) to assist in unloading and storing the merchandise. You are to tell him whether or not you will be able to do it by 3:00 P.M.

During lunch you remember the community league baseball game is scheduled for 6:00 P.M., and you decide to support the team and play the game rather than work the overtime. The opportunity cost associated with your decision is $30. This amount ($30) is the cost (value) of the opportunity forgone (unload the merchandise) by choosing to play the ball game.

Illustration of Cost Classifications

There are many interrelationships and overlaps in the preceding classifications. A given cost may appear in several different classifications. The key is to identify the cost object and then to classify the cost according to the cost objective. A short example will illustrate the interrelations and the classification process.

EXAMPLE

Julie Bean is the production manager for a garment manufacturer. A decision needs to be made about the type of fabric to be used to make a shirt. The fabric that has been used in the past cost $4.00 per yard, but it is currently unavailable. Similar fabric from another supplier will cost $5.00 per yard. The fabric cost can be classified as follows:

1. Time period: The $4.00 cost is an *historical cost,* whereas the $5.00 cost is a *budgeted cost*.
2. Management function: The fabric cost is a *manufacturing cost*.

3. Accounting treatment: Whatever is paid for the fabric will be capitalized as a *product cost* and carried in inventory until it is sold.
4. Traceability to product: The fabric is a *direct cost* because it represents a significant portion of the cost of the product and can be traced to a specific unit of finished product.
5. Cost behavior: Both the $4.00 and $5.00 costs per yard are *variable costs*. The total fabric cost increases proportionately with the number of yards purchased.
6. Decision significance: In making a purchase decision, the $4.00 cost is *irrelevant*. The $5.00 cost is *relevant* because it can be compared with the price of other fabrics of similar quality to select the best alternative.
7. Managerial influence: For Julie Bean this is a *controllable cost* because she is in charge of production and can control the amount produced and the quality of the fabric.
8. Other: The fabric is an *out-of-pocket cost* associated with producing additional shirts.

As can be seen from the list and preceding discussion, there are a variety of objectives for which costs can be measured. Figure 2.3 illustrates the cost objectives and classifications commonly used. Each of these will be discussed in more detail throughout the text as we apply them to cost accounting procedures and management decisions.

BASIC FINANCIAL STATEMENTS FOR A MANUFACTURING COMPANY

Financial statements for a manufacturing company are slightly different than financial statements for a merchandising or service organization. The basic difference is the presence of several inventories and a manufacturing process. Service organizations have no significant inventory and do no manufacturing. For example, law firms provide legal services and accounting firms provide accounting services. A service organization's costs are for the operating and administrative activities carried on in producing the service.

Merchandising organizations, such as wholesalers and retailers, purchase products in a saleable form and provide the products to others in convenient and attractive locations. During the holding period, product costs are recorded as finished goods inventory. Costs incurred by retailers are for selling, administration, and the cost of merchandise purchased for resale.

Manufacturing organizations perform selling and administrative functions similar to retail firms. However, instead of purchasing goods that are ready for resale, a manufacturing firm buys raw materials, labor, and other components needed to perform the manufacturing function of converting the raw materials into finished products. This difference shows up in the cost-of-goods-sold statements illustrated in figure 2.4. In addition, the balance sheet at the end of the period will show ending inventories for raw materials, work in process, and finished goods. Our objective here is to explain the computation of cost of goods manufactured and to illustrate the development of external financial statements for a manufacturing organization.

Accounting for the manufacturing process has the *finished product* as the primary *cost object*. The cost accounting system, when applied to the *cost finding* objective, is designed to accumulate the manufacturing costs and assign them to the units produced. We will first identify the terminology used for the different types of manufacturing costs and then illustrate how they are combined into a statement of cost of goods manufactured.

FIGURE 2.3

Cost Classifications and Terminology

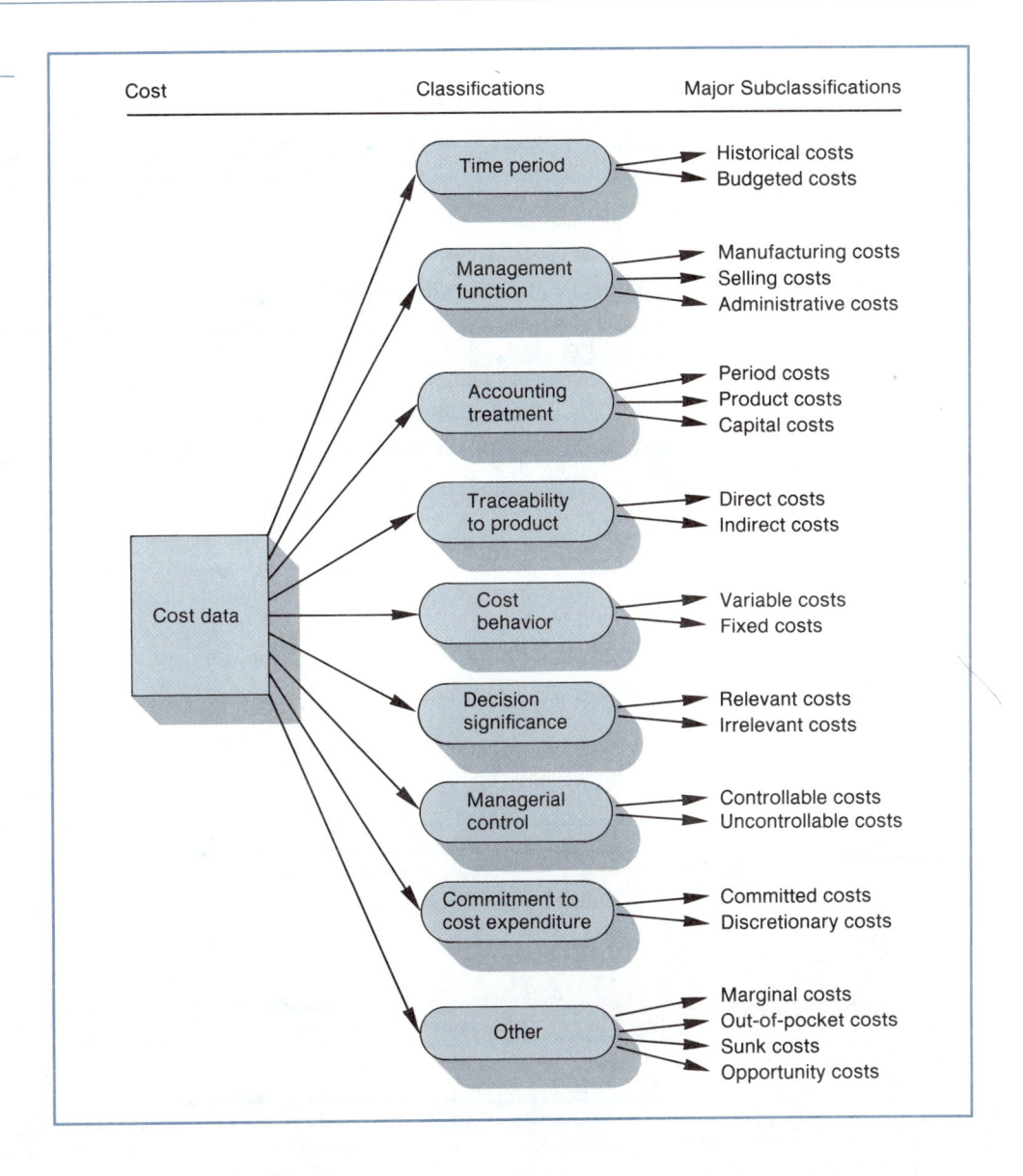

Cost	Classifications	Major Subclassifications
Cost data	Time period	Historical costs Budgeted costs
	Management function	Manufacturing costs Selling costs Administrative costs
	Accounting treatment	Period costs Product costs Capital costs
	Traceability to product	Direct costs Indirect costs
	Cost behavior	Variable costs Fixed costs
	Decision significance	Relevant costs Irrelevant costs
	Managerial control	Controllable costs Uncontrollable costs
	Commitment to cost expenditure	Committed costs Discretionary costs
	Other	Marginal costs Out-of-pocket costs Sunk costs Opportunity costs

FIGURE 2.4

Cost-of-Goods-Sold Statement for Merchandising and Manufacturing Firms

Merchandising

Beginning inventory	$125,000
Plus: Purchases (net)	675,000
Goods available for sale	$800,000
Less: Ending inventory	150,000
Cost of goods sold	$650,000

Manufacturing

Beginning finished-goods inventory	$ 75,000
Plus: Cost of goods manufactured	900,000
Goods available for sale	$975,000
Less: Ending finished-goods inventory	100,000
Cost of goods sold	$875,000

Product Costs

Product costs are classified for accounting purposes into direct material, direct labor, and indirect manufacturing costs. The criteria used in the classification are the type of cost, traceability to a particular unit of finished product, and materiality.

Direct Material Product costs that relate to the use of raw materials and supplies must be identified as either direct material or indirect material. **Direct material** includes the raw material components that can be physically identified with or traced to the finished product. It is distinguished from indirect material by the ability to identify it economically with a finished product. Indirect material lacks traceability to the finished product and is included as an element of indirect manufacturing costs.

The type of manufacturing process and the products being produced must be identified to evaluate whether a raw material input is direct or indirect. For example, paper used in a printing shop would be classified as direct material. The paper is a significant part of each printing job and can be easily identified with the finished product. However, paper used in a glass factory to pack around the finished products for shipping would probably be classified as indirect material. Here the paper is an insignificant part of the finished product, and it is not economically feasible to identify the quantity and cost of the paper used with each product. Other examples of direct materials include wheat in a flour mill, seats to be installed in manufacturing an airplane, and lumber in manufacturing wooden tables.

Direct Labor Salaries and wages properly classified as product costs must be separated into direct labor or indirect labor for accounting purposes. **Direct labor** includes the cost of employees who work directly on the product and whose efforts can economically be traced to a particular unit of finished product. The salary of a lathe operator in a machine shop and a mechanic's wage in an auto repair shop are examples of direct labor.

Indirect labor lacks traceability and is included as an element of indirect manufacturing costs.

Indirect Manufacturing Costs All manufacturing costs other than direct materials and direct labor are classified as **indirect manufacturing costs.** There are several other titles commonly used to describe this group of manufacturing costs, including *factory overhead, manufacturing overhead,* and *factory burden.* Although *indirect manufacturing* cost is more descriptive of the type of costs it includes, **factory overhead** is used more frequently in practice. Become familiar with each of these terms and recognize that they all refer to the same class of manufacturing costs.

Any product costs that cannot be classified as direct material or as direct labor are included in factory overhead and include the following:

1. indirect materials, such as glue, nails, screws, and sandpaper.
2. indirect labor, such as a supervisor's salary and janitorial services.
3. taxes on manufacturing facilities.
4. utilities for the manufacturing process.
5. depreciation on manufacturing facilities.

Factory overhead arises from various sources that can be grouped into three main categories: (*a*) current-period disbursements for items such as utility and telephone bills of the factory, (*b*) reassignments or regroupings from current asset or current liability accounts for indirect materials and indirect labor, and (*c*) end-of-period adjusting entries for depreciation, expired insurance, and other amortizations of previously incurred costs.

CHAPTER 2: BASIC COST CONCEPTS

FIGURE 2.5

Relationship of Manufacturing Costs

	Other Classifications	
Production Costs	*Prime Cost*	*Conversion Cost*
Direct material	★	
Direct labor	★	★
Factory overhead		★

Prime costs and conversion costs are two other terms used to describe production costs. **Prime costs** are the most important or significant costs traceable to units of finished product. They include direct material and direct labor. **Conversion costs** are those required to convert raw materials into a finished product and consist of direct labor and factory overhead. As noted earlier, the same cost may be given different titles and used for different purposes. Paper in a copy center, for example, would be classified as direct material for accounting purposes, but it would also be called a prime cost. These relationships are illustrated in figure 2.5.

Flow of Product Costs

Manufacturing enterprises typically have three inventory accounts to support the flow of costs through the production process—raw materials inventory, work-in-process inventory, and finished-goods inventory. The flow of costs through these manufacturing accounts is illustrated in a T-account form shown in figure 2.6.

Direct Material and Direct Labor Purchased raw materials are recorded in the raw materials inventory account and held there until they are requisitioned by a production super-

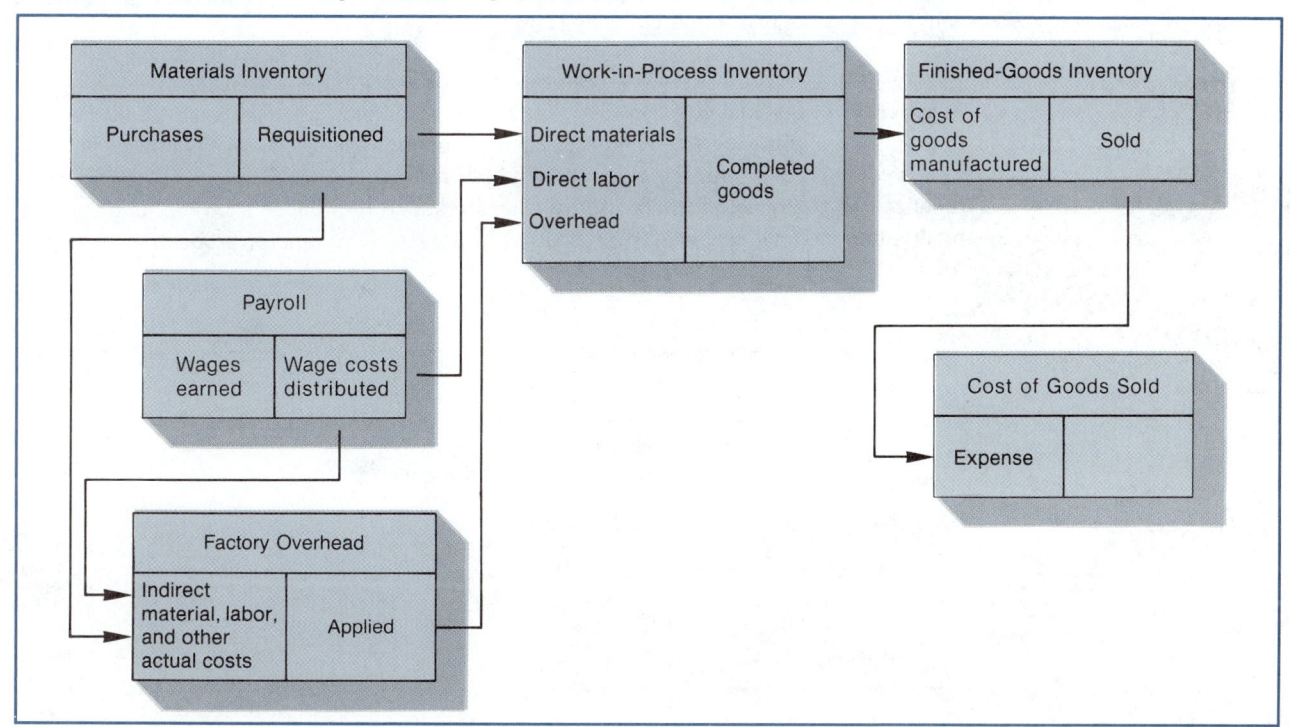

FIGURE 2.6 Flow of Costs Through Manufacturing Accounts

visor. Direct materials are transferred into the work-in-process inventory, whereas indirect materials are transferred to an account called factory overhead. Payroll obligations to production workers are paid through normal payroll channels. Direct labor is tranferred into work in process but indirect labor is transferred to factory overhead. The factory overhead account accumulates the actual indirect manufacturing costs as debit entries. Periodically, overhead is applied to work in process.

Factory Overhead Most firms find it necessary to make advance estimates of factory overhead and to use predetermined factory overhead rates to charge overhead into production. We will explain why this is done and illustrate how it is accomplished.

The input relationship of direct materials and direct labor costs to the product is generally one-to-one. As units of product are produced, the materials and labor costs must be incurred. Therefore, it is possible and logical to make a direct charge to the units for these costs as they are incurred. However, the situation is quite different for factory overhead, because those costs are indirect to the product, and the one-to-one relationship does not exist for most overhead items. For example, facilities costs (depreciation and taxes on equipment and buildings) are related to time periods, not to units produced. Therefore, special procedures are required to assign these costs to the units produced during a specific period of time. Also, many items of overhead that vary with the number of units produced are not found in a one-to-one variable relationship with the product. For example, annual repair and maintenance may vary according to the number of units produced. However, the pattern of weekly or monthly expenditures for repair and maintenance may not relate to the flow of units. Some firms, in fact, do only minimal maintenance when production is high, but they do large amounts of maintenance when production is low or down completely. This type of situation also creates a need for special handling of overhead.

Many firms use a *predetermined factory overhead rate* in an attempt to effectively manage overhead and to charge it to the units produced on an equitable and timely basis. The results of using a predetermined rate will be to charge overhead to the units produced on an *estimated* one-to-one basis; that is, the overhead is treated as if its relationship to the units is the same as material and labor costs.

EXAMPLE

Suppose direct material costs are $10.00 per unit and direct labor costs are $8.00 per unit to produce a chrome-legged, vinyl-seat chair. Suppose also that factory overhead is estimated at $150,000 for the year, and it is estimated that 10,000 chairs will be produced. An estimate of the factory overhead required to produce each unit is computed by dividing the total estimated overhead by the estimated volume of production as follows.

$$\text{Estimated overhead rate per unit of volume} = \frac{\text{Estimated total overhead}}{\text{Estimated volume of production}}$$
$$= \frac{\$150,000}{10,000 \text{ units}}$$
$$= \underline{\$15 \text{ per chair}}$$

Each chair will be charged with the following costs:

Materials	1 × $10 =	$10
Labor	1 × $ 8 =	8
Factory overhead	1 × $15 =	15
Total cost		$33

CHAPTER 2: BASIC COST CONCEPTS

Note that the estimates of overhead to be incurred and the number of units to be produced are made before the production period begins. Actual overhead or actual units produced may turn out to be different from the estimates. This gives rise to *over-* or *underapplication* of overhead, which is a problem we will address later in the text. The use of the predetermined rate enables the firm to do timely and equitable costing, which is not possible if such rates are not used.

Several decisions must be made and several steps taken in deriving predetermined overhead rates. The process includes the following:

1. Estimating factory overhead costs for the period.
2. Identifying an appropriate measure of volume. This is sometimes called an activity base or capacity base. Alternative measures include units produced, direct-labor hours worked, machine hours, and direct labor dollars. Units produced were used in the previous example.
3. Selecting an appropriate volume of output applicable for the production period.

Once the firm has established the overhead rate, it is in a position to charge overhead to work in process and to the product as production occurs.

EXAMPLE

ABC Company has developed the following information during its planning process for the coming year.

1. The estimate or budget of factory overhead is:

    Fixed costs   = $100,000
    Variable costs = $ 75,000 at 10,000 direct-labor hours.

2. The most appropriate capacity base for overhead application is direct-labor hours.
3. The estimate of a reasonable level of activity is 10,000 direct-labor hours.

The overhead rate would be:

$$\frac{\$175,000}{10,000 \text{ hours}} = \$17.50 \text{ per direct-labor hour.}$$

During June, if 1,500 direct-labor hours were worked, overhead applied or charged to production would be:

1,500 × $17.50 = $26,260.

During June, overhead incurred would be accumulated on the debit side of the factory overhead account. The amount allocated to work in process would be recorded as a credit to the factory overhead account. Suppose the total overhead incurred was $26,750. At the end of June, the factory overhead position is:

Factory overhead incurred	$26,750 (debits)
Factory overhead applied	26,250 (credits)
Factory overhead underapplied	$500 (debit balance)

The accounting, reporting, and analytical treatments of the over- or underapplied factory overhead will be presented in chapter 14.

Work in Process and Finished Goods The work-in-process inventory contains the cost associated with the units under construction. A "cost attach" concept is frequently used to describe the cost accumulation process while in the work-in-process inventory. Raw materials are changed into finished products as a result of the conversion costs. We account for these costs as if they "attach" to the raw materials. When the units are complete, a manufacturing cost per unit is computed by dividing total product costs by the units produced. The cost associated with the finished units is transferred to the finished-goods inventory account and held there until the units are sold. The cost associated with the units sold is then expensed as part of cost of goods sold.

Illustration of Financial Statements

Manufacturing companies have the same financial statements as other profit-oriented businesses—a balance sheet, an income statement, a statement of changes in owners' equity, and a statement of cash flows. The balance sheet and the income statement, however, must be modified slightly to include the additional inventories and the results of the manufacturing process.

The balance sheet of a manufacturing firm shows three inventory balances—raw materials, work in process, and finished goods. The income statement shows cost of goods manufactured in the cost-of-goods-sold sections and has a schedule to summarize the work-in-process activities for the period. It shows the beginning balance in work in process, plus direct material, direct labor, and factory overhead transferred into work in process during the period, and subtracts the ending balance of work in process to give the cost of goods manufactured.

A hypothetical company known as Basic Company will be used to illustrate the manufacturing statements. The Basic Company manufactures a single product called Basic. It is located in Basicville, just south of Chicago. It has a single manufacturing plant and a small company headquarters adjacent to the factory where selling and administrative activities occur. Basic is sold directly to selected retailers throughout the United States by Basic Company's own sales staff. There are two sales territories—an eastern division and a western division.

Results of operations for 19X1, the first year of operations, are summarized as follows:

1. *Production data*. There was no work in process at the beginning of the year. During the year the firm began the production of 12,000 units of Basic and incurred the following costs:

Direct material	$ 54,500
Direct labor	68,000
Factory overhead	136,000

   At the end of the year, there were 2,000 incomplete units still in work in process. These units are incomplete as to material, labor, and overhead. The following costs have been incurred on these unfinished units:

Direct material	$ 4,500
Direct labor	5,000
Factory overhead	10,000
Total	$19,500

CHAPTER 2: BASIC COST CONCEPTS

2. *Administrative costs.* The total administrative costs for the year were $75,000. Basic Company has several accounts to accumulate and control these costs, but we have lumped them together to simplify the example.
3. *Marketing activity and marketing cost data.* During the year 9,500 units of Basic were sold at $35.00 per unit, leaving 500 units in ending finished-goods inventory. Marketing costs totaled $30,000 for the year.

Figure 2.7 illustrates a schedule of cost of goods manufactured. Notice that this schedule summarizes the work-in-process account for the year. "Direct material," "direct labor," and "factory overhead" are combined into "total manufacturing costs." This number is added to "beginning work in process" to give "total work in process," and "ending work in process" is subtracted to give "cost of goods manufactured." Notice that the cost of goods manufactured is divided by the units completed for a "cost per unit."

The cost of goods manufactured is carried to the "cost of goods sold" section of the income statement, as illustrated in figure 2.8. "Cost of goods manufactured" is

FIGURE 2.7

Basic Company
Schedule of Cost of Goods Manufactured
Year Ending December 31, 19X1

Beginning work-in-process inventory		$ 0
Plus: Direct material	$ 54,500	
Direct labor	68,000	
Factory overhead (applied or actual)	136,000	
Total manufacturing costs		258,500
Total work in process		258,500
Less: Ending work in process		19,500
Cost of goods manufactured		$239,000
Cost per unit ($239,000 ÷ 10,000 units) = $23.90		

FIGURE 2.8

Basic Company
Income Statement
Year Ending December 31, 19X1

Sales (9,500 units @ $35)		$332,500
Less: Cost of goods sold		
Beginning finished-goods inventory	$ 0	
Plus: Cost of goods manufactured	239,000	
Goods available for sale	239,000	
Less: Ending finished-goods inventory	11,950[a]	
Cost of goods sold		227,050
Gross margin		105,450
Less: Administrative expenses	75,000	
Selling expenses	30,000	
Total		105,000
Net income before taxes		$ 450

[a]500 units at $23.90 each

FIGURE 2.9

Basic Company
Balance Sheet
December 31, 19X1

Assets

Current:		
Cash		$ 8,000
Accounts receivable		28,000
Inventories:		
Raw materials	$ 34,500	
Work in process	19,500	
Finished goods	11,950	65,950
Total current assets		$101,950
Fixed assets:		
Property, plant, and equipment (net)		570,050
Total assets		$672,000

Liabilities

Current:		
Accounts payable		$ 41,000
Wages payable		4,500
Payroll taxes payable		1,200
Total current liabilities		$ 46,700
Long term:		
Mortgage	120,000	
Bonds	240,000	360,000
Total liabilities		$406,700

Owners' Equity

Common stock	$264,850	
Retained earnings	450	
Total owners' equity		265,300
Total liabilities and owners' equity		$672,000

combined with "beginning finished-goods inventory" to give "goods available for sale." "Ending finished-goods inventory" is subtracted to give "cost of goods sold." Notice that the inventory is identified as finished goods to distinguish it from the inventories of raw materials and work in process. Some companies integrate the schedule of cost of goods manufactured into the cost-of-goods sold section of the income statement. The **gross margin** is computed on the income statement by subtracting cost of goods sold from sales revenue.

The balance sheet of Basic Company for December 31, 19X1, is shown in figure 2.9. Notice that the inventories of raw materials, work in process, and finished goods are included as current assets.

Accounting for the manufacturing activities of Basic Company as illustrated in these examples is part of the cost-finding function of cost accounting. The manufacturing cost per unit was used to value the ending finished-goods inventory and to measure the cost of goods sold.

SUMMARY

This chapter has described basic cost concepts and terminology. Cost is defined as a monetary measurement of the amount of resources used for some purpose. The different ways that costs may be classified and grouped or the different purposes for which costs are measured are called cost objectives.

In analyzing costs for accounting purposes, it is important to distinguish properly between assets and expenses. A cost should be classified as an asset when it has the potential to provide future benefits. These unexpired costs are capitalized as assets and reported on the balance sheet. A cost should be recorded as an expense when its benefits are used up. These expired costs are reported on the income statement.

Costs may be classified by many different objectives—by time period, by management function, by accounting treatment, by traceability to product, by cost behavior, by decision significance, by managerial control, and by commitment to expenditure. It is important to understand the criteria and terminology used in each of these classifications.

The basic financial statements used for a manufacturing company are the same as those used for merchandising and service organizations. However, minor modifications must be made to report additional inventories on the balance sheet and the results of operations in the income statement. The current assets section of the balance sheet reports three inventories: raw materials, work in process, and finished goods. The cost-of-goods-sold section of the income statement contains a schedule of cost of goods manufactured.

SELF-STUDY PROBLEM

Review Incorporated manufactures signs for retail outlets. The following information is available for November, 19X2.

	Inventories	
	November 1	November 30
Raw materials	$ 12,500	$15,000
Work in process	47,700	38,300
Finished goods	116,400	81,200

Raw materials purchased	$ 35,400
Direct-labor cost (5,440 hours @ $5)	27,200
Sales revenue	251,000
Marketing expenses	45,220
Administrative expenses	31,900
Factory overhead costs incurred	52,790

Factory overhead rate is $10 per direct-labor hour worked.

Required

1. Prepare a statement of cost of goods manufactured.
2. Prepare an income statement. Show the computation of cost of goods sold in detail.
3. Separate costs into period and product cost classifications. Compute total period costs and total product costs for November.
4. Was overhead over- or underapplied for November and by what amount?

Solution to the Self-Study Problem

Requirement 1

Review Incorporated
Statement of Cost of Goods Manufactured
November, 19X2

Manufacturing costs:		
Raw materials—Beginning inventory	$12,500	
Plus: Purchases	35,400	
Raw materials available	47,900	
Less: Ending inventory	15,000	
Raw materials used	$32,900	
Direct-labor cost	27,200	
Factory overhead (5,440 hours @ $10)	54,400	
Total manufacturing costs		$114,500
Beginning work-in-process inventory		47,700
Total work in process		162,200
Less: Ending work in process		38,300
Cost of goods manufactured		$123,900

Requirement 2

Review Incorporated
Income Statement
November, 19X2

Sales revenue		$251,000
Beginning finished-goods inventory	$116,400	
Plus: Cost of goods manufactured	123,900	
Goods available for sale	240,300	
Less: Ending finished-goods inventory	81,200	
Cost of goods sold		159,100
Gross margin		91,900
Less: Operating expenses		
Selling	45,220	
Administrative	31,900	
Total		77,120
Net income		$ 14,780

Requirement 3

Period costs:	
Marketing expenses	$ 45,220
Adminisrative expenses	31,900
Total	$ 77,120
Product costs:	
Raw materials used	$ 32,900
Direct-labor cost	27,200
Factory overhead costs incurred	52,790
Total	$112,890

Requirement 4

Factory overhead costs incurred	$ 52,790
Factory overhead costs applied	54,400
Overapplied	$ 1,610

SUGGESTED READINGS

American Management Association. *Direct Costing: A Look at Its Strengths and Weaknesses*. New York: American Management Association (Finance Division), 1964.

Beresford, Dennis R., and Neary, Robert D. "Allocation of Direct and Indirect Costs." *Financial Executive* 48 (August 1980): 10.

Demski, Joel S. *Cost Concepts and Implementation Criteria*. New York: American Institute of Certified Public Accountants, 1969.

Fremgen, James M. *Accounting for Managerial Analysis*. Homewood, Ill.: R.D. Irwin, 1972.

Goodman, Sam R., and Reece, James S. *Controller's Handbook*. Homewood, Ill.: Dow-Jones Irwin, 1978.

Howell, Robert and Soucy, Stephen R. *Cost Accounting in The New Manufacturing Environment*. Management Accounting (August, 1987): 42.

Mackey, Jim. *11 Key Issues in Manufacturing Accounting*. Management Accounting (Janaury, 1987): 32.

DISCUSSION QUESTIONS

Q2–1. Define *cost*.

Q2–2. What is a cost objective?

Q2–3. How does a cost objective differ from a cost object?

Q2–4. What are the basic criteria used to distinguish between expensing and capitalizing an expenditure? Explain the difference between an expense and a loss.

Q2–5. Are financial statements prepared according to generally accepted accounting procedures based primarily on historical costs or budgeted costs? Explain.

Q2–6. Are management reports prepared to assist managers in making wise decisions based primarily on historical costs or budgeted costs? Explain.

Q2–7. What is meant by the functional areas of an organization?

Q2–8. Distinguish between product and period costs.

Q2–9. What is a direct cost and how is it different from an indirect cost? Give five examples of direct costs, including a description of the product for which it would be considered direct.

Q2–10. What is means by cost behavior?

Q2–11. What criteria are used to distinguish between a relevant cost and an irrelevant cost?

Q2–12. During a performance evaluation a manager said, "Advertising is an uncontrollable cost?" Is this statement true or false? Explain.

Q2–13. When discussing committed as opposed to discretionary costs, are we talking about fixed costs or variable costs? How do budgeted costs and historical costs relate to the same issue?

Q2–14. Define *out-of-pocket cost*.

Q2–15. Define *sunk costs*.

Q2–16. What is an opportunity cost?

Q2–17. Describe the differences in the financial statements of a manufacturing and a merchandising organization.

EXERCISES

E2–1. Cost Terms Match the items in column 1 with the best choice in column 2.

1. Total fixed costs
2. "Incurred" costs
3. Prime costs
4. Cost of goods manufactured
5. Total manufacturing costs
6. Conversion costs
7. Unit variable costs
8. Costs not assigned to products
9. Expenses that are matched against revenues
10. Materials, labor, and factory overhead
11. Work-in-process control
12. Cost of goods sold

a. Costs incurred during a period
b. Total amount remains constant
c. What costs are expected to be
d. Control account for accumulating the costs of production
e. Expired costs
f. Direct materials and direct labor
g. Cost of completed production after adjustment for work-in-process inventories
h. Period costs
i. Direct labor and factory overhead
j. Added cost of a new product
k. Remains constant per unit
l. Costs of manufacturing (or costs of production)
m. Direct materials, direct labor, and factory overhead
n. Cost of goods manufactured adjusted for the finished-goods inventory change

E2–2. Income Statement Johnson Incorporated submits the following data for December 19X2:

Direct-labor cost is $60,000.
Cost of goods sold is $222,000.
Factory overhead is applied at the rate of 150 percent of direct-labor cost.

Inventory accounts showed these beginning and ending balances:

CHAPTER 2: BASIC COST CONCEPTS

	December 1	December 31
Finished goods	$30,000	$35,000
Work in process	19,200	26,000
Materials	14,000	14,800

Other data:

Marketing expenses	$ 28,200
General and administrative expenses	45,800
Sales for the month	364,000

Required

Prepare an income statement with a schedule showing cost of goods manufactured and sold.

E2–3. Income Statement—Profit Percentage

The Hardy Company's ledger shows the following information on August 31, 19X0:

Sales for the month	$157,000
Inventories, August 1:	
Finished goods	2,950
Work in process	2,300
Materials	1,900
Purchases of materials during August	70,000
Direct labor	33,676
Factory overhead is applied at 50% of direct-labor cost	
Inventories, August 31:	
Finished goods	4,635
Work in process	3,100
Materials	2,150
Other expenses incurred during August:	
Marketing expenses	11,560
Administrative expenses	8,840

Required

1. Prepare an income statement for the month of August.
2. Determine the percentage of income to sales, before income tax.

E2–4. Cost-of-Goods-Sold Statement (CPA)

The following data relate to the Barkley Corporation:

	Inventories	
	Ending	**Beginning**
Finished goods	$95,000	$110,000
Work in process	80,000	70,000
Direct materials	95,000	90,000

Costs incurred during the period were as follows:

Cost of goods available for sale	$684,000
Total manufacturing costs	584,000
Factory overhead	167,000
Direct materials used	193,000

Required

Prepare a cost-of-goods-sold statement.

E2-5. Cost-of-Goods-Sold Statement—Unit Cost Determination
The records of Raydeleh Incorporated present the following information on production costs as of May 31, this year (May 31st is the end of the fiscal year):

Materials used	$880,000
Direct labor	580,000
Indirect labor	92,000
Light and power	8,520
Depreciation	9,400
Repairs to machinery	11,600
Miscellaneous factory overhead	58,000
Work-in-process inventory, June 1, last year	82,400
Finished-goods inventory, June 1, last year	68,600
Work-in-process inventory, May 31, this year	85,000
Finished-goods inventory, May 31, this year	63,000

During the year 36,000 units were completed.

Required

Assume actual overhead is considered in requirements 1 and 2:

1. Prepare a cost-of-goods-sold statement for the year ending May 31, this year.
2. Determine the unit cost of goods manufactured for the year.
3. Determine the amount of over- or underapplied factory overhead if the company had applied factory overhead on the basis of 30 percent of direct labor.

E2-6. Costs Concepts (from CMA exam)

1. For a manufacturing company, which of the following is an example of a period rather than a product cost?
    a. depreciation on factory equipment
    b. wages of salespeople
    c. wages of machine operators
    d. insurance on factory equipment
2. Prime cost and conversion cost share what common element of total cost?
    a. variable overhead
    b. fixed overhead
    c. direct materials
    d. direct labor
3. Indirect materials are:
    a. a prime cost.
    b. a fixed cost.
    c. an irrelevant cost.
    d. a facory overhead cost.
4. Factory overhead:
    a. is a prime cost.
    b. can be a variable cost or a fixed cost.
    c. can only be a fixed cost.
    d. includes all factory labor

CHAPTER 2: BASIC COST CONCEPTS 41

5. Direct materials costs are a:

	Conversion Cost	Manufacturing Cost	Prime Cost
a.	Yes	Yes	No
b.	Yes	Yes	Yes
c.	No	Yes	Yes
d.	No	No	No

E2–7. Cost Analysis Potpourri—Multiple Choice

1. Use the following information for T Company to answer requirements a through c.

	Inventories	
	Ending	**Beginning**
Finished goods	$95,000	$110,000
Work in process	80,000	70,000
Direct materials	95,000	90,000

Costs Incurred during the Period

Total manufacturing costs	$584,000
Factory overhead	167,000
Direct materials used	193,000

    a. Direct materials purchased during the year were:
       a. $213,000.
       b. $198,000.
       c. $193,000.
       d. $188,000.
       e. none of the above or not determinable from these facts.
    b. Direct labor costs incurred during the period were:
       a. $250,000.
       b. $234,000.
       c. $230,000.
       d. $224,000.
       e. none of the above or not determinable from these facts.
    c. The cost of goods sold during the period was:
       a. $614,000.
       b. $604,000.
       c. $594,000.
       d. $589,000.
       e. none of the above or not determinable from these facts.

2. Information concerning the 19X7 projections of the Elston Manufacturing Company is as follows:

    Net sales of $100,000
    Fixed cost of sales of $100,000
    Variable cost of sales at 60 percent of net sales

What will the projected cost of sales be for 19X7?
    a. $700,000
    b. $600,000
    c. $400,000
    d. $300,000

3. For the year 19X5, the gross profit of Dumas Company was $96,000; the cost of goods manufactured was $340,000; the beginning inventories of goods in process and finished goods were $28,000 and $45,000, respectively; and the ending inventories of work in process and finished goods were $38,000 and $52,000, respectively. The sales of Dumas Company for 19X5 must have been:
   a. $419,000.
   b. $429,000.
   c. $434,000.
   d. $436,000.

4. The Carlo Company budgeted overhead at $255,000 for a period for Department A based on a budgeted volume of 100,000 direct-labor hours. At the end of the period, the factory-overhead control account for Department A had a balance of $270,000; actual direct-labor hours were $105,000.
   What was the overapplied (underapplied) overhead for the period?
   a. $2,250
   b. $(2,250)
   c. $15,000
   d. $(15,000)

E2–8. Basic Cost Analysis—Multiple Choice
Selected data concerning the past fiscal year's operations of the Televans Manufacturing Company are presented here (000's omitted).

	Inventories Beginning	Ending
Raw materials	$75	$ 85
Work-in-process	80	30
Finished-goods	90	110

Other data:

Raw materials used	$326
Total manufacturing costs charged to production during the year (includes raw materials, direct labor, and factory overhead applied at a rate of 60% of direct-labor cost)	686
Cost of goods available for sale	826
Selling and general expenses	25

Required

1. The cost of raw materials purchased during the year amounted to:
   a. $411.
   b. $360.
   c. $316.
   d. $336.
   e. Some amount other than those shown above.
2. Direct-labor costs charged to production during the year amounted to:
   a. $135.
   b. $225.
   c. $360.
   d. $216.
   e. Some amount other than those shown above.

3. The cost of goods manufactured during the year was:
   a. $636.
   b. $766.
   c. $736.
   d. $716.
   e. Some amount other than those shown above.

E2-9. Cost Analysis—Working Backwards For the extended Manufacturing Co. during March 19X1, the following facts were available to the controller:

1. Finished goods according to the perpetual inventory records had decreased by $15,000 from the beginning inventory of $120,000.
2. Sales were $700,000.
3. The payroll vouchered during the month was $220,000—all direct labor.
4. The accrual of month-end payroll was $14,000 greater than the previous month—all direct labor.
5. Beginning work-in-process inventory was $80,000. Ending work-in-process inventory was $90,000.
6. Factory overhead for the month was $177,000.
7. Ending inventory for direct materials was $100,000.
8. Cost of goods sold was $599,000.
9. There were no raw material purchases and no over- or underapplied factory overhead.

Required

The controller has asked you to put in good form the calculation of the value of the beginning raw materials inventory.

E2-10. Basic Statement Relationships (CMA) Selected data concerning the past fiscal year's operations of the Televans Manufacturing Company are presented here (000's omitted).

	Inventories	
	Beginning	Ending
Raw materials	$75	$ 85
Work in process	80	30
Finished goods	90	110

Other data:

Raw materials used	$326
Total manufacturing costs charged to production during the year (includes raw materials, direct labor, and factory overhead applied at a rate of 60% of direct-labor cost)	686
Cost of goods available for sale	826
Selling and general expenses	25

Required

Set up T-accounts and trace the flow of the previously given information through the accounts. Furnish missing information needed to complete the picture in the accounts. Among other missing information, be certain to show:

1. the cost of raw materials purchased during the year.
2. the direct-labor costs charged to production during the year.
3. the cost of goods manufactured during the year.
4. the cost of goods sold during the year.

PROBLEMS

P2–1. Classifications of Cost Several classifications and subclassifications may be used to describe costs. A list of subclassifications (not exhaustive) follows.

1. Historical costs
2. Budgeted costs
3. Period costs
4. Product costs
5. Direct costs
6. Indirect costs
7. Variable costs
8. Fixed costs
9. Committed costs
10. Discretionary costs
11. Manufacturing costs
12. Selling and administrative costs
13. Controllable costs
14. Uncontrollable costs
15. Sunk costs
16. Opportunity costs

The following are situations that involve costs:

1. Marshall Company has noticed that certain unit costs remain relatively constant over a wide volume range.
2. Nameless Company has assembled information about the costs of making blue jeans. The cost of denim was $5.00 per yard during the quarter. The cost of denim is forecast to be $5.25 during the fourth quarter of the year.
3. Stokes Company has manufacturing equipment in operation that was acquired for $300,000 four years ago.
4. Hales Company is reviewing its advertising program, which has cost an average of $300,000 annually over the past several years.
5. The Teller Company has a five-year contract with a janitorial service to clean the office for $500 per month.
6. The mixing department of the Archer Bakery receives services from the repairs and maintenance department. The cost department is trying to decide how to show the costs of repairs and maintenance in the performance reports of mixing departments, as well as for the manufacturing division as a whole.
7. Refer to situation 2. How should the cost of materials be shown on the financial report covering the third quarter?
8. The president of Affluent Company had the company acquire a Cessna jet plane for making trips to the various locations of the company's divisions. What are the costs of operating the jet?
9. You are exploring the possibility of opening a business that would rent live potted plants to various business offices and maintain them. Alternatively, you have an offer to work for an office design firm at a salary of $3,000 per month. You wonder if you should consider the $3,000 salary offer to be in any way connected with the decision to launch the plant business. Should you? If so, how should it be considered?

10. An analyst of the Dexter Company is working on a project that involves replacement of several items of manufacturing equipment with new state-of-the-art items. The analyst has determined that the equipment, which will be replaced if the project proceeds, has an undepreciated cost of $3,000,000. The analyst is puzzling about how to take the $3,000,000 into consideration in the project analysis. What advice would you offer the analyst?

Required

Indicate the cost classification(s) that relate(s) to each situation given and briefly explain your choice. Note that a given situation may have more than a single cost classification relating to it.

P2–2. Inventory Valuation—Cost of Goods Sold and Unit Costs

The cost department of the Randall Corporation prepared the following data and costs for the year:

	Inventories	
	January 1	December 31
Finished goods	$48,600	To be determined
Work in process	81,500	$ 42,350
Materials	34,200	49,300
Depreciation—factory equipment		21,350
Interest earned		6,300

Finished-goods inventory: January 1, 300 units; December 31, 420 units, all from current year's production

Sold during the year: 3,880 units at $220 per unit

Materials purchased	$364,000
Direct labor	162,500
Indirect labor	83,400
Freight in	8,600
Miscellaneous factory overhead	47,900
Purchase discounts	5,200

Required

Assume that Randall Corporation charges actual factory overhead to production.

1. Determine the unit cost of the finished-goods inventory, December 31.
2. Determine the total cost of the finished-goods inventory, December 31.
3. Determine the cost of goods sold.
4. Determine the total gross profit and the gross profit per unit.

P2–3. Income Statement—Cost and Profit Ratios

The records of the Yukon Refrigerator Company show the following information for the three months, ended March 31:

Materials purchased	$1,946,700
Inventories, January 1	
No unfinished work on hand	
Finished goods (100 refrigerators)	43,000
Materials	268,000
Direct labor	2,125,800
Factory overhead	764,000
Marketing expenses	516,000
General and administrative expenses	461,000
Sales (12,400 refrigerators)	6,634,000
Inventories, March 31	
No unfinished work on hand	
Finished goods (200 refrigerators)	
Materials	167,000

Required

Assume Yukon charges actual factory overhead to production and that a first-in, first-out inventory valuation is used for the finished-goods inventory.

1. Prepare an income statement for the period, with a complete backup for cost of goods manufactured and cost of goods sold.
2. Determine the number of units manufactured.
3. Determine the unit cost of refrigerators manufactured.
4. Determine the gross profit per unit sold.
5. Determine the income per unit sold.
6. Determine the ratio of gross profit to sales.
7. Determine the income to sales percentge.

P2–4. Manufacturing Statements—Product Costs and Period Costs

The following data were taken from the records of the Steward Company at the end of the fiscal year just completed.

Direct material pruchased	$102,000
Direct material used	90,000
Direct-labor costs	60,000
Factory supervision	10,000
Machine maintenance and repairs	8,000
Factory heat, light, and power	7,000
Depreciation of factory machinery and equipment	10,000
Factory rent	15,000
Miscellaneous factory costs	2,000
Sales revenue	295,000
Inventories of work in process:	
Beginning of year	25,000
End of year	35,000
Inventories of finished goods:	
Beginning of year	40,000
End of year	50,000
Marketing and administrative expenses	75,000

Required

Assume actual factory overhead is charged to production.

1. Prepare the following for the year just ended: *(a)* statement of cost of goods manufactured and *(b)* income statement, including a cost-of-goods-sold section.
2. Identify the product costs incurred for the year.
3. Identify the amount of product costs that are *(a)* prime costs and *(b)* conversion costs.
4. Identify the period costs for the year.

P2–5. Cost Statement

You have obtained the following information for the year ended December 31 from the Helper Corporation's books and records:

- Manufacturing costs incurred during 19X3 were $1,500,000.
- Cost of goods manufactured was $1,200,000.
- Factory overhead was 50 percent of the amount incurred for direct labor. Factory overhead for the year was 25 percent of manufacturing costs incurred.
- Beginning work-in-process inventory, January 1, was zero. Finished goods increased by $60,000.

Required

Prepare a schedule of cost of goods sold for the year ended December 31 for Helper Corporation. Show supporting computations in good form.

P2-6. Cost Relationships and the Costs of Production The following fragmentary information pertains to the operations of the Data's Missing Company for the year 19X9:

Materials Inventory

1/1 Balance	5,000	
12/31 Balance	2,000	

Work-in-Process Inventory

1/1 Balance	?	35,000 Cost of goods manufactured
Direct labor	20,000	
Factory overhead	10,000	
12/31 Balance	15,000	

Finished-Goods Inventory

1/1 Balance	15,000	
12/31 Balance	?	

Sales were $100,000, which produced a gross profit of 55 percent. Materials are one-third of the current total manufacturing costs.

Required

Bring the T-accounts completely up to date.

P2-7. Manufacturing Statements and Predetermined Overhead Rates Clout & Company applies factory overhead on a direct-labor cost basis. The application rate for the fiscal year 19X3 was obtained from the following budgeted costs:

Direct-labor cost	$2,400,000
Factory overhead	3,600,000

The following information was collected on July 31, 19X3 (balances in inventories):

	July 1	July 31
Work in process	$80,000	$100,000
Finished goods	50,000	40,000

During July, costs were recorded as follows:

Direct materials issued for production	$600,000
Direct-labor costs	240,000
Factory overhead costs	350,000

Required

1. Using the applied factory overhead costs, prepare: *(a)* a statement of cost of goods manufactured and *(b)* a statement of cost of goods sold.
2. Determine the under- or overapplied factory overhead for the month of July.
3. If the factory overhead account had a credit balance of $3,000 on July 1, determine the balance in the account on July 31.
4. Explain some possible reasons for the under- or overapplication of overhead during the month of July.

P2-8. Cost Terms and Concepts You have a job that pays $1,500 per month. While playing Pac Man for the hundredth time, you have an idea for a new video game. You think of resigning from your job and starting a new company to manufacture this game. Your company, Super Games Inc., will rent a small building for $100 a month. You have already paid $100 to assure that the building is available if you decide to go into business making the games. The material cost per unit is estimated to be $5, and the labor cost per unit will be $3. You will need to buy a new piece of equipment that will cost $2,000. A part-time worker will keep the books and make out billings. This worker will be paid $100 a week. A sales commission of $1 per game will also be paid. If you keep your current job, you could sell the rights to the idea to another company and receive a royalty of $1.00 per game.

With respect to your decision about whether you should go into business for yourself or keep your current job and contract with another company to produce the game, classify the costs identified below by placing checks in the appropriate columns.

Cost	Product Cost	Period Cost	Fixed Cost	Variable Cost	Prime Cost	Factory Overhead Cost	Sunk Cost	Opportunity Cost
1. Your current salary								
2. $100 advance rent								
3. Building rent								
4. Material cost								
5. Labor cost								
6. Depreciation on equipment								
7. Cost of part-time worker								
8. Sales commission								
9. Royalty								

P2-9. Summary Problem on Cost Classifications and Statements Using Predetermined Overhead Rates and Incomplete Data

The following information relates to the operations of the Jones Company for the year (000s omitted).

	Inventory/Balance	
	January 1	December 31
Raw materials	$ 750	$ 650
Work in process	400	450
Finished goods	1,250	1,100

Additional data:

Raw materials purchased	$ 500
Direct labor	?
Factory utilities	250
Factory rent	300
Indirect materials	150
Supplies used in shipping to customers	100
Foreman's salary (factory)	50
Finished-goods warehouse worker's salary	40
Total manufacturing costs added this period	2,080

Factory overhead is applied at the rate of $1.30 per dollar of direct-material cost used.

Required

Assume that the raw materials inventory includes direct materials only.

1. Prepare a statement of cost of goods manufactured and sold using applied overhead, with a separate schedule of factory overhead costs showing under- or overapplied overhead.
2. Identify and list the costs of production for the year. Of the production costs, identify prime costs and conversion costs.
3. Identify and list the period costs. Explain how period costs are treated in preparing a complete set of financial statements.

P2-10. Cost Statements and Inventory Determination—Incomplete Data

The recent killer storm that whipped through Denmark and Sweden early in January this year left massive ice jams on most lakes and rivers in the area. One major river overflowed its banks and flooded many areas along the banks in Denmark. Several homes and business establishments were destroyed. The Bluestone Company was one of the firms affected. Its manufacturing plant and all of its contents were virtually destroyed. Unfortunately, the records covering factory operations for the year recently ended were also destroyed in the flood.

Fortunately, the following fragmentary information has been obtained from material that the president of Bluestone Company happened to have in his briefcase:

Inventories at the beginning of last year:	
Materials and supplies	$ 36,000
Work-in-process	64,000
Finished goods	54,000
Purchases of materials and supplies	316,000
Sales	1,100,000
Gross profit % to sales	35%
Factory overhead costs for last year	270,000
Prime costs average 60% of the total manufacturing costs	
Direct labor is 40% of conversion costs	
Factory supplies used	15,000
Cost of goods available for sale	754,000

It is also fortunate that Bluestone carries flood insurance. After the flood, an analysis of partially finished production, held in another warehouse not affected by the flood, showed $25,000 worth of inventory on hand.

The relative proportions of the three cost components in work-in-process, finished goods, costs of goods manufactured, and cost of goods sold are consistent.

Required

The Copenhagen Mutual Insurance Co. needs to have reliable estimates of the costs of all of Bluestone Company's inventories destroyed in the flood in order to settle the insurance claim.

Determine your estimates of the cost of each inventory destroyed in the flood. Show your estimates in well-organized form, giving complete support where needed.

P2–11. Examining Statements for Errors—Revised Statements You and your cousin set up a computer chip manufacturing business (YYC) at the beginning of this calendar year. The year has been exciting, to say the least. Recruiting and training employees, customer relations, planning, and a host of other management activities have occupied both you and your cousin so extensively that you both get home most nights after midnight. You have been at your business before 6 A.M. on most mornings. Business seems to be going along so well that you have taken in another associate to enable you to spread the administrative load and spend more time at home. You sense that a strain has been placed on your marriage and family life.

One aspect of your business has been neglected. Sales, purchase, and expenditure documents have simply been accumulated in a file. The only attempts at formal record keeping have been for employee records and payroll taxes.

At year end, you have requested your cousin's son, who is taking his first accounting course, to sift through the files of financial documents and prepare an income statement for the company now known as YYC and Associate.

Three weeks later, you and your associates are presented the document that follows. You are also given the list of items that follows the document. Your cousin's son is uncertain about whether these items should be considered in presenting the income statement you requested. You have added a few notes of your own at the bottom of the list.

YYC and Associate
Operating Report
December 31, 19X1

Revenues:		
Sales to customers for cash	$175,000	
Partners' investment in the firm	105,000	$280,000
Expenses:		
Advertising	$ 10,000	
Office supplies purchased	3,000	
Rental of building	12,000	
Rental of equipment	2,400	
Heat, lights, power, and telephone	7,200	
Cash purchases of manufacturing materials	72,000	
Salaries and wages earned	96,000	
Purchase of manufacturing equipment	100,000	
Sales commissions	11,500	
Fees paid to product design contractor	12,000	$326,100
Loss		$ (46,100)

List of items of uncertain application:

Sales to customers on credit	$50,000
Accounts payable for purchases of manufacturing materials	35,000
Wages earned by manufacturing workers	80,000
Office supplies in the stock room	500
Raw materials on hand in the storeroom	26,000
Finished computer chips in the finished stockroom—about one-third of the total chips manufactured*	?

*This inventory level is within the range of the average inventory-to-sales level for the industry.

Your notes:

- The rental equipment is a small computer system used for customer billings and payroll.
- The manufacturing equipment has a ten-year expected useful life, and the costs of dismantling and disposal are expected to equal any residual value. Depreciation is expected to be about even throughout the ten years.
- The sales and administrative offices occupy approximately 10 percent of the total space in the building.

Required

1. Do you accept the report prepared by the student (your cousin's son)? Why or why not?
2. If you cannot accept the report, prepare your own report of operations. Be sure to include all schedules normally prepared for a manufacturer, including any support or backup for figures you derive.
3. What additional information, if any, would you like to have? Explain.

Chapter 3

Cost Behavior

Outline

RELEVANT TERMINOLOGY FOR
    MANUFACTURING COST BEHAVIOR
    ANALYSIS
Importance of Behavior Patterns to
    Management Decisions
Total and Unit Manufacturing Costs
COST PATTERNS
Fixed Cost
Variable Cost
Semivariable Cost
Step-variable Cost
Nonlinear Costs
  Increasing Cost
  Decreasing Cost
TOTAL MANUFACTURING COSTS
Product Cost Patterns
Total Cost Curve
Relevant Range of Production
ANALYSIS OF COST BEHAVIOR
Industrial-Engineering Approach
  Raw Materials
  Direct Labor
  Factory Overhead
Historical Cost Approach

Direct Costs: Materials and Labor
Factory Overhead
QUANTIFYING COST BEHAVIOR
Mathematical Properties of a Straight Line
  Fixed Cost Equation
  Variable Cost Equation
  Semivariable Cost Equation
Methods for Developing an Equation
  High-Low Method
  Scattergraph Method
  Least-Squares Method
  Computer Analysis of Cost Behavior
  Comparison of Methods
Application of Cost Patterns
SUMMARY
APPENDIX 3.1: ALTERNATIVE
    APPROACH TO LEAST-SQUARES
    REGRESSION ANALYSIS
SELF-STUDY PROBLEM
SUGGESTED READINGS
DISCUSSION QUESTIONS
EXERCISES
PROBLEMS

The way cost changes with time and with changes in volume is referred to as the cost's *behavior pattern*. Understanding cost behavior patterns is important in classifying and reporting costs, and it is essential in using cost data correctly in decision making. This chapter identifies various cost behavior patterns associated with the manufacturing process and the methods used to quantify them. After completing this chapter, you should be able to:

1. distinguish between total cost and unit cost.
2. identify the various cost patterns that are used to describe changes in cost when there are changes in the volume of output.
3. compute total manufacturing costs and develop a total manufacturing cost curve.
4. develop an equation from a set of data to mathematically express a linear cost relationship and plot it on a graph.

RELEVANT TERMINOLOGY FOR MANUFACTURING COST BEHAVIOR ANALYSIS

One of the cost objectives discussed in chapter 2 was the generally accepted accounting treatment, which includes product costs, period costs, and capital costs. Costs associated with the manufacturing process are called product costs and are capitalized as part of inventory. Product costs are subdivided further into direct material, direct labor, and factory overhead.

Direct material includes the raw material components that can be physically identified with or traced to the finished product. Direct labor is the labor time and corresponding dollars spent in converting the raw material into a finished product. Direct material and direct labor combined are the prime costs of a finished product.

Factory overhead includes all manufacturing costs other than direct material and direct labor. Indirect material, indirect labor, employee benefits, supervision, and depreciation on manufacturing equipment are examples of factory overhead. Factory overhead and direct labor are conversion costs associated with translating raw materials into a finished product.

This chapter uses these manufacturing costs to illustrate cost behavior patterns. Other costs, such as selling, general, and administrative costs, exhibit the same behavior patterns as illustrated for product costs. The procedures shown here for quantifying and graphing product cost patterns are applicable to any category of cost.

Before we begin to discuss behavior patterns and methods of quantifying them, we should explain why they are important and how they are useful to management. Another important item to discuss is the distinction between the total manufacturing cost and the unit manufacturing cost.

Importance of Behavior Patterns to Management Decisions

Cost accounting provides managers with relevant cost data to assist them in operating the business effectively. The management process includes developing an operating plan, implementing the plan, and evaluating the results of operations. Cost behavior patterns are particularly relevant in developing an operating plan and in evaluating the results of operations.

In developing an operating plan, it is essential to know how each cost will behave with respect to time and the volume of production. Some costs, such as rent on the manufacturing facility, will be fixed, and a constant amount must be paid each month. Other costs, such as direct materials, will be variable, depending on the amount of material to be purchased and used for the planned level of production. Costs such as heat and electricity in the factory will be part fixed and part variable. Such costs are called mixed costs or semivariable costs. Some heat and power must be used, even though nothing is produced. However, the usage of both will go up sharply as production increases. To prepare an accurate operating plan, the behavior patterns exhibited by these and other manufacturing costs must be known.

Actual operations seldom go exactly as planned. Perhaps management expected to produce 10,000 units of finished product, but because demand was stronger than anticipated, production was increased to 12,000 units. The actual cost to produce 12,000 units will not be the same as was planned for 10,000 units. In order to obtain meaningful data for evaluating the results of operations, adjustments need to be made in the budget for costs that vary according to the number of units produced. Cost behavior patterns must be known to adjust the variable costs for changes in the volume of production.

Knowledge of cost behavior patterns is also very useful for special management decisions. Suppose management planned to produce 10,000 units of finished product, but because demand is weak it has decided to cut production back to 6,000 units. A good cost analyst who knows the behavior of each cost will be able to advise management on which costs can be reduced and by how much. This will help managers concentrate their energies on reducing the right costs.

Total and Unit Manufacturing Costs

A manufacturing process generally produces numerous units of a product at the same time. Care must be taken in identifying the manufacturing cost as either a total or a unit cost. **Total cost** refers to all costs associated with a particular activity, generally the production of a group of finished products or the cost for a period of time. Total cost can also be limited to a specific category, such as total direct-material cost or total direct-labor cost. For example, total direct-labor cost refers to the total cost of all workers whose efforts are traceable to the finished products.

The **unit cost** is the cost associated with a single unit of product. Unit cost can also be limited to a specific cost category, such as direct material or direct labor. The unit cost of direct material is the cost of materials that are traceable to *one* unit of finished product. Total cost per unit refers to the **total manufacturing costs** (including direct material, direct labor, and factory overhead) required to produce *one* unit of finished product.

The unit cost is computed by dividing total cost by the number of units included in the group. An accurate label should always be associated with a cost, such as "total manufacturing cost" or "direct-labor cost per unit."

EXAMPLE

Bells Incorporated used $120,000 of direct materials, $84,000 of direct labor, and $42,000 of factory overhead to manufacture 10,000 units of finished product. Total and unit costs are represented as follows:

Total manufacturing cost:	$246,000
($120,000 + $84,000 + $42,000)	
Manufacturing cost per unit:	$24.60
($246,000 ÷ 10,000 units)	
Direct-labor cost per unit:	$8.40
($84,000 ÷ 10,000 units)	

Unit cost information is used in valuing the units in ending inventory and in determining the amount of cost of goods sold. Generally accepted accounting principles require manufacturing organizations to value their inventory at cost, which includes prime costs plus a proportionate share of factory overhead.

EXAMPLE

Bells Incorporated, in the previous example, produced 10,000 units at a cost of $24.60 per unit. If 7,000 units were sold during the period, the manufacturing cost would be reported as follows:

Finished-goods inventory: (3,000 units × $24.60)	$73,800
Cost of goods sold (7,000 units × $24.60)	$172,200

COST PATTERNS

Various costs behave differently with changes in time and in the volume of activity. Changes in volume generally have a different effect on total cost than they do on unit cost. There are a variety of behavior patterns commonly exhibited, which include fixed, variable, semivariable, and step variable. The nonlinearity of costs is also a relevant consideration.

Fixed Cost

A fixed cost is defined as a cost that remains constant in total regardless of the level of volume. The salary of a supervisor in a production department, for example, would be classified as a fixed cost. The salary is fixed at, say, $2,500 per month, regardless of the volume of production achieved by the department.

Fixed costs remain constant in total, but the cost per unit decreases with an increase in the number of units produced. In other words, fixed cost per unit varies inversely with volume. Suppose the production department produces 100 units in a given month. The cost per unit for the supervisor's salary is $25.00 ($2,500 ÷ 100 units). If production increased to 1,000 units, the cost per unit decreases to $2.50 ($2,500 ÷ 1,000). At 10,000 units per month, the cost goes down to $0.25 per unit ($2,500 ÷ 10,000 units).

Figure 3.1 illustrates the fixed cost pattern for both total cost and cost per unit when volume changes. The vertical axis represents dollars (total cost or cost per unit), and the horizontal axis represents volume (number of units produced).

Variable Cost

As defined in chapter 2, a variable cost is a cost that changes in total as the volume changes. Assuming a linear cost function, total variable cost increases proportionately with increases in volume. When volume decreases, there is a proportionate reduction in the total variable cost. The piece-rate of a seamstress in a pajama factory is an example of a variable cost. The seamstress is paid $2.00 for each pair of pajamas that are assembled. If 50 pairs are assembled in one day, the total labor cost for the seamstress is $100. If 100 pairs are assembled, the cost is $200

The cost per unit of variable cost remains constant regardless of the volume of production. In the preceding example the seamstress is paid $2.00 per unit, and that amount does not change regardless of the number of pajamas assembled. Figure 3.2 illustrates the cost pattern for both total variable cost and variable cost per unit as volume changes.

FIGURE 3.1 Graphic Representation of Fixed Costs

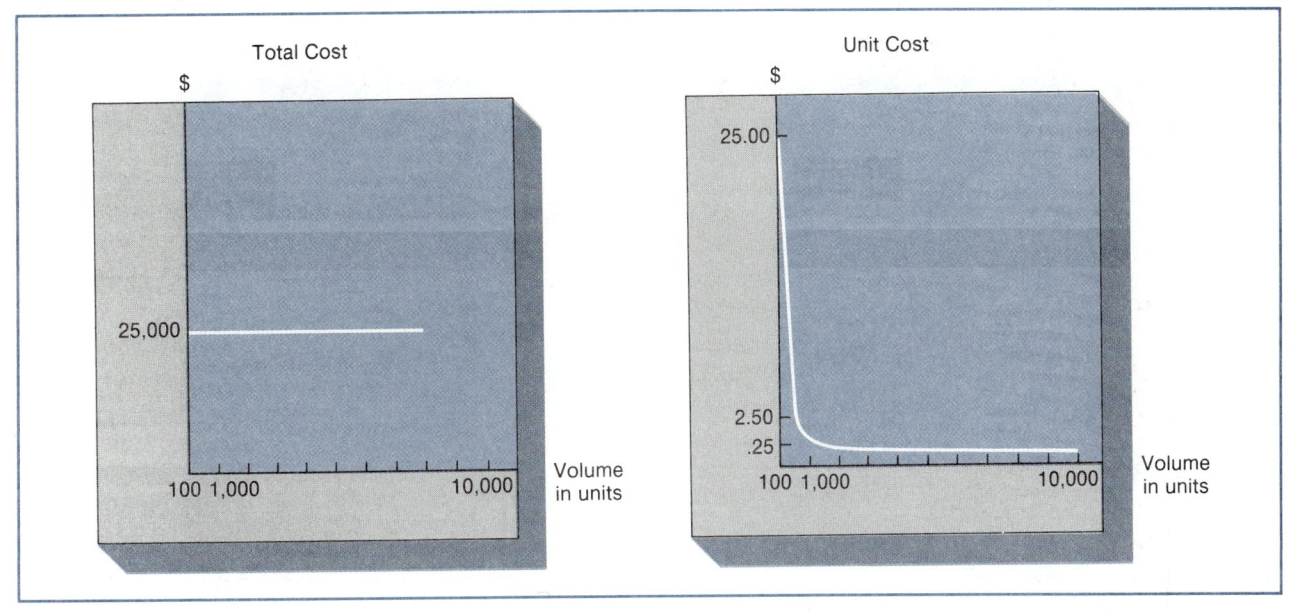

Notice that both total fixed cost and total variable cost were shown as a linear or straight-line relationship. Also, each example was descriptive of either a fixed cost or a variable cost but not both costs combined. There are several costs that do not follow the patterns described here either because they contain both a fixed and a variable element or because they do not follow a linear relationship.

Semivariable Cost

A **semivariable cost** is sometimes referred to as a **mixed cost** because it contains both a fixed cost portion and a variable cost portion. The fixed portion is the minimum cost required if no output is produced, but as output increases, cost also increases, as with a variable cost.

An example of a semivariable cost is the cost of natural gas that is used to heat a manufacturing facility. The pricing structure of some gas companies includes a flat fee, called a hook-up fee, plus an amount for each cubic foot of gas consumed. The price might

FIGURE 3.2 Graphic Representation of Variable Costs

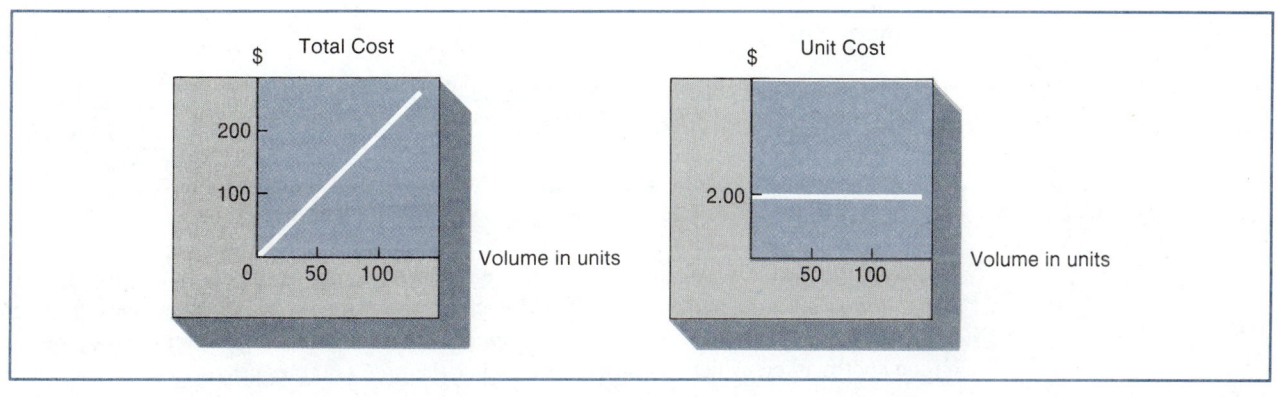

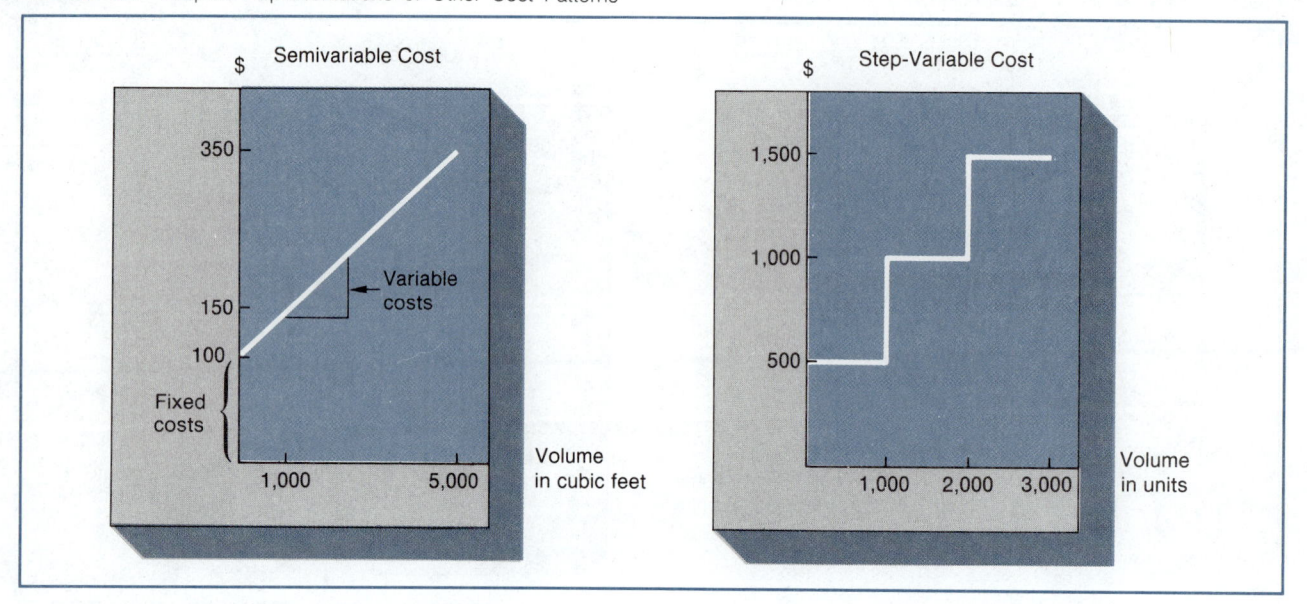

FIGURE 3.3 Graphic Representations of Other Cost Patterns

be $100 per month plus $0.05 per cubic foot of gas. The fixed element is $100 per month, which must be paid even if no gas is used, and the variable element is the $0.05 per cubic foot. If 1,000 cubic feet are consumed, the total cost is $150 ($100 + (1,000 × $0.05)). At 5,000 cubic feet the total cost is $350 [$100 + (5,000 × $0.05)]. Figure 3.3 shows a graphic representation of a semivariable cost.

Step-variable Cost

A **step-variable cost** is a variable cost that increases or decreases in "chunks" of cost with small changes in volume. A given amount of cost will sustain some increase in volume without any increase in cost. At some point, however, the cost must be increased by a fixed amount in order to continue to increase volume. Cost increases come in indivisible chunks and, therefore, the cost curve has a steplike pattern, as illustrated in figure 3.3.

An example of a step-variable cost is a supply clerk who has the responsibility of delivering raw materials to production workers. One clerk with a monthly salary of $500 can keep all production employees adequately stocked as long as production does not exceed 1,000 units per month. When this level is exceeded, an additional supply clerk must be employed at $500 per month, which raises the total cost for supply handling to $1,000. This pattern continues as the volume of production increases.

Nonlinear Costs

A linear cost is one that has a straight-line relationship with total cost remaining unchanged, or, if it changes, the change is in equal increments for all levels of volume. Some costs, however, do not follow this linear relationship. They may increase at a faster rate or a slower rate as volume increases. An example of each follows and is illustrated in figure 3.4.

Increasing Cost A gasoline refinery has established contracts to supply one billion barrels of crude oil at an agreed price of $22 each. If the company wants to increase production above the levels provided by these contracts, it must acquire the additional crude oil on the spot market, which is consistently higher than the contract price.

FIGURE 3.4 Graphical Representations of Nonlinear Costs

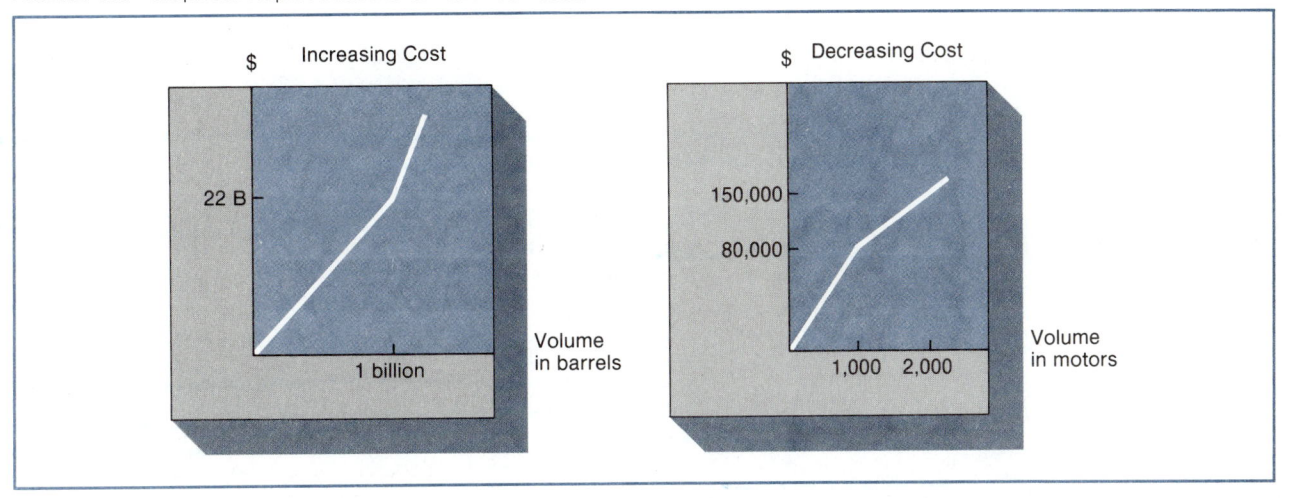

[Increasing Cost graph: $ vs Volume in barrels, showing 22 B at 1 billion]

[Decreasing Cost graph: $ vs Volume in motors, showing 80,000 at 1,000 and 150,000 at 2,000]

Decreasing Cost A mill manufacturer can receive a quantity discount on motors when the number of motors purchased each month exceeds 1,000. The first 1,000 motors cost $80 each, but additional motors cost only $70 each.

Accountants need to understand the various cost patterns and be able to correctly identify the pattern that any particular cost will follow when volume changes. Care must be taken to differentiate between total cost and cost per unit. This ability will be very valuable in understanding the manufacturing process and in using cost data correctly for all types of business decisions.

TOTAL MANUFACTURING COSTS

Product costs are categorized into direct material, direct labor, and factory overhead. Each of these costs follows one or more of the patterns described previously. Two approaches can be used to analyze and quantify cost behavior: *(a)* the industrial-engineering approach and *(b)* the historical cost analysis. In reality, some combination of the two approaches is generally followed. Separate analysis is frequently required on each cost, and sometimes with different analytical tools, to predict cost behavior. We will first discuss the behavior patterns commonly exhibited by each product cost and then discuss approaches to quantifying them.

Product Cost Patterns

Direct material is almost always a variable cost. Manufactured products are always made from some type of raw material, and there is generally a list of materials that specifies the quantities of each required to produce a finished product. Except for waste or dissipation of some raw materials, there is a one-to-one correspondence between the input of raw materials and the output of finished products.

Direct labor is also a variable cost for most companies. Employees typically perform the same function day after day, and there is high correlation between the amount of time worked and the number of finished products produced. However, some factors complicate the analysis of direct labor and make it more difficult to predict than direct material. In some industries, direct labor is relatively fixed within ranges of productivity. For example, one hundred direct laborers may be required to operate the factory when production is between 1,000 and 1,200 gallons per hour. As production increases, additional laborers are required. In these cases, direct labor is more like a step-variable cost, except the steps come in fairly small increments. Also, union contracts sometimes call for a guaranteed wage, which causes direct labor to exhibit a fixed cost pattern.

The presence of a learning curve is another complicating factor. A new employee generally cannot produce as much as an experienced employee. Over time, the speed with which an employee can produce a product increases, and more units of finished product can be produced within any given period of time. When this is measured and graphed, it is called the learning curve. At any point in time, a business will have employees at different points on the learning curve. As old employees leave the company, as new employees are hired, and as existing employees move up their learning curve, the average productivity of all employees will probably not change much over time. This is especially true when there are many employees. Therefore, the effects of the learning curve are generally ignored by companies that produce the same products continually.

Factory overhead is a combination of all cost patterns because it consists of many different kinds of cost. For example, straight-line depreciation on the equipment is a fixed cost. Indirect material is an example of a variable cost. Supervision and custodial work exhibit a step-variable pattern. When all the various costs are combined, the resulting cost curve is a semivariable cost pattern.

The most common pattern associated with each category is summarized as follows:

Manufacturing Cost	Cost Pattern
Direct material	Variable cost
Direct labor	Variable cost
Factory overhead	Semivariable cost

Total manufacturing cost is the combined total of the previously described product cost patterns. The resulting total cost curve is illustrated in figure 3.5. Notice that the total manufacturing cost curve is similar to the semivariable cost curve (see fig. 3.3) in that it contains both a fixed and a variable portion. The fixed portion is composed of the factory overhead costs that are not affected by different levels of production. These include such items as property tax and depreciation on the manufacturing facilities. The variable portion

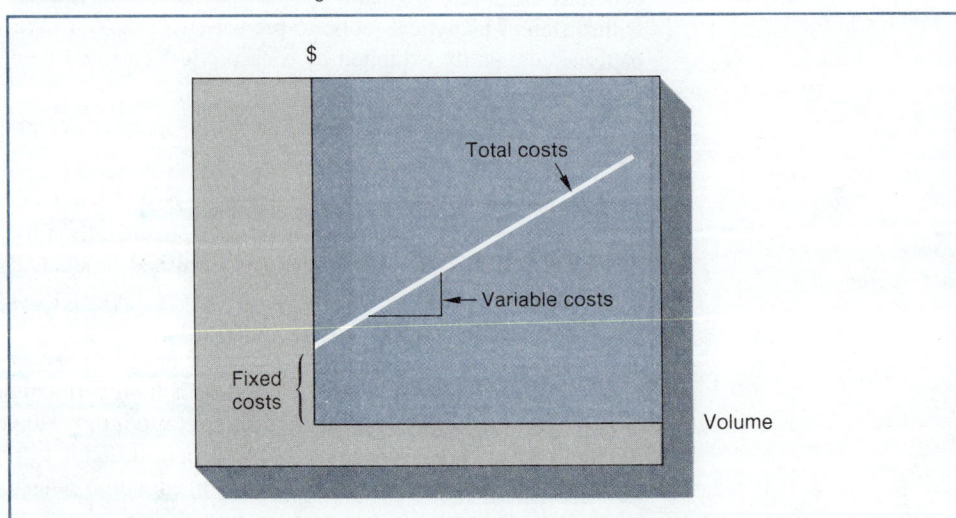

FIGURE 3.5 Total Manufacturing Cost Curve

CHAPTER 3: COST BEHAVIOR

is made up of direct materials, direct labor, and variable factory overhead, which are all dependent upon the volume of production.

Total Cost Curve

The total manufacturing cost curve is shown as a straight line. This is considered an average and a good approximation of all the product costs combined. It should be recognized that some individual costs have a step-variable pattern and others have an increasing or decreasing variable rate. Nevertheless, the major variable costs—including direct material, direct labor, and a large part of factory overhead—are linear. The deviation of other cost patterns is generally minor, and they very often counterbalance each other. Experience has shown that combining them into a straight line is a good representation of total manufacturing costs within the range of production normally achieved by an enterprise.

Relevant Range of Production

The range of operating volume within which the firm normally operates is called the **relevant range of production.** Within this range, the cost relationships can be expected to be reliable. At extremely low levels of production, some fixed costs can be avoided. For example, a supervisor's salary, which is considered part of fixed factory overhead, could be avoided by laying off the supervisor and having another supervisor cover both areas. One supervisor could do an adequate job because of fewer employees and lower production. When these types of cost reductions are employed, the total cost curve approaches zero as the volume of production approaches zero.

When attempting to achieve extremely high levels of volume, some costs will increase at a faster than normal rate. The increase in cost usually results from production problems such as excessive waste of raw materials, labor inefficiencies caused by congested work areas, and additional overhead costs due to excessive repair and maintenance on machinery that is overutilized. When these types of factors are considered, the total cost curve turns up as the volume of production approaches the maximum capacity. This type of analysis is normally employed by the economist. The typical total cost curve used in economic analysis is shown in figure 3.6. The figure also shows the economist's total cost curve with an accountant's total cost curve superimposed over it. Notice that the total

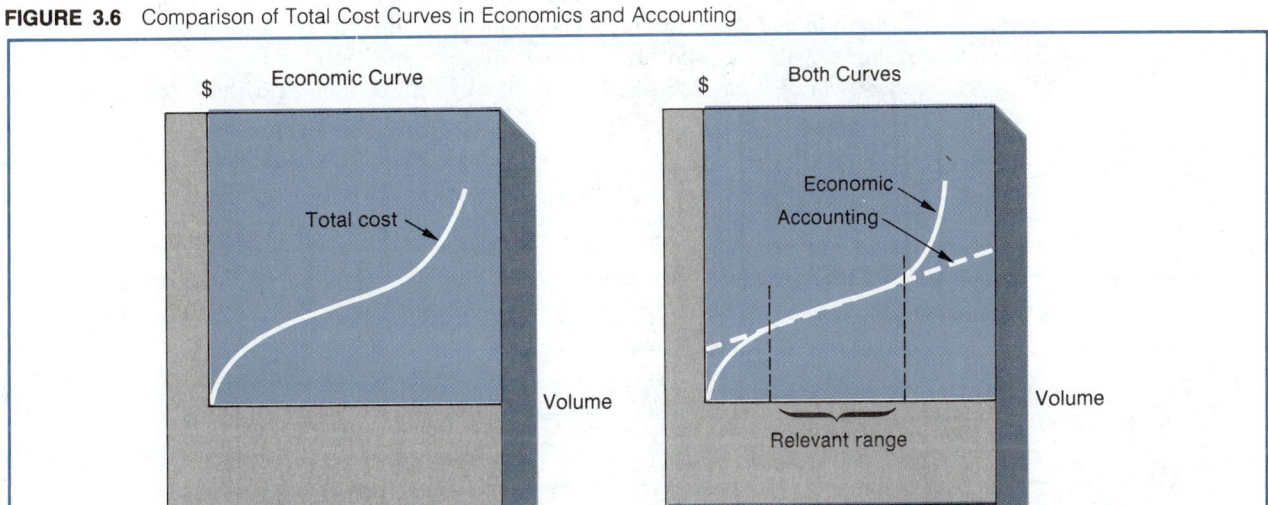

FIGURE 3.6 Comparison of Total Cost Curves in Economics and Accounting

ANALYSIS OF COST BEHAVIOR

Industrial-engineering analysis and *historical cost analysis* are two approaches to analyzing cost behavior. The objective is to develop a mathematical formula to describe each product cost as well as the total cost curve. Both approaches can be used on each product cost, but not with the same amount of ease. Typically, a combination of the two approaches is used in deriving the total cost curve.

Industrial-Engineering Approach

An industrial-engineering approach takes a forward look at the problem and attempts to quantify expected cost behavior. The basic issue is, What *should be* the amount of material, labor, or overhead required to produce a finished product given the production facilities of the enterprise? The total curve is based on the most efficient method of operations and the existing facilities. Therefore, the firm is limited in the short-run by the existing production facilities.

Industrial engineers utilize techniques such as time-and-motion studies and rely heavily on product specifications and raw material characteristics to develop a standard quantity of inputs required to produce one finished unit. They work closely with the financial people in the organization to price the various components of the production process. The price that is expected to be paid during the coming period is generally used.

The process followed by an industrial engineer in developing the individual product cost curves differs for each cost. Raw materials, direct labor, and factory overhead will be considered individually.

Raw Materials Product specifications are important in determining the type, quantity, and quality of raw materials. For example, a product that must be able to operate in temperatures of 40 degrees below zero will probably require raw materials that are much different than if the minimum operating temperature is 60 degrees above zero.

The form and shape of the raw material at the time of acquisition is also important. For example, if the required raw material is a round piece of aluminum 3 inches in diameter, there will be a considerable amount of scrap if the aluminum can be purchased only in large rectangular sheets.

The quality and condition of the raw materials must be closely correlated with the production process. Labor and machine time may be required when raw materials must be preprocessed into a usable form for normal production. For example, the labor standard as well as the raw material standard must be adjusted if the supplier of the 3-inch aluminum pieces mentioned before goes bankrupt and the company is forced to cut its own circles from large rectangular sheets. Labor and machine time that could have been used elsewhere are tied up in preparing the raw materials.

The result of the engineering study on direct materials will be a list of raw materials of a specific type, quality, and quantity required to produce each unit. The purchasing department then prices them at expected prices for the coming period and totals them. This is the raw material cost per unit and the variable cost of direct materials.

Direct Labor Time-and-motion studies are one of the more common techniques that identify the amount of direct-labor time required to perform the activities involved in producing a finished product. A complete time-and-motion analysis would include every job in the manufacturing process. The individual movements required by each worker to produce the product are first identified. Each movement is then timed, giving appropriate allowance for fatigue, breakdowns, and rest breaks. The times are accumulated by job classifications and priced at the expected wage rates for the coming period. The total amount is the variable cost of direct labor.

Factory Overhead Engineering analysis is least effective in making a direct estimate of the amount of factory overhead that should be incurred. Factory overhead is composed of many different types of costs. Individually these costs may be relatively small, but in total they account for a significant part of total production cost.

The various types of overhead costs can generally be identified, and some of them can be quantified as for direct materials or analyzed as for direct labor. Custodial service is an example. The size of the manufacturing facility can be measured, and studies can be performed to determine the number of custodians required, and hence, the amount of indirect labor incurred for custodial service.

Repair and maintenance cannot be analyzed in quite the same way. The amount of repair and maintenance will depend on the number of repair hours that will be worked during the period and the cost of the parts that are used. Studies of existing machines to determine which ones will break down and the amount of time and parts required to repair them probably will not be very accurate. The best information for estimating repair and maintenance for a period, assuming a consistent pattern of equipment replacement, is the amount of repair and maintenance required in prior periods. This utilizes the historical approach discussed in the next section.

A detailed study of each overhead cost would be very time consuming and costly. The resulting formula may be very accurate, yet it would probably be quite complex. The added precision is usually not worth the added complexity.

The industrial-engineering approach and the historical approach are generally combined to determine estimated factory overhead. Historical data is used as a starting point for projecting overhead costs and developing an overhead cost curve for the coming period. Engineering studies are then used to analyze the effects of anticipated changes in specific aspects of factory overhead on the cost curve. This makes the overhead cost curve easier to develop, yet applicable to the coming period.

Historical Cost Approach

An historical cost approach develops a total cost curve from cost data of prior operations. The first step is to collect the historical data to be used in the analysis. Operating data for the past year or two are commonly used. Any prior year or group of years could be used, but the time period selected should be representative of future operating results. The data should include *(a)* the amount of cost incurred for each production cost—direct material, direct labor, and factory overhead—and *(b)* the volume of activity, such as units produced. The data are broken down into short time intervals, such as months, weeks, or quarters, consistent with the reporting cycle of the company.

Direct Costs: Materials and Labor Direct costs for both materials and labor vary according to the number of units produced. Because no fixed costs are involved, the variable rate for each cost curve can be computed by dividing the total cost incurred by the number of units produced.

Factory Overhead Factory overhead is somewhat more complicated because it is composed of many different manufacturing costs that exhibit a variety of cost patterns. Individual cost data on each element of factory overhead may not be readily available for analysis. An approach is needed to analyze total factory overhead to develop a mathematical formula for a semivariable cost curve.

Three methods commonly used to separate total overhead into fixed and variable elements are the (a) high-low method, (b) scattergraph method, and (c) least-squares method. Before these methods are discussed and illustrated, we will review the mathematical properties of a straight line.

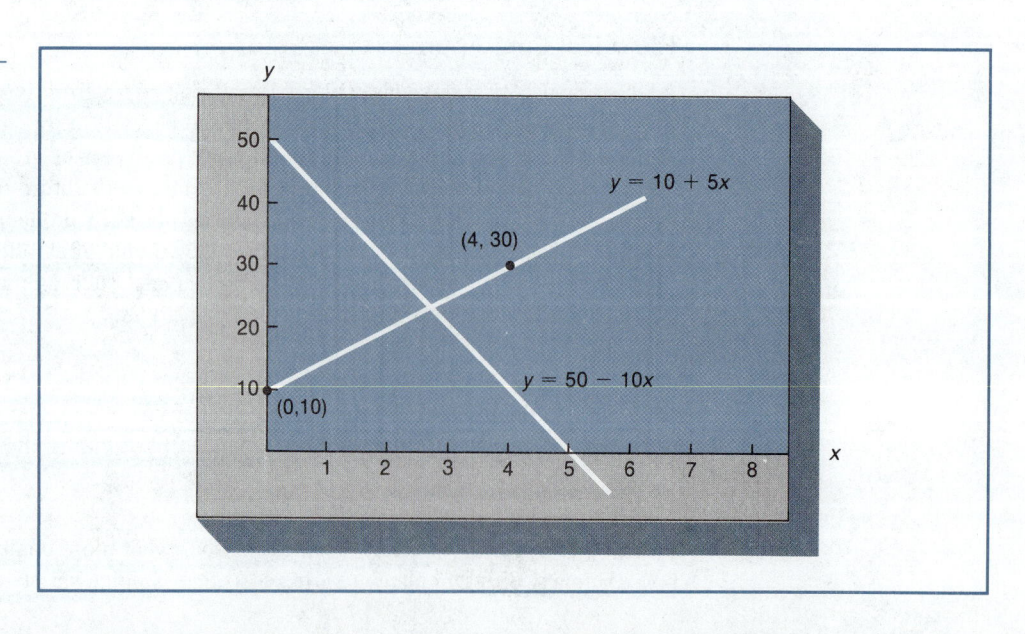

QUANTIFYING COST BEHAVIOR

It is useful when working with different costs and behavior patterns to be able to quantify them mathematically. Each of the product cost patterns can be represented by a mathematical equation. Because we assume linear relationships for almost all cost analysis in accounting, we will limit our discussion to the mathematical equation of a linear cost function. We will first discuss the mathematical properties of a straight line and then discuss several methods used within historical cost analysis for developing an equation from a given set of data.

Mathematical Properties of a Straight Line

Mathematically, a straight line can be described by the following equation:

$$y = a + bx$$

The symbols y and x represent variables. The symbol y is the **dependent variable,** which is the variable under investigation and is described by another variable. The symbol x is the **independent variable,** which is used to describe the dependent variable. The symbols a and b are constants for a given line; a is called the y-intercept and b is called the slope. The **y-intercept** identifies the amount of y when x is zero. The **slope** is the amount of change in y for each unit of x. For example, the equation $y = 10 + 5x$ describes a straight line with an intercept of 10 and a slope of 5. As shown in figure 3.7, the line intersects the vertical axis at 10 and slopes upward at a rate of 5 units of y for each unit of x.

FIGURE 3.7

Mathematical Properties of a Straight Line

When plotted on a graph, the vertical axis represents values of the dependent variable y, and the horizontal axis represents values of the independent variable x. Any two points on a line can be used to plot the straight line. One of the points often used is the y-intercept. For the preceding example, the coordinates of this point are (0, 10), representing the values of x and y, respectively. Another point may be obtained by selecting a value for x and solving the equation for y. For example, 30 is the value computed for y when 4 is selected as the value for x (10 + 5(4) = 30). The point representing the corresponding values of x and y (4, 30) is located on the graph, and the two points are connected with a ruler.

A line that slopes downward has a negative value for the slope. For example, the equation $y = 50 - 10x$ results in smaller values of y as x increases. Thus, y decreases by 10 for each unit increase in x. Since we will be working primarily with total costs that increase as volume increases, we will not be working much with negative-sloping lines.

The straight-line equation can be applied to the various manufacturing costs. The value of a represents the amount of fixed costs, and b represents the variable rate per unit of output. The independent variable x is a volume of output, such as units produced. The dependent variable y is the total cost, such as total direct labor, total factory overhead, or total manufacturing cost. This basic equation may be used as a cost formula to represent or predict total costs when volume changes.

$$y = a + bx$$
Total cost = Fixed cost + Variable rate per unit × Volume

Fixed Cost Equation A manufacturing cost such as a supervisor's salary, which consists of fixed cost entirely, would be represented by the following equation:

$$y = a + b(x)$$
Salary = \$2,500 + 0(x)

Figure 3.8 shows that the slope of the line is zero. Regardless of the volume of output, the supervisor's salary remains at \$2,500. Even when x is zero, the supervisor will continue to be paid \$2,500. Therefore, the line is horizontal and intersects the y axis at \$2,500.

FIGURE 3.8

Cost Equations

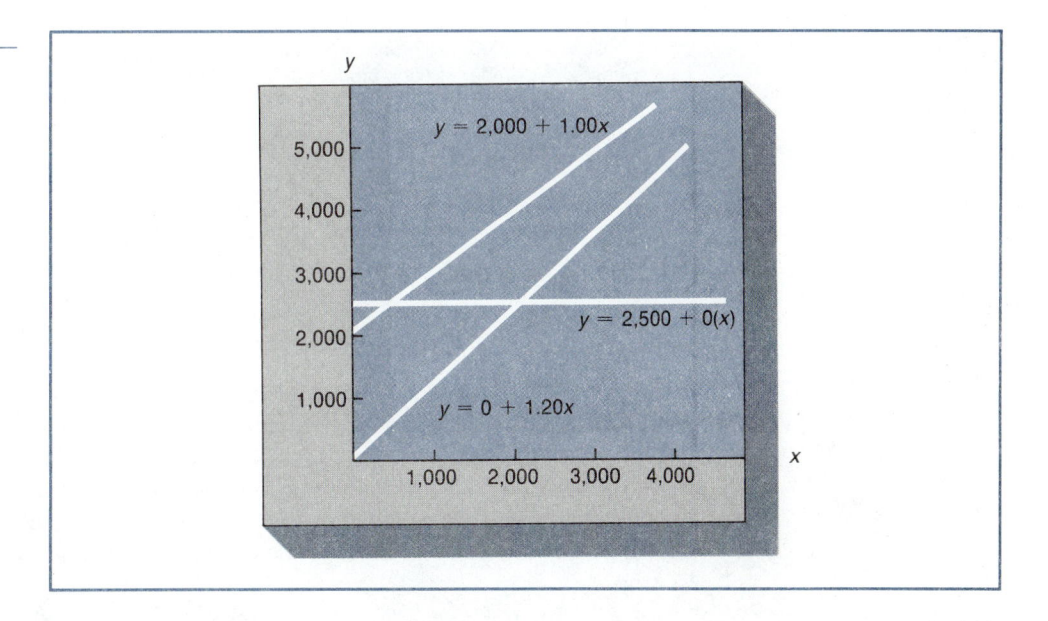

Variable Cost Equation

A manufacturing cost such as direct material, which is entirely variable, would be represented by the following equation:

$$y = a + b(x)$$
$$\text{Direct material} = 0 + \$1.20(x)$$

Figure 3.8 shows that y will be zero when x is zero, which means that no direct material cost will be incurred if nothing is produced. As x increases, y increases. Direct materials cost $1.20 for each unit of output. Therefore, the cost curve comes out of the origin and slopes upward at a rate of $1.20 per unit.

Semivariable Cost Equation

A semivariable cost has both a fixed and variable cost component. An example is an equipment lease that specifies a minimum monthly payment plus a variable amount based on usage. This cost would be represented by the following equation:

$$y = a + b(x)$$
$$\text{Lease cost} = \$2,000 + \$1.00(x)$$

The fixed cost is $2,000 per month and the variable rate is $1.00 per unit of output. Figure 3.8 shows the y-intercept at $2,000 with an upward slope.

Recall that the total manufacturing cost curve is similar to a semivariable cost curve. An equation for total manufacturing costs can be developed by adding the separate costs.

EXAMPLE

Milky Incorporated produced milk cans at the following cost:

Direct material	$12.50 per can
Direct labor	$7.50 per can
Overhead:	
Variable	$5.00 per can
Fixed	$6,000 per month

The total manufacturing cost equation is:

$$\text{Cost} = \$6,000 + \$25(x)$$
where x = number of cans produced.

The projected manufacturing cost to produce 200 milk cans in December is computed as follows:

$$\text{Cost} = \$6,000 + \$25(200) = \underline{\$11,000}$$

Methods for Developing an Equation

The preceding cost equations are useful in describing a cost's pattern of behavior and in evaluating the effect that various decisions will have on the cost of production. For any cost in a given situation, we may have some idea of its pattern but we may not know the exact equation. This is particularly true with factory overhead, which is composed of several different elements and different cost patterns. Given a set of data that includes the amount of cost incurred at various levels of output over time, we need a way to quantify

CHAPTER 3: COST BEHAVIOR 67

FIGURE 3.9

Hart Assembly Company
Summary of Factory Overhead
Six Months Ending December 31, 19X1

Month	Factory Overhead	Units Produced
July	$ 4,200	70
August	3,800	60
September	5,400	100
October	5,100	120
November	5,000	120
December	5,900	130
Total	$29,400	600

the values of the constants *a* and *b* for a cost equation. Three common estimation methods are the high-low method, the scattergraph method, and the least-squares method. Each of these methods will be explained and illustrated.

Figure 3.9 shows the amount of factory overhead incurred during the last six months of 19X1 for Hart Assembly Company. Also shown is the number of units manufactured each month. A factory overhead cost equation is desired to compute the amount of factory overhead that should be incurred at various levels of output. Factory overhead is the dependent variable *y*, and units produced is the independent variable *x*.

High-Low Method The **high-low method** selects a high level of volume and a low level of volume for use in developing the cost equation. Care must be exercised in examining the available data. It is important to determine that the high and low volume levels are representative of the firm's operations.

The variable rate *b* is determined by analyzing the change in cost that corresponds to the change in volume between the high and low points. Remember that fixed costs do not change in total with changes in volume. Therefore, the change in total cost that results from a change in volume is entirely due to variable costs. Variable cost is then subtracted from total cost at a particular volume of activity to compute fixed costs.

Using the data presented in figure 3.9, a cost equation can be developed for factory overhead. The following steps are used:

- **Step 1** Select the high and low points of activity. The highest level of activity was 130 units in December and the lowest level was 60 units in August. An analysis indicates that the data for December and August are representative of normal operations.
- **Step 2** The variable rate is computed by dividing the change in cost by the change in volume. The change in cost and the change in volume are first computed.

	Overhead Cost	Units Produced
High point	$ 5,900	130
Low point	3,800	60
Change	$ 2,100	70 units

The change in cost is then divided by the change in volume for the variable rate.

$$\text{Variable rate} = \frac{\text{Cost change}}{\text{Volume change}} = \frac{\$2,100}{70 \text{ units}} = \$30.00 \text{ per unit}$$

- **Step 3** Compute fixed cost by multiplying the variable rate times the volume at either the high or low point and subtracting that amount from total factory overhead at that point. Supposing the *high point* is selected, the fixed cost of $2,000 per month is computed as follows:

Factory overhead	$5,900
Variable cost ($30 × 130 units)	3,900
Fixed cost	$2,000 per month

Notice that the same answer is obtained if the *low point* is selected.

Factory overhead	$3,800
Variable cost ($30 × 60 units)	1,800
Fixed cost	$2,000 per month

- **Step 4** Develop the mathematical equation. Factory overhead is equal to fixed costs plus the variable rate multiplied by volume:

$$\text{Factory overhead} = \$2{,}000 + \$30.00(x)$$

The high-low method is easy to apply, but its accuracy is a potential problem. Most of the collected data are not used; the formula is based on only two points, and it will be biased if the points selected are not representative of the entire data set. As noted previously, care must be taken to select high and low points of activity that are representative of normal operations and are within the relevant range of activity. This can be seen by referring back to figure 3.6, which compares the accounting and economic cost curves. The economic cost curve is more accurate than the accounting cost curve outside the relevant range of production. If the high point and low point follow the economic cost curve and are both outside the relevant range, the cost curve developed by this method will have a steeper slope than is representative of normal operations within the relevant range.

Scattergraph Method The availability of the computer to aid analysis makes the scattergraph method archaic as a tool of cost analysis. The technique provides an effective visual picture of cost patterns, however, and it also demonstrates the characteristics of the results obtained from the other methods.

The **scattergraph method** plots the data on a graph, which is called a **scatter diagram** or **scattergraph**. A straight line, called a regression line, is inserted among the points on the graph by a visual fit. The line is intended to represent an average of the plotted points, so approximately half of the points will be on either side of the line. In drawing the line one should attempt to minimize the vertical distance between the plotted points and the line. The point at which the regression line intersects the vertical axis (y-intercept) determines the estimated amount of fixed costs, and the slope of the line determines the variable rate.

The scatter diagram in figure 3.10 presents the data from figure 3.9. The data from the figure have been plotted on the graph, and a regression line has been drawn by a visual fit. The point at which the regression line intersects the vertical axis represents the total fixed costs. As shown in figure 3.10, it is at approximately $2,200. The subjectivity involved in identifying the point of intersection indicates one of the weaknesses of this method.

An estimate of the variable rate can then be computed by subtracting the fixed costs from the total factory overhead at some point along the regression line and dividing the

FIGURE 3.10

Scattergraph

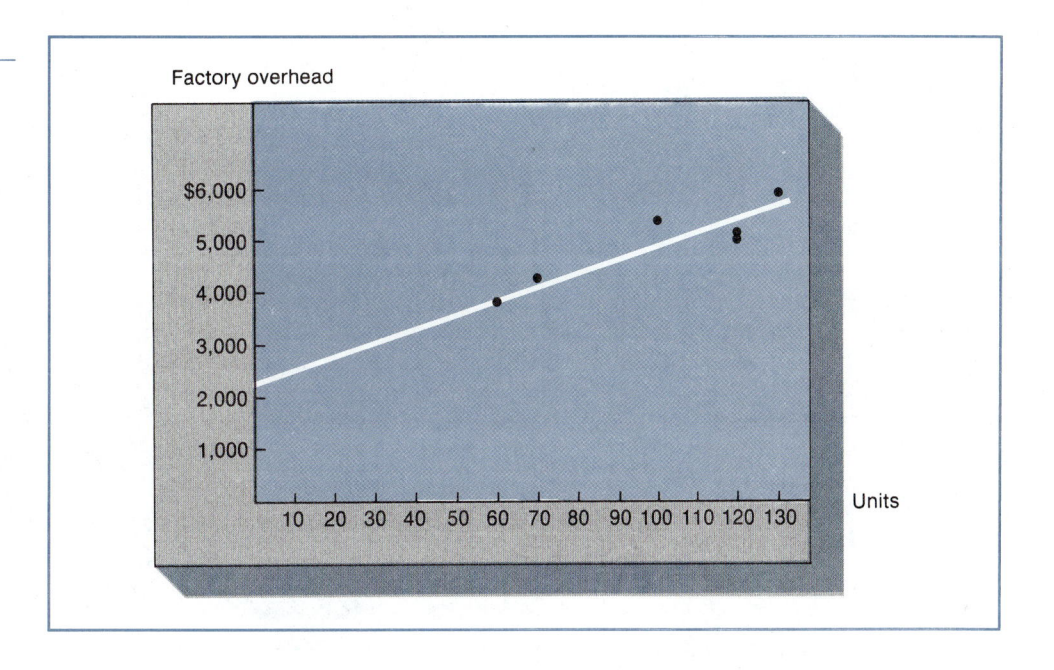

difference by the units produced. A point representing the August data (60 units at $3,800) is on the line and will be used to compute the variable rate.

Factory overhead	$3,800
Fixed cost	2,200
Variable cost	$1,600
Divided by units produced	÷ 70
Variable rate	$26.67 per unit

Cost equation:

Factory overhead = $2,200 + $26.67(x)
where x = units produced

Advantages of the scattergraph method are that it uses all the data in developing the formula and it is fairly quick and easy to apply. However, once again care must be taken to make appropriate adjustments for extraneous circumstances that cause abnormal fluctuations in cost behavior. Plotting the data on a graph helps to identify an abnormal bit of cost data. If one of the plotted points is way out of line with the others, it is probably the result of extraneous circumstances and should be ignored in visually fitting the regression line.

The biggest problem in using this method is in fitting a line to the plotted points. An accurate visual fit will provide a formula as accurate as if it were measured mathematically. However, a slight misplacement can cause a significant error in the y-intercept (fixed costs), the slope (variable rate), or both. Because the scattergraph method is subjective and imprecise and does not allow for more sophisticated statistical analysis, a least-squares regression analysis is often required.

Least-Squares Method The **least-squares method** uses a mathematical technique to fit the best line possible to the observed data. It identifies the formula for a regression line that minimizes the sum of the squares of the lengths of the vertical-line segments drawn from the observed data points on the scattergraph to the regression line. Figure 3.11 shows

FIGURE 3.11

Deviations of Observed Points from the Fitted Regression Line

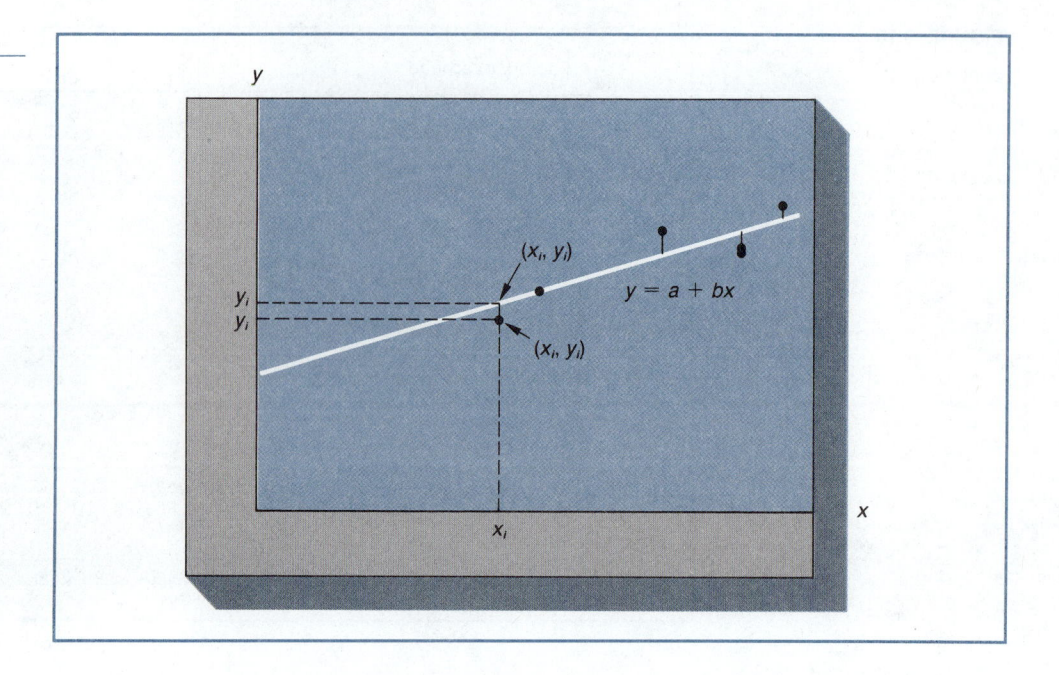

the vertical distance between the observed points and the regression line. The squared sum of *these* is minimized by this method. The idea is that the smaller the deviations of the observed values from this line (and consequently the smaller the sum of squares of these deviations), the better the fit of the line to the data points.

The following are the least-squares formulas to compute a and b. The point of intercept on the vertical axis and the slope, respectively, are:

$$a = \frac{(\Sigma y)(\Sigma x^2) - (\Sigma x)(\Sigma xy)}{n(\Sigma x^2) - (\Sigma x)^2}$$

$$b = \frac{n(\Sigma xy) - (\Sigma x)(\Sigma y)}{n(\Sigma x^2) - (\Sigma x)^2}$$

where Σx = the total of the observed values of the independent variable
Σy = the total of the observed values of the dependent variable
n = the number of observations
Σx^2 = the summation of the squared values of the independent variable
Σxy = the total of the products of the dependent variable multiplied by the independent variable.

The intermediate computations that are required to use the preceding formulas are illustrated in figure 3.12. The observed values of x (units produced) and y (factory overhead) are totaled for the values of Σx and Σy, respectively. The number of units produced is multiplied by the factory overhead for each month, and the products are totaled for the value of Σxy. The number of units produced each month is squared, and the results are totaled for the value of Σx^2. These values are substituted into the equations to compute the values of a and b.

$$a = \frac{(29,400)(64,200) - (600)(3,041,000)}{(6)(64,200) - (600)^2}$$

$$= \$2,495$$

CHAPTER 3: COST BEHAVIOR

FIGURE 3.12

Least-Squares Regression Analysis

Month	x Units Produced	y Factory Overhead	xy	x^2
July	70	$ 4,200	294,000	4,900
August	60	3,800	228,000	3,600
September	100	5,400	540,000	10,000
October	120	5,100	612,000	14,400
November	120	5,000	600,000	14,400
December	130	5,900	767,000	16,900
Total	600	$29,400	3,041,000	64,200

$$b = \frac{(6)(3,041,000) - (600)(29,400)}{(6)(64,200) - (600)^2}$$

$$= \$24.05$$

The resulting cost equation is:

Factory overhead = $2,495 + $24.05(x)
where x = units produced.

An alternative computation for the least-squares regression analysis is explained and illustrated in the appendix on page 94.

Computer Analysis of Cost Behavior The computer is a tool that can be used effectively in many aspects of accounting. Various cost accounting applications discussed in this text can be processed efficiently using various main-frame, as well as personal, computers. Students of cost accounting should have a basic knowledge of computers. A familiarity with some of the unique terminology associated with computers is assumed in the discussion that follows.

The formula for the least-squares method of cost behavior analysis can be efficiently manipulated by computer. Several programs are available for use on main-frame computers that aid in performing the least-squares analysis. The following discussion, however, centers on the personal computer. The least-squares method of cost analysis will be used to illustrate the application of personal computers to cost accounting.

Computer hardware is a term used to refer to the actual tangible equipment that makes up the computer. IBM, AT&T, Digital, and Wang are some of the more popular manufacturers of computer hardware.

Every computer must have an operating system, which is a set of computer instructions that directs the operation of the computer. The user of a personal (or micro-) computer interacts frequently with the operating system. One example of an operating system is DOS, or Disk Operating System. DOS is used in connection with the IBM PC.

The actual operation of an IBM PC is begun by placing a DOS disk in drive "A." When the computer is turned on, the operating system will automatically load itself into the memory of the computer. The system will ask the user to enter the current date and time, and then, after displaying certain copyright information, "A>" will be displayed. This indicates that the system is ready for further instructions.

Once the computer is ready to receive instructions, a user can model (i.e., create) a program or routine that uses the computer to reach an objective, such as the least-squares analysis discussed in this chapter. Alternatively, the user can use a packaged or pre-prepared program. Computer programs are referred to as *software*. Numerous packaged software products are available, including various word processing packages, accounting packages, and *electronic spreadsheets*. Spreadsheet software packages can be very effective for many cost accounting applications. Examples of spreadsheet software packages include Lotus 1-2-3, Visicalc, and Lotus Symphony.

A spreadsheet is simply the electronic computer equivalent of a pencil and a multiple-column paper worksheet. The electronic spreadsheet consists of rows and columns. Each intersection of a row and a column forms a cell into which data can be entered and stored. Each cell can accommodate labels, numeric values, or formulas.

The user of a spreadsheet enters data and formulas into the cells of the worksheet in much the same way that these items would be entered on a columnar paper worksheet. Because of this similarity, spreadsheets are easy to use and are potentially applicable to a variety of analyses.

The power of the spreadsheet comes from the ability to enter in a cell a formula that can reference and associate numbers or formulas from any number of other cells. This feature allows the user to change one value in a worksheet and see how the one change affects the rest of the worksheet.

The illustration presented in figure 3.12, which demonstrates the least-squares method by manual (i.e., pencil and paper worksheet) procedures, will be repeated in figure 3.13 in computer spreadsheet form.

FIGURE 3.13 Least-Squares Regression Analysis Using Lotus 1-2-3

Month	x Units Produced	y Factory Overhead	xy	x^2
July	70	$4,200	+B9*C9	+B9^2
August	60	3,800	+B10*C10	+B10^2
September	100	5,400	+B11*C11	+B11^2
October	120	5,100	+B12*C12	+B12^2
November	120	5,000	+B13*C13	+B13^2
December	130	5,900	+B14*C14	+B14^2
Total	@SUM(B14..B9)	@SUM(C14..C9)	@SUM(D14..D9)	@SUM(E14..E9)
a =	@ROUND(((C16*E16)−(B16*D16))/((6*E16)−(B16^2)),0)			
b =	@ROUND(((6*D16)−(B16*C16))/((6*E16)−(B16^2)),2)			

Factory Overhead = +B20   +   +B21   (x)

Month	x Units Produced	y Factory Overhead	xy	x^2
July	70	$4,200	294,000	4,900
August	60	3,800	228,000	3,600
September	100	5,400	540,000	10,000
October	120	5,100	612,000	14,400
November	120	5,000	600,000	14,400
December	130	5,900	767,000	16,900
Total	600	$29,400	3,041,000	64,200
a =	$2,495			
b =	$24.05			

Factory Overhead = $2,495   +   24.05   (x)

Comparison of Methods The previously described methods differ widely in their ease of application and in the precision of the resulting cost formula. Notice the difference in the results:

	Fixed Costs	Variable Rate
High-low method	$2,000	$30.00
Scattergraph method	2,200	26.67
Least-squares method	2,495	24.05

The least-squares method provides a regression line that, mathematically speaking, is the best fit for all the observed data points. The high-low method and the scattergraph method are intended only as approximations of the least-squares method.

However, the precision offered by the least-squares method is not always needed. Perhaps we are trying to estimate what factory overhead will be in the coming year and are looking at the prior year to give us some idea about what may be expected. Because economic conditions are never the same from year to year, an appoximation of the prior year's cost equation might be good enough. The important thing is to select a method that is adequate for its intended use.

Application of Cost Patterns

A clear understanding of the various cost patterns is essential. A significant part of the accountant's work is involved in identifying cost patterns, grouping them with other costs having similar patterns, and using them properly in making wise business decisions.

SUMMARY

This chapter identified the various cost patterns associated with the manufacturing process and described some of the ways that costs may be classified and quantified. Product costs include all costs associated with the manufacturing process, and are broadly classified into *(a)* direct materials, *(b)* direct labor, and *(c)* factory overhead. Materials and labor that are traceable to the finished product are classified as direct or prime costs. Indirect material and labor and all other manufacturing costs are included in factory overhead.

Manufacturing costs exhibit different patterns as volume changes. The most common patterns are called *(a)* fixed, *(b)* variable, and *(c)* semivariable. Care must be taken to distinguish between total cost and cost per unit when working with the various cost patterns. Fixed costs remain constant in total, but the cost per unit decreases as volume increases. Variable costs increase in total as volume increases, but the cost per unit remains constant. Semivariable costs have both a fixed and a variable cost element.

Total manufacturing costs combine the cost of direct labor, direct material, and factory overhead. The total manufacturing cost curve exhibits a semivariable cost pattern that can be represented by the following straight-line equation:

$$y = a + bx$$
where y = dependent variable or total cost
 x = independent variable or volume
 a = y-intercept or fixed cost
 b = slope or variable rate

Three commonly used methods of developing a cost equation from a set of data are the high-low, scattergraph, and least-squares methods. The amount of precision desired in the equation is important in selecting the method to be used. The least-squares method is the most difficult to apply but provides the best possible line for the observed data.

APPENDIX 3.1 Alternative Approach to Least-Squares Regression Analysis

This appendix explains and illustrates an alternate approach to the least-squares regression analysis. Recall that the objective of the least-squares method is to minimize the squared sum of the vertical distance between the observed points and the regression line. This concept is highlighted in the following equations. The least-squares formula to compute b, the slope of the line, is:

$$b = \frac{\sum_{i=1}^{n}(x_i - \bar{x})(y_i - \bar{y})}{\sum_{i=1}^{n}(x_i - \bar{x})^2}$$

where $\bar{x}$ = the sample mean of the independen variable
$\bar{y}$ = the sample mean of the dependent variable
x_i = the observed values of the independent variable from 1 to n
y_i = the observed values of the dependent variable from 1 to n

The least-squares formula for computing a, the point of intercept on the vertical axis, is:

$$a = \bar{y} - b\bar{x}$$

The steps in performing the calculations are as follows:

- **Step 1** Compute the sample means ($\bar{x}$ and $\bar{y}$) from the observed set of data. The mean is computed by summing the values of the variable and dividing by the number of observations.

$$\bar{x} = \frac{\sum_{i=1}^{n} x_i}{n}$$

Figure 3.14 shows these computations.

FIGURE 3.14 Least-Squares Regression Analysis (alternative computation)

Month	x Units Produced	y Factory Overhead	$x_i - \bar{x}$	$y_i - \bar{y}$	$(x_i - \bar{x})(y_i - \bar{y})$	$(x_i - \bar{x})^2$
July	70	$ 4,200	−30	−700	21,000	900
August	60	3,800	−40	−1,100	44,000	1,600
September	100	5,400	0	500	0	0
October	120	5,100	20	200	4,000	400
November	120	5,000	20	100	2,000	400
December	130	5,900	30	1,000	30,000	900
Total	600	$29,400			101,000	4,200
Divide by n	÷ 6	÷ 6				
Mean $\bar{x}$	100					
Mean $\bar{y}$		$ 4,900				

CHAPTER 3: COST BEHAVIOR

- **Step 2** Compute b, the slope or variable rate, using the preceding equation. Four intermediate computations are required.

  1. Compute the difference between the observed value of each *dependent* variable (x_i) with the sample mean ($\bar{x}$).
  2. Compute the difference between the observed value of each *independent* variable (y_i) with the sample mean ($\bar{y}$).
  3. Multiply the differences computed in numbers 1 and 2 for each observation [$(x_i - \bar{x})(y_i - \bar{y})$], and sum the products.
  4. Square the differences computed in number 1 for each observation, and sum the result. These computations are also shown in figure 3.14. The totals of the two columns on the right-hand side of the table are used in the equation.

$$b = \frac{101{,}000}{4{,}200} = \$24.05 \text{ per unit}$$

- **Step 3** Compute a, the vertical intercept or fixed cost, by entering the values computed before into the formula.

$$a = \bar{y} - b\bar{x}$$
$$a = 4{,}900 - 24.05(100) = \$2{,}495 \text{ per month}$$

- **Step 4** Develop the cost equation.

  Factory overhead = \$2,495 + \$24.05(x)
  where x = units produced

SELF-STUDY PROBLEM

The following set of data is available from the historical accounting records to develop a mathematical equation for factory overhead.

Month	Units Produced	Factory Overhead
January	15	$4,000
February	11	3,000
March	10	3,400
April	8	2,600
May	20	5,000

Required

Develop an equation in the form of $y = a + bx$ where y is factory overhead, a is the fixed element of factory overhead, and b is the variable element. Use each of the following methods:

1. High-low method
2. Scattergraph method
3. Least-squares regression analysis

Solution to the Self-Study Problem

Requirement 1

The high and low volumes are at 20 and 8 units, respectively. Using these two points, the variable cost is computed as follows:

	Factory Overhead	Units Produced
High point	$5,000	20
Low point	2,600	8
Change	$2,400	12 units

$$\text{Variable rate} = \frac{\$2,400}{12 \text{ units}} = \$200 \text{ per unit}$$

The fixed cost can then be determined by using one of the selected points. High point:

Factory overhead	$5,000
Variable cost ($200 × 20)	4,000
Fixed cost	$1,000

The factory overhead formula is:

Factory overhead = $1,000 + $200(x)
where x = units produced.

Requirement 2

The scattergraph method plots the data, as illustrated in figure 3.15, and visually fits a line to the data points.

FIGURE 3.15

Scattergraph Method

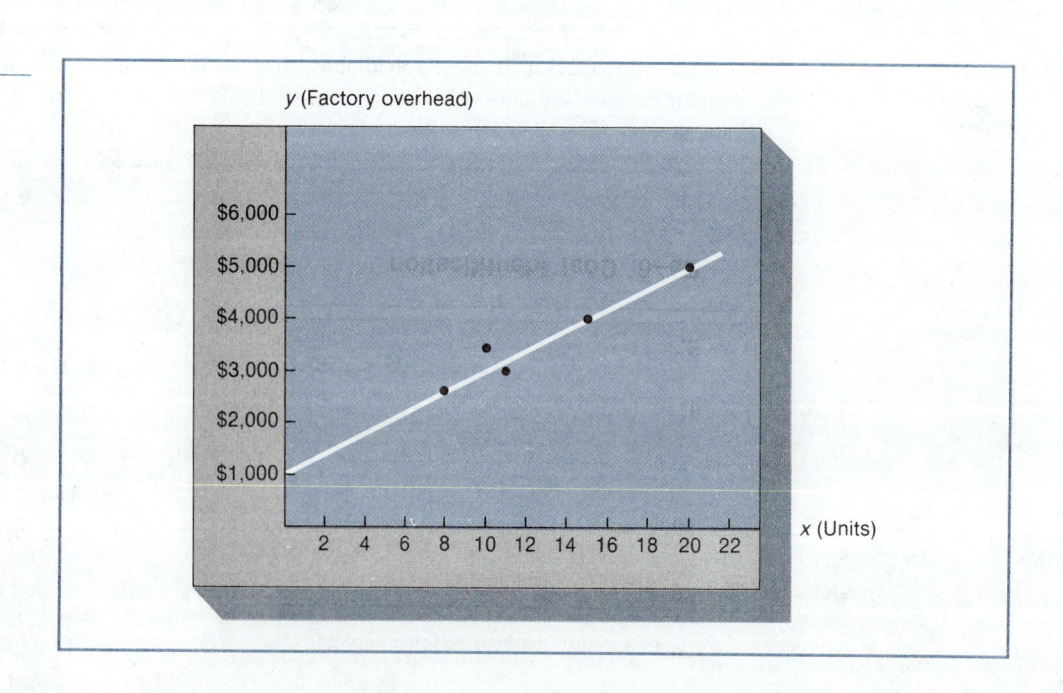

It appears that the factory overhead cost curve intersects the vertical axis at about $1,200 and passes through the April point of 8 units at $2,600 total overhead. Using these two points, the variable rate is computed as follows:

Factory overhead	$2,600
Fixed cost	1,200
Variable cost	$1,400
Divided by units produced	8
Variable rate	$175 per unit

The factory overhead formula is:

Factory overhead = $1,200 + $175(x)
where x = units produced.

Requirement 3

Figure 3.16 is developed to compute the intermediate values required for use in the least-squares equations.

The values computed in the table are substituted into the equations to compute *a* and *b*, the fixed cost and variable rate, respectively.

$$a = \frac{(\Sigma y)(\Sigma x^2) - (\Sigma x)(\Sigma xy)}{n(\Sigma x^2) - (\Sigma x)^2}$$

$$= \frac{(18,000)(910) - (64)(247,800)}{(5)(910) - (64)^2}$$

$$= \$1,147 \text{ fixed costs}$$

$$b = \frac{(n)(\Sigma xy) - (\Sigma x)(\Sigma y)}{n(\Sigma x^2) - (\Sigma x)^2}$$

$$= \frac{(5)(247,800) - (64)(18,000)}{(5)(910) - (64)^2}$$

$$= \$192 \text{ variable cost}$$

The factory overhead formula is:

Factory overhead = $1,147 + $192(x)
where x = units produced.

FIGURE 3.16

Least-Squares Method

Month	x Units Produced	y Factory Overhead	xy	x²
January	15	$ 4,000	$ 60,000	225
February	11	3,000	33,000	121
March	10	3,400	34,000	100
April	8	2,600	20,800	64
May	20	5,000	100,000	400
Total	64	$18,000	$247,800	910

SUGGESTED READINGS

Dean, Joel, *Statistical Cost Estimation*. Bloomington, Ind.: Indiana University Press, 1976.

Goodman, Sam R., and Reese, James S. *Controller's Handbook*. Homewood, Ill.: Dow-Jones Irwin, 1978.

Kleinbaum, David G., and Kupper, Lawrence L. *Applied Regression Analysis and Other Multivariable Methods*. North Scituate, Mass.: Duxbury Press, 1978.

Lesser, Frederic E. "Will the Real Cost Please Stand Up?" *Management Accounting* 68 (November 1986): 29–31.

McElroy, Elam E. *Applied Business Statistics*. 2d ed. San Francisco: Holden-Day, 1979.

Mason, Robert D. *Statistical Techniques in Business and Economics*. 4th ed. Homewood, Ill.: Richard D. Irwin, 1978.

National Association of Accountants. Accounting Practice Report #10. *Separating and Using Costs as Fixed and Variable*. New York: National Association of Accountants, 1960.

DISCUSSION QUESTIONS

Q3–1. What is meant by a cost's behavior pattern?

Q3–2. When someone says, "The cost per unit remains constant as volume increases," are they talking about a fixed cost or a variable cost? Explain.

Q3–3. When someone says, "The cost per unit decreases as volume increases," are they talking about a fixed cost or a variable cost? Explain.

Q3–4. Define *semivariable cost*.

Q3–5. Define *step-variable cost*.

Q3–6. How does a step-variable cost differ from a semivariable cost?

Q3–7. Describe the relevant range of production. Why is it important when talking about cost behavior from an accountant's perspective?

Q3–8. Describe the industrial-engineering approach to quantifying cost behavior for direct labor.

Q3–9. Describe the historical cost approach to quantifying cost behavior for direct labor.

Q3–10. In the formula $y = a + bx$, which symbol represents the dependent variable? Why is it called a dependent variable?

Q3–11. In the formula $y = a + bx$, which symbol represents the independent variable? Why is it called an independent variable?

Q3–12. Describe what is meant by y-intercept and slope when dealing with the mathematical properties of a straight line.

Q3–13. Why are the two points selected for the high-low method so important? Suppose the low point selected is higher than is representative of the data set. What will be the effect on the resulting cost curve?

Q3–14. What is the major benefit of using the least-squares method as opposed to the high-low or scattergraph methods? Under what circumstances could we justify using the high-low or scattergraph methods rather than the least-squares regression analysis?

CHAPTER 3: COST BEHAVIOR

Q3–15. Why is knowledge of a cost's behavior pattern important to a cost accountant?

Q3–16. Explain what a spreadsheet for computer analysis is. How may the computer be used in cost behavior analysis?

EXERCISES

E3–1. Cost Behavior Concepts (CMA) The assumptions, concepts, and terminology used by economists and accountants often differ and seem to conflict. For instance, the economist normally assumes that the functions for total revenue, variable (marginal) cost, and total cost have curvilinear characteristics, whereas the accountant traditionally assumes that these same functions behave in a linear fashion.

Required

1. Explain the economic concept behind the economist's assumption of curvilinear functions for the following:
   a. Total revenue
   b. Variable (marginal) cost
   c. Total cost
2. Explain why the accountant's assumption of linear functions need not invalidate accounting analyses.

E3–2. Cost Behavior—High-Low Method Jackson Incorporated is preparing a flexible budget for 19X1 and requires a breakdown of the cost of steam used in its factory into the fixed and variable elements. The following data on the cost of steam used and direct-labor hours worked are available for the last six months of 19X0:

Month	Cost of Steam	Direct-Labor Hours
July	$ 15,850	3,000
August	13,400	2,050
September	16,370	2,900
October	19,800	3,650
November	17,600	2,670
December	18,500	2,650
Total	$101,520	16,920

Required

1. Assuming that Jackson uses the high-low method of analysis, determine the variable cost of steam per direct-labor hour and the fixed cost total for steam cost.
2. Express your results in requirement 1 in $y = a + bx$ formula form.
3. Using Lotus, perform a least-squares regression analysis to determine the variable cost of steam per direct-labor hour and the fixed cost total for steam cost. Express the results in formula form.

E3–3. Separating Mixed Costs—Comparison of Methods Maywood Resort Lodge has the following data for its room upkeep costs and number of guest days of occupancy for the second half of the year:

	Room Upkeep Costs	Number of Guest Days of Occupancy
July	$4,585	10,500
August	4,628	10,750
September	4,475	9,850
October	4,780	11,650
November	4,508	10,050
December	4,750	11,450

Required

1. Separate the room upkeep costs into fixed cost per month and variable cost per guest day using the following methods:
   a. High-low
   b. Scattergraph
   c. Least-squares
2. Express the results you obtained in requirement 1c in equation form.
3. What amount of room upkeep costs would you estimate for 10,000 guest days?
4. Comment on the differences (if any) in the fixed and variable cost results when the different methods were applied in requirement 1. Why do the differences occur?

E3–4. Separating Mixed Costs by Using Different Alternative Methods

Mega Manufacturing's cost analyst is engaged in analyzing the power and light costs to determine the fixed element and the variable rate. Several activity bases have been tested. The analyst is about to test the power and light costs using direct-labor hours as the activity base. The following data have been assembled for the past six months:

Month	Power and Light Costs	Direct-Labor Hours
August	$3,096	594
September	2,810	482
October	3,334	700
November	3,068	560
December	3,270	570
January	3,400	710

Required

1. Determine the dollar amount of fixed power and light costs and the variable rate per direct-labor hour using the following methods:
   a. High-low
   b. Least-squares
2. Determine an estimate of expected power and light costs at the 600 direct-labor hour level of activity using the results you obtained in requirement 1a.
3. Identify two or three possible alternative activity bases that could be used instead of direct-labor hours, and briefly describe the desirable and undesirable aspects of using each as a base for cost estimation.

E3–5. Cost Behavior Identification

The following cost items are found in the cost ledger of the HLC Company:

1. Factory heat, light, and power
2. Rent on factory raw materials warehouse
3. Repairs to factory equipment

CHAPTER 3: COST BEHAVIOR

4. FICA taxes on direct-labor payroll
5. Factory supervisor
6. Custodial supplies
7. Direct labor
8. Indirect material
9. Depreciation on factory equipment
10. Fire and comprehensive insurance on the factory production facility

Required

1. Classify each item in the list according to cost behavior (fixed, variable, or semivariable). Briefly explain the reasons for your classifications.
2. Classify each item in the list of costs as being either direct or indirect with respect to units of product being produced.

E3-6. Cost Identification The Smallco Industries Company started business about five years ago. Recently the company made a significant shift in product emphasis. A new product has been designed that requires the following costs: direct materials, $25 per unit; direct labor, $35 per unit; production supervision, $1,500 per month; rental on warehouse for raw materials and finished-goods inventory storage, $1,000 per month; product advertising, $1,200 per month; sales commission, $8 per unit sold; and monthly depreciation on new factory equipment for production of new product, $400.

Required

Make a comprehensive classification of the cost items for the Smallco Industries Company's new product. Determine whether each item is variable, semivariable, or fixed in behavior pattern; whether it is a product (inventoriable) cost or a period cost; whether the product costs are direct or indirect to the new product; and whether the period costs are marketing or administrative costs.

E3-7. Cost Behavior Identification The following data have been assembled for the PDQ Company for the months of July and August.

Item	July	August
Amount of Sales (in thousands)	$ 1,500	$ 2,800
Cost 02230	35,000	50,000
Cost 02232	1,380	2,576
Cost 02233	16,000	16,000
Cost 02235	14,000	17,000
Cost 02238	67,500	126,000

Required

Without making a detailed quantitative analysis, identify the cost behavior pattern that best describes each cost. Give a brief explanation of the rationale for your choice.

E3-8. Cost Behavior—Tie to Cost Concepts Complete the schedule below by classifying each of the following costs as (1) fixed or variable (F or V) and (2) as period or product costs. If the cost is a period cost, indicate whether it would be part of selling cost or part of administrative cost; if it is a product cost, indicate whether it would be direct or indirect to units of product.

	Fixed or Variable	Period Cost Selling	Period Cost Adm.	Product Cost Direct	Product Cost Indirect
Example: Rent on sales office	F	X			
a. Plant security personnel	___	___	___	___	___
b. Executive office security personnel	___	___	___	___	___
c. Transportation-in costs on materials purchased	___	___	___	___	___
d. Transportation-in cost on manufacturing equipment	___	___	___	___	___
e. Assembly-line workers' wages	___	___	___	___	___
f. Supplies used in assembly work	___	___	___	___	___
g. Property taxes on work-in-process inventories	___	___	___	___	___
h. Sales taxes on equipment purchased	___	___	___	___	___
i. Salaries of administrative staff	___	___	___	___	___
j. Depreciation on factory building	___	___	___	___	___
k. Overtime premium for assembly workers	___	___	___	___	___
l. Factory heat and air conditioning	___	___	___	___	___
m. Varnish used for finishing product	___	___	___	___	___
n. Insurance on manufacturing plant	___	___	___	___	___

E3–9. Product versus Period Cost Classification One basic classification of costs is product versus period costs. Product costs are known as inventoriable costs, and period costs are expenses (i.e., are matched against revenue in the period of incurrence). The records of the Malcoa Company show the following items among a lengthy list of costs involved with the company's month-by-month operations.

1. Depreciation on the computerized telephone call transfer system
2. Factory heat, light, and power
3. Advertising expenditures
4. Boxes used to package the finished product
5. Lubricating materials for factory machines
6. Depreciation of salespersons' automobiles
7. Payroll of machine operators
8. Payroll of finished-goods warehouse employees
9. Depreciation of the president's jet aircraft
10. Costs incurred for reserving conference rooms at a resort hotel for the annual executives' conference

Required

1. Identify each cost item listed as a product (inventoriable) or period cost.
2. Explain the reasons for your classifications in requirement 1.
3. Explain why a company would be concerned with product versus period cost classifications.

E3–10. Least-Squares Regression Turfland Corporation provides commercial landscaping services. Linda Dake, the firm's owner, wants to develop cost estimates that she can use to prepare bids on jobs. After analyzing her costs, Dake has developed the following preliminary costs for each 1,000 square feet of landscaping.

Direct materials	$400
Direct labor (5 DLH @ $10/DLH)	50
Overhead (5 DLH @ $18/DLH)	90
Total cost per 1,000 square feet	$540

Dake is quite certain about the estimates for direct materials and direct labor. However, she is not as comfortable with the estimate for overhead, which is based on the overhead costs that were incurred during the past twelve months, as presented in the following schedule. The estimate of $18 per direct-labor hour (DLH) was determined by dividing the total overhead costs for the twelve month period ($648,000) by the total direct-labor hours (36,000).

	Total Overhead	Regular Direct-Labor Hours	Overtime Direct-Labor Hours	Total Direct-Labor Hours
January	$ 47,000	2,380	20	2,400
February	48,000	2,210	40	2,250
March	56,000	2,590	210	2,800
April	54,000	2,560	240	2,800
May	57,000	3,030	470	3,500
June	65,000	3,240	760	4,000
July	64,000	3,380	620	4,000
August	56,000	3,050	350	3,400
September	54,000	2,910	190	3,100
October	53,000	2,760	40	2,800
November	47,000	2,770	30	2,800
December	47,000	2,120	30	2,150
Total	$648,000	33,000	3,000	36,000

Dake believes that overhead is affected by total monthly direct-labor hours. The overtime premium, 50 percent of the direct-labor rate, is not included in total overhead. Instead, the overtime is regarded as a special item associated with each project.

Required

Perform a least-squares regression analysis of overhead using Lotus or some other electronic spreadsheet to develop the mathematical formula for predicting overhead cost. Print out a copy of the results, as well as a copy of the formulas used in the analysis.

E3–11. Least-Squares Regression Analysis

Westerlund, Inc. is preparing a flexible budget for next year's overhead. Data from the most recent year are as follows:

Month	Overhead Cost	Direct Labor	Machine Hours	Units
January	$21,159	11,204	10,244	895
February	35,458	24,439	22,582	1,555
March	27,888	22,456	20,177	1,258
April	24,569	20,465	20,105	1,586
May	28,045	25,782	23,852	2,100
June	19,723	22,801	21,423	1,483
July	20,430	21,750	20,783	1,250
August	15,580	24,460	23,500	1,850
September	12,458	20,380	19,480	1,605
October	16,850	18,700	17,500	1,480
November	18,700	20,850	19,000	1,500

Required

Using an electronic spreadsheet, develop a template to perform a least-squares regression analysis that uses each of the following as the independent variable for predicting overhead cost:

1. Direct-labor hours
2. Machine hours
3. Units of production

Include on the output the overhead formula for each of the independent variables.

PROBLEMS

P3–1. Cost Estimates from Cost Behavior Equations The Oxford Company's cost department has kept weekly records of production volume in units, electric power used, and direct-labor hours. For the past three months, production experience has ranged between 500 and 2,000 units per week. The production for the week just ended was 1,200 units. The following equations have been determined:

For electric power:

$$y = 1{,}000 + 0.4x$$
where y = electric power costs
x = number of units produced

For direct labor:

$$y = 100 + 1.2x$$
where y = direct-labor hours
x = number of units produced

Required

1. Estimate the electric power costs and direct-labor hours required for next week. The number of units produced is expected to run 200 units greater than production in the past week's period.
2. What assumptions were implicit in your analysis in requirement 1?
3. How reliable are the relationships that exist between the variables used in the equations determined by the cost department? What factors might cause the equations to be unreliable in predicting electric power costs and direct labor costs?

P3–2. Cost Behavior Determination The Alma Plant manufactures the industrial product line of CJS Industries. Plant management wants to have a good yet quick estimate of the manufacturing overhead costs that can be expected each month. The easiest and simplest way to accomplish this task seems to be to develop a cost formula for manufacturing overhead.

The plant's accounting staff suggested that simple linear regression be used to determine the cost behavior pattern of the overhead costs. The regression data could provide the basis for the cost formula. Sufficient evidence was available to conclude that manufacturing overhead costs vary with direct-labor hours. The actual direct-labor hours and the corresponding manufacturing overhead costs for each month during the last three years were used in the linear regression analysis.

The three-year period contained various occurrences not uncommon to many businesses. During the first year, production was severely curtailed for two months due to wildcat strikes. In the second year, production was reduced in one month because of material shortages and then increased (overtime scheduled) during two months to meet the units required for a one-time sale order. At the end of the second year, employee benefits were raised significantly as the result of a labor agreement. Production during the third year was not affected by any special circumstances.

Various members of Alma's accounting staff raised some issues concerning the historical data collected for the regression analysis. These issues were as follows:

1. Some members of the accounting staff believed that the use of data from all thirty-six months would provide the most accurate portrayal of the cost behavior. Although they recognized that any of the monthly data could include efficiencies and inefficiencies, they believed that these efficiencies and inefficiencies would tend to balance out over a longer period of time.
2. Other members of the accounting staff suggested that only data from those months that were considered normal should be used so that the regression would not be distorted.
3. Other members thought that only the past twelve months' data should be used, because they were the most current.
4. Some members questioned whether historical data should be used to form the basis for a budget formula.

The accounting department ran two regression analyses of the data—one used the data from all thirty-six months and the other used only the data from the past twelve months. The information derived from the two linear regressions follows:

Least-Squares Regression Analyses

	Data from All 36 Months	Data from Most Recent 12 Months
Coefficients of the regression equation:		
Constant	$123,810	$109,020
Coefficient of independent variable (dollars per direct labor hour)	$1.6003	$4.1977

Required

1. From the results of Alma Plant's regression analysis that used the data from all thirty-six months, do the following:
    a. Formulate the cost equation that can be employed to estimate monthly manufacturing overhead costs.
    b. Calculate the estimate of overhead costs for a month when 25,000 direct-labor hours are worked.
2. Repeat requirement 1 using the data for the most recent twelve months.
3. Considering only the results of the two regression analyses, explain which of the two results (twelve-month versus thirty-six month) you would use as a basis for the budget formula.
4. How would the four specific issues raised by Alma's accounting staff influence your willingness to use the results of the statistical analyses as the basis for the cost formula? Explain your answer.

P3-3. Cost Behavior Concepts—Least-Squares and High-Low Methods (CMA) Armer Company is accumulating data to use in preparing its annual profit plan for the coming year. The cost behavior pattern of the maintenance costs must be determined. The accounting staff suggests that linear regression and the high-low method of analysis be employed to test cost behavior and to derive an equation for maintenance costs in the form of $y = a + bx$. Data about maintenance hours and costs for the previous year are as follows:

	Hours of Activity	Maintenance Costs
January	480	$4,200
February	320	3,000
March	400	3,600
April	300	2,820
May	500	4,350
June	310	2,960
July	320	3,030
August	520	4,470
September	490	4,260
October	470	4,050
November	350	3,300
December	340	3,160

Required

Answer the following questions:

1. In the standard regression equation of $y = a + bx$, the letter b is best described as the
   a. independent variable.
   b. dependent variable.
   c. constant coefficient.
   d. variable coefficient.
   e. coefficient of determination.

2. The letter y in the standard regression equation is best described as the
   a. independent variable.
   b. dependent variable.
   c. constant coefficient.
   d. variable coefficient.
   e. coefficient of determination.

3. The letter x in the standard regression equation is best described as the
   a. independent variable.
   b. dependent variable.
   c. constant coefficient.
   d. variable coefficient.
   e. coefficient of determination.

4. If Armer Company uses the high-low method of analysis, the equation for the relationship between hours of activity and maintenance cost would be
   a. $y = 400 + 9.0x$.
   b. $y = 570 + 7.5x$.
   c. $y = 3,600 + 400x$.
   d. $y = 570 + 9.0x$.
   e. some equation other than those given above.

5. Based on the data derived for question 4, if 420 maintenance hours were budgeted for a given month, the budgeted maintenance cost would be
   a. $4,180.
   b. $7,380.
   c. $4,350.
   d. $3,720.
   e. some amount other than those given above.
6. Refer to the original data. Determine by the last-squares method the *a* and *b* values for the $y = a + bx$ equation.
7. If 420 maintenance hours were budgeted for a given month, how much should be budgeted for maintenance cost, considering your answers in requirement 6.?

P3–4. Cost Behavior and Cost Formulas—High-Low Method Records of Davis Company show the following total overhead costs and direct-labor hours for a four-month period:

Month	Labor Hours	Total Overhead Costs
July	100,000	$348,000
August	80,000	300,400
September	120,000	395,600
October	140,000	443,200

Suppose that for simplification purposes there are only three items of overhead. These three items have been analyzed for August at the 80,000 direct-labor hour level of volume, and the following behaviors and amounts have been identified:

Supplies (variable)	$104,000
Depreciation (fixed)	80,000
Equipment repairs (semivariable)	116,400

Required

1. Assume that the cost behavior relationships for total overhead remain the same in October as in August. Determine the dollar amount of supplies, depreciation, and equipment repairs for the $443,200 of total overhead in October.
2. Determine the variable and fixed portions of equipment repair costs.
3. Express the Davis Company's *total* overhead cost in formula form, $y = a + bx$.
4. Determine the estimate of total overhead costs at the 95,000 direct-labor hour level.

P3–5. Cost Behavior and Cost Statements The Cove Corporation had the following selected account balances for the year ending December 31:

Beginning materials inventory (Jan.1)	$ 50,000
Ending materials inventory (Dec. 31)	60,000
Direct materials used	266,000
Indirect materials used	24,000
Indirect labor	130,000
Property taxes on factory	46,000
Depreciation on factory equipment	72,000
Rent on factory building	120,000
Factory utilities	17,200
Insurance on factory facilities	10,400
Beginning work in process (Jan.1)	69,000
Beginning finished goods (Jan. 1)	230,600

The total direct-labor portion of the payroll for the year was lost in the computer and needs to be reconstructed. The ending inventories (Dec. 31) of work in process and finished goods need to be computed. Before the direct-labor cost total was lost, some processing totals had been determined that showed the following:

Total manufacturing costs	$ 937,600
Cost of goods available for sale	1,114,800
Cost of goods sold for the year	932,400

Cove Corporation does not use predetermined overhead rates.

Required

1. Set up a detailed schedule of the cost of goods manufactured, and extend the schedule to show the cost of goods sold. (Refer back to chapter 2 as needed.) Be sure that you find the missing direct-labor cost as well as the work-in-process and finished goods ending inventories.
2. Prepare a list classifying each manufacturing cost item as either variable or fixed. Note: Ignore the semivariable classification and select the cost behavior classification that best reflects the cost item.
3. Assume that during the past year there was no work in process at either the beginning or end of the year and that 40,000 units were produced during the year. Determine the applicable unit costs of materials, labor, and factory overhead for the year.
4. The marketing department has just released an analysis of expected market response for next year. It estimates Cove Corporation's unit sales next year to be 64,000 units. The production manager has requested that you provide her with an estimate of unit costs for materials, labor, and factory overhead for next year.
5. Explain to the production and marketing managers and Cove Corporation's president the reason(s) for any differences between unit costs in requirements 3 and 4.

P3–6. Cost Behavior—Comparison of Various Methods
Community Hospital reports the following nursing hours and operating costs in the emergency room during a five-month period:

Month	Nursing Hours	Operating Costs
March	1,500	$27,000
April	1,700	29,000
May	1,000	25,500
June	1,200	25,000
July	800	23,500

Required

1. Determine the variable operating costs per nursing hour and the fixed operating costs per month using the high-low method.
2. Determine the variable and fixed portions of cost using the least-squares method.
3. Estimate operating costs for 1,300 nursing hours using each of the results you obtained in requirements 1 and 2. Comment on your results.

P3–7. Cost Behavior—Alternative Volume Bases and Least-Squares Analysis
The Graybar Concrete Pipe Company is in the process of analyzing cost behavior for planning and decision-making purposes. An important issue is deciding on the best base to use as the volume variable. The cost department suggests direct-labor hours. The production superintendent doesn't think direct-labor hours relates very well to overhead costs, because the company produces several different sizes of pipe. Production suggests using

tons of pipe produced as a base. The controller suggests that repairs and maintenance, which has been identified as a mixed cost, should be analyzed with the least-squares method using tons of pipe and direct-labor hours alternatively.

The following information has been gathered for each quarter of the most recent two years:

	Tons of Pipe Produced	Direct-Labor Hours	Repairs and Maintenance Costs
Last year:			
First quarter	36,000	20,000	$200,000
Second quarter	50,000	18,000	210,000
Third quarter	60,000	16,000	170,000
Fourth quarter	56,000	22,000	240,000
Two years ago:			
First quarter	30,000	10,000	100,000
Second quarter	22,000	6,000	90,000
Third quarter	42,000	8,000	120,000
Fourth quarter	24,000	12,000	150,000

Required

1. Using the least-squares method and direct-labor hours as the volume variable, determine the variable rate and the fixed amount of repairs and maintenance costs. Express your results in formula form, $y = a + bx$.
2. Repeat requirement 1 using tons of pipe produced as the volume base.

P3–8. Identification of Cost Behavior Patterns (CPA)
Some cost-behavior patterns that might be found in a company's cost picture are shown in the following graphs. On each graph the vertical axis represents dollar cost and the horizontal axis represents level of activity (e.g., number of labor hours, number of units, etc.).

Required

For each of the following situations, identify the graph (see next page) that best depicts the cost behavior pattern described. A particular graph may be applicable to more than one situation.

1. Cost of materials. The cost decreases 5 cents per unit for each of the first 200 units purchased, after which the unit cost remains constant at $2 per unit.
2. Bill for power costs. There is a flat fixed charge plus a variable cost after a certain number of kilowatt hours are used.
3. Municipal water and sewer bill, computed as follows:

First 100,000 gallons or less	$100 flat charge
Next 1,000 gallons	0.003 per gallon
Next 1,000 gallons	0.006 per gallon
etc.	

4. Depreciation of equipment. The straight-line method is used. When the depreciation rate was established, the firm expected that the obsolescence factor would be greater than the wear-and-tear factor.
5. Rent on a factory facility donated by the city. The agreement calls for a fixed rental payment unless 100,000 or more labor hours are worked, in which case no rental will be paid.
6. Salaries of technicians, for which the following situations apply:

0 to 1,000 machine hours	one technician
1,001 to 2,000 machine hours	two technicians
etc.	

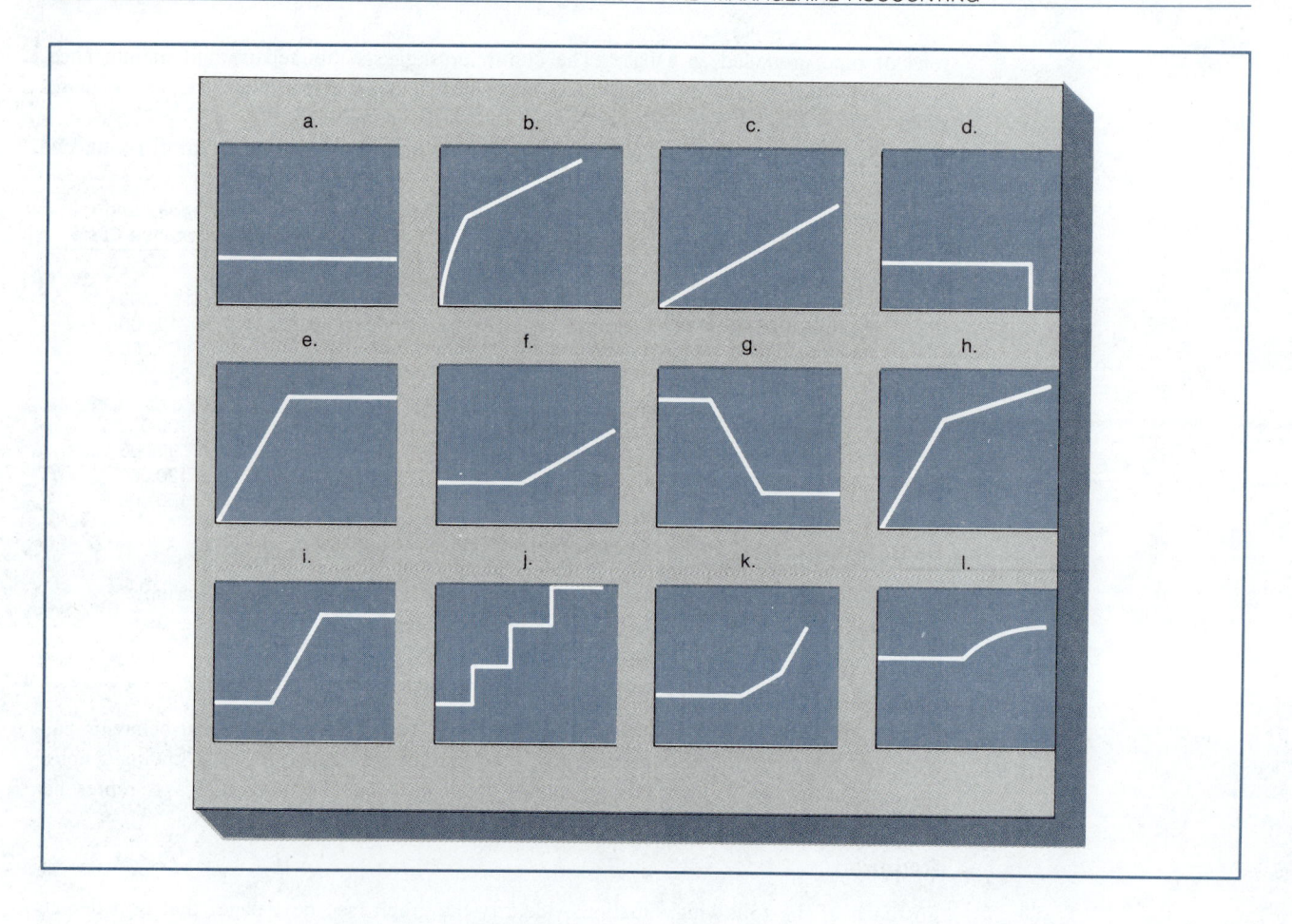

7. Cost of direct labor.
8. Rent on a building donated by the state to entice the firm to do business in the state. The agreement calls for a rental payment of $100,000, reduced by $1 for each direct-labor hour worked in excess of 200,000 hours, but a $20,000 minimum rental must be paid.
9. Lease payments on a machine. The lease agreement calls for a minimum payment of $1,000 up to 400 hours of machine time. An additional charge of $2 per hour is paid after 400 hours of machine time is used, up to a maximum charge of $2,000 per period.

P3–9. Cost Behavior Concepts—Summary of Chapters 2 and 3

Lundy Industries produces and sells chips used in microcomputers. The company purchases basic materials to specification from other suppliers, does a minimum of adaptation, and sells finished chips to computer component distributors. Information about Lundy's operations for the month of September is as follows:

1. Twenty thousand chips were produced at a cost of $1 each for basic materials and $0.75 each for out-of-pocket processing costs. Production capacity costs (i.e., depreciation, factory building and equipment, etc.) for September were $10,000. There were no beginning and ending work-in-process inventories.
2. One thousand finished chips were on hand September 1, carried at a cost of $2,250. Twelve hundred chips were on hand September 30.

3. Lundy has $2,200 of selling costs each month (for advertising, utilities, depreciation on selling equipment, etc.). Lundy also pays transportation on shipments to distributors, which averages $0.30 per chip, and a sales commission of 5 percent on a fixed sales price of $5 per chip.
4. Lundy's officers' salaries are $2,500 per month, and monthly office staff salaries are $1,000. Other administrative-type activities (i.e., mailing, communication, etc.) average $0.20 per chip sold.

Required

1. Determine the variable and fixed costs of production, marketing, and administration. Indicate in each category the totals for the month of September as well as the total variable and total fixed cost portions of the respective overall totals.
2. Prepare an income statement for the month of September that has appropriate sections showing the cost of goods manufactured, cost of goods sold, and operating expenses. Assume Lundy uses the first-in, first-out inventory costing method.

P3–10. Cost Behavior—Factory Overhead Application Calendar, Inc. is in the process of developing its overhead application rate for the coming year. Your assistant has developed the following data from the prior year's operations, which he thinks is representative of normal business operations.

	June	July	August
Units produced	1,600	1,500	2,000
Direct labor hours worked	2,800	3,000	4,200
Overhead costs:			
Cost #1	$ 7,300	$ 7,000	$ 8,500
Cost #2	1,200	1,200	1,200
Cost #3	5,600	5,250	7,000
Cost #4	12,750	11,500	14,500
Cost #5	900	800	1,000
Total	$27,750	$25,750	$32,200

Required

Use the high-low method to answer each of the following questions, and assume a linear relationship for cost behavior patterns.

1. With respect to *units produced,* what type of cost behavior pattern is exhibited by Cost #1?
2. With respect to *units produced,* what type of cost behavior pattern is exhibited by Cost #3?
3. With respect to *direct-labor hours worked,* what type of cost behavior pattern is exhibited by Cost #3?
4. Develop a mathematical equation that can be used to predict total manufacturing overhead costs each month, using units produced as the independent variable.
5. Suppose that the company decides to apply overhead to work in process based on units produced and that it expects 20,000 units to be produced during the coming year. What will be its overhead application rate?
6. Suppose further that the company used the rate you suggested in requirement 5 and incurred $300,000 of overhead but only produced 19,000 units. What is the over- or underabsorbed overhead for the year?

Chapter 4

Contribution Analysis: Alternative Cost Groupings and Relevant Cost Analysis for Decision Making

Outline

RELEVANT COST OBJECTIVES AND TERMINOLOGY FOR CONTRIBUTION REPORTING
Data Bank Concept
Relevant Cost Objectives
Management function
Cost behavior
Decision significance
Cost Groupings for Contribution Reporting
THE CONTRIBUTION MARGIN CONCEPT
Definition of Contribution Margin
Contribution Margin Ratio
Contribution Margin Versus Gross Margin
An Example of Contribution Reporting
Segment Margin Analysis
THE ROLE OF COST INFORMATION IN DECISIONS
Fallacy of Full Costs
RELEVANT COSTS IN DECISION PROBLEMS
Expected Future Costs
Costs that Differ Among Decision Alternatives

ANAYLSIS OF COST INFORMATION FOR TYPICAL NONROUTINE DECISIONS
Total Cost Approach
Contribution Approach
SOME EXAMPLES OF NONROUTINE DECISIONS
Make or Buy
Special Orders
Product Line Decisions
OTHER CONSIDERATIONS IN NONROUTINE DECISIONS
Short-run Versus Long-run Considerations
Taxes and the Time Value of Money
The Role of Qualitative Factors
SUMMARY
SELF-STUDY PROBLEMS
SUGGESTED READINGS
DISCUSSION QUESTIONS
EXERCISES
PROBLEMS

The basic objective of cost accounting is to accumulate manufacturing costs and to organize them in a meaningful way for management to use in the operation of the business and for external reporting in traditional financial statements. Chapter 2 identified several ways of classifying costs and illustrated the process by which costs are combined and prepared for external reporting. Chapter 3 focused on two cost objectives—generally accepted accounting treatment and cost behavior. Product costs were used to illustrate the various cost patterns and the methods used to analyze and quantify them.

This chapter focuses on internal uses of cost accounting data. It shows how cost information can be organized, classified, and reported to management in a format that is meaningful for many management decisions. This format is called *contribution reporting* and is based on the cost behavior and cost function classifications described in previous chapters.

After completing this chapter, you should be able to:

1. classify costs by both behavior and function.
2. describe the contribution reporting format and arrange costs within that format.
3. compute contribution margin.
4. prepare an income statement in a contribution reporting format.
5. define *relevant costs*.
6. apply relevant cost concepts in analyzing several short-run decision situations.

RELEVANT COST OBJECTIVES AND TERMINOLOGY FOR CONTRIBUTION REPORTING

Cost information that is assembled in the accounts and reported on the traditional cost-of-goods-manufactured statement for external users will generally be inadequate for internal uses. This is particularly true in large and complex manufacturing firms. The format of the external reports is not convenient for managers to use in planning, controlling, and evaluating operations. Also, information in conventional reports does not satisfy management's decision-making needs. The following section introduces a conceptual framework for capturing and recording cost data that can be used in a variety of reports. Cost data is stored in a company's data bank and extracted as needed for management reports.

Data Bank Concept

A data bank is a useful concept to bridge the gap from the traditional product-related format to other formats that may be more useful for internal purposes. The **data bank** contains information that relates to a particular organization. Try to picture a large collection device, like a memory bank in a computer, into which data flow. The data are coded according to several different classifications, such as management function, accounting treatment, traceability, and cost behavior. The data bank concept is illustrated in figure 4.1.

The data bank provides the capability of extracting data according to any cost objectives and assembling it into whatever format is most useful to management. There are a variety of reports that can be developed from the data bank. One possible format is an income statement with supporting schedules of cost of goods manufactured and cost of goods sold. Another possible format is a contribution report. This chapter describes the contribution report and illustrates its usefulness to management.

FIGURE 4.1 The Data Bank Concept

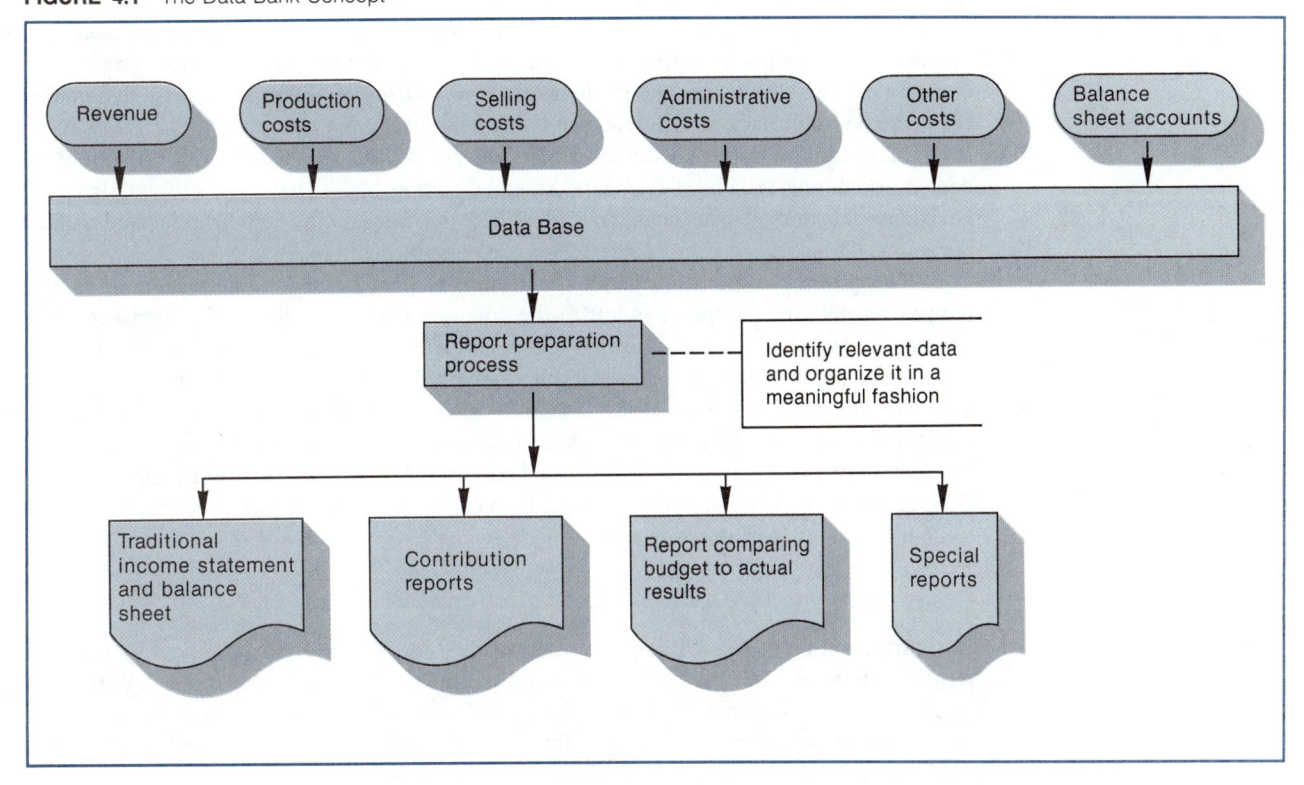

Relevant Cost Objectives

Chapter 2 provided an overview of cost objectives. There are three primary cost classifications that are used in developing a **contribution report**—management function, cost behavior, and decision significance. Each of these cost objectives will be briefly reviewed.

Management Function Management function identifies the functional area of the organization responsible for the activity that incurred the cost. The major functional areas for a manufacturing organization are manufacturing, marketing, and general administration. In preparing contribution reports we will combine marketing and general administrative costs into one category called "selling and administrative expenses" or some similar title.

Cost Behavior Cost behavior describes the way a cost changes as volume changes. The most common cost patterns are fixed, variable, and semivariable. A fixed cost remains relatively constant in total regardless of the level of production. Total variable costs vary proportionately with changes in production. Semivariable costs have both a fixed and variable element. The fixed portion is the amount incurred at a zero production level, and the variable portion is the increase that results as production increases. In preparing a contribution report we will split the semivariable cost into its fixed and variable components and combine them with other fixed and variable costs. Thus only fixed and variable costs will be included on the report.

Decision Significance Decision significance refers to the relevance of a cost in making a particular decision. Relevance is a key concept when drawing costs from the data bank for a special report. Important questions in determining relevance concern which costs are relevant to, make a difference in, or are likely to be influenced by the situation.

For management decision making, **relevant costs** are generally those future costs that differ among the alternatives. The typical situation with which managers must deal involves comparing the current situation with one or more alternatives. Certain costs change when embarking on one of the alternative courses of action. The costs that change are those that will make a difference and are, therefore, relevant costs.

In selecting costs for external reports, relevant costs are specified by generally accepted accounting principles (GAAP). Standard-setting bodies have tried to anticipate the decisions of external users and have identified the information that is relevant to those decisions. These information requirements are contained in GAAP.

The primary responsibility for identifying relevant costs for internal decisions that require special cost groupings is left to the cost accountant and the decision maker. They are free to draw information from the data bank, as well as from external sources such as general economics, statistics, and marketing analysis. The first thing that must be done in selecting relevant costs is to clearly identify the decision for which the cost data will be used. Two questions can then be asked in identifying relevant cost information: Is the information representative of *future* expected cost? and Is the cost information *different* from cost information that will exist regardless of the alternative chosen? A positive answer to both questions indicates a relevant cost.

Cost Groupings for Contribution Reporting

In contribution reporting the costs are grouped *first* by *cost behavior* and *then* by *management function*. A relevant cost is analyzed to see if it is fixed or variable. Within the behavioral classification it is then analyzed and grouped according to management function. Costs in each of these categories may be divided into product lines or operating units of a company, but that depends on the decision at hand.

The following variable and fixed categories, with the related product and nonproduct subdivisions, are used in contribution reporting.

I. Variable costs
  A. Manufacturing costs (product costs)
    1. Direct material
    2. Direct labor
    3. Variable factory overhead
  B. Other costs (nonproduct costs)
    1. Selling
    2. Administration

II. Fixed costs
  A. Manufacturing costs (product costs)
    1. Fixed factory overhead
  B. Other costs (nonproduct costs)
    1. Selling
    2. Administration

THE CONTRIBUTION MARGIN CONCEPT

Contribution margin has been developed for internal reporting to management. The same basic cost and revenue data that are reported externally are used in preparing contribution reports. The cost data are merely grouped differently to compute an intermediate number called contribution margin rather than the traditional gross margin. A key to the alternative groupings is the separation of costs into variable and fixed categories.

FIGURE 4.2

Income Statement Using Contribution Report Format

		%
Sales	$100,000	100
Less: Variable costs	60,000	60
Contribution margin	$ 40,000	40
Less: Fixed costs	25,000	25
Net income	$ 15,000	15

Definition of Contribution Margin

Contribution margin is defined as *revenue minus variable costs*. Fixed costs are subtracted from the contribution margin to equal net income. These relationships are illustrated in figure 4.2.

Contribution reporting emphasizes variable and fixed costs. The contribution margin represents the amount available after sales revenue has covered all variable costs, which include both product and nonproduct costs. The contribution margin is the amount available to cover fixed costs, both product and nonproduct, and provide net income.

Contribution reporting focuses on short-run profitability. Revenues and variable costs can generally be influenced by management decisions within a relatively short time period, such as an operating cycle of the business. Fixed costs generally cannot be changed in a short time period. Therefore, the contribution margin is the number that is most sensitive to management's decisions and that can help managers plan operations and evaluate results.

Contribution Margin Ratio

The **contribution margin ratio** is a ratio of the contribution margin to sales revenue. It can be computed on the contribution margin of the company as a whole, on individual divisions or segments of the company, or even on individual products. The formula to compute the contribution margin ratio for an entire company is:

$$\text{Company contribution margin ratio} = \frac{\text{Contribution margin}}{\text{Sales revenue}}$$

When the contribution margin ratio is computed for a single product, the contribution margin (sale price minus variable costs) is divided by the sale price of the product.

$$\text{Product contribution margin ratio} = \frac{\text{Sale price} - \text{Variable costs}}{\text{Sales price}}$$

In figure 4.2 the company's contribution margin ratio is shown as 40 percent. This figure also shows that 60 percent of the sales revenue goes to cover variable costs and 40 percent is available to cover fixed costs and provide net income.

Contribution Margin versus Gross Margin

The primary difference between contribution margin and gross margin is the cost objectives used in computing each intermediate result. Remember that revenues minus expenses equals net income in both statements. For internal contribution reports, however, the contribution margin is based on a cost behavior classification system. Revenues minus variable costs equals the contribution margin. Contribution margin minus fixed costs equals net income. The cost objective here is cost behavior (fixed/ variable).

For external income statements, an intermediate result called the gross margin is computed. Total product costs, both fixed and variable, are subtracted from sales to give the gross margin. Period costs are then subtracted from the gross margin to obtain net income. The cost objective here is accounting treatment (product/period).

An Example of Contribution Reporting

The following example will illustrate the data bank concept and show how alternative reports can be developed from the same basic set of data. Cost and revenue data for Hartshorn Incorporated are summarized as they might be contained in the data bank. A traditional income statement will be developed using the product/period cost classification. The contribution report will then be developed using the variable/fixed cost classification.

Hartshorn Incorporated manufactures and sells one style of briefcase. The following production, selling, and administrative data are for the year ending December 31, 19X1:

1. Production for the year was 100,000 briefcases at a cost of:

		Total	Per Unit
Direct material		$ 545,000	$ 5.45
Direct labor		925,000	9.25
Factory overhead			
Variable	$472,000		4.72
Fixed	318,000		3.18
Total factory overhead		790,000	
Total manufacturing cost		$2,260,000	$22.60

There were no beginning or ending work-in-process inventories.

2. Sales for the year totaled 100,000 units at $50 each. There were no beginning or ending finished-goods inventories.
3. Selling expenses were $1,200,000, of which $650,000 were fixed and $550,000 were variable.
4. Administrative expenses totaled $750,000, of which $270,000 were fixed and $480,000 were variable.

Figure 4.3 illustrates the traditional income statement based on the product/period cost classification. Cost of goods sold, which represents expired product costs, is

FIGURE 4.3

Hartshorn Incorporated
Income Statement—Traditional Format
Year Ending December 31, 19X1

Sales revenue (100,000 units @ $50)		$5,000,000
Less: Cost of goods sold (product costs)		
Beginning finished-goods inventory	$ 0	
Plus: Cost of goods manufactured	2,260,000	
Goods available for sale	$2,260,000	
Less: Ending finished-goods inventory	0	
Total cost of goods sold		2,260,000
Gross margin		$2,740,000
Less: Operating expenses (period costs)		
Selling expenses	$1,200,000	
Administrative expenses	750,000	
Total		$1,950,000
Net income		$ 790,000

FIGURE 4.4

Hartshorn Incorporated
Income Statement—Contribution Format
Year Ending December 31, 19X1

Sales revenue (100,000 units @ $50)		$5,000,000
Less: Variable costs		
Direct material (100,000 units @ $5.45)	$545,000	
Direct labor (100,000 units @ $9.25)	925,000	
Factory overhead (100,000 units @ $4.72)	472,000	
Selling	550,000	
Administrative	480,000	
Total variable costs		2,972,000
Contribution margin		2,028,000
Less: Fixed costs		
Factory overhead (100,000 units @ $3.18)	318,000	
Selling	650,000	
Administrative	270,000	
Total fixed costs		1,238,000
Net income		$ 790,000

subtracted from sales to obtain gross margin. This is the amount available to cover period costs and provide a net income.

Figure 4.4 illustrates the contribution report that is based on a variable/fixed cost classification. Variable costs are subtracted from sales revenue to obtain the contribution margin. This is the amount available to cover fixed costs and provide a net income. Notice that sales and net income are the same on both statements.

Remember that the contribution margin format focuses on the units sold. What was included as part of cost of goods sold under the traditional format is split between variable and fixed costs on the contribution report. Notice also that when you total the variable and fixed selling expenses on the contribution report, you have the same total operating expenses that were included on the traditional income statement.

Note that this example assumes no beginning or ending inventories of finished goods. Having inventory requires a cost flow assumption and a selection of direct or absorption costing, which is covered in detail in Chapter 19.

In summary, the same basic data used in preparing a traditional income statement are used in a contribution report. The costs are just grouped differently. Gross margin as presented on the income statement represents the amount of mark-up the company has on the products manufactured. The contribution margin represents the results that are most sensitive to management decisions in the short run.

Segment Margin Analysis

Another common measure of performance is the **segment margin,** which is the contribution margin of a segment minus all other direct fixed costs of the segment. The contribution margin differentiates between fixed and variable costs in the calculation of net income. However, when considering segment analysis, it is necessary to differentiate between avoidable fixed costs (those fixed costs that would be avoided if the segment was discontinued) and unavoidable fixed costs (those fixed costs that would continue even if the segment was discontinued), in addition to differentiating between fixed and variable costs.

Segment margin analysis is simply contribution margin analysis with the additional differentiation between avoidable and unavoidable fixed costs. It enables an evaluation of performance with a longer time perspective. Consider, for example, a company that uses

FIGURE 4.5

Segment Margin Analysis for Divisions

	Company Total	Division A	Division B
Sales	$550,000	$250,000	$300,000
Less: Variable expenses	300,000	100,000	200,000
Contribution margin	$250,000	$150,000	$100,000
Less: Direct fixed costs	25,000	10,000	15,000
Segment margin	$225,000	$140,000	$ 85,000
Less: Indirect fixed costs	20,000		
Net income	$205,000		

segment analysis to assess the performance of its two divisions. Figure 4.5 shows the numeric components of such an evaluation. The segment margin shows the amount each segment contributes toward the company's total fixed costs and net income. Figure 4.5 indicates the margin produced by each division after subtracting all directly traceable segment costs from the revenue directly produced by the division.

Depending on the detail desired by management, figure 4.5 may represent only the first level of segment analysis. For example, suppose that division B handles two important product lines. Segment analysis can be used to assess performance of these product lines, as shown in figure 4.6. The information in the figure indicates that up to $14,000 of direct fixed costs could be avoided, depending on the elimination or continuance of either one or both of the product lines—$8,000 related to product 1 and $6,000 to product 2. However, $1,000 of fixed costs are common or shared by both products and cannot be eliminated unless the entire division is eliminated. If division B was discontinued, a total of $15,000 of fixed costs would be avoided. The individual product segment margins calculated in Figure 4.6 represent the amount of the company's total net income that would change if that particular product line was discontinued. Remember that avoidable fixed costs are those that would be eliminated if a segment was discontinued.

The comparison of product segment margins in figure 4.6 provides some additional insights into segment analysis. Product 1 clearly contributes the most to divisional net income. Product 2 not only contributes less, but a negative segment margin raises questions about the product line's viability. This points out that segment analysis provides information for decisions that concern whether or not operations should be continued as well as information about relative performance.

A positive segment margin justifies continuing segment operations; a negative segment margin indicates that there may not be justification for continuing that segment. In such instances, an analysis of segment contribution margin may be helpful in making a final decision. For example, continuation of a segment with a negative segment margin

FIGURE 4.6

Segment Margin Analysis for Products

	Division B	Product 1	Product 2
Sales	$300,000	$250,000	$ 50,000
Less: Variable expenses	200,000	155,000	45,000
Contribution margin	$100,000	$ 95,000	$ 5,000
Less: Avoidable fixed costs (products)	14,000	8,000	6,000
Segment margin (products)	$ 86,000	$ 87,000	$ (1,000)
Less: Unavoidable fixed costs (division)	1,000		
Segment margin (division)	$ 85,000		

and a negative contribution margin should be seriously questioned. However, when considering discontinuance, other factors need to be considered. For example, is the situation expected to continue for a short or long period of time? Also, what effect will discontinuance have on the firm's other products?

In situations where the segment margin is negative and the contribution margin is positive, management may also consider discontinuing segment operations. A positive contribution margin indicates that variable costs are being covered, and a negative segment margin indicates that avoidable fixed costs are not being covered. Not only is the segment's viability in serious question, but because some fixed costs can be avoided, net income will increase if the segment is discontinued. However, because fixed costs are involved, how soon discontinuance can occur may depend on the time frame within which the firm's commitments to the segment's direct fixed costs can be avoided. This points out that when direct fixed costs are considered avoidable, it is important that the time required for avoidance be a criterion for classification.

THE ROLE OF COST INFORMATION IN DECISIONS

The types of decisions emphasized in this chapter are often referred to as **nonroutine decisions** because they are not directly related to the ordinary, repetitive production cycle of a firm. For example, discontinuing a product line, replacing present equipment with new machinery, making a component rather than buying one from outside vendors, and accepting a special order below customary prices are all examples of nonroutine decisions.

Accounting for **routine decisions,** on the other hand, relates to the accumulation and reporting of information for everyday control of operations and for ordinary product-costing purposes. This section develops concepts and procedures for handling decisions that arise only periodically in a firm's life and that are, therefore, called nonroutine decisions.

The primary function of information, including cost accounting information, in the process of making nonroutine decisions is to increase the knowledge level of the decision maker. **Knowledge** refers to one's understanding of reality or the true state of nature and concerns what is, what was, or what may be. Knowledge is vital in making all types of decisions. Because nonroutine decisions are infrequently made, however, most firms do not have built into their accounting systems the mechanisms for formulating all of the necessary information for these decisions. Therefore, the process of acquiring knowledge for nonroutine decisions is somewhat different than that for routine decisions.

Knowledge is vital in making nonroutine business decisions because it helps the decision maker to do the following:

1. Describe the problem or decision situation at hand.
2. Formulate alternative courses of action.
3. Reduce the possible courses of action to those that are actually viable alternatives.
4. Reduce the uncertainty related to the success or failure of each viable alternative.
5. Analyze the relevant information obtained in an appropriate model, which might be chosen from a number of analytical frameworks. The contribution income statement is an example.
6. Choose the course of action that appears most likely to accomplish organizational goals.

To illustrate how information facilitates the decision-making process, consider the following situation. The management of a firm is trying to decide whether or not to add a new product line or continue to operate with existing lines. In the process of considering this decision, management collects as much information as possible about other product lines and their potential impact on company operations. Cost accounting information is essential for such decisions. Information about the probable acceptance of each product in the marketplace, the forecasted sales of each new line, and the probable effect of new product lines on the sales of existing lines are examples of additional items that may be considered.

After accumulation, this information is analyzed by product line to provide a forecast of the expected contribution to earnings and the probability of success or failure for each product line. At this point, management has more knowledge with which to make a decision; that is, *(a)* the problem or decision situation has been described, *(b)* alternative courses of action have been formulated, and *(c)* the probable returns and uncertainty associated with each viable alternative are apparent. Cost accounting information has fulfilled its function by helping the decision maker acquire the knowledge necessary to make an appropriate decision.

The decision process then proceeds with management comparing the expected contribution from each project and making a decision. This is an abbreviated view of the actual decision process, but it illustrates that the role of cost accounting information in the decision-making process is to help the decision maker to *(a)* acquire some of the knowledge necessary for understanding the decision situation, *(b)* formulate the problem in a way that highlights the current state of knowledge, *(c)* analyze possible decision alternatives, and *(d)* increase the probability of selecting the best course of action.

Fallacy of Full Costs

There is a tendency toward the indiscriminate use of full-cost information for various purposes, including decision analysis. This can be dangerous because of the impossibility of obtaining a consistent and objective picture of full costs. It is important to keep in mind that to obtain full-cost results, some arbitrary allocations of certain costs are necessary. The most obvious problem in obtaining full-cost information arises with fixed manufacturing costs. For example, suppose a firm has $100,000 of fixed factory overhead. If the $100,000 is allocated over 20,000 units, the unit cost is $5. However, if only 10,000 units receive the allocation, the unit cost becomes $10.

The foolish and indiscriminate use of full costs is illustrated by a situation known to the authors. A firm that had experienced substantial growth and success had expanded into a number of product lines. The president decided it would be helpful to have information about the profitability of each product line. The accounting personnel, being schooled in traditional, full-cost procedures, prepared a conventional income statement showing operating results for the total company. The statement was then broken down for each of seven product lines. The president was shocked to discover that two of the seven product lines showed a net loss, and he ordered the losing lines to be discontinued. As a result, the firm's overall profits declined. The reason for the decline in profits was that certain manufacturing and administrative costs had to be arbitrarily allocated to each product line. Such costs were not eliminated when the two lines were discontinued.

RELEVANT COSTS IN DECISION PROBLEMS

There are various nonroutine decision situations and many types of cost accounting information. Variable costs, historical costs, standard costs, conversion costs, marginal costs, and opportunity costs are just some of the types discussed in this text. Determining which type of cost accounting information is actually relevant in a given business decision is one of the most important aspects of the decision-making process. Adding irrelevant information may confuse the decision maker or may draw attention away from other relevant information. In addition, there is always the danger that irrelevant information will be improperly used in analyzing decision alternatives, which may lead to the selection of a suboptimal course of action.

Relevant costs are simply the types of costs that are useful in a particular decision situation. As mentioned earlier, they can be identified by determining if they satisfy two necessary criteria—if they are *expected future costs* and if they *differ among decision alternatives.*

Expected Future Costs

Expected future costs are costs that are expected to be incurred in the future as a result of choosing a particular decision alternative. Management decisions are made and actions are taken to achieve specific goals. Because goals are achieved in the future, decisions must be made based on expected future circumstances that include expected future costs and revenues.

The "future" refers to the time period affected by the decision. For example, a manager evaluating whether to take or refuse a special order would consider the materials, labor, and overhead costs expected to be incurred as a result of taking the order. Historical or past costs incurred in making similar orders may be useful information for predicting what *might* be the cost of the special order. However, historical costs do not satisfy the criterion of expected future costs and are almost never relevant in decisions. Historical costs that are expected to continue at the same level into the future are actually expected future costs, not historical costs, and they are, therefore, relevant in decisions.

Costs That Differ Among Decision Alternatives

Only costs that differ among decision alternatives are relevant to a decision. For example, assume that the alternatives in a given decision situation are to purchase either machine *X* or machine *Y*. If the machines cost $10,000 and $12,000, respectively, their costs are relevant to the decision at hand because the prices differ between machines. The $2,000 difference between the cost of the machines is the relevant component of information. If both machines cost the same, however, their cost has no relevance for the decision.

Other information components, such as the disposal value of the machines or the future cost savings from purchasing the machines, might differ between machines and, as a result, constitute the relevant costs for this decision. When there are no cost (or revenue) differences among different alternatives, the decision maker may be indifferent about the choice of alternatives from an economic viewpoint. In such circumstances, the final decision may be based on nonquantifiable factors.

ANALYSIS OF COST INFORMATION FOR NONROUTINE DECISIONS

For a more detailed illustration of the application of the criteria for determining relevance, consider the following situation. A company is trying to decide if it should replace an old machine with a new, more efficient machine. Information about the old and new machines is as follows:

Old Machine

Original cost	$100,000
Book value	80,000
Current disposal value	30,000
Remaining life	5 years

New Machine

Current cost	$120,000
Disposal value in 5 years	0
Expected life	5 years

The new machine is expected to reduce total variable operating costs from $1,075,000 to $775,000. Total revenue from sales is expected to remain at $2,500,000 regardless of the machinery used.

At first management may consider the immediate effect on net income of replacing the old machine. With a book value of $80,000 and a current disposal value of only $30,000, an immediate effect would be the recognition of a $50,000 ($80,000 − $30,000) loss on disposal of the old macine. Management may be more inclined to continue with the old machine and show $16,000 depreciation expense on the income statement for the next five years rather than show such as large loss on disposal in the current year.

However, such a hasty and incomplete analysis rarely results in making the best decision from a cost viewpoint. A more complete analysis, as shown in figure 4.7, reveals that the most cost-effective decision is to purchase the new machine. In this example, the book value of the old machine is a historical cost and does not meet the criterion of a cost that differs between alternatives. Using historical costs, book values, or any other irrelevant information may cloud the decision analysis and lead to poor decisions. To avoid the pitfalls of using incomplete or irrelevant information, adoption of a thorough and systematic approach for making nonroutine decisions is suggested.

FIGURE 4.7

Five-year Analysis of Net Income for Decision to Keep Old Machine or Purchase New Machine

(000 omitted)

	Keep Old Machine	Purchase New Machine	Difference
Sales	$2,500	$2,500	$ 0
Variable operating expenses	(1,075)	(775)	300
Old machine:			
Book value written off by:			
Periodic depreciation	(80)		
or			0
Sump-sum sale		(80)	
Current disposal value		30	30
New machine:			
Current cost written off by:			
Periodic depreciation		(120)	(120)
Net income	$1,345	$1,555	$210

Calculation of loss on disposal of old machine:

Book value of old machine	$80
Current disposal value of old machine	30
Loss on disposal of old machine	$50

Total Cost Approach

The following set of procedures for making nonroutine decisions is referred to as the total cost approach to nonroutine decisions.

1. Accumulate all potentially relevant information about each alternative under consideration.
2. Eliminate those costs (revenues) that are not expected future costs (revenues).
3. Eliminate those costs (revenues) that do not differ among alternatives.
4. Evaluate alternatives based on the remaining relevant and differential information.

To illustrate the use of this approach, refer to the previous example concerning the possible replacement of an old machine. Figure 4.7 follows step 1 and gives a summary of potentially relevant information for the five-year period affected by the decision to replace the old machine.

After accumulating the potentially relevant information, the next step is to identify and eliminate costs and revenues that are not expected future costs. Forecasted sales and the current disposal value of the old machine are both expected future revenues, depending on which alternative is chosen. Variable operating expenses and the cost of the new machine are both expected future costs. The only cost that is not an expected future cost is the book value of the old machine; therefore, it should be eliminated from further consideration based on the future cost criterion of relevance.

The next step is to eliminate those costs and revenues that do not differ between decision alternatives. Sales do not differ between alternatives; neither does the book value of the old machine. Book value is handled in a different way in the accounting records, depending on which alternative is chosen. For example, if the old machine is retained, book value is written off by periodic depreciation charges over the machine's remaining useful life. If the new machine is acquired, the old machine's book value is written off as part of a sales transaction. However, this difference in accounting procedure does not alter the fact that book value does not differ between alternatives over the time period affected by the decision. Thus it fails to meet both criteria of relevance.

The final step in the analysis is to evaluate alternative courses of action based on the remaining differential information. The relevant items of information and the net effect on income are shown in the "difference" column in figure 4.7. Assuming that each alternative course of action has an equal probability of success or failure, the results indicate that the firm would be better off by $210,000 during the next five years by choosing to purchase the new machine.

Figure 4.7 illustrates a format that is useful for gathering and analyzing available information. It emphasizes the *differences* among alternatives, so that only those factors that should influence the final decision are highlighted. Yet all information related to the decision situation is openly and clearly presented, so there is no ambiguity about what information has been considered, how the analysis was made, and what information is actually relevant to the decision at hand.

The final report to management may contain only information that is relevant to the decision at hand. For example, using the data from figure 4.7 as supporting information, figure 4.8 illustrates a final report to management. When more than two decision alternatives are being considered, it is usually not helpful to calculate and show a number of "difference" columns. Rather, the relevant information for each alternative is reported, and the decision is based on a ranking of final total reults.

Capital budgeting principles that will be presented in chapters 23 and 24 apply to the calculation of costs and revenues that are assumed as "given" in this chapter. There are

FIGURE 4.8

Report to Management—Five-year Analysis of Net Income for Decision to Keep Old Machine or Purchase New Machine

	(000 omitted)
	Differential Revenues and Expenses
Decrease in variable operating expenses	$300
Disposal value of old machine	30
Cost of new machine	(120)
Increase in net income over the life of the new machine	$210

additional procedures, such as the calculation of present values of future cash flows, that may be necessary to determine the appropriate numbers to use in a decision analysis. However, the principles discussed in this chapter remain the same regardless of the detail involved in generating the basic information.

Contribution Approach

Contribution margin analysis, discussed earlier in this chapter, can be useful in making nonroutine decisions. A major feature of the contribution approach is that variable and fixed costs are clearly identified at the outset, which greatly simplifies the information analysis. This is especially useful in situations where all variable costs are relevant and all fixed costs are irrelevant. It should be emphasized, however, that variable costs may or may not be relevant and fixed costs may or may not be irrelevant. In each case it will depend on whether the cost or revenue is a future item that is expected to differ among alternatives. Variable costs should not be presumed to be relevant and fixed costs should not be presumed to be irrelevant.

In situations where relevance does not follow cost behavior patterns, the contribution approach is still a useful starting point. It also assists in analyzing the shot-run versus long-run effects of decisions.

When possible, the total cost approach and the contribution approach should be used simultaneously to verify the accuracy and validity of the information analysis. A characteristic of many nonroutine decisions is that the obvious is not always the best course of action. Using both approaches to compare results may uncover oversights and invalid reasoning. However, in some nonroutine decisions the contribution approach is a superior method of analysis, because an optimal solution using the total cost approach might require extended computations or even trial-and-error methods.

To illustrate the use of the contribution approach in making nonroutine decisions, consider the following situation. A company that manufactures two products wants to emphasize one product in its production and marketing efforts. The dilemma arises because both products use a particular metal alloy that is in scarce supply. Because a limited quantity of the metal alloy is available, management would like to promote the product that will contribute the most to company profits. Cost and revenue information for the two products is given in figure 4.9

Product *B* seems to be the logical choice for promotion because it has the larger contribution margin per unit. However, the supplier of the alloy indicates that only 5,000 pounds of the alloy will be available to the company during each accounting period for the foreseeable future. Therefore, the availability of the metal alloy, a *scarce resource,* is a *constraining factor* in this situation.

Scarce resources may include raw materials availability (as in this example), floor space, machine hours, labor hours, or budget constraints. When constraining factors are

FIGURE 4.9

Cost and Revenue Information for Competing Products

	Product A	Product B
Sales (per unit)	$20	$30
Variable costs (per unit)	15	21
Contribution margin	$ 5	$ 9

FIGURE 4.10

Scarce Resource Information for Competing Products

	Product A	Product B
Contribution margin per unit (fig. 4.9)	$5.00	$9.00
Pounds of alloy required to produce one unit	÷ 2	÷ 4
Contribution margin per pound of alloy	$2.50	$2.25
Total available pounds of alloy	× 5,000	× 5,000
Total contribution	$12,500	$11,250

involved, emphasis for maximizing profits shifts from contribution margin *per unit* to contribution margin *per unit of scarce resource*. For example, it takes 4 pounds of the alloy to produce one unit of *B,* and it takes 2 pounds of the alloy to produce one unit of *A*. Figure 4.10 shows the results of considering the contribution margin per unit of metal alloy.

This example shows how the contribution approach can provide important input into the solution of nonroutine decisions. A suggested procedure is to verify results found using one approach with the other approach. Figure 4.11 shows how the results obtained using the contribution approach can be verified by using the total cost approach.

The preceding example shows how to deal with a situation in which there is only one constraint—the limited availability of one scarce resource. However, a typical situation involves multiple constraints caused by the availability of a number of different resources. In such situations, an analytical tool called linear programming is necessary to make appropriate profit maximizing decisions. The use of linear programming is discussed in chapter 21.

FIGURE 4.11

Analysis of Information Under Constrained Conditions

Possible Production (in units) of Each Product

	Product A	Product B
Pounds of alloy available	5,000	5,000
Pounds of alloy required per unit	÷ 2	÷ 4
Potential production in units	2,500	1,250

Projected Income Statements for the Production of Each Product

	Product A Per Unit	Product A Amount	Product B Per Unit	Product B Amount	Dollar Difference
Sales	$20	$50,000	$30	$37,500	$12,500
Variable costs	15	37,500	21	26,250	11,250
Contribution margin		$12,500		$11,250	$ 1,250

SOME EXAMPLES OF NONROUTINE DECISIONS

The following are examples of nonroutine decisions that commonly occur in manufacturing operations. The types selected for illustration are intended to provide sufficient background to enable the application of solution principles in a wide variety of decision situations.

Make or Buy

A decision faced by many manufacturing firms is whether to make their own subassemblies and parts or to buy them from outside suppliers. For example, consider a company that produces a number of different subassemblies that eventually become part of a final product. The company has accumulated the following cost information concerning its annual production of one of these subassemblies.

	Cost per Unit	Total Cost for 5,000 Units
Direct materials	$ 4	$ 20,000
Direct labor	12	60,000
Variable overhead	8	40,000
Fixed overhead	6	30,000
Total	$30	$150,000

An external supplier has offered to provide the firm with its annual needs of this particular subassembly at a price of $29 per unit—an apparent savings of $1 per unit. Without the benefit of additional analysis, this $1 difference between the cost of making the subassembly and the price of buying the subassembly from the outside supplier might influence management to buy the subassemblies with the expectation of saving $5,000 each year. However, as previously illustrated, the best course of action in nonroutine decisions is rarely so obvious, and it is wise to develop a formal analysis rather than jump to a premature conclusion based on incomplete information.

Applying the concepts developed in this chapter, figure 4.12 presents an analysis of information using the total cost approach to making nonroutine decisions. All of the costs in figure 4.12 are expected future costs and satisfy the first criterion of relevance. The cost to buy externally and the variable manufacturing costs of making the subassembly differ between decision alternatives and satisfy the second criteria of relevance.

FIGURE 4.12

Analysis of Information for Make or Buy Decision

5,000 Units of a Certain Subassembly

	Make Internally	Buy Externally	Difference
Cost to buy externally @ $29		$145,000	$(145,000)
Cost to make internally:			
Direct materials @ $4	$20,000		20,000
Direct labor @ $12	60,000		60,000
Variable overhead @ $8	40,000		40,000
Fixed overhead[a]	30,000	20,000	10,000
Total	$150,000	$165,000	$ (15,000)

[a] $10,000 of fixed costs can be avoided if the subassemblies are purchased externally.

However, not all fixed overhead, such as insurance, depreciation, executive salaries, and property taxes, can be avoided if the decision is made to buy from the external supplier; that is, $20,000 of fixed overhead does not differ between decision alternatives. The difference of $10,000 is the only part of fixed overhead that satisfies both criteria of relevance and is, therefore, included in the difference column. The results of the analysis indicate that if the company purchases the subassemblies from the outside supplier, net income would not increase by $5,000 but would decrease by $15,000. Therefore, based on quantitative factors, the appropriate decision is to continue to manufacture the subassemblies.

Opportunity costs, which represent the measurable advantage of a foregone alternative, should also be considered in such circumstances. Opportunity costs essentially are expected future costs that will probably differ among decision alternatives. For example, a decision to satisfy needs internally rather than externally may also depend on whether the space and productive capacity now used to manufacture the subassemblies can be put to some alternative use. The opportunity cost of the capacity idled by discontinuing production of the subassemblies must be determined. If there are no alternative uses for the idled capacity, the opportunity cost is zero. If there is no opportunity cost, the decision to continue to manufacture the subassemblies is based on an analysis similiar to the previous illustration.

However, if the idle capacity could be used for another purpose, the contribution to net income generated by the alternative use should be considered in the analysis of the make or buy decision. For example, assume that the capacity used to produce the subassemblies illustrated in figure 4.12 could be used to produce a different product that would generate a contribution margin of $18,000 per year, as shown in figure 4.13. Note that the amount of avoidable fixed overhead may change under these conditions. For purposes of this example, however, avoidable fixed overhead is assumed to remain the same.

The $18,000 added contribution would result in an increase in net income of $3,000. Therefore, the appropriate decision would be to purchase the subassemblies from an outside supplier and use the idle capacity to produce the new product.

Special Orders

Management frequently faces the decision of accepting or rejecting special orders for the Company's product at a price below the usual selling price. For example, consider the

FIGURE 4.13

Analysis of Information for Make or Buy Decision

5,000 Units of a Certain Subassembly

	Make Internally	Buy Externally	Difference
Cost to buy externally @ $29		$145,000	$(145,000)
Cost to make internally:			
Direct materials @ $4	$ 20,000		20,000
Direct labor @ $12	60,000		60,000
Variable overhead @ $8	40,000		40,000
Fixed overhead[a]	30,000	20,000	10,000
Opportunity cost of idle capacity	18,000		18,000
Total	$168,000	$165,000	$ 3,000

[a] $10,000 of fixed costs can be avoided if the subassemblies are purchased externally.

FIGURE 4.14

Budgeted Income Statement

Based on Planned Production and Sales of 250,000 Units		
	Per Unit	**Amount**
Sales	$6.00	$1,500,000
Cost of goods sold	4.80	1,200,000
Gross profit	$1.20	$ 300,000
Selling expenses	0.40	100,000
Operating income	$0.80	$ 200,000

following situation in which a company produces a single product. The company's budgeted income statement is given in figure 4.14.

The company has received a special order from a foreign corporation for 15,000 units. It has been offered a price of $4.50 per unit, even though the customary selling price for this item is $6.00. The decision to accept or reject a special order such as this depends on several factors. The first consideration should be whether there is sufficient plant capacity available so that the special order can be produced without affecting production for regular sales. If the plant is operating at full capacity, the special order should be viewed as an alternative use of plant capacity. It is clear that accepting the special order at a price of $4.50 with the plant operating at full capacity would result in an unacceptable decline in gross profit of $22,500—the difference in selling price of $1.50 ($6.00 − $4.50) times 15,000 units.

If the plant is not operating at full capacity, the decision to accept or reject the special order should consider the opportunity cost of the idle capacity. Idle capacity usually has an opportunity cost greater than zero, because management is continuously searching for the most profitable ways to utilize available capacity. Therefore, there may be several alternatives under consideration at any one time. A special order may be simply one of many alternative uses of excess plant capacity.

In light of the availability of alternative choices, remember that the decision to accept a special order is typically a short-run decision, made on the expectation of increasing the current contribution margin rather than on the expectation of sustaining long-run profits. As a result, managment may be reluctant to accept a special order when there are other long-run opportunities for excess capacity, even though a special order may be more profitable in the short run. For example, a special order expected to contribute $10,000 to profits in the next year may be rejected in favor of a three-year contract that is expected to yield only $7,000 in the next year. This may be appropriate if the total expected contribution over the next three years is greater under the contract than with alternative short-run special orders.

Management in the previous illustration may be reluctant to accept the special order under any circumstances, because the offered price of $4.50 does not cover the per unit production cost of $4.80. Management realizes that the long-run survival of the firm is jeopardized unless the company can continue to cover *all* costs and provide a normal rate of return on employed capital.

Under appropriate circumstances, however, accepting the special order may benefit the firm in the short run without sacrificing long-run objectives. For example, assume that the company described in figure 4.14 has current excess plant capacity and that the excess capacity has no alternative uses. Additional information about the standard cost of producing each unit of this company's product is given in figure 4.15.

By examining the variable and fixed cost components of these operations, it becomes clear that if the special order is accepted even at a selling price of $4.50, a contribution

CHAPTER 4: CONTRIBUTION ANALYSIS

FIGURE 4.15

Standard Cost of Production

Based on a Relevant Range of Production of 250,000 to 300,000 Units

	Per Unit
Direct material	$ 2.00
Direct labor	1.60
Variable manufacturing overhead	0.50
Total variable costs	$ 4.10
Fixed manufacturing overhead	$175,000.00

will be made to cover fixed costs and gross profit. The amount of the contribution is $0.40 per unit ($4.50 selling price − $4.10 variable manufacturing costs). The total increase in gross profit from accepting this special order will be $6,000 ($0.40 per units × 15,000 units). The analysis of information in figure 4.16 verifies this calculation.

When there is excess plant capacity, the relevant costs in a special order decision include *sales* and *variable manufacturing costs*. For example, under the circumstances just illustrated, a comparison of the gross margin and the proposed selling price may lead to an inappropriate decision. This could happen because, unlike contribution margin, gross margin contains irrelevant information—fixed manufacturing costs.

In the preceding example, note that net income did not increase by the same amount as gross profit. Because selling expenses have a fixed as well as a variable component, part of selling expense is relevant information and must be included in the decision analysis. This illustrates the importance of collecting and analyzing *all* potentially relevant items of information so that the total effect on net income is known. For example, if variable selling expenses had been $0.40 per unit, the increase in gross margin from accepting the special order would have been offset by an increase in variable selling expense ($0.40 per unit × 15,000 units = $6,000). Net income would remain the same whether or not the

FIGURE 4.16

Analysis of Information for a Special Order Decision

	Order Not Accepted		Order Accepted		Total Difference
	Per Unit	Total	Per Unit	Total	
Sales:					
Regular (250,000)	$6.00	$1,500,000	$6.00	$1,500,000	
Special (15,000)			4.50	67,500	$ 67,500
Total	$6.00	$1,500,000		$1,567,500	$ 67,500
Cost of goods sold:					
Variable:					
Regular	4.10	1,025,000	4.10	1,025,000	
Special			4.10	61,500	61,500
Fixed	0.70	175,000		175,000	
Total	$4.80	$1,200,000		$1,261,500	$ 61,500
Gross profit	$1.20	$ 300,000		$ 306,000	$ 6,000
Selling expenses:					
Variable:					
Regular	$0.30	$ 75,000	0.30	$ 75,000	
Special			0.30	4,500	$ 4,500
Fixed	0.10	25,000		25,000	
Total	$0.40	$ 100,000		$ 104,500	$ 4,500
Net income	$0.80	$ 200,000		$ 201,500	$ 1,500

special order was accepted. This points out that costs other than manufacturing costs may be relevant in the special-order decision.

This example also illustrates the wisdom of comparing *total* amounts rather than *unit* amounts. For example, comparing the offered price of $4.50 against the production cost of $4.80 might result in the special order being unwisely rejected. The allocation of fixed costs to units of production is a necessary process for income determination and other purposes. However, in situations where total fixed costs are unaffected, they are irrelevant and their inclusion in the unit cost may lead to inappropriate decisions.

Product-Line Decisions

One of the most important nonroutine decisions managers must make is when to add new product lines and whether or not to continue to operate or discontinue existing product lines. These decisions are typically very critical, because they involve large amounts of capital and many employees in various departments of the company. A multitude of factors should be considered, ranging from the costs and revenues involved to the effect of losing trained employees and established markets. Reentering a market, hiring and training new employees, determining morale of other employees, and losing community goodwill are some factors that should be considered, even though such factors are not easily quantified.

The decision to discontinue a segment of a business is made primarily on the effect the decision will have on net income. However, great care should be exercised to avoid premature decisions. For example, consider the situation in which a company carries three major product lines, one of which is clearly unprofitable from a traditional accounting viewpoint. Cost and sales information for this company are given in figure 4.17. Amounts are given for each product line and for the company in total. Also, fixed costs are segregated into those that are avoidable and those that are unavoidable if that particular product line is discontinued.

It appears that the company's overall performance can be improved by dropping product *C*, due to its net loss of $10,000. However, this is another case in which the best course of action is not so obvious. First, if product *C* is dropped, the company will lose $30,000 of contribution margin that helps to cover fixed costs. Second, not all fixed costs can be avoided by discontinuing product *C*. Key management employees cannot be discharged, maintenance costs of buildings and equipment will continue, and taxes and insurance must be paid.

A fundamental principle in the decision to continue or discontinue a product line is the comparison of lost contribution margin with the amount of fixed costs that can be avoided. If the lost contribution exceeds avoided fixed costs, the decision should be to continue to operate the product line. If lost contribution is less than avoided fixed costs,

FIGURE 4.17

Sales and Cost Information by Product Line

	Total	Product A	Product B	Product C
Sales @ $1.00	$290,000	$130,000	$100,000	$ 60,000
Variable costs @ $0.50	145,000	65,000	50,000	30,000
Contribution margin @ $0.50	$145,000	$ 65,000	$ 50,000	$ 30,000
Fixed costs:				
Avoidable	$ 85,000	$ 20,000	$ 30,000	$ 35,000
Unavoidable	20,000	5,000	10,000	5,000
Total fixed costs	$105,000	$ 25,000	$ 40,000	$ 40,000
Net income (loss)	$ 40,000	$ 40,000	$ 10,000	$ (10,000)

CHAPTER 4: CONTRIBUTION ANALYSIS

FIGURE 4.18

Analysis of Information for Product Line Decision

	Continue Product C	Discontinue Product C	Difference
Sales	$60,000		$(60,000)
Less: Variable costs	30,000		(30,000)
Contribution margin	$30,000		$(30,000)
Less: Fixed costs			
Avoidable	$35,000		$(35,000)
Unavoidable	5,000	$ 5,000	
Total fixed costs	$40,000	$ 5,000	$(35,000)
Net income (loss)	$(10,000)	$ (5,000)	$ (5,000)

the decision should be to discontinue the product line. For example, figure 4.17 shows a lost contribution of $30,000, which is less than the avoided fixed costs of $35,000 by $5,000. Therefore, the appropriate decision is to discontinue product *C* so that there will be an increase in net income of $5,000. This result is verified in figure 4.18, which contains an analysis of relevant information.

If the amount of avoidable fixed costs in the preceding example had been $25,000 instead of $35,000, lost contribution would have been greater than the avoided fixed costs. Therefore, the appropriate decision would have been to continue to make product *C* to avoid an increase in net loss (decrease in net income) of $5,000. This situation is shown in figure 4.19.

As shown in figure 4.19, the company is attempting to minimize losses rather than maximize net income. In such situations it is helpful to determine at what volume of production and sales the loss will be greater or less than the level of unavoidable fixed costs. Because unavoidable fixed costs represent a cost of discontinuing a product, management should know the sales volume that must be maintained to justify the decision to continue to operate. In this situation the questions is, At what sales volume will the loss be greater than the cost of discontinuing the product line?

The answer to this question can be derived in two ways. Comparative income statement can be prepared at different levels of sales and production, as shown in figure 4.20. Then the level of production and sales at which the net loss exceeds the cost of discontinuance can be observed. In this example, the question to ask is, At what level of production does the $15,000 cost of discontinuance (the amount of unavoidable fixed costs) equal or exceed the operating loss? The **discontinue point** represents the level of production and

FIGURE 4.19

Analysis of Information for Product Line Decision

	Continue Product C	Discontinue Product C	Difference
Sales	$60,000		$(60,000)
Less: Variable costs	30,000		(30,000)
Contribution margin	$30,000		$(30,000)
Less: Fixed costs			
Avoidable	$25,000		$(25,000)
Unavoidable	15,000	$ 15,000	
Total fixed costs	$40,000	$ 15,000	$(25,000)
Net income (loss)	$(10,000)	$ (15,000)	$ 5,000

FIGURE 4.20
Comparative Income Statement for Product C

Units of production/sales	Dis-continue	25,000	50,000	75,000	80,000
Sales @ $1.00	0	$25,000	$50,000	$75,000	$80,000
Variable costs @ $0.50	0	12,500	25,000	37,500	40,000
Contribution margin @ $0.50	0	$12,500	$25,000	$37,500	$40,000
Less: Fixed costs					
Avoidable	0	$25,000	$25,000	$25,000	$25,000
Unavoidable	$15,000	$15,000	$15,000	$15,000	$15,000
Total fixed costs	$15,000	$40,000	$40,000	$40,000	$40,000
Net loss	$15,000	$27,500	$15,000	$ 2,500	0

sales at which the operating loss equals the cost of discontinuing the product. In this situation, the minimum volume of sales and production that is necessary for the company to continue to operate a product line is 50,000 units. If production and sales drop below 50,000 units, it would be desirable to drop the product line.

These results can also be found with logic and computations that parallel a breakeven analysis. For example, it is advisable to continue to operate as long as the contribution to fixed costs is at least equal to the amount of avoidable fixed costs—$25,000 in the previous situation. As shown in figure 4.17, each unit of product C contributes $0.50 to recovering avoidable fixed costs. Therefore, to recover $25,000 of the avoidable fixed costs, 50,000 units of product C must be sold.

$$\frac{\text{Avoidable fixed costs}}{\text{Contribution per unit}} = \text{Discontinue point}$$

$$\frac{\$25,000}{\$0.50} = 50,000 \text{ units}$$

The discontinue point is directly related to the breakeven point (see chapter 7). For example, the breakeven point represents the minimum volume of sales and production that is necessary for the company to cover total (avoidable and unavoidable) fixed costs. For product C, the breakeven point is 80,000 units. The *breakeven point* in figure 4.20 is the level of production at which the net income (loss) is zero.

$$\frac{\text{Total fixed costs}}{\text{Contribution per unit}} = \text{Breakeven point}$$

$$\frac{\$40,000}{\$0.50} = 80,000 \text{ units}$$

It should be pointed out that an organization may decide to operate below the discontinue point in the short run for a variety of rational economic and noneconomic reasons. For example, the costs of resuming production need to be considered before discontinuing the product as well as the effect that discontinuance has on other products.

OTHER CONSIDERATIONS IN NONROUTINE DECISIONS

Other topics affecting nonroutine decisions include the short-run versus the long-run aspects of decisions, the effect of the time value of money, and the role of qualitative factors in decisions.

Short-run versus Long-run Considerations

Many nonroutine decisions are long run rather than short run. Therefore, it is important for several reasons that the analysis of decision alternatives cover the total time period affected and not just the immediate future. Considering the total time period helps the decision maker to avoid maximizing short-run results to the detriment of long-run income. For example, the alternative in the chapters first illustration of keeping the old machine is attractive in the short run because it avoids a large loss on disposal. However, the short-run effect of keeping the old machine clearly conflicts with the long-run objective of maximizing net inocme.

This illustration also shows the importance of having the reward structure and other motivational factors affecting decision makers incorporate long-run as well as short-run performance measures. Otherwise, decision makers might be tempted to choose an alternative that is to their personal advantage but that suboptimizes company profits.

Another advantage of considering the long-run effect of nonroutine decisions is that it avoids the unwarranted assumption that all fixed costs are irrelevant and that all variable costs are relevant. Some types of costs if considered in the short run appear fixed when they are actually incremental or semivariable in the long run. The implication is that if only the short run is considered, a cost that is incremental and satisfies the criteria of relevance may be mistakenly considered to be irrelevant. For example, if production increases under a particular alternative, additional equipment, supervision, or other fixed cost items may have to be added, resulting in an incremental increase in what is normally considered fixed costs.

An assumption that variable costs are always relevant may lead to an inappropriate analysis, because the variable costs may not differ among alternatives. For example, a newly purchased delivery truck with a higher per-mile cost than the old truck may actually have the same total variable costs because it has more capacity and is driven fewer total miles. In this situation, the variable costs do not differ between alternatives and are irrelevant. Remember that variable costs may remain unchanged and that the fixed costs may change if the time period under consideration is long enough or if fixed cost items are affected by the decision.

Taxes and the Time Value of Money

Income tax payments are an expected future cost that will probably differ among decision alternatives. In most nonroutine decisions, income tax considerations are relevant. To preserve the simplicity of the previous examples, income tax considerations were not included. However, income tax information is readily incorporated in the decision analysis by applying the criteria of relevance and following the analysis steps outlined earlier in this chapter.

For example, if a new machine is acquired and a loss on the disposal of the old machine is anticipated, there will probably be a future tax saving. The amount of the tax saving depends on such factors as the similarity of the assets affected, the organization's effective tax rate, and the presence of any recapture provisions. Assuming a $50,000 loss on the disposal of an old machine when the effective tax rate is 50 percent and no other tax provisions apply, an income tax saving of $25,000 ($0.5 \times \$50,000$) will result. This is relevant information and should be considered in the analysis.

Note that when tax effects are considered, the book value of an old asset is still irrelevant information, even though book value is a component in the calculation determining the amount of future tax effects.

Another item of relevant information not included in this chapter's examples is the time value of money. Cash received today is worth more than the same amount of cash received at some future date. Because nonroutine decisions typically affect cash flows over a number of years, the present value of the cash flows should be used, not their future gross amounts.

For example, assume that the $25,000 tax saving in the previous situation is expected to be realized one year from now. Using an interest rate of 10 percent, the amount that should be considered in the decision analysis is $22,727.27 ($25,000 ÷ 1.10)—the present value of $25,000 one year discounted at 10 percent interest. The amount of $22,727.27 can be verified by reversing the calculation; that is, if the company had received a cash benefit of $22,727.27 today instead of a year from today, the cash could have been invested and earned a 10 percent return, giving the company $25,000 ($22,727.7 × 1.10) of cash one year from now.

The time value of money should be considered when making nonroutine decisions. The present values of future cash flows should be calculated and used in the decision analysis rather than simply using future gross amounts.

The Role of Qualitative Factors

Accountants, like mathematicians and statisticians, deal with numbers and tend to emphasize the quantitative aspects of decisions over the qualitative aspects. **Quantitative considerations** are those aspects of a decision situation that may be expressed in terms of numbers, such as dollars of cost, units of output, or years of life. **Qualitative considerations** are those aspects of a decision situation that are difficult to express in terms of numbers or other types of mathematical expression. For example, a proposed acquisition of a new machine may necessitate the relocation of several workers who are members of a local labor union. The union's reaction to the proposed acquisition may have a profound effect on management's final decision even though the union's impact may not be easily quantified.

There are several other classic examples of decision situations with important qualitative factors. The decision to continue to purchase certain components even though the part could be produced internally at a reduced cost may be made based on qualitative considerations, even though qualitative and economic considerations are not separate issues. For example, maintaining a long-run source of supply may be an overriding consideration when compared with temporary cost savings. As another example, the decision to reject a one-time order that would add to net income but at a price below that normally charged to regular customers could result from qualitative rather than quantitative factors. Even though accepting the special order might increase income, the effect on the company's regular customers of selling below customary prices may influence management's decision to reject the order even though the total impact is not quantifiable.

SUMMARY

This chapter focused on some of the internal uses of cost accounting data by showing how cost information needs to be organized, classified, and reported to help management make good decisions.

A contribution report is frequently used for internal reports to management. For this report, costs must first be categorized as either fixed or variable. Within these categories they can be further subdivided according to management function or, in the case of fixed costs, according to how easily they can be traced to products, departments, or other segments of the business.

Contribution margin is defined as revenue minus variable costs. It is the amount that is available to cover fixed costs and generate a profit. The contribution margin ratio is the contribution margin divided by sales revenue.

Relevant costs are those expected future costs that differ in amount among the decision alternatives being considered. When using cost accounting information in a decision analysis, it is not always clear which of the many different types of costs are relevant in a given decision situation. Also, many types of costs are not explicitly maintained in accounting records and must be quantified or predicted from available historical data. Memorized techniques must give way to the application of cost accounting and decision principles.

Successful accountants and decision makers exercise considerable judgment in gathering and analyzing cost information. Providing relevant costs for decisions is one of the accountant's most critical roles as a member of the firm's management team. To avoid confusion and poor decisions, accountants and decision makers should have a mutual understanding of what each cost concept means and how each relates to making nonroutine decisions.

The following is a list of common cost terms, their meanings, and a brief discussion on their relationship to the criteria of relevance.

	Cost Term	*Relationship to Decisions*
1.	Avoidable costs	Costs that can be reduced or eliminated by reducing the level of operations or by discontinuing some element of operations. They are expected future costs that may differ among decision alternatives. Also called *escapable cots*.
2.	Differential costs	a. The difference between the costs of separate decision alternatives. An expected future cost that represents the amount of difference among decision alternatives. Also called *incremental costs*. b. Changes in total historical costs that result from changes in operations. May be used as predictors of expected future costs.
3.	Discretionary costs	Costs that are not essential but that may be desirable to the accomplishment of a particular objective. If management intends to incur discretionary costs, they are future costs that may differ among decision alternatives. Otherwise, they are not future costs.
4.	Fixed costs	Costs that do not change in proportion to output. They are expected future costs (unless avoidable) that typically do not differ among alternatives. Fixed costs may be incremental costs in the long run.
5.	Imputed costs	Costs that represent the value in use of company resources. Imputed costs are hypothetical costs in that they do not require cash outlays nor do they appear in traditional accounting records. Examples include salaries of owner-operators, interest on invested capital, rental value of company properties, and the interest differential on loans made at rates below the current market rate. They are expected future costs that will probably differ among decision alternatives.
6.	Opportunity costs	Costs that represent the measurable advantage of a foregone alternative. They are expected future costs that will probably differ among decision alternatives.

Cost Term	Relationship to Decisions
7. Out-of-pocket costs	Costs that result in short-run cash expenditures due to making a particular decision. They are expected future costs that will probably differ among alternatives.
8. Outlay costs	Costs that result in cash expenditures. They are expected future costs that will probably differ among alternatives.
9. Postponable costs	Costs that may be shifted to the future with little or no effect on the efficiency of current operations. They constitute a deferral of costs rather than an avoidance. If management intends to incur a postponable cost within the period affected by the decision, they are future costs that may differ among alternatives. Otherwise, they are not future costs.
10. Sunk costs	Costs that are historical, irrevocable, and not recoverable. They are not future costs.
11. Unavoidable costs	Costs that cannot be reduced or eliminated by reducing the level of operations or by discontinuing some element of operations. They are future costs that do not differ among alternatives.
12. Variable costs	Costs that change in proportion to output. They are expected future costs that will probably differ among alternatives.

SELF-STUDY PROBLEMS

SP4–1. Contribution Income Statement–Special Offer Consideration

Pruning Incorporated manufactured and sold 2,500 machines during 19X5 through normal marketing channels. There were no beginning or ending inventories of work in process or finished goods for the year. During the year, the following costs were incurred:

Direct materials	$ 25,000
Direct labor	50,000
Factory overhead	100,000
Selling and administrative costs	60,000

Each machine sold for $100. Analysis of the cost data showed that 50 percent of the factory overhead and 40 percent of the selling and administrative costs were fixed.

Required

1. Perpare an income statement using the traditional format.
2. Prepare an income statement using a contribution margin format.
3. Suppose the company is operating at only 60 percent of capacity and that it has received a special offer from China to buy 1,000 machines at $55 each. The terms of the sale will specify FOB shipping point, and, therefore, Pruning will avoid half of the variable selling and administrative costs. Is this a profitable offer for the company?

Solution to the Self-Study Problem

Requirement 1

Pruning Incorporated
Income Statement—Traditional Format
Year Ending December 31, 19X5

Sales revenue (2,500 units × $100)	$250,000
Less: Cost of goods sold	175,000
Gross margin	75,000
Less: Selling and administrative	60,000
Net income	$ 15,000

Requirement 2

Pruning Incorporated
Income Statement—Contribution Format
Year Ending December 31, 19X5

Sales revenue (2,500 units × $100)		$250,000
Less: Variable costs		
Direct materials	$25,000	
Direct labor	50,000	
Factory overhead (50%)	50,000	
Selling and administrative (60%)	36,000	
Total variable costs		161,000
Contribution margin		$ 89,000
Less: Fixed costs		
Factory overhead (50%)	$50,000	
Selling and administrative (40%)	24,000	
Total fixed costs		74,000
Net income		$ 15,000

Requirement 3

The relevant costs on a unit cost basis are as follows:

Sale price		$55.00
Less: Variable costs		
Direct materials ($25,000 ÷ 2,500 units)	$10.00	
Direct labor ($50,000 ÷ 2,500 units)	20.00	
Factory overhead ($50,000 ÷ 2,500 units)	20.00	
Selling and administrative		
[($36,000 ÷ 2,500 units) × 50%]	7.20	
Total		57.20
Contribution margin (loss)		($2.20)

This is not a profitable offer for the company. They will lose $2.20 per unit.

SP4–2. Choice of Order to Accept Logan Company has excess capacity built into its current plant in anticipation of an expected increase in sales of its regular product line. To use this excess capacity in the most profitable way, Logan has solicited one-time orders for products from other companies. Two large orders have been received, and they appear to be profitable. However, only one of the orders can be accepted.

One of the orders is for 330,000 J-fittings at a price of $1.20 per unit. The other order is for 400,000 K-fittings at $1.40 per unit. The standard costs for these products are as follows:

	J-Fittings	K-Fittings
Materials	$0.50	$0.70
Direct labor	0.20	0.24
Factory overhead	0.40	0.36
	$1.10	$1.30

Factory overhead is applied to work in process on a machine-hour basis at $8.50 per hour. Factory overhead is estimated to be 25 percent variable and 75 percent fixed. There are no marketing costs associated with either of these orders, and the administrative costs are the same for each order.

Required

Which order should the Logan Company accept?

Solution to the Self-Study Problem

Logan Company should accept the order for K-fittings because it will provide the greater contribution margin.

	J-Fittings		K-Fittings	
Sales price per unit		$1.20		$1.40
Variable production costs per unit:				
Materials	$0.50		$0.70	
Direct labor	0.20		0.24	
Factory overhead (25% of standard)	0.10		0.09	
		0.80		1.03
Contribution margin per unit		$0.40		$0.37
Total contribution margin:				
J-Fittings (330,000 units × $.40)		$132,000		
K-Fittings (400,000 units × $37)				$148,000

SUGGESTED READINGS

Bartenstein, Edwin. "Different Costs for Different Purposes." *Management Accounting* 60 (August 1978): 42–47.

Ford, David, and Farmer, David. "Make or Buy—A Key Strategic Issue." *Long Range Planning* 19 (October 1986): 54–62.

Ford, Jerry L. "How to Communicate with Management." *Management Accounting* 60 (March 1979): 12–17.

Gambino, Anthony J. "The Make-or-Buy Decision." *Management Accounting* 62 (December 1980): 55–59.

Goodman, Sam R., and Reece, James S. *Controller's Handbook.* Homewood, Ill.: Dow-Jones Irwin, 1978.

Luoma, Gary A. "Accounting Information in Managerial Decision-Making in Small and Medium Manufacturers." *NAA Research Monograph #3.* New York: National Association of Accountants, 1968.

McCormick, Edmund J. "Sharpening the Competitive Edge for Profits." *Financial Executives* 43 (April 1975): 22–27.

DISCUSSION QUESTIONS

Q4–1. Explain why net income can be the same on an income statement prepared under the contribution margin format as when prepared under the traditional format.

Q4–2. Define *contribution margin* and explain its computation.

Q4–3. What is the contribution margin ratio, and how is it computed?

Q4–4. What is the benefit of a contribution margin report to managers in managing the business?

Q4–5. Is a contribution report based on cost behavior first and management function second, or management function first and cost behavior second? Explain.

Q4–6. Identify the general rule that should be used by management in a decision involving the discontinuance of a product line.

Q4–7. Identify the general rule that management should follow in a decision involving a special order at a reduced price.

Q4–8. Assuming a positive contribution margin, if sales price and variable costs both increase by the same percentage, will the contribution margin ratio increase, decrease, or remain the same? Explain.

Q4–9. Describe the difference between gross margin and contribution margin.

Q4–10. Is a contribution report focused more on the short run or the long run with respect to management decisions? Explain.

Q4–11. Describe the difference between routine and nonroutine decisions.

Q4–12. Define *knowledge* and explain the role of knowledge in the decision-making process.

Q4–13. Explain what constitutes a relevant cost for decisions. Explain the criteria for identifying relevant costs.

Q4–14. What are the steps involved in the total cost approach to decisions?

Q4–15. What are key elements of the contribution approach to decisions?

Q4–16. What constitutes a constraining factor in a decision analysis?

Q4–17. Define *opportunity cost* and tell when it is appropriate to include opportunity costs in a decision analysis.

Q4–18. What is a special order? Under what conditions should special orders be accepted?

Q4–19. Describe the role of fixed costs in the decision to continue or discontinue operations.

EXERCISES

E4–1. Basic Contribution Statement The Hardy Company has the following data covering the month of August:

Sales (11,000 units)	$160,000	
Inventories of finished goods—August 1	3,000[a]	(300 units)
August 31	?[a]	(500 units)
Materials used	62,000	
Direct labor	40,000	
Factory overhead	20,000	(50% fixed costs)
Marketing expenses	12,000	(60% variable)
Administrative expenses	10,000	(30% variable)

[a]Variable production costs only

There were no work-in-process inventories.

Required

Prepare a contribution income statement for the month of August.

E4–2. Basic Contribution Income Statements

The Lucky Company has capacity to produce 400,000 units each year. The materials, labor, and variable overhead production costs are $24 per unit. Variable selling expenses are $10 per unit, fixed factory overhead is $1,000,000 per year, and fixed selling expenses are $275,000 per year. All administrative expenses are fixed and amount to $325,000 per year. The firm produces and sells a single product at a current price of $48 per unit.

Required

1. Prepare an income statement on a contribution basis assuming that (a) there are no inventories at the beginning and end of the year and (b) operations are at capacity.
2. Assume that next year's operations are expected to drop by 25 percent from the capacity level because of a worldwide depressed market for the product produced by the Lucky Company. Determine the effect this expected drop-off will have on earnings. Assume cost and price relationships will remain as stated in the original data. Use the contribution approach.

E4–3. Contribution Income Statements

The Cheery-Hub Company produces novelty wheel covers for the Big Wheel Company. Last year 500,000 units were produced and sold. The following conventional income statement was prepared:

Sales	$1,000,000
Cost of goods sold	500,000
Gross margin	$ 500,000
Operating expenses	300,000
Net operating income	$ 200,000

Additional data:

1. The cost of goods sold includes 30 percent materials and 40 percent labor, and the rest is factory overhead. The factory overhead is two-thirds fixed costs.
2. Operating expenses include sales commissions of 5 percent of sales revenue. The remaining operating expenses tend to be stable in amount from year to year, even when volume moves up or down.

Required

Convert the income statement to a contribution statement.

E4–4. Contribution Reporting—Product Emphasis, Segment Consideration.
Assume that a division of the CHL Company has sales of two products as follows:

	Product A	Product B
Sales	$40,000	$20,000
Less: Variable expenses	30,000	10,000
Contribution margin	10,000	10,000
Less: Direct fixed expenses	2,000	3,000
Product-line margin	$ 8,000	$ 7,000

The CHL Company plans to spend $1,500 on advertising in the division for either product A or product B. If spent on product A, sales will increase by $5,000. If spent on product B, sales will increase by $4,000.

Required

1. On which product line should the company spend the advertising funds? Show your calculations.
2. Assume that the division has fixed costs of $12,000 that are common to all division operations. In the past this amount has been assigned to the two products on the basis of sales revenue. Do these common fixed costs have any bearing on which product the advertising fund should be spent? Explain.

E4–5. Contribution Reporting—Product-Line Performance
The Garrity Company experienced a loss for the second quarter, as shown by the following income statement.

Sales	$600,000
Less: Cost of goods sold	350,000
Gross margin	$250,000
Less: Operating expenses	$265,000
Net income (loss)	$(15,000)

To pinpoint the problem, the manager has asked for an income statement by product line. Accordingly, the accounting department has developed the following cost and revenue data:

	Product X	Product Y	Product Z
Sales	$200,000	$100,000	$300,000
Contribution margin ratio	30%	60%	45%
Direct fixed expenses	$ 65,000	$ 35,000	$ 90,000

Required

1. Prepare an income statement broken down by products, as desired by the manager. Explain to the manager the probable reasons for the net loss.
2. The marketing department believes that sales of product X could be increased by 50 percent if advertising were increased by $10,000 quarterly. Would you recommend the increased advertising? Show computations.

E4–6. Limitations of Conventional Costing Methods (CPA)
One of your clients operates a self-service discount store. Management of the store has consistently encountered difficulty in using traditional accounting data as a basis for decisions such as which departments to operate, which products to promote, and which marketing methods to use.

Required

Identify several overhead costs (or costs not applicable specifically to a particular aspect of operations, such as a department or a product) and explain how the existence of such costs may limit the use of traditional accounting data in making decisions in a discount store.

E4–7. Relevant Costs—Make or Buy Decision The blade division of Dana Company produces hardened steel blades. One third of the blade division's output is sold to the lawn products division of Dana; the remainder is sold to outside customers. The blade division's estimated sales and cost data for the fiscal year ending June 30 are as follows:

	Lawn Products	Outsiders
Sales	$15,000	$40,000
Variable costs	(10,000)	(20,000)
Fixed costs	(3,000)	(6,000)
Gross margin	$ 2,000	$14,000
Unit sales	10,000	20,000

The lawn products division has an opportunity to purchase 10,000 blades of identical quality from an outside supplier at a cost of $1.25 per unit on a continuing basis. Assume that the blade division cannot sell any additional products to outside customers.

Required

Should Dana allow its lawn products division to purchase the blades from the outside supplier? Provide support for your answer.

E4–8. Constraining Factors of Contribution Analysis Johnson Incorporated manufactures product X and product Y, which are processed as follows:

	Type A Machine	Type B Machine
Product X	6 hours	4 hours
Product Y	7.5 hours	5 hours

The contribution margin is $12 for product X and $7 for product Y. The available time daily for processing the two products is 120 hours for machine type A and 80 hours for machine type B.

Required

Do an analysis showing the contribution per machine hour generated by the two products.

E4–9. Cost Concepts

1. The type of costs presented to management for a special-order decision should be limited to
    a. relevant costs.
    b. standard costs.
    c. controllable costs.
    d. conversion costs.
2. In a make-or-buy decision,
    a. only variable costs are relevant.
    b. fixed costs that can be avoided in the future are relevant.
    c. fixed costs that will continue regardless of the decision are relevant.
    d. only conversion costs are relevant.

3. Argus Company, a manufacturer of lamps, budgeted sales of 400,000 lamps at $20.00 per unit. Variable manufacturing costs are $8.00 per unit, and fixed manufacturing costs are $5.00 per unit. A special order offering to buy 40,000 lamps for $11.50 each was received by Argus in April 19X0. Argus has sufficient plant capacity to manufacture the additional quantity of lamps; however, the production would have to be done by the present work force on an overtime basis at an estimated additional cost of $1.50 per lamp. Argus will not incur any selling expenses as a result of the special order. What would be the effect on operating income if the special order could be accepted without affecting normal sales?
   a. $60,000 decrease
   b. $80,000 increase
   c. $120,000 decrease
   d. $140,000 increase

4. The Reno Company manufactures part no. 498 for use in its production cycle. The cost data per unit for 20,000 units of part no. 498 are as follows:

Direct materials	$ 6
Direct labor	30
Variable overhead	12
Fixed overhead applied	16
	$64

The Tray Company has offered to sell 20,000 units of part no. 498 to Reno for $60 per units. Reno will decide to buy the part from Tray if there is a $25,000 savings for Reno. If Reno accepts Tray's offer, $9 per unit of the applied fixed overhead would be totally eliminated. Furthermore, Reno has determined that the released facilities could be used to save relevant costs in the manufacture of part no. 575. To have a savings of $25,000, the amount of relevant costs that would be saved by using the released facilities in the manufacture of part no. 575 would have to be
   a. $80,000.
   b. $85,000.
   c. $125,000.
   d. $140,000.

5. In deciding whether to manufacture a part or buy it from an outside vendor, a cost that is irrelevant to the short-run decision is
   a. direct labor.
   b. variable overhead.
   c. fixed overhead that will be avoided if the part is bought from an outside vendor.
   d. fixed overhead that will continue even if the part is bought from an outside vendor.

E4–10. Relevant Costs—Make or Buy Decisions

Plainfield Company manufactures part G for use in its production cycle. The costs per unit for 10,000 units of part G are as follows:

Direct materials	$ 3
Direct labor	15
Variable overhead	6
Fixed overhead	8
	$32

Verona Company has offered to sell Plainfield 10,000 units of part G for $30 per unit. If Plainfield accepts Verona's offer, the released facilities could be used to save $45,000 in relevant costs in the manufacture of part H. In addition, $5 per unit of the fixed overhead applied to part G would be totally eliminated.

Required

Determine which alternative (making or buying part G) is more desirable and by what amount it is more desirable.

E4–11. Relevant Costs—Special Order

Lincoln Company, a glove manufacturer, has enough idle capacity available to accept a special order of 20,000 pairs of gloves at $12 a pair. The normal selling price is $20 a pair. Variable manufacturing costs are $9 a pair, and fixed manufacturing costs are $3 a pair. Lincoln will not incur any selling expenses as a result of the special order.

Required

Determine the effect on operating income if the special order could be accepted without affecting normal sales.

PROBLEMS

P4–1. Contribution Analysis—Special Offer Decision

The Midland Company is a furniture manufacturer that has several product lines. Income data for one of the products for the year just ended follows.

		(in millions)
Sales (400,000 units @ $200 average price)		$80
Variable costs:		
Direct materials @ $70	$28	
Direct labor @ $20	8	
Variable factory overhead @ $10	4	
Sales commissions @ 15% of selling price	12	
Other variable costs @ $10	4	
Total variable costs @ $140		56
Contribution margin		$24
Fixed costs:		
Discretionary @ $30	12	
Committed @ $20	8	
Total fixed costs		$20
Operating income		$ 4

Near year end, the Odessa Company, a customer, offered $160 each for 3,000 units. This offer would be in addition to the 400,000 units already sold. The acceptance of this special order by Midland would not affect regular sales. As a sales commission, the salesperson negotiating the offer will accept a flat fee of $12,000 if the order is accepted.

Required

If the offer is accepted, what will be the effect on operating income?

P4–2. Contribution Reporting—Product Performance

The Charitable Company's most recent income statement, prepared on a contribution basis, showed the following:

Sales	$120,000
Less: Variable expenses	80,000
Contribution margin	$ 40,000
Less: Fixed expenses	35,000
Net income	$ 5,000

The president isn't happy with operating results of only 4.2 percent of sales and wants a thorough analysis of what can be done to improve results. As an expert analyst of operating results, you have determined the following:

1. The firm has two sales districts—northern and southern. The northern district produces 66 percent of total sales and incurs 54 percent of the variable expenses.
2. Of the fixed expenses, $20,000 is common to all operations of the company and $6,000 of the remaining $15,000 represents direct advertising and promotional efforts in the southern district. The balance is traceable to the northern sales district.

Required

1. Explain how you might proceed to analyze reasons for the Company's poor operating performance.
2. Prepare a segment report for each sales district tied to the report for the company as a whole.
3. Do the reports prepared in requirement 2 shed any light on where the company's operating problems exist? Explain.

P4–3. Relevant Costs of Operating a Copying Machine The costs of operating one office copier that makes 100,000 copies per year have been estimated as follows:

Inking materials	$ 500
Paper	500
Cleaning supplies	100
Feed rollers[a]	200
Maintenance contract	200
Depreciation (5,000 ÷ 5 yr life)	1,000
total	$2,500

[a]Parts that have to be replaced after about 20,000 copies to maintain consistent paper feed.

The cost per copy is 2 ½¢ (2,500 ÷ 100,000).

Required

1. If only 80,000 copies are made instead of 100,000, what would be the cost per copy? Provide support for your answer. What would be the cost per copy if 110,000 copies were made?
2. The office manager would like to have the convenience of having a copier in her home. Home use would probably involve about 25,000 copies. What would be your estimate of the cost per copy if the manager purchases one for home use? Provide support for your answer.
3. Identify alternatives that the office manager may consider for personal (home) copy needs. Describe the costs that are relevant to the alternatives.

P4–4. Reporting Format—Common Expense Allocations The Orem Company has three divisions. Performance in each division is evaluated on the basis of division net income before taxes. This net income figure includes an assignment of general corporate overhead based on the sales produced in each division. Statements covering operations for the third quarter are as follows (000s omitted):

	Total Company	L	M	N
Sales	$9,600	$4,000	$2,400	$3,200
Cost of goods sold	$4,460	$2,100	$1,080	$1,280
Division operating expense	1,070	500	250	320
Corporate expenses	1,920	800	480	640
Total expenses	$7,450	$3,400	$1,810	$2,240
Net income before taxes	$2,150	$ 600	$ 590	$ 960

The management team in division L is disgruntled with both the operating results and the form of presentation of those results. In that division, the managers have deliberately retained a line of products that account for 35 percent of sales but only 10 percent of the division profits. Division L's managers retained this low-margin product, until it could be replaced with a higher margin product, because they believed that the product was still contributing to profit. Now they think that the product might be an overall loser, considering that corporate general expenses are assigned on the basis of sales revenue.

Required

1. Recast the operating statements in a better format to show just what each division's contribution is. Include a breakdown in division L between the low-margin product and the remainder of its business.
2. Comment on the appropriateness of the base used for allocating the corporate general expenses.

P4–5. Relevant Cost Information for Decision Analysis—One Time Bid 110(CMA) Jenco Incorporated manufactures a combination fertilizer/weedkiller under the name Fertikil. This is the only product Jenco produces at this time. Fertikil is sold nationwide through normal marketing channels to retail nurseries and garden stores.

Taylor Nursery plans to sell a similar fertilizer/weedkiller compound through its regional nursery chain under its own private label. Taylor has asked Jenco to submit a bid for a 25,000 pound order of the private-brand compound. Although the chemical composition of the Taylor compound differs from Fertikil, the manufacturing pocess is very similar.

The Taylor compound would be produced in 1,000 pound lots. Each lot would require 60 direct-labor hours and the following chemicals:

Chemicals	Quantity in Pounds
CW–3	400
JX–6	300
MZ–8	200
BE–7	100

The first three chemicals (CW–3, JX–6, MZ–8) are all used in the production of Fertikil. BE–7 was used in a compound that Jenco has discontinued. This chemical was not sold or discarded because it does not deteriorate and there have been adequate storage facilities. Jenco could sell BE–7 at the prevailing market price less $0.10 per pound selling and handling expenses.

Jenco also has on hand a chemical called CN–5, which was manufactured for use in another product that is no longer produced. CN–5, which cannot be used in Fertikil, can be substituted for CW–3 on a one-for-one basis without affecting the quality of the Taylor compound. The quantity of CN–5 in inventory has a salvage value of $500.

Inventory and cost data for the chemicals that can be used to produce the Taylor compound are follows:

Raw Material	Pounds in Inventory	Actual Price per Pound When Purchased	Current Market Price per Pound
CW–3	22,000	$0.80	$0.90
JX–6	5,000	$0.55	$0.60
MZ–8	8,000	$1.40	$1.60
BE–7	4,000	$0.60	$0.65
CN–5	5,500	$0.75	(salvage)

The current direct-labor rate is $7.00 per hour. The manufacturing overhead rate is established at the beginning of the year and is applied consistently throughout the year using direct-labor hours as the base. The predetermined overhead rate for the current year, based on a two-shift capacity of 400,000 total direct-labor hours with no overtime, is as follows:

	Per Direct-Labor Hour
Variable manufacturing overhead	$2.25
Fixed manufacturing overhead	3.75
Combined rate	$6.00

Jenco's production manager reports that the present equipment and facilities are adequate to manufacture the Taylor compound. However, Jenco is within 800 hours of its two-shift capacity this month before it must schedule overtime. If need be, the Taylor compound could be produced on regular time by shifting a portion of Fertikil production to overtime. Jenco's rate for overtime hours is 1½ times the regular pay rate or $10.50 per hour. There is no allowance for any overtime premium in the manufacturing overhead rate.

Jenco's standard markup policy for new products is 25 percent of full manufacturing cost.

Required

Assume Jenco has decided to submit a bid for a 25,000-pound order of Taylor's new compound. The order must be delivered by the end of this month. Taylor has indicated that this is a one-time order. Determine the minimum bid amount for the Taylor order.

P4–6. Relevant Costs and Product Line Decisions (CMA) The Scio Division of Georgetown Incorporated manufactures and sells four related product lines. Each product is produced at one or more of the three manufacturing plants of the division. A product-line profitability statement for the year ending December 31, 19X7, shows a loss for the baseball equipment line. A similar loss is projected for 19X8.

The baseball equipment is manufactured in the Evanston plant. Some football equipment and all miscellaneous sports items also are processed through this plant. A few miscellaneous items are manufactured, and the remainder are purchased for resale. An item purchased for resale is recorded as materials in the records. A separate production line is used to produce the products of each product line.

A schedule on page 130 presents the costs incurred at the Evanston plant in 19X7. Inventories at the end of the year were substantially identical to those at the beginning of the year.

Product-Line Profitability
(000s omitted)

	Football Equipment	Baseball Equipment	Hockey Equipment	Miscellaneous Sports Items	Total
Sales	$2,200	$1,000	$1,500	$500	$5,200
Cost of goods sold:					
Materials	$ 400	$ 175	$ 300	$ 90	$ 965
Labor and variable overhead	800	400	600	60	1,860
Fixed overhead	350	275	100	50	775
Total	$1,550	$ 850	$1,000	$200	$3,600
Gross profit	$ 650	$ 150	$ 500	$300	$1,600
Selling expense:					
Variable	$ 440	$ 200	$ 300	$100	$1,040
Fixed	100	50	100	50	300
Corporate administration expenses	48	24	36	12	120
Total	$ 588	$ 274	$ 436	$162	$1,460
Contribution to corporation	$ 62	$ (124)	$ 64	$138	$ 140

Evanston Plant Costs—19X7
(000s omitted)

	Football Equipment	Baseball Equipment	Miscellaneous Sports Items	Total
Materials	$100	$175	$ 90	$ 365
Labor	$100	$200	$ 30	$ 330
Variable overhead:				
Supplies	$ 85	$ 60	$ 12	$ 157
Power	50	110	7	167
Other	15	30	11	56
Subtotal	$150	$200	$ 30	$ 380
Fixed overhead:				
Supervision[a]	$ 25	$ 30	$ 21	$ 76
Depreciation[b]	40	115	14	169
Plant rentals[c]	35	105	10	150
Other[d]	20	25	5	50
Subtotal	$120	$275	$ 50	$ 445
Total costs	$470	$850	$200	$1,520

[a]The supervision costs represent salary and benefit costs of the supervisors in charge of each product line.
[b]Depreciation cost for machinery and equipment is charged to the product line on which the machinery is used.
[c]The plant is leased. The lease rentals are charged to the product lines on the basis of square feet occupied.
[d]Other fixed overhead costs are the cost of plant administration and are allocated arbitrarily by management decision.

The management of Georgetown has requested a profitability study of the baseball equipment line to determine if the line should be discontinued. The marketing department of the Scio Division and the accounting department at the plant have developed the following additional data to be used in the study:

1. If the baseball equipment line is discontinued, the company will lose approximately 10 percent of its sales in each of the other lines.
2. The equipment now used in the manufacture of baseball equipment is quite specialized. It has a current salvage value of $105,000 and a remaining useful life of five years. This equipment cannot be used elsewhere in the company.

CHAPTER 4: CONTRIBUTION ANALYSIS

3. The plant space now occupied by the baseball equipment line could be closed off from the rest of the plant and rented for $175,000 per year.
4. If the line is discontinued, the supervisor of the baseball equipment line will be released. In keeping with company policy he would receive severance pay of $5,000.
5. The company has been able to invest excess funds at 10 percent per annum.

Required

1. Should Georgetown discontinue the baseball equipment line? Support your answer with appropriate calculations and qualitative arguments.
2. A member of the board of directors of Georgetown Incorporated has inquired whether the information about the discontinuance of product lines should be included in the financial statements on a regular monthly basis for all product lines. Draft a memorandum in repsonse to the board member's inquiry. Your memorandum should (a) state why or why not this information should be included in the regular monthly financial statement distributed to the board and (b) detail the reasons for your response.

P4-7. Contribution Reporting—Comparative Operating Results Dave Randell, president of Randell Incorporated, is frustrated and upset with the latest financial statement results for his company. He has just made the following comment to you and others in the accounting department: "These reports seem unbelievable. Our sales in the fourth quarter were up about 23 percent over the third quarter, yet this income statement shows a drop in net income for our latest quarter. Your accountants must be having problems getting the correct information through our new computer." The comparative income statements to which Randell is referring follow:

Randell Incorporated
Income Statements for the Last Two Quarters

	Third Quarter		Fourth Quarter	
Sales		$630,000		$774,900
Cost of goods sold				
Beginning finished-goods inventory	$100,000		$131,250	
Cost of goods manufactured	312,500		218,750	
Cost of goods available for sale	$412,500		$350,000	
Ending finished-goods inventory	131,250		4,063	
Cost of goods sold	$281,250		$345,937	
Plus: Underapplied overhead	0	281,250	60,000	405,937
Gross margin		$348,750		$368,963
Less: Selling and administrative expenses		258,000		282,840
Net income		$ 90,750		$ 86,123

After studying the statements further, Randell is certain that there must be a mistake somewhere in the fourth quarter figures and has asked you to identify the problem before the prelimnary operating results are released to the media.

You review the figures and report back to Randell that the problem is a drop-off in production in the fourth quarter because the manufacturing plant in Niagara experienced some unexpected problems with obtaining raw materials. You explain that his production decline caused the drop-off in earnings.

Randell is mystified by your explanation. He can't understand why an increase in sales should not be accompanied by an increase in net income unless costs went haywire somewhere, and he can't see any evidence of a cost problem. He concludes the conversation by saying, "If your statements can't show an earnings increase when sales increase by 23 percent, we had better call back those computer systems consultants and have them recheck our fancy new computerized information system."

Budgeted, unit sales and production for each quarter of the year are as follows:

	First	Seocnd	Third	Fourth
Budgeted sales	12,000	20,000	20,000	20,000
Actual sales	12,000	21,600	18,000	22,140
Budgeted production	20,000	20,000	20,000	20,000
Actual production	20,000	20,000	20,000	14,000

Fixed factory overhead is $200,000 each quarter, and variable costs of production are $5.625 per unit. Fixed factory overhead is applied to each unit produced at the rate of $10 per unit; any under- or overapplied overhead is disposed of directly to cost of goods sold each quarter. The company uses the first-in, first-out inventory costing method. Variable selling and administrative expenses are $6 per unit sold and the balance of selling and administrative expenses, is fixed expense.

Required

1. Explain the characteristics of the traditional costing procedures the company used that may have caused the drop in earnings when sales increased.
2. Prepare contribution income statements for each of the last two quarters and explain to Randell what these contribution statements show in comparison to the statements presented originally (if you haven't already included this explanation previously).

P4–8. Relevant Costs and Special Orders (CMA) Framar Incorporated manufactures automation machinery according to customer specifications. Framar is a relatively new firm and has grown each year. It operated at about 75 percent of practical capacity during the past fiscal year. The operating results for the most recent fiscal year are presented in the following income statement:

Framar Inc.
Income Statement
For the Year Ending September 30
(000s omitted)

Sales		$25,000
Less: Sales commissions		2,500
Net sales		$22,500
Expenses:		
Direct material		$ 6,000
Direct labor		7,500
Manufacturing overhead—variable		
Supplies	$ 625	
Indirect labor	1,500	
Power	125	2,250
Manufacturing overhead—fixed		
Supervision	$ 500	
Depreciation	1,000	1,500
Corporate administration		750
Total expenses		$18,000
Net income before taxes		$ 4,500
Income taxes (40%)		1,800
Net income		$ 2,700

Most of the management personnel has worked for firms in this type of business before joining Framar, but none of the top management has been responsible for overall corporate operations or for final decisions on prices. Nevertheless, Framar has been successful.

Framar's top management wants to have a more organized and formal pricing system to prepare quotes for potential customers. Therefore, it has developed the pricing formula shown below. The formula is based on the company's operating results achieved during the past fiscal year. The relationships used in the formula are expected to continue during the next year. Framar expects to operate at 75 percent of practical capacity during the next fiscal year.

APA Incorporated has asked Framar to submit a bid on some custom-designed machinery. Framar used the new formula to develop a price and submitted a bid of $165,000 to APA. The calculations to arrive at the bid price are given next to the pricing formula.

Pricing Formula

Details of Formula		APA Bid Calculations
Estimated direct-materials cost	$XX	$ 29,200
Estimated direct-labor cost	XX	56,000
Estimated manufacturing overhead calculated at 50% of direct labor	XX	28,000
Estimated corporate overhead calculated at 10% of direct labor	XX	5,600
Estimated total costs excluding sales commissions	$XX	$118,800
Add 25% for profits and taxes	XX	29,700
Suggested price (with profits) before sales commissions	$XX	$148,500
Suggested total price equals suggested price divided by 0.9 to adjust from 10% sales commissions	$XX	$165,000

Requried

1. Calculate the effect the order from APA Incorporated would have on Framar Incorporated's net income after taxes if Framar's bid of $165,000 were accepted by APA.
2. Assume APA has rejected Framar's price but has stated that it is willing to pay $127,000 for the machinery. Should Framar manufacture the machinery for the counteroffer of $127,000? Explain your answer.
3. Calculate the lowest price Framar can quote on this machinery without reducing its net income after taxes if it should manufacture the machinery.
4. Explain how profit performance next year would be affected if Framar accepted all of its work at prices similar to APA's $127,000 counteroffer described in requirement 2.

P4–9. Relevant Costs and Decisions (CPA)
Auer Company had received an order for a piece of special machinery from Jay Company. Just as Auer Company completed the machine, Jay Company declared bankruptcy, defaulted on the order, and forfeited the 10 percent deposit paid on the selling price of $72,500.

Auer's manufacturing manager identified the costs already incurred in the production of the special machinery for Jay as follows:

Direct materials used		$16,600
Direct labor incurred		21,400
Overhead applied:		
Manufacturing:		
Variable	$10,700	
Fixed	5,350	16,050
Fixed selling and administrative		5,405
Total cost		$59,455

Another company, Kaytell Corporation, is interested in buying the special machinery if it is reworked to Kaytell's specifications. Auer has offered to sell the reworked special machinery to Kaytell as a special order for a net price of $68,400. Kaytell has agreed to pay the net price when it takes delivery in two months. The additional indentifiable costs to rework the machinery to Kaytell's specifications are as follows:

Direct materials	$ 6,200
Direct labor	4,200
	$10,400

A second alternative available to Auer is to convert the special machinery to the standard model. The standard model lists for $62,500. The additional identifiable costs to convert the special machinery to the standard model are as follows:

Direct materials	$ 2,850
Direct labor	3,300
	$ 6,150

A third alternative for the Auer Company is to sell the machine as is as a special order, for a net price of $52,000. However, the potential buyer of the unmodified machine does not want it for sixty days. The buyer is offering a $7,000 down-payment, with final payment upon delivery.

The following additional information is available regarding Auer's operations:

1. The sales commission rate on standard models is 2 percent and the sales commission rate on special orders is 3 percent. All sales commissions are calculated on the net sales price (the list price minus cash discount, if any).
2. Normal credit terms for sales of standard models are 2/10, net/30. Credit terms for special orders are negotiated with the customer.
3. The application rates for manufacturing overhead and the fixed selling and administrative costs are as follows:

Manufacturing	
Variable	50% of direct-labor cost
Fixed	25% of direct-labor cost
Selling and administrative	
Fixed	10% of the total direct-material, direct-labor, and manufacturing overhead costs

4. Normal time required for rework is one month.
5. A surcharge of 5 percent of the sales price is placed on all customer requests for minor modifications of standard models.
6. Auer normally sells a sufficient number of standard models for the company to operate at a volume in excess of the breakeven point.

Auer does not consider the time value of money in analyses of special orders and projects whenever the time period is less than one year, because the effect is not significant.

Required

1. Determine the dollar contribution of each alternative. How much will each add to the Auer Company's before-tax profits?
2. If Kaytell makes Auer a counteroffer, what is the lowest price Auer should accept from Kaytell for the reworked machinery? Explain your answer.

3. Discuss the influence fixed factory overhead costs should have on the sales prices quoted by Auer Company for special orders.

P4-10. Contribution Analysis—Operating Performance MacCene Graybar is particularly elated over the Graycene Company's latest monthly operating results. The firm finally achieved the goal of leading the industry in the net income percentage of sales. As shown in the income statement, the company earned 6 percent on sales revenue, which is well above the industry average of 4.5 percent.

Graycene manufactures three products that are sold worldwide. The condensed income statement for the lastest month follows.

	$	%
Sales	600,000	100.0
Cost of goods sold	403,800	67.3
Gross margin	196,200	32.7
Operating expenses:		
Marketing	90,000	
Administrative	70,200 160,200	26.7
Net income	36,000	6.0

Ms. Graybar has been discussing these results and plans for the future with the controller. As they concluded their discussion, the controller commented, "By the way, Julia Bright, our new employee in accounting, the recent graduate from the Hampstead Professional School of Accountancy, has a head full of high sounding ideas about things that could be done in reporting operating results. She thinks costs should be broken down into fixed and variable, direct and common, etc., and that we should break our income statement down to show the performance of each of our three products. She has been doing all sorts of figuring. Well, for example, look at this sheet."

Product	Sales	Variable Production Costs	Marketing Expense, % of Sales	Fixed Production Expenses	Fixed Marketing Expense Direct to Product
X	$300,000	$165,000	6	$12,000	$18,000
Y	120,000	56,400	6	54,000	10,800
Z	180,000	63,000	6	53,400	6,000

"Julia proposes to use this kind of data to show how each product is contributing to the operating results of the company."

Ms. Graybar's response was, "We don't need to bother with such costly foolishness. The company is doing well, and besides, we know that product Y is the 'Cadillac' of that type of product in the industry. Tell Julia to get busy spending her time on more meaningful work."

Required

Do you agree with Ms. Graybar's perception of what Julia Bright proposes to do? What analysis could you do from Julia Bright's data that you could present to Ms. Graybar to demonstrate that Julia may know about some tools and methods that give useful insights? Prepare such a presentation. (Assume that all costs not referred to in Julia's breakdown are fixed and not identified directly with any of the three products.)

Part Two

PLANNING BUSINESS ACTIVITIES

Planning the activities of a business organization is covered in chapters 5 through 7. The budget is the final result of the planning process and provides an estimate of operating results for a future time period. Flexible budgeting is a tool that assists management in developing an accurate budget. It adjusts for different cost patterns so that estimated costs are consistent with the expected level of volume. Cost-volume-profit analysis is another planning tool that helps managers evaluate the relationships between costs and volume and their effect on profits.

Chapter 5

Budgeting

Outline

BUDGETING IN GENERAL
The Purpose of a Budget
  Coordination and Implementation
  Motivation
  Control and Evaluation
Budgeting Relative to Time
  Long-Range, Intermediate, and Short-Term Budgets
  Continuous Budgeting
Relationship of Budgets to Standards
Master Budgets
  Flexible Budgeting
  Capital Budgeting
  Performance Reporting
DEVELOPING A MASTER BUDGET
Budget Committee
Process of Developing a Budget
MASTER BUDGET EXAMPLE
Sales Forecast
Ending Inventory Levels
Production Budget
Raw Materials Purchases Budget
Cost-of-Goods-Sold Budget
Selling-Expense Budget
Administrative-Expense Budget
Cash Forecast of Receipts and Disbursements
  Cash Receipts
  Cash Disbursements
  Cash Balance
Budgeted Income Statement
Budgeted Balance Sheet
Analysis of the Budget
BUDGETING IN THE NOT-FOR-PROFIT SECTOR
Differences between Profit and Not-for-Profit Budgets
Budget Elements
  Estimating Revenues
  Planning Services and Allocating Resources
  Evaluating Effectiveness
BEHAVIORAL CONSIDERATIONS OF BUDGETING
SUMMARY
SELF-STUDY PROBLEM
SUGGESTED READINGS
DISCUSSION QUESTIONS
EXERCISES
PROBLEMS
CASE

Financially successful individuals and almost all business organizations find that the budgeting process is very useful in planning future activities. The budget itself is a document used to evaluate the success of those activities. This chapter identifies what a budget is, how it should be developed and utilized to make an organization successful, and how one can avoid the undesirable behavioral problems often associated with a budget.

After completing this chapter, you should be able to:

1. explain what a budget is and why it is important to an organization.
2. identify the procedures followed in developing a master budget.
3. develop a master budget with supporting schedules.
4. describe the procedures that should be followed in developing and implementing a budget so that behavioral problems are minimized and the budget is successful.
5. explain the basics of budgeting in the not-for-profit sector.

BUDGETING IN GENERAL

A **budget** is an itemized estimate of the operating results of an enterprise for a future time period. The form of the budget varies from organization to organization, but it is eventually summarized into the form of the normal financial statements. The major difference between the budget and the financial statements is the data used to develop each. Financial statements are based on actual results of past operations, whereas budgets are based on planned operations for a future time period. For this reason, budgets may be referred to as **pro-forma statements.**

The Purpose of a Budget

The purpose of the budget is to provide a blueprint or a *plan of operations* for the enterprise. The budgeting process provides a basis for *(a)* coordinating and implementing the plan, *(b)* motivating organizational members to perform well, and *(c)* controlling and evaluating the activities for the budgeted period.

Coordination and Implementation In large and diverse organizations, the problems of coordination become critical. An important role of budgeting is to improve the coordination among the various units of the organization. Planning or budgeting means establishing objectives in advance and identifying the steps by which the objectives are to be accomplished. The planning process initiates coordination and clarification of subgoals to achieve major enterprise goals. The coordinated plan or budget provides a blueprint for implementation and control.

Motivation Motivating organization members to perform well is generally associated with rewards and punishments rather than with budgeting. Yet the opportunities to participate in developing the budget and in other decision-making areas are highly rewarding and desirable to many employees. A budget also plays a potential role in motivation because of its goal-setting properties, and goal setting is related to performance. As individuals set higher performance goals, actual performance levels generally increase. If the budget is used properly, it can serve as a performance goal and, therefore, can be a significant factor in motivation. This motivational effect is not limited to production workers or supervisors. Top managers are key motivators as they commit themselves to certain performance levels for annual and long-term operating results.

CHAPTER 5: BUDGETING

Control and Evaluation Maintaining control over the activities occurring within an organization is an important responsibility of management. Fundamentally, managerial control consist of *(a)* defining what constitutes a standard or benchmark of acceptable performance, *(b)* measuring actual performance, *(c)* comparing the budget with the actual performance level, and *(d)* communicating the results to the applicable areas throughout the organization and taking corrective action if needed. Figure 5.1 illustrates the control cycle and the role of the budget as the standard for comparison.

The purpose of a budget in managerial control is to specify the level of acceptable performance. One cannot evaluate the acceptability of actual performance unless there is a standard for comparison. If an explicit standard has not been established in advance, it is likely that the individual examining the reports substitutes her or his own subjective standard. When this happens, those being evaluated are subject to capricious whims of the evaluator.

An understanding of organizational goals comes during the development of the budget as each manager develops a statement of attainable goals for her or his organizational unit. Initially the estimates of the individual subunits may not provide a coordinated plan, and revisions will be required as they are combined into a budget for the total enterprise. Nevertheless, these problems are resolved before actual operations begin. When the plan is implemented, the budget provides a basis for comparing actual results to maintain control over the operations.

Budgeting Relative to Time

Development of an annual budget is only one segment of the on-going planning process of a business. For the planning process to be most successful, there must be some long-range goals, intermediate objectives, and a short-term plan of action.

Long-Range, Intermediate, and Short-Term Budgets The long-range goals indentify the direction of the company over a five- to ten-year period. The goals are stated in general terms, but they deal with specific areas in which the company intends to be successful. Areas often covered in long-range planning include sales, research and

FIGURE 5.1

The Budget in the Control Cycle

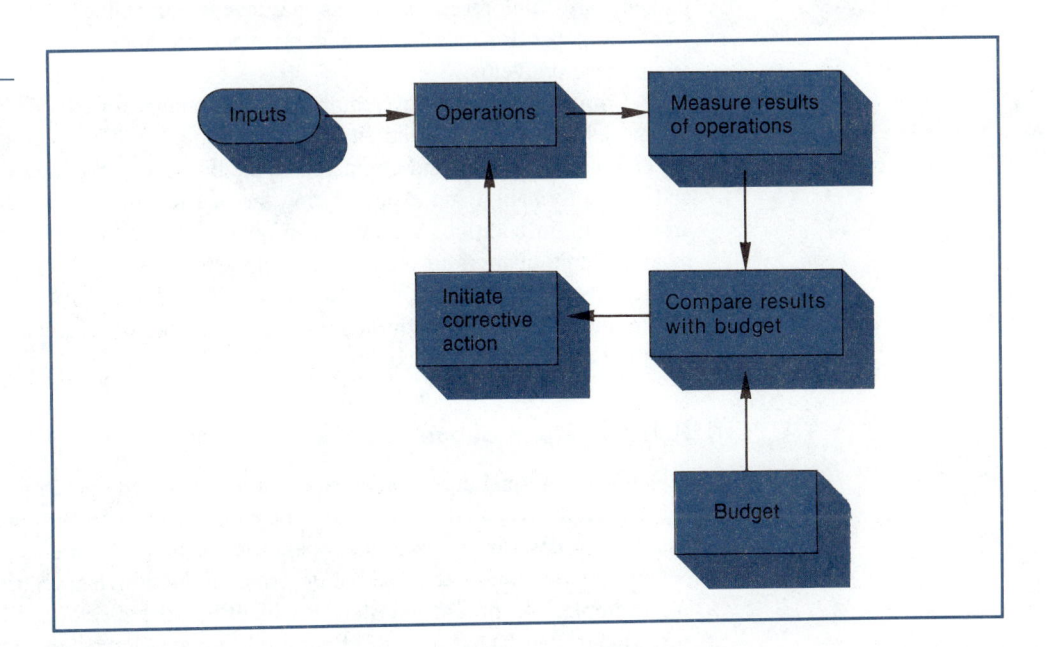

development, capital expenditures, personnel policies, and financial position. The following are some examples of long-range goals:

1. Increase the firm's share of the market from 30 to 35 percent.
2. Construct a new manufacturing facility complete with new equipment.
3. Develop a research and development team with an international reputation.
4. Improve the equity ratio from 40 to 45 percent.

Intermediate objectives identify the specific steps that will lead to accomplishing the long-term goals. They provide a link between the short-term plan and the long-term objectives. Too often an enterprise will develop grandiose ideas about how great and profitable it will be in the future without critically evaluating the feasibility of accomplishment. Long-range goals need to be broken down into workable steps that will lead to achieving the long-term objective. The long- and short-term plans are merged into an integrated strategic plan by the intermediate objectives. For example, the intermediate objectives required to increase the share of the market from 30 to 35 percent may include the following:

1. Introduce one new product each year.
2. Improve advertising coverage by introducing an advertising campaign on national television.
3. Improve the quality of the sales force by having an annual training seminar.

The short-term plan, called a budget or annual forecast, identifies the activities to be accomplished during the coming year. Most people think of the budgeting process as the development of this annual document. However, the development of the annual budget depends heavily on long-term and intermediate objectives. The remainder of this chapter focuses on the content of the annual budget and the process by which it is developed.

Continuous Budgeting   One of the problems in preparing a budget only once each year is the disruption of normal operations while the budget is being prepared. A large amount of time is required by many people throughout the organization to prepare a good budget. Also, unforeseeable events may occur during the year to make the budget a poor standard of performance. A technique called continuous budgeting has been developed to avoid these problems.

Continuous budgeting requires that the budget for the next fiscal year (four quarters) be revised and updated at the end of each quarter. Actual operating results are prepared at the end of each quarter and compared to the budget for that quarter. Based on these results and new information and events during the quarter, the budgets for the next three quarters are revised. In addition, a new fourth-quarter budget is developed and added to the remaining three quarters to maintain a budget for the next four-quarter period. Continuous budgeting spreads the time required to prepare the budget over the entire year and provides a more meaningful budget throughout the year. Figure 5.2 illustrates continuous budgeting and the time period that it covers.

Relationship of Budgets to Standards

A budget is a formal quantitative expression of planned operations for a future time period. It is generally prepared for an entire business organization; however, the term *budget* is also used to describe the expected operations of major segments of a business.

The term **standard** is used to describe production data relative to *one unit* of product. For example, the production standard identifies the *amount* and *cost* of direct material, direct labor, and factory overhead required to manufacture one unit of finished product.

FIGURE 5.2

Continuous Budgeting

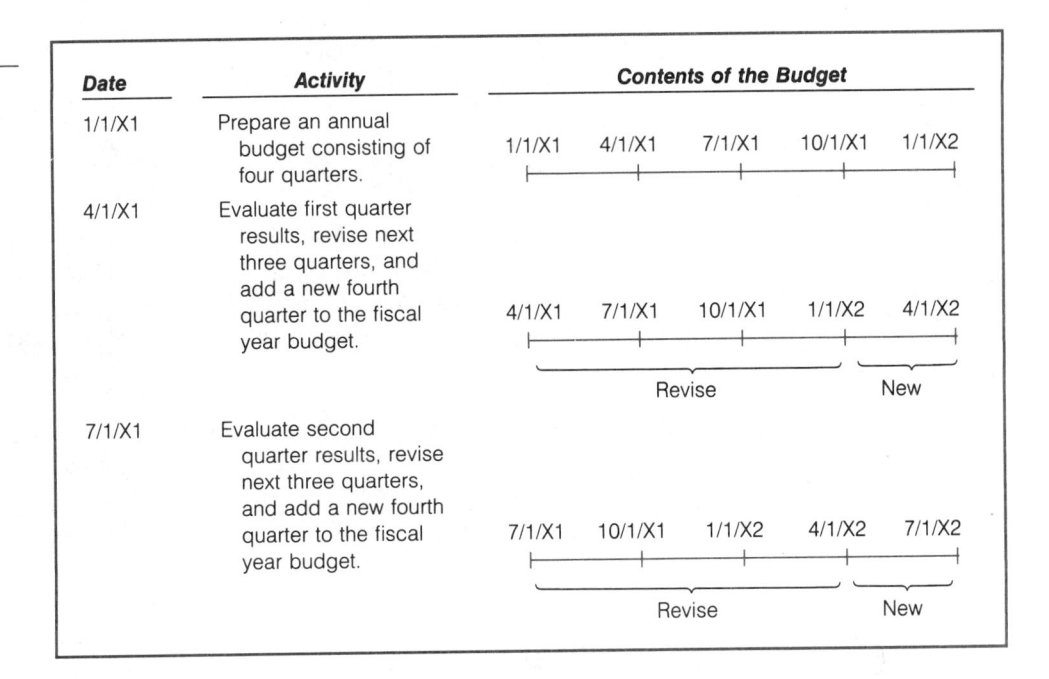

Date	Activity	Contents of the Budget
1/1/X1	Prepare an annual budget consisting of four quarters.	1/1/X1 — 4/1/X1 — 7/1/X1 — 10/1/X1 — 1/1/X2
4/1/X1	Evaluate first quarter results, revise next three quarters, and add a new fourth quarter to the fiscal year budget.	4/1/X1 — 7/1/X1 — 10/1/X1 — 1/1/X2 — 4/1/X2 (Revise / New)
7/1/X1	Evaluate second quarter results, revise next three quarters, and add a new fourth quarter to the fiscal year budget.	7/1/X1 — 10/1/X1 — 1/1/X2 — 4/1/X2 — 7/1/X2 (Revise / New)

Budgets and standards may be related. When the production budget is broken down on a unit basis, the unit amount is a standard. Standard costs then become manufacturing costs on a unit basis. However, the standards are generally developed first and then used as a basis for developing the budget. Standard cost data are also useful in controlling operations, which will be discussed in detail in chapters 15 and 16.

Master Budgets

The types of budgets and the extent of the budgeting activity vary considerably from organization to organization. In smaller organizations there may only be a sales forecast, a production budget, or a cash budget. Larger organizations generally prepare a master or comprehensive budget.

A **master budget** involves the development of a complete set of financial statements for the budget period, with supporting schedules. Figure 5.3 summarizes the budgets and schedules that should be included with a master budget.

Some aspects involved with the development and reporting of a master budget include (*a*) flexible budgeting, (*b*) capital budgeting, and (*c*) performance reporting. These will be discussed in more detail elsewhere in this text.

FIGURE 5.3

Master Budget

Budgeted Income Statement:	*Budgeted Balance Sheet:*
Sales forecast	Cash budget
Production budget	Cash receipts
Direct materials	Cash disbursements
Direct labor	Capital expenditure budget
Factory overhead	
Cost of goods sold	***Budgeted Statement of Changes***
Selling expense budget	***in Financial Resources***
Administrative expense budget	

Flexible Budgeting Flexible budgeting is used in the development of various cost budgets. Costs in many functional areas are composed of both fixed costs, which remain constant when volume changes, and variable costs, which increase as volume increases. Flexible budgeting is designed to determine the amount of cost that should be incurred at various levels of volume.

Capital Budgeting Capital budgeting is used to determine the desirability of investing in fixed assets. Such projects or decisions are substantial in amount and have a relatively long useful life. The time value of money is an important aspect of these decisions, and most capital-budgeting decision models use present value concepts to adjust for the time value of money.

Performance Reporting Performance reporting is a technique used to report the results of operations. The actual results are compared with budgeted expectations so that an individual's effectiveness can be evaluated. Critical to performance reporting is identifying who within the organization has the ability to control an item and therefore should be held responsible for it.

DEVELOPING A MASTER BUDGET

The primary responsibility for developing a master budget is given to the controller and her or his staff. In larger organizations, a special budget committee will be formed.

Budget Committee

The budget committee is composed of several key executives from various segments of the organization. People from finance, sales, purchasing, production, engineering, and accounting are usually represented. The procedures followed by this committee in developing the budget are largely determined (*a*) by the authority it has over the final budget and (*b*) by the amount of participation it allows from others within the organization.

The authority of the budget committee is determined by top management's philosophy. Top management may have a predetermined profit objective in mind and will look to the budget as a means to accomplish it. This objective may be stated in a variety of ways, such as a rate of return on net assets, earnings per share, or a specific amount of net income. It may be based on operating results of previous years adjusted for expectations about the coming year or some desired level of profitability. When top management has a predetermined profit objective, the budget committee must recognize it and develop a budget that will achieve it.

If top management has no specific profit level in mind, the budget committee must first develop some notion about what is a fair and reasonable expectation for the budget period. Without this, the budget process often turns into a "game" and much of the benefit is lost.

The budget committee may or may not invite other members in the organization to participate in developing the budget. In estimating sales for the coming period, for example, salespeople may be asked to project the number of units of each product they expect to sell in their territories. The sales representative on the budget committee would use these as a basis for developing the sales forecast for the entire company. Participation could be carried to the extreme, and every person in the organization could be asked to estimate productivity in her or his individual area. On the other extreme, the budget committee may allow no participation. It merely may develop a budget that will achieve the desired profit and pass it on as the standard of performance for the budget period. More will be said about the behavioral considerations associated with employee participation in developing the budget later in this chapter.

Process of Developing a Budget

The budget is developed in a step-by-step process, but it may take several iterations before the final budget is acceptable. Figure 5.4 illustrates the steps that are followed in developing the budget.

A *critical activity* must be identified for each enterprise. This is the area of the business or activity that limits its productivity or profitability. The selling process is the critical activity for most manufacturing organizations. These organizations can typically produce all the units they want, but finding someone to buy them at a price that provides a reasonable return on their investment is the limiting or critical factor. In organizations where there is a backlog of orders, production becomes the critical activity.

Emphasis should first be placed on estimating the critical activity's volume. This estimate is then used by other areas of the business to develop the supporting functions. These estimates are brought together to develop a master budget consisting of a complete set of pro forma statements. The resulting profitability is compared to the desired profitability. If the desired profitability is achieved, the budget is complete; if it is not achieved, estimates are changed and the budget is revised. Several iterations are often required to obtain a satisfactory budget.

FIGURE 5.4

Flowchart of Activities in Developing a Budget

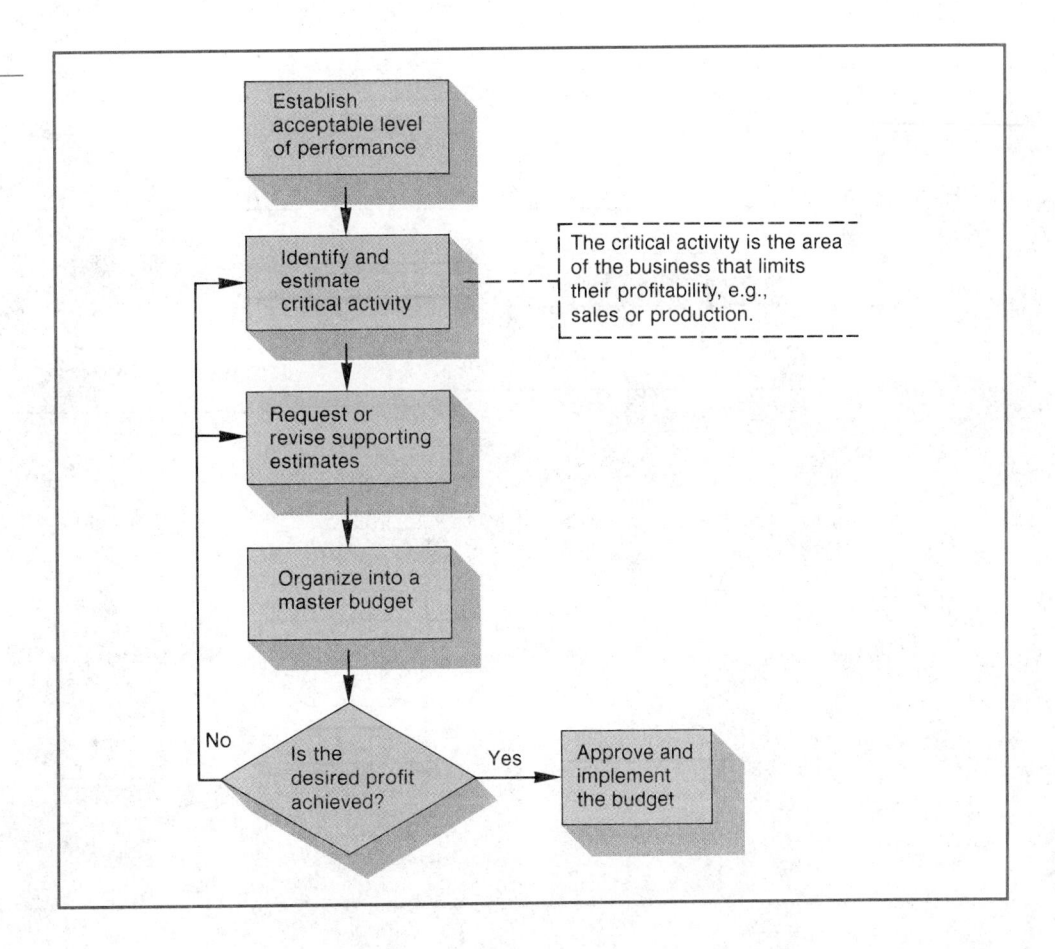

MASTER BUDGET EXAMPLE

L & M Incorporated will be used as an example to illustrate the development of a master budget. L & M Incorporated manufactures and sells one product called a Joe-go. It desires an aftertax rate of return of 18 percent on the average net assets employed during the year. Experience has shown that selling Joe-gos is its critical activity. The budget committee has outlined the following steps for developing its budget. Figure 5.5 illustrates the coordination among these steps.

- **Step 1** Prepare a sales budget by quarter, showing foreign sales separate from domestic sales.
- **Step 2** Determine the desired ending inventory levels of raw materials and finished goods for each quarter.
- **Step 3** Prepare a production budget that separately identifies the amount of materials, labor, and overhead.
- **Step 4** Prepare a direct-materials budget.
- **Step 5** Prepare a cost-of-goods-sold budget.
- **Step 6** Prepare a selling-expense budget.
- **Step 7** Prepare an administrative-expense budget.
- **Step 8** Prepare a cash budget of receipts and disbursements.
- **Step 9** Prepare a budgeted income statement.
- **Step 10** Prepare a budgeted balance sheet.

FIGURE 5.5

Coordinated Budgeting

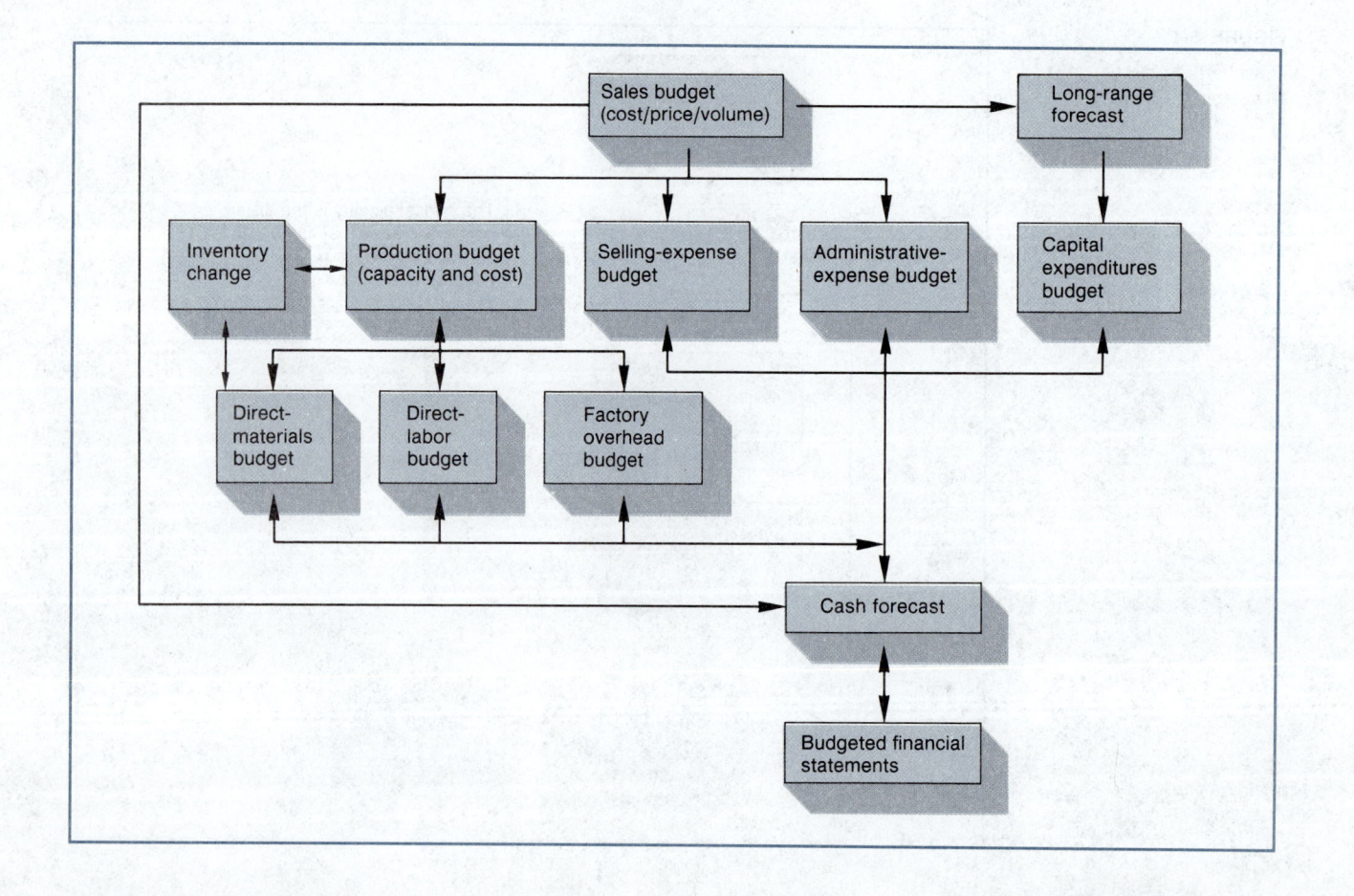

CHAPTER 5: BUDGETING

Figure 5.6 shows L & M Incorporated's balance sheet at the beginning of the current year. The notes to the balance sheet provide information about the composition of the accounts that is essential in developing the budget. The master budget will be developed according to the steps outlined here.

Sales Forecast

An accurate sales forecast for L & M Incorporated is critical, because most of the other budgets are at least partially based upon it. Factors to consider when estimating sales volume include general economic conditions, price, and actions of competitors.

The sales forecast for L & M Incorporated must separate domestic sales from foreign sales because of a sale price differential. A price of $4 per unit is charged for domestic sales and $5 per unit is charged for foreign sales. The sales forecast in units obtained from the sales managers of each territory is shown in figure 5.7. Estimates indicate that sales will take place uniformly throughout each quarter, and a total of 138,000 units will be sold during the year. Unit sales are priced at the appropriate dollar amounts to show sales in dollar amounts. Total sales for the year are expected to be $609,000.

FIGURE 5.6

L & M Incorporated
Balance Sheet
January 1, 19X1

Assets			Liabilities	
Current			Accounts payable	$ 7,000
Cash		$ 25,800	Taxes payable	3,000
Accounts receivable (net)		12,000	Mortgage payable	42,000
Raw materials inventory		8,000	Total	$52,000
Finished-goods inventory		19,200	**Owner's Equity**	
Total Current		65,000	Common stock (no par)	24,000
Fixed			Retained earnings	79,000
Land		40,000	Total	$103,000
Building and equipment	$60,000		Total liabilities and owners' equity	$155,000
Less: Accumulated depreciation	10,000	50,000		
Total assets		$155,000		

Notes:
1. Raw materials inventory consists of 20,000 units of material A at $0.25 per unit and 3,000 units of material B at $1.00 per unit.
2. Finished-goods inventory consists of 8,000 units of Joe-gos at $2.40 per unit.
3. Building and equipment consists of $36,000 of buildings with a useful life of 20 years and $24,000 of equipment with a useful life of 16 years. Straight-line method and zero salvage values are used. The building is used 50% for production and 50% for administration.
4. Taxes payable are due January 15, 19X2.
5. The mortgage is $40,000 with $2,000 of accrued interest. It carries a 10% interest rate. Accrued interest for the prior year and a $10,000 principal payment are due on June 30 of each year.

FIGURE 5.7

L & M Incorporated
Sales Forecast
Year Ending December 31, 19X1
and First Quarter of 19X2

	\multicolumn{5}{c	}{Quarters in 19X1 (in units and dollars)}	1st Quarter
	1	2	3	4	Total	19X2
Domestic						
East	10,000	12,000	15,000	15,000	52,000	12,000
West	6,000	6,000	10,000	7,000	29,000	8,000
Foreign	12,000	18,000	15,000	12,000	57,000	16,000
Total	28,000	36,000	40,000	34,000	138,000	36,000
Sales[a]						
Domestic	$ 64,000	$ 72,000	$100,000	$ 88,000	$324,000	
Foreign	60,000	90,000	75,000	60,000	285,000	
Total	$124,000	$162,000	175,000	$148,000	$609,000	

[a] Domestic sales are projected at $4.00 per unit and foreign sales at $5.00 per unit.

Ending Inventory Levels

There are two types of raw materials required for the production of a Joe-go—two units of raw material A and one unit of raw material B. Because the supply of both raw materials is expected to be tight throughout the year, the purchasing agents, with the approval of top management, have decided to maintain an inventory at the end of each quarter that is half the anticipated usage for the following quarter.

The demand for finished Joe-gos is fairly predictable and uniform throughout the year. Therefore, management has decided that the finished-goods inventory at the end of each quarter should be equal to one-fourth the expected sales of the following quarter. Figure 5.8 shows the desired amounts of raw materials and finished-goods inventories at the end of each quarter.

The desired ending inventory for raw material A in the first quarter is computed by multiplying the second quarter unit sales of 36,000 units (from fig. 5.7) by one-half and then multiplying by two units. Expected sales are multiplied by one-half in order to maintain an ending inventory at half the sales volume anticipated for the following quarter. It is then multiplied by two because two units of material A are required for each unit of finished product.

The computations for material B and finished goods follow a similar pattern. The footnote to figure 5.8 shows the first-quarter computations.

Production Budget

Enough finished goods must be available for sales and for the desired inventory levels outlined previously. Some finished goods are available in beginning inventory, but most of the goods will be manufactured during each quarter. The amount to be produced each quarter is computed as follows:

Expected sales + Desired ending inventory − Beginning inventory = Production

The number of units to be manufactured each quarter is shown in figure 5.9. It is expected that a total of 139,000 units will be manufactured during the year. Unit sales each quarter

FIGURE 5.8

L & M Incorporated
Desired Ending Inventories of Raw Materials
and Finished Goods
Year Ending December 31, 19X1

	Quarter 1	Quarter 2	Quarter 3	Quarter 4
Raw materials				
A	36,000[a]	40,000	34,000	36,000
B	18,000[b]	20,000	17,000	18,000
Finished goods	9,000[c]	10,000	8,500	9,000

[a] 36,000 × 1/2 × 2 units = 36,000
[b] 36,000 × 1/2 = 18,000
[c] 36,000 × 1/4 = 9,000

are obtained from figure 5.7, and the desired ending inventory is obtained from figure 5.8. Remember that the ending inventory in one quarter is the beginning inventory of the following quarter. Notice that the 139,000 units to be produced is 1,000 units more than expected sales because of the planned increase in ending finished-goods inventory.

The production costs must be developed for materials, labor, and overhead. The cost of raw materials is developed as part of the raw materials purchases budget discussed in the next section. Based on existing and anticipated market conditions, prices of $0.25 per unit and $1.00 per unit are anticipated for raw materials A and B, respectively. Remember that two units of material A ($0.25 × 2 = $0.50 per Joe-go) and one unit of raw material B are required to make each Joe-go.

The direct-labor cost is developed by estimating the amount of direct labor required to manufacture each unit of Joe-go and by pricing it at the expected direct-labor wage rate. Engineering and time-and-motion studies have shown that it takes five minutes of direct-labor time to produce each unit. The wage rate specified in the union contract is $7.20 per

FIGURE 5.9

L & M Incorporated
Production Budget
Year Ending December 31, 19X1

	Quarter 1	Quarter 2	Quarter 3	Quarter 4	Total
Units for sales	28,000	36,000	40,000	34,000	
Desired ending inventory	9,000	10,000	8,500	9,000	
Total needed	37,000	46,000	48,500	43,000	
Less: Beginning inventory	8,000	9,000	10,000	8,500	
Production (units)	29,000	37,000	38,500	34,500	139,000
Cost of production					
Raw materials					
A ($0.50/unit)	$14,500	$18,500	$19,250	$17,250	$ 69,500
B ($1.00/unit)	29,000	37,000	38,500	34,500	139,000
Direct labor ($0.60/unit)	17,400	22,200	23,100	20,700	83,400
Overhead ($0.40/unit)	11,600	14,800	15,400	13,800	55,600
Total	$72,500	$92,500	$96,250	$86,250	$347,500

FIGURE 5.10

L & M Incorporated
Overhead Production Budget
Calendar Year 19X1 at 139,000 Units of Production

Variable overhead costs		
Indirect materials	$10,000	
Indirect labor	8,800	
Utilities—variable portion	3,000	
Repair—variable portion	6,000	
Total variable cost		$27,800
Fixed overhead cost[a]		
Property tax and insurance	3,000	
Depreciation	2,400	
Supervision	15,000	
Utilities—fixed portion	2,000	
Repair—fixed portion	5,400	
Total fixed cost		27,800
Total overhead cost		$55,600
Overhead cost per unit ($55,600 ÷ 139,000)		$ 0.40

[a] Notice that the overhead is $27,800 of fixed cost plus $0.20 of variable cost for each unit produced ($27,800 ÷ 139,000 units = $0.20/unit).

---

hour. Therefore, the direct-labor cost to produce one Joe-go is expected to be $0.60 per unit ($7.20 ÷ 12 units per hours = $0.60).

The overhead costs expected to be incurred during the year 19X1 are summarized in figure 5.10. Notice that these are estimated for the entire year at the anticipated production level of 139,000 units. Since some overhead costs are fixed and some are variable, the length of time *and* the level of production are both important variables when projecting overhead. The overhead cost per unit at this level of production is $0.40.

Notice the relationship between the production standards and the production budget. The standards for manufacturing one Joe-go are shown in figure 5.11. The production budget is developed by applying the standards to the expected volume. Each manufacturing cost is multiplied by the number of units to be produced to compute the production cost for each quarter. The total production cost by quarter is shown in figure 5.9.

FIGURE 5.11

L & M Incorporated
Production Standards Per Unit of Joe-go
Year Ending December 31, 19X1

Production Component	Quantity of Component	Price of Component	Cost per Finished Unit
Raw materials			
A	2 units	$0.25/unit	$0.50
B	1 unit	1.00/unit	1.00
Direct labor	1/12 hour	7.20/hour	0.60
Overhead	1 unit	0.40/unit	0.40
Total			$2.50

FIGURE 5.12

L & M Incorporated
Raw Materials Purchases Budget

	Quarter 1	Quarter 2	Quarter 3	Quarter 4
Raw material A:				
Production needs[a] (units)	58,000	74,000	77,000	69,000
Desired ending inventory[b]	36,000	40,000	34,000	36,000
Total needed	94,000	114,000	111,000	105,000
Less: Beginning inventory	20,000	36,000	40,000	34,000
Quantity to be purchased	74,000	78,000	71,000	71,000
Price	$0.25	$0.25	$0.25	$0.25
Purchases—Material A	$18,500	$19,500	$17,750	$17,750
Raw material B:				
Production needs (units)	29,000	37,000	38,500	34,500
Desired ending inventory	18,000	20,000	17,000	18,000
Total needed	47,000	57,000	55,500	52,500
Less: Beginning inventory	3,000	18,000	20,000	17,000
Quantity to be purchased	44,000	39,000	35,500	35,500
Price	$1.00	$1.00	$1.00	$1.00
Purchases—Material B	$44,000	$39,000	$35,500	$35,500
Total purchases	$62,500	$58,500	$53,250	$53,250

[a]Two units are required for each unit of finished goods (2 × 29,000 = 58,000 units). See figure 5.9 for production needs.
[b]See figure 5.8 for desired ending inventory.

Raw Materials Purchases Budget

There are two important aspects to the raw materials purchases budget: the quantity to be purchased and the expected price. Enough raw material must be purchased to meet production needs and satisfy the desired level of ending inventory. However, some raw material is already available in the beginning inventory. The amount of raw material to be purchased each quarter is computed by adding the amount used in production to the desired ending inventory and subtracting the beginning inventory, as shown in figure 5.12.

The amount of raw material needed for production is based on the production budget (fig. 5.9). For example, in the first quarter, 29,000 units of finished product are to be produced. Each unit of finished product requires two units of raw material A, so 58,000 units of raw material A are needed for production. The desired ending inventory of each raw material was computed earlier and is shown in figure 5.8. The beginning inventory of each quarter is the ending inventory of the preceding quarter.

The expected purchase price is developed by the purchasing agent for each element of raw material. Factors that are considered in developing the price are the current price, expected supply and demand, and available quantity discounts. Prices of $0.25 per unit and $1.00 per unit are anticipated for raw materials A and B, respectively. The price multiplied by the quantity needed equals total purchases for each quarter.

Cost-of-Goods-Sold Budget

The cost-of-goods-sold budget is similar in form to the normal cost-of-goods-sold statement. Figure 5.13 shows a cost-of-goods-sold statement for the year ending December 31, 19X1.

FIGURE 5.13

L & M Incorporated
Cost-of-Goods-Sold Budget
Year Ending December 31, 19X1

Beginning finished-goods inventory[a]	$ 19,200
Plus: Cost of goods manufactured[b]	347,500
Goods available for sale	366,700
Less: Ending inventory[c]	22,500
Cost of goods sold	$344,200

[a]See figure 5.6
[b]See figure 5.9
[c](9,000 units × $2.50 = $22,500) See figure 5.8 and figure 5.11.

The beginning inventory of finished goods is taken from the January 1, 19X1, balance sheet shown in figure 5.6. Cost of goods manufactured is the result of the production budget illustrated in figure 5.9. Ending finished-goods inventory is based on the desired ending finished-goods inventory developed in figure 5.8 and the production standard developed in figure 5.11. The 9,000 units of ending inventory are valued at the production cost of $2.50, giving the ending inventory of $22,500.

Selling-Expense Budget

Selling expenses, which include sales commissions and freight-out, are developed by the sales managers and their staffs. Selling expenses are entirely variable, but the amounts differ for domestic and foreign sales. Domestic selling expenses are expected to be 10 percent of domestic sales, whereas foreign selling expenses are expected to be 20 percent of the foreign sales. Figure 5.14 shows the expected selling expenses by quarter for 19X1.

The expected sales in domestic and foreign areas as computed in the sales forecast (see figure 5.7) are used to determine the dollar amounts of selling expense each quarter. For example, foreign sales in the first quarter of 19X1 are expected to be $60,000. Of this amount, 20 percent equals the $12,000 of selling expenses budgeted for foreign sales.

Administrative-Expense Budget

The controller is responsible for developing the administrative-expense budget (also summarized in figure 5.14), which includes all expenses involved with the general management of the organization. Financing charges, uncollectable accounts receivable, and tax expenses are handled as separate items because of their interdepartmental relationship.

The controller estimates that salary and depreciation will be constant each quarter at $21,000 and $225, respectively. Other cash expenses will vary from quarter to quarter, as shown in the administrative budget, with slightly higher expenses occurring in the summer months.

Cash Forecast of Receipts and Disbursements

The cash budget is vital in forecasting cash needs and in planning short-term investments that effectively utilize surplus cash. A cash budget shows how the cash balance will change during a period of time for budgeted cash receipts and disbursements. The forecast starts with the beginning cash balance; cash receipts are added and cash disbursements are subtracted to compute the ending cash balance. It is important to break the cash budget into small time intervals, such as months or quarters, to identify periods when additional cash

FIGURE 5.14

L & M Incorporated
Selling- and Administrative-Expense Budget
Year Ending December 31, 19X1

	Quarter 1	Quarter 2	Quarter 3	Quarter 4	Total
Selling expenses:					
Domestic	$ 6,400	$ 7,200	$10,000	$ 8,800	$32,400
Foreign	12,000	18,000	15,000	12,000	57,000
Total	$18,400	$25,200	$25,000	$20,800	$89,400
Administrative expenses:					
Salary	$21,000	$21,000	$21,000	$21,000	$84,000
Depreciation	225	225	225	225	900
Other cash expenses	12,000	12,500	13,000	12,500	50,000
Total	$33,225	$33,725	$34,225	$33,725	$134,900

will be needed or when excess cash is available for short-term investments. To pinpoint any cash flow problems, a cash forecast will be prepared on a quarterly basis for L & M Incorporated.

Experience has shown that a minimum cash balance of $10,000 is required to maintain normal business operations. If this amount cannot be maintained during a quarter, the company will draw on its line of credit from the bank. The loan is made at the beginning of the quarter in which the shortage is expected to occur. The money is borrowed in multiples of $1,000 at an interest rate of 12 percent per year, and it can be paid back at the end of any quarter in which there is available cash, along with any accrued interest.

The accrual concept is ignored when developing the cash forecast. The criterion used in cash budgeting is receipt or payment of cash. Therefore, such items as interest on the mortgage are included in the cash forecast when they are paid, not as they are accrued. Such items as depreciation that do not involve cash are excluded in developing the cash forecast.

The collection and payment policies of a business are very important in developing the cash forecast. Most sales are on account, and the following schedule summarizes the timing of cash collections by L & M Incorporated:

- Ninety percent of each quarter's sales is collected in the quarter of sale.
- Nine percent is collected in the following quarter.
- One percent is uncollectible.

With the exception of raw materials purchases, all production costs and selling and administrative expenses are paid in the period incurred. Eighty percent of raw materials purchases are paid in the quarter of the purchase and 20 percent in the subsequent quarter. Figure 5.15 contains the cash forecast for 19X1. The computations followed in developing cash receipts, cash disbursements, and cash balance will be explained individually.

Cash Receipts Quarterly sales for L & M Incorporated must be separated into (a) the amount collected in the quarter of sale, (b) the amount collected in the following quarter, and (c) uncollectible accounts. Uncollectible accounts are noncash expenses that do not effect cash flows and are excluded from the sales forecast. Figure 5.16 illustrates a convenient format for performing these computations.

FIGURE 5.15

L & M Incorporated
Cash Forecast
Year Ending December 31, 19X1

	Quarter 1	Quarter 2	Quarter 3	Quarter 4
Beginning cash balance	$ 25,800	$ 10,450	$ 10,210	$ 13,630
Plus: cash receipts				
Sales[a]	123,600	156,960	172,080	148,950
Total cash	149,400	167,410	182,290	162,580
Less: Cash disbursements				
Material purchases[b]	57,000	59,300	54,300	53,250
Direct labor[c]	17,400	22,200	23,100	20,700
Overhead—variable[d]	5,800	7,400	7,700	6,900
Overhead—fixed[e]	6,350	6,350	6,350	6,350
Selling expenses[f]	18,400	25,200	25,000	20,800
Administrative expenses[g]	33,000	33,500	34,000	33,500
Interest—mortgage		4,000		
Mortgage		10,000		
Taxes payable	3,000	2,250	2,250	2,250
Total payments	140,950	170,200	152,700	143,750
Cash balance (deficiency)	8,450	(2,790)	29,590	18,830
Required loans	2,000	13,000		
Loan repayments			15,960	
Ending cash balance	$ 10,450	$ 10,210	$ 13,630	$ 18,830

[a]From figure 5.16.
[b]From figure 5.17.
[c]See figure 5.9.
[d]$0.20 per unit (fig. 5.10) times the units produced (fig. 5.9).
[e]25% of fixed factory overhead, excluding depreciation (fig. 5.10) each quarter.
[f]See figure 5.14.
[g]Administrative expenses (fig. 5.14) excluding depreciation.

 The $12,000 amount collected in the first quarter is the accounts receivable balance reported in the balance sheet of January 1, 19X1 (see figure 5.6). Of the first quarter sales of $124,000, $111,600 (90% × $124,000) will be collected in that quarter, $11,160 (9% × $124,000) will be collected in the second quarter, and $1,240 (1% × $124,000) is expected to be uncollectible. Sales in each subsequent quarter are separated in a similar manner.

Cash Disbursements Raw materials purchased by L & M Incorporated must be separated into *(a)* the amount paid in the quarter of purchase and *(b)* the amount paid in the following quarter. Figure 5.17 illustrates this computation.

 The $7,000 balance in accounts payable on January 1, 19X1, must be paid during the first quarter. Of the $62,500 of raw materials purchased in the first quarter, $50,000 ($62,500 × 80%) will be paid in that quarter and $12,500 ($62,500 × 20%) wil be paid in the next quarter. Purchases in each of the other quarters are separated in a similar manner. The total cash payments for raw materials are carried to the cash forecast in figure 5.15.

 Cash disbursements for most of the other manufacturing expenses are fairly straightforward. The quarterly amounts for direct labor are obtained from the production budget shown in figure 5.9. Factory overhead must be split into the variable and fixed components.

FIGURE 5.16

L & M Incorporated
Schedule of Cash Receipts
Year Ending December 31, 19X1

Quarter of Sale	Amount	Quarter of Collection 1	2	3	4	Year-End Accounts Receivable	Uncollectible Accounts
Prior year:							
4th Quarter		$ 12,000					
Current year:							
1st Quarter	$124,000	111,600	$ 11,160				$1,240
2d Quarter	162,000		145,800	$ 14,580			1,620
3rd Quarter	175,000			157,500	$ 15,750		1,750
4th Quarter	148,000				133,200	$13,320	1,480
Total		$123,600	$156,960	$172,080	$148,950	$13,320	$6,090

Variable overhead is $0.20 per unit (from figure 5.10) times the number of units produced (from figure 5.9). For example, in the first quarter, 29,000 units of production will result in $5,800 (29,000 units × $0.20) of variable overhead.

Fixed factory overhead totaling $27,800 (from figure 5.10) will be incurred uniformly throughout the year. The depreciation of $2,400, however, must be excluded because it is a noncash expense. Since the balance of $25,400 ($27,800 − $2,400) will be paid uniformly throughout the year, $6,350 ($25,400 × 25%) is budgeted for each quarter.

Selling expenses, as developed in figure 5.14, are carried directly to the cash forecast. Depreciation expense must be excluded from the administrative expenses before they are carried to the cash forecast. Also, the mortgage payment plus accrued interest must be paid at the end of the second quarter.

The $3,000 tax payment in the first quarter is the final payment for income tax due on 19X0 net income; this was the amount shown in the January 1, 19X1 balance sheet. The $2,250 tax payments in the second, third, and fourth quarters represent estimated income tax payments for 19X1. The estimated income tax is $8,985 (from figure 5.18), and tax laws require that at least 90 percent of this amount be deposited through timely quarterly payments.

FIGURE 5.17

L & M Incorporated
Schedule of Cash Disbursements for Material Purchases
Year Ending December 31, 19X1

Quarter of Purchase	Amount	Quarter of Payment 1	2	3	4	Year-end Accounts Payable
Prior year:						
4th Quarter		$ 7,000				
Current year:						
1st Quarter	$62,500	50,000	$12,500			
2d Quarter	58,500		46,800	$11,700		
3rd Quarter	53,250			42,600	$10,650	
4th Quarter	53,250				42,600	$10,650
Total		$57,000	$59,300	$54,300	$53,250	$10,650

Cash Balance The beginning cash balance of $25,800 is obtained from the balance sheet on January 1, 19X1 (see figure 5.6). It is increased by cash receipts and reduced by cash disbursements, both of which include any bank loans or repayments to maintain an adequate cash balance. The ending cash balance of one quarter is the beginning cash balance of the next quarter.

Notice that a cash shortage is expected in the first and second quarters, which will require the company to draw upon its line of credit from the bank. A loan of $2,000 will be needed at the beginning of the first quarter and $13,000 will be needed at the start of the second quarter to maintain the $10,000 minimum balance. Both loans will be paid back at the end of the third quarter, with interest computed as follows:

$$
\begin{aligned}
\$2,000 \times 12\% \times \tfrac{3}{4} &= \$180 \\
13,000 \times 12\% \times \tfrac{1}{2} &= \underline{780} \\
\text{Total interest} & \underline{\$960}
\end{aligned}
$$

Budgeted Income Statement

Most of the information for the income statement shown in figure 5.18 has already been developed. Sales, cost of goods sold, selling expenses, administrative expenses, and uncollectible accounts are all taken from previous schedules. Interest expense is computed on the mortgage and the line of credit from the bank as shown in the footnote for figure 5.18.

The average income tax rate for L & M Incorporated is expected to be 30 percent. If operations proceed as planned, the income tax expense and tax payable for the year will be $8,985 (30% × $29,950). Quarterly tax deposits of $2,250 are planned for the second, third, and fourth quarters, so taxes payable at the end of 19X1 will be only $2,235. This amount is shown as a current liability in the year-end balance sheet.

FIGURE 5.18

L & M Incorporated
Budgeted Income Statement
Year Ending December 31, 19X1

Sales		$609,000
Less: Cost of goods sold		344,200
Gross profit		264,800
Less: Other expenses		
Selling expenses	$ 89,400	
Administrative expenses	134,900	
Interest[a]	4,460	
Uncollectible accounts	6,090	
Total		234,850
Net income before taxes		29,950
Tax expense (30%)		8,985
Net income		$ 20,965

[a]Interest expense consists of:
$40,000 × 10% × 1/2 = $2,000
$30,000 × 10% × 1/2 = $1,500
$ 2,000 × 12% × 3/4 = $ 180
$13,000 × 12% × 1/2 = $ 780
$4,460

Budgeted Balance Sheet

All of the information for the balance sheet has been developed in the process of preparing the other schedules. However, some of the data must still be manipulated slightly to get them into a usable form. The footnotes to the budgeted balance sheet in figure 5.19 identify the sources of the data and any required computations.

Analysis of the Budget

The budget must be analyzed to see if it is complete and acceptable as a plan of operations for the coming year. The budget committee reviews the budget to make sure that no important items have been omitted and that it is internally consistent. The committee must also evaluate it to see if it provides a rate of return that is acceptable to top management.

Top management of L & M Incorporated has specified a desired after-tax rate of return of 18 percent on the average net assets employed during the year. The rate of return provided by this budget is 18.5 percent.

Average net assets	$113,480
($103,000 + $123,960 ÷ 2)	
Rate of return	18.5%
($20,965 ÷ $113,480)	

FIGURE 5.19

L & M Incorporated
Budgeted Balance Sheet
December 31, 19X1

Assets			Liabilities		
Cash[a]		$ 18,830	Current		
Accounts receivable (net)[b]		13,320	Accounts payable[e]		$ 10,650
Raw materials inventory[c]		27,000	Taxes payable		2,235
Finished-goods inventory[c]		22,500	Mortgage payable[f]		31,500
Total current		$ 81,650	Total		$ 44,385
Fixed			**Owners' Equity**		
Land	$60,000	40,000	Common stock (no par)		24,000
Building and equipment	13,300		Retained earnings:		
Less: Accumulated depreciation[d]		$ 46,700	Beginning	$79,000	
Total assets		$168,350	Plus: Net income[g]	20,965	$ 99,965
			Total		$123,965
			Total liabilities and owner's equity		$168,350

[a]See figure 5.15 ending balance.
[b]From figure 5.16.
[c]Estimated inventories from figure 5.8, priced at estimated cost.

(36,000 × $0.25 + 18,000 × $1.00 = $27,000)
(9,000 × $2.50 = $22,500)

[d]Accumulated depreciation from figures 5.10 and 5.14 plus the balance of January 1, 19X1.
[e]From figure 5.17.
[f]Mortgage balance, $30,000, plus accrued interest at 10% for 6 months.
[g]From figure 5.18.

The budget satisfies the profit objective for the coming year and will probably be acceptable to top management. If the firm is able to operate within the guidelines specified by the budget, it will achieve its desired growth and profitability.

If the budget does not meet top management's desired objectives, the budget committee must work with its people to identify areas in which changes can be made so that the objectives will be achieved. This is probably the most difficult aspect of budgeting. It generally requires someone to do something she or he would rather not do. The process by which the budget is changed is also very important. If the budget committee has encouraged broad participation by others within the organization in developing the budget to this point, and if it now changes the budget without involving the same people, those people are likely to believe that they had no real input in the first place. They will probably not be as willing to participate in developing future budgets, and their commitment to achieving the revised budget will probably not be as great because of their adverse feelings toward it.

BUDGETING IN THE NOT-FOR-PROFIT SECTOR

The not-for-profit sector of the economy has become more important over time as the number and size of federal, state, and local governmental agencies have grown. Churches and schools are other nonprofit organizations that account for a large part of the economy. Hospitals and health-care organizations have gone contrary to this trend by switching to a profit orientation during recent years.

In this section we will review the basic differences between profit and not-for-profit budgets and will identify the elements of budgeting in not-for-profit entities.

Differences between Profit and Not-for-Profit Budgets

Profit-oriented businesses have a bottom line called net income that helps keep everything else in focus. These organizations do everything possible (within legal and ethical constraints) to increase net income. Therefore, net income is the most commonly used measure to determine organizational effectiveness.

The primary objective of not-for-profit organizations is to provide as many services as possible with available resources. The services must be consistent with the objectives of the organization, and effectiveness is measured by the quantity and quality of services provided relative to the funds utilized. When shifting attention from profit to not-for-profit entities, one also must shift the focus from net income to services; rather than maximizing net income, the goal is to maximize services.

Most of the costs of profit-oriented companies, especially manufacturing organizations discussed earlier in the chapter, are *product* or *engineered costs*. The amount of material and labor required to produce each unit can be determined by engineers within rather close limits. Given a required level of production, little can be done to influence the amount of these costs. However, most of the costs of nonprofit organizations are classified as *discretionary costs*. Both the amount and time of occurrence are matters of managment choice. The amount to be spent can be varied within wide limits according to management's decisions.

Budgets in profit-oriented entities are tentative plans that often are updated on a quarterly basis. Continuous budgeting allows managers to react to unforeseen events. In contrast, most nonprofit organizations operate under more stable and predictable conditions.

Therefore, the annual budget can be a fairly accurate statement of available resources and how they are to be used during the period. A disadvantage of this stability is that managers of nonprofit organizations may develop a fixed mind-set so that they are not willing to change course when unforeseen events arise.

Budget Elements

The three main elements of budgeting in not-for-profit organizations are *(a)* estimating revenues, *(b)* planning services and allocating resources, and *(c)* evaluating effectiveness. These are not mutually exclusive activities. The results of one activity affect other activities. Each of these activities will be explained and illustrated.

Estimating Revenues The amount of revenue to be collected determines the potential services to be provided. Government organizations rely on tax revenues and fees charged for services. Other organizations, such as schools and churches, rely on fees charged to students, gifts, grants, endowment earnings, and contributions.

The organization's ability to collect revenue is partially affected by the quality of service provided. High-quality service and recognition of excellence facilitate the generation of revenue. Most organizations use all the fund-raising devices available to maximize revenues. Therefore, the tendency is to overcome a budget deficit by generating additional revenue. The danger in this tendency is that revenue requests may get out of control if there isn't a careful system of management accountability. The recent PTL scandals provide a case in point.

EXAMPLE

The University Accounting Society is a not-for-profit organization designed to inspire excellence and collegiality among accounting students. The one program that has consistently been offered in the past is a CMA preparation course. Activities, social events, and educational programs vary considerably from year to year. Revenues, which generally come from membership fees, registration for the CMA course, and donations from industrial organizations, are summarized here for the next school year.

Source	Amount
Membership (100 @ $25)	$2,500
CMA registration (40 @ $200)	8,000
Donations	9,500
Total	$20,000

Notice that one hundred members are expected to pay a $25 membership fee. Registration fee for the CMA course is $200, and forty people are expected to attend. Donations last year were $9,500, and the same amount is expected for this year.

Accurately estimating revenue is often a difficult task. The general state of the economy, earnings and profitability of individuals and organizations, propensity to save or spend, and tax rates all have an effect on most not-for-profit organizations. These items are quite difficult to predict. A variety of models are generally used to assist in revenue estimation.

Planning Services and Allocating Resources There are two general formats used for the spending portion of the budget: line-item budgets and program budgets.

A *line-item budget,* also called an object classification budget, focuses on expense elements such as wages, supplies, rent, transportation, and fringe benefits. (Note: line-item is not an accurate title for these budgets, because all budgets are arranged in lines.) A *program budget* focuses on programs, with expense elements categorized within each program.

EXAMPLE

The University Accounting Society has developed its proposed budget in both a line-item format and a program format. These are presented in figure 5.20. The total amount to be spent in each budget is the same, but the classification is quite different.

Line-item budgets generally make no reference to programs. For example, all personnel costs, regardless of the program incurring the cost, would be lumped together as one line-item. Likewise, all travel expenses, regardless of the program incurring the travel expense, would be grouped under the line-item called "travel."

The program budget first categorizes expenses by program. Notice that the speaker series to be sponsored by the University Accounting Society is expected to cost $2,000. This can be further broken down by expense elements, as follows:

Speaker Series	
Personnel	$1,250
Travel	500
Food	250
Total	$2,000

A program budget format is generally considered to be superior to the line-item budget because it permits the decision maker to judge the appropriateness of the resources allocated to each activity. It also allows actual spending to be matched with funds budgeted, and permits the effectiveness of the program to be evaluated relative to the resources committed to it. Although the popularity of program budgeting is growing, the majority of not-for-profit organizations still use line-item budgeting.

The amount of resources allocated to each area of the budget is extremely important to managers of not-for-profit organizations. The allocation these areas receive determines

FIGURE 5.20

University Accounting Society Alternative Budget Formats

Line-Item Format	
Personnel	$15,000
Travel	2,000
Supplies	700
Food	2,000
Miscellaneous	300
Total	$20,000

Program Format	
Speaker series	$ 2,000
Annual 5K fun run	500
CMA prep course	16,000
Awards banquet	1,500
Total	$20,000

the size and quality of their programs for the next period. Those managers allocating resources generally use an incremental approach or a rational approach based on program effectiveness.

An **incremental** approach gives each department, program, or agency the amount it had during the last budget period plus an extra fixed percentage, say 3 percent. Each department, program, or agency can request additional funds above the fixed percentage for program enhancements. For example, if the state expects revenues to increase by 5 percent this year over last year, 3 percent might be allocated as a fixed percentage increase for all areas and 2 percent might be used for program enhancements. This allows each area to build its budget step by step, with no sudden leaps or no deep cuts. The fixed percentage partially covers inflation and provides funds to reward areas for doing a good job or to allow them to take on new roles.

A **rational** approach based on program effectiveness is becoming more common. Its use is tied to the program budgeting format along with one or more measures of program effectiveness. This approach will be discussed in the next section.

Evaluating Effectiveness There are several different measures and budgeting techniques that can be used to evaluate program effectiveness and tie it into the allocation of resources. Each of these areas will be separately considered.

Measures used to evaluate program effectiveness include *(a)* results measures, *(b)* process measures, and *(c)* social measures. A brief description and example of each follow.

Results Measures These represent a measured output of organizational accomplishments that are consistent with the organization's objectives. For the University Accounting Society, for example, results measures could include an increased number of friends or an increased level of knowledge for its members. (Note: Results measures are frequently hard to identify and quantify.)

Process Measures These relate an activity of the organization to time, cost, or similar items. For example, the number of activities held per month or the cost per student preparing for the CMA exam are process measures for the University Accounting Society.

Social Indicators These represent a broad measure of the benefit to society resulting from the organization's actions. For example one may ask how much better off the university is because the members of the Accounting Society are friendlier and aspire to be successful. (Note: Social indicators are nebulous, difficult to obtain, and affected by external influences to such an extent that they are of little use in day-to-day management.

Techniques used to measure program effectiveness and to tie it into the allocation of resources include *(a)* performance budgets, *(b)* Planning-Programming-Budgeting Systems (PPBS), *(c)* management by objectives (MBO), and *(d)* zero base budgeting (ZBB).

Performance budgets report how well the organization performed in terms of work units or units of accomplishment. Process measures generally are used to evaluate each of the programs included in the budget. Figure 5.21 presents a performance budget for the University Accounting Society.

PPBS was created to help management focus on a rational allocation of resources. Its components include *(a)* analyzing goals, (b) identifying alternatives to accomplish the goals, *(c)* developing five-year cost projections, *(d)* analyzing the costs and benefits of alternatives, and *(e)* deciding about the mix of programs to be funded. PPBS takes a holistic approach to the budgeting problem; not only must the goals be identified, but

FIGURE 5.21

Performance Budget
University Accounting Society
Current Fiscal Year

Program	Cost	Effectiveness
Speaker series	$ 2,000	
Programs per month		2
Annual 5K fun run	500	
Cost per runner		$ 5
CMA prep course	16,000	
Cost per student		$400
Awards banquet	1,500	
Cost per person		$ 15
Total	$20,000	

alternatives to accomplish the goals and the cost and benefits of each alternative must also be identified.

EXAMPLE

There are several ways the University Accounting Society can inspire excellence and collegiality among members. The speaker series and CMA prep course are only two options to encourage excellence; field trips and service activities are other options. If the society believes that the CMA course is a desirable activity, sponsoring the course is only one alternative. Other options include contracting with another organization to sponsor the course or buying self-study books or cassette tapes that could be made available to members. The cost of each of these options would be explored using PPBS, a cost/benefit analysis would be performed, and a final decision would be made on the appropriate mix to achieve the overall objective.

Management by objectives (MBO) requires the development of quantified measures of results to be accomplished by each program. The planned objectives provide benchmarks by which actual performance is compared.

EXAMPLE

The following objectives were developed by the University Accounting Society for the CMA course:

- All course instructors will be assigned by May 1.
- Classes will begin by June 1.
- Class enrollment will be at least forty persons.
- Classes will be held weekly, with practice exams given monthly.
- 75 percent of class participants will pass all parts of the next CMA exam.

The term *zero base* in zero base budgeting (ZBB) is intended to be a direct challenge to incrementalism, suggesting that there is nothing sacrosanct about the current fiscal year as a base for next year's estimates. A series of decision packages is prepared under ZBB. The decision packages present a variety of activity levels, some below and some above the current year, so that decision makers have the option of expanding, cutting back, or eliminating a program. Each decision package should contain an estimated cost, a description of what it would buy, and the consequence if it is adopted.

EXAMPLE Decision packages for the University Accounting Society under ZBB might include the following:

Package	Cost	Provides	Consequences
3	$30,000	Speaker series, CMA course, banquet, 5K run, student lounge, and field trips	Students would have a place to socialize and be able to interact with professionals
2	$20,000	Speaker series, CMA course, banquet, 5K run	Basic program expected by most students
1	$10,000	CMA course with only 50% of material covered	Maintains traditional role of society but at reduced scale

BEHAVIORAL CONSIDERATIONS OF BUDGETING

A considerable amount of research has been conducted and material has been written about the behavioral implication of budgeting. Anyone who is closely involved with the budgeting process should study this research in some detail. Several important propositions or rules regarding the behavioral aspects of budgeting can be gathered from such literature. Several of the more notable conclusions will be summarized as follows:

- *Proposition No. 1.* Whether budgeting in an organization is constructive or destructive will depend largely on management's effectiveness in administering it. Budgets that are properly developed and administered can be of great assistance in planning, motivating, and controlling the activities of people. When improperly administered, budgets may cause increased tension, resentment, suspicion, fear, and mistrust among employees.
- *Proposition No. 2.* Planning is one of the most important parts of developing a good budget. Adequate preplanning allows everyone to be working on the same assumptions, targeted goals, and agenda. Employees must understand the limitations and constraints of their participation and the bounds of their decision making. The level of activity the organization expects to achieve within the coming year should be communicated to those individuals participating in the development of the budget. All involved individuals also should understand how their activity will fit into the entire organization and what constraints will be placed on them by upper-level administrative decisions.
- *Proposition No. 3.* Participation should be allowed and encouraged at each level within the organization. The activity of developing the budget should be structured so that the relevant people are included. The relevant people are those who are responsible for implementing the budget, who have the ability to control the item that is budgeted, and who will be rewarded according to its accomplishments. Emotional problems will be minimized if people are allowed to participate in setting their budget, if they are consulted when changes are made, and if they have ample opportunity to explain unfavorable variances from budgeted objectives. There are generally three benefits of allowing employees to participate in developing the budget: *(a)* employees tend to accept the budget as their own plan of action, *(b)* participation tends to increase morale among employees and goodwill toward management, and *(c)* employee cohesiveness is increased and productivity will also increase if dictated by the group norm.

- *Proposition No. 4.* Even though budgets are quantitative tools, considerable emotion is connected with both the controller and the controlled. The individual in control often uses the budget as a medium of personality expression. The people being controlled often have feelings of fear and anxiety because their success and promotions are tied directly to the budget. The climate for preparing the budget should be structured so that individuals feel free rather than anxious and defensive. Structuring the proper climate requires that each individual has the freedom and authority to influence and accept her or his own performance level as well as the responsibility for accomplishing it. This activity should be structured so that it is oriented to the problems and opportunities of the participant as well as the organization.
- *Proposition No. 5.* A major consideration in developing a budget or a standard is the *level of difficulty* that should be associated with successful achievement. The budget could be set too tight (difficult) that it will never be achieved, or it could be set very loose (easy) so that it will always be achieved. Since the budget is regarded as a standard of performance that the individual must reach to be successful, a budget that is set too high or too low fails to provide motivation. Optimal levels of motivation occur when the probability of successful achievement is about fifty–fifty; that is, when the chance of success and failure is approximately equal. Challenging but attainable goals, once achieved, produce feelings of success, confidence, and satisfaction. This, in turn, raises aspiration levels and produces feelings of self worth. The budget can still be difficult and challenging, but it should be attainable.
- *Proposition No. 6.* An important learning principle involved in budgeting is that people tend to perform acts that are rewarded and avoid doing those that are penalized. People want to know what is expected of them and what they must do to be rewarded. The budget is one of the most visible and widely used tools for identifying rewards and reward contingencies. Care must be taken when developing the budget to establish rewards that will lead to achieving organizational goals. Inappropriate reward contingencies will probably result in internal strife among departments and department managers.
- *Proposition No. 7.* Budgets are most effective when they are used to control costs at an efficient level of operation. A clear distinction should be maintained between the objectives of a budget and the objectives of a cost-cutting industrial-engineering study. An industrial-engineering study is very useful in developing some aspects of the budget, especially the type and quantity of direct-material and direct-labor requirements for a manufacturing process. It is also useful in identifying areas in which cost reduction is possible through changes in the manufacturing process. This change may be in the way a worker performs a job or in the equipment used in the process. A cost-reduction study, however, is a separate activity that may not have an immediate effect on the budget.

One major criticism of budgeting is that it is used as a cost-reduction tool rather than a cost-control tool. Budgeting may result in cost reductions by making people more aware of the need to control the costs. The mere process of measuring and reporting operating data may cause some people to improve their level of performance. However, if an individual is doing an efficient job under the current production process and is providing a fair day's work for the pay received, it is not reasonable to expect performance to improve and thereby reduce costs merely by tightening the budget. If additional cost reductions are required, engineering studies should be used to identify alternative production processes and techniques. The objective of the budget is to control costs at an efficient level of operation.

CHAPTER 5: BUDGETING

SUMMARY

Every organization has some type of plan that in reality is a budget. Some companies have a more elaborate budget and budgeting process than others, but all of them have some kind of budget. The critical problem is how to structure the budgeting process and how to prepare a budget that will help the organization achieve its goals and be successful.

A budget is an itemized estimate of an enterprise's operating results for a future time period. It provides a plan for coordinating and implementing activities, motivating people to perform well, and controlling and evaluating their results. The annual budget is part of a long-range planning process that includes long-range goals and intermediate objectives.

In developing the budget, the level of performance that is required to accomplish the intermediate and long-range goals should be established first. The organization must then identify and estimate the critical activity. Usually, selling is the most critical activity, but for some businesses, production is the limiting factor. Estimates are developed for other areas of the business that are required to support the critical activity, including raw materials purchases, production costs, selling and administrative expenses, and cash forecasts. These are developed as supporting schedules for the budgeted financial statements, including the income statement and balance sheet.

Budgeting for not-for-profit entities is increasingly important because the not-for-profit sector of the economy has grown in recent years. Estimating revenues, identifying programs, allocating resources, and evaluating program effectiveness are activities performed during the budgeting process. Incremental budgeting, Planning-Programming-Budgeting Systems, management by objectives, and zero base budgeting are techniques to assist managers in allocating resources and evaluating effectiveness.

Behavioral considerations in developing the budget are at least as important as the quantitative estimates. Because the success of the budget is largely determined by the way it is administered, the strategy to be used in preparing the budget is very important. Relevant people should participate in its development. The climate should be problem- or opportunity-oriented to reduce the emotional problems often associated with the budget. The budget should be difficult and challenging, yet it must be attainable. Care must also be taken to include rewards and reward contingencies that will lead to organizational goals.

SELF-STUDY PROBLEM (AICPA ADAPTED)

The January 31, 19X6, balance sheet of Shelpat Corporation follows:

Cash	$ 8,000
Accounts receivable (net of allowance for uncollectible accounts of $2,000)	38,000
Inventory	16,000
Property, plant, and equipment (net of allowance for accumulated depreciation of $60,000)	40,000
	$102,000
Accounts payable	$ 82,500
Common stock	50,000
Retained earnings (deficit)	(30,500)
	$102,000

Additional information:

1. Sales are budgeted as follows:
   February $110,000
   March $120,000
2. Collections are expected to be 60 percent in the month of sale, 38 percent the next month, and 2 percent uncollectible.
3. The gross margin is 25 percent of sales. Purchases each month are 75 percent of the next month's projected sales. The purchases are paid in full the following month.
4. Other expenses for each month, paid in cash, are expected to be $16,500. Depreciation each month is $5,000.

Required

1. Compute budgeted cash collections for February 19X6.
2. Prepare a pro forma income (loss) statement before income taxes for February 19X6.
3. Compute the projected balance in accounts payable on February 28, 19X6.

Solution to the Self-Study Problem

Requirement 1

Cash collections in February will come from February's sales and from accounts receivable collections for January's sales.

Month of Sale	Cash Collected	
January	$ 38,000	(Balance on accounts receivable)
February	66,000	($110,000 × 60%)
Total	$104,000	

Notice that the $38,000 balance in accounts receivable is net of the allowance for uncollectible accounts.

Requirement 2

Shelpat Corporation
Income Statement
February, 19X6

Sales		$110,000
Less: Cost of goods sold (75%)		82,500
Gross margin (25%)		27,500
Less: Other expenses		
Cash expenses	16,500	
Uncollectible accounts (2% × $110,000)	2,200	
Depreciation	5,000	
Total		23,700
Net income		$ 3,800

Requirement 3

The January 31 accounts payable balance of $82,500 will be paid in February. February purchases are 75 percent of expected sales in March, or $90,000 (75% × $120,000). Since purchases are paid in full the following month, the accounts payable balance on February 28, 19X6, will be $90,000.

SUGGESTED READINGS

Blanchard, Garth A.; Chow, Chee W.; and Noreen, Eric. "The Case of Hospital Budgeting under Rate Regulation." *The Accounting Review* 61 (January 1986): 1.

Brownell, Peter, and McInnes, Morris. "Budgeting Participation, Motivation, and Managerial Performance." *The Accounting Review* 61 (October 1986): 587.

Chenhall, Robert H. "Authoritarianism and Participative Budgeting—A Dyadic Analysis." *The Accounting Review* 61 (April 1986): 263.

Cherrington, David J., and Cherrington, J. Owen. "Participation, Performance, and Appraisal." *Business Horizons* 17 (December 1974): 35–45.

———. "The Role of Budgeting in Organizational Improvement." *Michigan Business Review* 27 (July 1975): 12–16.

———. "Budget Games for Fun and Frustration." *Management Accounting* 57 (January 1976): 28–33.

Collins, Frank; Munter, Paul; and Finn, Don W. "The Budgeting Games People Play." *The Accounting Review* 62 (January 1987): 29.

Gourley, Keith C., and Blecki, Thomas R. "Computerized Budgeting at Lord Corporation." *Management Accounting* 68 (August 1986): 37.

Schiff, Michael, and Lewin, Arie Y. "The Impact of People on Budgets." *The Accounting Review* 45 (April 1970): 259–268.

Umapathy, Srinivasan. "How Successful Firms Budget." *Management Accounting* 68 (February 1987): 25.

DISCUSSION QUESTIONS

Q5–1. Describe a budget.

Q5–2. Why is it so important for business organizations to have a budget?

Q5–3. How does an annual budget tie in with the long-term goals and intermediate objectives of an organization?

Q5–4. How does continuous budgeting differ from annual budgeting?

Q5–5. What are the major benefits of continuous budgeting?

Q5–6. Describe the relationship of a budget to a standard. What role may standards play in developing a budget?

Q5–7. What is a master budget, and how does it differ from flexible budgeting and capital budgeting?

Q5–8. What is the role of the budget committee in developing a budget?

Q5–9. Describe the process by which the budget is developed. Why is it important to identify the critical activity or limiting factor, and what part does it play in the development of the budget?

Q5–10. What are pro forma statements?

Q5–11. Why is planning in preparation for developing the budget so important?

PART TWO: PLANNING BUSINESS ACTIVITIES

Q5–12. Should a company allow broad-based participation in developing the budget? Why?

Q5–13. What is the meaning behind the following—the budget should be problem-oriented or opportunity-oriented rather than a finger-pointing device?

Q5–14. How difficult should the budget be? In order to achieve the optimal level of motivation, what should the probability of success be?

Q5–15. Why are the rewards associated with achieving the budget so important?

Q5–16. Is a budget a cost-control or a cost-reduction tool? Explain.

Q5–17. List and discuss three differences between profit and not-for-profit budgeting.

Q5–18. Why is estimating revenues for not-for-profit organizations such a difficult task?

Q5–19. Describe the difference between a line-item budget and a program budget. Which is considered superior? Why?

Q5–20. List the four ways described in the chapter in which budgeting is used to evaluate program effectiveness in not-for-profit organizations, and give a brief description of each.

EXERCISES

E5–1. Production Budget The estimated sales of Nesbit Company's three products for the third quarter of the year are as follows:

Product	Estimated Sales (units)
Zeon	32,000
Neon	36,000
Genon	54,000

Finished-goods inventories estimated at the beginning of the quarter and the target inventories at the end of the quarter are as follows:

Product	July 1	September 30
Zeon	6,000	6,600
Neon	11,000	9,500
Genon	14,000	12,500

Required

Prepare a production budget for the third quarter.

E5–2. Sales, Production, Direct-Materials, and Direct-Labor Budgets Cranston Company estimates the following unit sales in each of its five sales districts during the fourth quarter of the year:

	District				
Month	1	2	3	4	5
October	850	685	430	1,100	1,115
November	795	610	405	990	850
December	760	730	490	1,280	1,035

The sales price is $85 per unit.

Raw materials ending inventory is desired to be 45 percent of the following month's production. Raw materials inventory on October 1 is 2,800 units. January production is expected to be 2,600 units. Raw materials purchase price is $53 in October and $55 in November and December. Desired ending finished-goods inventory in units for October, November, and December is 3,000, 3,400, and 3,200, respectively. October 1 finished-goods inventory is 3,000 units.

It takes one unit of raw materials and 2.5 hours of direct labor at a cost of $10 per hour to complete one unit. One unit of direct materials is required for each unit of finished product.

Required

Prepare a sales budget, production budget, direct-materials purchase budget, direct-materials use budget, and direct-labor budget for the fourth quarter for Cranston Company. (Show both quantities and costs on the materials and labor budgets.)

E5–3. Production and Direct-Materials Budgets

Lamar Incorporated estimates sales for the second quarter as follows:

April	2,550 units
May	2,475 units
June	2,390 units

The target ending inventory of finished products is as follows for each month in the quarter:

April 1	2,000
April 30	2,230
May 31	2,190
June 30	2,310

Two units of material are required for each unit of finished goods. To start building inventory for the fall sales period, production for July is estimated at 2,700 units. Lamar's policy is to have a raw materials inventory at the end of each month equal to 60 percent of the following month's production needs in order to accommodate supplier and shipping lead time and to keep production on schedule.

Raw materials are expected to cost a uniform $4 per unit throughout the purchase period.

Required

1. Prepare a production budget.
2. Prepare a direct-materials purchase budget showing units and costs.
3. Prepare a direct-materials usage budget showing units and costs.

E5–4. Direct-Labor and Factory Overhead Budgets

Samson Corporation produces a product known as Samco. An acceptable productivity result to produce one Samco is two hours of direct labor. Because Samco requires moderate technical skill in the production process, the going labor rate is $12 per hour. Scheduled production for the third quarter is as follows:

July	2,200 units
August	2,500 units
September	1,800 units

Fixed factory overhead consists of $4,000 per month of items that come from adjusting entries, $3,500 of indirect materials and labor, and $2,300 of on-going current-period disbursement items.

Variable factory overhead includes $1.00 per labor hour of labor-related costs and $0.50 per labor hour of items that require current period disbursement.

Required

1. Prepare a direct-labor budget for each month in the third quarter, showing required hours and labor costs.
2. Prepare a factory overhead cost budget for each month in the third quarter that shows a breakdown of costs into sections covering variable costs and fixed costs, with a further breakdown in the variable and fixed costs sections into the broad overhead categories indicated in the facts.

E5–5. Selling Expense and Cost-of-Goods-Sold Budgets

Treewood Company estimates sales for the second quarter as follows:

April	$ 98,500
May	102,750
June	108,350

Selling expenses include fixed items of $6,500 per month, sales commissions of 5 percent of sales, and other items (such as travel and variable advertising) of 11 percent of sales.

The following production costs are estimated for the second quarter as a whole:

Direct materials	$35,000
Direct labor	45,000
Factory overhead	22,500

The monthly breakdown of quarterly production costs is expected to be as follows:

April	30%
May	45%
June	25%

Expected end-of-month finished-goods inventory are as follows:

March	$24,000
April	27,000
May	32,000
June	26,000

Required

1. Prepare selling expense budgets for each month in the second quarter.
2. Prepare monthly cost-of-goods-sold budgets, showing a breakdown of materials, labor, and factory overhead costs. Also prepare a monthly budget of pretax net income.

E5–6. Line-Item Budgeting in a Not-for-Profit Organization

Jefferson is a small city in the Northeast. The Jefferson Police Department's budgeted expenses for the current year are as follows:

	Fixed Expenses	Expenses that Vary with Population	Total Expenses
Salaries	$500,000		$500,000
Equipment repairs	26,250	$30,000	56,250
Vehicle purchases	62,500		62,500
Vehicle maintenance		12,500	12,500
Other expenses	17,500	20,000	37,500
	$606,250	$62,500	$668,750

Police salaries and purchase of police cruisers are listed as fixed expenditures. However, the city council has approved adding one new officer (at a starting salary of $15,000 per year) and one new cruiser (at a total cost of $15,625) with each 5 percent growth in population.

Analysts have predicted that the population will increase by 8 percent next year over the current year. An inflation rate of 5 percent is anticipated. Personnel currently on the payroll are scheduled to receive a salary increase amounting to 9 percent of their present rate.

Required

Prepare a line-item budget for the Jefferson Police Department for next year.

E5–7. Program Budget in a Not-for-Profit Organization
The National Society for Creative Anachronism is a national club for people with a particular interest in Medieval times. The society sponsors activities in different areas of the country throughout the year, holds a three-day annual national conference, and publishes a monthly newsletter and a quarterly magazine. Following is information for the society for the current year:

Publishing costs	
Magazine	$ 7,000
Newsletter	2,000
Mailing	4,170
Annual conference	89,200
Travel for officers	3,000
Lecture series	25,000
Regional jousting competitions	10,000
Publicity	2,000
Writing contest	2,000
Compensation of employees	30,000

This year's officers are trying to prepare next year's budget and have called you in to help. You have learned that next year's activities will be similar, except that the society has decided to expand the jousting competitions to an entire series of tournaments. This is expected to cost an additional $20,000. All other costs are to remain in the same proportion, but they should be adjusted for an expected inflation rate of 5.5 percent.

Required

Prepare a program budget for the society for next year.

E5–8. Cash Budgeting—Cash Receipts
Reid Company is developing a forecast of March cash receipts from credit sales. Credit sales for March are estimated to be $320,000. The accounts receivable balance at February 28 is $300,000; one-quarter of the balance represents January credit sales, and the remainder is from February sales. All accounts receivable from months prior to January have been collected or written off. Reid's history of accounts receivable collections is as follows:

In the month of sale	20%
In the first month after month of sale	50%
In the second month after month of sale	25%
Written off as uncollectible at the end of the second month after month of sale	5%

Required

Based on the preceding information, determine the cash receipts Reid Company is expecting from credit sales during March.

E5–9. Cash Budgeting—Cash Balance
Fields Corporation projects the following transactions for its first year of operations:

Proceeds from issuance of common stock	$1,000,000
Sales on account	2,200,000
Collections of accounts receivable	1,800,000
Cost of goods sold	1,400,000
Disbursements for purchases of merchandise and expenses	1,200,000
Disbursements for income taxes	250,000
Disbursements for purchase of fixed assets	800,000
Depreciation on fixed assets	150,000
Proceeds from borrowings	700,000
Payments on borrowings	80,000

Required

Determine the projected cash balance for December 31.

E5–10. Cash Budgeting—Cash Disbursement Mapes Corporation has estimated its activity for January. Selected data from these estimated amounts are as follows:

Sales	$1,400,000
Gross profit (based on sales)	30%
Increase in trade accounts receivable during month	$ 40,000
Change in accounts payable during month	$ 0
Increase in inventory during month	$ 20,000

- Variable selling, general, and administrative expenses include a charge for uncollectible accounts of 1 percent of sales.
- Total selling, general, and administrative expenses are $142,000 per month plus 15 percent of sales.
- Depreciation expense of $80,000 per month is included in fixed selling, general, and administrative expenses.

Required

What are the estimated cash disbursements for January?

E5–11. Production Budget P.C. Spreadsheet Analysis Val's Manufacturing Company produces two products, Altex and Burtex. Estimated sales for the fourth quarter for each product are as follows:

	Sales		
Product	October	November	December
Altex	23,000	27,000	24,000
Burtex	32,000	41,000	38,000

The finished-goods inventory balance on September 30 is 11,000 for Altex and 14,000 for Burtex. Val likes to have 55 percent of the following month's sales in the finished-goods inventory at the end of the month. Estimated sales for Altex and Burtex for January are 17,000 and 30,000, respectively.

Required

1. Using Lotus or some other spreadsheet program, prepare a production budget in units for both products for the months of October, November, and December. Print a copy of your results.
2. Assume the same sales projections as in requirement 1, but also assume that Val has now decided he wants to have 65 percent of the following month's sales in ending

finished-goods inventory. Change the worksheet you prepared in requirement 1 to reflect this change.

E5–12. Cash Budgeting—Cash Receipts PC Spreadsheet Analysis
Karen's Carpet Company is trying to develop a forecast of cash receipts for July. Karen, the owner, has asked you to help. The accountant has given you the following information:

- Credit sales for May and June were $25,000 and $28,000, respectively. Credit sales for July are estimated at $29,500.
- The accounts receivable balance on June 30 was $28,350. Collections of accounts receivables in the past have been as follows:

    30% in the month of sale
    35% in the first month after sale
    30% in the second month after sale
    5% written off as uncollectible at the end of the second month after sale.

Required

1. Using the preceding information and Lotus or another spreadsheet program, determine the expected cash receipts for Karen's Carpet Company for the month of July. Print a copy of your results.
2. Assume all the same information as in requirement 1, except now assume that Karen has just initiated a tighter collections policy. She has reduced uncollectible accounts to 2 percent. The extra 3 percent of receivables are collected in the second month after sale. What are the expected cash receipts for July. Print a copy of your results.

E5–13. Sales, Production, Direct-Materials, and Direct-Labor Budgets Spreadsheet Analysis
The Garrett Company has estimated unit sales for the first half of 19X9 to be as follows:

Month	Sales
January	700
February	760
March	730
April	790
May	850
June	840

The sales price for Garrett's product is $58 per unit.

The Garrett Company desires raw materials ending inventory to be 40 percent of the following month's production. Finished-goods ending inventory should be 60 percent of the following month's sales. December 31, 19X8, inventories for raw materials and finished goods are 600 units and 400 units, respectively. The raw materials purchase price is expected to be $23 for the first three months and $25 for the last three months of the six-month period. July's sales and production are expected to be 830 and 720 units, respectively.

It takes two units of raw materials and three direct-labor hours to produce one finished product. The cost per hour of direct labor is currently $8.50, and this is not expected to change. Overhead is charged out at $4.25 per unit.

Required

Using Lotus or another spreadsheet application, prepare for the Garrett Company a sales budget, production budget, direct-materials use budget, direct-materials purchase budget, and direct-labor budget by month for the first half of 19X9 (show both quantities and costs on all of the budgets except the direct-materials use budget).

PROBLEMS

P5-1. Budgeting—Basic Concepts and Procedures (CMA) The Russon Corporation is a retailer whose sales are all made on credit. Sales are billed twice monthly—on the 10th of the month for the last half of the prior month's sales, and on the 20th of the month for the first half of the current month's sales. The terms of all sales are 2/10, net 30. Based on past experience, the collection experience of accounts receivable is as follows:

Within the discount period	80%
On the 30th day	18%
Uncollectible	2%

The sales value of shipments for May 19X0 and the forecast for the next four months are as follows:

May (actual)	$500,000
June	600,000
July	700,000
August	700,000
September	400,000

Russon's average markup on its products is 20 percent of the sales price.

Russon purchases merchandise for resale to meet the current month's sales demand and to maintain a desired monthly ending inventory of 25 percent of the next month's sales. All purchases are on credit, with terms of net 30. Russon pays for one-half of a month's purchases in the month of purchase and the other half in the month following the purchase. All sales and purchases occur uniformly throughout the month.

1. How much cash can Russon Corporation plan to collect from accounts receivable collections during July 19X0?
    a. $574,000
    b. $662,600
    c. $619,000
    d. $608,600
    e. None of the above answers is correct.
2. How much cash can Russon plan to collect in September from sales made in August 19X0?
    a. $337,400
    b. $343,000
    c. $400,400
    d. $280,000
    e. None of the above answers is correct.
3. The budgeted dollar value of Russon's inventory on August 31, 19X0, will be
    a. $110,000.
    b. $80,000.
    c. $112,000.
    d. $100,000.
    e. Some amount other than those given above.

4. How much merchandise should Russon plan to purchase during June 19X0?
   a. $520,000
   b. $460,000
   c. $500,000
   d. $580,000
   e. None of the above answers is correct.
5. The amount Russon should budget in August 19X0 for the payment of merchandise is
   a. $560,000.
   b. $500,000.
   c. $667,000.
   d. $600,000.
   e. Some amount other than those given above.

P5–2. Sales, Production, and Raw Materials Purchases Budgets

Wisteria Products Company has estimated annual sales by region as follows:

	Annual Sales in Units
North	30,000
Central	18,000
South	40,000
Total	88,000

Wisteria has been growing steadily and has built into the sales projections a quarterly growth factor. The expected quarterly sales for each region is broken down as follows:

Quarter	Percentage of Annual Sales
1st	22
2d	24
3rd	26
4th	28
	100

For budgeting purposes the sales price per unit is estimated to be $2.50. This price is the same for each region and will remain constant throughout the year.

Required

1. Prepare a sales budget for each quarter and for the year broken down on a regional basis. Show quantity and dollar values in the budget.
2. Refer to your sales budget prepared for the Wisteria Products Company in requirement 1. Wisteria has found in previous years that it is necessary to have a quarterly ending inventory equal to 10 percent of the following quarter's sales. Production for all regions is done at one location, and the inventory shown at the beginning of the first quarter is 2,000 units. Assume that sales expectations for each year are the same as for the current budget year.

   Present to the management of Wisteria Products Company a production budget for each quarter and for the year.
3. Refer to the budgets you prepared in requirements 1 and 2. The product for which these budgets have been prepared is a room fragrance. The liquid raw material used in production is purchased from one supplier and costs $12 per gallon. Each unit produced requires 8 ounces of the fluid. Wisteria Company has discovered that the raw materials ending inventory for each quarter must be 20 percent of the following quarter's

production needs. Assume 250 gallons of the required liquid raw material are on hand at the beginning of the year.

Prepare a raw materials purchase budget for each quarter and give the year totals. Show unit production needs, purchase needs in gallons, and costs. Round dollar amounts to the nearest $1.00.

P5-3. Determining Change in Cash Balance
Sussex Company has budgeted its operations for February. No change in inventory level during the month is planned. Selected data from estimated amounts are as follows:

Net loss	$100,000
Increase in accounts payable	40,000
Depreciation expense	35,000
Decrease in gross amount of trade accounts receivable	60,000
Purchase of office equipment on 45-day credit terms	15,000
Provision for estimated warranty liability	10,000

Required

How much change in cash position is expected for February?

P5-4. Cash Budgeting (CMA)
United Business Education, Inc. (UBE), is a nonprofit organization that sponsors a wide variety of management seminars throughout the United States. In addition, it is heavily involved in research into improved methods of educating and motivating business executives. The seminar activity is largely supported by fees and the research program by member dues.

UBE operates on a calendar-year basis and is in the process of finalizing the budget for 19X1. The following information has been taken from approved plans, which are still tentative at this time.

Seminar Program

Revenue. The scheduled number of programs should produce $12,000,000 of revenue for the year. Each program is budgeted to produce the same amount of revenue, which is collected during the month the program is offered. The programs are scheduled so that 12 percent of the revenue is collected in each of the first five months of the year. The remaining programs, accounting for the remaining 40 percent of the revenue, are distributed evenly through the months of September, October, and November. No programs are offered in the other four months of the year.

Direct Expenses. The seminar expenses are made up of three segments:

1. Instructors' fees are paid at the rate of 70 percent of the seminar revenue in the month following the seminar. The instructors are considered independent contractors and are not eligible for UBE employee benefits.
2. Facilities fees total $5,600,000 for the year. They are the same for each program and are paid in the month the program is given.
3. Annual promotional costs of $1,000,000 are spent equally in all months except June and July, when there is no promotional effort.

Research Program

Research Grants. Many projects in the research program are nearing completion. The other main research activity this year includes the feasibility studies for projects to be started in 19X2. As a result, the total grant expense of $3,000,000 for 19X1 is expected to be paid out at the rate of $500,000 per month during the first six months of the year.

Salaries and Other UBE Expenses

Office Lease. Annual amount of $240,000, paid monthly at the beginning of each month

General Administrative Expenses. $1,500,000 annually, or $125,000 a month, for telephone, supplies, postage, etc.

Depreciation Expense. $240,000 a year

General UBE Promotion. Annual cost of $600,000, paid monthly

Salaries and Benefits:

Number of Employees	Annual Salary Paid Monthly	Total Annual Salaries
1	$50,000	$ 50,000
3	40,000	120,000
4	30,000	120,000
15	25,000	375,000
5	15,000	75,000
22	10,000	220,000
50		$960,000

Employee benefits amount to $240,000, or 25 percent of annual salaries. Except for the pension contribution, the benefits are paid as salaries are paid. The annual pension payment of $24,000, based on 2.5 percent of salaries (included in the total benefits and the 25 percent rate), is due April 15, 19X1.

Other Information

Membership income. UBE has 100,000 members, each of whom pays an annual fee of $100. The fee for the calendar year is invoiced in late June. The collection schedule is as follows:

July	60%
August	30%
September	5%
October	5%
	100%

Capital Expenditures. The capital expenditures program calls for a total of $510,000 in cash payments to be spread evenly over the first five months of 19X1.

Cash. Cash and temporary investments at January 1, 19X1, are estimated at $750,000.

Required

1. Prepare a budget of the annual cash receipts and disbursements for UBE for 19X1. Include data for each month.
2. Prepare a cash budget for UBE for January 19X1.
3. Using the information you developed in requirements 1 and 2, identify two important operating problems for UBE.

P5–5. Budgeted Income Statement (CMA) Rein Company, a compressor manufacturer, is developing a budgeted income statement for the calendar year 19X2. The president is generally satisfied with the projected net income of $700,000 for 19X1, resulting in an earnings-per-share figure of $2.80. However, next year the president would like the earnings per share to increase to at least $3.

Rein Company employs a standard absorption cost system. Inflation necessitates an annual revision in the standards, as evidenced by an increase in production costs expected in 19X2. The total standard manufacturing cost for 19X1 is $72 per unit produced.

Rein expects to sell 100,000 compressors at $110 each in the current year (19X1). Forecasts from the sales department are favorable, and Rein Company is projecting an annual increase of 10 percent in unit sales in 19X2 and 19X3. This increase in sales will occur even though a $15 increase in unit selling price will be implemented in 19X2. The selling price increase was absolutely essential to compensate for the increased production costs and operating expenses. However, management is concerned that any additional sales price increase would curtail the desired growth in volume.

Standard production costs are developed for the two primary metals used in the compressor (brass and a steel alloy), the direct labor, and manufacturing overhead. The following schedule represents the 19X2 standard quantities and rates for material and labor to produce one compressor.

Brass	4 pounds @ $5.35/pound	$21.40
Steel alloy	5 pounds @ $3.16/pound	15.80
Direct labor	4 hours @ $7.00/hour	28.00
Total prime costs		$65.20

The material content of the compressor has been reduced slightly, hopefully without a noticeable decrease in the quality of the finished product. Improved labor productivity and some increase in automation have resulted in a decrease in labor hours per unit from 4.4 to 4.0. However, the significant increases in material prices and hourly labor rates more than offset any savings from reduced input quantities.

The schedule of manufacturing overhead cost per unit has yet to be completed. Preliminary data are as follows:

	Activity Level (units)		
Overhead Items	**100,000**	**110,000**	**120,000**
Supplies	$ 475,000	$ 522,500	$ 570,000
Indirect labor	530,000	583,000	636,000
Utilities	170,000	187,000	204,000
Maintenance	363,000	377,500	392,000
Taxes and insurance	87,000	87,000	87,000
Depreciation	421,000	421,000	421,000
Total overhead	$2,046,000	$2,178,000	$2,310,000

The standard overhead rate is based on direct-labor hours and is developed by using the total overhead costs from the preceding schedule for the activity level closest to planned production. In developing the standards for the manufacturing costs, the two following assumptions were made.

1. Brass is currently selling at $5.65 per pound. However, this price is historically high, and the purchasing manager expects the price to drop to the predetermined standard early in 19X2.
2. Several new employees will be hired for the production line in 19X2. The employees will be generally unskilled. If basic training programs are not effective and improved labor productivity is not experienced, the production time per unit of product will increase by fifteen minutes over the 19X2 standards.

Rein employs a LIFO inventory system for its finished goods. Rein's inventory policy for finished goods is to have 15 percent of the expected annual unit sales for the coming year in finished-goods inventory at the end of the prior year. The finished-goods inventory at December 31, 19X1, is expected to consist of 16,500 units at a total carrying cost of $1,006,500.

Operating expenses are classified as selling, which are variable, and administrative, which are all fixed. The budgeted selling expenses are expected to average 12 percent of sales revenue in 19X2, which is consistent with the performance in 19X1. The administrative expenses in 19X2 are expected to be 20 percent higher than the predicted 19X1 amount of $907,850.

Management accepts the cost standards developed by the production and accounting departments. However, it is concerned about the possible effect on net income if the price of brass does not decrease or labor efficiency does not improve as expected. Therefore, management wants the budgeted income statement to be prepared using the standards as developed but considering the worst possible situation for 19X2. Each resulting manufacturing variance should be separately identified and added to or subtracted from budgeted cost of goods sold at standard. Rein is subject to a 45 percent income tax rate.

Required

1. Prepare the budgeted income statement for 19X2 for Rein Company as specified by management. Round all calculations to the nearest dollar.
2. Review the 19X2 budgeted income statement prepared for Rein Company and discuss whether the president's objectives can be achieved.

P5-6. Program Budget for City Government
Following is a line-item budget for the city of Lancaster, population 120,000:

Salaries and wages	$ 7,200,000
Supplies	600,000
Maintenance and repairs	720,000
Employee benefits	960,000
Capital expenditures	1,080,000
Miscellaneous	600,000
Total	$11,160,000

These expenditures provide city administration, police and fire protection, and sanitation services. The city has hired you to prepare a program budget that will show the cost per person of the services. A review of previous years has resulted in the following allocations of the line items:

	Administration	Police	Fire	Sanitation
Salaries and wages	30%	30%	20%	20%
Supplies	30	20	30	20
Maintenance and repairs	5	35	30	30
Employee benefits	30	30	25	15
Capital expenditures	15	35	30	20
Miscellaneous	Based on percentage of total allocations			

Required

1. Prepare a program budget for the city of Lancaster.
2. What will be the budget expenditure per person for each of the services provided?

P5-7. Budgets and Human Behavioral Considerations (CMA)
RV Industries manufactures and sells recreation vehicles. The company has eight divisions strategically located near major markets. Each division has a sales force and two to four manufacturing plants. These divisions operate as autonomous profit centers responsible for purchasing, operations, and sales.

John Collins, the corporate controller, described the divisional performance measurement system as follows: "We allow the divisions to control the entire operation from the purchase of raw materials to the sale of the product. We, at corporate headquarters, only get involved in strategic decisions, such as developing new product lines. Each division is responsible for meeting its market needs by providing the right products at a low cost on a timely basis. Frankly, the divisions need to focus on cost control, delivery, and services to customers in order to become more profitable.

"Although we give the divisions considerable autonomy, we watch their monthly income statements very closely. Each month's actual performance is compared with the budget in considerable detail. If the actual sales or contribution margin is more than 4 or 5 percent below the budget, we jump on the division people immediately. I might add that we don't have much trouble getting their attention. All of the management people at the plant and division level can add appreciably to their annual salaries with bonuses if actual net income is considerably greater than budget."

The budgeting process begins in August, when division sales managers, after consulting with their sales personnel, estimate sales for the next calendar year. These estimates are sent to plant managers, who use the sales forecasts to prepare production estimates. At the plants, production statistics (including raw material quantities, labor hours, production schedules, and output quantities) are developed by operating personnel. Using the statistics prepared by the operating personnel, the plant's accounting staff determines costs and prepares the plant's budgeted variable cost of goods sold and other plant expenses for each month of the coming calendar year.

In October, each division's accounting staff combines plant budgets with sales estimates and adds additional division expenses. "After the divisional management is satisfied with the budget," said Collins, "I visit each division to go over its budget and make sure it is in line with corporate stragtegy and projections. I really emphasize the sales forecasts because of the volatility in the demand for our product. For many years, we lost sales to our competitors because we didn't project high enough production and sales and couldn't meet the market demand. More recently, we were caught with large excess inventory when the bottom dropped out of the market for recreational vehicles.

"I generally visit all eight divisions during the first two weeks in November. After that, the division budgets are combined and reconciled by my staff, and they are ready for approval by the board of directors in early December. The board seldom questions the budget.

"One complaint we've had from plant and division managers is that they are penalized for circumstances beyond their control. For example, they failed to predict the recent sales decline. As a result, they didn't make their budget and, of course, they received no bonuses. However, I should point out that they are well rewarded when they exceed their budget. Furthermore, they provide most of the information for the budget, so it's their own fault if the budget is too optimistic."

Required

1. Identify and explain the biases that corporate management of RV Industries should expect in the communication of budget estimates by its division and plant personnel.
2. What sources of information can the top management of RV Industries use to monitor the budget estimates prepared by its divisions and plants?
3. What services could top management of RV Industries offer the divisions to help them in their budget development, without appearing to interfere with the division budget decisions?
4. The top management of RV Industries is attempting to decide whether it should get

more involved in the budget process. Identify and explain the variables management needs to consider in reaching its decision.

P5-8. Budget for a School District The White Mountains Regional School District is planning its budget for the ensuing year. Shown here are the total budgeted expenses for 19X7.

Teachers:		
Elementary	$900,000	
Secondary	400,000	
Special education	45,000	
Teachers' aides	30,000	
Substitutes	25,000	$1,400,000
Student transportation		32,000
Lunch program		150,000
Administration:		
School district	$ 80,000	
Elementary	210,000	
Secondary	120,000	
Secretarial	40,000	
Retirement, insurance, etc.	160,000	610,000
Physical facilities maintenance		250,000
Supplies		300,000
Other expenditures:		
Capital expenditures		180,000
Interest expense		150,000
Insurance		120,000
Total budget		$3,192,000

Other Information:

1. School board members estimate that the population in the district will increase by 1 percent next year and that one-half of that increase will be school-age children.
2. Teachers' salaries, transportation expenses, lunch-program expenses, and supplies expenses vary with the student population. All other expenses are fixed.
3. Inflation is expected to be 5 percent next year.
4. Average student enrollment in the district is 3,000, with 3 percent of those students in the special education program.
5. State grants to the district total $220 per student. The federal government matches the state grant at a rate of 75 percent, plus provides 50 percent of the lunch-program costs. In addition, the state grants $180 per student enrolled in the special education program.
6. The district has established a sinking fund to be used for replacement or refurbishing of outdated or inadequate buildings. Funds are to be deposited in the sinking fund at a rate of $250,000 per year.
7. Interest on the sinking funds and other temporary investments is expected to be $110,000. These funds are to be used for current capital expenditures.
8. All other needed funds are to be raised through taxation.

Required

1. Prepare the White Mountains Regional School District budget for 19X8.
2. Prepare a schedule showing how much money must be raised through taxation to meet the 19X8 requirements.

P5-9. Cash Budgeting—Summary Problem CMA Requirements 1 through 4 relate to data to be reported in the statement of changes in financial position for Debbie Dress Shops, Incorporated, based on the following information:

Debbie Dress Shops, Inc.
Balance Sheet

	December 31	
	19X1	19X0
Assets		
Current		
Cash	$ 300,000	$ 200,000
Accounts receivable (net)	840,000	580,000
Merchandise inventory	660,000	420,000
Prepaid expenses	100,000	50,000
Total current assets	1,900,000	1,250,000
Long-term investments	80,000	—
Land, buildings, and fixtures	1,130,000	600,000
Less: Accumulated depreciation	110,000	50,000
	1,020,000	550,000
Total assets	$3,000,000	$1,800,000
Equities		
Current liabilities:		
Accounts payable	$ 530,000	$ 440,000
Accrued expenses	140,000	130,000
Dividends payable	70,000	—
Total current liabilities	740,000	570,000
Note payable (due 19X4)	500,000	—
Stockholders' equity:		
Common stock	1,200,000	900,000
Retained earnings	560,000	330,000
	1,760,000	1,230,000
Total liabilities and stockholders' equity	$3,000,000	$1,800,000

Debbie Dress Shops, Inc.
Income Statement

	Year Ending December 31	
	19X1	19X0
Net credit sales	$6,400,000	$4,000,000
Cost of goods sold	5,000,000	3,200,000
Gross profit	1,400,000	800,000
Expenses (including income taxes)	1,000,000	520,000
Net income	$ 400,000	$ 280,000

Although the corporation will report all changes in financial position, management has adopted a format emphasizing the flow of cash.

All accounts receivable and accounts payable relate to trade merchandise. Accounts payable are recorded net and always are paid to take all discounts allowed. The allowance for doubtful accounts at the end of 19X1 was the same as at the end of 19X0; no receivables were charged against the allowance during 19X1.

The proceeds from the note payable were used to finance a new store. Capital stock was sold to provide additional working capital.

1. Cash collected during 19X1 from accounts receivable amounted to
   a. $5,560,000.
   b. $5,840,000.
   c. $6,140,000.
   d. $6,400,000.
2. Cash payments during 19X1 on accounts payable to suppliers amounted to
   a. $4,670,000.
   b. $4,910,000.
   c. $5,000,000.
   d. $5,150,000.
3. Cash receipts during 19X1 that were not provided by operations totaled
   a. $140,000.
   b. $300,000.
   c. $500,000.
   d. $800,000.
4. Cash payments for noncurrent assets purchased during 19X1 were
   a. $80,000.
   b. $530,000.
   c. $610,000.
   d. $660,000.

P5-10. Budgeting and Implementation Considerations (CMA) Springfield Corporation operates on a calendar-year basis. It begins the annual budgeting process in late August, when the president establishes targets for total dollar sales and net income before taxes for the next year.

The sales target is given to the marketing department, where the marketing manager formulates a sales budget by product line in both units and dollars. From this budget, sales quotas by product line in units and dollars are established for each of the corporation's sales districts.

The marketing manager also estimates the cost of the marketing activities required to support the target sales volume and prepares a tentative marketing expense budget.

The executive vice president uses the sales and profit targets, the sales budget by product line, and the tentative marketing expense budget to determine the dollar amounts that can be devoted to manufacturing and corporate office expense. The executive vice president prepares the budget for corporate expenses and then forwards to the production department the product-line sales budget in units and the total dollar amount that can be devoted to manufacturing.

The production manager meets with the factory managers to develop a manufacturing plan within the cost constraints set by the executive vice president. The budgeting process usually comes to a halt at this point, because the production department does not consider the financial resources allocated to be adequate.

When this standstill occurs, the vice president of finance, the executive vice president, the marketing manager, and the production manager meet together to determine the final budgets for each of the areas. This normally results in a modest increase in the total amount available for manufacturing costs, whereas the marketing expense and corporate office expense budgets are cut. The total sales and net income figures proposed by the president are seldom changed. Although the participants are seldom pleased with the compromise, these budgets are final. Each executive then develops a new detailed budget for the operations in her or his area.

None of the areas has achieved its budget in recent years. Sales often run below the target. When budgeted sales are not achieved, each area is expected to cut costs so that the president's profit target can still be met. However, the profit target is seldom met because costs are not cut enough. In fact, costs often run above the original budget in all functional areas. The president, who is disturbed that Springfield has not been able to meet the sales and profit targets, hired a consultant who has had considerable experience with companies in Springfield's industry. The consultant reviewed the budgets for the past four years and concluded that the product-line sales budgets were reasonable and that the cost and expense budgets were adequate for the budgeted sales and production levels.

Required

1. Discuss how the budgeting process as employed by Springfield Corporation contributes to the failure to achieve the president's sales and profit targets.
2. Suggest how Springfield Corporation's budgeting process could be revised to correct the problems.
3. Should the functional areas be expected to cut their costs when sales volume falls below budget? Explain your answer.

CASE

Case 5.1 Comprehensive Budgeting

Woody's Wood Specialty Manufacturing Company (WWSM), a partnership, started as a garage business a few years ago. Sales were $10,000 the first year. Last year sales topped $1 million.

Initially WWSM featured several wood novelties in its product line. One item, a replica of an antique automobile, captured such attention in the market that it accounted for 98 percent of the firm's sales by the end of the third business year. Market analysis indicated that the product had market acceptance as a "stand-alone" product, so the firm has concentrated production and sales efforts during the past two years on the single product.

Market analysis and projections indicate that sales acceptance will continue for at least five more years. Sales are made directly to exclusive novelty shops in high-priced urban and suburban shopping centers, and they are evenly spread throughout the year.

WWSM's management wants to get a better grasp of expected operating results and has requested a comprehensive budget for the month of June. It intends to review the budget carefully to assess whether it will provide needed operation guidance before investing in regular monthly, quarterly, and annual budgets.

The following operating data have been assembled from production, sales, finance, personnel, and accounting records. You have been assigned to analyze this information and to organize the results of your analysis into a comprehensive budget that is as complete as possible using the available data.

Monthly antique auto sales are expected to average 4,000 units at $25 each (manufacturer's list price subject to an 8 percent discount on orders of 400 or more from a particular customer). Credit terms are net 10 days from date of sale.

The finished-product inventory is expected to be 800 units on June 1. Management has targeted inventories at the end of each month to be 25 percent of the following month's projected sales.

Each auto requires two pieces of oak hardwood at a cost of $1.75/piece, from which the body and wheels are fashioned. Sixteen fir dowels that cost $0.02 each are used for top and door supports and for front and rear bumpers and axles. May 31 inventory of oak pieces and fir dowels is expected to be 900 and 6,500, respectively. Vendor and shipping company reliability can be counted on, so inventories of materials can be maintained at a minimum level sufficient to cover 10 percent of the next month's production. Vendors are offering WWSM exceptional purchase prices and in doing so have specified C.O.D. payment terms.

Production takes place in a small but adequate rented plant. Cutting and shaping, sanding, and finishing departments are set up to produce the product. Normally, departmental budgets for direct labor and factory overhead are expected, but management has suggested that the departments might be grouped for the test budget. The labor time to produce each unit averages one-fourth hour, and the average hourly rate is $7.80 for the three departments combined.

Factory overhead is applied to production at a predetermined rate based on labor time. The variable overhead rate averages $9.60 per labor hour. Fixed overhead averages $6.00 per labor hour. Normally, overhead budgets would be prepared for each department, showing detailed variable and fixed items. Management has suggested the preparation of overhead budgets in summary only for the test budget. You note that variable overhead includes items such as utilities and factory supplies that require monthly expenditures. Fixed overhead includes items (such as equipment depreciation) that come from monthly adjusting entries averaging 40 percent of the total. The remaining 60 percent includes items such as factory supervisory salaries.

Sales commissions are 5 percent of net sales. A minimum expenditure of $1,000 each month is made for a small one-eighth-page advertisement in a trade newspaper.

Management salaries are $16,000 per month. Depreciation on the sales manager's car is $250 per month. Other office expenses average $200 per month.

Management has requested that the test budget include a contribution statement of expected operating results, as well as a pro-forma operating statement in traditional format.

Just as you are about to begin your analysis, the president mentions two additional items: *(a)* The present capacity of production and the sales and administrative staff are considered adequate to sustain operations at the present and projected levels; and *(b)* the president is embarrassed to be seen in the 1941 Harper Arrow she drives on company business (not likely to become an antique). She proposes (already approved by the management group) to acquire a company car in June and believes the firm has done well enough to justify spending $25,200 for a new M-Z 90. These cars are "hot" sellers and are expected to appreciate in value over a three-year period.

You notice that the cash balance is expected to be $45,000 on June 1. Management targets a cash balance of at least $50,000 at month end.

Chapter 6

Flexible Budgeting and Responsibility Reporting

Outline

FLEXIBLE BUDGETING
Flexible Budgeting Defined
Flexible Budget Example
Flexible Budget Formula
DEVELOPING THE FLEXIBLE BUDGET FORMULA
Analyzing Cost Behavior in a Production Process
Direct Costs: Materials and Labor
Factory Overhead
   High-Low Method
   Scattergraph Method
   Least-Squares Regression and Correlation Analysis
Flexible Budgeting for Selling and Administrative Costs
RESPONSIBILITY ACCOUNTING
Responsibility Accounting Defined
Relationship to Segmented Reporting
Form and Content of Reports

Analysis of Budget Variances: Management by Exception
   Fixed Percentage of the Budget
   Statistical Analysis
Controllable versus Uncontrollable Costs
   Controllable Costs Defined
   Complete Versus Partial Control
BEHAVIORAL CONSIDERATIONS IN REPORTING
SUMMARY
APPENDIX 6.1: ALTERNATE COMPUTATIONS FOR COEFFICIENT OF CORRELATION AND COEFFICIENT OF DETERMINATION
SELF-STUDY PROBLEM
SUGGESTED READINGS
DISCUSSION QUESTIONS
EXERCISES
PROBLEMS

In chapter 5 we discussed the importance of a budget, procedures followed in developing a budget, and some of the behavioral problems associated with the development process. The budget developed there may be referred to as a *static budget* because no allowance was made to adjust budgeted expenditures for unexpected changes in the level of sales or the level of production. This creates a problem in evaluating the organization's effectiveness in meeting budgeted objectives whenever the level of sales or the level of production is not the same as outlined in the budget. A technique called *flexible budgeting* has been developed to assist in preparing the budget and in evaluating the operating results.

An important part of flexible budgeting is quantifying the various cost relationships and selecting a measure of volume that is a good predictor of the amount of cost that should be incurred. Chapter 3 discussed the high-low method, scattergraph method, and least-squares method for developing a cost equation. This chapter uses these methods to select from among alternative measures of volume the one that is the best predictor of cost.

The usefulness of both the budget and the results of operations is enhanced when they are presented together, with any significant deviations between them highlighted to attract management's attention. Reports for internal use should be broken down by segment, consistent with an individual's area of responsibility, and contain only those items that the individual can control. Such reports have an important effect on behavior because of the feedback they provide and because they are often used to evaluate performance.

This chapter introduces flexible budgeting and responsibility accounting and discusses some of the behavioral aspects of reporting. After completing this chapter, you should be able to:

1. describe what a flexible budget is and why it is useful.
2. prepare a flexible budget.
3. select the activity base or measure of volume that has the highest correlation with cost.
4. prepare meaningful performance reports.
5. discuss some of the important behavioral aspects of performance reporting.

FLEXIBLE BUDGETING

The annual or quarterly budget as developed by the procedures outlined in chapter 5 is referred to as a **static budget.** Generally it is prepared at the beginning of an accounting period and serves as an operating plan for the accounting period. This budget is static because it is relevant to only *one level of business activity*. For most manufacturing enterprises, selling is the critical activity, and the level of production is closely tied to expected sales. The most likely level of sales is projected, the production level is determined, and the production and sales budgets are developed for *that* level of business activity. If, however, the actual level of production or sales is not as planned, a comparison of the static budget with actual performance is not meaningful in evaluating the efficiency of the enterprise. There are two common factors that could account for the difference between budgeted data and actual operating data:

1. The change in the level of business activity. A higher (lower) level of production should result in higher (lower) production costs than budgeted merely because of the number of units involved. Likewise, selling more (less) units than expected will cause higher (lower) selling expenses than planned for in the budget.
2. The efficiency of the employees and managers. The efficiency with which workers perform their tasks can cause actual operating results to differ from the budget. For

example, production costs will be higher when production workers perform sloppy work or waste time in moving from one activity to the next.

A budget that eliminates the effects of a change in the level of business activity provides a meaningful evaluation of the efficiency of operations. This kind of budget is called a **flexible budget.**

Flexible Budgeting Defined

Flexible budgeting is a technique that is used to adjust the budget for *various levels of business activity*. Volume of business activity may be specified in a variety of ways, but one common measure is the number of units manufactured or the number of units sold. In developing the flexible budget, expected or budgeted cost relationships are quantified so that the budget can be easily adjusted to any level of business activity. In essence, the flexible budget says, "You tell me your level of business activity for the period, and I'll tell you what your costs should have been."

Flexible Budget Example

An example will illustrate how a flexible budget is used and why it is important for performance evaluations. Suppose that the expected cost of producing one unit of finished product consists of the following:

Manufacturing Costs	Standard	Cost per Unit
Direct material	(3 lbs. @ $1.20 per lb.)	$3.60
Direct labor	(1 hour @ $5.70 per hour)	5.70
Variable overhead	($2.00 per direct-labor hour)	2.00
Fixed overhead	($7,000 ÷ 10,000 units)	0.70
Total cost per unit		$12.00

Notice that the variable overhead is expected to vary in proportion to the number of direct-labor hours worked. Also notice that the fixed overhead is expected to be $7,000 for the year. At a planned production level of 10,000 units, the cost per unit is $0.70. Remember that fixed costs do not change when production changes, so $7,000 is expected to be spent on fixed overhead regardless of the actual level of production within the relevant range.

Figure 6.1 presents the budgeted cost data used in preparing the budget for 19X1. It shows the amount of cost that should be incurred at 9,000, 9,500, 10,000, and 10,500

FIGURE 6.1

Planning Schedule for Production Budget
Year Ending December 31, 19X1

Manufacturing Costs	Unit Cost	Volume of Production			
		9,000	9,500	10,000	10,500
Direct material	$ 3.60	$ 32,400	$ 34,200	$ 36,000	$ 37,800
Direct labor	5.70	51,300	54,150	57,000	59,850
Variable overhead	2.00	18,000	19,000	20,000	21,000
Variable costs	$11.30	$101,700	$107,350	$113,000	$118,650
Fixed costs		7,000	7,000	7,000	7,000
Total cost		$108,700	$114,350	$120,000	$125,650

FIGURE 6.2

Production Report
Year Ending December 31, 19X1

Manufacturing Costs	Budgeted Costs[a]	Actual Costs[b]	Variance Favorable (Unfavorable)
Direct material	$ 36,000	$ 41,500	($ 5,500)
Direct labor	57,000	61,900	(4,900)
Variable overhead	20,000	21,800	(1,800)
Fixed overhead	7,000	7,200	(200)
Total	$120,000	$132,400	($12,400)

[a]Budgeted costs are for 10,000 units of production.
[b]Actual production level was 11,000 units.

FIGURE 6.3

Revised Production Report
Year Ending December 31, 19X1

Manufacturing Costs	Budgeted Cost @ 10,000 Units	Budgeted Cost @ 11,000 Units	Actual Cost @ 11,000 Units	Variances[a] Production Level	Efficiency	Total
Direct material	$ 36,000	$ 39,600	$ 41,500	($ 3,600)	($1,900)	($ 5,500)
Direct labor	57,000	62,700	61,900	(5,700)	800	(4,900)
Variable overhead	20,000	22,000	21,800	(2,000)	200	(1,800)
Fixed overhead	7,000	7,000	7,200	0	(200)	(200)
Total	$120,000	$131,300	$132,400	($11,300)	($1,100)	($12,400)

[a]Variances are identified as favorable or unfavorable by the parenthesis—favorable, (unfavorable).

units of production. Because 10,000 units was considered to be the most likely level of production for 19X1, the data shown in that column were adopted and included in the master budget.

However, actual production during 19X1 was 11,000 units. Figure 6.2 shows the budgeted production cost data for 19X1 at the projected production level of 10,000 units. Also shown are the actual production costs incurred during the year at the 11,000 unit production level. The difference between actual and budgeted costs are shown as variances. When actual cost exceeds budgeted cost, it is considered an unfavorable variance and is enclosed within parentheses.

An initial review of the production report illustrated in figure 6.2 would lead a person to believe that the production process was very inefficient. However, a substantial part of the unfavorable variance resulted from the production level being higher than budgeted. Actual production was 11,000 units rather than 10,000 units as planned.

Figure 6.3 shows a revised production report. A column showing a revised budget for the actual production level is developed from the standard cost data shown earlier. The variance is also split between (a) the portion attributable to the effectiveness of the organization in increasing the production level and (b) the portion attributable to production efficiencies or inefficiencies.

Of the $12,400 ($132,400 − $120,000) unfavorable variance between actual and budgeted production costs, $11,300 of it is attributable to the change in production level. The other $1,100 relates to the efficiency of the production process. This is further divided into the various production components. Direct material and fixed overhead show unfavorable variances, whereas direct labor and variable overhead show favorable variances. Variance analysis (discussed in chapters 15 and 16) further divides the variances for individual components of production into a price variance and a usage (or efficiency) variance. For example, the $1,900 unfavorable direct-material variance may have resulted from *(a)* using more (less) than three pounds of raw material per unit, *(b)* paying more (less) than $1.20 per pound, or *(c)* some combination of *(a)* and *(b)*.

Flexible Budget Formula

The cost behavior exhibited by the various components of production was discussed in detail in chapter 3. Direct material and direct labor are both variable costs that increase proportionately with increases in the level of production. Factory overhead is a semivariable or mixed cost, because it includes both a fixed and a variable cost element. Assuming linear cost relationships, the total expected production cost can be represented by the following equations:

Mathematical formula for a straight line:

$y = a + b(x)$

Flexible budget formula:

Total cost = Fixed costs + Variable cost per unit of volume × Volume level
where y = dependent variable or total production cost
x = independent variable, representing a measure of volume or an activity base
a = point of intersection with the vertical axis or an estimate of the fixed costs
b = slope of the cost line or an estimate of the variable costs per unit, including direct materials, direct labor, and variable overhead

The total production cost formula in the preceding example is:

Total production cost = $7,000 + $11.30 (units).

At 10,000 units of production, the expected cost is $120,000.

$7,000 + $11.30 (10,000) = $120,000

At 11,000 units of production, the expected cost is $131,300.

$7,000 + $11.30 (11,000) = $131,300

Once it has been developed, the flexible budget formula is very useful in developing the budget and in evaluating the results of operations. A budget may be developed and revised several times before it is acceptable to top management. The flexible budget formula can assist in developing budget data for various levels of business activity assuming linear cost patterns. At the end of the accounting period, the flexible budget is useful in adjusting the budgeted data to the actual level of business activity achieved during the period. This is essential for correctly evaluating the efficiency or inefficiency of the enterprise during the period.

DEVELOPING THE FLEXIBLE BUDGET FORMULA

Flexible budgeting can be used in a variety of businesses to estimate and control costs. It is particularly useful in manufacturing enterprises for estimating both production costs and selling expenses. However, any enterprise with both fixed and variable costs can effectively use flexible budgeting. First we will focus on developing the flexible budget for the production process of a manufacturing firm. Then we will show how flexible budgets are used to estimate and control selling and administrative expenses.

Analyzing Cost Behavior in a Production Process

The industrial-engineering analysis and historical cost analysis are two approaches to analyzing costs and developing a flexible budget formula. The industrial-engineering approach looks forward and attempts to identify what the costs should be for the coming period using the most efficient method of operation in the existing facility. The historical cost approach uses prior operating cost data to predict future costs. In reality, some combination of the two approaches is generally used.

Chapter 3 discussed the high-low, scattergraph, and least-squares methods for identifying and analyzing cost patterns. We will focus on the historical cost analysis and show how these methods are used to develop the flexible budget formula and to select an activity base that is the best predictor of the amount of cost that should be incurred.

You will recall that the first step in using an historical cost analysis is to collect the historical data to be used. Any prior year or group of years could be used, but the period of time selected should be representative of future operating results. The data should include (a) the amount of cost incurred for each element of production—direct material, direct labor, and factory overhead—and (b) the volume of activity achieved for several alternative measures, such as units produced, machine hours worked, and direct-labor hours worked. The data are broken down into short time intervals, such as months, weeks, or quarters, consistent with the reporting cycle of the company.

Remember that direct material and direct labor are traceable to the product and vary according to the number of units produced. However, factory overhead is a mixed cost, the variable portion of which may vary according to a variety of **activity bases** or *volume measures*. These include such things as units produced, hours worked, and orders processed. It is important to identify the activity base that is the best predictor of factory overhead. Therefore, several measures of volume are usually identified, and data are collected on each of them.

Thompson Manufacturing Company will be used to illustrate the development of a flexible budget formula for material, labor, and overhead and the selection of the activity base that is the best predictor of factory overhead.

Figure 6.4 shows the cost data that was collected for Thompson Manufacturing Company during the last eight months of 19X4. The operations for 19X5 are expected to be similar to 19X4 with the exception of December. A bad winter storm caused power shortages and disrupted operations for almost two weeks. Overhead costs remained high, but productive output was almost zero. Therefore, the data from December are excluded from the analysis. The other seven months are considered useful in projecting and quantifying cost behavior patterns. The data show by month the number of sprinkler heads produced, the number of direct-labor hours worked, and the manufacturing costs incurred. Units produced and direct-labor hours worked are the activity bases to be studied.

FIGURE 6.4

Thompson Manufacturing Company
Manufacturing Cost Summary
Eight Months Ending December 31, 19X4

	Manufacturing Costs			Volume	
Month	Direct Material	Direct Labor	Factory Overhead	Units Produced	Direct-Labor Hours Worked
May	$1,920	$ 2,300	$ 4,200	1,600	840
June	1,440	1,740	3,500	1,200	670
July	1,080	1,310	3,100	900	460
August	720	880	2,200	600	320
September	960	1,170	2,600	800	390
October	1,680	1,740	3,900	1,400	620
November	1,860	2,140	3,600	1,550	860
December	—[a]	—[a]	—[a]	—[a]	—[a]
Total	$9,660[a]	$11,280[a]	$23,100[a]	8,050[a]	4,160[a]

[a] December data is not considered representative of normal operations and is excluded from the total and from any further analysis.

Direct Costs: Materials and Labor

Direct costs for both materials and labor vary according to the number of units produced. Because there are no fixed costs involved, the variable rate for the flexible budget formula can be computed by dividing the total cost incurred by the number of units produced.

The cost per unit of $1.20 for direct material is computed by dividing total material cost by the units produced, as follows:

$$\frac{\text{Total cost}}{\text{Units produced}} = \frac{\$9,660}{8,050} = \$1.20$$

The direct-material portion of the flexible budget formula is represented by the following equation:

$$\text{Direct-material cost} = 0 + \$1.20(x)$$
$$\text{where } x = \text{units produced}$$

Figure 6.5 illustrates in graphic form the observed data and the line that represents the preceding equation. Notice that the direct-material cost in each month is equal to $1.20 times the number of units manufactured. Thus each data point is on the line, and the cost per unit could have been computed by selecting any month and dividing the output into the cost incurred.

The direct-labor cost per unit is computed in the same manner and the direct-labor portion of the flexible budget formula looks as follows:

$$\frac{\text{Total cost}}{\text{Units produced}} = \frac{\$11,280}{8,050} = \$1.40 \text{ per unit}$$

$$\text{Direct-labor cost} = 0 + \$1.40(x)$$
$$\text{where } x = \text{units produced}$$

FIGURE 6.5 Direct Costs

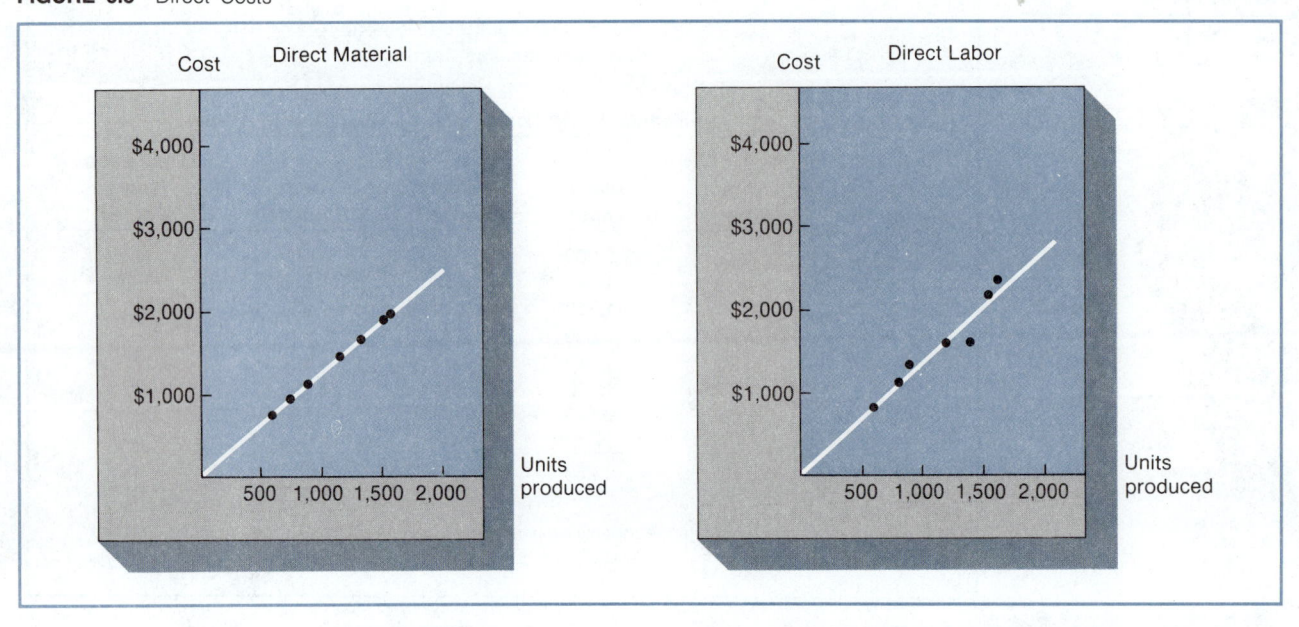

Figure 6.5 also shows in graphic form the observed direct-labor cost data and the line representing the preceding equation. Notice that there is some variability of the points around the line. Thompson Manufacturing Company employs a lot of part-time help, and the wage rate of each employee is determined by the length of employment with the company. Since the composition of the work force changes each week, the direct-labor cost relative to the number of units produced also changes. The $1.40 per unit is an average cost for the entire year and is probably the best predictor available for the coming year.

Factory Overhead

Factory overhead is somewhat more complicated, because it is composed of many different manufacturing costs exhibiting a variety of cost patterns. Some companies with a substantial portion of their manufacturing costs tied up in overhead find it useful to study each major element of overhead and prepare a separate formula for each. However, for many companies, the increased development cost and added complexity are not worth the added precision. Therefore, two assumptions are made:

1. The variable-cost portion of factory overhead is linear in relation to the activity base of the firm.
2. One activity base can be identified that will adequately predict variable overhead.

Our objective is to develop the overhead portion of the flexible budget formula that identifies the fixed cost in total and the variable rate for the activity base selected over the relevant range. Several activity bases are usually studied to select the one that is the best predictor of changes in variable overhead. The high-low method is not as useful as either the scattergraph method or a least-squares regression analysis in selecting the activity base.

High-Low Method The high-low method determines a variable overhead rate by analyzing the change in total factory overhead that corresponds to the change in *volume* of activity between the *high* and *low points*. Variable overhead is then subtracted from total overhead at a particular volume of activity to compute fixed overhead.

FIGURE 6.6

High-Low Point Analysis

	Factory Overhead	Units Produced	Direct-Labor Hours Worked
High point	$4,200	1,600	840
Low point	2,200	600	320
Change	$2,000	1,000	520

Variable rate:

$$\frac{\$2,000}{1,000} = \$2.00 \text{ per unit}$$

$$\frac{\$2,000}{520 \text{ hrs.}} = \$3.85 \text{ per hour}$$

Fixed cost:

	Units	Hours
Factory overhead	$4,200	$4,200
Variable cost:		
(1,600 units @ $2.00)	3,200	
(840 hours @ $3.85)		3,234
	$1,000	$ 966

Flexible budget equation for factory overhead:

Units:
    Factory overhead = $1,000 + 2.00(x)
    where x = units produced

Direct labor:
    Factory overhead = $966 + $3.85(x)
    x = number of direct-labor-hours worked

Using the data for Thompson Manufacturing Company, two flexible budget equations can be developed for factory overhead—one using units produced as the independent variable and the other using direct-labor hours worked. The computations are shown in figure 6.6.

A major weakness of this method is that it is not useful in selecting the activity base that is the best predictor of variable overhead. It is difficult to select between the flexible budget formula based on units produced as opposed to direct-labor hours worked in the Thompson Manufacturing Company example.

Scattergraph Method The scattergraph method plots the data on a scatter diagram with the overhead cost on the vertical axis and the activity base on the horizontal axis, as illustrated in figure 6.7. A regression line is inserted by a visual inspection, and the y-intercept and slope of the line are used to determine the fixed cost and the variable rate, respectively, in the flexible budget equation. A major problem with using the scattergraph method is the difficulty and subjectivity associated with developing the mathematical equation for the budget line drawn on the graph. Reading the y-intercept and any other point along the regression line is a subjective estimate at best.

A scattergraph method assists in selecting between alternative activity bases. The activity base that provides the best fit to the regression line should be selected. This can often be determined by a visual analysis of the scatter diagrams. The measure that has the plotted points clustered closest to the regression line provides the best fit. By studying the graphs in figure 6.7, it appears that the graph for units manufactured has the plotted points closer to the regression line and thus provides the best fit. The visual analysis, however, is subjective and cannot be quantitatively measured.

FIGURE 6.7 Scattergraph Method

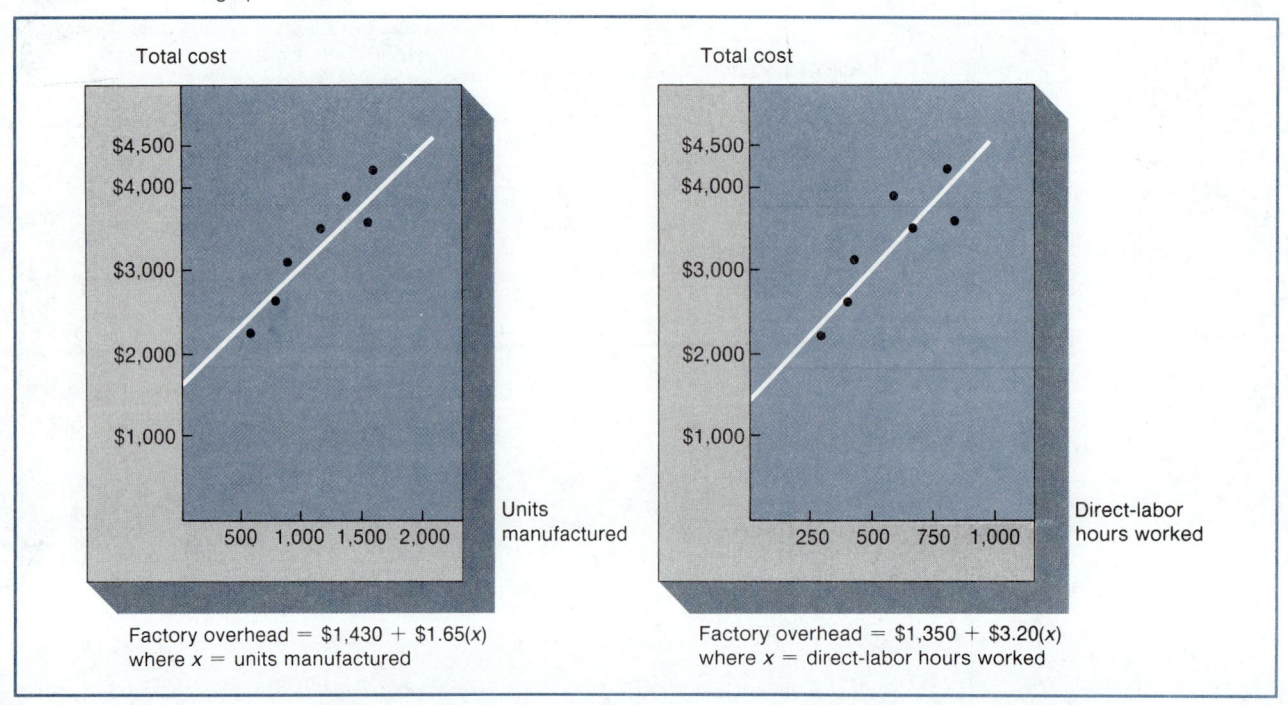

[Left graph: Total cost vs. Units manufactured, with data points and fitted line]
Factory overhead = $1,430 + $1.65(x)
where x = units manufactured

[Right graph: Total cost vs. Direct-labor hours worked, with data points and fitted line]
Factory overhead = $1,350 + $3.20(x)
where x = direct-labor hours worked

Least-Squares Regression and Correlation Analysis The least-squares regression analysis computes the *y*-intercept and slope of the regression line *mathematically* to minimize the sum of the squares of the lengths of the vertical line segments from the observed data points to the line itself. The computations for developing an overhead cost curve using units produced and direct-labor hours worked are shown in figures 6.8 and 6.9, respectively.

A desirable feature of a least-squares regression analysis is that a correlation analysis can be performed to determine quantitatively how good the regression line fits the data points. A **coefficient of correlation** (sometimes called a correlation coefficient) is computed that measures the linear association (correlation) between two variables—in our example, manufacturing overhead and an activity base. A high coefficient indicates greater linear assocation between the variables. This is extremely useful in selecting the activity base that is the best predictor of the amount of overhead cost that should be incurred.

A formula for computing *r,* the coefficient of correlation, is:

$$r = \frac{n(\Sigma xy) - (\Sigma x)(\Sigma y)}{\sqrt{[n\Sigma x^2 - (\Sigma x)^2][n\Sigma y^2 - (\Sigma y)^2]}}$$

An alternative computation is illustrated in the appendix to this chapter. The intermediate values developed for computing the values of *a* and *b* for the regression line can be substituted into the preceding equation to compute the value of *r*. The value of *r* using units produced as the activity base and direct-labor hours worked as the activity base is computed as follows:

Units produced as the activity base (numbers are obtained from figure 6.8):

$$r = \frac{(7)(28,150,000) - (8,050)(23,100)}{\sqrt{[(7)(10,172,500) - (8,050)^2][(7)(79,270,000) - (23,100)^2]}}$$
$$= \underline{0.95}$$

FIGURE 6.8

Thompson Manufacturing Company
Least-Squares Regression Analysis
Units Produced as Activity Base

Month	x Units Produced	y Factory Overhead	xy	x^2	y^2
May	1,600	$ 4,200	$ 6,720,000	2,560,000	$17,640,000
June	1,200	3,500	4,200,000	1,440,000	12,250,000
July	900	3,100	2,790,000	810,000	9,610,000
August	600	2,200	1,320,000	360,000	4,840,000
September	800	2,600	2,080,000	640,000	6,760,000
October	1,400	3,900	5,460,000	1,960,000	15,210,000
November	1,550	3,600	5,580,000	2,402,500	12,960,000
Total	8,050	$23,100	$28,150,000	10,172,500	$79,270,000

$$a = \frac{(\Sigma y)(\Sigma x^2) - (\Sigma x)(\Sigma xy)}{n(\Sigma x^2) - (\Sigma x)^2}$$

$$= \frac{(23,100)(10,172,500) - (8,050)(28,150,000)}{(7)(10,172,500) - (8,050)^2}$$

$$= \$1,308$$

$$b = \frac{n(\Sigma xy) - (\Sigma x)(\Sigma y)}{n(\Sigma x^2) - (\Sigma x)^2}$$

$$= \frac{(7)(28,150,000) - (8,050)(23,100)}{(7)(10,172,500) - (8,050)^2}$$

$$= 1.73$$

Flexible budget formula:
Overhead = $1,308 + 1.73(x)
where x = units produced

Direct-labor hours worked as activity base (numbers are obtained from figure 6.9):

$$r = \frac{(7)(14,675,000) - (4,200)(23,100)}{\sqrt{[(7)(2,815,000) - (4,200)^2][(7)(79,270,000) - (23,100)^2]}}$$

$$= 0.86$$

The possible values for r range from -1 to $+1$. It is a dimensionless quantity in that it is independent of the units of measurement of both x and y. Whether r is positive or negative depends on the slope of the regression line. Because the regression line for factory overhead generally slopes upward, the r value will be positive for this type of analysis.

The association between x and y increases as the absolute value of r increases. When applied to the factory overhead problem, a high absolute value of r indicates high correlation between factory overhead and the activity base being evaluated. When r is close to 1, for example, high factory overhead should be incurred during months of high production. Likewise, months in which a low number of units are produced should have low factory overhead. If r is close to zero, there is little, if any, linear association between the activity base being studied and factory overhead.

The value of r, the coefficient of correlation is often squared to compute a **coefficient of determination.** The coefficient of determination represents the amount of variation in y that is explained by x. For most people, r^2 is easier to interpret than r because it represents the *percentage* of variation in y that is explained by x.

The coefficient of determination (r^2) is computed below for each activity base being studied for Thompson Manufacturing Company.

FIGURE 6.9

Thompson Manufacturing Company
Least-Squares Regression Analysis
Direct-Labor Hours Worked as Activity Base

Month	x Direct-Labor Hours Worked	y Factory Overhead	xy	x^2	y^2
May	840	$ 4,200	$ 3,528,000	705,600	$17,640,000
June	670	3,500	2,345,000	448,900	12,250,000
July	460	3,100	1,426,000	211,600	9,610,000
August	320	2,200	704,000	102,400	4,840,000
September	390	2,600	1,014,000	152,100	6,760,000
October	620	3,900	2,418,000	384,400	15,210,000
November	900	3,600	3,240,000	810,000	12,960,000
Total	4,200	$23,100	$14,675,000	2,815,000	$79,270,000

$$a = \frac{(\Sigma y)(\Sigma x^2) - (\Sigma x)(\Sigma xy)}{n(\Sigma x^2) - (\Sigma x)^2}$$

$$= \frac{(23,100)(2,815,000) - (4,200)(14,675,000)}{(7)(2,815,000) - (4,200)^2}$$

$$= \$1,642$$

$$b = \frac{n(\Sigma xy) - (\Sigma x)(\Sigma y)}{n(\Sigma x^2) - (\Sigma x)^2}$$

$$= \frac{(7)(14,675,000) - (4,200)(23,100)}{(7)(2,815,000) - (4,200)^2}$$

$$= 2.76$$

Flexible budget formula:
Overhead = $1,642 + 2.76(x)
where x = direct-labor hours worked

Activity Base	r Coefficient of Correlation	r^2 Coefficient of Determination
Units produced	0.95	0.90
Direct-labor hours worked	0.86	0.74

A coefficient of determination of 0.90 for units manufactured as the activity base means that 90 percent of the variation in factory overhead can be explained by the number of units manufactured. An r^2 of 0.74 for direct-labor hours worked as the activity base means that 74 percent of the variation in factory overhead can be explained by the number of direct-labor hours worked.

The values of r and r^2 can be used to select the activity base that is the best predictor of factory overhead. The higher r value for units manufactured means that it is more highly correlated with factory overhead than direct-labor hours worked. The difference between the values of r^2 identifies how much better it is as a predictor. Units manufactured accounts for 16 percent (0.90 − 0.74) more of the variability in manufacturing overhead than direct-labor hours worked.

In summary, the methods for analyzing cost behavior are not equally applicable for selecting the activity base that is the best predictor of the cost that should be incurred. The scattergraph and least-squares regression methods provide useful information for this decision. However, a least-squares regression and correlation analysis is most useful because it quantifies the relationship between the variables and measures the variability in the dependent variable that is accounted for by changes in the independent variable.

Flexible Budgeting for Selling and Administrative Costs

Flexible budgeting is useful in estimating and controlling selling and administrative costs. In fact, it is useful for estimating any cost with both a fixed and variable element. A flexible budget formula is developed that identifies the fixed cost and the variable rate. The procedures for developing the flexible budget formula for selling and administrative costs are the same as illustrated for production costs. Several activity bases are generally studied to determine the one that has the highest correlation with the costs under consideration.

Once the flexible budget formula is developed, it can be used to estimate cost at a predicted level of operations as well as to identify the amount of cost that should have been incurred at the actual level of operations. This facilitates cost control and performance evaluations.

Thompson Manufacturing Company followed standard procedures to compute a flexible budget formula for selling and administrative expenses. Individual cost elements were identified, data were collected and analyzed, and the following results were obtained:

Cost Element	Fixed Cost per Month	Variable Rate per Unit Sold
Salary and wages	$1,250	$0.80
Office building	1,000	0.50
Freight out	0	0.20
Total	$2,250	$1.50

Formula:

Total cost = $2,250 + $1.50(x)
where x = units sold

During January 19X5, Thompson Manufacturing Company expected to sell 700 units. Total selling and administrative costs were expected to be $3,300.

Total cost = $2,250 + $1.50(700)
= $3,300

However, the actual cost in January was $3,200 and only 650 units were sold. Figure 6.10 shows an analysis of the difference between the actual costs incurred and the amounts that should have been incurred at 650 units of sales. Notice that costs for salary and wages

FIGURE 6.10

Thompson Manufacturing Company
Selling and Administrative Expense Analysis
January 19X5

Cost Element	Estimated Costs Fixed	Estimated Costs Variable[a]	Estimated Costs Total	Actual Cost	Variance Favorable (Unfavorable)
Salary and wages	$1,250	$520	$1,770	$1,950	($180)
Buildings	1,000	325	1,325	1,130	195
Freight	0	130	130	120	10
Total	$2,250	$975	$3,225	$3,200	$ 25

[a]The variable costs are based on the budgeted rate at 650 units sold.

were more than expected, but the costs of the office building and freight out were less than expected. The net effect was a $25 favorable variance between actual and estimated costs.

RESPONSIBILITY ACCOUNTING

An accounting system is useful if it helps to predict the costs that should be incurred, to accumulate the costs actually incurred, and to provide reports that summarize both budgeted and actual costs in a timely and meaningful way that allows corrective action to be taken. Accounting reports are an important part of performance evaluations. Therefore, care must be taken to identify responsibility for an item, and the reports should be consistent with that responsibility.

Responsibility Accounting Defined

Sound management practices and good internal controls require that someone be assigned to manage every activity that provides a revenue or incurs a cost. Theoretically, responsibility should rest on only one individual for each activity or cost. Each individual should understand his or her stewardship and should be held accountable for it. Cost considerations in operating the system usually preclude individual cost identification, however. The next best approach is to group several individuals who perform similar tasks into an activity center. Responsibility is then assigned and evaluated for the responsibility center. **Responsibility accounting** is a form of internal reporting that is based on the ability to control. Each responsibility center's report contains the items the center has the ability to control.

Relationship to Segmented Reporting

Segment reporting is the process of breaking up an enterprise into reportable segments and preparing financial information by segments. The segmented reports discussed here are used primarily for internal management use, but they may also be useful in developing the segmented reports that are required for external reporting.[1] Chapter 19 identifies various types of responsibility centers, discusses cost allocation as it relates to segmented reporting, and evaluates its usefulness in various decisions concerning the segment. Our objective here is to identify what responsibility reporting is, to explain how it relates to responsibility accounting, and to determine its effect on performance evaluations.

Form and Content of Reports

The accounting system and its reports should be consistent with the assignment of responsibility. Figure 6.11 shows an organization chart for Latham Products, Incorporated that identifies the key people who have responsibility for the company's operations and financial policies. If the company does well, they will receive the credit. When problems arise, it is their responsibility to identify and correct them.

    A **pyramid reporting** structure is used to report on each individual's area of responsibility. Individuals at the bottom of the organization chart receive reports on individual items within their area of control. Individuals at middle and upper levels of management receive reports containing summary information on the results of individual items over which they have control.

    The Latham Products example can be used to illustrate the pyramid reporting structure. Mr. Price, the production manager, should receive only production information on

---

1. The basic rules and procedures for external segmented reporting are specified by the Financial Accounting Standards Board in Statement No. 14. External segment reporting is covered in most financial accounting textbooks.

FIGURE 6.11

Latham Products, Inc., Organization Chart

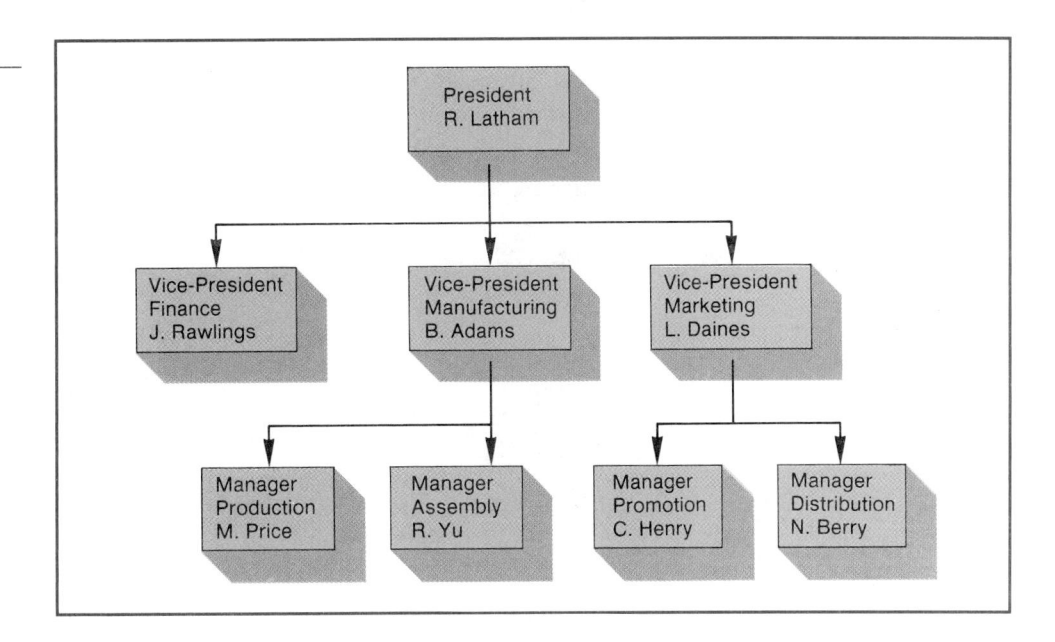

```
                        President
                        R. Latham
           ┌────────────────┼────────────────┐
    Vice-President    Vice-President    Vice-President
       Finance         Manufacturing      Marketing
      J. Rawlings        B. Adams         L. Daines
                    ┌──────┴──────┐   ┌──────┴──────┐
                 Manager       Manager  Manager    Manager
                Production    Assembly Promotion  Distribution
                 M. Price      R. Yu    C. Henry   N. Berry
```

his report, and it should be in enough detail to evaluate the production activities and to take corrective action as needed. Ms. Adams, the vice president of manufacturing and assembly, should receive summary information on both production and assembly as well as other manufacturing information that cannot be identified specifically with either production or assembly.

Figure 6.12 shows the reports that have been prepared for part of Latham Products. Notice the form of the reports and their relationship to each other. Summary information from lower levels is included on the president's and vice presidents' reports. If for some reason they need additional detail on a lower level, they merely request a copy of that report.

The form and content of the reports are important. Some basic rules include the following:

1. The title should clearly identify the area of responsibility and the time period covered.
2. The level of detail within the report should be appropriate for the level of the report within the organization. For example, a report for the production manager should detail each type of raw material and each class of direct labor required for production. The vice president of manufacturing, however, will only have summary data for each production area.
3. Actual operating data as well as budgeted operating data should be shown on the report. The budget identifies a level of business activity that will result in organizational success if that level is achieved. Therefore, it is an appropriate standard to which actual results can be compared so that areas of the operation in which management attention is needed can be identified.
4. Any significant deviations from the budget should be highlighted. Deviations from the budget can be shown as actual amounts (dollars or units) or as percentage amounts. Sound management practices suggest that managers should spend their time working in areas of the organization that are out of control or where the greatest benefit can be achieved. Accounting reports can help managers use their time effectively by identifying what is considered a material or significant deviation. The

FIGURE 6.12 Latham Products, Inc. Responsibility Center Reports

Company Cost Summary Report—President
September 19X3

	Budget		Actual		Variance	
Item	Month	Year to Date	Month	Year to Date	Month	Year to Date
Finance	$ 21,600	$ 194,400	$ 20,200	$ 190,000	$1,400	$ 4,400
Manufacturing	69,700	623,000	72,800	637,700	(3,100)	(14,700)
Marketing	37,200	334,800	46,300	338,900	(9,100)*	(4,100)
Political contributions	1,000	9,000	0	0	1,000 *	9,000 *
Interest	4,000	36,000	3,600	32,100	400	3,900
Depreciation	12,000	108,000	12,000	108,000	0	0
Total	$145,500	$1,305,200	$154,900	$1,306,700	($9,400)	($ 1,500)

Manufacturing Cost Summary—Vice President, Manufacturing
September 19X3

	Budget		Actual		Variance	
Item	Month	Year to Date	Month	Year to Date	Month	Year to Date
Production	$32,100	$288,900	$34,700	$295,000	($2,600)	($6,100)
Assembly	29,500	261,100	28,900	262,300	600	(1,200)
Indirect labor	6,000	54,000	5,800	53,400	200	600
Other	2,100	19,000	3,400	27,000	(1,300)*	(8,000)*
Total	$69,700	$623,000	$72,800	$637,700	($3,100)	($14,700)

Production Cost Summary—Production Manager
September 19X3

	Budget		Actual		Variance	
Item	Month	Year to Date	Month	Year to Date	Month	Year to Date
Material A	$ 9,000	$ 81,000	$ 9,400	$ 80,900	($ 400)	$ 100
Material B	6,000	54,000	5,700	55,000	300	(1,000)
Direct labor	15,000	135,000	15,500	138,000	(500)	(3,000)
Set up	2,100	18,900	4,100	21,100	(2,000)*	(2,200)*
Total	$32,100	$288,900	$34,700	$295,000	($2,600)	($6,100)

( )Parentheses indicate unfavorable variances
*Asterisk indicates significant deviations from the budget

variance between actual data and budgeted data is generally shown on the report with a star or asterisk, which indicates those areas in need of management's attention.

5. Noncontrollable items should be excluded from the report. If for some reason they are included, they should be separated from the controllable items and clearly labeled. This is necessary so the reports can be used for performance evaluations. An individual should not be held responsible for something over which there is little or no control.

Analysis of Budget Variances: Management by Exception

The concept of **management by exception** suggests that managers should concentrate their time on areas that deviate significantly from the budget or from normal operations.

Identifying significant deviations is not always easy. Two common approaches involve using (a) a fixed percentage of the budget and (b) a statistical analysis of current operations relative to prior operations.

Fixed Percentage of the Budget A fixed percentage of the budget is based on the concept of materiality. An item's materiality is generally based on its amount relative to another quantity. The budget is often used as the standard, and a fixed percentage between 5 percent and 10 percent is common.

EXAMPLE

Triple A productions uses 10 percent as the criterion for determining significant deviations from the budget. One of the following variances would be identified as material.

September 19X3

Cost	Budget	Actual	Variance[a] Favorable (Unfavorable)
Indirect labor	$30,000	$32,500	($2,500)
Supervision	21,000	20,000	1,000
Heat, light, and power	16,500	19,400	(2,900)[a]

[a]Indicates a material deviation from the budget.

This technique is fairly easy to apply and most people understand it. However, it does not consider normal fluctuation in an item.

Statistical Analysis A statistical analysis can be used to compare the results of this period's operations with budget to see if there is a significant deviation. Such an analysis is useful in identifying deviations that are material but not significant because the fluctuation is within what would be considered normal. Likewise, it is useful in identifying those items that may not be material but are significant because of the abnormal fluctuation.

Management science has extensively developed possible approaches to managing differences between actual results and budgets or standards. These approaches attempt to scientifically separate fluctuations from budgets or standards into random or normal and non-random or abnormal categories.

One such approach is drawn from the normal distribution technique of statistical analysis. A control chart is constructed by computing and plotting the means of small samples of operating results. Standard deviations from the means are computed using the process of analyzing a normal distribution. The standard deviations that are computed become the upper and lower control limits on the control chart.

The basic idea of the control chart is that fluctuations from the norm (in our case, the budget) can occur within the range between the upper and lower control limits because of random (uncontrollable) factors. Results that lie outside the control limits are outside normal expectations, and an investigation may identify a controllable cause.[2] Examples of control charts are shown in figure 6.13.

---

2. Several sources are available to pursue statistical quality control in greater depth. See, for example, some of the references at the end of the chapter.

Some accounting researchers have found only limited accounting applications of these statistical techniques compared with fairly extensive applications in engineering and operations management. See, for example, the Kaplan references in the list of suggested readings. We believe that even though the techniques are not widely used in accounting applications, they provide useful insights into the variance investigation process. They provide managers with an opportunity to employ a more refined and reliable technique as an alternative to the more widely used "percentage rule of thumb" approach.

FIGURE 6.13

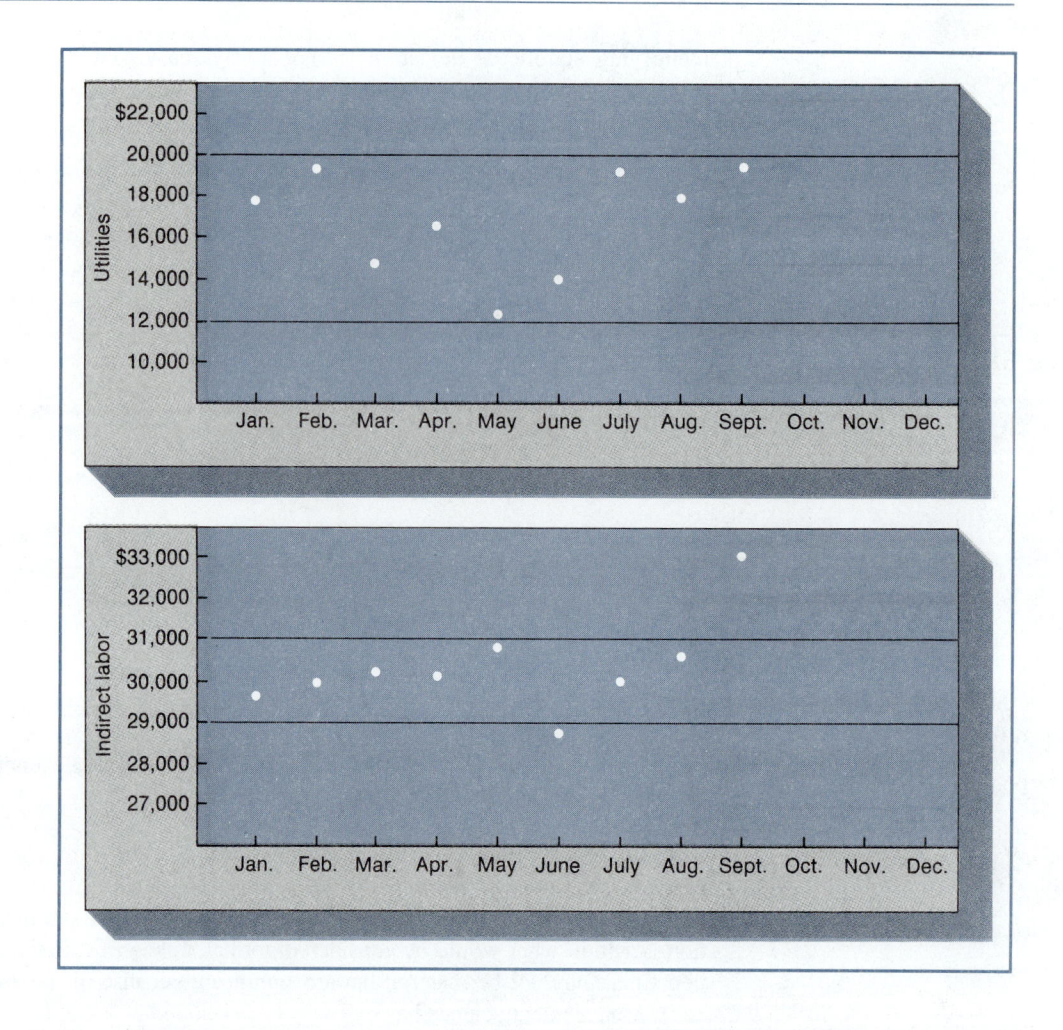

EXAMPLE

The charts shown in figure 6.13 are for utilities and indirect labor for Triple A Productions. The plotted points represent the results of operations for the previous nine months. The dotted lines above and below the data points identify an upper and lower limit based on a statistical analysis of the data. Notice that the September point for utilities is within the normal fluctuations for that cost. Management's time will probably be wasted in trying to improve performance in that area in the coming month. Notice also that the September data point for indirect labor lies outside of the normal fluctuation in cost. Management's attention will be more profitably spent investigating and improving this area because of its abnormal and significant fluctuation from normal operations.

Controllable versus Uncontrollable Costs

No cost is uncontrollable if the organization is viewed in its entirety over a long period of time. But as one looks at the organization in the short run or at separate segments within the organization, there are some costs that can be classified as uncontrollable. The concept of control is notable because of its importance to performance evaluations and the resulting effect on the form and content of reports.

Controllable Costs Defined A **controllable cost** is one that can be influenced to a considerable extent by an individual at a particular level of management within a specified period of time. Both parts of this definition are important—*(a)* the level of management and *(b)* the length of the time period.

A cost is considered controllable at a particular management level if that level has the power to authorize its incurrence. The person who has the most influence over the cost on a day-to-day basis or who has the most decision-making power over the activity in question is in control. For example, a production manager has control over the productivity of direct laborers because he or she assigns job tasks and motivates them to do a good job. However, the same manager may have no control over wages, because the hours and rates are fixed by union contracts that are negotiated by top management.

The length of time has a direct effect on the number of costs that are controllable. Over a long period of time an organization can change almost anything, from its advertising and marketing program to its production process. New buildings can be constructed and new equipment acquired if the time period is long enough. However, if the time period is short, say three months, it may be difficult to change even an advertising campaign because of existing contracts with the advertising agency.

Complete versus Partial Control We generally talk about control as if it were a "yes" or "no" decision. In reality, control varies in degrees from nearly complete to partial to little or to no control.

EXAMPLE

A purchasing agent has complete control over the acquisition of a raw material as long as it meets quality standards. It is complete control because the agent alone selects the raw materials vendor and negotiates the price.

A production manager has only partial control over equipment repairs and maintenance. The manager has some control over the care with which the machines are used, which is an important variable in determining the amount of repairs required. He or she has little or no control over how fast or how well the repair person performs preventive maintenance or repairs the machines.

The amount of property tax paid on the manufacturing facility is uncontrollable for the six production managers who operate within the facility. The amount of property tax is based on the value of the facility as determined by top management several years previously when the facility was constructed, and on a mill levy as determined by the tax assessment practices of the government unit.

Sometimes an individual will have control over acquisition or use but not over both. The purchasing agent described before may have complete control over the acquisition of the raw material but no control over its use, which is under the control of the production manager. This creates some problems in accurately reporting each person's responsibility. A standard cost system and variance analysis (discussed in chapter 15) is used to separate the effectiveness of the purchasing activity from the effectiveness of the using activity.

BEHAVIORAL CONSIDERATIONS IN REPORTING

Chapter 5 discussed some behavioral considerations in preparing and implementing a budget. There are also several behavioral considerations involved in developing reports and providing feedback on performance. Some of the more important conclusions are summarized.

1. Distinguishing between controllable and uncontrollable costs is important because behavioral implications are involved in using accounting reports to evaluate performance. An individual should not be held responsible for something over which there is no control. Such an evaluation is unfair because it does not relate to the individual's performance, and undesirable behavioral consequences generally result. As a rule, reports should contain only items for which an individual has partial or complete control. By including partially controllable items, the individual is encouraged to do everything possible to use them effectively.
2. Feedback on individual and group performance should be timely. The value of the report is inversely proportional to the amount of time a person must wait to receive it. Timely reports that are understandable to the workers and supervisors at the department level allow and encourage them to analyze their results and take corrective action where necessary.
3. Feedback is important in determining future levels of aspiration. **Level of aspiration** is a goal that has associated with it subjective feelings of success when achieved and subjective feelings of failure when not achieved. The stronger the success, the greater the probability of a rise in level of aspiration; the stronger the failure, the greater the probability of a lowering in level of aspiration. Feelings of success are a reward in themselves, and the level of aspiration is important in developing the budget for the subsequent period. Implementation of participatory budgeting can be valuable.
4. Reports should concentrate where possible on positive rewards for achieving the budget. The philosophy of management by exception tends to focus attention on the problem areas of the organization. This is valuable in using management's time effectively, but it should not mean that people are not rewarded when they achieve the budget. Also, management by exception should not lead to finger pointing. A responsibility accounting system merely identifies who has primary control over an item and where the investigation should begin.
5. Care must be taken to provide reports that are as accurate as possible given the time constraints under which they are developed. There is often a trade-off between timeliness and accuracy. Very accurate reports may take a long time to develop; however, late reports are not as useful. The developer, therefore, must be aware of the user's needs and provide timely and useful information. Users must be informed of estimates and approximations employed in developing the report so that they will use them appropriately.

SUMMARY

Flexible budgeting is a valuable tool for adjusting the budget to recognize unexpected changes in the volume of business activity. It helps management evaluate the difference between actual and budgeted costs. The variance that is attributable to the change in volume should be separated from the portion that is attributable to the efficiency of the employees. This facilitates accurate performance evaluations and assists in planning future operations.

The flexible budget formula is:

Total cost = Fixed cost + Variable cost per unit of volume × Volume level.

Important in developing the formula is the measure of volume or the activity base to be used. Several activity bases are generally studied and the one that is most highly correlated with cost is adopted. The scattergraph method and least-squares regression and correlation analysis are useful techniques in the selection process.

A responsibility accounting system is a form of segmented reporting in that it structures the organization into segments based on the ability to control. Reports are prepared consistent with the assignment of responsibility and include a comparison of budget and actual data. Significant deviations from the budget are highlighted to assist management in identifying areas of the organization that are out of control or where improvement is most likely. This practice is consistent with the philosophy of management by exception.

Behavioral considerations are important when developing reports and providing feedback on performance. Timely reports that relate to an individual's area of responsibility and that are understandable to the recipient encourage analysis of results and corrective action where necessary. This is an essential part of developing future levels of aspiration. Positive rewards should be provided where possible for achieving the budget. Estimates or approximation should be identified to assist the user in correctly using the information.

APPENDIX 6.1   *Alternate Computations for Coefficient of Correlation and Coefficient of Determination*

There are several formulas that can be used to compute the values of a, b, r, and r^2 in a least-squares regression and correlation analysis. Chapter 6 illustrated the computational formulas frequently used in connection with a statistical analysis. This appendix illustrates the formulas and computation used in a mathematical approach.

The data for Thompson Manufacturing Company that was used throughout chapter 6 also will be used to illustrate the alternate computations. Units produced will be used as the activity base for the analysis.

Figure 6.14 summarizes the historical cost data and illustrates the computation of a, and b, the y-intercept, and the slope of the flexible budget formula, respectively. These are the same formulas used in the alternate computation illustrated in the appendix for chapter 3.

The formula to compute r, the coefficient of correlation, is as follows:

$$r = \frac{\sum_{i=1}^{n}(x_i - x)(y_i - y)}{nS_xS_y}$$

where S_x = sample standard deviation of the independent variable x (computed as follows):

$$S_x = \sqrt{\frac{\sum x_i^2}{n} - (\bar{x})^2}$$

S_y = sample standard deviation of the independent variable y. (Use the preceding equation for the standard deviation but substitute the observed values of y.)

The standard deviations for x and y must be computed first. The numbers for these computations are taken from figure 6.15.

$$S_x = \sqrt{\frac{10{,}172{,}500}{7} - (1{,}150)^2} = \underline{361.51}$$

$$S_y = \sqrt{\frac{79{,}270{,}000}{7} - (3{,}300)^2} = \underline{659}$$

FIGURE 6.14

Thompson Manufacturing Company
Least-Squares Regression Analysis
Units Produced as Activity Base

Month	x Units Produced	y Factory Overhead	$(x_i - \bar{x})$	$(y_i - \bar{y})$	$(x_i - \bar{x})(y_i - \bar{y})$	$(x_i - \bar{x})^2$
May	1,600	$ 4,200	450	$ 900	$ 405,000	202,500
June	1,200	3,500	50	200	10,000	2,500
July	900	3,100	-250	-200	50,000	62,500
August	600	2,200	-550	-1,100	605,000	302,500
September	800	2,600	-350	-700	245,000	122,500
October	1,400	3,900	250	600	150,000	62,500
November	1,550	3,600	400	300	120,000	160,000
Total	8,050	$23,100			$1,585,000	915,000
$\bar{x}$		1,150				
$\bar{y}$				3,300		

$$\text{Slope } (b) = \frac{\sum_{i=1}^{n}(x_i - \bar{x})(y_i - \bar{y})}{\sum_{i=1}^{n}(x_i - \bar{x})^2} = \frac{1,585,000}{915,000} = 1.73$$

y intercept $(a) = \bar{y} - b(\bar{x}) = 3,300 - 1.73(1,150) = \underline{1,310}$

Flexible budget formula:

Overhead = $1,310 + 1.73(x)
where x = units produced

The summation of the product of the differences between the observed values of x and y and their means $[\Sigma(x_i - \bar{x})(y_i - \bar{y})]$ was computed in figure 6.14. This value, along with the standard deviations computed previously are substituted into the preceding equation to compute the value of r.

FIGURE 6.15

Computations for Sample Standard Deviations

Month	x Units Produced	x^2	y Factory Overhead	y^2
May	1,600	2,560,000	$ 4,200	$17,640,000
June	1,200	1,440,000	3,500	12,250,000
July	900	810,000	3,100	9,610,000
August	600	360,000	2,200	4,840,000
September	800	640,000	2,600	6,760,000
October	1,400	1,960,000	3,900	15,210,000
November	1,550	2,402,500	3,600	12,960,000
Total	8,050	10,172,500	$23,100	$79,270,000
Divide by n		÷ 7		÷ 7
$\bar{x}$		1,150		
$\bar{y}$			$ 3,300	

CHAPTER 6: FLEXIBLE BUDGETING AND RESPONSIBILITY REPORTING

Coefficient of correlation:

$$r = \frac{1{,}585{,}000}{(7)(361.51)(659)} = \underline{0.95}$$

The value of r is squared for the value of r^2.

Coefficinet of determination:

$$r^2 = 0.95^2 = \underline{0.90}$$

SELF-STUDY PROBLEM

Hawks Company began operations on July 1, 19X2. The first six months of operations were disappointing, primarily because the company's overhead costs were so much higher than had been anticipated. Management has asked you to assist them in developing a flexible budget formula and to identify the activity base that is the best predictor of overhead cost.

The accountant for Hawks Company has collected the following information for the first six months of operations:

Month	Overhead Cost	Units Produced	Days Worked
July	$ 4,000	5	120
August	7,000	10	200
September	9,000	15	290
October	8,000	11	170
November	10,000	20	400
December	7,500	8	220

Required

1. Using a least-squares regression analysis, prepare a flexible budget formula for each activity base under consideration.
2. Compute the coefficient of correlation and the coefficient of determination for each activity base.
3. Which activity base do you recommend and why?

Solution to the Self-Study Problem

Requirement 1

Figure 6.16 contains the intermediate computations required to prepare the flexible budget formula. The numbers computed there are substituted in the following equations:

Units produced as the activity base:

$$a = \frac{(\Sigma y)(\Sigma x^2) - (\Sigma x)(\Sigma xy)}{n(\Sigma x^2) - (\Sigma x)^2}$$

$$= \frac{(45{,}500)(935) - (69)(573{,}000)}{(6)(935) - (69)^2} = \underline{\$3{,}540}$$

$$b = \frac{n(\Sigma xy) - (\Sigma x)(\Sigma y)}{n(\Sigma x^2) - (\Sigma x)^2}$$

$$= \frac{(6)(573{,}000) - (69)(45{,}500)}{(6)(935) - (69)^2} = \underline{\$352}$$

FIGURE 6.16

Hawks Company
Computations for Correlation and Regression Analysis
Units Produced as the Activity Base

Month	x Units Produced	y Factory Overhead	xy	x^2	y^2
July	5	$ 4,000	$ 20,000	25	$ 16,000,000
August	10	7,000	70,000	100	49,000,000
September	15	9,000	135,000	225	81,000,000
October	11	8,000	88,000	121	64,000,000
November	20	10,000	200,000	400	100,000,000
December	8	7,500	60,000	64	56,250,000
Total	69	$45,500	$573,000	935	$366,250,000

Days Worked as the Activity Base

Month	x Employee Days Worked	y Factory Overhead	xy	x^2	y^2
July	120	$ 4,000	$ 480,000	14,400	$ 16,000,000
August	200	7,000	1,400,000	40,000	49,000,000
September	290	9,000	2,610,000	84,100	81,000,000
October	170	8,000	1,360,000	28,900	64,000,000
November	400	10,000	4,000,000	160,000	100,000,000
December	220	7,500	1,650,000	48,400	56,250,000
Total	1,400	$45,500	$11,500,000	375,800	$366,250,000

Flexible budget formula:

$$\text{Factory overhead} = \$3,540 + \$352(x)$$
$$\text{where } x = \text{units produced}$$

Days worked as the activity base:

$$a = \frac{(45,500)(375,800) - (1,400)(11,500,000)}{(6)(375,800) - (1,400)^2} = \underline{\$3,388}$$

$$b = \frac{(6)(11,500,000) - (1,400)(45,500)}{(6)(375,800) - (1,400)^2} = \underline{\$18}$$

Flexible budget formula:

$$\text{Factory overhead} = \$3,388 + \$18(x)$$
$$\text{where } x = \text{days worked}$$

Requirement 2

The values shown in figure 6.16 are also used to compute the coefficients of correlation (r) and determination (r^2).

Units produced as the activity base:

$$r = \frac{n\Sigma xy - (\Sigma x)(\Sigma y)}{\sqrt{[n\Sigma x^2 - (\Sigma x)^2][n\Sigma y^2 - (\Sigma y)^2]}}$$

$$r = \frac{(6)(573,000) - (69)(45,500)}{\sqrt{[(6)(935) - (69)^2][(6)(366,250,000) - (45,500)^2]}}$$

$$= \underline{0.908}$$

$$r^2 = 0.908^2 = \underline{0.824}$$

Days worked as the activity base:

$$r = \frac{(6)(11,500,000) - (1,400)(45,500)}{\sqrt{[(6)(375,800) - (1,400)^2][(6)(366,250,000) - (45,500)^2]}}$$

$$= \underline{0.865}$$

$$r^2 = 0.865^2 = \underline{0.749}$$

Requirement 3

Units produced is the best activity base. It accounts for 82.4 percent of the variation in factory overhead. Only 74.9 percent of the variation in factory overhead can be explained by the number of days worked.

SUGGESTED READINGS

Bierman, H., and Dyckman, T. R. *Managerial Cost Accounting*. New York: MacMillan, 1971.

Cherrington, David J., and Cherrington, J. Owen. "Participation, Performance, and Appraisal." *Business Horizons* 17 (December 1974): 35–45.

————. "The Role of Budgeting in Organizational Improvement." *Michigan Business Review* 27 (July 1975): 12–16.

Goodman, Sam R., and Reece, James S. *Controller's Handbook*. Homewood, Ill.: Dow-Jones Irwin, 1978.

Hays, William L. *Statistics*. New York: Holt, Rinehart and Winston, 1963.

Kaplan, R. S. "Optimal Investigation Strategies with Imperfect Information." *Journal of Accounting Research* 7 (Spring 1969): 32–43.

————. "The Significance and Investigation of Cost Variance Survey and Extensions." *Journal of Accounting Research* 13 (Autumn 1975): 311–337.

Sorensen, James E., and Franks, Davis D. "The Relative Contribution of Ability, Self-Esteem and Evaluative Feedback to Performance: Implications for Accounting Systems." *Accounting Review* 47 (October 1972): 735–746.

Weiss, Allen. "The Supervisor and the Budget, Part 3: How the Budget Affects You—How You Affect the Budget." *Supervisory Management* (July 1971): 5–8.

DISCUSSION QUESTIONS

Q6–1. Describe what a flexible budget is and explain how it differs from a static budget.

Q6–2. Why might it be misleading to compare actual results of operations with budget results when the actual volume of activity was not the same as the budgeted volume?

Q6–3. Is the high-low method useful in selecting the best activity base for the flexible budget formula? Explain.

Q6–4. Explain how to use the scattergraph method to select the best activity base for the flexible budget formula?

Q6-5. What is the range of possible values for the coefficient of correlation and what does it mean?

Q6-6. What is the range of possible values of the coefficient of determination and what does it mean?

Q6-7. Describe responsibility accounting.

Q6-8. Describe the relationship of responsibility accounting to segmented reporting.

Q6-9. What is meant by pyramid reporting?

Q6-10. What is management by exception, and how should reports be structured to facilitate management by exception?

Q6-11. Why is a statistical analysis better than a fixed percentage in determining a significant deviation of actual results from the budget?

Q6-12. What criteria should be used to determine which costs are controllable?

Q6-13. Should partially controllable costs be included in a manager's report under a responsibility accounting system? Explain.

Q6-14. What is the relationship between feedback and future levels of aspiration?

Q6-15. Why is a timely feedback important?

EXERCISES

E6-1. Fundamentals of Flexible Budgets A schedule format for a flexible budget is shown here. Complete the schedule by determining the amount that should be budgeted for each item for each indicated level of activity.

Overhead Category	Budget Rate	45,000	50,000	55,000	60,000
Variable costs (per direct-labor hour):					
Indirect labor	$2.00	$	$	$	$
Indirect materials	1.60				
Repairs	1.20				
Total variable cost					
Fixed costs					
Depreciation—machinery	$75,000	$	$	$	$
Insurance—factory	25,000				
Total fixed cost	$100,000	$	$	$	$
Total overhead budget		$	$	$	$

E6-2. Flexible Overhead Budget Sampson Corporation produces a product known as Samco. An acceptable productivity rate to produce one Samco is two hours of direct labor. Because Samco requires moderate technical skill in the production process, the going labor rate is $12 per hour. Scheduled production for the third quarter is as follows:

July	2,200 units
August	2,500 units
September	1,800 units

Fixed factory overhead consists of $4,000 per month of items that come from adjusting entries, $3,500 of indirect materials and labor, and $2,300 of ongoing current-period disbursement items.

Variable factory overhead includes $1.00 per labor hour of labor-related costs and $0.50 per labor hour of items that require current-period disbursement.

Required

Prepare a factory overhead cost budget for August adjusted on a flexible basis using intervals of 10 percent and 20 percent both up and down from the scheduled production for the month. Your budget will cover five possible production levels for August, with the costs broken down into variable and fixed cost sections.

E6–3. Cost Analysis—Choice of Activity Base

The Graybar Concrete Pipe Company is in the process of analyzing cost behavior for planning and decision-making purposes. An important issue is deciding on the best base to use as the volume variable. The cost department suggests direct-labor hours. The production superintendent doesn't think direct-labor hours relates very well to overhead costs, because the company produces several different sizes of pipe. Production suggests using tons of pipe produced as a base. The controller suggests that repairs and maintenance, which has been identified as a mixed cost, should be analyzed with the least-squares method using tons and direct-labor hours alternatively.

The following information has been gathered for each quarter of the most recent two years:

	Tons of Pipe Produced	Direct-Labor Hours	Repairs and Maintenance Costs
Last year:			
First quarter	36,000	20,000	$200,000
Second quarter	50,000	18,000	210,000
Third quarter	60,000	16,000	170,000
Fourth quarter	56,000	22,000	240,000
Two years ago:			
First quarter	30,000	10,000	100,000
Second quarter	22,000	6,000	90,000
Third quarter	42,000	8,000	120,000
Fourth quarter	24,000	12,000	150,000

Required

1. Using a least-squares regression analysis, prepare a flexible budget formula for repairs and maintenance costs using each of the activity bases under consideration.

2. Compute the coefficient of correlation and the coefficient of determination for each activity base.

3. Which activity base do you recommend and why?

E6–4. Flexible Budget Concepts

1. A flexible budget is
   a. appropriate for control of factory overhead but *not* for control of direct materials and direct labor.
   b. appropriate for control of direct labor but *not* for control of factory overhead.
   c. *not* appropriate when costs and expenses are affected by fluctuations in volume limits.
   d. appropriate for any level of activity.

2. Information needed to prepare a flexible budget includes
   a. total fixed costs, total variable costs, a capacity base, and information about the relevant range.
   b. unit fixed costs and unit variable costs.
   c. total fixed costs, variable costs per unit of capacity, several levels of activity, and an indication of the relevant range.
   d. total fixed costs and total variable costs only.
   e. total costs only.
3. Flexible budgets are useful for
   a. planning purposes only.
   b. planning, performance evaluation, and feedback control reporting.
   c. control of performance only.
   d. nothing at all. They are a waste of time and money because cost behavior is impossible to predict, and, in any case, results never agree with the budget.
4. A recent news report about a bankrupt firm indicated that the chief executive officer of the firm believed that budgetary controls shouldn't be used because they "stifle entrepreneurship" and threaten the ambience (pervading atmosphere) of the company. Your position is
   a. total agreement, because budgets, including flexible budgets, are known to destroy initiative and motivation.
   b. total disagreement, because budgets, including flexible budgets, are the only tool that can give effective guidance to a company in meeting objectives.
   c. total agreement, because all budgets are known to be used by top management to manipulate people as well as results.
   d. neither agreement nor disagreement, because the procedures used to create and operate a budget can cause the budget to stifle initiative and create a threatening environment in the company.

E6–5. Flexible Budget Fundamentals Maxwell Incorporated produces Maxis. The following costs were budgeted for the activity level of 95 percent of normal capacity:

Variable costs (based on the number of Maxis produced):	
Direct labor	$399,000
Direct materials	299,250
Indirect materials	99,750
Indirect labor	49,875
Repairs and maintenance	39,900
Heat, light, and power	19,950
Fixed costs:	
Supervision	$ 18,000
Depreciation on factory equipment	65,000
Rent on special equipment	10,000
Heat, light, and power	32,000
Property taxes	10,000

The normal production capability is 210,000 Maxis.

Required

1. Prepare a budget of factory overhead costs that covers the 90-percent, 100-percent, and 110-percent capacity levels.
2. Determine unit factory overhead costs and total production costs per unit at the three capacity levels in requirement 1.
3. Explain why the unit cost changed from one activity level to another, if there was a change.

4. Identify for Mrs. Maxwell, the company president, the true cost per unit of producing Maxis, which she might use in comparing her firm's cost position with the unit cost of other firms.

E6–6. Flexible Budget Formulas The following data reflect the results of analysis recently completed on the cost structure of the Hobart Company.

Item	Amount	Percentage of Total that Is Fixed
Machinery service	$15,000	100
Tools and dies	10,000	60
Production equipment depreciation	5,000	100
Factory heat, light, and power	12,000	40
Factory supervision	11,000	100
Direct labor	35,000	
Marketing salaries	45,000	
Direct materials	30,000	
Indirect materials	12,000	
Indirect labor	4,000	
Office supplies	1,500	
Depreciation on office equipment	5,000	100
Rental of automobiles for sales staff	3,000	100
Other marketing expenses	2,000	35
Other factory overhead	5,000	55

Required

1. Organize the cost information into functional budget form, assuming that marketing and administrative expenses are based on net sales of $350,000 and manufacturing costs are based on production of 20,000 units. Show separate sections in the functional budget for variable and fixed costs.
2. Set up budget formulas (with specific dollar amounts) for the following:
    a. Factory overhead
    b. Administrative expenses
    c. Marketing expenses

E6–7. Flexible Budget—Budget Formula for Different Ranges of Activity
Haymore Incorporated has obtained the following cost data:

	Amounts	
Item	Fixed	Variable per Labor Hour
Direct labor		$7.80
Direct materials		4.50
Indirect labor		2.70
Indirect materials		1.80
Rent of special equipment	$ 6,500	
Depreciation	15,000	
Heat, light, and power	1,800	0.80
Repairs and maintenance	6,200	0.30
Other factory overhead	600	0.10

Factory supervision costs are as follows:

Labor Hours	Costs
1–11,999	$1,000
12,000–23,999	2,000
24,000–35,999	3,000

Required

1. Set up flexible factory overhead budgets for 8,000, 14,000, and 26,000 direct-labor hours.
2. Show a *total* production cost formula for each of the three ranges of activity indicated in requirement 1.

E6–8. Static and Flexible Budgets, Performance, and Pyramid Reports

The Germaine Company prepared the following budget of costs for a typical month in which 9,000 units were produced and sold:

	Producing Departments		Factory Support	
	Preparation	Finishing	Repairs & Maintenance	Custodial
Direct labor	$5,400	$6,300	$2,700	$1,800
Direct materials	7,200	4,500	1,800	1,350
Indirect labor	3,600	2,700	—	—
Supplies	900	1,350	450	225
Supervision	2,000	2,200	1,500	1,300
Depreciation (straight-line)	1,500	1,250	800	500
Production managers (allocated equally)	1,000	1,000	1,000	1,000

	Marketing	Administrative
Commissions @ $5/unit	$45,000	$ —
Clerical salaries	15,000	20,000
Management salaries	7,000	12,000*
Supplies	1,800	720

*Including the president's salary. The president receives $144,000 per year.

During July, production and sales were targeted at 8,000 units. However, because of an unexpected material shortage of a critical component, only 7,500 units were produced and delivered to customers. The costs incurred were as follows:

	Producing Departments		Factory Support	
	Preparation	Finishing	Repairs & Maintenance	Custodial
Direct labor	$4,800	$5,500	$2,400	$1,650
Direct materials	6,200	3,900	1,350	1,050
Indirect labor	2,900	2,100	—	—
Supplies	790	1,300	400	—
Supervision	2,000	2,200	1,500	1,300
Depreciation (straight-line)	1,500	1,250	800	500
Production managers	1,200	1,200	1,200	1,200

	Marketing	Administrative
Commissions	$37,500	$ —
Clerical salaries	15,400	20,600
Management salaries	7,000	12,000
Supplies	1,750	750

Required

1. Prepare performance reports for the two producing departments, showing variances from a static budget based on targeted production for July.
2. Prepare performance reports for all responsibility centers based on flexible budget allowances for July's actual results.
3. Summarize the performance reports in pyramid form. (See the illustrated pyramid report in figure 6.12.)

E6-9. Budgeting Concepts (CMA)

1. A continuous budget
    a. drops the current month or quarter and adds a future month or a future quarter as the current month or quarter is completed.
    b. presents a statement of expectations for a period of time but does not present a firm commitment.
    c. presents the plan for only one level of activity and does not adjust to changes in the level of activity.
    d. presents the plan for a range of activity so that the plan can be adjusted for changes in activity levels.
    e. classifies budget requests by activity and estimates the benefits arising from each activity.

2. A static budget
    a. drops the current month or quarter and adds a future month or a future quarter as the current month or quarter is completed.
    b. presents a statement of expectations for a period of time but does not present a firm commitment.
    c. presents the plan for only one level of activity and does not adjust to changes in the level of activity.
    d. presents the plan for a range of activity so the plan can be adjusted for changes in activity levels.
    e. divides the activities of individual responsibility centers into a series of packages that are ranked ordinally.

3. A flexible budget
    a. classifies budget requests by activity and estimates the benefits arising from each activity.
    b. presents a statement of expectations for a period of time but does not present a firm commitment.
    c. presents the plan for only one level of activity and does not adjust to changes in the level of activity.
    d. presents the plan for a range of activity so that the plan can be adjusted for changes in activity levels.
    e. divides the activities of individual responsibility centers into a series of packages that are ranked ordinally.

4. When an organization prepares a forecast, it
    a. presents a statement of expectations for a period of time but does not present a firm commitment.
    b. consolidates the plans of the separate requests into one overall plan.
    c. presents the plan for a range of activity so that the plan can be adjusted for changes in activity levels.
    d. classifies budget requests by activity and estimates the benefits arising from each activity.

e. divides the activities of individual responsibility centers into a series of packages that are ranked ordinally.

E6–10. Flexible Budget—Review of the High-Low and Scattergraph Methods
Joplin Jumprope Company has recorded the following overhead amounts for the past six months. Because a causal relationship exists between overhead and direct-labor hours, you have also gathered labor information for the same period.

	Overhead Expenses	Direct-Labor Hours
January	$24,000	21,000
February	16,500	13,000
March	15,000	8,000
April	19,500	15,000
May	21,500	18,000
June	27,000	24,000

Required

1. Determine the flexible budget formula using the high-low method.
2. If direct-labor hours for July were 22,000 hours, what would the budgeted expense for overhead be?
3. Using the data given, plot a scattergraph of the overhead expense. Relate the expense to direct-labor hours. Fit a regression line to the plotted points by visual inspection.
4. Using the scattergraph, determine the approximate fixed cost per month and the variable cost per direct-labor hour.
5. Compare your results in requirements 1 and 4. If you were required to choose between only these methods for budgeting overhead costs, which would you choose? Why?

E6–11. Flexible Budgeting Fundamentals (Spread Sheet Analysis)
The Randall Company is trying to develop some standards for variable and fixed costs that top management can use to help evaluate the efficiency of the production department. The production budget states that production for June is expected to be 18,000 units. Based on this level of production, the variable and fixed costs are as follows:

Variable costs per unit:	
Direct materials	$1.20
Direct labor	1.85
Variable overhead	0.95
Total variable costs per unit	$4.00
Fixed overhead per unit	3.20
Total cost per unit	$7.20

Although production is expected to be 18,000 units, past experience has shown that production can fluctuate up to 2,000 units either way.

Required

Using a PC spreadsheet, prepare a flexible budget based on production levels of 16,000, 17,000, 18,000, 19,000, and 20,000 units. Print a copy of your results.

E6–12. Flexible Budget Equation and Choice of Activity Base (PC Spreadsheet)
The president and the controller of Wayne Companies Incorporated have recently been discussing the activity base used in the flexible budgeting formula for factory

overhead. The president believes that direct-labor hours has been a good base for the past fifty years, so it should be good enough for the next fifty years. The controller thinks that units produced is a better activity base, and she wants to change. The president has said that he will not budge until the controller can show him proof that units produced is a better activity base than direct-labor hours. The controller has done some preliminary studies of past data and has come up with the following information:

Month	Direct-Labor Hours	Units Produced	Factory Overhead
January	2,000	18,000	$52,500
February	1,925	17,500	49,850
March	2,050	16,900	47,600
April	2,200	18,750	53,200
May	2,350	21,500	55,000
June	2,250	23,000	56,300
July	2,275	21,100	54,000
August	2,100	17,800	51,400

Required

1. Using least-squares regression analysis, determine the flexible budget formula for factory overhead based on both direct-labor hours and units produced. Perform your analysis using a PC spreadsheet.
2. Compute the coefficient of correlation and the coefficient of determination for both activity bases. Include this computation on your spreadsheet, and print a copy of your results.
3. Do you agree with the president or the controller? Why?

E6-13. Flexible Budgeting Equation—High-Low and Scattergraph Methods

The controller of Romar Industries has provided you with the following information concerning units produced and factory overhead for 19X8:

Month	Units Produced	Factory Overhead
January	20	$2,300
February	40	2,500
March	39	2,500
April	35	2,460
May	33	2,445
June	45	2,550
July	48	2,562
August	33	2,440
September	23	2,325
October	23	2,370
November	30	2,400
December	10	1,850

The controller has asked you to determine the appropriate flexible budgeting equation for factory overhead.

Required

1. Using the high-low method, determine the factory overhead flexible budgeting equation using units produced as the activity base. Perform your analysis on Lotus, and print a copy of your results.
2. Using the Lotus graphics capabilities, plot the points in scattergraph form and then use the graph to develop a flexible budgeting equation.

3. Assuming that you can use only these two methods for calculating the flexible budgeting formula, which do you prefer.

PROBLEMS

P6-1. Flexible Budgets—Cost Breakdown

Abco is a service company operating in the western United States and Canada. Operations are typically at the 100-percent capacity level, which involves operating 120,000 hours. During the slack season of the year, capacity utilization is expected to drop to the 70-percent level; at that level, total budgeted overhead is $240,000. Variable costs are 60 percent of total costs at the 70-percent capacity level.

The overhead budget includes the following items at the percentages indicated:

Fixed Costs

Item	% of Total
Supervision	60%
Insurance	5
Taxes	5
Maintenance	15
Depreciation	10
Other	5
Total	100%

Variable Costs

Item	% of Total
Supplies	25%
Clerical wages	40
Custodial wages	20
Mailing and teletype expenses	10
Other	5
Total	100%

Required

1. Determine the flexible budget formula for total fixed costs and variable rate per hour. Show a breakdown of both fixed cost amounts and variable rates per hour for each cost item.
2. Prepare a flexible budget with details of cost items covering the 70-percent to 100-percent capacity levels at 10-percent intervals.

P6-2. Flexible Budget for Factory Overhead Costs

The production and sales managers for C & L, Incorporated have been uncertain about the quantity of components to produce. The recent production budget is for 150,000 components, and the overhead costs related to this budget are as follows:

Factory rent (fixed)	$ 3,000
Factory equipment depreciation (fixed)	5,500
Supervision (fixed)	45,000
Heat, light, and power (40% variable)	18,500
Indirect materials (variable)	225,000
Indirect labor (variable)	150,000
Supplies (variable)	1,500
Repairs (60% fixed)	1,500
Miscellaneous overhead expenses (50% fixed)	12,000

Required

1. Set up a flexible budget covering 100,000, 120,000, 140,000, 160,000, and 180,000 components. Show total variable costs, total fixed costs, and total costs. Also show unit costs for each variable cost and total unit variable cost.
2. Express the budget data in formula form.

3. How much would be budgeted for 150,000 components in total costs, total variable costs, and total fixed costs?

P6-3. Flexible Budget—Reporting Concepts (CMA) Pearsons is a successful regional chain of moderately priced restaurants, each with a carryout delicatessen department. Pearsons is planning to expand to a nationwide operation. As the chain gets larger and the territory covered becomes wider, managerial control and reporting techniques become more important.

The company's management believes that a budget program for the entire company as well as for each restaurant-deli unit is needed. The following budget has been prepared for a typical unit in the chain. Once a unit is in operation, it is expected to perform in accordance with the budget.

Typical Pearsons Restaurant-Deli
Budgeted Income
Year Ending December 31
(000 omitted)

	Delicatessen	*Restaurant*	*Total*
Gross sales	$1,000	$2,500	$3,500
Purchases	$ 600	$1,000	$1,600
Hourly wages	50	875	925
Franchise fee	30	75	105
Advertising	100	200	300
Utilities	70	125	195
Depreciation	50	75	125
Lease expense	30	50	80
Salaries	30	50	80
Total	$ 960	$2,450	$3,410
Net income before income taxes	$ 40	$ 50	$ 90

All units are approximately the same size, and the amount of space devoted to the carryout delicatessen is similar in each unit. The style of the facilities and the equipment used are all uniform. The unit operators are expected to carry out the advertising program recommended by the corporation. The corporation charges a franchise fee, which is a percentage of gross sales for the use of the company name, the building and facilities design, and the advertising advice.

The unit in Akron, Ohio, was selected to test the budget program. The Akron restaurant-deli's performance for the year ending December 31 is shown on page 222, with actual results compared to the typical budget for Pearsons.

The report was reviewed and discussed by company management. It concluded that a more meaningful comparison would result if a flexible budget analysis for each of the two lines was performed rather than just the single budget comparison, as in the test case.

Required

1. Prepare a schedule that compares a flexible budget for the deli line of the Akron restaurant-deli to its actual performance.
2. Would a complete report, comparing a flexible budget to the performance of each of the two operations, make the problems of the Akron operation easier to identify? Explain by using an example from the problem and your answer to requirement 1.
3. Should a flexible budget comparison to actual performance become part of the regular reporting system for the annual review or for a monthly review? Explain your answer.

Pearsons Restaurant-Deli, Akron, Ohio
Net Income
Year Ending December 31
(000 omitted)

	Actual Results				Over
	Delicatessen	Restaurant	Total	Budget	(Under) Budget
Gross sales	$1,200	$2,000	$3,200	$3,500	$(300)
Purchases	$ 780	$ 800	$1,580	$1,600	$(20)
Hourly wages	60	700	760	925	(165)
Franchise fee	36	60	96	105	(9)
Advertising	100	200	300	300	—
Utilities	76	100	176	195	(19)
Depreciation	50	75	125	125	—
Lease expense	30	50	80	80	—
Salaries	30	50	80	80	—
Total	$1,162	$2,035	$3,197	$3,410	$(213)
Net income before income taxes	$ 38	$ (35)	$ 3	$ 90	$(87)

P6–4. Flexible Budget—Performance Comparisons (CMA) The Jason Plant of Cast Corporation has been in operation for fifteen months. Jason employs a standard cost system for its manufacturing operations. The first six months' performance was affected by the usual problems associated with a new operation. Since that time the operations have been running smoothly. Unfortunately, the plant has not been able to produce profits consistently. As the production requirements to meet sales demand have increased, the profit performance has deteriorated.

The plant production manager held a staff meeting in which the plant general manager, the corporate controller, and the corporate budget director were in attendance. The production manager stated that the changing production requirements made it more difficult to control manufacturing expenses. He further noted that the budget for the plant, included in the company's annual profit plan, was not useful for judging the plant's performance because of the changes in operating levels. The meeting resulted in a decision to prepare a report that would compare the plant's actual manufacturing expense performance with a budget of manufacturing expense based on actual direct-labor hours in the plant.

The plant production manager and the plant accountant studied the cost patterns for recent months, as well as volume and cost data from other Cast plants. They then prepared the following flexible budget schedule for a month with 200,000 planned production hours that should result in 50,000 units of output. The corporate controller reviewed and approved the flexible budget.

	Amount	Per Direct Labor Hour
Manufacturing expenses		
Variable		
Indirect labor	$160,000	$0.80
Supplies	26,000	0.13
Power	14,000	0.07
		$1.00
Fixed		
Supervisory labor	64,000	
Heat and light	15,000	
Property taxes	5,000	
	$284,000	

The plant production manager was pleased with the manufacturing expense reports prepared for the first three months after the flexible budget program was approved. The reports showed that manufacturing expenses were in line with the flexible budget allowance. This was also reflected by the following report prepared for November, when 50,500 units were manufactured.

Jason Plant
Manufacturing Expenses
Month of November
220,000 Actual Direct-Labor Production Hours

	Actual Costs	Allowed Costs	(Over) Under Budget
Variable			
Indirect labor	$177,000	$176,000	$(1,000)
Supplies	27,400	28,600	1,200
Power	16,000	15,400	(600)
Fixed			
Supervisory labor	65,000	64,000	(1,000)
Heat and light	15,500	15,000	(500)
Property taxes	5,000	5,000	0
	$305,900	$304,000	$(1,900)

Required

1. Explain the advantages of flexible budgeting over fixed budgeting for cost-control purposes.
2. Present supporting computations for the allowed costs shown in the expense report for November.
3. Are there other approaches that could be used to show the performance for the month of November? Explain.

P6–5. Flexible Budget Completion The following is an incomplete flexible budget for one month:

Overhead Cost	Cost Formula	Machine-Hours Worked			
		3,000	4,000	5,000	6,000
Variable					
Maintenance			$1,440		
Indirect materials			880		
Indirect labor			640		
Total					
Fixed					
Depreciation			1,440		
Taxes			800		
Supervision			3,500		
Total					

Required

Complete the flexible budget by determining the missing information.

P6–6. Flexible Budget Preparation The Skinner Scanner Company wants a flexible budget for overhead expense. You have been assigned to assemble data from the past six months. Due to the nature of Skinner's business, machine-hours worked has been adopted as the activity base. Over a relevant range of 3,000 to 6,000 machine hours, you have determined the following flexible budget formula for overhead expenses:

Total overhead costs = $14,500 + ($0.60 × Machine-hours worked)

The fixed portion of this formula is broken down as follows:

Fixed Overhead Expense	Percentage
Depreciation	35%
Taxes	25
Insurance	10
Supervisor salaries	30

The variable portion of the cost formula is broken down as follows:

Variable Overhead Expense	Percentage
Maintenance	30%
Indirect materials	35
Lubricants	5
Power	30

Required

Prepare a flexible budget for the Skinner Scanner Company over the given relevant range in increments of 1,000 machine hours. Include variable as well as fixed overhead expenses broken down into their components.

P6-7. Performance Analysis—Static and Flexible Budgets

The following budget data have been prepared by the We're OK Now Company for the current year:

Selling and administrative expenses:	
Sales salaries (all variable)	$165,000[a]
Advertising (all variable)	22,000
Travel expenses (80% variable)	13,750
Depreciation (straight-line)	4,600
Executive salaries (fixed)	80,000
Taxes (fixed)	108,200
Insurance (fixed)	8,000
General expenses (40% variable)	41,250
Total selling and administrative expenses	$442,800
Manufacturing expenses:	
Direct labor (all variable)	$ 90,000
Direct materials (all variable)	99,000
Factory overhead:	
Indirect labor (all variable)	9,000
Indirect materials (all variable)	1,800
Supervision (fixed)	27,000
Rent (fixed)	2,000
Maintenance (60% variable)	15,000
Utilities (20% variable)	22,500
Total manufacturing expenses	$266,300
Total expenses	$709,100

[a]Selling and administrative expenses are based upon $1,100,000 sales dollars, and manufacturing expenses are based upon direct-labor dollars.

At year end, the records show the following actual results:

Sales salaries	$150,000[b]
Advertising	30,000
Travel expenses	12,000
Depreciation	4,600
Executive salaries	82,000
Taxes	108,000
Insurance	8,000
General expenses	42,000
Direct labor	100,000
Direct materials	99,000
Indirect labor	10,200
Indirect materials	2,000
Supervision	27,000
Rent	2,000
Maintenance	17,200
Utilities	23,500
Total expenses	$717,500

[b]Actual sales were $1,000,000

Required

1. Prepare a performance report comparing actual costs with the static budget. Include variances, and indicate whether each variance is favorable or unfavorable.
2. Using the information obtained from the static budget, prepare a flexible budget covering actual results.
3. Prepare a performance report comparing actual costs with the flexible budget. Include variances, and indicate whether each variance is favorable or unfavorable.

P6-8. Flexible Budget and the Performance Report

Dan Max has a fleet of snowmobiles. Dan's cost analyst has developed the following budget data for one year:

	Fixed	Variable per Mile Driven
Fuel		$0.25
Oil		0.10
Chassis and other lubricants	$ 1,000	0.05
Repairs	1,200	0.06
Parking fees	2,000	
State registration and licenses	600	
Property taxes	1,200	
Comprehensive and liability insurance	1,600	
Depreciation	2,500	
Total	$10,100	$0.46

Dan estimates operations of 20,000 miles in a typical year. During the year just ended, Dan's snowmobiles were drive 23,000 miles, and the following expenses were incurred:

Fuel	$6,210
Oil	2,415
Chassis and other lubricants	2,380
Repairs	2,695
Parking fees	2,100
State registration and license	650
Property taxes	1,400
Insurance	1,600
Depreciation	2,500

Required

1. Express the budget data in the form of the flexible budget formula ($y = a + bx$).
2. Prepare a performance report for the year comparing actual results with a flexible budget covering the year's actual operations. Include variances, and indicate whether each variance is favorable or unfavorable.

P6–9. Flexible Budgets—Performance and Pyramid Reports
The M&A Company has two major departments for which the following budget data have been developed for October:

	Department 1	Department 2
Direct-labor hours	7,000	
Machine hours	3,600	
Costs:		
Direct labor	$35,000	
Direct materials	21,000	
Indirect labor	20,300	
Repair labor wages		$13,320
Supervision	6,000	8,000
Supplies	5,250	5,950
Depreciation	4,000	1,800
Insurance—liability and property	1,000	800

During October, the following actual results were obtained:

	Department 1	Department 2
Direct-labor hours	6,500	
Machine hours	3,400	
Costs:		
Direct labor	$34,125	
Direct materials	$20,150	
Indirect labor	19,500	
Repair labor wages		$12,920
Supervision	6,200	7,800
Supplies	4,680	5,440
Depreciation	4,000	1,800
Insurance	1,100	900

Depreciation, supervision, and insurance are considered fixed expenses.

Department 1 is a producing department, and variable expenses are based on direct-labor hours. Department 2 is a repairs and maintenance service department, and variable expenses are based on machine hours in the producing department.

Required

1. Prepare a performance report for department 2, comparing actual costs with a flexible budget for October's actual operations. Include variances in your report.
2. Prepare two performance reports for department 1, comparing October's actual expenses against (*a*) the original budget and (*b*) a flexible budget for October's actual operations. Include variances from the budget in your report.
3. Comment on the usefulness of the two reports prepared in requirement 2.
4. Assume the production manager has responsibility for departments 1 and 2. The production vice president oversees a separate product-development group. You have already prepared the detailed report for product development, which shows totals for flexible budget amounts and actual costs of $73,300 and $75,500, respectively. You also have prepared detailed reports for marketing and administrative activities. The totals

reported are $135,000 budget and $127,300 actual for marketing and $92,600 budget and $90,000 actual for administrative activities. Prepare a summary report in pyramid form for all of the responsibility centers in the M&A Company for October. (See the model illustrated in figure 6.12.)

P6–10. Flexible Budget, Choice of Activity Base Luthy Construction Company is considering direct-labor hours and machine hours as activity bases for predicting overhead costs. Data for the last eight months are as follows:

Month	Overhead Cost	Direct-Labor Hours	Machine Hours
1	$24,800	740	650
2	27,500	1,150	1,100
3	26,900	920	850
4	24,400	960	790
5	29,100	1,350	1,200
6	25,700	840	800
7	21,300	790	750
8	23,600	770	640

Required

1. Prepare a flexible budget formula using the high-low method and the least-squares method for each activity base.
2. Compute the coefficient of correlation and coefficient of determination.
3. Which activity base would you recommend and why?

Chapter 7

Cost-Volume-Profit Analysis

Outline

BREAKEVEN ANALYSIS
Breakeven Analysis in Units
  Equation for Breakeven Point in Units
  Breakeven Charts
  Profit-Volume Graph
Breakeven Analysis in Sales Dollars
  Equation for Breakeven Point in Sales Dollars
  Breakeven Charts in Sales Dollars
Breakeven Analysis for Multiple Products
  Breakeven Analysis in Units for Multiple Products
  Breakeven Analysis in Sales Dollars for Multiple Products
  Breakeven Charts for Multiple Products
ASSUMPTIONS UNDERLYING COST-VOLUME-PROFIT ANALYSIS
Basic Assumptions
Economic Analysis
Sources of Data

APPLICATIONS OF COST-VOLUME-PROFIT ANALYSIS
Level of Volume Required to Achieve a Specified Profit
  Level of Volume in Units and Sales Dollars
  After-Tax Profit
Margin of Safety
Sensitivity Analysis
  Input Value Errors
  Substituting Fixed and Variable Costs
  Product Pricing
  Changes in Product Mix
SUMMARY
SELF-STUDY PROBLEM
SUGGESTED READINGS
DISCUSSION QUESTIONS
EXERCISES
PROBLEMS

Cost-volume-profit analysis is a study of the relationships between costs and volume and their effect on profit. Earlier in this text we discussed the relationship between costs and volume and identified various cost patterns, including fixed, variable, and semivariable. These relationships were used in chapter 6 to develop a flexible budget that can predict the amount of cost that should be incurred at various levels of output. In this chapter we add revenue to the analysis so that conclusions can be made about the profitability of the enterprise at various levels of output.

Cost-volume-profit analysis is primarily a planning tool to assist management in effectively utilizing resources in the short run. Management of a firm, a division, or a department is typically faced with a set of resources that are fixed or can be increased or decreased only slightly in the short run. Cost-volume-profit analysis assists in managing these resources and the fixed costs associated with them by providing answers to the following types of questions: How many units must be produced and sold to break even? What will be the effect on profit if price is changed? How will the breakeven point change if a machine, which adds additional fixed costs, is substituted for direct labor, which is a variable cost?

The analysis of costs, volume, and profit is static in that it is based on a given set of facts. If one or more of the facts are changed, a new analysis must be performed. It is also based on several assumptions that are made to keep the analysis as simple as possible, yet realistic in terms of the real-world environment. If one or more of the assumptions are not correct, the results of the analysis may be incorrect and misleading.

This chapter explains cost-volume-profit analysis, its uses, and its limitations. After completing this chapter, you should be able to:

1. compute the breakeven point in either units of production or sales dollars.
2. prepare a breakeven chart and a profit-volume graph.
3. identify the assumptions inherent in traditional breakeven analysis.
4. identify the revenue required to obtain a desired profit.
5. analyze the effects of a change in price, fixed costs, or variable costs on the breakeven point and on profit.
6. compute the breakeven point for a multiple-product entity and analyze the effect on the breakeven point for changes in the product mix.

BREAKEVEN ANALYSIS

A **breakeven analysis** is performed to identify the level of operation at which the entity has covered all costs but has not yet earned any profit. The **breakeven point** identifies the volume of activity at which total revenues equal total costs. This is often an important point to management, because it represents a minimum acceptable level of operations. Of course, the desirability of the project or the investment increases as profits increase, but profitable operations can only result when the level of activity exceeds the breakeven point.

The breakeven point is generally computed mathematically and is expressed in either *units of output* or *sales dollars*. Charts and graphs are frequently used to illustrate the breakeven point and to show the effect that changes in volume will have on profits. Our analysis will first consider entities with only a single product, but later it will be expanded to include multiple-product entities.

CHAPTER 7: COST-VOLUME-PROFIT ANALYSIS

Breakeven Analysis in Units

The breakeven point is defined as the level of operations at which total revenues equal total costs. The analysis can be for an entire firm, a division, or a separate department. Breakeven analysis utilizes the contribution margin approach, which separates costs into fixed and variable classifications.

Contribution Margin Format

Sales	$_____
Less: Variable costs	$_____
Contribution margin	$_____
Less: Fixed costs	$_____
New Income	$_____

Recall that the contribution margin approach first classifies expenses as fixed or variable and groups them together according to their pattern rather than their function. Therefore, both variable and fixed costs in this format contain selling and administrative costs as well as production costs. The basic analysis is based on an assumption that production and sales are equal.

Equation for Breakeven Point in Units

The breakeven point in units can be computed by dividing total fixed costs (*FC*) by the contribution margin provided by each unit.

$$\text{Breakeven point in units} = \frac{\text{Total fixed costs}}{\text{Contribution margin per unit}} = \frac{FC}{P - VC}$$

The contribution margin per unit is sales price per unit (*P*) minus variable cost per unit (*VC*). An example will illustrate the use of this formula:

EXAMPLE

Problem

Packard Incorporated manufactures and sells one type of calculator called Model Q. Model Q sells for $40, and the variable expenses associated with it are $20 for manufacturing and $5 for selling. Fixed costs are $75,000 for manufacturing and $15,000 for selling and administration. How many units must be produced and sold to break even?

Solution

$$\text{Breakeven point in units} = \frac{\text{Fixed cost}}{\text{Sale price per unit} - \text{Variable cost per unit}}$$

$$= \frac{\$90,000}{\$40 - \$25} = \underline{6,000 \text{ units}}$$

When the price *exceeds* the variable cost, as in the preceding example, each unit contributes something ($15) toward covering fixed costs and providing a profit. The breakeven point has been reached as soon as the cumulative amount of the contribution margin (6,000 × $15) equals the total fixed costs ($90,000).

If the price is ever *less than* the variable cost, the entity would maximize profits (minimize losses in this case) by producing nothing. In this situation it is not possible to have a breakeven point if there are any fixed costs.

EXAMPLE

Problem

All Grain Company produces home flour mills, which it sells for $120. Variable costs to produce and sell the mills are $125. Annual fixed costs total $75,000. What is the company's breakeven point?

Solution

The company cannot break even under current operating conditions. At zero production, the company will lose $75,000. At 10,000 units of production, the company will lose $125,000 [($125 − $120) × 10,000 + $75,000]. Because each additional unit increases the loss by $5, the optimal strategy is to produce nothing.

Breakeven Charts A **breakeven chart** is a graphic representation, drawn to scale, of the relationships between costs, revenues, and profits. It is developed by plotting the total cost curve and the total revenue curve on graph paper. The previous example for Packard will be used to illustrate the construction. The revenue and cost curves are as follows:

> Revenue = $40 (units)
> Cost = $90,000 + $25 (units)

These two lines are plotted on the graph illustrated in figure 7.1.

The breakeven point is the point at which the total revenue curve intersects the total cost curve. Sales above this level will provide a profit, whereas sales below this level will result in a loss. The amount of the profit or loss is shown by the *vertical distance* between the total revenue and total cost curves. These areas have been shaded and labeled on the graph.

Profit-Volume Graph As the name implies, a **profit-volume** (P/V) **graph** focuses entirely on the relationship between volume and profit. Many people find this graph more useful than the breakeven chart, because it shows the amount of profit directly rather than as the difference between the revenue and cost curves.

The profit-volume chart is constructed on a graph in which the vertical axis represents *net income* in dollars. The vertical axis is extended below the origin to show a net loss. The horizontal axis represents *volume*. The measure of volume can be in either units or sales dollars, but we will stay with units for now, as shown in figure 7.2. The profit (loss) line is plotted by computing the profit (loss) at several levels of output. These can be taken from the breakeven chart by analyzing the difference between the total revenue and total cost curves. The profit line is straight when both revenue and cost curves are linear and any two points can be used to plot it. The two most commonly used points are the zero production level and the breakeven point. At an output of zero, the loss will equal the amount of fixed costs. Using our data for Packard, the coordinates of this point are (0, −90,000). The profit line slopes upward to the right and crosses the horizontal axis at the breakeven point. The coordinates of this point are (6,000, 0).

The formula for the profit line is:

> Net income = −a + bx
> where a = (y-intercept) fixed cost
> b = (slope) contribution margin per unit
> x = (independent variable) volume in units or sales dollars.

FIGURE 7.1

Breakeven Charts

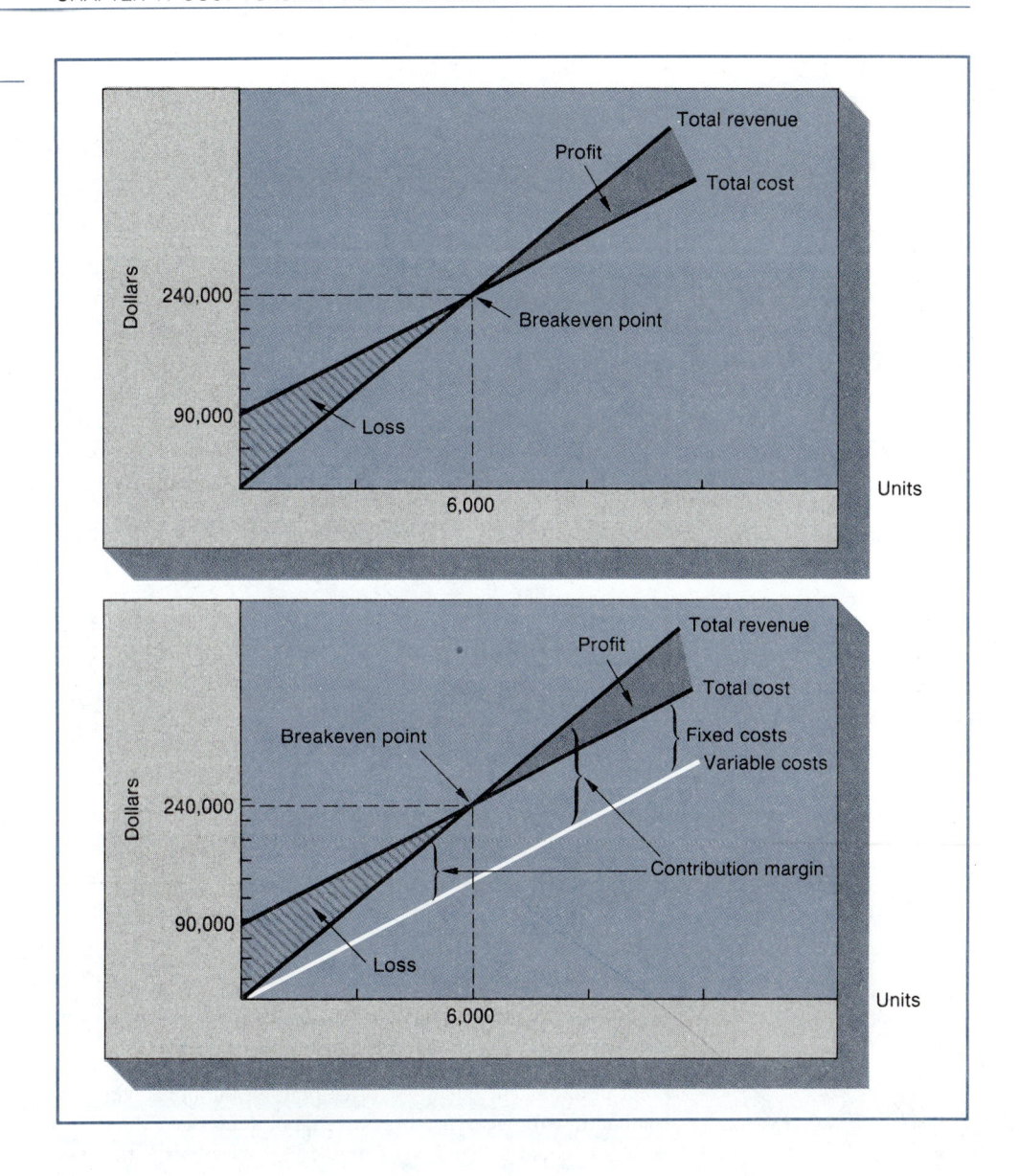

Notice that the *slope* of the profit line is equal to the *contribution margin*. Profit increases (loss decreases) by the amount of each unit's contribution margin. Notice also that the profit line represents the *cumulative contribution margin* in dollars at various volume levels. When the profit line crosses the horizontal axis, the cumulative contribution margin is enough to cover fixed costs. Operations above that point provide an income to the company.

Breakeven Analysis in Sales Dollars

The concept of the breakeven point does not change when the analysis is performed in sales dollars. The breakeven point merely identifies the amount of *sales dollars* that is required to cover all costs but that generates no profit.

FIGURE 7.2

Profit-Volume Graph

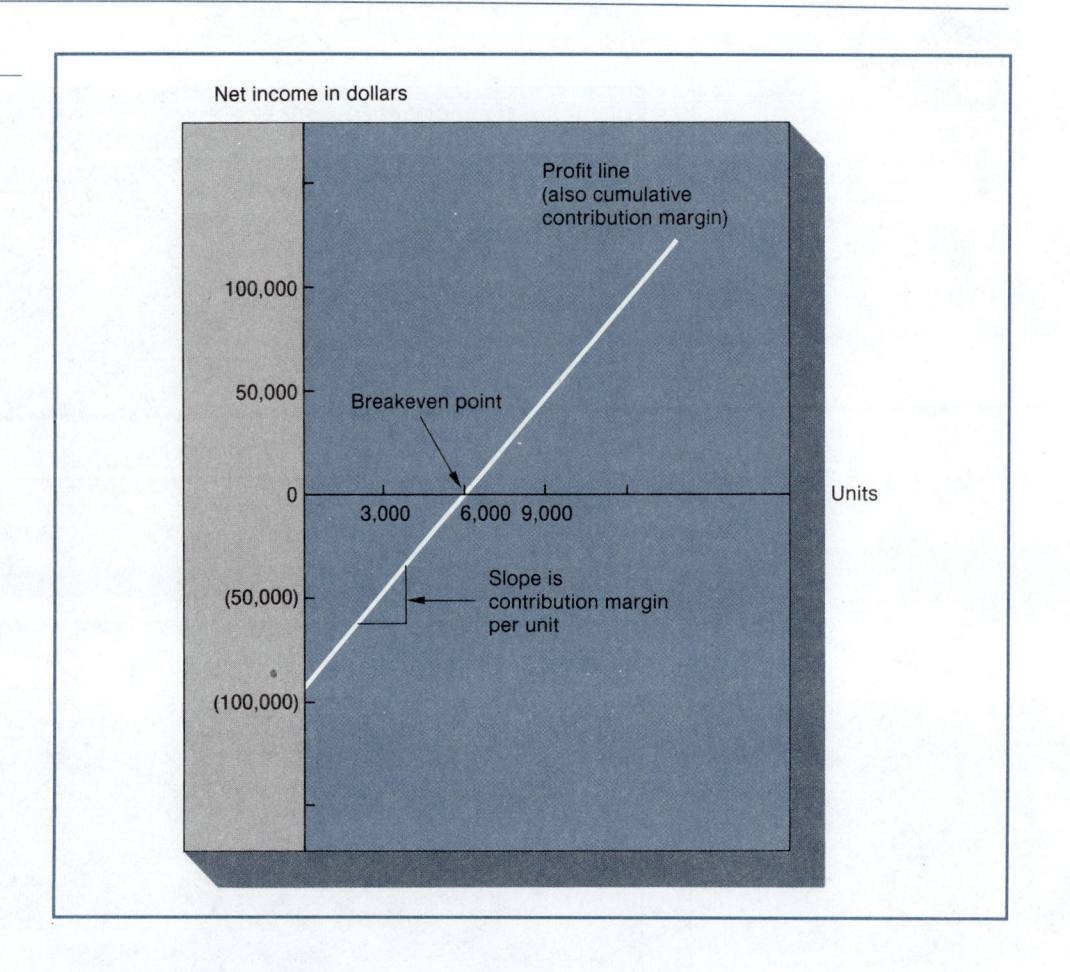

```
Net income in dollars

100,000                    Profit line
                           (also cumulative
                           contribution margin)

 50,000
              Breakeven point
      0  ┼────────┬────┬────┬──────── Units
          3,000  6,000 9,000

(50,000)         Slope is
                 contribution margin
                 per unit

(100,000)
```

Equation for Breakeven Point in Sales Dollars One method of computing the breakeven point in sales dollars is to compute the breakeven point in units and multiply the number of units by the sales price per unit. However, sometimes it may not be convenient or efficient, because of the way the data are given, to first compute the breakeven point in units. The equation for computing the breakeven point in units can be manipulated so that it will yield the breakeven point in sales dollars. The breakeven point in sales dollars is equal to fixed costs divided by the contribution margin ratio.

$$\text{Breakeven point in sales dollars} = \frac{\text{Fixed costs}}{\text{Contribution margin ratio}}$$

By definition, the **contribution margin ratio** is the ratio of the contribution margin to sales. The **contribution margin** is the sale price minus variable costs, and the ratio is computed by dividing contribution margin by the sales price.

$$\text{Contribution margin ratio} = \frac{\text{Sale price per unit} - \text{Variable costs per unit}}{\text{Sale price per unit}}$$

or

$$= \frac{\text{Total sales} - \text{Total variable costs}}{\text{Total sales}}$$

EXAMPLE

Problem
All Time Company manufactures and sells a watch for $25. Variable costs are $20 per unit and fixed costs total $100,000 per year. What is the required sales revenue for the company to break even? The contribution margin ratio is first computed and then divided into the total fixed costs.

Solution

$$\text{Contribution margin ratio:} \frac{\$25 - \$20}{\$25} = \underline{0.20 \text{ or } 20\%}$$

$$\text{Breakeven point in sales dollars:} \frac{\$100,000}{0.20} = \underline{\$500,000}$$

Breakeven Charts in Sales Dollars The breakeven chart does not change when the analysis is performed in sales dollars rather than in units. The breakeven point in sales dollars is obtained by reading the dollar amount on the *vertical axis* that corresponds to the breakeven point. Remember that the number of units is obtained by reading the amount on the *horizontal axis* that corresponds to the breakeven point.

When a profit-volume graph in sales dollars is developed, sales dollars is substituted for units as the volume measure on the horizontal axis. The profit line is the difference between the total revenue and total cost curves for various levels of sales dollars.

Breakeven Analysis for Multiple Products

Our analysis so far has assumed that only one product was being produced and sold, which is not very realistic for most companies. Breakeven analysis can still be performed using either units of production or sales dollars by assuming that the company's sales mix will remain constant.

Sales mix refers to the ratio or relative combination of each product's sales to total sales. It is the composition of total sales broken down among various products or product lines.

EXAMPLE

Multi Products Incorporated has three products—model X, model Y, and model Z. Sales on a monthly basis are expected to be as follows:

	Model X	Model Y	Model Z	Total
Units sold:	1,000	1,500	2,500	5,000
Ratio:	20%	30%	50%	100%

Product mix is usually stated in the form of a ratio, such as (2:3:5) for models X, Y, and Z, respectively. This means that for every 2 units of model X that are sold, there are 3 units of model Y and 5 units of model Z sold. Another way of viewing sales mix is to imagine a **market basket** that represents the average expected sales of a company. Within that basket, representing one product mix, Multi Products would have 2 units of model X, 3 units of model Y, and 5 units of model Z, for a total of 10 units.

Breakeven Analysis in Units for Multiple Products A market-basket approach can be used to compute a breakeven point in units. A market basket representing the average sales mix is developed. The contribution margin provided by the basket is used to compute the number of baskets that must be sold to break even. The number of individual products required to fill the baskets at the breakeven point is then determined.

EXAMPLE

Problem

Multi Products Incorporated has a sales ratio of 2:3:5: (i.e, $2x + 3y + 5z = 1$ sales unit) for models X, Y, and Z, respectively. Total fixed costs for the year are $200,000. The sale price, variable costs, and contribution margin associated with each product are as follows:

	(2) Model X	(3) Model Y	(5) Model Z	(10) Total	Average
Sales price/unit	$50	$25	$10	$225	$22.5
Variable cost/unit	30	15	8	145	14.5
Contribution margin/unit	$20	$10	$ 2	$ 80	$ 8.0

Solution

The average market basket is based on the sales ratio and consists of 10 units with a total contribution margin of $80 [(2 × $20) + (3 × $10) + (5 × $2)]. The breakeven point in market baskets is computed using the formula for the breakeven point in units

$$x = \frac{\$200,000}{\$80} = 2,500 \text{ baskets or}$$

$$\frac{\$200,000}{\$8} = 25,000 \text{ composite units of } X, Y, \text{ and } Z$$

In order to fill 2,500 baskets, it will take the following amounts for each model:

Model X   5,000 units (2,500 × 2)
Model Y   7,500 units (2,500 × 3)
Model Z   12,500 units (2,500 × 5) or

Proportion of total composite units:
X: 25,000 × 0.2 = 5,000
Y: 25,000 × 0.3 = 7,500
Z: 25,000 × 0.5 = 12,500

This, then is the breakeven point in units as long as the sales mix stays at (2:3:5).

Breakeven Analysis in Sales Dollars for Multiple Products The breakeven point in sales dollars for a multiple-product entity can be computed by using an average contribution margin ratio, which can be computed on a per-unit basis or developed from the income statement. In both cases, the fixed costs are divided by the average contribution margin ratio, but the difference is in the level of aggregation in computing this ratio.

When computed on a unit basis, the average unit sale price is divided into the average unit contribution margin.

EXAMPLE

Using the preceding data for Multi Products Incorporated, the average sale price is computed by multiplying the sales ratio by the sale price for individual products and

CHAPTER 7: COST-VOLUME-PROFIT ANALYSIS

summing the results. The average contribution margin is computed in a similar manner, and the contribution margin ratio is the average contribution margin divided by the average sale price.

Average sale price:

$$(20\% \times \$50) + (30\% \times \$25) + (50\% \times \$10) = \$22.50$$

Average contribution margin:

$$(20\% \times \$20) + (30\% \times \$10) + (50\% \times \$2) = \$8.00$$

Average contribution margin ratio:

$$(\$8.00 \div \$22.50) = 35.555\%$$

Breakeven point in sales dollars:

$$\frac{\$200,000}{35.555\%} = \$562,500 \text{ per year}$$

An average contribution margin ratio can also be developed from an income statement once the fixed and variable costs have been identified. The contribution margin format is most useful for this type of analysis.

EXAMPLE

Problem
C. M. Incorporated has twenty products, and the contents of an average market basket are not known. The firm reported the following net income for January 19X1. The sales mix and costs for January are expected to continue throughout the coming year. Management was disappointed with the results and wants to know the sales level required to break even.

Sales	$120,000	100%
Variable costs	90,000	75%
Contribution margin	30,000	25%
Fixed costs	40,000	
Net income (loss)	($10,000)	

Solution
The average contribution ratio is 25 percent ($30,000 ÷ $120,000) and the breakeven point in sales dollars is $160,000 ($40,000 ÷ 25%). Assuming the product mix and costs remain the same as in January, C. M. Incorporated must sell $160,000 per month to break even.

Breakeven analysis in sales dollars is generally easier to compute than breakeven analysis in units for multiple-product entities, because it does not require a knowledge of the product mix and the average market basket. A contribution margin ratio can be developed from the income statement for use in the breakeven analysis.

Breakeven Charts for Multiple Products A breakeven chart for a multiple-product entity is similar to that for a single-product entity in that it shows dollars on the vertical axis and volume on the horizontal axis. If volume is specified in units, the market-basket approach must be followed. One unit is equal to one market basket containing the normal sales mix of the company.

A profit-volume graph is useful in showing the contribution that each product provides to total company profit. A profit-volume chart for Multi Products Incorporated shown in figure 7.3 has two profit lines—one shows each product's contribution and one shows the average for all products.

Suppose that management of Multi Products expects sales to be $675,000 (3,000 baskets @ $225 each) for the year. The contribution margin provided by each product to cover fixed costs and to provide a profit is plotted as a solid line. Segments X, Y, and Z represents X, Y, and Z, respectively. The dashed line is the average profit line for all products.

The profit line for an individual product is plotted by computing the sales and contribution margin as if only that product was produced and sold. For example, if only model X is produced and sold, there will be 6,000 units (3,000 baskets @ 2 each) with total sales of $300,000 (6,000 × $50) and a contribution margin of $120,000 (6,000 × $20). The company's net loss, if only model X is sold, will be $80,000. The coordinates of this point are (300,000, −80,000).

Model Y is considered next. Sales of model Y will be 9,000 units (3,000 baskets @ 3 each) or $225,000 (9,000 × $25), with a contribution margin of $90,000 (9,000 × $10). The cumulative sales for models X and Y combined are $525,000, and the profit is $10,000. These numbers provide the coordinates of this point.

FIGURE 7.3

Profit-Volume Chart for Multiple Products

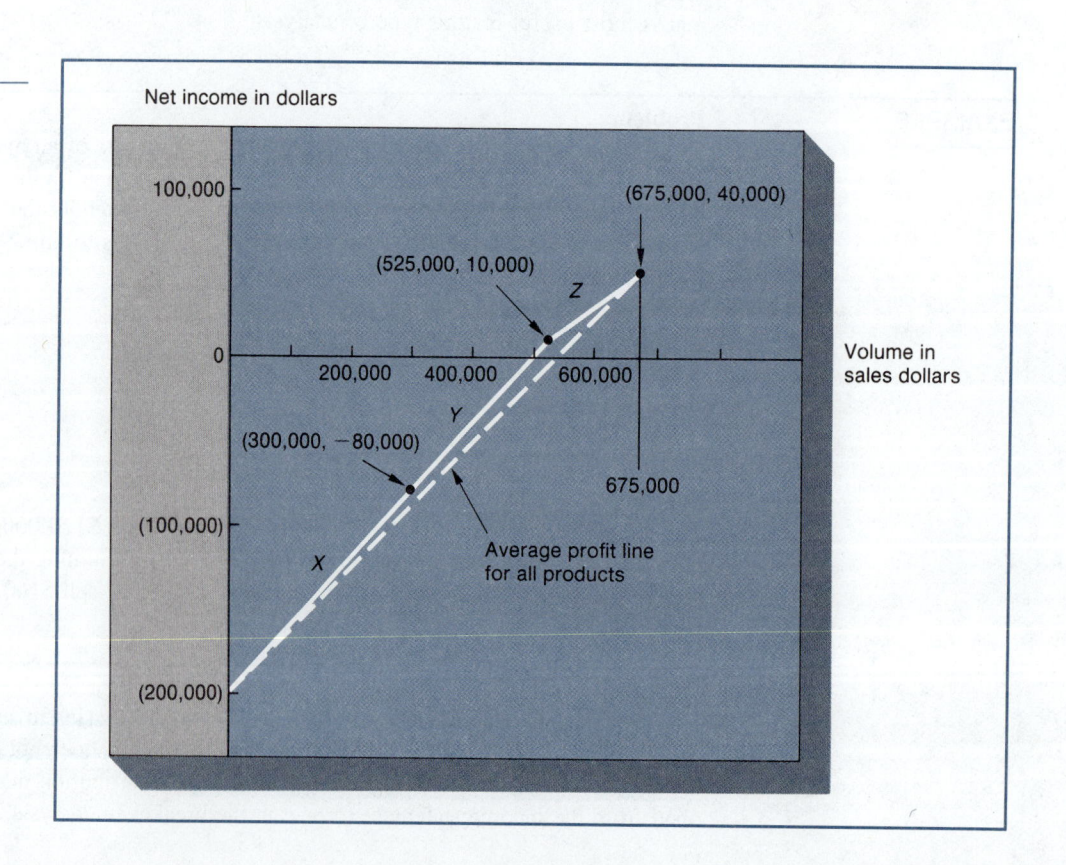

By adding model Z with 15,000 units, $150,000 of sales, and $30,000 of contribution margin, we arrive at a total sales and profit for the year of $675,000 and $40,000, respectively. The products can be considered in any order. However, a different order will change the shape of the profit line. The beginning and ending points will not change, and the average profit line for all products will remain the same.

ASSUMPTIONS UNDERLYING COST-VOLUME-PROFIT ANALYSIS

Although the cost-volume-profit analysis is a valuable tool in making a variety of decisions, the analysis is based on several assumptions, and, if the assumptions are not realistic, the analysis will be misleading. Cost-volume-profit analysis is relatively simple to understand and work with, and, if the assumptions are not grossly violated, its results will approximate actual results. A more sophisticated analysis is required when the assumptions are relaxed or changed.

Basic Assumptions

The following list summarizes the basic assumptions underlying cost-volume-profit analysis:

1. Cost data are available for manufacturing, selling, and administrative activities. Costs can be classified as either fixed or variable.
2. Variable costs change at a linear/constant rate per unit.
3. Fixed costs remain constant.
4. Volume is the only factor that affects cost.
5. Unit selling prices do not change as the unit sales volume changes.
6. There is only one product, or, if there are multiple products, the sales mix remains constant.
7. There are no constraints on either production or marketing.
8. Productivity remains constant. This is required for cost functions to be linear.
9. All units that are produced are sold in the same period. In other words, there is no significant change in inventory levels between periods. The analysis assumes that all costs incurrred during the period are also expensed in the same period. For example, if production exceeds sales, some costs will be carried in inventory rather than expensed.
10. There is a relevant range of validity for these and other underlying assumptions and concepts. The relevant range establishes the limits within which the volume of activity can vary and the sales and cost relationships remain valid.

The relevant range is one of the most important assumptions and is basic to several other assumptions. Within a fairly narrow range of activity, the assumptions are generally valid. If the analysis is extended beyond that range, a new chart must be developed with new cost and revenue curves or a more sophisticated analysis must be employed using parabolic cost and revenue curves.

Economic Analysis

An economic analysis of cost, volume, and profit avoids many of the preceding assumptions by using parabolic (nonlinear) cost and revenue curves. Figure 7.4 shows a typical economic analysis.

FIGURE 7.4

Economic Breakeven Analysis

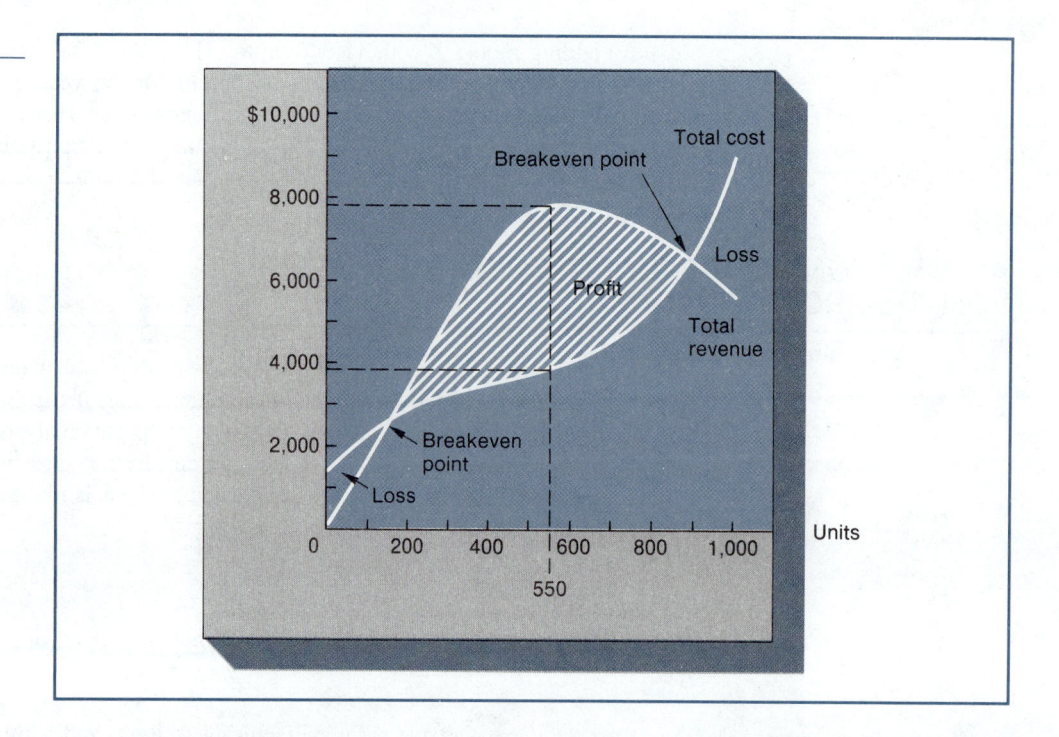

Notice that the revenue curve comes out of the origin, rises quickly, levels off, and finally declines. When only a few units are available, a premium price can be charged; however, price must be reduced to sell larger quantities. The point of diminishing returns indicates where total revenue begins to decline. The increase in the number of units sold is not enough to offset the loss due to a reduction in the sales price.

The total cost curve intersects the vertical axis at $1,250, rises initially, then levels off, but rises sharply at higher levels of volume. Some, but not all, fixed costs can be avoided in the short run at very low levels of output; in the example, $1,250 of fixed costs are unavoidable. The initial rise in the cost curve results from discretionary fixed costs that were avoided at zero output and from production inefficiencies associated with low levels of output. As output increases, fixed costs remain relatively constant. However, because of improvements in production efficiency, there is a decline in the rate of increase in the cost curve. Total costs increase rapidly as output approaches plant capacity. Additional fixed costs must be incurred, and production inefficiencies result in higher per-unit variable costs.

The two points at which total revenues equal total costs are the breakeven points. One is at a relatively low level of output and the other at a relatively high level. A profit will be earned by operating within this range. The areas of profit and loss have been shaded and labeled in figure 7.4.

One of the benefits of this analysis is that it identifies the optimal level of output. Profit will be maximized at the point where there is the maximum vertical distance between the total revenue and total cost curves. This can also be determined by identifying the point at which the slope of the two curves are equal. Output of 550 units in figure 7.4 results in the maximum profit of $4,000 ($7,900 − $3,900).

Sources of Data

Essential data for computing cost-volume-profit analysis include the selling price of the product(s), sales mix for multiple-product entities, and costs broken down into fixed and variable classifications. The budget is the best source of this information for companies that have a formal one. The budget is typically developed by studying historical operating data and adjusting them for expected changes during the coming period. As such, it is directly applicable to current decisions relating to costs, volume, and profit.

The sales portion of the budget contains the selling price of the product(s). The sales mix can be developed from the number of units of each product that are expected to be sold. The flexible budget provides total fixed costs and a variable rate. An adjustment, however, is required if the measure of volume associated with the variable rate is something other than units. Because breakeven analysis is unit based, the variable rate must also be specified in units. For example, if the variable portion of the flexible budget is based on direct-labor hours worked, it would first need to be converted to a variable rate per unit by using the standard for direct-labor hours required to produce each unit.

Companies without a formal budget must go through some of the same analysis as those with a formal budget in collecting the information required for breakeven analysis. Historical cost data can be analyzed using such techniques as the high-low point method, scattergraph method, or least-squares regression analysis to separate fixed and variable costs and to quantify the cost functions. Sales reports can be used to identify sales prices and sales mix. Remember that adjustments may be required to these historical data to make them meaningful for decisions on current and future operations.

Data collection is most difficult for products with which the company has had little or no experience. In these situations, industrial-engineering studies are most useful in providing an estimate of the cost data, and market studies can provide relevant information on sales price and product mix.

APPLICATIONS OF COST-VOLUME-PROFIT ANALYSIS

The breakeven analysis discussed previously is only one application of cost-volume-profit analysis. Cost-volume-profit analysis can provide useful information for product pricing, for analyzing the effect of changes in the product mix or changes in the cost structure by substituting fixed costs for variable costs, and for determining the volume of output required to yield a specified profit.

Level of Volume Required to Achieve a Specified Profit

A breakeven point is important because it identifies the level of operation that will avoid a loss. However, investors and managers are generally not satisfied with breaking even. A level of profit that provides an adequate return on investment must be achieved in the long run to make the product or project attractive.

Level of Volume in Units and Sales Dollars Our equation for computing the breakeven point can be adjusted to compute the volume of sales dollars or units required to provide a specified profit. This is done by adding the desired profit to the fixed costs and dividing by the contribution margin (for units) or the contribution margin ratio (for sales dollars).

$$\text{Volume in units} = \frac{\text{Fixed costs} + \text{Desired profit}}{\text{Contribution margin per unit}}$$

$$\text{Volume in sales dollars} = \frac{\text{Fixed costs} + \text{Desired profit}}{\text{Contribution margin ratio}}$$

EXAMPLE

Problem

Packard Incorporated sells its model Q calculator for $40. Fixed costs are $90,000 per month, and variable costs are $25 per unit. How many units must be sold to provide $30,000 net income (before income tax)? What is the sales volume associated with the before-tax net income of $30,000?

Solution

$$\text{Sales in units} = \frac{\$90{,}000 + \$30{,}000}{\$40 - \$25} = 8{,}000 \text{ units}$$

$$\text{Sales in dollars} = \frac{\$90{,}000 + \$30{,}000}{(\$40 - \$25)/\$40} = \frac{\$120{,}000}{37.5\%} = \$320{,}000 \text{ sales dollars}$$

Notice that the breakeven point in units multiplied by the sale price (8,000 units × $40) equals $320,000.

After-Tax Profit In the previous example, the desired profit was specified as a before-income-tax amount. Income tax is a *tax on income* and income results only after all costs have been covered. Remember that both fixed and variable costs include manufacturing, selling, and administrative costs required to produce and sell the product. No allowance has been made for any income tax on profits.

The income tax problem must be considered with the addition of the profit factor, and the desired profit must be specified as either before or after income tax. When the desired profit is specified as a *before-income-tax amount,* we ignore the tax and include that amount of profit in the equations as illustrated on page 000. If the profit figure is specified as an *after-tax amount,* it must first be converted to a before-tax amount for inclusion in the equation.

The net income before tax can be computed by working backwards from the desired net income after tax and the tax rate. Remember that net income before tax, multiplied by the tax rate, gives the amount of income tax that is subtracted in deriving the after-tax profit.

EXAMPLE

Problem

Packard Incorporated desired an after-tax net income of $18,000, and it is subject to an average income tax rate of 34 percent. What is its desired before-tax income?

Solution

The after-tax net income is divided by one minus the tax rate (1 − 0.34) to give the before-tax net income. This can be generalized into equation form and used to compute the before-tax net income.

$$\text{Before-tax net income} = \frac{\text{After-tax net income}}{(1 - \text{Tax rate})} = \frac{\$18{,}000}{(1 - 0.34)} = \$27{,}273$$

Margin of Safety

The **margin of safety** identifies the amount of reduction in sales that could occur without sustaining a loss. It is the excess of actual or budgeted sales over sales at the breakeven point. The margin of safety may be specified in units of output, in sales dollars, or as a percentage of sales. When it is expressed as a percentage of sales, it is called a *margin of safety ratio*.

Margin of safety in sales dollars = Current Sales − Breakeven sales

$$\text{Margin of safety ratio} = \frac{\text{Current sales} - \text{Breakeven sales}}{\text{Current sales}}$$

EXAMPLE

Problem

Marginal Manufacturing Company produces filing cabinets that it sells for $120. Monthly fixed costs are $75,000, and variable costs are $90 per unit. Sales for the past few months have averaged $350,000. Compute the margin of safety in sales dollars and the margin of safety ratio.

Solution

$$\text{Breakeven point:} \frac{\$75,000}{(\$120 - \$90)/\$120} = \$300,000$$

Margin of safety: $350,000 − $300,000 = $50,000

$$\text{Margin of safety ratio:} \frac{\$350,000 - \$300,000}{\$350,000} = 14.3\%$$

Sales of Marginal Manufacturing Company can be reduced by $50,000 or 14.3 percent before a loss sustained.

Sensitivity Analysis

Sensitivity analysis is a "what if" analysis that examines the effect on the outcome of changes in one or more input values. The input values for cost-volume-profit analysis include the sales mix, sale price, units, variable cost per unit, and total fixed cost. A change in any of these items will cause a change in the breakeven point and a change in the amount of profit (loss) at any given level of sales. Remember that the values for these inputs are often only estimates. Also, management may be considering a change in the manufacturing or selling process that would have an effect on one or more of the values. A technique is needed to determine the impact on the breakeven point and on profit of errors in estimating the values or of changes in the production or selling process. Cost-volume-profit analysis with breakeven charts and profit-volume graphs is often used.

Input Value Errors Suppose management is considering a new product that must be priced at $40 in order to be competitive in the market. Costs to produce and sell the product are expected to be $30 per unit variable and $100,000 per month fixed. For the first two years, management expects to capture 10 percent of a total market of 130,000 units. Should management pursue the new product?

If its cost estimates are correct, the answer is probably yes. The breakeven point is 10,000 units [$100,000 ÷ ($40 − $30)], which is less than its expected sales of 13,000 units (10% × 130,000).

Remember, however, that the cost data provided by management are only estimates and that management has had no prior experience with this product. It admits that its cost estimates for both fixed and variable costs could be as much as 10 percent high or 10 percent low, but the probability that the costs would exceed those limits is remote.

Sensitivity analysis can be used to analyze the effect on the expected breakeven point for the most optimistic and pessimistic estimates.

Optimistic breakeven point: (10% reduction in costs)	$\dfrac{\$90{,}000}{\$40 - \$27}$ =	6,923 units
Pessimistic breakeven point: (10% increase in costs)	$\dfrac{\$110{,}000}{\$40 - \$33}$ =	15,714 units

The profit-volume graph in figure 7.5 shows the optimistic, most likely, and pessimistic outcomes.

Additional analysis could be performed to determine the amount of increase in cost above the estimate that can be sustained and still break even, assuming the new product is able to capture 10 percent of the market, or 13,000 units. Management's cost estimates can be as much as 6 percent low and still break even by capturing only 10 percent of the market. The computations are as follows with x representing the percentage increase in costs:

$$\frac{\$100{,}000(x)}{\$40 - \$30(x)} = 13{,}000 \text{ units}$$

Solving the equation for x

x = 1.0612, or 6.1% increase

There appears to be a reasonable probability that costs will exceed the estimates. If the company expects to capture only 10 percent of a 130,000-unit market, a loss will be sustained if costs exceed the estimates by more than 6.1 percent. Management may want

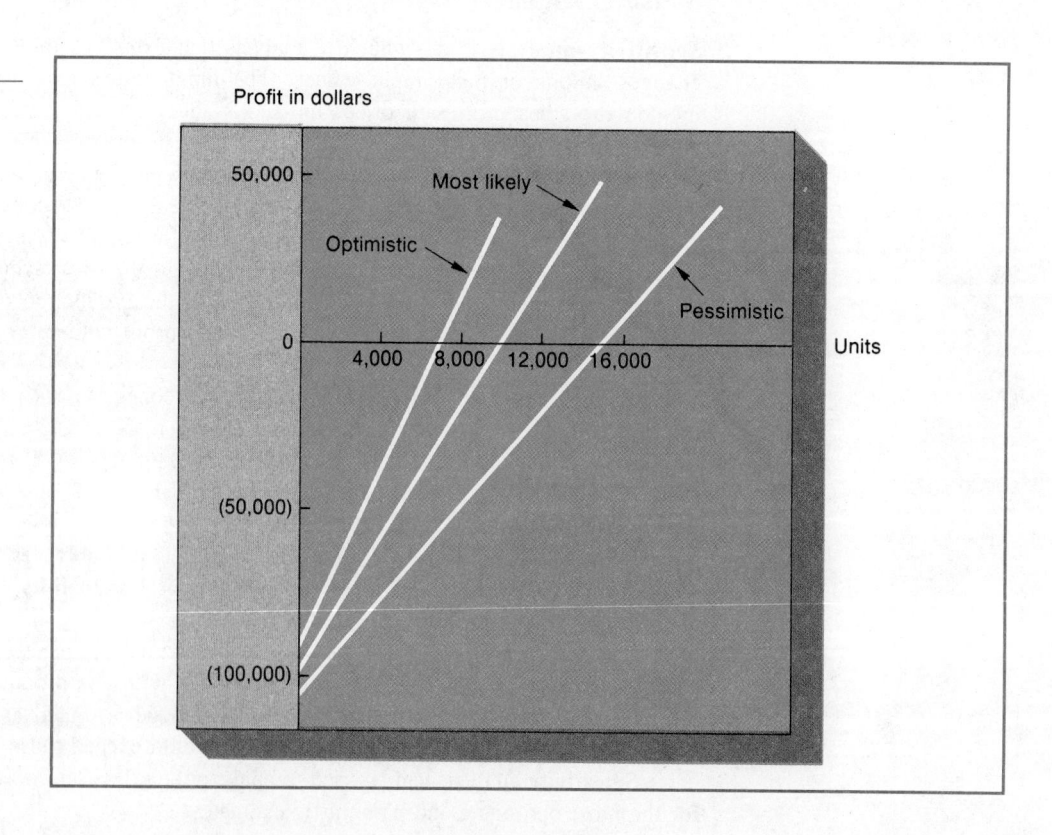

FIGURE 7.5

Sensitivity Analysis—New Product Decision

CHAPTER 7: COST-VOLUME-PROFIT ANALYSIS

to consider additional cost or market studies before a final decision is made. Additional cost studies can be used to forecast the actual costs of producing and selling the product more accurately and with more confidence. Market studies can provide information on the total market size and the likelihood of capturing 10 percent or more of it.

Substituting Fixed and Variable Costs Costs often change as a result of a decision to change the procedures used to produce or sell a product. An analysis of the change's impact is often desired to assist in the decision-making process. Some changes either increase or decrease fixed or variable costs, or both. Often management is faced with a decision to substitute a fixed cost for a variable cost, or vice versa. Sensitivity analysis can be used to study the effect on the breakeven point and profit for these types of changes.

EXAMPLE

Problem

Merge Incorporated is a multiple-product entity considering the acquisition of a new machine that would replace two direct-labor workers. Wages for these two individuals currently constitute about 20 percent of the variable costs. The new machine will initially be used at only 50 percent capacity but will add about $40,000 per year of fixed costs. The following statement shows the current operating results:

Sales	$350,000	100%
Variable costs	189,000	54%
Contribution margin	161,000	46%
Fixed costs	140,000	
Net income	$ 21,000	

What will be the effect on net income and the breakeven point if the machine is acquired?

Solution

If sales continue at the current level and the machine is acquired, net income will decrease by $2,200.

Additional fixed costs	$40,000
Savings in variable costs	
(20% × $189,000)	37,800
Increase in total costs	$ 2,200

The breakeven point with a new machine is $316,901, which is slightly higher than the existing breakeven point of $304,348.

$$\text{Current breakeven point} = \frac{\$140,000}{46\%} = \$304,348$$

$$\text{New breakeven point} = \frac{\$180,000}{56.8\%^a} = \$316,901$$

$$^a\text{Contribution margin ratio} = \frac{350,000 - 151,200}{350,000} = 56.8\%$$

If sales are expected to increase, the new machine may be a very profitable investment. Figure 7.6 shows profit lines under the existing conditions and assuming the new

FIGURE 7.6

Sensitivity Analysis—New Machine Acquisition

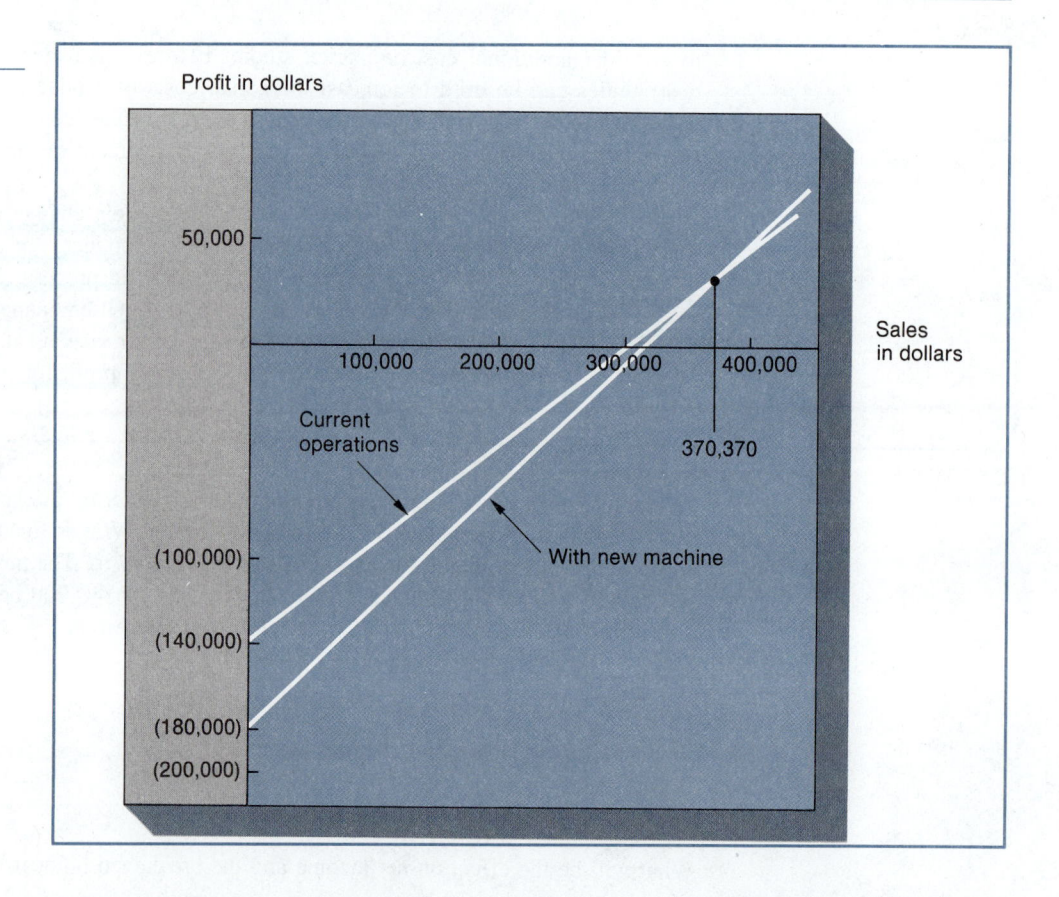

piece of equipment is acquired. Notice that the profit line with the new machine has a steeper slope. The new machine will be profitable when sales exceed $370,370 per year. This is determined by computing the point at which the two lines intersect, as follows:

$$-140{,}000 + 0.46x = -180{,}000 + 0.568x$$
$$0.108x = 40{,}000$$
$$x = \$370{,}370$$

This type of analysis considers only the impact of the machine during its first year of operations and should not be used as the sole criterion in the acquisition decision. Capital budgeting techniques (discussed in chapter 23 and 24) consider the contribution of the machine over its entire life and should be used in connection with the preceding analysis.

Product Pricing Management does not have much influence over product pricing when the product is sold in a competitive market environment. Market forces of supply and demand dictate to a large extent the price that can be charged for the product. However, the sales price has an important effect on the breakeven point and on profit. Sensitivity analysis is useful in projecting the effects of price fluctuation on company profitability.

EXAMPLE

Problem

Western Sales Company currently sells its dishwashers for $350. Costs are $100,000 per month fixed and $200 per unit variable. Currently the company is selling 800 units per month. However, the economy is in a slight recession, and to maintain the same sales level Western must cut the selling price by 10 percent. If the current price is maintained, Western estimates a 10 percent loss in sales. What is the breakeven point with each pricing strategy, and which strategy would you recommend?

Solution

The breakeven points under the existing price and alternative price are:

$$\text{Existing price} = \frac{\$100{,}000}{\$350 - \$200} = \underline{\underline{667 \text{ units}}}.$$

$$\text{Alternative price} = \frac{\$100{,}000}{\$315 - \$200} = \underline{\underline{870 \text{ units}}}.$$

As shown in figure 7.7, maintaining the current price will result in a breakeven point of 667 units. Estimated sales will drop to 720 units (800 × 90%) and profits will be lower than under normal conditions. But at least the company can expect to earn a profit.

A 10 percent cut in price results in a breakeven point of 870 units, and estimated sales remain at 800 units. This will result in a loss and is therefore an undesirable alternative. The current pricing policy should be continued.

Changes in Product Mix Sales mix is the composition of total sales broken down among various products or product lines. A change in the product mix generally results in a different breakeven point and level of profitability. Sensitivity analysis can be used to evaluate the effects on sales and profits for alternative sales mixes.

FIGURE 7.7

Sensitivity Analysis—Product Pricing

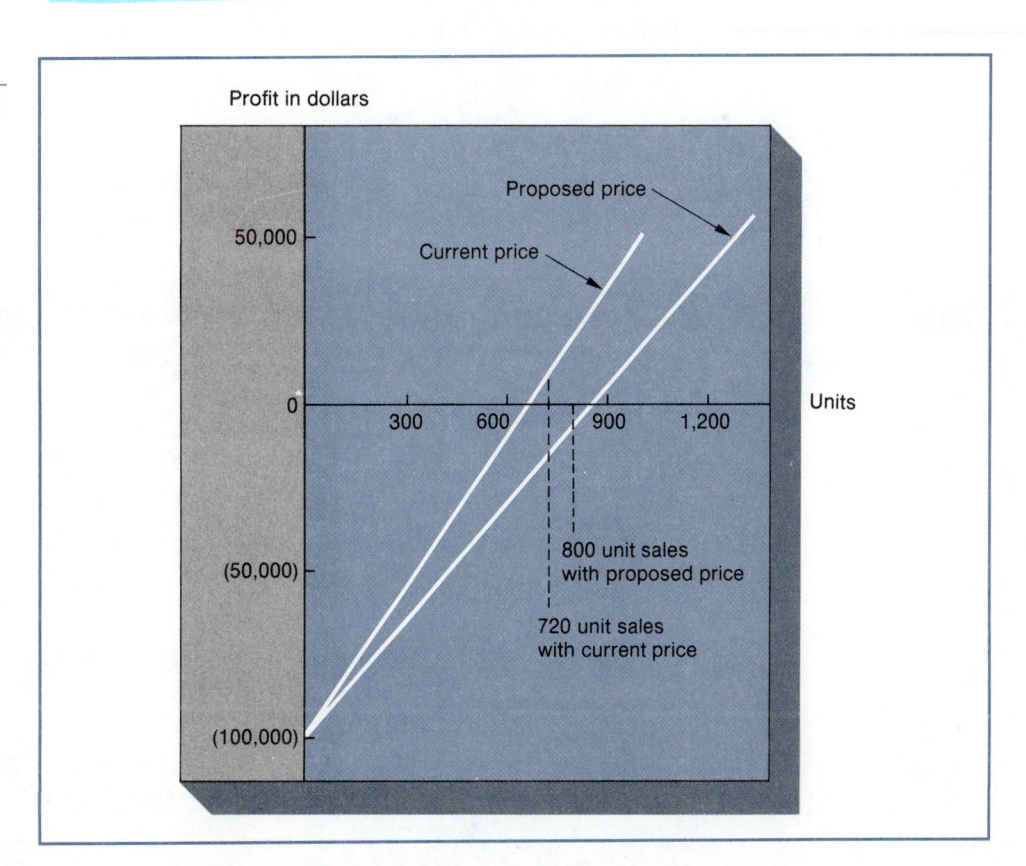

EXAMPLE

Problem

Beckhard Company has three product lines called Regular, Lite, and Draft with annual fixed costs of $280,000. Over the next year the company expects a 20 percent decrease in sales of Regular, with about half of those customers switching to Lite and half to Draft. You have collected the following information:

	Lite	Regular	Draft	
Sale price per case	$4.00	$3.00	$5.00	
Variable costs	2.20	1.80	2.50	
Contribution margin	$1.80	$1.20	$2.50	
Current data:				**Total Cases**
Sales per month (cases)	40,000	100,000	60,000	200,000
Sales ratio	20%	50%	30%	100%

What will be the effect on the breakeven point and on profits if the product mix changes as anticipated?

Solution

Figure 7.8 shows the profit line for the existing and anticipated conditions. Because the shift in product mix is from the product with the lowest contribution margin ratio to products with higher contribution margin ratios, the new breakeven point will be lower. The average contribution margin will be higher, and even though there is no change in the total cases sold, both profits and dollar sales will be higher by $19,978 and $30,000, respectively.

The computations for developing the profit lines follow:

Current Sales Mix:

Average sales price = (20% × $4.00) + (50% × $3.00) + (30% × $5.00) = $3.80
Average contribution margin = (20% × $1.80) + (50% × $1.20) + (30% × $2.50) = $1.71
Average contribution margin ratio = ($1.71 ÷ $3.80) = 45%

Breakeven point = $\frac{\$280,000}{45\%}$ = $622,222

Sales = ($4 × 40,000) + ($3 × 100,000) + ($5 × 60,000) = $760,000
Profit = [(45% × $760,000) − $280,000] = $62,000

Anticipated Sales Mix:

	Lite	Regular	Draft	Total
Revised sales (cases)	50,000	80,000	70,000	200,000
Sales ratio	25%	40%	35%	100%

Average sales price = (25% × $4.00) + (40% × $3.00) + (35% × $5.00) = $3.95
Average contribution margin = (25% × $1.80) + (40% × $1.20) + (35% × $2.50) = $1.81
Average contribution margin ratio = ($1.81 ÷ $3.95) = 45.82%

Breakeven point = $\frac{\$280,000}{45.82\%}$ = $611,086

Sales = ($4 × 50,000) + ($3 × 80,000) + ($5 × 70,000) = $790,000
Profit = [(45.82% × $790,000) − $280,000] = $81,978

FIGURE 7.8

Sensitivity Analysis—Change in Product Mix

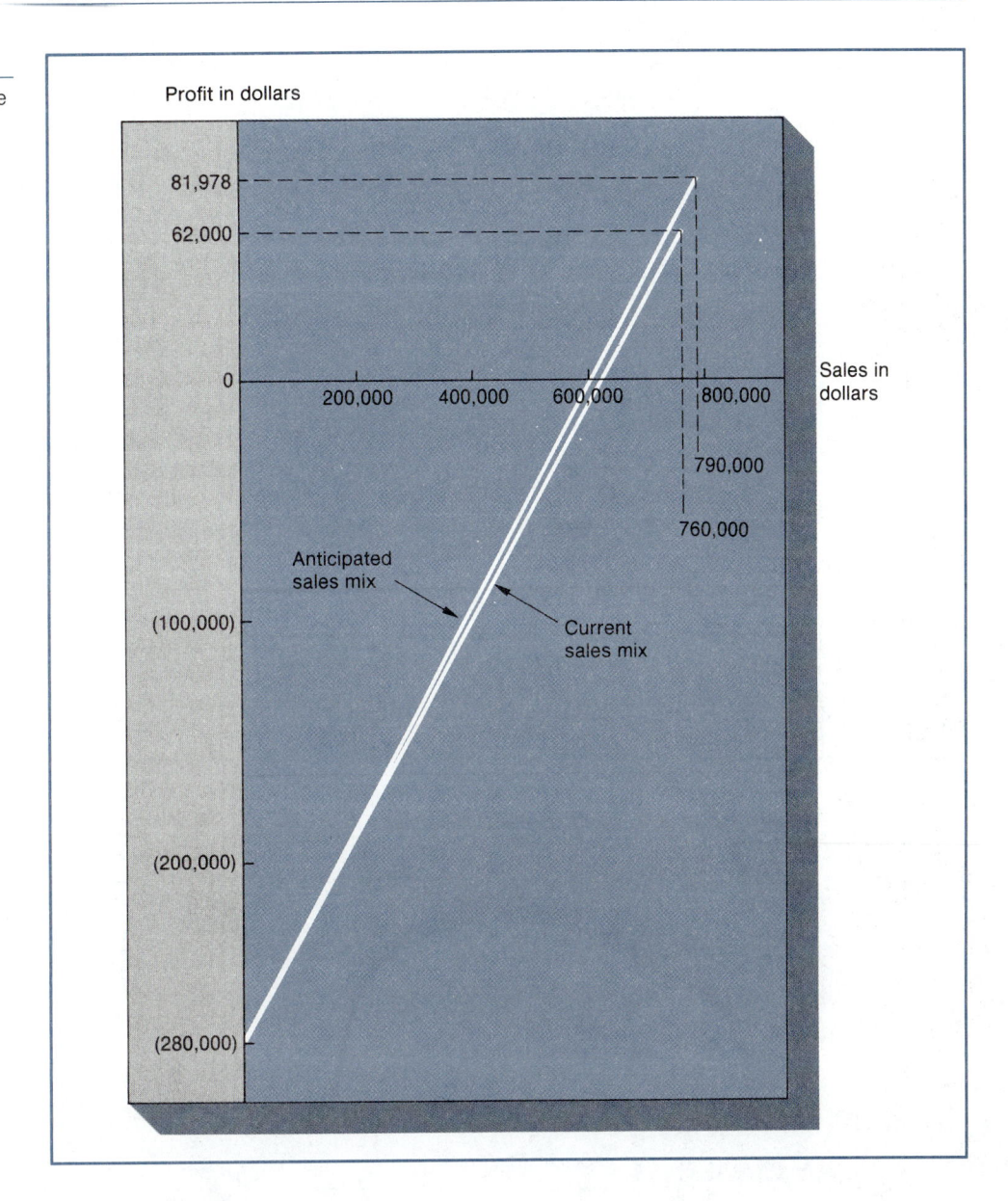

[Graph showing Profit in dollars vs Sales in dollars. Two lines labeled "Anticipated sales mix" and "Current sales mix" extend from approximately (0, -280,000) through the x-axis and up to points showing 81,978 and 62,000 profit at sales of 790,000 and 760,000 respectively. Y-axis shows values: 81,978, 62,000, 0, (100,000), (200,000), (280,000). X-axis shows: 200,000, 400,000, 600,000, 800,000.]

SUMMARY

This chapter focused on cost-volume-profit analysis, its uses, and its limitations. Cost-volume-profit analysis is a study of the relationships between costs and volume and their effect on profit. One of the most common analyses is breakeven analysis, which identifies the breakeven point. This point is the level of sales volume, specified in either units or sales dollars, at which total revenues equal total expenses and the business has neither earnings nor a loss. The equations to compute the breakeven point are as follows:

$$\text{Breakeven point in units} = \frac{\text{Fixed costs}}{\text{Sale price per unit} - \text{Variable cost per unit}}$$

$$\text{Breakeven point in sales dollars} = \frac{\text{Fixed costs}}{\text{Contribution margin ratio}}$$

Breakeven and profit-volume charts are useful in graphically illustrating the cost-volume-profit relationships. A breakeven chart contains a total revenue curve and a total cost curve. The point of their intersection identifies the breakeven point. Operations above that point result in a profit; operations below that point result in a loss. The amount of profit or loss is equal to the vertical distance between the total revenue and total cost curves. The profit-volume chart focuses on profit and its relationship to volume. A profit line is developed that is equal to the vertical distance between the total revenue and total cost curves on the breakeven chart.

Cost-volume-profit analysis is useful in providing information for a variety of decisions. Margin of safety identifies the excess of actual or budgeted sales over the breakeven point. It is the amount by which sales could decrease before losses occur. Sensitivity analysis is a "what if" analysis that examines the effect on the outcome when one or more of the input values are changed. Cost-volume-profit analysis can be used to evaluate the effect on the breakeven point or profits of changes in the input values. This is useful in evaluating potential errors in the input data, the substitution of fixed or variable costs, alternate pricing strategies, and changes in the product mix.

There are several assumptions typically used by accountants that underlie breakeven analysis. Most of the assumptions relate to the linearity of cost and revenue functions within a relevant range of activity. More sophisticated analysis using nonlinear curves is required when the assumptions are not satisfied.

SELF-STUDY PROBLEM

Even Products Company manufactures a product it calls MARKY. The following financial projections have been made.

Even Products Company
Financial Projection for Product MARKY
Year Ending December 31, 19X7

Sales (100 units at $200 a unit)		$20,000
Manufacturing cost of goods sold:		
Direct labor	$3,000	
Direct materials used	2,800	
Variable factory overhead	2,000	
Fixed factory overhead	1,000	
Total		8,800
Gross margin		$11,200
Selling expenses:		
Variable	$1,200	
Fixed	2,000	
Administrative expenses:		
Variable	1,000	
Fixed	2,000	
Total		6,200
Operating income		$ 5,000
Income taxes (40%)		2,000
Net income		$ 3,000

Required

1. How many units of MARKY must be sold to break even?
2. What would operating income be if sales increase 25 percent?
3. Compute sales at the breakeven point if fixed factory overhead increases by $3,400.

4. How many units of MARKY must be sold to realize an after-tax net income of $4,800? Assume fixed costs remain at the level shown in the preceding financial statement.

Solution to the Self-Study Problem

Requirement 1

Breakeven in units can be computed by the following equation:

$$\text{Breakeven point in units} = \frac{\text{Fixed costs}}{\text{Sale price per unit} - \text{Variable cost per unit}}$$

The fixed costs and variable costs are as follows:

Costs	Fixed	Variable
Manufacturing	$1,000	$ 7,800
Selling	2,000	1,200
Administration	2,000	1,000
Total	$5,000	$10,000

Variable cost per unit is $100 ($10,000 ÷ 100 units).

$$\text{Breakeven point} = \frac{\$5,000}{\$200 - \$100} = \underline{50 \text{ units}}$$

Requirement 2

The contribution margin ratio is 50 percent.

$$\text{Contribution margin ratio} = \frac{\text{Sales price per unit} - \text{Variable costs per unit}}{\text{Sales price per unit}}$$

$$= \frac{\$200 - \$100}{\$200} = \underline{50\%}$$

Therefore, the contribution margin will increase at a rate of $0.50 for each $1 increase in sales. Fixed costs will not change.

Operating income:
Current level	$5,000
Increased sales ($20,000 × 25% × 50%)	2,500
Total	$7,500

Requirement 3

An increase of $3,400 in fixed factory overhead brings the total fixed cost to $8,400 ($3,400 + $5,000). The contribution margin ratio computed in requirement 2 is used in the following equation to compute the breakeven point in sales dollars:

$$\text{Breakeven point in sales dollars} = \frac{\text{Fixed costs}}{\text{Contribution margin ratio}}$$

$$= \frac{\$8,400}{50\%} = \underline{\$16,800}$$

Requirement 4

To realize an after-tax profit of $4,800, operating income must be $8,000.

$$\text{Before-tax net income} = \frac{\text{After-tax net income}}{(1 - \text{Tax rate})} = \frac{\$4,800}{(1 - 0.40)} = \underline{\$8,000}$$

This amount is included in the following equation to compute the number of units that must be sold to realize an after-tax net income of $4,800.

$$\frac{\text{Fixed costs + Desired profit}}{\text{Sales price per unit - Variable costs}} = \frac{\$5,000 + \$8,000}{\$200 - \$100} = \underline{130 \text{ units}}$$

Suggested Readings

Goodman, Sam R., and Reece, James S. *Controllers' Handbook.* Homewood, Ill.: Dow-Jones Irwin, 1978.

Goulet, Peter G. "Attacking Business Decision Problems with Breakeven Analysis." *Management Aids for Small Manufacturers,* no. 234. Washington, D.C.: U.S. Small Business Administration, 1978.

Grossman, Steven, D.; Plum, Charles W.; and Welker, Robert B. "New Dimensions to the Cost-Volume-Profit Technique." *Managerial Planning* 27 (March/April 1979): 35–38

Hartl, Robert J. "The Linear Total Revenue Curve in Cost-Volume-Profit Analysis." *Management Accounting* 56 (March 1975): 49.

Sinclair, Kenneth P., and Talbott, James A. Jr. "Using Breakeven Analysis When Cost Behavior is Unknown." *Management Accounting* 68 (July, 1986): 52.

DISCUSSION QUESTIONS

Q7–1. Define *cost-volume-profit analysis*.

Q7–2. What is meant by the breakeven point?

Q7–3. What is the relationship between a breakeven chart and a profit-volume chart?

Q7–4. Assume a company has no ability to change its sales price, fixed costs, or variable costs. Is the company guaranteed a breakeven point merely by increasing sales? Explain.

Q7–5. Describe a sales mix. Why is sales mix important in cost-volume-profit analysis?

Q7–6. Describe the typical cost-volume-profit graph used in economic analysis.

Q7–7. One of the assumptions made by accountants when performing a cost-volume-profit analysis is that productivity remains constant. What will be the effect on the cost or revenue curves if this assumption is not valid?

Q7–8. One of the assumptions made by accountants when performing cost-volume-profit analysis is that all units produced are sold in the same period. What will be the effect on the analysis if this assumption is not valid?

Q7–9. Why is the relevant range an important assumption to the accountant's cost-volume-profit analysis?

CHAPTER 7: COST-VOLUME-PROFIT ANALYSIS

Q7–10. Where will an accountant generally obtain the data required for a cost-volume-profit analysis?

Q7–11. Why is before-tax net income versus after-tax net income relevant when identifying the amount of sales revenue required to achieve a desired profit level?

Q7–12. Define *margin of safety*.

Q7–13. How is the margin of safety ratio computed?

Q7–14. What is sensitivity analysis? How is it relevant to cost-volume-profit analysis?

Q7–15. Assume a change is made in the production process, substituting fixed costs for variable costs. Will the breakeven point increase or decrease? Will operating income increase or decrease? Explain.

EXERCISES

E7–1. Basic Concepts of Cost-Volume-Profit Analysis The following statements relate to cost-volume-profit analysis. Indicate whether each statement is true or false, and write a brief explanation supporting your answer.

1. Breakeven calculations have little practical value because most managers have to do better than break even.
2. In the breakeven chart in figure 7.1, total fixed costs cannot be identified.
3. If you decided to rent a truck for $3,600 a year for all mileage up to 10,000 miles and 10 cents for each additional mile, truck rental would be a semivariable cost of the user.
4. If fixed costs are $5,000 a year, variable costs are 15 cents per unit, and the selling price is 20 cents per unit, it will be necessary to sell 1,000,000 units to break even.
5. The breakeven chart in figure 7.1 indicates that there will be a profit if 6,200 units are sold by the firm and there will be a loss if only 5,800 units are sold.
6. The main purpose of cost-volume-profit analysis is to pinpoint the position at which the firm neither makes a profit nor suffers a loss.
7. Data for breakeven analysis can be taken directly from the conventionally prepared (absorption cost) income statement.
8. A successful business manager should set a goal of achieving the breakeven point in each period's operations.

E7–2. Advanced Concepts of Cost-Volume-Profit Analysis The following statements relate to several concepts of cost-volume-profit relationships. Indicate whether you agree or disagree with each statement, and give a brief explanation supporting your answer.

1. The variable cost ratio is determined by dividing sales revenue by variable costs, and the ratio is the complement of the contribution margin ratio.
2. Breakeven sales in units can be computed by dividing total dollar fixed costs by the contribution margin per unit.
3. The breakeven chart can be regarded as a dynamic analysis in the sense that total fixed costs and the relationship between variable costs and sales revenue will hold true for *any* and *all* levels of sales.
4. In applying cost-volume-profit analysis, managers should understand that an increase in fixed costs will cause both the breakeven point and the contribution margin ratio to increase.

5. The unit profit-volume graph in figure 7.2 shows that as the number of units sold increases, the fixed costs per unit will also increase.
6. A fundamental concept in cases of multiple products is that changes in the breakeven point are caused by changes in sales prices and are not affected by any changes in the sales mix of the various products.

E7–3. Concepts of Cost-Volume-Profit Analysis For each of the following numbered items, identify the item in the right-hand column that best matches the numbered item. No item in the right-hand column should be used more than once.

1. Indicates the point at which the company neither makes a profit nor incurs a loss.
2. A graphic analysis of the relationship of costs and sales revenue to profit.
3. Determined by dividing the dollar contribution margin by dollar sales revenue.
4. Determined by dividing total fixed costs by the contribution margin ratio.
5. Determined by dividing fixed costs by the contribution margin per unit.
6. The amount of total fixed costs and unit variable costs, as well as the slope of the revenue line, are meaningful only within this area.
7. When a shift in this aspect occurs, a change in profit can also be expected unless the same contribution margin ratio is realized on all products.
8. Indicates how much sales may decrease from a particular sales figure before a loss is incurred.
9. The margin of safety expressed as a percentage of sales.
10. This change will not necessarily lead to an increase in volume sufficient to increase profits.
11. A measure of the effect of price changes on volume sold.
12. Products make a favorable contribution as long as the sales revenue exceeds this.

a. Relevant range
b. Unit profit-volume graph
c. Departmentalization
d. Cost-volume-profit analysis
e. Price reduction
f. Variable cost
g. Breakeven chart
h. Breakeven analysis
i. Margin of safety ratio
j. Margin of safety
k. Contribution margin ratio
l. Sales mix
m. Breakeven point in dollars
n. Elasticity of demand
o. Breakeven point in units

E7–4. Simple Cost-Volume-Profit Analysis Calculations The following data have been determined for the Rollerberry Company for each month.

Normal plant capacity	1,500 units
Fixed costs	$10,000
Unit sales price	$16
Unit variable costs	7

Required

1. Determine the breakeven point in units. Use the contribution margin technique.
2. Determine the breakeven point in dollars, using the contribution margin technique.
3. Determine the necessary sales volume for the first quarter of the year if the target profit for the quarter is $12,000.

E7–5. Cost-Volume-Profit Analysis—Margin of Safety Considerations
Data for one month's normal operations for the Gamble Company are as follows:

Sales	$100,000
Variable costs	35,000
Fixed costs	30,000
Normal plant capacity	50,000 units

Required

1. Determine the net income for a normal month.
2. Determine the breakeven point in dollars, units, and percent of capacity.
3. If operations are at normal capacity, determine the margin of safety and the margin of safety ratio.

E7–6. Cost-Volume-Profit and Sensitivity Analysis
Refer to the data in exercise 7.5.

Required

1. Determine the new breakeven point if the sales price is reduced to $1.80 and the other data remain the same as in the original case.
2. What net profit will be earned at normal capacity if fixed costs increase by $10,000 and the other factors remain as in the original case?
3. If the contribution margin ratio changes to 60 percent, determine the effects of this change on fixed costs.
4. If the contribution margin per unit changes to $1.20, what must sales be to earn the same net income in a normal month as determined for the original data?

E7–7. Cost-Volume-Profit Analysis—Effect of Changes in Cost
The income statement for Hansen & Company was as follows for the year:

Sales		$200,000
Less: Expenses		
Variable expenses	150,000	
Fixed expenses	80,000	230,000
Net profit (loss)		$(30,000)

Required

Assume that the variable expenses will always remain the same percentage of sales.

1. What amount of sales will cause Hansen & Company to break even if fixed expenses are increased by $60,000?
2. What amount of sales will cause Hansen & Company to realize a net profit of $25,000, assuming the increase in fixed expenses?

E7–8. Basic Considerations of Cost-Volume-Profit Analysis
Kevin has recently decided to sell toy planes at a local carnival. He can buy these planes at $1.25 each and retains the option of returning all unsold planes. The cost for leasing the booth is $360. Kevin has decided to sell these planes for $2.00 each.

Required

1. Determine the number of planes Kevin must sell to break even.
2. Kevin wants to earn $150.00 to buy a video game. How many planes must be sold to reach his goal?

E7–9. Basic Procedures of Cost-Volume-Profit Analysis (CMA) The following data apply to items 1 through 7.

Siberian Ski Company recently expanded its manufacturing capacity, allowing it to produce up to 15,000 pairs of cross-country skis of the mountaineering model or the touring model. The sales department assures management that it can sell between 9,000 and 13,000 pairs of either product this year. Because the models are very similar, Siberian Ski will produce only one of the two models.

The following information was compiled by the accounting department.

	Mountaineering	Touring
Selling price per pair	$88.00	$80.00
Variable costs per pair	52.80	52.00

Fixed costs will total $369,600 if the mountaineering model is produced and $316,800 if the touring model is produced. Siberian Ski Company is subject to a 40-percent income tax rate.

Required

1. The contribution margin ratio of the touring model is
   a. 40.0%.
   b. 66.0%.
   c. 51.5%.
   d. 34.0%.
   e. some amount other than those given above.

2. If Siberian Ski Company desires an after-tax net income of $24,000, how many pairs of touring model skis will the company have to sell?
   a. 13,118
   b. 12,529
   c. 13,853
   d. 4,460
   e. Some amount other than those given above.

3. The total sales revenue at which Siberian Ski Company would make the same profit or loss regardless of the ski model it decided to produce is
   a. $880,000.
   b. $422,400.
   c. $924,000.
   d. $686,400.
   e. some amount other than those given above.

4. If the Siberian Ski Company sales department could guarantee the annual sale of 12,000 pairs of either model, Siberian would
   a. produce touring skis because they have a lower fixed cost.
   b. be indifferent about the model sold because each model has the same variable cost per unit.
   c. produce only mountaineering skis because they have a lower breakeven point.
   d. be indifferent about the model sold because both are profitable.
   e. produce mountaineering skis because they are more profitable.

5. How much would the variable cost per unit of the touring model have to change before it had the same breakeven point in units as the mountaineering model?
   a. $2.68/pair increase
   b. $4.53/pair increase
   c. $5.03/pair decrease

d. $2.97/pair decrease
e. Some amount other than those given above.
6. If the variable cost per unit of touring skis decreases by 10 percent, and the total fixed cost of touring skis increases by 10 percent, the new breakeven point will be
   a. unchanged from 11,648 pairs, because the cost changes are equal and offsetting.
   b. 10,730 pairs.
   c. 13,007 pairs.
   d. 12,812 pairs.
   e. some amount other than those given above.
7. Which of the following statements is *not* an assumption made when employing a cost-volume-profit study for decision analysis?
   a. Volume is the only relevant factor affecting costs.
   b. Changes in beginning and ending inventory levels are insignificant in amount.
   c. Sales mix is variable as total volume changes.
   d. Fixed costs are constant over the relevant volume range.
   e. Efficiency and productivity are unchanged.

E7–10. Cost-Volume-Profit Concepts and Procedures (CMA) The following income statement for Davann Company represents the operating results for the fiscal year just ended. Davann had sales of 1,800 tons of product during the current year. The manufacturing capacity of Davann's facilities is 3,000 tons of product.

Davann Company
Income Statement
Year Ending December 31

Sales	$900,000
Variable costs	
Manufacturing	$315,000
Selling	180,000
Total variable costs	$495,000
Contribution margin	$405,000
Fixed costs	
Manufacturing	$ 90,000
Selling	112,500
Administration	45,000
Total fixed costs	$247,500
Net income before income taxes	$157,500
Income taxes (40%)	63,000
Net income after income taxes	$ 94,500

Required

1. The breakeven volume in tons of product for the year was
   a. 420 tons.
   b. 1,100 tons.
   c. 495 tons.
   d. 550 tons.
   e. some amount other than those shown above.
2. If the sales volume is estimated to be 2,100 tons in the next year, and if the prices and costs stay at the same levels and amounts next year, the after-tax net income that Davann can expect next year is
   a. $135,000.
   b. $110,250.

c. $283,500.
d. $184,500.
e. some amount other than those shown above.

3. Davann has a potential foreign customer who has offered to buy 1,500 tons of product at $450 per ton. Assume that all of Davann's costs would be at the same levels and rates as last year. What net income after taxes would Davann make if it took this order and rejected some business from regular customers so as not to exceed capacity?
   a. $297,500
   b. $252,000
   c. $211,500
   d. $256,500
   e. Some amount other than those shown above.

4. Davann plans to market its product in a new territory. Davann estimates that an advertising and promotion program costing $61,500 annually would need to be undertaken for the next two or three years. In addition, a $25 per ton sales commission over and above the current commission to the sales force in the new territory would be required. How many tons would have to be sold in the new territory to maintain Davann's current after-tax income of $94,500?
   a. 307.5 tons
   b. 1,095.0 tons
   c. 273.333 tons
   d. 1,545.0 tons
   e. Some amount other than those shown above.

5. Davann is considering replacing a labor-intensive process with an automatic machine. This would result in an increase of $58,500 annually in fixed manufacturing costs. The variable manufacturing costs would decrease by $25 per ton. The new breakeven volume in tons would be
   a. 990 tons.
   b. 1,224 tons.
   c. 1,854 tons.
   d. 612 tons.
   e. some amount other than those shown above.

6. Ignore the facts presented in item 5. Now assume that Davann estimates that the per-ton selling price would decline 10 percent next year. Variable costs would increase $40 per ton and fixed costs would not change. What sales volume in dollars would be required to earn an after-tax net income of $94,500 next year?
   a. $1,140,000
   b. $825,000
   c. $1,500,000
   d. $1,350,000
   e. Some amount other than those shown above.

E7-11. Cost-Volume-Profit Sensitivity Analysis (PC Analysis) The Evans Crouton Company has determined the following budget data for next year:

Sales	$34,000,000
Fixed costs	21,000,000
Variable costs	11,500,000

Required

Determine the expected profit for the Evans Crouton Company given the following independent changes from budget. Compute your results using a PC spreadsheet, and print a copy of each output.

1. A 10% increase in sales revenue (due to sales price increase)
2. A 6% increase in fixed costs
3. A 10% increase in variable costs
4. An 8% decrease in sales revenue
5. A 4% decrease in fixed costs
6. A 5% increase in sales revenue and a 10% increase in fixed costs
7. A 5% decrease in fixed costs and a 5% increase in variable costs
8. A 6% increase in all three variables

E7–12. Cost-Volume-Profit Analysis (PC Analysis)
Lynette Companies Incorporated (LCI) reported the following cost-revenue data for the past year for product x.

Sales price	$8.00
Fixed costs	$36,000
Variable cost per unit	$5.50

Required

1. Using a PC spreadsheet and the preceding information, set up a worksheet that will compute the breakeven point in units and dollars. Print a copy of your result.
2. Assume the following independent changes from last year's results, and compute the new breakeven sales in units and dollars. After each computation, print a copy of your results.
    a. Sales price increases $0.50.
    b. Fixed expenses increase by $5,000.
    c. Variable costs increase $0.25.

PROBLEMS

P7–1. Basic Cost-Volume-Profit Analysis
Hickman Company produces a single product for which the following data have been determined:

Unit sales price	$24.00
Unit variable cost	$18.00
Annual fixed costs	$48,000

Required

Consider each of the following situations to be independent of the others.

1. Determine the contribution margin for the product, per unit and as a ratio.
2. Using the contribution margin technique, determine breakeven sales for a year in units and in dollars.
3. Hickman estimates that sales will increase by $40,000 during the next year. If other relationships remain the same, by how much should the contribution margin increase? What effect should the sales increase have on net income?
4. Last year Hickman Company sold 10,500 units. Market research indicates that a 5-percent cut in selling price accompanied by a $10,000 addition in advertising would result in a 40-percent increase in unit sales. Should the action suggested by marketing be undertaken? Prepare contribution income statements for last year and for the proposed change to support your conclusion.
5. Assume last year's sales were 10,500 units. An alternative to the price reduction is to leave the price as is and increase sales commissions by $1.00 per unit, accompanied by some increase in advertising. Marketing research indicates sales may be increased by

40 percent because of these changes. If profits were maintained at last year's level, by how much could advertising be increased?

6. Assume that sales for this year are running at last year's level. A Canadian customer wants to purchase 2,500 units at a special price. If Hickman wants to double current profits, what price must be quoted to the Canadian customer?

P7–2. Cost-Volume-Profit Analysis—Sales Mix Considerations

The Margets Company sells three products. Budgeted sales by product and in total are as follows for one month:

	Lino	Malo	Nema	Total
Percent of total sales	25%	40%	35%	100%
Sales	$40,000	$64,000	$56,000	$160,000
Less: Variable expense	24,000	41,600	22,400	88,000
Contribution margin	$16,000	$22,400	$33,600	$ 72,000
Contribution margin ratio	40%	35%	60%	45%
Less: Fixed expenses				50,700
Net income				$ 21,300

$$\text{Breakeven sales} = \frac{\$50,700}{0.45} = \$112,667$$

Assume that actual sales for July are Lino—$48,000, Malo—$96,000, and Nema—$16,000.

Required

1. Prepare an income statement for July based on actual data. Use the contribution format shown in the budget. Assume the individual product variable cost relationship to sales is the same as budgeted and that the fixed costs are as budgeted.
2. Determine breakeven sales based on actual results.
3. Considering Margets met the $160,000 sales budget for July, explain why net income and breakeven sales are different from the budget.

P7–3, Cost-Volume-Profit Analysis—Breakeven and Profit Considerations

You have observed that many of your neighbors have joined the home gardening trend. You have also noticed that the soil in your area is very high in clay content and is so compact that many neighbors get poor plant growth and, as a result, a poor yield. The costs of seed, care, fertilizing, and watering hardly seem justified.

You get a bright idea that you could assist your neighbors and make some money to help finance your education if you invest in a power soil aerator and do custom soil-conditioning work during the summer. The power aerator costs $450. You estimate that a $25 charge for each garden-conditioning job is reasonable (for a typical-size garden spot). You estimate that fuel for the aerator and other supplies will cost $3 for each garden and that you can do six gardens each day.

Required

1. Determine how many gardens you will need to aerate to break even. How many days' work will be required?
2. You estimate that if you can clear $5,000 during the summer, you can cover your costs of attending school next year, since you have a scholarship to finance part of the costs. If you can earn that much, you wouldn't need support from your father. How many garden jobs will you need to do to clear $5,000? How many days will it take to do this?

3. Suppose your estimate of $25 to do each garden is 10 percent high (even though professional yard-care firms charge $35) for a new operation getting established and that your estimate of fuel and other costs is 25 percent low. You believe that your estimate of the cost of equipment is close because you have estimated a 15-percent increase in price above that charged for similar equipment last year. What effect will these changes in estimates have on your answers to requirements 1 and 2?

4. Identify any factors of cost or revenue that you haven't taken into account previously (focus on items, not amounts). Describe how you would obtain information about dollar amounts for these factors.

P7–4. Cost-Volume-Profit Analysis and Sensitivity Analysis Romney Produce Company operates four warehouses in the southwestern part of the United States. It has recently provided you with the following company budget data for next year:

Sales	$25,000,000
Fixed expenses	15,500,000
Variable expenses	8,500,000

Required

Determine from the preceding data the expected profit for each of the following changes, considering each change independently:

1. A 15% increase in fixed costs
2. A 10% increase in total contribution margin (sales remain constant)
3. An 8% increase in total sales
4. An 8% decrease in fixed costs
5. A 10% decrease in total contribution margin (sales remain constant)
6. A 15% decrease in total sales
7. A 5% increase in total sales and 10% increase in fixed costs
8. A 10% decrease in variable costs and 10% increase in fixed costs

P7–5. Cost-Volume-Profit Analysis and Sensitivity Analysis The Barlow Company operates a chain of women's apparel boutiques. This chain sells a variety of clothing packs, including blouses, scarves, and jewelry pins, for $40 per pack. Up to this point, Barlow Company has been relatively successful in this area of sales and is presently evaluating the possibility of opening up another store that would possess the following revenue and expense relationships:

	Per Pack
Selling price	$40.00
Invoice cost of a pack	$32.00
Sales commissions	2.00
	$34.00

Annual fixed expenses:

Rent	12,400
Salaries	110,000
Utilities	9,500
Other	23,500
	$155,400

Required

Consider each question independently.

1. What is the annual breakeven point in dollars and units?
2. If 30,000 packs were sold, what would be the store's net income (loss)?
3. If sales commissions were increased another 50¢ per pack, what would be the store's beakeven point in dollars and units?
4. If, instead of increasing sales commissions, fixed salaries were increased by $24,000, what would be the annual breakeven point in dollars and units? Is this alternative desirable over the alternative described in requirement 3?
5. Now suppose that in addition to the regular $2.00 commission per pack, the store manager is paid 75¢ for each pack sold in excess of the breakeven point. What would be the store's net income if 40,000 packs were sold?

P7–6. Cost-Volume-Profit Analysis Concepts (CMA) The SAB Company uses a profit-volume graph similar to the one shown here to represent the cost-volume-profit relationships of its operations. The vertical (y-axis) is the profit in dollars and the horizontal (x-axis) is the volume in units. The diagonal line is the contribution margin line.

Required

1. Point A on the profit-volume graph represents
   a. the point at which fixed costs equal sales.
   b. the point at which fixed costs equal variable costs.
   c. a volume level of zero units.
   d. the point at which total costs equal total sales.
   e. the point at which the rate of contribution margin increases.
2. The vertical distance from the dotted line to the contribution margin line denoted as B on the profit-volume graph represents
   a. the total contribution margin.
   b. the contribution margin per unit.
   c. the contribution margin rate.
   d. total sales.
   e. the sum of the variable and fixed costs.

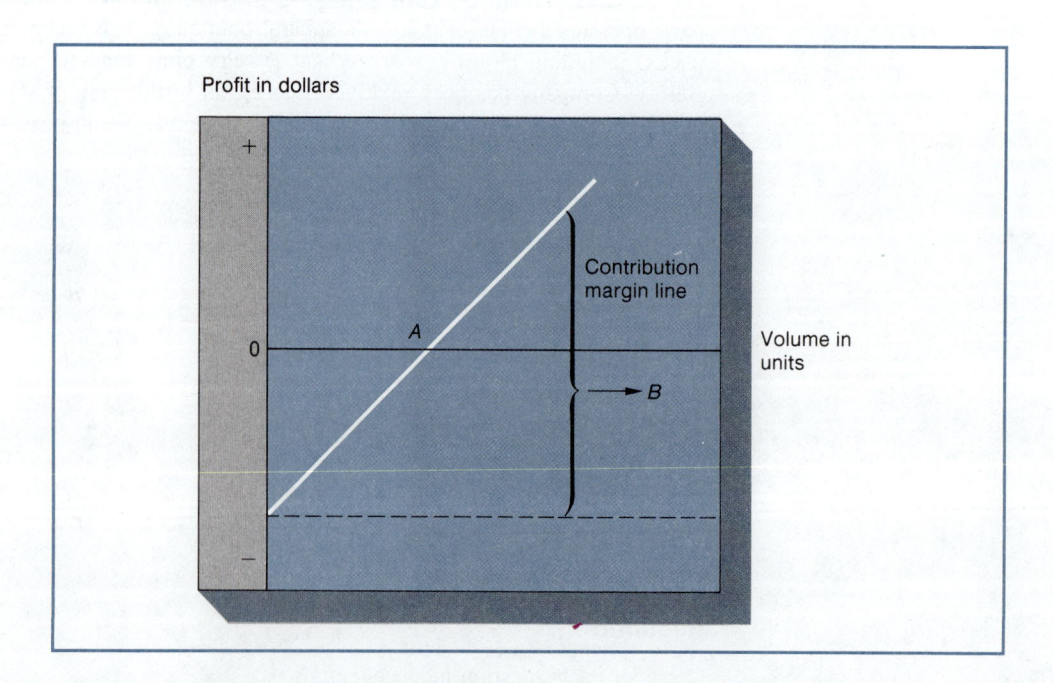

3. If SAB Company's fixed cost were to increase,
   a. the contribution margin line would shift upward parallel to the present line.
   b. the contribution margin line would shift downward parallel to the present line.
   c. the slope of the contribution margin line would be more pronounced (steeper).
   d. the slope of the contribution margin line would be less pronounced (flatter).
   e. the contribution margin line would coincide with the present contribution margin line.
4. If SAB Company's variable costs per unit were to increase but its unit selling price stayed constant,
   a. the contribution margin line would shift upward parallel to the present line.
   b. the contribution margin line would shift downward parallel to the present line.
   c. the slope of the contribution margin line would be more pronounced (steeper).
   d. the slope of the contribution margin line would be less pronounced (flatter).
   e. the slope of the contribution margin line probably would change, but how it would change is not determinable.
5. If SAB Company decided to increase its unit selling price to exactly offset the increase in the variable cost per unit,
   a. the contribution margin line would shift upward parallel to the present line.
   b. the contribution margin line would shift downward parallel to the present line.
   c. the slope of the contribution margin line would be more pronounced (steeper).
   d. the slope of the contribution margin line would be less pronounced (flatter).
   e. the contribution margin line would coincide with the present contribution margin line.

P7-7. Cost-Volume-Profit and Sensitivity Analysis (CMA) Pawnee Company's normal operating capacity is 50,000 units of a single product. Sales and production for the current year totaled 40,000 units at an average price of $20 per unit. Variable manufacturing costs were $8 per unit, and variable marketing costs were $4 per unit sold. Fixed costs were incurred uniformly throughout the year and amounted to $188,000 for manufacturing and $64,000 for marketing. There was no year-end work-in-process inventory.

Required

1. Determine Pawnee's breakeven point in sales dollars for the current year.
2. If Pawnee is subject to an income tax rate of 30 percent, determine the number of units required to be sold in the current year to earn an after-tax net income of $126,000.
3. Pawnee's variable manufacturing costs are expected to increase 10 percent in the coming year. Determine Pawnee's breakeven point in sales dollars for the coming year.
4. If Pawnee's variable manufacturing costs do increase 10 percent, determine the selling price that would yield Pawnee the same contribution margin ratio in the coming year.

P7-8. Concepts and Procedures of Cost-Volume-Profit Analysis (CPA) Each of the following short cases (1 through 4) are independent of each other. Answer the questions indicated.

1. Pitt Company is considering a proposal to replace existing machinery used for the manufacture of product A. The new machines are expected to result in increased annual fixed costs of $120,000; however, variable costs should decrease by 20 percent due to a reduction in direct-labor hours and more efficient usage of direct materials. Before this

change was under consideration, Pitt had budgeted product A sales and costs for a year as follows:

Sales	$2,000,000
Variable costs	70% of sales
Fixed costs	$400,000

Assuming that Pitt implemented the proposal by January 1, what would be the increase in budgeted operating profit for product A for the year?

2. Lindsay Company reported the following results from sales of 5,000 units of product A for the month of June:

Sales	$200,000
Variable costs	120,000
Fixed costs	60,000
Operating income	20,000

Assume that Lindsay increases the selling price of product A by 10 percent on July 1. How many units of product A would have to be sold in July to generate an operating income of $20,000?

3. Birney Company is planning its advertising campaign for the year and has prepared the following budget data based on a zero advertising expenditure:

Normal plant capacity	200,000 units
Sales	150,000 units
Selling price	$25.00 per unit
Variable manufacturing costs	$15.00 per unit
Fixed costs:	
Manufacturing	$800,000
Selling and administrative	$700,000

An advertising agency claims that an aggressive advertising campaign would enable Birney to increase its unit sales by 20 percent. What is the maximum amount that Birney can pay for advertising and obtain an operating profit of $200,000?

4. In planning its operations for the year based on a sales forecast of $6,000,000, Wallace Incorporated prepared the following estimated data:

	Costs and Expenses	
	Variable	Fixed
Direct materials	$1,600,000	
Direct labor	1,400,000	
Factory overhead	600,000	$ 900,000
Selling expenses	240,000	$ 360,000
Administrative expenses	60,000	140,000
	$3,900,000	$1,400,000

What would be the amount of sales dollars at the breakeven point?

P7–9. Cost-Volume-Profit Analysis—Comprehensive Analysis (CMA)

The following data are used in requirements 1 through 3. Refer to those data for each question asked.

Pralina Products Company is a regional firm with three major product lines—cereals, breakfast bars, and dog food. The income statement for the year ending April 30 is shown below. The statement was prepared by product line using full absorption costing. Explanatory data related to the items presented in the income statement follow.

CHAPTER 7: COST-VOLUME-PROFIT ANALYSIS 265

Pralina Products Company
Income Statement
Year Ending April 30
(000 omitted)

	Cereals	Breakfast Bars	Dog Food	Total
Sales in pounds	2,000	500	500	3,000
Revenue from sales	$1,000	$400	$200	$1,600
Cost of sales				
Raw materials	$ 330	$160	$100	$ 590
Direct labor	90	40	20	150
Factory overhead	108	48	24	180
Total cost of sales	$ 528	$248	$144	$ 920
Gross margin	$ 472	$152	$ 56	$ 680
Operating expenses				
Selling expenses				
Advertising	$ 50	$ 30	$ 20	$ 100
Commissions	50	40	20	110
Salaries and related benefits	30	20	10	60
Total selling expenses	$ 130	$ 90	$ 50	$ 270
General and administrative expenses				
Licenses	$ 50	$ 20	$ 15	$ 85
Salaries and related benefits	60	25	15	100
Total general and administrative expenses	$ 110	$ 45	$ 30	$ 185
Total operating expenses	$ 240	$135	$ 80	$ 455
Operating income before taxes	$ 232	$ 17	($ 24)	$ 225

1. *Cost of sales.* The company's inventories of raw materials and finished products do not vary significantly from year to year. The inventories at April 30 this year were essentially identical to those at April 30 last year.

   Factory overhead was applied to products at 120 percent of direct-labor dollars. The factory overhead costs for the fiscal year were as follows:

Variable indirect labor and supplies	$ 15,000
Variable employee benefits on factory labor	30,000
Supervisory salaries and related benefits	35,000
Plant occupancy costs	100,000
	$180,000

   There was no overapplied or underapplied overhead at year-end.

2. *Advertising.* The company has been unable to determine any direct causal relationship between the level of sales volume and the level of advertising expenditures. However, because management believes advertising is necessary, an annual advertising program is implemented for each product line. Each product line is advertised independently of the others.

3. *Commissions.* Sales commissions are paid to the sales force at the rates of 5 percent on the cereals and 10 percent on the breakfast bars and dog food.

4. *Licenses.* Various licenses are required for each product line. These are renewed annually for each product line.

5. *Salaries and related benefits.* Sales and general and administrative personnel devote time and effort to all product lines. Their salaries and wages are allocated on the basis of management's estimates of time spent on each product line.

Required

1. The controller of Pralina Products Company has recommended that the company do a cost-volume-profit analysis of its operations. As a first step, the controller has requested that you prepare a revised income statement for Pralina Products Company, employing a product contribution margin format that will be useful in cost-volume-profit analysis. The statement should show the profit contribution for each product line and the net income before taxes for the company as a whole.
2. What effect, if any, would there be on net income before taxes determined in requirement 1 if the inventories as of April 30 this year had increased significantly over the inventory levels of April 30 last year? Explain your answer.
3. The controller of Pralina Products Company is going to prepare a report that she will present to the other members of top management explaining cost-volume-profit analysis. Identify and explain the following points that the controller should include in the report.
   a. The advantages that cost-volume-profit analysis can provide to a company.
   b. The difficulties Pralina Products Company could experience in the calculations involved in cost-volume-profit analysis.
   c. The dangers that Pralina Products Company should be aware of in using the information derived from the cost-volume-profit analysis.

P7–10. Spreadsheet Application for Cost-Volume-Profit Analysis Hicks Incorporated produces a single product for which the following data have been determined:

Unit sales price	$24.00
Unit variable cost	$18.00
Annual fixed costs	$48,000

Required

1. Use a computerized spreadsheet application such as Lotus or Visicalc to prepare a cost-volume-profit analysis. The worksheet should be set up so that by entering the unit sales price, unit variable cost, and annual fixed cost, the program automatically will compute (a) breakeven points in units and (b) breakeven points in sales dollars. Enter the preceding data, and print out the results.
2. Hicks Incorporated is also considering a 5-percent cut in selling price and a $10,000 addition to the advertising budget. What is the effect on the breakeven point if these changes are made? Print out the modified results.
3. Hicks Incorporated is also considering a change in the production process that would replace direct-labor workers with a new machine. Referring back to the original data, if this change is made, variable costs will decrease by $3.00 per unit and fixed costs will increase by $8,000 per year. What is the effect on the breakeven point if these changes are made? Once again, print out the result.

Part Three

COST DETERMINATION

A major part of cost accounting is accumulating manufacturing costs and identifying them with the units produced. This process is called cost determination or cost finding and is the topic covered in chapters 8 through 14.

Manufacturing processes can be broadly classified into two types—job order and process costing. Separate accounting procedures are required for each manufacturing process. Special accounting procedures are also required for processes that produce more than one product. These products are called joint products and may be subdivided into main products, by-products, scrap, and waste.

Manufacturing costs can also be broken down into the separate elements of material, labor, and overhead, which provides management with the cost information necessary to effectively control operations.

Chapter 8

Job-Order Cost Systems

Outline

MANUFACTURING ACCOUNTING SYSTEMS
Chart of Accounts
   Control Accounts and Subsidiary Ledgers
   Clearing Accounts
   Example of Payroll Summary
Flow of Costs Through the Manufacturing Accounts
Financial Statements
JOB-ORDER VERSUS PROCESS COST SYSTEMS
JOB-ORDER COST SYSTEMS—MANUFACTURING FIRMS
Job-Order Cost Sheet
Flow of Costs in Job-Order Cost System
   Transferring Raw Materials to Work in Process
   Recording Labor to Work in Process
   Allocating Factory Overhead to Work in Process
   Balance Between Subsidiary Ledger and General Ledger
   Transferring Finished Goods from Work in Process
JOB-ORDER COST SYSTEMS—SERVICE ORGANIZATIONS
COMPLICATIONS TO THE MANUFACTURING ACCOUNTING SYSTEM
Multiple Work in Process Accounts
Multiple Departments
Departmental Overhead Accounts and Rates
Overhead Applied Account
Split Ledger System
Reporting for Partially Completed Jobs
Revenue Recognition for Partially Completed Jobs
SUMMARY
SELF-STUDY PROBLEM
SUGGESTED READINGS
DISCUSSION QUESTIONS
EXERCISES
PROBLEMS
CASE

A primary objective of cost accounting is to provide managers with information that will assist them in operating a business successfully. The management process includes activities such as setting objectives and formulating a plan of operation, implementing the plan and monitoring operating activity on a day-to-day basis, and evaluating the results to see if the objectives of the organization are being accomplished. Chapters 1 through 7 have dealt mainly with planning business operations. Cost analysis, budgeting, flexible budgeting, and cost-volume-profit analysis are important topics in planning business activities.

This chapter and several that follow focus on the cost accounting aspects of implementing the plan and measuring the results of operations, which is the next phase of the management cycle. These activities are typically referred to as *cost determination* or *cost finding*. The objective of cost finding is to account for the costs associated with producing a good or providing a service. In a manufacturing environment, the end object is the manufacturing cost per unit of finished product. In a service organization, such as a CPA firm, the objective is to determine the costs associated with each client project. A cost per project or a cost per client is necessary when evaluating project profitability for management control and for billing and collection purposes. It is also useful in the cost analysis function to evaluate efficiency and to make pricing and budgeting decisions.

Two different accounting systems have been developed to account for two different types of processes. One is called a *job-order accounting system* and the other is called a *process cost accounting system*. This chapter distinguishes between these two types of accounting systems, identifies the criteria to be used in selecting one of them, and describes the job-order cost accounting system in detail.

Manufacturing processes will be used initially to introduce the difference between job-order and process costing and to illustrate a job-order cost system. The example of a CPA firm will then be used to illustrate the application of these concepts to service organizations. After completing this chapter, you should be able to:

1. explain the flow of costs through the accounts of a manufacturing organization.
2. distinguish between job-order and process cost accounting systems.
3. identify manufacturing processes that are applicable to a job-order cost system.
4. describe the accounting procedures followed in a job-order cost system.
5. distinguish between control accounts and clearing accounts, and properly use a subsidiary ledger for the work-in-process account of a job-order cost system.
6. prepare journal entries for the administrative office and factory under a split-ledger accounting system.

MANUFACTURING ACCOUNTING SYSTEMS

Manufacturing organizations buy raw materials, labor, and other required manufacturing components and convert them into finished products. The manufacturing process complicates the accounting process because of the additional inventories for raw materials and work in process and because of the need to account for the product costs as the units flow through the production process. Financial statements must be adjusted to reflect the results of the manufacturing process and the additional inventories.

Journalizing the flow of costs through the manufacturing process and preparing a cost-of-goods-manufactured statement introduces the cost-finding phase of cost accounting. The chart of accounts used by a manufacturing organization is an integral part of the accounting system.

Chart of Accounts

Every company must have a **chart of accounts** that lists all the accounts used by a company in its accounting system. A coding system is usually developed, and each account is given a unique number. An account may be referred to by its name (for example, raw materials inventory) or by its number (for example, #115). A common numbering system identifies assets with numbers between 100 and 199, liabilities with numbers between 200 and 249, and owner's equity with numbers between 250 and 299. Similar groups of numbers are identified for revenues and the different types of expenses.

Figure 8.1 contains a chart of accounts for a manufacturing organization. Accounts that are unique to manufacturing enterprises have a letter *a* by the account number. Notice that the major differences are in the additional inventories shown as current assets, factory machinery and equipment, and overhead accounts.

The number of accounts required to accumulate manufacturing costs and compute a unit cost is very small. However, external reporting is only one objective of cost accounting. Additional accounts and elaborate coding structures may be developed to accumulate useful information for management decisions. Further refinement and additional sophistication are for the benefit of the users, who should be heavily involved in developing the system.

Several refinements and additional accounts will be discussed in the latter sections of this chapter. Keep in mind that the chart of accounts will most likely be unique to each company. The type of business organization, products manufactured, services rendered, organizational structure, and the decision-making process are all important factors in determining the appropriate accounts for a company.

Control Accounts and Subsidiary Ledgers All of the accounts listed in the chart of accounts are control accounts. A **control account** is a summary account in the general ledger that is supported in detail by individual accounts in a subsidiary ledger. Therefore, a **subsidiary ledger** provides a detailed breakdown of the contents of a control account.

Financial accounting uses control accounts extensively. For example, accounts receivable is a control account used to record the sale of merchandise on account. Any time merchandise is sold on account the debit is to accounts receivable, and any collections on account are recorded as credits to accounts receivable. Balances owed by any individual customer are not reflected in the control account. A subsidiary ledger for accounts receivable is required to keep track of individual customer balances that make up the total accounts receivable balance.

Control accounts and subsidiary ledgers are also used extensively in cost accounting. Raw materials inventory, work-in-process inventory, and finished-goods inventory, are all control accounts. A subsidiary ledger is required for each inventory account to keep track of the items in inventory and the costs associated with each item. If the accounting is performed properly, the total cost of the items in the subsidiary ledger will equal the balance in the inventory control account.

The factory overhead account is also a control account. A subsidiary ledger is generally maintained for factory overhead to break down the total overhead cost into subcategories that are meaningful to management for planning and control. Remember that factory overhead includes all manufacturing costs other than direct material and direct labor. This includes several different kinds of costs, some of which will be fixed, some variable, and some semivariable. If overhead costs are unusually high, management will be at a loss to know what went wrong without a meaningful cost breakdown.

Figure 8.2 shows the detailed coding system for the factory overhead subsidiary ledger. The control account is number 400. The subsidiary ledger accounts are also a 400

FIGURE 8.1 Typical Chart of Accounts for a Manufacturing Organization

Balance Sheet Accounts (100–299)

Assets (100–199)
Current Assets (100–129)
- 100 Cash in bank
- 104 Marketable securities
- 106 Accounts receivable
- 107 Allowance for doubtful accounts
- 110 Notes receivable
- 115[a] Raw-materials inventory
- 120[a] Work-in-process inventory
- 125[a] Finished-goods inventory
- 129 Prepaid expenses

Investments (130–139)
- 130 Stock investments
- 135 Bond investments

Property, Plant, and Equipment (140–169)
- 140 Land
- 142 Buildings
- 143 Accumulated depreciation—buildings
- 145[a] Factory equipment
- 146[a] Accumulated depreciation—factory equipment
- 150 Office furniture and fixtures
- 151 Accumulated depreciation—office furniture and fixtures

Intangible Assets (170–179)
- 170 Goodwill
- 175 Patents
- 178 Franchise and licenses

Other Assets (180–199)

Liabilities and Owners' Equity (200–299)
Current Liabilities (200–239)
- 200 Accounts payable
- 205 Notes payable
- 210 Accrued payroll
- 215 Other accrued liabilities
- 220 Payroll taxes payable
- 225 Current portion of long-term debt
- 230 Dividends payable

Long-Term Liabilities (240–249)
- 240 Bonds payable
- 245 Other long-term debt
- 248 Deferred income tax payable

Capital (250–299)
- 250 Common stock
- 260 Additional paid-in capital
- 270 Retained earnings
- 275 Treasury stock

Income Statement Accounts (300–899)

Sales (300–349)
- 300 Sales revenue
- 310 Sales returns and allowances
- 320 Sales discounts

Cost of Goods Sold (350–399)
- 350 Cost of goods sold

Factory Overhead (400–499)
- 400[a] Factory overhead

Marketing Expenses (500–599)
- 500 Sales supervision salaries
- 510 Sales employees salaries
- 520 Freight out
- 530 Employer payroll taxes on marketing salaries
- 540 Supplies
- 550 Utilities
- 560 Telephone
- 570 Postage
- 580 Travel
- 590 Advertising

Administrative Expenses (600–699)
- 600 Administrative salaries
- 605 Administrative clerical salaries
- 610 Employer payroll taxes on administrative salaries
- 620 Supplies
- 630 Light and power
- 640 Telephone
- 650 Postage
- 660 Insurance
- 670 Legal and accounting
- 680 Donations
- 690 Uncollectible accounts receivable

Other Expenses (700–799)
- 710 Interest
- 720 Other losses

Other Income (800–899)
- 800 Investment income
- 810 Rental income
- 820 Other gains

[a]Indicates accounts unique to a manufacturing enterprise.

FIGURE 8.2

Subsidiary Ledger for Factory Overhead

Factory Overhead	
400	Factory-overhead control
400.1	Indirect materials
400.2	Indirect labor
400.3	Freight in
400.4	Overtime premium
400.5	Employer's payroll taxes (factory wages)
400.6	Fuel—factory
400.7	Light and power
400.8	Telephone and telegraph
400.9	Defective work
400.10	Insurance expense
400.11	Depreciation expense—buildings
400.12	Depreciation expense—machinery and equipment
400.13	Repairs and maintenance of building and equipment
400.14	Rent of equipment
400.15	Property tax
400.16	Amortization of patents on company products

number, but they are differentiated by a decimal number. For example, indirect materials are identified with a .1 decimal number.

Clearing Accounts A **clearing account** facilitates the accounting process. Generally a clearing account is used to hold cost data until they can be transferred or distributed to other accounts. Clearing accounts may or may not be shown in the chart of accounts.

The income summary account used in financial accounting to close revenue and expense accounts into owners' capital or retained earnings is an example of a clearing account. The net income for the accounting period is recorded in the income summary account as the revenue and expense accounts are closed. This clearing account holds the net income data until they are distributed to the owners' capital accounts (for a partnership) or transferred to retained earnings (for a corporation).

Factory overhead is an example of a clearing account for a manufacturing organization. Actual indirect manufacturing costs (manufacturing costs excluding direct costs) are recorded as debits in the factory overhead account. Then they are transferred into work in process by crediting the factory overhead account using the factory overhead rate. Thus the factory overhead account holds the indirect manufacturing costs until they are allocated to work in process and distributed to specific units of production.

Occasionally a clearing account is used for payroll costs and costs associated with major pieces of equipment. In both cases the concept is the same—an account is needed to hold cost data until a detailed analysis can be performed to determine the amount of direct cost that should be assigned to work in process and the amount of indirect cost that should be assigned to factory overhead.

Example of Payroll Summary Auxiliary Maintenance has a group of employees who spend some time as direct laborers and some time as indirect laborers. Several days are required after the end of the pay period to analyze the time cards and break down the amount of time spent in each area. A Payroll Summary account holds the payroll costs until the analysis is complete.

Assuming the payroll for the current period is $12,500, the following entry would record the cash payment to employees. (Payroll taxes are ignored to highlight the payroll summary account.)

Payroll summary	12,500	
Cash		12,500

Entry to record payroll payment to employees.

The time card analysis reveals that $10,000 was for work classified as direct labor and $2,500 was for indirect labor. The following entry transfers the direct labor into work in process and the indirect labor into factory overhead.

Work-in-process inventory	10,000	
Factory overhead	2,500	
Payroll summary		12,500

Entry to record payroll distribution.

Flow of Costs through the Manufacturing Accounts

The **cost cycle** refers to the steps taken in tracing the flow of manufacturing costs through the accounts. The objective of the cost cycle is to systematically accumulate the cost of material, labor, and factory overhead incurred in producing a finished product. When the product is sold, the production costs are expensed as cost of goods sold. The sale of the product provides funds for the acquisition of raw materials and other inputs needed for the production process, and the cycle is repeated.

Inventory accounts for raw materials, work in process, and finished goods are used to account for the *flow of costs* as the units being produced flow through the production process. These accounts are descriptive of the activity or process that occurs. Figure 8.3 summarizes the flow of the costs through the production process.

An example for Marko Plastics Company will illustrate the journal entries required to account for the manufacturing process. At the beginning of January 19X2, Marko Plastics Company had a balance in raw-materials inventory of $22,000. The work-in-process inventory had a balance of $34,000, and there was $18,000 of finished goods on hand. During January, $57,000 of raw materials were purchased, part paid in cash and part paid on account. The journal entry to record these purchases is as follows:

a.	Raw-materials inventory	57,000	
	Cash		11,400
	Accounts payable		45,600

Record purchases of raw materials

The manufacturing supervisor requested $63,000 of raw materials for use in the production process during January. Of this amount, $7,500 could not be traced to individual products. The journal entry transfers the direct materials into work in process, but the indirect materials go to factory overhead.

b.	Work-in-process inventory	55,500	
	Factory overhead	7,500	
	Raw-materials inventory		63,000

Record the use of raw materials.

Factory payroll for the month totaled $115,000, with $90,000 as direct labor and $25,000 as indirect labor. Once again the direct costs go into work in process and the indirect costs go into factory overhead.

FIGURE 8.3 Flow of Costs through Manufacturing Accounts

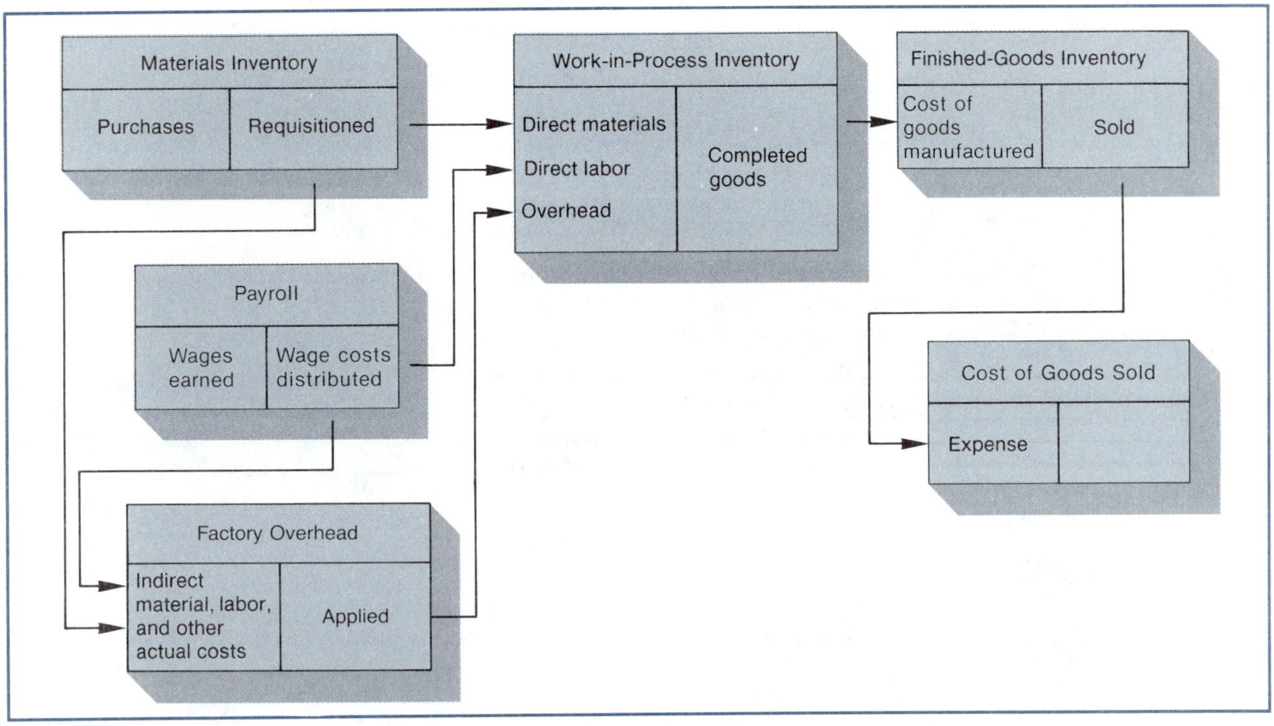

	c. Work-in-process inventory	90,000	
	Factory overhead	25,000	
	Wages payable		115,000
	Record factory payroll.		

Other factory overhead costs for the month included equipment rental at $6,300, equipment repairs at $2,200, depreciation on factory building at $4,700, depreciation on factory equipment at $1,200, light and power at $7,800, insurance at $700, and employer's payroll taxes at $12,400. Part of these were paid in cash ($14,800), part were on account, and others were adjusting entries. However, all of them are debited to factory overhead. The subsidiary ledger for factory overhead would break the total down by type and accumulate each of the amounts with others of the same type.

	d. Factory overhead	35,300	
	Accumulated depreciation—factory equipment		1,200
	Accumulated depreciation—factory building		4,700
	Cash		14,800
	Payroll taxes payable		12,400
	Accounts payable		2,200
	Record other factory overhead.		

Marko Plastics Company uses a predetermined factory overhead rate of 80 percent of direct-labor cost to allocate factory overhead to work in process. The overhead rate was predetermined at the beginning of the year by estimating the total overhead cost ($480,000) and the total direct-labor cost ($600,000) for the year. The factory overhead rate was then computed as follows:

$$\text{Factory overhead rate} = \frac{\text{Estimated factory overhead}}{\text{Estimated volume}}$$

$$= \frac{\$480,000}{\$600,000} = 80\%$$

This rate is used to allocate the factory overhead to work-in-process inventory.

e. Work-in-process inventory	72,000	
Factory overhead		72,000
Allocate factory overhead to work in process (80% × $90,000).		

Notice from the preceding journal entries that the actual factory overhead costs total $67,800—indirect material ($7,500) + indirect labor ($25,000) + other overhead ($35,300). The amount allocated to the work-in-process inventory is $72,000, leaving a $4,200 credit balance in the factory overhead account. This means that factory overhead has been overapplied during the month. However, the $4,200 credit balance is left in the factory overhead account to be offset by underapplied amounts in later months of the year. If operations go as planned for the entire year, the balance in the factory overhead account at the end of the year will be zero.

During January, the manufacturing process was completed on $146,000 of work. Also, merchandise costing $152,000 was sold to customers.

f. Finished-goods inventory	146,000	
Work-in-process inventory		146,000
Transfer completed units to finished-goods inventory.		
g. Cost of goods sold	152,000	
Finished-goods inventory		152,000
Record the cost of units sold.		

Parts of these journal entries that relate to the manufacturing process are posted in T-accounts, as shown in figure 8.4.

FIGURE 8.4 Flow of Costs through Manufacturing Accounts

Marko Plastics Company
January 19X2

Raw Materials Inventory

Bal.	$22,000		
a.	57,000	63,000	b.
Bal.	$16,000		

Work-in-Process Inventory

Bal.	$34,000	146,000	f.
b.	55,500		
c.	90,000		
e.	72,000		
Bal.	$105,500		

Finished-Goods Inventory

Bal.	$ 18,000		
f.	146,000	152,000	g.
Bal.	$ 12,000		

Wages Payable

	115,000	c.

Cost of Goods Sold

g.	$152,000	

Factory Overhead

b.	$ 7,500	72,000	e.	
c.	25,000			
d.	35,300			
		$ 4,200	Bal.	

FIGURE 8.5

Marko Plastics Company
Cost-of-Goods-Sold Statement
January 19X2

Finished-goods inventory—January 1, 19X2		$ 18,000
Cost of goods manufactured:		
Work in process—beginning	$ 34,000	
Plus:		
Direct materials $55,500		
Direct labor 90,000		
Factory overhead 72,000		
Total manufacturing costs	217,500	
Total work in process	251,500	
Less: Ending work in process	105,500	
Cost of goods manufactured		146,000
Goods available for sale		164,000
Less: Ending finished-goods inventory		12,000
Cost of goods sold		$152,000

Financial Statements

A manufacturing organization's financial statements include the additional assets associated with the manufacturing process and a statement of cost of goods manufactured that summarizes the results of the production process. Inventories associated with raw materials, work in process, and finished goods are included among the current assets of the business. Building, machinery, and equipment used in the production process are reported as part of property, plant, and equipment.

A cost-of-goods-manufactured statement may be reported separately or included as part of the statement of cost of goods sold. Either way, it summarizes the flow of costs through the work-in-process inventory account for the accounting period. Figure 8.5 contains a cost-of-goods-sold statement for Marko Plastics Company for January 19X2. The cost of goods manufactured is integrated into this statement.

JOB-ORDER VERSUS PROCESS COST SYSTEMS

Job-order and process cost are two types of accounting systems that have been developed to account for two different types of processes. Job-order costing is used for manufacturing processes that produce products in batches. One or more units of one product are produced in a batch. When that batch is completed, another product is produced in a different batch, and the process moves from batch to batch, each batch being a different product.

Job-order costing is also used in service organizations. Here each client, or separate problem for a client, represents one job. When the problem is solved or the client is satisfied, the company moves on to other problems or a new client.

A **job-order cost system** is commonly used by companies with products that are unique and divisible. Examples of businesses that use job-order costing include construction companies, furniture manufacturers, printing firms, repair shops, and service organizations. An automobile repair shop provides a good example of a job-order cost system. When you take your car into the garage to be repaired or tuned up, it becomes a batch or a job. Costs associated with the mechanic's time, parts, and overhead are accumulated for this job and are used as a basis for developing the fee for the services rendered. The following are other examples of projects or processes that are applicable to job-order cost systems:

Organization	Type of Batch or Job
Construction	Each house is a separate job because each house has different characteristics.
Furniture manufacturing	Each style of furniture is one batch. For example, several units of one style of chair will be produced in one batch.
Printing	Each item to be printed, whether it is a class handout, book, or advertising flyer, is a separate job.
Service	A CPA firm is an example of a service organization. Each client is a separate job, and time and other resources used to satisfy the client's needs are accumulated as the cost of the job.

Process cost systems are used for manufacturing processes that produce a single product or a single mix of products continuously for an extended period of time. Changes in the product are not made or are made only infrequently. Products that lend themselves to a process cost accounting system include cement, petroleum products, flour, beer, glass, steel, textiles, and food.

One of the objectives of the job-order and process cost systems is the same—to determine the cost per unit of the finished product. This is used to value ending inventory, value cost of goods sold, control costs, develop pricing strategies, and make similar management decisions. A job or a batch is the center of a job-order cost system, but the department or cost center is the center of the process cost system. The differences between the two systems are shown in figure 8.6.

The decision to use a job-order cost or a process cost system is determined by the type of product and the production process. Job-order costing is mandatory for many service, heavy manufacturing, and construction firms. Process costing is a must for most homogeneous products. Light manufacturing occasionally provides an option by which either method could be used. It should not be assumed that one company would use only one system throughout the entire organization. For example, a process cost system may be used on the main product and a job-cost system on occasional products or one-shot efforts such as a major repair or a capital improvement.

FIGURE 8.6

Comparison of Job-Order and Process Cost Systems

	Job Cost	Process Cost
Type of product	Diversified product line in which products are produced in batches, with each batch representing a unique product	Homogeneous product produced continuously
Cost accumulation	By job for a specified number of units	By department or cost center for a specified period of time
Cost per unit	Costs accumulated by job divided by units in job; computed when job is complete	Costs accumulated by cost center divided by equivalent units of production during a period of time
Reporting	By job	By cost center or department

CHAPTER 8: JOB-ORDER COST SYSTEMS

This chapter focuses on the procedures used in a job-order cost system. Chapters 9 and 10 will cover the process cost system.

JOB-ORDER COST SYSTEMS—MANUFACTURING FIRMS

A job-order cost system is used to determine the costs associated with projects or groups of units in a production process that are done in separate and distinct batches of product. Other names for a job-order cost system are *specific order cost system* or simply *job cost system*.

Job-Order Cost Sheet

A critical part of the job-order cost system is the job-order cost sheet, which *accumulates the manufacturing costs* associated with a particular job or batch of units in a job-order cost system. In a manual accounting system, there is a separate sheet of paper for each job. The amount of materials, labor, and overhead required to complete the process are manually posted to the job-order cost sheet. Figure 8.7 shows an example of such a job-order cost sheet. The concepts are exactly the same for computerized systems, except that the job-order cost sheet is a separate file in the computer system and the computer does the posting. Either way, each job is assigned a number, and manufacturing costs associated with the job are accumulated on the job-order cost summary.

Flow of Costs in a Job-Order Cost System

Manufacturing costs in a job-order cost system flow through the manufacturing accounts in the usual way. A separate inventory is maintained for raw materials. Direct materials and direct labor used in producing the finished product are accumulated in the work-in-process account. Overhead costs are accumulated in an overhead account and are allocated to work in process using a predetermined overhead rate. Finished goods are shipped to the customer, if they have been made to order, or are transferred to finished-goods inventory and held there until they are sold. At that time their cost is assigned to the cost-of-goods-sold account.

The unique feature of a job-order cost system is the assignment of a production cost to individual jobs. Each time direct material, direct labor, or factory overhead is assigned to the work-in-process inventory, the costs must also be assigned to a particular job. The job-order cost sheet accumulates the costs associated with that particular job. It acts as a subsidiary ledger for the work-in-process inventory account. Also, when units are completed and the costs are transferred to the finished-goods inventory account, the job-order cost sheet for the completed job must be removed from the subsidiary ledger. Therefore, the total of the costs on the job-order cost sheets in the work-in-process subsidiary ledger should equal the balance in the work-in-process inventory account.

These accounting procedures will be illustrated using the Marko Plastics Company data summarized earlier for January 19X2. Marko Plastics Company would be classified as a light manufacturing company. It produces a variety of plastic containers and uses a job-order cost system. The work-in-process inventory on January 1, 19X2, consisted of one job, number 244, to produce 10,000 five-gallon plastic containers. The job-order cost sheet for Job #244 on January 1, 19X2, is shown in figure 8.8. Three more jobs (numbers 245, 246, and 247) were begun in January, and two jobs were completed.

The journal entries illustrated earlier do not change when the job-order cost system is in use. We merely add the job-order cost sheets as a subsidiary ledger of work in

FIGURE 8.7

Typical Job-Order Cost Sheet

Reynolds Manufacturing
Job-Order Cost Sheet

Customer _____ Job Order # _____
Product _____ Date Started _____
Quantity _____ Date Completed _____

Direct Materials			Direct Labor			Factory Overhead	
Date	Type	Amount	Date	Hours	Amount	Date	Amount

Cost Summary:	Amount	Actual Unit Cost	Budgeted Unit Cost	Variance
Direct material	$	$	$	$
Direct labor				
Factory overhead				
Total job	$	$	$	$

Explanation of variance:

process. There must be a correspondence between the amounts posted to the work-in-process inventory and the subsidiary ledger. The timing of the recording may vary from organization to organization. For example, some firms post entries to the subsidiary ledger daily and make summary entries to the general ledger weekly. The important thing is to maintain the balance between the two ledgers. This is illustrated by reanalyzing the four entries to work-in-process inventory and by providing additional information on the allocation of costs to each job. In this example, we will assume that posting to the general ledger and the subsidiary ledger occurs simultaneously.

Transferring Raw Materials to Work in Process Raw materials are transferred from the raw materials inventory into the work-in-process inventory by a materials requisition form prepared by an authorized manufacturing supervisor. The raw materials requisition form serves as the source document for entries in the accounting system. Materials that are to be used for a specific job are classified as direct materials, and the job-order number is shown on the requisition form. This is used as a basis for posting to the job-order cost

FIGURE 8.8
Work in Process Subsidiary Ledger, January 1, 19X2

Marko Plastics Company
Job-Order Cost Sheet

Customer	Inventory	Job Order #	244
Product	5 gallon containers	Date Started	12/5/X1
Quantity	10,000	Date Completed	

Direct Materials		Direct Labor		Factory Overhead	
Date	Amount	Date	Amount	Date	Amount
12/5/X1	$14,200	12/31/X1	$11,000	12/31/X1	$8,800

Total cost to date $34,000

---

sheets. Materials that are not used on any one job are classified as indirect materials and transferred to factory overhead.

A total of $63,000 of materials wre transferred into work in process during January: $7,500 was indirect materials and $55,500 was direct material. An analysis of the requisition forms showed the following distribution:

Job Number	Amount
244	$ 2,000
245	15,500
246	18,200
247	19,800

The general journal entry is the same.

Work-in-process inventory	55,500	
Factory overhead	7,500	
Raw materials inventory		63,000
Record the use of raw materials.		

In addition, the debit to the work-in-process inventory is posted to the job-order cost sheets in the subsidiary ledger, as illustrated in figure 8.9.

Recording Labor to Work in Process Individual workers and their supervisors are responsible for identifying their time as either direct labor or indirect labor. This is accomplished in a manual system by the use of time cards or a job assignment sheet and a time clock. The employees' time tickets serve as the source documents for entries made in the accounting records, including postings to the job-order cost sheets. Each time workers move from one task to another, they punch their time cards into the time clock, which records the time on the card. The employees write the type of task to which they are going next to the time. If they are going to work on a particular job, they would write the job-order number by the time. If the task is part of general factory labor not associated with any particular job, they would write "overhead." The payroll accounting department is responsible for periodically accumulating the labor hours, pricing them, and allocating them to factory overhead and to individual jobs in work in process.

Computer data processing facilitates the allocation of labor cost to individual jobs or to factory overhead. With a computer system in place, employees merely insert their badge

FIGURE 8.9 Work in Process Subsidiary Ledger–January, 19X2

Job # 244	Units 10,000				
Direct Materials		**Direct Labor**		**Factory Overhead**	
Date	Amount	Date	Amount	Date	Amount
12/5/X1	$14,200	12/31/X1	$11,000	12/31/X1	$8,800
1/31/X2	2,000	1/31/X2	10,000	1/31/X2	8,000
Total	$16,200		$21,000		$16,800

Total cost $54,000
Cost per unit $5.40
($54,000 ÷ 10,000 units)

Job # 245	Units 15,000				
Direct Materials		**Direct Labor**		**Factory Overhead**	
Date	Amount	Date	Amount	Date	Amount
1/31/X2	$15,500	1/31/X2	$32,000	1/31/X2	$25,600

Total cost to date $73,100

Job # 246	Units 20,000				
Direct Materials		**Direct Labor**		**Factory Overhead**	
Date	Amount	Date	Amount	Date	Amount
1/31/X2	$18,200	1/31/X2	$41,000	1/31/X2	$32,800

Total cost $92,000
Cost per unit $4.60
($92,000 ÷ 20,000 units)

Job # 247	Units 5,000				
Direct Materials		**Direct Labor**		**Factory Overhead**	
Date	Amount	Date	Amount	Date	Amount
1/31/X2	$19,800	1/31/X2	$7,000	1/31/X2	$5,600

Total cost to date $32,400

card into a computer badge-card reader when they move to a new job. A magnetic strip on the back of the card identifies the employee to the computer. The only input required by the employee is the job number of the new job (or the overhead account number if the work is classified as indirect labor). The computer uses it's internal clock to record the start time on the new job and to compute the amount of time spent on the previous job. The employee's wage rate is read from a file and is multiplied by the time spent on the job, and the charge is posted to the job cost file.

A labor analysis for Marko Plastics Company for January 19X2 showed the following labor distribution schedule:

Activity/Job	Amount
Overhead	$ 25,000
Work in process:	
244	10,000
245	32,000
246	41,000
247	7,000
Total	$115,000

Once again the general journal entry does not change, but the debit to the work-in-process inventory is posted to the job-order cost sheets as shown in figure 8.9. The general journal entry is as follows:

CHAPTER 8: JOB-ORDER COST SYSTEMS

Work-in-process inventory	90,000	
Factory overhead	25,000	
Wages payable		115,000
Record factory payroll.		

Allocating Factory Overhead to Work in Process

The predetermined factory overhead rate is used to allocate overhead to individual jobs in work in process. The basis used to allocate overhead to work in process must be known for each job. For example, if machine hours are used, the accounting system must accumulate machine hours by job. When overhead is allocated on the basis of units, direct-labor hours, or direct-labor dollars, the amount for each job is known or developed as a by-product of other computations.

Marko Plastics Company allocates overhead to work in process using an overhead rate of 80 percent of direct-labor cost. The amount of overhead assigned to each job is 80 percent of the direct-labor cost identified previously. This is computed as follows:

Job	Direct Labor	×	Overhead Rate	=	Overhead Allocation
244	$10,000		80%		$ 8,000
245	32,000		80%		25,600
246	41,000		80%		32,800
247	7,000		80%		5,600
Total					$72,000

The general journal entry is as follows:

Work-in-process inventory	72,000	
Factory overhead		72,000
Allocate factory overhead to work in process.		

The $72,000 debit to the work-in-process inventory recorded in the general journal is posted to the job-order cost sheets in the subsidiary ledger shown in figure 8.9.

Balance between Subsidiary Ledger and General Ledger

The balance in work in process is $251,500 after the transfer of materials, labor, and overhead.

Beginning balance	$ 34,000
Direct material	55,500
Direct labor	90,000
Factory overhead	72,000
Total	$251,500

A schedule of the subsidiary ledger of work in process is also $251,500 (see figure 8.10). If the accounting has been performed properly, these balances should always be equal.

Transferring Finished Goods from Work in Process

At the completion of a job, the costs of materials, labor, and overhead are totaled and combined for a total job cost. The cost per unit is computed by dividing the units produced into the total job cost. For major jobs, actual costs are compared to budgeted costs, and the variances are computed. Significant variances should be investigated immediately, and an explanation should be included on the job-order cost sheet. This is useful in evaluating performance and for future reference when budgeting, bidding for work, and making pricing decisions.

The costs accumulated on the job-order cost sheets for completed jobs are transferred into finished-goods inventory. The unit cost is used to value the units while in inventory and to value cost of goods sold as the units are sold. During January 19X2, Marko Plastics

FIGURE 8.10

Marko Plastics Company
Schedule of Work-in-Process Subsidiary Ledger
January 19X2

Job Number	Total Costs to Date
244	$ 54,000
245	73,100
246	92,000
247	32,400
Total	$251,500

Company completed Jobs #244 and #246. The general journal entry debits the finished-goods inventory and credits the work-in-process inventory for $146,000. The job-order cost sheets are removed from the subsidiary ledger at this time.

Jobs #245 and #247 continue in process at the end of January 19X2. Notice that the combined total of these jobs ($73,100 + $32,400 = $105,500) is equal to the balance in the work-in-process inventory account at the end of the month.

JOB-ORDER COST SYSTEM—SERVICE ORGANIZATIONS

The principles of job-order costing do not change when moving from manufacturing to service organizations. Rather than producing a good, a service is provided. Each client is considered to be a separate job or project. Costs are accumulated by project, and reports show costs and revenues by project.

Some minor differences exist in job-order cost systems for service organizations. Service firms generally do not have an inventory of raw materials or finished goods. A CPA firm, for example, has no raw materials inventory. Direct materials are usually a minor part of the service provided, and any required direct materials are bought specifically for each project. Services generally cannot be inventoried. It is not possible, for example, to have an inventory of prepared audits or federal income tax returns because each service must be tailored to the client's needs. Also, the service comes as an indivisible chunk. Therefore, number of units and a cost per unit are not meaningful.

Direct labor is the most important cost for service organizations like CPA firms or engineering firms. Each employee is required to maintain a time and expense log. Each hour worked either is assigned to a job and ultimately billed to a client or is charged to overhead. The percent of unbillable time (i.e., the overhead portion) is an important element in performance evaluations. Expenses that relate specifically to a job are charged to that job, whereas indirect expenses are charged to overhead. Any direct materials purchased, such as books, equipment, or supplies, are charged directly to the job.

Overhead is allocated to individual jobs using a predetermined overhead rate. Generally, overhead is allocated as a percentage of labor costs or total direct costs.

Project cost sheets provide the subsidiary ledger for projects in process. Once again, there must be a balance between the cost in the projects-in-process account and the total costs on the uncompleted project cost sheets.

When a project is completed, revenues are compared with project costs to determine project profitability. Project costs are removed from the projects-in-process account and charged to a project-cost expense account.

COMPLICATIONS TO THE MANUFACTURING ACCOUNTING SYSTEM

There are many items that can complicate the accounting procedures described in this chapter for organizations using a job-order cost system. Multiple work-in-process accounts, multiple departments, departmental overhead accounts and rates, the overhead applied account, the split-ledger system, reporting on partially completed jobs, and revenue recognition using the percentage of completion method are some of the more common problems. Each of these will be briefly discussed.

Multiple Work-in-Process Accounts

So far we have used one work-in-process account that contains the costs of direct materials, direct labor, and factory overhead for units in process. Some organizations find it useful to have three work-in-process accounts, one for each element of manufacturing cost. The journal entries for Marko Plastics Company will be used to illustrate this approach.

Work-in-process direct material	55,500	
Factory overhead	7,500	
Raw materials inventory		63,000
Record the use of raw materials.		
Work-in-process direct labor	90,000	
Factory overhead	25,000	
Wages payable		115,000
Record factory payroll.		
Work-in-process factory overhead	72,000	
Factory overhead		72,000
Allocate factory overhead to work-in-process (80% × $90,000).		

The journal entry to transfer completed products to finished goods is the most complicated.

Finished goods inventory	146,000	
Work-in-process direct materials		34,400
Work-in-process direct labor		62,000
Work-in-process factory overhead		49,600
Transfer finished units to finished-goods inventory.		

This method provides additional detail on the content of work in process. However, one notable disadvantage is that the subsidiary ledger of jobs in process does not directly tie into the balance of one account. Each element of cost on the job cost sheets must be totaled separately to verify the balance in each work-in-process account.

Multiple Departments

Some firms that use a job-order cost system have two or more departments that are involved in producing the goods or providing the services. For example, a production process may be divided into assembly, finishing, and packaging, with separate departments for each. A survey firm may have separate departments for engineering and land survey. Such organizations usually find it easier to control costs and to obtain meaningful cost reports when separate work-in-process accounts are maintained for each department.

Alternative cost-flow patterns increase as the number of departments increase. Sometimes a product must go through each production department (e.g., assembly, finishing, and packaging). However, another product may require assembly and packaging but may

FIGURE 8.11

Cost Flow in Multiple Departments

Engineering Work-in-Process

Labor	3,000	7,500	Transferred Out
Overhead	4,500		

Survey Work-in-Process

Transferred In	7,500	20,000	Transferred Out
Labor	5,000		
Overhead	7,500		

Completed Project Expense

20,000	

not require the finishing department's services. One job in a survey firm may require engineering work, another may require land survey work, and some may require both.

When a job moves from one department to another, all costs accumulated on that job in the prior department are called *transferred-in costs* to the new department. Additional materials, labor, and overhead are assigned to the job in the new department. As these costs are transferred to subsequent departments, they also become transferred-in costs to those departments.

Corner Survey, Inc. has two departments—engineering and survey. Project 545 will be used to illustrate the flow of costs through the work-in-process accounts and finally into an expense account when the project is completed. Direct labor on project 545 was $3,000 in engineering and $5,000 in survey. There were no direct materials associated with the job. Overhead was allocated at 150 percent of direct-labor cost. Figure 8.11 illustrates the flow of these costs through the accounts.

Departmental Overhead Accounts and Rates

In this discussion we have assumed that each organization has one overhead account and one overhead application rate. When a firm has more than one production or service department, separate overhead accounts for each department may provide better information for cost planning and control. Overhead should be allocated to work in process using the activity base that is the best predictor of change in variable overhead cost. This may require a separate activity base in each department.

Corner Survey, Inc. in the preceding example has found that direct-labor hours is the best predictor of overhead cost for engineering, but that mileage driven is the best predictor of overhead cost for the survey department. The overhead rates in each department were developed at the beginning of the period as follows:

$$\text{Engineering rate} = \frac{\text{Estimated overhead}}{\text{Estimated direct-labor hours}} = \frac{\$90,000}{\$60,000}$$

$$= \$1.50/\text{direct-labor hour}$$

$$\text{Survey rate} = \frac{\text{Estimated overhead}}{\text{Estimated mileage}} = \frac{\$150{,}000}{30{,}000}$$

$$= \$5.00/\text{mile}$$

The $1.50 rate would be used to allocate overhead from the engineering department's overhead account into that department's work-in-process account. A $5.00 rate per mile driven for each job would be used to allocate overhead from the survey department's overhead account into its work-in-process account.

Overhead Applied Account

So far one overhead account that contains both actual and applied overhead has been used. The actual overhead cost has been recorded as a debit in the account, and the applied overhead has been recorded as a credit. A debit balance in the account represents underapplied overhead, and a credit balance represents overapplied overhead, as illustrated here.

Overhead	
Actual Overhead	Applied Overhead
Underapplied	Overapplied

As discussed earlier, the factory overhead account is a control account, and a subsidiary ledger should be maintained to break down the overhead costs into meaningful categories for cost planning and control. One weakness in the approach we have used thus far is that the subsidiary ledger for overhead cost (as illustrated in figure 8.2) does not correspond with the balance in the control account. That balance represents the under- or overapplied overhead, and it does not equal the total of the actual costs summarized in the subsidiary ledger.

An alternative approach is to have two accounts: overhead control and overhead applied. With this procedure, the actual overhead costs are recorded as debits in the overhead control account, and applied overhead is recorded as a credit in the overhead applied account. By separating these two activities into two accounts, the balance in the overhead control account should always equal the total in the overhead subsidiary cost ledger.

The balances in the two accounts must be compared to determine over- or underapplied overhead.

Overhead Control		Applied Overhead	
Actual Cost $17,500			$16,000 Applied Cost
Balance $17,500			$16,000 Balance

Overhead control	$17,500
Overhead applied	16,000
Underapplied overhead	$ 1,500

Split-Ledger System

An accounting system in which the administrative office maintains the general ledger and the factory maintains a factory ledger is called a **split-ledger system.** Such a system may be required when the administrative offices are physically separated from the factory or when there are several factories and it is not possible for the administrative offices to do all the accounting on one general ledger. When the factory is responsible for business transactions of its own, it is often more convenient and information is more timely if it maintains its own limited set of financial records.

The amount of record keeping that is performed at the factory depends upon the factory's autonomy and the type of business transactions over which it has control.

Factory Responsible for:	*Accounts Included in the Factory Ledger*
Sales, billing, and collection of accounts receivable	Sales, accounts receivable, and cash
Sales and billing only	Sales account
Purchase and payment of raw materials	Raw material inventory, accounts payable, and cash
Purchase of raw materials only	Raw materials inventory
Purchase and use of buildings, machinery, and equipment used for manufacturing	Property, plant, and equipment account
Accrual and payment of payroll but not payroll taxes	Payroll account and payroll checking account

The responsibilities of the factory and the administrative office must be specified in advance and the appropriate accounts established. The accounting performed on each set of books must be coordinated for transactions that affect both ledgers. This is accomplished through a factory ledger account on the general ledger at the administrative office and a general ledger account on the ledger maintained by the factory. Each time the factory enters into a transaction that requires some action by the administrative office, it will debit or credit the general ledger account and send an interoffice memo to the administrative office describing the action taken. Likewise, any time the administrative office enters into a transaction that affects the ledger maintained by the factory, it will debit or credit the factory ledger account.

EXAMPLE

Suppose the factory is responsible for sales but the administrative office is responsible for collections of accounts receivable. When the factory makes a sale, it will record the following:

General ledger	$22,000	
Sales		$22,000

The administrative office will record the following:

Accounts receivable	$22,000	
Factory ledger		$22,000

The balance in the general ledger account should always equal the balance in the factory ledger account. The general ledger account on the factory ledger is like an owner's equity; it represents the administrative office's equity in the net assets of the factory. The factory ledger account is like an investment account on the administrative office books; it represents the home office's investment in the factory.

Several transactions for Floss Manufacturing Company will illustrate the split-ledger system. Because the administrative offices are some distance from the factory, it was decided to give the factory the responsibility for maintaining the inventory of raw materials,

FIGURE 8.12

Floss Manufacturing Company
Split-Ledger System

		General Ledger		Factory Ledger	
a.	Purchase of raw materials by factory.				
	Factory ledger	15,000		Raw materials	15,000
	Accounts payable		15,000	General ledger	15,000
b.	Transfer raw materials into work in process.				
				Work in process	12,000
	No entry			Factory overhead	2,000
				Raw materials	14,000
c.	Calculate and record payroll by the factory. The factory uses a payroll clearing account.				
	Factory ledger	20,000		Payroll	20,000
	Payroll payable		20,000	General ledger	20,000
d.	Allocate payroll to jobs and to factory overhead.				
				Work in process	14,000
	No entry			Factory overhead	6,000
				Payroll	20,000
e.	Employer payroll taxes are computed by the home office, and the amount is communicated to the factory. It is considered to be part of factory overhead.				
	Factory ledger	3,000		Factory overhead	3,000
	Payroll taxes payable		3,000	General ledger	3,000
f.	Allocate overhead to individual jobs in work in process.				
				Work in process	13,500
	No entry			Factory overhead	13,500
g.	Transfer jobs that are complete to finished-goods inventory.				
				Finished-goods inventory	40,000
	No entry			Work in process	40,000
h.	Sale of $35,000 of finished-goods inventory for $60,000.				
	Accounts receivable	60,000		General ledger	60,000
	Factory ledger		60,000	Cost of goods sold	35,000
				Sales	60,000
				Finished-goods inventory	35,000
i.	Collection of cash by the general office.				
	Cash	60,000			
	Accounts receivable		60,000	No entry	

work in process, and finished goods. Furthermore, it is responsible for all purchases of materials, labor, and overhead as well as for sales, but all cash receipts and payments are to be made by the administrative office. Figure 8.12 lists the journal entries for both home office and factory for a variety of transactions.

Notice in figure 8.12 that each time the factory ledger account is debited on the general ledger, the general ledger account is credited on the factory ledger, and vice versa. This maintains the equality of the accounts.

Reporting for Partially Completed Jobs

Projects accounted for by the job-order cost system frequently extend over several months and even several years. Management needs periodic reports throughout the project to monitor progress and to take corrective action where necessary. Figure 8.13 illustrates the type of report format that is frequently used to provide progress reports on partially completed jobs.

FIGURE 8.13 Report Format For Partially Completed Jobs

Cost Classification		Base Estimate	Revised Estimate	Cost This Period	Cumulative Cost to Date	Estimated Costs to Complete	Forecasted Total	Variance
Code	Description							
10	Direct labor (type)	$500,000	$550,000	$100,000	$300,000	$275,000	$575,000	($25,000)
50	Direct materials (type) etc.	750,000	750,000	50,000	450,000	290,000	740,000	10,000

Cost classifications are listed on the report in meaningful categories. At lower levels of management the cost categories are small and very specific. As summary reports are prepared for middle and upper levels of management, the cost categories are combined to keep the length of the report manageable and the significant data more prominent.

As seen in figure 8.13, the cost categories listed across the report show budgeted data, actual data, and variances. The budget is broken down into an original or base estimate and a revised estimate, which is the original estimate plus or minus change orders from the customer or a redistribution of cost estimates due to a change in the processing method.

Actual costs are broken down by *(a)* costs incurred this period, *(b)* cumulative costs to date, and *(c)* estimated costs to complete this project. The forecasted total cost is the combined total of cumulative costs to date and the estimated costs to complete the project.

The total forecasted costs are compared with the revised estimate to compute a variance. For management, the variance is a key number in identifying the areas of the project that are going well and those that are not going so well.

Revenue Recognition for Partially Completed Jobs

Long-term construction contracts, such as those for buildings, ships, and defense, are usually accounted for by a job-order cost system. There are two generally accepted methods to account for revenues on long-term construction contracts—the completed contract method and the percentage of completion method.

Under the completed contract method of revenue recognition, no income is recognized until the contract is completed. At that time all the costs of the project are known, and the income can be computed as the difference between total revenues and total costs. A problem with this method is that it does not recognize income as it is earned. For example, if a project extends over a two-year period, no income would be recognized in the first year because the project is not completed. All of the income would be recognized in the second year. Thus profits flow to the income statement in an erratic pattern and frequently with substantial fluctuations.

The percentage of completion method recognizes revenue as the contract progresses toward completion. A frequently used method to measure progress toward completion compares the costs incurred to date relative to the total costs required to complete the project. This percentage-of-completion measure is used to compute the amount of profits to be recognized.

EXAMPLE

Magleby Incorporated is a contractor with a contract that will extend over two years. The price of the contract is fixed at $500,000. During the first year, $168,000 of the total estimated cost of $420,000 was incurred. Management believes that the $420,000 original estimate continues to be an accurate estimate of total costs to complete the project. Therefore, the project is 40-percent complete ($168,000 ÷ $420,000), and Magleby Incorporated should recognize $32,000 (40% × ($500,000 − $420,000)) of profit.

The criteria that need to be satisfied in order to use the percentage of completion method and the journal entries involved in its application are financial accounting issues covered in most intermediate accounting textbooks. Cost accounting issues include accurate cost estimation and accumulation. The budgeting procedures outlined in chapters 5 and 6 and the job-order cost system discussed in this chapter are critical in developing accurate cost data for the percentage of completion method.

SUMMARY

This is the first of several chapters dealing with the cost-finding aspects of cost accounting. The primary objectives of cost finding are to account for manufacturing costs and to determine the cost per unit of a finished product. This information is an integral part of both internal and external reports.

The manufacturing process combines materials, labor, and overhead into a finished product. The journal entries used to account for acquiring these components and transferring them through the accounts as the products move through the production process were explained and illustrated in this chapter.

The job-order and process cost accounting systems have been developed to account for two different types of production processes. A job-order cost system is used in manufacturing processes that produce a variety of products, one product at a time, in batches. The batch is the focus of this accounting system; both cost accumulation and reporting are batch-oriented. A process cost accounting system is used when only one product is produced for an extended period of time. The department or cost center is the focus of this system; costs are accumulated and reports are prepared for individual departments.

A job-order cost sheet is used in a job-order cost system to accumulate the direct materials, direct labor, and factory overhead used on a job. For jobs in process these cost sheets serve as a subsidiary ledger for the work-in-process inventory account. The jobs in the subsidiary ledger must be updated for each journal entry that has a debit or credit to the work-in-process inventory.

Some organizations that use a job-order cost system have several departments involved in producing a good or providing a service. These firms may have separate work-in-process accounts for each element of cost or each department, separate departmental overhead accounts and rates, and even separate accounts for actual overhead and applied overhead. Accountants need to be familiar with these alternatives and be able to design and use the system that best meets the organization's needs.

A split-ledger accounting system is frequently used when the general office is physically separated from the factory or when there are several factories. The general ledger is maintained at the administrative offices, whereas a factory ledger is maintained at the factory to account for selected business transactions over which it has control. The factory ledger account on the general ledger is a reciprocal account to the general ledger account on the factory ledger. These accounts are used each time there is a transaction on one ledger that needs to be picked up and recorded on the other ledger.

SELF-STUDY PROBLEM

Job-O Company uses job-order costing. Factory overhead is applied to production at a predetermined rate of 200 percent of the direct-labor cost. Any over- or underapplied overhead is left in the factory overhead account until the end of the year. Additional information follows:

1. Job #100 was the only job in process on February 1, 19X2, with accumulated costs as follows:

Direct material	$5,000
Direct labor	1,000
Factory overhead	2,000
Total	$8,000

2. Jobs #101 and #102 were started during February.
3. Material requisitions for February totaled $33,000 ($5,000 for #100, $10,000 for #101, $15,000 for #102, and $3,000 for general factory use.)
4. Labor costs of $25,000 were incurred in February ($4,000 for #100, $7,000 for #101, $9,000 for #102, and $5,000 for general factory work.)
5. Other actual factory overhead costs for February totaled $30,000.
6. The only job still in process on February 28, 19X2, was #102.

Required

1. Prepare a job-order cost sheet for Job #102.
2. Prepare a statement of cost of goods manufactured for February.
3. Prepare general journal entries for:
   a. Raw materials requisitioned.
   b. Allocation of overhead to work in process.
   c. Transfer of finished goods into the finished-goods inventory.
4. What is the over- or underapplied overhead for February?

Solution to the Self-Study Problem

Requirement 1

Job-O Company
Job-Order Cost Sheet   Job #102

Direct Materials	Direct Labor	Factory Overhead
$15,000	$9,000	$18,000

Total cost $42,000

Requirement 2

Job-O Company
Statement of Cost of Goods Manufactured
February 19X2

Direct materials	$30,000	
Direct labor	20,000	
Factory overhead ($20,000 × 200%)	40,000	$90,000
Plus: Beginning work in process		8,000
Total work in process		$98,000
Less: Ending work in process		42,000
Cost of goods manufactured		$56,000

Requirement 3

a. Raw materials requisitioned:
   Work-in-process inventory   30,000
   Factory overhead   3,000
      Raw materials inventory   33,000
b. Allocation of overhead to work in process:
   Work-in-process inventory   40,000
      Factory overhead   40,000
c. Transfer of finished goods into the finished-goods inventory:
   Finished-goods inventory   56,000
      Work-in-process inventory   56,000

Requirement 4

Actual overhead costs incurred:	
Indirect materials	$ 3,000
Indirect labor	5,000
Other factory overhead	30,000
Total	$38,000
Allocated to work in process	40,000
Overapplied overhead	$ 2,000

SUGGESTED READINGS

Carbone, Frank J. "Automated Job Costing Helps Mulach Steel Stay Competitive." *Management Accounting 61* (June 1980): 29.

Clough, Richard H. *Construction Project Management.* New York: John Wiley & Sons, 1972.

Dellinger, Roy E. "Job Cost Reporting for Construction Companies." *Cost and Management 48* (July–August 1974): 24.

Goodman, Sam R., and Reece, James S. *The Controller's Handbook.* Homewood, Ill.: Dow-Jones Irwin, 1978.

Hunt, R.; Garrett, L.; and Merz, C. M. "Direct Labor Cost Not Always Relevant at H-P." *Management Accounting 66* (February 1985): 58–62.

Kaplan, R. S. "Measuring Manufacturing Performance: A New Challenge for Managerial Accounting Research." *The Accounting Review 63* (October 1983): 686–705.

Niles, Timothy J., and Dowis, Robert H. "Accounting for New Plant Construction." *Management Accounting 55* (July 1974): 35.

Possett, R. W. "Measuring Productive Costs in the Service Sector." *Management Accounting 62* (October 1980): 16–24.

Wood, T. D., and Sweet, F. H. "Using Job Order Cost in a Small Manufacturing Plant." In *Modern Accounting Principles and Practices.* Englewood Cliffs, N. J.: Prentice-Hall, 1978.

DISCUSSION QUESTIONS

Q8-1. Identify the accounts used to trace the flow of costs associated with the manufacturing process and describe the flow of costs through those accounts.

Q8-2. What is a job-order cost sheet and why is it used?

Q8-3. Describe the job-order cost sheet's relationship to the flow of costs through the manufacturing accounts.

Q8-4. What is job-order costing and for what types of manufacturing processes is it applicable?

Q8-5. What is process costing and for what types of manufacturing processes is it applicable?

Q8-6. Under a job-order cost system, are reports prepared by job or by department? Explain.

Q8-7. Under a job-order cost system, are costs accumulated by job or by department? Explain.

Q8-8. What is a chart of accounts? Which accounts are unique to a manufacturing organization?

Q8-9. Identify three accounts that are associated with the manufacturing process and that are control accounts with a subsidiary ledger.

Q8-10. What is the difference between a control account and a clearing account?

Q8-11. Why is cost data so important when recognizing revenue on long-term construction contracts on a percentage of completion basis?

Q8-12. Why does a company use a split-ledger accounting system?

Q8-13. Describe the relationship between the factory ledger account and the general ledger account under a split-ledger accounting system.

Q8-14. What source documents are used to post direct materials, direct labor, and factory overhead to the job-order cost sheets?

Q8-15. What types of errors will cause an inequality between the balance in the work-in-process inventory account and the total costs on the job-order cost sheets in the subsidiary ledger? How would you go about identifying the discrepancy?

EXERCISES

E8-1. Job-Order Cost Entries Stewart Company uses a job-order cost system. Transactions completed during the first month of operations were as follows:

1. Purchased raw materials and supplies for $19,380.
2. Materials and supplies were used as follows:

Direct materials:			
Job 1		$3,200	
Job 2		4,600	
Job 3		800	$8,600
Indirect materials			200

3. The factory payroll was as follows:

Direct labor:
Job 1	$2,800	
Job 2	3,200	
Job 3	500	$6,500
Indirect labor		2,500

4. Miscellaneous factory overhead costs totaled $2,800.
5. Factory overhead was applied on a direct-labor cost basis using a rate of 70 percent.
6. Job 1 (200 units) and Job 2 (300 units) were completed and transferred to finished goods.
7. Shipments to customers were as follows:
   100 units from Job 1
   200 units from Job 2

Required

Set up T-accounts for the following accounts and record the transactions for the month in the T-accounts.

Factory Ledger	Job Ledger
Materials and supplies	Job 1
Work in process	Job 2
Finished goods	Job 3
Cost of goods sold	
Factory overhead costs applied	
Factory overhead costs control	

E8–2. Job-Order Cycle Entries—Control and Subsidiary Accounts Medford Incorporated provided the following data for January.

Materials and supplies:	
Inventory, January 1	$10,000
Purchases on account	30,000
Labor:	
Accrued, January 1	$ 3,000
Paid during January (ignore payroll taxes)	25,000
Factory overhead costs:	
Supplies (issued from materials)	$ 1,500
Indirect labor	3,500
Depreciation	1,000
Other factory overhead costs	14,200[a]

Work in process:

	Job 1	Job 2	Job 3	Total
Work in process, Jan. 1	$1,000	—	—	$ 1,000
Job costs during Jan:				
Direct materials	4,000	$6,000	$5,000	15,000
Direct labor	5,000	8,000	7,000	20,000
Applied factory overhead	5,000	8,000	7,000	20,000

Job 1 started in December, finished during January. Sold to a customer for $21,000 cash in January.

Job 2 started in January, not yet finished.

Job 3 started in January, finished during January, and now is in the finished-goods warehouse awaiting sale.

Finished-goods inventory, January 1

[a]Includes items like 0 utility bills, which are set up for payment in a payable account.

Required

Record the journal entries, with detail for the respective job orders and factory overhead subsidiary records, for all January events.

E8-3. Job-Order Costing—Basic Procedures Tillman Corporation uses a job-order cost system and has two production departments, *M* and *A*. Budgeted manufacturing costs for 19X0 are as follows:

	Department M	Department A
Direct materials	$700,000	$100,000
Direct labor	200,000	800,000
Manufacturing overhead	600,000	400,000

The actual material and labor costs charged to Job no. 432 during 19X0 were as follows:

Direct materials		$25,000
Direct labor:		
Department *M*	$ 8,000	
Department *A*	12,000	20,000

Tillman applies manufacturing overhead to production orders on the basis of direct-labor cost, using departmental rates based on the annual budget predetermined at the beginning of the year.

Required

Determine the total manufacturing cost associated with Job no. 432 for 19X0.

E8-4. Job-Order Costing—Cost Statement The Rebecca Corporation manufactures special machines made to customer specifications. All production costs are accumulated by means of a job-order costing system. The following information is available at the beginning of the month of October 19X0.

Direct-materials inventory, October 1	$16,200
Work-in-process, October 1	3,600

A review of the job-order cost sheets revealed the composition of the work-in-process inventory on October 1, as follows:

Direct materials	$1,320
Direct labor (300 hours)	1,500
Factory overhead applied	780
	$3,600

Activity during the month of October was as follows:

Direct materials costing $20,000 were purchased.
Direct labor for job orders totaled 3,300 hours at $5 per hour.
Factory overhead was applied to production at the rate of $2.60 per direct-labor hour.

On October 31, inventories consisted of the following components:

Direct-materials inventory	$17,000
Work-in-process inventory:	
Direct materials	$4,320
Direct labor (500 hours)	2,500
Factory overhead applied	1,300
	$8,120

Required

Using Lotus, prepare a detailed statement of the cost of goods manufactured for the month of October.

E8–5. Cost of Goods Manufactured The Wonder Manufacturing Corporation uses the job-order cost system. On April 1, the following jobs are estimated to be in process.

	Job X-61	Job X-62
Materials	$1,200	$ 900
Labor	1,800	3,100
Overhead	1,200	1,600
	$4,200	$5,600

Overhead is applied to work in process at the rate of 40 percent of prime costs. During April the following materials requisitions are expected to be filled:

Job X-62	$ 600
Job X-63	800
Job X-64	1,400
	$2,800

Also during the month, job labor tickets are expected to be as follows:

Job X-61	$ 500
Job X-62	1,000
Job X-63	600
Job X-64	2,400
	$4,500

Only Jobs X-63 and X-64 are expected to be in work in process at the month's end.

Required

1. Assume Wonder Manufacturing Corporation is trying to budget its cost of goods manufactured for April, and the information given here is based on its initial best estimate. Develop a cost of goods manufactured statement on Lotus using these estimates. Print out a copy of your statement. Include on your Lotus template a subsidiary ledger of work in process. Print out a copy of this also.
2. Develop three more statements of cost of goods manufactured using the following assumptions:
   a. Labor costs for Job X-62 and Job X-64 are 15 percent higher than expected.
   b. In addition to (a), materials costs on Job X-62 and Job X-64 are 10 percent higher than expected.
   c. Job X-64 is the only job that is not complete by the end of the period.

E8–6. Journal Entries—Job-Order Cost System with Two Ledgers The Binderman Manufacturing Company uses a factory ledger and a general ledger to record cost data. Applied factory overhead rates are in use.

The following transactions were recorded for August 19x2.

1. Materials purchased—$35,000 for the factory and $8,000 for the office.
2. Freight incurred and paid by the home office on materials received at the factory—$385.
3. Materials put into process—direct, $22,000; factory supplies, $3,000.

4. Purchased factory equipment

List price	$10,000
Trade discount	20%
Cash discount	5%
Transportation costs	$100

5. Payroll for period:

Direct labor (gross pay)	$60,000
Indirect labor (gross pay)	15,000
Office payroll (gross pay)	25,000
FICA tax (withholding)	7,000
Federal withholding tax	18,000

6. Employers portion of payroll taxes

FICA tax	$7,000
Federal unemployment	4,000

7. Depreciation

Office equipment	$7,500
Factory equipment	14,000

8. Overhead applied

50% of direct-labor cost

9. Goods finished during period $80,000

10. Sales $90,000
      Cost of goods sold   80,000

Required

Prepare journal entries for the preceding transactions. Assume the inventories for direct materials, work in process, and the factory overhead accounts are at the factory.

E8–7. Journal Entries—Job-Order Costing with Two Ledgers The Carson Company completed the following transactions during the month of October 19X7:

Oct 3   Materials requisitioned—direct, $2,000; indirect, $1,000.
     4   Raw materials purchased—$10,000. Terms 2/10, net/30.
     7   Weekly factory payroll of $1,000 was allocated as follows: direct labor, $940; maintenance, $60. Income taxes were $90; FICA taxes were $45.
   10   Completed factory job with the following costs: direct labor, $480; materials, $225; factory overhead, 75 percent of direct labor.
   12   Shipped completed job to customer per instructions of home office. Billing—$1,150.
   13   Home office vouchered and paid miscellaneous factory overhead, $400.

Required

Prepare journal entries in the general and factory journals for the preceding transactions. Assume the inventory and factory overhead accounts are kept at the factory.

E8–8. Journal Entries—Job-Order Cost System Sloane Manufacturing Company uses a job-order cost system and compiled the following data for 19X1. (They also use a perpetual inventory system.)

Materials and supplies purchased	$242,000
Direct material used	190,000
Supplies used	20,000
Direct labor	150,000
Other labor	35,000
Utility costs for the year	65,000
Miscellaneous overhead	40,000
Depreciation, equipment	22,000
Depreciation, buildings	8,000
Applied factory overhead (20% of direct labor)	?
Cost of goods completed	326,000
Material ($170,000)	
Labor ($130,000)	
Sales	500,000
Cost of goods sold	326,000
Selling and administrative expenses	110,000

Assume that two jobs, Jobs 208 and 209, were in process during the period. One was completed (Job 208) and the other (Job 209) is still in process at year end.

Required

1. Prepare the appropriate journal entries covering these data.
2. Set up T-accounts covering all transactions indicated and post your journal entries to the T-accounts. Include work-in-process and factory overhead control and subsidiary accounts.
3. Determine end-of-period balances in the accounts as appropriate.
4. Prepare a statement of cost of goods manufactured in as much detail as the data permits.
5. Prepare an income statement for the year.

E8–9. Job Order Costing-Accounting for Overhead The Navajo Company has a fiscal year that runs from July 1 to June 30. The company uses a job-order accounting system for its production cost. A predetermined overhead rate based on direct-labor hours is used to apply overhead to individual jobs. A budget of overhead costs was prepared for the 19X4–19X5 fiscal year as follows:

Direct-labor hours:	120,000	Variable overhead costs	$390,000
		Fixed overhead costs	216,000
		Total overhead	$606,000

The following information is for November 19X4. Jobs 50 and 51 were completed during November.

Inventories, November 1, 19X4

Raw materials & supplies	$ 10,500
Work-in process (Job 50)	54,000
Finished goods	112,500

Purchases of Raw Materials & Supplies

Raw materials	$135,000
Supplies	15,000

Materials and Supplies Requisitioned for Production

Job 50	$ 45,000
Job 51	37,500
Job 52	25,500
Supplies	12,000 OH
Total	$120,000

Direct-Labor Hours		Labor Costs	
Job 50	3,500	Direct-labor wages	$51,000
Job 51	3,000	Indirect-labor wages	
Job 52	2,000	(4,000 hours)	15,000 OH
	8,500	Supervisory salaries	6,000 OH
		Total	$72,000

Building Occupancy Costs (heat, light, depreciation, etc.)		Factory Equipment Costs	
Factory facilities	$6,500 OH	Power	$4,000 OH
Sales offices	1,500	Repairs & maintenance	1,500 OH
Administrative offices	1,000	Depreciation	1,500 OH
	$9,000	Other	1,000 OH
			$8,000

Assume all direct-labor workers receive the same hourly rate.

Required

1. Calculate a predetermined overhead rate to be used to apply overhead to individual jobs during the 19X4–19X5 fiscal year.
2. Assume the company uses two overhead accounts, overhead control and overhead applied. Prepare T-accounts for these two accounts and post the appropriate amounts to the accounts for the November 19X4 transactions.
3. Calculate over- or underapplied overhead.
4. Prepare a job-cost sheet for Job 50 and compute total job cost.

E8–10. Journal Entries-Split-Ledger Accounting System Lonn Corporation uses a general ledger and a factory ledger. Inventory accounts (materials, work-in-process, finished goods), a payroll clearing account for factory employees, and a factory overhead account are kept at the factory; plant asset, revenue, and expense accounts and accounts payable are part of the general office books. The following transactions took place:

Aug. 2 Purchased materials for the factory for $10,000, with terms of 2/10, net/30.
    4 Requisitions of $3,000 of direct materials and $1,000 of indirect materials were filled from the stockroom.
    9 Factory payroll of $1,500 ($1,320 direct labor and $180 indirect labor) for the week was made up at the home office; $1,230 in cash was sent to the factory. FICA tax withheld was $90, and income tax withheld was $180.
   14 Depreciation of $300 for factory equipment was recorded.
   14 A job was completed in the factory, with $800 of direct labor and $375 of direct materials being previously charged to the job. Factory overhead is to be applied at a rate of 75 percent of direct labor when a job is completed.
   15 Miscellaneous factory overhead of $650 was paid by the home office and transferred to the factory.
   16 The job completed on August 14 was shipped to Weber Company on instructions from the home office. Customer was billed for $2,500.

Required

Prepare journal entries on the factory books and the general office books.

E8–11. Job-Cost Sheet
Job # 47 for Ross Foundation incurred the following costs during May 19X4.

Direct labor:
    Employee #7455   20 hours @ $6.85 per hour
    Employee #6947   16 hours @ $10.75 per hour
    Employee #9443   47 hours @ $12.50 per hour
Direct materials:
    Type 47A Requisition #1964 $647.50
    Type 94M Requisition #1969   463.00

Overhead is allocated at 150 percent of direct-labor cost.

Required

Post the May charges to Job #47 and compute total job cost to date. Print out a copy of the job-cost sheet. (A partially completed job-cost sheet on the Lotus disk is available for your use.)

PROBLEMS

P8–1. Job-Order Costing Entries—Work-in-Process Inventories
The Joy Manufacturing Corporation uses a job-order cost system. The three following jobs were in process on August 1, 19X7.

	75-A	65-B	68-C
Materials	$12,500	$ 7,800	$10,700
Labor	2,800	1,200	5,400
Overhead	4,200	1,800	8,100
	$19,500	$10,800	$24,200

The following costs were incurred during August.

Job	Materials	Labor
75-A		$ 3,200
65-B	$ 3,100	1,800
68-C		1,000
69-B	7,500	6,000
72-A	5,500	1,200
74-C	2,300	200
	$18,400	$13,400

Jobs 72-A and 74-C are still in process on August 31. Overhead is applied at the rate of 150 percent of direct-labor costs. Actual factory overhead was equal to applied factory overhead.

Required

1. Prepare summary journal entries for the month of August.
2. Prepare a work-in-process subsidiary ledger for each job in process during August.
3. Determine the August 1st and August 31st balances in work in process.
4. Prepare a cost-of-goods-manufactured statement.

P8-2. Job-Order Costing—Work-in-Process Inventory

Brahms Manufacturing Company uses a job-order cost system. Overhead is applied at the rate of 150 percent of direct-labor costs. Work in process at July 1, 19X0, was as follows:

	C-21	F-15	N-75
Direct materials	$1,200	$1,800	$ 750
Direct labor	1,100	800	600
Applied overhead	1,650	1,200	900
Total	$3,950	$3,800	$2,250

Total work in process: $10,000.

The following materials and labor costs were incurred during July:

Job	Materials	Labor
D-53	$1,500	$ 700
C-21	200	300
F-69	1,000	1,800
F-15		200
Z-83	1,500	500
N-75	500	300
R-48	1,000	400
	$5,700	$4,200

Actual factory overhead costs were $6,300. Jobs Z-83 and R-48 were incomplete at the end of the month.

Required

1. Compute the work in process inventory at July 31, 19X0.
2. Prepare a cost-of-goods-manufactured statement.

P8-3. Job-Order Costing—Complete and Incomplete Job Costs

Jolley Printing Company uses a job-order cost system. The following jobs were in process at the beginning of 19X7:

	65-A	75-B
Material	$ 6,500	$ 7,500
Labor	9,400	8,000
Overhead	4,700	4,000
Total	$20,600	$19,500

Total work in process: $40,100

The following costs were incurred during 19X7:

	Materials	Labor
65-A	—	$ 2,200
75-B	$ 2,000	1,400
85-C	7,500	8,400
95-D	5,500	6,800
05-E	2,500	3,000
	$17,500	$21,800

Overhead is applied at the rate of 50 percent of direct-labor cost. Jobs 65-A, 75-B, 85-C, and 95-D were completed and sold. There was no beginning or ending finished-goods inventory. Selling and administrative expenses were $18,500. The jobs were sold for the following:

65-A	$ 26,000
75-B	31,000
85-C	28,000
95-D	35,000
	$120,000

Required

1. Compute the cost of completed jobs.
2. Compute the ending work-in-process inventory.
3. Compute the net income for the year.

P8–4. Job-Order Costing—Journal Entries Lind Manufacturing Company uses a perpetual inventory system and a job-order cost system. The following data were compiled for 19X5 (the current costs of production apply 70 percent to Job 307 and 30 percent to Job 308):

Payroll costs	$150,000
($125,000—direct labor; ignore payroll taxes)	
Direct materials purchased	116,000
Direct materials used	85,000
Factory rent	3,000/month
Depreciation, factory building	10,000
Indirect supplies used	15,000
Miscellaneous factory overhead	18,000
Sales	350,000

Factory overhead is applied at the rate of 80 percent of direct-labor costs. There was no beginning or ending work-in-process inventory. The over- or underapplied factory overhead is not considered material and is charged directly to cost of goods sold at year end. Job 307 was completed and sent to the finished-goods warehouse. On Job 307, shipments were made to customers for 95 percent of the units produced.

Required

1. Prepare summary journal entries for the preceding information.
2. Prepare a subsidiary ledger for work in process.
3. Prepare a T-account for factory overhead to show the computation of over- or underapplied overhead.

P8-5 Journal Entries of a Split Ledger Tinker Manufacturing Company records transactions on a general journal and factory journal. Tinker uses a perpetual inventory system. The following transactions occurred during April 19X0:

Gross wages:	
Direct labor	$10,000
Indirect labor	2,000
Office salaries	3,000
Withholdings:	
FICA	$ 900
Federal income tax	2,000
Employer taxes:	
FICA	900
Federal unemployment	100
State unemployment	500
Materials purchased	25,000
Freight-in on materials purchased	500
Materials used	21,000
Depreciation	
Office equipment	5,000
Factory equipment	4,000
Rent	
Factory	3,000
Office	5,000
Miscellaneous factory expenses	2,000
(Factory overhead is applied at 60% of direct-labor costs)	
Cost of completed goods	50,000
Cost of goods sold	45,000
Sales	75,000

Required

Prepare summary journal entries for the preceding transactions on both the factory and general journals. Assume that all accounts are maintained in the general ledger except the inventories and the factory overhead account. Also assume that employer payroll taxes on factory labor are classified as overhead costs.

P8-6. Job-Order Costing—Split Ledger The Dearden Manufacturing Company incurred the following costs during July 19X8. The company uses a split ledger with the materials, work-in-process, and finished-goods inventories at the factory. The factory has a factory overhead control and factory payroll account.

Payroll:	
Direct labor	$30,000
Indirect labor	4,000
FICA taxes	600
Federal withholding taxes	2,400
(ignore the employer's share of taxes)	
Materials:	
Purchased	25,000
Used (5% indirect)	28,000
Factory overhead:	
Factory rent	8,000
Depreciation	4,000
Miscellaneous	2,000
Cost of completed jobs	45,000
Cost of goods sold	55,000
Sales	82,000
Applied factory overhead	50% of direct-labor cost

Required

Prepare summary journal entries for the preceding transactions on the general journal and the factory journal.

P8–7. Job-Order Cost System—Cost Schedules Scanlon Printing Company uses a periodic inventory system to account for its printing operations. Because jobs are produced under contract specifications, the cost of completed jobs is immediately included in cost of goods sold. Overhead is applied to each job at a rate of 200 percent of direct-labor charges. Work in process on November 1, 19X3, consisted of the following job analysis:

Total Work in Process

Job	Materials	Labor	Applied	Process
B-743	$ 430	$207	$ 414	$1,051
P-418	125	150	300	575
D-017	350	250	500	1,100
A-411	240	175	350	765
	$1,145	$782	$1,564	$3,491

During November, a tabulation of materials requisition forms and labor time tickets showed costs for individual jobs to be as follows:

Requisition	Job	Material Cost	Time Ticket	Job	Labor Cost
1101	B-743	$ 120	2001	D-017	$ 190
1102	D-017	150	2002	A-411	270
1103	A-411	260	2003	D-017	100
1104	R-218	318	2004	B-743	348
1105	C-100	474	2005	P-418	200
1106	F-041	230	2006	C-100	350
1107	A-415	319	2007	R-218	420
1108	G-200	450	2008	F-041	230
1109	P-504	618	2009	P-504	429
1110	X-219	144	2010	X-219	237
1111	Z-001	275	2011	F-400	820
1112	F-400	760	2012	A-415	910
		$4,118	2013	G-200	560
					$5,064

On November 30, Jobs Z-001, A-415, and X-219 were incomplete. All remaining jobs were delivered to customers at cash prices equal to 150 percent of assigned costs. Actual overhead costs for the month were $11,500.

Required

1. Prepare a schedule to compute the work-in-process inventory balance at November 30.
2. Prepare a schedule to compute cost of goods sold for November.
3. Compute the amount of underapplied or overapplied overhead.

P8–8. Job-Order Cost System—Cost Determination Power Manufacturing Corporation uses a job-order cost system to trace the cost of production. During 19X1, the indicated costs were incurred on the following jobs:

Work in Process Beginning

Job #	Materials	Labor	Factory Overhead	Total
L1670	$1,500	$6,000	$8,000	$15,500
J1901	5,000	8,000	4,000	17,000

Direct Materials		Direct Labor		
Job #	Cost	Job #	Hours	Cost
H702	$16,872	L1670	200	$ 800
G901	10,980	J1901	3,000	9,600
B168	5,670	H702	500	1,575
		G901	600	1,200
		B168	90	180

Factory Overhead

Applied at $2.00 per direct-labor hour

Jobs Completed During the Year

#L1670, #J1901, #H702, #G901
Selling and administrative expenses: $25,510

Sales	
Job #	Selling Price
L1670	$ 18,000
J1901	45,000
H702	28,000
G9001	25,000
	$116,000

Required

1. Compute the ending work in process.
2. Compute the cost of completed jobs.
3. Compute the net operating income for the year.
4. Journalize the cost transactions that occurred in the Power Manufacturing Company during 19X1.
5. Set up in T-account form the ledger accounts that are needed to reflect all the cost transactions that occurred. Include accounts for the job subsidiary. Post the transactions to both control and subsidiary accounts.

P8–9. Job Order Costing—Financial Statement Preparation The Pierre LaMontte Company designs and builds custom yachts on a fixed-price contract basis. The company uses a job-order cost system and recognizes revenue using the completed contract method. On January 1, the following jobs were in progress.

Job A1	$250,000
Job A7	76,500
Job A9	123,750

Overhead is applied at the rate of 150 percent of direct labor. During the year the following labor costs were incurred:

Job A1	$ 93,000
Job A7	125,000
Job A9	85,000
Job B1	100,000
Job B2	55,000
Job B3	14,700

During the year the following material requisitions were filled:

Job A7	$ 25,000
Job B1	203,000
Job B2	155,000
Job B3	33,700

Only Jobs B2 and B3 were in process at the end of the year. All other jobs were delivered to customers.

An evaluation of the contract file reveals the following contract pricing structure (the negotiated sales price of each yacht):

Job A1	$550,000
Job A7	525,000
Job A9	450,000
Job B1	500,000
Job B2	480,000
Job B3	600,000

Administrative expenses for the year were $45,000. Marketing expenses were $55,000.

Required

1. Prepare a cost-of-goods-manufactured statement.
2. Prepare an income statement.

P8–10. Comprehensive Job-Order Cost Problem (CPA) The Custer Manufacturing Corporation, which uses a job-order cost system, produces various plastic parts for the aircraft industry. On October 9, 19X2, production was started on Job #487 for a hundred front bubbles (windshields) for commercial helicopters.

Production of the bubbles begins in the Fabricating Department, where sheets of plastic (purchased as raw material) are melted down and poured into molds. The molds are placed in a special temperature and humidity room to harden the plastic. The hardened plastic bubbles are then removed from the molds and hand-worked to remove imperfections.

After fabrication, the bubbles are transferred to the Testing Department, in which each bubble must meet rigid specifications. Bubbles that fail the tests are scrapped, and there is no salvage value.

Bubbles passing the tests are transferred to the Assembly Department, where they are inserted into metal frames. The frames, purchased from vendors, require no work before installing the bubbles.

The assembled unit is then transferred to the Shipping Department for crating and shipment. Crating material is relatively expensive and most of the work is done by hand.

The following information concerning Job #487 is available as of December 31, 19X2 (the information is correct as stated):

1. Direct materials charged to the job:
   a. The Fabricating Department was charged for 1,000 sq. ft. of plastic at $12.75 per sq. ft. This amount was to meet all plastic material requirements of the job, assuming no spoilage.
   b. The Assembly Department was charged for 74 metal frames at $408.52 each.
   c. Packing material for 40 units at $75 per unit was charged to the Shipping Department.
2. Direct-labor charges through December 31, 19X2, were as follows:

	Total	Per Unit
Fabricating Department	$1,424	$16
Testing Department	444	6
Assembly Department	612	12
Shipping Department	256	8
	$2,736	

3. Differences between actual and applied manufacturing overhead for the year ending December 31, 19X2, were immaterial. Manufacturing overhead is charged to the four production departments by various allocation methods, all of which you approve. Manufacturing overhead charged to the Fabricating Department is allocated to jobs based on heat-room hours; the other production departments allocate manufacturing overhead to jobs on the basis of direct-labor dollars charged to each job within the department. The following reflects the manufacturing overhead rates for the year ending December 31, 19X2:

	Rate Per Unit
Fabricating Department	$0.45 per hour
Testing Department	0.68 per direct-labor dollar
Assembly Department	0.38 per direct-labor dollar
Shipping Department	0.25 per direct-labor dollar

4. Job #487 used 855 heat-room hours during the year ending December 31, 19X2.
5. Following is the physical inventory for Job #487 as of December 31, 19X2:

    Fabricating Department:
    a. 50 sq. ft of plastic sheet.
    b. 8 hardened bubbles, ¼ complete as to direct labor.
    c. 4 complete bubbles.

    Testing Department
    a. 15 bubbles that failed testing when ⅖ of testing was complete. No others failed.
    b. 7 bubbles complete as to testing.

    Assembly Department:
    a. 13 frames with no direct labor.
    b. 15 bubbles and frames, ⅓ complete as to direct labor.
    c. 3 complete bubbles and frames.

    Shipping Department:
    a. 9 complete units, ⅔ complete as to packing material, ⅓ complete as to direct labor.
    b. 10 complete units; 100 percent complete as to packing material; 50 percent complete as to direct labor.
    c. 1 unit complete for shipping was dropped off the loading docks. There is no salvage.
    d. 23 units have been shipped before December 31, 19X2.
    e. There was no inventory of packing materials in the shipping department on December 31, 19X2.

6. Following is a schedule of equivalent units in production by department for Job #487 as of December 31, 19X2:

CHAPTER 8: JOB-ORDER COST SYSTEMS

Custer Manufacturing Corporation
Schedule of Equivalent Units in Production for Job Number 487
December 31, 19X2

Fabricating Department

	Plastic (sq. ft.)	Bubbles (units) Materials	Labor	Overhead
Transferred in from raw materials	1,000			
Production to date	(950)	95	89	95
Transferred out to other departments		(83)	(83)	(83)
Spoilage				
Balance at December 31, 19X2	50	12	6	12

Testing Department (units)

	Bubbles Transferred in	Labor	Overhead
Transferred in from other departments	83		
Production to date		74	74
Transferred out to other departments	(61)	(61)	(61)
Spoilage	(15)	(6)	(6)
Balance at December 31, 19X2	7	7	7

Assembly Department (units)

	Transferred In	Frames	Labor	Overhead
Transferred in from raw materials		74		
Transferred in from other departments	61			
Production to date			51	51
Transferred out to other departments	(43)	(43)	(43)	(43)
Balance at December 31, 19X2	18	31	8	8

Shipping Department (units)

	Transferred In	Packing Material	Labor	Overhead
Transferred in from raw materials		40		
Transferred in from other departments	43			
Production to date			32	32
Shipped	(23)	(23)	(23)	(23)
Spoilage	(1)	(1)	(1)	(1)
Balance at December 31, 19X2	19	16	8	8

Required

Prepare a schedule for Job #487 of ending inventory costs for *(a)* raw materials by department, *(b)* work in process by department, and *(c)* cost of goods shipped. All spoilage costs are charged to cost of goods shipped.

CASE

Case 8.1 Job-Order Costing with General and Factory Ledgers On December 31, 19X6, after posting the closing entries, the general and factory ledgers of the Stocks Manufacturing Company contained these accounts and balances:

Cash	$84,000	Accounts payable	$ 50,000
Accounts receivable	60,000	Common stock	80,000
Finished goods*	33,000	Retained earnings	142,275
Work in process*	10,175	Factory ledger	83,275
Materials*	40,100	General ledger*	83,275
Machinery (net)	45,000		

*Maintained in the factory ledger.

Details of the three inventories are as follows:

Finished-Goods Inventory

Item L—1,500 units @ $14.00	$21,000
Item M—1,500 units @ 8.00	12,000
Total	$33,000

Work-in-Process Inventory	**Job 88**	**Job 89**
Direct materials:		
400 units of C @ $6.00	$2,400	
300 units of S @ 4.50		$1,350
Direct labor:		
450 hours @ $8.00	3,600	
200 hours @ 6.00		1,200
Factory overhead applied at the rate of $2.50/hour	1,125	500
Total	$7,125	$3,050

Materials Inventory

Material C—2,700 units @ $6.00	$16,200
Material S—4,200 units @ 4.50	18,900
Indirect materials	5,000
Total	$40,100

During January 19X6, the following transactions were completed:

a. Payroll totaling $140,000 was paid. Of the total payroll, $30,000 was for administrative salaries. Payroll deductions consisted of $20,500 for employees' income tax and 7.15% for FICA tax. The factory uses payroll summary account.

b. The payroll is to be distributed as follows: Job 88, 5,000 direct-labor hours @ $8.00; Job 89, 6,000 direct-labor hours @ $6.00; Job 90, 4,000 direct-labor hours @ $3.50; indirect labor, $20,000; administrative salaries, $30,000. Employer's payroll taxes are FICA, 7.15 percent; state unemployment, 2.7 percent; and federal unemployment, 0.7%.

c. Materials purchased on account: Material C, 8,000 units @ $6.50; Material S, 14,000 units @ $5.10; and indirect materials, $22,500.

d. Materials were issued on a FIFO basis in the following order:

Material C:	2,000 units to Job 88	
	5,000 units to Job 90	
	3,000 units to Job 89	
Material S:	5,000 units to Job 90	
	4,000 units to Job 89	
	1,000 units to Job 88	

Indirect materials amounting to $7,520 were issued.

e. Factory overhead was applied to Jobs 88, 89, and 90 based on a rate of $2.50 per direct-labor hour.

f. Jobs 88 and 89 were completed and transferred to finished-goods inventory. Job 88 was for 5,000 units of Item L, and Job 89 was for 10,000 units of Item M.

g. Units sold on account consisted of 5,500 units of Item L for $20 per unit and 9,500 units of Item M for $16 per unit. FIFO inventory method is also used for the finished-goods inventory.

h. Collections on accounts receivable totaled $280,000.

i. Administrative expenses (other than salaries) paid during the month amounted to $24,000. Miscellaneous factory overhead of $18,800 was paid and transferred to the factory. Depreciation on machinery was $2,600.

j. Payments on account were $90,000.

Required

1. Prepare two trial balances as of January 1, 19X6—one for the general ledger and one for the factory ledger.
2. Set up T-accounts for each of the general ledger and factory ledger accounts recorded on the January 1 trial balance. Record the beginning balances.
3. Prepare general journal entries for the January transactions.
4. Post January transactions to the general ledger, factory ledger, and subsidiary ledgers for materials, work in process, finished goods, and factory overhead incurred.
5. Prepare trial balances for the general ledger and the factory ledger as of January 31, 19X6, and reconcile control accounts with the subsidiary ledgers.
6. Prepare a statement of cost of goods sold for January 19X6.

Chapter 9

Process Costing:
Basic Procedures

Outline

CHARACTERISTICS OF PROCESS
   COSTING
PROCEDURES FOR PROCESS COSTING
Weighted Average Method
First-In, First-Out Method
Modified Methods
  Operation Costing

Simplified Costing
SUMMARY
SELF-STUDY PROBLEM
SUGGESTED READINGS
DISCUSSION QUESTIONS
EXERCISES
PROBLEMS

Process costing is a method used for costing inventories in industries characterized by the continuous mass production of similar finished units. For example, oil, canning, steel, rubber, chemical, textile, glass, cement, paint, mining, shoe, electronic, and food processing industries all use some form of process costing.

Each unit of output in a process-costing environment receives essentially the same input of materials, labor, and overhead as any other unit. The large numbers of similar units in a continuous production process make it impractical, if not impossible, to maintain cost accounting records for *each unit* of production. This is unlike the production situation in which relatively small numbers of dissimilar outputs make it practical and useful to identify production by individual units or batches. For example, producers of certain types of heavy machinery or mobile homes identify production by individual units. Job-order costing (as discussed in chapter 8) is used in manufacturing environments in which each unit or batch of output receives varying amounts of materials, labor, and overhead.

This chapter describes basic process-costing procedures. After completing this chapter, you should be able to:

1. identify the characteristics of a manufacturing environment in which process costing is appropriate.
2. apply process-costing techniques using:
    a. the weighted-average method.
    b. the first-in, first-out method.
    c. other modified methods.
3. prepare cost of production reports.

CHARACTERISTICS OF PROCESS COSTING

From an accounting viewpoint, it is important to understand that process costing is simply a method for *averaging* costs over a number of homogeneous or similar units of production. When job-order costing is used, manufacturing costs are identified with specific units of production. In a continuous or mass-production environment this is not realistic because of the large numbers of units involved. Therefore, a multi-step procedure called process costing is used to identify costs with units of production.

In a continuous or mass-production environment, each product typically passes through a series of production steps called *processes* or *departments*. When using process costing, the first phase of accounting is to assign costs to these processes or departments, which are often referred to as responsibility or cost centers. Next, the total cost assigned to each process or department is divided by a measure of the total productive effort expended in that process or department during the accounting period. This results in an average per-unit cost of production, which is finally applied to inventory quantities to derive total inventory costs.

The major difference between job-order and process costing is that with job-order costing, manufacturing costs are identified with one or a few units composing a job, but with process costing, manufacturing costs are first identified with a process or department and then averaged over the total productive effort of that process or department. Using these averages, costs are then assigned to inventory.

The accounting focus of process costing is on departments or processes; materials, labor, and overhead are accumulated and analyzed by department for product-costing purposes. For planning and control purposes, the general cost-accounting principles and procedures discussed in other chapters apply equally well to either job-order or process-costing situations.

Because of the departmentalization of costs and different cost-flow patterns that are possible in process-costing environments, there are some unique characteristics of product flow and related cost-accounting procedures that should be considered. First, process costing is typically visualized as a **sequential flow** of products from one process or department to the next. For example, in the manufacture of bone china, pieces typically proceed in sequence through mixing, molding, cleaning, glazing, and firing departments. Although this is the typical situation, there are other possible product-flow patterns, such as parallel flows and network flows.

Parallel flow characterizes the situation in which various parts are first processed in different departments and then are brought together in subsequent departments to form a finished good. For example, in the electronics industry several different circuit boards may be needed as components in one finished unit. These circuit boards may be manufactured simultaneously in different departments operating parallel to one another. Then these various circuit boards are brought together in an assembly department to form the finished product.

Another pattern is **network flow,** in which products pass through various departments as needed. For example, in a packing house operation, parts of the carcass may be sent to different departments in different sequences, depending on the desired output. Boxed steaks may flow directly from cutting to packing. However, smoked sausages may go through grinding, mixing, stuffing, smoking, and then packing. Any number of other combination of flows may exist for other products.

The essential principle is that all product flows must be identified to insure proper cost accounting, because *inventory cost flows track the product flows*. Once the product flows are identified, the differences between accounting for a complex network flow and a simple sequential flow mainly relate to the amount of detail involved. The reassuring feature of process costing is that regardless of the complexity of the production situation, the basic process-costing principles remain the same.

The sequence of journal entries that follows illustrates the flow of costs from the acquisition of raw materials through the sale of finished goods. In this situation, products move sequentially through two departments, assembly and testing, to finished-goods inventory. Figure 9.1 diagrams the cost flows implicit in these journal entries.

Close attention should be given to these cost flows and to related journal entries, because they portray a basic pattern that underlies even the most complex parallel or network flow. More detail is involved when accounting for complex flows, but the basic principles of process costing remain the same. Once again, cost accounting for planning and control purposes is the same whether using job-order costing or process costing; only the costing aspects are different. However, the departmentalization of costs in a process-costing system does add an additional dimension to the accounting system that aids in planning and control. These additional aspects of departmental accounting are discussed in other chapters.

The first four journal entries outline the cost-acounting procedures for materials, labor, and factory overhead. The same accounts are used in process-costing systems as in any other system, except for the added detail of using separate departmental accounts for work in process.

1. **Purchase of materials:**

Raw materials inventory	80,000	
Accounts payable		80,000

FIGURE 9.1

Cost-Flow Diagram

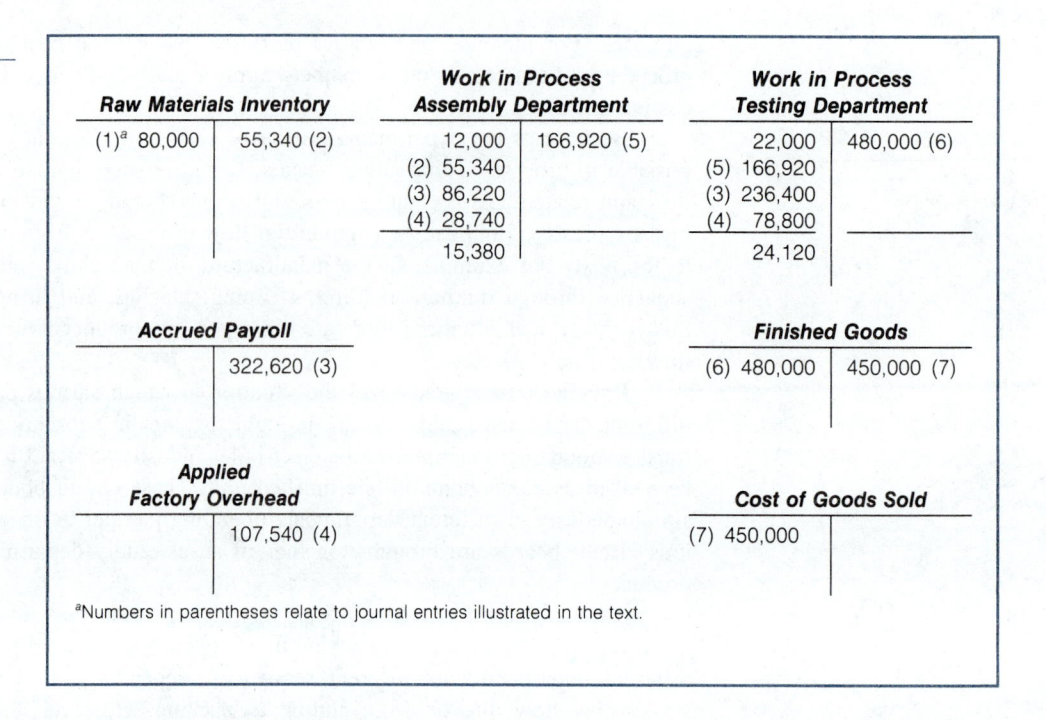

Raw Materials Inventory		Work in Process Assembly Department		Work in Process Testing Department	
(1)[a] 80,000	55,340 (2)	12,000	166,920 (5)	22,000	480,000 (6)
		(2) 55,340		(5) 166,920	
		(3) 86,220		(3) 236,400	
		(4) 28,740		(4) 78,800	
		15,380		24,120	

Accrued Payroll		Finished Goods	
	322,620 (3)	(6) 480,000	450,000 (7)

Applied Factory Overhead		Cost of Goods Sold	
	107,540 (4)	(7) 450,000	

[a] Numbers in parentheses relate to journal entries illustrated in the text.

2. **Issuance of materials:**

Work in process—assembly department	55,340	
Raw materials inventory		55,340

3. **Payroll costs:**

Work in process—assembly department	86,220	
Work in process—testing department	236,400	
Accrued payroll		322,620

4. **Overhead costs:**

Work in process—assembly department	28,740	
Work in process—testing department	78,800	
Factory overhead—applied		107,540

Factory overhead is applied in all departments on the basis of one-third of payroll costs. For example, the amount of overhead applied in the assembly department is $28,740, which is one-third of $86,220, the amount of payroll cost incurred in the assembly department. Journal entries 5 and 6 are unique to departmentalization because they represent cost flows between production departments and between a production department and finished-goods inventory. These journal entries result from the physical transfer of goods. Assigned to these physical units are the material, labor, and overhead costs incurred to that point. The next section of this chapter explains the basis for assigning costs to physical units of production in a process-costing environment.

5. **Transfer of Goods—assembly department to testing department:**

Work in process—testing department	166,920	
Work in process—assembly department		166,920

6. **Transfer of goods—testing department to finished goods:**

Finished-goods inventory	480,000	
Work in process—testing department		480,000

7. **Sales:**

Accounts receivable	560,000	
Sales		560,000
Cost of goods sold	450,000	
Finished-goods inventory		450,000

PROCEDURES FOR PROCESS COSTING

The application of process costing has a two-fold objective: to value goods manufactured and transferred out either to the next department or to finished-goods inventory during an accounting period; and to value work-in-process inventory remaining in production at the end of an accounting period. To accomplish this, a five-step procedure is described and a cost of production worksheet and reporting format is illustrated. Remember that, in practice, these procedures are followed for each department each accounting period.

The five-step process-costing procedure is intended to provide a logical method for accumulating production and cost information in a way that minimizes potential procedural errors. There are many opportunities for taking shortcuts, and several of these will be illustrated. However, care should be taken to thoroughly understand each step before taking shortcuts. The five steps in process costing are as follows:

1. Account for the physical flow of units processed during the period, and determine the percentage completion of work-in-process inventory at the end of the period.
2. Determine the total costs for which an accounting must be made.
3. Compute the work effort of the department for the period in terms of equivalent units of production.
4. Compute costs per equivalent unit of production.
5. Compute total costs for (a) work completed and transferred out of the department during the period and (b) work-in-process inventory at the end of the period.

The following company situation illustrates the application of these steps. An electronics company purchases component parts and assembles and tests them for subsequent resale and ultimate use in larger pieces of equipment. For accounting purposes, the company has two processes—assembly and testing. Raw material is put in process at the beginning of the assembly process, and no material is added during testing. Labor costs are uniformly utilized throughout both processes, and overhead costs are applied at the rate of one-third of labor costs. The manufacturing process is sequential; after assembly, all goods are transferred to the testing department and finally to finished-goods inventory. Data taken from production records of the assembly department for a typical month of operations are as follows:

Production Statistics—Assembly Department

	Units
Work in process, beginning inventory	6,000
(Materials 100% complete; labor and overhead 75% complete)	
Started in process	80,000
Completed and transferred out	78,000
Work-in-process, ending inventory	8,000
(Materials 100% complete; labor and overhead 85% complete)	

Accounting data for both the assembly and testing departments are given in figure 9.1 and recorded in the journal entries beginning on page 316. In practice, the only data available at this stage in the accounting process are those contained in the production statistics plus the accounting data generated through journal entry 4; that is, raw materials would have been acquired and materials cost of $55,340 would have been placed in process in the assembly department. Payroll expenses would also have been incurred, with $86,220 utilized in the assembly department. Manufacturing overhead would have been incurred, with $28,740 being applied in the assembly department. These costs, added to the $12,000 of costs previously assigned to work-in-process beginning inventory, result in a present balance in the work-in-process account of $182,300 before journal entry 5 is made.

The next step in the accounting process is to determine how much of the total costs accumulated in the work-in-process account are associated with *(a)* goods transferred out of the assembly department to the testing department and *(b)* work-in-process inventory remaining in the assembly department. The five steps of process costing are used to make these determinations, which provide the information for journal entries 5 and 6 for the assembly and testing departments, respectively.

There are some minor variations in applying the five steps of process costing that depend on which of two basic methods is used—the weighted-average method or the first-in, first-out method. The five steps of process costing are illustrated in following sections of this chapter.

Weighted-Average Method

The general procedure when using the **weighted-average method** is to determine an average cost per unit from the cost of work-in-process beginning inventory plus the cost of current production. This average cost is then used to determine the total cost of work finished during the period and work still in process at the end of the period. The weighted-average method is relatively easy to apply and is widely used in practice. The steps of process costing using the weighted-average method are as follows:

- **Step 1:** *Account for the physical flow of units processed during the period, and determine the percentage completion of work-in-process inventory at the end of the period.* Data concerning the physical flow of units are typically available in the production records of each department. The stage or percentage of completion of work-in-process inventory is usually estimated by engineering or production personnel. These estimates depend on the *proportion* of total effort that has already been applied to the units in process relative to the total effort required to bring these units to completion.

Some processes have a relatively uniform flow and consistent content of materials, labor, and overhead in process at any particular time.

Other processes may have wide fluctuations of materials, labor, and overhead in process at any one time. For example, oil refineries and cement factories typically have the same percentage of completion at the end of each accounting period. In such instances, the same percentage-of-completion statistics are used from period to period, with only occasional investigation to validate their reasonableness. However, an assembly operation may have widely fluctuating materials and labor content at any particular moment in time.

The practice of using a percentage-of-completion estimate from period to period is justified, because the cost of investigation and estimation to obtain more accurate data each accounting period is usually greater than the benefits of having slightly more accurate percentages. Estimating the degree of materials completion is often easier than estimating labor and overhead completion. The physical and visual properties of materials are usually easier to measure than the labor component and certainly are easier to measure than virtually invisible overhead. For this reason, labor and overhead are sometimes combined and accounted for as conversion costs when process costing is used.

Production data that describes the unit flows in the assembly department and data concerning the degree of completion of work-in-process inventories follow.

Accounting for Units

	Physical Units	Percentage Completion		
		Material	Labor	Overhead
Units to account for:				
Work in process, beginning	6,000	100%	75%	75%
Transferred in this period	80,000			
Total units to account for	86,000			
Units accounted for as follows:				
Completed and transferred out	78,000	100%	100%	100%
Work in process, ending	8,000	100%	85%	85%
Total units accounted for	86,000			

There are 6,000 units in process at the beginning of the period plus 80,000 units started in process during the period, giving a total of 86,000 units to account for. Because there are 8,000 units still in process at the end of the period, 78,000 units (86,000–8,000) must have been completed and transferred out of the department during the period. The number of units transferred out is derived in this illustration. In practice, however, units transferred out are usually physically counted. This could result in a situation in which a number derived as described previously may differ from a physical count. Reasons for such discrepancies and accounting for lost or spoiled units are discussed in subsequent chapters.

- **Step 2:** *Determine the total costs for which an accounting must be made.* This step is accomplished by extracting and summarizing information from departmental work-in-process accounts. At this point in the accounting cycle materials, labor, and overhead costs have been applied to work in process. Data extracted from figure 9.1 and associated journal entries relating to the assembly department indicate that the current balance in the work-in-process account is $182,300 ($12,000 + $55,340 + $86,220 + $28,740). These data are derived as follows:

Total Costs to Account For

	Total	Material	Labor	Overhead
Work in process, beginning	$ 12,000	$ 4,000	$ 6,000	$ 2,000
Costs of the current period	170,300	55,340	86,220	28,740
Total costs to account for	$182,300	$59,340	$92,220	$30,740

The task at hand is to determine how much of the total cost ($182,300) that has been accumulated in the assembly department should be assigned to goods transferred to the testing department and how much should be assigned to the work-in-process ending inventory remaining in the assembly department. This is accomplished by multiplying the number of units transferred out and the number of units still in process by an average cost per unit, as is explained in the following process-costing steps.

- **Step 3:** *Compute the work effort of the department for the period in terms of equivalent units of production.* An **equivalent unit,** as used in process costing, is a measure of work effort expended on units of production. To illustrate, if 1,000 units are 100-percent complete, then 1,000 equivalent units of work effort have been expended on them. However, if another 1,000 units are only 60-percent complete, only 600 equivalent units (0.60 × 1,000) of work effort have been expended on them. These partially completed units will require 40 percent (1.00 − 0.60) or 400 equivalent units of work effort to complete them. If these 1,000 partially completed units are in ending work-in-process inventory, then 600 equivalent units of work effort were expended in the current accounting period and 400 equivalent units of work effort will be expended in the next accounting period to complete them.

Assume that the preceding description of equivalent units applies to a department or process that has started and completed 1,000 units plus has 1,000 units 60-percent complete in work-in-process inventory at the end of the period. The result is that the department has expended 1,600 (1,000 + 600) equivalent units in production during the period.

The determination and use of equivalent units of production is probably the most important aspect of process costing, because equivalent units are the basis for assigning costs at the end of each accounting period to completed units and to work-in-process ending inventory. Equivalent units of production are used to measure exactly how much work effort has been expended in a department during an accounting period. Once the total work effort is known in terms of equivalent units, a cost per equivalent unit can be calculated and used as the basis for allocating costs. For appropriate costing of inventories, there must be an assignment of costs to partially completed units as well as to work fully completed during the period. The use of equivalent units helps accomplish this without the necessity of maintaining voluminous records concerning each completed and partially completed unit in all possible stages of production.

When using the weighted-average method, equivalent units are calculated for units that are completed during the period as well as for units that are started but not completed at the end of the period. Also, equivalent units of production are typically calculated for each cost category—materials, labor, and overhead—as illustrated for the assembly department in the following schedule.

Equivalent Units of Production

	Physical Units	Material	Labor	Overhead
Completed and transferred out	78,000	78,000 (100%)	78,000 (100%)	78,000 (100%)
Work in process, ending	8,000	8,000 (100%)	6,800 (85%)	6,800 (85%)
Total	86,000	86,800	84,800	84,800

The units that were completed and transferred from the assembly department to the testing department during the period, which included the work-in-process beginning inventory, were 100-percent complete as to work units expended in all cost categories. Therefore, 78,000 (1.00 × 78,000) equivalent units of effort were generated.

Equivalent units of work-in-process ending inventory is a measure of the number of physical units that could have been brought to completion *if* all attention and effort had been expended to finish as many units as possible. The work-in-process ending inventory of the assembly department consists of 8,000 physical units. They are 100-percent complete with regard to materials. Therefore, there have been 8,000 (1.00 × 8,000) equivalent units of production in the materials category. However, these same physical units are only 85-percent complete with regard to labor and overhead. This means that if all labor and overhead *had been* expended to bring as many units as possible to completion, 6,800 (0.85 × 8,000) equivalent units would have been produced. This gives a total work effort for the department of 86,000 equivalent units (78,000 + 8,000) for materials and 84,800 equivalent units (78,000 + 6,800) for labor and overhead.

Equivalent units provide the basis for assigning costs to physical units of production. This is accomplished by relating costs and equivalent units to obtain costs per equivalent unit of production, as illustrated in the following step.

CHAPTER 9: PROCESS COSTING: BASIC PROCEDURES

- **Step 4:** *Compute costs per equivalent unit of production.* A cost per equivalent unit of production is computed for each cost category by dividing the total costs to account for by the total equivalent units of production as follows:

Cost per Equivalent Unit of Production

	Total	Material	Conversion Costs — Labor	Conversion Costs — Overhead
(1) Total costs to account for		$59,340	$92,220	$30,740
(2) Total equivalent units		86,000	84,800	84,800
Cost per equivalent unit (1) ÷ (2)	$2.140	$ 0.690	$ 1.088	$ 0.362

Total conversion costs per unit ($1.088 + $0.362) = $1.450

It should be noted that the total cost per equivalent unit of $2.140 is found by adding $0.690, $1.088, and $0.362 costs per equivalent unit and *not* by dividing the total cost to account for by some total number of equivalent units.

Costs per equivalent unit of production provide a way to assign costs to units completed and to work-in-process inventory based on the amount of work effort actually received by each unit. Since *totals* are used in the calculation of costs per equivalent unit, this is essentially an averaging process as opposed to specific identification, which is the procedure used in job-costing. The characteristics of a process-costing environment make this the most acceptable method.

- **Step 5:** *Compute total costs for work completed and transferred out of the department during the period and for work-in-process inventory at the end of the period.* The actual assignment of costs is accomplished by multiplying equivalent units of production found in step 3 by costs per equivalent unit found in step 4. The following illustration shows these calculations. Costs are first assigned to units completed and transferred out of the department during the period and then are assigned to partially completed work remaining in the department at the end of the period. These computations are usually made by cost category, as follows.

Accounting for Costs

	Total	Material	Labor	Overhead
Costs transferred out:				
Equivalent units of production		78,000	78,000	78,000
Cost per equivalent unit		× $0.690	× $1.088	× $0.362
Total	$166,920	$53,820	$84,864	$28,236
Work in process, ending:				
Equivalent units		8,000	6,800	6,800
Cost per equivalent unit		× $0.690	× $1.088	× $0.362
Total	15,380	$ 5,520	$ 7,398	$ 2,462
Total costs accounted for	$182,300	$59,340	$92,262	$30,698

There are two features that readers should observe in the preceding calculations. First, process costing is a self-checking procedure. Comparing the total costs accounted for $182,300 with the total costs to account for of $182,300 can verify the accuracy of arithmetic. The second feature is that the total cost of goods transferred out can be found by multiplying the equivalent units of goods transferred out by the *total* cost per equivalent unit rather than by the cost per equivalent unit for each cost category. This is a valid shortcut for costing work in process at the end of the period only when equivalent units are identical for each cost category. The self-checking feature and shortcut, when appropriate, are used in all other illustrations of process costing in this chapter.

Now that cost assignments have been made in the final step of process costing, information is available to make the journal entry to transfer costs to the next department in the process. Journal entry number 5 on page 316 accomplishes the task. The debit of $166,920 to "work in process—testing department" transfers the costs associated with the movement of physical units to the testing department. The credit to "work in process—assembly department" results in an ending balance of $15,380 in the acount. This amount represents the costs associated with the physical units still in process in the assembly department at the end of the accounting period.

To facilitate learning, the five steps of process costing were presented separately in this text discussion. In practice, however, the results of process costing are brought together in departmental cost of production reports, as shown in figure 9.2. The cost of production report summarizes the process costs to be accounted for during the period, the

FIGURE 9.2

Assembly Department
Cost of Production Report
(Weighted-Average Method)

	Physical Units	Material	Labor	Overhead
		\multicolumn{3}{c}{Percentage Completion}	
Units to account for:				
Work in process, beginning	6,000	100%	75%	75%
Transferred in this period	80,000			
Total units to account for	86,000			
Units accounted for as follows:				
Completed and transferred out	78,000	100%	100%	100%
Work in process, ending	8,000	100%	85%	85%
Total units accounted for	86,000			

	Total	Material	Labor	Overhead
Costs to account for:				
Work in process, beginning	$ 12,000	$ 4,000	$ 6,000	$ 2,000
Costs of the current period	170,300	55,340	86,220	28,740
(1) Total costs to account for	$182,300	$ 59,340	$ 92,220	$ 30,740
Equivalent units of production:				
Completed and transferred out		78,000	78,000	78,000
Work in process, ending		8,000	6,800	6,800
(2) Total equivalent units		86,000	84,800	84,800
Cost per equivalent unit, (1) ÷ (2)	$ 2.140	$ 0.690	$ 1.088	$ 0.362
Costs accounted for as follows:				
Costs transferred out:				
Equivalent units of production		78,000	78,000	78,000
Cost per equivalent unit		× $0.690	× $1.088	× $0.362
Total	$166,920	$ 53,820	$ 84,864	$ 28,236
Work in process, ending				
Equivalent units		8,000	6,800	6,800
Cost per equivalent unit		× $0.690	× $1.088	× $0.362
Total	15,380	$ 5,520	$ 7,398	$ 2,462
Total costs accounted for	$182,300	$ 59,340	$ 92,262	$ 30,698

units completed and transferred out, the computation of per-unit costs, the costs assigned to work in process at the end of the period, and the costs assigned to units completed and transferred out during the period.

All columns on a typical cost of production report, other than the total column, are necessary to make the computations. However, only a total column is usually presented on the final report to management.

Now that the accounting and reporting work is complete for the assembly department, attention is shifted to the next department in the production process—the testing department. Production records of the testing department for the current period provide the following data:

Production Statistics—Testing Department

	Units
Work-in-process beginning inventory	7,000
(Materials 100% complete; labor and overhead 60% complete)	
Transferred in from the assembly department	78,000
Completed and transferred to finished goods	80,000
Work-in-process ending inventory	5,000
(Materials 100% complete; labor and overhead 70% complete)	

Apart from the quantities involved, the production statistics for the testing department are different from the assembly department's in two ways. First, goods are transferred to finished-goods inventory from the testing department rather than to another department for additional processing. The cost at which units are transferred out of the testing department is the cost at which the units are carried in finished-goods inventory. This includes all costs—testing department costs plus assembly department costs.

There are some fundamental differences between departments in which work is initiated (such as the assembly department) and departments that perform subsequent processing (such as the testing department). First, note that costs are accumulated from a zero basis in the assembly department, but work coming into the testing department already has had effort applied and a cost assigned for all of the work previously performed in the assembly department. These costs are called *transferred-in costs,* and they represent the accumulated cost of materials, labor, and overhead applied in all prior departments. For example, the transferred-in costs for goods received by the testing department during the current period are $166,920; this is the total amount transferred out of the assembly department as shown in figure 9.2. The important thing about transferred-in costs is that they are handled in the process-costing steps and in the cost of production report *as though they are another cost category, like materials, labor, or overhead.* A separate column is added to the cost of production report to handle transferred-in costs.

Rather than discuss each step of process costing for the testing department, the cost of production report for the department is presented in its entirety in figure 9.3. The unique features of process cost accounting for subsequent departments as illustrated by the testing department are then discussed.

Assume that any defective units found in the testing department are corrected with simple adjustments made by the testing technician and that no units are lost. Accounting for lost units in a process-costing environment is discussed in chapter 10.

Note that figure 9.3 has a separate column to account for transferred-in costs. The amount of $166,920 transferred out of the assembly department, as shown in figure 9.2, appears as a transferred-in cost of the testing department in figure 9.3. Notice also that the work-in-process beginning inventory of the testing department contains $9,880 of transferred-in costs. This represents all of the materials, labor, and overhead costs incurred from work performed on these units before they were transferred into this department. Continuing

FIGURE 9.3

Testing Department
Cost of Production Report
(Weighted Average Method)

	Physical Units	Percentage Completion		
		Transferred In	Material	Labor and Overhead
Units to account for:				
Work in process, beginning	7,000	100%		60%
Transferred in this period	78,000			
Total units to account for	85,000			
Units accounted for as follows:				
Completed and transferred out	80,000	100%		100%
Work in process, ending	5,000	100%		70%
Total units accounted for	85,000			

	Total	Transferred In	Material	Labor and Overhead
Costs to account for:				
Work in process, beginning	$ 22,000	$ 9,880		$ 12,120
Costs of the current period	482,120	166,920		315,200
(1) Total costs to account for	$504,120	$176,800		$327,320
Equivalent units of production:				
Completed and transferred out		80,000		80,000
Work in process, ending		5,000		3,500
(2) Total equivalent units		85,000		83,500
Cost per equivalent unit, (1) ÷ (2)	$ 6.000	$ 2.080		$ 3.920
Costs accounted for as follows:				
Costs transferred out	$480,000	(80,000 × $6.000)		
Work in process, ending:				
Transferred-in costs	$ 10,400	(5,000 × $2.080)		
Labor and overhead	13,720	(3,500 × $3.920)		
Total	$ 24,120			
Total costs accounted for	$504,120			

the inspection of the transferred-in column, equivalent units and cost per equivalent unit are computed for transferred-in costs just as for other cost categories.

It should be noted that the cost per equivalent unit of $2.080 for transferred-in costs in the testing department is not the same as the total cost per equivalent unit of $2.140 in the assembly department. Even though it seems as if they should be equal, they differ because of the difference in per-unit cost of work-in-process beginning inventory and the per-unit cost of goods transferred in this period. If the cost of production in a prior department remains the same through successive accounting periods, transferred-in costs per equivalent unit will also remain the same in subsequent departments.

Finally, examine the assignment of costs to units transferred to finished goods and to work-in-process ending inventory to see that transferred-in costs are also assigned to inventories as though they represent another cost category.

Another important difference between the cost of production reports of the assembly and testing departments is that the materials column is vacant in the testing department's report because no materials are added in the testing department. All prior materials costs are carried as part of the transferred-in costs accounted for in the testing department. Materials can be added to processes subsequent to the first process; this feature is simply not a part of this particular example but is illustrated in chapter 10.

Another difference between the reports of the two departments is that labor and overhead costs are combined into one column on the testing department's cost of production report. When overhead is applied as a function of labor, as in this example, it is common practice to combine labor and overhead into a single conversion-cost category in one column of the report.

Once again, the purpose of the cost of production report is to provide information for costing inventories. Journal entries 5 and 6 on page 000 illustrate how the information generated in the testing department's cost of production report is used in the accounting cycle.

Before proceeding to the next section, review the process-costing steps for both the originating and subsequent departments. A clear understanding is important at this point because the remainder of this chapter and chapter 10 will expand on the basics of process costing presented here.

First-in, First-out Method

The **first-in, first-out (FIFO) method** is simply another way of calculating product costs in a continuous or mass-production environment. The five process-costing steps and the basic format of the cost of production report are essentially the same whether using the weighted-average or FIFO method. The major differences between the two methods are in calculating equivalent units of production, determining costs per equivalent unit, and applying costs per equivalent unit to inventories. To illustrate these differences, the information for the assembly department used to illustrate the weighted-average method is recast in figure 9.4 using the FIFO method. All production and cost statistics are the same; only the process-costing method is different.

The calculation of equivalent units using the FIFO method separates the costs associated with work-in-process beginning inventory from the costs related to work performed in the current period. In contrast, the weighted-average method is based on averaging the costs of all work performed, regardless of whether the work was performed in the current period or in prior periods. Because the FIFO method distinguishes between work done in the current period and work done in prior periods, it is necessary to calculate equivalent units of production for work effort expended on *(a)* completing work-in-process beginning inventory; *(b)* starting, completing, and transferring out work during the period; and *(c)* bringing work-in-process ending inventory to its current level of completion.

This is why the equivalent-units section of the cost of production report in figure 9.4 contains equivalent-unit calculations for effort used to complete work-in-process beginning inventory, plus effort relating to units started and completed during the period, plus effort relating to work-in-process ending inventory. In contrast, when using the weighted-average method, equivalent-unit calculations are made only for units completed plus work-in-process ending inventory. For example, the equivalent-units-of-production section in figure 9.4 contains 1,500 equivalent units necessary to complete work-in-process inventory. This number is found by determining that if work-in-process inventory is 75-percent complete at the beginning of the period, there is 25 percent of the total effort yet required to complete the units in the current period. Multiplying 6,000 physical units by 25 percent yields 1,500 equivalent units of production expended during the current period to complete work-in-process beginning inventory.

There were 72,000 (1.00 × 72,000) equivalent units started, completed, and transferred out of the department during the current period. The total number of units actually

FIGURE 9.4

Assembly Department
Cost of Production Report
(First-in, First-out Method)

	Physical Units	Percentage Completion		
		Material	Labor	Overhead
Units to account for:				
Work in process, beginning	6,000	100%	75%	75%
Transferred in this period	80,000			
Total units to account for	86,000			
Units accounted for as follows:				
Completed and transferred out	78,000	100%	100%	100%
Work in process, ending	8,000	100%	85%	85%
Total units accounted for	86,000			

	Total	Material	Labor	Overhead
Costs to account for:				
Work in process, beginning	$ 12,000[a]			
(1) Costs of the current period	170,300	$55,340	$86,220	$28,740
Total costs to account for	$182,300[a]			
Equivalent units of production:				
Complete work in process, beginning			1,500	1,500
Started and completed		72,000	72,000	72,000
Work in process, ending		8,000	6,800	6,800
(2) Total equivalent units		80,000	80,300	80,300
Cost per equivalent unit, (1) ÷ (2)	$ 2.124	$ 0.692	$ 1.074	$ 0.358
Costs accounted for as follows:				
Costs transferred out:				
Work in process, beginning	$ 12,000			
Work completed on work in process, beginning:				
Labor	1,611	(1,500 × $1.074)		
Overhead	537	(1,500 × $0.358)		
Work started and completed	152,928	(72,000 × $2.124)		
Total	$167,076			
Work in process, ending:				
Materials	$ 5,536	(8,000 × $0.692)		
Labor	7,303	(6,800 × $1.074)		
Overhead	2,434	(6,800 × $0.358)		
Total	$ 15,273			
Total costs accounted for	$182,300	(Rounded from $182,349)		

[a]Detail and totals for material, labor, and overhead are omitted to emphasize the FIFO method.

transferred out was 78,000. However, 6,000 of these units were already in process at the beginning of the period and receive a separate accounting. Therefore, only 72,000 units (78,000 − 6,000) were started and completed during the period.

The calculation of equivalent units for work-in-process ending inventory is the same for weighted-average and FIFO methods.

The calculation of cost per equivalent unit of production also follows the FIFO assumption that costs associated with work-in-process beginning inventory are not mingled with the cost of work done in the current period; that is, to derive costs per equivalent unit of production using the FIFO method, "costs of the *current* period" rather than the "*total* costs to account for" are divided by total equivalent units of production. In this way, costs incurred in prior periods are segregated from costs incurred in the current period as assumed by the FIFO method.

The final differences between weighted-average and FIFO methods concern the assignment of costs to inventories. First, costs incurred during prior periods associated with work-in-process beginning inventory are carried as though they are a "batch" of costs associated with beginning inventory. For example, the $12,000 total cost of work-in-process beginning inventory is a separate item in the determination of total costs to transfer out, or to finished goods. Added to the cost of work-in-process beginning inventory are the current costs necessary to complete these units. For example, 1,500 equivalent units of labor and overhead were required to complete the beginning inventory. Multiplying 1,500 equivalent units by the cost per equivalent unit for labor and overhead ($1.074 and $0.358, respectively) gives the productive effort expended this period to complete beginning work in process. Remember that the work-in-process beginning inventory is already complete as to materials. The cost of materials is contained in the $12,000 cost of beginning work in process.

The last portion of the total cost transferred out consists of current costs for materials, labor, and overhead assigned to units started and completed during the current period. This amount is simply computed using the 72,000 equivalent units for work started and completed this period multiplied by the $2.124 total cost per equivalent unit, as shown in figure 9.4.

The cost of work-in-process ending inventory is also found by multiplying equivalent units of production for materials, labor, and overhead by their respective costs per equivalent unit, as shown in figure 9.4. This completes the process-costing procedure for the assembly department using the FIFO method and provides the information necessary for recording the transfer of costs to the testing department. The transfer of costs is accomplished with the following journal entry:

Work in process—testing department	167,076	
Work in process—assembly department		167,076

Tracing costs to the next department, the amount of $167,076 transferred out of the assembly department to the testing department is shown as an element of costs of the current period on the testing department's cost of production report, as shown in figure 9.5.

Note that a separate column is used to account for transferred-in costs when using the FIFO method, just as when using the weighted-average method (see figure 9.3). Transferred-in costs are handled in the same way as described for the weighted-average method. The calculation of equivalent units for work-in-process beginning inventory and the assignment of costs to complete work-in-process beginning inventory are also similar to the procedures used with the FIFO method in the assembly department. Recording of the transfer of costs from the testing department to finished-goods inventory is as follows:

Finished-goods inventory	479,671	
Work in process—testing department		479,671

A theoretical question about whether or not process costing using the FIFO method represents strict adherence to FIFO or a modified FIFO method arises for two reasons. First, each department in a multiprocess environment is treated as a separate entity, and

FIGURE 9.5

Testing Department
Cost of Production Report
(First-in, First-out Method)

	Physical Units	Percentage Completion Transferred In	Material	Labor and Overhead
Units to account for:				
Work in process, beginning	7,000	100%		60%
Transferred in this period	78,000			
Total units to account for	85,000			
Units accounted for as follows:				
Completed and transferred out	80,000	100%		100%
Work in process, ending	5,000	100%		70%
Total units accounted for	85,000			

	Total	Transferred In	Material	Labor and Overhead
Costs to account for:				
Work in process, beginning	$ 22,000			
(1) Costs of the current period	$482,276	$167,076		$315,200
Total costs to account for	$504,276[a]			
Equivalent units of production:				
Complete work in process, beginning				2,800
Started and completed		73,000		73,000
Work in process, ending		5,000		3,500
(2) Total equivalent units		78,000		79,300
Cost per equivalent unit, (1) ÷ (2)	$ 6.117	$ 2.142		$ 3.975
Costs accounted for as follows:				
Costs transferred out:				
Work in process, beginning	$ 22,000			
Completed work in process	11,130	(2,800 × $3.975)		
Started and completed	446,541	(73,000 × $6.117)		
Total	$479,671			
Work in process, ending:				
Transferred-in costs	$ 10,710	(5,000 × $2.142)		
Labor and overhead	13,913	(3,500 × $3.975)		
Total	$ 24,623			
Total costs accounted for	$504,276	(Rounded from $504,294)		

[a] Detail and totals for transferred-in, labor, and overhead costs omitted to emphasize the FIFO method.

the accounting method used in any one department is independent of the method used in any other department. Therefore, unless the FIFO costing method is used for all departments, it is doubtful whether strict FIFO costing is present.

    Second, all units transferred into a department during an accounting period are carried at the same unit cost, even though there may be a number of batches transferred in at different times during the period. Therefore, it may be argued that if strict FIFO costing is desired, beginning work-in-process and all other batches started at various times during a period should receive separate accountings. However, such a strict adherence to the FIFO concept would quickly become overly complicated and burdensome except in the very simplest production environment. Therefore, the departmental FIFO method illustrated in this chapter is typically used when FIFO inventory costing is desired.

Modified Methods

The endless variety of types of industries, products, and processes presents a situation more complex than two costing methods can satisfy. In reality, job-order costing and process costing provide general accounting methods that satisfy requirements at two ends of a continuum of manufacturing types. However, there are many ways to modify these basic methods to satisfy conditions in specific industries, companies, or processes. Two such modifications to process costing are discussed in this section.

Operation Costing When batches of goods that have some common and some unique characteristics are processed, a modified method called *operation costing* is used. The common characteristics usually involve the manufacturing operations, and the unique characteristics usually include the materials used or the routing of goods through various possible processing operations. For cost-accounting purposes, an operation-costing system handles materials costs as in job-order costing and conversion costs as in process costing. In other words, the cost of direct materials is assigned directly to the product (usually a batch), as in job-order costing. However, direct labor and factory overhead are accumulated by operation or department, and they are then assigned to the physical units passing through that operation or department based on an average per-unit cost, as in process costing. Two examples of operation costing are given in this section.

The first example of operation costing deals with a maker of commemorative medallions. Each type of medallion passes through the same punching, stamping, finishing, and packaging operations. However, some medallions are made of gold, some of silver, and others of a nickle alloy. A great difference in material costs but identical processing requirements has led this particular company to account for the cost of materials on a job-order costing basis and to account for the cost of labor and overhead on a process costing basis. Each type of medallion is identified as a batch or production run, and the cost of materials is assigned directly to that batch. Labor and overhead costs are accumulated by department using the customary process-costing methods, and each medallion is assigned a portion of these costs based on the average cost per medallion for each process.

To illustrate, consider the following hypothetical information for the production of two batches of medallions consisting of 50 Type G medallions and 100 Type N medallions.

	Type G	Type N
Direct materials	$ 7,500	$ 500
Conversion costs:		
Punching ($6 per unit)	300	600
Stamping ($6 per unit)	300	600
Finishing ($14 per unit)	700	1,400
Packaging ($30 per unit)	1,500	3,000
Total	$10,300	$6,100
Cost per unit	$ 206	$ 61

A second example of operation costing deals with a manufacturer of microprocessor chips. Although a variety of different types of chips are produced, the cost of the principal direct material, a silicon wafer, is essentially the same. However, different types of chips are routed through various operations and receive different amounts of additional materials and conversion costs, depending on the design of that particular chip. Product costs are accumulated by batch, where a batch consists of 100 wafers of a particular type of chip.

Initial direct materials are specifically identified with a batch; direct labor and factory overhead are accumulated by process. An average per-unit conversion cost is calculated and applied to batches based on the processing operations required for that particular type of chip.

To illustrate, consider the following hypothetical information for the production of one batch of each of two types of chips. A Type I chip requires processing in operations 1 and 4, whereas a Type II chip requires processing in all operations.

	Type I	Type II
Direct materials ($35 per unit)	$3,500	$3,500
Conversion costs:		
Operation 1 ($6 per unit)	600	600
Operation 2 ($4 per unit)	—	400
Operation 3 ($10 per unit)	—	1,000
Operation 4 ($15 per unit)	1,500	1,500
Total	$5,600	$7,000
Cost per unit	$ 56	$ 70

Simplified Costing In this text, *simplified costing* describes a modified method of cost accounting used when a manufacturing company *(a)* operates in a repetitive manufacturing environment and *(b)* uses a just-in-time (JIT) production philosophy. Repetitive manufacturing, also called constant flow manufacturing, refers to a production environment where a high volume of standardized units are fabricated, machined, assembled, and tested in a continuous flow.[1] Repetitive manufacturing and traditional process costing environments are similar, except that repetitive manufacturing refers to the production of separate and distinct physical units, such as circuit boards or machine parts, as opposed to products in fluid or powder form. Also, repetitive manufacturing takes place in a highly automated plant characterized by computer controlled machines, robots, and automated materials handling.

The implication for cost accounting is that direct-labor cost, as a component of total product costs, appears to be much lower in repetitive manufacturing situations than it is in traditional job-order or process costing situations. For example, one company that uses repetitive manufacturing reports that direct labor composes only 3 to 5 percent of total product costs.[2]

Just-in-time (JIT), as discussed in chapter 12, has an additional implication for cost accounting. JIT is synonymous with zero inventories, for which the basic philosophy is that finished goods are produced just in time to be sold, subcomponents are produced just in time to be assembled into finished goods, and raw materials are purchased just in time to be transformed into subassemblies. The overall goal of JIT is improved manufacturing productivity, but the important result of using JIT for cost accounting is that inventories are significantly reduced or eliminated.

The traditional process-costing environment typically has inventories large enough to require a separate accounting. In fact, much of the effort of process costing illustrated in this chapter is directed toward proper inventory valuation. However, in repetitive manufacturing or JIT situations, the reduction in inventories and direct-labor component has prompted some companies to reassess their cost accounting procedures. For example, one company has made several simplifying changes. First, direct labor has been eliminated as a separate cost category and is accounted for as part of manufacturing overhead. The

---

1. Definition by the American Production and Control Society.
2. Patrick Linnen, "No Inventory—No Cost System," *Hewlett-Packard Financial Notes* 10 (September 1983): 1.

company indicates that labor has become such a small part of the total product cost that the cost of maintaining a separate, detailed accounting for direct labor exceeds its benefit.

A second simplifying change made by this company is that overhead is treated as a period expense by charging it directly to cost of goods sold, rather than charging it to work in process and then tracking it through various departments to finished goods and, finally, to cost of goods sold. The company indicates that with a minimum level of inventories on hand at the end of an accounting period, virtually all overhead has already flowed through to the cost-of-goods-sold account. Management concluded that tracking overhead through department work-in-process accounts to finished-goods inventory and finally to cost of goods sold provided little useful information for decisions. However, the company does track the cost of materials through department work-in-process accounts into finished-goods inventory. For financial reporting, labor and overhead costs are included in work-in-process and finished-goods inventories at the end of an accounting period by making adjusting entries to reclassify part of cost of goods sold as work-in-process and finished-goods inventories.

Figure 9.6 shows the difference between the cost flows using traditional cost accounting and the simplified costing system described here.

Operation costing and simplified costing are only two examples of many possible modified methods used in manufacturing environments where the traditional job-order and process approaches do not have a perfect fit. Before deciding if job-order, process, or some form of modified method should be used, cost accountants should thoroughly evaluate the underlying production processes and the information needs of management in each particular production situation. Only then can a system be designed that is relevant for the needs of management.

FIGURE 9.6

Comparison of Cost Flows

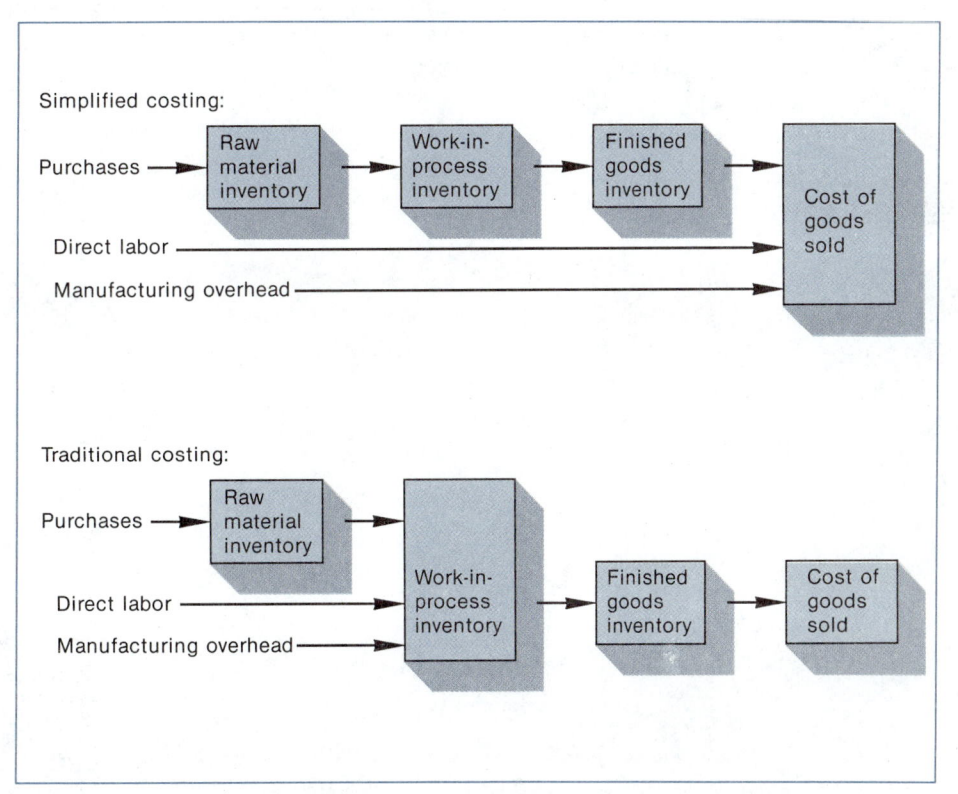

Adapted from Rick Hunt, Linda Garrett, and C. Mike Merz, "Direct Labor Cost Not Always Relevant at H–P," *Management Accounting* 66 (February 1985): 60.

SUMMARY

Process costing is a method used to assign costs to inventory in manufacturing operations characterized by the continuous mass production of similar finished units. There are five basic steps in process costing:

1. Accounting for the physical flow of production and estimating the percentage completion of work-in-process ending inventory.
2. Determining the total costs for which an accounting must be made.
3. Computing equivalent units of production.
4. Determining costs per equivalent unit of production.
5. Assigning costs to completed units and to work-in-process ending inventory.

The concept of equivalent units is the key to process costing. Equivalent units are measures of the work effort expended in a department or process during an accounting period. Costs per equivalent unit are used to assign costs to finished work and work in process.

There are two general methods used to apply process costing—the weighted-average method and the first-in, first-out (FIFO) method. The weighted-average method is easiest to apply and most widely used. It differs from the FIFO method in that it averages costs of the prior period contained in the work-in-process beginning inventory with costs of the current period. The FIFO method does not mingle costs of the current period with costs incurred in prior periods.

Process-costing procedures are often modified to accommodate unique characteristics of different manufacturing environments. Basic process-costing procedures are used to account for the continuous mass-production component of operations, whereas elements of job-order costing are incorporated to account for the unique features in the processing environment. Two types of modifications, operation costing and simplified costing, are described in this chapter.

SELF-STUDY PROBLEM

Wood Products Company uses a fabrication process in the initial construction of its cabinets for mantel clocks. The rough cabinet is then sent to the finishing department for the next phase of processing. Production and accounting statistics summarized from fabrication department records for the current period are as follows:

Production Statistics

	Units
Work-in-process beginning inventory	1,800
(Materials 100% complete; labor 50% complete; and overhead 60% complete)	
Units of wood placed in process	76,000
Work-in-process ending inventory	800
(Materials 100% complete; labor 40% complete; and overhead 50% complete)	

Accounting Statistics

Work-in-process beginning inventory:		
Materials	$	47,000
Labor		3,600
Overhead		1,000
Total	$	51,600
Costs of the current period:		
Materials		$1,976,000
Labor		315,200
Overhead		77,000
Total		$2,368,200
Total costs to account for		$2,419,800

Required

Using the first-in, first-out method, calculate the following:

1. The cost of work transferred out of the fabrication department during the current period.
2. The cost of work-in-process ending inventory.

Present your results in the form of a cost of production report suitable for management use.

Solution to the Self-Study Problem

**Fabrication Department
Cost of Production Report
(First-in, First-out Method)**

	Physical Units	Percentage Completion		
		Material	Labor	Overhead
Units to account for:				
Work in process, beginning	1,800	100%	50%	60%
Transferred in this period	76,000			
Total units to account for	77,800			
Units accounted for as follows:				
Completed and transferred out	77,000	100%	100%	100%
Work in process, ending	800	100%	40%	50%
Total units accounted for	77,800			

	Total	Material	Labor	Overhead
Costs to account for:				
Work in process, beginning	$ 51,600			
(1) Costs of the current period	2,368,200	1,976,000	315,200	77,000
Total costs to account for	$2,419,800			
Equivalent units of production:				
Complete work in process, beginning			900	720
Started and completed		75,200	75,200	75,200
Work in process, ending		800	320	400
(2) Total equivalent units		76,000	76,420	76,320
Cost per equivalent unit, (1) ÷ (2)	$ 31.134	$ 26.000	$ 4.125	$ 1.009

Costs accounted for as follows:		
Costs transferred out:		
Work in process, beginning	$51,600	
Completed work in process:		
Labor	3,713	(900 × $ 4.125)
Overhead	727	(720 × $ 1.009)
Work started and completed	2,341,277	(75,200 × $31.134)
Total	$2,397,317	
Work in process, ending:		
Materials	$ 20,800	(800 × $26.000)
Labor	1,320	(320 × $ 4.125)
Overhead	404	(400 × $ 1.009)
Total	$ 22,524	
Total costs accounted for	$2,419,800	(Rounded from $2,419,841)

SUGGESTED READINGS

Cummins, Peter. "Process Costing Calculations: An Alternative Layout." *Australian Accountant* 55 (September 1985): 69–71.

Mong, Han Kang. "Control Theory Approach to Process Costing." *Accounting and Business Research* 15 (Spring 1985): 129–133.

Sandretto, Michael J. "What Kind of Cost System Do You Need?" *Harvard Business Review* 63 (January–February 1985): 110–118.

DISCUSSION QUESTIONS

Q9–1. What is process costing and in what types of industries is it used?

Q9–2. Discuss characteristics of process costing that differentiate it from job-order costing.

Q9–3. Describe three different cost-flow patterns that may occur among departments in a process-costing environment.

Q9–4. Describe the flow of costs from the acquisition of raw materials through the sale of products in a typical process-costing company. Also, give the typical journal entry(s) made at each phase in the cost-flow cycle.

Q9–5. What is the two-fold objective of process costing?

Q9–6. Discuss the steps of process costing.

Q9–7. What is an equivalent unit of production?

Q9–8. How are costs assigned to completed work and work-in-process ending inventory using the weighted-average method?

Q9–9. What are the differences between the weighted-average method and the first-in, first-out method?

Q9–10. How are costs assigned to completed work and work-in-process ending inventory using the first-in, first-out method?

Q9–11. What is the purpose of the cost of production report? Discuss the purpose of each section.

Q9–12. What differences, if any, are there between process-costing procedures for initial departments in which products are started in process and accounting procedures for subsequent departments?

Q9–13. Why is it a bad idea to shortcut the assignment of costs to work-in-process ending inventory?

Q9–14. Describe two modified methods that may be used in a company that does not exactly match either a job-order or process-costing situation.

EXERCISES

E9–1. Concepts and Procedures—Weighted-Average and FIFO Methods

Make the equivalent-unit calculations for department A that are necessary to answer the questions in each of the following independent situations.

1. Sussex Corporation's production cycle starts in department A. The following information is available for the month of April:

	Units
Work in process, April 1 (50% complete)	40,000
Started in April	240,000
Work in process, April 30 (60% complete)	25,000

Materials are added in the beginning of the process in department A. Using the weighted-average method determine the equivalent units of production for the month of April.

2. Department A is the first stage of Mark Company's production cycle. Conversion costs for this department were 80-percent complete as to the beginning work in process and 50-percent complete as to the ending work in process. Information about conversion costs in the cutting department for January is as follows:

	Units	Conversion Costs
Work in process at January 1	25,000	$ 22,000
Units started and costs incurred during January	135,000	$143,000
Units completed and transferred to next department during January	100,000	

Using the FIFO method, determine the equivalent units of production for work transferred out and work-in-process inventory at January 31.

3. A company uses a first-in, first-out method of costing in a process-costing system. Material is added at the beginning of the process in department A, and conversion costs are incurred uniformly throughout the process. Work-in-process beginning inventory on April 1 in department A consisted of 50,000 units estimated to be 30-percent complete. During April, 150,000 units were started in department A, and 160,000 units were completed and transferred to department B. Work-in-process ending inventory on April 30 in department A was estimated to be 20-percent complete. What were the total equivalent units in department A for April for materials and conversion costs, respectively?

4. The Ace Company had computed the flow of physical units for department A for the month of April 19X9 as follows:

Units completed:	
From work in process on April 1, 19X9	10,000
From April production	30,000
	40,000

Materials are added at the beginning of the process. There were 8,000 units of work in process at April 30, 19X9. The work in process at April 1, 19X9, was 80-percent complete as to conversion costs and at April 30, 19X9, was 60-percent complete as to conversion costs. What were the equivalent units of production for materials and conversion costs for the month of April 19X9 using the FIFO method?

5. Walton Incorporated had 8,000 units of work in process in department A on October 1, 19X8, that were 60-percent complete as to conversion costs. Materials are added at the beginning of the process. During the month of October, 34,000 units were started and 36,000 units completed. Walton had 6,000 units of work in process on October 31, 19X8, that were 80-percent complete as to conversion costs. By how much did the equivalent units for the month of October using the weighted-average method exceed the equivalent units for the month of October using the first-in, first-out method?

E9-2. Equivalent Units—FIFO versus Weighted-Average Costing Harrow Company uses a process-costing system. The following information is available for department A:

	Units
Work in process, July 1	25,000
Work in process, July 31	20,000
Units started in process	40,000
Units transferred to Department B	45,000

	Percentage of Completion	
	July 1	July 31
Materials	80%	70%
Labor	50%	40%
Overhead	30%	20%

Required

1. Determine the equivalent units of production using the weighted-average cost method.
2. Determine the equivalent units of production using the FIFO cost method.

E9–3. Equivalent Units—FIFO versus Weighted-Average Costing The following data relate to the activities of the manufacturing department of Hanlock Company during September 19X5:

	Units
Work in process, September 1 (100% complete as to materials; 60% complete as to conversion costs)	25,000
Work in process, September 30 (100% complete as to materials; 40% complete as to conversion costs)	15,000
Units started in process	60,000
Units transferred to the finishing department	70,000

Required

1. Compute the equivalent units of production using the weighted-average method.
2. Compute the equivalent units of production using the FIFO method.

E9–4. Equivalent Unit Computations Gerry Incorporated has four departments—cutting, building, sanding, and finishing. Gerry uses a process-costing system to account for the costs. The following information is available about Gerry's work-in-process inventory at the end of the fiscal year, August 31, 19X8:

1. Cutting: 2,500, 60-percent complete as to raw materials
2. Building: 1,200, 70-percent complete as to conversion costs
3. Sanding: 1,800, 30-percent complete as to conversion costs
4. Finishing: 3,200, 80-percent complete as to conversion costs

Required

1. Determine the number of equivalent units of raw materials in all inventories at August 31, 19X8. All materials are added in the cutting department.

2. Determine the number of equivalent units of the building department's conversion costs in all inventories at August 31, 19X8.
3. Determine the number of equivalent units of the finishing department's conversion costs in all inventories at August 31, 19X8.

E9-5. Process Costing Basic Procedures—Weighted-Average Method

Morkiss Company uses a mixing process to prepare the base ingredient for its lipsticks and other lip products. The mixed chemicals are then sent to other processes, depending on the desired final product. The following are equivalent-unit and cost-per-equivalent unit data for the mixing process for the month of April.

Equivalent Units of Production

	Materials	Labor	Overhead
Completed and transferred out	500	500	500
Work in process, ending	20	10	10
Total	520	510	510
Cost per equivalent unit	$8.00	$6.00	$12.00

Required

Using the weighted-average method:
1. Calculate the cost of work transferred out of the mixing department during the month of April.
2. Calculate the cost of work-in-process ending inventory at the end of April.
3. What was the total cost to account for in the mixing process for April?
4. Prepare the journal entry to record the transfer of costs out of the mixing department.

E9-6. Process Costing Basic Procedures—FIFO Method

Lenwood Company makes an industrial cleaning powder. Information concerning equivalent units and costs per equivalent unit for the month of June for department 1, Lenwood Company's first stage of production, is as follows:

Equivalent Units of Production

	Materials	Labor	Overhead
Complete work in process, beginning	0	1,000	1,000
Started and completed	40,000	40,000	40,000
Work in process, ending	2,000	1,500	1,500
Total	42,000	42,500	42,500
Cost per equivalent unit	$3.00	$2.00	$2.00
Cost of work in process, beginning	$6,000	$4,000	$4,000

Required

Using the FIFO method:
1. Calculate the cost of work transferred out of department 1 during June.
2. Calculate the cost of work-in-process ending inventory for department 1 at the end of June.
3. What was the total cost to account for in department 1 for June?
4. Prepare the journal entry to record the transfer of costs out of department 1 to department 2.

E9-7. Materials Cost Determination

Maurice Company adds materials at the beginning of the process in the forming department, which is the first of two stages in its production cycle. Information concerning the materials used in the forming department in April is as follows:

	Units	Materials Costs
Work in process at April 1	12,000	$ 6,000
Units started during April	100,000	$51,120
Units completed and transferred to next department during April	88,000	

Required

Using the weighted-average method, determine the materials cost of the work in process at April 30.

E9–8. Materials Cost Determination Lucas Company adds materials at the beginning of the process in the forming department, which is the first of two stages in its production cycle. Information concerning the materials used in the forming department in October is as follows:

	Units	Materials Costs
Work in process at October 1	6,000	$ 3,000
Units started during October	50,000	$25,560
Units completed and transferred to next department during October	44,000	

Required

Using the weighted-average method, determine the following:
1. The materials cost per equivalent unit.
2. The total materials cost of units transferred to the next department during October.
3. The total materials cost of units in process at October 31.

E9–9. Equivalent Units—FIFO Method Alpha Company uses a process-costing system. On September 1, 19X2, the manufacturing department had 8,000 units in process, which were 80-percent complete as to materials costs and 40-percent complete as to conversion costs. During September, 25,000 units were started in process and 28,000 units were transferred to the next department. On September 30, 19X2, work in process was 70-percent complete as to materials costs and 60-percent complete as to conversion costs.

Required

Prepare an electronic spreadsheet to assist in answering the following questions. Print a copy of the results.

1. Would the amount of equivalent units for materials costs differ if the first-in, first-out method were used instead of the weighted-average method?
2. Would the amount of equivalent units for conversion costs differ if the first-in, first-out method were used instead of the weighted-average method?

E9–10. Equivalent Units and Unit Costs—Weighted-Average Method Lyman Company uses a process-costing system. The following information is available for the finishing department, the second and last department in Lyman's system:

Beginning work in process, November 1, 19X4:
Transferred in from manufacturing department	$20,000
Materials	8,400
Labor	4,000
Factory overhead	2,000

Costs added during November
Transferred in	$43,000
Labor	7,040
Factory overhead	6,280

Percentage of completion of work in process:

	November 1	November 30
Materials	100%	100%
Conversion costs	50%	40%

Production statistics:
Units in process, Nov. 1	10,000
Units in process, Nov. 30	4,000
Units transferred in	20,000
Units shipped	26,000

Lyman accounts for the costs by the weighted-average method.

Required

1. Determine the equivalent units of production for materials and conversion costs for the month of November.
2. Determine the cost per equivalent unit for materials, labor, and factory overhead costs.

E9-11. Simplified Costing Hunt Manufacturing Company is considering the use of a simplified costing system that charges all manufacturing costs directly to cost of goods sold. At the end of each accounting period, an adjusting entry would be made to reclassify part of cost of goods sold as work-in-process and finished-goods inventory.

The following relates to Hunt's operations for the month of July.

Work in process, beginning:	
Materials	$2,000
Labor	3,000
Overhead	4,500
Total	$9,500

The following manufacturing costs were incurred during July. Hunt had no beginning or ending inventories of raw materials or finished goods.

Materials	$60,000
Labor	$90,000

Overhead is applied at the rate of 150 percent of direct-labor costs. Actual factory overhead was equal to applied facory overhead. Work in process at the end of July consisted of the following cost components.

Materials	$1,000
Labor	1,500
Overhead	2,250
Total	$4,750

Required

1. Explain the major difference between traditional costing and simplified costing. In what type of manufacturing environment is simplified costing most effective?

2. Prepare summary journal entries for Hunt Manufacturing for July using traditional costing methods.
3. Prepare summary journal entries for Hunt Manufacturing for July using its simplified costing method.
4. Explain what makes simplified costing simpler than traditional costing.

PROBLEMS

P9–1. Essays on Process-Costing Concepts An important concept in process costing is that of equivalent units.

Required

1. Describe the difference between units placed in process for a period and equivalent units for a period when there is no work-in-process beginning inventory and the work-in-process ending inventory is 50-percent complete.
2. Describe the difference between units completed for a period and equivalent units for a period when there is no work-in-process beginning inventory and the work-in-process ending inventory is 50-percent complete.
3. Describe how equivalent units for a period are used to compute the cost of the work-in-process ending inventory.

P9–2. FIFO and Average Costing Procedures (from CPA exam)

1. Information concerning department A of Stover Company for the month of June is as follows:

	Units	Materials Costs
Work in process, beginning	17,000	$12,800
Started in June	82,000	69,700
Units completed	85,000	
Work in process, ending	14,000	

All materials are added at the beginning of the process.

Required

Using the weighted-average method, determine the cost per equivalent unit for materials cost.

2. Department 1 is the first stage of Drucker Company's production cycle. The following information is available for conversion costs for the month of April:

	Units
Work in process, beginning (40% complete)	40,000
Started in April	320,000
Completed in April and transferred to department 2	340,000
Work in process, ending (60% complete)	20,000

Required

Using the FIFO method, determine the equivalent units for conversion cost calculation.

P9-3. Equivalent Unit Computations

The Jorcano Company uses a process-costing system to account for the costs of its only product, product D. Production begins in the fabrication department, where units of raw material are molded into various connecting parts. After fabrication is complete, the units are transferred to the assembly department. After assembly is complete, the units are transferred to the packaging department, where packing material is placed around the units. The packaging department is considered a production department. When the units are ready for shipping, they are sent to the shipping area.

At year end, the following inventory of the product is on hand:

1. No unused raw material or packing material.
2. Fabrication department—300 units, 1/3 complete as to raw material and 1/2 complete as to direct labor.
3. Assembly department—1,000 units, 2/5 complete as to direct labor.
4. Packaging department—100 units, 3/4 complete as to packing material and 1/4 complete as to direct labor.
5. Shipping area—400 units.

Required

1. Determine the number of equivalent units of raw material in all inventories at year end.
2. Determine the number of equivalent units of fabrication department direct labor in all inventories at year end.
3. Determine the number of equivalent units of packing material in all inventories at year end.

P9-4. Process Costing—Weighted-Average Method

On April 1, the Collins Company had 6,000 units of work in process in department B, the second and last stage of its production cycle. The costs attached to these 6,000 units were $12,000 of costs transferred in from department A, $2,500 of materials costs added in department B, and $2,000 of conversion costs added in department B. Materials are added in the beginning of the process in department B. Conversion was 50-percent complete on April 1. During April 14,000 units were transferred in from department A at a cost of $27,000, and material costs of $3,500 and conversion costs of $3,000 were added in department B. On April 30, department B had 5,000 units of work in process 60-percent complete as to conversion costs. Costs attached to these 5,000 units were $9,750 of costs transferred in from department A, $1,500 of material costs added in department B, and $833 of conversion costs added in department B.

Required

1. Using the weighted-average method, determine the equivalent units for the month of April for all cost components.
2. Using the weighted-average method, determine the cost per equivalent unit for all cost components.
3. Prove that the costs assigned to the 5,000 units of ending work-in-process inventory are correct.

P9-5. Cost of Production Report—FIFO Method

Melody Corporation is a manufacturing company that produces a single product known as Jupiter. Melody uses the first-in, first-out (FIFO) process-costing method for both financial statement and internal management reporting.

Data for the month of April are as follows:

1. The beginning inventory consisted of 2,500 units, which were 100-percent complete as to raw material and 40-percent complete as to direct labor and factory overhead.
2. An additional 10,000 units were started during the month.
3. The ending inventory consisted of 2,000 units, which were 100-percent complete as to raw material and 40-percent complete as to direct labor and factory overhead.
4. There were 10,500 units completed and transferred to finished goods.
5. There was $55,200 in the work-in-process account on April 1.
6. Costs applicable to April production were as follows:

	Actual Cost
Raw material used	$121,000
Direct labor	105,575
Factory overhead	31,930

Required

1. For each element of production for April (raw material, direct labor, and factory overhead), compute the following:
    a. equivalent units of production
    b. cost per equivalent unit of production
2. Prepare a cost of production report.

Show supporting computations in good form.

P9–6. Cost of Production Report—Weighted-Average Method
You are engaged in an audit of the January 31 financial statement of Spirit Corporation, a manufacturer of a digital watch. You are attempting to verify the costing of the ending inventories of work in process and finished goods, which were recorded on Spirit's books as follows:

	Units	Costs
Work in process (50% complete as to labor overhead)	300,000	$ 660,960
Finished goods	200,000	$1,009,800

Materials are added to production at the beginning of the manufacturing process, and overhead is applied to each product at the rate of 60 percent of direct-labor costs. There was no finished-goods inventory on January 1.

A review of Spirit's inventory cost records disclosed the following information:

		Costs	
	Units	Materials	Labor
Work in process, January 1 (80% complete as to labor and overhead)	200,000	$ 200,000	$ 315,000
Units started in production	1,000,000		
Material costs		1,300,000	
Labor costs			1,995,000
Units completed	900,000		

Required

Prepare a cost of production report for Spirit Corporation for January using the weighted-average method.

P9-7. Cost of Production Report—FIFO Method Crews Company produces a chemical agent for commercial use. The company accounts for production in two cost centers—cooking and mix-pack. In the first cost center, liquid substances are combined in large cookers and boiled. After the batch is cooked, it is transferred to a second cost center.

Material is added at the beginning of production in each cost center, and labor is added equally during production. Overhead is applied on the basis of 80 percent of labor cost. The FIFO method is used to cost inventories.

The following information is available for the month of October:

Cost Information	Cooking
Work in process, October 1	
Materials	$ 990
Labor	100
Month of October	
Materials	$39,600
Labor	10,050

Inventory and production records show that cooking had 1,000 gallons 40-percent processed on October 1 and 800 gallons 50-percent processed on October 31. Production reports for October show that cooking started 40,000 gallons into production and completed and transferred 40,200 to mix-pack.

Required

Prepare a cost of production report for the cooking department.

P9-8. Cost of Production Report—Weighted-Average Method Prepare a cost of production report for Elko Corporation. All production is done in one department. The following information is available.

	Units
Beginning work in process (100% complete for materials, 75% complete for conversion costs)	10,000
Started in process during the period	70,000
Transferred to finished goods	65,000
Completed and still on hand	2,000
Ending work in process (100% complete for materials, 40% complete for conversion costs)	13,000

	Costs	
Opening work in process:		
Materials	$ 2,000	
Labor	3,000	
Factory overhead	1,000	$ 6,000
Added during the period:		
Materials	50,000	
Labor	170,000	
Factory overhead	80,000	300,000

Required

Prepare an electronic spreadsheet to generate a cost of production report using the weighted-average costing method. Print a copy of the report.

P9-9. Cost of Production Report—FIFO Method Sparks Corporation uses process-costing techniques to account for its chemical division. The following production information is available for the chemical division for the month of June.

	Units
Beginning work in process (100% complete for materials, 85% complete for conversion costs)	1,000
Started in process during the period	23,000
Transferred to finished goods	?
Ending work in process (100% complete for materials, 50% complete for conversion costs)	2,000

	Costs
Work in process, beginning:	
Materials	$ 2,800
Labor	7,000
Overhead	3,500
Added during the period:	
Materials	59,800
Labor	181,630
Overhead	90,815

Required

1. Prepare a cost of production report using the FIFO method.
2. Prepare the journal entry necessary to transfer costs from work-in-process to finished-goods inventory.

P9–10. Cost of Production Report—Weighted-Average Method

Kats Manufacturing Company produces a petroleum compound used to seal asphalt surfaces against moisture penetration. The company accounts for production in three cost centers—blending, cooking, and packing. In the first cost center, liquid ingredients are combined in large vats and mixed. After the proper blend of ingredients is achieved, the liquid is transferred to cooking for further processing.

Materials are placed in process at the beginning of the blending process, and labor is utilized uniformly during processing. Overhead is applied on the basis of 110 percent of direct-labor cost.

The following information is available for the month of August.

Blending Department	Costs
Work in process, August 1:	
Materials	$ 2,600
Labor	460
Month of August:	
Materials	79,400
Labor	23,900

Production and inventory records indicate that blending had 2,000 gallons 60-percent processed on August 1 and 1,600 gallons 50-percent processed on August 31. There were 80,000 gallons started in production in blending and 80,400 gallons transferred to cooking.

Required

1. Prepare an electronic spreadsheet to generate a cost of production report for August for the blending department using the weighted-average method. Print a copy of the report.
2. Prepare the journal entry necessary to transfer costs from the blending department to the cooking department.

Chapter 10

Process Costing: Additional Features

Outline

ADDITION OF MATERIALS IN PROCESSES SUBSEQUENT TO THE FIRST PROCESS
No Change in Units
Increase in Units
ACCOUNTING FOR LOST UNITS
COST FLOWS AND PROCESS-COSTING PROCEDURES
Weighted-Average Method
  Lost Units Detected at the End of the Process
  Lost Units Detected During the Process
  Lost Units Detected Near the Beginning of the Process
FIFO Method
  Lost Units Detected at the End of the Process
  Lost Units Detected During the Process
  Lost Units Detected Near the Beginning of the Process
Other Considerations
SUMMARY
SELF-STUDY PROBLEM
SUGGESTED READINGS
DISCUSSION QUESTIONS
EXERCISES
PROBLEMS

A number of features, in addition to the basic procedures discussed in chapter 9, are necessary for proper implementation of process costing in specific production situations. For example, materials may be added in processes subsequent to the first process. The addition of materials results in either no change or an increase in the number of units in process. In either event there is an effect on product costs for which an accounting must be made.

Another situation requiring special accounting is the loss of units in process due to, for example, spoilage or shrinkage. This leaves fewer units to absorb total manufacturing costs. This chapter examines process-costing techniques used to account for manufacturing costs in these special types of situations. After completing this chapter, you should be able to:

1. account for material additions in processes subsequent to the first process when:
   a. there is no change in the number of units in production.
   b. there is an increase in the number of units in production.
2. explain why units are lost during production.
3. distinguish between normal and abnormal losses.
4. account for the cost of lost units in a process-costing environment.

ADDITION OF MATERIALS IN PROCESSES SUBSEQUENT TO THE FIRST PROCESS

Materials are often added in processes subsequent to the first process. For example, paint, handles, or other trimmings may be added to furniture in a finishing process subsequent to the assembly process. When materials are added in subsequent processes, it is important to determine if the number of units of production remains the same or if it increases because of the addition.

If the number of units remains the same, accounting for the cost of additional materials is the same in subsequent processes as in the initial process. However, if the number of units in production increases as a result of adding materials in subsequent processes, care must be taken to properly assign costs to these additional units. Accounting in each of these situations is illustrated in the following sections.

No Change in Units

The number of units in process remains the same if the materials simply add to the units already in process. For example, applying decals to plastic toys or placing cabinets on television components represents an addition of materials but not an increase in the number of units in production.

When there is no change in the number of units, the basic process-costing procedures are the same in subsequent processes as in an initial process. To illustrate, consider the following situation. A manufacturer of a certain chemical uses two processes—mixing and blending. Basic ingredients are combined in the mixing department and transferred to the blending department for further processing.

The blending department had 20,000 pounds of product in process at the beginning of the current accounting period. These units were 80-percent complete as to materials and 60-percent complete as to labor and overhead. There were 25,000 pounds transferred from mixing to blending during the period. There were 33,000 pounds of chemical completed and transferred from blending to finished-goods inventory. Work-in-process inventory at the end of the period consisted of 12,000 pounds, which were 90-percent complete as to materials and 50-percent complete as to labor and overhead.

Costs recorded by the blending department for the current period are as follows:

Accounting Data

Work-in-process beginning inventory:	
Transferred-in costs	$28,000
Materials	10,632
Labor and overhead	6,540
Total	$45,172
Costs of the current period:	
Transferred-in costs	$56,000
Materials	21,000
Labor and overhead	21,000
Total	$98,000

The cost of production report in figure 10.1 illustrates the accounting for materials costs when materials are added in subsequent processes with no increase in the number of units. All materials costs from the mixing department are contained in the transferred-in costs of the blending department. Materials costs added by the blending department in the prior period are contained in the work-in-process beginning inventory in the amount of $10,632. Finally, materials costs added by the blending department in the current period are $21,000.

In summary, the basic process-costing procedures remain the same when materials are added in subsequent processes and the number of units in process remains the same. The only difference is that a column for materials is added to the cost of production report. Because the basic process-costing procedures are also the same when using the FIFO method in this situation, a cost of production report is not given to illustrate the FIFO method.

Increase in Units

Adding materials in subsequent processes may result in an increase in the number of units in production. For example, adding hardening and drying agents when making paint increases the number of gallons in process. The accounting for these additional units is only slightly more complicated than when there is no increase in units.

To illustrate, consider the information in the previous example but assume that additional chemicals are added in the blending process, resulting in an increase of 15,000 units in process. Also assume that the cost of these additional chemicals is $6,000, resulting in total materials costs of $27,000 added during the current period. Figure 10.2 contains the cost of production report using the weighted-average method in this situation.

Observe in figure 10.2 that the increase in the number of units in process simply increases the total units to account for. This increase is also reflected in the equivalent-unit calculations and in the number of units completed and transferred out. Notice also that the costs per equivalent unit decreased in this situation because there are more units over which to spread the costs.

The basic process-costing procedures remain unchanged when using the FIFO method to account for material additions in subsequent processes when there is an increase in units. Like the weighted-average method, the additional units to account for must be included in equivalent-unit and other calculations as appropriate. A cost of production report using the FIFO method in this situation is illustrated in figure 10.3.

FIGURE 10.1

Materials Added in Subsequent Departments—No Change in Units
Cost of Production Report
(Weighted-Average Method)

	Physical Units	Transferred In	Material	Labor and Overhead
Units to account for:				
Work in process, beginning	20,000	100%	80%	60%
Transferred in this period	25,000			
Total units to account for	45,000			
Units accounted for as follows:				
Completed and transferred out	33,000	100%	100%	100%
Work in process, ending	12,000	100%	90%	50%
Total units accounted for	45,000			

	Total	Transferred In	Material	Labor and Overhead
Costs to account for:				
Work in process, beginning	$ 45,172	$ 28,000	$10,632	$ 6,540
Costs of the current period	98,000	56,000	21,000	21,000
(1) Total costs to account for	$143,172	$ 84,000	$ 31,632	$ 27,540
Equivalent units of production:				
Completed and transferred out		33,000	33,000	33,000
Work in process, ending		12,000	10,800	6,000
(2) Total equivalent units		45,000	43,800	39,000
Cost per equivalent unit, (1) ÷ (2)	$ 3.295	$ 1.867	$ 0.722	$ 0.706
Costs accounted for as follows:				
Costs transferred out	$108,735	(33,000 × $3.295)		
Work in process, ending:				
Transferred-in costs	$ 22,404	(12,000 × $1.867)		
Materials	7,798	(10,800 × $0.722)		
Labor and overhead	4,236	(6,000 × $0.706)		
Total	$ 34,438			
Total costs accounted for	$143,172	(Rounded from $143,173.)		

Whether using the weighted-average or the FIFO method, an increase in the number of units in process can be viewed as resulting in a decrease in the per-unit cost for units transferred in. In this example there were 25,000 units transferred into the blending department at a total cost of $56,000. Transferred-in costs were therefore $2.24 per unit ($56,000 ÷ 25,000 units). Since 15,000 units were added in the blending department, there are now 40,000 units available to absorb manufacturing costs. An increase in the number of units over which the same costs are spread results in a decrease in per-unit transferred-in costs from $2.24 to $1.40 ($56,000 ÷ 40,000 units).

One advantage of using the form of the cost of production report presented in this text is that there is no need to explicitly calculate an adjusted per-unit cost from the preceding department. Rather, the form of the report implicitly recalculates per-unit transferred-in costs, averaging current production costs with work-in-process costs of the prior period.

FIGURE 10.2

Materials Added in Subsequent Departments—Increase in Units
Cost of Production Report
(Weighted-Average Method)

	Physical Units	Percentage Completion		
		Transferred In	Material	Labor and Overhead
Units to account for:				
Work in process, beginning	20,000	100%	80%	60%
Transferred in this period	25,000			
Increase from added materials	15,000			
Total units to account for	60,000			
Units accounted for as follows:				
Completed and transferred out	48,000	100%	100%	100%
Work in process, ending	12,000	100%	90%	50%
Total units accounted for	60,000			

	Total	Transferred In	Material	Labor and Overhead
Costs to account for:				
Work in process, beginning	$ 45,172	$ 28,000	$ 10,632	$ 6,540
Costs of the current period	104,000	56,000	27,000	21,000
(1) Total costs to account for	$149,172	$ 84,000	$ 37,632	$ 27,540
Equivalent units of production:				
Completed and transferred out		48,000	48,000	48,000
Work in process, ending		12,000	10,800	6,000
(2) Total equivalent units		60,000	58,800	54,000
Cost per equivalent unit, (1) ÷ (2)	$ 2.550	$ 1.400	$ 0.640	$ 0.510
Costs accounted for as follows:				
Costs transferred out	$122,400	(48,000 × $2.550)		
Work in process, ending:				
Transferred-in costs	$ 16,800	(12,000 × $1.400)		
Materials	6,912	(10,800 × $0.640)		
Labor and overhead	3,060	(6,000 × $0.510)		
Total	$ 26,772			
Total costs accounted for	$149,172			

ACCOUNTING FOR LOST UNITS

Inputs to a manufacturing process do not always result in good output. Virtually all manufacturing processes experience some amount of waste, scrap, spoilage, spillage, dehydration, evaporation, or defective work. One of the concerns with process costing is accounting for the cost of units that are lost during the production process, whatever the cause. Accounting for lost units is important so that there can be a proper assignment of costs to good units produced and so that the quality of production can be effectively monitored for control purposes. This chapter focuses on the product-costing procedures typically used in a process-costing environment when units are lost during production. Chapter 12 examines additional aspects of accounting for scrap, waste, and defective units. Finally, chapters 15

FIGURE 10.3

Materials Added in Subsequent Departments—Increase in Units
Cost of Production Report
(First-in, First-out Method)

	Physical Units	Percentage Completion		
		Transferred In	Material	Labor and Overhead
Units to account for:				
Work in process, beginning	20,000	100%	80%	60%
Transferred in this period	25,000			
Increase from added materials	15,000			
Total units to account for	60,000			
Units accounted for as follows:				
Completed and transferred out	48,000	100%	100%	100%
Work in process, ending	12,000	100%	90%	50%
Total units accounted for	60,000			

	Total	Transferred In	Material	Labor and Overhead
Costs to account for:				
Work in process, beginning	$ 45,172			
(1) Costs of the current period	104,000	56,000	27,000	21,000
Total costs to account for	$149,172			
Equivalent units of production:				
Complete work in process, beginning			4,000	8,000
Started and completed		28,000	28,000	28,000
Work in process, ending		12,000	10,800	6,000
(2) Total equivalent units		40,000	42,800	42,000
Cost per equivalent unit, (1) ÷ (2)	$ 2.531	$ 1.400	$ 0.631	$ 0.500
Costs accounted for as follows:				
Costs transferred out:				
Work in process, beginning	$ 45,172			
Work completed on work in process, beginning:				
Material	2,524	(4,000 × $0.631)		
Labor and overhead	4,000	(8,000 × $0.500)		
Work started and completed	70,868	(28,000 × $2.531)		
Total	$122,564			
Work in process, ending:				
Transferred-in costs	$ 16,800	(12,000 × $1.400)		
Materials	6,815	(10,800 × $0.631)		
Labor and overhead	3,000	(6,000 × $0.500)		
Total	$ 26,615			
Total costs accounted for	$149,172	(Rounded from $149,179.)		

and 16 emphasize the control aspects of accounting for such costs when using a standard cost system.

One of the challenges of accounting for lost units is that there needs to be a differentiation between normal and abnormal rates of loss. A **normal rate of loss** is the rate of loss that is expected to occur under efficient operating conditions. Most production processes will generate bad units along with good ones. It may be technologically possible to reduce the probability of generating bad units to very low levels. However, as loss rates are reduced, costs of production usually increase. Production is efficient when the cost of lowering loss rates is greater than the benefit derived from having additional good output.

On the other hand, an **abnormal rate of loss** is the rate of loss that is not expected to occur under efficient operating conditions. It is that part of total loss that falls outside normal or expected limits. Abnormal loss may result from a bad batch of materials, machine malfunction, carelessness, or accidents. For example, the cost of bent nails in excess of a 7-percent expected loss rate or broken bottles in excess of a 4-percent expected breakage rate is considered abnormal loss.

The implications for management between normal and abnormal losses are that losses within normal limits are indicative of a controlled situation, but the presence of abnormal losses suggests that the process is not adequately controlled. Because normal losses are inherent in the manufacturing process, no amount of remedial action aside from measuring and reporting the cost of lost units needs to be taken.

COST FLOWS AND PROCESS-COSTING PROCEDURES

The general rule is that (a) the costs of normal versus abnormal losses are identified and segregated in the accounting system, (b) the cost of normal loss is inventoried (assigned to good units produced) and follows those units through subsequent processes into finished-goods inventory, and (c) the cost of abnormal loss is removed from work in process, assigned to a loss account, and reported as such in the current period. The cost of abnormal loss is typically identified with the creating process or department to assist management in recognizing and solving problems. These cost flows are depicted in figure 10.4.

Another factor to consider when accounting for lost units is that losses may occur at various points in the production process. However, losses usually are not identified for accounting purposes except at specific points of inspection. The typical situation is that losses are discovered during final inspection at the end of a process, immediately before goods are transferred out. However, inspection may occur at the beginning of a process, at some point during the process, or at the end of a process.

The general rule is that the cost of normal losses should be assigned to the good units that have passed the point of inspection during that accounting period. If all units passing inspection have been transferred to the next process or to finished goods, the total cost of normal loss should be transferred out with those good units. However, if units in ending work in process have also passed the inspection point, they should be considered "good units produced" and should be allocated a proportionate share of the cost of normal loss along with the good units transferred out.

Given the possibility of (a) normal and abnormal losses, (b) inspection at various points during the production process, and (c) use of the weighted-average or FIFO methods of accounting, there is a large variety of different process-costing situations. A number of these situations are illustrated in the following sections. First, accounting for normal and abnormal losses is illustrated using the weighted-average method, with inspection at the end of the process; during the process with work in process having been inspected; and at the beginning of the process. Second, accounting for normal and abnormal losses is illustrated using the FIFO method, with inspection at the end of the process, and during the process with work in process having been inspected. The following assumed information about Pottery Company is used for these illustrations.

FIGURE 10.4 Cost Flow of Normal Versus Abnormal Losses

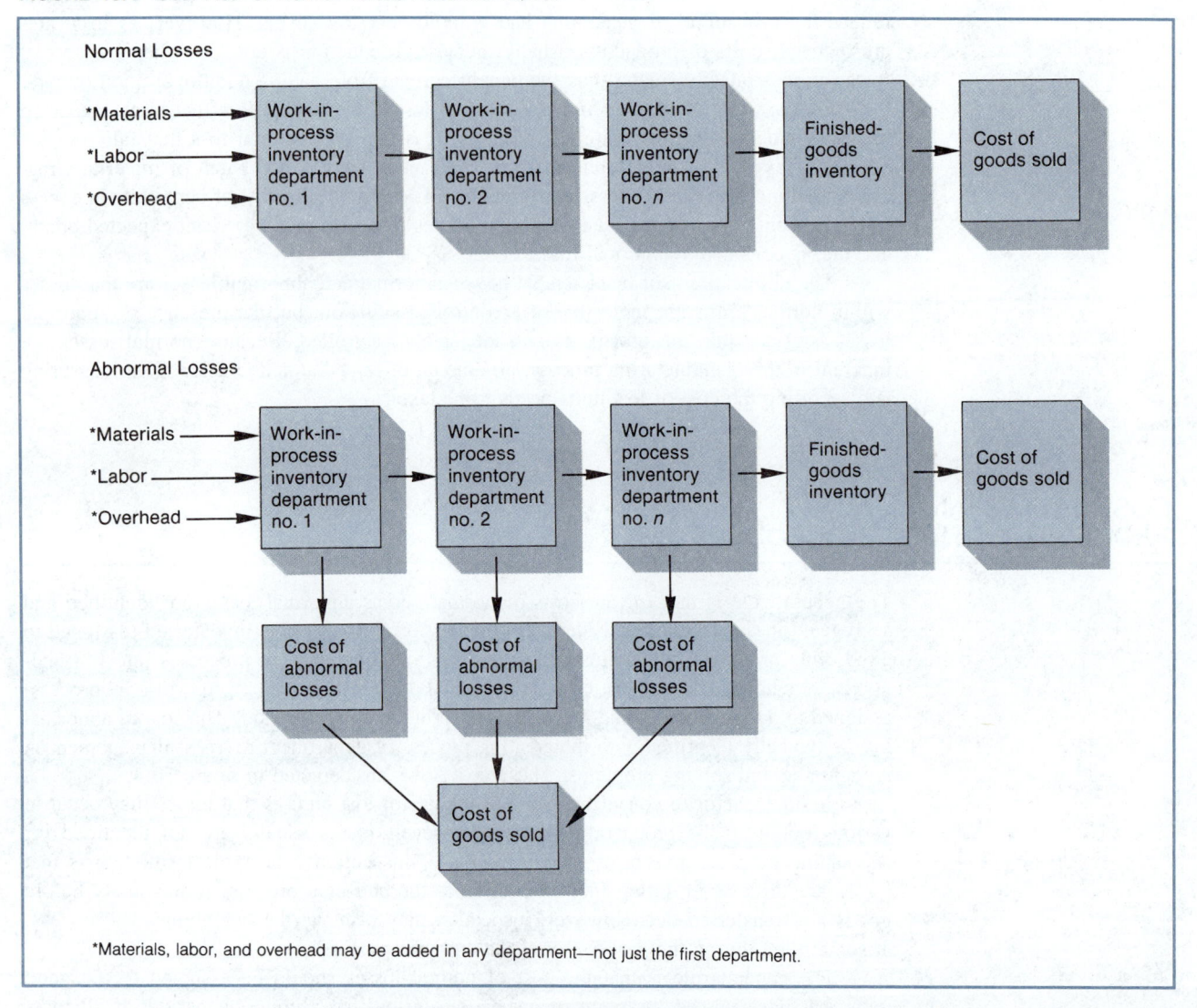

*Materials, labor, and overhead may be added in any department—not just the first department.

Pottery Company uses process-costing techniques to accumulate the costs of glazing one of its products. The major portion of materials are placed in production at the beginning of processing in the glazing department, with a minor amount of materials being added at various times through the first half of the process. There is no change in the number of units as a result of the addition of materials. Labor and overhead costs are incurred evenly throughout the process. Some of the pottery pieces are spoiled because of misapplication of glaze or improper machine handling. Production records show that the normal loss rate is 10 percent of good units produced.

At the beginning of the accounting period, work-in-process inventory for this product was $106,550, representing 8,000 pieces with $48,000 of transferred-in costs, $50,000 of materials costs (85% completed), and $8,550 of labor and overhead costs (50% completed).

During the period, 19,000 pieces were transferred in from the prior process at a cost of $114,000. Materials costing $143,500 were placed in process during the current period, and direct labor of $26,000 was charged to the glazing department. Manufacturing overhead of $20,800 was applied to production at the rate of 80 percent of direct-labor cost. Therefore, total labor and overhead costs of $46,800 ($26,000 + $20,800) were charged to the glazing department during the period.

The work-in-process ending inventory consisted of 4,000 units, 70-percent complete as to materials and 40-percent complete as to labor and overhead. There were 20,000 good units transferred to finished goods after final inspection. Lost units totaled 3,000 units. Normal losses of 10 percent of good output or 2,000 units were expected, which means that there were 1,000 units of abnormal spoilage.

Lost Units Detected at the End of the Process If the ending work-in-process inventory has *not* been inspected, the cost associated with normal loss is transferred out with the completed units to finished-goods inventory. Figure 10.5 contains a cost of production report for the glazing department using the weighted-average method in this situation. Notice that the entire cost associated with the normal loss is transferred out with the good units completed and transferred out during the period.

Several features of figure 10.5 are important to review. First, to eliminate ambiguity and to provide information for management control purposes, differentiation is made throughout the report between normal and abnormal losses. Second, equivalent units of production must be calculated for bad as well as good units to enable appropriate cost assignments. Since bad units are not discovered in this situation until final inspection after all processing is complete, 100 percent of transferred-in, materials, labor, and overhead costs are included in the equivalent unit computation.

For convenience in making journal entries, the $315,000 cost allocated to good production is added to the $31,500 cost of normal losses to obtain a total cost of $346,500, which is transferred to finished-goods inventory. The $15,750 cost of abnormal losses is transferred to a loss account and shown on the income statement of the current period. The journal entries that follow relate to the operations of the glazing department and should be reviewed in the context of the cost flows shown in figure 10.4 and the cost of production report in figure 10.5.

Finally, care should be taken to reflect the proper per-unit cost of items transferred to finished-goods inventory. The per-unit cost of goods transferred to finished-goods inventory is found by dividing the *total* cost of goods transferred to finished goods by the number of *good* units transferred. In this case, the cost per unit of items completed and transferred is $17.325 per unit ($346,500 ÷ 20,000 units).

The following summary journal entries would be made to record the activity of the glazing department reported in figure 10.5.

1. To establish total costs to account for in the glazing department:

Work in process—glazing department	410,850	
Various accounts		410,850

2. Transfer of goods, glazing department to finished goods:

Finished-goods inventory	346,500	
Work in process—glazing department		346,500

   $315,000 (cost of good production transferred out) + $31,500 (cost of normal losses)
   = $346,500

3. Abnormal losses charged to a loss account:

Cost of abnormal losses	15,750	
Work in process—glazing department		15,750

FIGURE 10.5

Glazing Department
Cost of Production Report
(Weighted-Average Method—With Lost Units)
(Work in process has not been inspected)

	Physical Units	Percentage Completion Transferred In	Material	Labor and Overhead
Units to account for:				
Work in process, beginning	8,000	100%	85%	50%
Transferred in this period	19,000			
Total units to account for	27,000			
Units accounted for as follows:				
Completed and transferred out	20,000	100%	100%	100%
Normal loss	2,000	100%	100%	100%
Abnormal loss	1,000	100%	100%	100%
Work in process, ending	4,000	100%	70%	40%
Total units accounted for	27,000			

	Total	Transferred In	Material	Labor and Overhead
Costs to account for:				
Work in process, beginning	$106,550	$ 48,000	$ 50,000	$ 8,550
Costs of the current period	304,300	114,000	143,500	46,800
(1) Total costs to account for	$410,850	$162,000	$193,500	$55,350
Equivalent units of production:				
Completed and transferred out		20,000	20,000	20,000
Normal loss		2,000	2,000	2,000
Abnormal loss		1,000	1,000	1,000
Work in process, ending		4,000	2,800	1,600
(2) Total equivalent units		27,000	25,800	24,600
Cost per equivalent unit, (1) ÷ (2)	$ 15.750	$ 6.000	$ 7.500	$ 2.250

Costs accounted for as follows:		
Costs transferred out:		
Good production	$315,000	(20,000 × $15.750)
Normal loss	31,500	(2,000 × $15.750)
To finished goods	$346,500[a]	
Abnormal loss	15,750	(1,000 × $15.750)
Total costs transferred out	$362,250	
Work in process, ending:		
Transferred-in costs	$ 24,000	(4,000 × $ 6.000)
Materials	21,000	(2,800 × $ 7.500)
Labor and overhead	3,600	(1,600 × $ 2.250)
Total	$ 48,600	
Total costs accounted for	$410,850	

[a] The cost per unit of goods transferred to finished-goods inventory is $17.325 ($346,500 ÷ 20,000 units).

There is an alternative approach to recording the cost of lost units. First, the total cost of lost units is segregated from the cost of good production. This is accomplished, using the preceding data, by debiting a separate "cost of lost units" account for $47,250 ($31,500 + $15,750), the sum of normal and abnormal losses. This treatment highlights the total problem of lost units and provides a monitoring vehicle for management. Second, the part of the total cost of lost units that is abnormal, $15,750 in this case, is transferred to a "cost of abnormal losses" account and the cost of normal loss, $31,500 in this case, is transferred to finished-goods inventory along with the $315,000 cost of good units finished and transferred.

The emphasis of the more practical approach first illustrated is on product costing, whereas the emphasis of the more conceptually oriented approach is on planning and control. Regardless of the accounting techniques used, a well-designed cost of production report can present information in a form that will meet the needs of both product costing and management control.

Lost Units Detected During the Process If the ending work-in-process inventory *has* been inspected, the cost associated with normal loss is allocated between *(a)* units completed and transferred out and *(b)* units in ending work in process. The amount allocated is based on the relative number of units in each category.

Figure 10.6 contains a cost of production report prepared under the assumption that ending work in process has been inspected in the glazing department. Assume that inspection takes place at a point when 60 percent of materials have been added and conversion costs are at a 30-percent stage of completion. All other costs and quantities are assumed to be the same as previously illustrated for the glazing department. Notice that 83.3 percent (20,000 ÷ 24,000) of the normal loss is allocated to the 20,000 units completed and transferred out and 16.7 percent (4,000 ÷ 24,000) of the loss is allocated to units in the ending work-in-process inventory.

The following is a summary journal entry that illustrates the transfer of costs out of the glazing department for the situation in figure 10.6.

Finished-goods inventory	345,608	
Cost of abnormal losses	11,458	
Work in process—glazing department		357,066

As indicated before, the cost of normal loss is allocated based on the relative number of units completed and transferred out and the number of units in work in process. In this example, beginning work in process is 50-percent complete, indicating that these units were inspected in the prior period and found to be good. Therefore, if there had been a normal loss in the prior period, these units would have been allocated a portion of that loss. It may seem as if these units are being given a "double dose" of loss by allocating part of the current-period loss to them because they are completed and transferred out this period. However, this is consistent with the weighted-average method, which allocates all costs of the current period to the units worked on during the period. The same allocation procedure would have been used had the beginning work in process been inspected during the current period.

Lost Units Detected Near the Beginning of the Process Accounting for lost units when inspection occurs near the beginning of a process follows the same general rules as for losses detected during the process. The critical factor is determining whether or not the ending work-in-process inventory has been inspected. If ending work in process has been inspected (which is the likely situation, because inspection is near the beginning of the process), the accounting for losses is like that illustrated in figure 10.6. If the ending work in process has not been inspected, the accounting for losses is like that illustrated in figure 10.5.

A shortcut method can be used in the unique situation where all losses are normal and occur at the beginning of the process. By leaving the lost units out of the equivalent-unit calculation, the cost associated with these units will automatically be spread over the good units produced. This is sometimes called the *method of neglect*. Figure 10.7 illustrates this shortcut, assuming, for simplicity, that all of the lost units in the glazing

FIGURE 10.6

Glazing Department
Cost of Production Report
(Weighted Average Method—With Lost Units)
(Work in process has been inspected)

	Physical Units	Percentage Completion		
		Transferred In	Material	Labor and Overhead
Units to account for:				
Work in process, beginning	8,000	100%	85%	50%
Transferred in this period	19,000			
Total units to account for	27,000			
Units accounted for as follows:				
Completed and transferred out	20,000	100%	100%	100%
Normal loss	2,000	100%	60%	30%
Abnormal loss	1,000	100%	60%	30%
Work in process, ending	4,000	100%	70%	40%
Total units accounted for	27,000			

	Total	Transferred In	Material	Labor and Overhead
Costs to account for:				
Work in process, beginning	$106,550	$ 48,000	$ 50,000	$ 8,550
Costs of the current period	304,300	114,000	143,500	46,800
(1) Total costs to account for	$401,850	$162,000	$193,500	$55,350
Equivalent units of production:				
Completed and transferred out		20,000	20,000	20,000
Normal loss		2,000	1,200	600
Abnormal loss		1,000	600	300
Work in process, ending		4,000	2,800	1,600
(2) Total equivalent units		27,000	24,600	22,500
Cost per equivalent unit, (1) ÷ (2)	$ 16.326	$ 6.000	$ 7.866	$ 2.460

department are normal; that all costs to account for are the same as given in figure 10.5; and that no material, labor, or overhead has been expended in the glazing department on units lost at the beginning of the process.

It should be observed that ignoring lost units as in figure 10.7 may not give results as accurate as when lost units are explicitly included in the calculations. Ignoring lost units has the effect of decreasing the total number of units to be accounted for, which in turn results in a higher cost per equivalent unit. The effect is to allocate different total costs to units transferred out and to ending work-in-process inventory, even though the total cost to be allocated remains the same. To illustrate, figure 10.8 contains a summary comparison of the costs allocated when using the shortcut method compared with an explicit accounting for lost units with 50% of materials and conversion costs added.

FIFO Method

Lost Units Detected at the End of the Process Once again, if ending work in process *has not been inspected,* the cost associated with normal loss is assigned only to units completed and transferred out to finished-goods inventory. The process-costing pro-

FIGURE 10.6 Continued

Glazing Department
Cost of Production Report
(Weighted Average Method—With Lost Units)
(Work in process has been inspected)

Costs accounted for as follows:
  Costs transferred out:

Good production	$326,520	(20,000 × $16.326)
Normal loss	19,088	(0.833 × $22,915[a])
To finished goods	$345,608	
Abnormal loss	11,458[b]	
Total costs transferred out	$357,066	

Work in process, ending:

Transferred-in costs	$ 24,000	(4,000 × $ 6.000)
Materials	22,025	(2,800 × $ 7.866)
Labor and overhead	3,936	(1,600 × $ 2.460)
Normal loss	3,827	(0.167 × $22,915[a])
Total	$ 53,788	
Total costs accounted for	$410,850	(Rounded from $410,854.)

[a]Cost of normal loss:

Transferred-in costs	$ 12,000	(2,000 × $ 6.000)
Materials	9,439	(1,200 × $ 7.866)
Labor and overhead	1,476	(600 × $ 2.460)
	$ 22,915	

[b]Cost of abnormal loss:

Transferred-in costs	$ 6,000	(1,000 × $ 6.000)
Materials	4,720	(600 × $ 7.866)
Labor and overhead	738	(300 × $ 2.460)
	$ 11,458	

[c]The cost per unit of goods transferred to finished-goods inventory is $17.2802 ($345,604 ÷ 20,000 units).

cedures using the FIFO method in this situation are illustrated in figure 10.9. Note the similarities between figure 10.5, which illustrates the weighted-average method, and figure 10.9, which illustrates the FIFO method in the same situation.

Lost Units Detected During the Process Once again, if the ending work in process has been inspected, the cost associated with normal losses is allocated to the good units that have passed the inspection point. The period in which units in beginning work-in-process inventory are inspected is important in this allocation when using the FIFO method. For example, if inspection occurs at the midpoint of processing, all units passing this point during the current period are allocated a portion of the cost of normal losses. This means that beginning work in process that is less than 50-percent complete at the beginning of the period passed the midpoint during the current period, as do any units started and completed during the period. Also, ending work in process that is at least 50-percent complete has also passed the inspection point. Therefore, all of these units should be allocated a portion of the cost of normal losses. However, if units in beginning work in process passed the inspection point in the prior period, they would not be allocated any portion of the current period's normal losses.

This accounting is consistent with the FIFO method, in which prior period costs are separated from current period costs. Beginning work in process that has passed the inspection point in a prior period has a normal inspection loss already allocated to it and is not

FIGURE 10.7

Glazing Department
Cost of Production Report
(Weighted-Average Method—With Lost Units)
(Work in process inspected—method of neglect)

	Physical Units	Percentage Completion		
		Transferred In	Material	Labor and Overhead
Units to account for:				
Work in process, beginning	8,000	100%	85%	50%
Transferred in this period	19,000			
Total units to account for	27,000			
Units accounted for as follows:				
Completed and transferred out	20,000	100%	100%	100%
Normal loss	3,000	NA[a]	NA	NA
Work in process, ending	4,000	100%	70%	40%
Total units accounted for	27,000			

	Total	Transferred In	Material	Labor and Overhead
Costs to acount for:				
Work in process, beginning	$106,550	$ 48,000	$ 50,000	$ 8,550
Costs of the current period	304,300	114,000	143,500	46,800
(1) Total costs to account for	$410,850	$162,000	$193,500	$55,350
Equivalent units of production:				
Completed and transferred out		20,000	20,000	20,000
Work in process, ending		4,000	2,800	1,600
(2) Total equivalent units		24,000	22,800	21,600
Cost per equivalent unit, (1) ÷ (2)	$ 17.800	$ 6.750	$ 8.487	$ 2.563

Costs accounted for as follows:
Costs transferred out	$355,985[b]	(20,000 × $17.800)
Work in process, ending:		
Transferred-in costs	$ 27,000	(4,000 × $6.750)
Materials	23,764	(2,800 × $8.487)
Labor and overhead	4,101	(1,600 × $2.563)
Total	$ 54,865	
Total costs accounted for	$410,850	

[a] NA = not applicable.
[b] Adjusted from $356,000 due to rounding.

FIGURE 10.8

Comparison of Results—
Shortcut versus Explicit Accounting for Units Lost

	Costs Transferred Out	Work in Process Ending	Total
Shortcut method	$355,985	$ 54,865	$410,850
Explicit accounting	355,018	55,832	410,850
Difference	$ (967)	$ 967	$ 0

allocated any current-period cost of normal losses. If the units in beginning work in process pass inspection during the current period, a portion of the normal loss of the current period is considered a necessary cost to complete these units.

Figure 10.10 shows a cost of production report using the FIFO method that was prepared under the assumption that inspection occurs when the units are 40-percent complete as to conversion costs. This means that ending work in process has been inspected. It also means that beginning work in process was inspected in the prior period and is not allocated any part of the current period's normal loss. Therefore, in this situation, the cost of normal loss is allocated between units started and completed and ending work-in-process inventory. The ratio of distribution is 75 percent (12,000 ÷ 16,000) to units started and completed and 25 percent (4,000 ÷ 16,000) to ending work in process.

FIGURE 10.9

Glazing Department
Cost of Production Report
(First-in, First-out Method—With Lost Units)
(Work in process has not been inspected)

	Physical Units	Transferred In	Material	Labor and Overhead
Units to account for:				
Work in process, beginning	8,000	100%	85%	50%
Transferred in this period	19,000			
Total units to account for	27,000			
Units accounted for as follows:				
Completed and transferred out:				
Beginning inventory	8,000	100%	85%	50%
Started and completed	12,000	100%	100%	100%
Normal loss	2,000	100%	100%	100%
Abnormal loss	1,000	100%	100%	100%
Work in process, ending	4,000	100%	70%	40%
Total units accounted for	27,000			

	Total	Transferred In	Material	Labor and Overhead
Costs to account for:				
Work in process, beginning	$106,550			
(1) Costs of the current period	304,300	$114,000	$143,500	$46,800
Total costs to account for	$410,850			
Equivalent units of production:				
Complete work in process, beginning			1,200	4,000
Started and completed		12,000	12,000	12,000
Normal loss		2,000	2,000	2,000
Abnormal loss		1,000	1,000	1,000
Work in process, ending		4,000	2,800	1,600
(2) Total equivalent units		19,000	19,000	20,600
Cost per equivalent unit, (1) ÷ (2)	$ 15.825	$ 6.000	$ 7.553	$ 2.272

(continued on next page)

FIGURE 10.9 Continued

Glazing Department
Cost of Production Report
(First-in, First-out Method—With Lost Units)
(Work in process has not been inspected)

Costs accounted for as follows:		
Costs transferred out:		
Work in process, beginning	$106,550	
Work completed on work in process, beginning:		
Material	9,064	(1,200 × $ 7.553)
Labor and overhead	9,088	(4,000 × $ 2.272)
Good units started and completed	189,900	(12,000 × $15.825)
Normal loss	31,650	(2,000 × $15.825)
To finished goods	$346,252[a]	
Abnormal loss	15,825	(1,000 × $15.825)
Total costs transferred out	$362,077	
Work in process, ending:		
Transferred-in costs	$ 24,000	(4,000 × $ 6.000)
Materials	21,148	(2,800 × $ 7.553)
Labor and overhead	3,635	(1,600 × $ 2.272)
Total	$ 48,783	
Total costs accounted for	$410,850	(Rounded from $408,860)

[a]The cost per unit of goods transferred to finished-goods inventory is $17.313 ($346,252 ÷ 20,000 units).

Note in figure 10.10 that if both beginning work in process and ending work in process had passed the inspection point in the current period, each (along with units started and completed) would have been allocated a portion of the cost of normal loss in the following percentages:

	Units	Percent
Work in process, beginning	8,000	33.3%
Started and completed	12,000	50.0
Completed and transferred out	20,000	83.3%
Work in process, ending	4,000	16.7
Total	24,000	100.0%

Lost Units Detected Near the Beginning of the Process As with the weighted-average method, accounting for lost units when inspection occurs at the beginning of a process follows the same general rules as for losses detected during the process. The critical factor is determining the point of inspection and deciding whether or not work-in-process inventories have passed the point of inspection during the current period. Once this is determined, the cost of normal loss is allocated between work in process and units transferred out as previously discussed or illustrated.

Other Considerations

There are several additional concepts that should be considered when accounting for lost units. First, a separate allocation of the cost of normal loss could be made for each component of manufacturing costs; that is, the transferred-in portion of the normal loss could

FIGURE 10.10

Glazing Department
Cost of Production Report
(First-in, First-out Method—With Lost Units)
(Work in process has been inspected)

	Physical Units	Percentage Completion Transferred In	Material	Labor and Overhead
Units to account for:				
Work in process, beginning	8,000	100%	85%	50%
Transferred in this period	19,000			
Total units to account for	27,000			
Units accounted for as follows:				
Completed and transferred out:				
Beginning inventory	8,000	100%	85%	50%
Started and completed	12,000	100%	100%	100%
Normal loss	2,000	100%	70%	40%
Abnormal loss	1,000	100%	70%	40%
Work in process, ending	4,000	100%	70%	40%
Total units accounted for	27,000			

	Total	Transferred In	Material	Labor and Overhead
Costs to account for:				
Work in process, beginning	$106,550			
(1) Costs of the current period	304,300	$114,000	$143,500	$46,800
Total costs to account for	$410,850			
Equivalent units of production:				
Complete work in process, beginning			1,200	4,000
Started and completed		12,000	12,000	12,000
Normal loss		2,000	1,400	800
Abnormal loss		1,000	700	400
Work in process, ending		4,000	2,800	1,600
(2) Total equivalent units		19,000	18,100	18,800
Cost per equivalent unit, (1) ÷ (2)	$ 16.417	$ 6.000	$ 7.928	$ 2.489

(continued on next page)

be allocated based on the relative number of transferred-in equivalent units completed and those in ending work in process. Likewise, the direct material, direct labor, and factory overhead portions of the normal loss could be similarly allocated. This would result in a more precise allocation. However, the additional accuracy is not generally believed to be worth the added effort. All elements of the cost of normal loss are generally allocated using the same allocation percentage based on total units in work-in-process inventory and units transferred out during the period.

Second, care should be taken to use a proper base for the calculation of normal losses. This base is usually determined as part of a budgetary or planning process before actual operations begin for the accounting period. There are two acceptable bases—good output, and normal input for good output actually produced. Actual input should not be used as a base for computing *normal* losses, because actual input may contain abnormal as well as normal losses. To illustrate, assume that under normal conditions 11,000 units of input result in 10,000 units of good output, or a normal loss of 1,000 units. This represents

FIGURE 10.10 Continued

Glazing Department
Cost of Production Report
(First-in, First-out Method—With Lost Units)
(Work in process has been inspected)

Costs accounted for as follows:

Costs transferred out:		
Work in process, beginning	$106,550	
Work completed on work in process, beginning:		
Material	9,514	(1,200 × $7.928)
Labor and overhead	9,956	(4,000 × $2.489)
Good units started and completed	197,004	(12,000 × $16.417)
Normal loss	18,818	(0.75 × $25,090[a])
To finished goods	$341,842	
Abnormal loss	12,546[b]	
Total costs transferred out	$354,388	
Work in process, ending:		
Transferred-in costs	$24,000	(4,000 × $6.000)
Materials	22,198	(2,800 × $7.928)
Labor and overhead	3,982	(1,600 × $2.489)
Normal loss	6,272	(0.25 × $25,090[a])
Total	$56,452	
Total costs accounted for	$410,850	(Rounded from $410,840.)

[a] Normal loss:

Transferred-in costs	$12,000	(2,000 × $6.000)
Materials	11,099	(1,400 × $7.928)
Labor and overhead	1,991	(800 × $2.489)
Total	$25,090	

[b] Abnormal loss:

Transferred-in costs	$6,000	(1,000 × $6.000)
Materials	5,550	(700 × $7.928)
Labor and overhead	996	(400 × $2.489)
Total	$12,546	

a normal loss rate of approximately 9.1 percent based on normal input or a 10-percent loss rate based on good output. Figure 10.11 illustrates these relationships.

The difficulty with using total input as a base can be illustrated by assuming that during a particular period, it actually took 11,500 units to produce 10,000 units of good output. Because the numbers have been kept quite simple, it is apparent that there are 500 units of abnormal loss in this situation—1,500 units of total loss minus 1,000 units of normal loss. However, applying a loss rate of either 9.1 or 10 percent to total input does not result in an accurate finding of 500 units of abnormal loss. In fact, because the relationship among normal input, good output, and normal loss is predetermined, the only unknown quantity is abnormal loss. This means that it is not possible to develop a loss rate (before actual results are available) that can be applied to total input to accurately uncover abnormal loss. Without an expected or predetermined loss rate, it is not possible to differentiate between normal and abnormal loss.

It is most convenient to apply a single loss rate when calculating normal loss. Because of random influences in virtually all production processes, however, actual loss rates

FIGURE 10.11

Bases for Calculating Expected Normal Losses

	Units	Bases for Calculating Normal Losses	
		Good Output	Normal Input
Normal input	11,000	90.0%	100.0%
Good output	10,000	100.0	90.9
Normal loss	1,000	10.0%	9.1%

typically fluctuate around some average value. This should be kept in mind as abnormal losses are analyzed and loss rates revised. For example, assume that a given loss rate is used throughout a year when, from an engineering perspective, there have been no abnormal losses. In comparing actual losses with expected normal losses, small differences probably will still occur. Sometimes actual losses will be less than expected normal losses, and sometimes they will be greater. The net difference over a number of periods is expected to be zero if the normal loss rate accurately represents the manufacturing process.

Since losses in excess of expected normal losses are defined as abnormal, small abnormal losses will occasionally occur even though the process is not out of control and there is no need to stop or adjust operations. If this is the case, how persistent and how large must abnormal losses be before they indicate a process that is truly out of control and where investigation is warranted? Chapter 16 answers this and other questions about how to determine when indicators such as abnormal losses actually signal an out-of-control condition that requires management intervention.

Another consideration in accounting for lost units because of spoilage or shrinkage concerns the point in the process at which losses are discovered. Typically an inspection or quality control check is made at the end of a process, immediately before goods are transferred to the next process or to finished goods. However, in some processes spoilage or shrinkage may be detected at intermediate stages in the process.

SUMMARY

A number of unique accounting problems arise when using process-costing procedures. When materials are added in processes subsequent to the first process, there may be no change in the number of units in process or there may be an increase in the number of units. When there is no change in the number of units, accounting procedures remain the same except for the addition of materials cost as another cost category in that process. When the number of units increase, the additional units are added to the number of units for which an accounting must be made. In so doing, the cost per equivalent unit for transferred-in costs and all other cost categories is automatically adjusted when using the form of the cost of production report illustrated in this chapter. Otherwise, revised per-unit transferred-in costs must be calculated. With adjusted unit costs, process-costing procedures relating to the assignment of costs remain the same.

Spoilage and shrinkage may result in a decrease in the number of units in process. Nearly every manufacturing process operates with some level of lost units; preventing all losses is usually impossible except at a very high cost. How the cost of lost units is handled depends on whether losses are considered to be normal or abnormal. The cost of normal losses is assigned to inventory and eventually charged to cost of goods sold in the period of sale. The cost of abnormal losses is charged to a separate loss account and reported on the income statement in the period in which the abnormal loss is incurred.

SELF-STUDY PROBLEM

Chemco Incorporated manufactures a single product that passes through four sequential processes. Accounting and production data for department 3 of the operation are as follows for the current accounting period:

Production Statistics

	Units
Work-in-process beginning inventory	2,000
(Materials 100% complete; labor and overhead 40% complete)	
Received from department 2	50,000
Started in process due to the addition of materials	20,000
Transferred to department 4	64,000
Work-in-process ending inventory	6,000
(Materials 100% complete; labor and overhead 30% complete)	

Accounting Data

Work-in-process beginning inventory:

Transferred-in costs	$ 5,600
Materials	2,500
Labor and overhead	500
Total	$ 8,600

Costs of the current period:

Transferred-in costs	$206,500
Materials	91,000
Labor and overhead	244,550
Total	$542,050

Materials are added at the beginning of the process. All losses are discovered at final inspection just before units are transferred to department 4. Department 3 has a normal loss rate of 2.5 percent of good units produced.

Required

Prepare a cost of production report for department 3 using the FIFO method of process costing. Prepare journal entries to record the cost of abnormal losses and to transfer costs to department 4.

Solution to the Self-Study Problem

The following journal entries are derived from given information and the accompanying cost of production report.

1. To establish total costs to account for in department 3 (not required):

Work in process—department 3	550,650	
Various accounts		550,650

2. Transfer of goods, department 3 to department 4:

Work in process—department 4	515,420	
Work in process—department 3		515,420

3. Abnormal losses charged to a loss account:

Cost of abnormal losses	3,160	
Work in process—final department		3,160

CHAPTER 10: PROCESS COSTING: ADDITIONAL FEATURES

Department 3
Cost of Production Report
Lost Units Are Discovered at Final Inspection
(First-in, First-out Method)

	Physical Units	Percentage Completion		
		Transferred In	Material	Labor and Overhead
Units to account for:				
Work in process, beginning	2,000	100%	100%	40%
Transferred in this period	50,000			
Placed in process	20,000			
Total units to account for	72,000			
Units accounted for as follows:				
Completed and transferred out:				
Beginning inventory	2,000	100%	100%	40%
Started and completed	62,000	100%	100%	100%
Normal loss	1,600[a]	100%	100%	100%
Abnormal loss	400[b]	100%	100%	100%
Work in process, ending	6,000	100%	100%	30%
Total units accounted for	72,000			

	Total	Transferred In	Material	Labor and Overhead
Costs to account for:				
Work in process, beginning	$ 8,600			
(1) Costs of the current period	542,050	206,500	91,000	244,550
Total costs to account for	$550,650			
Equivalent units of production:				
Completed work in process, beginning				1,200
Started and completed		62,000	62,000	62,000
Normal loss		1,600	1,600	1,600
Abnormal loss		400	400	400
Work in process, ending		6,000	6,000	1,800
(2) Total equivalent units		70,000	70,000	67,000
Cost per equivalent unit, (1) ÷ (2)	$ 7.900	$ 2.950	$ 1.300	$ 3.650
Costs accounted for as follows:				
Costs transferred out:				
Work in process, beginning	$ 8,600			
Work completed on work in process, beginning	4,380	(1,200 × $ 3.650)		
Work started and completed	489,800	(62,000 × $ 7.900)		
Normal loss	12,640	(1,600 × $ 7.900)		
To department 4	$515,420			
Abnormal loss	3,160	(400 × $ 7.900)		
Total costs transferred out	$518,580			
Work in process, ending:				
Transferred-in costs	$ 17,700	(6,000 × $ 2.950)		
Materials	7,800	(6,000 × $ 1.300)		
Labor and overhead	6,570	(1,800 × $ 3.650)		
Total	$ 32,070			
Total costs accounted for	$550,650			

[a](0.025 × 64,000 units)
[b]Found by subtraction.

SUGGESTED READINGS

Arthur Andersen & Company. *Inventory Shrinkage: A Guide to Analysis and Resolution.* Chicago: Arthur Andersen & Co., 1981.

Kaplan, Robert S. *Advanced Management Accounting.* Englewood Cliffs, N.J.: Prentice-Hall, 1982.

National Association of Accountants. "Cost Control of Spoiled Work." *Accounting Practice Report No. 12.* New York: National Association of Accountants, 1971.

Richards, Jim E. "Salvaging Your Company's Scrap-Disposal Procedures." *Internal Auditor* 39 (August 1982): 18–20.

Shaw, Robert J., and Gordon, Paul N. "Cut Down on Inventory Shrinkage with an In-Depth Analysis Program." *Corporate Accounting* 1 (Winter 1983): 85–88.

DISCUSSION QUESTIONS

Q10–1. When materials are added in processes subsequent to the first process, what are the possible outcomes with respect to the number of units in process?

Q10–2. What is the effect on the per-unit cost of production when the number of units in process increases as a result of adding materials in processes subsequent to the first process?

Q10–3. Explain how materials costs are handled in a cost of production report when they are added in processes subsequent to the first process and there is no increase in the number of units.

Q10–4. What change is necessary in the cost of production report when there is an increase in the number of units in process due to materials being added in processes subsequent to the first process?

Q10–5. Why is it usually not necessary to specifically calculate a revised per-unit cost for transferred-in costs when using the form of cost of production report illustrated in this chapter?

Q10–6. Explain the difference between normal and abnormal rates of loss.

Q10–7. Are normal and abnormal losses controllable by management? Explain.

Q10–8. Discuss the cost flows for normal versus abnormal losses, and give journal entries to illustrate these cost flows.

Q10–9. What are two acceptable bases for the calculation of normal losses? Why is actual input not an acceptable base?

Q10–10. What is the general rule for deciding whether the cost of normal losses should be allocated only to units transferred out or to work-in-process ending inventory *and* units transferred out?

EXERCISES

E10–1. Materials Added in Subsequent Processes (CPA) Information concerning department *B* of the Toby Company is as follows:

CHAPTER 10: PROCESS COSTING: ADDITIONAL FEATURES

	Units	Costs
Beginning work in process	5,000	$ 6,300
Units transferred in	35,000	58,000
	40,000	$64,300
Units completed	37,000	
Ending work in process	3,000	

Costs

	Transferred In	Materials	Conversion	Total Costs
Beginning work in process	$ 2,900		$ 3,400	$ 6,300
Units transferred in	17,500	$25,500	15,000	58,000
	$20,400	$25,500	$18,400	$64,300

Conversion costs were 20-percent complete as to beginning work in process and 40-percent complete as to ending work in process. All materials are added at the end of the process. Toby uses the weighted-average method.

Required

1. Prepare a cost of production report for department *B*.
2. Prepare the journal entry or entries to transfer costs out of department *B*.

E10-2. Materials Added in Subsequent Processes JDL Company makes a certain liquid product for its consumer market. During the last process, the final quality control check is made and a filler chemical is added to give bulk to the product. Materials are placed in production near the end of this final process, with labor and overhead costs uniformly applied throughout the process. Data for the current accounting period for this last process are as follows:

Production Statistics

	Units
Work-in-process beginning inventory	1,000
(Materials 40% complete; labor and overhead 60% complete)	
Transferred in	12,000
Increase in units from added materials	3,000
Work-in-processes ending inventory	800
(Materials 50% complete; labor and overhead 50% complete)	

Accounting Data

Work-in-process beginning inventory:	
Transferred-in costs	$ 8,480
Materials	400
Labor and overhead	1,792
Total	$ 10,672
Costs of the current period:	
Transferred-in costs	$120,000
Materials	15,980
Labor and overhead	50,000
Total	$185,980

Required

Prepare an electronic spreadsheet to generate a cost of production report for JDL Company's final process, using the weighted-average method of process costing. Print a copy of the report.

E10–3. Equivalent Units—FIFO versus Average Costing

Blakely Incorporated uses a process-costing system to account for the costs of its two departments, manufacturing and packing. The following information is available for the month of March 19X2:

	Units	
	Manufacturing	**Packing**
In process at beginning	3,000	5,000
Started in process	25,000	
Received from preceding department		20,000
Transferred to next department	20,000	
Transferred to finished goods		17,000
Completed and on hand	2,000	
Still in process	5,000	7,000
Lost at end of process	1,000	1,000

	Percentage Completion of Work in Process	
	Manufacturing	**Packing**
Beginning inventory		
Materials	80%	
Conversion costs	20%	50%
Ending inventory		
Materials	100%	
Conversion costs	30%	70%

Required

1. Determine the equivalent units of production for the manufacturing department's materials and conversion costs, using:
   a. the FIFO method.
   b. the weighted-average method.
2. Determine the equivalent units of production for the packing department's material and conversion costs, using:
   a. the FIFO method.
   b. the weighted-average method.

E10–4. Basic Procedures for Normal and Abnormal Spoilage

The following data are available for one of the processes of Weight Control Products, Inc. The company uses the weighted-average method of process costing and inspects products at the end of this process.

Beginning work in process, ⅗ complete	100 units
Transferred in	620 units
Normal loss	40 units
Abnormal loss	60 units
Good units transferred out	540 units
Ending work in process, ¾ complete	80 units
Conversion costs in beginning work in process	$2,000
Conversion costs, current period	$9,200

Required

Determine the following items, showing supporting computations in good form.

1. Equivalent units for conversion costs.
2. Cost per equivalent unit for conversion costs.
3. Total conversion costs for normal loss.
4. Total conversion costs for abnormal loss.
5. Total conversion costs trransferred out to the following process.
6. Total conversion costs in the ending work-in-process inventory.

E10–5. Weighted-Average Cost Procedures (CMA)

JC Company employs a process-costing system. A unit of product passes through three departments—molding, assembly, and finishing—before it is completed.

The following activity took place in the finishing department during May:

	Units
Work-in-process inventory—May 1	1,400
Units transferred in from the assembly department	14,000
Units lost	700
Units transferred out to finished-goods inventory	11,200

Raw material is added at the beginning of the process in the finishing department without changing the number of units being processed. The work-in-process inventory was 70-percent complete as to conversion on May 1 and 40-percent complete as to conversion on May 31. All loss was discovered at final inspection before the units were transferred to finished goods; 560 of the units lost were within the limit considered normal.

JC Company employs the weighted-average costing method. The equivalent units and the current costs per equivalent unit of production for each cost factor are as follows:

	Equivalent Units	Current Costs per Equivalent Unit
Cost of prior departments	15,400	$5.00
Raw materials	15,400	1.00
Conversion cost	13,300	$9.00
	3.00	

Required

1. Determine the cost of production transferred to the finished-goods inventory.
2. Determine the cost assigned to the work-in-process inventory on May 31.
3. If the total costs of prior departments included in the finishing department's work-in-process inventory on May 1 amounted to $6,300, determine the total cost transferred in from the assembly department to the finishing department during May.
4. Determine the cost associated with the abnormal loss.
5. Determine how the cost associated with the abnormal loss ordinarily would be treated.

E10–6. Cost of Production Report—Normal and Abnormal Loss

The Zigler Company uses process costing. In department C, conversion costs are incurred uniformly during the process. Materials are added at the end of the process after an inspection is made. Normal losses are expected to be 5 percent of good output.

The following information is evident for department C for January:

	Units	$ Amount
Received from department B	24,000	$168,000
Transferred to finished goods	18,000	
Ending inventory (75% complete)	4,000	
Department C materials costs		36,000
Department C conversion costs		91,200

Required

Prepare a complete cost of production report for department C, including a quantity schedule (i.e., a schedule accounting for units) and an equivalent-unit schedule.

E10–7. Normal and Abnormal Losses—FIFO Method with Work in Process Inspected Mint Products, Inc. accumulated the following information for its final process for the current month.

Units:

Beginning work in process (40% complete as to conversion costs)	200
Transferred in	800
Transferred out	600
Ending work in process (50% complete as to conversion costs)	300
Normal loss	80
Abormal loss	20

Costs:

Beginning work-in-process inventory:		
Transferred in	$1,400	
Direct materials	800	
Conversion costs	500	$ 2,700
Transferred in during the current period:		6,200
Added this period:		
Direct materials	$4,400	
Conversion costs	2,900	7,300
Total to account for		$16,200

Materials are added at the beginning of this process, and inspection occurs when units are 35-percent complete as to conversion costs. Mint Products, Inc. uses the FIFO method of product costing.

Required

Determine the following items, showing supporting computations in good form.

1. Equivalent units for conversion costs.
2. Cost per equivalent unit for conversion costs.
3. Total conversion costs for normal loss.
4. Total conversion costs for abnormal loss.
5. Total conversion costs transferred out to the following process.
6. Total conversion costs in the ending work-in-process inventory.

E10–8. Equivalent Units—Normal Spoilage Kopper Incorporated began business on April 1, 19X9. Kopper has two departments, A and B, and uses a process-costing system. During April, Kopper incurred $80,000 of materials costs and $45,000 of conversion costs. Of the 45,000 units started in process, 5,000 were lost in process, 30,000 were transferred to department B, and 10,000 were still in process. The ending work-in-process units were 100-percent complete as to materials costs and 60-percent complete as to conversion costs. All losses are considered normal. Inspection occurs at the end of the process.

Required

1. Determine the equivalent units of production.
2. Determine the cost per equivalent unit for materials and conversion costs.
3. Determine the total costs transferred to department B.

E10-9. Quantity Schedule—Equivalent Units Poole Incorporated produces a chemical compound by a unique chemical process that Poole has divided into two departments, A and B, for accounting purposes. The process functions as follows:

1. The formula for the chemical compound requires one pound of chemical X and one pound of chemical Y. In the simplest sense, one pound of chemical X is processed in department A and transferred to department B for further processing. In department B one pound of chemical Y is added when the process is 50-percent complete. When the processing is complete, the finished chemical compound is transferred to finished goods. The process is continuous, operating twenty-four hours a day.
2. Normal spoilage occurs in department A. During the first few seconds of processing 5 percent of chemical X is lost.
3. No spoilage occurs in department B.
4. In department A, conversion costs are incurred uniformly throughout the process and are allocated to good pounds produced because spoilage is normal.
5. In department B, conversion costs are allocated equally to each equivalent pound of output.
6. The following data are available for the month of October:

	Department A	Department B
Work in process, October 1	8,000 pounds	10,000 pounds
Stage of completion of beginning inventory (one batch per department)	3/4	3/10
Started or transferred in	50,000 pounds	?
Transferred out	46,500 good pounds	?
Work in process, October 31	?	12,000
Stage of completion of ending inventory (one batch per department)	1/3	1/5
Total equivalent pounds of material added in department B	—	44,500 pounds

Required

1. Prepare a quantity schedule (schedule accounting for units) for both departments.
2. Determine the equivalent units of production for material and conversion costs.

E10-10. Normal and Abnormal Loss The Klammer Company uses process costing in accounting for production. Two materials are used. Material A is added at the beginning of the process. Inspection is at the 90-percent stage; material B is then added to the good units. Normal-loss units amount to 5-percent of good output.

Company records contain the following information for January:

Started during the period	20,000 units
Material A	$26,740
Material B	$ 9,000
Direct-labor cost	$75,160
Factory overhead	$93,950
Transferred to finished goods	14,000 units
Ending inventory (95% complete)	4,000 units

Required

Prepare an electronic spreadsheet to generate a cost of production report for Klammer Company using the weighted-average method of process costing. Print a copy of the report.

PROBLEMS

P10–1. Cost of Production Report—Normal Loss Orson Incorporated began a new process on July 1, 19X2; a single product is manufactured in two departments. The finishing department is the last department before the product is transferred to finished goods. The accounting department has gathered the following information about the finishing department.

Units received from preceding department	75,000 units
Units transferred to finished goods	60,000 units
Units completed and on hand	5,000 units
Units still in process (50% complete as to conversion costs)	8,000 units
Units lost in process	2,000 units
Transferred from preceding department	$61,050
Costs added by department:	
Labor	$20,925
Factory overhead	$27,900

Normal loss is 5-percent of units completed during the month. Approximately one half of the losses occur at the 25-percent stage and one half occur at the 75-percent stage. No additional work is done on lost units. Lost units are scrapped.

Required

Prepare a cost of production report for the finishing department for July 19X2, using the weighted-average method.

P10–2. Normal and Abnormal Losses—Various Assumptions Slurrey Corporation has the following data for the current year:

Units:		
Beginning work-in-process inventory		
(40% complete as to conversion costs)	100	
Transferred in	900	
Transferred out	800	
Ending work-in-process inventory		
(45% complete as to conversion costs)	100	
Loss	100	
Costs:		
Beginning work-in-process inventory:		
From prior department	$ 600	
Direct materials	200	
Conversion costs	100	$ 900
Transferred in		6,000
Added this period:		
Direct materials	$1,800	
Conversion costs	1,300	3,100
		$10,000

Required

Make the required calculations in each of the following independent situations. Assume that all materials are added at the beginning of the process.

1. If the loss is normal, inspection is at 90-percent of processing, and the FIFO method is used, what is the cost transferred out to finished goods?
2. If the loss is abnormal, inspection is at 20-percent of processing, and the weighted-average method is used, what is the cost assigned to ending work-in-process inventory?
3. If the loss is 50-percent normal and 50-percent abnormal, inspection is at 90-percent of processing, and the weighted-average method is used, what is the cost transferred to finished goods?
4. If the loss is 50-percent normal and 50-percent abnormal, inspection is at the beginning of processing (just before direct materials are added in this department), and the weighted-average method is used, what is the cost assigned to ending work-in-process inventory?

P10-3. Cost of Production Report—Normal and Abnormal Losses Lakeview Corporation is a manufacturer that uses the weighted-average process-costing method to account for costs of production. Lakeview manufactures a product that is produced in three separate departments—molding, assembling, and finishing. The following information was obtained for the assembling department for the month of June.

Work in process, June 1—2,000 units, composed of the following:

	Amount	Degree of Completion
Transferred in from the molding department	$32,000	100%
Costs added by the assembling department		
Direct materials	$20,000	100%
Direct labor	7,200	60%
Factory overhead applied	5,500	50%
	$32,700	
Work in process, June 1	$64,700	

The following activity occurred during the month of June:

10,000 units were transferred in from the molding department at a cost of $160,000.
$150,000 of costs were added by the assembling department:

Direct materials	$ 96,000
Direct labor	36,000
Factory overhead applied	18,000
	$150,000

There were 7,000 units completed and transferred to the finishing department. There were 1,000 units lost at final inspection in the assembling department just before they were to be transferred to the finishing department. Losses are 80-percent normal and 20-percent abnormal.

On June 30, there were still 4,000 units in work in process. The degree of completion of work in process on June 30 was as follows:

Direct materials	90%
Direct labor	70%
Factory overhead applied	35%

Required

1. Prepare a cost of production report for the assembling department for the month of June.
2. Prepare the summary journal entry or entries to transfer costs out of the assembling department for June.

P10–4. Cost of Production Report—Normal Losses

Joy Company manufactures product X in a two-stage production cycle in departments A and B. Materials are added at the beginning of the process in department B. Joy uses the weighted-average method. Conversion costs for department B were 50-percent complete as to the 6,000 units in the beginning work in process and 75-percent complete as to the 8,000 units in the ending work in process. There were 11,800 units completed and transferred out of department B during February. Normal losses of 200 units were discovered at an inspection point where 60-percent of the processing had been completed as to conversion costs.

An analysis of the costs relating to work in process and production activity in department B for February is as follows:

	Transferred In	Materials Costs	Conversion
Work in process, February 1:			
Costs attached	$12,000	$2,500	$1,000
February activity:			
Costs added	29,000	5,500	5,000

Required

1. Prepare a cost of production report for department B for the month of February.
2. Prepare the summary journal entry or entries to transfer costs out of department B for February.

P10–5. Cost of Production report—FIFO Method, Lost Units

Carman Incorporated has developed a process that produces widgets. The widgets are assembled in the assembly department and packaged for sale in the packaging department. Packaged widgets are moved to the finished goods storeroom until they are sold. The accounting department has gathered the following cost and production data for the month of March 19X3:

	Assembly	Packaging
Work-in-process beginning inventory:		
Cost from preceding department		17,500
Materials (100% complete)	13,750	5,450
Labor (50% complete, assembly; 60% complete, packaging)	7,500	6,900
Factory overhead (50% complete, assembly; 50% complete, packaging)	5,450	7,700
Costs added during the month		
Materials	75,680	24,800
Labor	43,008	39,650
Factory overhead	36,864	42,700
Work-in-process ending inventory, % of completion		
Materials	100%	100%
Conversion costs	30%	70%
Units in process at beginning	6,500 widgets	4,300 widgets
Units started in process	35,400	
Units transferred to next department	31,000	27,900
Units still in process	9,900	7,400
Units lost in process	1,000	—

CHAPTER 10: PROCESS COSTING: ADDITIONAL FEATURES

The units lost in the assembly department are lost near the beginning of the assembly process. None of the lost units are from the beginning work in process and all losses are normal.

Required

Prepare a cost of production report for all departments for March 19X3, using the FIFO method.

P10–6. Equivalent Unit Calculations for Lost Units

Clifford Company, Inc. produces a single plastic product. In department B, empty molds (one per unit of production) are received from department A and are immediately inspected. Units that pass the first inspection are processed by being cleaned and oiled.

When 60-percent of the cost of processing has been applied, the plastic material is poured into the molds. The units are inspected a second time immediately after the material is added. Units that pass the second inspection are stripped from the molds, cleaned, and polished. Just before the units are transferred to department C, a final inspection occurs.

During March, the following molds (units) were involved in department B:

Beginning inventory, 70% processed		10,200
Received from department A		120,800
		131,000
Completed and transferred out	110,500	
Lost—didn't pass inspection	9,800	
		120,300
Ending inventory		10,700

Required

For each of the following assumptions: (a) compute equivalent units of production for transferred-units, materials, and conversion costs, using the weighted-average method; and (b) explain what disposition should be made of the cost of lost units.

1. Ending inventory is 80-percent processed, all losses are considered normal, and all losses are detected at the first inspection.
2. Ending inventory is 80-percent processed, all losses are abnormal, and all losses are detected at the final inspection.
3. Ending inventory is 80-percent processed, all losses are normal, and all losses are detected at the final inspection.
4. Ending inventory is 40-percent processed, all losses are abnormal, and all losses are detected at the second inspection.
5. Ending inventory is 40-percent processed, 1,000 units of the losses are normal, and this 1,000 units was detected at the second inspection. The remainder of the loss is normal and was detected at the final inspection.

P10–7. Normal and Abnormal Losses

Paul, Inc. manufactures a chemical compound, utilizing a continuous process where units pass first through department A and then through department B. Material and conversion costs are added uniformly during processing in department B. At the end of the process in department B, normal losses occur due to evaporation. Normal losses amounted to 200 units during the current month.

There were 6,600 units of the chemical compound transferred from department A to department B during the month. All units that were completed in department B were transferred to finished-goods inventory. The following production information for department B is available for the current month:

Costs Incurred	Units	Prior Department Costs	Material Added This Department	Conversion Costs
Beginning work in process		$ 8,500	$ 3,000	$ 4,500
Current month		21,400	31,600	24,500

Physical Flow		Percentage Completion		
Beginning work in process	2,000	100%	20%	50%
Ending work in process	800	100%	40%	60%

Required

1. Compute the equivalent units of production for all cost elements, using (a) the FIFO method and (b) the weighted-average method.
2. Compute the cost of goods transferred to finished-goods inventory, using the FIFO method.
3. Assume for this part that the 200 units lost in department B were abnormal rather than normal losses. Using the weighted-average method, show the journal entry to remove the costs from the work-in-process inventory of department B at the end of the current month.

P10–8. Lost Units at Various Points During a Process

Swizzle, Inc. accumulated the following for its assembly division during the month of April. Materials added in the assembly division are added at the beginning of the process. Swizzle, Inc. uses the weighted-average method of process costing.

Units:

Beginning work in process (40% complete as to conversion costs)	200
Transferred in	800
Transferred out	600
Ending work in process (50% complete as to conversion costs)	300
Loss	100

Costs:

Beginning work-in-process inventory:		
Transferred in	$1,400	
Direct materials	800	
Conversion costs	500	$ 2,700
Transferred in during the current period		6,200
Added this period:		
Direct materials	$4,400	
Conversion costs	2,900	7,300
Total to account for		$16,200

Required

Prepare a cost of production report and appropriate journal entry or entries to transfer costs out of the assembly division to finished-goods inventory under each of the following assumptions:

1. The entire 100-unit loss is normal, and inspection occurs when units are 60-percent complete as to conversion costs.
2. The entire 100-unit loss is normal, and inspection occurs when units are 30-percent complete as to conversion costs.

3. The loss of 100 units is 60-percent normal and 40-percent abnormal, and inspection occurs when units are 35-percent complete as to conversion costs.

P10–9. Cost of Production Report—FIFO and Weighted-Average Methods—Loss with Recovery Value (from CPA exam) The Minsky Processing Company manufactures one product through two processes. For each unit of Process no. 1 output, two units of material A are put in at the start of processing. For each unit of Process no. 2 output, three cans of material B are put in at the end of processing. Two pounds of Process no. 1 output are put in at the start of Process no. 2 for each unit of finished goods started.

Loss generally occurs in process no. 2 when processing is approximately 50-percent complete. The company uses FIFO costing for Process no. 1 and weighted-average costing for Process no. 2.

Data for March:

1. Units transferred:

From Process no. 1 to Process no. 2	2,200 pounds
From Process no. 2 to finished goods	900 gallons
From finished goods to cost of goods sold	600 gallons

2. Units spoiled in Process no. 2: 100 gallons.
3. Materials unit costs: A, $1.51 per unit; B, $2 per can.
4. Conversion costs: Process no. 1, $3,334; Process no. 2, $4,010.
5. Spoilage recovery: $100 (treated in Process no. 2 as a reduction in the cost that came from Process no. 1).
6. Inventory data:

	Process no. 1 Beginning	Process no. 1 Ending	Process no. 2 Beginning	Process no. 2 Ending
Units	200	300	200	300
Fraction complete, conversion cost	1/2	1/3	1/2	2/3
Costs:				
Materials	$560			
Conversion cost	108		$ 390	
Prior department cost			2,200	

Required

Prepare a cost of production report with a quantity schedule for March for both processes.

P10–10. Cost of Production Reports—Lost Units Dartmouth Manufacturing began business July 1, 19X5. Dartmouth uses a process-costing system for the company's two departments—department A and department B. The following information is available for department B:

Cost of units transferred:	$105,000
Cost added by department:	
Labor	$ 35,200
Factory overhead	$ 26,400
Transferred from department A	20,000 units
Transferred to finished goods	12,000 units
Ending inventory (60% complete as to conversion costs)	6,000 units

The units are inspected at the 75-percent stage. Normal loss is considered to be 8-percent of good units inspected. Lost units are not processed further.

Required

1. Prepare a cost of production report for department *B*, using the weighted-average method.
2. Prepare a cost of production report for department *B*, assuming that ending inventory is 90-percent complete, using the weighted-average method.

P10–11. Cost of Production Reports—Multiple Departments The Mintz Corporation manufactures seven-inch rulers in three departments—mixing, shaping, and finishing. A process-costing system is used to account for the goods manufactured. The following information is available:

	Departments		
Units	**Mixing**	**Shaping**	**Finishing**
Opening work in process			
Mixing (all materials, 30% conversion)	10,000		
Shaping (all materials, 60% conversion)		18,000	
Finishing (all materials, 45% conversion)			5,000
Started in process during the period	90,000		
Transferred out	?	?	?
Completed and still on hand	4,000	2,000	6,000
Closing work in process			
Mixing (all materials, 75% conversion)	7,000		
Shaping (all materials, 35% conversion)		8,000	
Finishing (all materials, 75% conversion)			9,000
Costs			
Opening work in process			
Materials	$ 15,000		
From preceding department		$ 9,620	$ 11,630
Labor	8,075	13,954	6,531
Overhead	10,215	9,792	4,650
Total	$ 33,290	$33,366	$ 22,811
Added during the period			
Materials	$195,000		
Labor	100,000	$40,000	$ 60,000
Overhead	40,000	35,000	45,000
Total	$335,000	$75,000	$105,000

Required

1. Prepare an electronic spread-sheet to generate a cost of production report for all three departments, using the weighted-average costing method. Print your results.
2. Prepare an electronic spread-sheet to generate a cost of production report for all three departments, using the FIFO costing method. Print your results.

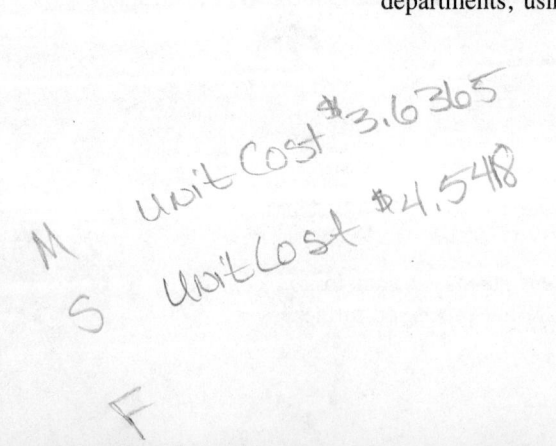

Chapter 11

Joint Products and By-Products: Cost Allocations and Decisions

Outline

THE JOINT PRODUCT ENVIRONMENT
JOINT PRODUCT COST ALLOCATION
   METHODS
Physical Measures
Market Measures
   Relative Sales Value
   Net Realizable Value
ALTERNATIVES TO MAKING JOINT
   PRODUCT COST ALLOCATIONS
ACCOUNTING FOR BY-PRODUCTS
Assigning a Cost to By-Products at the
   Time of Production

Recognizing the Cost of By-Products at
   the Time of Sale
Comparison of the Two Methods
JOINT COSTS AND MANAGEMENT
   DECISIONS
SUMMARY
SELF-STUDY PROBLEM
SUGGESTED READINGS
DISCUSSION QUESTIONS
EXERCISES
PROBLEMS
CASE

Joint products and by-products are a part of many manufacturing operations in which one product cannot be produced without the simultaneous production of one or more other products. For example, copper mining, oil refining, cheese making, lumber milling, and vegetable canning all produce joint products and by-products. The equitable assignment of total manufacturing costs to various joint products and by-products is often a difficult and complicated accounting problem. However, the assignment of joint costs is important for inventory costing, income determination, and financial reporting purposes. Also, appropriate costing of joint products and by-products provides management with data for evaluating profit performance and for planning and control purposes. This chapter explains how to account for joint product costs and how joint product costs are used in management decisions. After completing this chapter, you should be able to:

1. identify joint product costs.
2. differentiate between joint products and by-products.
3. allocate joint product costs using either physical measures or market measures as an allocation base.
4. account for the cost of by-products.
5. use joint product and by-product costs in management decisions.

THE JOINT PRODUCT ENVIRONMENT

Whenever a resource or input results in more than one useful output, with each having relatively substantial value, **joint products** are produced. For example, hogs represent a single input to a meat packing operation in which pork chops, roasts, bacon, ham, and any number of other useful items are produced. A distinguishing characteristic of joint product operations is that no single group of joint products may be produced without the production of other joint products. For example, it is not reasonable to expect the only output from the slaughter of cattle will be steaks; a hide, hamburger, and various other cuts of meat are also supplied. Joint products may be produced in various proportions (for example, steaks can be ground into hamburger), but the economic and physical characteristics inherent in such operations naturally result in the production of joint products.

A **by-product** is basically a joint product with a relatively minor sales value when compared with other joint products. A by-product can be thought of as a secondary product that is produced during the manufacture of a primary product. Examples of by-products include hides from processing cattle, seeds from processing cotton, and silver from processing copper. Silver may be considered a by-product when mining copper because even though silver has a higher unit price than copper, the total value per ton of ore processed is typically much less for silver than for copper.

It is not always clear what constitutes a joint product and what constitutes a by-product, because judgment must be exercised in determining what constitutes a "relatively minor sales value." Also, shifts in the relative sales values of products may result in the need to reclassify by-products. For example, there are products that result from the manufacture of cheese and photographic film that once were considered by-products. However, these by-products are now classified as joint products because of newly discovered uses and their increased relative importance in the joint product group.

Various terms are used in accounting practice for joint products, by-products, scrap, and waste. Usage varies depending on the business environment and management viewpoint. For example, some sewage plants consider their output as waste, whereas others have developed recycling programs and account for their output as by-products. Some metal fabrication plants treat salable trimmings as scrap, whereas others account for trimmings as by-products. The distinction between waste and by-products is that waste usually

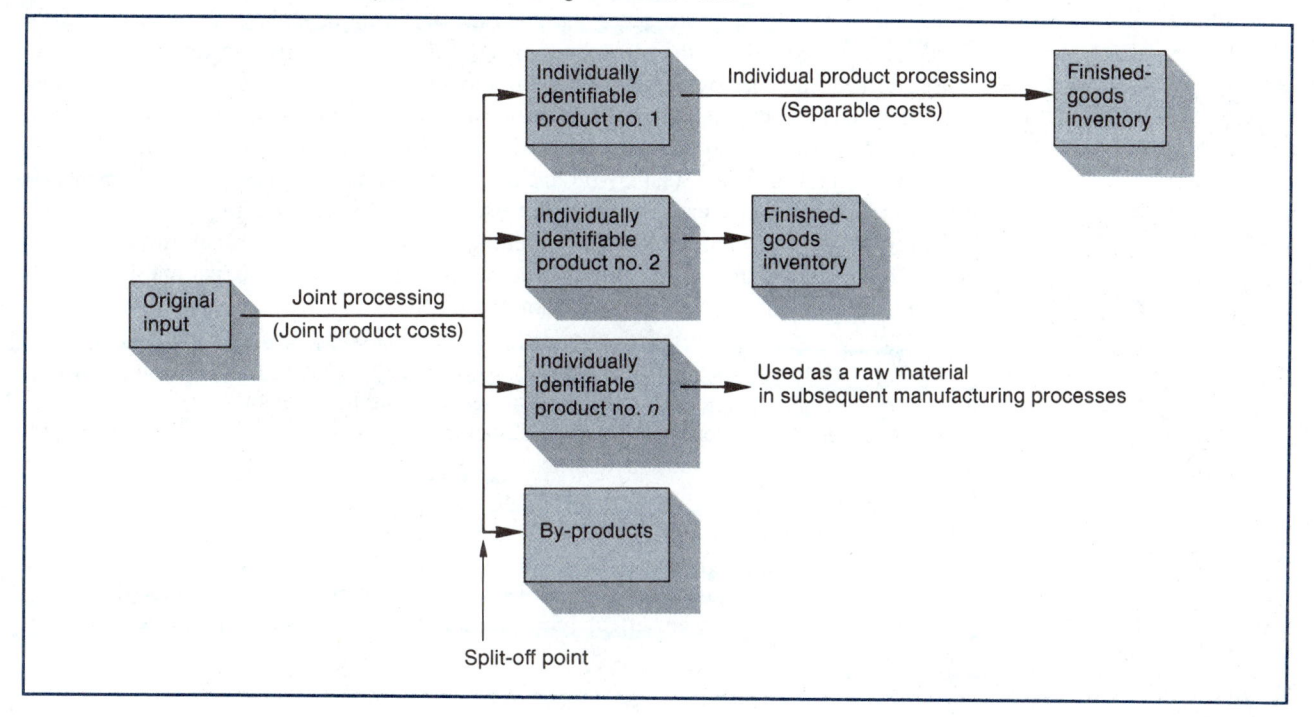

FIGURE 11.1 Joint Product and By-Product Processing and Cost Flows

does not have a sales value. The distinction between scrap and by-products is that by-products have a relatively higher sales value than scrap. Also, by-products may require additional processing to be marketable. These differences are not merely a matter of semantics for accountants. An accountant who makes the proper distinction between joint products, by-products, scrap, and waste overcomes potential cost allocation problems and develops appropriate inventory values and related information for financial statement users and company managers.

Joint product costs, also called joint or common costs, are those manufacturing costs incurred during the processing of original inputs before the point where joint products become individually identifiable. Joint costs are a type of common or shared cost in that they cannot be assigned directly to joint products. For example, all material, labor, and overhead costs incurred to process the carcass of a hog to the point where it is divided into its various categories of dressed meat are considered joint or common costs. At the point of division, which is called the **split-off point,** joint product categories such as sides for bacon and shoulders for roasts become individually identifiable.

Costs incurred after the split-off point are assigned to individual products and are classified as **separable** or **direct product costs.** For example, the costs of trimming, slicing, and packaging bacon are separable costs assigned solely to bacon, because it is an individually identifiable joint product in the processing cycle. The *total* cost of bacon consists of an allocated portion of joint costs plus the separable costs of processing bacon beyond the split-off point. Figure 11.1 illustrates the difference between joint costs and separable costs in a joint product manufacturing environment.

As shown in figure 11.1, there are several different possibilities for production and cost flows. Product no. 1, which could be bacon, undergoes individual processing beyond the split-off point before it is inventoried and sold. However, product no. 2 is not processed further and is simply inventoried and sold. For example, whole sides of bacon could be sold as soon as they are divided from the main carcass without additional trimming, slicing, or packaging.

384 PART THREE: COST DETERMINATION

Another possibility for joint product cost and production flow is the situation in which a joint product is reintroduced into the manufacturing process as a raw material. For example, coal and gas are the major raw material inputs in the manufacture of coke. Gas is used to heat the coal, which results in the production of many joint products including coke, benzol, tar, and coke oven gas. The gas recovered from the coking process is then typically reintroduced into the coking process to heat subsequent batches of coal.

Figure 11.1 indicates that by-products can be generated at the split-off point or at any stage of the manufacturing process. For example, hides and entrails occur rather early in a packing house operation, whereas trimmings usually result from final dressing operations. These various production and cost flow possibilities in joint product and by-product environments present unique cost allocation problems.

There are several reasons why joint product cost allocations are important. First, all product costs must be assigned to inventory to meet requirements for financial reporting, regulatory accounting, and income tax purposes. The assignment of costs to inventories provides for the proper identification of manufacturing costs with cost-of-goods-sold, work-in-process, and finished-goods inventories. Second, for some industries production costs are assigned to goods and services sold in order to derive a selling price. For example, the prices charged by regulated utilities are usually related to the cost of supplying the services. Therefore, accountants should understand the joint product manufacturing environment and know *(a)* what methods are available for allocating joint product costs, *(b)* how to account for by-products, and *(c)* what effect joint product cost allocations have on management decisions.

JOINT PRODUCT COST ALLOCATION METHODS

There are several ways to allocate joint costs to products. These cost allocations are made for purposes of inventory valuation and subsequent income determination. Inventory values are important because they affect *(a)* financial position through the amount of inventory shown on the balance sheet and *(b)* net income through a company's cost of goods sold shown on the income statement.

The following situation illustrates the various accounting methods available for allocating joint product costs. In one of its operations, Chemical Company uses Alpha as primary input and produces two products, Beta and Gamma. Alpha is refined in a common process that produces unfinished Beta and Gamma. Unfinished Beta can be sold for $0.34 per pound or further refined in a separate process to yield finished Beta, which is salable at $1.60 per pound. Unfinished Gamma can be sold at a price of 0.26 per pound or receive additional work in a separate process yielding finished Gamma, which has a sales price of $1.80 per pound.

Approximately 400,000 pounds of Alpha are processed each accounting period, with Beta and Gamma being produced in the following proportions:

Product	Quantity (lbs)
Beta	250,000
Gamma	150,000
Total	400,000

At a normal level of processing, the following manufacturing costs are typical when both unfinished Beta and Gamma are refined beyond the split-off point. Remember that the costs incurred beyond the split-off point that are identifiable with specific joint products are called separable costs or direct product costs.

	Joint Product Costs	Separable Costs Beta	Separable Costs Gamma
Materials	$ 60,000	$ 64,700	$ 14,600
Labor	25,000	139,300	146,000
Overhead	15,000	42,000	29,400
	$100,000	$246,000	$190,000

The preceding situation is modified in the next section as required to illustrate various cost allocation alternatives associated with physical and market measures. Regardless of what method is used, the question is, How should the $100,000 joint product cost of processing Alpha be allocated to the resulting joint products Beta and Gamma?

Physical Measures

Physical measures such as units, weight, or volume may be used as bases for allocating joint costs. For example, assume that the Chemical Company uses pounds of output as the basis for allocating joint costs. Since the company produces 400,000 total pounds of Beta and Gamma, $250/400_{ths}$ and $150/400_{ths}$ of the total joint cost of $100,000 is allocated, respectively, to Beta and Gamma. By expressing the allocation formula as an average unit cost, common costs are allocated to the joint products at the rate of $0.25 per pound ($100,000 ÷ 400,000 pounds). The following general formula can be used to make this computation:

$$\text{Cost per unit of physical measure} = \frac{\text{Total joint product cost}}{\text{Units of physical measure (i.e., weight, volume, etc.)}}$$

The amount of joint product cost allocated to each joint product is then calculated by multiplying the cost per unit of physical measure by the total units of physical measure for each product, as follows:

Joint Product	Pounds Produced	Cost per Pound	Joint Costs Allocated
Beta	250,000	$0.25	$ 62,500
Gamma	150,000	0.25	37,500
			$100,000

The following is a partial income statement using the joint cost allocations of $62,500 for Beta and $37,500 for Gamma, which were calculated previously using pounds of output as the allocation base. For simplicity, assume that there are no beginning inventories and that all production is sold during the current period.

Partial Income Statement
(Joint Product Costs Allocated Using a Physical Measure)

	Total	Beta	Gamma
Sales	$124,000	$85,000	$39,000
Cost of goods sold	100,000	62,500	37,500
Gross profit	$ 24,000	$22,500	$ 1,500
Gross profit rate	19%	26%	4%

Care should be exercised to insure that the same unit of measure is used for allocation of costs to joint products. For example, joint products for export may be measured in liters or kilograms whereas other joint products may be measured in pounds or cubic feet. In those instances where joint products are measured using different units of measure, it is necessary to convert them to a common term before cost allocation. For example, in the manufacture of coke, gas measured in cubic feet and liquids measured in gallons are converted to pounds per ton of coal processed before joint costs are allocated.

A variation in the use of physical measures as an allocation base is to assign relative weights to each joint product. These weights are intended to reflect important factors in the production process that relate to the amount of joint cost that should be allocated to each product. The amount of time consumed, the type of labor utilized, the difficulty of the process, the size of the product, or the amount of material consumed may all be relevant weighting factors. To implement this technique, relative weights in the form of "points" are assigned to each product and then are used as multiplication factors in the joint cost allocation process. For example, assume that Beta and Gamma are assigned weights of 8 and 20 because of the relative difficulty of handling each product. Using weighted pounds produced as the allocation base, joint costs are allocated as follows:

Joint Product	Pounds Produced	Weight (points)	Weighted Units	Joint Costs Allocated
Bets	250,000	8	2,000,000	$ 40,000[a]
Gamma	150,000	20	3,000,000	60,000[b]
			5,000,000	$100,000

[a] (2,000,000 ÷ 5,000,000) × $100,000 = $40,000
[b] (3,000,000 ÷ 5,000,000) × $100,000 = $60,000

The use of a physical measure is easy to apply and accomplishes the task of spreading the cost of production in proportion to physical units produced. However, physical measures typically have no relationship with the revenue producing potential of individual joint products. Therefore, some observers believe that using a market measure for joint cost allocations is a better approach, because it gives more realistic costs for product costing and decision making. However, managers and accountants are cautioned that analysis of product profitability should not be based on data containing joint cost allocations. The allocation process is inherently arbitrary and may produce results that give a distorted view of the relative profitability of different products. Such distortions may lead to improper management decisions. For example, if weight were used to allocate the joint costs of slaughtering cattle, then steak would have the same per-pound cost as tongue, tail, or hamburger. Because of this, some cuts may consistently be very profitable, whereas other cuts may consistently show losses inconsistent with economic reality. A valid evaluation of economic profitability in a joint cost situation depends on all costs and all revenues being evaluated together.

Market Measures

Market measures are the most popular basis for allocating joint product costs. Two market measures commonly used are relative sales value and net realizable value. The popularity of these measures arises from the belief that costs should be allocated on a basis related to the revenue-generating power of the joint products. The assumption is that the greatest proportion of joint product costs should be assigned to the joint product with the highest revenue-generating power. The least joint product cost should be assigned to the joint products with the lowest revenue-generating power.

Underlying the use of market measures is the notion that value in the marketplace is somehow indicative of the actual costs incurred to produce each joint product. If this view is taken, joint costs should be allocated based on relative market values. However, even if there is no relationship between a market measure and actual production costs, a market measure may be very useful for another reason; that is, gross profit percentages remain the same for all joint products when using market measures. This means that gross profit percentages do not become biased by joint cost allocations when market measures are used. This feature is very important for proper appraisal of profit performance, as illustrated in the following section.

Relative Sales Value A common market measure used to allocate joint costs is the predicted **relative sales value** of joint products in the ordinary course of business measured at the split-off point. A product's relative sales value is its estimated selling price less any estimated costs of completion and sale. To illustrate, assume that Chemical Company sells both Beta and Gamma as unfinished products and uses their relative sales value as the basis for allocating joint costs. The predicted market value for Beta is $85,000 (250,000 units × $0.34 per unit) and for Gamma is $39,000 (150,000 units × $0.26 per unit). This gives a total predicted market value of $124,000 ($85,000 + $39,000), of which Beta represents 68.5 percent ($85,000 ÷ $124,000) and Gamma represents 31.5 percent ($39,000 ÷ $124,000). Based on these percentages, the joint product cost of $100,000 incurred in the common process is allocated as follows:

Joint Product	Pounds Produced	Market Price (per pound)	Market Value	Percentage Weighting	Joint Costs Allocated
Beta	250,000	$0.34	$ 85,000	68.5%	$ 68,500
Gamma	150,000	0.26	39,000	31.5%	31,500
			$124,000	100.0%	$100,000

The following is a partial income statement using a market measure as the allocation base and joint cost allocations of $68,500 for Beta and $31,500 for Gamma calculated in the previous example.

Partial Income Statement
(Joint Product Costs Allocated Using a Market Measure)

	Total	Beta	Gamma
Sales	$124,000	$85,000	$39,000
Cost of goods sold	100,000	68,500	31,500
Gross profit	$ 24,000	$16,500	$ 7,500
Gross profit rate	19%	19%	19%

When products are not processed beyond the split-off point, note that each joint product has the same gross profit rate when relative sales value is used as the allocation base. This is typically not the case when using physical measures, as can be shown by comparing the gross profit percentages obtained for Chemical Company in the previous illustrations. When using a physical measure, the gross profit rates for Beta and Gamma are 26 percent and 4 percent, respectively. When using a market measure, the gross profit rates for Beta and Gamma are both 19 percent, which is also the combined gross profit rate.

It should be remembered that joint cost allocations are inherently arbitrary, and gross profit percentages can be significantly different when using different joint cost allocation methods. If management is not aware of this phenomenon when deciding which method to use, the effects of joint cost allocations may be mistakenly attributed to some factor other than the joint cost allocations themselves. This, in turn, may lead to improper conclusions about individual product profitability.

Net Realizable Value There may *not* be a market for joint products at the split-off point, and management may have no choice but to process beyond the split-off point. However, management may decide to process products beyond the split-off point for economic reasons, even though there may be a market for these joint products at the split-off point. When joint products are processed beyond the split-off point, the relative market values of the joint products *at the split-off point* should still be used as the market measure for allocating joint costs. When price quotations are not available for joint products at the split-off point, however, the best alternative basis for allocating joint costs is the net realizable value of the joint products at the split-off point.

Net realizable value is defined, for purposes of joint cost allocations, as the ultimate predicted selling price of a joint product minus reasonably predictable costs of completion and sales. Net realizable values are found by first calculating the ultimate expected market value of joint products and working backwards to obtain net realizable values at the split-off point. Joint product costs are then allocated based on net realizable values *as though* they are actual market values at the split-off point. Thus, net realizable value actually represents a hypothetical market value at the split-off point.

Assume that in the Chemical Company situation there is no market for either unfinished Beta or unfinished Gamma. This indicates that both products require additional processing to place them in a marketable condition. The expected costs of separate processing beyond the split-off point (also referred to as separable costs) are $246,000 for Beta and $190,000 for Gamma at the normal production volume of 250,000 pounds of Beta and 150,000 pounds of Gamma. The ultimate selling price for Beta is $1.60 per pound and for Gamma is $1.80 per pound. From these data it is possible to calculate the net realizable value of Beta and Gamma as follows:

Joint Product	Pounds Produced	Ultimate Market Price (per pound)	Ultimate Market Value	Less: Costs Beyond Split-off Point	Net Realizable Value
Beta	250,000	$1.60	$400,000	$246,000	$154,000
Gamma	150,000	1.80	270,000	190,000	80,000
					$234,000

If there are marketing or administrative costs incurred after the split-off point that are associated with individual joint products, such costs are handled the same as manufacturing costs beyond the split-off point and also should be subtracted to arrive at a product's net realizable value.

After calculation, the net realizable values of joint products are used on a percentage basis to allocate joint costs in the same fashion as when using actual market values. To illustrate, the joint cost of $100,000 to process Alpha into Beta and Gamma is allocated as follows when using net realizable value as an allocation base:

Joint Product	Net Realizable Value	Percentage Weighting	Joint Costs Allocated
Beta	$154,000	65.8%	$ 65,800
Gamma	80,000	34.2	34,200
	$234,000	100.0%	$100,000

Remember that net realizable values are actually hypothetical or artificial market values and represent only a next best alternative to using actual market values at the split-off point. This means that whenever a market exists for intermediate products at the split-off point, relative sales values should be used. This guide should be followed even though some joint products may have a market at the split-off point, whereas others must be processed further before a market is available. Therefore, actual market values may be used along with hypothetical market values (net realizable values) as the basis for allocating joint costs.

The following partial income statement presents the results of joint cost allocations when there is processing beyond the split-off point. Once again it is assumed for simplicity that there are no beginning inventories and that all production is sold in the current period.

Partial Income Statement

	Total	Beta	Gamma
Sales	$670,000	$400,000	$270,000
Cost of goods sold:			
Joint costs	$100,000	$ 65,800	$ 34,200
Costs beyond split-off	436,000	246,000	190,000
Total costs of goods sold	$536,000	$311,800	$224,200
Gross profit	$134,000	$ 88,200	$ 45,800
Gross profit rate	20%	22%	17%

Note that in the previous illustration, gross profit rates for joint products are different even though a market measure is used as an allocation base. Gross profit rates remain the same only when there is no processing beyond the split-off point. If management does not want joint cost allocations to bias gross profit statistics, the following modification can be made to the joint cost allocation process. First, the overall gross profit rate is calculated to determine what gross profit rate should be assigned to each joint product. Then, joint cost allocations are determined by subtracting from the ultimate market value of joint products (a) the amount of gross profit, using the overall gross profit rate, and (b) costs beyond the split-off point. The following schedule illustrates this calculation, using information and the overall gross profit rate of 20 percent from the previous example:

	Total	Beta	Gamma
Ultimate market value	$670,000	$400,000	$270,000
Less: Gross profit of 20%	134,000	80,000	54,000
Total cost	$536,000	$320,000	$216,000
Less: Costs beyond split-off	436,000	246,000	190,000
Joint cost allocation	$100,000	$ 74,000	$ 26,000

The joint product cost allocation of $74,000 for Beta and $26,000 for Gamma derived in the previous illustration is used in the following partial income statement to show that this revised allocation process results in the same gross profit rate for each joint product. Sales amounts and assumptions are the same as in previous partial income statements.

Partial Income Statement

	Total	Beta	Gamma
Sales	$670,000	$400,000	$270,000
Cost of goods sold:			
Joint costs	$100,000	$ 74,000	$ 26,000
Costs beyond split-off	436,000	246,000	190,000
Total cost of goods sold	$536,000	$320,000	$216,000
Gross profit	$134,000	$ 80,000	$ 54,000
Gross profit rate	20%	20%	20%

ALTERNATIVES TO MAKING JOINT PRODUCT COST ALLOCATIONS

Even though there are difficulties with each of the joint cost allocation methods, firms subject to the full cost reporting requirements of the Securities and Exchange Commission, Financial Accounting Standards Board, Cost Accounting Standards Board, Federal Trade Commission, Internal Revenue Service, and other such bodies must make cost allocations where appropriate to value inventories. Although there are a number of acceptable ways to allocate joint costs, the choice of methods affects the reported results of operations, as demonstrated in this chapter. In addition, because of the arbitrary nature of cost allocations, information about a company can be improperly interpreted, resulting in inappropriate decisions. For these reasons joint cost allocations are avoided whenever possible by the management of many companies.

The main purpose for making joint cost allocations is to determine inventory values. Therefore, if cost allocations are avoided, other methods for valuing inventories that do not rely on joint cost allocations must be found. Several alternatives are available for making such inventory valuations. One alternative is to carry inventories at their sales value at the split-off point or, if price quotations are unavailable, at their net realizable value minus a normal gross profit. As separable costs are incurred, they are added to this initial inventory value to obtain the total inventory value at any point during processing.

The use of this method has some merit in situations where products experience a rapid turnover or where profit margins are very small. Where there is rapid turnover and the time between products being inventoried and sold is short, the probability that products will be sold at prevailing prices is quite high. Some companies in the mining, produce, and meat packing industries use this method to value inventories.

To illustrate this method, assume that Chemical Company has 10,000 pounds of Beta in inventory at the end of the period and uses its sales value minus a normal gross profit of 20 percent of sales to value its inventory. The following schedule shows how the Beta inventory would be valued, assuming a market price of $0.34 per pound for Beta:

Sales value of Beta (10,000 units × $0.34 per pound)	$3,400
Less: Normal gross profit (0.20 × $3,400)	680
Inventory carrying value	$2,720

ACCOUNTING FOR BY-PRODUCTS

A by-product, by definition, has a relatively minor sales value when compared with the main joint products. As a result, accounting for by-products is quite different from accounting for joint products. This difference revolves around the question of whether or not any inventory cost should be assigned to by-products before they are sold. Some people believe that by-products should be assigned part of the joint manufacturing costs and accounted for as any other joint product. However, others think that since, by definition, by-products have a minor value, no costs should be assigned to them at the time of production. Rather, at the time by-products are sold the net amount realized should be shown on the income statement, either as revenue or as a reduction in manufacturing costs. These differing views, the accounting procedures necessary to implement them, and some practical and theoretical considerations for deciding which approach to adopt are discussed in the following sections.

Assigning a Cost to By-Products at the Time of Production

Assigning a cost to by-products at the time of production most nearly resembles the accounting used for joint products. When this method is used, the cost assigned to by-products is typically the net realizable value of by-products produced. The accounting procedure is to debit a by-product inventory account and credit work in process. Any subsequent processing and disposal costs are added to the by-product inventory account.

(Note that the journal entry to record by-product inventory reduces the amount of joint product costs to be allocated among joint products. The remaining joint product costs are allocated to joint products using one of the methods previously discussed in this chapter.)

To illustrate this accounting procedure, consider the following situation. Chemical Company uses Alpha as a primary input to produce two joint products, Beta and Gamma, and a by-product, Sigma. After some additional processing subsequent to split-off, Sigma can be sold for $0.50 per pound. Assume for simplicity that Beta and Gamma are sold at the split-off point for $0.34 and $0.26 per pound, respectively. Assume that production is in the following proportions:

Product	Quantity (pounds)
Beta	250,000
Gamma	150,000
	400,000
Sigma	50,000
Total	450,000

The joint manufacturing costs incurred in the common process to produce these quantities of Beta, Gamma, and Sigma total $100,000. Separable costs required to further process Sigma beyond the split-off point are as follows:

	Cost (per pound)
Material	$0.05
Labor	$0.03
Overhead	$0.02
	$0.10

Using the net realizable value of Sigma as a basis, the task at hand is to assign a cost to the 50,000 pounds of Sigma produced in the common process. The net realizable value of Sigma at the time of production is $20,000 [50,000 pounds produced × $0.40 ($0.50–$0.10) per pound]. Therefore, $20,000 of work in process is reclassified as by-product inventory, the cost associated with the by-product produced during the current period.

Also assume that 48,000 pounds of Sigma are sold during the period. If there is no beginning by-product inventory, 2,000 pounds of Sigma will remain in inventory at the end of the period. The ending balance in the inventory account is then $800 (2,000 pounds × $0.40 per pound). The following journal entries illustrate the accounting process:

1. At the time of production, the by-product inventory account is charged with the net realizable value of the by-products produced.

By-product inventory	20,000	
Work in process		20,000

2. As subsequent processing costs are incurred to place the by-products in a marketable condition, actual manufacturing costs are charged to the by-product inventory account. It is assumed that (a) 48,000 pounds of Sigma have been processed and sold, and (b) no additional costs have been incurred to further process the 2,000 units of ending by-product inventory.

By-product inventory	4,800	
Material (48,000 × 0.05)		2,400
Payroll (48,000 × 0.03)		1,440
Overhead applied (48,000 × 0.02)		960

3. There are 48,000 pounds of Sigma sold for cash at $0.50 per pound.

Cash	24,000	
By-product inventory (48,000 × 0.50 = 24,000)		24,000

The following ledger account summarizes the preceding transactions and verifies that the ending balance in the by-product inventory account is $800, as previously calculated.

By-Product Inventory

(1)	20,000	24,000	(3)
(2)	4,800		
	24,800	24,000	
Bal.	800		

For simplicity, this illustration assumes that the 2,000 pounds of Sigma on hand at the end of the period have not been processed beyond the split-off point. If these units had received additional processing or if other disposal costs had been incurred on their behalf, the by-product inventory account would include the net realizable value of the by-products *plus* any other separable manufacturing or disposal costs incurred *beyond* the split-off point.

An income statement using this method of accounting for by-products is shown in figure 11.2. To clearly illustrate how using this method of accounting for by-products affects the amount of production costs being inventoried, it is assumed that 95 percent of each joint product produced during the period is sold at the split-off point.

FIGURE 11.2

Income Statement—Cost Assigned at the Time of Production

Sales, joint products		$117,800[a]
Cost of goods sold:		
Gross production costs		$100,000
Less: Net realizable value of by-products produced		20,000
Net production costs		$ 80,000
Less: Ending inventory of joint products		4,000[b]
Cost of goods sold		$ 76,000
Gross margin		$ 41,800
Less: Marketing/administrative expenses		10,000
Income from operations		$ 31,800

[a]Sales: Beta—250,000 × 0.95 × $0.34 = $ 80,750
        Gamma—150,000 × 0.95 × $0.26 =   37,050
                                      $117,800

[b]0.05 × $80,000 = $4,000.

Note in figure 11.2 that the net sales value of by-products is deducted from the total cost of joint products produced, resulting in a reduced amount to allocate between Beta and Gamma, the joint products in this situation. As a result, $80,000 is allocated to the joint products Beta and Gamma rather than $100,000 that would have been allocated if by-products were not assigned an inventory value. This results in a reduced per-unit cost for joint products. Even though a balance sheet is not illustrated, the by-product inventory is treated in the same way on the balance sheet as finished-goods inventory.

Recognizing the Cost of By-Products at the Time of Sale

Another approach to by-product accounting is simply to maintain memorandum records of the physical amount of by-products produced and on hand without assigning any cost to by-product inventory. Then, when by-products are sold, the amount of net revenue actually realized is reported on the income statement, either as revenue or as a reduction of total manufacturing costs of joint products.

This method avoids time-consuming and often complicated cost allocations and is justified with the rationale that the production of by-products is simply a coincidental result of manufacturing the main joint products. Since no manufacturing costs are directly incurred for the purpose of producing by-products, no part of the joint costs incurred should be allocated to by-products. Rather, net revenue received from the sale of by-products is handled on the income statement as either *(a)* additional sales revenue, *(b)* a reduction in the cost of production, *(c)* a reduction in the cost of sales, or *(d)* other income.

The amount of net revenue from by-products *sold* is the amount of gross revenue received minus *(a)* any separable costs incurred beyond the split-off point to place the by-products in a salable condition and *(b)* any other costs incurred to dispose of the by-products.

To illustrate, assume the same facts about Sigma as contained in the preceding illustration. As previously calculated, gross revenue from the sale of Sigma is $24,000 (48,000 pounds × $0.50 per pound). Separable manufacturing costs applicable to by-products sold is $4,800 (48,000 pounds × $0.10 per pound). Therefore, the net revenue realized from the sale of by-products is $19,200 ($24,000 − $4,800). Figure 11.3 shows how the net revenue of $19,200 is presented on an income statement using each of the four alternative methods of accounting.

There is no balance sheet illustrated. Even though there are 2,000 pounds of Sigma on hand at the end of the period, there is no financial disclosure required when this method is used because no manufacturing costs are assigned to by-products unless separable processing costs have been incurred. The manufacturing costs that would have been assigned to by-products when using the previous method are instead part of the costs associated with the joint products either sold during the period or in ending inventory. However, note in figure 11.3 that when by-product costs are shown as a reduction of the cost of production, the joint product ending inventory is less than under other accounting treatments, resulting in slightly lower net income.

Comparison of the Two Methods

There are practical as well as theoretical considerations in selecting which method to use to account for by-products. Theoretically, assigning a net realizable value to by-products at the time of production has the most appeal, because it results in a better matching of costs and revenues. However, the additional effort involved in making cost allocations and maintaining inventory valuation records may encourage the recognition of by-product values at the time of sale rather than at the time of production. Another drawback when

FIGURE 11.3

Income Statement—Cost Assigned at the Time of Sale

	As Sales Revenue	As a Reduction of the Cost of Production	As a Reduction of the Cost of Sales	As Other Income
Sales, joint products	$117,800	$117,800	$117,800	$117,800
Sales, by-products	19,200			
Total	$137,000	$117,800	$117,800	$117,800
Cost of goods sold:				
Gross production costs	$100,000	$100,000	$100,000	$100,000
Less: Sales of by-products		19,200		
Net production costs	$100,000	$ 80,800	$100,000	$100,000
Less: Ending inventory of joint products	5,000[a]	4,040[b]	5,000	5,000
Cost of goods sold (gross)	$ 95,000	$ 76,760	$ 95,000	$ 95,000
Less: Sales of by-products			19,200	
Cost of goods sold (net)	$ 95,000	$ 76,760	$ 75,800	$ 95,000
Gross margin	$ 42,000	$ 41,040	$ 42,000	$ 22,800
Less: Marketing/administrative expenses	10,000	10,000	10,000	10,000
Income from operations	$ 32,000	$ 31,040	$ 32,000	$ 12,800
Revenue from sale of by-products				19,200
Income before taxes	$ 32,000	$ 31,040	$ 32,000	$ 32,000

[a] 0.05 × 100,000 = 5,000
[b] 0.05 × 80,800 = 4,040

assigning an inventory value to by-products is that there is no assurance that the by-products can be sold at the same market price that prevailed when the inventory value was established. Therefore, as a practical matter, the stability of the market for by-products and the reliability of estimates of future market prices favor recognizing the value of by-products at the time of sale.

Timing effects related to the recognition of revenues and expenses represent the major difference between the accounting results when using these methods; that is, each method will usually result in a different net income being reported in any given accounting period. However, if by-product inventories are sold within two accounting periods, net income will be the same using either method when the two periods are taken together. Because the basic difference between the two methods is timing, some people think that by-product value should be recognized at the time of sale in business situations where by-product quantities are relatively constant from period to period and where by-product prices are relatively stable.

JOINT COSTS AND MANAGEMENT DECISIONS

There are a number of manufacturing situations in which management must decide whether joint products should be processed beyond the split-off point or simply sold at the split-off point. For example, meat packers must decide whether to sell meat as cut or to continue

FIGURE 11.4

Comparison of Incremental Costs and Revenues

Incremental Price from Selling Finished versus Unfinished Products

Product	Price for Unfinished Product	Price for Finished Product	Incremental Price
Beta	$0.34	$1.60	$1.26
Gamma	0.26	1.80	1.54

Incremental Revenue

Product	Incremental Price	Units of Production	Incremental Revenue
Beta	$1.26	250,000	$315,000
Gamma	1.54	150,000	231,000

Comparison of Incremental Costs with Incremental Revenue

Product	Incremental Revenue	Incremental Costs[a]	Profit (Loss)
Beta	$315,000	$246,000	$ 69,000
Gamma	231,000	190,000	41,000
Total	$546,000	$436,000	$110,000

[a]Amounts are developed in a prior illustration.

the curing and packing process. Petroleum refiners must decide what combination of processes and final products will yield the most profit.

The decision to sell or process further hinges on expected future costs and revenues and *not* on how joint costs are allocated or on the method used to account for by-products. Joint cost allocations are simply not relevant to the decision to sell or process further. Relevant costs and revenues (or, in economic terms, incremental costs and incremental revenues) are expected future costs that differ among decision alternatives (see chapter 4). The key to making appropriate management decisions is to compare expected future costs (incremental costs) with expected future revenues (incremental revenues). The focus is on the *future* and on *incremental* costs and revenues. Since joint costs are *past* costs at the split-off point, they are not relevant to the decision to sell or process further.

Although it is true, for example, that joint manufacturing costs are relevant for the decision by Chemical Company to engage in the business of processing Alpha, once that decision has been made, the decision to process Beta and Gamma beyond the split-off point does not depend on joint costs but rather on expected future costs and expected future revenues. To illustrate, let's examine the situation presented earlier and determine if it is in fact an appropriate decision to process Beta and Gamma beyond the split-off point. Expected future costs are assumed to consist only of separable manufacturing costs relating to Beta and Gamma of $246,000 and $190,000, respectively. Figure 11.4 contains an analysis of expected future costs and revenues in this situation.

From the analysis in figure 11.4, it is clear that the company should process both Beta and Gamma beyond the split-off point. By doing so, net income will increase by a total of $110,000 over what it would be if the joint products are sold at the split-off point. The analysis also indicates that neither joint costs nor the method used to allocate joint costs is relevant, because they are not future or incremental costs. These results can be verified by comparing an income statement assuming sale at the split-off point with an

FIGURE 11.5
Comparison of Incremental Costs and Revenues

Incremental Price from Selling Finished versus Unfinished Products

Product	Price for Unfinished Product	Price for Finished Product	Incremental Price
Beta	$0.34	$1.60	$1.26
Gamma	0.26	1.65	1.39

Incremental Revenue

Product	Incremental Price	Units of Production	Incremental Revenue
Beta	$1.26	250,000	$315,000
Gamma	1.39	150,000	208,500

Comparison of Incremental Costs with Incremental Revenue

Product	Incremental Revenue	Incremental Costs[a]	Profit (Loss)
Beta	$315,000	$246,000	$ 69,000
Gamma	208,500	190,000	18,500
Total	$523,500	$436,000	$ 87,500

[a]Amounts are developed in a prior illustration.

income statement assuming sale after further processing and examining net income under each assumption.

The difficulty encountered if joint costs are considered in such decisions is illustrated by assuming that *finished* Gamma has a selling price of $1.65 rather than $1.80, a reduction of $0.15 per unit in incremental revenues. Repeating the analysis shows that even at this lower price it is profitable to process Beta beyond the split-off point, as indicated in figure 11.5.

However, if the analysis is made by evaluating the profitability of Gamma in isolation on a total cost basis (which includes joint costs) rather than on an incremental cost basis (which excludes joint costs), there are conflicting results, depending on which joint cost allocation method is used. For example, assume that a physical measure using relative weights is used to allocate joint costs. As illustrated earlier, the amount of allocated joint costs is $60,000 and the amount of separable costs of processing beyond the split-off point is $190,000. Using these data, an analysis indicates (in error) that processing Gamma beyond split-off is unprofitable, as shown here:

Total market value of Gamma ($1.65 × 150,000 units)		$247,500
Total cost to produce Gamma:		
Allocated joint costs	$ 60,000	
Separable costs of further processing	190,000	250,000
Loss from processing Gamma		$ (2,500)

If the physical measure of units of production is used to allocate joint costs, the amount of allocated joint costs is $31,500 (as illustrated earlier) rather than $60,000. The separable costs of processing beyond the split-off point remain at $190,000 using either assumption. However, because of different allocated joint costs, the results in this situation indicate that it is profitable to process Gamma, as indicated here:

Total market value of Gamma ($1.65 × 150,000 units)		$247,500
Total cost to produce Gamma:		
Allocated joint costs	$ 31,500	
Separable costs of further processing	190,000	221,500
Gain from processing Gamma		$ 26,000

This inconsistency shows how reliance on irrelevant information such as joint cost allocations may interfere with the decision process. In this situation, management could become confused and decide not to process Gamma beyond the split-off point, when in reality not doing so would cause net income to decline. Therefore, joint cost allocations should not be used when deciding whether a product should be sold at the split-off point or processed further. Neither should joint costs be used in an analysis of the relative profitability of different product lines.

SUMMARY

Joint products, and thus joint product costs, are part of a large variety of manufacturing environments. Accounting for joint product costs focuses on three general questions. First, how should joint costs be allocated to joint products and by-products? Second, what are the available methods of accounting for by-products? Finally, what effect, if any, do joint product costs have on deciding whether a product should be sold at the split-off point or processed further?

There are two general bases used to allocate joint product costs—physical measures and market measures. Physical measures include units, weight, or volume as the basis for allocating joint product costs. A variation in the use of physical measures involves assigning relative weights to each joint product in addition to using units, weight, or volume as the allocation base. Market measures use the market value of the joint products at the split-off point as the allocation base. If there is no available market for the joint product at the split-off point, a hypothetical net realizable value may be used as an allocation base. Because joint product cost allocations are inherently arbitrary, some firms avoid making cost allocations wherever possible. In such instances, inventory carrying values for joint products are usually set equal to their expected sales values minus a normal gross profit.

There are two general methods of accounting for by-products. First, by-products are assigned a value at the time of production equal to their estimated net realizable value. Second, no inventoriable costs other than direct subsequent processing costs are assigned to by-products; rather, net revenue realized from the sale of by-products is recognized on the income statement of the period of sale. There are many practical and theoretical questions to consider when deciding which method of accounting is appropriate for a given business situation.

Joint product cost allocations are made for purposes of product costing and income determination. Joint product costs are not relevant in the decision to process beyond the split-off point. Such a decision should be based on expected future costs, which differ between the decision to process further or to sell at the split-off point.

SELF-STUDY PROBLEM

Lester Company processes Wizon in department 1, where it is split off into products *X, Y,* and *Z*. Product *X* is sold at the split-off point with no further processing. Products *Y* and *Z* require further processing to finish them before they can be sold. Product *Y* is finished in department 2, and product Z is finished in department 3. The following is a summary of costs and other related data for the year ending December 31, 19X2.

	Department		
	1	2	3
Direct labor	$28,000	$ 90,000	$130,000
Manufacturing overhead	20,000	42,000	98,000
	$48,000	$132,000	$228,000

	Product		
	X	Y	Z
Gallons processed	60,000	60,000	120,000
Gallons on hand at December 31, 19X2	20,000	0	30,000
Sales (in dollars)	$60,000	$192,000	$283,500

The cost of Wizon purchased during the year was $192,000. There were no inventories on hand on January 1, 19X2, and there was no Wizon on hand on December 31, 19X2. All products on hand at year end were complete as to processing, and there were no cost variances.

Required

1. Calculate the total amount of joint costs to allocate among products X, Y, and Z at December 31, 19X2.
2. Allocate total joint costs to products X, Y, and Z using market measures as an allocation base.
3. What is the total cost of product Y sold during the year?
4. Product X could have been processed in department 4 at a total separable cost of $1.20 per unit. The market price for finished product X is $2.50 per unit. Did management make the appropriate decision to sell product X at the split-off point?

Solution to the Self-Study Problem

Requirement 1

The total joint costs to be allocated:

	Department 1
Materials (cost of Wizon)	$192,000
Direct labor	28,000
Manufacturing overhead	20,000
Total	$240,000

Requirement 2

The allocation of joint costs based on market measures:

Product	Units Produced	Ultimate Market Price (per unit)	Ultimate Market Value	Less: Costs Beyond Split-off Point	Net Realizable Value
X	60,000	$1.50[a]	$ 90,000	$ 0	$ 90,000
Y	60,000	3.20[b]	192,000	132,000	60,000
Z	120,000	3.15[c]	378,000	228,000	150,000
					$300,000

[a] $60,000 ÷ (60,000 − 20,000 = 40,000 units) = $1.50 per unit
[b] $192,000 ÷ 60,000 units = $3.20 per unit
[c] $283,500 ÷ (120,000 − 30,000 = 90,000 units) = $3.15 per unit

Product	Net Realizable Value	Percentage	Joint Costs Allocated
X	$ 90,000	30%	$ 72,000
Y	60,000	20%	48,000
Z	150,000	50%	120,000
	$300,000	100%	$240,000

Requirement 3

Total cost of product Y sold for the year:

	Costs
Joint costs allocated	$ 48,000
Costs beyond split-off	132,000
Total	$180,000

Requirement 4

Decision to sell product X at the split-off point:

	Product X (per unit)
Ultimate selling price	$2.50
Selling price at split-off	1.50
Incremental price	$1.00
Less: Incremental cost	1.20
Difference	$(0.20)

Yes, management made the correct decision to sell product X at the split-off point, because incremental costs exceed the incremental price for further processing.

SUGGESTED READINGS

Amey, Lloyd R. "Joint Product Decisions, The Fixed Proportions Case: A Note." *Journal of Business Finance and Accounting* 11 (Autumn 1984): 295–300.

Barton, M. Frank. "Practical Alternatives to Joint Cost Allocation." *Woman CPA* 47 (July 1985): 24–26.

Biddle, Gary C. "Allocations of Joint and Common Costs." *Journal of Accounting Literature* 3 (Spring 1984): 1–45.

Cats-Baril, William L.; Gatti, James F.; and Grinnel, D. Jacque. "Joint Product Costing in the Semiconductor Industry." *Management Accounting* 67 (February 1986): 28–31, 34–35.

Steinwurtzel, Samuel L. "Current Developments on Joint Costs of Not-for-Profit Organizations." *CPA Journal* 56 (March 1986): 65–67.

Zimmerman, Jerold L. "The Cost and Benefits of Cost Allocation." *The Accounting Review* 54 (July 1979): 504–521.

DISCUSSION QUESTIONS

Q11–1. Define and contrast *joint product, by-product,* and *scrap*. Give examples of each.

Q11–2. Describe the effect changing market values might have on the classification of and accounting for joint products and by-products.

Q11-3. Define and contrast *joint cost* and *separable cost,* and tell at what stage in the manufacture of joint products each typically occurs.

Q11-4. Explain the relationship of the split-off point to joint costs and separable costs.

Q11-5. Discuss the general methods available for the allocation of joint costs, and describe the strengths and weaknesses of each.

Q11-6. When weights are used in connection with a physical measure to allocate joint costs, what do these weights represent?

Q11-7. If management believes that the allocation of joint costs should have no effect on the firm's gross profit rate, what allocation method should be used? Why?

Q11-8. Define *net realizable value,* and describe the market condition that would lead to its use in the allocation of joint costs.

Q11-9. Describe how costs that are incurred beyond the split-off point are incorporated in the calculation of net realizable values.

Q11-10. Discuss the alternatives available for costing inventories if joint cost allocations are not made.

Q11-11. Describe how sales prices may be adjusted when they are used as the basis for assigning a cost to joint product inventories.

Q11-12. Describe two possible methods for accounting for by-products. Which method is most closely related to accounting for joint costs?

Q11-13. Discuss the various income statement presentations that would be made when using either method of accounting for by-products.

Q11-14. Describe some theoretical and practical considerations to consider in deciding which method of accounting for by-products should be adopted in a particular business situation.

Q11-15. Why do joint cost allocations have limited usefulness for planning and control decisions? What type of costs are relevant for planning and control decisions?

Q11-16. Describe the method of cost analysis that yields valid results when management needs to decide if a joint product should be processed beyond the split-off point.

EXERCISES

E11-1. Joint Cost Allocation (CPA) The Rote Company manufactures products *C* and *R* from a joint process. The total joint costs are $60,000. The sales value at the split-off point was $75,000 for 8,000 units of product *C* and $25,000 for 2,000 units of product *R*. Assuming that total joint costs are allocated using the relative sales value at split-off approach, what were the joint costs allocated to product *C*?

E11-2. Joint Cost Allocations Gilbert Manufacturing Company manufactures two products, Alt and Bat. Initially, they are processed from the same raw material, and then, after split-off, they are further processed separately. Additional information is as follows:

	Alt	Bat	Total
Final sales value	$9,000	$6,000	$15,000
Joint costs prior to split-off point	?	?	6,600
Costs beyond split-off point	3,000	3,000	6,000

Required

Prepare an electronic spreadsheet to assign joint costs to Alt and Bat, using the relative sales value method. Print your results.

E11-3. Joint Cost Allocations (CPA)
Forward Incorporated manufactures products P, Q, and R from a joint process. Additional information is as follows:

	Product			
	P	Q	R	Total
Units produced	4,000	2,000	1,000	7,000
Joint costs	$36,000	?	?	$60,000
Sales value at split-off	?	?	$15,000	$100,000
Additional costs if processed further	$7,000	$5,000	$3,000	$15,000
Sales value if processed further	$70,000	$30,000	$20,000	$120,000

Required

1. Assuming that joint costs are allocated using the relative sales value at split-off approach, what are the joint costs allocated to products Q and R?
2. Assuming that joint costs are allocated using the relative sales value at split-off approach, what is the sales value at split-off for product P?

E11-4. Joint Cost Allocation (CPA)
Superior Company manufactures products A and B from a joint process, which also yields the by-product X. Superior accounts for the revenues from its by-product sales as miscellaneous revenue. Additional information is as follows:

	Product			
	A	B	X	Total
Units produced	15,000	9,000	6,000	30,000
Joint costs	?	?	?	$270,000
Sales value at split-off	$290,000	$150,000	$10,000	$450,000

Required

Assuming that joint product costs are allocated using the relative sales value at split-off approach, determine the joint cost allocated to each product produced.

E11-5. Joint Cost Allocation—Relative Sales Value Method
Sideways Company manufactures products A, B, and C from a joint process. Additional information is as follows:

	Product			
	A	B	C	Total
Units produced	8,000	4,000	2,000	14,000
Joint costs	$72,000	?	?	$120,000
Sales value at split-off	?	?	$30,000	$200,000
Additional costs if processed further	$14,000	$10,000	$6,000	$30,000
Sales value if processed further	$140,000	$60,000	$40,000	$240,000

Required

Assuming that joint costs are allocated using the relative sales value at split-off approach, determine the sales value at split-off for product A.

E11-6. Joint Cost Allocation—Comparison of Methods and Decision to Process Further

Bott Chemical Company purchases chemical A and processes it into more refined products B and C. Chemical B is sold at the split-off point. Chemical C is processed further to produce product D, which is then sold. During the current accounting period, 1,000 pounds of A were purchased at a cost of $3,000. Joint conversion costs incurred to produce B and C were $5,000. Separable costs associated with processing C were $1,000. Production and sales information are as follows:

Product	Production	Sales	Sales Price (per pound)
B	600 lbs.	600 lbs.	$14.00
C	400 lbs.	400 lbs.	$ 9.00

There were no beginning inventories.

Required

1. Calculate how the joint cost of producing B and C should be allocated under each of the following methods: *(a)* pounds of production; *(b)* constant gross profit percentage.
2. Assume that all of product C was processed further, even though there is an active market that could have absorbed all of C at the split-off point at a price of $7.00 per pound. Evaluate management's decision to process C beyond the split-off point.

E11-7. By-Product Accounting

Beck Company makes a product called Bionate that it sells for $4.00 per pound. The manufacturing process also yields a similar product called Calcate. With further processing, Calcate can be sold for $1.00 per pound. During the month, total joint manufacturing costs up to the split-off point consisted of the following:

Direct materials	$600,000
Direct labor	480,000
Factor overhead	120,000

Production for the month totaled 880,000 pounds of Bionate and 120,000 pounds of Calcate. There were no beginning or ending inventories of Bionate or Calcate. Further processing costs incurred during the month to complete Calcate were as follows:

Direct materials	$8,000
Direct labor	6,000
Factory overhead	2,000

Required

1. Prepare the journal entries for Calcate for the month, assuming that Calcate is accounted for as a by-product that is assigned a cost at the time of production.
2. Prepare the journal entries for Calcate for the month, assuming that Calcate is accounted for as a by-product whose value is recognized at the time of sale as a reduction in total manufacturing costs.
3. Prepare the journal entires for Calcate for the month, assuming that it is accounted for as a joint product and that joint costs are allocated on the basis of pounds produced.

E11-8. Joint Cost Allocations—Alternative Methods (CPA)

Vreeland Incorporated manufactures products X, Y, and Z from a joint process. Joint product costs were $60,000. Assume all products are processed further. Additional information is as follows:

Product	Units Produced	Sales Value at Split-off	Sales Values	Additional Costs
X	6,000	$40,000	$55,000	$9,000
Y	4,000	35,000	45,000	7,000
Z	2,000	25,000	30,000	5,000

Sales Values and Additional Costs if Processed Further

Required

1. Prepare an electronic spreadsheet to assign joint costs to products X, Y, and Z under each of the following assumptions. Print your results.
   a. Joint product costs are allocated using the physical measures (units produced) approach.
   b. Joint product costs are allocated using the physical measures approach where the relative weights of 4, 6, and 6 are assigned to products X, Y, and Z, respectively.
   c. Joint product costs are allocated using the relative sales value at split-off approach.
2. Comment on the magnitude of differences in joint cost allocations using each of the preceding approaches.

E11-9. Joint Cost Allocation by Relative Sales Value Method (CPA)
Miller Manufacturing Company buys zeon for $0.80 a gallon. At the end of processing in department 1, zeon splits off into products A, B, and C. Product A is sold at the split-off point with no further processing. Products B and C require further processing before they can be sold; product B is processed in department 2 and product C is processed in department 3. The following is a summary of costs and other related data for the year ending June 30.

	Department 1	Department 2	Department 3
Cost of zeon	$96,000	—	—
Direct labor	$14,000	$45,000	$65,000
Factory overhead	$10,000	$21,000	$49,000

	Product A	Product B	Product C
Gallons sold	20,000	30,000	45,000
Gallons on hand at June 30	10,000	—	15,000
Sales in dollars	$30,000	$96,000	$141,750

There were no inventories on hand at the beginning of the year, and there was no zeon on hand at June 30. All gallons on hand at June 30 were complete as to processing. There were no factory overhead variances. Miller uses the relative sales value method of allocating joint costs.

Required

1. For allocating joint costs, determine the relative sales value of product A for the year ending June 30.
2. Determine the joint costs to be allocated for the year ending June 30.
3. Determine the cost of product B sold for the year ending June 30.
4. Determine the value of the ending inventory for product A.

E11-10. Joint Cost Procedures—Sales Value Determination (CPA) Stellar Corporation manufactures products R and S from a joint process. Additional information is as follows:

	Product R	Product S	Total
Units produced	4,000	6,000	10,000
Joint costs	$36,000	$ 54,000	$ 90,000
Sales value at split-off	?	?	?
Additional costs if processed further	$ 3,000	$ 26,000	$ 29,000
Sales value if processed further	$63,000	$126,000	$189,000
Additional margin if processed further	$12,000	?	$ 40,000

Required

Assuming that joint costs are allocated on the basis of relative sales value at split-off, determine the sales value at the split-off point for product S.

PROBLEMS

P11-1. Joint Cost Allocation—Sales Value at Split-off Point Barker Electric Incorporated manufactures products G, H, and I. Additional information follows:

	G	H	I	Total
Units produced	?	5,000	8,000	16,000
Joint cost	?	$25,000	?	$ 80,000
Sales value at split-off	?	?	$72,000	$120,000

Required

Fill in the missing blanks, assuming Barker used the sales value at split-off point for allocating joint costs.

P11-2. Joint Cost Allocation—Relative Sales Value Method The Harrison Corporation produces three products—Alpha, Beta, and Gamma. Alpha and Gamma are joint products, whereas Beta is a by-product of Alpha. No joint cost is to be allocated to the by-product. The production processes for a given year are as follows:

In Department One, 110,000 pounds of raw material, Rho, are processed at a total cost of $120,000. After processing in Department One, 60 percent of the units are transferred to Department Two and 40 percent of the units (now Gamma) are transferred to Department Three.

In Department Two, the material is further processed at a total additional cost of $38,000. Then 70 percent of the units (now Alpha) are transferred to Department Four, and 30 percent emerge as Beta, the by-product, to be sold at $1.20 per pound. Selling expenses related to disposing of Beta are $8,100.

In Department Four, Alpha is processed at a total additional cost of $23,660. After this processing, Alpha is ready for sale at $5 per pound.

In Department Three, Gamma is processed at a total additional cost of $165,000. In this department, a normal loss of units of Gamma occurs that equals 10 percent of the good output of Gamma. The remaining good output of Gamma is then sold for $12 per pound.

Required

Using the relative sales value approach, prepare a schedule showing the allocation of the $120,000 joint cost between Alpha and Gamma. The net realizable value of Beta should be treated as an addition to the sales value of Alpha.

P11–3. Joint Cost Allocation (CPA)   Two independent situations follow:

1. Andy Company manufactures products *N*, *P*, and *R* from a joint process. The following information is available:

	\multicolumn{3}{c	}{Product}	
	N	P	R	Total
Units produced	12,000	?	?	24,000
Sales value at split-off	?	?	$50,000	$200,000
Joint costs	$ 48,000	?	?	$120,000
Sales value if processed further	$110,000	$90,000	$60,000	$260,000
Additional costs if processed further	$ 18,000	$14,000	$10,000	$ 42,000

Required

Assuming that joint product costs are allocated using the relative sales value at split-off approach, determine the sales value at split-off for products *N* and *P*.

2. Kyle Company manufactures products *S* and *T* from a joint process. The sales value at split-off was $50,000 for 6,000 units of product *S* and $25,000 for 2,000 units of product *T*.

Required

Assuming that the portion of the total joint costs properly allocated to product *S* using the relative sales value at split-off approach was $30,000, what were the total joint costs?

P11–4. Joint Products and Decision Analysis (CPA)   From a particular joint process, Watkins Company produces three products—*X*, *Y*, and *Z*. Each product may be sold at the split-off point or processed further. Additional processing requires no special facilities, and production costs of further processing are entirely variable and traceable to the products involved. In 19X3, all three products were processed beyond split-off. Joint production costs for the year were $60,000. Sales values and costs needed to evaluate Watkins's 19X3 production policy follow:

Product	Units Produced	Sales Value at Split-off	Sales Values (If Processed Further)	Added Costs (If Processed Further)
X	6,000	$25,000	$42,000	$9,000
Y	4,000	41,000	45,000	7,000
Z	2,000	24,000	32,000	8,000

Joint costs are allocated to the products in proportion to the relative physical volume of output.

Required

1. For units of *Z*, determine the unit production cost most relevant to a decision to sell or process further.

2. To maximize profits, determine which products Watkins should subject to additional processing.

P11-5. Joint Cost Allocation—Alternative Methods Johnson Electronics Corporation manufactures two products—A and B. The following information is available:

	A	B	Both
Joint manufacturing costs			$250,000
Direct costs	$75,000	$100,000	
Per-unit sales value at split-off point	$8	$8	
Per-unit sales value after further processing	$10	$15	
Unit production	15,000	10,000	

The same number of units were sold as produced during 19X2. The products are considered to be joint products.

Required

Prepare an electronic spreadsheet to determine total cost and unit cost of product A and product B under each of the following assumptions. Print your results.

1. Joint costs are allocated using sales value at the split-off point.
2. Joint costs are allocated using the average units produced method.

P11-6. Joint Cost Allocations—Alternative Methods Jefferson, Incorporated manufactures products X, Y, and Z from a joint process. Joint product costs were $120,000. The products are processed further. Additional information is as follows:

			Sales Values and Additional Costs If Processed Further	
Product	Units Produced	Sales Value at Split-off	Sales Values	Additional Costs
X	9,000	$90,000	$120,000	$18,000
Y	4,500	60,000	80,000	15,000
Z	4,500	50,000	65,000	6,000

Required

1. Determine the total costs assigned to products X, Y, and Z using the relative sales value at split-off approach.
2. Determine the total costs assigned to products X, Y, and Z using the units produced approach.
3. Assume that products X, Y, and Z have been assigned the following weights: $X = 3$, $Y = 6$, $Z = 4$. Determine the total costs assigned to products X, Y, and Z with a physical measures approach using relative weights.
4. Determine the total costs assigned to products X, Y, and Z so that the gross profit rate will be the same for each product.

P11 7. Joint Product Costing—Determining Total and Unit Costs Doolittle Company produces two products from a single process. Product X, a liquid, can be sold for $2.35 per gallon at the split-off point and for $5 per gallon as a finished product. Product Y, a solid, can be sold for $3.25 per pound at the split-off point and for $4 per pound as a finished product.

During last year 400,000 gallons of X and 100,000 pounds of Y were produced. Joint costs were $1,200,000. Separate, or direct, processing costs for the year were $600,000 for X and $120,000 for Y.

Required

Assume that X and Y are treated as joint products. Determine the total and unit costs for X and Y using the sales value at split-off point method. Evaluate the decision to process the joint products beyond the split-off point.

P11-8. Analysis of Further Processing Decisions—Joint Products (CMA)

The Clean Corporation produces a variety of cleaning compounds and solutions for both industrial and household use. Although most of its products are processed independently, a few are related.

Grit 337 is a coarse cleaning powder with many industrial uses. It costs $1.60 a pound to make and has a selling price of $2.00 a pound.

A small portion of the annual production of this product is retained for futher processing in the mixing department, where it is combined with several other ingredients to form a paste that is marketed as a silver polish selling for $4.00 per jar. This further processing requires ¼ pound of Grit 337 per jar. Other ingredients, labor, and variable overhead associated with this further processing cost $2.50 per jar. Variable selling costs amount to $0.30 per jar. If the decision were made to cease production of the silver polish, $5,600 of fixed mixing department costs could be avoided. Assume that the demand for Grit 337 is very poor and the company is considering alternative uses.

Required

Determine the minimum number of jars of silver polish that would have to be sold to justify further processing of Grit 337.

P11-9. Sell at Split-off or Process Further Considerations

The two following situations are independent of each other.

1. Yardley Corporation uses a joint process to produce products A, B, and C. Each product may be sold at its split-off point or processed further. Additional processing costs are entirely variable and are traceable to the respective products produced. Joint production costs for 19X5 were $50,000 and are allocated by Yardley using the relative sales value at split-off approach. Relevant data follow:

Product	Units Produced	Sales Value at Split-off	Sales Values (Processed Further)	Additional Costs (Processed Further)
A	20,000	$ 45,000	$60,000	$20,000
B	15,000	75,000	98,000	20,000
C	15,000	30,000	62,000	18,000
		$150,000		

Required

Determine which products Yardley should subject to further processing to maximize profits.

2. A company manufactures two joint products at a joint cost of $1,000. These products can be sold at the split-off point or they can be further processed at an additional cost and sold as higher-quality items at a higher price.

Required

Describe the criteria a company like this one should use in deciding whether to sell each product at the split-off point or to process each product further. Include in your discussion reference to the role of the joint costs.

P11–10. Joint Costs—Evaluation of Costing Results (CMA)

Doe Corporation grows, processes, cans, and sells three main pineapple products—sliced pineapple, crushed pineapple, and pineapple juice. The outside skin is cut off in the cutting department and processed as animal feed. The skin is treated as a by-product. Doe's production process is as follows:

1. Pineapples first are processed in the cutting department. The pineapples are washed and the outside skin is cut away. Then the pineapples are cored and trimmed for slicing. The three main products (sliced, crushed, juice) and the by-product (animal feed) are recognizable after processing in the cutting department. Each product is then transferred to a separate department for final processing.
2. The trimmed pineapples are forwarded to the slicing department, in which the pineapples are sliced and canned. Any juice generated during the slicing operation is packed in the cans with the slices.
3. The pieces of pineapple trimmed from the fruit are diced and canned in the crushing department. Again, the juice generated during this operation is packed in the can with the crushed pineapple.
4. The core and surplus pineapple generated from the cutting department are pulverized into a liquid in the juicing department. There is an evaporation loss equal to 8 percent of the weight of the good output produced in this department. This loss occurs as the juices are heated.
5. The outside skin is chopped into animal feed in the feed department.

The Doe Corporation uses the net realizable value method to assign costs of the joint process to its main products. The by-product is inventoried at its market value.

A total of 270,000 pounds of pineapple was entered into the cutting department during May. The following schedule shows the costs incurred in each department, the proportion by weight transferred to the four final processing departments, and the selling price of each end product.

Processing Data and Costs
May 19X1

Department	Costs Incurred	Proportion of Product by Weight Transferred to Departments	Selling Price per Pound of Final Product
Cutting	$60,000	—	none
Slicing	4,700	35%	$0.60
Crushing	10,580	28	0.55
Juicing	3,250	27	0.30
Animal feed	700	10	0.10
Total	$79,230	100%	

Required

1. The Doe Corporation uses the net realizable value method to determine inventory values for its main products and by-products. Calculate the following:

a. The pounds of pineapple that result as output for pineapple slices, crushed pineapple, pineapple juice, and animal feed.
  b. The net realizable value at the split-off point of the three main products.
  c. The amount of the cost of the cutting department assigned to each of the three main products and to the by-product in accordance with corporate policy.
  d. The gross margins for each of the three main products.
2. Comment on the importance to management of the gross margin information by main product.
3. In the production of joint products, either a by-product or scrap could be generated.
  a. Distinguish between a by-product and scrap.
  b. Would the proper accounting treatment for scrap differ from that for by-products? Explain your answer.

CASE

CASE 11-1. Joint Cost Allocations (NAA adapted) The National Manufacturing Company produces and markets many different kinds of memory devices for use in the computer industry. Memory chips, the major component of memory devices, result from a single process. Although identical in composition, the chips are separated after production into good chips and defective chips. Through testing, the good chips are further divided into various grades according to their performance characteristics.

Because the different grades are produced simultaneously, only the total cost of the process, and not that of the individual chips, is known. The cost incurred for any specific chip cannot be separately traced.

The average cost (good chips divided by the total cost of the process) does not provide a satisfactory cost allocation if consideration is given to the performance characteristics and the relative market value of the individual chips. Two grades of chips are considered for purposes of this problem: (1) good high-quality chips and (2) good low-quality chips. Good high-quality chips are worth far more in the market than good low-quality chips. The differences in value are masked in the manufacturing process. However, both grades of chips are profitable.

The final product, memory devices, is obtained from two basic manufacturing processes: chip fabrication and testing and device assembly and testing. Refer to figure 11.6 for a diagram of the basic manufacturing processes. A raw silicon wafer is the input to the chip fabrication and testing process. Each wafer yields multiple chips of identical design but of different quality, as mentioned before.

After several hundred different manufacturing steps performed during chip fabrication, the finished chips are ready for testing in the chip fabrication & testing process. The finished chips are first tested to distinguish between the good chips and the defective chips. Subsequently, good chips are classified according to the number of good memory bits on each chip and the time required to access the good bits. The chip testing process can determine only the number of good memory bits and the speed of each chip. Reliability is determined when testing the completed memory devices. The cost of the chips constitutes approximately 80 percent of the cost of the completed memory devices.

Good chips of various densities and speeds are the input to the device assembly and testing process, where the chips are processed through a series of separable manufacturing operations. Costs can be identified for each device assembly operation and for each part number.

FIGURE 11.6
Memory Device Manufacturing Process

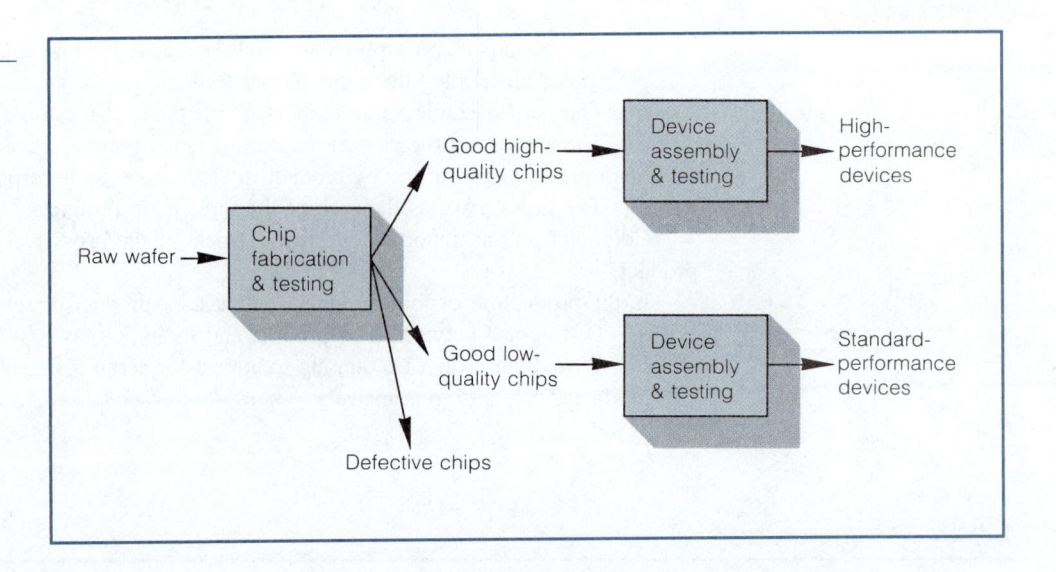

The output of the device assembly process, as determined by the final device test, consists of memory devices of different quality that are priced accordingly in the marketplace. Figure 11.7 contains information about production, cost, and product characteristics.

Required

What cost allocation methodology will properly value each memory device for profitability and inventory valuation? Support your conclusion with appropriate calculations.

FIGURE 11.7
Production, Cost, and Product Characteristics for a Batch of Memory Devices

Production Quantity Data:

Devices:	
Standard performance	500
High performance	500
Chips:	
High quality	800
Low quality	500

Production Cost Data:

Total separable costs:	
High performance	$2,000
Standard performance	$1,000
Chips (total fabrication cost)	$20,000
Market value:	
High performance	$45
Standard performance	$20

Product Characteristics Data:

Reliability of device	
High performance	100,000 hours
Standard performance	80,000 hours
Speed of device:	
High performance	150 nanoseconds
Standard performance	200 nanoseconds

Chapter 12

Materials and Labor: Costing and Control

Outline

MATERIALS COSTING
Materials Received
  Purchase Discounts
  Freight-In
  Material-Related Costs
Materials Issued
Spoilage and Quality
  Normal and Abnormal Spoilage
  Scrap
  Waste
MATERIALS CONTROL
Materials Control—General
Two-Bin System
ABC Method
Economic Order Quantity (EOQ)
Materials Requirements Planning (MRP)
    and Manufacturing Resource Planning
    (MRP II)
Just-In-Time (JIT)
LABOR COSTING

LABOR CONTROL AND LEARNING
    CURVES
Learning Curves
SUMMARY
APPENDIX 12.1: MATERIALS CONTROL
    PROCEDURES
Purchasing Materials
Maintaining and Issuing Materials
APPENDIX 12.2: LABOR CONTROL
    PROCEDURES
APPENDIX 12.3: THE MATHEMATICS OF
    THE ECONOMIC ORDER QUANTITY
    AND LEARNING CURVE
SELF-STUDY PROBLEMS
Economic Order Quantity
Learning Curve
SUGGESTED READINGS
DISCUSSION QUESTIONS
EXERCISES
PROBLEMS

A major objective of cost accounting is to accumulate and assign costs to cost objects such as units of production, departments, or other activities for which management desires a separate measurement or evaluation. This accounting effort is referred to as **costing. Control** is the ongoing process of implementing management's plans and providing feedback of actual results so that managers can evaluate performance and make needed adjustments to keep operations in line with plans and objectives. Costing and control are interrelated, because costing provides a fundamental component of feedback needed for management control. Together with planning and budgeting they provide the basis for an effective cost accounting system.

Chapters 12, 13, and 14 present an in-depth examination of costing and control aspects of each manufacturing cost element—materials, labor, and overhead. These chapters explain how a cost accounting system can be designed to provide management with appropriate cost information necessary for the effective control of operations. After completing this chapter, you should be able to:

1. handle purchase discounts, freight-in, and other material-related costs.
2. distinguish between defective units, scrap, waste, normal spoilage, and abnormal spoilage, and be able to apply the appropriate accounting treatment for each of these, depending on the particular production situation.
3. use the two-bin system, ABC method, economic order quantity, materials requirements planning, and just-in-time philosophy in controlling the size of inventories
4. use learning curves and budgetary concepts in controlling labor costs.

MATERIALS COSTING

The cost of materials received is typically not the amount shown on a vendor invoice. For example, cash discounts and materials handling costs represent possible modifications to the invoice price. Also, the cost of materials received may not be the same as the cost of materials issued because of adjustments made for scrap, waste, or defective units. Therefore, it is important to understand how materials costs are accumulated and assigned so that accounting records reflect the actual costs of production.

Materials Received

The vendor's invoice provides one basis for determining the cost of materials entered on the inventory records.[1] It provides a description of each item, the quantity shipped, individual prices, freight charges, and the terms of sale. Trade and quantity discounts may also appear on the vendor's invoice.

The general rule is that the cost of materials includes the invoice amount plus other costs paid to put the materials in place ready for use at the production facility. These costs typically include:

- The invoice amount
- Shipping costs (freight-in)
- Sales taxes
- Cost of delivery containers (pallets, spools, etc.) net of return refunds
- Duty on international shipments

---

1. Standard costs, as discussed in chapter 15, provide another basis for recording the cost of materials.

- Material-related costs such as purchasing, receiving, inspection, storage, and issuing costs

Trade discounts, quantity discounts, purchase (cash) discounts, rebates, and purchase returns should not be included in the cost of materials. Several of the items listed above are discussed in more detail in the following sections.

Purchase Discounts The terms of sale typically include any available **purchase discounts,** also referred to as cash discounts. For example, a vendor may specify terms such as 2/15, net/30, which means that the buyer may deduct 2 percent from the total invoice price if payment is made within the discount period—in this example, 15 days after the invoice date. Otherwise, the total invoice amount is due within the payment period—in this example, 30 days. It is usually profitable to pay the invoice within the discount period, because purchase discounts are designed to make prompt payment an attractive alternative for the buyer. For example, with terms 2/10, net/30 on a $100 purchase, the discount or cash price is $98 ($100 − $2 discount). Not taking the discount results in borrowing $98 for 20 (30 − 10) days and paying $2 for the privilege. Since there are approximately eighteen 20-day periods in a year, the effective interest rate is approximately 37 percent (2/98 × 18). Therefore, the company should take the cash discount if it has the cash or can borrow money at an interest rate less than 37 percent.

The decision whether or not to take purchase discounts is a financing decision, and materials should be recorded at the invoice price minus the amount of purchase discounts permitted whether they are taken or not. This procedure is known as recording purchases net of discounts. Lost discounts are not considered an inventoriable cost; rather, they should be treated as a separate item and shown on the income statement as a financing expense. For example, if a $1,000 purchase offering the terms 2/10, net/30 is paid after the discount period, the following journal entry would be made if the payable had been recorded net of discounts:

Accounts payable	980	
Purchase discounts lost	20	
Cash		1,000

This procedure is designed to provide proper disclosure for management review of the total financing activity. Some firms elect to record purchases at the gross invoice amount and then record the amount of purchase discounts taken. However, this procedure does not automatically provide exception-type information, which is usually preferred for management control.

Freight-in Accounting theory recognizes that freight-in is an ordinary and necessary cost of purchasing materials. However, there are many different ways to handle freight charges, depending on the business situation. For example, if the number of items received is relatively small or individually identifiable, such as when new automobiles are received at a dealership, it may be appropriate to calculate the transportation cost applicable to each item. When there are different items received representing various commodity classes and transportation rates, such as when lawn care equipment is shipped with garden chemicals, it may be very difficult to trace freight charges to specific items. In such instances it may be necessary to compute the relationship between the number of pounds in the shipment and allocate freight charges on a per-pound basis. For example, if the freight charge on a shipment is $250 and the total weight of the items is 625 pounds, the average freight cost is $0.40 per pound ($250 ÷ 625 pounds). Therefore, if a specific item weighed 130 pounds, it would be assigned a $52 freight charge.

If the number of items received is very large, procedures that are sound in theory do not always work in practice because of the volume of clerical operations that might be involved. A common practice in accounting for freight charges is to accumulate all freight cost in a single freight-in account, and, as materials are issued and charged to work-in-process inventory, a portion of freight-in is also charged to the work-in-process inventory. The amount of freight going to work in process is based on previously estimated amounts of freight-in and total materials cost for an accounting period. For example, if total freight-in is estimated to be $8,000 and the total materials cost is estimated to be $160,000 during the next year, freight-in would be applied to the work-in-process inventory at the rate of 5 percent of materials cost, as follows:

$$\frac{\$8,000 \text{ estimated freight-in}}{\$160,000 \text{ estimated materials cost}} = 5\% \text{ application rate}$$

As materials are issued, the work-in-process inventory is debited with the cost of materials plus 5 percent for transportation costs. Freight-in is credited for 5 percent of the cost of materials issued. Assuming the freight-in application rate is 5 percent, the following journal entries are made when (a) $5,000 of materials are received with terms 2/10, net/30 and a freight charge of $275 and (b) $1,000 of materials are issued to production:

1. Receipt of incoming materials recorded net of discounts.

Freight-in	275	
Materials inventory (0.98 × 5,000)	4,900	
Accounts payable		5,175

2. Issue of materials to production.

Work-in-process inventory	1,050	
Materials inventory		1,000
Freight-in (0.05 × 1,000)		50

This same principle applies for indirect materials, except that factory overhead is debited rather than the work-in-process inventory. At the end of the accounting period, any balance remaining in the freight-in account is usually allocated between inventories and cost of goods sold or is simply closed to cost of goods sold.

Another method of accounting for freight is to estimate the total freight costs for the period and to include this amount in the calculation of the factory overhead application rate. Using this method, the freight-in account is a subsidiary of the factory overhead control account, as explained in chapters 13 and 14.

Material-related Costs There are certain costs that are closely related to the quantities of materials purchased or used but that like freight-in have some practical limitations on the extent to which they can be assigned directly to items received. The clerical expense required to make cost allocations with a high degree of accuracy may not justify the benefits received from a detailed accounting. Material-related costs usually arise from the following functions:

- Purchasing
- Receiving
- Inspection
- Storage (prior to entering production)
- Issuing

One procedure that may be used to assign other acquisition costs to materials is to compute an application rate similar to the overhead application rate and use it to assign costs in an approximate fashion. A rate is calculated for each material-related function, such as purchasing, receiving, and warehousing. The rate is then used to apply other acquisition costs to the materials account.

Depending on which function is involved, there are a number of allocation bases that may be used to allocate other acquisition costs. For example, the cost of operating the purchasing department might be allocated to materials based on the estimated number of purchase orders processed or the estimated dollar volume of purchases. Receiving department costs might be allocated on the basis of the number of items or the tonage of materials received. Warehousing costs might be allocated on the basis of the dollar value of items or the amount of square footage occupied. The selection of an appropriate base should be made on the strength of the relationship between each possible base and the actual utilization of material-related costs. Direct-labor cost or direct-labor hours is usually not an acceptable base.

To illustrate the use of this method, data for a materials handling situation are presented here. The cost application rates for each department are found by dividing the estimated costs for the period by the estimated application base.

Department	Estimated Cost for the Period	Estimated Application Base	Application Rate
Purchasing	$100,000	5,000 purchase orders	$20 per purchase order
Receiving	50,000	$1,400,000 value received	$0.04 per dollar value received
Warehousing	160,000	100,000 square feet	$1.60 per square foot

Assume that during the current month there were 420 purchase orders processed, $110,000 worth of materials received, (based on invoice prices), and 8,500 square feet occupied. Under these conditions, the following journal entry would be made to record the application of other materials costs to the materials inventory:

Materials inventory	26,400	
Applied purchasing department expenses		8,400
(420 × $20 = $8,400)		
Applied receiving department expenses		4,400
($110,000 × $0.04 = $4,400)		
Applied warehouse department expenses		13,600
(8,500 × $1.60 = $13,600)		

Actually distributing the $26,400 among different items or purchases could be very involved and time-consuming. Typically materials acquisition costs are applied to each product or to each invoice as it is processed. Therefore, the preceding journal entry may represent a summary of individual cost applications made for each invoice that was processed during the period.

The actual expenditures made to operate each of the material-related departments are accumulated in an "actual" departmental expense account. Because of forecast error or unexpected operating results, the debit balance in the actual account may not equal the credit balance in the applied account. These differences are called overapplied materials acquisition costs if the applied amount is greater than actual costs or underapplied materials acquisition costs if the reverse is the case. Insignificant over- or underapplied amounts may not require management attention; however, substantial amounts should trigger management review and analysis.

Over- or underapplied materials acquisition costs are closed at the end of an accounting period to inventory accounts, or the cost-of-goods-sold account. To illustrate, assume that the total actual cost of operating the purchasing department is $98,000 and that 5,100 purchase orders were processed during the period, resulting in an applied amount of $102,000 (5,100 × $20). Assuming that the overapplied amount of $4,000 ($102,000 − $98,000) is closed to the cost-of-goods-sold account, the following journal entry is made for the purchasing department:

Applied purchasing department expenses	102,000	
Actual purchasing department expenses		98,000
Cost of goods sold		4,000

Rather than using two accounts—an applied and an actual account—many firms simply use a departmental expense control account, with debits to the account representing actual expenditures and credits to the account representing applied amounts. Any balance in the account at the end of an accounting period represents over- or underapplied acquisition costs. The end results are the same regardless of the account structure used.

Materials Issued

Accounting for materials issued is quite simple. For example, if materials requisitioned during the week total $8,000 for direct materials and $2,000 for indirect materials, the following journal entry is made:

Work-in-process inventory	8,000	
Factory overhead	2,000	
Materials inventory		10,000

Difficulties in accounting for materials issued arise when materials are purchased at different times at different prices. This results in different costs for essentially the same materials. When this situation occurs, an assumption must be made about the flow of costs through the materials account. An intuitive approach would be to have the flow of costs coincide with the physical flow of units, but this is not a requirement. For example, one cost flow assumption may be used for internal management accounting whereas another may be used for financial statements and income tax purposes. The assumption used should give an accurate reflection of periodic income when costs are subtracted from revenues. There are three facets underlying this notion: first, the proper matching of costs and revenues; second, the costing of materials inventories transferred from period to period; and third, the provision of relevant information for evaluating company policies relating to the purchase, manufacture, and sale of materials.

There are three generally accepted cost flow assumptions that may be applied to inventories, whether they are materials, work in process, or finished goods. The method selected, however, must be consistently applied for similar categories of materials. The three basic cost flow assumptions are first-in, first-out (FIFO), last-in, first-out (LIFO), and average cost.

The **FIFO** method assumes that the cost flow of materials resembles a cafeteria line—the first in are the first out. The cost of the first materials received is assumed to be the cost of the first materials issued. The assumption is that the oldest materials in stock are issued first.

The **last-in, first-out (LIFO) method** assumes that the cost flow of materials resembles a situation in which materials are figuratively placed in a barrel when they are received. As materials are requisitioned they are withdrawn from the top of the barrel, with the last items received being the first items out. Therefore, the cost of the last materials received is assumed to be the cost of the first materials issued. The assumption is that the newest materials in stock are issued first.

The **average-cost method,** as the name implies, uses the average cost of materials purchased to determine the cost of materials issued. The average cost of materials purchased can be calculated in several ways, depending on how often the cost figure is to be revised. For example, a moving average could be calculated after each purchase of materials by dividing the total cost of materials available by the number of units on hand. Issues of materials are then recorded at that cost until the next purchase, when a new moving average is calculated. Or an average purchase cost for materials could be calculated monthly or quarterly and applied to materials issued during the corresponding future period.

Spoilage and Quality

There are a number of ways that materials can be spoiled or lost during production. **Spoilage** is a general term that refers to materials that have become bad or unfit for their intended use. Spoilage is the term generally used when referring to defective units. **Defective units** are products that do not meet quality standards. They may be reworked and sold at or near regular prices or they may be disposed of for salvage value, depending on the manufacturing situation. **Scrap** is material residue from a manufacturing operation that has some value in excess of disposal costs. Scrap may have relatively minor value, as in the case of steel, or may have significant value, as in the case of gold. **Waste** is material that is lost through shrinkage or evaporation or is material residue from a manufacturing operation that has little or no value in excess of disposal costs. The disposal of some types of waste, such as nuclear fuel, is very costly.

Information about spoilage, scrap, and waste is used for product costing and cost control. Each of these purposes is discussed briefly in this section, followed by a more detailed explanation of accounting for normal and abnormal spoilage, scrap, and waste.

The general rule for product costing is that the cost of direct materials includes the cost of scrap, waste, and normally anticipated spoilage that occurs in the ordinary course of production activities. Unanticipated or abnormal amounts of scrap, waste, and spoilage should be expensed in the period incurred or, in some situations, may be included in factory overhead. Additional guidance concerning the details of accounting for normal and abnormal amounts of defective units, scrap, and waste is contained in the following sections.

Management typically strives to use the most economical methods possible to produce consistently high-quality products. High-quality production is a prerequisite for effective competition in today's national and international markets. Advertising slogans such as "quality is job one" and "quality is our business" indicate the importance many firms place on quality. Aggressive, quality-conscious companies may set quality goals such as "parts per million scrap" or "zero defects," for example. Progress toward such quality goals is measured, in part, by how well the cost of scrap, waste, and defective units is controlled.

Quality is defined as the degree of conformance of a product (or service) to a prespecified or preannounced standard. The costs of spoilage, scrap, and waste are measures associated with poor quality. Other costs of poor quality include the cost of returned merchandise, warranty costs, product liability costs, customer ill will, and lost markets. The cost of improving quality includes the costs of preventive maintenance, machine tooling, employee training, and equipment design changes.

There has been considerable discussion and research into the relative costs and benefits of high-quality production. Much of the attention given to quality production is because foreign firms have been very successful in penetrating American markets. Many observers believe that one reason for this successful penetration is that foreign companies have offered superior-quality products. There is concern that, in many instances, American manufacturers have not invested in better quality because of inadequate cost-benefit evaluations. For example, one firm appeared to make a sound decision when it rejected a proposed investment in a new machine that would have improved product quality because the expected return on investment (ROI) did not meet cut-off criteria. However, the evaluation was flawed because it did not fully consider the revenue impact of a loss of market share to a competitor who guaranteed a higher-quality product. The company has now decided to make the investment in an attempt to regain market share.

The message is that management and cost accountants must be alert to all costs and benefits when considering decisions to improve quality. Particular attention should be given to those cost categories requiring subjective judgment.

A more detailed discussion of quality is beyond the scope of this chapter. It is sufficient for our purposes to point out that there seems to be mounting evidence that better quality, as indicated by such measures as less spoilage, scrap, and waste, leads to lower overall costs and higher sales. The suggested readings at the end of the chapter should be consulted by those interested in more detail concerning quality and measures of quality. The following sections focus on the product-costing aspects of spoilage.

Normal and Abnormal Spoilage

The level of spoilage that is expected to occur in the ordinary course of efficient operations is called *normal spoilage*. The cost of normal spoilage is considered to be a necessary cost of good units produced. Normal spoilage, by definition, is not controllable in the current accounting period; it is an inherent part of the manufacturing process. This definition should not be construed to mean that management should not strive to reduce or eliminate spoilage. Rather, normal spoilage simply reflects management's expectation concerning the prevailing state of affairs.

To understand accounting for normal spoilage, consider, for example, a company in which a quantity of material is lost in a production process through evaporation. The amount of material that is lost can be predicted with reasonable accuracy and is an expected occurrance. In this situation the cost of evaporated materials is included in the cost of good units produced. As another example, consider a company in which engineering estimates are made each accounting period that give the percentage of defective units expected from a production process. These estimates are reasonably accurate because of factors inherent in the production process, so the cost of defective units is included in the cost of good units produced.

Abnormal spoilage constitutes unanticipated quantities of scrap, waste, or defective units, and accounting for it depends on the reason it occurred. If abnormal spoilage occurs because of unusual or unexpected factors, such as exacting specifications or difficult processing requirements that can be identified with a specific job or batch, the cost of abnormal spoilage should be charged to that particular job or batch. However, if abnormal spoilage occurs because of an oversight or error on the part of workers, its cost should be charged to an expense account in the period incurred.

To illustrate accounting for normal and abnormal spoilage that does *not* result from exacting manufacturing specifications, consider the following situation. A company plans to produce 102,000 units of a particular product to obtain 100,000 units of good output. Costs of production are expected to be as follows:

	Per Unit
Materials	$0.50
Labor	0.60
Factory overhead (200% of direct labor)	1.20
	$ 2.30

Given these costs, the following journal entry summarizes the costs of placing 102,000 units into production:

Work-in-process inventory	234,600	
Materials (102,000 × $0.50)		51,000
Labor (102,000 × $0.60)		61,200
Factory overhead—applied (102,000 × $1.20)		122,400

On final inspection at the end of the process, 3,000 units were found to be defective. The abnormal spoilage of 1,000 units was identified with a careless worker. Journal entries to record the cost of spoiled goods are as follows:

Cost of normal spoilage (2,000 × $2.30)	4,600	
Cost of abnormal spoilage (1,000 × $2.30)	2,300	
Work-in-process inventory		6,900
Finished-goods inventory	4,600	
Cost of normal spoilage		4,600

An obvious alternative in the preceding situation is to make one journal entry and to simply debit cost of abnormal spoilage and credit work-in-process inventory for $1,200. However, the explicit recognition of normal spoilage when making two journal entries helps keep management aware of the problem of production quality.

In some situations defective units can be sold for some salvage value. For example, assume that the defective units in the previous situation can be sold for $0.80 each. The following journal entries illustrate accounting for the $1.50 ($2.30 − $0.80) per-unit cost not recovered.

Spoiled-goods inventory (3,000 × $0.80)	2,400	
Cost of normal spoilage (2,000 × $1.50)	3,000	
Cost of abnormal spoilage (1,000 × $1.50)	1,500	
Work-in-process inventory		6,900
Finished-goods inventory	3,000	
Cost of normal spoilage		3,000
Cash or accounts receivable	2,400	
Spoiled-goods inventory		2,400

Rather than junking or selling the units, assume that the company in this situation reworks the defective units and sells them at regular prices. The cost of rework is generally assigned to factory overhead. This treatment implies that a certain amount of normal rework has been considered in production plans and is included in the factory-overhead application rate. If rework is identified with a particular job or batch, however, the cost of rework is charged directly to that specific job or batch.

Charging the cost of rework to factory overhead has the effect of spreading the cost over all good units produced. To illustrate this situation, refer to the basic facts in the previous situation and assume that the factory-overhead application rate of $1.20 includes an allowance for the cost of rework. The following journal entries would be made in this situation. Note that assumed amounts are used for the cost of rework for materials and labor.

Work-in-process inventory	234,600	
Materials (102,000 × $0.50)		51,000
Labor (102,000 × $0.60)		61,200
Factory overhead—applied (102,000 × $1.20)		122,400
Factory overhead—actual (cost of rework)	2,100	
Materials		900
Labor		600
Factory overhead—applied		600
Finished goods inventory	234,600	
Work-in-process inventory		234,600

If the cost of rework had been identified with specific jobs, the following journal entries would have been made.

Work-in-process inventory	234,600	
Materials (102,000 × $0.50)		51,000
Labor (102,000 × $0.60)		61,200
Factory overhead—applied (102,000 × $1.20)		122,400
Work-in-process-inventory	2,100	
Materials		900
Labor		600
Factory overhead—applied		600
Posting to work-in-process subsidiary ledger:		
Job no. 13–976 800		
Job no. 14–808 900		
Job no. 15–509 400		
Finished-goods inventory	236,700	
Work-in-process inventory		236,700

Rework should not be undertaken unless the units' incremental value received from their sale as good units over their sale as defective units equals or exceeds the additional cost of rework. Refer to chapter 4 for additional guidance in making such decisions.

A final illustration of accounting for spoilage concerns abnormal spoilage associated with exacting specifications for a particular job. Assume the same basic cost data as in the previous illustrations, except that a special order for 2,000 units was processed with unusually strict specifications. Production records indicate that the normal spoilage rate increased when attempting to meet such specifications. As a result, 2,300 units were actually placed in production to obtain the required 2,000 good units of output. The proper accounting procedure under these circumstances is to charge the cost of spoiled units directly to the job rather than spreading the cost of spoiled units over all units produced. Therefore, to properly assign the cost of lost units to this job, the number of units charged to this job would not be the 2,000 good units delivered but the 2,300 total units produced to obtain the 2,000 good units.

The following summary journal entry would be made to record the total costs placed into production for this particular job. Assume that spoiled units were not discovered until the end of the manufacturing process.

Work-in-process inventory	5,290	
Materials (2,300 × $0.50)		1,150
Labor (2,300 × $0.60)		1,380
Factory overhead—applied (2,300 × $1.20)		2,760

As in the previous example, these spoiled units can be sold for $0.80 each. Given this information, the following journal entry would be made:

Spoiled materials inventory (300 × $0.80)   240
    Work-in-process inventory   240

Finally, the cost of the 2,000 good units relating to this job would be transferred to the finished-goods inventory with the following journal entry:

Finished-goods inventory ($5,290 − $240)   5,050
    Work-in-process inventory   5,050

Scrap As mentioned earlier, scrap is material residue from a manufacturing operation that has some value. Examples of scrap include shavings from the manufacture of furniture, borders from the stamping of steel, and remnants from the production of garments. Although scrap usually has a minor recovery value, as in the case of cloth remnants, it may have a substantial value, as in the case of platinum.

For control purposes and to prevent manipulation or theft, scrap should be weighed or counted and returned to the storeroom or other controlled area as soon as it is practical. Maintaining records of scrap recovery is important, because the production of excessive scrap may indicate inefficient operations. Many firms maintain quantity statistics for scrap because of its importance in quality control even if the scrap's dollar value is immaterial for financial accounting. Actual amounts of scrap should be compared with standard or anticipated amounts, and corrective action should be taken if there are unacceptable deviations from expectations.

For product-costing purposes, the total amount of materials assigned to work in process includes any anticipated scrap. For example, when a part is stamped from a sheet of steel, the cost of material lost in the borders can be predicted with reasonable accuracy and should be included in the material cost of the part. In practice, the total cost of materials issued is charged to work in process; this process automatically includes the cost of normally anticipated scrap in the cost of direct materials. The net realizable value of any scrap recovery is subsequently withdrawn from work in process if it can be linked to specific jobs or batches. Although this is the most appropriate treatment, implementing such a procedure may present some problems. For example, associating scrap with each individual job or production run may not be feasible. The amount involved may not justify the additional accounting necessary to identify costs with jobs. However, if a significantly different amount of scrap is expected to occur because of individual job characteristics or if customers expect ''scrap credits'' on their individual jobs, identifying scrap with individual jobs is the appropriate accounting treatment.

When a normal, uniform amount of scrap results from manufacturing operations, it may be accurate enough to consider scrap as part of the cost of general manufacturing operations included in factory overhead. Instead of linking scrap with particular jobs, all production benefits from scrap recovery by incorporating the expected offset to factory overhead as part of the predetermined factory overhead application rate. The predetermined overhead application rate is reduced by the amount of the expected sales. This treatment, which is widely used in practice, eliminates the clerical burden of assigning scrap value to particular jobs.

Another element in deciding how to account for scrap relates to whether the value of scrap is recorded at the time it occurs or at the time it is sold or used. Deciding on the appropriate time to record the value of scrap depends on such factors as whether or not the value of the scrap is known or can be reasonably estimated, the relative significance of the total value of scrap, the availability and stability of a market for scrap, and the expected

FIGURE 12.1

Journal Entries for Methods of Accounting for Scrap

Costing Treatment	Method 1 (Value assigned when scrap occurs)	Method 2 (Value assigned when scrap sold)
1. Scrap is linked to particular jobs or products	Scrap is returned to storeroom: Scrap material inventory Work-in-process inventory Scrap is sold: Cash or accounts receivable Scrap material inventory	Scrap is returned to storeroom: No entry made Scrap is sold: Cash or accounts receivable Work-in-process inventory
2. Scrap is an offset to factory overhead	Scrap is returned to storeroom: Scrap materials inventory Factory overhead Scrap is sold: Cash or accounts receivable Scrap materials inventory	Scrap is returned to storeroom: Memorandum entry only Scrap is sold: Cash or accounts receivable Factory overhead

time lag between the occurrence and sale of scrap. Scrap is typically recorded at the time it occurs if the value of scrap is known and the total value of scrap is significant.

Two methods for assigning scrap value (when scrap occurs or when it is sold) and two costing treatments (linking scrap to particular jobs or products or treating scrap as an offset to factory overhead) result in four possible ways to account for scrap. Figure 12.1 contains an outline of the journal entries that would be made under each alternative.

Waste Material that is lost through shrinkage or evaporation or material residue from a manufacturing operation that has little or no value in excess of disposal costs is called waste. Normal or expected levels of waste do not receive a separate accounting but are simply included as a component of the cost of materials issued. Abnormal levels of waste are usually indicated when materials are placed in production in excess of planned amounts. For example, if a process requires 1,000 square feet of material to produce 900 units of good output, the engineering specification would indicate a 90-percent yield rate. An actual yield rate of 85 percent, therefore, may indicate that excessive waste is present in the process. The cost of abnormal waste should be charged to expense or to factory overhead, as for spoilage and scrap.

Accounting for waste is directly related to materials quantity variances, overhead efficiency variances, and production yield variances, which are calculated when using a standard cost system. These topics are discussed in chapters 15, 16, and 17.

MATERIALS CONTROL

Materials control has many important aspects. Materials of the desired quality must be on hand at the appropriate time and in the right location to support manufacturing operations. The procedures for handling materials should guard against waste, misuse, spoilage, obsolescence, and theft. There are also several important ways in which the size of investment in inventory can be controlled. General procedures typically used to purchase, maintain, and issue materials are discussed in appendix 12.1 at the end of this chapter. In the following sections a number of systems used to manage the makeup and size of inventories are discussed. These methods include a two-bin system, the ABC method, economic order quantity (EOQ), materials requirements planning (MRP and MRP II), and just-in-time (JIT).

Materials Control—General

Materials control is a vital concern for management because a relatively large investment is carried in inventories. Depending on the type of industry and the characteristics of individual firms, a manufacturing company may have as much as one third of its total investment in inventories. No wonder managers are concerned with minimizing the cost of acquiring, handling, and maintaining inventories. However, management is also concerned with having sufficient inventories available to cushion the effects of uneven flows in the receipt, production, and sale of goods. These and other factors influence the cost-benefit trade-offs that make inventory control especially challenging. For example, when considering the cost of carrying sufficient inventory to facilitate production and sales, management must include the following costs in its decision making:

1. Investment of working capital or interest on borrowed capital
2. Storage or warehousing
3. Handling
4. Deterioration, shrinkage, or obsolescence
5. Property taxes and insurance

However, the cost of *not* carrying sufficient inventories includes the following:

1. Idle time, overtime, and extra setup time because of disruptions in production caused by stockouts.
2. Higher prices and extra purchasing, transportation, and handling costs because of frequent small orders.
3. Lost sales and loss of customer goodwill.
4. Extra managerial and clerical burden to handle stockout and back-order situations.

Materials management requires a trade-off between the conflicting costs of carrying sufficient inventories and the costs of *not* carrying them. To make management's task even more difficult, some of these costs, such as the cost of lost sales and the loss of customer goodwill, are difficult to quantify. Materials management is so important that many techniques for planning and controlling inventories have been developed. These techniques typically focus on fundamental questions about *when* and *how much* inventory to order. Some techniques used for low-volume, low-cost inventories are simple, easily implemented, and require little cost to operate. Others used for high-volume, high-cost inventories are rather complex and rely on computer technology to implement.

Two-Bin System

A simple but effective technique used to manage low-value, noncritical items is called a two-bin system. Using this method, inventory is separated by some means into two bins—a main bin and a reserve bin. To begin the cycle, both bins are filled and materials are issued from the main bin. The reserve bin contains enough inventory to satisfy requirements from the time an order is placed for more inventory until the time goods are received. When the main bin becomes empty, a purchase requisition is initiated and the reserve bin is tapped until the order arrives. When the materials arrive, both bins are replenished and another inventory cycle begins.

ABC Method

The ABC method is an inventory control technique that provides for easier management of very large inventories. It divides inventory into groups (A, B, and C) and then applies different control techniques to each group. The ABC method is based on the common situation that a relatively small percentage of inventory items will account for a relatively large percentage of the total cost and activity in the inventory. For example, grocery stores, automobile parts houses, and hardware distributors may have inventories in excess of 60,000 items, but only 6,000 items may account for as much as 80 percent of the cost of the inventory. Those items are put in the inventory category that receives the most attention with the most sophisticated techniques, because it has the greatest potential for affecting the overall inventory situation. The other categories receive lesser degrees of attention because of their minor effect on the overall situation.

Economic Order Quantity (EOQ)

Another, more sophisticated approach involves calculating an economic order quantity (EOQ) to determine *how much* should be purchased at a time. Production and sales schedules are then used to determine *when* orders of this size should be placed.

EOQ is the order quantity that minimizes the *total* of the cost of ordering plus the cost of carrying inventory. Finding the point at which the total of these costs is at a minimum requires knowledge of how these costs behave. The cost of ordering and the cost of carrying inventory have an inverse relationship. As order size is increased, the average amount of inventory on hand also increases and the cost of handling and carrying inventory increases. As order size is increased, however, fewer orders are needed to satisfy total requirements, and the cost of placing and receiving orders decreases. With one cost increasing and the other cost decreasing as a function of order size, there is an ideal order size at which the cost of ordering plus the cost of carrying inventory is at a minimum. The order size where this occurs is called the **economic order quantity (EOQ).** These cost relationships and a graphic determination of EOQ are presented in figure 12.2.

In addition to a graphic approach, EOQs can be calculated by using either a tabular approach for approximate results or a formula for exact results. The following EOQ calculations illustrate both of these approaches.

The data items required to calculate the EOQ for a particular inventory item are:

1. A forecast of the total quantity of units required during an accounting period.
2. The cost of placing an order.
3. The cost of carrying one unit of inventory in stock for one accounting period.

For example, a company uses a particular item for which the following statistics have been gathered:

Annual materials requirements	5,000 units
Cost of placing an order	$18 per order
Carrying costs	$2 per unit per year

When using the tabular approach, the first step is to arbitrarily select a number of order sizes near what is thought to be the EOQ. Then, the number of orders that are required to satisfy total requirements is calculated by dividing total requirements by each respective order size. The total costs of ordering and carrying inventories are then calculated using the procedures outlined in figure 12.3.

CHAPTER 12: MATERIALS AND LABOR: COSTING AND CONTROL   425

FIGURE 12.2

Economic Order Quantity (EOQ)

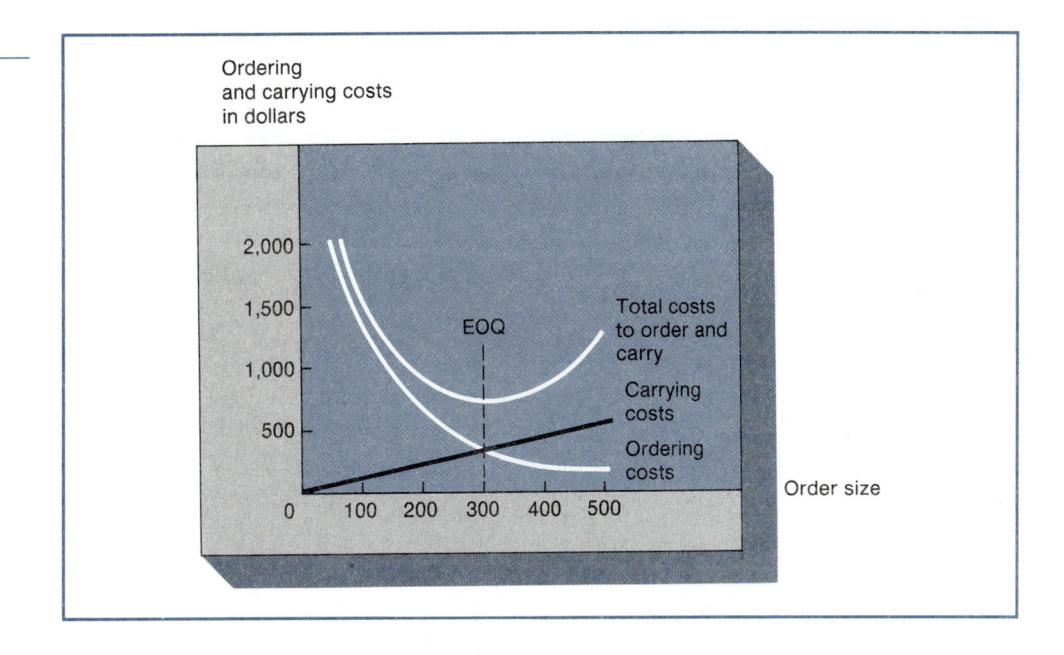

The final step is to select the order size with the minimum total cost, which is the EOQ. The minimum in this case is $606 at an EOQ of approximately 300 units. Note that the graphic solution in figure 12.2 and the tabular solution in figure 12.3 relate to the same inventory situation.

A formula that can be used to calculate a precise EOQ is as follows:

$$EOQ = \sqrt{\frac{2RO}{C}}$$

where
R = Total materials requirements for one period
O = Cost of placing an order
C = Cost of carrying one unit of inventory for one period

The mathematical determination of this formula and certain assumptions underlying its use are explained in appendix 12.3 at the end of this chapter. When using the EOQ formula, the same time period should be used for both R and C. Also, for firms that

FIGURE 12.3

Tabular Calculation of Economic Order Quantity (EOQ)

Annual requirement	5,000	5,000	5,000	5,000	5,000
Order size	100	200	300	400	500
Number of orders (annual requirement ÷ order size)	50	25	17	13	10
Total ordering costs (number of orders × $18 per order)	$ 900	$ 450	$ 306	$ 234	$ 180
Average inventory (order size ÷ 2)	50	100	150	200	$ 250
Total carrying costs (average inventory × $2 per unit)	$ 100	$ 200	300	$ 400	$ 500
Total ordering and carrying costs	$1,000	$ 650	$ 606	$ 634	$ 680

express carrying cost as a percentage of unit cost, C can be replaced with "unit cost times carrying cost percentage."

Finally, the cost of carrying inventory, C, may include an amount representing the desired rate of return on the investment in inventory. For example, if an item costs $30.00 per unit and the minimum desired rate of return for the company is 15 percent, then $4.50 (0.15 × $30.00) should be included as part of the cost of carrying inventory.

Using the data presented earlier, with R = 5,000 units, O = $18 per order, and C = $2 per unit, the EOQ is determined to be 300 units as follows:

$$\sqrt{\frac{2 \times 5{,}000 \times 18}{2}} = 300$$

The EOQ of 300 units found with both methods is simply the result of a chance selection of the right order size when using the tabular method.

As presented here, the EOQ model has a major shortcoming in that it does not contain all relevant costs that affect the order-size decision. For example, neither the total purchase price nor a provision for quantity discounts are included in this model. Such items are important if, for example, a firm does not have adequate financing or if for other reasons it may need to purchase in quantities less than the EOQ. Also, the availability of quantity discounts may shift the EOQ to a larger order size. To illustrate, assume that the following discount schedule is available for the EOQ situation shown in figure 12.3:

Order Size (units)	Quantity Discount
0–99	0%
100–199	4
200–299	5
300–399	6
400+	8

Incorporating these quantity discounts causes the EOQ to shift from 300 to approximately 400 units, as indicated by the order size with the minimum total annual cost in figure 12.4. There are advanced models that are used when such factors are considered, but they are not presented in this text.

EOQ answers the question *how much* to order. Several other factors must be considered before answering the question *when* to order. Typically, what happens is that a **reorder point** is established so that as the number of units on hand declines, a purchase requisition is triggered when the reorder point is reached. The order point is set depending on **lead time,** the time between placing an order and having the materials delivered; **safety stock,** an added cushion of inventory maintained to protect against stockouts; and the

FIGURE 12.4

Calculation of Economic Order Quantity (EOQ) with Quantity Discount

Order size	100	200	300	400	500
Total ordering and carrying costs[a]	$ 1,000	$ 650	$ 606	$ 634	$ 680
Total cost of materials (5,000 units × $3 per unit)	$15,000	$15,000	$15,000	$15,000	$15,000
Less: Applicable discount	600	750	900	1,200	1,200
Net cost of materials	$14,400	$14,250	$14,100	$13,800	$13,800
Total annual cost	$15,400	$14,900	$14,706	$14,434	$14,480

[a]From figure 12.3

average rate of inventory usage. To illustrate how the order point is set, consider the previous situation, with annual usage equal to 5,000 units and an EOQ of 300 units. Assuming that there are fifty productive weeks in a year, the weekly usage of this item is 100 units per week (5,000 units ÷ 50 weeks). By examining records of prior purchases, it is determined that there is an average lead time of two weeks for the delivery of this item. Therefore, if there is no requirement for safety stock, the order point is set at 200 units (2 weeks × 100 units per week). As inventory declines, a purchase requisition is initiated when the quantity on hand reaches 200 units. Inventory continues to decline for the next two weeks while the order is processed and goods are in transit. The inventory level finally reaches zero just as the new order is received. However, if the order is delayed for some reason or if there is an unexpectedly high usage for this item, a stockout situation will exist until the order is received. Therefore, management may decide that one week's supply of this item should be maintained as *safety stock* to protect against stockouts. This would increase the order point to 300 units (1 + 2 = 3 weeks × 100 units per week). The relationships among lead time, safety stock, and inventory usage are illustrated in figure 12.5.

In figure 12.5 it is assumed that 400 units are on hand at the beginning of the inventory cycle. Inventory declines from that point to the order point, 300 units, by the end of the first week of operations, and an order is placed. The order is received in two weeks as expected, the total inventory quantity is restored to its beginning level, and the cycle starts over. The layer of safety stock provides a one-week cushion for delayed orders or other unexpected usage of this item.

Several observations should be noted about EOQ. First, with only slight modification, the EOQ formula and procedures are equally appropriate in computing the optimum size of a production run. The formula used to obtain an EOQ for a production run is as follows:

$$EOQ = \sqrt{\frac{2RS}{C}}$$

where
R = Total production requirements for one period
S = Setup costs for a production run (adjust machines, etc.)
C = Cost of carrying one unit of inventory for one period

Second, EOQ is based on the assumption that usage or demand for materials or products is uniform through time, as shown by the straight lines in figure 12.5. However, seasonal factors or lumpy demand are common in many product situations and require materials management to go beyond EOQ calculations to answer questions about when and how much to purchase. This is when materials management becomes even more complex and when computer technology is required for proper control.

Finally, many companies are discovering that in the current era of high technology manufacturing, the cost of carrying inventories has increased dramatically. Most of these increases are associated with intangible costs or costs that were considered insignificant in traditional manufacturing environments. For example, some of the costs of holding larger inventories result from longer lead times, poorer due-date performance, slower response to needed engineering changes, poorer quality, and obsolescence.

Some retailers have long recognized the magnitude of inventory carrying costs in their unique situations and have adjusted their purchasing practices accordingly. For example, retailers of meat, produce, and other perishable goods have very high holding costs because of spoilage and, as a result, make frequent (daily) purchases of goods. Some manufacturers of electronic components, automobiles, and toys have recognized the effect of increased carrying costs and have also altered their purchasing practices.

FIGURE 12.5

Rate of Usage, Lead Time, and Order Point

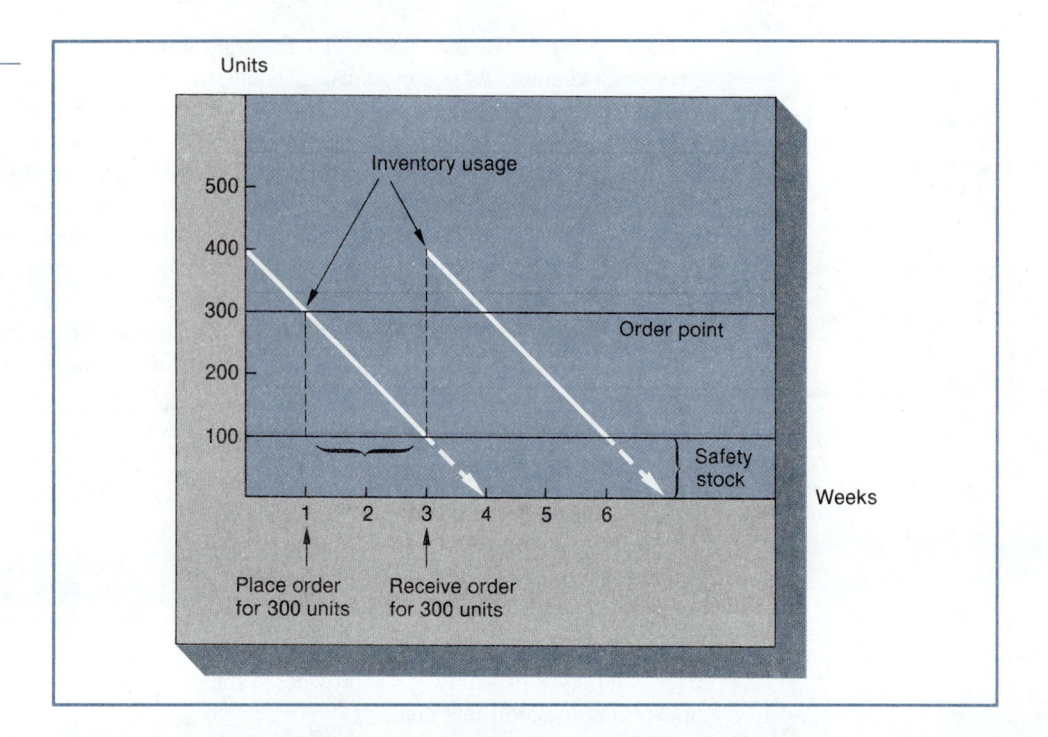

In addition, companies operating in just-in-time (JIT) environments typically have long-term purchase agreements with a few select vendors. The effect of these agreements is to reduce ordering costs that are included in the EOQ formula. The combined effect of increased carrying costs and reduced ordering costs is a reduction in EOQ, as illustrated in Figure 12.6. This is one reason companies in JIT environments use small order sizes for purchasing and small lot sizes for manufacturing.

Material Requirements Planning (MRP) and Manufacturing Resource Planning (MRP II)

Material requirements planning (MRP) in its simplest form is a system for developing a plan to purchase materials. The system works backwards, starting with the development of a production schedule that meets the demand for finished goods. From this schedule the amount and timing of purchases for raw materials are determined. MRP answers questions about when and how much to order in a more accurate way than when EOQ and an order point based on lead time and safety stock is used. However, the complexity of MRP also requires a computer to operate the system in a realistic time frame.

The basic MRP approach consists of determining (a) what is to be produced, (b) what raw materials are required to produce it, (c) what raw materials are on hand, and (d) what raw materials need to be purchased. The basic MRP system uses a bill of materials that contains an "explosion"—a detailed listing of each raw material and subcomponent that is included in each type of finished product. By combining materials requirements from bills of materials for all products to be made during an accounting period and comparing that with the current status of raw materials and work-in-process inventories, it is possible to develop a plan for ordering materials.

Over a period of years the basic MRP concept has evolved to the point where it has become a comprehensive manufacturing resource planning (MRP II) system. The first stage

FIGURE 12.6

Economic Order Quantity (EOQ)—With Cost Shifts

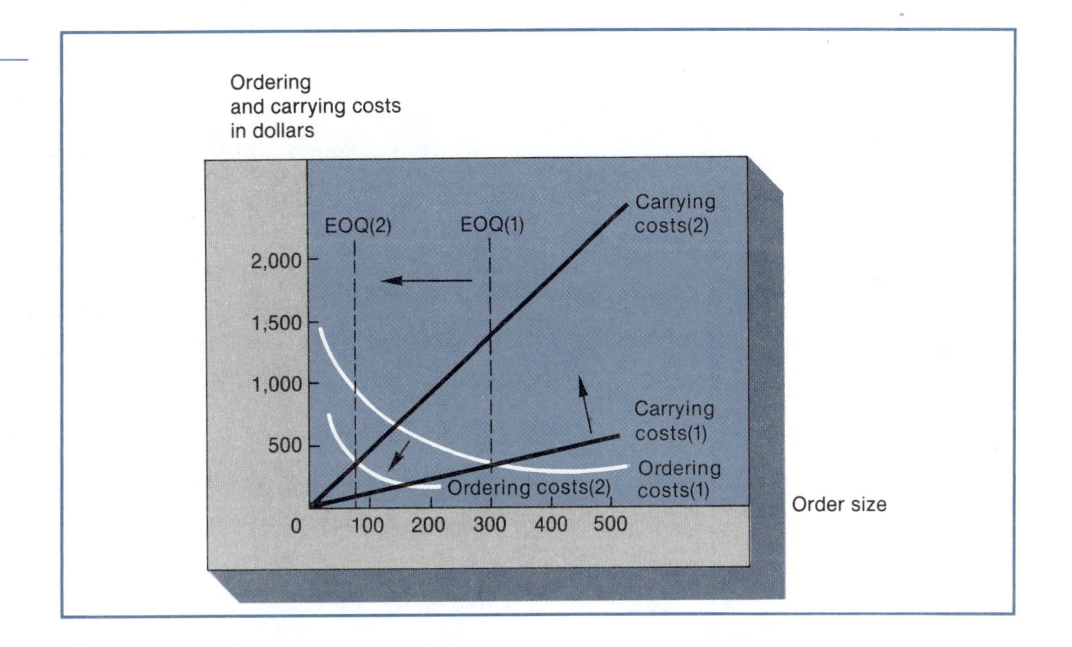

of evolution involved the addition of "need dates" and scheduling to the system; that is, elements were added to the basic MRP concept concerning (a) when the goods need to be delivered and (b) what production schedule is required to meet the need dates. As a result, MRP became both a plan for ordering materials and a master production schedule.

The next step in the evolution of MRP was the addition of capacity planning to materials requirements planning and scheduling. It is useful to know what materials are needed and when, but if plant capacity is not available, the materials cannot be utilized and should not be purchased. The most recent step in MRP's evolution has been the inclusion of overall business planning along with the other components. MRP II is intended to help management give overall guidance to the operation of a manufacturing company. Figure 12.7 presents a graphic view of the components in an MRP II system.

A refinement to MRP II is a system called OPT (Optimized Production Technology), which is intended to help with the management of constrained resources or bottlenecks. MRP II considers the effect of constraints on the manufacturing process, but OPT helps synchronize operations to achieve maximum throughput from the total manufacturing process. Additional detail about the operation of MRP or OPT is beyond the scope of this text; suggested readings at the end of this chapter describe each of these systems in detail.

It is important for cost accountants to understand systems such as MRP and OPT for several reasons. First, cost accountants should be intimately involved with the design and operation of such systems because they provide much of the basic data and cost functions used in the systems' operation. For example, engineers and accountants typically provide the basic data for the bill of materials in MRP; engineers provide the parts explosion (itemized listing of required parts and raw materials) and accountants provide the cost data. Also, accountants provide a host of cost factors for the operation of such systems, such as the costs of holding inventory, of downtime, and of acquiring additional plant capacity. Accountants are probably the source of most of the production statistics used for planning and control purposes within the cost accounting function. The reliability and usefulness of systems such as the MRP model depend on the information inputs to the system.

FIGURE 12.7

Components of an MRP II System

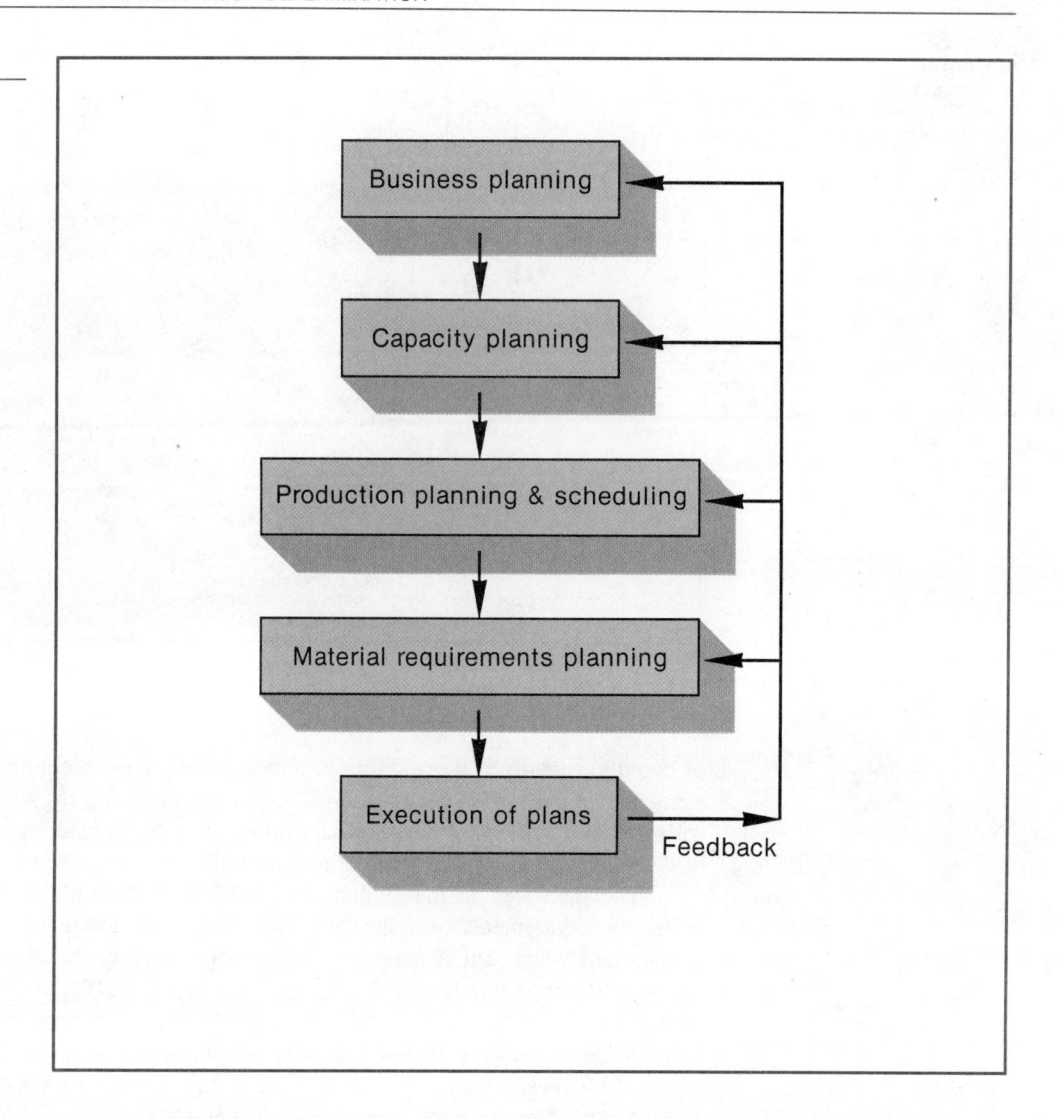

[Figure: Flowchart showing Business planning → Capacity planning → Production planning & scheduling → Material requirements planning → Execution of plans, with Feedback arrows returning to each prior stage]

Just-in-Time

Just-in-time (JIT) is a manufacturing philosophy that promotes the simplest, least costly means of production. The ideal production system is one that produces:

- only what customers want
- at the rate of customer demand
- with perfect quality
- with no unnecessary lead time
- with no waste
- with zero idle inventory.

Producing only what the customers want and at the rate of customer demand means making each day only what is needed—nothing more. It also means that production facilities have the flexibility to switch quickly from one product to another and to economically run large or small lot sizes as required. Perfect quality means no rework, no overproduction to allow for defective units, and no damage in handling or in transit. No unnecessary lead time means that no inventory just sits and that equipment operates only for productive purposes. No waste means that all material is converted to product and that there are no errors or defective units to rework. Finally, zero idle inventory means that raw materials and finished-goods inventories are eliminated. Work-in-process inventories are minimized so that there is zero idle inventory except just before capacity-constrained or bottleneck operations.

JIT is an ideal not attainable in most situations, but the ideal provides a goal for continual improvements in production systems. Companies that ascribe to the JIT philosophy have found that significant progress can be made toward the ideal by focusing on two primary areas: managing and minimizing inventories, and striving for total quality control (TQC) in manufacturing operations.

Managing and minimizing inventories relates to the JIT philosophy that inventory is an "evil" that should be eliminated if at all possible. Eliminating inventories is thought to be synonymous with removing a security blanket that covers up operating problems in the production system. For example, backup inventories may be justified as insurance against unexpected delays or shortages when, in fact, they may simply shield poor planning and control. It is believed that efforts to reduce inventories uncover production problems so that corrective action can be taken to move the company closer to the ideal production system. Because of this strong emphasis on controlling inventories, JIT is sometimes mistakenly thought of as simply another program to reduce the size of investment in inventories to increase return on investment (ROI); it is, in fact, much more.

When using JIT techniques, goods are produced only on a "demand pull" or synchronized basis; that is, finished goods are produced just in time to be sold, subcomponents are produced just in time to be assembled into finished goods, and raw materials are purchased just in time to be transformed into subassemblies. The overall volume of production is geared to customer demand. The rate of production for individual departments is determined by the needs of each succeeding department, working backwards from the final process to the first process. Inventory buffers with predetermined maximum sizes are used between departments to signal when a department should be working. The general rule is that when the inventory buffer ahead of a department is empty, the department should work; when the inventory buffer ahead of a department is filled, the department should stop work. In this way excess work-in-process inventories are eliminated.

Raw materials are delivered just in time with a guaranteed high level of quality so that they can bypass inspection and temporary storage and go directly to the production line. Thus raw-materials inventories are reduced or eliminated. The delivery of high-quality goods in the exact quantity ordered at the right time requires tight coordination of purchasing and production. A special relationship typically exists between JIT companies and their vendors. JIT usually leads to long-term purchase agreements between the company and a few selected vendors, in contrast to the company making periodic purchases from a large number of vendors. One of the benefits of this shift in purchasing practice is to substantially reduce the cost of purchase requisitions, purchase orders, receiving reports, and many other purchase-order costs.

Striving for total quality control (TQC) with JIT has two key elements: involving all employees in quality control, and stopping the production process whenever something goes wrong. Employee involvement is essential for quality control in a JIT environment. Production processes are so tightly synchronized that when something goes wrong, it becomes immediately apparent to workers on the production line, who must then act as part of a total company team to identify and solve the problem. Without employee involvement in a TQC effort, it is doubtful if JIT can work effectively.

Whenever defective parts are discovered or materials or parts are absent in a JIT environment, production stops until the problem is remedied *and* steps are taken to avoid the same problem in the future. This practice emphasizes the high cost of defective units and poor inventory management. In a JIT environment, defective units are not simply treated as a problem for which someone must be found to blame; they are treated as signposts or signals to be studied so that management can learn from them how to refine the production process to come closer to the ideal.

Benefits of JIT and TQC are both tangible and intangible. The tangible benefits include the following:

1. Lower inventory handling and carrying costs

   - less investment in inventories
   - less warehouse and factory space
   - less risk of obsolesence and spoilage

2. Lower manufacturing costs

   - less scrap and rework
   - less paperwork
   - improved quality
   - more quantity discounts because of buying from fewer vendors

Substantial intangible benefits come from a JIT environment because of the company's ability to be more responsive to the marketplace. There are virtually no inventories to be cleared through the system before changes can be implemented. For example, a company may want to initiate an engineering change that will significantly improve the function of a particular product. However, if the company must wait two months for current work-in-process and finished-goods inventories to be processed and sold before the change can affect current sales, the competitive advantage may be lost to a JIT company that can respond in two weeks.

Another intangible benefit relates to quality control. If work-in-process inventories are low when defective work is discovered, *(a)* there are fewer potentially defective units already produced, *(b)* the process with a problem can be fixed before additional units are placed in production, and *(c)* because immediate attention is given to the problem's solution, it is probable that the cause can be found and fixed quickly. This situation is much different than finding a defect in production after an entire batch has been processed and after the opportunity has been lost for quickly identifying the problem and minimizing its effect on production.

Other claimed benefits of JIT when compared with traditional inventory management systems include: the ability to earn higher margins because less overtime premium is paid; a lower investment in plant assets per unit of production because facilities are used more effectively; better due-date performance because production is more reliable; and shorter lead times because of better scheduling.

LABOR COSTING

The cost of labor includes more than the amounts computed for each employee on an hourly or piece-work basis. There are numerous additional labor-related costs, including payroll taxes, pension contributions, hospitalization insurance, bonuses, and vacation pay, just to mention a few. Because payments to employees take many forms, it is important that these costs are properly accumulated and matched with the appropriate period and production of that period. There are three general categories of labor costs—labor benefits, fringe benefits, and employer taxes.

Labor benefits include wages, salaries, and compensation from incentive plans. Wages represent payments based on hourly or piece rates; salaries are fixed periodic payments made to employees; and incentive compensation is based on employee performance that exceeds predetermined goals or standards. These types of labor costs are distinguished from fringe-benefit costs in that fringe benefits are generally paid indirectly to employees. However, the cost of fringe benefits is a component of total labor costs and represents a significant cost of doing business. Examples of fringe benefits include holiday pay for certain days during the year, vacation pay for a specific number of days off each year based on the employee's tenure, and retirement pay set aside for future pension payments. Also included as fringe benefit costs are the costs of various stock and thrift plans in which employees are allowed to buy company stock at favorable prices or borrow company funds at favorable interest rates.

Employer payroll taxes include social security (FICA) and unemployment taxes. The employer must pay an amount equal to the FICA taxes withheld from employees. Unemployment taxes are levied by state and federal governments to provide unemployment compensation to workers who are laid off.

Since our purpose here is to present the unique cost accounting aspects of labor costs in manufacturing operations, the financial accounting aspects of payroll accounting are greatly simplified. The examples of payroll in this text do not include the detail work of paying different payrolls at different times for numerous individual employees.

There are two general sets of journal entries required to account for labor costs. The first set records the cost and payment of labor benefits, including salaries, wages, and incentive plans. The debit side of the journal entry, which is most important for cost accounting purposes, contains the distribution of labor costs among various cost categories that represent the purposes for which labor costs were incurred. These categories and accounts include work in process for the cost of direct labor, factory overhead for the cost of indirect labor, marketing expense for the cost of marketing labor, and administrative expense for the cost of administrative labor. The credit side of the journal entries to record labor costs contains the liability to employees for net earnings plus all other liabilities related to payroll withholding. For example, the first set of journal entries records the cost and payment of payroll as follows:

Work-in-process inventory	4,600	
Factory overhead	1,400	
Marketing expense	800	
Administrative expense	1,000	
FICA tax payable		470
Federal income tax payable		1,800
State income tax payable		400
Union dues payable		250
Medical insurance payable		360
Payroll payable		4,520
Payroll payable	4,520	
Cash		4,520

The second set of journal entries records the cost and payment of the employer's payroll expenses arising from FICA and federal and state unemployment taxes. Payroll expenses applicable to direct labor should be assigned to work in process, and payroll expenses applicable to indirect labor should be assigned to factory overhead. Payroll expenses applicable to selling and administrative labor should be assigned to their respective expense accounts, as follows:

Work-in-process inventory	432	
Factory overhead	134	
Marketing expense	76	
Administrative expense	94	
FICA tax payable		470
State unemployment tax payable		234
Federal unemployment tax payable		32

This is generally recognized as the correct approach. However, because of the extra effort involved in distinguishing between payroll expenses for direct versus indirect labor, some employers accumulate payroll taxes for *all* factory personnel in the factory overhead account. When this procedure is followed, an estimate of total payroll expenses is included in the overhead application rate.

For simplicity, the basic payroll journal entries illustrated previously do not contain provisions for vacation, overtime, or other similar types of pay. Accounting for vacation pay is illustrative of benefits that are earned throughout the year but that are usually paid only once during the year. To insure that vacation pay, for example, is spread over the entire year and is not recognized in total in the period when it is paid, special accrual procedures must be followed. The procedure most widely used is to include an estimate of vacation pay as part of the factory overhead application rate and to charge the actual cost of vacation pay to the factory overhead account as part of the regular payment of payroll.

To illustrate, assume that a factory employee earns $50 a day and in addition receives ten working days of paid vacation as part of the employment agreement. The $500 cost of vacation pay (10 days × $50 per day) should be spread over the entire year and not totally recognized in the payroll period when it is actually paid. To accomplish this, a portion of the total cost is recognized in each pay period. For simplicity, it is assumed that there are fifty pay periods in a year with five working days in each period. The following journal entry is made each pay period for this employee:

Work-in-process inventory (5 days × $50 per day)	250	
Factory overhead ($500 ÷ 50 pay periods)	10	
Accrued vacation pay		10
Payroll and withholdings payable		250

The debit to the factory overhead account recognizes that part of total vacation pay is applicable to the current period. Similar entries made for all employees each pay period result in total vacation pay being recognized in the appropriate periods during the year.

When an employee actually takes the vacation and vacation pay is made, the following journal entries are prepared:

Accrued vacation pay	500	
Withholdings payable		205
Payroll payable		295
Payroll payable	295	
Cash		295

Notice that rather than debiting an expense account when vacation pay is paid, the accrued vacation pay account is debited. The debit in the previous journal entry to factory overhead records the actual cost of vacation pay.

Overtime pay is required for most workers engaged in interstate commerce who work more than forty hours per week. When overtime is paid, gross earnings are divided into two parts—regular earnings and an overtime premium. The overtime premium is found by multiplying the overtime hours by the overtime rate. If the overtime premium occurred because of specific job requirements, the overtime cost should be assigned to the specific jobs. However, when overtime cannot be attributed to specific jobs because of general factory conditions, it should be charged to the factory overhead account.

LABOR CONTROL AND LEARNING CURVES

Effective control over labor and labor-related costs is achieved through *(a)* planning of production requirements, *(b)* use of labor time and wage standards, *(c)* labor performance reports, and *(d)* appropriate payment for labor. Accountants share responsibility with management for all aspects of labor control.

General procedures typically used to account for labor costs are discussed in appendix 12.2 of this chapter. Learning curves as they are used to plan and control labor costs are discussed in this section.

The debit to the factory overhead account recognizes that part of total vacation pay is applicable to the current period. Similar entries made for all emplooyees each pay period result in total vacation pay being recognized in the appropriate periods during the year.

When an employee actually takes the vacation and vacation pay is made, the following journal entries are prepared:

Accrued vacation pay	500	
Withholdings payable		205
Payroll payable		295
Payroll payable	294	
Cash		295

Learning Curves

Learning curves are important for planning and controlling labor costs because they provide a mechanism for predicting the labor time required to perform repetitive production work. Learning curves are based on the observed fact that as workers gain experience in performing tasks, they become more proficient and take less time to complete the same task. Case studies have found a predictable relationship between the number of times repetitive work is performed and the rate of learning that takes place.

The rate of learning and the related improvement in job performance is so regular that labor requirements, budget allowances, performance standards, and cost estimates can be made with a high degree of accuracy. A **learning curve** is the graphic (mathematical) representation of the relationship between labor time and production quantity. It shows that when new products or processes are begun, learning also begins. Thereafter, efficiency improves in a nonlinear manner until learning is essentially complete and a "steady state" prevails. Figure 12.8 illustrates a learning curve sometimes called an experience or improvement curve.

In more precise terms, a learning curve illustrates a time and cost relationship: as *cumulative* production increases, the *average* time and cost per unit systematically decline. Case studies reveal that each time the cumulative quantity of production is doubled, the cumulative average hours per unit are reduced by a constant percentage. The mathematics of a learning curve are given in appendix 12.2 at the end of this chapter.

Learning curve percentages typically range from 60 percent to 90 percent. For example, an 80-percent learning curve indicates that doubling output will result in the cumulative average per-unit time of production being 80 percent of the previous cumulative average time.

To illustrate the learning curve, assume that it takes 50 labor hours to produce the first 2 units of a particular product. This results in a cumulative average of 25 hours per unit produced (50 cumulative hours ÷ 2 units of production). If another batch of 2 units is produced (a doubling of production), it is expected that the cumulative average hours of production for the 4 units will be 80 percent of 25 hours, or 20 hours. Therefore, total production time for the total of 4 units is expected to be 80 hours (20 hours average per

FIGURE 12.8

Learning Curve

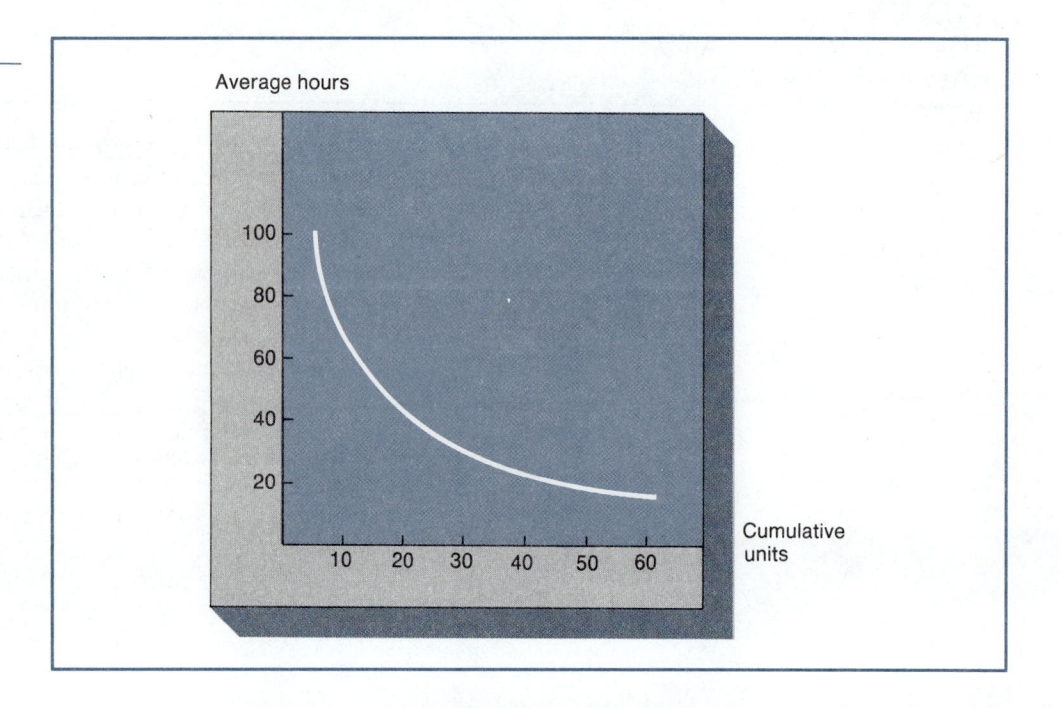

unit × 4 units). The following schedule shows the relationship between the number of items produced, the cumulative average hours, and the total hours, using an 80-percent learning curve:

Cumulative Number of Units	Cumulative Average Hours	Total Hours
2	25	50 (2 × 25)
4	20 (0.8 × 25)	80 (4 × 20)
8	16 (0.8 × 20)	128 (8 × 16)

The value in the learning curve theory is that if still another batch of 4 units (another doubling of output to a total of 8 units) is contemplated, it is possible to accurately predict the additional labor requirement with surprising accuracy. For example, if the company is submitting a competitive bid for the manufacture of these items, it may be very important to predict the learning curve effects so that an appropriately low bid can be submitted. This can be done quite easily. If output is doubled, the cumulative average hours required should be 80 percent of the prior cumulative average. In this instance, 16 hours (0.80 × 20 hours) are the cumulative average hours expected to produce the total of 8 units. Therefore, total production time for the 8 units is estimated to be 128 hours (16 hours cumulative average × 8 units). Since total production time for the first 4 units is 80 hours and the total time for 8 units is expected to be 128 hours, the time required on the last 4 units is 48 hours (128 hours for 8 units − 80 hours for 4 units). If the effect of learning had been ignored, the predicted labor requirement would probably have been much higher and the company may have lost the bid.

Learning curves can be applied to labor-related costs as well as to labor hours. Costs such as overhead, waste, and spoilage may vary in proportion to labor hours and be predicted with learning curves, but costs such as taxes, insurance, and management salaries may not be predictable with learning curves. To illustrate, assume that a company produced a prototype aircraft costing $1.8 million. A total of $1.0 million is considered to be labor-related costs. The company receives an order for 16 of these aircraft, including the prototype. What are the total expected labor-related costs for this order, assuming a 90-percent learning curve?

Number of Aircraft	Cumulative Average Costs
1	$1,000,000
2	900,000 (0.9 × $1,000,000)
4	810,000 (0.9 × $ 900,000)
8	729,000 (0.9 × $ 810,000)
16	656,100 (0.9 × $ 729,000)

The total labor-related costs for 16 aircraft equal $10,497,600 (16 aircraft × $656,100 average cost per aircraft). This is almost $6 million less than if no learning is assumed in building the aircraft.

When learning is substantially complete a *steady state* is achieved. The average cost per unit during the last increment before the steady state is achieved is typically used for budgeting future production.

SUMMARY

Materials typically represent a substantial capital investment and make up a large percentage of the cost of production. Therefore, it is important that they are properly costed and carefully controlled. The accounting department has primary responsibility for cost determination, including assigning costs to materials purchased, maintaining records of the internal flow of materials-related costs, and assigning costs to materials used.

There are two primary questions relating to the costing of materials—what costs should be included as part of the cost of materials received, and what costs should be assigned to materials issued? The purchase price is included as a cost of materials, but purchase discounts are not. In addition, the costs of freight, receiving, inspection, storage, insurance, and similar acquisition costs should also be considered as costs of materials. The difficulty in accounting for these materials-acquisition costs is finding an economical method for assigning them to individual items purchased. Rather than following some tedious procedure of direct assignment to individual items, acquisition and handling costs usually are allocated to materials inventory using some predetermined application rate.

The question of what costs to assign to materials issued is answered in the selection of an inventory cost flow assumption. Three basic assumptions are available—first-in, first-out (FIFO), last-in, first-out (LIFO), and average cost.

Additional costing and control problems arise from the need to account for defective units, scrap, and waste. The general rule for product costing is that the cost of direct materials includes the costs of scrap, waste, and normally anticipated spoilage that occur in the ordinary course of production activities. Unanticipated or abnormal amounts of scrap, waste, and spoilage should be expensed in the period incurred or, in some situations, may be included in factory overhead.

There are several different methods used to control inventories. The two-bin system is a mechanical method used with small inventories, whereas the ABC method helps in the control of very large inventories. The economic order quantity (EOQ) model helps determine the most cost-effective size of inventory orders. Materials requirements planning (MRP) and manufacturing resource planning (MRP II) help coordinate inventory control with overall manufacturing activities. Just-in-time (JIT) is a manufacturing philosophy that advocates zero inventories as the ideal situation.

Labor costs also represent a substantial portion of the cost of production. Labor costs include not only wages and salaries but also various payroll and fringe benefit costs. The accounting department cooperates with personnel, timekeeping, and production departments to insure that labor is properly authorized, paid, assigned to production, and reported for management review. The details of payroll accounting are primarily financial accounting functions; however, the costing and control of the labor component of production is a major concern of the cost accountant.

Finally, learning curves have been developed from results of numerous case studies to explain the relationship between the number of times repetitive work is performed and the rate at which learning takes place. The rate of learning and improvement are so predictable that labor budgets, standards, and cost estimates can be made with a high degree of accuracy using learning curves.

APPENDIX 12.1 Materials Control Procedures

The following are general procedures typically used to purchase, maintain, and issue materials.

Purchasing Materials

Procedures for acquiring materials should be established with the following objectives in mind. First, materials should be purchased only when a need exists. Second, materials of the desired quality should be purchased at the most favorable price. Third, payment for materials should be approved only on materials received and in good condition. Finally, someone should be responsible for physically safeguarding materials from the time of receipt. To accomplish these objectives, the organization should provide a clear description of responsibilities and an accounting system with built-in checks and balances. Typically, five organizational functions are involved in the materials acquisition cycle—stores, purchasing, receiving, and accounting. Figure 12.9 outlines the relationships and functions of these organizational areas.

The purchasing cycle typically begins with a *purchase requisition,* which is usually initiated in the stores department. The need to order materials usually results from a physical check or a computer system that is programmed to indicate that the quantity of materials on hand is at the reordering minimum. Other purchase requests may come from engineering, research, or other departments when there are special needs for nonproduction materials. Also, requests may come from job managers and supervisors who foresee unusual quantity demands. In any event, all acquisition requests should be processed through one department such as the stores department, with purchase requisitions approved by various department heads providing initial authorization for purchases.

The materials requisition contains descriptions, quantities, stock numbers, and other necessary purchasing information. It is sent to the purchasing department, where the actual ordering takes place. The stores department keeps a copy of the purchase requisition to verify, at a later date, that all purchase requests have been processed and that materials have been received. The purchasing department then prepares a *purchase order,* which is a written authorization, to a vendor to supply materials. A purchase order should be issued for every materials acquisition, even if the order is placed by telephone or with a sales representative. The purchase order is a prenumbered document that contains a complete description of items ordered, prices, terms, shipping instructions, required delivery dates, and other information needed to identify materials of the desired specifications and quality.

The original purchase order is sent to the vendor. Additional copies are generated and distributed internally for control purposes. For example, a copy is usually supplied to the originator of the purchase requisition as evidence that a purchase order has been pro-

FIGURE 12.9

Materials Purchasing Procedures

Stores	Purchasing	Receiving	Accounting
Initiates purchase requisition	Prepares purchase order	Verifies materials received	Receives vendor's invoice
Verifies purchase orders		Verifies receiving	Compares data, verifies liability, and approves payment
Verifies receiving		Prepares receiving report	
Maintains and issues materials		Transfers materials to stores	

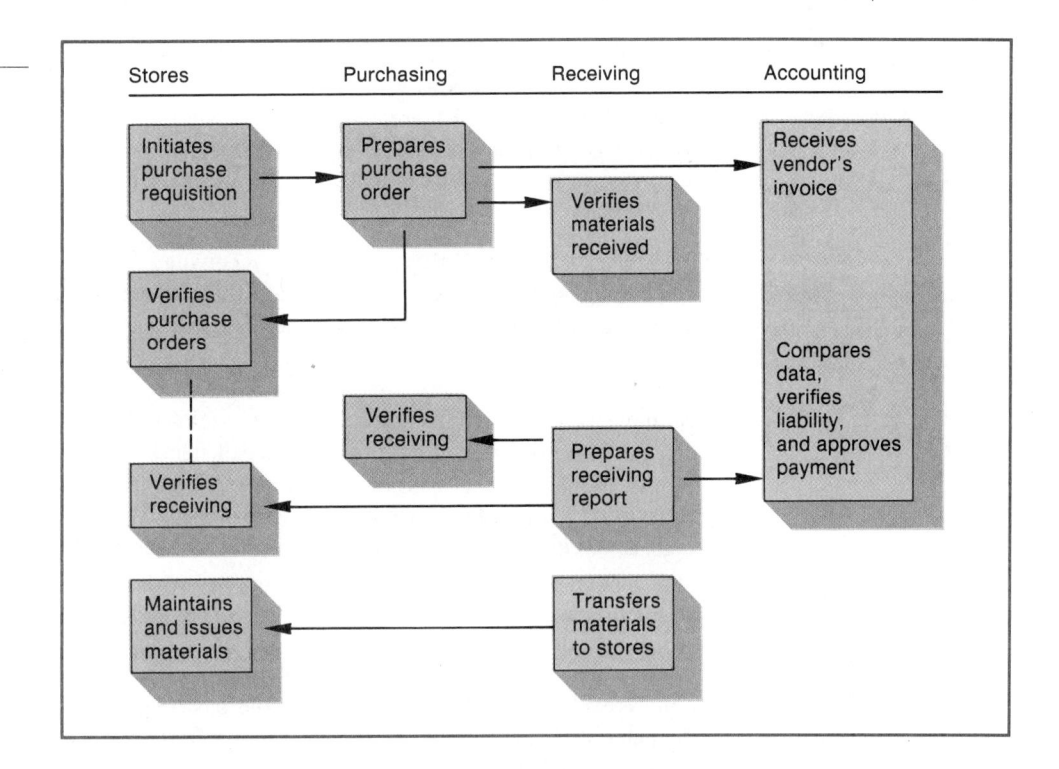

cessed and as a cross-check on the accuracy of information. The receiving and accounting department also receive copies in anticipation of their role when materials are received and payment is made. Finally, the purchasing department keeps a copy to verify, at a later date, that all items ordered have been received.

Upon receipt of materials, the receiving department prepares a *receiving report,* which details what items were actually received and indicates if any damage occurred in transit. Bills of lading, packing lists, and a copy of the original purchase order are attached to the receiving report to be used for cross-checking and as support for transportation or other acquisition costs to be paid.

The receiving department keeps a copy of the receiving report and sends all primary documents to the accounting department, where they are matched with the vendor's invoice. A copy of the receiving report is also sent to the purchasing department to verify that materials ordered have been received. If all items on a purchase order are not received, there should be follow-up by the receiving department to determine if the purchase order should be kept open, anticipating that the remainder of the order will be received, or if it should be cancelled. If cancelled, a new purchase order may need to be executed with the same or another vendor who can and will supply the needed materials. A copy of the receiving information is also sent with the materials to the stores department. Sometimes the copy sent to accounting is first sent with the materials to stores to verify the transfer of goods from receiving to stores. The receiving information is used to update inventory records.

The accounting department assembles a copy of the purchase order, the receiving report, and the vendor's invoice. It compares prices, terms, and quantities and checks for arithmetic accuracy. If materials have been received as ordered, the invoice is approved for payment, and the finance department issues a check.

The size of the company or the type of business may result in more extensive or modified purchasing procedures. For example, some hardware wholesalers perform only cursory counts in the receiving department, because the cost of detailed counts (such as counting each nut and bolt) would be unreasonably expensive. Occasional check counts of important items as well as reliance on the basic integrity of vendors and the firm's own accounting system is usually the most cost effective approach.

Maintaining and Issuing Materials

The stores department is responsible for receiving, safeguarding, handling, issuing, and maintaining appropriate accounting records for materials. Materials are typically safeguarded by designating individuals to be responsible for them, by using secured areas for storage, and by issuing materials only to authorized persons for authorized purposes. The primary accounting concern relates to the record keeping that should accompany the physical movement of materials. As materials are delivered to the stores department, inventory records should be updated with the quantity of items and the date received. Records in the form of bin cards, ledger sheets, or computer files are typically maintained for each individual item if a perpetual inventory system is used. Materials are issued based on a *materials requisition,* which is an authorized order to issue or deliver materials for a particular purpose or job. The completed materials requisition has two purposes. First, it is the basis for accumulating the cost of materials charged to work-in-process inventory. When materials are issued for maintenance or other general factory usage, the materials requisition is the basis for charges to the actual factory overhead account. Second, the materials requisition, as well as the receiving report, is the basis for maintaining physical accountability for materials in inventory. A copy of the materials requisition is sent to the accounting department for recording of costs.

APPENDIX 12.2 *Labor Control Procedures*

The following are general procedures typically used to handle payroll processing.

Payroll procedures for controlling labor costs should insure that *(a)* persons are authorized to work, *(b)* persons receiving wages have performed services, and *(c)* persons employed have worked efficiently. Just as for materials, the organization should provide a clear description of payroll responsibilities and an accounting system with built-in checks and balances. Typically, five organizational functions are involved in payroll accounting—personnel, timekeeping, production, payroll, and accounting. Figure 12.10 outlines the relationships and functions of these organizational areas.

In situations in which employees work on an hourly or piece-work basis, payroll procedures typically begin in the personnel department with the hiring of workers and the establishment of pay rates. The personnel department acts in close cooperation with the production departments to provide a number of employee services. From an accounting control viewpoint, the personnel department also acts as a check on the authorization and the granting of appropriate pay rates.

Direct supervision and timekeeping are the responsibility of individual production departments. The payroll cycle actually begins in the production department with the preparation of a *time* or *clock card*. The time card provides for the identification of each individual employee, the amount of time worked each payroll period, and an indication of time off or overtime. Time cards should be reviewed and authorized by production department supervisors before they are sent to the timekeeping department for subsequent processing. Also, either as part of the time card or on a separate *job ticket,* work performed on specific jobs or production runs is normally recorded by each employee.

FIGURE 12.10 Payroll Procedures

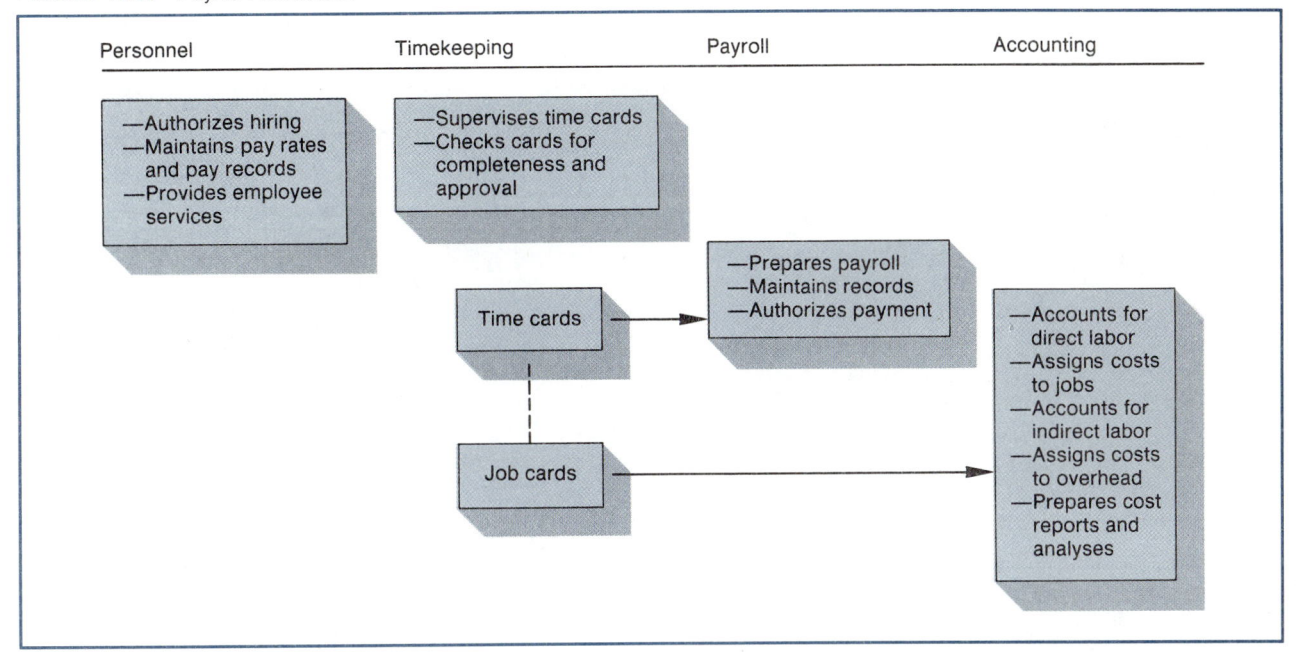

Personnel	Timekeeping	Payroll	Accounting
—Authorizes hiring —Maintains pay rates and pay records —Provides employee services	—Supervises time cards —Checks cards for completeness and approval	—Prepares payroll —Maintains records —Authorizes payment	—Accounts for direct labor —Assigns costs to jobs —Accounts for indirect labor —Assigns costs to overhead —Prepares cost reports and analyses

Time cards → Payroll
Job cards → Accounting

Authorized time cards are sent to the timekeeping department, which typically performs two main functions. First, using the time card as its data source, total hours worked by each employee are accumulated so that earnings can be calculated by the payroll department. Second, timekeeping usually accumulates labor hours by job to facilitate distribution of costs to individual jobs (direct labor) or to factory overhead (indirect labor) by the cost accounting department. In large operations the timekeeping function is best handled by specially trained personnel in a separate organizational function. In some cases, however, the employee performs the timekeeping function.

Time card data are periodically transmitted to the payroll department, where the detailed work of payroll and check preparation takes place. The payroll department computes gross and net pay for each worker, computes the total payroll, and maintains individual earnings records. Payroll payments are usually made by check.

The results of payroll computations are then transmitted in the form of a payroll distribution report to the cost accounting department, where individual jobs, products, processes, or departments are charged with labor costs. Cost accounting is also responsible for reconciling job cost data with payroll data as a check on the integrity of the payroll system.

APPENDIX 12.3 *The Mathematics of the Economic Order Quantity and Learning Curve*

Economic Order Quantity

The determination of economic order quantity is based on ordering, carrying, and total costs expressed as follows:

$$\text{Ordering costs} = O\frac{R}{Q}$$

$$\text{Carrying costs} = C\frac{Q}{2}$$

$$\text{Total costs} = O\frac{R}{Q} + C\frac{Q}{2}$$

where
R = Total materials requirements for one period
O = Cost of placing an order
C = Cost of carrying one unit of inventory for one period
Q = Order size (in units)

Using calculus to find the minimum total, the total costs function is differentiated with respect to Q and set equal to zero, as follows:

$$\frac{dTC}{dQ} = \frac{-OR}{Q^2} + \frac{C}{2} = 0$$

Solving for Q yields:

$$Q = \sqrt{\frac{2RO}{C}} = \text{Economic order quantity (EOQ)}.$$

The EOQ formula is based on the following assumptions:

1. Demand is known with certainty.
2. Demand is continuous over time rather than discrete.
3. Lead time is known with certainty.
4. Lead time is constant.
5. Ordering costs and carrying costs are constant.
6. The system is never out of stock (stockout costs are infinite).

Learning Curve

A learning curve is expressed mathematically as follows:

$$Y = IX^b$$

where
X = Cumulative total units produced
I = Input quantity required to produce the first unit of output
r = Learning rate
b = Index of learning, $b = \dfrac{\log r}{\log 2}$

SELF-STUDY PROBLEMS

Economic Order Quantity (EOQ)

Lakewood Hardware Company has provided the following information about one of its products. Sales statistics indicate that usage is quite uniform, so average inventory is assumed to equal one-half of the order quantity.

Usage	400 units per month
Ordering costs	$18 per order
Inventory carrying costs	$0.50 per unit per month
Safety stock	150 units
Lead time	2 weeks

Required

Calculate the following:

1. Economic order quantity
2. Reorder point

Solution to the Self-Study Problem

Requirement 1

$$EOQ = \sqrt{\frac{2 \times 400 \times 18}{0.50}} = 170$$

Requirement 2

	Units
Usage during lead time	200
(400 units per month ÷ 2 weeks)	
Safety stock	150
Reorder point	350

Learning Curve

Alpha-Macro Company, specialists in machine manufacture and design, received an order for a unique type of materials handling machine. The customer presented blueprints and specifications and asked Alpha-Macro to prepare a bid for the manufacture of four machines. Alpha-Macro suggested that the total contract price be postponed until after the first machine was built and that the final price include (a) the cost of materials, (b) labor and labor-related overhead costs based on an 80-percent learning curve, and (c) a 40-percent markup on materials and labor costs.

The customer agreed, and the first machine was built with the following costs:

Materials	$10,000
Direct labor (500 hours × $12)	6,000
Labor-related overhead (500 × $8)	4,000
Total	$20,000

Required

Prepare a price quotation for the four machines based on the experience of making the first machine.

Solution to the Self-Study Problem

Number of Machines Produced	Cumulative Average Hours	Total Hours Worked
1	500	500
2	400 (0.8 × 500)	800 (2 × 400)
4	320 (0.8 × 400)	1,280 (4 × 320)

Therefore, the total hours required to manufacture four machines is predicted to be 1,280 (4 machines × 320 average hours per machine).

Price Quotation

Materials (4 × $10,000)	$40,000
Direct labor (1,280 hours × $12)	15,360
Labor-related overhead (1,280 hours × $8)	10,240
Total	$65,600
Markup (0.4 × $65,600)	26,240
Bid	$91,840

SUGGESTED READINGS

Backes, Robert W. "Cycle Counting: A Better Method of Achieving Accurate Inventory Records." *Management Accounting* 61 (January 1980): 42–46.

Deming, W. Edwards. *Quality, Productivity, and Competitive Position.* Cambridge, Mass. Massachusetts Institute of Technology, 1982.

Gillespie, Jackson F. "An Application of Learning Curves to Standard Costing." *Management Accounting* 63 (September 1981): 63–65.

Goldratt, Eliyahu M., and Fox, Robert E. *The Race.* Milford, Conn. Creative Output Inc., 1986.

Hall, Robert W. *Zero Inventories.* Homewood, Ill. Dow Jones-Irwin, 1983.

National Association of Accountants. *Cost Accounting for the 90s.* Montvale, N.J.: National Association of Accountants, 1986.

Wight, Oliver W. *MRP II: Unlocking America's Productivity Potential.* Williston, V.: Oliver Wight Limited Publications, Inc., 1981.

DISCUSSION QUESTIONS

Q12–1. Define *costing* and *control*. Explain the role of the accounting department in the costing and control of materials and labor.

Q12–2. What expenditure items should be included in the cost of materials purchased? What items are excluded from the cost of materials purchased?

Q12–3. What are the three basic cost flow assumptions used when accounting for materials issued? Describe the cost flows each assumes for costing purposes.

Q12–4. What is the major problem with assigning materials acquisition costs to units received? What accounting procedure is typically used to overcome this difficulty?

Q12–5. Define *spoilage, defective units, scrap,* and *waste*.

Q12–6. What are the general methods and considerations concerning accounting for normal versus abnormal spoilage?

Q12–7. Discuss the differences in accounting for detective units that are scrapped and defective units that are reworked.

Q12–8. Describe the general procedures used to account for the cost of defective and spoiled units if these costs are not attributable to any partiular job. How do these proce-

CHAPTER 12: MATERIALS AND LABOR: COSTING AND CONTROL

dures differ if defective and spoiled units are the result of exacting specifications on specific jobs?

Q12-9. Briefly describe economic order quantity, materials requirements planning, and just-in-time, and tell how each helps answer questions about when and how much to buy.

Q12-10. Define *lead time, reorder point,* and *safety stock.*

Q12-11. What are some of the costs of carrying inventory? What are some of the costs of not carrying enough inventory?

Q12-12. What expenditures are properly recorded as part of labor costs?

Q12-13. What special accounting treatment is given holiday and vacation pay? Why?

Q12-14. Some people think that payroll expenses on direct labor should be charged to work in process, whereas others charge payroll expenses to factory overhead. Give the theoretical and practical reasons for this difference.

Q12-15. What is the difference between the journal entry to record the payroll and the journal entry to record payroll expenses?

Q12-16. What is the basic theory behind the learning curve?

Q12-17. Describe how the learning curve might be used in *(a)* budgeting labor costs, *(b)* establishing standards for labor performance, or *(c)* bidding on specific jobs.

EXERCISES

E12-1. Journal Entries for Raw Materials Cressall Manufacturing Company uses a special type of finishing material called Plycor for some of its products. At the beginning of the month there were 1,000 sheets of Plycor on hand that had been purchased at a price of $5.00 per sheet. The company uses the FIFO method for inventory costing.

The following documents and information relate to the acquisition and use of Plycor during the month.

1. A receiving report shows that 100 sheets had been received at a cost of $5.00 per sheet.
2. Stores requisitions show the following: 200 pieces were issued for Job 137; 325 pieces were issued for Job 138; and 10 pieces were issued to fix defective work. The defective work is considered to be within normal limits. A scrap recovery report indicates that Plycor recovered from defective work had a net realizable value of $10.
3. A materials credit slip shows that 20 pieces were not used on Job 137 and were returned to inventory.
4. Cash receipts indicate that Plycor scrap was sold for its scrap value.
5. Inventory count sheets indicate that there were 500 sheets of Plycor on hand at the end of the month. Any shortage is considered abnormal.

Required

Prepare journal entries for the preceding Plycor transactions.

E12-2. Pricing Issues of Materials Lindon Company maintains perpetual inventory records for each of its raw materials. Information about one of these materials for the month of July is as follows:

Date	Action	Units	Per Unit	Total
July 1	Balance	2,000	$10.20	$20,400
July 3	Issue	1,900	?	?
July 10	Purchase	1,600	$10.40	16,640
July 15	Purchase	2,000	$10.60	21,200
July 28	Issue	3,000	?	?
July 31	Balance	700	?	?

Required

Calculate the values missing on the perpetual inventory card using each of the following cost flow assumptions: *(a)* FIFO; *(b)* LIFO; and *(c)* average cost. Average cost is based on beginning inventory plus purchases during the month.

E12–3. Spoiled Units
Garrison Components makes stereo products. Production lot number 85–38 calls for the manufacture of 2,800 cabinet speakers. These speakers have the following unit costs:

Direct materials	$ 39.20
Direct labor	34.40
Factory overhead (includes $2 allowance for spoiled work)	29.60
	$103.20

After completion of the lot, 140 speakers did not pass inspection (a normal amount). These speakers were sold for $31.20. Each cost element of the production phase has a separate work-in-process account.

Required

1. Make the journal entries necessary if the loss is considered a cost of all production.
2. Make the journal entries necessary if the loss is charged specifically to lot number 85–38.

E12–4. Defective Units
Biddie Company has received a special order for 50 custom water pumps. Because of the customization, spoilage is expected to exceed normal rates. The cost of materials for the pumps is $66 per unit; labor cost is $72 per unit; and factory overhead is applied at 100 percent of labor cost. During production, 7 units were found to be defective. These units were reworked with the following additional per-unit costs: materials, $5; labor, $9; and overhead, again applied at 100 percent of labor rate. Of the 50 units reaching completion, 3 were classified as not meeting the specifications of the client. These were sold separately for $175 each, which was credited to the special order. The client accepted the order as being complete with the delivery of 47 pumps.

Required

Determine the correct unit cost of the delivered pumps.

E12–5. EOQ Concepts and Procedures
The Fan-tas-tic Company produces a household cleanser. The principal chemical material used in the cleanser is purchased in gallon containers from the Pon Do Company. Fan-tas-tic has gathered the following data about the chemical material:

Annual requirement	4,000 gallons
Costs per gallon	$1.50
Administrative clerical costs	$1.30 for each purchase order
Stationery, postage, etc.	$1.00 for each purchase order
Insurance and inventory property taxes	$0.15 per gallon per year
Minimum desired return on inventory investment	10%

Required

1. Identify the total cost of placing each order and the total cost, in dollars, of carrying a gallon in inventory for the year.
2. Determine the economic order quantity, using the formula method.

E12–6. Basic EOQ Analysis The Nashville Company manufactures small electric power tools. It has assembled data that indicate a typical annual usage of 4,000 six-inch circular saw blades. Inventory carrying costs are estimated to be 10 percent of average inventory cost. Each saw blade costs $2. The cost to place a purchase order is $6.

Required

1. Using the formula method, determine the EOQ for saw blades.
2. Using the economic order quantity determined in requirement 1, determine how many orders Nashville will need to place each year.

E12–7. Payroll Entries The Aster Company has completed the computation of wages earned during the payroll period ending May 31. Summary information follows:

Factory wages	$52,500[a]
Administrative salaries	28,000
Marketing salaries	16,000
FICA tax rate	7.51%
Federal Income taxes	9,650
State unemployment tax rate	6.2%
Federal unemployment tax rate	0.8%
Credit union savings	1,200

[a]$40,000 direct labor

Required

1. Prepare journal entries to set up, pay, and distribute the payroll.
2. Assume no employee has earned over $6,000 since January 1. Make the entry to record the employer's payroll tax liability.

E12–8. Basic Payroll Procedures The Mills Manufacturing Company has a weekly payroll. The following summary covers the company payroll for the week ending February 18:

Employee	Hours or Function Worked In	Hourly or Weekly Rate
Harold Zapel	Factory: 36 direct, 4 indirect	$8 per hour
John Yazzie	Factory: 40 direct	$10 per hour
Kenneth Walch	Factory: 38 indirect	$7 per hour
Lewis Vincent	Sales	$400 per week
Monte Uhlman	Sales	5% of sales $
Nona Tresnak	Administrative	$350 per week

Monte Uhlman took firm sales orders of $6,000.

FICA taxes are 7.51 percent, and federal income taxes average 20 percent of gross wages.

Required

1. Determine each employee's gross earnings, witholdings, and net pay for the week.
2. Prepare a payroll analysis showing the amount of gross pay and employer FICA that should be classified as direct labor, indirect labor, marketing, and administrative costs, respectively.

3. Prepare the journal entry to record employee's salaries and wages and the distribution of labor costs.
4. Prepare the journal entry to record the employer's payroll expenses.

E12–9. Basic Learning Curve Analysis Integrated Electronics Company has developed a new computer component. It took thirty direct-labor hours to produce the first component. The labor rate is $12 per hour. The steady state is expected to occur when 16 components have been produced. The firm has determined that a 90-percent learning curve is applicable in the production of components.

Required

1. Compute the cumulative average labor time needed up to the steady-state point.
2. Determine the average labor cost per component at the steady state.

E12–10. Learning Curve The Signal-Sell Company produces a special part used in satellite tracking devices. Recently it has been asked to submit a bid on a contract for 900 units of this special part. Production of the first 300 parts with the specifications required for the potential contract involved the following costs for labor and factory overhead:

Direct labor—12,000 hours @ $10/hr. = $120,000
Factory overhead—applied @ 100% of direct-labor cost[a]

[a]Factory overhead is 60% variable. The fixed portion of overhead is primarily depreciation on equipment and other capacity costs.

The Signal-Sell Company has analyzed operations and has ascertained that an 80-percent learning curve is applicable.

Required

Determine an estimate of the labor and overhead costs that could be used in submitting a minimum bid on the contract for 900 units (including the first 300 units) of the special part.

E12–11. Basic Materials Ordering Procedures Watson Company's production plans specify the following needs for material 29–N:

July	3,200 units
August	2,900 units
September	3,500 units

On July 1, the inventory of 29–N was 2,800 units. Materials on order show contracted delivery in July of 3,200 units and contracted delivery in August of 2,900 units. A minimum reserve of 70 percent of the July 1 inventory is required to be maintained throughout the year.

Required

Using an electronic spreadsheet, prepare a schedule of inventory requirements for July, August, and September.

E12–12. Basic Learning Curve Analysis The Champion Chip Company has developed a new computer chip. It took three direct-labor hours to produce the first chip. The labor rate is $6 per hour. The steady state is expected to occur when 16 chips have been produced. The firm has determined that a 90-percent learning curve is applicable in the production of chips.

Required

Prepare an electronic spreadsheet to (1) compute the cumulative average labor time needed and the output of chips per hour up to the steady-state point and (2) compute the average labor cost per chip at the steady state. Print your results.

E12–13. The Francom Company produces a lawn and garden chemical. The principal ingredient used in the chemical is purchased by the gallon at a cost of $13.00 per gallon. Francom has gathered the following data about the principal ingredient:

Annual requirement	5,000 gallons
Total cost of placing an order	$15.00
Cost of carrying a gallon in inventory for one year	$3.50

Required

Prepare an electronic spreadsheet to determine the economic order quantity for the principal ingredient. Print your results.

PROBLEMS

P12–1. Inventory Control—Estimating Theft Loss (AICPA adapted) The president of Merlin Manufacturing Company is concerned that there has been a theft of raw materials from the plant. A production manager has not been at work for several days and cannot be found. It appears that an unknown quantity of raw materials is missing along with the production manager.

The company keeps perpetual inventory records, but these are unreliable because the production manager has had complete control over the production and inventory records. The missing raw material is high-strength metal tubing used to make lawn chairs. The chair frame requires a 72-inch length of tubing; each of the four legs requires a length of 24 inches. Experience shows that the scrap loss from cutting to size has consistently averaged about 10 percent of the material issued for production.

From a physical inventory taken directly after the disappearance of the production manager and from audited statements of the preceding year, you determine the following inventories:

	December 31, 19X7	April 1, 19X8
Metal tubing (feet)	100,000	95,000
Finished chairs (units)	5,000	10,000

Your examination of the accounting records reveals that purchases of metal tubing during the first three months of 19X8 amounted to 1,425,000 feet and that 85,000 chairs were sold during the same period. There were no work-in-process inventories.

Required

1. Prepare an estimate of the quantity of tubing apparently stolen by the production manager. State any assumptions or qualifications that should be attached to your estimate.
2. Suggest changes that should be made to Merlin's inventory control system.

P12–2. Journal Entries for Scrap, Spoilage, and Defective Units The following transactions (unless specified) have not been recorded. All took place during the current period.

1. Materials for production were erroneously recorded as a $480 charge to supplies.
2. Goods with a cost of $750 were returned by a customer and erroneously recorded as a debit to materials and a credit to accounts receivable at the cost amount. The sales price for the units was $1,100.
3. Scrap materials were returned to the storeroom. They were valued at an estimated sales price—$70 from supplies and indirect materials, and $135 from direct materials.
4. A job order of 800 units required additional work to be done on 20 units. Costs per unit applied in the reworking were materials, $5; labor, $3; and $4 for factory overhead, which includes a $0.50 allowance for rework of defective units. The company uses one of the two following assumptions in recording such costs:
   a. Reworking cost is charged to the specific job.
   b. Reworking cost is allocated to all production.
5. Normal spoilage of 150 units occurred in the finishing department. The 150 units have a total estimated sales value of $900. These units had been charged with $1,000 of materials, $600 of labor, and $400 of factory overhead. The following assumptions must be looked at alternatively.
   a. Spoilage cost is charged to the specific job.
   b. Spoilage cost is allocated to all production.

Required

Make the journal entries to correctly record each of the transactions listed. Where alternatives exist, make the entries under each alternative separately. Assume that perpetual inventory records are kept and that there is only one work-in-process account.

P12–3. Journal Entries for Spoiled Units

The Proctor Company manufactures product C at a per-unit cost of $6 that consists of $1 for materials, $2 for labor, and $3 for factory overhead. During May, 1,000 units were spoiled that can be sold for $0.60 each. The accountant said that the entry for these 1,000 spoiled units could be one of these four:

1.	Spoiled goods	600	
	Work in process—materials		100
	Work in process—labor		200
	Work in process—factory overhead		300
2.	Spoiled goods	600	
	Factory overhead control	5,400	
	Work in process—materials		1,000
	Work in process—labor		2,000
	Work in process—factory overhead		3,000
3.	Spoiled goods	600	
	Loss on spoiled goods	5,400	
	Work in process—materials		1,000
	Work in process—labor		2,000
	Work in process—factory overhead		3,000
4.	Spoiled goods	600	
	Accounts receivable	5,400	
	Work in process—materials		1,000
	Work in process—labor		2,000
	Work in process—factory overhead		3,000

Required

List the circumstances under which each of the preceding entries would be appropriate.

P12–4. Spoiled Goods—Revision of Contract Billing The Space Magic Company just completed a contract with NASA covering the production of 250 special components used in space rocket boosters.

Materials costs for each component were $47.50. There were 5,260 direct-labor hours used on the contract at a cost of $8 per labor hour. The direct-labor time on the contract included ten hours required to correct defects in one component. Factory overhead was applied at the rate of $4 per direct-labor hour.

During final inspection, 11 components were discovered to have been spoiled or defective during production. Of these units, 10 could not be corrected and had to be sold as scrap for $50 each. Additional materials costing $15 were used to correct the defects in the one component. NASA agreed to accept 240 components as completion of the contract.

Space Magic submitted the following billing to NASA:

Materials	$11,810.75
Labor	41,799.45
Factory overhead	20,899.80
Total manufacturing costs	$74,510.00
5% to cover administrative overhead and profit	3,725.50
Total billing (240 components)	$78,235.50

NASA submitted the billing to the disbursement audit division for review and payment. Audit has challenged the billing from Space Magic on the grounds that the cost of the spoiled components (reduced by the scrap recovery value) as well as the costs of correcting defects on the one component have been charged to the contract. Audit claims that contract regulations require costs of spoilage and correcting defects to be spread over all products produced by a company.

Required

1. Compute a corrected billing to submit to NASA.
2. Reconstruct all journal entries the Space Magic Company has made that relate to the data shown in the original billing.
3. Make the journal entries needed to bring the records into agreement with the corrected billing.

P12–5. Concepts of Inventory Models (CMA) ROAT Company is a regional manufacturing company that operates a typical manufacturing plant utilizing a raw material, work-in-process, and finished-goods inventory system. Raw materials are purchased and stored until their introduction into the manufacturing process. Upon completion, the finished products are stored in the company's warehouse until their final sale.

ROAT's controller recently read an article, which stated that the annual cost of carrying inventory from the raw material phase through the finished-goods phase can cost between 15 and 30 percent of the average value of the total inventory. As a consequence of the article, the controller asked the company's cost accounting department to prepare an analysis and estimate of ROAT's inventory carrying cost. The analysis indicated that ROAT's carrying costs were greater than 25 percent of the average inventory value. The study confirmed the controller's belief that inventory carrying costs might be an excellent area to implement cost reductions.

At a management meeting, the production manager suggested that the inventory carrying costs be shifted to suppliers and customers. This could be accomplished by not requesting raw materials from suppliers until needed in the manufacturing process and by transferring the finished goods to customers immediately following completion.

Required

1. Identify three types of inventory carrying costs and give specific examples of each type of cost.
2. The production manager of ROAT Company has suggested that inventory carrying costs be shifted to suppliers and customers. Identify and discuss the circumstances that would have to exist to make such a proposal feasible with respect to:
   a. raw materials inventories.
   b. finished-goods inventories.
3. Suppose ROAT Company is successful in shifting a portion of its inventory carrying costs to suppliers and customers.
   a. Identify the inventory carrying costs ROAT might be able to reduce by shifting the inventory burden.
   b. Identify possible areas of increased costs that could offset, in whole or part, the reduction of inventory carrying costs.

P12–6. Concepts and Procedures for Materials

The two following situations are independent of each other.

1. The following information is available for Digby Company's material *Y*:

Annual usage in units	10,000
Working days per year	250
Normal lead time in working days	30
Maximum lead time in working days	70

Required

Assuming that the units of material *Y* will be required evenly through the year, determine the reorder point.

2. Several key estimates are necessary to compute the economic order quantity.

Required

List and describe these key estimates.

P12–7. Economic Order Quantity and Safety Stock (CMA)

SaPane Company is a regional distributor of windshields. With the introduction of the new subcompact car models and the expected high level of consumer demand, management recognizes a need to determine the total inventory cost associated with maintaining an optimal supply of replacement windshields for the new subcompact cars introduced by each of the three major manufacturers. SaPane is expecting a daily demand for 36 windshields. The purchase price of each windshield is $50.

Other costs associated with ordering and maintaining an inventory of these windshields are as follows:

1. The historical ordering costs incurred in the purchase order department for placing and processing orders are as follows:

Year	Orders Placed and Processed	Total Ordering Costs
19X1	20	$12,300
19X2	55	12,475
19X3	100	12,700

Management expects the order costs to increase 16 percent over the amounts and rates experienced during the last three years.

2. A clerk in the receiving department receives, inspects, and secures the windshields as they arrive from the manufacturer. This activity requires eight hours per order received. This clerk has no other responsibilities and is paid at the rate of $9 per hour. Related variable overhead costs in this department are applied at the rate of $2.50 per hour.

3. Additional warehouse space will have to be rented to store the new windshields. Space can be rented as needed in a public warehouse at an estimated cost of $2,500 per year plus $5.35 per windshield.

4. Breakage cost is estimated to be 6 percent of the unit cost.

5. Taxes and fire insurance on the inventory are $1.15 per windshield.

6. The desired rate of return on the investment in inventory is 21 percent of the purchase price.

Six working days are required from the time the order is placed with the manufacturer until it is received. SaPane uses a 300-day work year when making economic order quantity computations. The economic order quantity formula is:

$$EOQ = \sqrt{\frac{2 \text{ (Annual demand) (Ordering cost)}}{\text{Storage cost}}}$$

Required

Calculate the following values for SaPane Company.

1. The value for ordering cost that should be used in the EOQ formula
2. The value for storage cost that should be used in the EOQ formula
3. The economic order quantity
4. The minimum annual relevant cost at the economic order quantity point
5. The reorder point in units

P12–8. EOQ—Setup and Carrying Costs (CMA) Pointer Furniture Company manufactures and sells office furniture. To compete effectively in different quality and price markets, it produces several brands of office furniture. The manufacturing operation is organized by the item produced rather than by the furniture line. Thus, the desks for all brands are manufactured on the same production line. For efficiency and quality control reasons, the desks are manufactured in batches. For example, 10 units of a high-quality desk might be manufactured during the first two weeks in October and 50 units of a lower-quality desk during the last two weeks. Because each model has its own unique manufacturing requirements, the change from one model to another requires the factory's equipment to be adjusted.

Pointer's management wants to determine the most economical production run for each item in its product lines. The manager of the cost accounting department is going to adapt the economic order quantity (EOQ) inventory model for this analysis.

One of the cost parameters that must be determined before the model can be employed is the setup cost incurred when there is a change to a different furniture model. The cost accounting department has been asked to determine the setup cost for the desk (model JE 40) in its junior executive line as an example.

The equipment maintenance department is responsible for all changeover adjustments on production lines in addition to the preventive and regular maintenance of all the production equipment. The equipment maintenance staff has a forty-hour workweek; the size of the staff is changed only if there is a change in the workload that is expected to persist for an extended period of time. The equipment maintenance department had 10 employees last year, and each employee averaged 2,000 hours for the year. They are paid $9.00 an hour, and employee benefits average 20 percent of wage costs. The other departmental costs, which include items such as supervision, depreciation, insurance, etc., total $50,000 per year.

Two workers from the equipment maintenance department are required to make the change on the desk line for model JE 40. They spend an estimated five hours in setting up the equipment as follows:

Machinery changes	3 hours
Testing	1 hour
Machinery readjustments	1 hour
Total	5 hours

The desk production line on which model JE 40 is manufactured is operated by five workers. During the changeover these workers assist the maintenance workers when needed and operate the line during the test run. However, they are idle for approximately 40 percent of the time required for the changeover.

The production workers are paid a basic wage rate of $7.50 an hour. Two overhead bases are used to apply the indirect costs of this production line, because some of the costs vary in proportion to direct-labor hours whereas others vary with machine hours. The overhead rates applicable for the current year are as follows:

	Based on Direct-Labor Hours	Based on Machine Hours
Variable	$2.75	$ 5.00
Fixed	2.25	15.00
	$5.00	$20.00

These department overhead rates are based on an expected activity of 10,000 direct-labor hours and 1,500 machine hours for the current year. This department is not scheduled to operate at full capacity, because production capability currently exceeds sales potential at this time.

The estimated cost of the direct materials used in the test run totals $200. Salvage material from the test run should total $50.

Required

1. Prepare an estimate of Pointer Furniture Company's setup cost for desk model JE 40 for use in the economic production run model. For each cost item identified in the problem, justify the amount and the reason for including the cost item in your estimate. Explain the reason for excluding any cost item from your estimate.

2. Identify the cost items that would be included in an estimate of Pointer Furniture Company's cost of carrying the desks in inventory.

P12–9. Budgeting Departmental Payroll Costs Optek Instruments prepares monthly payroll budgets for each of its production departments to assist in pricing products and making cash flow projections. Information for budgeting payroll for the grinding department follows. Optek prepares its budgets based on a forty-hour week and a fifty-week year.

The grinding department is made up of a foreman who earns $22,000 per year and five machine operators who earn $8 per hour. Optek pays machine operators time and a half for overtime. Each machine operator receives eighty hours of regular pay for holidays and vacations during the year. Machine operators are also paid for any time that they are idle because of machine maintenance and repair. Idle time, overtime premium, and vacation and holiday pay are considered factory overhead.

Production is scheduled during the coming year that will require 10,200 hours. It is expected that the time required for machine maintenance and repair will be 1,000 hours.

Tax rates for the next year are expected to be as follows:

FICA	7.51%
State unemployment	6.20%
Federal unemployment	0.80%
Federal income withholding	20.00%

Required

Prepare a departmental payroll budget for the year, giving the estimated amount to be charged to the work-in-process and factory overhead accounts. Payroll expenses for direct labor are charged to factory overhead.

P12–10. Labor Costs and the Learning Curve (CMA)

The Kelly Company plans to manufacture a product called Electrocal, which requires a substantial amount of direct labor on each unit. Based on the company's experience with other products that required similar amounts of direct labor, management believes that there is a learning factor in the production process used to manufacture Electrocal.

Each unit of Electrocal requires 50 square feet of raw material at a cost of $30 per square foot for a total material cost of $1,500. The standard direct-labor rate is $25 per direct-labor hour. Variable manufacturing overhead is assigned to products at a rate of $40 per direct-labor hour. The company adds a markup of 30 percent on variable manufacturing cost in determining an initial bid price for all products.

Data on the production of the first two lots (16 units) of Electrocal is as follows:

1. The first lot of 8 units required a total of 3,200 direct-labor hours.
2. The second lot of 8 units required a total of 2,240 direct-labor hours.

Based on prior production experience, Kelly anticipates that there will be no significant improvement in production time after the first 32 units. Therefore, a standard for direct-labor hours will be established based on the average hours per unit for the rest of the units.

Required

1. What is the basic premise of the learning curve?
2. Based on the data presented for the first 16 units, what learning rate appears to be applicable to the direct labor required to produce Electrocal? Support your answer with appropriate calculations.
3. Calculate the standard for direct-labor hours that Kelly Company should establish for each unit of Electrocal.
4. After the first 32 units have been manufactured, Kelly Company was asked to submit a bid on an additional 96 units. What price should Kelly bid on this order of 96 units? Explain your answer.
5. Knowledge of the learning curve phenomenon can be a valuable management tool. Explain how management can apply the learning curve in the planning and controlling of business operations.

Chapter 13

Factory Overhead: Costing and Control I

Outline

FACTORY OVERHEAD COST CONCEPTS
Factory Overhead Costs
Variable, Fixed, and Mixed Overhead Costs
OVERHEAD APPLICATION FOR PRODUCT COSTING
Overhead Application
Concepts Underlying the Overhead Application Process
Selection of an Activity Base
Time Period Considerations
Capacity Concepts
GENERAL LEDGER ACCOUNTING
The Accounting Process
Analysis of Budgeted Versus Actual Overhead

Disposition of Under-or Overapplied Overhead
MANAGEMENT REPORTING OF OVERHEAD FOR PLANNING AND CONTROL
Variable Overhead Reporting
Fixed Overhead Reporting
SUMMARY
SELF-STUDY PROBLEM
SUGGESTED READINGS
DISCUSSION QUESTIONS
EXERCISES
PROBLEMS

Factory overhead costs are given special consideration in this chapter and chapter 14. Accounting for factory overhead differs from accounting for direct material and direct labor because factory overhead costs have some unique characteristics. First, the total amount of factory overhead that should be assigned to goods produced during an accounting period may not be known until the end of an accounting period, long after some goods are finished and sold. In contrast, the cost of direct materials and direct labor typically is known at the time of production. Also, factory overhead may fluctuate considerably from month to month because of factors other than the volume of production; the cost of direct materials and direct labor usually fluctuates with the volume of production. Finally, factory overhead typically consists of both fixed and variable costs, unlike direct-materials and direct-labor costs, which are typically variable.

This chapter explains how to account for these unique aspects of factory overhead costs. It reviews and refines some cost concepts discussed in previous chapters, examines methods for recording and applying overhead costs, discusses the handling of over- and underapplied overhead, and illustrates management reporting of overhead costs. After completing this chapter, you should be able to:

1. define *factory overhead costs*.
2. differentiate between variable and fixed factory overhead.
3. apply factory overhead costs to units of production.
4. select an activity base appropriate for the application of factory overhead in particular manufacturing situations.
5. account for factory overhead costs in the general ledger.
6. prepare meaningful factory overhead cost reports for management use.

FACTORY OVERHEAD COST CONCEPTS

A complete understanding of two cost concepts is necessary before developing additional principles of factory overhead costing and control. These cost concepts include a definition of factory overhead costs and an analysis of the various cost behavior patterns that factory overhead costs may exhibit.

Factory Overhead Costs

Although the origin of the term **overhead** is not clear, it has become a common brief expression for indirect manufacturing costs. The terms *indirect manufacturing costs, factory overhead costs,* or simply *overhead* are defined as all manufacturing costs other than direct materials and direct labor. The cost of materials that physically become part of work in process represents a direct-materials cost. However, the cost of indirect materials, such as the cost of lubricating oil that does not become an identifiable part of work in process but is necessary for factory operations, represents an indirect manufacturing cost. The wages of a machine operator whose work is directly associated with the production of finished goods are considered direct labor costs. However, the labor cost of a repair and maintenance person is only indirectly related to the cost of finished goods and is considered an indirect manufacturing cost.

Other terms, such as *factory burden* and *manufacturing expense,* are also used to refer to overhead costs. However, the use of such terms is discouraged because they tend to be ambiguous and misleading. For brevity, the term *factory overhead* or simply *overhead* is used throughout this text to refer to indirect manufacturing costs.

FIGURE 13.1 Examples of Cost Behavior Patterns

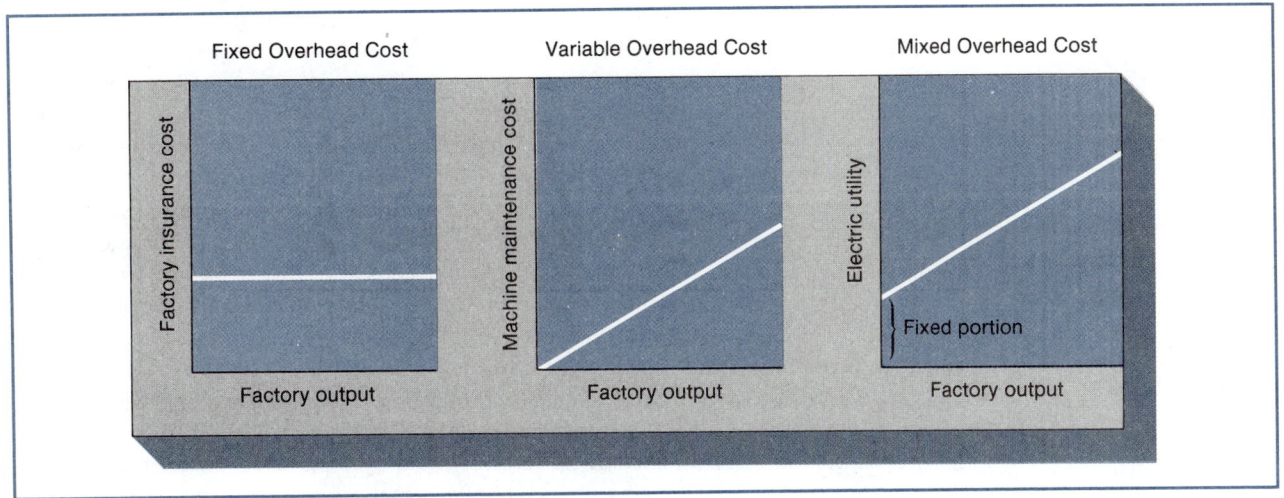

Variable, Fixed, and Mixed Overhead Costs

To provide managers with appropriate information for purposes of product costing, planning, and control, it is useful to determine how overhead costs behave when there are changes in the level of production. There are three general categories used to classify overhead cost behavior—variable overhead costs, fixed overhead costs, and mixed overhead costs.

Variable overhead costs are factory overhead costs that vary in proportion to the level of manufacturing activity. Examples of variable overhead include manufacturing supplies and certain energy-related costs.

Fixed overhead costs are factory overhead costs that remain constant or fixed as the volume of manufacturing activity changes. Examples of fixed overhead include factory depreciation and factory supervisory salaries.

Mixed overhead costs are indirect manufacturing costs that have both a fixed and a variable cost component. For example, a utility cost may include a fixed "connect fee" plus a per-unit charge for services. This type of rate structure results in the total utility bill being a mixed cost. Mixed costs are usually separated into variable and fixed components and reported in these respective cost categories on budgets and management reports. Figure 13.1 illustrates different types of costs and their behavior patterns.

The determination of whether specific costs are actually variable, fixed, or mixed depends on an examination of the cost behavior of each type of expenditure in relation to the volume of manufacturing output. In chapter 5 specific techniques for categorizing overhead costs into behavior categories were discussed. A number of benefits are derived from a behavioral analysis of overhead costs. The principal benefit, discussed later in this chapter, is that a cost analysis according to cost behavior develops more useful information for management control than would otherwise be available.

OVERHEAD APPLICATION FOR PRODUCT COSTING

One role of overhead accounting is to give managers reasonably accurate and timely information about the total actual costs incurred to operate a manufacturing facility over a period of time. Then, by the use of some rational allocation procedure, the total per-unit manufacturing costs are determined and used to value inventories and calculate cost of goods sold. The full cost of manufacturing a product, which includes factory overhead costs, is also useful to management in such ways as evaluating the long-term economic viability of a product, determining an appropriate selling price for a product, or deciding if a certain item included in a product should be purchased or manufactured in-house. These types of decisions are discussed in chapter 21. Because product costs are used for so many purposes, it is important that they be as accurate and timely as possible.

Obtaining accurate and timely product cost information for direct materials and direct labor is relatively easy. By their very nature, direct costs can be traced to specific units of production. For example, the cost of a kitchen appliance is readily identified with the cost of manufacturing a particular mobile home. Also, the labor cost of the worker who installs the appliance is easily identified with the cost of producing the mobile home. However, unlike direct-materials and direct-labor costs, it is difficult, if not impossible, to trace indirect or overhead costs to specific units of production. To illustrate, maintenance expenditures on factory equipment are recognized manufacturing costs, but it is difficult to identify the specific units of production that are benefited by a particular maintenance expenditure. Rather, it is more representative of the actual situation to view such costs as *benefiting all units of production over a given period of time.*

Selecting an appropriate time period to use as the basis for budgeting and applying overhead is sometimes difficult. The most common time period is a year, but it is also possible to use a month, a quarter, or another time period for calculating and using overhead application rates. The selection of an appropriate time period is discussed later; for now, an annual time period is assumed.

Overhead Application

Total overhead costs may not be known with certainty until the end of an accounting period. This would be the case if property taxes are assessed and paid near the end of a company's fiscal year. However, managers usually cannot wait until the end of an accounting period to make a number of decisions dependent on full cost information.

Also, overhead costs may fluctuate considerably from month to month during an accounting period. For example, a machine may require many repairs in one month and no repair in another month.

It would be unrealistic and result in improperly fluctuating product costs to charge the cost of items such as machine repair incurred in a given month only to that month's production rather than to the total period benefited.

To deal with these unique characteristics of overhead costs and to provide management with timely, reasonably accurate, and consistent product cost information, accountants have developed a procedure referred to as **overhead application** for determining what overhead to assign to units of production.

Overhead application is accomplished with the following steps:

1. Overhead costs are identified and categorized as either variable or fixed, and a forecast of total overhead cost is made. Methods of budgeting total overhead costs were discussed in chapters 6 and 7. Figure 13.2 illustrates a manufacturing overhead budget developed using flexible budget concepts.
Note that in figure 13.2 the variable costs per unit are determined and then are multiplied by the anticipated volume of production (70,000 units in this case) to calculate total budgeted variable costs. Fixed costs are then added to variable costs to arrive at the total budgeted overhead.
2. An activity base is selected to be used as the basis for assigning overhead costs to units of production. An *activity base* is a measure of productive activity that most

FIGURE 13.2

Manufacturing Overhead Budget

(Based on 70,000 units of production at 1 hour of direct labor per unit.)
For the year ending December 31, 19X8

	Amount per Unit	Total Amount
Budgeted overhead:		
Variable items:		
Indirect labor	$1.00	$ 70,000
Repair and maintenance	0.30	21,000
Utilities (variable portion)	0.20	14,000
Idle time	0.05	3,500
Other variable overhead	0.05	3,500
	$1.60	$112,000 ÷ 70,000 = $1.60
Fixed items:		
Supervisory salaries		$ 50,000
Depreciation		28,000
Insurance		10,000
Utilities (fixed portion)		4,000
Other fixed overhead		6,000
		$ 98,000 ÷ 70,000 = 1.40
Total budgeted overhead		$210,000 $3.00 per hour

nearly explains the variation in amount of actual overhead absorbed by units of production.

Typically, an activity base is chosen about which data is readily available and routinely recorded during the manufacturing process. For example, direct-labor hours, direct-labor cost, machine hours, direct-material cost, and units of production are common activity bases.

3. A budget is made to show the activity base's *total expected volume* for the coming period. For example, if direct-labor hours are chosen as the activity base, the total number of direct-labor hours expected to be employed is budgeted for the next year.

When budgeting for an activity base (direct-labor hours in this instance), it is important to understand what is being assumed about plant capacity. For example, it should be clear whether the activity level being forecasted assumes a plant operating at peak engineering efficiency or whether the capacity assumption takes into consideration such realities as maintenance, down time, and holidays. Budgets based on different assumptions of plant capacity have important implications for analyzing end-of-the-period results. Plant capacity concepts will be discussed later.

4. An overhead application rate is calculated by dividing total budgeted overhead by the total budgeted activity level. This rate is then used to apply overhead costs to units of production.

To illustrate the calculation and use of an overhead rate, figure 13.2 indicates a situation in which total expected overhead is budgeted to be $210,000. The activity base chosen in this situation is direct-labor hours. Each unit of product requires one hour of direct labor, for a total budget of 70,000 hours for the year. Given this information, the overhead application rate is calculated as follows:

$$\frac{\text{Total budgeted overhead}}{\text{Total budgeted activity base}} = \frac{\$210,000}{70,000} = \$3.00 \text{ per direct-labor hour.}$$

This rate is a **predetermined overhead application rate** because it is determined in advance as part of the budgetary process rather than determined from the results of actual operations after they occur.

FIGURE 13.3

Job Cost Summary

Job No. A136-4 Date Started: 5/15/19X8

Cost Category	Hours	Rate	Cost
Materials	—	—	$4,500.00
Direct labor	200	$6.50	1,300.00
Overhead applied	200	3.00	600.00
Total cost			$6,400.00

5. Overhead costs are applied to production using the overhead rate that was determined in steps 1 through 4. For example, consider the job cost information summarized in figure 13.3.

   Materials and labor costs are determined as the job moves through the production process. However, unlike direct costs, overhead is applied to jobs using the predetermined overhead rate—$3.00 per direct-labor hour in this example. This particular job required 200 direct-labor hours, resulting in $600 (200 hours × $3.00 per hour) of overhead being assigned. The total cost for the job of $6,400 represents the full cost of production when using this overhead application procedure.

   Before proceeding to refine these concepts, note that the $3.00 application rate is actually the total of a variable overhead application rate of $1.60 ($112,000 ÷ 70,000) plus a fixed overhead application rate of $1.40 ($98,000 ÷ 70,000). The full significance of a variable plus a fixed rate is discussed later in this chapter and in chapter 14.

   In the preceding illustration, direct-labor hours were used as the activity base, but machine hours could have been used instead. For example, assume that total budgeted machine hours are 50,000 and that 140 machine hours are used on the job shown in figure 13.3. The new overhead rate based on machine hours is:

$$\frac{\text{Total budgeted overhead}}{\text{Total budgeted activity base}} = \frac{\$210,000}{50,000} = \$4.20 \text{ per machine hour.}$$

   Using this different overhead rate would result in applying $588.00 (140 machine hours × $4.20 per machine hour) to the job in figure 13.3 rather than applying $600.00 when direct-labor hours are used. This difference is expected because of the nature of the overhead application process when different activity bases are used. The selection of an appropriate activity base is an important matter, because an inappropriate base could result in the improper assignment of costs to jobs. This example emphasizes that an activity base is intended to provide a common denominator for productive activity among units produced.

Concepts Underlying the Overhead Application Process

Several concepts that underlie the overhead application process include the selection of an activity base, time period considerations, and capacity concepts.

Selection of an Activity Base An activity base has two major functions. First, it provides the foundation for the development of a flexible budget, and, second, it provides the basis for applying overhead costs to work in process. The activity base must provide a high correlation between actual production costs and the amount of overhead incurred by each unit of production. For example, if overhead costs relate mainly to machine operation, machine hours is a more appropriate activity base than materials cost.

The cost of measuring and administering an activity base is another factor that should be considered in its selection. Recent developments in automated data acquisition and processing technology have greatly lowered the clerical costs of budgetary and overhead accounting. However, when several different activity bases provide essentially the same results, the most cost-effective base should be chosen.

There are any number of measures that could be used as an activity base. However, the five following bases represent those most commonly used.

Machine Hours This method is appropriate when machine operation is an important part of the manufacturing process and when there is a direct relationship between machine activity and overhead used. The advent of flexible manufacturing systems, robotics, and computer-integrated manufacturing has resulted in machine hours being more widely used as an activity base. However, additional record keeping to accumulate the information needed to apply overhead to work in process typically is required.

Overhead is applied using a rate per machine hour. For example, if total budgeted overhead is $360,000 and the total budgeted machine hours are 400,000 hours, overhead is applied to each unit of production at the rate of $0.90 ($360,000 ÷ 400,000 hours) per machine hour.

Direct-Labor Hours Direct-labor hours is a popular activity base, but its use is declining in highly automated factories where direct labor is a small part of total manufacturing costs. The use of direct-labor hours is appropriate when labor operations are a major factor in the manufacturing process. One reason for the popularity of direct-labor hours is that information for its use is routinely accumulated for purposes other than overhead application. Therefore, the use of direct-labor hours as an overhead base adds little in incremental costs to the operation of the cost accounting system.

Direct-labor hours is usually preferred over direct-labor cost when workers are paid different rates for the same type of work. For example, a person with seniority may be paid more than another even though he or she performs the same task. In this situation, the use of direct-labor cost would result in a disproportionate share of overhead applied to the units of production.

With the direct-labor hour base, overhead is applied using a rate per direct-labor hour. For example, if total budgeted overhead is $360,000 and if there are 200,000 total budgeted direct-labor hours, overhead is applied to each unit of production at the rate of $1.80 ($360,000 ÷ 200,000 hours) per direct-labor hour.

Direct-Labor Cost This is another base that is easy to use because necessary information is readily available in payroll records. Direct-labor cost is an appropriate activity base when there is a close relationship between the cost of labor and the amount of overhead used in manufacturing a product. However, direct-labor cost may be inappropriate as an activity base when jobs that use essentially the same amount of overhead require labor having different skill levels, thus resulting in different labor costs for each job.

With direct-labor cost as the base, overhead is applied using a rate per dollar of labor cost. For example, if the total budgeted overhead is $360,000 and the total budgeted direct-labor cost is $1,000,000, overhead is applied to each unit of production at the rate of $0.36 ($360,000 ÷ $1,000,000) per dollar of direct-labor cost. If a particular job has $900 of direct-labor cost, $324 ($900 × $0.36) is applied to work in process.

Units of Production This base is convenient because units of production are routinely part of the information in a cost accounting system. The units of production base is typically used when there is only one product produced or when the different products manufactured are quite homogeneous. Otherwise, the application of overhead may result in unrealistic product costs. For example, in a job-costing environment, a major job that produces only a few units would receive less applied overhead than a minor job that produces may units.

With the units of production base, overhead is applied using a rate per unit of production. For example, if total budgeted overhead is $360,000 and there are 180,000 total budgeted units of production, overhead is applied to each unit of production at the rate of $2.00 ($360,000 ÷ 180,000 units) per unit produced.

Materials Costs This base is appropriate when there is a high correlation between the cost of materials and the amount of overhead used in production. This situation typically occurs when a single product is produced or when all products are homogeneous in terms of materials used. However, if one product uses higher priced materials than another but the amount of overhead used is approximately the same, the use of materials cost as an activity base would result in an inappropriate amount of overhead being applied to work in process.

With materials cost as a base, overhead is applied using a rate per dollar of materials cost. For example, if total budgeted overhead is $360,000 and total budgeted cost of direct materials is $1,440,000, overhead is applied to each unit of production at the rate of $0.25 ($360,000 ÷ $1,440,000) per dollar of direct-materials cost. If a particular job has $2,000 of direct-materials cost, $500 ($2,000 × $0.25) is applied to work in process.

Time Period Considerations

Instead of using an annual time period, it is possible to use a monthly, quarterly, or other time period for calculating and using overhead application rates. When deciding what time period to use for an overhead rate, two major considerations are fluctuations in the volume of activity and the uniformity of overhead expenditures through time.

Fluctuations in the volume of activity have little effect on unit production costs for materials, labor, and variable overhead; however, the unit cost of fixed overhead will change with the level of production. For example, if fixed overhead costs are expected to be $10,000 per month and the volume of production in January is 10,000 units, the fixed cost portion of the overhead rate is $1.00 per unit. If the production forecast for February is set at 8,000 units, however, the fixed cost portion of the overhead rate is computed to be $1.25. Thus overhead rates may differ from month to month due *only* to monthly changes in the volume of production. Therefore, the selection of an annual, monthly, or other period of time for applying the activity base should depend on how well the derived overhead rate represents actual, typical, or normal per-unit production costs.

The second major consideration in selecting a base period is the uniformity of overhead expenditures through time. Expenditures for overhead items may range from being highly uniform through time to being highly erratic. For example, monthly rent on the factory building is stable from month to month, but other expenditures may be seasonal, as in the case of air-conditioning costs, or once per year, as in the case of property taxes. Under these circumstances, it seems unrealistic to have the cost of production of units made in March be more or less than those made in July simply because property taxes are paid in March rather than in July. This type of monthly fluctuation in overhead costs is the major reason for computing overhead rates on a time period longer than a week or a month.

In most situations it is thought that a rate based on the *operating cycle* of a business (which is usually an annual cycle) provides an average of activity that is most representative of the actual or normal costs of production.

Capacity Concepts When budgeting the expected level of an activity base, it is important to understand the meaning of plant capacity. The discussion to this point has been based on an expected level of activity as a measure of plant capacity. However, the term "expected level of activity" is ambiguous because it is not clear if it refers to the activity level attainable if the plant is operating at peak engineering efficiency or if it takes into consideration such realities as unavoidable delays or expected idle time.

When a factory is first built, it has a basic level of productive capacity. Determining initial plant size is essentially a capital budgeting decision (see chapters 23 and 24). Once the basic productive capabilities of a factory are in place, another notion of capacity is the extent to which the available capacity is expected to be utilized. In this connection, there are four capacity concepts that may be considered: theoretical, practical, normal, and expected. Note that theoretical capacity and practical capacity relate to production capabilities of a firm. In contrast, normal capacity and expected capacity relate the level of production to consumer demand.

1. **Theoretical capacity** refers to the upper limit of production capabilities from an engineering and economic viewpoint. It includes operating the plant at full potential with 100-percent efficiency. No interruptions are contemplated for such things as breakdowns or maintenance. Theoretical capacity could also include additional levels of output achievable by using overtime or subcontracting to augment production if they are economically feasible. Because theoretical capacity does not allow for normal interruptions and unavoidable delays, it is typically not used as a basis for measuring capacity.

2. **Practical capacity** refers to the more realistic production level at which machine breakdowns, machine maintenance, and other idle-time events are considered to be a normal part of operations. This capacity level is often used to apply overhead costs.

3. **Normal capacity** is the level of production volume that is expected to meet average consumer demand over some specified period of time—often three to five years. Normal capacity is essentially a long-run measure of expected average sales activity that takes into consideration seasonal and cyclical fluctuations in demand. Since normal capacity is long-run in nature, budgeted overhead could be greater than actual overhead in some years and less than actual overhead in other years. The net effect over a period of years is expected to be equal and offsetting.

    The use of normal capacity is beneficial when management wants to have long-run criteria for product costing and control. However, when normal capacity is used, care should be taken to ensure that all concerned fully understand and can evaluate the potential effect of using a long-run concept in the short run. For example, over- or underapplied overhead should be evaluated realizing that on a year-by-year basis it may have resulted simply because a long-run capacity concept was used to make short-run cost application.

4. **Expected capacity** is the level of plant activity that is expected to meet consumer demand for the next planning period—usually one year. It is usually the basis of the annual master budget for a company. Under this concept, overhead costs are budgeted on a year-by-year basis, taking into consideration cyclical and trend patterns anticipated to affect only the upcoming year. The use of an expected capacity concept tends to place unit production costs at more realistic levels in the short run, makes cost accounting more responsive to the current business environment, and provides less ambiguous information for management control of overhead costs. Therefore, expected capacity is a common capacity concept for both product-costing and management control purposes.

GENERAL LEDGER ACCOUNTING

Accounting for overhead costs has two major purposes. First, overhead costs are accumulated and applied to estimate how much it actually costs to produce each unit of output: this is referred to as the product-costing objective. In addition, overhead costs are accumulated and reported to help management make planning and control decisions. *Both* of these objectives should be kept in mind as the general ledger accounting for overhead is examined.

We reemphasize this matter because although the traditional orientation of general ledger accounting for overhead costs has tended to focus on the product-costing objective, the importance of planning and control cannot be overemphasized. A well-founded information system centered on the general ledger and supplemented with other procedures and reports can provide meaningful information for planning and control as well as for product-costing purposes.

The Accounting Process

The calculation of the overhead rate is part of the budgetary process that takes place before any actual overhead costs are incurred or recorded. Because of timing and uneven expenditure patterns, the overhead rate is used to apply overhead to units of production independent of the incurrence of actual overhead costs. This peculiarity in overhead accounting gives rise to the following typical account structure. A **factory overhead control account** is used to accumulate the *actual* overhead costs incurred. A **factory overhead applied account** is used to record the amount of overhead *applied* to work in process by using the predetermined overhead application rate. Sometimes only a *factory overhead account* is used, with the debit side representing actual overhead costs and the credit side representing applied overhead costs.

The factory overhead control account is so designated because it serves as the control account over the *factory overhead subsidiary ledger*. Just as the accounts receivable control account has a subsidiary ledger of individual customer accounts, the factory overhead control account has a subsidiary ledger that consists of accounts representing individual categories of actual overhead expenditure. Figure 13.4 lists typical overhead cost categories that could be used as subsidiary account titles.

As actual overhead costs are incurred, the factory overhead control account is debited. The offsetting credit is made to either a liability account, the cash account, or some other appropriate asset account. Also, the amount of actual expenditure is posted to the

FIGURE 13.4

Factory Overhead Subsidiary Accounts

Typical Overhead Cost Categories

Supervisor/foreman salaries	Repairs and maintenance
Other indirect labor	Factory supplies
Overtime premium	Oil and gas
Idle time	Electricity
Vacation/holiday expense	Water
FICA taxes	Depreciation—factory building
Unemployment taxes	Depreciation—machinery
Group/hospitalization insurance	Property taxes
Pension plan expense	Fire and casualty insurance
Manufacturing supplies	Small tools

appropriate account in the factory overhead subsidiary ledger. For example, a cash expenditure of $250.00 for factory supplies would result in the following journal entry and subsidiary posting:

General Ledger:

Factory overhead control   250.00
    Cash   250.00
To record expenditure for factory supplies.

Factory Overhead Subsidiary Ledger:

Factory supplies   250.00
To post to subsidiary ledger.

The recording of actual overhead costs continues throughout the accounting period as costs are incurred and is independent of the application of overhead costs to work in process. Only at the end of a specified accounting period are differences between actual costs and applied costs compared and analyzed.

The application of overhead costs to work in process is based on the use of a predetermined overhead application rate. To illustrate, refer to the job statistics in figure 13.3. During the production process, 200 direct-labor hours were expended on the job. Using the predetermined overhead rate of $3.00 per direct-labor hour, total overhead applied to work in process for this job is $600.00. The journal entry to record the application of overhead for this job is as follows:

General Ledger:

Work-in-process control   600.00
    Factory overhead applied   600.00
To record the application of overhead to work in process for job number A136–4.

Analysis of Budgeted versus Actual Overhead

Since the recording of actual overhead and applied overhead are carried on as separate accounting functions, the probability is remote that the balance in the factory overhead control account will ever be the same as the balance in the factory overhead applied account. In fact, the difference at various times during the accounting period may be quite large because of the uneven nature of some types of overhead expenditures. However, at the end of an accounting period (usually a year), the balances in the two accounts should be nearly equal.

Any difference between balances in the two accounts at the end of an accounting period represents the amount by which budgeted (applied) amounts differed from actual expenditures. Unexpected changes in the cost of maintenance supplies or the unexpected use of more labor to perform maintenance functions could result in actual amounts being different from applied amounts. An analysis of any differences between applied and actual overhead provides important information for management planning and control.

An analysis of differences between these accounts begins with the computation of under- or overapplied overhead. **Underapplied overhead** occurs when the balance in the factory overhead applied account is less than (under) the balance in the factory overhead control account. **Overapplied overhead** occurs when the balance in the factory overhead applied account is greater than (over) the balance in the factory overhead control account. To illustrate, part *a* of figure 13.5 shows that actual overhead expenditures made during the period amounted to $212,000, in comparison with overhead applied to work in process during the period of $213,000. The application of overhead resulted from an assumed

FIGURE 13.5

Recording of Under- or Overapplied Overhead

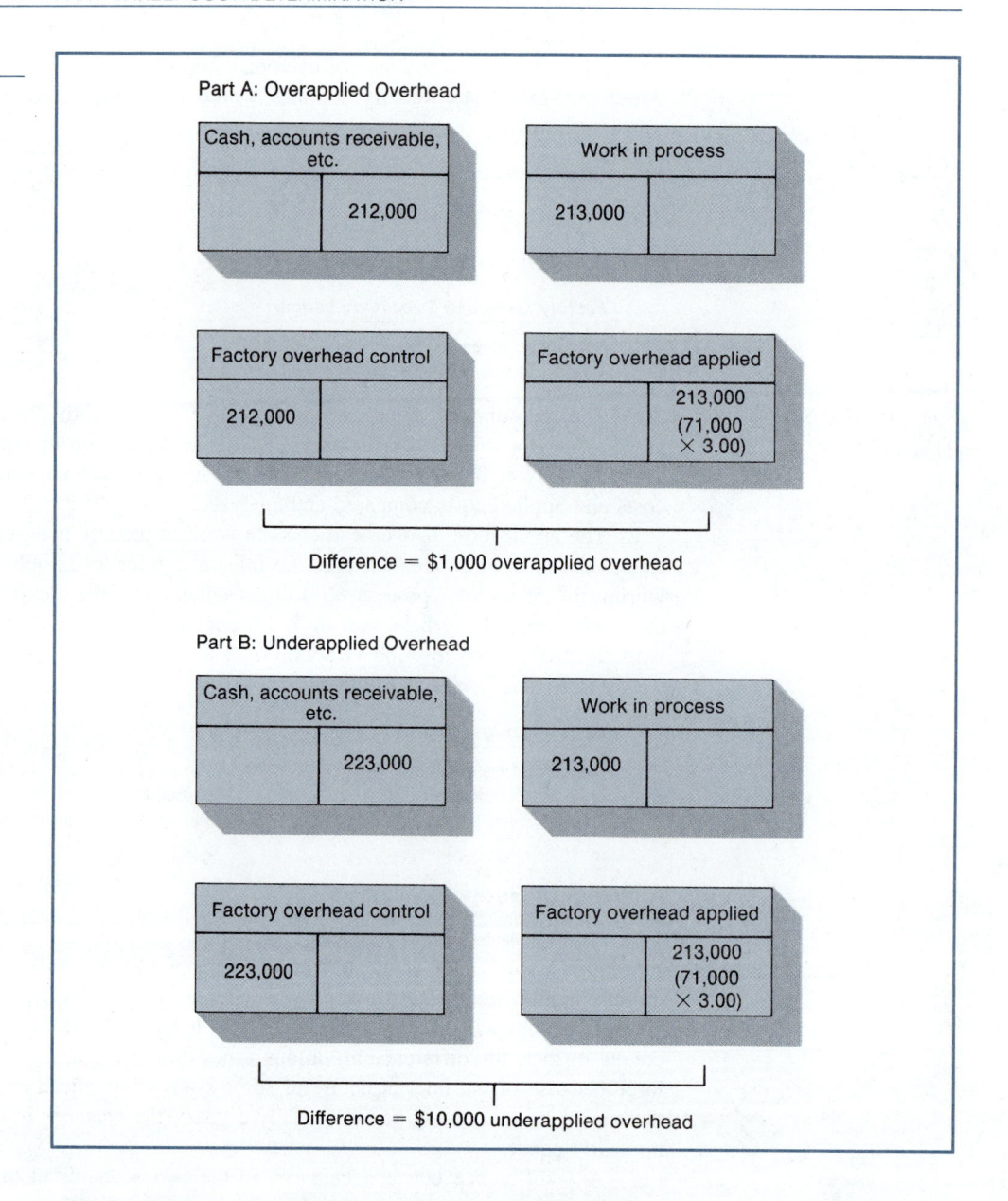

Part A: Overapplied Overhead

Cash, accounts receivable, etc.
212,000

Work in process
213,000

Factory overhead control
212,000

Factory overhead applied
213,000 (71,000 × 3.00)

Difference = $1,000 overapplied overhead

Part B: Underapplied Overhead

Cash, accounts receivable, etc.
223,000

Work in process
213,000

Factory overhead control
223,000

Factory overhead applied
213,000 (71,000 × 3.00)

Difference = $10,000 underapplied overhead

activity level of 71,000 direct-labor hours with an overhead application rate of $3.00 per direct-labor hour. The difference of $1,000 between actual and applied accounts represents overapplied overhead.

If instead of 71,000 direct-labor hours only 70,000 direct-labor hours had been expended, then only $210,000 (70,000 hours × $3.00 per hour) would have been applied to work in process. In this case there would have been a difference of $2,000 between the accounts, which would represent *underapplied* overhead.

Disposition of Under- or Overapplied Overhead

It is almost inevitable that there will be some amount of under- or overapplied overhead. In addition, unexpected changes in business conditions may result in very large amounts of under- or overapplied overhead.

The relative magnitude of any under- or overapplied overhead influences how the overhead accounts are closed at the end of an accounting period and what disposition is made of any under- or overapplied amount. If, by some chance, the ending balances in the factory overhead control and factory overhead applied accounts are equal, these accounts can be closed against each other with an equal credit and debit, respectively, and no additional accounting is necessary. However, a more likely situation is that a difference in account balances will exist. If the amount of under- or overapplied overhead is immaterial, a widely accepted practice at year end is to simply close the overhead accounts against each other with the difference going as an adjustment to cost of goods sold. Using this approach, the following journal entry closes the overhead accounts illustrated in figure 13.5, part a:

Factory overhead applied	213,000	
Factory overhead control		212,000
Cost of goods sold		1,000

To close overhead accounts and charge overapplied overhead to cost of goods sold.

If overhead had been underapplied during the period, the closing entry would have resulted in a debit (increase) to the cost-of-goods-sold account.

When under- or overapplied overhead amounts are large, as would be the case when there is a large and unexpected change in prices for overhead items, it is best to use a more accurate procedure in handling them. Theoretically, if there is under- or overapplied overhead at the end of an accounting period, the amount of overhead charged to individual jobs during the period is in error and should be adjusted.

This procedure results in a precise, after-the-fact correction of the application of overhead. However, most firms do not go to this much corrective detail even for substantial amounts of over- or underapplied overhead. Rather, the typical procedure is to prorate under- or overapplied overhead to work in process, finished goods, and cost of goods sold based on the amount of overhead component in each account.

To illustrate this procedure, assume that in figure 13.5, part b, actual overhead amounted to $223,000 because of unexpected increases in overhead costs. With the amount of overhead applied remaining at $213,000, the result is $10,000 of underapplied overhead rather than $1,000 of overapplied overhead as previously illustrated.

Figure 13.6 shows assumed amounts of overhead in work-in-process, finished-goods, and cost-of-goods-sold accounts at the end of the year. Relative proportions are also calculated in figure 13.6.

The adjustment amounts shown in figure 13.6 are found by multiplying the relative proportions times the $10,000 underapplied overhead. The journal entry to close the overhead accounts under these circumstances and using this allocation procedure is as follows. The amounts debited to work in process and finished goods are posted to individual job cost sheets for proper job costing.

Work in process	300	
Finished goods	2,200	
Cost of goods sold	7,500	
Factory overhead applied	213,000	
Factory overhead control		223,000

To close overhead accounts and charge underapplied overhead to work in process, finished goods, and cost of goods sold.

Allocating under- or overapplied overhead using this procedure assumes that the proportion of direct-materials, direct-labor, and overhead costs are relatively uniform among jobs or products produced. In most situations this is a valid assumption. However, if this assumption is not warranted, the procedure illustrated will result in an improper allocation

FIGURE 13.6

Allocation of Underapplied Overhead

Account	Amount of Overhead in Account	Proportion of Total	Adjustment Amount
Work in process	$ 72,000	0.03	$ 300
Finished goods	528,000	0.22	2,200
Cost of goods sold	1,800,000	0.75	7,500
Total	$2,400,000	1.00	$10,000

of under- or overapplied overhead and it may be necessary to resort to the detail of job-by-job cost adjustments previously discussed.

Under- or overapplied overhead may also be handled using a total cost approach. With this method, any under- or overapplied overhead is closed to work in process, finished goods, and cost of goods sold based on the balance of total costs in each account. Although this method is not as precise, it is easier to apply because only ending balances are required for its use. In many instances the choice of accounting method depends on an evaluation of the relationship between the cost of greater precision and the benefit derived from improved management decisions.

MANAGEMENT REPORTING OF OVERHEAD FOR PLANNING AND CONTROL

A principal benefit of the budgetary and accounting procedures discussed in this chapter is that information is made available for management to assess the quality of past performance as a basis for future planning and control. Whether examining the entire firm or each individual department, analysis of past performance begins with a detailed examination of the causes of any under- or overapplied overhead.

The difference between actual overhead incurred and the amount of overhead applied to work in process is the result of two possible conditions. First, under- or overapplied overhead results if more or less overhead costs than originally budgeted are incurred for the number of units produced. This may happen because of unexpected fluctuations in the price of overhead items or unexpected changes in overhead used. A second condition is the production of more or fewer units than originally budgeted.

The first cause is identified with both variable and fixed overhead, whereas the second cause is identified with fixed overhead only. This situation makes it appropriate to provide management with overhead analysis reports that separately analyze variable and fixed overhead costs. The combined analysis explains why total overhead is under- or overapplied. Such reports typically show company-wide results and detailed reports are then developed for each job or department.

Variable Overhead Reporting

The variable overhead portion of a performance report consists of a detailed listing of overhead items or accounts. For each overhead item, amounts are given for (a) the budgeted cost, (b) the actual costs incurred, (c) the difference between budgeted and actual costs, and (d) an indication whether actual expenditures are greater than or less than the budgeted amount. Figure 13.7 shows such a report. The information contained in the report is extracted from the illustrations in this chapter. The variable overhead items and rates are

FIGURE 13.7

Comparison of Budgeted and Actual Overhead

Flexible budget based on 71,000 direct-labor hours

	Variable Rate per Direct-Labor Hour	Budgeted Amount	Actual Amount	Variance from Budget
Variable items:				
Indirect labor	$1.00	$ 71,000	$ 71,600	$ 600 U[a]
Repair and maintenance	0.30	21,300	20,900	400 F
Utilities (variable portion)	0.20	14,200	14,250	50 U
Idle time	0.05	3,550	3,450	100 F
Other variables	0.05	3,550	3,700	150 U
Total	$1.60	$113,600	$113,900	$ 300 U
Fixed overhead		$ 98,000	$ 98,100	100 U
Total		$211,600	$212,000	$ 400 U
Volume variance [(71,000 − 70,000) × $1.40[b]]				1,400 F
Overapplied overhead				$1,000 F

[a] F = Favorable
U = Unfavorable
[b] Fixed overhead application rate: $3.00 total − $1.60 variable = $1.40 fixed
  Variable items:
    Favorable = Actual amount is less than budgeted amount
    Unfavorable = Actual amount is greater than budgeted amount
  Volume variance = Fixed overhead rate × (Budgeted hours − Actual hours)
    Favorable = Actual activity base used is greater than the budgeted activity base
    Unfavorable = Actual activity base used is less than the budgeted activity base
  Overapplied overhead = Favorable
  Underapplied overhead = Unfavorable

those given in figure 13.2. The variable rates per direct-labor hour developed in figure 13.2 are based on 70,000 hours of direct labor. The budgeted cost in figure 13.7 is calculated using flexible budget procedures at the *actual level of production* of 71,000 direct-labor hours.

This type of report makes it possible to quickly pinpoint how well specific variable overhead items are being utilized in the production process. For example, the unfavorable variance for indirect labor may have been the result of an unexpected machine breakdown that required more maintenance labor than had been expected. This information provides the point of departure for investigation into the causes of deviations from budget and the formulation of remedies or rewards for poor or good performance as appropriate.

The type of analysis in figure 13.7 has a critical limitation, however, in that it does not indicate if the over- or under budget amounts are caused by unexpected prices paid for overhead items or by the efficiency with which overhead items are utilized. For example, is the $50 unfavorable variance for utilities caused by an increase in utility rates or the result of the utilities being inefficiently used? Or is the $50 amount caused by a combination of such factors? Even though this report is quite useful, a more comprehensive comparison of budgeted and actual variable overhead would be helpful. Such a report is developed in chapters 15 and 16 in connection with the use of standard costs.

Fixed Overhead Reporting

The fixed overhead portion of the performance report shown in figure 13.7 shows actual expenditures exceeding budgeted expenditures by $100. This seems inconsistent with the notion that fixed costs remain fixed, yet in reality there will probably be differences between budgeted and actual fixed costs. For example, the cost of insurance, generally a fixed cost, may unexpectedly increase. Remember that a fixed cost is one that does not change with changes in the volume of production. Also, fixed costs are expected to remain unchanged during a given budgetary period. However, fixed costs can and do change. The self-study problem at the end of this chapter illustrates another situation in which actual fixed costs exceeded the budgeted amount. In addition, chapter 14 discusses other aspects of accounting and reporting for changes in fixed costs.

There is another feature of fixed overhead that needs special attention. Even though fixed and variable overhead have different cost-behavior patterns, it is generally accepted practice to apply fixed overhead, along with variable overhead, *as though* it is a variable cost. In other words, the inclusion of fixed overhead in the predetermined factory overhead application rate causes the total amount of fixed overhead *applied* to work in process to fluctuate with the level of production as though it were a variable cost. The amount of fixed overhead applied to work in process equals budgeted fixed overhead *only* at the budgeted level of activity. Thus there is over- or underappplied overhead whenever the actual volume of activity differs from the budgeted volume of activity, regardless of any price or efficiency differences.

This phenomenon is accounted for by calculating a **volume variance,** which shows the difference between the budgeted amount of fixed overhead and the amount of fixed overhead applied to work in process that results from differences in volume. To illustrate, fixed overhead is applied in the previous example at the rate of $1.40 per direct-labor hour, whereas the variable overhead rate is $1.60 per hour. Therefore, the amount of fixed overhead applied will equal budgeted overhead only at the activity level of 70,000 hours, which was used to calculate the predetermined overhead application rate. Figure 13.8 graphically indicates this point.

By examining figure 13.8 it can be seen that budgeted fixed overhead remains the same for various levels of production. However, fixed overhead applied to production on a per-unit basis behaves as though it is a variable cost. If actual production equals budgeted production of 70,000 direct-labor hours, the amount of fixed overhead applied to work in process is also equal to budgeted fixed costs of $98,000. However, if 71,000 direct-labor hours were actually utilized, as in the preceding example, the result is $99,400 (71,000 hours × $1.40 per hour) of fixed overhead applied to work in process. The difference of $1,400 is the amount of the volume variance. A volume variance will occur whenever the actual level of activity differs from the budgeted activity level used to calculate the overhead application rate. The formula for calculating the volume variance is:

$$\text{Volume variance} = \left[\begin{array}{c} \text{Budgeted level} \\ \text{of production} \end{array} - \begin{array}{c} \text{Actual level} \\ \text{of production} \end{array} \right] \times \begin{array}{c} \text{Fixed part of} \\ \text{overhead rate.} \end{array}$$

The volume variance has nothing to do with the price paid or the efficiency of usage of fixed overhead. Also, because the volume variance is simply the result of the actual level of activity differing from the budgeted level of activity, it can be controlled only at higher levels of management where production volume is controlled. For these reasons, the volume variance is shown on managerial reports only as a balancing number to indicate that all over- or underapplied overhead has been accounted for.

Further discussion about the volume variance and the analysis of fixed overhead costs requires a more refined analysis that depends on the use of standard costs, which are discussed in chapters 15 and 16.

FIGURE 13.8 Volume Variance

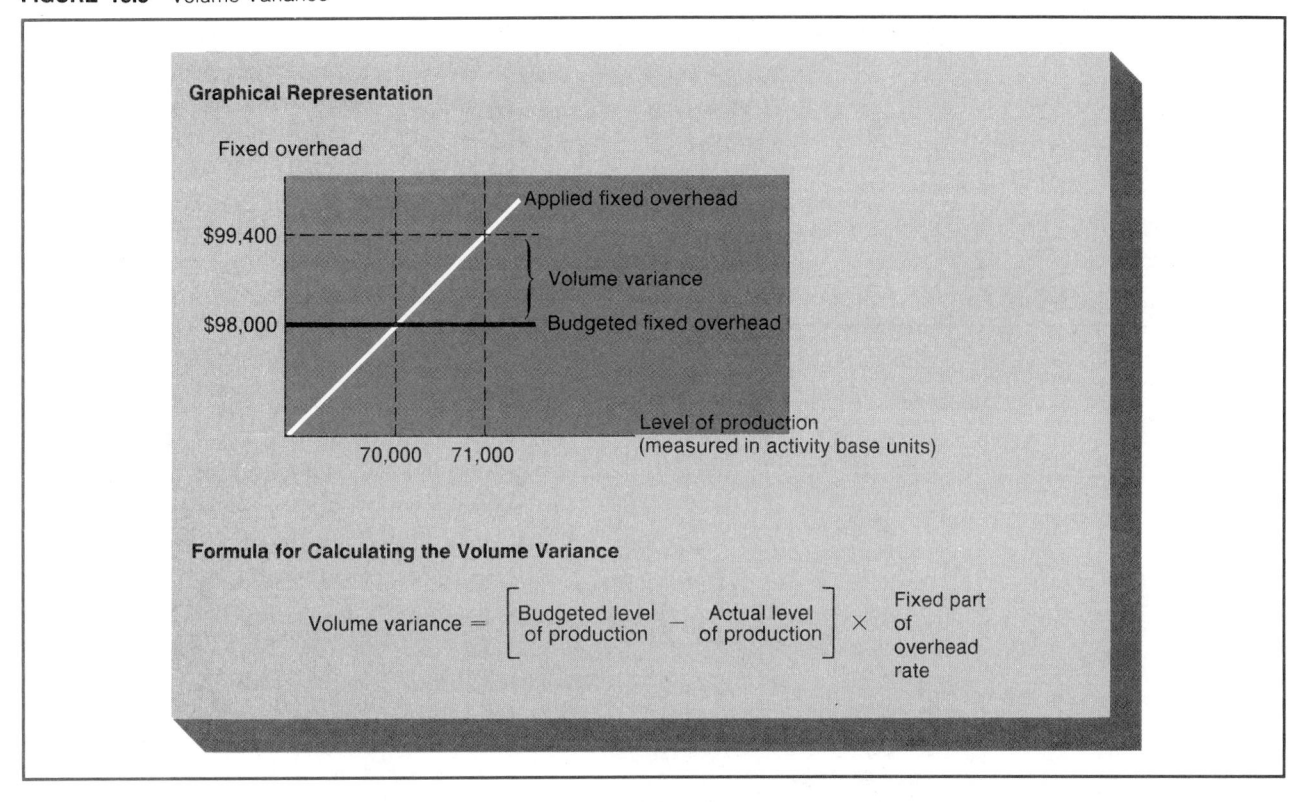

Graphical Representation

Fixed overhead

$99,400 ---- Applied fixed overhead

Volume variance

$98,000 ---- Budgeted fixed overhead

Level of production (measured in activity base units)

70,000   71,000

Formula for Calculating the Volume Variance

$$\text{Volume variance} = \left[\text{Budgeted level of production} - \text{Actual level of production} \right] \times \text{Fixed part of overhead rate}$$

SUMMARY

Accounting for factory overhead has a number of unique features that require procedures different from those for direct materials and direct labor. Because the amount of actual overhead is not known with certainty until the end of an accounting period, overhead costs are assigned to work in process by using a predetermined overhead application rate. This rate is found by dividing total budgeted overhead by a total budgeted activity base.

An activity base is a measure of productive activity that represents the relationship between units of production and the amount of overhead costs absorbed by those units. There are a number of activity bases that may be used, depending on the manufacturing situation; for example, direct-labor hours and machine hours are common activity bases. The activity base chosen should accurately represent the amount of overhead costs absorbed by units of production.

The development of an overhead application rate is part of the budgetary process, and two aspects of this process relate especially to overhead costs. First, total overhead typically consists of fixed as well as variable costs. Proper identification and classification of fixed and variable costs are vital for correct overhead accounting and management reporting. Second, an understanding of plant capacity and the consequences of using theoretical, practical, normal, or expected capacity assumptions are important for appropriate reporting and control of overhead costs.

When accounting for overhead in the general ledger, an overhead *applied* account is used to record the amounts of overhead assigned to work in process, and an *actual* account is used to record actual expenditures for overhead items. At the end of an accounting period, the actual and applied totals are compared. Any under- or overapplied overhead is reported and is either closed to cost of goods sold or prorated among the work-in-process inventory, the finished-goods inventory, and the cost-of-goods-sold accounts.

The procedures outlined in this chapter provide a meaningful way to assign overhead costs to units of production, as well as a way to provide useful information for management planning and control of operations.

SELF-STUDY PROBLEM

Bridgerland Products, a manufacturing company, recently began operations. The firm's budgeted and actual overhead costs for the past month are shown by its accounting records:

Overhead Account	Variable Rate	Budget	Actual
Variable Overhead:			
Indirect materials	$1.20	$ 3,600	$ 3,200
Indirect labor	1.30	3,900	4,200
Payroll-related costs	0.90	2,700	3,000
Utilities	0.40	1,200	1,400
Miscellaneous	0.20	600	400
	$4.00	$12,000	$12,200
Fixed:			
Supervisor's salary		2,000	2,000
Depreciation		3,500	3,600
Property tax		300	300
Insurance		200	200
		$ 6,000	$ 6,100
Total		$18,000	$18,300

The company uses direct-labor hours to calculate a predetermined rate to apply manufacturing overhead. Budgeted direct-labor hours are 3,000, but 3,100 hours of direct labor were actually worked. Since the company has been in business for only a short period of time, it uses a monthly rate to apply overhead to work in process.

During the past month, Bridgerland worked on a number of different jobs. Statistics for two of these jobs are as follows:

	Job 12	Job 15
Materials cost	$6,000	$8,000
Direct-labor cost	$9,000	$12,000
Direct-labor hours	1,000	800

Required

1. Calculate the predetermined overhead application rate, using direct-labor hours as the base.
2. Give the journal entries to record (a) overhead applied to work in process and (b) actual overhead expenditures. In the explanation of the first journal entry, indicate how much overhead is applied to Jobs 12 and 15 this month.

3. How much over- or underapplied overhead resulted from this month's operations?
4. Prepare a flexible budget for variable overhead at the 3,100-hour level of activity.
5. Calculate the portion of the predetermined overhead application rate that is applicable to fixed costs.
6. Calculate the volume variance. Tell if it is favorable or unfavorable, and explain its importance to management.
7. Prepare a management report comparing budgeted and actual overhead.

Solution to the Self-Study Problem

1. Predetermined overhead application rate:

$$\frac{\$18,000 \text{ total budgeted overhead}}{3,000 \text{ total direct-labor hours}} = \$6.00 \text{ per hour}$$

2. *(a)* Entry to record overhead applied to work in process:

    Work-in-process control   18,600
        Factory overhead applied   18,600
    To record the application of overhead based on 3,100 direct-labor hours at $6.00 per hour.

    Job 12: 1,000 hrs. × $6 per hour = $6,000
    Job 15:   800 hrs. × $6 per hour = $4,800

    (b) Entry to record actual overhead:

    Factory overhead control   18,300
        Cash, etc.   18,300
    To record actual expenditures for manufacturing overhead.

3. Over- or underapplied overhead:

Overhead applied to work in process	$18,600
Actual overhead expenditures	18,300
Overapplied overhead	$ 300

4. Flexible budget for manufacturing overhead:

	Rate	Budgeted Amount (3,000 hrs.)	Budgeted Amount (3,100 hrs.)
Variable items:			
Indirect materials	$1.20	$3,600	$3,720
Indirect labor	1.30	3,900	4,030
Payroll-related costs	0.90	2,700	2,790
Utilities	0.40	1,200	1,240
Miscellaneous	0.20	600	620
	$4.00	$12,000	$12,400
Fixed items	2.00	6,000	6,000
Total	$6.00	$18,000	$18,400

5. Fixed overhead application rate:

$$\frac{\$6,000}{3,000} = \$2.00 \text{ per hour}$$

6. Volume variance:

Actual direct-labor hours	3,100
Budgeted direct-labor hours	3,000
Difference	100
Fixed overhead application rate	× $2
Volume variance	$ 200 Favorable

The volume variance indicates the amount of difference between actual fixed overhead and applied fixed overhead caused by working more or less hours than budgeted. In this situation more hours were worked, resulting in a favorable volume variance (overapplied overhead) of $200F. Working more of an activity base than was planned is considered a favorable outcome.

7. Comparison of budgeted and actual overhead:

	Variable Rate	Budgeted Amount	Actual Amount	Variance from Budget
Variable Items:				
Indirect materials	$1.20	$3,720	$3,200	$520 F
Indirect labor	1.30	4,030	4,200	170 U
Payroll-related costs	.90	2,790	3,000	210 U
Utilities	.40	1,240	1,400	160 U
Miscellaneous	.20	620	400	220 F
Total	$4.00	$12,400	$12,200	$200 F
Fixed overhead		$6,000	$6,100	$100 U
Total		$18,400	$18,300	$100 F
Volume variance				200 F
Overapplied overhead				$300 F

SUGGESTED READINGS

Beresford, Dennis R., and Neary, Robert D. "Allocation of Direct and Indirect Costs." *Financial Executive* 48 (August 1980): 10.

Grinnell, D. Jacque, and Mills, John R. "Management Strategies for Allocating Fixed Overhead Costs to Production." *Managerial Planning* 33 (March–April 1985): 36–40, 45.

Hakala, Gregory. "Measuring Costs with Machine Hours." *Management Accounting* 67 (October 1985): 57–61.

Howell, Robert A., and Soucy, Stephen R., "The New Manufacturing Environment: Major Trends for Management Accountants." *Management Accounting* 69 (July 1987): 21–27.

Schwarzbach, Henry R. "Impact of Automation on Accounting for Indirect Costs." *Management Accounting* 67 (December 1985): 45–50.

Skinner, Wickham. "The Productivity Paradox." *Harvard Business Review* 64 (July–August 1986): 55–59.

DISCUSSION QUESTIONS

Q13–1. Define *overhead* and explain the difference between fixed, variable, and mixed overhead.

Q13–2. Describe three types of wages that are usually considered to be indirect manufacturing costs.

Q13–3. What are some difficulties encountered in obtaining timely overhead costs?

Q13–4. Describe the processes of overhead accumulation and overhead application.

Q13–5. What is the function of an activity base? What are the major criteria for selecting an appropriate activity base?

Q13–6. Name the five most common activity bases. Describe a situation in which each would be the most appropriate activity base to use.

Q13–7. What is the purpose of a predetermined overhead application rate? What is the formula for its calculation?

Q13–8. When choosing a base period for allocating overhead, why do managers often prefer an annual rate to a monthly or quarterly rate?

Q13–9. Define *theoretical capacity, normal capacity,* and *expected capacity.* Explain why these concepts are important for overhead application.

Q13–10. What purposes are served by keeping departmental subsidiary ledgers for overhead?

Q13–11. Why might there be differences between the factory overhead control account and the factory overhead applied account? At what point in the accounting cycle should such differences be smoothed?

Q13–12. What are the terms used to describe the net differences that may occur between budgeted versus actual overhead?

Q13–13. Explain why fixed overhead rates might fluctuate from period to period even though fixed costs remain unchanged.

Q13–14. Define *volume variance.* What importance does it have for the management and control of overhead costs?

Q13–15. When associated with overhead variances, the terms *favorable* and *unfavorable* have unique meanings. What are their meanings when associated with variable overhead variances? What are their meanings when associated with the volume variance?

EXERCISES

E13–1. Factory Overhead Rates and Application of Overhead to Jobs
The cost department of the Park Company made the following estimates for the year.

Factory overhead	$212,500
Materials cost	$425,000
Labor cost	$125,000
Production in cases	22,000
Labor hours	110,000

Required

1. Determine the factory overhead rate based on *(a)* labor cost, *(b)* labor hours, and *(c)* materials cost.
2. Determine the amount of overhead to be charged to Job 829 by each rate in requirement 1, given the following information about Job 829:

	Job 829
Materials cost	$10,500
Labor cost	$ 7,400
Labor hours	3,700

E13–2. Basics of Factory Overhead and the Uses of Predetermined Rates

Capital Company uses a flexible budget system and prepared the following information for last year:

	Percent of Capacity	
	80%	90%
Direct-labor hours	48,000	54,000
Variable factory overhead	$48,000	$54,000
Fixed factory overhead	$96,000	$96,000
Total factory overhead rate per direct labor hour	$3.00	$2.78

Capital Company operated at 80 percent of capacity during last year. It applied factory overhead based on the 90-percent capacity level. The actual costs were $49,000 for variable overhead and $97,000 for fixed overhead.

Required

1. Determine the amount of over- or underapplied overhead for the year.
2. Prepare a report showing variances from budget and the amount of over- or underapplied overhead.

E13–3. Factory Overhead Costing Results—Over- or Underapplied

Peters Company uses a flexible budget system and prepared the following information for the year:

	Percent of Capacity	
	80%	90%
Direct-labor hours	24,000	27,000
Variable factory overhead	$48,000	$54,000
Fixed factory overhead	$108,000	$108,000
Total factory overhead rate per direct-labor hour	$6.50	$6.00

Peters operated at 80 percent of capacity last year, but applied factory overhead was based on the 90-percent capacity level. Actual factory overhead was $158,000 for the year.

Required

1. Determine the amount of overhead applied for the year.
2. Determine the amount of under- or overapplied overhead for the year.
3. Prepare a report showing variances from budget. Does your report agree with the amount of over- or underapplied overhead calculated in requirement 2?

E13–4. Factory Overhead Concepts—Review of Cost Behavior Determination

Handy Company has estimated overhead of $96,000 for 6,000 labor hours per month and $144,000 for 14,000 labor hours per month. The company is preparing to handle factory overhead by using predetermined overhead rates instead of the practice that has been used—waiting until year-end and assigning actual overhead to production.

Handy estimates that 12,000 labor hours represent normal capacity operation.

Required

1. Determine the variable overhead rate per labor hour in the overhead estimates. Use the high-low method described in chapter 3 for this requirement and for requirement 2.
2. Determine the fixed cost overhead total in the overhead estimates.
3. Determine a predetermined overhead rate for normal capacity.

E13–5. Factory Overhead—Analysis of Over- or Underapplied Overhead

Factory overhead for a company has been estimated as follows for the month of March:

Fixed factory overhead	$ 50,000
Variable factory overhead	$150,000
Estimated direct-labor hours	100,000

Production for March reached 80 percent of the estimated level, and actual factory overhead totaled $175,000. Actual fixed overhead was $51,000.

Required

1. Determine the overhead application rates and the amount of overhead applied to work in process for March.
2. Prepare an electronic spreadsheet to calculate the volume variance and the amount of under- or overapplied overhead for March.

E13–6. Factory Overhead and Year-End Disposition of Overhead Balances

At the end of the last fiscal year, Bailey Company had the following account balances:

Factory overhead	$ 1,000 (credit balance)
Cost of goods sold	980,000
Work-in-process inventory	38,000
Finished goods inventory	82,000

Required

1. List and briefly describe the various possible methods for disposing of over- or underapplied overhead.
2. Determine the disposition of the $1,000 overapplied overhead for Bailey Company if the amount is prorated (allocated) to the work-in-process and finished-goods inventories and to cost of goods sold.
3. Show the disposition you obtained in requirement 2 in general journal form.
4. Which method of disposition of the year-end overapplied overhead would you recommend for Bailey Company? Explain your recommendation.

E13–7. Factory Overhead and End-of-Period Results

Boley, Inc. has a variable overhead application rate of $15.00 per machine hour based on a 3,000-hour activity level. Total fixed overhead costs are budgeted at $51,000. Actual factory overhead for the month was $93,000 at an actual volume of 2,800 machine hours. Actual expenditures for fixed overhead exceeded the budget by $1,000.

Required

Determine the following:

1. Applied factory overhead.
2. Over- or underapplied factory overhead.
3. Variance from budget.
4. Volume variance.

E13–8. Factory Overhead Concepts and Variance Analysis Contadora Company has set a factory overhead rate of $9.00 per hour. Budgeted overhead for 3,000 hours per month is $48,000 and for 7,000 hours is $72,000. Actual factory overhead for the month of July was $54,000, and the actual volume was 5,000 hours.

Required

Determine the following:

1. Variable overhead in the overhead rate, using the high-low method described in chapter 3.
2. Budgeted fixed overhead.
3. Normal volume or normal capacity hours.
4. Applied factory overhead.
5. Over- or underapplied factory overhead.
6. Variance from budget.
7. Volume variance.

E13–9. Factory Overhead A summary of accounts has been prepared for the LHC Company at the end of June. The work-in-process and factory overhead accounts follow:

Work in Process

June 1 balance	3,580	64,480	Cost of goods manufactured
Direct materials	21,600		
Direct labor	25,000		
Factory overhead	27,500		

Factory Overhead

Indirect materials	5,160	27,500	Charged to production at a predetermined percentage of direct-labor cost
Indirect labor	12,500		
Supervision	2,000		
Repairs and maintenance	1,540		
Utilities	1,200		
Other	5,700		

Required

1. Determine the work-in-process ending inventory in total and broken down into individual amounts of materials, labor, and factory overhead. Materials costs in the inventory amount to $3,960.
2. Determine the total factory overhead incurred during June and the amount of under- or overapplied overhead.

E13–10. Factory Overhead and Journal Entries Wonder Company produces and sells Wundra software materials for personal computers. Wonder uses a predetermined overhead rate in all departments. Direct-labor hours are used in the final assembly department to apply overhead to production.

The following transactions occurred during May in the final assembly department:

1. The payroll was recorded and distributed. The total for the department was $15,000, of which $3,000 was indirect. The FICA rate is 7.51 percent, and federal income taxes average 10 percent of gross earnings. All workers earn $10 per hour.
2. Supplies for specific use in the department were purchased on account for $3,500. These supplies are accounted for in the department's own inventory account.
3. Materials used in production included $8,000 direct and $1,800 indirect materials and supplies. The indirect materials and supplies came from the department's own inventory account.
4. The employer's payroll taxes were recorded as factory overhead. The rates are FICA, 7.51 percent; state unemployment, 6.2 percent; and federal unemployment, 0.8 percent.
5. The following costs were recorded during May to be paid: repairs, $125; equipment rental, $325; and utilities, $350.
6. Adjusting entries were recorded. They included depreciation on equipment of $750 and expired insurance of $125.
7. Overhead was applied to work in process. The rate used in the department is $5.50 per direct-labor hour.

Required

1. Set up journal entries to record the preceding transactions for the final assembly department for the month of May.
2. Summarize the total overhead incurred during May and determine the amount of under- or overapplied overhead.

E13–11. Overhead Variance Reporting Henry Manufacturing Company had the following budgeted and actual rates and amounts for the month of July.

Budget Item	Amount/Rate Budgeted	Actual
Direct-labor (DL) hours	10,000 hours	10,200 hours
Variable overhead:		
Indirect material	$5.80 per DL hour	$59,000
Indirect labor	9.20 per DL hour	94,000
Other variable overhead	6.00 per DL hour	61,000
Fixed overhead:		
Depreciation	$ 80,000	$ 82,000
Other fixed overhead	120,000	119,000

Henry uses direct-labor hours to calculate a predetermined rate for applying factory overhead. The company uses a monthly rate to apply overhead to work in process.

Required

1. Using an electronic spreadsheet, prepare a management report to compare budgeted and actual overhead. Include the volume variance and over- or underapplied overhead in the report. Construct the spreadsheet so that the flexible budget, variances, and under- or overapplied overhead are automatically calculated.
2. Using the spreadsheet prepared for requirement 1, assume that 9,900 hours were actually worked during the month. What happened to the volume variance? What happened to under- or overapplied overhead?

PROBLEMS

P13–1. Factory Overhead and Job Costs Using Different Bases
During the past month, the Bigelow Company had the following costs:

Materials used	$39,000
Direct labor	48,000
Indirect materials	6,000
Indirect labor	8,000
Supervisor's salary (factory operations)	6,000
Labor fringe cost (factory labor)	5,600
Depreciation on factory building	2,000
Factory machinery depreciation	4,000
Property tax on factory facilities	600
Selling and administrative expense	7,000
Insurance on factory facilities and inventory	400
Miscellaneous factory overhead	2,400
Power and light (factory operations)	1,000
Advertising	3,000

During the past month, Bigelow worked on three orders. Costs and other pertinent data in connection with these orders are as follows:

	Job 221	Job 222	Job 223
Materials cost	$12,000	$16,000	$11,000
Direct-labor hours	1,950	2,700	975
Machine hours	1,600	1,800	600
Direct-labor cost	$16,000	$24,000	$8,000

Required

1. Determine the total actual factory overhead for the past month.
2. Determine the total cost of each job, using each of the following as the basis for charging factory overhead:
   a. Direct-labor costs
   b. Direct-labor hours
   c. Machine hours

P13–2. Factory Overhead and End-of-Period Results
Robotics, Inc., a manufacturing company, uses the following data as the basis for its monthly factory overhead budget.

Overhead Category	Rate per Machine Hour
Variable	
Indirect materials	$2.00
Indirect labor	3.00
Other variable	5.00
Fixed	**Amount**
Supervisory salaries	$ 4,000
Depreciation	6,000
Other fixed	10,000

Robotics uses machine hours to calculate a predetermined rate for applying factory overhead to work in process. Budgeted machine hours were 5,000, but 4,900 machine hours were actually utilized. The following actual costs were incurred:

Indirect materials	$12,000
Indirect labor	14,000
Other variable overhead	27,000
Supervisory salaries	4,000
Depreciation	6,000
Other fixed overhead	11,000

Required

1. Calculate the predetermined overhead application rate.
2. Give the summary journal entries to record *(a)* actual overhead expenditures and *(b)* overhead applied to work in process.
3. Prepare a management report showing budgeted and actual results, variances for each cost item plus the volume variance, and the amount of under- or overapplied overhead.

P13–3. Factory Overhead and End-of-Period Results Pinewood Products has prepared the following overhead budget for its factory operations for June.

Account	Variable Rate	Budget
Variable overhead:		
Labor	$12.00	$24,000
Materials	8.00	16,000
Miscellaneous	6.00	12,000
		$52,000
Fixed overhead:		
Depreciation		$11,000
Taxes		6,000
Miscellaneous		3,000
		$20,000
Total		$72,000

The company uses direct-labor hours as its budgetary base. Payroll records indicate that there were 2,200 direct-labor hours worked during June. The following summary journal entries were made during June with regard to factory overhead costs.

(a) To record expenditures for overhead incurred:
    Factory overhead control   77,300
        Cash/accounts payable   77,300

Postings to overhead subsidiary ledger:

Labor	$26,000
Materials	18,100
Miscellaneous (variable)	13,300
Depreciation	11,000
Taxes	6,200
Miscellaneous (fixed)	2,700

(b) To record overhead applied to work in process:
    Work in process   79,200
        Factory overhead applied   79,200

Required

1. Calculate the predetermined overhead application rate, showing the variable and fixed portions, for the month of June.
2. Prepare a management report comparing budgeted and actual overhead for each

overhead cost item. Also, show the volume variance and over- or underapplied overhead in your report.

3. Explain the meaning of the volume variance. Draw a graph showing fixed and variable overhead amounts for June. Label the volume variance on your graph.

4. Explain what alternatives are available for the disposition of over- or underapplied overhead. What method would you recommend Pinewood Products use for June? Explain.

P13-4. Overhead Variance Reporting Holman Scientific, Inc., a manufacturing company, produces a variety of electronic sensors for military applications. The firm's budgeted and actual overhead costs for the month of September, as shown by its accounting records, are as follows:

Overhead Account	Variable Rate	Budget	Actual
Variable overhead:			
Indirect material	$ 6.00	$ 90,000	$ 90,300
Indirect labor	6.50	97,500	99,000
Repair and maintenance	4.50	67,500	68,000
Other variable	3.00	45,000	45,000
	$20.00	$300,000	$302,300
Fixed overhead:			
Depreciation		$ 85,000	$ 85,000
Insurance		33,000	34,000
Other fixed		6,750	6,000
		$124,750	$125,000
Total		$424,750	$427,300

Holman uses machine hours to calculate a predetermined rate for applying factory overhead. The budget is based on 15,000 hours, but 15,100 hours were actually worked. The company uses a monthly rate to apply overhead to work in process.

During the month of September, Holman worked on a number of different jobs. Machine-hour statistics for two jobs are as follows:

	Machine Hours
Job X	5,000
Job Z	4,000

Required

1. Calculate the predetermined overhead application rate, using machine hours as the base.
2. Give the journal entries to record (a) actual overhead expenditures and (b) overhead applied to work in process. How much overhead was applied to Jobs X and Z? By how much was overhead over- or underapplied?
3. Using an electronic spreadsheet, prepare a management report to compare budgeted and actual overhead. Include the volume variance and over- or underapplied overhead in the report. Construct the spreadsheet so that the flexible budget, variances, and under- or overapplied overhead are automatically calculated.
4. Using the spreadsheet prepared for requirement 3, assume that (a) 15,200 hours and (b) 14,900 hours were actually worked during September. What happened to the volume variance in each instance? What happened to under- or overapplied overhead in each instance?

P13-5. Factory Overhead Application and Analysis of Variances The Duncan Company's factory overhead for April is summarized in the following table. Normal ca-

CHAPTER 13: FACTORY OVERHEAD: COSTING AND CONTROL I   485

pacity is used as the activity level for computing the predetermined factory overhead rate. Normal capacity is 1,600 hours. During April actual activity was 80 percent of normal.

Expense	Estimated Factory Overhead at 100% of Normal	Estimated Factory Overhead at 80% of Normal	Actual Factory Overhead
Superintendence	$1,100	$1,100	$1,100
Depreciation	650	650	650
Property tax	720	720	720
Rent	900	900	900
Power	600	480	530
Maintenance labor	840	672	790
Insurance	350	350	350
Factory supplies	480	384	425
Indirect labor	960	768	710
Payroll taxes	280	224	234
Total	$6,880	$6,248	$6,409

Required

1. Determine the predetermined overhead rate and the overhead applied during April.
2. Determine the over- or underapplied factory overhead.
3. Determine the volume variance.
4. Prepare a report showing the variance from budget for each variable overhead item, the volume variance, and the amount of over- or underapplied overhead.

P13–6. Factory Overhead and Job Costing Baehr Company is a manufacturing company with a fiscal year that runs from July 1 to June 30. Baehr uses a job-order accounting system for its production costs.

A predetermined overhead rate based on direct-labor hours is used to apply overhead to individual jobs. A flexible budget of overhead costs was prepared for the fiscal year, as shown here:

Direct-labor hours	100,000	120,000	140,000
Variable overhead costs	$325,000	$390,000	$455,000
Fixed overhead costs	216,000	216,000	216,000
Total overhead	$541,000	$606,000	$671,000

Although the annual ideal capacity is 150,000 direct-labor hours, Baehr's officials have determined 120,000 direct-labor hours as normal capacity for the year.

The following information is for November, during which Jobs 77–50 and 77–51 were completed.

Inventories, November 1	
Raw materials and supplies	$ 10,500
Work in process (Job 77–50)	54,000
Finished goods	112,500
Purchase of raw materials and supplies	
Raw materials	$135,000
Supplies	15,000
Materials and supplies requisitioned for production	
Job 77–50	$ 45,000
Job 77–51	37,500
Job 77–52	25,500
Supplies	12,000
	$120,000

Factory direct-labor hours (incurred this month)
Job 77–50	3,500 hours
Job 77–51	3,000 hours
Job 77–52	2,000 hours

Labor costs
Direct-labor wages	$ 51,000
Indirect-labor wages (4,000 hours)	15,000
Supervisory salaries	6,000

Building occupancy costs (heat, light, depreciation, etc.)
Factory facilities	$6,500
Sales offices	1,500
Administrative offices	1,000
	$9,000

Factory equipment costs
Power	$4,000
Repairs and maintenance	1,500
Depreciation	1,500
Other	1,000
	$8,000

Required

1. Determine the predetermined overhead rate to be used to apply overhead to individual jobs during the fiscal year.
2. Using the rate you obtained in requirement 1, determine the amount of overhead applied to all jobs during November.
3. Determine the *total cost* of Job 77–50.
4. Determine the factory overhead costs applied to Job 77–52 during November.
5. Determine the actual factory overhead incurred during November.

P13–7. Determining Overhead Rates and Evaluating Overhead Information

Tastee-Treat Company prepares, packages, and distributes six frozen vegetables in two different sized containers. The different vegetables and different sizes are prepared in large batches. Tastee-Treat employs an actual job-order costing system with factory overhead assigned to batches by a predetermined rate on the basis of direct-labor hours. The factory overhead costs incurred by Tastee-Treat during two recent years (adjusted for changes using current prices and wage rates) are presented here:

	Year 1	Year 2
Direct-labor hours worked	2,760,000	2,160,000
Factory overhead costs incurred		
Indirect labor	$11,040,000	$8,640,000
Employee benefits	4,140,000	3,240,000
Supplies	2,760,000	2,160,000
Power	2,208,000	1,728,000
Heat and light	552,000	552,000
Supervision	2,865,000	2,625,000
Depreciation	7,930,000	7,930,000
Property taxes and insurance	3,005,000	3,005,000
Total overhead costs	$34,500,000	$29,880,000

Required

Tastee-Treat Company expects to operate at a 2,300,000 direct-labor hour level of activity next year. Using the preceding data, calculate the rate Tastee-Treat should employ to assign manufacturing overhead to its products. State any assumptions you make about cost behavior, and back up your answer with a schedule showing your estimate of overhead costs, by overhead item, for the 2,300,000 direct-labor hour level of activity.

P13-8. Determination and Use of Overhead Rates Using Different Bases

The Mann Company's budget data for March are as follows:

Estimated factory overhead	$360,000
Production scheduled	40,000 units
Direct-labor hours scheduled	100,000 hours
Estimated direct-labor cost	$500,000
Machine hours scheduled	120,000 hours

Required

1. Compute the overhead rate using the various bases indicated.
2. Assume that the total overhead estimate is composed of a variable estimate of $240,000 and a fixed estimate of $120,000. Compute variable and fixed overhead rates using machine hours.
3. Prepare the journal entry that would charge the overhead to production using the labor hour rate determined in requirement 1, assuming that 99,000 labor hours were used during the period.
4. Supply the missing account name in the following journal entry for overhead incurred:

?	359,200	
Stores control (factory supplies)		65,000
Accumulated depreciation—machinery		80,000
Prepaid insurance—factory inventory and equipment		20,000
Payroll (indirect labor)		156,200
Accounts payable (overhead from current period disbursements)		38,000

5. Was the factory overhead over- or underapplied during March and by how much?
6. Assume that the $359,200 overhead incurred consisted of $120,500 of fixed costs and $238,700 of variable costs. Determine the over- or underapplied variable and fixed overhead for the period.

P13-9. Factory Overhead—Variances and Job Results (CMA)

The following data apply to the operations of Mack Incorporated:

Department 203—Work in Process—Beginning of Period

Job No.	Material	Labor	Overhead	Total
1376	$17,500	$22,000	$33,000	$72,500

Department 203 actual costs for the year:

Incurred by Jobs	Material	Labor	Other	Total
1376	$ 1,000	$ 7,000	—	$ 8,000
1377	26,000	53,000	—	79,000
1378	12,000	9,000	—	21,000
1379	4,000	1,000	—	5,000
Not incurred by Jobs				
Indirect materials and supplies	15,000	—	—	15,000
Indirect labor	—	53,000	—	53,000
Employee benefits	—	—	$23,000	23,000
Depreciation	—	—	12,000	12,000
Supervision	—	20,000	—	20,000
Total	$58,000	$143,000	$35,000	$236,000

Department 203 overhead rate for the year:

Budgeted overhead	
Variable—Indirect materials	$ 16,000
Indirect labor	56,000
Employee benefits	24,000
Fixed—Supervision	20,000
Depreciation	12,000
Total	$128,000
Budgeted direct-labor dollars	$80,000
Rate per direct-labor dollar ($128,000 ÷ 80,000)	160%

Required

1. Determine the actual overhead for Department 203 for the year.
2. Determine for Department 203 the overhead applied to each job, the total applied, and the amount of over- or underapplied overhead.
3. Analyze the over- or underapplied overhead into budget and volume variances.
4. Job No. 1376 was the only job completed and sold during the year. Determine the amount included in cost of goods sold for this job.
5. Determine the cost of work-in-process inventory at the end of the year.
6. If underapplied overhead was distributed between cost of goods sold and work-in-process inventory, how much of the underapplied overhead was charged to the year-end work-in-process inventory?

P13-10. Factory Overhead—Comprehensive Evaluation of Procedures (CMA)

The Herbert Manufacturing Company manufactures custom-designed restaurant and kitchen furniture. Herbert Manufacturing uses a job-order cost accounting system. Actual overhead costs incurred during the month are applied to the products on the basis of actual direct-labor hours required to produce the products. The overhead costs consist primarily of supervision, employee benefits, maintenance costs, property taxes, and depreciation.

Herbert Manufacturing recently won a contract to manufacture the furniture for a new fast-food chain that is expanding rapidly in the area. In general, this furniture is durable but of a lower quality than the company normally manufactures. To produce this new line, Herbert Manufacturing must purchase more molded plastic parts for the furniture than for its current line. Through innovative industrial engineering, an efficient manufacturing process for this new furniture has been developed that requires only minimum capital investment. Management is very optimistic about the profit improvement the new product line will bring.

At the end of October, the start-up month for the new line, the controller has prepared a separate income statement for the new product line. On a consolidated basis, the gross profit percentage was normal; however, the profitability for the new line was less than expected.

At the end of November the results were somewhat improved. Consolidated profits were good, but the reported profitability for the new product line still was less than expected. John Herbert, president of the company, is concerned that knowledgeable stockholders will criticize his decision to add this lower-quality product line at a time when profitability appeared to be increasing with the firm's standard product line.

The results presented below are for the first nine months of the current year and for October and November. Additional data about operations for October and November are presented on page 490.

Herbert Manufacturing Company
(000 omitted)

	Fast-Food Furniture	Custom Furniture	Consolidated
Nine months year-to-date			
Gross sales	—	$8,100	$8,100
Direct material	—	$2,025	$2,025
Direct labor			
Forming	—	758	758
Finishing	—	1,314	1,314
Assembly	—	558	558
Overhead	—	1,779	1,779
Cost of sales	—	$6,434	$6,434
Gross profit	—	$1,666	$1,666
Gross profit percentage	—	20.6%	20.6%
October 19X8			
Gross sales	$400	$ 900	$1,300
Direct material	$200	$ 225	$ 425
Direct labor			
Forming	17	82	99
Finishing	40	142	182
Assembly	33	60	93
Overhead	60	180	240
Cost of sales	$350	$ 689	$1,039
Gross profit	$ 50	$ 211	$ 261
Gross profit percentage	12.5%	23.4%	20.1%
November 19X8			
Gross sales	$800	$ 800	$1,600
Direct material	$400	$ 200	$ 600
Direct labor			
Forming	31	72	103
Finishing	70	125	195
Assembly	58	53	111
Overhead	98	147	245
Cost of sales	$657	$ 597	$1,254
Gross profit	$143	$ 203	$ 346
Gross profit percentage	17.9%	25.4%	21.6%

Caroline Jameson, cost accounting manager, has stated that the overhead allocation based only on direct-labor hours is no longer appropriate. On the basis of a recently completed study of the overhead accounts, Jameson believes that only supervision and employee benefits should be allocated on the basis of direct-labor hours, and the balance of the overhead should be allocated on a machine-hour basis. In her judgment the increase in the profitability of the custom design furniture is because of a misallocation of overhead in the present system.

The actual direct-labor hours and machine hours for the past two months are as follows:

	Fast-Food Furniture	Custom Furniture
Machine Hours		
October		
Forming	660	10,700
Finishing	660	7,780
Assembly	—	—
	1,320	18,480
November		
Forming	1,280	9,640
Finishing	1,280	7,400
Assembly	—	—
	2,560	17,040
Direct-Labor Hours		
October		
Forming	1,900	9,300
Finishing	3,350	12,000
Assembly	4,750	8,700
	10,000	30,000
November		
Forming	3,400	8,250
Finishing	5,800	10,400
Assembly	8,300	7,600
	17,500	26,250

The actual overhead costs for the past two months were as follows:

	October	November
Supervision	$ 13,000	$ 13,000
Employee benefits	95,000	109,500
Maintenance	50,000	48,000
Depreciation	42,000	42,000
Property taxes	8,000	8,000
All other	32,000	24,500
Total	$240,000	$245,000

Required

1. Based on Mrs. Jameson's recommendation, reallocate the overhead for October and November using direct-labor hours as the allocation base for supervision and employee benefits. Use machine hours as the base for the remaining overhead costs.
2. Develop a revised statement of operating results for October and November, incorporating the revised overhead amounts you determined in requirement 1.
3. Support or criticize Mrs. Jameson's conclusion that the increase in custom design profitability is caused by a misallocation of overhead. Use the answers you developed in requirements 1 and 2 to support your analysis.
4. Mrs. Jameson has also recommended that consideration be given to using predetermined overhead application rates calculated on an annual basis rather than allocating actual cost over actual volume each month. She stated that this is particularly applicable now that the company has two distinct product lines. Discuss the advantages of predetermined overhead rates prepared on an annual basis.

Chapter 14

Factory Overhead: Costing and Control II

Outline

DEPARTMENTALIZATION OF OVERHEAD COSTS
Production and Service Departments
Service Department Cost Allocation
Accumulating Overhead Costs by Department
Selection of an Allocation Base
Allocation Methods
  Direct Method
  Step Method
  Reciprocal Method
ADVANTAGES OF DEPARTMENTALIZATION
THE NUMBER AND CONFIGURATION OF DEPARTMENTS
Homogeneity of Costs
Production Departments
Service Departments
ALLOCATION OF COSTS BY BEHAVIOR
Variable Costs
Fixed Costs

SUMMARY
APPENDIX 14.1: APPLICABLE STANDARDS OF THE COST ACCOUNTING STANDARDS BOARD
Standard 402: Consistency in Allocating Costs Incurred for the Same Purpose
Standard 403: Allocation of Home Office Expenses to Segments
Standard 410: Allocation of Business Unit General and Administrative Expenses to Final Cost Objectives
Standard 418: Allocation of Indirect Cost Pools
APPENDIX 14.2: RECIPROCAL ALLOCATIONS USING MATRIX ALGEBRA
SELF-STUDY PROBLEM
SUGGESTED READINGS
DISCUSSION QUESTIONS
EXERCISES
PROBLEMS

In chapter 13, principles of factory overhead accounting were discussed using a factory-wide perspective in which *(a)* one factory-wide predetermined overhead application rate is calculated, *(b)* one set of accounts is used to record applied and actual overhead, and *(c)* one set of reports is used to analyze under- or overapplied overhead. This chapter develops additional aspects of overhead accounting using a departmental rather than a factory-wide perspective; *separate departmental* overhead application rates, accounts, and reports are used rather than just one factory-wide rate, set of accounts, and reports.

The additional detail of departmental accounting has several advantages. Departmentalization usually provides more meaningful cost allocations to jobs and products than factory-wide accounting does. Also, the potential usefulness of information for planning and control is enhanced by having costs accumulated and reported at a department level rather than at a factory level.

This chapter explains overhead accounting principles that relate to departmentalization in manufacturing companies. After completing this chapter, you should be able to:

1. explain the meaning of departmentalization and give advantages and disadvantages of departmentalization for product costing and management control.
2. define production and service departments and explain how they are related.
3. apply various methods of allocating service department costs.
4. determine the number and configuration of service and production departments in a particular factory operation.
5. apply departmental overhead costs by behavior.

DEPARTMENTALIZATION OF OVERHEAD COSTS

Departmental accounting for overhead costs is simply an extension of the overhead accounting principles discussed in chapter 13. The processes of budgeting, computing a predetermined overhead application rate, and applying overhead to work in process are the same whether using factory-wide or departmental accounting. Only the added detail of departmental accounting and certain cost allocation concepts are different.

A **department,** for cost accounting purposes is a subunit of a manufacturing firm for which a separate measurement of costs is made. The objective of subdividing operations into departments is to facilitate more accurate product costing and more effective cost control. Terms other than *department* that might be used when referring to the same subunit concept are cost object, cost center, cost pool, and factory segment.

Production and Service Departments

Departments within a factory operation can be classified as either production departments or service departments. **Production departments** include those departments that are directly engaged in the manufacturing activity and that contribute to the content and form of the finished product. Examples of typical production departments include cutting, assembly, and finishing departments. Other examples of production departments are given in figure 14.1.

Service departments, as their name suggests, provide services or assistance to other departments. They contribute to the production process in an indirect manner and do not directly shape or form the finished product. Examples of service departments include personnel, cafeteria, and maintenance departments.

A distinction can be made between service and administrative departments. Service departments provide specific types of services to other specified units of an organization,

FIGURE 14.1

Typical Production and Service Departments

Production Departments	
Assembly	Milling
Cutting	Mixing
Finishing	Packing
Knitting	Refining
Matching	

Service Departments	
Accounting	Personnel
Administration	Planning
Cafeteria	Purchasing
Custodial/Grounds	Receiving
First Aid/Medical	Scheduling
General Factory	Security
Internal Auditing	Shipping
Production Control	Stores
Quality Control	Utilities
Maintenance	

whereas administrative departments provide general services for the benefit of the organization as a whole. Recognizing this difference can be useful; however, the underlying principles of cost allocation are the same for service and administrative departments. Therefore, administrative departments are included with service departments in the discussion in this chapter. Figure 14.1 lists typical service departments in manufacturing firms.

Service department costs are used in an organization to provide information in greater detail for more accurate product costing and more effective cost control than would otherwise be available. The costs incurred in service departments, although not directly expended in the production process, are generally thought to be as much a cost of production as are direct materials, direct labor, and factory overhead that is incurred as a direct cost of a production department. In fact, service department costs are simply overhead costs that are accumulated in separately designated service departments rather than in production departments.

Service Department Cost Allocation

Service department costs can be accumulated using three different cost constructs, depending on how the product cost information is used. These cost constructs are *(a)* full costs, *(b)* responsibility costs, and *(c)* differential costs. Each method of accumulating product costs is briefly described in this section, followed by an in-depth discussion of service department accounting in a full-cost context.

Full costs are defined as the sum of direct materials and direct labor plus a fair share of all indirect costs. From a full-cost perspective, costs incurred in service departments should be included as components of the total cost to produce a product. Full costs are used for external reporting according to the guidelines of the Financial Accounting Standards Board (FASB), Securities and Exchange Commission (SEC), and other regulatory bodies; analysis of long-term economic profitability of a product or company; and the determination of product prices, as in the case of regulated utilities. Full costs are the focus of this chapter.

Responsibility costs are intended to encourage managers to make decisions that are consistent with the overall goals of the company. Costs are accumulated by responsibility center and compared against budgeted or planned costs. According to the underlying principle of responsibility for costs, service department costs should be allocated to responsibility centers only if: they can be controlled or influenced by the responsibility center manager; they provide a valid indication of the amount of company resources absorbed by the responsibility center; and they improve the comparability of responsibility centers' performance. Responsibility costs are emphasized in chapter 20.

Differential costs are future costs that are expected to differ depending on which alternative course of action is taken. They may be calculated to compare the relative profitability of two proposed new product lines, for example. Because differential cost accumulations relate to specific decision alternatives, service department costs are included only when they contribute to the difference between specific proposals. Differential costs are emphasized in chapter 4.

As mentioned before, the way service department costs are handled depends on the type of cost accumulation that is needed. The focus for the remainder of this chapter is on accounting for service department costs in a full-cost context.

Including service department costs as costs of production is accomplished by allocating the costs incurred in each service department to benefiting production departments. Amounts allocated to each production department are usually based on the relative quantity of services each production department receives from the various service departments. Allocated service department costs are then added to the overhead costs directly incurred by each production department. Finally, total overhead accumulated in each production department is allocated to units of production as a component of each production department's predetermined overhead application rate. Figure 14.2 illustrates potential overhead cost flows among three service departments and two production departments.

FIGURE 14.2 Allocation of Service Department Costs to Units of Production

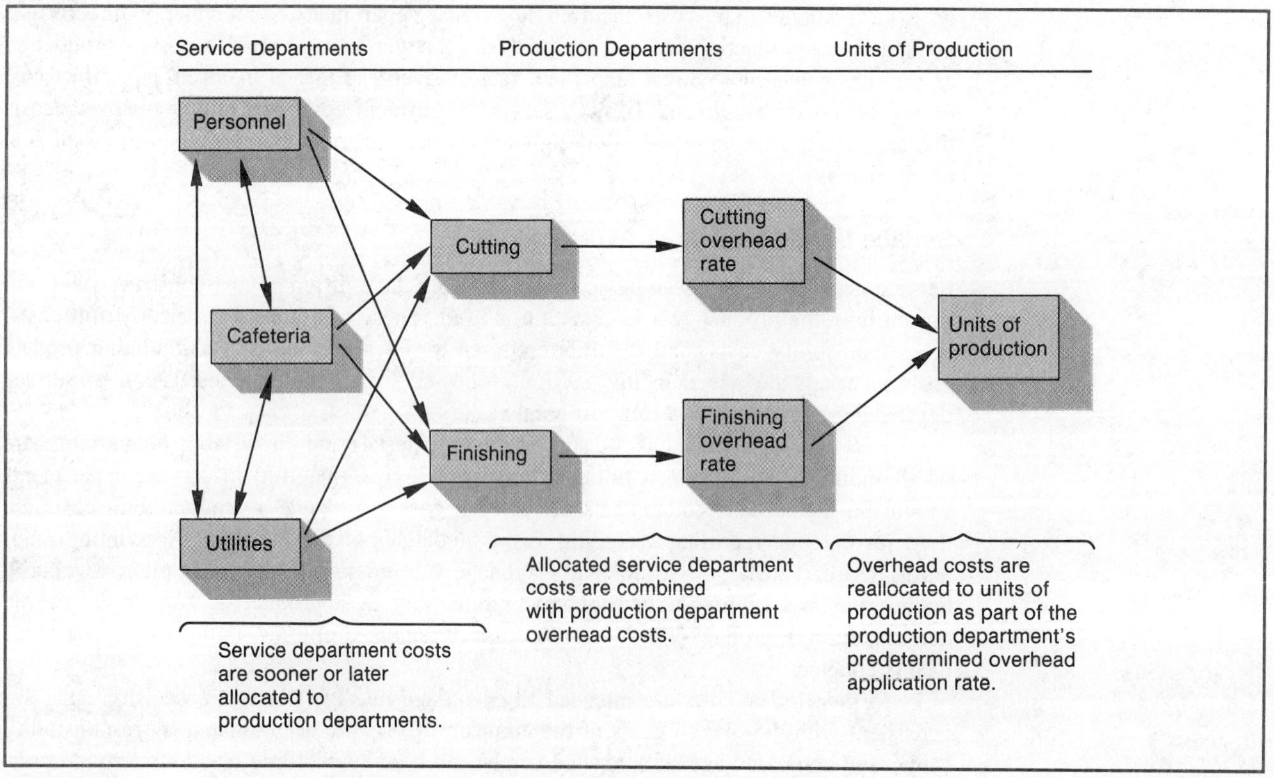

Note in figure 14.2 that service departments may provide assistance to other service departments as well as to production departments. Figure 14.2 does not include some types of costs that may be incurred by a manufacturing company. Costs incurred for purposes far removed from the production process or that do not have a direct connection with the production process, such as general corporate expenses, interest, and taxes, are treated as period expenses rather than charged to factory departments and then to units of production. Such costs appear on the income statement in accounts other than cost of goods manufactured or cost of goods sold.

The process of allocating service department costs to production departments generally takes place twice during an accounting period. Budgeted service department costs are allocated to production departments when departmental manufacturing budgets are prepared before the start of the accounting period. Then actual service department costs are allocated to production departments when end-of-period results are accounted for. However, the process is essentially the same whether done at the beginning of an accounting period using budget data, or done at the end of an accounting period using actual data. Although the illustrations that follow could relate to either time, they deal primarily with the budgetary process because of its fundamental importance in developing predetermined overhead application rates.

Before costs can be properly accumulated and allocations made, each activity for which an accounting is to be made must be identified with a particular department. Otherwise, there would not be a clear basis for either product costing or cost control. Principles relating to the definition of departments and assignment of activities are discussed later in this chapter. For now, assume that various production and service departments are in place and focus on the proper accumulation of overhead costs in departments.

Accumulating Overhead Costs by Department

The concept of *traceability of costs* is important when deciding which costs should be assigned to which departments. Usually, this decision is not very complicated. If a custodial department is selected as a service department, for example, the costs associated with the custodial function are identified with and accumulated in the custodial department accounts. Custodial salaries, fringe benefits, supplies, and depreciation on custodial equipment that originate within the custodial function should become part of the costs associated with that department.

In other instances, however, cost accumulation may be more complicated. For example, the cost of utilities like electricity may directly benefit some departments while they indirectly benefit all departments. In such situations, a company may use meters or other devices to measure departmental consumption, and each department would be assigned its direct share of the cost of the electrical bill. However, the plant probably also incurs electrical costs that are not directly traceable to any specific department. For example, the cost of lighting the outside of the building is usually not traceable to specific departments. This type of overhead cost is typically accumulated in a service department, probably a utilities department in this example. Then a portion of the total cost is allocated to each benefiting department on some rational basis, such as the proportion of total space lighted.

As used in the previous illustration, the terms *direct* and *indirect* are associated with overhead in terms of its traceability to departments. Direct overhead refers to those overhead costs that are traceable directly to specific departments. Indirect overhead refers to those overhead costs that are first accumulated in service departments and then assigned to other departments through an allocation process. Therefore, the use of service departments results in part of the overhead costs of a production department being considered direct overhead and part being considered indirect overhead. Figure 14.3 contains the factory overhead budget for the weaving department of a textile company.

Figure 14.3 shows that the total budgeted overhead of $210,000 is the total direct overhead cost of the weaving department before the allocation of any indirect or service department costs. An addition to the overhead budget by the amount of allocated service department costs is then made.

Once departments have been identified and total costs have been accumulated in each department, the basis used to allocate service department costs to production departments should be determined.

Selection of an Allocation Base

Service department costs are allocated to production departments by using an allocation base in much the same way that overhead costs in production departments are allocated to work in process by using a predetermined overhead application rate. One difference is that the base suggested for allocating overhead is sometimes not appropriate for allocating service department costs. For example, direct-labor hours may be an appropriate base for allocating overhead to units of production but may not be an appropriate base for allocating service department costs to production departments.

The general rule is that the base selected for allocating service department costs should reflect as accurately as possible the relationship between the quantity of services provided by service departments and the amount received by the various other benefitted departments. The allocation bases listed in figure 14.4 exhibit cost-benefit relationships.

Each service department may use a different allocation base, depending on the nature of services rendered. For example, the base used to allocate legal department costs may be

FIGURE 14.3

Weaving Department Factory Overhead Budget

(Based on 70,000 units of production at 1 hour of direct-labor per unit.)
For the year ending December 31, 19X8

	Amount per Unit	Total Amount
Budgeted overhead:		
Variable items:		
Indirect labor	$1.00	$ 70,000
Repair and maintenance	0.30	21,000
Utilities (variable portion)	0.20	14,000
Idle time	0.05	3,500
Other variable overhead	0.05	3,500
	$1.60	$112,000
Fixed items:		
Supervisory salaries		$ 50,000
Depreciation		28,000
Insurance		10,000
Utilities (fixed portion)		4,000
Other fixed overhead		6,000
		$ 98,000
Total budgeted overhead before allocated amounts		$210,000
Total allocated from service departments		$ 39,500
Total budgeted overhead		$249,500
Predetermined overhead application rate (Based on 70,000 direct-labor hours)		$3.56/hr.

the number of hours of legal services used. However, the base used to allocate custodial costs may be the square footage of space occupied by each department served. Sometimes bases are modified so that they result in a more fair and equitable allocation of costs. For example, when one production department produces shavings during processing and others do not, square footage of space occupied may not provide an equitable allocation of costs. In such instances, the manufacturing department producing shavings may be charged a fee in addition to the charge based on square footage of space occupied.

When it is difficult to identify a cause-benefit relationship, a base which represents some level of overall plant activity may be used. For example, sales dollars of product produced or gross margin are overall measures of plant activity that could be used to allocate service department costs. However, the use of this type of base should be avoided whenever there is a base available which exhibits a cause-benefit relationship.

Note that figure 14.4 does not contain the allocation bases that were used in chapter 13 to allocate production department overhead. They are excluded from figure 14.4 simply to distinguish between the process of allocating service department costs to production departments and the use of predetermined overhead application rates to assign total overhead costs accumulated in production departments to work in process. Allocation bases such as direct-labor hours or machine hours may, in fact, be appropriate. However, care should be taken when using them to allocate service department costs.

When a service department's costs are fixed, the use of a variable allocation base, as determined by production department activity, should be avoided because of the potential for inaccurate allocations. For example, the number of machine hours worked may have little correlation with the cost of services received from the personnel department. The use

FIGURE 14.4

Commonly Used Service Department Allocation Bases

Basis	Type of Costs to be Allocated: Department/Cost Category

Number of employees	Personnel-related costs:
	    Personnel department
	    Payroll preparation
	    Cafeteria
	    First aid/medical

Labor cost	Payroll-related costs:
	    Pensions
	    Fringe benefits
	    Payroll taxes

Material cost/material quantity	Material-related costs:
	    Purchasing
	    Material handling
	    Storage

Square (cubic) footage of space occupied	Space-related costs:
	    Insurance
	    Depreciation
	    Maintenance of buildings

Metered usage or installed horsepower	Energy-related costs:
	    Electricity
	    Heating
	    Steam

Hours of services rendered	Time-related costs:
	    Accounting
	    Legal
	    Maintenance
	    Research and development

of machine hours in this example may result in an inequitable allocation of personnel department costs.

Another consideration in the selection of an allocation base is the availability of data and the ease with which allocations are made. The cost of elaborate measurement systems and complex computations may exceed the benefits received from such systems. An accountant should try to use a base for which data are already available or are easily gathered and maintained. Allocation schemes should be well understood and acceptable to the department managers who must rely on them for decision-making information.

Allocation Methods

There are three methods used to allocate service department costs—the *direct method*, the *step method* (sometimes called multi-step or step-down method), and the *reciprocal method* (sometimes called the algebraic or linear algebra method). To illustrate the use of each of these methods, assume a plant situation in which there are two production departments (cutting and finishing) and three service departments (personnel, cafeteria, and utility). Assumed departmental statistics are given in figure 14.5.

Direct Method The **direct method** is used to allocate service department costs directly to production departments with no allocation of service department costs to any other service department. Although this method is the easiest to apply, it should be used only when service departments do not in fact render service to other service departments or when such service is considered immaterial in its effect on final product costs. For example, if the direct method is used to allocate service department costs in the situation illustrated in figure 14.5, the potential service of the custodial department to the cafeteria is assumed to be either nonexistent or immaterial in its effect on product costs.

Each service department illustrated in this example uses a different base to allocate costs. The base used to allocate personnel department costs is the number of personnel transactions processed for each production department. The base used to allocate cafeteria costs is the number of employees in each production department. The base used to allocate utilities costs is the amount of floor space occupied by each production department.

Using the direct method, service department costs are allocated based on the relative proportion or percentage of the allocation base associated with each production department. Figure 14.6 shows the calculation of these percentages for the cutting and finishing departments.

FIGURE 14.5

Factory Statistics for Service Department Cost Allocation

Department	Personnel Transactions Processed	Number of Employees	Space Occupied (square feet)
Production:			
Cutting	150	400	60,000
Finishing	250	600	60,000
Total	400	1,000	120,000
Service:			
Personnel	20	15	4,000
Cafeteria	40	20	10,000
Utilities	60	120	—
Total	120	155	14,000
Grand total	520	1,155	134,000

FIGURE 14.6

Direct Method of Allocation: Factory Statistics and Percentages

Department	Personnel Transactions Processed Number	Percent	Number of Employees Number	Percent	Space Occupied (square feet) Number	Percent
Cutting	150	37.5%	400	40.0%	60,000	50.0%
Finishing	250	62.5	600	60.0	60,000	50.0
	400	100.0%	1,000	100.0%	120,000	100.0%

Using the relative percentages calculated in figure 14.6, service department costs are allocated directly to production departments, as illustrated in figure 14.7.

Step Method The **step method** is used to allocate service department costs when service departments provide services to *other service departments* as well as to production departments. Ultimately, all service department costs find their way to production departments. The step method simply recognizes the cost of services provided by one service department to another and provides for a more precise ultimate application of overhead costs.

To apply the step method, a sequence for allocating service department costs must first be chosen. This sequence is usually determined by applying some rational or systematic criteria. For example, the first service department chosen may be the one that provides the most service to others, the second may provide the next amount of services, and so forth. Such a ranking gives guidance as to which service department's costs are to be allocated first, second, third, and so forth. In this example, assume that after applying some criteria, it is determined that the personnel, cafeteria, and utilities departments are to be ranked in that order for purposes of allocating service department costs.

FIGURE 14.7

Direct Method of Allocation: Allocation Procedure

	Service Departments			Production Departments	
	Personnel	Cafeteria	Utilities	Cutting	Finishing
Overhead costs Before allocation	$20,000	$30,000	$40,000	$210,000	$300,000
Allocation:					
Personnel {Percent}	(20,000) {100.0%}			7,500 {37.5%}	12,500 {62.5%}
Cafeteria {Percent}		(30,000) {100.0%}		12,000 {40.0%}	18,000 {60.0%}
Utilities {Percent}			(40,000) {100.0%}	20,000 {50.0%}	20,000 {50.0%}
Total production department overhead after allocation				$249,500	$350,500
Predetermined overhead application rates:					
Cutting ($249,500 ÷ 70,000 direct-labor hours)				$3.56/hr.	
Finishing ($350,500 ÷ 90,000 direct-labor hours)					$3.89/hr.

Using this sequence, the process begins with the allocation of personnel department costs to the other service and production departments. It continues in a step-by-step fashion with the allocation of total cafeteria costs to utilities and production departments. Finally, the utilities department's costs are allocated to production departments.

Before actual cost allocations are made, it is necessary to determine the percentage of each service department's cost that is to be allocated to a certain service and production department. Percentages are calculated using overhead application bases as with the direct method; however, the step-wise process must be taken into consideration when calculating these percentages. To illustrate, assume that personnel department costs are allocated on the basis of the number of personnel transactions processed, that cafeteria department costs are allocated on the basis of the number of employees in each department, and that utilities department costs are allocated on the basis of space occupied. Figure 14.8 gives factory statistics for each of these bases and illustrates the calculation of percentages for each production and service department.

Because personnel department costs are allocated first, zero personnel department costs are allocated to themselves. Therefore, factory statistics are not applicable, and 0% is shown for the personnel department in figure 14.8. Also, note that this same general principle applies to subsequent departmental allocations consistent with the step method.

Now that percentage allocation numbers have been developed, actual cost allocations can be made, as shown in figure 14.9.

Personnel department costs are first allocated to all other service departments *and* to production departments. Next, cafeteria costs plus allocated personnel department costs are allocated to the utilities department and to production departments. Finally, utilities costs plus previously allocated costs are allocated to production departments. Through this process, all service department costs are eventually assigned to production departments.

When using the step method as compared to the direct method, there could be a significant difference in the amount of costs that ultimately reach production departments. Such differences directly effect the amount of costs assigned to each unit of production and could consequently have a substantial effect on the firm's operations when costs of production are used in management decisions. Therefore, it is vital that the allocation method chosen is representative of the actual cost of producing each product.

Reciprocal Method The **reciprocal method** is used when service departments render service to one another in a mutual or complementary relationship. This situation is typical of most service department relationships and represents the most theoretically accurate

FIGURE 14.8

Step Method of Allocation: Factory Statistics and Percentages

Department	Personnel Transactions Processed Number	Percent	Number of Employees Number	Percent	Space Occupied (square feet) Number	Percent
Production:						
Cutting	150	30%	400	36%	60,000	50%
Finishing	250	50	600	53	60,000	50
Service:						
Personnel	na	0	na	0	na	0
Cafeteria	40	8	na	0	na	0
Utilities	60	12	120	11	na	0
	500	100%	1,120	100%	120,000	100%

na = not applicable (Costs of service departments are not allocated to themselves when using the step method.)

CHAPTER 14: FACTORY OVERHEAD: COSTING AND CONTROL II   501

FIGURE 14.9

Step Method of Allocation: Allocation Procedure

	Service Departments			Production Departments	
	Personnel	**Cafeteria**	**Utilities**	**Cutting**	**Finishing**
Overhead costs					
Before allocation	$20,000	$30,000	$40,000	$210,000	$300,000
Allocation:					
Personnel	(20,000)	1,600	2,400	6,000	10,000
{Percent}	{100%}	{8%}	{12%}	{30%}	{50%}
Cafeteria		(31,600)	3,476	11,376	16,748
{Percent}		{100%}	{11%}	{36%}	{53%}
Utilities			(45,876)	22,938	22,938
{Percent}			{100%}	{50%}	{50%}
Total production department overhead after allocation				$250,314	$349,686
Predetermined overhead application rates:					
Cutting ($250,314 ÷ 70,000 direct-labor hours)				$3.58/hr.	
Finishing ($349,686 ÷ 90,000 direct labor hours)					$3.89/hr.

method. It is a rare manufacturing situation in which all service departments serve only production departments and do not simultaneously serve other service departments. The step method goes part way in recognizing these reciprocal relationships, but its results only approximate a theoretical solution when reciprocal relationships are present. Such approximations may be adequate in some company situations, but in other situations more precision is desirable.

The application of the reciprocal method relies on the use of simultaneous equations. To illustrate the procedure, let's begin with a simple situation and assume that a firm has only two service departments (department A and department B) and two production departments (department 1 and department 2). Department A provides services to department B as well as to both production departments based on the percentage of space occupied by each department. Department B provides services to department A and to both production departments based on the number of employees in each of these departments.

These relationships and associated percentages are outlined in figure 14.10 along with the respective departmental costs before allocation. Remember that the objective of this

FIGURE 14.10

Reciprocal Method of Allocation: Factory Statistics and Percentages

	Depart B Number of Employees		Department A Space Occupied		Overhead Costs before Allocation
Department	**Number**	**Percent**	**Square Feet**	**Percent**	
Production:					
Department 1	30	20%	15,000	30%	$ 40,000
Department 2	105	70	25,000	50	60,000
					$100,000
Service:					
Department A	15	10	na	0	8,000
Department B	na	0	10,000	20	12,000
					$ 20,000
	150	100%	50,000	100%	$120,000

Note: The objective is to allocate total service department costs of $20,000 to the production departments.

procedure is to allocate total service department costs of $20,000 ($8,000 for department A plus $12,000 for department B) to the production departments.

Once the relationships illustrated in figure 14.10 are determined, the next step in applying the reciprocal method is to formulate total cost functions for the service departments, *taking into consideration their reciprocal relationships*. For example, the total cost to be allocated by department A is $8,000 plus 10 percent of department B's costs. The total cost to be allocated by department B is $12,000 plus 20 percent of department A's costs. Stated algebraically, this reciprocal relationship is shown as follows:

Let A = total costs of department A
B = total costs of department B

(1) $A = \$8,000 + 0.1B$
(2) $B = \$12,000 + 0.2A$

The next step in the reciprocal method is to solve the preceding equations simultaneously for either A or B. This can be done by substituting the value of B in equation (2) for B in equation (1) and solving for A. Then the value of A can be substituted for A in equation (2) and solved for B, as follows:

Substituting in (1):
$A = \$8,000 + 0.1(\$12,000 + 0.2A)$
$A = \$8,000 + \$1,200 + 0.02A$
$0.98 A = \$9,200$
$A = \$9,388$

Substituting in (2):
$B = \$12,000 + 0.2(\$9,388)$
$B = \$13,878$

The final step in the reciprocal method is to allocate the total cost for each service department calculated in the preceding process to other service departments and to the production departments based on the percentage of services provided. Figure 14.11 illustrates this final step.

The mathematical technique shown here can be used to allocate service department costs in two-department situations. However, in more involved situations it may be necessary to use matrix algebra to find the solution. Appendix 14.2 at the end of this chapter discusses the use of matrix algebra to make reciprocal allocations.

FIGURE 14.11

Reciprocal Method of Allocation: Allocation Procedure

	Service Departments		Production Departments	
	A	B	1	2
Overhead costs before allocation	$8,000	$12,000	$40,000	$60,000
Allocation of reciprocal costs				
Department A	(9,388)	1,878	2,816	4,694
{Percent}	{100%}	{20%}	{30%}	{50%}
Department B	1,388	(13,878)	2,776	9,714
{Percent}	{10%}	{100%}	{20%}	{70%}
Total	0	0	$45,592	$74,408
Predetermined overhead application rates:				
Department 1: Based on 9,000 direct-labor hours			$5.07/hr.	
Department 2: Based on 11,000 direct-labor hours				$6.76/hr.

Remember, the reason for making these computations is to provide the information needed to develop manufacturing overhead budgets and to make an ultimate assignment of actual overhead to work in process for full-cost purposes.

ADVANTAGES OF DEPARTMENTALIZATION

The segregation of factory overhead costs by department has several advantages over factory-wide overhead accounting. The first advantage is that the costs assigned to each job or unit of production may be more representative of actual production costs when departmental accounting is used. This is especially true when various departments have different cost characteristics and provide different levels of input to each job. For example, consider a plant with two production departments. If one department is capital intensive and the other department is labor intensive, and if each job that passes through the plant spends a different amount of time in each department, a factory-wide overhead application rate will probably give inaccurate cost allocations. The use of several department overhead application rates in such a situation will probably result in more accurate product costs than if a single factory-wide rate had been used. A factory-wide rate may obscure the unique contribution made by each department to various types of products.

The second advantage of departmentalized accounting is that overhead expenditures can be more easily identified with the specific managers or supervisors who control such costs, which in turn may encourage more efficient and effective use of overhead than when accounting takes place at a factory-wide level. Also, a comparison of actual expenditures with budgeted amounts at the department level provides management with an important tool for monitoring and controlling overhead expenditures.

A major disadvantage of departmentalization is that it requires an expanded accounting system to accumulate, allocate, and report departmental detail. However, management may find that the added benefits derived from the more detailed information more than offset the additional costs of operating an expanded accounting system.

THE NUMBER AND CONFIGURATION OF DEPARTMENTS

The extent to which manufacturing operations should be subdivided into departmental categories is a common dilemma for company executives. For example, a plant manager may wonder if it is adequate to have one factory-wide department for indirect overhead accumulation or if there should be a number of service departments created for this purpose.

In a small plant where all units of production pass uniformly through all departments, a single factory-wide rate may be an appropriate and accurate way to allocate overhead costs. On the other hand, if the processing of each job or unit of production is unique, individual overhead costs should be allocated using individual overhead rates. In practice, most manufacturing operations are not so involved as to require allocations with individual-cost rates, yet most are sufficiently involved to require more detailed allocations than provided by factory-wide rates. The question is, where on this continuum from individual-cost to factory-wide allocations is the appropriate place for an allocation scheme to operate? Stated another way, how many departments should be created in an individual situation to give adequate information for product costing and cost control?

The major disadvantage of using a factory-wide overhead accumulation is that any pooling of overhead costs results in the *averaging* of costs before they are allocated. Such averaging inevitably yields less accurate product-costing information than if costs had been individually allocated. How many (if any) cost pools should be created beyond a factory-wide pool to optimize the cost-benefit relationship that exists in each factory situation?

The application of economic theory to this question tells us that the creation of more detailed cost pools (that is, moving along the continuum from factory-wide to individual-cost allocations) should continue until the expected increase in costs resulting from more detailed allocations is greater than the expected benefits derived from them. Because such measurements are often very difficult to make, it may be necessary to develop additional guidelines for determining the appropriate extent of departmentalization. Several considerations in formulating such guidelines follow.

Homogeneity of Costs

A pervasive concept affecting the degree of departmentalization is the homogeneity of overhead costs. In factory overhead accounting, **homogeneity of overhead costs** refers to the similarity of costs that permits their grouping for accumulation and allocation without compromising the accuracy of product costing.

One of the best ways to determine whether overhead costs are homogeneous is to compare the actual cost allocations made to units of production when costs are applied with a factory-wide rate or applied with multiple departmental rates. If the amount of overhead costs assigned to each unit of production using factory-wide rates equals the amount assigned using multiple departmental rates, the individual costs are considered to be homogeneous, and there is no justification for the extra accounting involved in the use of departmental rates. If the use of departmental rates results in different costs being assigned to units of production, this indicates that individual costs are heterogeneous and are appropriate candidates for departmentalization.

For example, consider two overhead cost pools—pool A and pool B. Should the pools be kept separate and individual allocations made for each pool or should the two pools be combined into a larger pool and one cost allocation made? Assume that each product or job is routed through or receives benefits from each pool. Pool A consists of costly automatic equipment and little labor, whereas pool B is labor intensive and requires a great deal of skilled workmanship in its processes. Thus, simply because of the differences in the amount of depreciation expense in each pool, it can be expected that overhead costs would be relatively large in pool A and relatively small in pool B. Finally, the overhead costs of the pools are allocated based on direct-labor hours. Figure 14.12 depicts the numeric details of this situation.

Now consider the overhead costs that would be allocated to two different jobs routed through pools A and B. Job 1 requires 10 hours of pool A time and 2 hours of pool B time. Job 2 requires 4 hours of pool A time and 8 hours of pool B time. If separate cost pools are used to make the allocation, job 1 is allocated $72.00 of overhead whereas job 2 is allocated only $36.00 of overhead—a significant difference. However, if cost pools A and B are combined, both jobs would be allocated $48.00 of overhead—no difference. The disparity between allocated costs using an aggregated cost pool and separate cost pools indicates that the costs in pools A and B are heterogeneous and should not be combined for product costing.

The preceding illustration indicates that the extent of factory-wide versus departmental accounting depends mostly on the homogeneity of the costs involved. When costs are homogeneous, they may be combined into a factory-wide rate with little loss in the accuracy of product-costing information. However, using a factory-wide rate when costs are heterogeneous results in less accurate cost allocations. Reliance on such data may also result in less reliable management decisions.

FIGURE 14.12

Homogeneity of Cost Pools

	Separate Cost Pools		Combined Cost Pool
	Pool A	Pool B	(Pool A/B)
Budgeted overhead amount	$105,000	$15,000	$120,000
Direct-labor hours	15,000	15,000	30,000
Overhead application rate per direct-labor hour	$7.00	$1.00	$4.00

Overhead application to jobs:	
Job #1:	
Pool A: 10 hrs. @ $7.00/hr.	$70.00
Pool B: 2 hrs. @ $1.00/hr.	2.00
Total	$72.00
Combined cost pool: 12 hrs. @ $4.00/hr.	$48.00
Job #2:	
Pool A: 4 hrs. @ $7.00/hr.	$28.00
Pool B: 8 hrs. @ $1.00/hr.	8.00
Total	$36.00
Combined cost pool: 12 hrs. @ $4.00/hr.	$48.00

Production Departments

The number and configuration of production departments in a given plant depends mainly on the physical characteristics of the manufacturing process, which may include the type of processes or operations involved, the amount and type of machinery used, the physical location of each operation relative to other operations, and the product-flow relationships of processes. Generally speaking, departmental boundaries should be made at points that logically separate functional operations, at points that recognize natural breaks in the production flow, and at points where the physical control of production units is important.

The relative emphasis that management places on cost control also influences the number and configuration of production departments. For example, a desire for tighter cost control usually leads to a larger number of production departments, which in turn makes for more explicit cost control assignments. It is not uncommon in such situations to find departments organized around the operation of a single machine. A full discussion of cost centers and responsibility accounting is contained in chapter 20.

Service Departments

Since all service department costs constitute indirect production costs, the focus for determining the number and configuration of service departments should be cost control rather than product costing. Therefore, the selection of an organizational structure that facilitates effective cost control should be the foremost consideration. Usually service departments are selected on the basis of functional supervisory responsibility. This provides a desirable coordination of functional and cost responsibility necessary for effective cost control.

Other important considerations include the type of services involved, the number of employees in each service function, the total cost of providing each service, and the physical location of each service function. Based on these considerations, management concepts rather than accounting concepts should guide the organization of service departments. In some situations, management philosophy and homogeneity of costs may dictate that only one department, called "general factory," represent a cost pool of all service functions.

ALLOCATION OF COSTS BY BEHAVIOR

Often it may be advisable to separate service department costs into their fixed and variable components and then to make a separate allocation of each component. This approach avoids inequitable allocations when fixed and variable cost components constitute heterogeneous cost pools. From a managerial viewpoint, the analysis of overhead costs into their fixed and variable components is also useful for more effective planning and control of departmental operations.

Variable Costs

Variable service department costs fluctuate in proportion to the level of services provided. For example, supplies in a data-processing department are typically considered a variable cost. Variable service department costs should be allocated to production departments in proportion to the actual level of usage by each receiving department. If the costs of preparing management reports varies in proportion to the machine hours used to prepare them, the variable costs of data processing could be allocated on the basis of machine hours spent preparing reports for other departments.

This type of allocation system actually represents a "charge for services" concept rather than a traditional cost allocation concept. Charging for services rendered, when departments have the choice of consuming as much or as little as they want, also encourages more efficient utilization of such services and provides more accurate cost allocations. However, if departments do not have the choice of consuming as much or as little as they want, as is usually the case with fixed service department costs, a different method of allocation is appropriate.

Fixed Costs

Fixed service department costs do not fluctuate in proportion to the level of services provided. For example, depreciation on computer equipment is usually considered a fixed cost. As a general rule, fixed costs should be allocated based on predetermined activity levels. To illustrate, consider the example of a data-processing department. Before purchasing the machinery a study was conducted to determine the capacity that should be built into the equipment to handle the expected current demand for data-processing services as well as to accommodate anticipated future increases in demand during the useful life of the equipment. Based on the information from this study, the proportion of total capacity built into the equipment was identified with each department. This makes it possible to allocate the fixed data-processing costs to departments based on the percentage of total capacity identified with each department. Since in the long run both the costs and capacity relationships are fixed in such situations, the allocation takes the form of a lump-sum amount that remains constant through time until there are changes in the capacity or service relationships of the departments.

SUMMARY

This chapter expanded on the principles of overhead accounting discussed in chapter 13 by examining departmental accounting. Manufacturing operations are typically subdivided into various departments to provide more detail for product costing and management control. Production departments are directly engaged in the actual manufacturing process, whereas service departments provide assistance to other departments. For example, cutting and assembly are typical production departments, and personnel and maintenance are typical service departments.

Service department costs represent overhead costs accumulated in departments other than production departments. When using a full-cost approach these costs are assigned in some equitable way to units produced. The assignment is accomplished by using a procedure in which service department costs are first allocated to production departments and then reallocated to units of production along with other production department overhead costs.

Service department costs are allocated to production departments in much the same way as overhead costs are allocated to units passing through a production department. However, different allocation bases are usually used to allocate service department costs than are used to allocate overhead of production departments. Typical bases for allocating service department costs include the number of reports processed, floor space occupied, or the number of employees working in a department.

Methods that might be used to allocate service department costs include the direct method, step method, and reciprocal method. The direct method allocates service department costs directly to production departments with no allocation of service department costs to any other service department. The step method allocates service department costs to other service departments when they render services to each other as well as to production departments. The reciprocal method is used to allocate service department costs when service departments provide services to one another in a mutual or complementary relationship.

The extent to which manufacturing operations are departmentalized depends on a number of factors. First, from a conceptual viewpoint, similar (homogeneous) costs should be grouped together. Second, from a situational viewpoint, production departments should be selected based on the physical characteristics of the manufacturing process. The emphasis is on both product costing and cost control when organizing production departments. However, when organizing service departments, cost control should be the major consideration.

Service department costs may be allocated as one amount or they may be subdivided into their fixed and variable components and allocated in two amounts by cost behavior. Allocation by cost behavior requires more detailed computations and is primarily done to provide more information for management control. Many firms find that the added benefits of allocating costs by behavior exceed the additional computational costs.

APPENDIX 14.1 Applicable Standards of the Cost Accounting Standards Board

Several *cost accounting standards* of the Cost Accounting Standards Board (CASB) are directly related to the problems of overhead accounting. Even though these standards are only required of firms engaged in certain types of government contracts, there are several theoretical and practical principles associated with their use that all cost accountants should understand.

The overall objective of cost accounting standards is to help derive a fair price for goods or services when a market price is not available by providing for an equitable assignment of costs to work performed. The general rule is that only costs of performing work under a particular contract should be assigned to that contract. However, it may be difficult to decide what service department costs are appropriately assigned to a particular contract when a company is working on several contracts simultaneously and when some work is being done for commercial customers and some work is being done for the government. The CASB provides guidelines for making cost allocations in these situations. Several CASB standards that relate to accounting for service department costs are outlined in the following sections.

STANDARD 402: Consistency in Allocating Costs Incurred for the Same Purpose

This standard ensures that each cost is assigned *only once* to products or services acquired by the government. This standard guards against double counting some types of costs. It specifies that all costs incurred for the same general purpose must be treated as either direct costs or as indirect costs when such costs are assigned to products or services acquired by government contract; that is, if some costs are treated as indirect costs, other costs incurred for the *same general purpose* cannot be treated as direct costs.

For example, consider a contractor who places all travel costs into an indirect cost pool and then allocates this pool to government contracts using direct-labor hours as an allocation base. This standard requires the travel costs incurred by personnel whose salaries are considered direct-labor costs of a government contract to be placed in the travel cost pool and allocated with other travel costs rather than charged directly to the contract. All costs incurred for the *same purpose* must be either allocated or directly assigned. Therefore, the possible combination of directly assigning some travel costs to contracts and allocating other travel costs via an indirect cost pool is not allowed. Requiring consistency in how costs incurred for the same purpose are assigned to government contracts is expected to reduce the possibility of some costs being assigned to a contract twice.

STANDARD 403: Allocation of Home Office Expenses to Segments

A home office is an office that is responsible for managing or directing other parts of the business. Home offices may perform supervisory, managerial, or administrative functions. They may also perform service functions similar in character to those previously discussed in this chapter.

A **segment** is a subdivision of a business that has a service or reporting relationship to the home office. Subsidiaries, product lines, and plants could all be considered segments of a business. Segments usually produce a product or service and are responsible for profits.

Standard 403 specifies that home office expenses are to be allocated to segments based on a beneficial or causal relationship existing between them. In addition, the standard states that home office costs should be *directly assigned* to segments to the maximum extent possible. Other costs not amenable to direct assignment are to be placed in homogeneous cost pools and allocated to segments in the same way that service department costs are allocated to production departments. The standard specifies what some of these cost pools might contain and what bases might be appropriate for their allocation. Figure 14.13 lists the suggested pools and bases.

After examining the home office cost pools and associated allocation bases in figure 14.13, it is evident that the concepts and procedures for allocating home office expenses are virtually the same as those already examined with regard to the allocation of service department costs. Only the level in the organization hierarchy is different. For example, home office expenses may be allocated to a plant, which also has a number of service and production departments. At the plant level, allocated home office expenses are reallocated to units of production in much the same way as service department costs incurred at the plant level are allocated to units of production. Thus, the full cost of a government contract using this procedure includes direct materials, direct labor, allocated service department costs, and allocated home office expenses.

FIGURE 14.13

Home Office Expenses and Allocation Bases

Home Office Expense/Function	Illustrative Allocation Bases
Centralized Service Functions:	
1. Personnel administration	1. Number of personnel, labor hours, payroll, number of hires
2. Data-processing services	2. Machine time, number of reports
3. Centralized purchasing and subcontracting	3. Number of purchase orders, values of purchases, number of items
4. Centralized warehousing	4. Square footage, value of material, volume
5. Company aircraft service	5. Actual or standard rate per hour, mile, passenger mile, or similar unit
6. Central telephone service	6. Usage costs, number of instruments
Staff Management and Specific Activities:	
1. Personnel management	1. Number of personnel, labor hours, payroll, number of hires
2. Manufacturing policies (quality control, industrial engineering, production scheduling, tooling, inspection and testing, etc.)	2. Manufacturing cost input, manufacturing direct labor
3. Engineering policies	3. Total engineering costs, engineering direct labor, number of drawings
4. Material/purchasing policies	4. Number of purchase orders, value of purchases
5. Marketing policies	5. Sales, segment marketing costs
Central Payments or Accruals:	
1. Pension expenses	1. Payroll or other factor on which total payment is based
2. Group insurance expenses	2. Payroll or other factor on which total payment is based
3. State and local income taxes and franchise taxes	3. Any base or method that results in an allocation equal or approximate to a segment's proportionate share of the tax imposed by the jurisdiction in which the segment does business, as measured by the same factors used to determine taxable income for that jurisdiction

Source: *Cost Accounting Standards Board Standards, Rules and Regulations*, U.S. Government Printing Office, Washington, D.C. 20402.

STANDARD 410: Allocation of Business Unit General and Administrative Expenses to Final Cost Objectives

This standard specifies the criteria for allocating general and administrative (G&A) expenses and home office expenses to final cost objectives. A *final cost objective* is defined as an object of final cost accumulation. It is typically a contract, but it could also be the cost of services rendered or the cost of units produced.

The first general provision of this standard specifies that allocations of home office expenses should be included in the G&A expense pool of the receiving organizational unit.

For example, consider a firm that consists of a home office and three manufacturing plants. The home office expenses are first allocated to each plant as outlined in Standard 403. Then, allocated home office expenses are placed in the G&A expense pool of each plant. Finally, the G&A expense pool in each plant is allocated to final cost objectives as outlined in Standard 410.

The second general provision of this standard specifies that G&A expense pools will be allocated *only* to final cost objectives. This allocation is to be based on a measure of total cost inputs, such as direct-labor or direct-materials cost. For example, a G&A expense pool, which includes allocated home office expenses, is appropriately allocated directly to units of production using total direct-labor cost as the basis for the allocation.

STANDARD 418: Allocation of Indirect Cost Pools

This standard specifies a hierarchy of preferable allocation bases for companies working on certain government contracts. It should be noted that for companies not engaged in government contracting, the selection of an allocation base is entirely up to the company. Any rational and systematic allocation method can be used. However, the hierarchy specified by the CASB may be useful to any firm trying to decide how to allocate service department costs.

The first category of allocation bases specified by the CASB represents a measure of the activity (input) of the providing department. For example, square footage or hours of service rendered constitute measures of service department activity. Activity measures provide an appropriate allocation base when there is a direct and definitive relationship between the activity of the providing department and the benefits flowing to the receiving department.

The second category of bases in the CASB hierarchy represents measures of output of the providing department. These measures are preferred when activity measures do not provide a direct and definitive linkage or when such measures are unavailable or impractical to obtain. Output is generally measured in terms of units of product (services) rendered by the service department. Examples of output measures include the number of hours spent by the maintenance department and the amount of steam supplied by the boiler department.

When there is no practical measure of either activity (input) or output, the CASB prefers the use of surrogate measures. A surrogate measure is any quantifiable measure of activity in the *receiving* department that is representative of the amount of services received. Such measures typically vary with the level of services received. For example, suppose that the services provided by a personnel department cannot be adequately measured on either an activity or output basis. As a surrogate measure, the number of employees in receiving departments may be representative of the benefits received and might be an appropriate allocation base.

The final category of preferred allocation bases is the measure of overall plant activity. Examples include total materials cost, machine hours, or labor hours. Resorting to an overall activity measure is justified when there is no other base to provide a clear cause-benefit relationship among departments. For example, the plant manager's salary or cost of property taxes may not have a direct or definitive relationship to benefiting departments. In such instances, the CASB prefers the selection of a base that is representative of overall management or plant activity.

The allocation of period costs, as well as inventoriable costs, to government contracts means that the contractor typically performs additional accounting to allocate some types of costs to contracts that may not be allocated to products under other circumstances. For example, general and administrative expenses are not usually allocated to products but are shown on the income statement as period expenses. However, a firm working on government contracts allocates a portion of general and administrative costs to each contract. Such allocations may be made by memorandum only and not recorded by journal entry because their main purpose is simply to establish the full cost of a government contract.

Only the general provisions of these standards are outlined here. Before application, the actual standards and CASB literature should be consulted for specific provisions and application guidelines.

APPENDIX 14.2 Reciprocal Allocations Using Matrix Algebra

To demonstrate the use of matrix algebra techniques, figure 14.14 illustrates a situation that involves three service departments providing reciprocal services. These are actually the same data used to demonstrate the direct and step methods shown in the chapter.

To apply the reciprocal method in this situation, it is necessary to develop three simultaneous equations, as follows:

Let P = total costs of Personnel service department
C = total costs of Cafeteria service department
U = total costs of Utilities service department

(1) $P = \$20{,}000 + 0P + 0.07C + 0.04U$
(2) $C = \$30{,}000 + 0.08P + 0C + 0.16U$
(3) $U = \$40{,}000 + 0.12P + 0.10C + 0U$

These equations have been formulated by reading across the rows of percentages for service departments in figure 14.14. This figure assumes that none of the service departments has a reciprocal relationship with itself, which is why each equation has a zero as the coefficient in its own department's cost function. For example, equation (1) has a zero as the coefficient of P, indicating that the personnel department renders no services to itself. If a service department has a reciprocal relationship with itself (as would actually be expected with the personnel department, processing transactions for its own employees), the zero in equation (1) would be replaced with the appropriate percentage of services rendered to itself.

FIGURE 14.14

Reciprocal Method of Allocation: Factory Statistics and Percentages

Department	Personnel Transactions Processed Number	Percent	Number of Employees Number	Percent	Space Occupied (square feet) Number	Percent
Production:						
Cutting	150	30%	400	33%	60,000	40%
Finishing	250	50	600	50	60,000	40
Service:						
Personnel (P)	na	0	80	7	6,000	4
Cafeteria (C)	40	8	na	0	24,000	16
Utilities (U)	60	12	120	10	na	0
	500	100%	1,200	100%	150,000	100%

na = not applicable

The next step when using matrix algebra techniques is to simplify the service department equations and put them in a form amenable to matrix manipulations, as follows:

(1) $\quad P - 0.07C - 0.04U = 20{,}000$
(2) $-0.08P + \quad C - 0.16U = 30{,}000$
(3) $-0.12P - 0.10C + \quad U = 40{,}000$

Proceeding to matrices:

Let: A = the matrix of coefficients
B = the vector of service department costs before allocation
X = the vector of reciprocal service department costs (the unknown amounts in this situation)

$$\begin{array}{ccc} A & X & = & B \end{array}$$

$$\begin{bmatrix} 1 & -0.07 & -0.04 \\ -0.08 & 1 & -0.16 \\ -0.12 & -0.10 & 1 \end{bmatrix} \begin{bmatrix} P \\ C \\ U \end{bmatrix} = \begin{bmatrix} 20{,}000 \\ 30{,}000 \\ 40{,}000 \end{bmatrix}$$

To solve for X, the matrix A must be inverted and multiplied by vector B:

$$X = A^{-1} B$$

The next four steps are used to invert A. The adjoint determinant method for inverting matrices is illustrated here; however, there are other methods available for inverting matrices.

- **Step 1:** Obtain the *minor* for each element in A. This is done by calculating the determinant of each submatrix of A, obtained by deleting the i_{th} row and j_{th} column. For example, the submatrix found after deleting the first row and first column of A is:

$$\begin{bmatrix} 1 & -0.16 \\ -0.10 & 1 \end{bmatrix}$$

The *determinant* of this submatrix can be calculated by subtracting the product of the *cross-diagonal* elements from the product of the *main diagonal* elements, as follows:

$$\{(1 \times 1) - (-0.10 \times -0.16)\} = 0.984$$

Repeating this process for all elements of A results in the following:

$$\begin{bmatrix} \begin{bmatrix} 1 & -0.16 \\ -0.10 & 1 \end{bmatrix} & \begin{bmatrix} -0.08 & -0.16 \\ -0.12 & 1 \end{bmatrix} & \begin{bmatrix} -0.08 & 1 \\ -0.12 & -0.10 \end{bmatrix} \\ \begin{bmatrix} -0.07 & -0.04 \\ -0.10 & 1 \end{bmatrix} & \begin{bmatrix} 1 & -0.04 \\ -0.12 & 1 \end{bmatrix} & \begin{bmatrix} 1 & -0.07 \\ -0.12 & -0.10 \end{bmatrix} \\ \begin{bmatrix} -0.07 & -0.04 \\ 1 & -0.16 \end{bmatrix} & \begin{bmatrix} 1 & -0.04 \\ -0.08 & -0.16 \end{bmatrix} & \begin{bmatrix} 1 & -0.07 \\ -0.08 & 1 \end{bmatrix} \end{bmatrix} =$$

$$\begin{bmatrix} 0.9840 & -0.0992 & 0.1280 \\ -0.0740 & 0.9952 & -0.1084 \\ 0.0512 & -0.1632 & 0.9944 \end{bmatrix} = \text{the matrix of minors for each element of } A$$

- **Step 2:** Convert the minors for each element in A into *cofactors* by multiplying each

FIGURE 14.15

Reciprocal Method of Allocation: Allocation Procedure

	Service Departments			Production Departments	
	Personnel	Cafeteria	Utilities	Cutting	Finishing
Overhead costs					
Before allocation	$20,000	$30,000	$40,000	$210,000	$300,000
Allocation:					
Personnel	(24,639)	1,971	2,956	7,392	12,320
{Percent}	{100%}	{8%}	{12%}	{30%}	{50%}
Cafeteria	2,763	(39,475)	3,947	13,027	19,738
{Percent}	{7%}	{100%}	{10%}	{33%}	{50%}
Utilities	1,876	7,504	(46,903)	18,761	18,762
{Percent}	{4%}	{16%}	{100%}	{40%}	{40%}
	0	0	0	$249,180	$350,820

Predetermined overhead application rates:

Cutting ($249,180 ÷ 70,000 direct-labor hours) $3.56/hr.

Finishing ($350,820 ÷ 90,000 direct-labor hours) $3.90/hr.

---

element by $(-1)^{i+j}$, where i and j are the subscripts of each element. This step yields the following matrix:

$$\begin{bmatrix} 0.9840 & 0.0992 & 0.1280 \\ 0.0740 & 0.9952 & 0.1084 \\ 0.0512 & 0.1632 & 0.9944 \end{bmatrix}$$

- **Step 3:** Calculate the *determinant* of A by *(a)* multiplying the elements in *any* column (or *any* row) of the original matrix A by their corresponding cofactors computed in step 2 and *(b)* summing their products. Any row or column will yield the same result. For example, the determinant of A (that is $|A|$) using:

Column 1: $(1)(0.9840) + (-0.08)(0.0740) + (-0.12)(0.0512) = 0.97194$
Row 3: $(-0.12)(0.0512) + (-0.10)(0.1632) + (1)(0.9944) = 0.97194$

- **Step 4:** *Transpose* the A matrix of cofactors by making its rows into columns. This yields the *adjoint matrix,* which is then divided by the determinant of A to obtain the inverse matrix A^{-1}.

$$\frac{\begin{bmatrix} 0.9840 & 0.0740 & 0.0512 \\ 0.0992 & 0.9952 & 0.1632 \\ 0.1280 & 0.1084 & 0.9944 \end{bmatrix}}{0.97194} = \begin{bmatrix} 1.0124 & 0.0761 & 0.0527 \\ 0.1021 & 1.0239 & 0.1679 \\ 0.1317 & 0.1115 & 1.0231 \end{bmatrix} = A^{-1}$$

Having inverted matrix A, all that remains to the solution of the equation $X = A^{-1}B$ is to multiply A^{-1} by B to obtain X as follows:

$$X = \begin{bmatrix} 1.0124 & 0.0761 & 0.0527 \\ 0.1021 & 1.0239 & 0.1679 \\ 0.1317 & 0.1115 & 1.0231 \end{bmatrix} \times \begin{bmatrix} 20,000 \\ 30,000 \\ 40,000 \end{bmatrix} = \begin{bmatrix} 24,639 \\ 39,475 \\ 46,903 \end{bmatrix} = \begin{bmatrix} P \\ C \\ U \end{bmatrix}$$

The results indicate that the reciprocal costs for allocation by the personnel, cafeteria, and utilities departments are, respectively, $24,639, $39,475, and $46,903. The allocation procedure in figure 14.15 shows the final results using the reciprocal service department costs calculated in the preceding procedure.

As this illustration demonstrates, the computations using the reciprocal method can become quite tedious when there are a number of service departments involved. Therefore, it is suggested that computations involving more than three service departments be left to acomputer because of the time involved and the probability of error using manual methods.

SELF-STUDY PROBLEM

Perpotkin Corporation is trying to decide whether to use the direct, step, or reciprocal method to allocate service department costs to production departments. The corporation has three service and three production departments with reciprocal service arrangements. The balances in the departmental accounts before distribution of service department costs are given in the following schedule. Also contained in the following schedule are statistics for each service department's allocation base:

Allocation Base and Statistics

Department	Balance in Department Overhead Accounts	Personnel Department: Personnel Transactions	Maintenance Department: Maintenance Hours	General Department: General Hours
Producing:				
Layout	$125,000	2,500	3,500	2,500
Assembly	90,000	2,500	3,000	2,000
Finishing	105,000	2,000	2,000	2,000
Service:				
Personnel	16,000	0	1,000	2,000
Maintenance	29,500	1,000	0	1,500
General	42,000	2,000	500	0

Production departments assign costs to work process using direct-labor hours as the allocation base. Direct-labor hours worked for the layout, assembly, and finishing departments for the current period are, respectively, 90,000, 65,000, and 70,000 hours.

Required

Prepare schedules allocating service department costs using the direct, step, and reciprocal methods. Which method do you suggest management use to allocate service department costs? Why?

Solution to the Self-Study Problem

Direct Method of Allocation: Factory Statistics and Percentages

Department	Transactions Processed Number	Percent	Maintenance Hours Number	Percent	General Hours Number	Percent
Layout	2,500	36%	3,500	41%	2,500	38%
Assembly	2,500	36	3,000	35	2,000	31
Finishing	2,000	28	2,000	24	2,000	31
	7,000	100%	8,500	100%	6,500	100%

CHAPTER 14: FACTORY OVERHEAD: COSTING AND CONTROL II

Allocation Procedure Using Direct Method

	Service Departments			Production Departments		
	Personnel	Maintenance	General	Layout	Assembly	Finishing
Overhead costs before allocation	$16,000	$29,500	$42,000	$125,000	$90,000	$105,000
Allocation:						
Personnel	(16,000)			5,760	5,760	4,480
{Percent}	{100%}			{36%}	{36%}	{28%}
Maintenance		(29,500)		12,095	10,325	7,080
{Percent}		{100%}		{41%}	{35%}	{24%}
General			(42,000)	15,960	13,020	13,020
{Percent}			{100%}	{38%}	{31%}	{31%}
Total production department overhead after allocation				$158,815	$119,105	$129,580

Predetermined overhead application rates:

Layout ($158,815 ÷ 90,000 direct-labor hours) $1.76/hr.

Assembly ($119,105 ÷ 65,000 direct-labor hours) $1.83/hr.

General ($129,580 ÷ 70,000 direct-labor hours) $1.85/hr.

Step Method of Allocation: Factory Statistics and Percentages

	Transactions Processed		Maintenance Hours		General Hours	
Department	Number	Percent	Number	Percent	Number	Percent
Production:						
Layout	2,500	25%	3,500	39%	2,500	38%
Assembly	2,500	25	3,000	33	2,000	31
Finishing	2,000	20	2,000	22	2,000	31
Service:						
Personnel	na	0	na	0	na	0
Maintenance	1,000	10	na	0	na	0
General	2,000	20	500	6	na	0
	10,000	100%	9,000	100%	6,500	100%

Allocation Procedure Using Step Method

	Service Departments			Production Departments		
	Personnel	Maintenance	General	Layout	Assembly	Finishing
Overhead costs before allocation	$16,000	$29,500	$42,000	$125,000	$90,000	$105,000
Allocation:						
Personnel	(16,000)	1,600	3,200	4,000	4,000	3,200
{Percent}	{100%}	{10%}	{20%}	{25%}	{25%}	{20%}
Maintenance		(31,100)	1,866	12,129	10,263	6,842
{Percent}		{100%}	{6%}	{39%}	{33%}	{22%}
General			(47,066)	17,885	14,590	14,591
{Percent}			{100%}	{38%}	{31%}	{31%}
Total production department overhead after allocation				$159,014	$118,853	$129,633

Predetermined overhead application rates:

Layout ($159,014 ÷ 90,000 direct-labor hours) $1.77/hr.

Assembly ($118,853 ÷ 65,000 direct-labor hours) $1.83/hr.

General ($129,633 ÷ 70,000 direct-labor hours) $1.85/hr.

Reciprocal Method of Allocation: Factory Statistics and Percentages

Department	Transactions Processed Number	Percent	Maintenance Hours Number	Percent	General Hours Number	Percent
Production:						
Layout	2,500	25%	3,500	35%	2,500	25%
Assembly	2,500	25	3,000	30	2,000	20
Finishing	2,000	20	2,000	20	2,000	20
Service:						
Personnel	na	0	1,000	10	2,000	20
Maintenance	1,000	10	na	0	1,500	15
General	2,000	20	500	5	na	0
	10,000	100%	10,000	100%	10,000	100%

Allocation Procedure Using Reciprocal Method

Let: P = personnel; M = maintenance; G = general
(1) $P = 16{,}000 + 0.10M + 0.20G$
(2) $M = 29{,}500 + 0.10P + 0.15G$
(3) $G = 42{,}000 + 0.20P + 0.05M$

Rewriting equations (1) through (3):
(1) $\quad\quad P - 0.10M - 0.20G = 16{,}000$
(2) $-0.10P + \quad\quad M - 0.15G = 29{,}500$
(3) $-0.20P - 0.05M + \quad\quad G = 42{,}000$

Multiplying equation (2) by 10 and adding to equation (1):
$$P - 0.10M - 0.20G = 16{,}000$$
$$\underline{-P + 10.00M - 1.50G = 295{,}000}$$
$$\quad\quad 9.90M - 1.70G = 311{,}000$$

Multiplying equation (3) by 5 and adding to equation (1):
$$P - 0.10M - 0.20G = 16{,}000$$
$$\underline{-P - 0.25M + 5.00G = 210{,}000}$$
$$\quad -0.35M + 4.80G = 226{,}000$$

Eliminating M between the resulting equations:
$$9.90M - 1.70G = 311{,}000$$
$$-0.35M + 4.80G = 226{,}000$$
$$(0.35)(9.90M) - (0.35)(1.70G) = (0.35)(311{,}000)$$
$$(9.90)(-0.35M) + (9.90)(4.80G) = (9.90)(226{,}000)$$
$$3.465M - 0.595G = 108{,}850$$
$$\underline{-3.465M + 47.520G = 2{,}237{,}400}$$
$$46.925G = 2{,}346{,}250$$
$$G = 50{,}000$$

Substituting $G = 50{,}000$ into a previous equation:
$9.90M - 1.70G \quad\quad\quad = 311{,}000$
$9.90M - 1.70(50{,}000) = 311{,}000$
$\quad\quad\quad 9.90M = 396{,}000$
$\quad\quad\quad\quad\quad M = 40{,}000$

Substituting $M = 40{,}000$ and $G = 50{,}000$ into a previous equation:
$P - 0.10M \quad\quad - 0.20G \quad\quad = 16{,}000$
$P - 0.10(40{,}000) - 0.20(50{,}000) = 16{,}000$
$\quad\quad\quad\quad\quad\quad\quad P = 30{,}000$

Allocation Procedure Using Reciprocal Method

	Service Departments			Production Departments		
	Personnel	Maintenance	General	Layout	Assembly	Finishing
Overhead costs before allocation	$16,000	$29,500	$42,000	$125,000	$90,000	$105,000
Allocation:						
Personnel	(30,000)	3,000	6,000	7,500	7,500	6,000
{Percent}	{100%}	{10%}	{20%}	{25%}	{25%}	{20%}
Maintenance	4,000	(40,000)	2,000	14,000	12,000	8,000
{Percent}	{10%}	{100%}	{5%}	{35%}	{30%}	{20%}
General	10,000	7,500	(50,000)	12,500	10,000	10,000
{Percent}	{20%}	{15%}	{100%}	{25%}	{20%}	{20%}
Total production department overhead after allocation	0	0	0	$159,000	$119,500	$129,000

Predetermined overhead application rates:
  Layout ($159,000 ÷ 90,000 direct-labor hours) $1.77/hr.
  Assembly ($119,500 ÷ 65,000 direct-labor hours) $1.84/hr.
  General ($129,000 ÷ 70,000 direct-labor hours) $1.84/hr.

Solution

The direct method is recommended for allocating service department costs because it gives essentially the same results in this case as the other methods but it is easier to calculate.

SUGGESTED READINGS

Blanchard, Garth A., and Chow, Chee W. "Allocating Indirect Costs for Improved Management Performance." *Management Accounting* 64 (March 1983): 38–41.

Fultz, Jack F. *Overhead, What It Is and How It Works*. Cambridge, Mass.: Abt Books, 1980.

National Association of Accountants. *Allocation of Service and Administrative Costs*. New York: National Association of Accountants, 1985.

National Association of Accountants. *The Allocation of Corporate Indirect Costs*. New York: National Association of Accountants, 1981.

Singhvi, Surendra S. "Corporate Budgeting and Financial Management." *Journal of Accounting, Auditing, and Finance* 2 (Spring 1978): 290–293.

Zimmerman, Jerold L. "The Cost and Benefits of Cost Allocation." *The Accounting Review* 54 (July 1979): 504–521.

DISCUSSION QUESTIONS

Q14–1. What is a department? What are some of the advantages of departmentalization?

Q14–2. Describe the difference between production and service departments and give examples of each.

Q14–3. Describe the allocation process through which service department costs become part of the cost of units of production.

Q14–4. What is the purpose of an allocation base? Give several examples of allocation bases. For each example, tell which type of service department is likely to be the user.

Q14-5. Name three methods used to allocate service department costs.

Q14-6. Describe the direct method of allocation and give some of its advantages and disadvantages.

Q14-7. Describe the step method of allocation and give some of its advantages and disadvantages.

Q14-8. Describe the reciprocal method of allocation and give some of its advantages and disadvantages.

Q14-9. What difference is there between using factory-wide versus departmental rates for allocating service department costs?

Q14-10. What are the advantages and disadvantages of using factory-wide versus departmental rates?

Q14-11. What is a homogeneous cost pool? How is the allocation of service department costs connected with the homogeneity of cost pools?

Q14-12. Describe any differences that exist between cost allocations when fixed versus variable costs are involved.

Q14-13. What are the general provisions of cost accounting Standard 402?

Q14-14. Define the terms *home office* and *segment*.

Q14-15. According to Cost Accounting Standard 403, what are the preferred methods of allocating home office expenses?

Q14-16. Define *final cost objective*.

Q14-17. According to Cost Accounting Standard 410, how should general and administrative expenses be allocated to final cost objectives?

Q14-18. Describe the Cost Accounting Standards Board's hierarchy of preferred allocation bases.

EXERCISES

E14-1. Basic Concepts for Production and Service Departments For each description listed here, put a check in the blank indicating whether the description is or is not a proper inference.

	Proper	Not Proper
1. Production departments render a service that relates directly to the production of a product.	____	____
2. Examples of production departments include production control, machinery repairs, and shipping.	____	____
3. A departmentalized factory is usually divided along lines of identifiable responsibility centers.	____	____
4. When relatively few employees are involved, service activities are frequently combined to gain more effective cost control.	____	____
5. Direct departmental expenses do not originate with any specific departments but rather are incurred for all departments.	____	____

6. The overtime premium portion of overtime paid to direct-labor employees should always be charged to work in process. _____ _____

7. Indirect departmental expenses include factory costs such as power, light, and maintenance. _____ _____

8. Factory expenses such as depreciation, property tax, and insurance should be allocated by using the number of factory employees as a distribution base. _____ _____

9. It is not unusual to use different distribution bases for allocating the overhead of the different service departments to other service and production departments. _____ _____

10. A factory survey produces the underlying data for allocating indirect departmental expenses to production departments. _____ _____

11. The expenses of production departments must be allocated to service departments to establish predetermined factory overhead rates. _____ _____

12. Service department costs may be allocated only to production departments if no material differences in final production department costs result. _____ _____

13. The expenses of the service department with the largest factory overhead costs should always be distributed first when using the step method. _____ _____

14. Once costs for a service department are allocated, that department is usually considered closed and no further distributions are made to it when using the direct or the step methods. _____ _____

15. Departmental expense analysis sheets are not needed as long as specific expense accounts are kept in the ledger. _____ _____

E14-2. Service Department Allocation—Direct Method (CMA)

Barrylou Corporation is developing departmental overhead rates based on direct-labor hours for its two production departments—molding and assembly. The molding department employs twenty people and the assembly department employs eighty people. Each person in these two departments works 2,000 hours per year. The production-related overhead costs for the molding department are budgeted at $200,000, and the assembly department costs are budgeted at $320,000. Two service departments—repair and power—directly support the two production departments and have budgeted costs of $48,000 and $250,000, respectively. The production departments' overhead rates cannot be determined until the service departments' costs are properly allocated. The following schedule reflects the use of the repair department's and power department's output by the various departments.

	Repair	Power	Molding	Assembly
Repair hours	0	1,000	1,000	8,000
Kilowatt hours	240,000	0	840,000	120,000

Required

1. Calculate the overhead rates per direct-labor hour for the molding department and the assembly department, using the direct allocation method to charge the production departments for service department costs.

2. Allocate the service departments' overhead to each other and to the production departments, using the reciprocal method.

3. Calculate overhead rates per direct-labor hour for the two production departments, using your results from requirement 2.
4. Compare the results obtained in requirements 2 and 3 with the results in requirement 1. Discuss the arguments that are made in support of the reciprocal method.

E14-3. Allocation of Service Department Costs—Step Method

The factory overhead worksheet for Brandon Incorporated had the following columnar totals after the direct overhead departmental expense assignments had been made:

Service departments:	A—$36,000
	B—$28,000
	C—$20,000
Production departments:	D—$80,000
	E—$75,000

Required

Complete a schedule showing the allocation of overhead to the production departments if the service department costs are allocated to the production and other service departments as follows:

Department A costs: 20% to B, 15% to C and E, 50% to D
Department B costs: 35% to C, 35% to D, 30% to E
Department C costs: 40% to D, 60% to E

E14-4. Service Department Allocation—Reciprocal Method

Jerry Corporation uses machine hours to compute overhead application rates and to allocate overhead to units of production in its two production departments, casting and assembly. During the past accounting period, the casting department used 10,000 machine hours and the assembly department used 40,000 machine hours. The production-related overhead costs are budgeted at $50,000 for the casting department and $80,000 for the assembly department. Two service departments—repair and power—directly support the production departments and have budgeted costs of $12,000 and $62,500, respectively. The production departments' overhead rates cannot be determined until the service departments' costs are properly allocated. The following schedule reflects the use of the repair department's and power department's output by various other departments.

	Department			
	Repair	Power	Casting	Assembly
Repair hours	0	500	500	4,000
Kilowatt hours	60,000	0	210,000	30,000

Required

1. Prepare an electronic spreadsheet to allocate the service departments' overhead to each other and to the production departments, using the reciprocal method.
2. Calculate overhead rates per machine hour for the two production departments, using the results obtained in requirement 1.
3. Assume that if the step method of allocation is used, the overhead application rates are $10.602 and $2.462 for the casting and assembly departments, respectively. Compare these rates with those determined in requirement 2, and discuss any arguments that might be made in support of the reciprocal method.

E14-5. Allocation of Service Department Costs—Step Method

Outfitter Manufacturing, Inc. has developed the following overhead costs by department.

Production departments:	A—$90,000
	B—$80,000
Service departments:	X—$40,000
	Y—$32,000
	Z—$24,000

Service department costs are allocated to the production departments and other service departments in the sequence X, Y, and Z, as follows.

Department X costs: 20% to Y, 10% to Z and B, 60% to A.
Department Y costs: 40% to Z, 30% to A, 30% to B.
Department Z costs: 40% to A, 60% to B.

Required

1. Complete a schedule showing the allocation of overhead to the production departments, using the step method.
2. Determine the overhead application rates for departments A and B based on direct-labor hours if each department works 10,000 hours.

E14–6. Allocation of Service Department Costs—Reciprocal Method

Osberg Company has gathered the following statistics concerning its factory operations.

Department	Personnel Transactions Processed	Number of Employees	Space Occupied (square feet)
Production:			
Cutting	80	608	60,000
Finishing	140	800	30,000
Service:			
Personnel	na	80	2,000
Cafeteria	20	na	8,000
Utilities	10	112	na

Overhead costs budgeted for each department for the next accounting period are as follows:

Cutting	$80,000
Finishing	60,000
Personnel	10,000
Cafeteria	20,000
Utilities	30,000

Required

1. Develop the three simultaneous equations necessary to allocate service department costs using the reciprocal method.
2. Develop an electronic spreadsheet to solve the simultaneous equations developed for requirement 1. (Hint: Place each formula in the cell indicated and perform a number of iterative recalculations.)
3. With the results found in requirement 2, use the electronic spreadsheet to allocate service department costs to production departments.
4. Calculate overhead application rates, using 20,000 and 15,000 direct-labor hours, respectively, for the cutting and finishing departments.

E14–7. Job Cost Results from Using Alternative Allocation Methods

The controller of Cadcom Corporation has been using the direct method to allocate service department costs to production departments. However, she wonders if the step method will provide a more realistic allocation of service department costs. The following schedule contains overhead application rates for Cadcom's two service departments, using the direct and step methods of allocation.

	Rate	
Department	Using Step Method	Using Direct Method
A	$3.72	$3.65
B	$2.70	$2.75

During May, jobs 108 and 109 were produced. Job 108 required 600 labor hours in department A and 800 labor hours in department B. Job 109 required 1,000 and 1,500 labor hours in departments A and B, respectively.

Required

1. Determine the overhead costs applied to jobs 108 and 109 using overhead rates obtained from the step method.
2. Determine the overhead costs applied to jobs 108 and 109 using the rates obtained from the direct method.
3. Comment on the results you obtained in requirements 1 and 2, and make a recommendation to the controller of Cadcom Corporation concerning the use of the direct method or step method of allocation.

E14–8. Evaluation of the Proper Basis for Allocating Service Department Costs

Maxwell Company has four production and two service departments. Each production department produces an individual product through all steps from design implementation and materials preparation to final finishing. The service departments—design support and repairs and maintenance—have for years had their costs allocated to the production departments on the basis of sales revenue produced.

Recently, a new university accounting graduate was hired in cost accounting. Her assignment was to allocate service department costs to the four production departments. After the first month on the job, she suggested to the production manager and the controller that sales revenue was not a good basis for service department cost allocation. The following information, which might be useful in evaluating an alternative allocation approach, was presented:

	Service Departments		Production Departments			
	Design Support	Repairs and Maintenance	1	2	3	4
Direct overhead	$26,000	$8,000	$40,000	$35,000	$52,000	$45,000
Design hours	—	300	600	450	700	500
Repairs and maintenance hours	200	—	600	250	350	500

Required

1. Do you agree with the new cost accountant's criticism of sales revenue as a base for service department cost allocation? Explain. Are there possible circumstances that justify the use of sales revenue as an allocation base for service department costs? Explain.
2. What basis would you recommend the Maxwell Company use for service department cost allocation? Explain.

E14–9. Step Method Allocation of Service Department Costs

The following information about departmental direct overhead for the production and service departments is available for the Edwardian Company:

CHAPTER 14: FACTORY OVERHEAD: COSTING AND CONTROL II

Direct Factory Overhead

Service Departments			Production Departments	
G	H	I	A	B
$24,960	$28,000	$22,000	$38,000	$56,000

An analysis indicates the following proportions of service rendered by each service department:

Department G: 30% to H, 20% to I, 20% to A, and 30% to B
Department H: 30% to I, 35% to A, and 35% to B
Department I: 50% to each A and B

Required

1. Set up a schedule showing service department overhead allocations, using the step method. (Round to the nearest dollar.)
2. Determine overhead rates for departments A and B, assuming that direct-labor hours is used as a base and that 20,000 and 35,000 hours are estimated for A and B, respectively. (Carry rates to 5 decimals.)
3. Set up a schedule showing allocation of service department costs to production departments, using the direct method.
4. Determine overhead rates for departments A and B assuming the direct-labor hours indicated in requirement 2.

E14–10. Service Department Overhead Allocation—Step Method

Pitt Manufacturing Company has two operating departments—A and B—and three service departments—X, Y, and Z. The controller for Pitt prepared the following projection of operations for the coming year:

Department	Direct Materials	Direct Labor	Factory Overhead	Total
A	$241,000	$1,401,000	$498,000	$2,140,000
B	285,000	898,000	802,000	1,985,000
X	0	48,000	49,000	97,000
Y	25,000	72,000	41,000	138,000
Z	0	54,000	36,000	90,000

Using various allocation bases, the controller developed the following estimates of percentages of effort devoted to other departments by service departments.

	% of Effort				
Service to	X	Y	Z	A	B
Service by					
X	0%	10%	8%	48%	34%
Y	5	0	11	36	48
Z	2	8	0	40	50

Required

1. Prepare a schedule showing the allocation of service department costs using the step method. Begin with the department that performs the largest percentage of service for other *service* departments.
2. Determine the total overhead rates as a percentage of labor cost for each operating department.
3. If at the end of the year the *total* factory overhead amounts to $1,650,000, and if departments A and B had direct-labor costs of $1,420,000 and $913,000, respectively, what can you say about the company's over- or underapplied factory overhead *in total*?

E14-11. Allocation of Service Department Costs—Reciprocal Method

SDL Manufacturing, Inc. has developed the following overhead costs by department.

Production departments:	P1—$100,000
	P2—$ 90,000
Service departments:	S1—$ 50,000
	S2—$ 42,000

SDL has gathered the following statistics concerning its factory operations.

Department	Allocation Base (S1)	Allocation Base (S2)
Production:		
P1	300	1,216
P2	600	1,600
Service:		
S1	na	384
S2	100	na

Required

Prepare an electronic spreadsheet to calculate overhead application rates for each production department, using 40,000 and 30,000 direct-labor hours, respectively, for P1 and P2.

PROBLEMS

P14-1. Departmental Overhead Distribution—Direct Method

Marshall Incorporated applies factory overhead on the following bases:

In department F, 45% of F's material cost
In department G, $4.70 per direct-labor hour in G

The following accounts and their balances at month's end are as follows:

Work in process—materials	$50,000
Work in process—direct labor	28,000
Work in process—applied factory overhead	26,000
Indirect labor	15,000
Factory office	4,000
Depreciation and insurance on building	5,000
Power plant expenses	3,000

	Production Departments		
Other information	F	G	Power Plant
Direct materials	$28,000	$22,000	
Direct labor	11,000	16,500	
Direct-labor hours	2,600	3,200	
Power used	56%	44%	
Floor space occupied	1,100 sq. ft.	500 sq. ft.	400 sq. ft.

Indirect labor and factory office are apportioned in the ratio of direct-labor cost. No service department costs are allocated to other service departments, except for the appropriate portion of depreciation and insurance that is applicable to the power plant.

Required

1. Prepare a distribution sheet showing the distribution of service department factory overhead costs to production departments.

2. Determine the over- or underapplied factory overhead in total and for each production department after all overhead has been allocated to the production departments.

P14–2. Factory Overhead Distribution Schedule and Rate Calculation

Cassel Chemical Company consists of three production departments and four service departments. For the purpose of creating factory overhead rates, the accountant prepared the cost distribution sheet that follows. It contains operational data gathered by the accountant.

Data	Total	Preparation	Mixing	Packaging	Utilities	Maintenance	Materials Handling	Factory Office
Operational Data:								
Floor space (sq. ft.)	53,000	10,000	12,000	16,000	3,000	3,000	5,000	4,000
Maintenance hours	6,820	1,860	2,480	930	620		620	310
Metered hours (in hundreds)	4,000	1,400	1,600	320		200	320	160
Expenses:								
Indirect labor	$22,000	$3,800	$2,600	$2,400	$3,500	$4,000	$3,300	$2,400
Payroll taxes	2,522	440	532	420	230	355	320	225
Indirect materials	5,703	700	938	2,300	920	150	150	545
Depreciation	850	100	150	50	100	200	200	50
Total	$31,075	$5,040	$4,220	$5,170	$4,750	$4,705	$3,970	$3,220

For the distribution of the service departments' expenses, the following procedures were decided on:

1. Utilities: 80% on metered hours of power
   20% on square footage of floor space
2. Maintenance: maintenance hours excluding utilities
3. Materials Handling: 48% to preparation, 32% to mixing, and 20% to packaging—pounds handled is 395,300 in preparation and 262,850 in mixing
4. Factory Office: preparation, 40%; mixing, 30%; packaging, 30%

Required

1. Complete a cost distribution sheet using the step method. No reciprocal charging should take place. (Round off all amounts to the nearest dollar.)
2. Determine the factory overhead rates based on pounds handled in preparation and mixing, and on the direct-labor cost of $86,000 in packaging. (Round off to the nearest cent.)

P14–3. Allocation of Service Department Costs—Step Method

The Wing Company has three production departments and three service departments. The following information was given for August:

Department	Direct Departmental Expenses	Square Feet	Employees	Equipment in $
Cutting	$17,000	1,200	25	$ 60,000
Forming	34,000	2,000	30	100,000
Finishing	20,000	800	15	80,000
Building service	8,000	400	10	10,000
Health service	5,000	300	10	2,000
Repairs service	12,000	300	10	30,000
Total	$96,000	5,000	100	$282,000

The bases for distributing expenses of the service departments are as follows:

Building service = area occupied
Health service = number of employees
Repairs service = investment in equipment

Wing Company assigns service department expenses to other service departments. However, after a department's expenses are allocated, no expenses are allocated back to it.

Required

Distribute the expenses of the service departments, beginning with the building service, then the health service, and then the repairs service. (Round to the nearest dollar.)

P14-4. Factory Overhead—Service Department Allocations (CPA)

Marker Manufacturing Company has two production departments—fabrication and assembly—and three service departments—general factory administration, factory maintenance, and factory cafeteria. The following summarizes the costs and other data for each department before allocation of service department costs for the year ending June 30:

	Fabrication	Assembly	General Factory Administration	Factory Maintenance	Factory Cafeteria
Direct-labor costs	$1,950,000	$2,050,0000	$90,000	$82,100	$87,000
Direct-material costs	$3,130,000	$950,000	—	$65,000	$91,000
Factory overhead costs	$1,650,000	$1,850,000	$70,000	$56,100	$62,000
Direct-labor hours	562,500	437,500	31,000	27,000	42,000
Number of employees	280	200	12	8	20
Square footage occupied	88,000	72,000	1,750	2,000	4,800

The costs of the general factory administration department, factory maintenance department, and factory cafeteria are allocated on the basis of direct-labor hours, square footage occupied, and number of employees, respectively. Round all final calculations to the nearest dollar.

Required

1. Assuming that Marker elects to distribute service department costs directly to production departments without interservice department cost allocations, determine the amount of factory maintenance department costs that would be allocated to the fabrication department.
2. Assuming the same method of allocation as in requirement 1, determine the amount of general factory administration department costs that would be allocated to the assembly department.
3. Assuming that Marker elects to distribute service department costs to other service departments (starting with the service department with the greatest total costs) as well as to the production departments, determine the amount of factory cafeteria costs that would be allocated to the factory maintenance department. (Note: Once a service department's costs have been allocated, no subsequent service department costs are recirculated back to it.)
4. Assuming the same method of allocation as in requirement 3, determine the amount of factory maintenance department costs that would be allocated to the factory cafeteria.

P14-5. Reciprocal Distribution of Factory Overhead

The estimated departmental factory overhead for production departments A and B and service departments L, M, and N (before any service department allocations) are as follows:

Production Departments		Service Departments	
A	$120,000	L	$40,000
B	$180,000	M	$40,000
		N	$20,000

The reciprocal services performed by each department for other departments are as follows:

	Services Provided		
Departments	L	M	N
Production—A	—	30%	40%
Production—B	50%	40	30
Service—L	—	20	—
Service—M	20	—	—
Service—N	30	10	—
Sales	—	—	20
General administration	—	—	10
	100%	100%	100%

Required

1. Determine the final amount of estimated overhead for each service department after reciprocal transfer costs have been calculated, using the reciprocal method.
2. Determine total factory overhead for each production department and the amount of department N cost assigned to the sales department and to general administration.

P14–6. Reciprocal Distribution of Factory Overhead (Computer) The financial vice president of the Manville Company has instructed the cost department to use an algebraic procedure for allocating service department costs to production departments. The firm's three production departments are served by three service departments, each of which consumes part of the services of the other two. After the direct departmental costs have been determined, the account balances of the service departments and interdependence of the departments were as follows:

Department	Department Overhead before Distribution of Service Departments	Service Provided		
		Powerhouse	Cafeteria	Custodial
Smelting	$250,000	25%	35%	25%
Concentrating	180,000	25	30	20
Refining	210,000	20	20	20
Powerhouse	32,000	—	10	20
Cafeteria	59,000	10	—	15
Custodial	84,000	20	5	—
	$815,000	100%	100%	100%

Required

1. Develop the three simultaneous equations necessary to allocate service department costs using the reciprocal method.
2. Using subtraction and substitution, solve the simultaneous equations algebraically. Verify these results by developing an electronic spreadsheet to solve the simultaneous equations developed in requirement 1. (Hint: Place each formula in a cell and perform a number of iterative recalculations.)

3. Set up a schedule showing the allocation of overhead costs to production departments.

P14–7. Cost Allocation—Evaluation of Allocation Bases (CMA)

Columbia Company is a regional office supply chain with twenty-six independent stores. Each store has been responsible for its own credit and collections. The assistant manager in each store is responsible for credit activities, including the collection of delinquent accounts, because the stores do not need a full-time employee assigned to credit activities. The company has experienced a sharp rise in uncollectibles during the last two years. Corporate management has decided to establish a collections department in the home office to be responsible for the collection function company-wide. The home office of Columbia Company will hire the necessary full-time personnel. The size of this department will be based on the historical credit activity for the stores.

The new centralized collections department was discussed at a recent management meeting. A method to assign the costs of the new department to the stores has been difficult to determine, because this type of home office service is somewhat unique. Alternative methods are being reviewed by top management.

The controller favored using a predetermined or standard rate for charging the costs to the stores. The predetermined rate would be based on budgeted costs. The vice president of sales preferred an actual cost charging system.

In addition, the basis for the collection charges to the stores was discussed. The controller identified the four following measures of services (allocation bases) that could be used:

1. Total dollar sales
2. Average number of past-due accounts
3. Number of uncollectible accounts written off
4. The cost equally divided between all the stores

The executive vice president stated that he would like the accounting department to prepare a detailed analysis of the two charging methods and the four service measures (allocation bases).

Required

1. Evaluate the two methods identified—predetermined (standard) rate versus actual cost—that could be used to charge to the individual stores the costs of Columbia Company's new collections department in terms of the following:
   a. Practicality of application and ease of use
   b. Cost control
   Also indicate whether a centralized or decentralized type of organizational structure would be more conducive for each charging method.
2. For each measure of service (allocation base) identified by the controller, do the following:
   a. Discuss whether the service measure (allocation base) is appropriate to use in this situation.
   b. Identify the behavioral problems, if any, that could arise as a result of adopting the service measure (allocation base).

P14–8. Cost Allocation—Government Requirements (CMA)

The Anderson Company, a moderate-sized manufacturing firm, was awarded a negotiated defense contract of $4,000,000 on May 1. Anderson has never been subject to cost accounting standards that cover defense contracts because it had no defense contracts before the $4,000,000 award. Management wants to continue with the company's present cost accounting practices, but it is not sure that these practices are in compliance with defense contract requirements. The accounting department has been asked to review its cost accounting practices for compliance with government standards for defense contracts.

The Huron Division, which will perform the contract, is one of four segments of the Anderson Company. The review disclosed that the Huron Division includes selling costs as part of its general and administrative expenses. In negotiating the contract, the division had used cost of sales as a base for allocating general and administrative expenses to the contract to arrive at the final contract amount.

The applicable defense contract cost standard to which Anderson Company must comply in this situation is Cost Accounting Standard 410, "Allocation of Business Unit General and Administrative Expenses to Final Cost Objectives." This standard defines general and administrative expenses as any management, financial, and other expenses that are incurred by or allocated to a business unit and are for the general management and administration of the business unit as a whole.

Cost Standard 410 requires the use of a cost input base for allocation of general and administrative expenses to a cost objective (such as a defense contract). Cost input is defined as the cost that for contract costing purposes is allocable to the production of goods or services during a cost accounting period.

Required

1. Did the Huron Division of Anderson Company comply with the provisions of Cost Accounting Standard 410 as discussed here when it used a cost of sales base for allocating general and administrative expenses? Explain why or why not.
2. According to the provisions of the standard, is the classification of selling costs used by Huron Division appropriate? Explain.

P14-9. Factory Overhead and Journal Entries Backman Foundry produces manhole and sewer covers. Three production operations are needed. There are no service departments. Support activities needed by production departments, such as custodial and maintenance, are either provided directly to production departments or contracted for with outside providers. Thus all overhead costs are charged directly to production department overhead control accounts.

Before the current year began, management initiated the use of predetermined overhead rates for the first time. These rates were to be used for the first six months of the year. At the end of June, a thorough review of results was to be made. Revisions in rates were to be affected as indicated by the review of results.

The production departments and the overhead rates set for the first six months are as follows:

Casting	$5 per machine hour
Stamping	$3 per direct-labor hour
Finishing	60% of direct-labor cost

During the first six months, the summary operating data are as follows:

Department	Actual Operating Statistics	Factory Overhead Incurred
Casting	3,200 machine hours	$22,000
Stamping	9,600 direct-labor hours	30,000
Finishing	$75,000 of direct-labor costs	40,000

The June 30 review indicates that the operations and the overhead incurred during the first six months can be expected to be typical for the remainder of the year under expected conditions.

Required

1. Determine the overhead applied to production during the first six months in each department, and indicate the over- or underapplied overhead.
2. Make summary journal entries to record the overhead incurred and overhead applied to production for the first six months of the year.
3. Determine revised overhead rates for each department based on the operating data for the first six months of the year.

P 14–10. Cost Allocation—Evaluation of Assertions Made in a Dialogue

The following discussion was printed in the Lybrand Journal in 1960, as well as in numerous other sources. The original source is unknown.

In discussing the cost incident to various types of operation, the following analogy was drawn. A restaurant adds a rack of peanuts for the counter, intending to pick up a little additional profit in the usual course of business. Consider the actual problem faced by the restauranteur (Joe) as revealed by his accountant–efficiency expert.

Eff Ex: Joe, you said you put in these peanuts because some people ask for them, but do you realize what this rack of peanuts is costing you?

Joe: It ain't gonna cost. It's gonna be a profit. Sure, I had to pay $25 for a fancy rack to hold bags, but the peanuts cost 6¢ a bag and I sell 'em for 10¢. Figger I sell 50 bags a week to start. It'll take 12½ weeks to cover the cost of the rack. After that I gotta clear profit of 4¢ a bag. The more I sell the more I'll make.

Eff Ex: This is an antiquated and completely unrealistic approach, Joe. Fortunately, modern accounting procedures permit a more accurate picture that reveals the complexities involved.

Joe: Huh?

Eff Ex: To be precise, those peanuts must be integrated into your entire operation and be allocated their appropriate share of business overhead. They must share a proportionate part of your expenditures for rent, heat, light, equipment depreciation, decoration, salaries for waitresses, cook, . . .

Joe: The cook? What's he gotta do with peanuts? He don't even know I got 'em!

Eff Ex: Look, Joe, the cook is in the kitchen. The kitchen prepares the food. The food is what brings people in here, and the people ask to buy peanuts. That's why you must charge a portion of the cook's wages, as well as a part of your own salary to peanut sales. This carefully calculated cost analysis sheet indicates the peanut operation should pay exactly $1,278 per year toward these general overhead costs.

Joe: The Peanuts? $1,278 a year for overhead? The nuts?

Eff Ex: It's really a little more than that. You also spend money each week to have the windows washed and to have the place swept out in the mornings. Keep soap in the washroom and provide free cokes to the police. That raises the total to $1,313 per year.

Joe: (thoughtfully) But the peanut salesman said I'd make money. Put 'em on the end of the counter, he said, and get 4¢ a bag profit.

Eff Ex: (with a sniff) He's not an accountant. Do you actually know what the portion of the counter occupied by the peanut rack is worth to you?

Joe: Ain't worth nothing. No stool there, just a dead spot at the end.

Eff Ex: The modern cost picture permits no dead spots. Your counter contains 60 square

Joe: feet and the counter grosses $15,000/year, so the square foot of space occupied by the peanut rack is worth $250 per year. Since you have taken area away from general counter use, you must charge the value of the space of the occupant.

Joe: You mean I gotta pay $250 a year more to the peanuts?

Eff Ex: Right. That raises their share of the general operation costs to a grand total of $1,563 per year. Now then, if you sell 50 bags of peanuts per week, these allocated costs will amount to 60¢ per bag.

Joe: What?

Eff Ex: Obviously, to that must be added your purchase price of 6¢ per bag, which brings the total to 66¢. So you see, by selling peanuts at 10¢ per bag you are losing 56¢ on every sale.

Joe: Somethin's crazy?

Eff Ex: Not at all! Here are the figures. They prove your peanut operation cannot stand on its own feet.

Joe: (brightening) Suppose I sell lotsa peanuts, thousand bags a week 'stead of fifty?

Eff Ex: (tolerantly) Joe, you don't understand the problem. If the volume of peanut sales increases your operating costs will go up. You'll have to handle more bags, with more time, more depreciation, more everything. The basic principle of accounting is firm on that subject—the bigger the operation, the more general overhead costs that must be allocated. No, increasing the volume of sales won't help.

Joe: Okay. You are so smart. You tell me what I gotta do.

Eff Ex: (condescendingly) Well, you could first reduce operating expenses.

Joe: How?

Eff Ex: Move to a building with cheaper rent. Cut salaries. Wash the windows biweekly. Have the floor swept only on Thursday. Remove the soap from the washrooms. Decrease the square foot value of your counter. For example, if you can cut your expenses 50 percent, you will reduce the amount allocated to peanuts from $1,563 down to $781.50 per year. Reducing the cost to 36¢ per bag.

Joe (slowly) That's better?

Eff Ex: Much, much better. However, even then you would lose 26¢ per bag if you charge only 10¢. Therefore, you must also raise your selling price. If you want a net profit of 4¢ per bag, you would have to charge 40¢.

Joe: (flabbergasted) You mean after I cut operating costs 50 percent I still gotta charge 40¢ for a 10¢ bag of peanuts? Nobody's that nuts about nuts? Who's gonna buy 'em?

Eff Ex: That's a secondary consideration. The point is at 40¢ you'd be selling at a price based upon a true and proper evaluation of your then reduced costs.

Joe: (eagerly) Look! I gotta better idea. Why don't I just throw the nuts out. Put 'em in a trash can?

Eff Ex: Can you afford it?

Joe: Sure. All I got is about 50 bags of peanuts. It cost about three bucks, so I lost $25 on the rack. But I'm out of this nutsy business and no more grief.

Eff Ex: (shaking head) Joe, it isn't quite that simple. You are in the peanut business! The minute you throw those peanuts out, you are adding $1,563 of annual overhead to the rest of your operation. Joe, be realistic. Can you afford to do that?

Joe: (completely crushed) It's unbelievable! Last week I made money. Now I'm in trouble, just because I think peanuts on a counter is a gonna bring me some extra profit, just because I believe 50 bags of peanuts a week is easy.

Eff Ex: (with raised eyebrow) That is the object of modern cost studies, Joe, to dispel those false illusions.

Required

1. What is Joe's operating result on the peanut business? Is he losing 56¢ on the sale of every bag of peanuts? Explain.
2. Has the efficiency expert identified some relevant issues in his discussion with Joe? Explain.
3. If the volume of peanut sales is increased, does more cost have to be assigned to that aspect of operations? Explain.
4. Should Joe get out of the peanut business? Why or why not?

Part Four

COST CONTROL

Cost control is critical in order to achieve the desired profit outlined in the budget. The various techniques used to control costs are outlined in chapters 15 through 19.

A standard cost system is a cost control technique that identifies the costs that should be incurred during normal operations. At the end of a time period, actual costs are compared with the standard costs and any differences are called variances. Variance analysis highlights areas of the operation in which corrective action is needed.

The development of a good cost accounting system is critical for effective cost control. The advent of the computer has had a significant impact on cost accounting systems. A variety of reports can be provided by the system to assist management in controlling costs. Some of the most frequently used reports include gross margin analysis, segment performance reports, and reports based on variable costing.

Chapter 15

Standard Costs for Materials and Labor

Outline

COST CONTROL SYSTEMS
STANDARD COSTS DEFINED
Materials Standards
Labor Standards
STANDARDS AS BUDGETARY GOALS AND PERFORMANCE BENCHMARKS
MATERIALS AND LABOR VARIANCES
RESPONSIBILITY FOR VARIANCES
Materials
Labor
RECORDING MATERIALS AND RELATED VARIANCES
Recognizing Price Variance at Time of Purchase
Recognizing Price Variance at Time of Issue
RECORDING LABOR AND RELATED VARIANCES
DISPOSITION OF VARIANCES
INVESTIGATION OF VARIANCES
DEVELOPMENT OF STANDARDS
Standard-Setting Philosophies
Physical Standards
SUMMARY
APPENDIX 15.1: A HYBRID METHOD FOR RECOGNIZING MATERIALS PRICE VARIANCES
SELF-STUDY PROBLEM
SUGGESTED READINGS
DISCUSSION QUESTIONS
EXERCISES
PROBLEMS

Budgets provide a formal mechanism for comparing actual results with plans and goals. Flexible budgets, as discussed in chapter 7, provide the key element of responsibility accounting, by which plans and actions of responsible persons are coordinated and monitored by higher levels of management. A flexible budget is both a planning tool and a criterion against which actual performance can be evaluated. Standard or predetermined costs greatly enhance the effectiveness of flexible budgets and are widely used as the basis for their development and for providing feedback to management.

This chapter explains how standard costs are used in cost accounting systems. After completing this chapter, you should be able to:

1. define *standard costs* and explain their role in providing feedback for cost control.
2. use materials and labor standards in the development of budgets.
3. record materials and labor costs using a standard cost system.
4. calculate materials and labor variances.
5. explain who is responsible for materials and labor variances.
6. develop appropriate standards for materials and labor.
7. determine when it is appropriate to investigate variances.

COST CONTROL SYSTEMS

Just as manufacturing enterprises grow and mature, their managerial control systems evolve with the volume and complexity of operations. A system of control often begins with a set of historical records that compares the results of operations for two succeeding periods. Financial results of the current period are compared with results of the prior period, differences are noted, and causes of differences are investigated. Following such an analysis, managerial action can be taken to correct unfavorable situations or to promote favorable results.

The usefulness of simple historical comparisons is limited, however, because it is often difficult to precisely identify specific causes of differences. For example, assume that the volume of sales for a particular company remained the same from one period to the next but that cost of goods sold increased, resulting in a decrease in operating income. Management wants to know what caused the increase in the cost of goods sold and discovers that the cost of materials increased. However, without more specific information, management may not be able to determine the relative effect of changes in materials prices compared with, say, changes in the efficiency with which materials were used.

The comparison of flexible budgets based on standard costs with actual results of operations provides additional information to answer questions about the effect of *(a)* changes in prices paid for materials, *(b)* changes in rates paid for labor, *(c)* the efficiency with which materials were utilized, and *(d)* the efficiency with which labor was utilized. With this feedback, management is better equipped to make meaningful decisions about the future conduct of operations.

Note that standard costs are used in conjunction with either job-order or process costing systems. The use of standard costs does not constitute another accounting system; rather, standard costs are applicable to both job-order and process-costing systems in the same way that budgets are applicable to both systems. Standard costs are simply used as the basis for developing manufacturing budgets, whichever basic system is used. These budgets are then used as a criteria against which to judge the quality of actual performance.

STANDARD COSTS DEFINED

A **standard** is a criterion for measurement. In cost accounting the term refers to an expected quantity or price to be paid for the materials and labor required to make a product or provide a service. Standards are expressed in terms of specific items of input—the units of materials, the hours of labor, the price of materials, the rate of labor, and the percent of plant capacity required to manufacture one unit of output. A **cost,** as related to standard costs, is the dollar outlay or sacrifice that is incurred for each unit of output.

The combination of the terms *standard* and *cost* into **standard cost** refers to the dollar outlays expected to be incurred to manufacture a particular product in a given manufacturing situation. Typically, a standard cost is a cost per unit that the firm should try to achieve if the results of operations are to be as desired. Management's underlying philosophy dictates what targeted or expected costs should be. For example, management may expect the lowest costs possible under ideal manufacturing conditions, or it may consider the consequences of factors such as lost time for maintenance as part of what is expected. Different philosophies and the development of standards will be discussed later in this chapter.

As actual production takes place, standard costs are compared with actual costs incurred, and any differences or variances are recorded. The variance between actual costs incurred and projected standard costs can be used as feedback to management for control purposes.

Standard costs are developed for each manufacturing cost component—materials, labor, and overhead. Standard costs for materials and labor are discussed in this chapter; whereas those for factory overhead are discussed in chapter 16.

Two components—a quantity standard and a price standard—make up a standard cost. Multiplying the quantity standard times the price standard gives the standard cost. To illustrate, figure 15.1 contains the standard cost calculations for the manufacture of one type of bronze bookend. The use of these standards is discussed throughout this chapter.

Materials Standards

As shown in figure 15.1, a materials standard consists of two components—a *materials quantity standard* and a *materials price standard*. Multiplying the price standard times the quantity standard gives the standard materials cost per unit. For example, to manufacture

FIGURE 15.1

Standard Costs for Bronze Bookends

Materials				
Quantity standard	×	Price standard	=	Standard cost
3 pounds per bookend	×	$4.00 per pound	=	$12.00 per bookend

Labor				
Efficiency standard	×	Rate standard	=	Standard cost
1 hour per unit	×	$7.00 per hour	=	$7.00 per bookend

Combined Standard Costs per Unit

Materials	$12.00
Labor	7.00
Total	$19.00

one bookend, three pounds of materials per bookend (the material quantity standard) are expected to be required at an expected cost of $4.00 per pound (the material price standard), giving a materials standard cost per unit of $12.00.

The materials quantity standard is developed from a combination of engineering design studies and previous manufacturing experience. Materials quantity standards may take into consideration acceptable levels of spoilage, waste, shrinkage, and evaporation. After the product has been through a developmental stage, current production experience may be the best guide for adjusting quantity standards to accurately reflect expected materials usage. Additional guidance for the development of material standards is given later in this chapter.

The materials price standard should reflect the market prices that are expected to prevail during the budgeted accounting period. Determination of an appropriate price standard is complicated, because prices are largely controlled by factors that are external to the firm and that are subject to unexpected change. Suppliers' price lists and the judgment of the firm's purchasing agents can provide the basis for setting cost standards. A suggested rule is to review price standards at the beginning of each budgetary period and make adjustments as appropriate.

Labor Standards

Just like materials standards, labor standards consist of two components. Although the underlying concept is the same, the accepted terminology for labor differs slightly from that used for materials. As illustrated in figure 15.1, a *labor efficiency standard* is used instead of a quantity standard to indicate how efficiently the available hours of labor are utilized. Instead of a cost standard, a *labor rate standard* is used to indicate the cost of labor based on a per-hour rate.

Multiply the rate standard times the efficiency standard gives the standard labor cost per unit. For example, one bookend requires one hour of labor (the labor efficiency standard) at an expected rate of $7.00 per hour (the labor rate standard), giving a labor standard cost per unit of $7.00.

The labor efficiency standard is usually determined through time and motion studies of actual worker performance. Taking into consideration personal needs, fatigue, and production factors outside the control of the individual worker, the average effort of workers with average skills may be used to develop efficiency standards. Additional guidance for the development of labor standards is given later in this chapter.

The labor rate standard is based on employment agreements. Labor rates may be determined by individual employees' agreements with the firm's personnel department or by collective bargaining agreements under which a number of employees are covered by union contract. In either event, the agreed hourly or piece rates and bonus agreements provide the basis for labor rate standards.

STANDARDS AS BUDGETARY GOALS AND PERFORMANCE BENCHMARKS

Standard costs relate to one unit of production and can be thought of as representing a unit concept. On the other hand, budgets portray an aggregate concept in that the budget is derived by multiplying standard costs by the planned level of output. Therefore, standard costs are literally basic building blocks of manufacturing budgets.

FIGURE 15.2

Materials and Labor Budget for Bronze Bookends (for 5,000 Units of Production)

	Standard Costs	Budgeted Costs
Materials	$12.00	$60,000
Labor	7.00	35,000
Total	$19.00	$95,000

Alternative computations:
Materials: 5,000 units × 3 pounds per unit × $4.00 per pound = $60,000
Labor: 5,000 units × 1 hour per unit × $7.00 per hour = $35,000

Unless standard costs are visualized as a *unit* concept and budgets are visualized as an *aggregate* concept, the more detailed aspects of standard cost systems will seem confusing. Figure 15.2 illustrates this relationship and provides a materials and labor budget for a manufacturer of bronze bookends.

Figure 15.2 shows that the total standard cost for materials and labor for each bookend is $19.00. If the level of activity is 5,000 bookends, the total budgeted standard cost of materials and labor is $95,000.

As indicated before, standard costs provide the foundation of a feedback and control system in manufacturing operations. Figure 15.3 shows data from accounting records concerning the production of bookends for one period. The term *total standard costs allowed* is alternate terminology for *total budgeted costs* when using flexible budgets.

Actual results of operations can be compared with budgeted results to provide management with feedback about the attainment of goals and to serve as a benchmark against which to evaluate performance. This can be done in successive levels of detail. As shown in figure 15.4, an overall or total budget variance can be calculated to show how much total actual results differed from total budgeted results.

Budget variances indicate the total deviation of actual costs from expected costs. In figure 15.4, total actual costs exceeded budgeted costs, resulting in an unfavorable total budget variance. However, the total actual cost of materials was less than expected, resulting in a favorable budget variance for materials. Total labor costs exceeded the budget and resulted in an unfavorable budget variance for labor. The combination of the favorable budget variance for materials and the unfavorable budget variance for labor resulted in the unfavorable total budget variance.

FIGURE 15.3

Production Results

Units produced	5,000	
Materials:		
Pounds of materials purchased	15,000	
Pounds of materials used	14,740	
Price per pound paid for materials	× $4.05	
Total materials cost		$59,697
Labor:		
Hours of labor used	5,060	
Rate per hour paid to labor	× $7.00	
Total labor cost		$35,420
Total materials and labor costs		$95,117

FIGURE 15.4

Budget Variances

	Budgeted[a] Costs	Actual[b] Costs	Budget Variance
Direct materials	$60,000	$59,697	$303 F
Direct labor	35,000	35,420	420 U
Total	$95,000	$95,117	$117 U

F = Favorable
U = Unfavorable
[a] See figure 15.2.
[b] See figure 15.3.

MATERIALS AND LABOR VARIANCES

Budget variances do not give the complete story about deviations between budgeted and actual results; that is, it is not yet clear in figure 15.4 what contributed to the favorable materials variance. By visually comparing production results in figure 15.3 with the standards in 15.1, it can be observed that the firm paid more for raw materials than expected, which would have contributed to an unfavorable materials variance. Fewer raw materials were used in production than expected, which would have contributed to a favorable materials variance. However, the relative effect of these price and quantity differences is not clear without further investigation. This same type of ambiguity also exists in the analysis of the budget variance for labor.

To completely and meaningfully analyze the total budget variance, each component of standard costs must be analyzed; that is, materials variances are analyzed in terms of the materials price standard and the materials quantity standard. The labor variances are analyzed in terms of the labor rate standard and the labor efficiency standard. This level of analysis results in *(a)* a *materials price variance* that identifies the effect of differences in prices paid for materials, *(b)* a *materials quantity (usage) variance* that identifies the effect of differences in the quantities of materials used, *(c)* a *labor rate variance* that identifies the effect of differences in the rates paid workers, and *(d)* a *labor efficiency (usage) variance* that identifies the effect of differences in the quantities of labor used. Figure 15.5 shows formulas that are used to calculate these variances.

The rationale underlying the variance formulas is that by holding one of the cost components constant, it is possible to isolate the effect of differences in the other standard cost component. For example, if the quantity of materials is held constant at the level of actual usage, and it is multiplied by the difference between the standard price and the actual price of materials, it is possible to isolate the effect of differences in prices. Also, if the price of materials is held constant at the standard price, and it is multiplied by the difference between budgeted and actual usage of materials, it is possible to isolate the effect of differences in quantities. This underlying principle is also used to calculate labor variances.

Figure 15.6 shows an application of the variance formulas. The data used in figure 15.6 are the standard costs for bronze bookends given in figure 15.1 and the results of operations given in figure 15.3.

An alternative to the use of formulas is a tabular approach to the calculation of variances. This approach is actually based on an expansion and comparison of the variance formulas in figure 15.5. For example, expanding the materials variance formulas by multiplication results in the following (see fig. 15.5 for an explanation of the formula's abbreviations):

FIGURE 15.5 Formulas for Computing Materials and Labor Variances

Materials

Price variance:

$$\left[\begin{array}{c}\text{Standard price of materials} \\ \text{(per unit)}\end{array} - \begin{array}{c}\text{Actual price of materials} \\ \text{(per unit)}\end{array}\right] \times \begin{array}{c}\text{Actual quantity of materials} \\ \text{purchased or used}^a\end{array}$$

Quantity (usage) variance:

$$\left[\begin{array}{c}\text{Standard quantity of materials} \\ \text{for units produced}\end{array} - \begin{array}{c}\text{Actual quantity of materials} \\ \text{used}\end{array}\right] \times \begin{array}{c}\text{Standard price of materials} \\ \text{(per unit)}\end{array}$$

Labor

Rate variance:

$$\left[\begin{array}{c}\text{Standard rate for labor} \\ \text{(per hour)}\end{array} - \begin{array}{c}\text{Actual rate paid for labor} \\ \text{(per hour)}\end{array}\right] \times \begin{array}{c}\text{Actual hours of labor} \\ \text{used}\end{array}$$

Efficiency (usage) variance:

$$\left[\begin{array}{c}\text{Standard hours of labor} \\ \text{for units produced}\end{array} - \begin{array}{c}\text{Actual hours of labor} \\ \text{used}\end{array}\right] \times \begin{array}{c}\text{Standard rate for labor} \\ \text{(per hour)}\end{array}$$

Formulas

	where	and
$PV = (SP - AP) \times AQ$	PV = Price variance	AH = Actual hours of labor used
$QV = (SQ - AQ) \times SP$	QV = Quantity variance	AP = Actual price (per unit) of materials
$RV = (SR - AR) \times AH$	RV = Rate variance	AQ = Actual quantity of materials (purchased or used)
$EV = (SH - AH) \times SR$	EV = Efficiency variance	AR = Actual rate paid (per hour) for labor
		SH = Standard hours of labor for units produced
		SP = Standard price (per unit) of materials
		SQ = Standard quantity of materials for units produced
		SR = Standard rate for labor

[a] Materials price variances are typically recognized at the time of purchase. However, they may be recognized at the time of issue as illustrated in figure 15.7 and discussed on page 000.

FIGURE 15.6

Materials and Labor Variances for Bronze Bookends

Materials

Price variance: (purchased) ($4.00 − $4.05) × 15,000 pounds =	$ 750 U
Price variance: (issued) ($4.00 − $4.05) × 14,740 pounds =	$ 737 U
Quantity variance: (15,000 pounds − 14,740 pounds) × $4.00 =	1,040 F
Budget variance	$ 303 F

Labor

Rate variance: ($7.00 − $7.00) × 5,060 hours =	$ 0
Efficiency variance: (5,000 hours − 5,060 hours) × $7.00 =	420 U
Budget variance	$ 420 U

Price variance = [(AQ)(SP) − (AQ)(AP)]
Quantity variance = [(SQ)(SP) − (AQ)(SP)]

Both variance formulas contain a common expression—*(AQ)(SP)*. This feature, which also occurs with labor variances, makes it possible to use the framework in figure 15.7 to calculate materials and labor variances.

FIGURE 15.7 Framework for Analysis of Variances

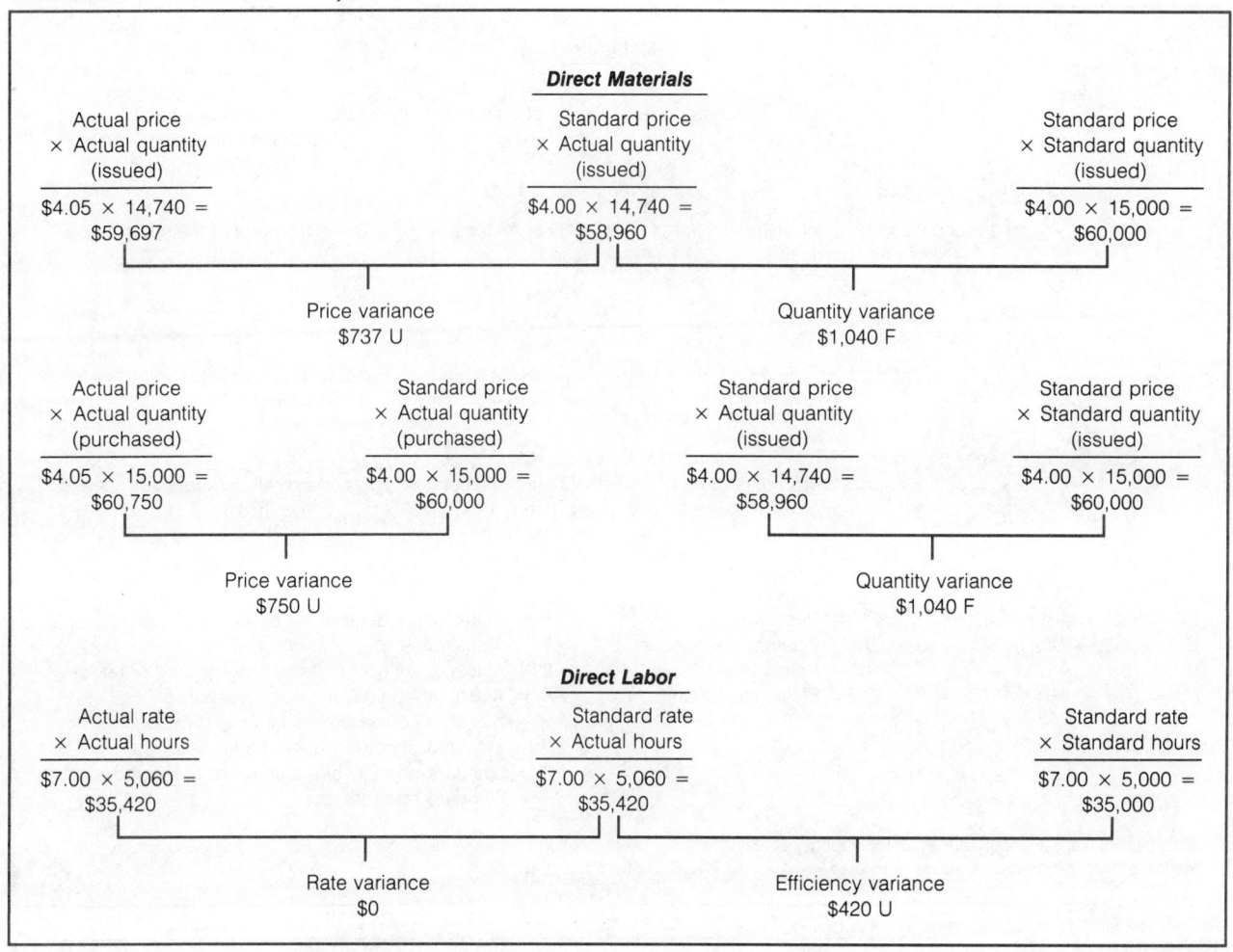

Direct Materials

Actual price × Actual quantity (issued)	Standard price × Actual quantity (issued)	Standard price × Standard quantity (issued)
$4.05 × 14,740 = $59,697	$4.00 × 14,740 = $58,960	$4.00 × 15,000 = $60,000

Price variance $737 U   Quantity variance $1,040 F

Actual price × Actual quantity (purchased)	Standard price × Actual quantity (purchased)	Standard price × Actual quantity (issued)	Standard price × Standard quantity (issued)
$4.05 × 15,000 = $60,750	$4.00 × 15,000 = $60,000	$4.00 × 14,740 = $58,960	$4.00 × 15,000 = $60,000

Price variance $750 U   Quantity variance $1,040 F

Direct Labor

Actual rate × Actual hours	Standard rate × Actual hours	Standard rate × Standard hours
$7.00 × 5,060 = $35,420	$7.00 × 5,060 = $35,420	$7.00 × 5,000 = $35,000

Rate variance $0   Efficiency variance $420 U

You may prefer to use the tabular approach to calculate variances. However, when doing so remember that the tabular approach is simply a convenient way to apply the basic variance formulas and not a different calculation. Note that in figure 15.7 the materials variances are calculated on two bases: *(a)* materials purchased and *(b)* materials issued. The importance of this difference is discussed later in this chapter.

RESPONSIBILITY FOR VARIANCES

The objective of a standard cost system and the calculation of variances is to provide feedback for planning and cost control. To achieve *effective* cost control, each reported variance must be associated with a responsible person. The person given the responsibility must also have the authority to control that item of material or labor in the production process. If a definite linkage does not exist between reported variances and a manager who is responsible and able to exercise control, the effectiveness of a standard cost system will be compromised.

Depending on the production environment, variance reports may be needed on an hourly, daily, weekly, or monthly basis. For example, control over material usage for a fast-moving, continuous process such as generating instant cake mixes may require hourly monitoring, but control over material usage for ship building may require only weekly or monthly reporting.

In some high technology manufacturing environments, the occurrence and reporting of variances are virtually simultaneous events. For example, one company using computer-integrated manufacturing and just-in-time techniques (described in chapter 12) has various colored lights that report situations needing attention as they occur on its production line. A blue light flashes if raw materials are getting low. A yellow light flashes if automatic testing equipment discovers a defective unit. A red light flashes if a computer-controlled machine has gone out of adjustment. Depending on the severity of the situation, the production line is automatically shut down until the situation is corrected. This type of reporting is much more effective than waiting to investigate variances until cost variance reports are generated at the end of an accounting period. However, each manufacturing situation is unique, and this type of reporting may not be technologically available or necessary in every situation.

The reporting of major variances may trigger an investigation by responsible persons in an attempt to identify causes and implement improvements in operations. The question of when variances are significant enough to warrant investigation is treated in a later section of this chapter and in chapter 17.

Materials

The head of the purchasing department is generally responsible for materials price variances. Production supervisors are responsible for materials quantity variances. However, there may be times when part of a materials price variance is the responsibility of a production supervisor. For example, a price variance may result because a supervisor is permitted to specify that certain materials should be purchased from a specific vendor. Price variances in such situations should be attributed to the requesting person.

In some instances price variances should be a shared responsibility. For example, consider the situation in which additional materials must be purchased at an unfavorable price because a production supervisor is inefficient. It could be reasoned that the production supervisor is not only responsible for the resulting unfavorable quantity variance but also responsible for all or part of any associated price variance.

Sometimes an unfavorable variance may be tolerated to obtain an even larger favorable variance. For example, the opportunity may arise to acquire a batch of raw materials of exceptionally high quality but at a price that is above standard. Even though an unfavorable price variance will result, the materials can be used very efficiently, resulting in an even larger favorable quantity variance because of production efficiencies and improved quality.

There are a number of reasons materials variances occur. For example, price variances may occur because of unexpected vendor price changes, because of the availability of quantity discounts, or simply because of changes in the bargaining power of the purchasing agent. Quantity variances may result from faulty workmanship, careless handling, or the purchase of inferior materials. Finally, there may be instances in which materials price variances are not relevant simply because they do not occur. For example, a firm using just-in-time techniques may have long-term purchase contracts with a few selected vendors. This means that materials standards are based on firm price commitments and price variances do not occur while these agreements are in effect. This situation is quite different than purchasing from any one of numerous potential vendors based on minimum price quotations.

Labor

Department supervisors are responsible for both labor rate and labor efficiency variances. However, labor rates usually are not subject to the same degree of control as labor efficiency variances. They are typically the result of union contract negotiations or come from individual employment agreements. Because of this, standard rates may simply be a function of actual labor rates. If standard rates for labor reflect actual labor rates, labor rate variances should be relatively small and are the responsibility of individual supervisors.

When standard rates for labor are not kept current with actual labor rates, labor rate variances may be relatively large. In such instances, it may be difficult to determine what part of the rate variance is the responsibility of individual supervisors and what part is the responsibility of contract negotiators. Therefore, to maintain the accountability of supervisors for rate variances, it is recommended that labor rate standards be adjusted as employment agreements change, usually on an annual basis.

Labor variances could occur for a number of reasons. For example, labor rate variances could result from a supervisor's use of workers with different rates than originally specified for particular jobs. Labor efficiency variances could be caused by such factors as unexpected changes in the quality of materials, unexpected differences in the technological level of machinery, or unexpected rates of spoilage and rework.

RECORDING MATERIALS AND RELATED VARIANCES

Information furnished by purchasing, accounts payable, and raw materials inventory provides the basis for recording materials costs and related price and quantity variances. The following data concerning materials for bronze bookends are used to illustrate recording materials costs and their related variances.

Standard price	$4.00/pound
Purchase price	$4.05/pound
Amount purchased	20,000 pounds
Amount placed in production	14,740 pounds
Budgeted usage	15,000 pounds

There are three important concepts to remember about materials when using a standard cost system. First, materials are placed in the work-in-process inventory at standard cost, and the work-in-process inventory is carried at standard cost. Second, the materials quantity variance is recognized when materials are issued and placed in production. Third, the materials price variance can be recognized either when materials are purchased or when materials are issued. Therefore, depending on when the materials price variance is recognized, the materials inventory will be carried at either actual cost or standard cost. The following sections illustrate each method of recognizing the materials price variance and the related effect each has on the carrying cost of materials inventory.

Recognizing Price Variance at Time of Purchase

When the materials price variance is recognized at the time of purchase, the following journal entries are made. The first journal entry records the receipt of materials, the incurrence of a liability, and the recognition of any price variance.

Materials inventory ($4.00/lb × 20,000 lbs.)	80,000	
Materials price variance ([$4.00 − $4.05] × 20,000 lbs.)	1,000	
Accounts payable ($4.05 × 20,000 lbs.)		81,000

The second journal entry is made when materials are issued and placed in production along with the recognition of any materials quantity variance.

Work in process ($4.00 × 15,000 lbs.)	60,000	
Materials quantity variance ([15,000 lbs. − 14,740 lbs.] × $4.00)		1,040
Materials inventory ($4.00 × 14,740 lbs.)		58,960

Recognizing Price Variance at Time of Issue

When the materials price variance is recognized at the time materials are placed in production, the following journal entry is made at the time of purchase.

Materials inventory ($4.05 × 20,000 lbs.)	81,000	
Accounts payable		81,000

The following journal entry is made when materials are issued and placed in production.

Work in process ($4.00 × 15,000 lbs.)	60,000	
Materials price variance ([$4.00 − $4.05] × 14,740 lbs.)	737	
Materials quantity variance ([15,000 lbs. − 14,740 lbs.] × $4.00)		1,040
Materials inventory ($4.05 × 14,740 lbs.)		59,697

Note that materials costs are added to the work-in-process inventory at the standard rate for the actual number of units produced. Thus the work-in-process inventory is carried at standard cost when using either system.

Recognizing materials price variances at the time of purchase rather than the time of issue has several advantages. One advantage is that price variances are reported on a more timely basis, which permits faster response by management to unfavorable situations. If price variances were not revealed until materials were placed in production, the time may have passed when the most effective corrective action could have been taken.

Another advantage of recording price variances at the time of purchase is that the materials inventory is maintained at standard cost. This means that the inventory records can be maintained by recording only quantities, which could result in some clerical savings. However, if it is important to carry inventories at actual cost rather than at standard cost, recognition of price variances may be delayed until materials are placed in production. The work-in-process inventory is usually carried at standard cost, whether or not the materials inventory is maintained at standard cost. To provide consistency by carrying all inventories at standard cost, recognizing price variances at the time of purchase is preferred.

Finally, if price variances are recognized when materials are placed in production, an additional difficulty arises in deciding which purchase price to use when materials have been purchased at more than one price. The choice of which cost flow assumption to use—LIFO, FIFO, or average cost—may affect the usefulness of materials price variances. For example, if the FIFO method is used during a period of rapidly changing prices, the inventory items that are issued may carry relatively old prices. Using old prices against current standards may result in variances that are difficult to interpret in terms of current business conditions.

A third method that can be used to record materials and recognize materials variances is a hybrid of the two general methods already described. When using this third method, a *purchase price variance* is recorded when materials are purchased and a *usage price variance* is recorded when materials are placed in production. To avoid confusion with the methods already described, this third method is illustrated in appendix 15.1 at the end of this chapter.

RECORDING LABOR AND RELATED VARIANCES

Information furnished by the payroll department provides the basis for recording labor costs and related rate and efficiency variances. The hours and rates previously used in the bronze bookend example illustrate the recording of labor.

Actual hours used	5,060
Budgeted hours allowed	5,000
Actual rate paid	$7.00
Standard rate	$7.00

The following journal entry is made to record labor costs and recognize the labor efficiency variance.

Work in process (5,000 hrs. × $7/hr.)	35,000	
Labor efficiency variance		
([1 hr./unit × 5,000 units] − 5,060 hrs.) × $7	420	
Wages payable (5,060 hrs. × $7.00)		35,420

If the actual rate paid had been $7.10 per hour instead of $7.00 per hour, an unfavorable labor rate variance would have resulted. The following journal entry would have been used to record labor costs and related rate and efficiency variances under this new assumption.

Work in process (5,000 hrs. × $7/hr.)	35,000	
Labor efficiency variance	420	
Labor rate variance ([$7.00/hr. − $7.10/hr.] × 5,060 hrs.)	506	
Wages payable ($7.10/hr. × 5,060 hrs.)		35,926

Just as for materials, labor costs are added to the work-in-process inventory at the standard rate for the actual number of units produced. Labor rate and efficiency variances compose the difference between standard (budgeted) labor costs and the actual payroll liability.

DISPOSITION OF VARIANCES

Two methods are available for handling the balances in variance accounts at the end of an accounting period. Although each method is briefly discussed and illustrated here to complete the accounting cycle for materials and labor, a more comprehensive discussion, including overhead cost variances, is contained in chapter 16.

Standard cost variances may be closed at the end of the period to cost of goods sold. This method is used when variances are considered insignificant or immaterial and when standard costs are believed to be representative of actual costs of production. The following journal entry illustrates the disposition of variances when this method is used.

Cost of goods sold (income summary)	623	
Materials quantity variance	1,040	
Materials price variance		737
Labor rate variance		506
Labor efficiency variance		420

Standard cost variances may also be prorated among inventories and cost of goods sold. This method is used when variances are significant or when standard costs are not considered representative of actual manufacturing costs. The basis for proration is usually the proportion of total manufacturing costs in each cost category. To illustrate, the following schedule contains assumed quantities and percentages of materials and labor costs in work in process, finished goods, and cost of goods sold:

| | Materials and Labor ||
Account	Amount	Percent
Work in process	$ 40,000	25%
Finished goods	16,000	.10
Cost of goods sold	104,000	65
Total	$160,000	100%

Based on these proportions, the following schedule indicates how the variances are to be prorated:

	Total Amount (100%)	Work in Process (25%)	Finished Goods (10%)	Cost of Goods Sold (65%)
Materials price variance	$ 737.00	$184.25	$ 73.70	$479.05
Materials quantity variance	(1,040.00)	(260.00)	(104.00)	(676.00)
Labor rate variance	506.00	126.50	50.60	328.90
Labor efficiency variance	420.00	105.00	42.00	273.00
Total	$ 623.00	$155.75	$ 62.30	$404.95

Using the amounts in this schedule, the following journal entry is made to allocate standard cost variances:

Work in process	155.75	
Finished goods	62.30	
Cost of goods sold	404.95	
Materials quantity variance	1,040.00	
Materials price variance		737.00
Labor rate variance		506.00
Labor efficiency variance		420.00

Numerous proration schemes are more detailed than the procedure just illustrated. For example, it may be desirable to allocate variances in a step-wise fashion by first allocating the materials price variance to the materials efficiency variance and raw materials inventory, as well as to work in process, finished goods, and cost of goods sold. Then the remaining variances are allocated to work in process, finished goods, and cost of goods sold. Whether using a simple allocation as illustrated or a complex allocation scheme, the basic principles remain the same.

INVESTIGATION OF VARIANCES

How does a manager know whether a specific variance is large enough to warrant investigation? This question arises in standard cost systems because, by intuition, one would expect that some variances will occur even though the production process is performing within satisfactory limits. Random favorable and unfavorable variances occur under normal conditions simply because of chance variations in the production environment.

If this is true, a more fundamental question concerns the magnitude of the range or tolerance limits within which variances may be allowed to fluctuate without investigation. Once such tolerance limits are established, management can proceed on an exception basis to investigate variances. For some classes of materials or labor, small variances may require investigation, whereas relatively large variances may be required to justify investigation for other items. Therefore, variance analysis and the decision to investigate should be subjected to a cost-benefit analysis in the same way that other elements of a management reporting system are evaluated. Two common ways to set tolerance limits for variance control are to develop rules of thumb or to use statistical techniques.

Rules of thumb arise from past experience or intuition. They take the form of rules such as "investigate all individual materials variances in excess of $1,000" or "investigate variances for each category of labor exceeding 20 percent of total standard costs." From such rules of thumb a range of acceptable variances can be calculated. For example, using the first rule of thumb suggested for materials, a materials quantity variance falling within a plus or minus $1,000 region will be assumed to have arisen because there are random variations in the production process, and the added costs of investigation and corrective action are not warranted.

Statistical techniques utilize probability theory and past performance to establish acceptable ranges within which variances are allowed to fluctuate without investigation. When using statistical techniques, the boundaries of the acceptable region for fluctuations are referred to as *control limits*. For example, if the statistical method employed indicates that the control limits for a labor efficiency variance should be plus or minus $1,500, a variance of $1,600 would indicate that the production process is out of control and should be investigated. However, variances within the $1,500 limit would indicate that the production process is operating in control and no investigation is required. Additional guidance concerning variance investigation is given in chapter 17.

DEVELOPMENT OF STANDARDS

Standard setting is primarily the responsibility of supervisors, department managers, and other line personnel directly involved with operations. Standard setting is usually an integral part of an organization's budgetary process. Accountants, industrial engineers, market researchers, and other technical advisers extend advice and assist in the development of both standards and the budget. However, line personnel are ultimately responsible for departmental performance and should make the major decisions about standards.

Higher management must provide the basic guidelines for the development of standards and then review standards for reasonableness and adherence to established guidelines. Typically, the standard-setting process involves a great amount of discussion, bargaining, and even arbitration among those involved. Central to the process, however, are some basic concepts and guidelines.

Standard-Setting Philosophies

Standard setting is based on basic philosophies that concern how demanding standards should be. One philosophy holds that **ideal standards** should be set with perfect manufacturing conditions in mind. Standards based on this philosophy relate to the lowest possible costs that can be expected under the best conceivable manufacturing conditions. Existing equipment and specifications are considered from an ideal perspective.

If management's philosophy is that standards set for maximum efficiency provide the best goals for motivation, ideal standards are appropriate. However, remember that all variances will probably be unfavorable when such a philosophy is used. This is because ideal or perfect manufacturing conditions rarely occur in practice. As a result, operating personnel may become frustrated by not being able to achieve perfect standards if they are not aware that ideal standards have been formulated.

An alternative philosophy holds that **currently attainable standards** should be set under efficient operating conditions. Currently attainable standards, which are less demanding than ideal standards, allow for ordinary equipment failure, normal lost time, and normal spoilage. They are usually set tightly enough so that they can be achieved with a reasonable effort on the part of workers. As a result, operating personnel may feel a sense of accomplishment when currently attainable standards are achieved or if favorable variances are produced.

Currently attainable standards seem to provide better motivation for operating personnel than other possible philosophies. If line managers believe *(a)* that the standard is indeed attainable, *(b)* that they are in control of the variables the standard measures, and *(c)* that data are reported accurately, the standard is usually accepted as a norm for behavior. The ability to generate favorable variances with somewhat more than expected efficiency may motivate operating personnel, especially if bonuses are contingent on achieving attainable standards.

A final point about standard-setting philosophies is that variances do not answer questions; they are attention directors for management. Variances are intended to raise questions and draw attention to situations that should be examined. In the examination process, the variances generated from applying standards provide clues for pinpointing causal relationships. From this viewpoint, considering the magnitude and complexity of interrelationships in most organizations, management should not jump to conclusions about favorable or unfavorable variances. Rather, conclusions about a situation being favorable or unfavorable should follow proper investigation. Variances provide feedback and clues, not answers.

Physical Standards

Physical standards are also an integral part of a standard cost system. They come from physical estimates based on engineering standards. For example, physical standards for materials are usually expressed in terms of pounds, gallons, or units of input for each unit of output produced. For labor, physical standards are typically expressed in terms of hours or minutes of labor per unit of output produced. Multiplying the physical standard by the price expected to be paid for materials and labor results in the standard cost. The importance of this process should not be overlooked, because the result in *dollars,* instead of pounds or hours, is the common denominator and measuring stick in a standard cost system and provides for uniformity and consistency in planning and controlling manufacturing operations.

Physical standards for materials are derived from product specifications usually contained in blueprints. Along with product specifications, consideration is given to the production method, normal waste, and unavoidable spoilage. Physical standards are often refined using test production runs under conditions that are as close to normal as possible. The test runs will avoid standards being based on artificially inefficient or extraordinarily efficient results. There also probably will be a refinement period in which the results of actual operations will be used to adjust physical standards.

Physical standards for labor are developed using time and motion studies. Predicting the human element in a production environment is a difficult task, thus increasing the likelihood of disputes about establishing physical standards for labor. Therefore, to be an effective base for standards, the conditions under which labor performance is measured are critically important. Both the manufacturing operation itself and the manufacturing environment must be considered. Instructions and training for the worker, materials availability, materials handling requirements, equipment, and organization of the work space also must be considered.

Allowances are usually made in labor standards for learning, rest time, and fatigue. Because there is a potential for disagreement and disputes, a delicate balance usually exists

FIGURE 15.8

Standard Cost Card

Standard Cost Card

Product: XYZ Fitting   Date: Jan. 1, 19X8

Materials

Inventory number	Standard quantity	Standard unit cost	Total
C1351	2	$6.70	$13.40
B4962	1	1.20	1.20
2853	4	2.35	9.40
		Total	$24.00

Labor

Department number	Standard hours	Standard hourly rate	Total
1	2	$4.00	$ 8.00
3	3	4.10	12.30
4	1	4.65	4.65
		Total	$24.95

| | | Total materials and labor | $48.95 |

among labor standards that are too loose, attainable, or unattainable. For example, if a bonus system is based on the attainment of standard performance, the time standard should be set at a level that is fair to the firm in terms of value received as well as fair to the workers in terms of rewarding above-average performance. After taking into consideration all of these factors through study and observation, time and motion engineers set labor efficiency standards.

Physical standards for materials and labor along with their cost components are usually represented on a *standard cost card,* as shown in figure 15.8. Standard cost cards are maintained for each product and show the quantities and prices for all productive inputs, including overhead.

SUMMARY

Manufacturing costs are affected by factors over which management can exercise control. An important role of cost accounting is to facilitate management's efforts by providing information for effective control decisions. A widely accepted procedure is to use flexible budgets based on standard costs as the criterion against which actual results are compared. Standard costs are the dollar outlays expected to be incurred to manufacture a particular product in a given manufacturing environment. Differences between standard and actual

This journal entry is identical to the first journal entry made when recognizing the materials price variance at the time of purchase, except for the title of the price variance account. Entries to the materials purchase price variance account provide recognition of variances at the time of purchase, and the balance in the account at any moment in time provides a valuation amount to reflect the cost of materials inventory. For example, a partial balance sheet immediately after the purchase would take the following form:

Materials inventory at standard cost	$80,000
Plus: Unfavorable purchase price variance	1,000
Materials inventory at cost	$81,000

When using this method, there are two journal entries made when materials are issued and placed in production. These journal entries are:

Work in process ($4.00 × 15,000 lbs.)	60,000	
Materials quantity variance ([15,000 lbs. − 14,740 lbs.] × $4.00)		1,040
Materials inventory ($4.00 × 14,740 lbs.)		58,960

and

Materials usage price variance	737	
Materials purchase price variance ([4.00 − $4.05] × 14,740 lbs.)		737

The first journal entry is identical to the journal entry made when placing materials into production and recognizing materials price variances at the time of purchase. The second journal entry is used to indicate the amount of price variance related to materials placed into production, as well as to properly value the amount of purchase price variance relating to materials still in the materials inventory. For example, a partial balance sheet immediately following the issuance of materials would be as follows:

Materials inventory at standard cost	$21,040[a]
Plus: Unfavorable purchase price variance	263
Materials inventory at cost	$21,303[b]

[a] 20,000 lbs. − 14,740 lbs. issued = 5,260 lbs. at $4.00 = $21,040.
[b] 5,260 lbs. at $4.05 = $21,303.

This combination of methods provides for both the immediate recognition of price variances when materials are received and the valuation of materials inventory at cost and standard cost. The advantages of this method should be balanced with the extended amount of record keeping necessary to support it.

SELF-STUDY PROBLEM

Karen Company uses flexible budgets and a standard cost system to control materials and labor costs. Information from the standard cost card for one of its products, ABC Fasteners, follows:

Materials

Inventory Number	Standard Quantity	Standard Unit Cost	Total
AA1	4	$2.00	$ 8.00
BB2	6	5.00	30.00
	Total materials		$38.00

costs, referred to as variances, can be used to determine why results differed from plans. Significant variances can be investigated so that either corrective action can be taken or beneficial results can be rewarded.

Variances can isolate the effect of differences between planned and actual *(a)* prices paid for materials (materials price variance), *(b)* usage of materials (materials quantity variance), *(c)* rates paid for labor (labor rate variance), and *(d)* usage of labor (labor efficiency variance). Formulas and a tabular approach are available for calculating each of these variances.

The effectiveness of a standard cost system depends on the assignment of responsibility to company managers and supervisors. Responsibility for each variance should be assigned to the person who has the authority to control that material or labor item in the production process. The purchasing agent is usually responsible for the materials price variance. Supervisors are responsible for the materials and labor usage variances and may also be responsible for labor rate variances. However, labor rates are often set through contract negotiations or by agreement with the personnel department.

Variances are recorded in the general ledger using appropriately titled accounts. The materials price variance is usually recorded at the time materials are purchased, even though it could be recorded when materials are placed in production. The materials quantity variance is recorded when materials are placed in production. Labor variances are recorded when the payroll liability is recorded. Variance accounts are closed at the end of the accounting period in one of two ways. If variances are insignificant, they are closed directly to cost of goods sold. If variances are significant, they are prorated among inventories and cost of goods sold.

Management must determine when a variance is significant enough to warrant further investigation. Rules of thumb and statistical techniques are used to establish control limits within which variances are allowed to fluctuate without further investigation. However, a variance falling outside of control limits indicates that the process is out of control and investigation is warranted.

There are several philosophies underlying the development of standards. Currently attainable standards are thought to be most effective for management control. Ideal standards based on perfect conditions are often frustrating because they may not be attainable. Loose standards do not provide motivation for quality behavior.

In conclusion, standard costs provide a valuable planning and control tool for management. However, the standard cost system is not complete until standard costs for overhead are included.

APPENDIX 15.1 *A Hybrid Method for Recognizing Materials Price Variances*

This method provides for the recognition of a materials *purchase price variance* and a materials *usage price variance*. It also provides for the disclosure of materials inventory at cost and standard cost. This is accomplished by having two materials price variance accounts. A materials *purchase price variance* account records price variances when materials are received and serves as an inventory valuation account. A materials *usage price variance* account is used to record the price variance associated with materials placed into production. The journal entry to record materials received, using data from the chapter illustration, is as follows:

Materials inventory ($4.00 × 20,000 lbs.)	80,000	
Materials purchase price variance ([$4.00 − $4.05] × 20,000 lbs.)	1,000	
Accounts payable ($4.05 × 20,000 lbs.)		81,000

CHAPTER 15: STANDARD COSTS FOR MATERIALS AND LABOR

Labor

Department Number	Standard Hours	Standard Hourly Rate	Total
1	2	$7.50	$15.00
2	1	9.00	9.00
		Total labor	$24.00
		Total materials and labor	$62.00

Two materials are used in the production of ABC Fasteners—AA1 and BB2. Production takes place in two departments with different standard labor rates. Production for the past week resulted in 6,000 good fasteners being produced.

Materials purchased during the past week were:

AA1: 26,000 units at $2.04 per unit = $ 53,040
BB2: 37,000 units at $4.98 per unit = $184,260
$237,300

Actual materials used to produce the 6,000 good units were:

AA1: 23,500 units
BB2: 36,100 units

Actual labor costs for the past week were:

Department 1: 12,100 hrs. at $7.50/hr. = $ 90,750
Department 2: 5,990 hrs. at $9.10/hr. = $ 54,509
$145,259

Assume that Karen Company recognizes materials price variances at the time of purchase and that the purchasing department is responsible for materials price variances. Individual department managers are responsible for the materials quantity variance as well as the labor rate and efficiency variances. Material AA1 is placed in production in department 1 and material BB2 is placed in production in department 2.

Required

1. Prepare a schedule showing the budget variances resulting from the past week's operations.
2. Compute the materials price variance, the materials quantity variance, the labor rate variance, and the labor efficiency variance.
3. Show the journal entries to record the preceding variances.
4. Prepare a responsibility report for the managers of departments 1 and 2 and give a brief analysis of each department's performance.

Solution to the Self-Study Problem

Requirement 1

	Budgeted Costs	Actual Costs	Budget Variances
Direct materials	$228,000(1)	$227,500(3)	$ 500 F
Direct labor	144,000(2)	145,259(4)	1,259 U
Total	$372,000	$372,759	$ 759 U

(1) 6,000 good units × $38.00 standard materials cost per unit

(2) 6,000 good units × $24.00 standard labor cost per unit

(3) Standard price × Actual quantity*
AA1: $2.00/unit × 23,500 units used = $ 47,000
BB2: $5.00/unit × 36,100 units used = $180,500
Total materials budget $227,500

(4) Actual rate × Actual hours
Dept. 1: $7.50/hr. × 12,100 hrs. = $ 90,750
Dept. 2: $9.10/hr. × 5,990 hrs. = $ 54,509
Total labor budget $145,259

*Note that the materials budget uses standard prices rather than actual prices, because the firm recognizes the materials price variance when materials are purchased. This results in the materials budget variance being synonymous with the materials quantity variance.

Requirement 2

Materials price variance:

AA1: ($2.00 − $2.04) × 26,000 = $1,040 U
BB2: ($5.00 − $4.98) × 37,000 =   740 F
                                 $ 300 U

Materials quantity variance:

AA1: (24,000 − 23,500) × $2.00 = $1,000 F
BB2: (36,000 − 36,100) × $5.00 =   500 U
                                 $ 500 F

Labor rate variance:

Department 1: ($7.50 − $7.50) × 12,100 =   0
Department 2: ($9.00 − $9.10) × 5,990 = $599 U
                                         $599 U

Labor efficiency variance:

Department 1: (12,000 − 12,100) × $7.50 = $750 U
Department 2: (6,000 − 5,990) × $9.00 =   90 F
                                          $660 U

Requirement 3

(a) To record materials acquisition

Materials inventory	237,000[a]	
Materials price variance	300	
Accounts payable		237,300

[a] (26,000 × $2.00) + (37,000 × $5.00)

(b) To record materials placed in production

Work in process	228,000[a]	
Materials quantity variance		500
Materials inventory		227,500[b]

[a] (24,000 × $2.00) + (36,000 × $5.00)
[b] (23,500 × $2.00) + (36,100 × $5.00)

(c) To record labor costs

Work in process	144,000[c]	
Labor rate variance	599	
Labor efficiency variance	660	
Wages payable		145,259

[c] (12,000 × $7.50) + (6,000 × $9.00)

Requirement 4

Department 1	Direct Materials	Direct Labor	Total
Budgeted costs	$ 48,000	$ 90,000	$138,000
Controllable variances:			
Materials quantity	1,000 F		1,000 F
Labor rate		0	0
Labor efficiency		750 U	750 U
Total controllable costs	$ 47,000	$ 90,750	$137,750
Department 2			
Budgeted costs	$180,000	$ 54,000	$234,000
Controllable variances:			
Materials quantity	500 U		500 U
Labor rate		599 U	599 U
Labor efficiency		90 F	90 F
Total controllable costs	$180,500	$ 54,509	$235,009
Grand total	$227,500	$145,259	$372,759

Note that the responsibility report contains only those costs that are controllable by each department manager. Remember that the materials price variance is the responsibility of the purchasing manager. Therefore, the materials price variance does not appear on this report.

Department 1 experienced a favorable materials quantity variance and an unfavorable labor efficiency variance. Workers could have exercised extra caution during the week in handling materials in an effort to reduce waste, which could have resulted in the favorable materials quantity variance. However, additional caution may have also required more total time in the production process, resulting in an unfavorable labor efficiency variance.

Department 2 experienced an unfavorable materials quantity variance, an unfavorable labor rate variance, and a favorable labor efficiency variance. This could have resulted from adding more skilled labor to the production process than previously planned. Using more skilled labor could have resulted in both the unfavorable labor rate variance and the favorable labor efficiency variance. An improperly adjusted machine could have been responsible for the unfavorable materials quantity variance.

Taken as a whole, the production process seems to be within acceptable control limits. For example, the largest unfavorable variance is the materials quantity variance of $1,000, which is less than one half of 1 percent of total materials cost.

SUGGESTED READINGS

Calvasina, Richard V., and Calvasina, Eugene J. "Standard Costing Games That Managers Play." *Management Accounting* 45 (March 1984): 49–51, 71.

Dorward, Neil. "Variance Analysis: Pitfalls of Present Costing Techniques." *Accountancy* (Eng.) 96 (November 1985): 204–206.

Hall, Robert W. "Zero Inventory Crusade—Much More Than Materials Management." *Production and Inventory Management* 24 (Third Quarter 1983): 1–9.

Lere, John C. "Explaining Alternative Standard Cost Entries." *Journal of Accounting Education* 3 (Fall 1985): 187–193.

Ross, Timothy, and Bullock, R. J. "Integrating Measurement of Productivity into a Standard Cost System." *Financial Executive* 48 (October 1980): 34–36.

Siegel, Joel G., and Rubin, Mathew S. "Corporate Planning and Control Through Variance Analysis." *Managerial Planning* 33 (September–October 1984): 35–39, 49–50.

DISCUSSION QUESTIONS

Q15–1. Define *standard cost* and explain how standard costs are used in connection with flexible budgets and responsibility accounting.

Q15–2. Is the use of standard costs equally applicable to job-order and process costing systems?

Q15–3. Explain the components of a materials or labor standard.

Q15–4. What is a variance?

Q15–5. List each materials and labor variance, give the formula for its calculation, and explain the meaning of each variance.

Q15–6. Outline the tabular approach to calculating materials and labor variances and explain the basis for its use.

Q15–7. Explain why responsibility for particular variances should be assigned to individual managers.

Q15–8. List the managers who are typically responsible for each materials and labor variance.

Q15–9. Explain why the materials price variance may be recognized at different points in the accounting cycle.

Q15–10. Outline the journal entries for recording variances, assuming that *(a)* the materials price variance is recognized at the time of purchase and *(b)* the materials price variance is recognized at the time of issue.

Q15–11. List the alternative accounting procedures that could be used to close the variance accounts at the end of an accounting period. Under what conditions should each be used?

Q15–12. Does every variance indicate that the production process is out of control? Explain.

Q15–13. What are two common methods used to determine when a variance should be investigated?

Q15–14. What are two philosophies that management could use when setting standards?

Q15–15. Explain how physical standards are established for *(a)* materials and *(b)* labor.

Q15–16. Sketch a standard cost card and explain its contents and use.

EXERCISES

E15–1. Standard Cost Concepts and Procedures for Material Costs Durable Company installs shingle roofs on residential houses. The standard materials cost for a type R house is $1,250, based on 1,000 units at a cost of $1.25 each. During April Durable installed roofs on 20 type R houses, using 22,000 units of material at a cost of $1.20 per unit and a total cost of $26,400.

Required

1. Determine the materials price variance for Durable Company for April.
2. Determine the materials quantity variance for Durable Company for April.

E15–2. Materials Standards and Variances Dallas Company had budgeted 25,000 units of output requiring 50,000 units of raw materials at a total materials cost of $150,000. Actual output was 25,000 units of finished product requiring 50,100 units of raw materials at an actual cost of $3.10 per unit of raw materials. Assume that Dallas Company had no beginning or ending inventories of raw materials.

Required

1. Calculate the budget variance for materials.
2. Calculate the direct materials price variance and quantity variance. Reconcile the sum of the variances calculated in this requirement with the budget variance calculated in requirement 1.

E15–3. Materials and Labor Standards and Variances Morse Manufacturing Company has the following materials and labor standards:

Cost Category	Standard Quantity	Standard Unit Cost	Total
Materials	5 units	$20.00	$100.00
Labor	9 hours	$15.00	135.00
			$235.00

There were 16,000 units of raw materials purchased during the month of April at a total cost of $312,000. There were 18,000 units of raw materials used to produce 3,500 units of good output during April. The total payroll of $470,400 was paid during April based on 32,000 hours of actual work performed. Morse records the materials price variance at the time of purchase.

Required

1. Calculate the standard cost variances for materials and labor for the month of April.
2. Prepare journal entries to record the preceding variances.

E15–4. Standard Costs and Variances for Materials During March, Younger Company's direct-materials costs for the manufacture of product T were as follows:

Actual unit pruchase price	$6.50
Standard quantity allowed for actual production	2,100
Quantity purchased and used for actual production	2,300
Standard unit price	$6.25

Required

1. Prepare an electronic spreadsheet to calculate Younger's materials price and usage variances for March.
2. Identify the department that is customarily held responsible for materials usage variances. Explain why.

E15–5. Standard Cost Concepts and Procedures for Labor Costs
Sullivan Corporation's direct-labor costs for the month of March were as follows:

Standard direct-labor hours	42,000
Actual direct-labor hours	40,000
Direct-labor rate variance—favorable	$8,400
Standard direct-labor rate per hour	$6.30

Required

1. Determine Sullivan's total direct-labor payroll for the month of March.
2. Determine Sullivan's direct-labor efficiency variance for March.

E15–6. Labor Standards and Variances—Journal Entries
Information on Barber Company's direct-labor costs for the month of January is a follows:

Actual direct-labor hours	34,500
Standard direct-labor hours	35,000
Total direct-labor payroll	$241,500
Direct-labor efficiency variance—favorable	$3,200

Required

1. Determine Barber Company's labor rate variance.
2. Explain what a direct-labor efficiency variance means.
3. Make journal entires to record the direct-labor payroll and to charge labor costs to production, assuming that standard labor costs are charged to inventory.

E15–7. Determination of Materials Standards and Cost (CMA)
Danson Company is a chemical manufacturer that supplies industrial users. Danson plans to introduce a new chemical solution and needs to develop a standard product cost for this new solution.

The new chemical solution is made by combining a chemical compound (nyclyn) and a solution (salex), boiling the mixture, adding a second compound (protet), and bottling the resulting solution in 10-liter containers. The initial mix, which is 10 liters in volume, consists of 12 kilograms of nyclyn and 9.6 liters of salex. However, a 20-percent reduction in volume occurs during the boiling process. The solution is then cooled slightly before 5 kilograms of protet are added; the addition of protet does not affect the total liquid volume and no protet is lost during processing.

The purchase prices of the raw materials used in the manufacture of this new chemical solution are as follows:

Nyclyn	$1.30 per kilogram
Salex	1.80 per liter
Protet	2.40 per kilogram

Required

Determine the standard initial quantity for each raw material needed to produce a 10-liter container of finished product of Danson Company's new chemical solution.

E15–8. Materials and Labor Variances—Standard Cost System (CMA)
The Lonn Manufacturing Company produces two primary chemical products that are used as base ingredients for a variety of products. The 19X8 budget (000s omitted) for the two products was as follows:

	X-4	Z-8	Total
Production output in gallons	600	600	1,200
Direct materials	$1,500	$1,875	$3,375
Direct labor	900	900	1,800
Total prime manufacturing cost	$2,400	$2,775	$5,175

The following planning assumptions were used for the budget:

Direct-materials yield of 96%.
Direct-labor rate of $6 per hour.

The actual direct-production cost (000s omitted) for 19X8 was as follows:

	X-4	Z-8	Total
Production output in gallons	570	658	1,228
Direct materials	$1,368.00	$2,138.50	$3,506.50
Direct labor	936.00	1,092.00	2,028.00
Total prime manufacturing cost	$2,304.00	$3,230.50	$5,534.50

The actual production yield was 95 percent for *X-4* and 94 percent for *Z-8*. The direct-labor cost per hour for both products was $6.50.

Required

1. Calculate the following, for product *X-4:*
   a. The direct-materials price variance
   b. The direct-materials efficiency variance
2. Calculate the following for product *Z-8:*
   a. The direct-labor rate variance
   b. The direct-labor efficiency variance

E15–9. Entries for Direct Materials and Direct Labor
The Krazy Kradle Company produces unique baby cradles. During June, 11,200 standard cradles were produced. Five units of materials at a cost of $1.80 per unit are required for each cradle produced. During June, 57,500 units of materials were used in production. During June, 60,000 units of materials were purchased at a cost of $1.78 each.

The payroll for direct labor during June was $138,000. The average wage rate was $6 per hour. To produce one cradle, two hours of labor are required at a standard rate of $5.80 per hour.

Assume that there were no beginning inventories of direct materials or work in process and that all production of cradles during June was completely finished.

Required

1. Determine the number of units and the cost assigned to the ending direct-materials inventory, assuming that
   a. materials inventory is kept at actual cost.
   b. materials inventory is kept at standard cost.

2. Prepare journal entries for the purchase and use of direct materials, assuming that
   a. the materials account is kept at actual cost.
   b. the materials account is kept at standard cost.
3. Prepare all journal entries for recording and distributing the payroll. Ignore payroll taxes.

E15–10. Standard Cost Variance Disposition

Nanron Company has a process standard cost system for all its products. All inventories are carried at standard cost during the year. The inventories and cost of goods sold are adjusted for all variances considered significant at the end of the fiscal year for financial statement purposes. All products are considered to flow through the manufacturing process to finished goods and ultimate sale in a FIFO pattern.

The standard cost of one of Nanron's products manufactured in the Dixon Plant, unchanged from the prior year, is shown below:

Raw materials	$2.00
Direct labor (0.5 direct-labor hour @ $8.00)	4.00
Manufacturing overhead	3.00
Total standard cost	$9.00

There is no work-in-process inventory of this product due to the nature of the product and the manufacturing process.

The following schedule reports the manufacturing and sales activity measured at standard cost for the current fiscal year:

	Units	Dollars
Product manufactured	95,000	$855,000
Beginning finished-goods inventory	15,000	135,000
Goods available for sale	110,000	$990,000
Ending finished-goods inventory	19,000	171,000
Cost of goods sold	91,000	$819,000

The manufacturing performance relative to standard costs both this year and last year was not good. The balance of the finished-goods inventory—$140,800—reported on the balance sheet at the beginning of the year included a $5,800 adjustment for variances from standard cost. The unfavorable standard cost variances for labor for the current fiscal year consisted of a wage rate variance of $32,000 and a labor efficiency variance of $20,000 (2,500 hours @ $8.00). There were no other variances from standard cost for this year.

Required

Assume that the unfavorable labor variances totaling $52,000 are considered significant by management and are to be allocated to the finished-goods inventory and to cost of goods sold. Determine the amount that will be shown on the year-end balance sheet for the finished-goods inventory, as well as the amount that will be shown for the cost of goods sold on the income statement prepared for the fiscal year.

E15–11. Labor Standards and Variances

Skousen Manufacturing Company has the following labor standards for the manufacture of one of its products:

Standard hours = 8.4 per unit
Standard rate = $12.60 per hour

Actual results for the month of June are as follows:

Units produced = 4,000
Actual hours = 8.5 per unit
Actual rate = $12.50 per hour

Required

1. Prepare an electronic spreadsheet to calculate labor rate and efficiency variances for the month of June.
2. Prepare the journal entries to record the direct-labor payroll and to charge labor costs to production, assuming standard labor costs are charged to work in process.

E15–12. Materials and Labor Standards and Variances

Brackner Manufacturing Company has the following materials and labor standards for the manufacture of one of its products:

	Materials	Labor
Standard quantity	14 units	18 hours
Standard unit cost	$29 per unit	$24 per hour

Actual results for the period are as follows:

	Materials	Labor
Quantity used	97,000 total units	129,500 total hours
Quantity purchased	95,000 total units	129,500 total hours
Actual cost	$28.50 per unit	$24.25 per hour

There were 7,000 units of good output produced during the accounting period. Brackner records the materials price variance at the time of purchase.

Required

1. Prepare an electronic spreadsheet to calculate the standard cost variances for materials and labor for the current accounting period.
2. Prepare journal entries to record the preceding variances.

PROBLEMS

P15–1. Materials and Labor Variances

The following data have been extracted from the records of Flora Company at the end of the current accounting period.

Direct Materials
Standard cost per unit = $2.00
Standard units allowed for good production = 600,000
Quantity variance = $200,000 U
Price variance = $70,000 F

Direct Labor
Actual total payroll = $468,000
Rate variance = $13,000 U
Efficiency variance = $35,000 U
Actual hours worked = 65,000

Flora Company uses standard costs and applies overhead based on direct-labor hours. Normal capacity is 50,000 hours. Standard hours allowed for actual production are 60,000 hours. The materials price variance is recognized when the materials are issued to the production process.

Required

1. Prepare answers to each of the following questions:
   a. How many units of direct materials were actually used during the year?
   b. What was the actual unit price of direct materials?
   c. What was the actual rate paid per direct-labor hour?
   d. What was the standard rate per direct-labor hour?
2. Prepare journal entries to record the materials and labor variances.

P15–2. Standard costs and Labor Variances

Landeau Manufacturing Company uses a process cost accounting system. An analysis that compares the actual results with both a monthly plan and a flexible budget is prepared monthly. The standard direct-labor rates used in the flexible budget are established each year when the annual plan is formulated and are held constant for the entire year.

The standard direct-labor rates in effect for the fiscal year ending June 30 and the standard hours allowed for output for the month of April are shown in the following schedule:

	Standard Direct-Labor Rate Per Hour	Standard Direct-Labor Hours Allowed for Output
Labor class III	$8.00	500
Labor class II	$7.00	500
Labor class I	$5.00	500

The wage rates for each labor class increased on January 1, under the terms of a new union contract negotiated in December. The standard wage rates were not revised to reflect the new contract.

The actual direct-labor hours worked and the actual direct-labor rates per hour experienced for the month of April were as follows:

	Actual Direct-Labor Rate Per Hour	Actual Direct-Labor Hours
Labor class III	$8.50	550
Labor class II	$7.50	650
Labor class I	$5.40	375

Required

1. Calculate the dollar amount of the total direct-labor variance for April for Landeau Manufacturing Company. Analyze the total variance into the following components:
   a. Direct-labor rate variance
   b. Direct-labor efficiency variance
2. Discuss the advantages and disadvantages of a standard cost system in which the standard direct-labor rates per hour are not changed during the year to reflect events such as a new labor contract.

P15–3. Labor Variances and Job-Order Costing (CMA)

Mary's Pie Company produces pies in quantity for various fast-food restaurants. The labor standard for each pie calls for ¼ hour at $4 per hour.

CHAPTER 15: STANDARD COSTS FOR MATERIALS AND LABOR 563

During May, the following job orders (among others) were put into production:

Job Order #	# of Pies
206	500
207	350
208	300 (⅔ complete on May 31)

The actual payroll for May by job was as follows:

Job Order #	Actual Hours	Actual Cost
206	128	$524.80
207	85	344.25
208	27	106.50

Required

1. Determine the labor rate and efficiency variances for each job order and in total for the month.
2. Make journal entries for the total payroll to show the setup and distribution of labor costs.

P15–4. Standard Costs, Materials and Labor, and Variances Fashions Unlimited manufactures ladies blouses of one quality, produced in lots to fill each special order from its customers, which comprise department stores located in various cities. Fashions sews the particular store's labels on the blouses. The standard costs for a dozen blouses are as follows:

Direct materials	24 yards @ $1.10	$26.40
Direct labor	3 hours @ $4.90	14.70
Manufacturing overhead	3 hours @ $4.00	12.00
Standard cost per dozen		$53.10

During June, Fashions worked on three orders, for which the month's job cost records disclose the following:

Lot No.	Units in Lot (dozens)	Fabric Used (yards)	Hours worked
22	1,000	24,100	2,980
23	1,700	40,440	5,130
24	1,200	28,825	2,890

The following information is also available:

1. Fashions purchased 95,000 yards of fabric during June at a cost of $106,400. The materials price variance is recorded when goods are purchased. All inventories are carried at standard cost.
2. Direct labor during June amounted to $55,000. According to payroll records, production employees were paid $5.00 per hour.
3. Manufacturing overhead during June amounted to $45,600.
4. A total of $576,000 was budgeted for manufacturing overhead for the year based on estimated production at the plant's normal capacity of 48,000 dozen blouses annually. Manufacturing overhead at this level of production is 40 percent fixed and 60 percent variable. Manufacturing overhead is applied on the basis of direct-labor hours.
5. There was no work in process on June 1. During June, lots 22 and 23 were completed. All material was issued for lot 24, which was 80-percent completed as to direct labor.

Required

1. Prepare a schedule of lots 22, 23, and 24 for June, showing the computation of total material, labor, and overhead at standard cost.
2. Prepare a schedule showing the computation of the materials price variance for June. Indicate whether the variance is favorable or unfavorable.
3. Prepare a schedule showing, for each lot produced during June, the computations of the
   a. materials quantity variance in yards.
   b. labor efficiency variance in hours.
   c. labor rate variance in dollars.

   Indicate whether each variance is favorable or unfavorable.

P15-5. Standard Costs for Materials and Labor The Jensen Company, which manufactures a single product, began operations at the beginning of the current year. The company has adopted a standard cost system but plans to adjust all inventories to actual cost for financial reporting purposes at the end of each accounting period. Under the standard cost system used by Jensen, the materials price variance is recognized when raw materials are issued. Work in process is carried at standard cost. Variance accounts are used to record all variances as they are identified.

One-half of the raw materials for each unit of output is put into production at the beginning of the process and the remainder is added when the processing is one-third completed.

Standard costs are based on normal capacity of 280,000 direct-labor hours with a production of 2,800 units. The standards for a unit of product are as follows:

Materials (50 pieces at $6.00 per piece)	$ 300
Direct labor (100 hours at $6.00 per hour)	600
Factory overhead (100 hours at $3.00)	300
Total	$1,200

A summary of transactions and other statistics for the year ended December 31 are as following:

Materials purchased (126,000 pieces at $6.20)	$781,200
Direct labor (242,200 hours at $6.30)	$1,525,860
Materials issued to production (pieces)	125,800
Units completed	2,300
Units one-half complete	150
Units one-fourth complete	100

Required

1. Prepare a schedule showing the equivalent units of production for materials and labor.
2. Determine the total amount debited to raw materials inventory during the period.
3. Determine the total debit to work in process for materials put into production during the period.
4. Calculate the materials quantity variance.
5. Determine the total debit to work in process for labor this period.
6. Calculate the labor efficiency variance.
7. Determine the amount of the adjustment to finished-goods inventory for the materials price variance at the end of the period.

P15-6. Standard Costs—Materials and Labor (CMA) Dash Company adopted a standard cost system several years ago. The standard costs for its single product are as follows:

Material	8 kilograms @ $5.00 per kilogram	$40.00
Labor	6 hours @ $8.20 per hour	$49.20

The following operating data was taken from the records for November:

1. In process beginning inventory—none
2. In process ending inventory—800 units, 75% complete as to labor; material issued at the beginning of processing
3. Units completed—5,600 units
4. Budgeted output—6,000 units
5. Purchases of materials—50,000 kilograms
6. Total actual labor costs—$300,760
7. Actual hours of labor—36,500 hours
8. Materials usage variance—$1,500 unfavorable
9. Total materials variance—$750 unfavorable

Required

1. Determine the labor rate variance for November.
2. Determine the labor efficiency variance for November.
3. Determine the actual kilograms of material used in the production process during November.
4. Determine the actual price paid per kilogram of material during November.
5. Show journal entries to record the purchase of materials and payroll and the charging of materials and labor costs to production.

15-7. Standard Costs and Motivation (CMA) The Kristy Company has grown from a small operation of 50 people to 200 employees during a ten-year period. Kristy designs, manufactures, and sells environmental support equipment. In the early years, each item of equipment had to be designed and manufactured to meet each customer's requirements. The work was challenging and interesting for the employees because innovative techniques were often needed in the production process to complete an order according to a customer's requirements. In recent years Kristy has been able to develop several components and a few complete units that can be used meet the requirements of several customers.

The early special design and manufacture work has given the Kristy Company a leadership position in its segment of the pollution control market. Kristy takes great pride in the superior quality of its products, and this quality has contributed to its dominant role in this market segment. To help ensure high-quality performance, Kristy hires the most highly skilled personnel available and pays them above the industry average. This policy has resulted in a labor force that is very efficient, stable, and positively motivated toward company objectives.

The recent increase in government regulations requiring private companies to comply with specific environmental standards has made this market very profitable. Consequently, several competitors have entered the market segment once controlled by Kristy. Although Kristy still maintains a dominant position in its market, it has lost several contracts to competitors who offer similar equipment to customers at a lower price.

The Kristy manufacturing process is very labor intensive. The production employees played an important role in the early success of the company. As a result, management gave employees a great deal of freedom to schedule and manufacture customers' orders. For example, when the company increased the number of orders accepted, more employees were hired rather than pressuring current employees to produce at a faster rate. In management's view, the intricacy of work involved required ample time to ensure the work was done right.

Management introduced a standard cost system that it believed would be beneficial to the company. The managers thought it would identify the most economical way to manufacture much of the equipment, would give management a more accurate picture of the costs of the equipment, and could be used in evaluating actual costs for cost control. Consequently, the company should become more price competitive. Although the introduction of standards would probably lead to some employee discontent, management thought that the overall result would be beneficial. The standards were introduced on June 1 of this year.

During December, the production manager reported to the president that the new standards were creating problems in the plant. The employees had developed bad attitudes, absenteeism and turnover rates had increased, and standards were not being met. In the production manager's judgment, employee dissatisfaction has outweighed any benefits management thought would be achieved by the standard cost system. The production manager supported this contention with the following data; derived when monthly production was at normal volume levels.

Exhibit A
Kristy Company
Labor and Materials Operating Data

	J	F	M	A	M	J	J	A	S	O	N
Absenteeism rates:	1%	1%	1%	1%	0.5%	1%	2%	4%	6%	8%	11%
Turnover rate:	0.2%	0.5%	0.5%	0.5%	0.3%	0.8%	0.7%	1.4%	1.9%	2.5%	2.9%
Direct labor Efficiency Variance: (Unfavorable)	—	—	—	—	—	$(10,000)	$(11,500)	$(14,000)	$(17,000)	$(20,500)	$(25,000)
Direct materials Usage variance: (Unfavorable)	—	—	—	—	—	$(4,000)	$(5,000)	$(6,500)	$(8,200)	$(11,000)	$(14,000)

Required

1. Explain the general features and characteristics associated with the introduction and operation of a standard cost system that make it an effective cost control tool.
2. Discuss the apparent effect of Kristy Company's cost system on the following:
    a. Cost control
    b. Employee motivation
3. Discuss the probable causes for employee dissatisfaction with the new cost system.

P15-8. Standard Costs and Performance Reports (CMA)

The Kalman Company, a subsidiary of the Camper Corporation, submits interim financial statements. Camper combines these statements with similar statements from other subsidiaries to prepare its quarterly statements. The following data are taken from the records and accounts of the Kalman Company.

CHAPTER 15: STANDARD COSTS FOR MATERIALS AND LABOR

1. Sales forecasts for the year are:

Quarter	Stove Units	Percent
First	450,000	30%
Second	600,000	40
Third	150,000	10
Fourth	300,000	20
	1,500,000	100%

Sales have been achieved as forecasted in the first and second quarters of the current year.

2. Management is considering increasing the selling price of a stove from $30 to $34. However, management is concerned that this increase may reduce the already low sales volume forecasts for the third and fourth quarters.

3. The production schedule calls for 1,500,000 stoves this year. The manufacturing facilities can produce 1,720,000 units per year or 430,000 units per quarter during regular hours. The quarterly production schedule that follows was developed to meet the seasonal sales demand and is being followed as planned.

Quarter	Scheduled Production (in Units)	Percent
1	465,000	31%
2	450,000	30
3	225,000	15
4	360,000	24
	1,500,000	100%

4. The standard manufacturing cost of a stove unit, as established at the beginning of the current year, is shown below. This standard cost does not incorporate any charges for overtime.

Materials	$ 4.00
Labor	9.00
Variable overhead	2.00
Fixed overhead	3.00
Standard cost per stove	$18.00

5. A significant and permanent price increase in the cost of raw material resulted in a materials price variance of $270,000 for the materials used in the second quarter.

6. There was a $120,000 unfavorable direct-labor variance in the second quarter due in part to overtime pay to meet the heavy production schedule. An overtime premium equal to 0.5 times the standard labor rate is paid whenever production requires working beyond regular hours. The remaining amount of the labor variance during the quarter occurred as a result of unexpected inefficiencies.

7. The second quarter unfavorable overhead variance of $36,000 was entirely related to the excess direct-labor costs.

8. Total fixed overhead expected to be incurred and budgeted for the year is $4,500,000. Through the first two quarters, $2,745,000 of fixed overhead had been absorbed into the production process. Of this amount, $1,350,000 was absorbed in the second quarter. The high production activity resulted in a total fixed overhead volume variance of $495,000 for the first two quarters.

9. Selling expenses are 10 percent of sales and are expected to total $4,500,000 for the year.

10. Administrative expenses are $6,000,000 annually and are incurred uniformly throughout the period.
11. Inventory balances as of the end of the second quarter are as follows:

Raw material—at actual cost	$400,000
Work in process, 50% complete—at standard cost	72,000
Finished goods—at standard cost	900,000

12. The stove product line is expected to earn $7,500,000 before taxes this year. The estimated state and federal income tax expenses for the year are $4,500,000.
13. Any unplanned variances that are significant and permanent in nature are prorated to the applicable accounts during the quarter in which they are incurred.

Required

Prepare the second quarter interim income statement for the Kalman subsidiary of Camper Corporation.

P15–9. Standard Costs and Control Reports (CMA) The Ashley Company manufactures and sells a household product that is marketed through direct mail and advertisements in home improvement and gardening magazines. Although similar products are available in hardware and department stores, none are as effective as Ashley's model.

Ashley uses a standard cost system in its manufacturing accounting. The standards have not undergone a thorough review in the past eighteen months. The general manager has seen no need for such a review for the following reasons.

1. The materials quality and unit costs were fixed by a three-year purchase commitment signed in July 19X9.
2. A three-year labor contract had been signed in July 19X9.
3. There have been no significant variations from standard costs for the past three quarters.

The standard cost for the product, as established in July 19X9, is as follows:

Materials	0.75 lb. @ $1.00 per lb.	$0.75
Direct labor	0.3 hrs. @ $4.00 per hour	1.20
Overhead	0.3 hrs. @ $7.00 per hour	2.10
Standard manufacturing cost per unit		$4.05

The standard for overhead costs was developed from the following budgeted costs based on an activity level of 1.0 million units (300,000 direct-labor hours).

Variable manufacturing overhead	$ 600,000
Fixed manufacturing overhead	1,500,000
Total manufacturing overhead	$2,100,000

The earnings statement and the factory costs for the first quarter are shown on the next page. The first quarter results indicate that Ashley probably will achieve its sales goal of 1.2 million units for the current year. A total of 320,000 units were manufactured during the first quarter to increase inventory levels needed to support the growing sales volume.

ACTION Hardware, a national chain, recently asked Ashley to manufacture and sell a slightly modified version of the product, which ACTION would distribute through its stores. ACTION has offered to buy a minimum quantity of 200,000 units each year over the next three years and has offered to pay $4.10 for each unit, f.o.b. shipping point.

Ashley Company
First Quarter Earnings
Period Ending March 31, 19Y1

Sales (300,000 units)		$2,700,000
Cost of goods sold		
Standard cost of goods	$1,215,000	
Variation from standard costs	12,000	1,227,000
Gross profit		$1,473,000
Operating expenses		
Selling		
Advertising	$ 200,000	
Mailing list costs	175,000	
Postage	225,000	
Salaries	60,000	
Administrative		
Salaries	120,000	
Office rent	45,000	
Total operating expenses		825,000
Income before taxes		$ 648,000
Income taxes (45%)		291,600
Net income		$ 356,400

Ashley Company
Factory Costs
For the Quarter Ending March 31, 19Y1

Materials	$ 266,000
Direct labor	452,000
Variable manufacturing overhead	211,000
Fixed manufacturing overhead	379,000
Total manufacturing costs	$1,308,000
Less: Standard cost of goods manufactured	1,296,000
Unfavorable variation from standard cost	$ 12,000

Ashley's management is interested in the proposal because it represents a new market. Ashley has the capacity to meet the production requirements. However, in addition to the possible financial results of taking the order, Ashley must consider carefully the other consequences of this departure from its normal practices. The president asked the assistant general manager to estimate the financial aspects of the proposal for the first twelve months.

The assistant recommended that the order not be accepted and presented the following analysis to support the recommendation.

Sales Proposal of ACTION Hardware
First Twelve Months' Results

Proposed sales (200,000 @ $4.10)	$820,000
Estimated costs and expenses	
Manufacturing (200,000 @ $4.05)	$810,000
Sales salaries	10,000
Administrative salaries	20,000
Total estimated costs	$840,000
Net loss	$ (20,000)

Note: None of the regular selling costs are included because this is a new market. However, a 16.6% increase in sales and administrative salaries has been incorporated because sales volume will increase by that amount.

Required

1. Review the financial analysis of the ACTION hardware proposal prepared by the assistant general manager.
   a. Criticize the first year's financial analysis.
   b. Using only the data given, present a more suitable analysis for the first year of the order.
2. Identify the additional financial data Ashley Company would need to prepare a more comprehensive financial analysis of the ACTION proposal for the three-year period.
3. Discuss the nonfinancial issues Ashley's management should address in considering the ACTION proposal.

P15–10. Materials and Labor Standards The Lenco Company employs a standard cost system as part of its cost control program. The standard cost per unit is established at the beginning of each year. Standards are not revised during the year for any changes in materials or labor inputs or in the manufacturing processes; any revisions in standards are deferred until the beginning of the next fiscal year. However, to recognize such changes in the current year, Lenco includes planned variances in the monthly budgets prepared after such changes have been introduced.

The following labor standard was set for one of Lenco's products effective July 1, the beginning of the fiscal year.

Class I labor 4 hrs. @ $ 6.00	$24.00
Class II labor 3 hrs. @ 7.50	22.50
Class V labor 1 hr. @ 11.50	11.50
Standard labor cost per 100 units	$58.00

The standard was based on the quality of materials that had been used in previous years and what was expected to be available for the current fiscal year. The labor activity is performed by a team consisting of four persons with class I skills, three persons with class II skills, and one person with class V skills. This is the most economical combination for the company's processing system.

The manufacturing operations occurred as expected during the first five months of the year, and standard costs contributed to effective cost control during this period. However, there were indications that changes in the operations would be required in the last half of the year. Lenco had received a substantial increase in orders for delivery in the spring. Because an inadequate number of skilled workers was available to meet the increased production, the production teams, beginning in January, would be made up of more class I labor and less class II labor than the standard required. The teams would consist of six class I persons, two class II persons, and one class V person. This labor team would be less efficient than the normal team. The reorganized teams work more slowly, so only 90 units would be produced in the same time period that 100 units normally would have been produced. No raw materials will be lost as a result of the change in the labor mix. Completed units have never been rejected in the final inspection process as a consequence of faulty work; this is expected to continue.

In addition, Lenco was notified by its materials supplier that a lower quality material would be supplied after January 1. One unit of raw material is required normally for each good unit produced. Lenco and its supplier estimated that 5 percent of the units manufactured would be rejected on final inspection because of defective material. Normally, no units are lost because of defective material.

Required

1. How much of the lower quality material must be entered into production to produce 42,750 units of good production in January with the new labor teams? Show your calculations.
2. How many hours of each class of labor will be needed to produce 42,750 good units from the material input? Show your calculations.
3. What amount should be included in the January budget for the planned labor variance due to the labor team and material changes? What amount of this planned labor variance can be associated with *(a)* the materials change and *(b)* the team change? Show your calculations.

Chapter 16

Standard Costs for Factory Overhead

Outline

STANDARD COSTS FOR FACTORY OVERHEAD
THE OVERHEAD BUDGET
OVERHEAD APPLICATION AND GENERAL LEDGER ACCOUNTING
SPECIAL CONSIDERATIONS IN FIXED OVERHEAD ACCOUNTING
ANALYSIS OF OVERHEAD VARIANCES
Framework for Overhead Variance Analysis
Two-Way Analysis
Three-Way Analysis

Four-Way Analysis
Reporting Variances
DISPOSITION OF STANDARD COST VARIANCES
Treated as Period Expenses
Treated as Inventoriable Costs
SUMMARY
APPENDIX 16.1: PROCESS COSTING AND STANDARD COSTS
SELF-STUDY PROBLEM
SUGGESTED READINGS
DISCUSSION QUESTIONS
EXERCISES
PROBLEMS

This chapter continues the discussion of standard costs begun in chapter 15. Just as for direct materials and direct labor, standard costs for factory overhead help management to plan, coordinate, and monitor manufacturing operations. Standard costs for factory overhead provide the third and final cost element in a responsibility accounting system in which flexible budgets are used for planning and control. They are also used with standard costs for direct materials and direct labor for product costing.

Separate attention is given to standard costs for factory overhead because they possess two unique characteristics. First, unlike direct materials and direct labor, overhead costs cannot be traced to individual units of production. Second, whereas direct materials and direct labor are typically variable, total factory overhead includes *both* variable and fixed costs. Therefore, the budgetary and variance analysis procedures used for standard costs for factory overhead differ from those used for direct materials and direct labor.

This chapter reviews selected flexible budget and factory overhead topics and explains how to account for factory overhead when using standard costs. After completing this chapter, you should be able to:

1. develop a flexible budget for factory overhead.
2. calculate standard overhead application rates.
3. calculate standard costs for factory overhead.
4. perform general ledger accounting for factory overhead when using standard overhead application rates.
5. analyze factory overhead variances using several alternative analysis techniques.
6. account for the disposition of factory overhead variances.

STANDARD COSTS FOR FACTORY OVERHEAD

As defined in chapter 13, *factory overhead* consists of all costs incurred in a manufacturing operation other than direct materials and direct labor. The traceability of costs determines whether they are classified as direct materials and direct labor or as factory overhead. Direct materials and direct labor can be traced to specific units of production, but factory overhead cannot. It includes such items as insurance, taxes, supplies, maintenance, repairs, idle time, and factory depreciation. Even though overhead costs cannot be traced to specific units of production, overhead is still a manufacturing cost and needs to be assigned as part of the full cost of each unit produced. In a standard cost system, the mechanism for making this assignment is a predetermined or standard overhead application rate.

The term *standard cost*, as defined in chapter 15, has the same meaning when applied to overhead as it does when applied to materials or labor; that is, a *standard cost for overhead* is expressed as the per-unit amount of factory costs (other than direct materials and direct labor) that is expected to be incurred to produce one unit of output. As actual production takes place, standard costs are compared with actual costs, analyzed, and used as feedback to management for planning and control. Standard costs are also used during the period to assign costs to units of production.

The following steps describe the accounting process when using standard costs for factory overhead:

1. Develop a factory overhead flexible budget based on standard costs.
2. Calculate standard overhead application rates for fixed and variable overhead costs.
3. Calculate standard costs using standard overhead application rates.
4. Assign costs to units of production.
5. Compare total actual overhead with the flexible budget (standard costs).
6. Analyze any differences or variances between actual costs and standard costs.

THE OVERHEAD BUDGET

As discussed in chapter 15, a flexible budget for direct materials and direct labor typically begins with the development of per-unit standard costs for materials and labor, which are then multiplied by the expected volume of production to determine total budgeted standard costs for the period. However, because overhead costs have unique characteristics, the budgetary procedure for overhead is different in that *total* factory overhead is estimated first. Standard overhead application rates are then calculated by dividing total budgeted costs by the total expected volume of activity. Activity is measured using a base such as direct-labor hours or machine hours, as discussed in chapters 13 and 14. Finally, standard costs are calculated by multiplying the standard overhead application rate by the standard amount of the activity base allowed to produce each unit of output.

The budgetary procedure is different for factory overhead because overhead costs are not traceable to specific units of production. For example, it is relatively easy to determine how much metal should be used in the production of a bronze bookend. However, it is not readily apparent how much factory depreciation should be assigned to each bookend. Therefore, the budgetary procedure for overhead costs is first to compile total expected costs and then to derive per-unit standard costs.

Another important feature of overhead budgets using standard costs is that they should distinguish between fixed factory overhead and variable factory overhead. Variable overhead costs fluctuate with the level of production in the same way as direct materials and direct labor. Fixed overhead costs remain constant for different activity levels within a relevant range of total expected activity.

The distinction between fixed and variable overhead is maintained in the budgetary process so that standard costs are calculated for *both* fixed and variable overhead. This distinction is also carried through the remainder of the accounting process so that information is provided about why actual overhead costs may have deviated from budgeted amounts.

A *flexible budget for factory overhead* is illustrated for a hypothetical factory department in figure 16.1. The overhead budget is compiled at several different levels of expected output, which is consistent with the concept of flexible budgeting. Note that a clear distinction is made between fixed and variable overhead costs.

FIGURE 16.1

Flexible Budget for Factory Overhead

Department 1			
Standard direct-labor hours	10,000	12,000	14,000
Variable factory overhead:			
Indirect labor	$10,000	$12,000	$14,000
Supplies	2,200	2,640	3,080
Repairs	800	960	1,120
Total	$13,000	$15,600	$18,200
Fixed factory overhead:			
Supervision	$ 5,000	$ 5,000	$ 5,000
Insurance	1,300	1,300	1,300
Depreciation	500	500	500
Taxes	200	200	200
Total	$ 7,000	$ 7,000	$ 7,000
Total factory overhead	$20,000	$22,600	$25,200

The expected level or volume of production for the coming accounting period is referred to as the **standard activity level.** The choice of a standard activity level results from a process best described as "judgmental forecasting," which requires consideration of such factors as expected sales, inventory levels, and plant capacity. The activity level of 10,000 direct-labor hours in figure 16.1 is used as the standard activity level in the rest of the illustrations in this chapter.

Although direct-labor hours is the activity base used in this chapter to illustrate the standard activity level, measures such as machine hours or units of output can also be used as an activity base.

OVERHEAD APPLICATION AND GENERAL LEDGER ACCOUNTING

The next step in the budgetary process is to calculate standard overhead application rates for (a) variable overhead, (b) fixed overhead, and (c) total overhead costs. This is done by dividing budgeted overhead by the standard activity level, as indicated by the following general formula:

$$\text{Factory overhead (variable, fixed, or total)} \div \text{Standard activity level} = \text{Standard overhead application rate}$$

Figure 16.2 contains overhead application rates based on the flexible budget shown in figure 16.1. Remember that the standard activity level is 10,000 direct-labor hours.

The final step in the budgetary process is to calculate the standard cost of overhead using the standard overhead application rates. In general, this is accomplished by multiplying the standard overhead application rates for variable and fixed overhead by the standard amount of the activity base allowed for each unit of production. For example, the standard variable overhead application rate of $1.30 per direct-labor hour is multiplied by 2 standard hours allowed for each unit, giving a standard cost for variable overhead of $2.60 per unit. The standard fixed overhead application rate of $0.70 per direct labor hour is multiplied by 2 standard hours allowed for each unit, giving a standard cost for fixed overhead of $1.40 per unit.

From a total cost perspective, the standard costs for overhead are combined with standard costs for materials and labor to give the total standard cost for a particular product. Figure 16.3 shows a simplified standard cost card for ABC Fasteners that contains all standard cost elements.

Now that standard costs for overhead have been calculated, we can show their use in accounting for overhead. To illustrate the accounting for overhead in a standard cost sys-

FIGURE 16.2

Calculation of Standard Overhead Application Rates

Standard variable overhead application rate:
$13,000 variable overhead ÷ 10,000 hours = $1.30 per direct-labor hour

Standard fixed overhead application rate:
$7,000 fixed overhead ÷ 10,000 hours = $0.70 per direct-labor hour

Total standard overhead application rate:
$20,000 total overhead ÷ 10,000 hours = $2.00 per direct-labor hour

FIGURE 16.3

Simplified Standard Cost Card

ABC Fasteners	
Direct materials (6 pounds at $4.00 per pound)	$24.00
Direct labor (2 hours at $4.00 per hour)	8.00
Variable overhead (2 hours at $1.30 per hour)	2.60
Fixed overhead (2 hours at $0.70 per hour)	1.40
Total	$36.00

tem, consider the following information for ABC Fasteners during the current accounting period. Budget and standard cost data from figures 16.1 and 16.3 are also repeated for convenient reference:

Data Concerning Actual Costs and Production Volume

Actual overhead incurred (variable)	$15,000
Actual overhead incurred (fixed)	$ 7,900
Actual direct-labor hours used	12,100 hours
Fasteners produced this period	6,000 units

Budget and Standard Cost Data

Budgeted overhead (variable)	$13,000
Budgeted overhead (fixed)	$ 7,000
Standard overhead application rate (total)	$ 2.00 per hour

The journal entries used to illustrate the accounting process represent an aggregation of many individual journal entries and many individual postings to subsidiary ledgers that are typically made during an entire accounting period.

The following journal entries record (a) actual expenditures made during the period for overhead items and (b) overhead applied to work in process during the period using the standard cost for overhead.

The amount of actual expenditures for factory overhead is given at $22,900 ($15,000 variable + $7,900 fixed). The following journal entry is made to record this actual overhead incurred.

Factory overhead	22,900	
Cash, accounts payable, etc.		22,900

The total standard overhead applied to work in process is calculated by multiplying the units of good output by the standard cost per unit for overhead as follows:

Formula for Application of Standard Variable Factory Overhead

Units of good output × Standard cost for overhead = Standard overhead to apply to work in process

Variable:	6,000 units	×	$2.60	=	$15,600
Fixed:	6,000 units	×	$1.40	=	$ 8,400
			$4.00		$24,000

The following journal entry is made to record the application of factory overhead to work in process.

Work in process	24,000	
Factory overhead		24,000

An alternative method of computation is to multiply the units of good output (6,000 units) by the number of standard direct-labor hours allowed per unit (2 hours), which gives the number of *standard hours allowed* for the good output (12,000 hours). Then the total standard hours allowed (12,000 hours) is multiplied by the standard overhead application rate ($2.00 per hour = $1.30 variable + $0.70 fixed) to give the total standard variable overhead to apply to work in process.

Any balance in the factory overhead control account at the end of an accounting period represents over- or underapplied overhead. In the preceding illustration there is $1,100 of overapplied factory overhead. The analysis and disposition of over- or underapplied overhead will be discussed after a more detailed examination of fixed overhead accounting.

SPECIAL CONSIDERATIONS IN FIXED OVERHEAD ACCOUNTING

By definition, budgeted fixed factory overhead remains constant for all levels of output over the relevant range of productive activity. However, as illustrated in chapter 15, the accepted practice is to treat fixed overhead as though it is a variable cost. This is done by assigning fixed overhead to units of production using a fixed overhead application rate.

Using a per-unit rate to apply fixed overhead in the same way that variable factory overhead is applied creates a situation that deserves special consideration, because reported results of operations could be misinterpreted. The reason for concern is immediately apparent when one compares the behavior of budgeted fixed and variable overhead costs with the behavior of applied overhead costs. Figure 16.4 contains graphs of budgeted and applied variable and fixed overhead costs. These graphs are derived from the data presented in previous illustrations.

Note in figure 16.4 that the graph for budgeted variable overhead is identical to the graph of applied variable overhead; that is, applied variable overhead is equal to budgeted variable overhead at each level of output. All truly variable costs will exhibit these same cost behavior patterns. Graphs for direct materials and direct labor would show this same general relationship between budgeted and applied costs.

It is a different situation with fixed costs. The graph for budgeted fixed costs is horizontal, indicating that fixed overhead is expected to be the same for each level of output within the relevant range. If fixed overhead is assigned to work in process on a per-unit basis, however, the graph of applied fixed overhead resembles the behavior of a variable cost. As a result, budgeted fixed overhead is equal to applied fixed overhead only at one level of output—the *standard activity level*.

To illustrate, if the number of standard hours allowed for good output for the period turns out to be 10,000 direct-labor hours, then $7,000 (10,000 hours × $0.70 per hour = $7,000) of fixed overhead will be applied to work in process, which, as expected, is the amount of budgeted fixed costs. However, if the actual volume of activity turns out to be 12,000 rather than 10,000 direct-labor hours, $8,400 (12,000 hours × $0.70 per hour = $8,400) of fixed overhead will be applied to work in process—a difference of $1,400 ($8,400 − $7,000) between budgeted fixed overhead and applied fixed overhead. This means that fixed overhead will be either under- or overapplied to work in process simply because the level of actual activity is not equal to the standard level of activity. In this case, fixed overhead is overapplied by $1,400.

To emphasize this concept, figure 16.4 shows that applied fixed overhead is equal to budgeted fixed overhead *only* at the standard activity level. Also, compare the variable overhead graphs with the fixed overhead graphs to see that this phenomenon is unique to fixed overhead.

FIGURE 16.4 Comparison of Variable and Fixed Overhead

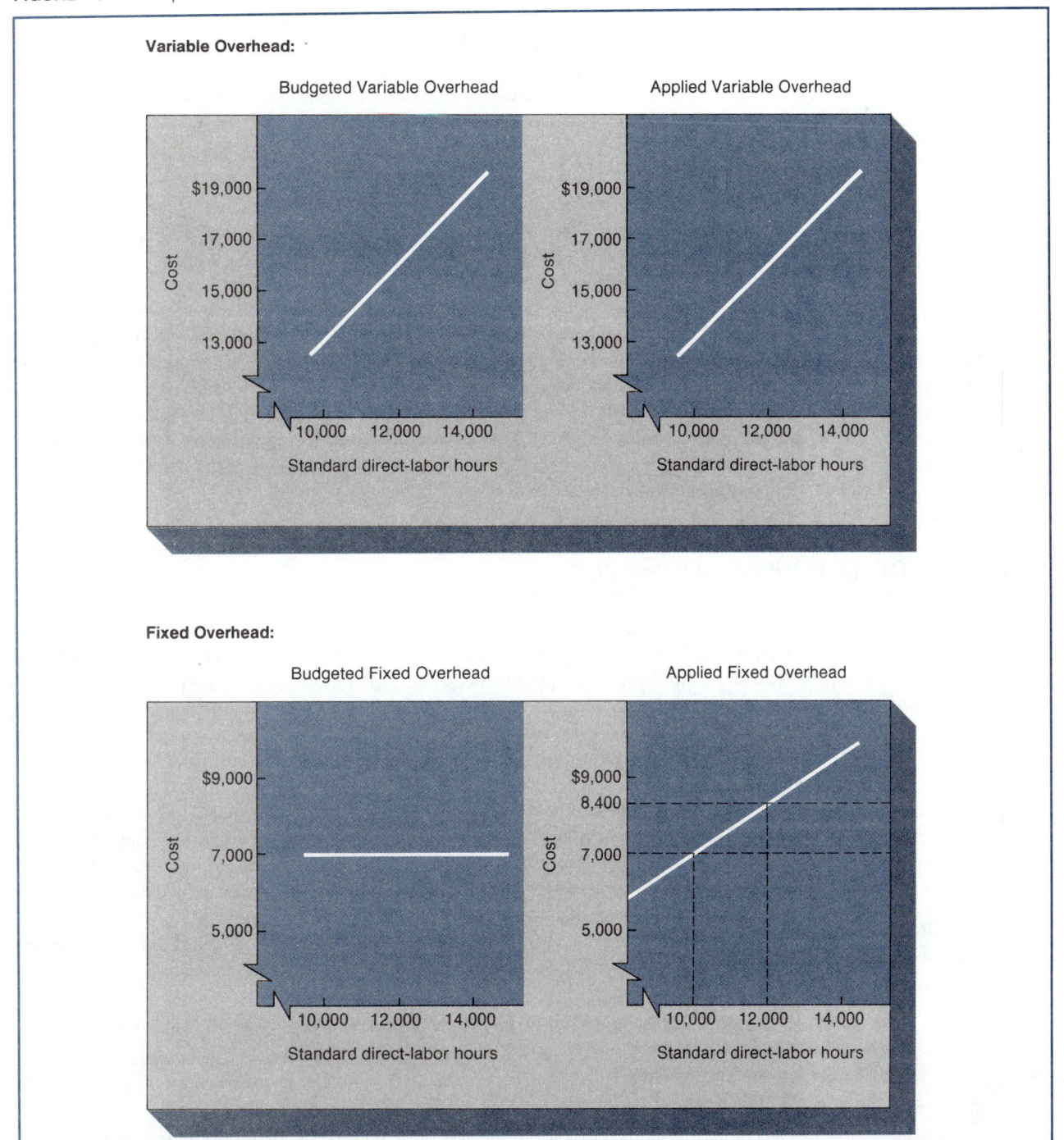

The difference between budgeted fixed factory overhead and applied fixed factory overhead is called the production volume variance or simply the **volume variance.** Mathematically the volume variance is found in the following way:

$$\left[\begin{array}{c}\text{Predetermined standard} \\ \text{activity level}\end{array} - \begin{array}{c}\text{Standard hours allowed} \\ \text{for good output}\end{array}\right] \times \begin{array}{c}\text{Standard fixed costs} \\ \text{per unit}\end{array} = \text{Volume variance}$$

$$[10{,}000 \text{ hours} - 12{,}000 \text{ hours}] \times \$0.70 \text{ per hour} = \$1{,}400$$

In reality, the probability is very low that the actual activity level will equal the standard activity level. Therefore, it is almost certain that firms using a standard cost system will experience a volume variance.

The volume variance is designated favorable (F) if actual activity exceeds the budgeted or standard activity level. The volume variance is designated unfavorable (U) if the opposite occurs. The terms *favorable* and *unfavorable* when applied to the volume variance are not intended to render a qualitative judgment. Rather, a favorable variance simply indicates that more plant capacity was utilized than originally budgeted, and an unfavorable variance indicates that less plant capacity was utilized than originally budgeted. Whether or not either variance is judged good or bad depends on top management's assessment relative to overall company goals. The volume variance usually is the concern of managers responsible for overall utilization of plant capacity.

ANALYSIS OF OVERHEAD VARIANCES

Overhead accounting in a standard cost system has two general purposes—to provide data for product costing and to provide information for planning and control decisions. Overhead application emphasizes product costing. This section stresses the planning and control aspects of overhead accounting by which standard costs provide a budgetary benchmark against which actual performance can be compared. Actual costs incurred are compared with standard or expected costs, and differences are analyzed to provide guidance for management.

The analysis of overhead variances begins with the *total overhead variance,* which is the difference between total actual overhead incurred and total overhead applied to work in process. In the ABC Fastener example, there is a total overhead variance of $1,100 F. Overapplied overhead is designated a favorable variance and underapplied overhead is designated an unfavorable variance.

Simply reporting an overhead variance of $1,100 F provides very little information. Management needs some indication why this deviation from the budget occurred, whether this deviation is good or bad, and who, if anyone, can control its causes. There are several common methods for analyzing the total overhead variance and breaking it down into its causal components.

Framework for Overhead Variance Analysis

Depending on the level of detail desired by management, there are three general ways to analyze the total overhead variance. Minor differences in terminology and computational techniques exist among different firms and authors. However, the following framework incorporates the most widely used methods and uses what seems to be the most widely accepted terminology.

Analysis of an overhead variance can be done using a two-way analysis, a three-way analysis, or a four-way analysis, as shown in figure 16.5.

FIGURE 16.5 General Framework for Overhead Variance Analysis

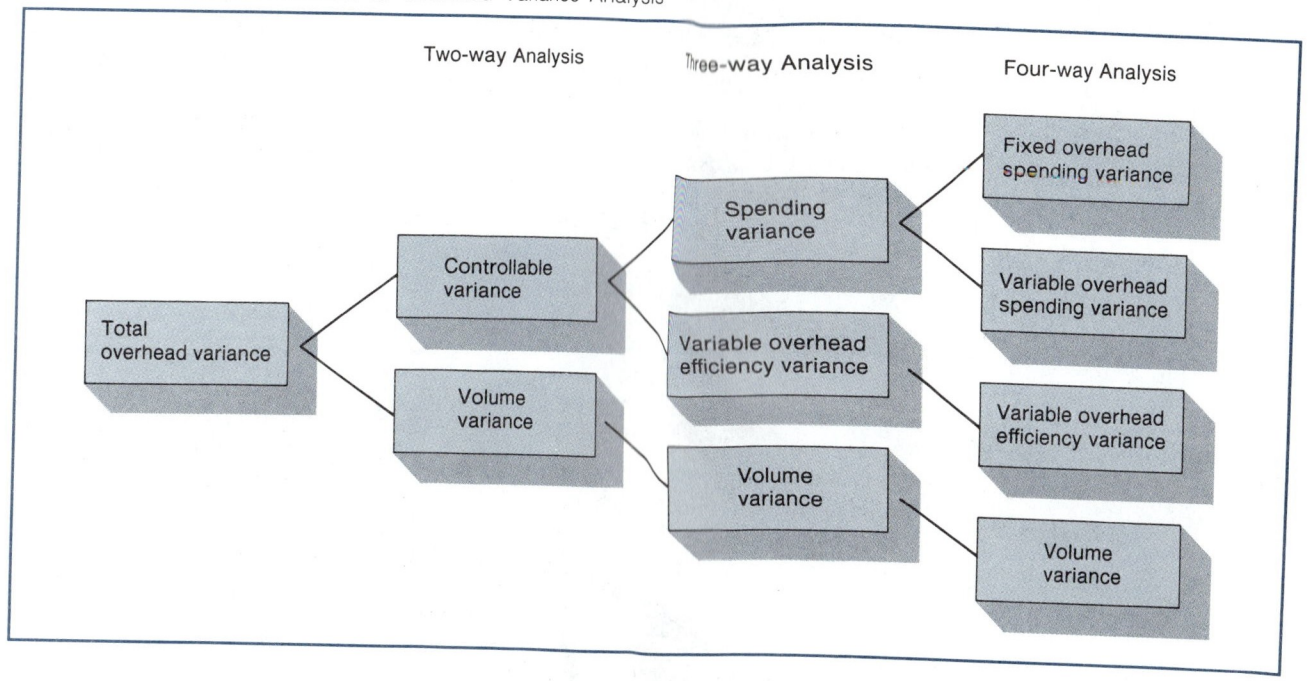

Each method of analyzing the total overhead variance simply represents more detail as one progresses from the two-way to the four-way analysis. The more detailed the analysis, the more apparent the opportunities for fine-tuning factory operations.

A quick scan of the variances and their descriptions indicates the cost area involved and the type of information provided by each. The most thorough analysis is obtained with the four-way analysis, but the two-way or three-way methods may suffice in many factory situations. In any event, the discussion that follows begins with the $1,100 F total overhead variance and progressively analyzes it at each level of detail. Do not jump ahead to the four-way analysis, because there are conceptual and computational foundations built along the way that will help you to understand and interpret four-way analysis of variances.

Two-Way Analysis

The two-way analysis of overhead variances separates what is called a controllable variance and the volume variance. Calling one variance controllable may give the impression that the volume variance is uncontrollable. However, both variances are controllable, but at different levels in the organization. Because the volume variance relates to *total* manufacturing activity, the factors affecting it are probably controlled only at higher levels of management. On the other hand, the **controllable variance** relates to factors such as the price paid for overhead items (custodial supplies and insurance, for example) as well as the efficiency with which overhead items are utilized. These factors are typically controlled at lower levels in an organization—usually at the departmental level and most often in the purchasing department. Therefore, the segregation between the controllable variance and the volume variance simply makes it possible to place responsibility for the controllable variance with lower-level supervisors who control daily operations and to place the responsibility for the volume variance with higher-level managers who control overall plant activity.

A two-way analysis can be performed quite simply by calculating the volume variance as previously illustrated, then finding the controllable variance by taking the difference between the volume variance and the total overhead variance. For example, the volume variance calculated in the previous illustrations is $1,400 F. The difference between a $1,400 U volume variance and a $1,100 F total overhead variance is a $300 U controllable variance.

For conceptual reasons and to lay the foundation for the three-way and four-way analysis techniques, let's look at a tabular approach to performing a two-way analysis. Figure 16.6 contains an outline for calculating the controllable and volume variances. Formulas that underlie this analysis are also given in figure 16.6.

FIGURE 16.6

Controllable and Volume Variances—Two-Way Analysis

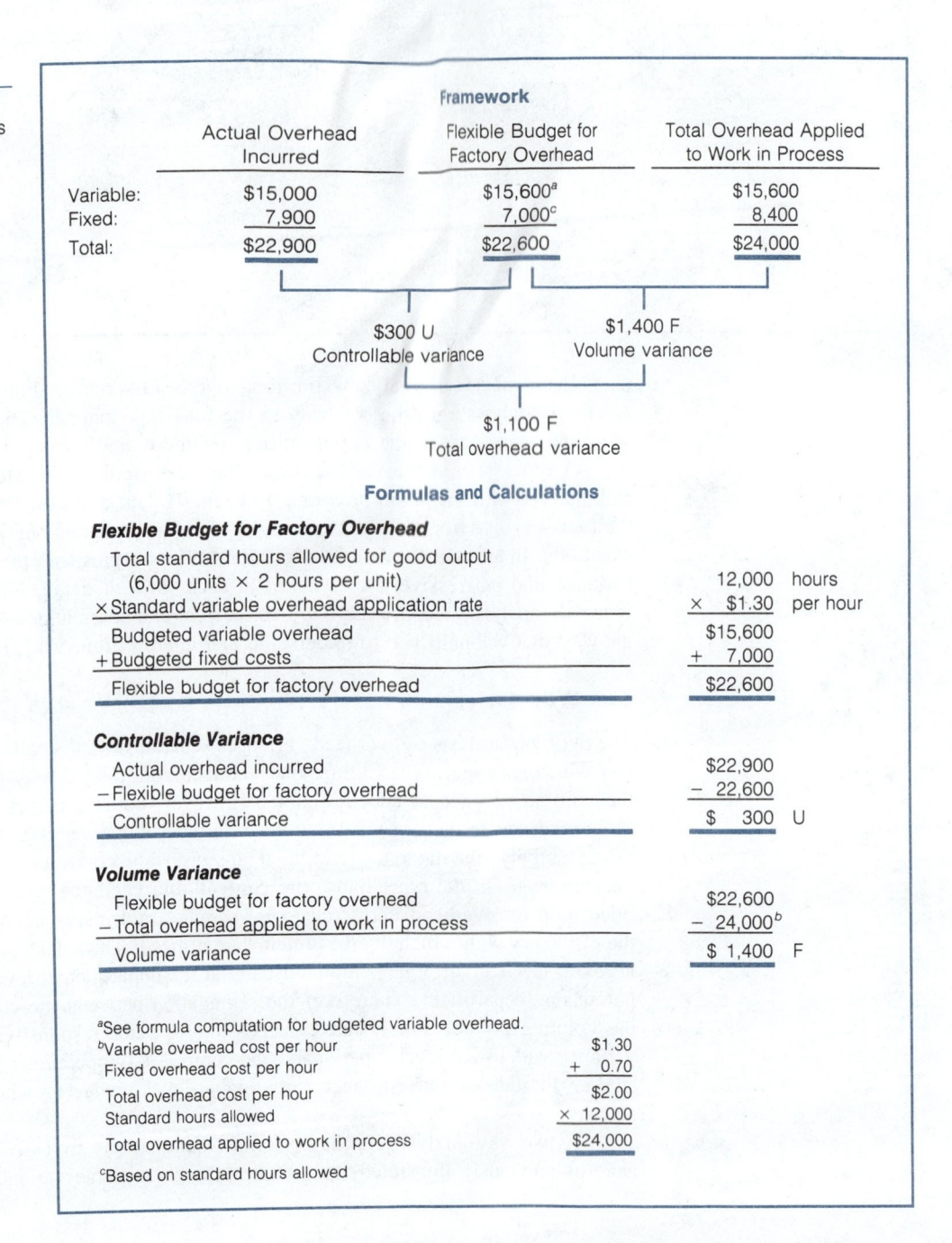

Framework

	Actual Overhead Incurred	Flexible Budget for Factory Overhead	Total Overhead Applied to Work in Process
Variable:	$15,000	$15,600[a]	$15,600
Fixed:	7,900	7,000[c]	8,400
Total:	$22,900	$22,600	$24,000

$300 U Controllable variance $1,400 F Volume variance

$1,100 F Total overhead variance

Formulas and Calculations

Flexible Budget for Factory Overhead

Total standard hours allowed for good output (6,000 units × 2 hours per unit)	12,000	hours
× Standard variable overhead application rate	× $1.30	per hour
Budgeted variable overhead	$15,600	
+ Budgeted fixed costs	+ 7,000	
Flexible budget for factory overhead	$22,600	

Controllable Variance

Actual overhead incurred	$22,900
− Flexible budget for factory overhead	− 22,600
Controllable variance	$ 300 U

Volume Variance

Flexible budget for factory overhead	$22,600
− Total overhead applied to work in process	− 24,000[b]
Volume variance	$ 1,400 F

[a] See formula computation for budgeted variable overhead.

[b]
Variable overhead cost per hour	$1.30
Fixed overhead cost per hour	+ 0.70
Total overhead cost per hour	$2.00
Standard hours allowed	× 12,000
Total overhead applied to work in process	$24,000

[c] Based on standard hours allowed

The calculations for both the controllable and the volume variance utilize the flexible budget for factory overhead. For this reason, figure 16.6 contains a formula for computing the flexible budget for factory overhead based on an actual activity level equal to the standard hours allowed for actual good output.

A formula is useful at this time because the flexible budget calculated before operations began probably did not contain calculations at the actual level of activity. For example, figure 16.1 contains the factory overhead flexible budget for the 10,000-, 12,000-, and 14,000-hour levels of activity. If the actual standard hours allowed for good output turns out to be one of these levels of activity, the total overhead budget can be read directly from the previously computed budget in figure 16.1. However, the standard hours allowed probably will not coincide exactly with one of the levels of activity included in the flexible budget. For example, if 5,500 good ABC Fasteners had been produced, the number of standard hours allowed would have been 11,000 hours (5,500 units × 2 hours per unit = 11,000 hours). The 11,000-hour level of activity is not included in the budget in figure 16.1. Therefore, the formula in figure 16.6 represents a convenient computational tool to derive the total overhead budget at the end of the period when variances are analyzed.

The unfavorable controllable variance indicates that there may be ways to improve the efficiency and effectiveness of some overhead items. To be able to specifically pinpoint areas for evaluation, a more detailed analysis of the controllable variance is needed.

Three-Way Analysis

The three-way analysis of overhead variances provides an additional level of detail for the controllable variance. The volume variance is the same for the two-way analysis and three-way analysis, and its calculation is not repeated in this discussion.

The controllable variance can be further analyzed in terms of a variable overhead efficiency variance and a spending variance. The **variable overhead efficiency variance** helps in evaluating the efficiency with which the activity base is utilized. If direct-labor hours is used as the activity base, the variable overhead efficiency variance will vary in the same direction as the labor efficiency variance. If machine hours is used as the activity base, the variable overhead efficiency variance will help to evaluate the efficiency with which machine hours were utilized. The **spending variance** is an indicator of how well actual overhead expenditures were kept within the budget independent of the efficiency with which the activity base was utilized. A complete explanation of the spending variance is developed in the discussion of the four-way analysis.

A three-way analysis requires that a flexible budget for factory overhead is calculated based on the total actual hours used. Comparing a flexible budget based on the *total actual hours* used with a flexible budget based on the *total standard hours allowed for good output* helps to isolate the amount of total overhead variance relating to the efficiency with which labor was utilized. If machine hours had been the activity base, the variable overhead efficiency variance would be calculated using flexible budgets based on the total actual machine hours and standard machine hours allowed.

Figure 16.7 contains the framework and related formulas for computing the spending and variable overhead efficiency variances.

Supervisors and other line personnel have the responsibility for the variable overhead efficiency variance because they are usually the ones responsible for activity bases such as direct labor or machine hours.

Four-Way Analysis

The four-way analysis of overhead variances produces an additional level of detail and understanding for the spending variance. The volume variance and the variable overhead efficiency variance remain the same for the three-way analysis and four-way analysis.

FIGURE 16.7

Spending and Variable Overhead Efficiency Variances—Three-Way Analysis

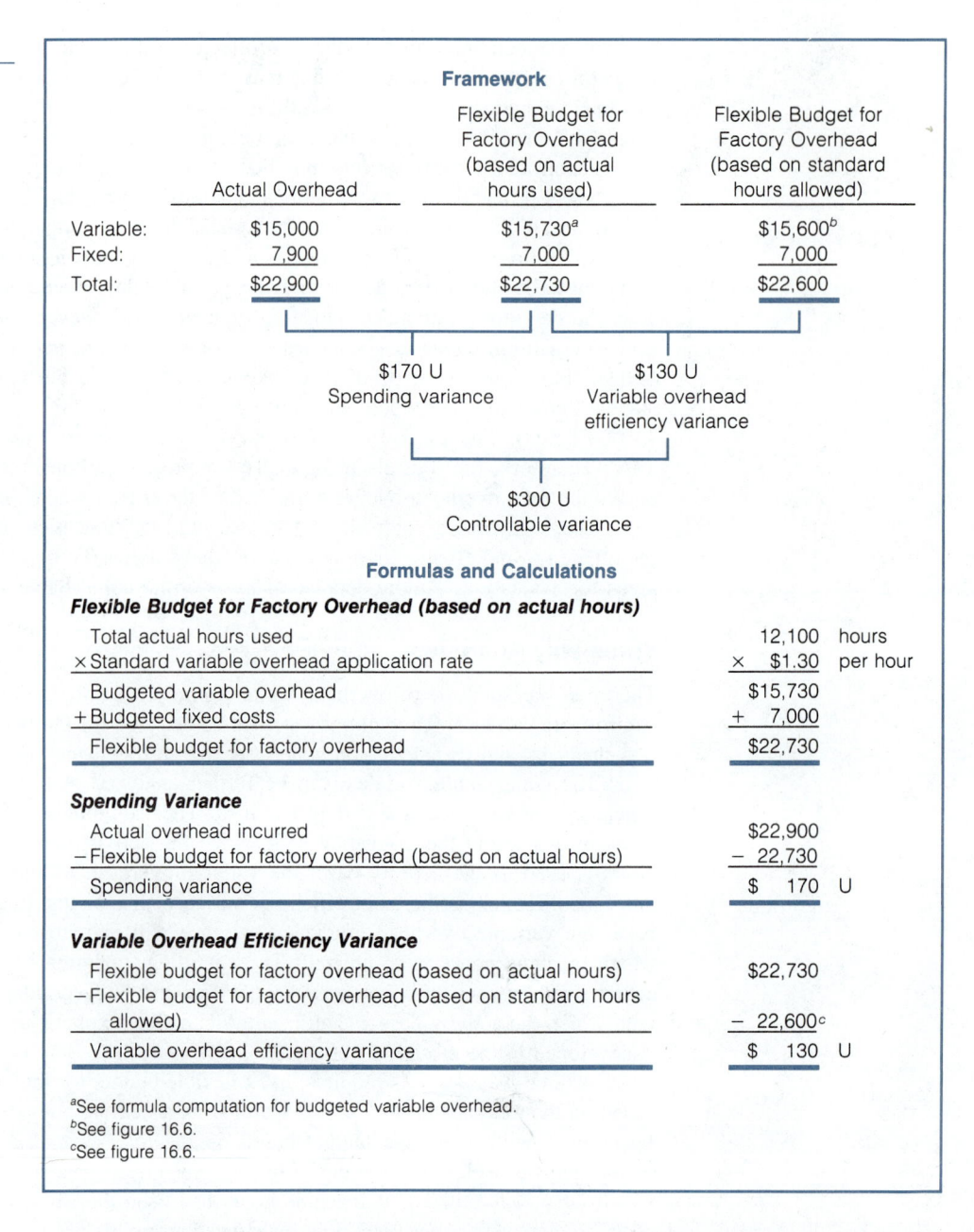

Framework

	Actual Overhead	Flexible Budget for Factory Overhead (based on actual hours used)	Flexible Budget for Factory Overhead (based on standard hours allowed)
Variable:	$15,000	$15,730[a]	$15,600[b]
Fixed:	7,900	7,000	7,000
Total:	$22,900	$22,730	$22,600

$170 U Spending variance

$130 U Variable overhead efficiency variance

$300 U Controllable variance

Formulas and Calculations

Flexible Budget for Factory Overhead (based on actual hours)

Total actual hours used	12,100 hours
× Standard variable overhead application rate	× $1.30 per hour
Budgeted variable overhead	$15,730
+ Budgeted fixed costs	+ 7,000
Flexible budget for factory overhead	$22,730

Spending Variance

Actual overhead incurred	$22,900
− Flexible budget for factory overhead (based on actual hours)	− 22,730
Spending variance	$ 170 U

Variable Overhead Efficiency Variance

Flexible budget for factory overhead (based on actual hours)	$22,730
− Flexible budget for factory overhead (based on standard hours allowed)	− 22,600[c]
Variable overhead efficiency variance	$ 130 U

[a] See formula computation for budgeted variable overhead.
[b] See figure 16.6.
[c] See figure 16.6.

As indicated before, the spending variance can be further analyzed in terms of a fixed overhead spending variance and a variable overhead spending variance. The **variable overhead spending variance** gives any difference between actual expenditures for variable overhead and budgeted expenditures caused by differences in prices. The variable overhead spending variance is somewhat like the materials price variance or the labor rate variance. The **fixed overhead spending variance** gives any difference between actual fixed overhead incurred and budgeted fixed overhead.

The framework for calculating these variances is essentially the same as that used to determine the spending variance in the three-way analysis. The only difference between the three-way and the four-way analyses is that calculations are made separately for variable and fixed overhead costs; that is, the variable overhead spending variance relates only to variable costs and the fixed overhead spending variance relates only to fixed costs. Figure 16.8 presents the framework and related formulas for computing the variable and the fixed overhead spending variances. The figure also contains the calculation of the variable overhead efficiency variance and the controllable variances so that the framework can be easily related to the three-way analysis.

The unfavorable fixed overhead spending variance indicates that more was expended for fixed cost items than was expected. The fact that there are cost differences in the fixed cost items may appear irregular unless it is remembered that fixed costs may change even though they were expected to remain the same at the time the original budget was prepared. However, fixed costs do not change in proportion to the volume of output. For example, property tax assessments may change, insurance coverage may be altered, and depreciation charges may increase, leading to a change in costs that otherwise are properly classified as fixed.

To conclude this section on the calculation of overhead variances, figure 16.9 presents a total framework for calculating all of the variances using either two-way, three-way, or four-way analysis methods. Figure 16.9 combines figures 16.6, 16.7, and 16.8.

Finally, figure 16.10 shows the conceptual relationship of overhead variances by presenting the general framework for overhead variances contained in figure 16.5 along with the dollar amounts for all of the variances illustrated in this chapter. Note that the total of the variances using any analysis method always equals the total overhead variance.

Reporting Variances

It is important that reports are prepared that detail individual overhead items. Such reports give management the item-by-item information necessary to effectively control future overhead costs. Figure 16.11 contains an overhead report relating the examples of this chapter.

The overhead report in figure 16.11 contains both variable and fixed costs. In reality, the fixed cost portion may be omitted, depending on whether or not fixed costs are controllable at the departmental level. The responsibility for fixed overhead budget variances and the volume variance usually resides at higher levels of management. However, lower-level managers may be able to control fixed overhead expenditures to the extent that they are discretionary fixed costs. Thus, lower-level managers should be held responsible for all costs that are controllable at the departmental level.

DISPOSITION OF STANDARD COST VARIANCES

There are two general ways to handle standard cost variances at the end of an accounting period. Depending on the situation and management's conceptual viewpoint, either of these two methods could be used. First, standard cost variances may be *treated as period expenses* with the variance accounts being closed directly to cost of goods sold or to income summary. Second, standard cost variances could be *treated as inventoriable costs* with the variance accounts being allocated among inventories and cost of goods sold.

The accounting procedures for each of these methods are illustrated on the following pages. Figure 16.12 contains a schedule of standard cost variances used in these illustrations. Remember that favorable variances are represented in general ledger accounts by credit balances and unfavorable variances by debit balances. It is assumed that all variances have been recorded in the general ledger and that all overhead transactions have been recorded in one factory overhead account.

FIGURE 16.8

Fixed Overhead Budget and Variable Overhead Spending Variances—Four-Way Analysis

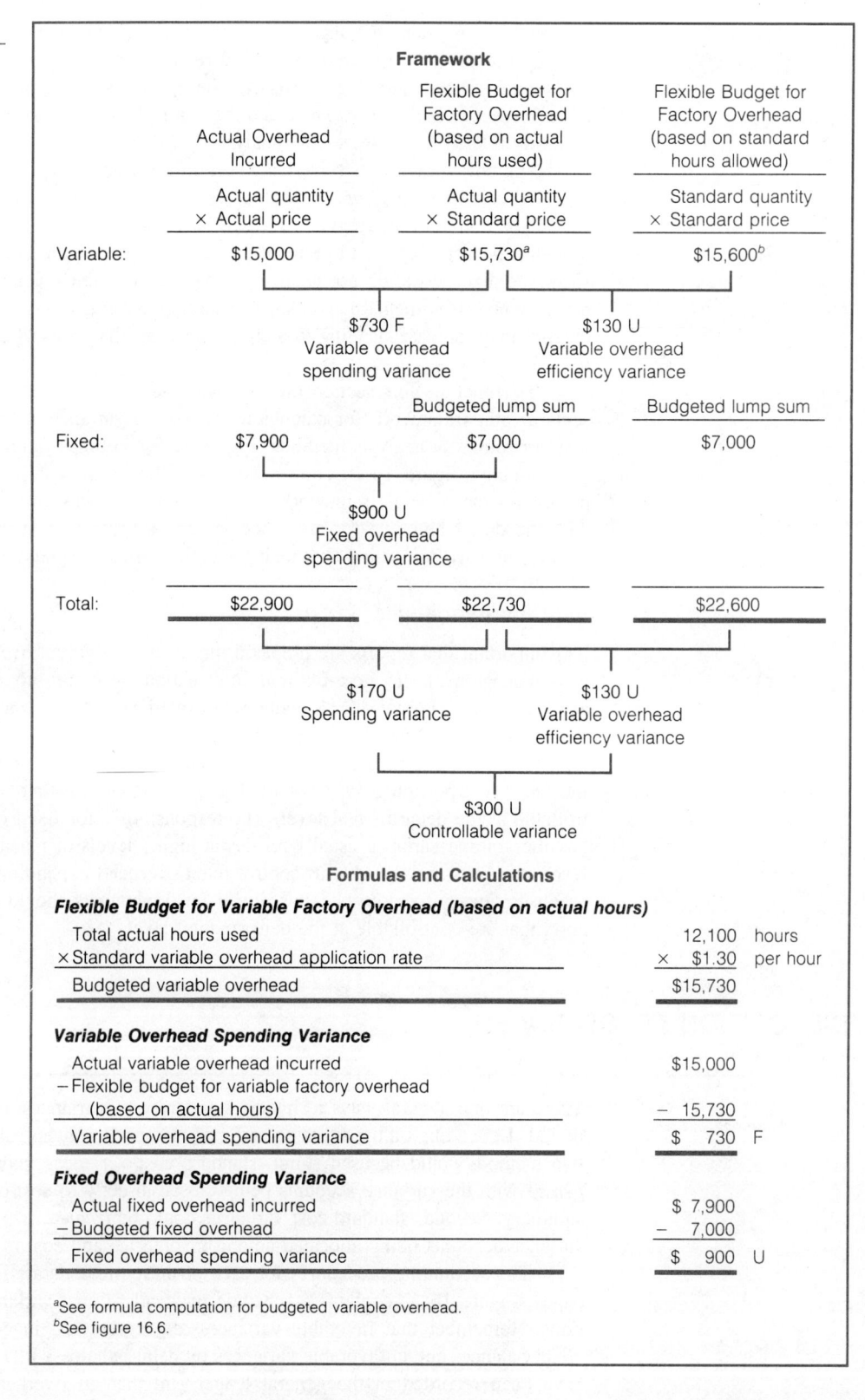

Framework

	Actual Overhead Incurred	Flexible Budget for Factory Overhead (based on actual hours used)	Flexible Budget for Factory Overhead (based on standard hours allowed)
	Actual quantity × Actual price	Actual quantity × Standard price	Standard quantity × Standard price
Variable:	$15,000	$15,730[a]	$15,600[b]

$730 F Variable overhead spending variance

$130 U Variable overhead efficiency variance

		Budgeted lump sum	Budgeted lump sum
Fixed:	$7,900	$7,000	$7,000

$900 U Fixed overhead spending variance

| Total: | $22,900 | $22,730 | $22,600 |

$170 U Spending variance

$130 U Variable overhead efficiency variance

$300 U Controllable variance

Formulas and Calculations

Flexible Budget for Variable Factory Overhead (based on actual hours)

Total actual hours used	12,100 hours
× Standard variable overhead application rate	× $1.30 per hour
Budgeted variable overhead	$15,730

Variable Overhead Spending Variance

Actual variable overhead incurred	$15,000
− Flexible budget for variable factory overhead (based on actual hours)	− 15,730
Variable overhead spending variance	$ 730 F

Fixed Overhead Spending Variance

Actual fixed overhead incurred	$ 7,900
− Budgeted fixed overhead	− 7,000
Fixed overhead spending variance	$ 900 U

[a] See formula computation for budgeted variable overhead.
[b] See figure 16.6.

CHAPTER 16: STANDARD COSTS FOR FACTORY OVERHEAD

FIGURE 16.9 Analysis of Total Overhead Variance

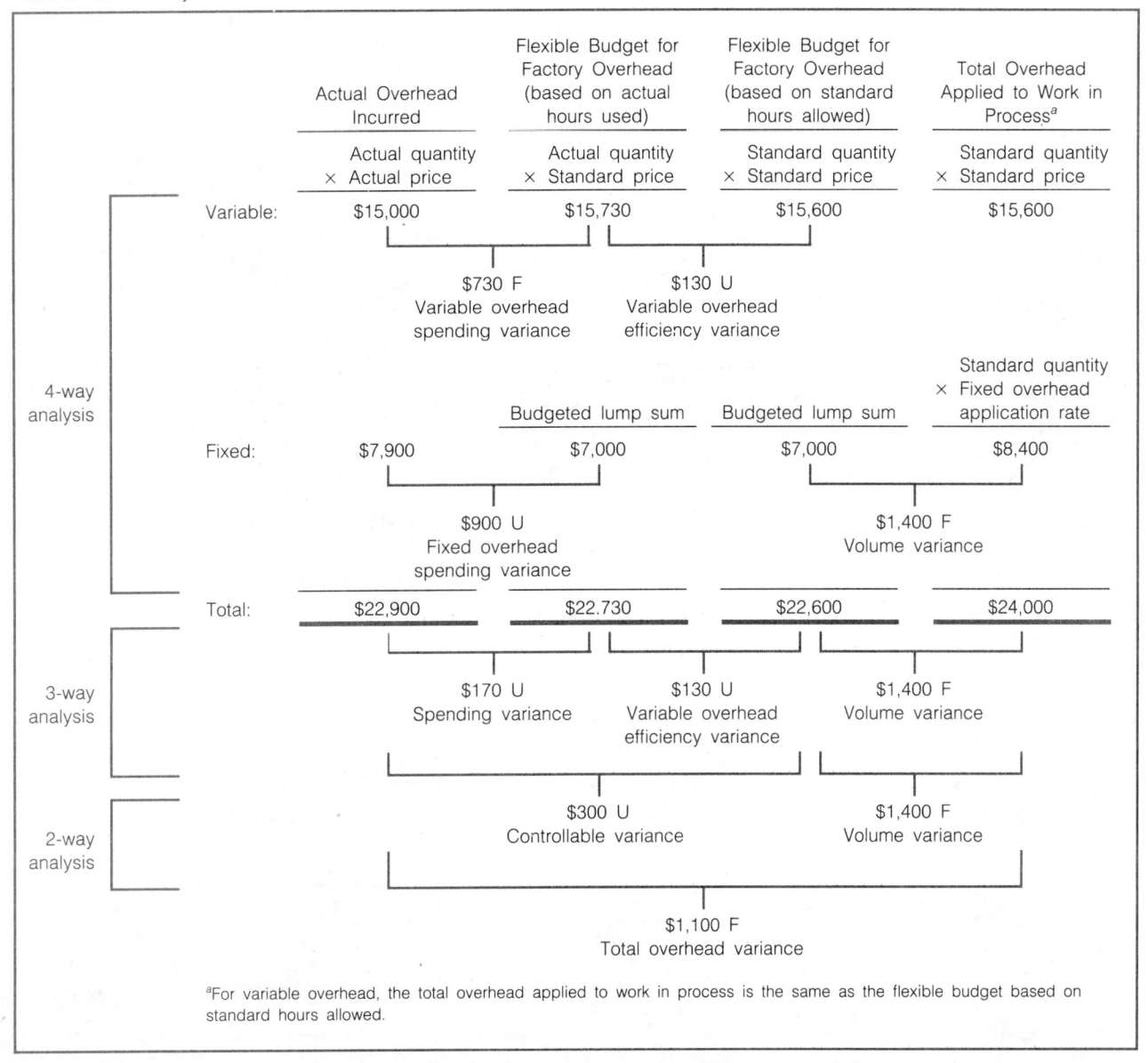

	Actual Overhead Incurred	Flexible Budget for Factory Overhead (based on actual hours used)	Flexible Budget for Factory Overhead (based on standard hours allowed)	Total Overhead Applied to Work in Process[a]
	Actual quantity × Actual price	Actual quantity × Standard price	Standard quantity × Standard price	Standard quantity × Standard price
Variable:	$15,000	$15,730	$15,600	$15,600

$730 F Variable overhead spending variance
$130 U Variable overhead efficiency variance

		Budgeted lump sum	Budgeted lump sum	Standard quantity × Fixed overhead application rate
Fixed:	$7,900	$7,000	$7,000	$8,400

$900 U Fixed overhead spending variance
$1,400 F Volume variance

| Total: | $22,900 | $22,730 | $22,600 | $24,000 |

3-way analysis:
$170 U Spending variance
$130 U Variable overhead efficiency variance
$1,400 F Volume variance

2-way analysis:
$300 U Controllable variance
$1,400 F Volume variance

$1,100 F Total overhead variance

4-way analysis applies to the first set of variances above.

[a]For variable overhead, the total overhead applied to work in process is the same as the flexible budget based on standard hours allowed.

Treated as Period Expenses

One viewpoint is that standard costs represent a close approximation to the actual or "true" cost of inventories and cost of goods sold. It is almost impossible to determine the true cost of inventories, but carefully developed standard costs may be the best estimate that management has of the actual cost of production. If this is the case, abnormal deviations from standard costs may be considered to be period expenses rather than inventoriable costs, and variance accounts are closed directly to cost of goods sold or to income summary. In reality, whatever view is taken, insignificant or immaterial variances are also treated as period expenses because of the simplicity of this accounting method.

When cost variances are considered to be period expenses, all variance accounts are closed to either cost of goods sold or to an income summary account. For example, the

FIGURE 16.10 General Framework for Overhead Variance Analysis

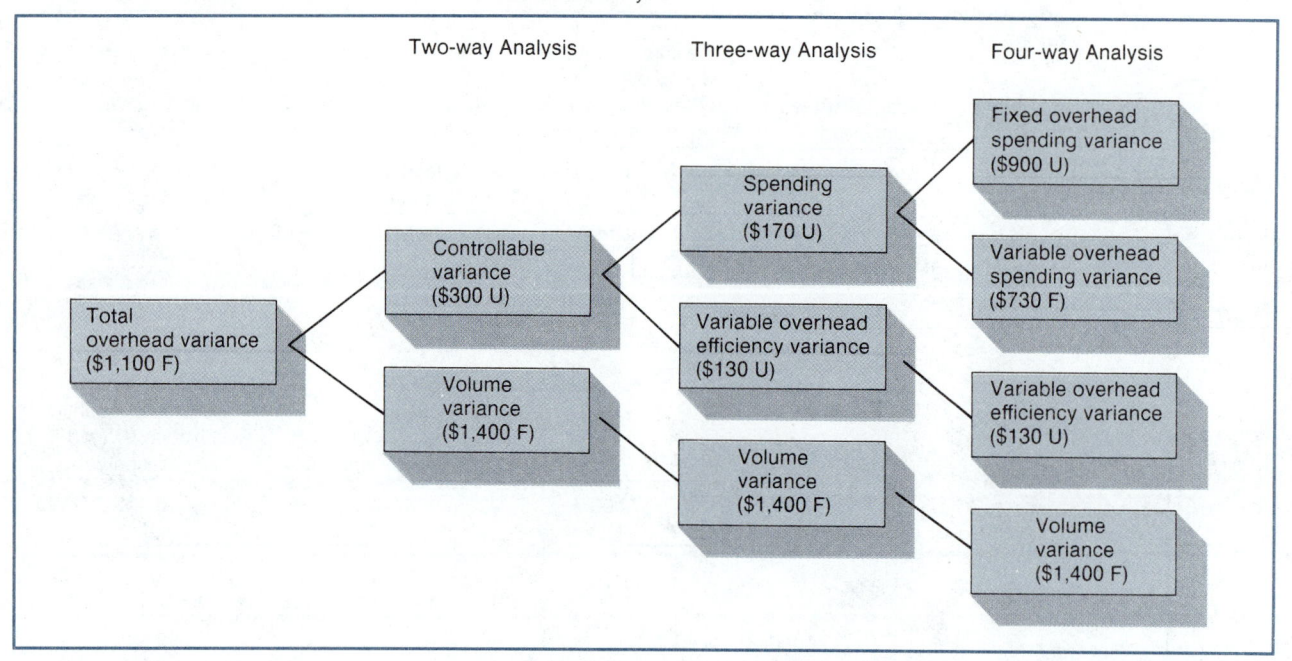

Two-way Analysis | Three-way Analysis | Four-way Analysis

- Total overhead variance ($1,100 F)
  - Controllable variance ($300 U)
    - Spending variance ($170 U)
      - Fixed overhead spending variance ($900 U)
      - Variable overhead spending variance ($730 F)
    - Variable overhead efficiency variance ($130 U)
      - Variable overhead efficiency variance ($130 U)
  - Volume variance ($1,400 F)
    - Volume variance ($1,400 F)
      - Volume variance ($1,400 F)

FIGURE 16.11 Overhead Report

Department 1
Variable Overhead Spending Variance

Item	Actual Expenditure	Flexible Budget for Variable Overhead (based on actual hours used)	Variance
Indirect labor	$11,500	$12,050	$550 F
Supplies	2,460	2,680	220 F
Repairs	1,040	1,000	40 U
Total	$15,000	$15,730	$730 F

Fixed Overhead Spending Variance

Item	Actual Expenditure	Budgeted Amount	
Supervision	$ 5,700	$ 5,000	700 U
Insurance	1,500	1,300	200 U
Depreciation	500	500	0
Taxes	200	200	0
Total	$ 7,900	$ 7,000	$900 U
Variable overhead efficiency variance			$ 130 U
Volume variance			1,400 F
Total overhead variance			$ 1,100 F

FIGURE 16.12

Schedule of Variances

Materials price variance	$ 500 U
Materials usage variance	700 F
Labor rate variance	1,000 U
Labor efficiency variance	400 F
Total overhead variance	1,100 F
Total	$ 700 F

journal entry to close the variance accounts given in figure 16.12 using this method is as follows:

Materials usage variance	700	
Labor efficiency variance	400	
Factory overhead	1,100	
Cost of goods sold (income summary)		700
Materials price variance		500
Labor rate variance		1,000

Figure 16.13 illustrates the financial statement presentation when cost variances are closed to income summary. Note that all inventories are carried on the balance sheet at standard cost.

A refinement of this procedure is to recognize that part of the materials price variance relates to materials inventory at the end of the accounting period. For example, part of the $500 materials price variance in the preceding example relates to materials that are still in the materials inventory. The accounting procedure may be modified by prorating the materials price variance between the materials inventory and the income summary. To illustrate, assume that the balance of the materials inventory account at the end of the period

FIGURE 16.13

Financial Statement Presentation When Variances are Closed to Income Summary

Partial Income Statement
For the Period Ending December 31, 19X8

Sales		$580,000
Cost of goods sold (at standard)		360,000
Gross profit (at standard)		$220,000
Plus: Net standard cost variances		700
Gross profit (adjusted)		$220,700
Less: Distribution expenses	$110,000	
General and administrative expenses	50,000	160,000
Income from operations		$ 60,700

Partial Balance Sheet
December 31, 19X8

Inventories (at standard):	
Finished goods	$ 40,000
Work in process	34,000
Materials	20,000
Total	$ 94,000

represents 10 percent of the purchases made during the period. To prorate the materials price variance and close variance accounts, the following journal entry could be made:

Materials inventory (10% of $500)	50	
Materials usage variance	700	
Labor efficiency variance	400	
Factory overhead	1,100	
Cost of goods sold (income summary)		750
Materials price variance		500
Labor rate variance		1,000

Treated as Inventoriable Costs

The alternative to treating cost variances as period expenses is to treat them as inventoriable costs. The purpose of prorating variances as inventoriable costs is to adjust the standard cost to an actual cost. This is the most theoretically correct method, and it is used when variances are significant or material in size. This method is also used when standard costs are thought to be artificial and do not represent the actual cost of production and cost of goods sold.

When this method is used, cost variances are allocated among inventories (materials, work in process, and finished goods) and cost of goods sold. Then the cost of goods sold at standard cost plus a prorated share of standard cost variances is closed to income summary. With this method, inventories appear on the balance sheet at their standard cost plus a prorated share of standard cost variances.

Several methods can be used to allocate overhead variances. Care should be taken to avoid using a more involved method than the benefits from it justify. One method, which is illustrated on page 000, adopts the rationale that cost variances should be prorated in proportion to the standard-cost balances in the related inventory and cost-of-goods-sold accounts. For example, the materials price variance is allocated to the materials inventory, work in process, finished goods, and cost of goods sold in proportion to the amount of standard materials cost in each account. The materials quantity variance is allocated to work in process, finished goods, and cost of goods sold in proportion to the amount of standard materials cost in these accounts.

The rationale for not allocating any materials quantity variance to materials inventory is that the quantity variance relates to the *usage* of materials and not to the *acquisition* of materials. Therefore, the allocation of materials quantity variance to materials inventory would not be appropriate.

Labor and overhead variances are allocated to work in process, finished goods, and cost of goods sold in proportion to the amount of the respective labor and overhead standard costs in each of these accounts.

The procedure, percentage computations, and variance allocations for this method are shown in figure 16.14. Account balances and variance amounts are either assumed or are taken from the example in this chapter.

The journal entry to record the disposition of standard cost variances in accordance with the allocations in figure 16.14 is as follows:

Materials	66	
Materials usage variance	700	
Labor efficiency variance	400	
Factory overhead	1,100	
Work in process		61
Finished goods		69
Cost of goods sold		636
Materials price variance		500
Labor rate variance		1,000

FIGURE 16.14

Percentages of Costs in Inventories and Cost of Goods Sold

Percentages of Costs in Inventories and Cost of Goods Sold

Item		Materials Inventory	Work in Process	Finished Goods	Cost of Goods Sold	Total/ Percent
Materials:						
—(Including materials inventory)	Amount:	$20,000	$10,200	$12,000	$108,000	$150,200
	Percent:	{13.3%}	{6.8%}	{8.0%}	{71.9%}	{100.0%}
—(Excluding materials inventory)	Amount:		$10,200	$12,000	$108,000	$130,200
	Percent:		{7.8%}	{9.2%}	{83.0%}	{100.0%}
Labor:	Amount:		$14,200	$16,800	$151,000	$182,000
	Percent:		{7.8%}	{9.2%}	{83.0%}	{100.0%}
Overhead:	Amount:		$ 9,600	$11,200	$101,000	$121,800
	Percent		{7.8%}	{9.2%}	{83.0%}	{100.0%}
Total amount		$20,000	$34,000	$40,000	$360,000	

Proration of Variances Based on Preceding Percentages

Allocated to:

Variance	Amount	Materials Inventory	Work in Process	Finished Goods	Cost of goods Sold
Materials price	$ 500 U	$66	$ 34	$ 40	$ 360
Materials usage	700 F		(55)[a]	(64)	(581)
Labor rate	1,000 U		78	92	830
Labor efficiency	400 F		(32)	(36)	(332)
Overhead	1,100 F		(86)	(101)	(913)
Total	$ 700 F	$66	$(61)	$(69)	$(636)

[a] Amounts in parentheses indicate credit items necessary to close favorable variance account balances.

The financial statement presentation that would result when standard cost variances are allocated in this fashion is shown in figure 16.15.

A comparison of income from operations obtained when variances are treated as period expenses (figure 16.13) and when variances are treated as inventoriable costs (figure 16.15) shows a difference of $64 ($60,700 − $60,636) more income when variances are allocated. This difference can be reconciled by computing the difference between inventory balances in the examples. Thus there is a potential impact on financial statements of closing cost variances to income summary versus allocating cost variances to inventories and cost of goods sold. The difference in this example is immaterial in amount; however, in other situations the difference could be quite substantial.

As a final note, budgeted fixed factory overhead, by definition, remains constant at all levels of output over the relevant range of productive activity. Therefore, it would seem reasonable to treat fixed factory overhead as a lump sum period expense rather than as an inventoriable cost like direct materials, direct labor, and variable factory overhead. In fact, there is an accounting method explained in chapter 19 known as direct costing that does treat fixed overhead as a period expense. However, direct costing is only used for internal

FIGURE 16.15

Financial Statement Presentation When Variances are Allocated to Inventories and Cost of Goods Sold

Partial Income Statement
For the Period Ending December 31, 19X8

Sales		$580,000
Cost of goods sold		359,364
Gross profit		$220,636
Less: Distribution expenses	$110,000	
General and administrative expenses	50,000	160,000
Income from operations		$ 60,637

Partial Balance Sheet
December 31, 19X8

Inventories:	
Finished goods	$ 39,931
Work in process	33,940
Materials	20,066
Total	$ 93,937

management purposes. Generally accepted accounting principles for external reporting require all factory overhead to be assigned to units of production. The method of accounting that is used to assign all overhead to units of production is called *full or absorption costing*. It is so named because inventory is assigned the full cost of production, including the cost of fixed overhead, as illustrated in this chapter.

SUMMARY

Standard costs for factory overhead are used in the same general way that standard costs for materials and labor are used. When developing a flexible budget for factory overhead, however, the process is slightly different. Because of the indirect nature of overhead costs, total overhead is first compiled and standard overhead application rates are then calculated. Finally, these standard overhead application rates are used to develop standard costs for factory overhead.

The use of standard costs for factory overhead makes it possible to analyze why actual expenditures for factory overhead may have differed from budgeted or expected amounts. The total difference, called the total overhead variance, can be analyzed at various levels of detail.

The first level of detail, called a two-way analysis, breaks down the total overhead variance into a controllable variance and a volume variance. The volume variance gives the difference between budgeted fixed factory overhead and applied fixed factory overhead. A volume variance results because the actual level of activity differs from the budgeted level of activity. The controllable variance relates to factors such as the price paid for overhead items and the efficiency with which overhead items are utilized.

The next level of detail, called a three-way analysis, separates the controllable variance into a spending variance and a variable overhead efficiency variance. The variable overhead efficiency variance helps to evaluate the efficiency with which the activity base (such as direct labor) is utilized. The spending variance indicates how well actual overhead expenditures were kept within the budget independent of the efficiency with which the activity base was utilized.

The final level of detail, called a four-way analysis, divides the spending variance into a variable overhead spending variance and a fixed overhead spending variance. The variable overhead spending variance gives the difference between budgeted expenditures and actual expenditures for variable overhead that were caused by differences in prices. This variance is somewhat like the materials price variance or the labor rate variance. The fixed overhead spending variance gives any difference between actual fixed overhead incurred and budgeted fixed costs.

There are two ways to account for standard cost variances at the end of an accounting period. First, standard cost variances may be treated as period expenses. When this treatment is used, variance accounts are simply closed to either the cost-of-goods-sold or the income summary account.

The second method of handling standard cost variances is to treat them as inventoriable costs. When using this treatment, the balances in the variance accounts are allocated among inventories (materials, work in process, and finished goods) and cost of goods sold.

These principles of accounting for standard costs for factory overhead are intended to accomplish the dual objectives of providing information for product costing and providing feedback to management for planning and control.

APPENDIX 16.1 Process Costing and Standard Costs

With process-costing methods, standard costs take the place of costs per equivalent unit of production. To illustrate, figure 16.16 presents a cost production report that uses standard costs. The following data are also needed to develop the cost of production report.

Standard Costs

Per Unit

Materials	$0.70
Labor	0.80
Overhead	0.60
Total	$2.10

Production Statistics

	Units
Work-in-process beginning inventory	6,000
(Materials 100% complete; labor and overhead 75% complete)	
Started in process	80,000
Completed and transferred out	78,000
Work-in-process ending inventory	8,000
(Materials 100% complete; labor and overhead 85% complete)	

Accounting Statistics

Work-in-process beginning inventory:	
Materials	$ 4,200
Labor	3,600
Overhead	2,700
Total	$ 10,500
Costs of the current period:	
Materials	$ 55,340
Labor	65,760
Overhead	49,200
Total	$170,300
Total costs to account for	$180,800

The most important thing to observe in figure 16.16 is that costs per equivalent unit are not calculated as they are when using either weighted-average or FIFO methods. Stan-

FIGURE 16.16

Assembly Department
Cost of Production Report
(using standard costs)

	Physical Units	Percentage Completion		
		Materials	Labor	Overhead
Units accounted for as follows:				
Work in process, beginning	6,000	100%	75%	75%
Transferred in this period	80,000			
Total units to account for	86,000			
Completed and transferred out	78,000			
Work in process, ending	8,000	100%	85%	85%

	Total	Materials	Labor	Overhead
Costs to account for:				
Work in process, beginning	$ 10,500	$ 4,200	$ 3,600	$ 2,700
Costs of the current period	170,300	55,340	65,760	49,200
Total costs to account for	$180,800	$59,540	$69,360	$51,900
Equivalent units of production:				
Complete work in process, beginning			1,500	1,500
Started and completed		72,000	72,000	72,000
Work in process, ending		8,000	6,800	6,800
Total equivalent units		80,000	80,300	80,300
Cost per equivalent unit	$ 2.100	$ 0.700	$ .800	$ .600
Costs accounted for as follows:				
Costs transferred out:				
Work in process, beginning	$ 10,500	$ 4,200	$ 3,600	$ 2,700
Work completed on work in process, beginning	2,100		1,200[1]	900[2]
Work started and completed	151,200	50,400[3]	57,600[4]	43,200[5]
Total	$163,800	$54,600	$62,400	$46,800
Work in process, ending	15,120	5,600[6]	5,440[7]	4,080[8]
Total standard costs	$178,920	$60,200	$67,840	$50,880
Total costs to acount for	180,800	59,540	69,360	51,900
Cost variances	$ 1,880 U	$ 660 F	$ 1,520 U	$ 1,020 U

1. 1,500 × $0.80 = $ 1,200
2. 1,500 × $0.60 = $ 900
3. 72,000 × $0.70 = $50,400
4. 72,000 × $0.80 = $57,600
5. 72,000 × $0.60 = $43,200
6. 8,000 × $0.70 = $ 5,600
7. 6,800 × $0.80 = $ 5,440
8. 6,800 × $0.60 = $ 4,080

dard per-unit costs are used in place of costs per equivalent unit. This results in goods transferred out and work-in-process ending inventory being costed at standard rather than at actual costs, which facilitates the comparison of actual with budgeted results. For example, actual costs incurred by the department contained in "total costs to account for" and budgeted amounts contained in "total standard costs" are compared to determine what differences incurred, if any. This is done by subtracting the "total standard costs" from the "total costs to account for," resulting in "cost variances" as shown on the report.

A final observation about the mechanics of constructing a cost of production report with standard costs is that costs are assigned to inventories as with the FIFO method. This emphasizes the results of current-period operations and facilitates the analysis of variances because costs of two periods are not mingled.

The use of standard costs is a completely general procedure relative to job-order, process, or hybrid costing systems; in other words, it is a modification of each of these basic systems rather than a separate or different type of costing system. Comparing the usefulness of standard costs to the various basic costing systems makes it apparent that standard costs and process costing form the best partnership. The continuous-flow, mass-production environment of process costing lends itself best to the use of budgets as a tool for management control. Variances provide valuable information for analyzing and adjusting mass-production processes.

The use of standard costs also overcomes many of the conflicts between weighted-average and FIFO methods. This is especially true in manufacturing situations in which there are several ways that inputs can be combined to produce a variety of similar products. For example, a manufacturer of bone china uses various clays, finishing processes, and glazes on product pieces with varying finishes, shapes, and sizes. When many such combinations are possible, the averaging inherent in process costing may not provide sufficient detail for product costing or control purposes. However, it may not be practical to modify process-costing procedures because of the many possible alternatives that may arise. In such situations, standard costs provide a more reasonable approach to providing useful cost information.

SELF-STUDY PROBLEM

Bloomington Products specializes in the production of a single component used in automobile transmissions. Engineering estimates and financial forecasts have yielded the following standard costs per unit:

Materials (10 pounds @ $3 per pound)	$30
Labor (2 hours @ $12 per hour)	24
Variable overhead (2 hours @ $2 per hour)	4
Fixed overhead (2 hours @ $4 per hour)	8
Total standard cost per unit	$66

The total flexible budget for factory overhead indicates that the company expects total overhead to be $120,000 at a standard activity level of 20,000 direct-labor hours.

Actual expenditures for the period are listed below. There were no beginning or ending inventories of materials.

Materials	$450,000
Labor	332,000
Variable overhead	48,000
Fixed overhead	82,000
Total costs	$912,000
Actual units produced	12,000
Actual cost per unit	$ 76

When the shop foreman saw that the actual cost of production was $76 per unit, he explained that his operation had performed beyond expectations and that others in the organization were responsible for the large cost overrun. For example, he pointed out that purchasing had paid $3.60 for materials that were expected to cost only $3.00 per pound, and that personnel had conceded to a wage increase resulting in the average wage rate being $13.28 rather than $12.00. The shop foreman remarked, "I am responsible for all quantity and efficiency variances, but it is clear that we have done our job or else the cost overrun would be even larger than it is!"

Required

You have been asked to analyze the situation and prepare a brief report indicating how much of the responsibility for the large cost overrun, if any, rests with the shop foreman.

Solution to the Self-Study Problem

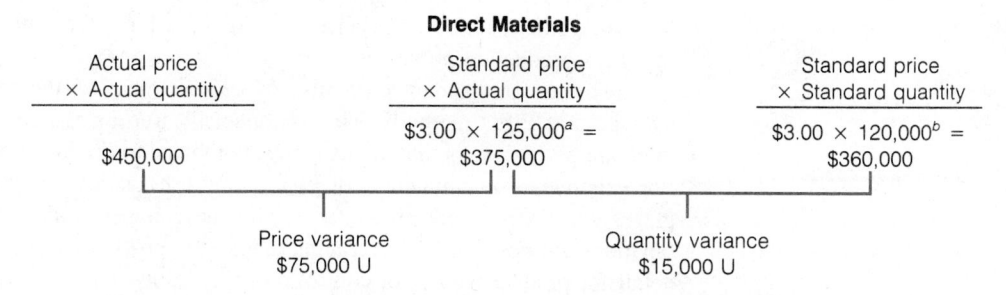

Direct Materials

Actual price × Actual quantity	Standard price × Actual quantity	Standard price × Standard quantity
$450,000	$3.00 × 125,000[a] = $375,000	$3.00 × 120,000[b] = $360,000

Price variance $75,000 U

Quantity variance $15,000 U

[a]Actual materials purchased and used = $450,000 ÷ $3.60 per pound = 125,000 pounds.
[b]Standard materials allowed for 12,000 units of output = 12,000 units × 10 pounds allowed per unit = 120,000 total pounds allowed.

Direct Labor

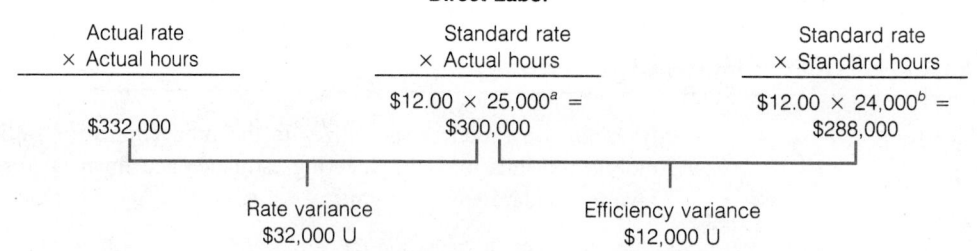

Actual rate × Actual hours	Standard rate × Actual hours	Standard rate × Standard hours
$332,000	$12.00 × 25,000[a] = $300,000	$12.00 × 24,000[b] = $288,000

Rate variance $32,000 U

Efficiency variance $12,000 U

[a]Actual labor hours used = $332,000 ÷ $13.28 per hour = 25,000 hours.
[b]Standard hours allowed for 12,000 units = 12,000 units × 2 hours per unit = 24,000 hours.

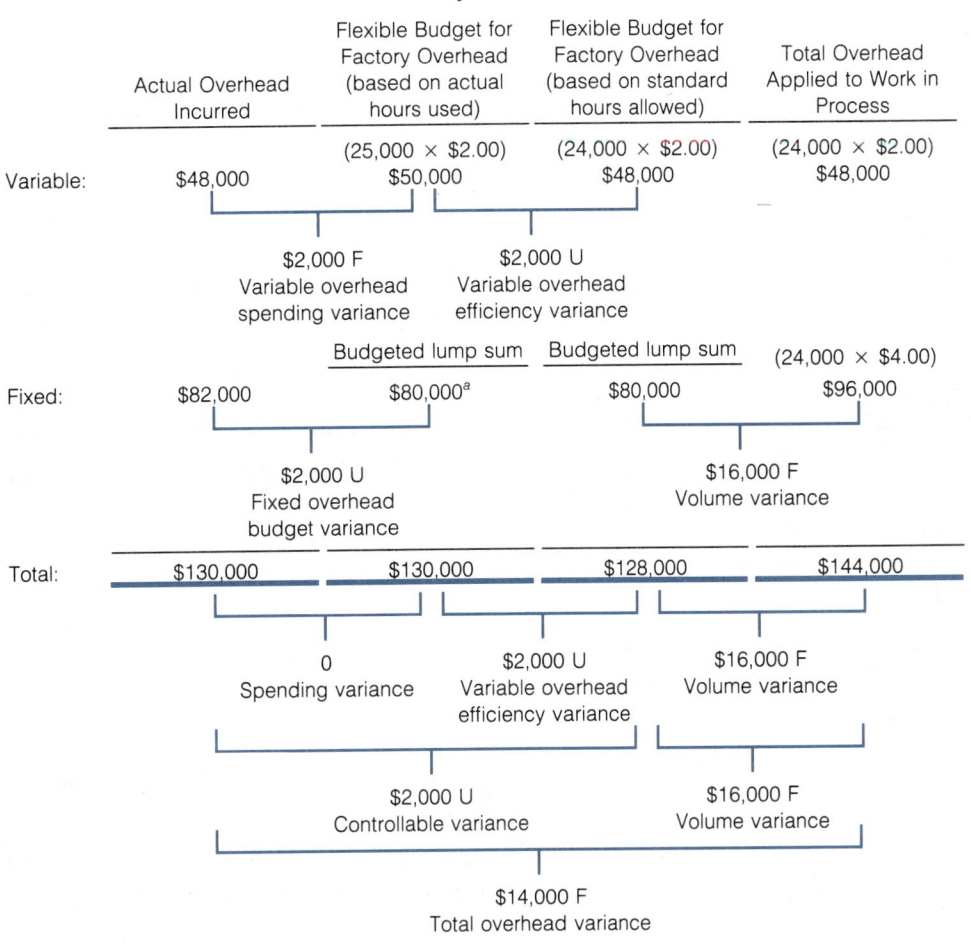

Factory Overhead

	Actual Overhead Incurred	Flexible Budget for Factory Overhead (based on actual hours used)	Flexible Budget for Factory Overhead (based on standard hours allowed)	Total Overhead Applied to Work in Process
Variable:	$48,000	(25,000 × $2.00) $50,000	(24,000 × $2.00) $48,000	(24,000 × $2.00) $48,000

$2,000 F Variable overhead spending variance
$2,000 U Variable overhead efficiency variance

		Budgeted lump sum	Budgeted lump sum	(24,000 × $4.00)
Fixed:	$82,000	$80,000[a]	$80,000	$96,000

$2,000 U Fixed overhead budget variance
$16,000 F Volume variance

| Total: | $130,000 | $130,000 | $128,000 | $144,000 |

0 Spending variance
$2,000 U Variable overhead efficiency variance
$16,000 F Volume variance

$2,000 U Controllable variance
$16,000 F Volume variance

$14,000 F Total overhead variance

[a] $120,000 @ 20,000 direct labor hours
   − 40,000 variable overhead (20,000 hours × $2.00 per hour)
   $ 80,000

Summary of Variances Controllable by Department Managers

Controllable by Shop Foreman

Materials quantity variance	$15,000 U	
Labor efficiency variance	12,000 U	
Variable overhead efficiency variance	2,000 U	
Total controllable by shop foreman	$29,000 U	21%

Controllable by Other Department Managers

Materials price variance	$75,000 U	
Labor rate variance	32,000 U	
Variable overhead spending variance	2,000 F	
Total	$109,000 U	79%
Total controllable by department managers	$138,000 U	100%

SUGGESTED READINGS

Aggarwal, Sumer C. "Manager, Manage Thyself." *Business Horizons* 26 (January–February 1983): 25–30.

Bulloch, James. "Analysis of Standard Cost Variances." In *Accountants' Cost Handbook,* 3rd ed. New York: John Wiley 1983, 10-1–10-51.

Inman, Mark Lee. "Overhead Absorption Variance Analysis: Compounding the Problem?" *Management Accounting* 63 (Eng.) (September 1985): 30–31.

Miller, Jeffrey G., and Vollmann, Thomas E. "Hidden Factory." *Harvard Business Review* 63 (September–October 1985): 142–150.

Mister, William G. "Note on the Interpretation of Standard Cost Variances." *Journal of Accounting Education* 1 (Fall 1983): 51–56.

DISCUSSION QUESTIONS

Q16–1. What are standard costs for overhead? Explain how they relate to standard costs for materials and labor.

Q16–2. Outline the accounting process for using standard costs for overhead.

Q16–3. What is a standard activity level and how is it used?

Q16–4. Explain the general procedure used to develop a flexible budget for factory overhead.

Q16–5. What are standard overhead application rates and how are they used?

Q16–6. What is the relationship between standard overhead application rates and standard costs?

Q16–7. Give journal entries with hypothetical numbers to record actual and applied *(a)* variable overhead and *(b)* fixed overhead.

Q16–8. "Fixed overhead is applied to work in process as though it is a variable cost." Explain this concept and provide graphs of budgeted and applied fixed costs to support your explanation.

Q16–9. What are the consequences of using a fixed overhead application rate to apply fixed overhead to work in process as though it is a variable cost?

Q16–10. Define *volume variance* and explain what is responsible for its incurrence.

Q16–11. What is a favorable volume and an unfavorable volume variance?

Q16–12. Define *total overhead variance* and sketch the general framework for its analysis.

Q16–13. Present the framework and related formulas for analyzing the total overhead variance using *(a)* a two-way analysis, *(b)* a three-way analysis, and *(c)* a four-way analysis.

Q16–14. Give an outline of an overhead variance report suitable for management reporting. How might this report be different if fixed overhead variances are controllable only at higher levels of management?

Q16–15. Explain two methods of accounting for standard cost variances at the end of an accounting period.

Q16–16. What is the difference between full costing and direct costing?

EXERCISES

E16–1. Overhead Spending and Efficiency Variances
The following information has been obtained for the Barkley Company:

	Budget per Standard Direct-Labor Hour	Actual Costs
Direct labor	$1.55	$37,200
Direct materials	1.40	32,400
Controllable overhead costs:		
Indirect materials	0.90	21,360
Indirect labor	0.75	18,240
Supplies	0.20	4,800
Lubricants	0.16	4,800
Maintenance	0.14	3,120
Repairs	0.21	4,800
Other	0.09	2,160

Normal capacity: 25,750 direct-labor hours
Standard direct-labor hours allowed: 25,000
Actual direct-labor hours: 24,000

Required

Determine the efficiency and spending variances for overhead. Indicate whether the variances are favorable or unfavorable.

E16–2. Standard Cost Concepts and Procedures—Two-way Analysis
Information on Ripley Company's overhead costs for January production activity is as follows:

Budgeted fixed overhead	$75,000
Standard fixed overhead rate per direct-labor hour	$3
Standard variable overhead rate per direct-labor hour	$6
Standard direct labor allowed for actual production	24,000 hours
Actual total overhead incurred	$220,000

Ripley has a standard cost and flexible budgeting system and uses the two-way analysis method for overhead variances.

Required

Determine the overhead controllable and volume variances for January.

E16–3. Standard Cost Variance for Overhead
Union Company uses a standard cost accounting system. The following overhead costs and production data are available for August:

Standard fixed overhead rate per direct-labor hour	$1.00
Standard variable overhead rate per direct-labor hour	$4.00
Normal monthly direct-labor hours	40,000 hours
Actual direct-labor hours worked	39,500 hours
Standard direct-labor hours allowed for actual production	39,000 hours
Overall overhead variance—favorable	$2,000

Required

1. Determine the amount of overhead applied for August.
2. Determine the amount of actual overhead incurred during August.
3. Assume that the Union Company uses the three-way variance method. Determine the overhead spending, efficiency, and volume variances.

E16–4. Standard Cost Concepts—Two-way Analysis
Dickey Company had total underapplied overhead of $15,000 during March. Additional information is as follows:

Variable Overhead

Applied based on standard direct-labor hours allowed	$42,000
Budgeted based on standard direct-labor hours	42,000

Fixed Overhead

Applied based on standard direct-labor hours allowed	$30,000
Budgeted based on standard direct-labor hours	27,000

Required

1. Determine the actual total overhead incurred during March.
2. Assume the Dickey Company uses the two-way analysis method. Determine the overhead controllable and volume variances.

16–5. Standards for Factory Overhead—Three-way Analysis
Miriam Company uses a standard cost system to monitor its overhead costs. For the month of June, the following data have been extracted from Miriam Company's records:

Overhead budget (based on 6,000 hours)	
Fixed overhead	$6,600
Variable overhead	$10,200
Results for June:	
Actual overhead (variable)	$10,400
Actual overhead (fixed)	$6,500
Actual direct-labor hours	6,100 hours
Standard hours allowed for good output	6,200 hours

Required

1. Prepare an electronic spreadsheet to calculate overhead variances for Miriam Company, using a three-way analysis.
2. Prepare journal entries to record overhead expenses and overhead variances in separate ledger accounts for June.

E16–6. Standards and Variable Factory Overhead Variances (CMA)
Modelo Company has developed overhead costs based on a capacity of 180,000 direct-labor hours as follows:

Standard costs per unit:		
Variable portion	2 hours @ $3 =	$ 6
Fixed portion	2 hours @ $5 =	10
		$16

During April, 85,000 units were scheduled for production, but only 80,000 units were actually produced. The following data relate to April:

1. The actual direct-labor cost incurred was $644,000 for 165,000 actual hours of work.
2. The actual overhead incurred totaled $1,378,000—$518,000 variable and $860,000 fixed.
3. All inventories are carried at standard cost.

Required

1. Determine the variable overhead spending variance for April.
2. Determine the variable overhead efficiency variance for April.

3. Determine the fixed overhead spending variance for April.
4. Determine the overhead volume variance for April.

E16–7. Standards and Variable Factory Overhead Variances

King Company estimates that it will operate its manufacturing facilities at 800,000 direct-labor hours for the year. The estimate for total budgeted overhead is $2,000,000. The standard variable overhead rate is estimated to be $2 per direct-labor hour or $6 per unit. The actual data for the year are as follows:

Actual finished units	250,000 units
Actual direct-labor hours	764,000 hours
Actual variable overhead	$1,610,000
Actual fixed overhead	$392,000

Required

1. Determine the variable overhead spending variance for the year.
2. Determine the variable overhead efficiency variance for the year.
3. Determine the fixed overhead spending variance for the year.
4. Determine the overhead volume variance for the year.

Refer to the following data for exercises 8 through 11.

McQueen Furniture Creations uses a standard cost approach in its accounting system. For the month of April, the following information has been collected:

Normal capacity (in direct-labor hours)	4,000 hours
Total overhead at normal capacity	
Fixed	$ 6,400
Variable	9,600
Total	$16,000
Overhead rate per direct-labor hour	
Fixed	$ 1.60
Variable	2.40
Total	$ 4.00
Actual overhead	$15,200
Actual direct-labor hours	3,475 hours
Standard hours allowed for actual production	3,400 hours

E16–8. Standard Costs and Overhead Variances—Two-way Analysis

Refer to the preceding data.

Required

1. Determine the manufacturing overhead variances for McQueen Furniture Creations using a two-way analysis.
2. Prepare journal entries for the overhead expenses and overhead variances in separate ledger accounts in April using a two-way variance analysis.

E16–9. Standards for Factory Overhead—Three-way Analysis

Refer to the preceding data.

Required

1. Determine the manufacturing overhead variances for McQueen Furniture Creations using a three-way analysis.
2. Prepare journal entries for the overhead expenses and overhead variances in separate ledger accounts in April using a three-way variance analysis.

E16–10. Standards for Factory Overhead—Four-way Analysis
Refer to the preceding data. Also assume that actual fixed overhead is $6,600 of the $15,200 total actual overhead.

Required

1. Determine the manufacturing overhead variances for McQueen Furniture Creations using a four-way analysis.
2. Prepare journal entries for the overhead expenses and overhead variances in separate ledger accounts in April using a four-way variance analysis.

E16–11. Standards for Factory Overhead—Four-way Analysis
Refer to the preceding data. Also assume that the variable portion of total actual overhead expenditures made during April amounted to $8,600.

Required

Prepare an electronic spreadsheet to calculate manufacturing overhead variances for McQueen Furniture Creations using a four-way analysis.

E16–12. Overhead Variances
The following data have been made available from the records of JDL Manufacturing Company. Budgeted production was 1,000 units. Actual production was 1,200 units.

```
Standard:
    Direct labor       — 2 hours per unit at $5.00 per hour
    Factory overhead — $1 per direct-labor hour (variable) $500 (fixed)
Actual:
    Direct labor       — 2,100 hours at $4.00 per hour
    Factory overhead — $2,010 (variable)  $ 505 (fixed)
```

Required

Prepare an electronic spreadsheet to calculate the following overhead variances:

- Controllable variance
- Volume variance
- Variable overhead spending variance
- Variable overhead efficiency variance
- Fixed overhead spending variance

PROBLEMS

P16–1. Materials, Labor, and Factory Overhead Standards and Variances
Armando Corporation manufactures a product with the following standard costs:

Direct materials—20 yards @ $1.35 per yard	$27
Direct labor—4 hours @ $9.00 per hour	36
Factory overhead—applied at 5/6 of direct labor	
Ratio of variable costs to fixed costs: 2 to 1	30
Total standard cost per unit of output	$93

Standards are based on normal monthly production involving 2,400 direct-labor hours (600 units of output).

The following information pertains to the month of July:

Direct materials purchased—18,000 yards @ $1.38 per yard		$24,840
Direct materials used—9,500 yards		
Direct labor—2,100 hours @ $9.15 per hour		19,215
Actual factory overhead		16,650

In July, 500 units of the product were actually produced.

Required

1. Prepare schedules computing the following:
    a. Variable factory overhead rate per direct-labor hour
    b. Total fixed factory overhead based on normal activity
2. Prepare the following schedules for the month of July, indicating whether each variance is favorable or unfavorable:
    a. Materials price variance (based on purchases)
    b. Materials usage variance
    c. Labor rate variance
    d. Labor efficiency variance
    e. Controllable factory overhead variance
    f. Factory overhead volume variance

P16–2. Standard Costs, Materials, Labor, and Factory Overhead

Eastern Company manufactures special electrical equipment and parts. Eastern employs a standard cost accounting system with separate standards established for each product.

A special transformer is manufactured in the transformer department. Production volume is measured by direct-labor hours in this department, and a flexible budget system is used to plan and control department overhead.

Standard costs for the special transformer are determined annually in September for the coming year. The standard cost of a transformer was computed to be $67, as shown here:

Direct materials		
Iron	5 sheets @ $2.00	$10.00
Copper	3 spools @ $3.00	9.00
Direct labor	4 hours @ $7.00	28.00
Variable overhead	4 hours @ $3.00	12.00
Fixed overhead	4 hours @ $2.00	8.00
Total		$67.00

Overhead rates were based on normal monthly capacity of 4,000 direct-labor hours. Practical capacity for this department is 5,000 direct-labor hours per month. Variable overhead costs are expected to vary with the number of direct-labor hours actually used.

During October, 800 transformers were produced. This was below expectations because a work stoppage occurred during contract negotiations with the labor force. Once the contract was settled, the department scheduled overtime in an attempt to catch up to expected production levels.

The following costs were incurred in October:

Direct Materials	Direct Materials Purchased	Materials Used
Iron	5,000 sheets @ $2.00 per sheet	3,900 sheets
Copper	2,200 spools @ $3.10 per spool	2,600 spools
Direct labor		
Regular time:	2,000 hours @ $7.00	
	1,400 hours @ $7.20	
Overtime:	600 of the 1,400 hours were subject to overtime premium. The total overtime premium of $2,160 is included in variable overhead in accordance with company accounting practices.	
Variable overhead:	$10,000	
Fixed overhead:	$8,800	

Required

1. Indicate and explain the most appropriate time to record any variation of actual material prices from standard.
2. Determine the total materials quantity variance for October.
3. Determine the labor rate (price) variance for October.
4. Determine the variable overhead spending variance for October.
5. Determine the efficiency variance for variable overhead for October.
6. Determine the spending variance for fixed overhead for October.
7. Determine the fixed overhead volume variance for October.
8. Explain the most common cause of an unfavorable fixed overhead volume variance.

P16–3. Materials, Labor, and Overhead Variances

Howard & Sons, Co. has the following standards for its single product, which is processed in one department.

		Per Unit
Direct materials: 0.5 pounds at $3.20		$1.60
Direct labor: 0.1 hours at $7.00		0.70
Factory overhead:		
Fixed—$8 per labor hour	$0.80	
Variable—$4 per labor hour	0.40	1.20
		$3.50

Normal production for a month is 15,000 units or 1,500 hours.

During August, 14,800 units were completed and transferred out. There were 4,000 units in process at August 31 that were 100-percent complete for direct materials and 40-percent complete for conversion costs. Actual costs for August were as follows:

Direct materials:	8,050 pounds at $3.30	= $26,565
Direct labor:	1,420 hours at $7.00	= $ 9,940
Factory overhead:		= $17,410

Required

Compute the following for the month of August:

- Materials quantity variance
- Labor efficiency variance

CHAPTER 16: STANDARD COSTS FOR FACTORY OVERHEAD

- Factory overhead controllable variance
- Factory overhead volume variance
- Standard cost of goods completed and transferred to finished-goods inventory

P16–4. Materials, Labor, and Overhead Variances

The Rapid Manufacturing Company has the following unit standard costs at a normal activity level of 5,000 direct-labor hours per month:

Direct materials (2 kilograms at $5)	$10
Direct labor (1 hour at $6)	6
Factory overhead:	
Variable (1 direct-labor hour at $2)	2
Fixed (1 direct-labor hour at $5)	5
	$23

Budgeted monthly fixed factory overhead is $25,000.

On November 1, work in process consisted of 800 units of product that were 100-percent complete as to materials and 40-percent complete as to conversion costs, with a total assigned standard cost of $12,160. During November the following events occurred:

a. 12,000 kilograms of raw materials were purchased on account at a net delivered cost of $58,800, and 11,000 kilograms were issued to production. Raw materials are inventoried at standard cost.
b. 5,500 units of product were started.
c. 5,700 direct-labor hours were used at a total cost of $35,340.
d. 4,800 units were completed and transferred to finished-goods inventory.
e. Variable overhead costs incurred were $11,200, and fixed overhead costs incurred were $26,500.

The work in process inventory at November 30 consisted of 1,500 units, 100-percent complete as to materials and 70-percent complete as to conversion costs.

Required

Compute the following for the month of November:

- Materials price variance
- Materials quantity variance
- Labor efficiency variance
- Variable overhead efficiency variance
- Factory overhead spending variance
- Volume variance
- Over- or underapplied overhead
- Standard cost of ending work-in-process inventory

P16–5. Standard Costs and Journal Entries

The Frivolous Manufacturing Co. has the following standard costs for a component it produces that is used in the manufacture of large aircraft.

Materials: 10 linear feet of aluminum at $1.00 per foot
Labor: 3 hours at $8 per hour
Overhead: Variable—3 hours at $2 per hour
           Fixed—$2 per hour
Normal capacity is 2,500 direct-labor hours per month.

The following are results of the most recent month's activity:

700 components were produced.
7,500 linear feet of materials were purchased at a cost of $9,000.
7,200 linear feet of materials were used in production.
2,300 labor hours were worked at a cost of $18,860.
Actual factory overhead was $5,200 variable and $5,100 fixed.

Required

Prepare journal entries to record the following:

- Purchase and use of materials, assuming that *(a)* materials are carried at standard cost and *(b)* materials are carried at actual cost
- Labor used in production
- Factory overhead *(a)* incurred and *(b)* charged to production (See the next requirement before making these entries.)
- Overhead variances. Also, prepare journal entries to close the overhead control account assuming that *(a)* two-way variance analysis is used and *(b)* four-way variance analysis is used.

P16-6. Standard Cost Concepts and Procedures

Owl-Wobber Manufacturing Company uses a standard cost system to account for the cost of production of its only product—product A. The standards for the production of one unit of product A are as follows:

Direct materials: 10 feet of item 1 at $0.75 per foot and 3 feet of item 2 at $1 per foot.
Direct labor: 4 hours at $15 per hour.
Factory overhead is applied at 150% of standard direct-labor costs.

There was no inventory on hand at May 1, 19X2. The following is a summary of cost-related data for the production of product A during the year ended April 30, 19X3:

100,000 feet of item 1 were purchased at $0.78 per foot.
30,000 feet of item 2 were purchased at $0.90 per foot.
8,000 units of product A were produced, which required 78,000 feet of item 1, 26,000 feet of item 2, and 31,000 hours of direct labor at $16 per hour.
6,000 units of product A were sold.

At April 30, 19X3, there are 22,000 feet of item 1, 4,000 feet of item 2, and 2,000 completed units of product A on hand. All purchases and transfers are "charged in" at standard cost.

Required

1. Determine for the year ending April 30, 19X3, the total debits to the raw materials account for the purchase of item 1.
2. Determine for the year ending April 30, 19X3, the total debits to the work-in-process account for direct labor.
3. Determine for the year ending April 30, 19X3, the total debits to the work-in-process account for factory overhead.
4. Determine the balance in the materials efficiency variance account for item 2.
5. If all standard variances are prorated to inventories and cost of goods sold, determine the amount of materials efficiency variance for item 2 to be prorated to the raw materials inventory.
6. If all standard variances are prorated to inventories and cost of goods sold, determine

the amount of materials price variance for item 1 to be prorated to the raw materials inventory.

P16–7. Standard Costs and Flexible Budgets Oldetta Huffy, production manager for C. H. L. Incorporated, evaluates the performance of the production departments by comparing budget and standard costs with actual costs. The following data were collected for department 88 during last year:

	Budget Data		Actual Data	
Factory Overhead	Variable	Fixed	Variable	Fixed
Indirect labor	$31,500		$33,000	
Indirect materials	22,400		25,300	
Supplies	1,910		2,200	
Maintenance	2,020	800	2,200	800
Repairs	1,740	1,200	1,980	1,200
Depreciation		4,800		4,800
Supervision		19,800		19,800
Rent		1,510		1,510
Miscellaneous	430	890	440	890
Total	$60,000	$29,000	$65,120	$29,000

The overhead rate, used to apply the preceding overhead budget to work in process, is computed by using a normal capacity base equivalent to 80 percent of theoretical capacity.

Theoretical capacity (100 percent) for department 88 is 25,000 direct-labor hours, and the standard number of direct-labor hours allowed is 21,000. Department 88 actually incurred 22,000 direct-labor hours during the year.

Required

1. Develop a flexible budget for the following capacity levels: 70, 80, 90, and 100 percent. Include unit costs for variable overhead, fixed overhead, and total overhead.
2. Assuming that the fixed costs are not controllable, prepare a performance report comparing the flexible budget with actual results for department 88. Include variances and indicate whether they are favorable or unfavorable.
3. Since the company maintains a standard cost system, determine the following variance *only* for total overhead costs (not for each overhead item):
    a. Spending variance
    b. Volume variance
    c. Variable efficiency variance

P16–8. Standard Cost Concepts and Motivation Issues The Kelly Company, founded twenty years ago, has achieved a moderate degree of success. Kelly manufactures and sells pottery items. All manufacturing takes place in one plant with four departments and each manufacturing department produces only one product. The Kelly Company's four products are plaques, cups, vases, and plates. The president and founder credits the company's success to the well-designed, quality products and to an effective cost-control system. The system was installed early in the firm's existence to improve cost control and to serve as a basis for planning.

Kelly Company establishes standard costs for material and labor with the participation of plant management. Each year the plant manager, the department heads, and the time-study engineers are invited by top management to recommend changes in the standards for the next year. Top management reviews these recommendations and the records of actual performance for the current year before setting the new standards. As a general rule, tight standards representing very efficient performance are established. Top management does this so that no inefficiency or slack will be included in cost goals. The plant manager and department heads are charged with cost-control responsibility, and the variances from standard costs are used to measure their performance in carrying out this charge.

No standards are set for factory overhead because the management believes it is too difficult to predict and relate overhead to output. The actual factory overhead for the departments and the plant is accumulated in one pool. The actual overhead is then allocated to the departments on the basis of departmental output. The following schedule is a three-year summary of overhead allocation among the departments.

	19X5		19X6		19X7	
Department	Units Produced	Allocated[a] Overhead	Units Produced	Allocated[a] Overhead	Units Produced	Allocated[a] Overhead
Plaques	300,000	$120,000	330,000	$126,000	180,000	$ 60,000
Cups	250,000	100,000	270,000	103,091	360,000	120,000
Vases	200,000	80,000	220,000	84,000	300,000	100,000
Plates	250,000	100,000	280,000	106,909	360,000	120,000
Totals	1,000,000	$400,000	1,100,000	$420,000	1,200,000	$400,000

[a]Dollar amounts are rounded to the nearest dollar.

Kelly's executives are convinced that more effective cost control can be obtained than is currently being realized from the standard cost system. A review of cost performance for recent years disclosed several factors that led them to this conclusion. The following factors were disclosed:

1. Unfavorable variances were the norm rather than the exception, although the size of the variances was quite uniform.
2. Department managers took steps that, although benefiting their own departments, were detrimental to overall company performance.
3. Employee motivation, especially among firstline supervisors, appeared to be low.

Required

1. What are the probable effects, if any, on the motivation of the plant managers and department heads from (a) the participative standard cost system and (b) the use of tight standards? Explain the reasons for your conclusions.
2. What effect, if any, will the practice of applying actual overhead costs on the basis of the actual units produced have on the motivation of department heads to control overhead costs? Explain your answer.

P16–9. Standard Costs—Reconstructing Data from Given Variances

The Sherman Company has the following budget and standard data for its single product:

Materials—3 gallons at $3 per gallon
Variable factory overhead budget of $160,000 for 80,000 direct-labor hours
Fixed overhead budget of $240,000
Budgeted direct-labor cost for 80,000 hours—$640,000
Labor—2 hours per unit

During May production was below budget, and the following variances from standard were noted:

1. Labor efficiency variance	$16,000 U
2. Materials quantity variance	6,000 U
3. Materials price variance based on purchases ($0.05 per gallon)	5,500 U
4. Labor rate variance	7,200 U
5. Variable overhead spending variance	1,000 U
6. Variable overhead efficiency variance	4,000 U
7. Fixed overhead spending variance	2,000 F
8. Fixed overhead volume variance	30,000 U

Required

1. Determine how many units were produced during May.
2. Determine the actual quantity of materials purchased.
3. Determine the actual labor hours and actual payroll cost.
4. Determine the actual variable and actual fixed overhead incurred.
5. Determine the fixed overhead applied to production.
6. Determine the number of excess gallons and excess labor hours used during May above standard.

P16–10. Overhead Variances, Process Costing, and Variance Disposition

Lundberg Company uses a process-costing system tied to standard costs. The finishing department adds labor and overhead costs to the products received from the blending department.

The standard costs per unit in finishing are as follows:

Labor (one hour)	$6.00
Factory overhead	
Variable	2.50
Fixed	1.25

The standard capacity is 10,000 units.

During March, the finishing department completed and sent to finished goods 9,500 units. It received 9,600 units from blending during March, and it had 500 units in process on March 1 that were ¼ complete and 600 units in process on March 31 that were ⅔ complete.

There were 300 units of finished product in stock on March 31 and none on March 1.

During March, 9,850 labor hours were used; $25,000 of variable overhead was incurred; and $12,400 of fixed overhead was incurred. The actual labor rate was at standard.

Required

1. Determine the variances for labor and factory overhead for March. Use the three-way method of analysis for overhead. Clearly identify the equivalent units produced.
2. Prepare journal entries to record actual labor and overhead costs charged to production, including the variances incurred.
3. Determine the ending inventory standard cost for work in process, finished goods, and cost of goods sold.
4. Assume that Lundberg adjusts all accounts to actual cost for financial statement purposes at the end of each month. Determine the disposition of the labor efficiency variance at March 31 and show the disposition in journal-entry form.

Chapter 17

Mix, Yield, and Variance Investigation

Outline

PRODUCTION MIX AND YIELD
Direct-Materials Mix and Yield Variances
Direct-Labor Mix and Yield Variances
VARIANCE REPORTS
INVESTIGATION OF VARIANCES
Why Variances Occur
Techniques for Deciding When to
    Investigate Variances
Cost-Benefit Evaluation of Investigation

BEHAVIORAL CONSIDERATIONS
SUMMARY
SELF-STUDY PROBLEMS
Mix and Yield
Variance Investigation
SUGGESTED READINGS
DISCUSSION QUESTIONS
EXERCISES
PROBLEMS

A primary objective of cost accounting is to provide information to assist management in planning and controlling operations. The use of standard costs and the analysis of variances in a standard cost system provide important feedback to management for these purposes. The fundamentals of using standard costs for materials and labor were discussed in chapter 15. This chapter examines standard costs for materials and labor in a more complex environment where mix and yield are important considerations.

Variance reports are used along with other types of information to determine which, if any, parts of the manufacturing process may require management's attention and possible corrective action. The decision to investigate a manufacturing process is often difficult, because the presence of a variance does not necessarily indicate an out-of-control situation that requires attention. Some basic guidelines for deciding when a variance indicates a condition that warrants investigation were discussed in chapter 15. In this chapter, statistical techniques that are useful as decision aids for determining when to investigate variances are examined.

After completing this chapter, you should be able to:

1. explain the meaning of mix and yield as they relate to the use of materials and labor in a standard cost system.
2. calculate mix and yield variances for materials and labor.
3. explain how each variance is useful for management.
4. use statistical techniques to determine when it is appropriate to investigate variances.

PRODUCTION MIX AND YIELD

Mix refers to the relative proportion of components in a mixture. There are two general categories of mix that are of concern in cost accounting. First, *production mix* refers to the relative proportion of different types of direct materials or direct labor used to manufacture a given product. Second, *sales mix* refers to the relative proportion of each product sold when the company manufactures and sells more than one product. Sales mix is discussed in chapter 19; production mix is discussed in this chapter.

Yield refers to the quantity of finished output obtained from a given amount of input. For example, if 10,000 pounds of materials are placed in production and the result is 8,500 pounds of finished output, the manufacturing process is said to have an 85-percent yield.

Production mix and yield are important for planning and control when there are multiple inputs of either materials or labor to a manufacturing process. For example, plastics and metals can be combined in different proportions in certain machine parts; cotton, wool, and polyester can be combined in different proportions in some textiles; and labor teams with different levels of training and experience can be used to build houses.

The mix of inputs, such as direct materials, is fixed for the manufacture of many products. For example, one maker of quality cheeses uses only Grade A pasteurized milk, even though other grades of milk and milk products can be substituted. When no discretion regarding mix is allowed, whether by the decree of management or by the physical requirements of the product, it is usually sufficient to calculate individual standard cost variances for each type of material and each class of labor as illustrated in chapter 15. However, when materials can be substituted for each other, the mix and efficiency with which they are used may also change. For example, production managers may change the mix of material inputs to take advantage of a lower price for one type of material, even though the lower grade of the material may not be as efficient to use. Management hopes that there will be a positive cost-efficiency trade-off in this situation. In addition to planned changes in mix, uncontrolled conditions such as temperature or purity of materials may also affect the relationship between inputs and outputs.

If the quality and salability of a product is unaffected by substituting less expensive materials, for example, there should be complete substitution to minimize costs. Under such conditions, mix is not important. However, when only partial substitutability is possible while keeping quality within acceptable limits, information about mix may be important to management for planning and control purposes.

When the mix of inputs is likely to change, for whatever reason, it is important to analyze quantity variances (in the case of materials) and efficiency variances (in the case of labor) in more detail by calculating mix and yield variances.

Mix is measured relative to a standard proportion of inputs and has two components: *materials mix*, which is analyzed by calculating a *materials mix variance;* and *labor mix*, which is analyzed by calculating a *labor mix variance*.

Yield is measured relative to a standard amount of good output for a given amount of input such as direct labor. Yield also has two components: *materials yield*, which is analyzed by calculating a *materials yield variance;* and *labor yield*, which is analyzed by calculating a *labor yield variance*.

The calculation of mix and yield variances is simply the application of standard costs for materials and labor in a more complex manufacturing environment. Therefore, students should be familiar with the standard cost concepts and variance analysis calculations for materials and labor discussed in chapter 15 before proceeding with the next two sections.

Direct-Materials Mix and Yield Variances

To illustrate the calculation of materials mix and yield variances, consider the following situation. A chemical company produces a product by using three material inputs—M1, M2, and M3. These materials are interchangeable within certain limits without reducing the overall quality of the finished product. The process has a standard yield of 95 percent; that is, 1,000 pounds of input materials should result in 950 pounds of good output. Also, materials are purchased on a just-in-time basis, resulting in no inventory of materials on hand at the end of the period. The following is the standard cost card for materials.

Standard Cost for Materials
(per 1,000 pounds of input)

Type of Material Input	Standard Mix Ratio	Standard Price (per pound)	Standard Cost (per pound of input)
M1	0.40	$5.00	$2.00
M2	0.40	3.00	1.20
M3	0.20	3.00	0.60
	1.00		$3.80

Standard cost per pound of *output* = $3.80 ÷ 0.95 = $4.00

Note that a standard yield of 95 percent results in a standard cost of $3.80 per pound of *inputs* but a standard cost for good *output* of $4.00 per pound ($3.80 ÷ 0.95 = $4.00). Also note that the standard mix ratios could be expressed as a unit relationship, such as 4:4:2, rather than as a percentage relationship as in this illustration.

Suppose that one of the suppliers of material M1 reduces its price to $4.90 and that the sole supplier of material M3 raises its price to $3.20. As a result, the production manager decides to use more M1, the same amount of M2, and less M3 during the next production cycle in a ratio of 5:4:1. Actual results in this situation are as follows:

Actual Results for Materials
(good output = 9,215 pounds)

Materials	Cost per Pound	Pounds Used	Total Actual Cost
M1	$4.90	5,000	$24,500
M2	3.00	4,000	12,000
M3	3.20	1,000	3,200
		10,000	$39,700

The management team uses a standard cost system and variance analysis as tools to help it understand the relative significance of the results of each production cycle. One level of analysis using standard costs that higher-level management can use involves the calculation of a budget variance showing aggregate results, as described in chapter 6. The budget variance is simply the difference between the flexible budget and actual results. The flexible budget for materials at a level of 9,215 pounds of good output at a standard cost per pound of $4.00 is $36,860 ($4.00 × 9,215 pounds). Comparing actual results with the flexible budget indicates that there is an unfavorable budget variance of $2,840 U, as indicated here.

Budget Variance for Materials

Budget for materials	$36,860
Actual cost of materials	39,700
Budget variance for materials	$ 2,840 Unfavorable

Although this level of analysis may be satisfactory for higher-level managers who are interested only in aggregate results, production managers typically require more detail to be able to make meaningful decisions about the production process itself. Another level of detail would be provided by employing variance analysis applicable in a standard cost system, as described in chapter 15, *without* considering the effect of mix or yield. This level of analysis showing total price and quantity variances for materials is presented in the top section of figure 17.1 and is similar to that shown in figure 15.7 on page 542.

The calculation of standard quantity for each class of materials is made by multiplying the standard mix ratio times the quantity of input expected to be placed in process given the amount of good output produced. In this example, 9,215 pounds were produced. At a standard yield rate of 95 percent, 9,700 pounds (9,215 ÷ 0.95) of input are expected to have been placed in process.

Observe that the calculations "standard price times actual quantity" and "standard price times actual mix times actual total quantity" are the same calculation, except that "actual quantity" has been expanded to "actual mix times actual total quantity" in the latter calculation.

The calculations shown in figure 17.1 indicate that the materials budget variance consists of a total favorable price variance of $300 F but a total unfavorable quantity variance of $3,140 U. It appears that even though the decision to use more of material M1 resulted in a small favorable price variance, it also may have contributed to a large unfavorable quantity variance. However, even with this level of analysis, it is unclear whether the unfavorable quantity variance resulted from a change in mix, a change in yield, or both. At this point one can observe that using more of material M1 obviously changed the mix and that the yield also declined from the 95-percent standard to 92.15 percent (9,215 pounds of output ÷ 10,000 pounds of input). However, more detailed calculations are

FIGURE 17.1 Calculation of Materials Price and Quantity Variances

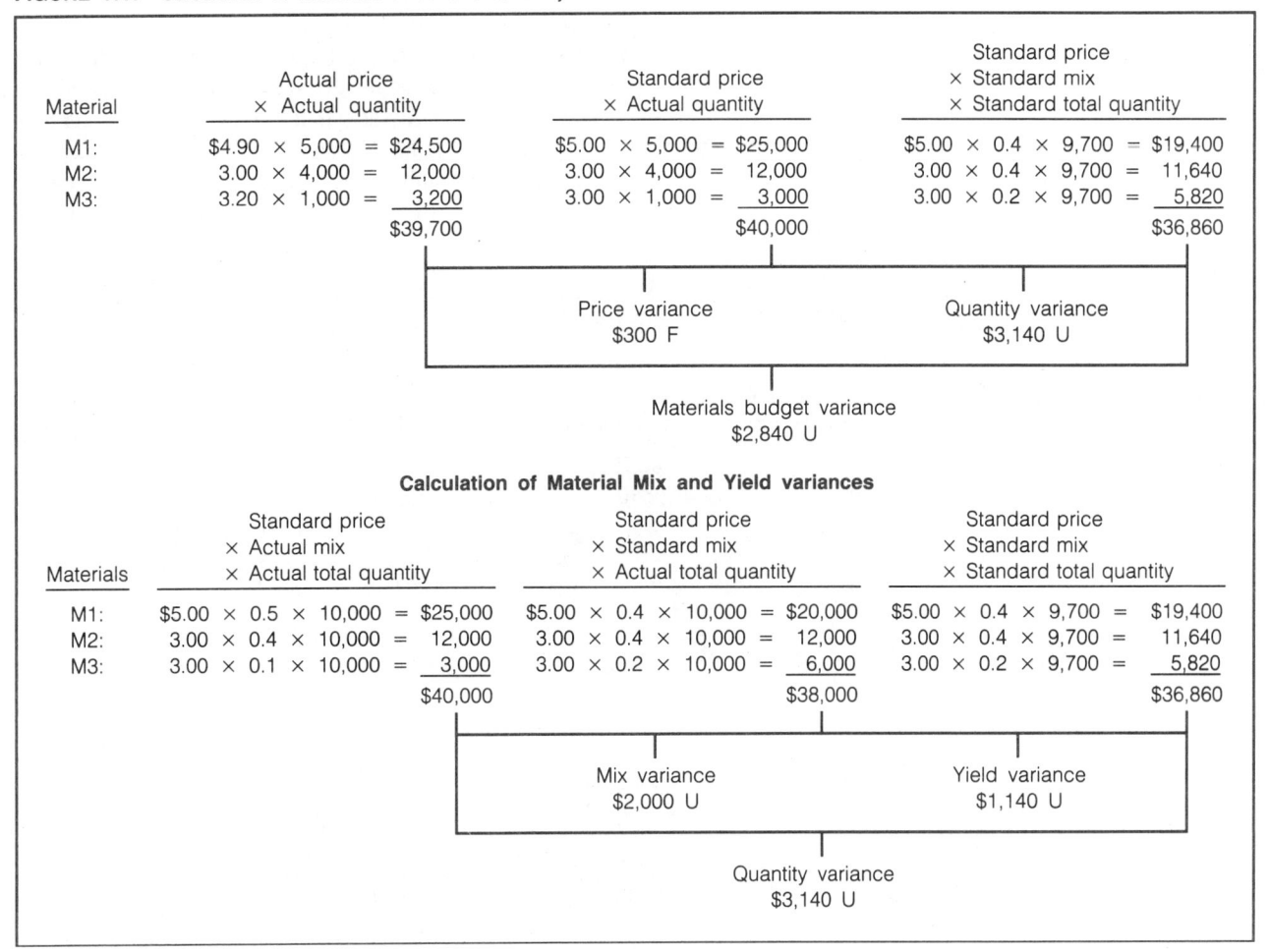

Material	Actual price × Actual quantity	Standard price × Actual quantity	Standard price × Standard mix × Standard total quantity
M1:	$4.90 × 5,000 = $24,500	$5.00 × 5,000 = $25,000	$5.00 × 0.4 × 9,700 = $19,400
M2:	3.00 × 4,000 = 12,000	3.00 × 4,000 = 12,000	3.00 × 0.4 × 9,700 = 11,640
M3:	3.20 × 1,000 = 3,200	3.00 × 1,000 = 3,000	3.00 × 0.2 × 9,700 = 5,820
	$39,700	$40,000	$36,860

Price variance $300 F   Quantity variance $3,140 U

Materials budget variance $2,840 U

Calculation of Material Mix and Yield variances

Materials	Standard price × Actual mix × Actual total quantity	Standard price × Standard mix × Actual total quantity	Standard price × Standard mix × Standard total quantity
M1:	$5.00 × 0.5 × 10,000 = $25,000	$5.00 × 0.4 × 10,000 = $20,000	$5.00 × 0.4 × 9,700 = $19,400
M2:	3.00 × 0.4 × 10,000 = 12,000	3.00 × 0.4 × 10,000 = 12,000	3.00 × 0.4 × 9,700 = 11,640
M3:	3.00 × 0.1 × 10,000 = 3,000	3.00 × 0.2 × 10,000 = 6,000	3.00 × 0.2 × 9,700 = 5,820
	$40,000	$38,000	$36,860

Mix variance $2,000 U   Yield variance $1,140 U

Quantity variance $3,140 U

required to measure the relative effect of these changes in dollars. Together, changes in mix and yield explain the quantity variance.

The procedures for calculating mix and yield variances are similar to the procedures for calculating price and quantity variances: hold one of the factors constant, allow the other factor to change, and isolate the effect of the changed factor. The calculation of mix and yield variances in the previous example is illustrated in the bottom part of figure 17.1. The mix variance is calculated by holding price and quantity constant and varying the mix ratios. In a similar manner, the yield variance is calculated by holding price and mix constant and varying quantities.

In the preceding illustration it is apparent that the substitution of the higher priced material M1 for the less expensive material M3 resulted in a substantial unfavorable mix variance, even though M1's price had declined. The substitution also had a negative effect on yield, as indicated by the unfavorable yield variance. Clearly, the substitution of M1 in this situation did not produce the desired results.

The actual reason the yield declined is not uncovered by the preceding calculations. Further investigation into the production process, the materials used, or other factors affecting yield is required; yet further investigation also costs more money. Whether or not it is cost effective to investigate a variance further is discussed later in this chapter. The point here is that the yield variance has served as an attention-directing device for management. In general, variances help to identify problems, not to solve them.

An alternative method of calculating materials mix and yield variances that uses formulas is illustrated in figure 17.2. These formulas are derived from the framework for analysis presented in figure 17.1. The "actual quantity at standard mix" is simply the total amount of input (10,000 pounds in this situation) at the standard mix ratio. Also, "standard quantity at standard mix" is the total amount of input expected to be used at the standard yield rate to produce the actual amount of output (9,215 ÷ 0.95 = 9,700) at the standard mix ratio.

Direct-Labor Mix and Yield Variances

The calculation of direct-labor mix and yield variances parallels the calculation of direct-materials mix and yield variances. To illustrate, the following standard cost information is for the chemical company described in the previous section.

Standard Cost for Labor
(per 100 pounds of output per hour)

Type of Labor Input	Workers Required	Standard Mix Ratio	Rate per Hour	Total per Hour
L1	1	0.2	$18	$18
L2	3	0.6	16	48
L3	1	0.2	14	14
	5	1.0		$80

Standard labor cost per pound of *output* at 100 pounds per hour = $0.80 ($80 ÷ 100)

Suppose that during the current period, category L1 workers were called away for part of the time to solve a problem in another part of the plant. To keep the process going, L1 workers were replaced with category L3 workers, who were somewhat less experienced. Asssume also that category L3 workers were paid $1 more per hour this period than originally budgeted. Actual results in this situation are as follows:

Actual Results for Labor
(good output = 9,215 pounds)

Labor	Hours Worked	Mix Ratio	Rate paid	Total Cost
L1	40	0.08	$18	$ 720
L2	270	0.56	16	4,320
L3	170	0.36	15	2,550
	480	1.00		$7,590

Just as for materials, a budget variance for labor can be calculated. The flexible budget for labor for 9,215 pounds of good output at a standard cost of $0.80 per pound is $7,372 ($0.80 × 9,215). Comparing actual results with the flexible budget indicates that there is a $218 unfavorable budget variance, as indicated here.

Budget Variance for Labor

Budget for labor	$7,372
Actual cost of labor	7,590
Budget variance for labor	$ 218 Unfavorable

FIGURE 17.2

Formula Calculation of Materials Mix and Yield Variances

Materials Mix Variance

$$\begin{bmatrix} \text{Actual quantity} \\ \text{at actual mix} \end{bmatrix} - \begin{bmatrix} \text{Actual quantity} \\ \text{at standard mix} \end{bmatrix} \times \text{Standard price} = \text{Mix variance}$$

M1:	(5,000	−	4,000)	× $5.00	=	$5,000 U
M2:	(4,000	−	4,000)	× $3.00	=	0
M3:	(1,000	−	2,000)	× $3.00	=	$3,000 F
	10,000		10,000			$2,000 U

Materials Yield Variance

$$\begin{bmatrix} \text{Actual quantity} \\ \text{at standard mix} \end{bmatrix} - \begin{bmatrix} \text{Standard quantity} \\ \text{at standard mix} \end{bmatrix} \times \text{Standard price} = \text{Yield variance}$$

M1:	(4,000	−	3,880)	× $5.00	=	$ 600 U
M2:	(4,000	−	3,880)	× $3.00	=	$ 360 U
M3:	(2,000	−	1,940)	× $3.00	=	$ 180 U
	10,000		9,700			$1,140 U

Alternate Formula for Yield Variance

(Total actual quantity − Total standard quantity) × Weighted average Standard price per unit of *input* = Yield variance

(10,000 − 9,700) × $3.80 = $1,140 U

The budget variance for labor can be further analyzed by calculating a labor rate variance and a labor efficiency variance, as shown in figure 17.3. Similar calculations are shown in figure 15.7 on page 542. This type of analysis *does not* consider the effect of mix and yield, but it is useful for understanding the orderly progression of detail of analysis and the role of mix and yield in a standard cost system.

The calculation of standard hours for each class of labor is made by multiplying the standard mix ratio times the total standard hours expected to be worked given the amount of good output produced. In this example, the standard hours allowed to produce 9,215 pounds at 100 pounds per hour is 92.15 hours (9,215 ÷ 100). With five workers employed in the process, the total standard hours allowed is 460.75 (92.15 × 5).

The results in figure 17.3 indicate that the labor budget variance consists of a total unfavorable rate variance of $170 U and a total unfavorable efficiency variance of $48 U. The need to use less experienced category L3 labor to temporarily replace category L1 labor reduced the expected efficiency of labor for this period. Also, the unbudgeted increase in wages for category L3 workers produced an unfavorable rate variance.

The next level of detail requires analyzing the efficiency variance to determine the relative impact of mix and yield. The substitution of the lower-paid category L3 workers for higher-paid L1 workers should have resulted in a favorable mix variance. However, the number of hours actually worked exceeded the standard hours allowed, which should have resulted in an unfavorable yield variance. The relative magnitude of these variances can be calculated with the same general procedures used to calculate materials mix and yield variances, as illustrated in the bottom part of figure 17.3. As expected, there is a

FIGURE 17.3

Calculation of Labor Rate and Efficiency Variances

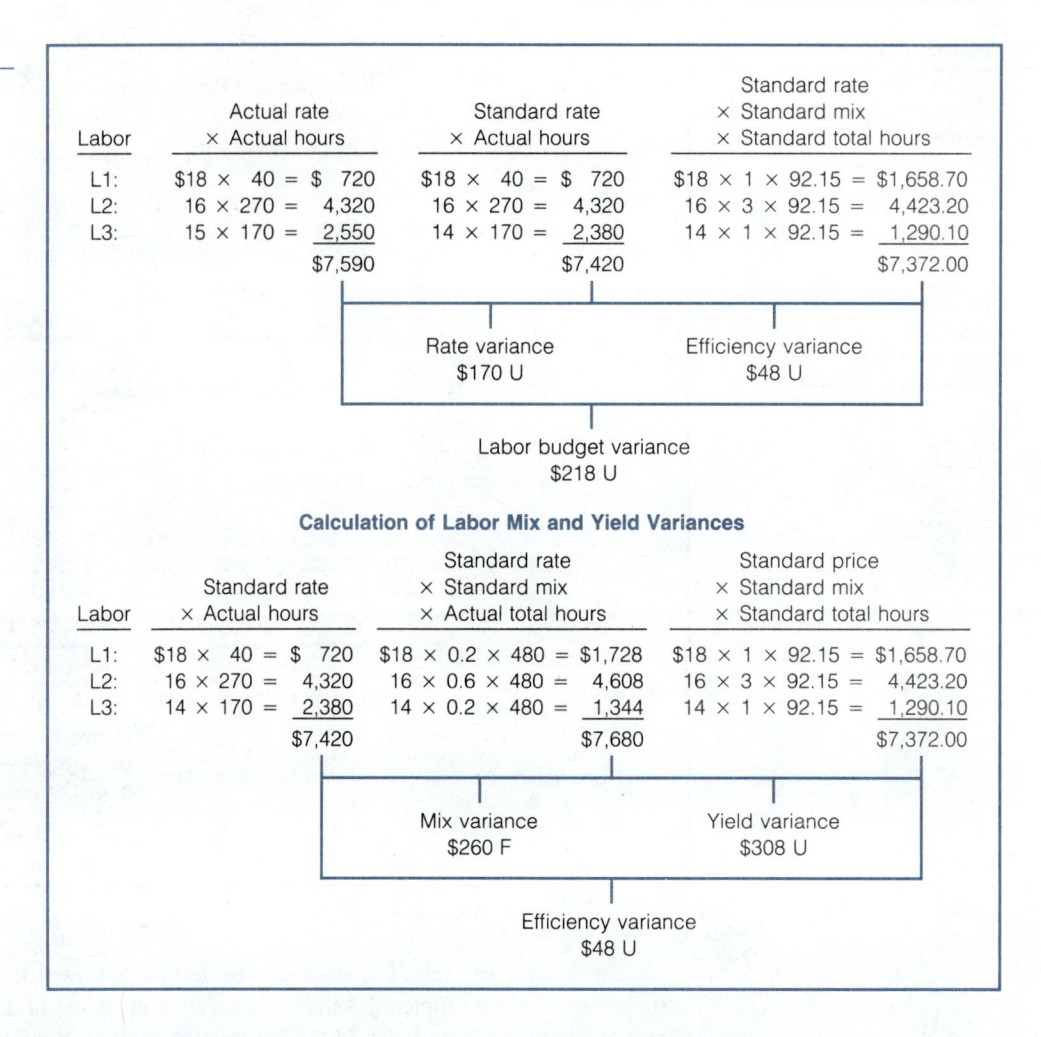

Labor	Actual rate × Actual hours	Standard rate × Actual hours	Standard rate × Standard mix × Standard total hours
L1:	$18 × 40 = $ 720	$18 × 40 = $ 720	$18 × 1 × 92.15 = $1,658.70
L2:	16 × 270 = 4,320	16 × 270 = 4,320	16 × 3 × 92.15 = 4,423.20
L3:	15 × 170 = 2,550	14 × 170 = 2,380	14 × 1 × 92.15 = 1,290.10
	$7,590	$7,420	$7,372.00

Rate variance $170 U   Efficiency variance $48 U

Labor budget variance $218 U

Calculation of Labor Mix and Yield Variances

Labor	Standard rate × Actual hours	Standard rate × Standard mix × Actual total hours	Standard price × Standard mix × Standard total hours
L1:	$18 × 40 = $ 720	$18 × 0.2 × 480 = $1,728	$18 × 1 × 92.15 = $1,658.70
L2:	16 × 270 = 4,320	16 × 0.6 × 480 = 4,608	16 × 3 × 92.15 = 4,423.20
L3:	14 × 170 = 2,380	14 × 0.2 × 480 = 1,344	14 × 1 × 92.15 = 1,290.10
	$7,420	$7,680	$7,372.00

Mix variance $260 F   Yield variance $308 U

Efficiency variance $48 U

favorable labor mix variance of $260 and an unfavorable labor yield variance of $308—apparently the result of substituting one category of labor for another.

Labor mix and yield variances can also be calculated by means of formulas, as illustrated in figure 17.4.

VARIANCE REPORTS

Variance reports are prepared in numerous ways, depending on the needs of management. Factors affecting the form and content of variance reports include the following:

1. the level in the organization at which the report is being used
2. the persons responsible for the variances that appear on the report
3. whether management by exception is being used
4. the level of aggregation desired
5. the nature of the products being manufactured
6. the number of materials and labor inputs
7. the frequency with which reports are developed

Figure 17.5 contains a sample variance report that uses data from this chapter.

FIGURE 17.4

Formula Calculation of Labor Mix and Yield Variances

Labor Mix Variance

$$\left[\begin{array}{c}\text{Actual hours} \\ \text{at actual mix}\end{array} - \begin{array}{c}\text{Actual hours} \\ \text{at standard mix}\end{array}\right] \times \text{Standard rate} = \text{Mix variance}$$

L1: (40 − (0.2 × 480)) × $18 = $1,008 F
L2: (270 − (0.6 × 480)) × 16 =   288 F
L3: (170 − (0.2 × 480)) × 14 = 1,036 U
       480                              $ 260 F

Labor Yield Variance

$$\left[\begin{array}{c}\text{Actual hours} \\ \text{at standard mix}\end{array} - \begin{array}{c}\text{Standard hours} \\ \text{at standard mix}\end{array}\right] \times \text{Standard rate} = \text{Yield variance}$$

L1: (96 − (0.2 × 460.75)) × $18 = $ 69.30 U
L2: (288 − (0.6 × 460.75)) × 16 = 184.80 U
L3: (96 − (0.2 × 460.75)) × 14 =   53.90 U
       480                             $308.00 U

Alternate Formula for Yield Variance

(Total actual hours − Total standard hours) × Weighted average standard labor rate = Yield variance

(480 − 460.75) × $16 = $308 U

FIGURE 17.5

Sample Variance Report

Material Variances:

Price variances:
M1	$ 500 F	
M2	0	
M3	200 U	
		$ 300 F

Mix variance:
M1	$5,000 U	
M2	0	
M3	3,000 F	
		2,000 U
Yield variance		1,140 U
Budget variance		$2,840 U

Labor variances:

Rate variances:
L1	$ 0	
L2	0	
L3	170 U	
		$ 170 U

Mix variances:
L1	$1,008 F	
L2	288 F	
L3	1,036 U	
		260 F
Yield variance		308 U
Budget variance		$ 218 U

There are several useful features of variance reports not illustrated in figure 17.5 that should be noted. First, it may be useful to include variances from several reporting periods in a comparative format on the variance reports. Including past variances helps to put current-period performance in proper perspective. Some firms also use graphs that highlight the relative changes in variances over several accounting cycles. Graphs help identify trends and unusual or unexpected conditions that might need attention.

Another item that could be included in the variance report is some indication of when a variance has triggered a management-by-exception rule. This feature may be more useful at higher levels of management than at lower levels. For example, the number of items on a foreman's variance report will probably be less than the number of items on a plant manager's variance report. Thus, although the foreman may be able to easily discern which variances are significant, the plant manager may need some device for highlighting variances that should be studied in detail.

Finally, the person or department responsible for each variance should be indicated in some way on the variance report. This can be done explicitly by associating a person or department with each variance, or it can be done implicitly by including only those variances on a report that are controllable by the person or department receiving the report.

INVESTIGATION OF VARIANCES

Standard cost variances occur whenever there is a difference between budgeted and actual results. Because budgets are based on expected *future* prices and quantities, it is unlikely that actual results will ever exactly equal the budgeted amounts. As a result, variances will probably be reported for every direct-material, direct-labor, and overhead item for which standards are used. One can expect that some variances will be insignificant and not indicative of any real problem, but other variances may be very large and clearly indicate the presence of a problem that requires immediate attention. The dilemma for management is in deciding which variances (aside from the obvious ones) indicate that there is a high enough probability that a real problem exists to warrant investigation.

There are no generally accepted procedures or decision rules for deciding which variances should be further investigated. However, there are some basic concepts and techniques that are useful when developing a model for deciding when to investigate variances. First, an understanding of the reasons variances occur gives insight into whether some variances should or should not be investigated. Second, an understanding of some decision techniques, such as statistical quality control, provides a framework for developing rules about when to investigate variances. Finally, an understanding of how probabilities, expected costs, and expected benefits can be incorporated in the decision process helps ensure that the decision to investigate will be cost effective.

Why Variances Occur

Variances occur for many reasons. The most important categories of reasons include *(a)* normal random fluctuations, *(b)* inaccurate data, *(c)* inappropriate standards, *(d)* efficient operations, and *(e)* out-of-control operations.

Normal random fluctuations are inherent in virtually all manufacturing processes. For example, the efficiency of a particular milling machine may be affected by its own vibration, or the yield from a certain compound may be affected by temperature changes between batches. It is hoped that this type of fluctuation can be eliminated or at least controlled within minimum acceptable limits. However, some types of fluctuations will persist because they are either inherent in the manufacturing process and cannot be eliminated or because they are very costly to eliminate altogether.

Another factor contributing to normal random fluctuations is the fact that standards are typically set at a single expected price or quantity when a range of possible prices or quantities may be more representative of actual expectations. For example, in one situation it was expected that between thirty-three and thirty-five hours of direct labor were required for each unit of output. Rather than use a range of values, the standard was set at thirty-four hours. Variances occuring in this type of situation should be analyzed relative to a range of acceptable values rather than relative to a single value.

Variances that result from normal random fluctuations do not require investigation because there is no need, by definition, for corrective action. The obvious problem is in deciding whether a particular variance is simply the result of normal random fluctuations or if there is another problem requiring corrective action.

Inaccurate data because of either human or mechanical failure may contribute to standard cost variances. An information system must operate with integrity for variances to be reliable. To illustrate, consider the situation of one company that implemented a standard cost system. Management decided to take the dollar values for its variance calculations from accounting data and the quantity values from production statistics. Accounting data had a high degree of integrity because of rigorous internal controls, but the production statistics were not well controlled and, unknown to management, contained many errors. As a result, management found that conditions requiring its attention were not indicated on a timely basis and that many variances were being investigated when no corrective action was necessary. The solution was to implement additional internal controls so that *both* production and accounting data were reported with a high degree of integrity. Thus variance analysis became an effective management tool for planning and control.

Sources of inaccurate data, once discovered, can usually be corrected. The remaining question is whether the cost of correction can be offset by the savings from improved operations. For example, adjustment of a pressure sensing device on a stamping machine may have a large cost-benefit trade-off, but the cost of modifying the structure of a data base may be prohibitive when the derived benefits are considered.

Inappropriate standards may guarantee the presence of standard cost variances. For example, industrial robots can substantially reduce the amount of direct labor expended on a product. If standards are not adjusted for this kind of change, however, variances will occur simply because the standard is inappropriate. Management should revise standards as often as conditions dictate. Otherwise, the effect of technological changes, for example, will be combined with other effects, and it will be difficult, if not impossible, for management to differentiate among causes of significant variances. A variance indicating a condition that needs attention could be masked by the use of inappropriate standards.

Using an "ideal" philosophy to set standards, as discussed in chapter 15, may also guarantee the presence of standard cost variances. Ideal standards with perfect manufacturing conditions in mind are set at the lowest possible prices and quantities. If the ideal is not attainable, unfavorable variances will result, along with the danger that the built-in variances may mask conditions requiring management's attention. Also, from a personnel management perspective, the inability to operate at standard, let alone produce favorable variances, may have important negative motivational outcomes.

Very efficient operations may create substantial favorable variances. The decision to investigate favorable variances may not seem logical: Why be concerned with things that are going well? Yet favorable variances may signal areas that require management's attention just as surely as negative variances do. For example, the pressure to meet a shipping deadline may cause workers to speed production, resulting in a decline in the finished product's quality. Efficiency variances may be favorable in such instances, but lost customers, recalls, or other quality problems may more than offset any gains in efficiency.

On the positive side, favorable variances may signal improved methods of operation. For example, a study of mechanics in a large machine shop showed that they spent considerable time waiting in line for parts at the parts room. Methods within the parts room were changed, thus allowing the mechanics to spend more time doing repair work. The effects of improvements in the parts room were confirmed by favorable efficiency variances for direct labor.

Workers with appropriate incentives may voluntarily suggest changes in operations to improve productivity. The people who are the closest to the work typically know the most about how to improve it. When a worker's initiative and creativity are properly measured and appropriately rewarded within a standard cost system, an environment exists for continual improvements in productivity.

Out-of-control operations occur for many reasons, ranging from fatigued or disinterested workers to worn or damaged machinery. Out-of-control operations require corrective action. To be most useful, variances should serve as attention-directing devices that point to potential or emerging problems on a timely basis. Cost variances verifying that an out-of-control condition existed during the past reporting period are certainly useful. However, the timeliness and form of reporting of variances cannot be over emphasized. For example, it is more cost effective to sense that there is a drift in the standard mix of a product and discover through investigation that a valve is beginning to malfunction than to have the valve deteriorate to the point where finished goods are spoiled before variances are investigated.

Techniques for Deciding When to Investigate Variances

The actual decision processes that managers use to decide when a variance should be investigated are not clearly understood. It appears that there is heavy reliance on intuition and personal judgment developed over many years of experience. Because of the large number of variables in a manufacturing environment and their complex interrelationships, it has been difficult to develop decision models that are useful in all situations. Perhaps expert systems or artificial intelligence techniques discussed in chapter 25 will become useful for variance analysis. For now, however, there are several principles that can provide a frame of reference for ascertaining when to investigate variances.

The first intuitive step in deciding whether to investigate a variance is to determine whether the variance resulted from normal random fluctuations or from another cause that might require investigation. Fundamental to this determination is the *size* of the variance, any apparent *trend* in the data, and the range or *control limits* within which variances are allowed to fluctuate without assuming that a condition needing attention exists. To illustrate, consider the monthly variances for an assembly operation plotted in figure 17.6.

For much of the year, it was likely that the size and lack of trend of variances in figure 17.6 indicated nothing more than normal random fluctuations in the assembly operation. However, a trend of increases appeared late in the year, and within three months, management decided that these variances probably indicated that something was amiss.

A new machine had been installed in the product flow just before the assembly operation. The new machine was much more efficient than the old machine, which caused a buildup of work-in-process inventory at the assembly process. Investigation revealed that the inventory buildup was so great that workers had to spend extra time sorting through the work in process to find what was needed next in the assembly operation, thus reducing the process's efficiency. The flow of product through the factory was adjusted, allowing the assembly process to return to normal efficiency. This pattern is confirmed in figure 17.6 by the reduction in variances for the last two months of operation.

An important thing to learn from the preceding example is that management may use simple tools to make complex decisions. For example, management used a graph as the

FIGURE 17.6

Monthly Plot of Variances

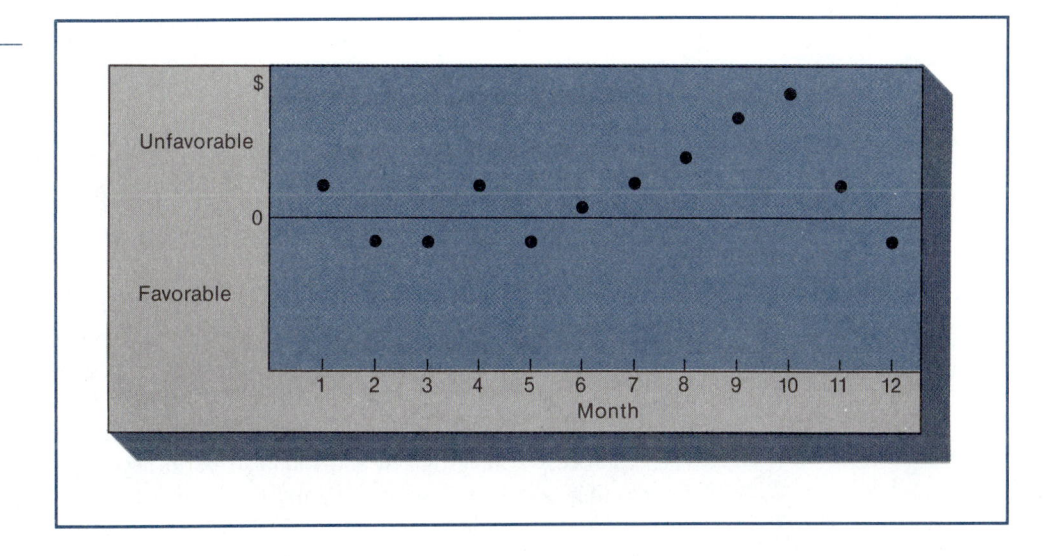

basic tool for analysis in this situation. It may be that a few minutes spent examining a graph of monthly or weekly variances will answer most questions about whether or not a variance should be investigated. Experienced managers' ability to spot significant trends or unusual fluctuations by observation should not be underestimated.

In the previous example, note that variances were allowed to fluctuate within an acceptable range before management thought a limit had been exceeded and there was now a strong probability that something other than normal random fluctuations was affecting the assembly process. Such limits are critical to the question of whether or not to investigate a variance, and there are several ways in which they can be set. First, such limits can be based on intuition, as in this illustration. Second, management may develop informal rules of thumb. Last, management may use formal statistical techniques for identifying situations that require attention.

Rules of thumb are developed from past experience and personal judgment. They are usually based on the size of the variance. Typical examples are rules such as "investigate materials price variances in excess of $500" or "investigate all deviations greater than 15 percent of the total standard cost." Variances within these exception regions are assumed to have arisen because of normal random fluctuations in the production process, and, therefore, the added costs of investigation and corrective action are not warranted.

Statistical techniques constitute a more formal approach to identifying variances that represent more than normal random fluctuations. Past performance and the application of probability theory are important elements of most statistical approaches. The statistical quality control technique, which is used primarily to identify nonrandom fluctuations in a production process, may be used in some situations to analyze fluctuations in standard cost variances. Statistical quality control is applied by taking samples from the manufacturing process every hour, for example, and plotting the mean and range of the sample observations on a special graph called a quality control chart. Each chart contains previously calculated control limits based on the probability that management is willing to accept that the process is in control. The assumption is that if the plot of a sample falls outside the control limits, something other than normal random fluctuations is causing the deviation, and the process is investigated.

Statistical inference may be applied to variance analysis to calculate the probability that a particular price or quantity has resulted from something other than normal random fluctuations. Regression analysis, discussed in chapter 6, is yet another method to determine when a particular price or quantity has deviated beyond acceptable limits. Students interested in these advanced techniques for analyzing variances should consult the suggested readings at the end of the chapter.

Cost-Benefit Evaluation of Investigation

A decision table is useful for understanding the cost-benefit trade-offs of variance investigation. As shown in figure 17.7, the decision to investigate is a two-state, two-action situation. The two states of the process being evaluated are (1) needs investigation and (2) does not need investigation; the two actions that management can take are (1) investigate and (2) do not investigate. There are four possible outcomes—two correct and two in error.

There is a cost associated with each possible outcome in figure 17.7. The cost of investigation *(A)* includes the cost of labor and supplies that may be used to do the actual investigation plus the cost of lost production if the process must be stopped for evaluation. When a process is investigated and found to be in need of adjustment or repair, the cost of correcting whatever is wrong *(B)* must be added to the cost of investigation *(A)*. The cost of correction could be very small if all that is needed is a twist of a knob, but it could be very great if a machine must be replaced.

The cost of allowing the process to run when it needs attention *(C)* could include the cost of lost units, rework, dissatisfied customers, or even liability claims from injured customers. The cost of not investigating a process that does not need attention is assumed to be zero. The actual calculation of these costs can be highly subjective and may require a great deal of judgment and the use of estimates. Management must try to quantify all costs that are relevant to the decision to investigate.

The decision to investigate is made under conditions of uncertainty. In other words, there is a probability that one or the other state of the production process is the actual state of affairs at that moment. For example, the probability that a process needs investigation

FIGURE 17.7

Decision Table for Variance Investigation

Management Decision	True state of the Production Process	
	Does not need investigation $P(1)$	Needs investigation $P(2)$
Investigate	Error(A)	Correct ($A + B$)
Do not investigate	Correct (0)	Error(C)

A = cost of investigation
B = cost of correcting whatever needs attention
C = cost of allowing the process to run when it needs investigation
$P(1)$ = probability that the true state is that the process does not need investigation
$P(2)$ = probability that the true state is that the process needs investigation
$P(1) + P(2) = 1$

Expected Costs

Investigate = $P(1)A + P(2)(A + B)$
Do not investigate = $P(1)0 + P(2)C = P(2)C$
Indifference probability = $\dfrac{A}{C - B}$

may be 5 percent. This, in turn, means that the probability is 95 percent that the process does not need investigation.

The goal to minimize the expected cost of investigation is accomplished by combining costs and probabilities to calculate expected values for *(a)* the cost of investigating and *(b)* the cost of not investigating a variance. To illustrate, consider the following situation. Management has concluded that a particular variance indicates a 10-percent probability that a process is out of control and needs investigation. The cost to investigate variances has averaged $300 during the past year. When a process actually needs correction, the additional cost of spare parts and adjustment has averaged $500. Management estimates that the present value of the costs incurred when a condition that needs investigation is not investigated averages $4,000. Should management investigate this variance? The calculation of expected costs indicates that the least-cost alternative is to investigate.

Investigate: 0.90 ($300) + 0.10 ($800) = $350
Do not investigate: 0.10 ($4,000) = $400

For each situation there is a critical level of probability, called the breakeven or indifference level, where the expected costs are equal. This level of probability is dependent on the relative costs in each situation. For example, the indifference probability in the preceding situation is 8.6 percent, as calculated here.

$$\text{Indifference probability} = \frac{\$300}{\$4,000 - \$500} = 0.086$$

An indifference probability is particularly useful to management, because there is usually a direct relationship between the size of a variance and the probability that the variance indicates a condition needing attention. Therefore, rather than calculate expected costs for each variance, it may be more useful to first calculate the indifference probability for a variance and then to use that probability in connection with a rule of thumb or statistical inference. For example, assume that the probability an investigation is needed in the previous situation in a future period is found by statistical inference to be 7 percent. Because the indifference probability is greater than 7 percent the appropriate decision is to not investigate the variance.

BEHAVIORAL CONSIDERATIONS

The objective of a standard cost system is to provide information to help management plan and control manufacturing operations. The system's effectiveness depends on how its standard cost variances are used by managers as they work with subordinates and other managers. Variances can be used in a positive way to identify opportunities for improvement or commendation, or they can be used in a negative way to fix blame and determine penalties. It is the experience of many companies that a positive approach leads to greater gains in productivity than a negative approach.

A fundamental rule is that those persons who are assigned responsibility for a variance are also those who have control over the cost and quantity factors used to calculate that variance. Improper matching of responsibility and control can lead to frustration and ineffective action, even when there is a pressing problem that needs a solution. Therefore, variance reports should include an indication of the department or person that is responsible for each variance. When departmental reports are prepared, it is important that only those variances controllable within that specific department are included on that department's report or that they are clearly identified as someone else's responsibility.

SUMMARY

This chapter explained the role of production mix and yield in a standard cost system. Production mix refers to the relative proportion of different types of direct materials or direct labor used to manufacture a product. Yield refers to the quantity of finished output obtained from a given amount of input.

Production mix and yield are important considerations, because management may, either by design or because of economic conditions, make trade-offs among inputs, anticipating that potential savings will exceed potential costs. Also, factors that affect production, such as humidity and temperature, may not be completely controlled, resulting in changes in mix. Whether the result of planned trade-offs or uncontrolled environmental conditions, mix and yield variances for both materials and labor inputs can be used in a standard cost system to evaluate the relationship between inputs and outputs in a multiple input environment.

Some basic guidelines for deciding when to investigate variances were also discussed. Management typically receives reports that contain variances for every direct-material, direct-labor, and overhead item for which standards have been set, but it does not investigate why every variance occurred. The cost of labor used for the investigation as well as the cost of lost production when the process must be stopped for inspection motivate managers to investigate only variances that have a high probability of being caused by something needing attention.

On the other hand, ignoring the control features of a standard cost system also has its negative consequences. The cost of not investigating variances resulting from something needing attention may include costs of scrap, rework, lost customers, or even product liability claims.

Management faces the dilemma of deciding which variances are cost effective to investigate. To aid in the decision, management typically develops rules of thumb or uses statistical techniques to identify which variances should be investigated.

To utilize variances in a positive, productive way, a verbal analysis could be conducted at the time variance reports are issued. This can help in several ways. First, a verbal analysis provides an opportunity for higher-level managers to express appreciation for what is being accomplished. Second, taking time to discuss what is going on is a subtle way to communicate respect and appreciation for subordinates. Finally, face-to-face discussion can often clarify a situation more efficiently and effectively than written communication.

SELF-STUDY PROBLEMS

Mix and Yield

Wescor, Inc. produces a compound called Quickset that is added to wet cement to reduce setup time. To make this compound, two different materials, Amfol and Byzon, are used in the proportions 4/10 and 6/10, respectively, at standard. Their standard costs are $3.00 and $10.00 per gallon, respectively. Production reports indicate that during the past few months, the standard yield has been at 90 percent for 100 gallons of input. The company does not keep any Amfol or Byzon on hand because of its toxic nature.

Last week the company produced 80,100 gallons of Quickset at a total raw materials cost of $600,750. The actual number of gallons used and costs per gallon for the two materials are as follows:

	Gallons	Cost (per gallon)
Amfol	45,000	$ 3.10
Byzon	45,000	10.25
	90,000	

Required:

1. Calculate the standard cost per gallon of output for Quickset.
2. Calculate the budget variance for materials and analyze it in terms of price, quantity, mix, and yield.

Solution to the Self-Study Problem

Standard Cost of Material Inputs

40 gallons of Amfol at $3.00 =	$120
60 gallons of Byzon at $10.00 =	600
	$720

Standard cost per gallon of output = $720 ÷ 90 = $8.00

Materials Budget Variance

Budget for materials ($8.00 × 80,100)	$640,800
Actual cost of materials	600,750
Budget variance for materials	$ 40,050

Calculation of Materials Price and Quantity Variances

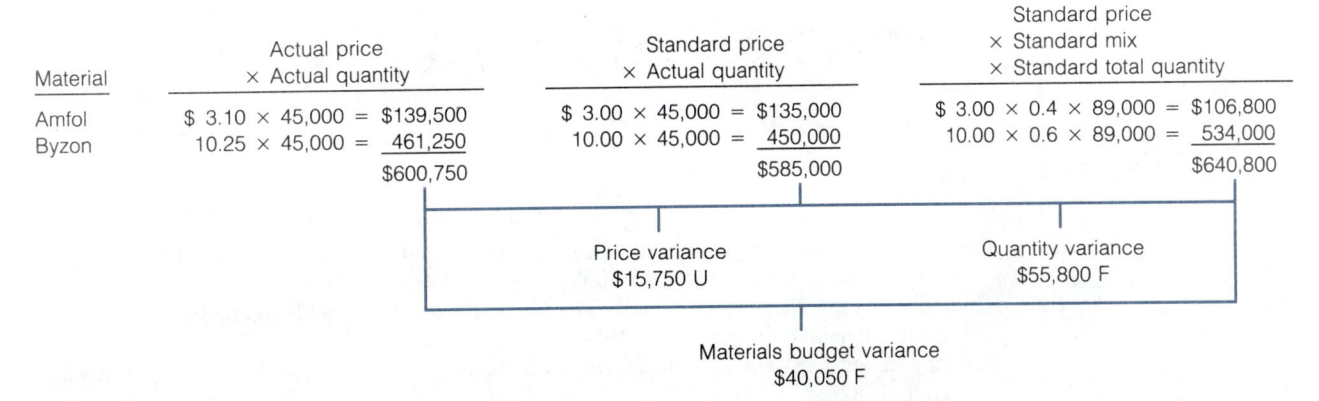

Material	Actual price × Actual quantity	Standard price × Actual quantity	Standard price × Standard mix × Standard total quantity
Amfol	$ 3.10 × 45,000 = $139,500	$ 3.00 × 45,000 = $135,000	$ 3.00 × 0.4 × 89,000 = $106,800
Byzon	10.25 × 45,000 = 461,250	10.00 × 45,000 = 450,000	10.00 × 0.6 × 89,000 = 534,000
	$600,750	$585,000	$640,800

Price variance $15,750 U

Quantity variance $55,800 F

Materials budget variance $40,050 F

Calculation of Materials Mix and Yield Variances

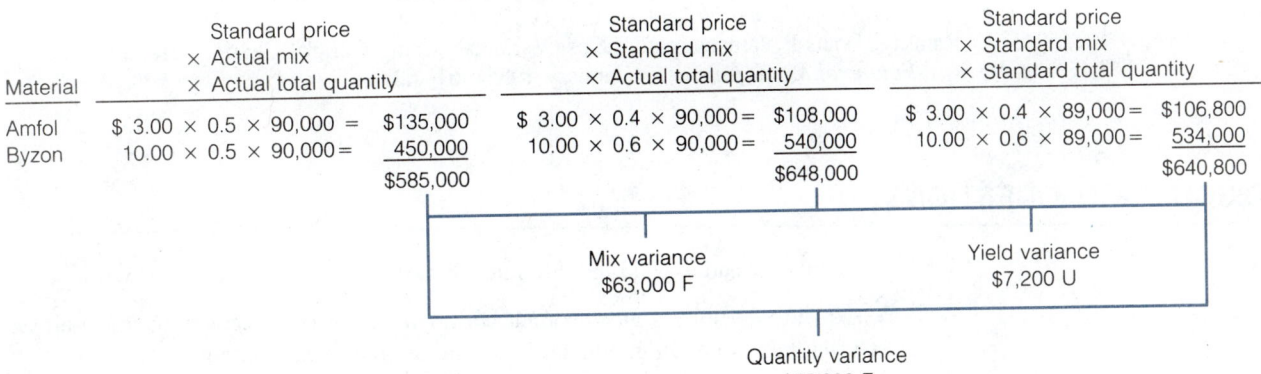

Material	Standard price × Actual mix × Actual total quantity	Standard price × Standard mix × Actual total quantity	Standard price × Standard mix × Standard total quantity
Amfol	$ 3.00 × 0.5 × 90,000 = $135,000	$ 3.00 × 0.4 × 90,000 = $108,000	$ 3.00 × 0.4 × 89,000 = $106,800
Byzon	10.00 × 0.5 × 90,000 = 450,000	10.00 × 0.6 × 90,000 = 540,000	10.00 × 0.6 × 89,000 = 534,000
	$585,000	$648,000	$640,800

Mix variance $63,000 F

Yield variance $7,200 U

Quantity variance $55,800 F

Variance Investigation

Simex, Inc. uses statistical inference to evaluate its materials usage. Management has determined that a particular process has an 8 percent probability of needing investigation. The cost of investigation averages $2,100 and the cost of making corrections averages $400. The present value of the costs incurred when a condition that needs investigation is not investigated is estimated to be $6,400. Management needs to know if it is cost effective to investigate this process.

Required

1. Based on your calculation of the indifference probability, should management investigate?
2. Verify your response to requirement 1 by calculating expected costs of investigation and no investigation.

Solution to the Self-study Problem

1. Management should not investigate because the indifference probability is greater than the probability that the process needs investigation (0.35 > 0.08).

$$\text{Indifference probability} = \frac{2,100}{6,400 - 400} = 0.35$$

2. The calculation of expected costs verifies that the expected cost of investigation is greater than the expected cost of no investigation ($2,132 > $512).

$$\text{Investigate: } 0.92(\$2,100) + 0.08(\$2,100 + \$400) = \$2,132$$
$$\text{Do not investigate: } 0.08(\$6,400) = \$512$$

SUGGESTED READINGS

Deming, W. Edwards. *Quality, Productivity, and Competitive Position.* Cambridge, Mass.: Massachusetts Institute of Technology, 1982.

Goldratt, Eliyahu M., and Cox, Jeff. *The Goal: Excellence in Manufacturing.* Milford, Conn.: Creative Output, Inc., 1984.

Kaplan, Robert S. *Advanced Management Accounting.* Englewood Cliffs, N.J.: Prentice-Hall, 1982.

Lambert, Richard A. "Variance Investigation in Agency Settings." *Journal of Accounting Research* 23 (Autumn 1985): 633–647.

Ramsay, Louis P. "Investigating Cost Variances Using Control Charts." *Healthcare Financial Management* 39 (January 1985): 61–62.

DISCUSSION QUESTIONS

Q17-1. Define *mix* and explain the difference between sales mix and production mix.

Q17-2. Explain why mix is an important consideration in cost accounting. Give an example of when mix is not an important consideration in cost accounting.

Q17–3. Define *yield* and explain why it is important in cost accounting. Give an example of when yield is not an important consideration in cost accounting.

Q17–4. What variances are used to evaluate mix and how are they calculated?

Q17–5. What variances are used to evaluate yield and how are they calculated?

Q17–6. Explain the relationship of mix and yield to the materials quantity variance and the labor efficiency variance.

Q17–7. Explain some of the factors that should be considered when preparing variance reports.

Q17–8. "Every variance should receive equal consideration." Do you agree? Discuss.

Q17–9. Explain some of the reasons that variances occur.

Q17–10. Explain how the size, range, and trend of variances may be useful for deciding when to investigate a process.

Q17–11. How are rules of thumb and statistical techniques used to decide whether a process should be investigated?

Q17–12. The decision to investigate has four possible outcomes. Explain these possible outcomes and tell what costs and benefits are associated with each.

Q17–13. What is an indifference probability? How is it useful for variance investigation?

Q17–14. Suggest some ways in which variances can be used in a positive way to promote productive behavior among workers.

EXERCISES

E17–1. Materials Mix and Yield Hightop Company makes a product from two materials that can be mixed in different proportions. The materials costs for 100 units of output at standard are as follows:

Material P 300 lbs. at $2.00 per pound	$ 600
Material Q 300 lbs. at $3.00 per pound	900
600 lbs.	$1,500

During a recent production run, 100 units of good output with the following materials costs were produced:

Material P 340 lbs. at $2.20 per pound	$ 748
Material Q 280 lbs. at $3.10 per pound	868
620 lbs.	$1,616

Required

1. Calculate the materials price and materials quantity variances for this production run.
2. Calculate the materials mix and materials yield variances for this production run, and verify that together they equal the materials quantity variance.

E17–2. Labor Mix and Yield Varion Products, Inc. has the following standard labor cost for one of its products:

Labor (category A)	6 hours at $8.00 per hour	$48
Labor (category B)	2 hours at $6.00 per hour	12
	8 hours	$60

During a recent month, the labor cost to complete 100 units was as follows:

Labor (category A)	620 hours at $8.00	$4,960
Labor (category B)	240 hours at $6.20	1,488
	860 hours	$6,448

Required

1. Calculate the labor rate variance and the labor efficiency variance for this month's activity.

2. Calculate the labor mix and labor yield variances for this month's activity, and verify that together they equal the labor efficiency variance.

E17–3. Material and Labor Yield Variances Jasper Chemical Company processes 1,000-gallon batches of a single raw material to obtain 900 gallons of good output per batch. Standard costs for materials and labor are as follows:

Materials—$6.00 per gallon of input
Labor   —$2.00 per gallon of input

During the period, 20 batches of raw materials were placed into production, and a total of 18,450 gallons of good output were produced. There were 20,000 gallons of materials used and 20,000 hours of labor worked. Material costs were $122,000, and labor costs were $40,000.

Required

Calculate the materials and labor yield variances. Use the alternate formula for calculating yield variances.

E17–4. Mix and Yield—Materials and Labor Miffin Manufacturing Company has the following direct-material and direct-labor standards for one of its products. The process that manufactures this product has a 98-percent standard yield rate.

Material	Mix ratio	Cost (per gallon)
S	40%	$ 4.00
T	60%	$10.00

Labor	Hours (per 100 gallons)	Cost (per hour)
Type I	3	$8.00
Type II	2	$6.00

During the last production cycle, 9,900 gallons of good output were produced from an input of 10,000 total gallons of raw materials. Costs were as follows:

Material	Mix Ratio	Cost (per gallon)
S	50%	$3.85
T	50%	$9.90

CHAPTER 17: MIX, YIELD, AND VARIANCE INVESTIGATION

Labor	Total Hours	Cost (per hour)
Type I	29,000	$8.00
Type II	19,800	$6.00

Required

Prepare an electronic spreadsheet to calculate the mix and yield variances for materials and labor.

E17–5. Materials Mix and Yield

Fancy Foods, Inc. manufactures white flour for use in delicate pastries. Two types of wheat are used: hard red and soft white. These types of wheat can be mixed in various proportions without severely harming the quality of the pastries. The standard input for 100 pounds of white flour is as follows:

Hard red wheat	(65 lbs. at $0.07 per lb.)	$4.55
Soft white wheat	(55 lbs. at $0.05 per lb.)	$2.75
		$7.30

During the current month, 20,000 pounds of white flour were manufactured using the following quantities and prices:

Hard red wheat	(13,500 lbs. at $0.071 per lb.)	$ 958.50
Soft white wheat	(10,700 lbs. at $0.049 per lb.)	524.30
		$1,482.80

Required

1. Compute the materials price and materials quantity variances.
2. Compute the materials mix and materials yield variances.
3. Analyze the composition of the mix variance by individual input component.

E17–6. Reasons Variances Occur

There are five general reasons that differences between budgeted and actual results may occur. The chapter described them as follows:

a. Normal random fluctuations
b. Inaccurate data
c. Inappropriate standards
d. Efficient operations
e. Out of control operations

The following list presents some examples of events in a manufacturing situation that could affect the evaluation of standard cost variances.

1. A worker develops a different way of organizing materials so that they can be loaded into a heat treating machine in less time.
2. The cost of maintenance supplies is charged to expense when purchased rather than when used.
3. The foreman is complaining about a 2 percent variance, even though all production quotas and quality measures are within reasonable limits.
4. The installation of a computer-controlled milling machine results in a very favorable labor efficiency variance.
5. The salvage value from scrap is not included in the calculation of standard costs.

6. A worker is sick but keeps working because there is no replacement available. As a result, the rate of defective units increases through the day.

7. A worker records production statistics at the end of the month according to his best recollection. Variances in this department have wide fluctuations.

8. A labor-intensive operation experiences large efficiency variances in its first three months of operation. Standards were set at the average labor efficiency rate for a three-year production run.

9. A machine has a worn part that results in a relatively large number of defective units. However, workers are not willing to replace the part because stopping the machine to make repairs will reduce the daily efficiency more than having some defective units. "It can wait until the next shift," they claim.

10. The quality of raw materials has steadily improved, allowing certain machine operations to be speeded up.

Required

For each event, assign the most likely reason the variances occur.

E17–7. Graphic Evaluation of Variances
Simtex Chemical Company uses a standard cost system. The plant manager requests that all standard cost variances be reported graphically as well as numerically. A variance is investigated when it goes outside the predetermined limits for that variance. The following graph presents the recent history of a particular materials yield variance.

```
                                                          *
Upper limit  _____*___*___
                                                    *
                                                *
              *         *   *       *              *
Standard yield _____*_____*_____
                 *              *       *
                     *                *

Lower limit  _____
```

Required

Discuss when it would be appropriate to investigate this variance. Explain the role of human judgment versus statistical rules in variance investigation.

E17–8. Decision to Investigate: Expected Costs
Harris Products, Inc. has been experiencing some difficulty with one of its processes. After reviewing the last variance report, the plant manager has estimated that there is a 40-percent probability that this particular process is out of control. The cost to investigate the process is $200, the cost of correcting the process, if it is out of control, is expected to be $900, and the present value of the future cost savings from correction are estimated to be $2,000.

Required

1. Calculate the expected costs for investigating and not investigating the process. Should the process be investigated?

2. What is the indifference probability for investigating this process?

3. Discuss the relationship between the size of a variance and the probability that a variance is out of control.

4. Discuss the relationship between the size of a variance and the potential savings obtained from investigating and correcting a process.

E17-9. Cost Savings Necessary to Investigate The manager of High Impact Plastics, Inc. is 90-percent sure that the main production process is in control. The cost of correcting an out-of-control process is $1,000. The cost of investigating and testing the process to determine if it is actually out of control is $4,000. Because the cost of investigating the process is so high, the plant manager wants to make sure that the benefits of correcting the process exceed the costs.

Required

1. Determine what the minimum amount of cost savings must be before the plant manager should be advised to investigate the process.
2. If the plant manager desires a $1,000 "cushion" to allow for estimation errors in determining future benefits from investigation, what would be his or her indifference probability for investigation?

E17-10. Decision to Investigate: Expected Costs Karikor Inc. uses a computer-controlled machine in one of its processes that rarely goes out of control. The manager supervising this process has received a variance report that makes her believe there is a 10-percent probability that the process is out of control. It will cost $900 to stop and investigate the process. The cost of correcting any difficulties in the process have averaged $2,500 per out-of-control occurrence. The present value of the cost savings from correcting an out-of-control process is estimated to be $10,000.

Required

1. Prepare an electronic spreadsheet that automatically calculates (a) the expected cost of investigating, (b) the expected cost of not investigating, and (c) the indifference probability.
2. From a cost-benefit standpoint, should this process be investigated? Explain.

PROBLEMS

P17-1. Materials Mix and Yield Variances DeCarries Company produces a special mouthwash used for the prevention of cavities. To make this mouthwash, three different ingredients are used. A-Flor, B-Flor, and C-Flor are mixed in the proportions 4:3:3, respectively, at standard, and their standard costs are $12.00, $7.00, and $5.00 per liter, respectively. Reports indicate that the yield for the mixing process has produced 90 liters for each 100 liters of input for the past few months; therefore, 90 percent has been adopted as the standard yield rate. The company uses just-in-time inventory techniques and does not carry any inventories at the end of a period. The production budget indicates that 8,000,000 liters of mouthwash are planned for production this period.

Last week the company produced 150,000 liters of mouthwash at a total raw materials cost of $500,000. The actual number of liters used and costs per liter for the three ingredients are as follows:

Ingredient	Liters	Cost (per liter)
A-Flor	90,000	$11.00
B-Flor	70,000	8.40
C-Flor	40,000	5.50

Required

Compute the materials price, yield, and mix variances for each of the three ingredients. Reconcile these variances with the total materials budget variance.

P17–2. Labor Mix and Yield Variances Taber Clothing Company specializes in the manufacture of quality suits for men. The following standard direct labor rates are in effect for the company's main production activities.

Labor Category	Rate (per hour)	Hours (per item)
Cutting	$10.00	0.10
Assembly	$ 8.00	0.80
Sewing	$ 8.00	0.80
Finishing	$ 6.00	0.30

During the current accounting period, the labor cost to complete 1,000 suits was as given below. There was no work-in-process inventory at either the beginning or the end of the period.

Labor Category	Rate (per hour)	Total Hours Worked
Cutting	$10.05	500
Assembly	$ 8.00	470
Sewing	$ 7.80	520
Finishing	$ 7.10	540

Required

Compute the labor rate, yield, and mix variances for each category of labor. Reconcile these variances with the total labor budget variance.

P17–3. Materials Price, Mix, and Yield Variances Nibley Company uses a standard cost system. The standard cost card for inputs for the production of a special soil treatment compound shows the following materials standards:

Material	Kilograms	Cost (per kilogram)
Calcor	60	$1.40
Demrel	20	1.00
Ecktem	80	0.50

The standard 150 kilogram mix is expected to produce 147 kilograms of finished compound. During a recent production run, 500,000 kilograms of materials were used as follows:

Material	Quantity and Unit Cost
Calcor	230,000 kilograms at $1.50
Demrel	50,000 kilograms at $0.95
Ecktem	220,000 kilograms at $0.60

The output of finished compound from the process was 495,000 kilograms.

Required

Develop a standard cost analysis showing materials price, mix, and yield variances.

P17–4. Labor Mix and Yield Variances (CMA) KnitsPlus Manufacturing Company uses a process cost accounting system. An analysis that compares the actual results with a flexible budget is prepared monthly. The standard direct-labor rates used in the flexible budget are established each year at the time the annual plan is formulated. They are then held constant for the entire year.

The standard direct-labor rates in effect for the fiscal year ended June 30, 19X7, and the standard hours allowed for output for the month of April are shown in the following schedule:

Direct Labor	Rate (per hour)	Hours Allowed (for output)
Labor (category I)	$8.00	500
Labor (category II)	$7.00	500
Labor (category III)	$5.00	500

The wage rate for each labor category increased on January 1, 19X7, under the terms of a new union contract negotiated in December 19X6. The standard wage rates were not revised to reflect the new contract.

The actual direct-labor hours worked and the actual direct-labor rates per hour experienced for the month of April were as follows:

Direct Labor	Rate (per hour)	Actual Hours
Labor (category I)	$8.50	550
Labor (category II)	$7.50	650
Labor (category III)	$5.40	375

Required

1. Calculate the dollar amount of the direct-labor budget variance for the month of April for KnitsPlus Manufacturing Company and analyze the total variance into the following components:
    a. direct-labor rate variance
    b. direct-labor efficiency variance
    c. direct-labor mix variance
    d. direct-labor yield variance
2. Discuss the advantages and disadvantages of a standard cost system in which the direct-labor rates per hour are not changed during the year to reflect events such as a new labor contract.

P17–5. Mix and Yield; Materials and Labor Perry Industries has the following standard materials and direct-labor costs for a batch of input that typically results in one unit of good output. Materials can be substituted for each other within a limited range. Because of the special training required for category Y labor, it is not interchangeable with category Z labor.

Materials:
    Material W—4 units at $3.00 per unit = $12.00
    Material X —16 units at $2.00 per unit = $32.00
                                                                          $44.00

Labor:
    Category Y—4 hours at $10.00 per hour = $40.00
    Category Z—4 hours at $ 6.00 per hour = $24.00
                                                                          $64.00

During the period, 50 batches of input were placed in production, with good output equaling only 45 units. Costs were as follows:

Materials:
 Material W—235 units at $2.90 per unit = $ 681.50
 Material X —705 units at $2.50 per unit = 1,762.50
                $2,444.00

Labor:
 Category Y—200 hours at $10.00 per hour = $2,000
 Category Z—200 hours at $ 6.00 per hour = 1,200
                $3,200

Required

1. Prepare an electronic spreadsheet to calculate mix and yield variances for materials and labor.
2. Use the spreadsheet developed for requirement 1 to determine what the results would have been for materials if the standard total quantity of materials had been used at the actual mix ratio.

P17–6. Decision to Investigate: Expected Costs The plant manager of Everflow Corporation is evaluating a $4,000 unfavorable variance and cannot decide if the process should be investigated. The plant manager estimates that a variance of this magnitude indicates a 20-percent chance that the process is out of control and should be investigated. The cost to investigate is $700. If the process is out of control, it will cost an estimated $500 to correct the problem. It is almost certain that next month's variance will be zero if the process is stopped and corrected this month. If the process is out of control but not corrected, next month's variance is expected to be the same as this month's variance. However, company policy indicates that a variance of this magnitude must be investigated if it occurs two months in a row. Therefore, the only loss due to delaying investigation is the expected reoccurrence of the $4,000 variance next month.

Required

1. What is the plant manager's indifference level of probability for investigating this variance? Assume that the total $4,000 unfavorable variance will be eliminated through investigation and correction.
2. Assume that $500 of the total $4,000 variance is caused by normal random fluctuations. Should the plant manager investigate the process? Support your conclusion with calculations.

P17–7. Variance Investigation: Indifference Numerical Control Products, Inc. has estimated that the probability of its welding robots being in a controlled state is 98 percent. Thus the probability of the robots operating in an out-of-control situation is 2 percent. Because of the nature of the products involved and the nature of the welds made by the robots, investigating an out-of-control situation is expected to result in cost savings of approximately $15,000 a year for the next five years. Costs of investigation average about $8,000, and costs to correct out-of-control situations average $9,000.

Required

1. Determine whether the company should investigate any out-of-control situations. Assume a cost of capital of 12 percent.
2. If the cost of investigation can be reduced by $2,000, what would be the plant manager's indifference probability?

P17–8. Decision to Investigate a Variance Harden Machine Company has an $84,000 standard cost for producing a Model X-55 milling machine. Last month several milling machines were produced at an average materials cost of $102,000. The production manager is at a loss to explain exactly what happened, but she believes that there is an 80-percent chance that the process is out of control.

The production manager anticipates that if nothing is done and the process actually is out of control, the present value of the extra costs (in excess of those caused by normal random fluctuations) over the planning horizon will be $16,000. The cost to investigate is $1,200. The cost to correct the process, if it is out of control, is estimated to be $2,400.

Required

1. Prepare a report for the production manager that shows whether or not the process should be investigated. Your report should contain all relevant cost-benefit calculations.
2. What level of probability that the process is in control would be necessary to make the production manager indifferent about investigating the process?
3. If the process is out of control, why is the present value of the extra costs over the planning horizon less than the current difference between standard and actual costs?

P17–9. Variance Investigation: Expected Values (AICPA adapted)

Crest Oil Company currently sells three grades of gasoline: regular; unleaded; and premium unleaded, which has a higher octane rating than regular unleaded. Premium unleaded is advertised as being "at least 15 percent more powerful than regular unleaded." Although any unleaded gasoline with a 15 percent or higher octane rating than regular unleaded could be sold as premium unleaded, it is less costly to have the octane level be exactly 15 percent higher. The percentage of octane in premium unleaded is determined by one small valve in a refinery blending process. If the valve is properly adjusted, the process provides premium unleaded that is 15 percent higher in octane. If the valve is out of adjustment, the process provides premium unleaded that is 25 percent higher in octane.

Once the process is started, it must continue until 100,000 gallons of premium unleaded have been produced. The following cost data are available:

Cost per gallon:	
Regular	$0.60
Unleaded	0.70
Premium unleaded (15% higher octane)	0.80
Premium unleaded (25% higher octane)	0.90
Cost of checking the valve	$500
Cost of adjusting the valve	$250

Estimates of the probabilities of the valve's condition are as follows:

Event	Probability
Valve in adjustment	0.7
Valve out of adjustment	0.3

Required

1. What is the expected cost of checking the valve and adjusting it, if necessary?
2. What is the expected cost of not checking the valve?
3. At what probability would Crest Oil be indifferent about whether or not to investigate?

P17–10. Behavioral Considerations of Variance Analysis (CMA)

WesTek Company, manufacturer of biochemical products, has been in operation for five years. Although the first few years were difficult, the company has been very successful, with an average annual growth rate based on sales of 35 percent. However, the company is experiencing some concerns about its management of direct labor, and it is considering adopting a standard cost system to help control labor and other costs.

WesTek Company hired an engineering consultant to help establish labor standards. After a complete study of the work processes, the consultant recommended a labor standard of 3 units of production per hour, or 24 units of production per day per worker. The consultant further advised WesTek that its labor rates were below the prevailing rate of $8.00 per hour.

WesTek's production vice president thought that this labor standard was too tight and that employees would be unable to attain it. From his experience with the labor force, he believed a labor standard of 20 units per day for each worker would be more reasonable.

The president of WesTek believed that the standard should be set at a high level to motivate the workers, but he also recognized the standard should be set at a level that would provide adequate information for control and reasonable cost comparisons. After much discussion, management decided to use a dual standard. The labor standard recommended by the engineering consultant of 24 units per day would be employed in the plant as a motivational device, and the cost standard of 20 units per day would be used for reporting purposes. Management also concluded that the workers would not be informed of the cost standard used for reporting purposes. The production vice president conducted several sessions before implementation in the plant, informing the workers of the new standard cost system and answering questions. The new standards were not related to incentive pay but were introduced at the same meeting in which wage increases to $8.00 per hour were announced.

The new standard cost system was implemented in January of the current year. At the end of six months of operation, the following statistics on labor efficiency were presented to the president.

Month	Production (units)	Direct Labor (hours)	Variance from Labor Standard	Variance from Cost Standard
January	5,100	3,000	$1,350 U	$1,200 F
February	5,000	2,900	1,200 U	1,300 F
March	4,700	2,900	1,650 U	700 F
April	4,500	3,000	2,250 U	0
May	4,300	3,000	2,550 U	400 U
June	4,400	3,100	2,700 U	500 U

Materials, labor mix, and other variances, as well as plant conditions, have not changed to any great extent during the six-month period.

Required

1. Discuss the apparent effect on motivation of adopting labor standards in WesTek's plant.
2. Evaluate the decision to use dual standards in WesTek's standard cost system.

Chapter 18

Accounting Systems for Management Planning and Control

Outline

THE COMMON BODY OF KNOWLEDGE FOR MANAGEMENT ACCOUNTANTS
Management Decision Process
Cost Accounting as a Subsystem of the Management Information System
Fully Integrated Management Information System
  Strategic Decisions
  Nonprogrammed Decisions
  Repetitive Decisions
HOW MUCH INFORMATION?
Required Information
Cost Benefit Analysis of Additional Information
DEVELOPING A COST ACCOUNTING SYSTEM
Master Plan
Systems Analysis and Design Life Cycle
  Systems Analysis Phase
  General Systems Design Phase
  Detailed Systems Design Phase
  Review and Decision Points
  Implementation
  Evaluation and Maintenance
Behavioral Considerations
DATA VERSUS INFORMATION
Report Preparation
Types of Reports
  Operational Report
  Planning Report
  Control Report
  Performance Report
  Legal Compliance Reports
Designing Output Reports
COST ACCOUNTING SYSTEM INTERNAL CONTROLS
Administrative Controls
  Separation of Duties and Responsibilities
  Rotation of Personnel
  Mandatory Vacations
  Standard Operating Procedures
  Performance Evaluations
  Terminations and Exit Interviews
Input Controls
  Control Totals
  Capturing Data in Machine-Readable Form
  Originating Department Approval
Processing Controls
  Limit and Reasonableness Test
  Crossfooting
  Control Totals
Output Controls
SUMMARY
SELF-STUDY PROBLEM
SUGGESTED READINGS
DISCUSSION QUESTIONS
EXERCISES
PROBLEMS

The procedures and practices discussed in this text need to be integrated into a cost accounting system. Recent developments in mini- and microcomputer technology have made computers available to both medium- and smaller-sized organizations. They have also resulted in decentralization of much of the data processing in larger organizations. The computer has now become an integral part of many people's jobs. Few manual cost accounting systems will remain in existence because of the new technology, reduced processing costs, additional computational power, and added capacity provided by the computer. Also, many of the applications that assist management in the decision functions of the organization are now computerized.

To a large extent, management accounting personnel are responsible for the development, operation, and control of a major portion of an organization's information systems. An extensive knowledge of computers and computer data processing will greatly benefit someone pursuing a career in management or cost accounting. There are many courses and many text books on computers and computer data processing, and a complete coverage of the requisite knowledge is beyond the scope of this text. However, a review of the required systems topics for a management accountant is appropriate. After completing this chapter, you should be able to:

1. identify the major systems topics contained in the common body of knowledge for management accountants.
2. identify the role of the cost accounting system within a fully integrated management information system.
3. describe the process used to design, implement, and maintain internal reporting systems.
4. explain the internal controls required to ensure the integrity of an organization's financial information.

THE COMMON BODY OF KNOWLEDGE FOR MANAGEMENT ACCOUNTANTS

The National Association of Accountants (NAA) through its Management Accounting Practices Committee periodically issues statements referred to as Statements on Management Accounting (SMA). One of the more recent statements, titled *The Common Body of Knowledge for Management Accountants,* was issued to do the following:

1. Guide academic institutions in structuring a curriculum for management accountants.
2. Describe management accounting knowledge in enough detail to assist students in making career decisions.
3. Guide practicing management accountants in expanding or updating their professional knowledge.
4. Provide a basis for NAA and other professional associations to structure pertinent continuing education programs.
5. Establish a foundation from which the Certified Management Accountant program can continue to evolve.

The statement has three core-of-knowledge areas: *(a)* information and decision processes, *(b)* accounting principles and functions, and *(c)* entity operations. Each of these areas has one or more sections dealing with the design, operation, or control of a managerial or cost accounting system in a computer data-processing environment. The accounting systems topics can be classified into four broad areas:

1. The role of management accountants and management accounting information in the management process.
2. The design, implementation, and maintenance of an internal reporting system.
3. Internal controls required to ensure the integrity of an organization's financial information.
4. Concepts, processes, and security aspects of information and communication systems.

The knowledge requirements and the major concepts associated with each of these four areas will be reviewed in this chapter and in chapter 25.

Management Decision Process

The management accountant's role in the management decision process is described as follows in the NAA *Common Body of Knowledge* statement:

> At various levels in the organization, management accountants participate in decision processes which establish, implement, and revise short-term, intermediate, or long-term plans. Management accountants also help coordinate decision-making activities for an entire organization. They therefore develop and maintain reporting systems that are aligned with organizational structures and that provide decision-useful information on an organization's performance.

If a management accountant is to adequately perform in this area, he or she must understand the relationship of the cost accounting system to the management information system, the various categories of management decisions, and the computer applications that are useful for each category of decisions.

Cost Accounting as a Subsystem of the Management Information System

A **management information system** may be defined as a computer-based information processing system that supports an organization's operation, management, and decision functions. The management information system must be able to support all the functional areas within the organization, including marketing, manufacturing, personnel, and finance.

Within the management information system there is a subsystem commonly called the accounting information system, which comprises all activities involved with recording, classifying, summarizing, and reporting business transactions. It includes external reporting to stockholders, creditors, and governmental agencies as well as internal reporting to management.

Examples of systems that are included in a management information system but are not part of the accounting information system are the personnel information system and the marketing information system. A personnel information system may include information on educational training, medical history, prior job experience, fluency in foreign languages, results on performance evaluations, and character references. Typically these things are of no interest to the users of the accounting information system. However, information such as marital status and number of exemptions is relevant to both accounting and personnel information systems.

Cost accounting is a subsystem of the accounting information system, which is designed to assist management in operating the business smoothly and profitably. The cost accounting system can be split into two functions—cost determination and cost analysis. Cost determination seeks to identify the cost of individual products, product components, or services provided. In a manufacturing environment, this information is used to evaluate the manufacturing process, to value ending inventories, and to determine the cost of goods sold. Cost analysis uses the cost data along with other data that are collected or developed as needed to help management make decisions that relate to current and future operations.

Figure 18.1 shows the relationship of the management information system to the management cycle. The management cycle encompasses the activities performed by management from one planning period to the next. An operating plan is developed at the beginning of the period. Throughout the period, management attempts to implement the plan. Corrective action is taken to control the activity whenever actual operations differ significantly from planned operations. A final evaluation is performed at the end of the period and is used as a basis for developing a new plan for the coming period.

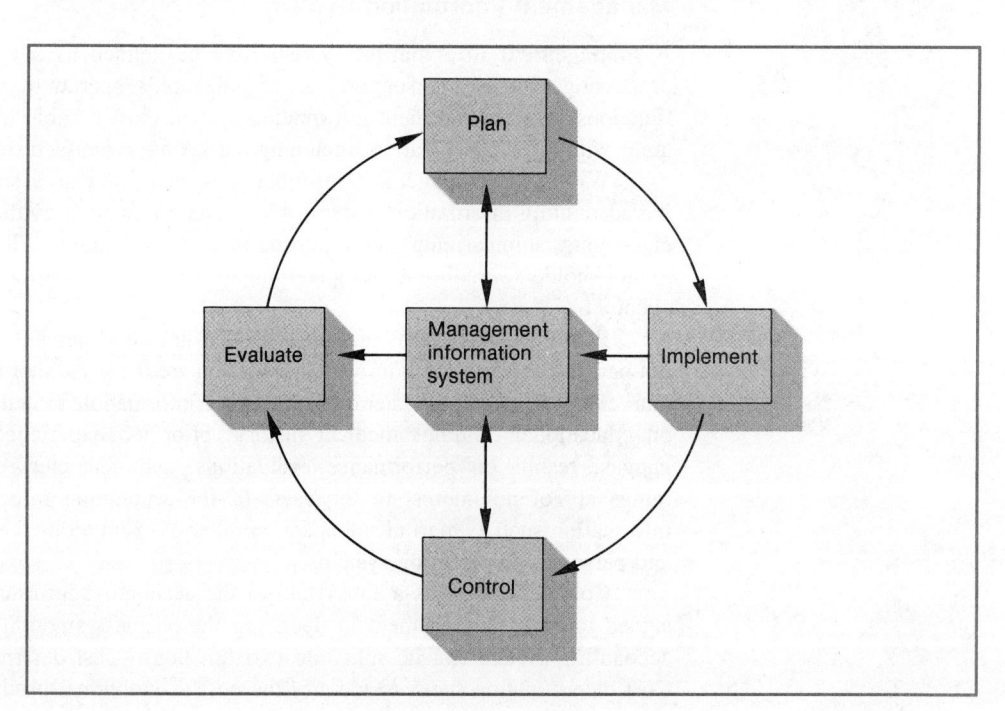

Note that the management information system is central to all activities. It provides management with the data required to develop the plan or budget for the coming period. As the plan is executed, data are collected on the results of operations. These are compared to the budget to compute the variances that help management to identify areas of the business in which corrective action is required. The information system provides the final results for the period that are used to evaluate performance and serve as a basis for developing the plan for the next operating cycle.

Fully Integrated Management Information System

A management information system is considered to be fully integrated when the informational needs of each subsystem are coordinated and each draws information from a common source called the **data base.** A fully integrated management information system enters data into the system only once. Information that is collected in any area of the business is immediately made available to all other areas of the business through the common data base. All records and files are updated for the new information regardless of where it is captured.

FIGURE 18.1

The Management Information System Relative to the Management Cycle

The subsystems of a management information system usually correspond with the functional areas of the organization. Figure 18.2 shows several functional areas and their relationships to the fully integrated system. Each functional area has special informational needs at each level of management. Top management is concerned primarily with strategic planning, whereas middle and lower management is responsible for operational planning and control reporting. These different levels of management decisions have been broadly classified in the NAA *Common Body of Knowledge* statement into three categories: *(a)* strategic, *(b)* nonprogrammed, and *(c)* repetitive. Each functional area and each level of management decision must be supported, in part at least, by the common data base.

FIGURE 18.2

Components of a Management Information System

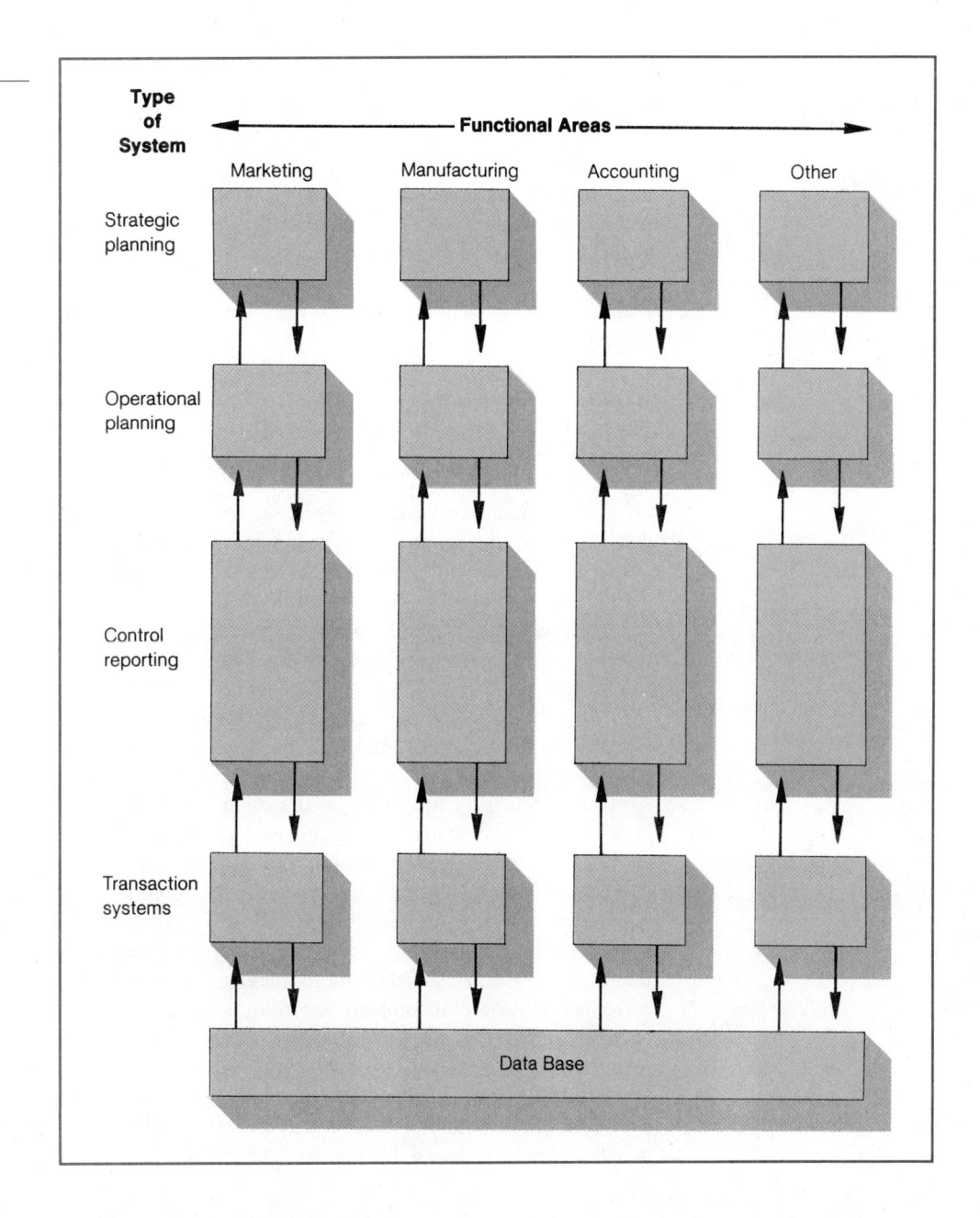

Strategic Decisions Strategic decisions involve planning the direction and undertaking the actions needed to achieve an entity's long-range goals and objectives. The scope of an entity's businesses and its market share, sales, profitability, financial risks, and technological positions are some of the factors considered in strategic decision making. Management accountants integrate knowledge from an organization's environment, its history, and its principal operations to help management develop alternatives and to track strategic plans.

Much of the strategic planning data, as well as the computer programs required to analyze the data, are not available within the organization. Special task forces may be organized to collect the required data. Generalized software applications such as Lotus, Visacalc, or Multimate may be used, or computer programs may be written specifically for analyzing the data.

Nonprogrammed Decisions Some events cannot be anticipated; reports and judgments about optimal courses of action must be made as the need arises. Management accountants have to be able to quickly apply analytical skills and reporting techniques to supply relevant information for nonprogrammed decision making. Innovative and creative approaches are often needed to provide the proper perspective.

Information required for making nonprogrammed decisions is generally available within the organization; however, the programs to analyze the data will usually not be available and the appropriate decision rules may not be clear. Once again, generalized software may be used, or special programs may be developed to perform the required analysis. Management accountants are often relied on to provide the appropriate decision rule.

Repetitive Decisions This area of decision making requires knowledge of an organization's routine operations as governed by management policies and procedures. Management accountants assist in setting policies and objectives and in monitoring their implementation.

The information system must be set up to routinely collect and process the necessary data to provide the information that is required for the repetitive decisions. The traditional cost accounting systems, including job-order or process costing systems, will typically be used. These systems may have built into them the use of standard costs, variance analysis, and exception reporting to help managers identify the operating areas requiring their attention.

A fully integrated management information system, with a well-designed data base, is a primary goal of most organizations. It provides much of the data as well as the computer programs for processing the data for each functional area and level of management. A major benefit of a fully integrated system is that data are entered into the system only once and then are shared among all uses and users. Other benefits generally include reduced personnel for data processing, reduced rate of operator error, and less time devoted to error correction. Information is more timely, more accurate, and consistent across functional areas. There is also less redundancy of information in the enterprise's files.

The process of hiring a new employee illustrates the operation of a fully integrated information system and some of its benefits. Suppose a new employee is hired by the personnel division of a company according to a job description developed by the manufacturing supervisor. At the time of hiring, the personnel department collects the information required for the employee's file. Among other things this includes the pay rate, marital status, and number of dependents. The employee's record becomes part of the company's data base that is available to authorized users in other functional areas. This information is subsequently accessed by the cost accounting function when posting direct labor to individual job tickets and when preparing the employee's paycheck. By sharing these data, cost accounting did not have to contact the employee and collect the same data again. It also avoided having to develop and maintain its own personnel file.

The major problem with a fully integrated information system is in designing a data base that is flexible to the changing needs of the organization yet that satisfies the needs of all users at each level of management and within each functional area. The controller or a representative from the cost accounting function plays a key role in the development of the data base and the entire information system. Accounting for financial transactions is required for all functional areas. Therefore, the cost accountant must be knowledgeable not only about accounting but also about computer processing and the development and implementation of computerized information systems.

HOW MUCH INFORMATION?

The objective of an accounting information system is to provide information that is useful to both internal and external parties who have an interest in the organization. Some information provided by the cost accounting system is required by law or by generally accepted accounting principles. However, much of the information provided for management decisions is not required but is given with the hope that it will assist management in operating the business more profitably. Questions that continually must be asked when providing nonrequired information include: "How much information should be provided?" and "Is the benefit of additional information worth its cost?"

Let's first identify some of the information that must be provided by the cost accounting system to be in compliance with the law and with generally accepted accounting principles. Then we will consider the cost-benefit analysis of additional information.

Required Information

Public Law Number 95–213, titled the Foreign Corrupt Practices Act, was passed by the United States Congress in December 1977. There are three major sections of the act, two of which identify what constitutes foreign corrupt practices and penalties associated with them. The other section identifies accounting standards that must be met by every company, domestic or foreign, that is subject to the Securities Act of 1934.

This act requires a company to (a) make and keep books, records, and accounts that, in reasonable detail, accurately and fairly reflect the transactions and dispositions of the assets of the issuer; and (b) devise and maintain a system of internal accounting controls that will provide reasonable assurance of the following:

1. Transactions are executed in accordance with management's general or specific authorization.
2. Transactions are recorded as necessary (a) to permit preparation of financial statements in conformity with generally accepted accounting principles or any other criteria applicable to such statements and (b) to maintain accountability for assets.
3. Access to assets is permitted only in accordance with management's general or specific authorizations.
4. The recorded accountability for assets is compared with the existing assets at reasonable intervals and appropriate action is taken with respect to any differences.

The implementation of controls required by this act for a cost accounting system will be discussed later in this chapter. First we will focus on the information that must be provided by the system to prepare financial statements in accordance with generally accepted accounting principles and with Internal Revenue Service (IRS) requirements.

The major objective of generally accepted accounting principles in accounting for inventory is to obtain an appropriate matching of costs against revenues to properly determine realized income. The inventory at any given date is the balance of costs applicable to goods on hand that remain after the matching of absorbed costs with concurrent revenues. This balance is carried forward to future periods.

Generally accepted accounting principles identify the primary basis of accounting for inventory as *cost,* which has been defined as the price paid or consideration given to acquire an asset. As applied to inventories, cost means the sum of the applicable expenditures and charges *directly* or *indirectly* incurred to bring an article to its existing condition and location. This has special meaning for a manufacturing organization because of its indirect manufacturing costs that we call overhead. The exclusion of overhead from an inventory cost does not constitute an acceptable accounting procedure.

The Internal Revenue Code also specifies the full cost method (sometimes called the absorption method) of inventory costing:

> In order to conform as nearly as may be possible to the best accounting practices and to clearly reflect income, both direct and indirect production costs must be taken into account in the computation of inventoriable costs in accordance with the "full absorption" method of inventory costing.

Thus, to provide financial statements that are in accordance with generally accepted accounting principles and to satisfy reporting requirements with the IRS, the cost accounting system must be based on the full cost method of inventory valuation. Under this method, production costs must be allocated to goods produced during the period, whether sold during that period or in inventory at the close of the period. Thus inventoriable costs include all direct production costs (direct materials and direct labor) as well as indirect production costs (manufacturing overhead). A manufacturing overhead rate or a standard cost method is generally used to allocate manufacturing overhead to the units produced.

Cost-Benefit Analysis of Additional Information

Additional information should be provided as long as the marginal value of the new information exceeds its marginal cost. The *value* of additional information is often difficult to measure, but conceptually it is defined as the improvement in management's decisions as a result of the new information. The cost of information is the amount paid to capture, store, process, and report it to management.

Value of information = Benefit from improved decisions − Cost of providing information

An example will illustrate the type of analysis that is required to evaluate the costs and benefits of additional information. Suppose Nebeker Incorporated manufactures two products, malt and silt, from a common raw material. Somewhere during the production process, each product becomes separately identifiable. However, no separate accounting has been made of production costs by product after the split-off point because both products have been saleable only in a finished state.

An offer has just been received from a foreign company to purchase 100,000 pounds of malt at the split-off point for $4.00 per pound over the next year. Malt currently sells for $5.00 per pound, and selling and administrative expenses will not be affected by this

FIGURE 18.3

```
                    Nebeker, Inc.
              Projected Income Statement
           Assuming all Sales to U.S. Customers
```

Sales revenue:		
Malt (200,000 lbs. @ $5.00/lb.)		$1,000,000
Silt (50,000 lbs. @ $7.50/lb.)		375,000
Total		$1,375,000
Manufacturing costs:		
Materials	$400,000	
Labor	600,000	
Overhead	200,000	
Total	$1,200,000	
Selling and administrative expenses	100,000	
Total		1,300,000
Net income		$ 75,000

decision. Figure 18.3 shows the results of operations for the year just ended. Operations for the coming year are anticipated to be about the same, assuming the foreign offer is rejected.

Management thought that it had inadequate information with which to make a decision, but intuition suggested that it should reject the offer. After all, $4.00 was rather low, and a gut feeling told the managers that their profit would be greater if the malt was processed to a finished state and sold through normal market channels within the United States. One young executive disagreed, however, and suggested that they hire a consulting firm to determine the amount of processing costs that were incurred on malt after the split-off point. "If it costs more than $1 to process the malt after the split-off point," she argued, "we would be further ahead to sell the malt to the foreign company." The management team reluctantly agreed to contact a consulting firm and obtain an estimate of the consulting fee for such a study.

A reputable consulting firm was contacted and a proposal was obtained from it. The proposal identified two phases to the study:

Phase	Cost	Scope
I	$5,000	Analyze direct materials and direct labor to identify the cost to process malt after the split-off point.
II	$5,000	Analyze manufacturing overhead to identify the amount that could be avoided if 100,000 pounds of malt were not processed after the split-off point.

The young executive was successful in convincing other members of management to commit themselves to the project one phase at a time. The results of phase I could be obtained and analyzed before they committed themselves to phase II.

After a few days the consulting firm submitted the phase I report, which indicated that $0.70 of direct materials and $0.50 of direct labor per pound are incurred in processing malt after the split-off point. Based on this information, the young executive argued that the foreign offer should be accepted and that phase II of the study should be eliminated. The added $1.00 ($5.00 − $4.00) from processing the product and selling it in its finished state was less than the $1.20 ($0.70 + $0.50) of direct costs required to process the malt to a finished state. The elimination of any overhead costs would simply make it more desirable to sell the malt in its raw state to the foreign company. Once again management adopted the young executive's suggestion and accepted the foreign offer.

For illustrative purposes, note that if phase II of the consulting firm's proposal had been pursued, the firm would have found that $10,000 of overhead would be eliminated by not processing 100,000 pounds of malt to a finished state. This $10,000 savings will be achieved during the year that the company sells the malt in its raw state. The point is that the $10,000 savings is a result of this decision even though management didn't know the amount at the time it made the decision. Let's assume we know this amount in order to compute the value of the information provided by the consultants.

The young executive thought a personal victory had been achieved, but she was concerned that the consultant's fee had used up a major portion of the additional earnings from the foreign sale. In the quiet of her office she prepared a revised forecast for the coming year, which is shown in figure 18.4. From this she computed the value of the information provided by the consulting firm. Without the additional information, Nebeker, Inc. would have rejected the foreign offer and earned $75,000 of net income. With the additional information it accepted the offer and will have $105,000 of net income. The benefit of the improved decision is the $30,000 increase in net income.

Benefit of an improved decision = $105,000 − $75,000
= $30,000

The cost to capture, store, analyze, and report the information to management was all contained in the $5,000 consulting fee.

Cost of the information = $5,000

The organization is $25,000 better off by having the information provided by the consulting firm. The young executive felt satisfied that her contribution to the company was greater than her salary for the week.

FIGURE 18.4

Nebeker, Inc.
Projected Income Statement
Assuming Foreign Offer is Accepted

Sales revenue:			
Malt (100,000 lbs. @ $5.00/lb.)			$ 500,000
Silt (50,000 lbs. @ $7.50/lb.)			375,000
Foreign sales—Malt (100,000 lbs. @ $4.00/lb.)			400,000
Total			$1,275,000
Manufacturing costs:			
Material	$330,000		
Labor	550,000		
Overhead	190,000[a]		
Total		$1,070,000	
Selling and administrative expenses		100,000	
Total			1,170,000
Net income			$ 105,000

[a] The overhead amount recorded here is net of the savings achieved by selling malt in its raw state. If phase II of the consultant's project was not pursued, this would not be known until the end of the year. However, let's assume that management knows it now in order to compute the value of the information.

```
Value of information     = Benefit of improved decisions − Cost of the information
Value of the information = $30,000 − $5,000
                         = $25,000
```

There are two questions to consider at this point: Would the company have been better off if it had allowed the consultants to complete phase II of the study? What would the value of the information be if the additional processing costs for malt after the split-off point had been lower—say, $0.80 per pound ($0.40 per pound for direct material, $0.30 per pound for direct labor, and $10,000 of overhead for 100,000 pounds)?

The company would have been $5,000 worse off by having the consultants complete phase II of the study. The decision would have still been to sell the malt to the foreign company, but the cost of the information would have been $10,000. The net benefit to the firm would be only $20,000 rather than $25,000 as computed previously.

```
Value of information = $30,000 − $10,000
                     = $20,000
```

If the results of the study had shown additional processing costs to be only $0.80 per pound, the company should reject the foreign offer. The additional processing costs of $0.80 per pound provide $1.00 of extra revenue when the product is processed to its finished state and sold through normal market channels. Since operations do not change and net income remains at $75,000, the benefit from this decision alternative is zero. However, management still must pay the consulting firm $10,000 for both phases of the study. The net result to the company would be a $10,000 loss.

```
Value of information = 0 − $10,000
                     = ($10,000)
```

In summary, the value of information is equal to the benefit provided by the improvement in the decision-making process minus the cost of providing it. If the decision is not changed, there is no benefit to having the information, other than the comfort it provides management to know that it has made a good decision. Additional information should be provided as long as management is able to use it to make better decisions and as long as the improvement exceeds the cost associated with providing it.

DEVELOPING A COST ACCOUNTING SYSTEM

As mentioned before, the development of a cost accounting system must be integrated with the entire information system of an organization. The management accountants' primary responsibilities are to design, implement, and maintain internal reporting systems. Such systems should be designed to contribute to effective decision making and to monitor managerial policies. Once implemented, reporting systems should be reviewed continually and revised as needed to ensure that they properly reflect internal requirements. Management accountants, then, synthesize, analyze, and edit data and convey the resulting information to management in a usable form.

The structure of the information system and how it is to be developed is planned and documented in a master plan. Standard procedures are then followed in developing individual applications identified in the master plan. These procedures are typically called the *systems analysis and design life cycle*.

The required skills identified in the NAA *Common Body of Knowledge* statement for the management accountant include the following:

- An important part of a management accountant's knowledge is a familiarity with how systems are designed. This would include concepts and techniques relating to a system's life cycle; design; installation; implementation; operation; modification; and evaluation.
- Organizing and analyzing information involves deciding what data elements are important, knowing how they should be accumulated, understanding user needs and preferences, and transforming data into meaningful information.
- An understanding of how to assemble and convey information is necessary for effective communication.

In this section we will identify the contents of the master plan and explain how it is developed, as well as discuss the individual steps included in the systems analysis and design life cycle. Data will be distinguished from information, and some of the rules for good report preparation will be reviewed.

Master Plan

The objectives of the information system and the order in which they are developed are laid out in an information systems master plan. The **master plan** contains a summary of the information system's current capabilities as well as a projection of future requirements for labor, hardware, software, and financial resources. It generally covers a two-to-five year time period but places greatest emphasis on the planned activities of the coming year. Development activities as well as activities and requirements associated with operating the system are included in the master plan.

The development of the information system is broken down into subsystems called *applications*. Examples of individual applications include (a) the accounts receivable and billing system, (b) the fixed asset accounting system, (c) the cost accounting system, and (d) the personnel information system. The development portion of the master plan includes new applications that have been made by various user departments and important modifications to existing applications. Once an application has been developed and is operational, it becomes part of the operating section of the master plan. Figure 18.5 shows the master plan and its contents.

The first step in developing a computerized cost accounting system or in modifying an existing system is to get an approved project included in the organization's master plan. The controller, or a responsible individual from that division, works with the director of information systems to develop a *proposal for application development*. This is included along with other application modification and development requests in the annual update to the master plan prepared by the company's information systems division. The revised master plan is then reviewed by a standing steering committee composed of a variety of information-system users at middle and upper levels of management. This group reviews each application being made with special emphasis on the priority in which they are to be developed. Top management ultimately reviews, modifies, and approves the master plan.

Generally, the criteria used to rank the applications in the master plan are based heavily on a quantitative analysis of the expected costs and benefits. Because the life of most applications extends beyond one year, the cost-benefit analysis is a capital budgeting problem, which will be discussed in detail in chapters 23 and 24. Qualitative factors, such as an orderly development of the information system and effective utilization of data-processing personnel, may also be relevant.

Once the cost accounting application moves to the top of the priority list of applications for development, the information systems division organizes a project team to

FIGURE 18.5

Master Plan Contents

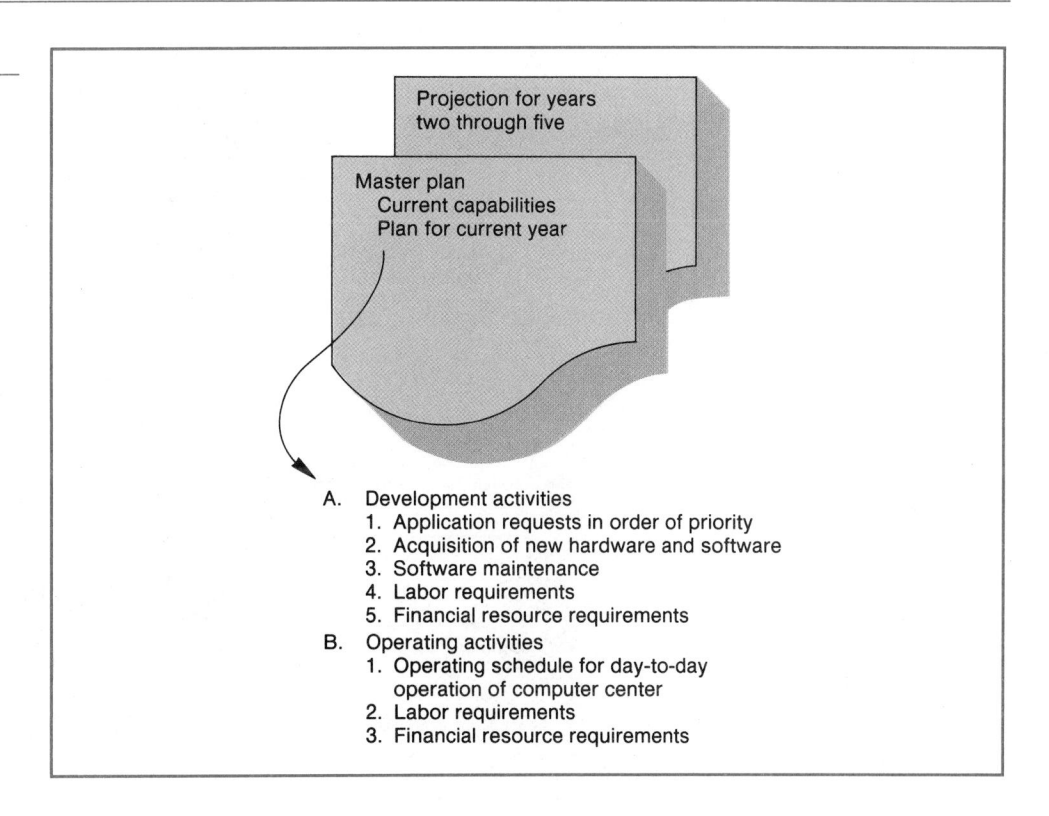

Projection for years two through five

Master plan
　Current capabilities
　Plan for current year

A. Development activities
　1. Application requests in order of priority
　2. Acquisition of new hardware and software
　3. Software maintenance
　4. Labor requirements
　5. Financial resource requirements
B. Operating activities
　1. Operating schedule for day-to-day operation of computer center
　2. Labor requirements
　3. Financial resource requirements

develop and implement the application. The project team is headed by a project director and includes one or more analysts or programmers or both, depending on the nature of the project. Also, a special steering committee is appointed whose members come from other user departments that may be affected by the application. For example, if a change is being made in the process-costing system to account for direct materials, a representative would probably be appointed to the steering committee from the financial reporting division, manufacturing division, raw materials storeroom, and perhaps the finished-goods warehouse. The objective of the committee is to provide broad-based input for the development of the application and to keep all interested departments informed of the development and implementation activities.

Figure 18.6 shows that the project director has supervisory responsibility over the project. Much of the preliminary investigation of the problem and the development of the application proposal may have been done by the person ultimately appointed as project director. The systems analysts are responsible for working with the users to identify the information desired, the decision rules that are to be used, and the sources of input data. Flowcharts, report layouts, and input forms are used to document their work. These are then used as a basis for designing a system to process the inputs and provide the necessary information. Programmers receive program specifications from the systems analysts and develop instructions in the form of code to control the computer's operation.

The primary responsibilities of the cost accountants are to provide information to the systems analysts and to critically review their work. The systems analysts frequently provide the cost accountants with a copy of their flowcharts to be sure that they accurately reflect the existing system. Cost accountants are also asked to review report layouts and input forms to see if they contain all the necessary information and if they are in a convenient format. The cost accountants can do these things if they know something about the systems analysis and design life cycle.

FIGURE 18.6

Systems Development Project Team

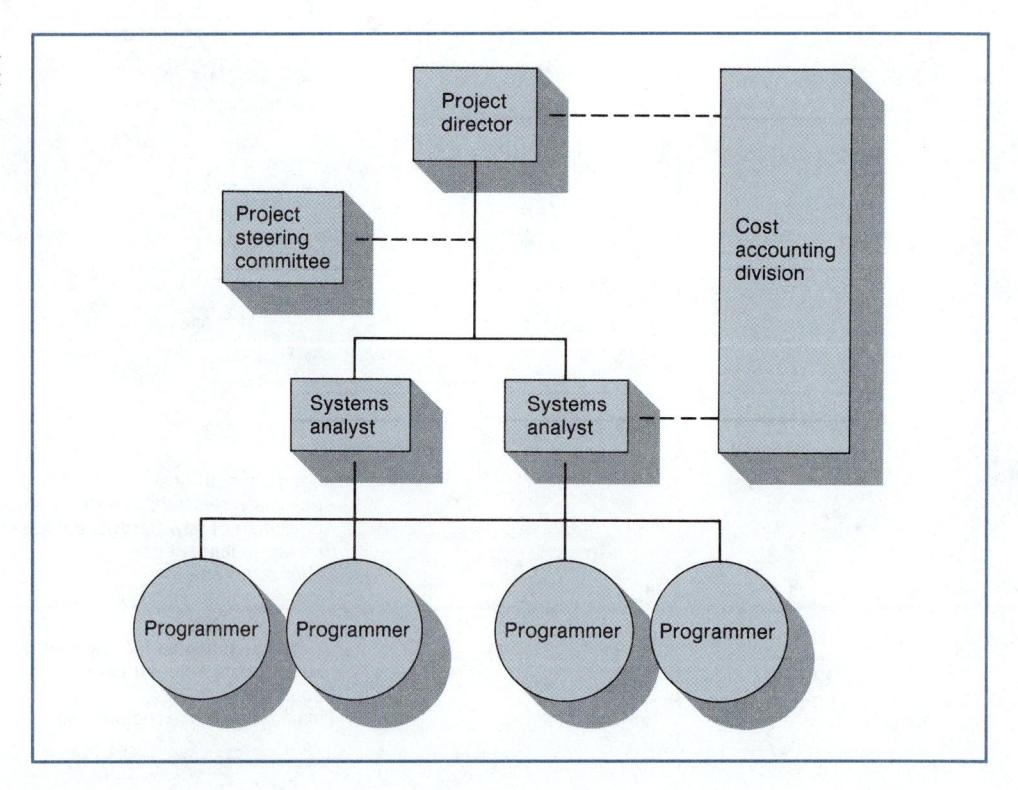

Systems Analysis and Design Life Cycle

The systems analysis and design life cycle comprises the activities that occur in the development of an approved application. This is a multistep process that contains several review and decision points. The reviews are intended to verify that adequate progress is being made toward the desired result and that the planned system will meet the needs of the users. The steps included in the cycle are shown in figure 18.7.

Systems Analysis Phase Usually a problem or a perceived opportunity initiates the application request. During the initial phase the project team must obtain a clear understanding of the problem or the opportunity and identify how the system operates. Generally this phase is a fact-finding process that takes the form of interviews, group meetings, and document analysis. The results of these activities are documented in the form of interview notes, copies of documents in use, and flowcharts.

Flowcharting is commonly used to summarize the flow of documents and information during this phase of the analysis and design life cycle. Once developed, flowcharts are useful in analyzing the strengths and weaknesses of the existing system and in structuring the new system and programs during the systems design phase.

The following are the three major types of flowcharts:

1. *Document/procedural flowcharts* show the flow and control of documents through a system and the major activities performed on them. These are the most general of all flowcharts, and they can be applied to both manual and computer operations.
2. *System flowcharts* show the relationship of the inputs to the various computer files and programs used to process the data, update the files, and provide output reports. These flowcharts apply only to computer processing.

FIGURE 18.7

Systems Analysis and Design Life Cycle

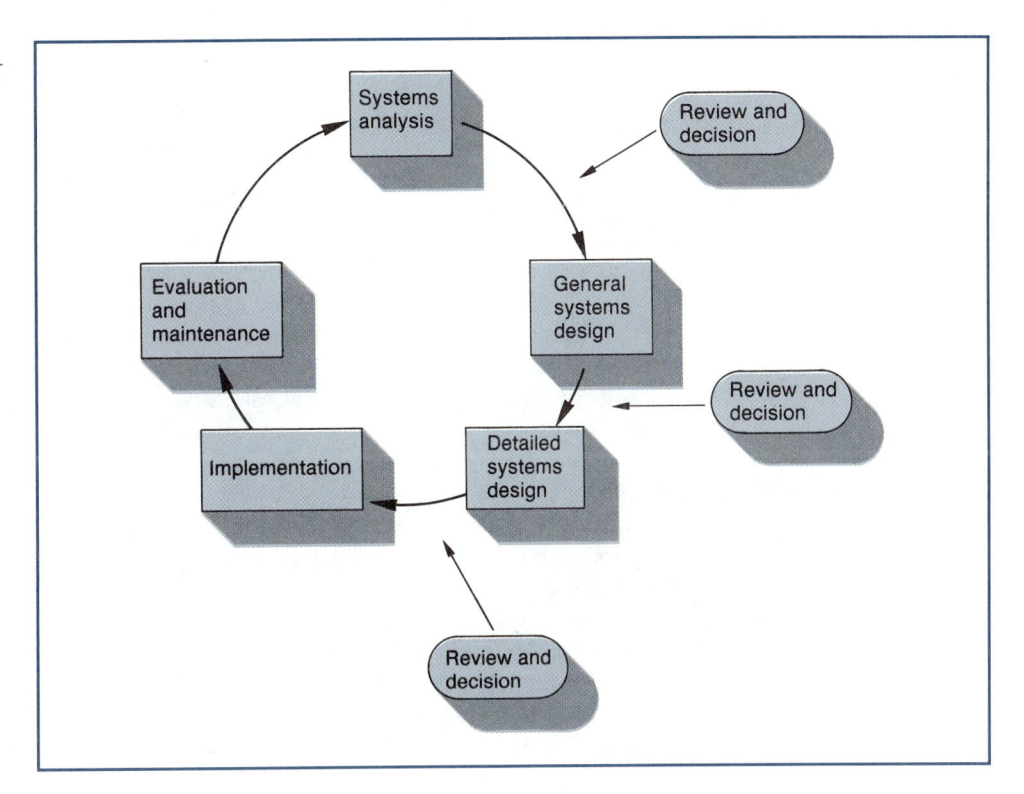

3. *Program flowcharts* provide the detailed logic of individual computer programs. They illustrate the sequence followed in reading transactions, opening and closing files, performing mathematical computations, making decisions, and loops within a program.

General Systems Design Phase Systems design can be defined as the drawing, planning, sketching, or arranging of many separate elements into a viable, unified whole. The general systems design stage focuses on determining the most desirable alternative or problem solution identified in the last stage and on designing the system to meet the users' requirements. Decisions at this phase include: Should the system be centralized or decentralized? Where will the inputs originate, and how will they be converted into machine readable form for processing by the computer? Where will output be made available, and in what form will it be provided? Remember that the general systems design phase provides only a conceptual model of the system, in much the same way that a blueprint is a conceptual model of a house. The actual construction begins during the detailed systems design phase.

Some results of the general systems design phase are documented in the form of revised document/procedure flowcharts and systems flowcharts. The development of the new system frequently results in a proposed change in the flow of documents through the system and the activities performed on them. Revised document flowcharts illustrate these changes. Systems flowcharts are frequently used to document the computerized portion of the proposed system. They show the relationship of the inputs to the computer process that updates the files and prepares the reports or other outputs from the system.

Detailed Systems Design Phase The actual development of the system takes place during the detailed systems design phase. This includes acquisition of required hardware, acquisition or development of software, and development of support materials such as operating procedures manuals.

The decision to acquire packaged software externally or to develop it internally is a critical one. Both time and cost usually are reduced when packaged software is purchased externally, but in many cases packaged software cannot be located to fit the exact needs of the organization. In such situations it must be decided whether it is easier and cheaper to buy a package that comes close to fitting the organization's needs and to modify it as required, or to start from scratch and develop an entirely new package. Regardless of the decision, it never hurts to investigate the market to identify what is available.

Different approaches can be taken to acquiring hardware and software, but the best approach is to develop a *request for proposal (RFP)* and to send it to several potential vendors. Vendors who think that they can satisfy the needs identified in the RFP respond in the form of a proposal. The proposals are reviewed and analyzed, and two or three that seem to be the most attractive are selected. These vendors are invited to make formal presentations of their hardware or software, as shown in figure 18.8. The vendor of the most desirable product is selected, and final negotiations are completed for the purchase.

Software that is developed internally starts with a report layout. The cost accountant should provide a great deal of input at this point to identify both the form and content of the desired information. It is critical that this be well thought out and reviewed carefully. This is so important that frequently the systems analyst will ask the accountant to sign a document stating that he or she has reviewed the report layouts and that they are satisfactory for the system's needs. The content of the input into the system, the files, and the processing all depend upon the output desired. A subsequent change in the report layout,

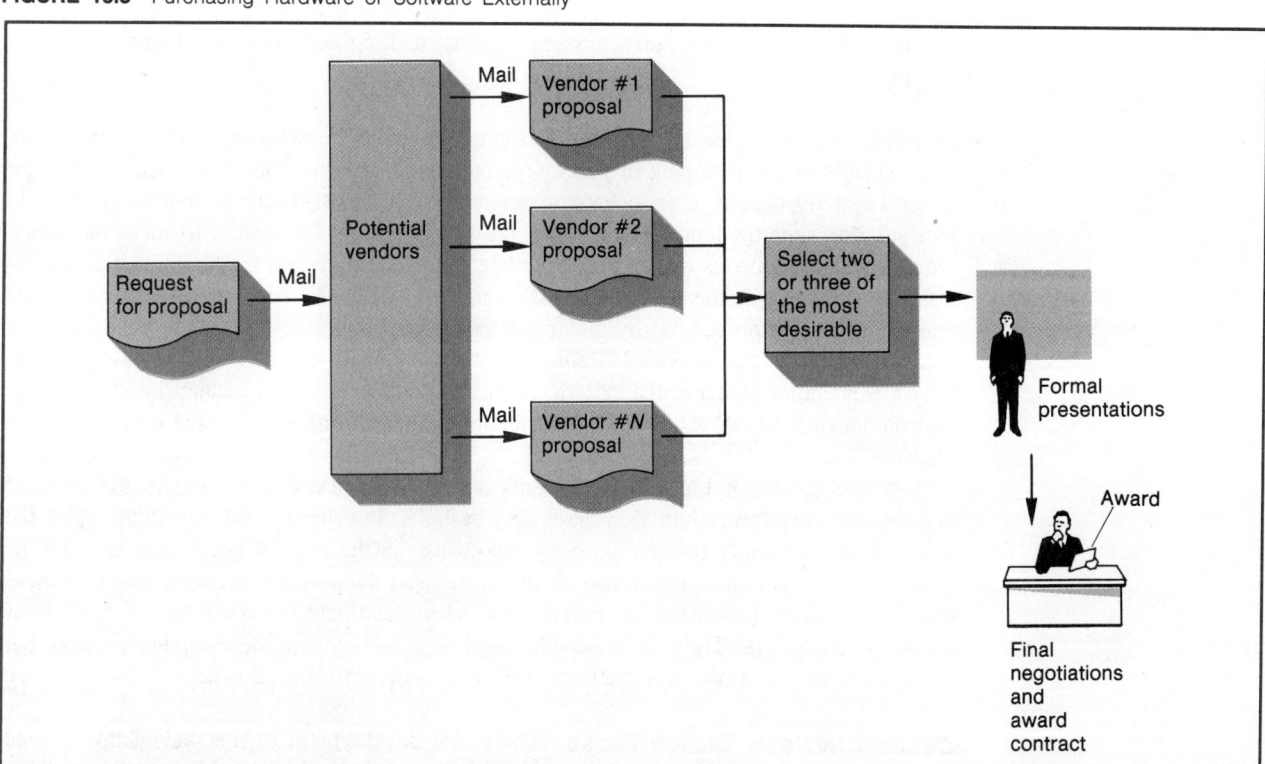

FIGURE 18.8 Purchasing Hardware or Software Externally

as minor as it may seem, may require substantial rework in the design of input forms, file layouts, and program codes.

Operating procedures manuals also must be developed during the detailed systems design phase. The operating procedures manuals describe in detail the procedures that must be followed to input data into the system and to get reports from it. These manuals are extremely important for training employees during the implementation phase and for training new employees during the on-going operation of the system. Only authorized personnel should have access to the operating procedures manuals. Otherwise, unauthorized personnel could get access to sensitive information and manipulate the accounting records to defraud the company.

Review and Decision Points The users and the steering committees review the results of each of the three previously discussed development stages before proceeding to the next phase. The reviews provide a checkpoint on the adequacy of documentation and on the feasibility of the system.

Documentation consists of forms, records, worksheets, flowcharts, and other documents that describe the procedures followed in developing the system as well as the procedures to be followed in operating the system. The system should be documented throughout the analysis and design life cycle. Systems analysts and programmers should provide complete documentation of the work that is performed, the results that are accomplished, and the systems that are developed. Documentation provides some assurance that the system has been carefully designed.

It is essential to have good documentation when attempting to modify an existing system. Without it, a simple modification can be almost as costly as developing an entirely new system. Users should follow up on documentation to make sure it is complete and accurate.

A feasibility analysis is performed to verify that the new system will measure up to expectations. The measures of feasibility and some typical questions asked in the analysis are summarized as follows:

1. Economic feasibility—Are the expected benefits from the new system worth the costs required to design, implement, and operate it? (This is a cost-benefit analysis that involves the use of capital budgeting techniques, which will be discussed in chapters 23 and 24).
2. Technical feasibility—Does the organization have the technical capability (hardware and personnel) to carry out the project? If not, can the required technical capability be obtained within the outlined cost constraints?
3. Operational feasibility—Will the system be used by the people for whom it is intended?
4. Legal feasibility—Are there conflicts between the proposed system and the organization's legal obligations?
5. Scheduling feasibility—Can the project be implemented by the required date?

A negative response to any of these questions at any of the review and decision points can terminate the project. The most detailed feasibility analysis is done just before implementation. The decision to implement is the final decision, and once implementation begins it is difficult to turn back without significant disruption to organizational stability.

Implementation Implementation of the new system involves converting from the existing system to the new system. The people whose jobs will be affected by the new system must be retrained. New hardware and software are installed, and existing files are converted to the format required by the new system. A system test, which generally is performed just before formally adopting the new system, requires the newly trained people who will be using the system to enter and process fictitious data (called test data) through the system. Accurate results and smooth processing during the system test indicate that the system is ready for formal implementation. Frequently, both the old system and the new system are operated for a short time in what is called *parallel processing*. Parallel processing provides a check on the accuracy of the new system and a back-up system in case the new system fails. At some point, however, the use of the old system must be discontinued.

Evaluation and Maintenance After the system has been implemented and allowed to operate for a short period of time, it should be evaluated to see if the anticipated benefits have in fact been achieved. This includes not only a check on the realization of cost savings or increased revenue but also a check on the adequacy of the information for the users' needs.

Program maintenance refers to the program modifications required to keep the system current. For example, some values, such as the manufacturing overhead rate, may have been included in the computer programs as a constant. As the overhead rate changes from year to year, the programs must be modified. Changes in input and file content also require program modifications.

Behavioral Considerations

Behavioral problems often occur during the analysis, design, and implementation phases of a computerized cost accounting system. The primary cause for the behavioral problems is resistance to change. Occasionally someone will lose his or her job when a new system is implemented, but most people who desire to remain with the company can do so as long as they are willing to be retrained for employment within the new system or in some other part of the organization. Aggression, avoidance, and projection are behavioral problems commonly encountered.

Aggression, in this context, is defined as an attack intended to beat or destroy the system. This type of behavior sometimes is exhibited by manufacturing personnel who are required to enter input data into the system. For example, direct laborers may be required by the new system to input the job number and the times they start and stop working on the job into a computer terminal located on the manufacturing floor. Aggressive behavior is exhibited when the terminal is mysteriously run over by a forklift truck or when honey is poured between the keys on the keyboard.

Projection entails blaming the new system for causing difficulties that are in fact caused by something else. This type of behavior is commonly exhibited by people who work with the system. A comment such as, "The system doesn't give me the information I need when I need it," may be a problem with the system. But more likely the problem is that the individual has not learned where to look on the report to get the needed information.

Avoidance occurs when a person withdraws from the system development activities or does not use the new system. People who have had little or no experience with the computer generally avoid becoming involved. This frequently happens to accountants and management at middle and upper levels. For example, a controller who does not understand computer processing might say to the director of information system, "You go ahead and computerize our accounting records but don't bother me. Just make sure the data is 100-percent accurate and the reports look about like the ones we have now." Or a vice president with a terminal on his desk that can help him in a dozen ways to do his job better might say, "I'm not going to use this thing because typing is a waste of my time." What he is really saying is, "I don't know how to use this thing and if I try and make a mistake, I'll be embarrassed."

Although these behavioral problems are occasionally exhibited during the analysis and design phases, most frequently they are exhibited during the implementation phase. By that time, however, it is generally too late to avoid them. Most steps to eliminate or reduce behavioral problems must be taken during the analysis and design phases; these include participation, planning, communication, retraining, and system testing.

Participation is one of the most effective techniques for avoiding behavioral problems. Those people who will be affected by the system should be allowed to participate in its development. There are several benefits that participation provides to the design and implementation of a system, and many of them are the same benefits that result from allowing people to participate in developing the budget.

1. Participation is ego-enhancing and builds self-esteem, which results in more favorable attitudes.
2. Participation can be challenging and intrinsically satisfying, leading to positive attitudes.
3. Users who participate in developing the system are more knowledgeable about its technical aspects and are better trained to use it.
4. Participation usually results in more commitment to the change, which insures that the new system will be used.
5. Because user participants know more about the old system and the needs of the new system than the information systems personnel do, the users' participation will make the new system better.

The steering committee that was discussed earlier is important in making sure that the system is well planned and well communicated to those affected by it. Open communication establishes trust between the users and designers of the system.

Retraining and system testing are performed during implementation of the system. It is extremely important that employees are well trained and that the system is well tested before implementation. The system will probably fail if it is implemented without these things being accomplished, and it will be much more difficult to get people to use the system a second time. Even if the new system is completely free of errors and the people know exactly how to use it, they will still resist because of the bad experience they had earlier.

By making sure there is proper planning, good communication, and participation and by following the other steps outlined in the analysis and design life cycle, most behavioral problems associated with system changes can be either minimized or avoided.

DATA VERSUS INFORMATION

The ultimate objective of the analysis and design process is to provide information to management. The information is used to make decisions—decisions about which products to produce, how much to produce, and when it should be produced.

The terms *data* and *information* are often used interchangeably, but they have different meanings. The term **data** refers to the input into the information system, characters, symbols, facts, and figures that have little or no meaning, taken by themselves, to the user. Therefore, they are not useful in a decision-making activity. **Information** is data that have been processed and transformed into understandable intelligence that is useful in a current or prospective decision-making activity. The processing of the data includes activities such as modeling, formatting, organizing, summarizing, and filtering.

For information to be useful, it must provide facts that were not previously known or must add assurance through the reduction of uncertainty. Technically, an item is not information if it is not decision-compelling. This means that if after receiving the item we do nothing, the item is not information. However, if on receipt we apply a decision rule and take some action, the item is information.

EXAMPLE

Suppose I tell you, "John was drinking last night and wrecked the truck!" Is this data or information? The answer probably depends on who John is and what his relationship is to you. If John is an unknown individual, this is data. You may accumulate this fact along with similar data on drunk driving. Whether you will ever be able to use the data in a meaningful decision-making activity is currently unknown. If, on the other hand, you are the supervisor of warehouse and delivery, John is one of the truck drivers you supervise, and John was on duty last night when the accident occurred, this is information to you. You will apply a decision rule and take appropriate action.

The relationships among data, information, and decision making are illustrated in figure 18.9.

Report Preparation

Reports communicate information to management and provide a sound basis for decision making. For them to be useful, they must communicate meaningful and useful information in an understandable format.

FIGURE 18.9

Data Versus Information

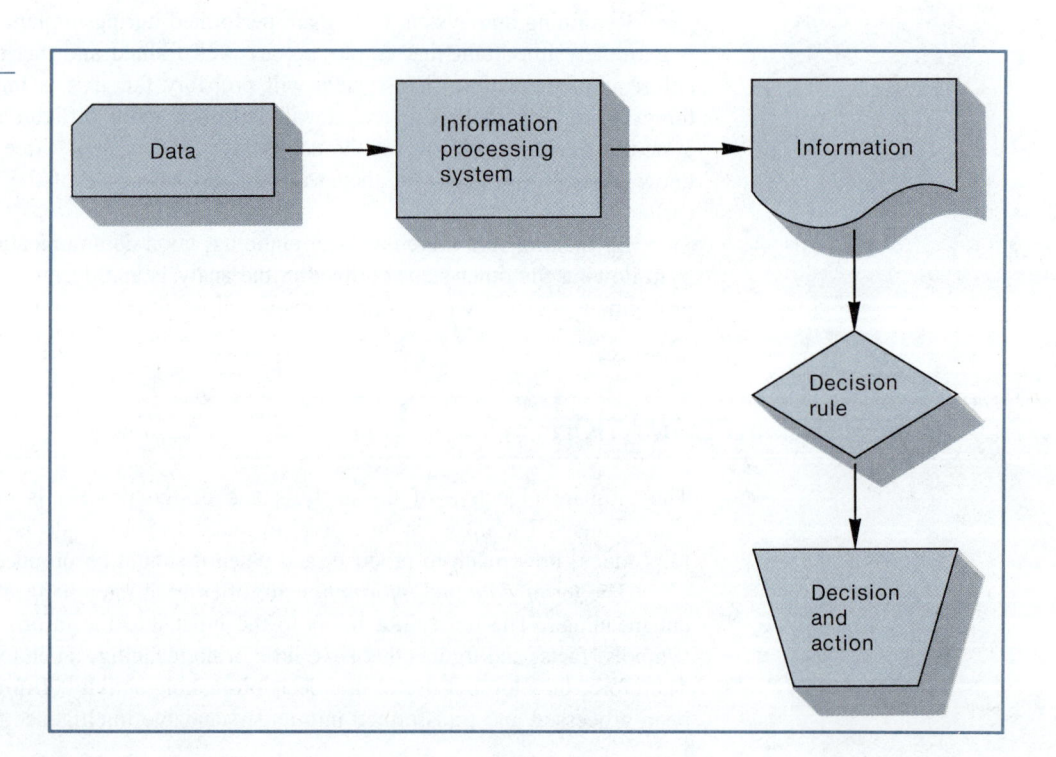

Accountants have always been active participants in report design. Some reports are standardized and, once developed, do not change for an extended period of time. Specialized reports can now be obtained from data bases, data base management systems, report generators, and other specialized software packages. Cost accountants are now able to develop tailor-made reports with a few wisely selected key strokes.

In this section we identify the different types of reports that are frequently developed and summarize some basic rules for developing good reports.

Types of Reports

Reports may be classified into a variety of categories. Figure 18.10 lists six classifications and identifies several options within each. Note that these are not mutually exclusive categories; in fact, some accounting reports can be included in every classification.

The description of many of the options within each category is self-explanatory. For example, under the "format" classification there are two basic options—hard copy, which is any report printed on paper, and terminal display (soft copy), which is a report presented on a computer display. Narrative reports, graphic reports, and tabular reports can be provided on either paper or computer display.

Because the "purpose" classification is perhaps the most important, each option within that classification will be reviewed.

Operational Report Operational reports reflect past events and current status. They support operations by initiating actions to implement decisions made during the planning process, and they also provide reference information.

Examples of operational reports include balance sheets, income statements, statements of changes in financial position, agings and analyses of accounts receivable, back-order reports, payroll registers, and distribution reports.

FIGURE 18.10

Classification Plan for Reports

Classification	Options
Purpose	Operational report
	Planning report
	Control report
	Performance report
	Legal compliance report
Scope	Firm wide report
	Divisional report
	Departmental report
	Cost center report
Conciseness	Detailed report
	Summary report
	Exception report
Occurrence	Scheduled periodic report
	Demand report
	Event-triggered report
Time frame	Historical report
	Forecast report
Format	Hard copy report
	Terminal display
	Narrative report
	Graphic report
	Tabular report

Planning Report Planning reports project expected activities or status at some point in the future. They aid management in planning for the future and selecting the most desirable alternatives.

Planning reports include budgets and forecasts. More specifically, a budgeted income statement, budgeted balance sheet, sales forecast, production scheduling report, and planned raw materials usage report would all be classified as planning reports.

It is not always easy to classify a particular report into only one category. For example, a segment report showing last year's contribution margin by segment would be classified as an operational report. However, if it is used as a basis to delete one or more unprofitable segments of the business, it would be a planning report. Therefore, a report may be considered a planning report if it contains estimated costs or future values or contains past costs or values that are good predictors of estimated future values.

Control Report A control report compares actual performance against a benchmark, such as expected performance, actual performance during the same period for the prior year, ratios based on industry averages, or actual performance of a similar operational center. As explained in earlier chapters, differences between actual performance and the benchmark are called variances. Variances may be reported as a dollar amount, a percentage of the budget, or both.

Examples of control reports include the following:

1. Inventory control reports that compare actual quantities on hand with the reorder point.
2. Equipment utilization reports that compare total usage time with planned usage time.
3. Delivery reports that compare actual deliveries with scheduled deliveries.

The usefulness of a control report increases as it becomes more discriminating, more timely, more concise, and more understandable. A report pinpointing activities by individual employees or machines within a department is more useful than a report showing the entire department's productivity. A materials usage report on yesterday's production needs to be available today, not next week, to be most useful. Finally, a report that highlights significant variances will help management focus its attention an areas of greatest need.

Performance Report A performance report shows the items under the control of a particular individual. It is used to evaluate how well that individual has performed his or her assigned stewardship.

A performance report is generally used in conjunction with the responsibility accounting system. Under a responsibility accounting system, the organization, including its activities and assets, is divided according to areas of responsibility and the individuals who have control over them. Internal reporting is then based on ability to control. Each individual's report contains the items he or she controls. A pyramid or hierarchical reporting structure (see figure 6.12) is generally used to report on each individual's area of responsibility.

Legal Compliance Reports People often speculate on the purpose of many of the reports that must be filed with various state and federal government agencies. The reporting requirements are extensive and reports must be filed on time to avoid late penalties and interest charges. Examples include, among many others, Form 10-K with the SEC and Forms 1120, 940, and 941 with the IRS.

Designing Output Reports

Although there are many outputs from the computer, the types of output we want to discuss are the reports and statement used by management to plan and control business operations.

The form and content of reports are important because reports influence behavior. Managers will make decisions and take action based on the information contained in the reports. Some rules for designing good reports include the following:

1. The report title should clearly identify the area of responsibility, the time period covered, the date the report was prepared, and the units of measure.
2. Each page or section should have a brief descriptive title.
3. Report pages should be numbered. If a report is not distributed in entirety but is divided and distributed to several individuals according to areas of responsibility, each section should begin with page 1.
4. Headings should appear across the top and down the left-hand side, whereas totals are placed along the right-hand side and at the bottom of the report. Columnar headings should be repeated on each page as necessary and should be brief but descriptive. Any abbreviations should be explained on the report unless they are standard abbreviations that all users understand.
5. The report should be structured so that the items are read from left to right and from top to bottom.
6. The most important information on the report should be the easiest to locate.
7. Overcrowding by including too much on a single page should be avoided. White space can be used to enhance the appearance and readability of the report.
8. The level of detail within the report should be appropriate for the report recipient's hierarchical level within the organization. For example, a report for the production manager should detail each type of raw material and each class of direct labor required for production. The vice president of manufacturing, however, will receive only summary data for each production area.
9. Actual operating data, benchmark data, and variances between the two should be shown on the report.
10. Any significant deviations should be highlighted. Deviations can be shown as actual amounts (dollars or units) or as percentages.
11. Noncontrollable items should generally be excluded from the report. If for some reason they are included, they should be separated from the controllable items and clearly labeled. This is necessary so that the reports can be used for performance evaluations. An individual should not be held responsible for something over which there is little or no control.
12. Information overload should be avoided by classifying, summarizing, and filtering what is reported. Even managers have a limit to the amount they can absorb.

COST ACCOUNTING SYSTEM INTERNAL CONTROLS

Federal law requires companies that are subject to the Securities Act of 1934 to have an adequate system of controls. Internal control encompasses plans, methods, and measures adopted by an entity to safeguard assets, check the accuracy and reliability of accounting data, promote operational efficiency, and encourage adherence to management policies. According to the common body of knowledge statement by NAA:

. . . management accountants are expected to understand the purpose of internal control and develop the techniques for employing it within organizations. They participate in the process by designing internal control systems, including the control aspects of computer-based systems, and by undertaking internal audits.

The concept of controls is the same regardless of the method used to process the data. In general, an internal control system is a series of checks and balances used to verify that things are as they should be. This control system has various requirements, such as the following:

1. There should be separation of duties and responsibilities so that the work of one individual is checked by another individual.
2. Production and work standards should identify the amount of expected output. Standard output will be compared to actual output, and management will then follow up on significant variances.
3. Physical counts of inventories at periodic intervals should identify actual quantities on hand that can be compared with recorded quantities.
4. Responsibility accounting systems should identify the individual with the greatest ability to control an item. Accounting records and reports will be developed to show each individual's area of responsibility and the results of her or his activities.

The types of checks and balances that are built into a computerized accounting system are different than some of those used in a manual accounting system. For example, one small computer can do the work of several individuals. Therefore, there is not as much separation of duties and responsibilities in a computerized system as in a manual system. Also, people can be relied on to ask questions or get clarification on transactions that do not look reasonable. The computer does not have that capability, however, unless it has been specifically included as an input, output, or program control.

In this section, the controls that are relevant to a computerized cost accounting system are identified. The purpose of having these controls is to reduce unidentified errors and the probability of fraud.

Administrative Controls

Getting the right people into the right jobs initially and managing them effectively during their employment with the firm require **administrative controls.**

When hiring an employee for a cost accounting position, it is extremely important that the individual is honest and ethical and is technically qualified for the job. Individuals who have access to the company's assets or to the accounting records are in the best position to defraud the company. A high standard of personal integrity is a major factor in determining honesty. Substantial progress has been made recently in developing test instruments that can be used as part of the employment screening process to measure personal integrity. Feedback on past job performance and character references should also be obtained. There is always the chance, however, that if financial pressures become very great or if the opportunity to defraud the company seems easy, an otherwise honest individual will perform a dishonest act. For these reasons, it is always wise to bond employees who are in sensitive accounting positions.

Formal training programs should be a normal part of an employee's work. It is extremely important that new employees are properly trained in their job responsibilities. During an in-house training program the new employees are taught the company's way of doing things. Over time, considerable changes continue to occur in generally accepted accounting principles, and new techniques are constantly being developed to assist management in the decision functions of the business. Cost accountants must keep current with these changes to continue to be valuable contributors to the organization.

Technical capability is usually assessed by college degrees and by obtaining feedback on performance from previous jobs. Qualifying oneself to receive a Certificate in Management Accounting (CMA) or as a Certified Public Accountant (CPA) is also evidence of technical capability. To date, companies have not typically required a CMA or CPA as minimum qualifications for a cost accounting position. However, it is expected that the CMA will become as important to cost and managerial accounting as the CPA is to public accounting. Any individual who is seriously considering cost accounting as a career path should pursue the CMA.

Personnel administration deals with effectively managing an individual once the person is employed with the firm. This includes adequate separation of duties and responsibilities, rotation of personnel, mandatory vacations, standard operating procedures, performance evaluations, and termination and exit interviews.

Separation of Duties and Responsibilities The cost accountant must make sure that people who have access to the assets of the company do not also have access to the accounting records. If they do, there needs to be some system to verify that all assets have been used for legitimate company purposes.

EXAMPLE

Under the old manual accounting system, Short Company had a group of cost accountants maintain a perpetual inventory of the raw materials storeroom. Materials were issued only on receipt of a written requisition from the production supervisor. The requisition was prepared in triplicate. The production supervisor kept one copy, the cost accountants were sent another copy, and the original went to the raw materials storeroom clerk. After the requisition was filled, the clerk sent the original copy to the cost accountants. They matched the original with the copy received from the production supervisor and made the entry to update the accounting records.

When Short Company computerized the cost accounting system, it was decided to eliminate several cost accountants and to have the raw material storeroom clerk enter the items issued into a computer terminal, which automatically updated the inventory records. The clerk soon found that he could take inventory for personal use (and sell it on the black market). To cover up the theft, he made an entry into the system to reduce inventory and charge indirect materials. That way the stock of raw materials was always in balance with the perpetual inventory. The result of the fraud was not discovered until the end of the year, when it then showed up as an unabsorbed overhead item that no one could easily trace back to the storeroom clerk. No investigation was initiated the first year because it was considered abnormal. After two years and a time-consuming investigation, the problem was identified. Before the investigation was completed, however, the clerk had quit his job and left the country.

The problem was resolved by not allowing the new storeroom clerk to input changes to the inventory records. The terminal was changed so that it would provide only output in the form of inventory balances on hand. All input was keyed into the system by a keypunch clerk in the data-processing division. Requisition forms prepared by the manufacturing supervisor and filled by the storeroom clerk were used as a basis for the input.

Rotation of Personnel Most computer frauds require an individual to be in a particular position for an extended period of time to be able to take advantage of the system. First the employee must learn the system and all the controls thoroughly to identify a weakness in it. The person then uses his or her position to take advantage of the system's weakness and defraud the company.

Many frauds are like an invisible window into the system that no one can see except the person who built it. The person manipulating the system may pass large amounts of assets through the window over an extended time period. Rotation of personnel at periodic intervals will discourage fraudulent schemes from being developed initially and will terminate most of those that have been developed.

Note that this control, as with most controls, is not without a cost to administer. Employees must be retrained each time they are moved to a new job, and they will be less productive initially because they are at the low point of their learning curve.

Mandatory Vacations Because most computer frauds require the person to perform a specific activity at a regular time interval, most frauds can be uncovered if the person is absent for an extended time, such as two weeks. It is important for the individual to be physically absent from work for the entire vacation period and for problems associated with his or her job to be handled by someone else. Most computer frauds are discovered by someone else investigating a problem situation. If the problems are accumulated until the individual returns from vacation, the fraud can be perpetuated by the way the problem is handled.

EXAMPLE

A $21.3 million bank fraud against Wells Fargo Bank was perpetuated by an operations officer for more than two years, even though the bank had a mandatory two-week vacation requirement. Each Friday afternoon of the vacation period, the officer would slip into the office under some guise and in ten minutes would complete the necessary paperwork to perpetuate the fraud. If he had not been allowed into the office, the fraud would have been detected the following week.

Standard Operating Procedures Standard operating procedures outline in detail the steps to be followed in performing a job. Standardization of jobs helps to insure that every job is performed completely and accurately and that the work of many people is coordinated. It provides a standard that others can rely on and that can be used as a basis for performance evaluations.

Performance Evaluations The primary objective of performance evaluations is to provide feedback and reward incentives to help individuals perform their jobs well and accomplish the organization's goals.

The performance of each individual on the cost accounting staff should be evaluated periodically. The evaluation should be based, as much as possible, on quantitative data, such as timeliness and accuracy of reports, quantity of output, and the amount of money and time required to complete a task. Subjective evaluations should be applied to other areas that are important to the job, such as the ability to delegate and supervise, the ability to cope with unexpected obstacles, the effectiveness of oral and written communications, poise, appearance, and maturity.

Terminations and Exit Interviews Terminating an individual is never a pleasant task, but the procedures followed in terminating someone who has access to accounting records maintained on the computer are very important. Occasionally, individuals will think that they have been treated unfairly and will do something drastic to get even with the company.

EXAMPLE	A computer operator was informed that her services would no longer be needed and that the company was giving her the two-week notice required by their employment contract. During her last two weeks on the job, she systematically erased all of the company's accounting files, including backup copies. The company had to spend much time and money to reconstruct its files.

Generally, individuals should not have access to the computer, accounting programs, or files after they have been given their termination notice. They should clean out their desk in the presence of a security guard and be asked to leave the premises. The company should not expect any benefit from the required severance pay.

An exit interview should be held with anyone who voluntarily terminates employment with the company. It creates goodwill with the individual, verifies that all manuals and other materials belonging to the company are left with the company, and frequently uncovers problems with the job or company in general.

Input Controls

To verify that the required input into the computer process is complete and accurate, that no additional data have been added, and that the data have been accurately converted into machine-readable form for processing by the computer, **input controls** are designed.

As a general rule, all data should originate outside the data-processing center. For example, a computer operator should never be able to originate and input a transaction into the system. Cost accounting personnel in the various operating departments should identify the data to be processed, accumulate it, and submit it to the data-processing division to be processed. The form of submission may be batch or on-line, depending on the processing mode used by the company.

EXAMPLE	Bill was a very conscientious employee in the manufacturing division of a company. As a reward for his efforts, he was promoted to the cost accounting staff and changed from a wage-earning employee to a salaried employee. One of Bill's responsibilities as a salaried employee was to prepare for all wage-earning employees in the division the payroll summary that showed each employee's name, number, and hours worked. Each pay period Bill prepared the payroll list and gave it to the manufacturing supervisor for her review and signature on the bottom of the last page. Bill's job then required him to take the form to the data-processing department, where the data were entered into the computer. Before Bill submitted it, however, he added his name and a normal number of hours on the bottom of the list of wage-earning employees. The computer performed all the extensions, maintained the files, prepared the checks, and mailed them directly to the employees. Thus Bill was paid twice—once as a wage-earning employee and once as a salaried employee. The computer programs were not designed to compare salaried and wage-earning employees to verify that an individual was not being paid as both. Adequate input controls should have prevented this.

Some of the most important input controls include control totals, capturing data in machine-readable form, and approval of input data in the originating department.

Control Totals   A control total identifies the total amount of input to be processed. The control total may be one of several types:

1. A financial control total is the total dollar amount of the input, such as the total payroll for the period.
2. A hash control total is the total of some numbers that are not a normal part of the processing. A total of the employees' numbers is an example.
3. A record count control total is the total number of input transactions or records to be processed. If a record count of the number of employees to be paid in the preceding example had been developed and checked by the supervisor, Bill would not have been able to insert his fraudulent data.

The control totals often are used during the processing of the data to verify that all data are present and processed. For example, as the computer prepares checks in a payroll run, the number of checks prepared can be counted as a control total and compared with the number of employees authorized to be paid by the department supervisor. A control clerk who receives the output from the computer can compare the control totals before sending the checks to the employees.

Capturing Data in Machine-Readable Form Data should be collected in machine-readable form whenever possible to reduce processing errors. Each human process increases the probability of error and allows fraudulent data to be inserted. Turnaround documents capture the output of one process in machine-readable form, which then can be used as input for a subsequent process. Turnaround documents should be used whenever possible.

Originating Department Approval The originating department should code, review, and approve all input transactions. Also, sensitive documents such as checks, purchase orders, and requisition forms should be prenumbered and controlled.

Processing Controls

A broad category that includes all controls connected with the processing of data by the computer, processing controls include built-in hardware controls, operating system controls, file reconstruction capability, and controls to prevent or detect computer operator errors. In addition, they include programmed controls to check the reasonableness of the data and accuracy of the processing in much the same way as a person would do when processing the data manually. Based on previous experience and a knowledge of the process, a person can look at the amount of a transaction and see if it is within normal limits. She or he also develops techniques to check the computations for accuracy and can look at the results to see if they are reasonable.

Checkpoints, called edit checks, need to be built into the computer programs so that the computer can perform the same kinds of tests that a person would perform. It is primarily the responsibility of the cost accountant to identify the computer tests that should be included in the programs and to see that they are included by the systems analysts and programmers. Remember that although the analysts and programmers know a great deal about computers, data processing, and programming, they are not cost accountants and do not understand cost accounting systems. Major problems generally occur when the cost accountant does not work closely with the analysts and programmers in developing the system.

EXAMPLE

The managers of a relatively new manufacturing company were pleased with the company's preaudit net income of $1 million. Their joy turned to disappointment, however, when the auditors required a physical count of the raw materials inventory and a $2 million shortage was identified. The $1 million profit went to a $1 million loss with one adjusting entry. The cause of the discrepancy was an error in the program to account for the raw materials inventory. The inventory was increased for items shown on the purchase orders rather than for items shown on the receiving reports. Items that were ordered but never received and items on back order were never taken out of the inventory balance. This error had also caused numerous disruptions to the manufacturing process because of out-of-stock items, but management never could identify the cause until the audit and a thorough investigation. The perpetual inventory system showed an item in stock, but it could not be located when requisitioned for a production run. The production run would have to be delayed while the item was ordered from the supplier.

Some of the most common program controls include limit and reasonableness tests, crossfooting, and control totals.

Limit and Reasonableness Test A computer program can be written to compare the input amount with predefined limits. As long as the input amount is within the limits, it is processed normally. Input that exceeds the defined limits must be processed on an exception basis. Tests also can be performed on the output to see if it is reasonable in relation to the process or activity being performed. Output that is not reasonable is highlighted for further investigation.

EXAMPLE

Young Company is a manufacturing organization that uses a job-order cost system. Experience has shown that 95 percent of the jobs take between 50 and 90 direct-labor hours to complete. These amounts could be used as a limit test on the amount of direct labor charged to the job. Experience also has shown that the total cost of the job is between 300 percent and 350 percent of the total direct-labor cost. These amounts could be used as reasonableness checks on the total job cost.

Crossfooting Footing is the process of totaling a column of numbers. Crossfooting is the process of comparing several column totals to verify that they are in balance. For example, several materials and labor charges are typically posted to each job in a job-order cost system. Totaling the materials charges, direct-labor charges, and overhead charges is footing. Combining these amounts and comparing the total to a running balance of the total job cost is crossfooting. As long as these amounts are equal, the computer does nothing. The computer should be instructed to print out an error message whenever the crossfooting does not balance so that the mistake can be identified and corrected.

Control Totals The same type of control totals that are developed by the department preparing the input should also be built into the computer programs. Output from the computer process should include the control totals developed for the computer program. For example, if the computer is preparing the payroll checks for the manufacturing division of a company, the computer could count the number of checks prepared as a record count control total and the total amount of all checks prepared as a financial control total.

Output Controls

To assure that the output is complete and that no errors were identified during processing, **output controls** are necessary. As a general rule, the output should not be given back to the person who prepared the input. That would allow the individual to cover up mistakes or hide fraudulent entries before the output is distributed to other users. A control clerk should receive the output, check its accuracy, and distribute it only to authorized personnel.

Control clerks reconcile the control totals prepared by the inputting department with those prepared by the computer. They must follow up on any discrepancies between the control totals. They also have the responsibility to follow up on errors identified by the computer in processing the data. Each computer run should have an error report listing the transactions it was unable to process. The control clerk must identify the source and cause of the error and enter a correction into the computer system.

The output from the computer system frequently contains sensitive information. The control clerk should control the dissemination of documents and information to authorized personnel only.

SUMMARY

Changes in computer technology have made the cost of data processing so inexpensive that most companies are computerizing their information systems. An integrated information system provides many benefits to the organization, including less redundancy in the data files and more accurate, uniform, and timely information in all functional areas. The cost accounting portion of the system supports other functional areas and draws from the data that they collect.

The cost accountant plays a key role during the analysis and design of the information system. Systems analysts and programmers frequently look to the controller when identifying the types of decisions that need to be made, the information needed to make those decisions, and the operation of the existing systems. The controller also provides valuable input for identifying the types of controls that need to be built into the system.

Behavioral considerations are important in determining the long-term success of a systems project. Regardless of how good the information system is, it will fail if it does not have the support of those whom it is intended to serve. Participation in the development of the system is one of the most effective techniques for avoiding behavioral problems. Effective communication between the designers and potential users during the development process is also very important.

SELF-STUDY PROBLEM (CMA)

Business organizations must modify or replace a portion or all of their financial information systems to keep pace with their growth and to take advantage of improved information technology. The process involved in modifying or replacing an information system, especially if computer equipment is involved, requires a substantial commitment of time and resources. When an organization undertakes a change in its information system, a series of steps, or phases, is initiated that includes the following:

1. Survey of the existing system
2. Analysis of information collected in the survey and development of recommendations for corrective action
3. Design of a new or modified system
4. Equipment study and acquisition
5. Implementation of a new or modified system

These phases tend to overlap rather than being separate and distinct. In addition, the effort required in each phase varies from one system to another, depending on such factors as the extent of the changes or the need for different equipment.

Required

1. Explain the purposes and reasons for surveying an organization's existing system during a systems study.
2. Identify and explain the general activities and techniques that are commonly used during the systems survey and analysis phases of a systems study conducted for a financial information system.
3. The systems survey and analysis phases of a financial information systems study are often carried out by a project team composed of a systems analyst, a management accountant, and other persons in the company who would be knowledgeable and helpful in the study. What would be the role of the management accountant in these phases of a financial information systems study?

Solution to the Self-Study Problem

1. The *purposes* for surveying an organization's existing system during a systems study include the following:
    a. To determine how the existing system functions and how the work is accomplished
    b. To determine the feasibility of redesigning and converting the existing system to new hardware
    c. To determine the constraints of the current system

The *reasons* for surveying an organization's existing system during a systems study include the following:
    a. To assess the effectiveness and weaknesses of the existing system
    b. To gain an understanding of the existing system, which will provide benefits later during any revision or redesign
    c. To provide a source for design ideas and identify the resources that are available

2. The general activities and techniques that are commonly used during the systems survey and analysis phases of a systems study include the following:
    a. The study and review of the existing organization structure to determine how it functions
    b. The review and collection of internal documents and reports to determine design, content, use, frequency of preparation, and so forth
    c. The development and use of questionnaire forms to determine processing frequencies, input and output volumes, and other information useful to the systems study
    d. The conducting of personal interviews with operating personnel to confirm and expand on data gathered from the questionnaire
    e. The development of flowcharts for both the system and documents

3. The systems survey and analysis phases of a financial information systems study would probably be dominated by the systems people. However, the management accountant would be of assistance in assessing management's needs for required reports as well as their formats. The management accountant could also provide information about the following aspects of the system:
    a. The source documents in use
    b. The relevance, reliability, and timeliness of input and output data
    c. The internal controls that exist and that should be incorporated into any new or redesigned system

SUGGESTED READINGS

Burch, John G., and Grudnitski, Gary. *Information Systems: Theory and Practice*, 4th ed. New York: John Wiley & Sons, 1986.

Cushing, Barry E., and Romney, Marshall B. *Accounting Information Systems and Business Organizations*, 4th ed. Reading, Mass.: Addison-Wesley, 1987.

Moscove, Stephen A., and Simkin, Mark G. *Accounting Information Systems*, 3rd ed. New York; John Wiley & Sons, 1987.

National Association of Accountants. "NAA Issues SMA 10: The Common Body of Knowledge for Management Accountants." *Management Accounting* 68 (August 1986): 56–61.

Schoderbek, Charles G.; Schoderbek, Peter P.; and Kefalas, Asterios G. *Management Systems: Conceptual Considerations*, rev. ed. Dallas, Tex.: Business Publications, Inc., 1980.

Willinson, Joseph W. *Accounting Information Systems*, 2nd ed. New York: John Wiley & Sons, 1986.

DISCUSSION QUESTIONS

Q18–1. What is the difference between a management information system and an accounting information system?

Q18–2. What is a fully integrated management information system?

Q18–3. Identify the major benefits and problems associated with a fully integrated information system.

Q18–4. What effect does the Foreign Corrupt Practices Act have on the development of a cost accounting system?

Q18–5. Describe the value of additional information. If the additional information does not change the decision, does it have any value?

Q18–6. What is the information system master plan? Why is the master plan important when developing an accounting information system?

Q18–7. What is the primary objective of the systems analysis phase of the systems analysis and design life cycle?

Q18–8. Distinguish between program flowcharts, systems flowcharts, and document/procedure flowcharts.

Q18–9. In which phase of the systems analysis and design life cycle is the conceptual model of the system developed?

Q18–10. What does RFP stand for and why is it used?

Q18–11. Why are the output reports the first items to be developed for any particular application?

Q18–12. What is meant by *feasibility analysis* and why is it used? What are the most common measures of feasibility?

Q18–13. What is parallel processing and in which phase of the systems analysis and design life cycle is it used?

Q18–14. What are the most common behavioral problems encountered during the computerization of a cost accounting system?

Q18-15. Why is it important for the controller to be involved in identifying the controls that should be built into the cost accounting system?

Q18-16. What types of control totals can be developed? Are control totals input controls, output controls, or processing controls? Explain.

Q18-17. What is a limit and reasonableness test? Is it used as an input control, output control, or processing control? Explain.

EXERCISES

E18-1. General Concepts of Information Systems (CMA) Select the best answer for each of the multiple choice questions that follow.

1. Which of the following is *not* a general objective of all information systems?
   a. A system should provide information that is timely and relevant for decision making by management and operating personnel.
   b. The output of a system should be highly accurate.
   c. A system should have sufficient capacity to accommodate levels of normal activity; any additional capacity proves too costly in the long run.
   d. A system should be as simple as permitted so that its structure and operation can be easily understood and its procedures easily accomplished.
   e. A system should be flexible to accommodate changes of reasonable magnitude when required.

2. When designing a computer-based information system, the initial step in the systems design process is to determine the
   a. required output.
   b. source documents that serve as the basis for input.
   c. processing required.
   d. decisions for which data will be required.
   e. file information required during processing.

3. A source document with an invalid number of hours worked for one week, such as 93 hours instead of 39, would be best detected by
   a. keypunching controls.
   b. a limit test in an edit run.
   c. a hash total of hours worked.
   d. a record count total.
   e. a key verifying control.

4. A systems analysis or survey is the process of obtaining an accurate perspective on the existing system so that weaknesses can be identified and corrected in the new system. Which one of the following steps is *not* considered part of this system survey?
   a. Interviews are conducted with operating people and managers.
   b. The complete documentation of the system is obtained and reviewed.
   c. Measures of processing volume are obtained for each operation.
   d. Equipment sold by various computer manufacturers is reviewed in terms of capability, cost, and availability.
   e. Work measurement studies are conducted to determine the time required to complete various tasks or jobs.

5. In conducting a feasibility study, technical feasibility refers to whether or not
   a. a proposed system is attainable, given the existing technology.
   b. the systems' manager can coordinate and control the activities of the systems department.

c. an adequate computer site exists for the proposed system.
d. the proposed system will produce economic benefits that will exceed its costs.
e. the system will be effectively used within the operating environment of an organization.

6. In conducting a feasibility study, operational feasibility refers to whether or not
   a. a proposed system is attainable, given the existing technology.
   b. a system's manager can coordinate and control the activities of the systems department.
   c. an adequate computer site exists for the proposed system.
   d. the proposed system will produce economic benefits that will exceed its costs.
   e. the system will be used effectively within the operating environment of an organization.

7. In the life cycle of systems development and implementation, the optimal timing for completing the documentation of a computer-based system would be
   a. after the entire systems project is completed but before the post audit is conducted.
   b. after the post-audit phase of the systems project is completed.
   c. in time for the go or no-go decision phase of the systems planning committee.
   d. before starting the programming phase.
   e. as each phase of the systems life cycle is completed.

8. In recent years many businesses have formed a common information source within their business organization called a data base. One advantage of building data bases is the simultaneous updating of files with common data elements. Another major advantage of the data-base concept is that
   a. data-base systems can be used as efficiently with microprocessors as with large computers.
   b. data-base systems are simple to install and maintain.
   c. data-base systems are generally less expensive than separate file maintenance systems.
   d. less duplication of data occurs with a data-base system.
   e. fewer skilled people are required to run a data-base system than any other system.

9. Jones Auto Parts Company, a small sole proprietorship, has decided to change from manual to computerized inventory management. Frequently, in implementing a new system, both the old and new systems are maintained during a shakedown period. This changeover technique is called
   a. parallel running conversion.
   b. pilot testing.
   c. back-up system conversion.
   d. debugging.
   e. systems conversion management.

10. Many customers, managers, employees, and suppliers blame the computer for making errors. In reality, computers make very few mechanical errors. Most likely, errors in a fully operational computer-based system are due to errors in
    a. programming.
    b. operator actions.
    c. systems analysis.
    d. processing.
    e. input.

11. One primary purpose of a data-base information system is to
    a. eliminate multiple access to a particular piece of stored data.

b. eliminate redundancy in the data base of a company.
c. lessen the integration of information-producing activities so that a given department may easily ascertain its current status.
d. provide each application program with its own fixed data file.
e. make it possible to have data compatible with a variety of computer hardware.

12. Which one of the following control functions normally would *not* be the responsibility of the input/output control group of the data-processing department?
   a. Review of the efficiency and effectiveness of systems design
   b. Scanning of the console log
   c. Review and distribution of computer output
   d. Maintenance of an error log
   e. Resolution of control totals

13. For a routine management report produced on the computer, which of the following control duties is most likely to be the sole responsibility of the user department?
   a. Scanning the report for garbled output
   b. Checking input totals against report totals
   c. Determining that figures in the report are reasonable
   d. Verifying record count totals
   e. Checking the console listing for improper operator procedures

14. Which of the following methods of control is *not* applicable to computer systems?
   a. Control totals
   b. Reasonableness checks
   c. Limit checks
   d. Edit checks
   e. None of the above

E18–2. Value of Information

Suppose you have $1,000 to invest and you have identified three investments: *A*, *B*, and *C*. Without doing any research on the likely payoffs of each, you estimate the following:

Investment	Expected Payoff
A	$200 per year
B	300 per year
C	150 per year

If you had to make a decision on only this much information, you would probably select investment *B*.

Required

1. Suppose someone could do an investment analysis (look into a crystal ball) and tell you with 100-percent certainty what the real payoff will be. How much would you pay this person for the information? Would you pay $80, more than $80, or less than $80? Explain why.
2. Suppose further that the investment analysis was performed and it predicted the following payoffs (which turned out to be what they actually paid):

Investment	Predicted Payoffs
A	$180 per year
B	200 per year
C	340 per year

What decision would you make, and what is the benefit provided by the information?
3. Using the information provided in requirement 2, if you had paid $80 for the information, what would be the value of the information?

4. Suppose that you paid $80 for the investment analysis and it provided the following projections (which turned out to be what they actually paid):

Investment	Predicted Payoffs
A	$250 per year
B	290 per year
C	180 per year

What is the value of this information?

E18–3. Input, Output, and Process Controls (CMA)
A well-designed management information system using electronic data-processing equipment will include methods of assuring that the data are appropriate to the situation and are accurate.

Required

1. Describe procedures that should exist in order to assure that the input data are accurate and appropriate.
2. Describe procedures that would assure that all data were processed and processed properly.
3. Describe procedures that would assure that the output data are accurate and appropriate.

E18–4. Systems Design—Feasibility Analysis
A request has been made to design a corporate distribution system to be used in both long-range planning and daily management of operations. Cost data on the present distribution system are scanty and out of date. Substantial cost savings are expected, but they are not included in the proposal. Responsibility for distribution lies with the marketing vice president, a man who has made no major changes in distribution policy or practices for fifteen years and who has a well-earned reputation for being hostile to innovation. Perhaps understandably, he has not been consulted on the proposal, yet his support would obviously be indispensable to its success.

Required

1. Without reference to the preceding situation, identify what feasibility analysis is and the factors that should be considered.
2. With reference to the preceding situation, which areas of feasibility analysis would you study most? Why?

E18–5. Systems Analysis and Design Life Cycle (CMA)
Curtis Company operates in a five-county industrial area. The company employs a manual system for all of its record keeping except payroll; the payroll is processed by a local service bureau. Other applications have not been computerized because they could not be cost justified previously.

The company's sales have grown substantially during the past five years. With this growth rate, a computer-based system seemed more practical. Consequently, Curtis Company engaged the management consulting department of its public accounting firm to conduct a feasibility study for converting the record-keeping system to a computer-based system. The accounting firm reported that a computer-based system would improve the company's record-keeping system and still provide material cost savings.

Therefore, Curtis Company decided to develop a computer-based system for its records. Curtis wants to hire a person with experience in systems development as manager of systems and data processing. This person's responsibilities will be to oversee the entire systems operation, with special emphasis on the development of the new system.

Management knows that you are familiar with the analysis and design of information systems and has asked you to prepare a brief memo to inform it of what should be expected.

Required

Describe the major steps that will be undertaken to develop and implement Curtis Company's new computer-based system.

E18-6. Systems Design—Identifying Documents and Document Flow (CMA)
Wooster Company is a beauty and barber supplies and equipment distributorship servicing a five-state area. Management generally has been pleased with overall operations of the company until now. The present purchasing system has evolved through practice rather than having been formally designed. Consequently, it is inadequate and needs to be redesigned.

A description of the present purchasing system is as follows. Whenever the quantity of an item is low, the inventory supervisor phones the purchasing department with the item description and the quantity to be ordered. A purchase order is then prepared in duplicate in the purchasing department. The original is sent to the vendor, and the copy is retained in the purchasing department and filed in numerical order. When the shipment arrives, the inventory supervisor sees that each item received is checked off on the packing slip accompanying the shipment. The packing slip is then forwarded to the accounts payable department. When the invoice arrives, the packing slip is compared with the invoice in the accounts payable department. Once any differences between the packing slip and the invoice are reconciled, a check is drawn for the appropriate amount and is mailed to the vendor with a copy of the invoice. The packing slip is attached to the invoice and is filed alphabetically in the paid invoice file.

Wooster Company intends to redesign its purchasing system from the time an item needs to be ordered until the time payment is made. The system should be designed to ensure that all of the proper controls are incorporated into the system.

Required

1. Identify the internally and externally generated documents that would be required to satisfy the minimum requirements of a basic system and indicate the number of copies of each document that would be needed.
2. Explain how all of these documents should interrelate and flow among Wooster's various departments, including the final destination or file for each copy.

E18-7. Report Preparation and Decision Making
The Reaman Computer Corporation has asked you to develop a computerized report to analyze product sales by dealer. The company sells its three major lines of computers through retail outlets across the country. The computer lines are called Big Blue, Flash, and Junior. All dealers carry all three models.

The one constraint that management has placed on the report is that it not exceed eight columns across the width of the page. The report can be as long as required, and there is no constraint concerning the number of lines of information that may be reported on a dealer.

Assume that any data required for the report will be contained in the data base.

Required

1. Prepare a report that you believe will be useful for management. Provide standards and variances where appropriate.

2. Identify the types of decisions that you think your report will help management to make.

E18–8. Distinguishing Between Data and Information Jim Kemp, a 55-year-old purchasing agent for J & J Equipment Company, was recently given the economic order quantity (EOQ) formula by the new president of the company. The president had picked it up at a management training seminar at the local university. When the president gave it to Jim, she said, "Here is the information that you need to cut down the total cost of inventory ordering and storage. I assume that if a manager is given the information that he or she needs, that manager will have no problem in using it effectively."

Jim didn't really understand what the abbreviations meant under the square root sign. He also had trouble calculating a square root. So he filed the formula in his drawer until he could get the accountant to explain it to him. In the meantime he thought he would start to monitor the cost of ordering and carrying inventory items.

Some months later, the president was very upset to find that Jim was not regularly using the EOQ formula and that the company had not saved large amounts of money in purchasing and storing inventory.

Required

1. Do you agree with the statement that the president made when she gave the EOQ formula to Jim? Explain.
2. Obviously Jim was not able to measure up to the president's expectations. Who was at fault in this situation? Was it Jim, who did not use the information given to him, or was it the president, who did not teach Jim to use the information?
3. How should the EOQ have been given to Jim in the first place?

E18–9. Distinguishing Between Data and Information Campbell Scientific Inc. is a small family-owned manufacturing company that produces data monitors. Paulette Campbell is the operations manager in charge of manufacturing.

A data monitor is an electronic device designed to collect data, such as wind speed, temperature, moisture level, etc., in computer-processable form. The data monitors are made in batches according to a customer's specifications. There are usually twelve direct-labor employees in the manufacturing department.

Required

1. Distinguish between data and information.
2. Identify five messages that would be considered information to Paulette Campbell. For each message, identify the type of decision that it would facilitate.

E18–10. An Example of Inadequate Controls[1] The following correspondence (battle) was reported to have taken place between an accounts receivable computer in a department store and one of the store's customers.

---

1. Adapted from *Saturday Review,* August 13, 1965.

CHAPTER 18: ACCOUNTING SYSTEMS FOR MANAGEMENT PLANNING AND CONTROL

August 17

Dear Madam:

Our records show an outstanding balance of $2.98 on your account. If you have already remitted this account, kindly disregard this notice.

THIS IS A BUSINESS MACHINE CARD.
PLEASE DO NOT SPINDLE OR MUTILATE.

August 19

Gentlemen,

I do *not* have an outstanding balance. I attached a note with my payment advising you that I have been billed *twice* for the same amount: once under my first name, middle initial, and last name; and then under my first initials and my last name. (The former is correct.) Please check your records.

September 17

Dear Madam:

Our records show a delinquent balance of $2.98 on your account. Please remit $3.40. This includes a handling charge.

THIS IS A BUSINESS MACHINE CARD.
PLEASE DO NOT SPINDLE OR MUTILATE.

September 19

Dear Machine,

You're not paying attention! I am NOT delinquent. I do *not* owe this money. I was billed TWICE for the same purchase. Please look into this.

October 17

Dear Madam:

Our records show you to be delinquent for three months. Please remit the new charges of $13.46, plus $4.10. (This includes a handling charge.) May we have your immediate attention to this matter.

THIS IS A BUSINESS MACHINE CARD.
PLEASE DO NOT SPINDLE OR MUTILATE.

October 19

Dear Machine,

My attention! You want MY attention! Listen here, YOU ARE WRONG!!! I don't owe you $4.10. CAN YOU UNDERSTAND THAT? I also DON'T owe you the new charge of $13.46. You billed ME for my MOTHER'S purchase. Please correct this statement at once!

> November 17
>
> Dear Madam:
>
> Our records now show you to be delinquent for four months in the total amount of $17.56, plus $1.87 handling charges.
>
> Please remit in full in ten days or your account will be turned over to our Auditing Department for collection.
>
> THIS IS A BUSINESS MACHINE CARD.
> PLEASE DO NOT SPINDLE OR MUTILATE.

> November 19
>
> Dear Human Machine Programer,
> DEAR ANYONE HUMAN,
> WILL YOU PLEASE TAKE YOUR HEAD OUT OF THE COMPUTER LONG ENOUGH TO READ THIS? I DON'T OWE YOU THIS MONEY!!! I DON'T OWE YOU <u>ANY</u> MONEY. <u>NONE</u>.

> December 17
>
> Dear Madam:
>
> Is there some question about your statement? Our records show no payments on your account since August. Please call DI7-9601 and ask for Miss Gilbert at your earliest convenience.
>
> THIS IS A BUSINESS MACHINE CARD.
> PLEASE DO NOT SPINDLE OR MUTILATE.

December 18

    . . . deck the halls with boughs of holly . . . "Good afternoon. Carver's hopes you have enjoyed its recorded program of carols. May I help you?"

    "Hello. Yes . . . My bill is . . . should I wait for a 'beep' before I talk?"

    "About your bill?"

    "Yes. Yes, it's my bill. There's a mistake . . ."

    "One moment, please. I'll connect you with Adjustments!"

    "Good afternoon and Merry Christmas. This is a recorded message. All our lines are in service now. If you will please be patient, one of our adjusters will be with you as soon as the line is free. Meanwhile, Carver's hopes you will enjoy its program of Christmas carols" . . . deck the halls with boughs of holly . . .

> December 26
>
> Dear Machine,
> I tried to call you on December 18. Also on the 19th, 20th, 21st, and the 23rd and the 24th. But all I got was a recorded message and those Christmas carols. Please, oh, please, won't you turn me over to a human? Any human?

> January 17
>
> Dear Madam:
>
> Our Credit Department has turned your delinquent account over to us for collection. Won't you please remit this amount now? We wish to cooperate with you in every way possible, but this is considerably past due. May we have your check at this time?
>
> Very truly yours,
> Henry J. Hooper, Auditor

CHAPTER 18: ACCOUNTING SYSTEMS FOR MANAGEMENT PLANNING AND CONTROL

> *January 19*
>
> Dear Mr. Hooper,
> You doll! You gorgeous HUMAN doll! I refer you to letters I sent to your department dated the 19th of August, September, October, and November, which should clarify the fact that I owe you nothing.

> February 17
>
> Dear Madam:
>
> According to our microfilm records, our billing was in error. Your account is clear; you have no balance.
> We hope there will be no further inconvenience to you. This was our fault.
>
> Very truly yours,
> Henry J. Hooper, Auditor

> *February 19*
>
> Dear Mr. Hooper,
> Thank you! Oh, thank you, thank you, thank you!

> March 17
>
> Dear Madam:
>
> Our records show you to be delinquent in the amount of $2.98, erroneously posted last August to a nonexistent account. May we have your remittance at this time?
>
> THIS IS A BUSINESS MACHINE CARD.
> PLEASE DO NOT SPINDLE OR MUTILATE.

> *March 19*
>
> Dear Machine,
> I give up. You win. Here's a check for $2.98. Enjoy yourself.

> April 17
>
> Dear Madam:
>
> Our records show an overpayment on your part of $2.98. We are crediting this amount to your account.
>
> THIS IS A BUSINESS MACHINE CARD.
> PLEASE DO NOT SPINDLE OR MUTILATE.

Required

Discuss the issues evident in the narrative that relate to automated accounting systems, and recommend the design changes you believe would enable avoidance of the problems that occurred.

PROBLEMS

P18–1. The Value of Information A projected income statement for Shields Manufacturing Company for 19X6 is shown below. Products A, B, and C all come from a joint process. Products A and B are classified as main products, whereas product C is classified as a by-product. To date, all products have been sold at the split-off point. No value has been assigned to product C until it is sold, and the revenue has been reported as other income. Joint costs are allocated using their relative sales value at split-off.

Shields Manufacturing Company
Projected Income Statement
Year Ending December 31, 19X6

Sales revenue:		
Product A (100,000 units @ $7.70/unit)		$ 770,000
Product B (80,000 units @ $6.00/unit)		480,000
Total		$1,250,000
Manufacturing costs:		
Direct materials	$250,000	
Direct labor	300,000	
Factory overhead	450,000	
Total	$1,000,000	
Selling and administrative expenses	225,000	1,225,000
Income from main products		25,000
Other income—sale of product C		
(20,000 units @ $2.00/unit)		40,000
Net income—before tax		$ 65,000

A proposal has been received to buy all 20,000 units of product C in a finished state for $10 per unit. Considerable manufacturing costs would need to be incurred to process product C beyond the split-off point; the amount of cost, however, is not known. Rather than investigate the proposal, top management is tempted to turn it down and continue to run the business as usual.

Suppose that you believe there is potential profit in the proposal and you would like to have a study completed to accurately determine the additional processing costs associated with product C. Management is willing to commission the study but insists that it must be cost justified. It also insists that if product C is processed further, it must be classified as a main product.

Required

1. How much are you willing to pay for the study? Explain.
2. Assume that the study is completed at a cost of $20,000 and that the study reveals additional processing costs of $7.00 per unit. How much better or worse off is the company by having completed the study?
3. Assume that the study is completed at a cost of $30,000 and that it reveals additional processing costs of $4.00 per unit. How much better or worse off is the company by having completed the study?

P18–2. The Value of Information Side Street Blues manufactures portable stereos that sell for $150 per unit. The current manufacturing and distribution process requires fixed costs of $120,000 and variable costs of $75 per unit. Last year the company had an after-tax net income of $60,000.

In an attempt to improve net income, management has decided to buy a new machine at a cost of $40,000 that will replace several manual laborers. The net result will be a $10

After several months the production people started complaining that raw materials items shown as being in stock were not in stock. Planned production runs had to be postponed until the required parts could be rush ordered. This increased the cost of the materials because they were not bought in quantity, and the rush orders had much higher freight bills than normal. Also, there was a fair amount of wasted time by production personnel in setting up and taking down for jobs that were never run. However, the workers did not dare to question the accuracy of the computer system for fear they would display their lack of systems knowledge publicly.

At year end, an external accounting firm was hired to audit the company's financial statements, which showed a $1 million profit. When the physical count of the raw materials inventory was complete, the $1 million profit turned into a $1 million loss because of an inventory shortage. Further investigation identified the problem to be a programming error. The computer program had been written to record the inventory in stock at the time it was ordered, not when it was received. Cancelled and unfilled orders during the period since the system had been installed had resulted in an overstatement in inventory of approximately $2 million dollars.

When the warehouse manager was asked why he had not questioned the accuracy of the system earlier, he responded, "I felt incompetent to do so."

Required

1. Who was at fault for the error and the resulting cost associated with it?
2. Who had the responsibility to verify the accuracy of a data processing system: the programmer, analyst, purchasing agent, warehouse manager, cost accountant, or someone else?
3. What steps should have been taken to prevent the problem described here?

P18-7. Flowchart, File, and Output Design (CMA) Huron Company manufactures and sells eight major product lines with fifteen to twenty-five items in each product line. All sales are on credit, and orders are received by mail or telephone. Huron Company has a computer-based system that employs magnetic disks as a file medium.

All sales orders received during regular working hours are typed into an intelligent terminal that performs two functions—(a) prepares a sales order immediately and (b) stores the relevant data on a disk for shipment or back order, billing and update of accounts receivable, and update of inventory. However, the activities are done on an after-hours basis on the mainframe computer. After closing, the information is transferred to the mainframe computer by communication lines. Processing is completed during the night to update the files for the current day's activities and to facilitate the shipment of goods the following day. In other words, an order received one day is processed that night and shipped the next day.

The daily processing that has to be accomplished at night includes the following activities:

1. Preparing the invoice to be sent to the customer at the time of shipment
2. Updating the accounts receivable file
3. Updating finished-goods inventory
4. Listing all items that are back-ordered and short

Each month the sales department would like to have a sales summary and analysis. At the end of each month the statements should be prepared and mailed to customers. Management also wants an aging of accounts receivable each month.

Required

1. Identify the master files that Huron Company should maintain in this system to provide for the daily processing. Indicate the data content that should be included in each file and the order in which each file should be maintained.
2. Describe *(a)* the items that should appear in the monthly sales analysis reports the sales department should have and *(b)* the input data and master files that would have to be maintained to prepare these reports.

P18-8. Data-Processing Controls (CMA)

The Vane Corporation is a manufacturer that has been in business for the past eighteen years. During this period, the company has grown from a very small family-owned operation to a medium-sized manufacturer with several departments. Despite the growth, a substantial number of the procedures employed by Vane Corporation have been in effect since the business was started. Just recently Vane Corporation has computerized its payroll function.

The payroll function operates in the following manner. Each worker picks up a weekly time card on Monday morning and writes in her or his name and identification number. These blank cards are kept near the factory entrance. The workers write on the time card their daily arrival and departure times. On the following Monday the factory supervisors collect the completed time cards for the previous week and send them to data processing.

In data processing the time cards are used to prepare the weekly time file. This file is processed with the master payroll file, which is maintained on magnetic tape according to worker identification number. The checks are written by the computer on the regular checking account and imprinted with the treasurer's signature. After the payroll file is updated and the checks are prepared, the checks are sent to the factory supervisors, who distribute them to the workers or hold them for the workers to pick up later if they are absent.

The supervisors notify data processing of new employees and terminations. Any changes in hourly pay rate or any other changes affecting payroll are usually communicated to data processing by the supervisors.

The workers also complete a job time ticket for each individual job they work on each day. The job time tickets are collected daily and sent to cost accounting, where they are used to prepare a cost distribution analysis.

Further analysis of the payroll function reveals the following:

1. A worker's gross wages never exceed $300 per week.
2. Raises never exceed $0.55 per hour for the factory workers.
3. No more than 20 hours of overtime is allowed each week.
4. The factory employs 150 workers in ten departments.

The payroll function has not been operating smoothly for some time, but even more problems have surfaced since the payroll was computerized. The supervisors have indicated that they would like a weekly report indicating worker tardiness, absenteeism, and idle time so that they can determine the amount of productive time lost and the reason for the lost time. The following errors and inconsistencies have been encountered in the past few pay periods:

1. A worker's paycheck was not processed properly, because he had transposed two numbers in his identification number when he filled out his time card.
2. A worker was issued a check for $1,531.80 when it should have been $153.18.
3. One worker's paycheck was not written, and this error was not detected until the paychecks for that department were distributed by the supervisor.

4. One worker received a paycheck for an amount considerably larger than she should have. Further investigation revealed that 84 had been punched instead of 48 for hours worked.

5. In processing nonroutine changes, a computer operator included a pay rate increase for one of his friends in the factory. This was discovered by chance by another employee.

Required

1. Identify three ways that the company either has been defrauded or could easily be defrauded without anyone detecting it because of the manner in which payroll is being handled. Also, identify what should be done to minimize or prevent the types of fraud you identify.

2. For each of the five numbered errors and inconsistencies listed in the problem, identify the control weakness in the payroll procedure and in the computer processing system as it is now conducted, and recommended any changes required to correct for them in the future.

P18–9. Computer Data Processing—Behavioral Problems (CMA)

Audio Visual Corporation manufactures and sells visual display equipment. The company is headquartered near Boston. The majority of sales are made through seven geographical sales offices located in Los Angeles, Seattle, Minneapolis, Cleveland, Dallas, Boston, and Atlanta. Each sales office has a warehouse located nearby to carry an inventory of new equipment and replacement parts. The remainder of the sales are made through manufacturers' representatives.

Audio Visual's manufacturing operations are conducted in a single plant that is highly departmentalized. In addition to the assembly department, there are several departments responsible for various components used in the visual display equipment. The plant also has maintenance, engineering, scheduling, and cost accounting departments.

Early in 19X5, management decided that its management information system (MIS) needed upgrading. As a result, the company ordered an advanced computer in 19X5, which was installed in July 19X6. The main processing equipment is still located at corporate headquarters, and each of the seven sales offices is connected with the main processing unit by remote terminals.

The integration of the new computer into the Audio Visual information system was carried out by the MIS staff. The MIS manager and the four systems analysts who had the major responsibility for the integration were hired in the spring of 19X6. The department's other employees—programmers, machine operators, and key-punch operators—have been with the company for several years.

During its early years, Audio Visual had centralized decision making; top management formulated all plans and directed all operations. As the company expanded, some of the decision making was decentralized, although the information processing was still highly centralized. Departments had to coordinate their plans with the corporate office but they had more freedom in developing their sales programs. However, as the company expanded, information problems developed. As a consequence, the MIS department was given the responsibility to improve the company's information processing system when the new equipment was installed.

The MIS analysts reviewed the information system in existence before the acquisition of the new computer and identified weaknesses. They then redesigned old applications and designed new applications in developing the new system to overcome the weaknesses. During the eighteen months since the acquisition of the new equipment, the following applications have been redesigned or developed and are now operational—payroll, production scheduling, financial statement preparation, customer billing, raw materials usage in production, and finished-goods inventory by warehouse. The operating departments of Audio Visual affected by the systems changes were rarely consulted or contacted until the system was operational and the new reports were distributed to the operating departments.

The president of Audio Visual is very pleased with the work of the MIS department. During a recent conversation the president stated, "The MIS people are doing a good job and I have full confidence in their work. I touch base with the MIS people frequently, and they have encountered no difficulties in doing their work. We paid a lot of money for the new equipment and the MIS people certainly cost enough, but the combination of the new equipment and new MIS staff should solve all of our problems."

Recently, two other conversations regarding the computer and information system have taken place. One was between Jerry Adams, plant manager, and Bill Taylor, the MIS manager; the other was between Adams and Terry Williams, the new personnel manager.

Taylor-Adams Conversation

Adams: "Bill, you're trying to run my plant for me. I'm supposed to be the manager, yet you keep interfering. I wish you would mind your own business."

Taylor: "You've got a job to do but so does my department. When we analyzed the information needed for production scheduling and by top management, we saw where improvements could be made in the work flow. Now that the system is operational, you can't reroute work and change procedures because that would destroy the value of the information we're processing. And while I'm on that subject, it's getting to the point where we can't trust the information we're getting from production. The mark sense cards we receive from production contain a lot of errors."

Adams: "I'm responsible for the efficient operation of production. Quite frankly, I think I'm the best judge of production efficiency. The system you installed has reduced my work force and increased the work load of the remaining employees, but I don't see that this has improved anything. In fact, it might explain the high error rate in the cards."

Taylor: "This new computer costs a lot of money and I'm trying to be sure that the company gets its money's worth."

Adams-Williams Conversation

Adams: "My best production assistant, the one I'm grooming to be a supervisor when the next opening occurs, came to me today and said he was thinking of quitting. When I asked him why, he said he didn't enjoy the work anymore. He's not the only one who is unhappy. The supervisors and department heads no longer have a voice in establishing production schedules. This new computer system has taken away the contribution we used to make to company planning and direction. We seem to be going way back to the days when top management made all the decisions. I have more production problems now than I used to. I think it boils down to a lack of interest on the part of my management team. I know the problem is within my area but I thought you might be able to help me."

Williams: "I have no recommendations for you now but I've had similar complaints from purchasing and shipping. I think we should get your concerns on the agenda for our next plant management meeting."

Required

1. Apparently the development of and transition to the new computer-based system has created problems among the personnel of Audio Visual Corporation. Identify and briefly discuss the apparent causes of these problems.
2. How could the company have avoided the problems? What steps should be taken to avoid such problems in the future?

P18-10. Data Processing—Report Design (CMA) Denny Daniels is production manager of the Alumalloy Division of WRT Incorporated. Alumalloy has limited contact with outside customers and has no sales staff. Most of its customers are other divisions of WRT. All sales and purchases with outside customers are handled by other corporate divisions. Therefore, Alumalloy is treated as a cost center for reporting and evaluation purposes rather than as a revenue or profit center.

Daniels perceives the accounting department as a historical number generating process that provides little useful information for conducting his job. Consequently, the entire accounting process is perceived to be a negative motivational device that does not reflect how hard or how effectively he works as a production manager. Daniels tried to discuss these perceptions and concerns with June Scott, the controller for the Alumalloy Division. Daniels told Scott, "I think the cost report is misleading. I know I've had better production over a number of operating periods, but the cost report still says I have excessive costs. Look I'm not an accountant, I'm a production manager. I know how to get a good quality product out. Over a number of years, I've even cut the raw materials used to do it. But the cost report doesn't show any of this. Basically, it's always negative, no matter what I do. There's no way you can win with accounting or the people at corporate who use those reports."

Scott gave Daniels little consolation. Scott stated that the accounting system and the cost reports generated by headquarters are just part of the corporate game and almost impossible for an individual to change. "Although these accounting reports are pretty much the basis for evaluating the efficiency of your division and the means corporate uses to determine whether you have done the job they want, you shouldn't worry too much. You haven't been fired yet! Besides, these cost reports have been used by WRT for the last twenty-five years."

Daniels perceived from talking to the production manager of the Zinc Division that most of what Scott said was probably true. However, some minor cost reporting changes of Zinc had been agreed to by corporate headquarters. He also knew from the trade grapevine that the turnover of production managers was considered high at WRT, even though relatively few were fired. Most seemed to end up quitting, usually in disgust, because of beliefs that they were not being evaluated fairly. The following are typical comments of production managers who had left WRT:

> "Corporate headquarters doesn't really listen to us. All they consider are those misleading cost reports. They don't want them changed and they don't want any supplemental information."

> "The accountants may be quick with numbers but they don't know anything about production. As it was, I either had to ignore the cost reports entirely or pretend they were important even though they didn't tell how good a job I had done. No matter what they say about not firing people, negative reports mean negative evaluations. I'm better off working for another comany."

A recent copy of the cost report prepared by corporate headquarters for the Alumalloy Division follows. Daniels does not like this report because he believes it fails to reflect the division's operations properly, thereby resulting in an unfair evaluation of performance.

**Allumalloy Division
Cost Report
for the Month of April, 19X0
(000 omitted)**

	Master Budget	Actual Cost	Excess Cost
Aluminum	$ 400	$ 437	$ 37
Labor	560	540	(20)
Overhead	100	134	34
Total	$1,060	$1,111	$ 51

Required

1. Comment on Denny Daniel's perception of the following:
   a. June Scott, the controller
   b. corporate headquarters
   c. the cost report
   d. himself as a production manager

   Discuss how this perception affects his behavior and probable performance as a production manager and employee of WRT.

2. Identify and explain three changes that could be made in the cost information presented to the production managers that would make the information more meaningful and less threatening to them.

Chapter 19

Variable Costing and Contribution Margin Analysis

Outline

VARIABLE COSTING
Comparison of Variable Costing and
    Absorption Costing
Variable Costing as a Management Tool
External Reporting Considerations
CONTRIBUTION MARGIN ANALYSIS
Isolating the Components of Variance
Calculating the Variances
  Sales Price Variance
  Sales Mix Variance
  Sales Volume Variance
  Cost Price Variance
Gross Margin Analysis
Gross Margin Variance

Sales Price Variance
Sales Mix Variance
Sales Volume Variance
Cost Price Variance
SUMMARY
SELF-STUDY PROBLEMS
Variable Costing
Contribution Margin Analysis
SUGGESTED READINGS
DISCUSSION QUESTIONS
EXERCISES
PROBLEMS
CASE

There are two important ways in which cost accounting systems can be augmented to provide additional useful information for management decisions. First, *variable costing*, also called direct costing, can be used as an alternative method of product costing and income determination. Second, *gross margin analysis* can be used to analyze differences between budgeted and actual results. Both tools are widely used in cost accounting systems. This chapter explains how to apply variable costing and gross margin analysis and how to interpret their results. After you have completed this chapter, you should be able to:

1. define *variable* or *direct costing* and how it relates to the traditional cost accounting system known as absorption or full costing.
2. apply variable costing to provide useful information for management decisions.
3. explain why variable costing is not used for reporting to users of financial statements who are external to the company.
4. define contribution margin analysis.
5. apply contribution margin analysis to help explain why deviations occurred between budgeted and actual contribution margin.
6. apply contribution margin analysis to help explain why deviations occurred between contribution margins of succeeding years.

VARIABLE COSTING

Also called direct costing, **variable costing** is an alternative approach to product costing and income determination. It is similar to the traditional product costing method discussed elsewhere in this text (known as absorption, full, or conventional costing), with one important exception—when variable costing is used, fixed manufacturing overhead is *not* included as an inventoriable cost. Instead, fixed manufacturing overhead is charged off as a period expense. Because of the effect of this change on operating income and inventory values and for other philosophical reasons, accounting standard setting and regulatory bodies such as the Securities and Exchange Commission deny the use of variable costing for *external* reporting purposes. However, it is widely accepted by management for *internal* reporting as a powerful tool for management decision making.

It is important to understand what happens when fixed manufacturing overhead is charged as an expense in the income statement in the period when the cost is incurred rather than as part of cost of goods sold in a subsequent period of sale. Figure 19.1 contrasts the cost flows of absorption costing versus variable costing.

When variable costing is used, the assumption is that only those manufacturing costs that fluctuate directly with the volume of production should be inventoried. All other costs, which are fixed costs and are a function of time, are assumed to be more closely related to the capacity to produce each year than to the production of specific units of output in a year. Therefore, it is argued that such costs should be charged as current period costs rather than being inventoried, carried forward in time, and finally expensed in a future period when the inventory is ultimately sold. On the other hand, the assumption with **absorption costing** is that all manufacturing costs, whether variable or fixed, are necessary to produce goods and should be inventoried. Under this assumption all manufacturing costs are charged as costs of goods sold in the period of sale.

Comparison of Variable Costing and Absorption Costing

The concept of variable costing is deceptively simple and at face appears to be redundant to a discussion on the contribution approach. However, the use of variable costing has a

FIGURE 19.1 Comparison of Cost Flows—Variable Costing versus Absorption Costing

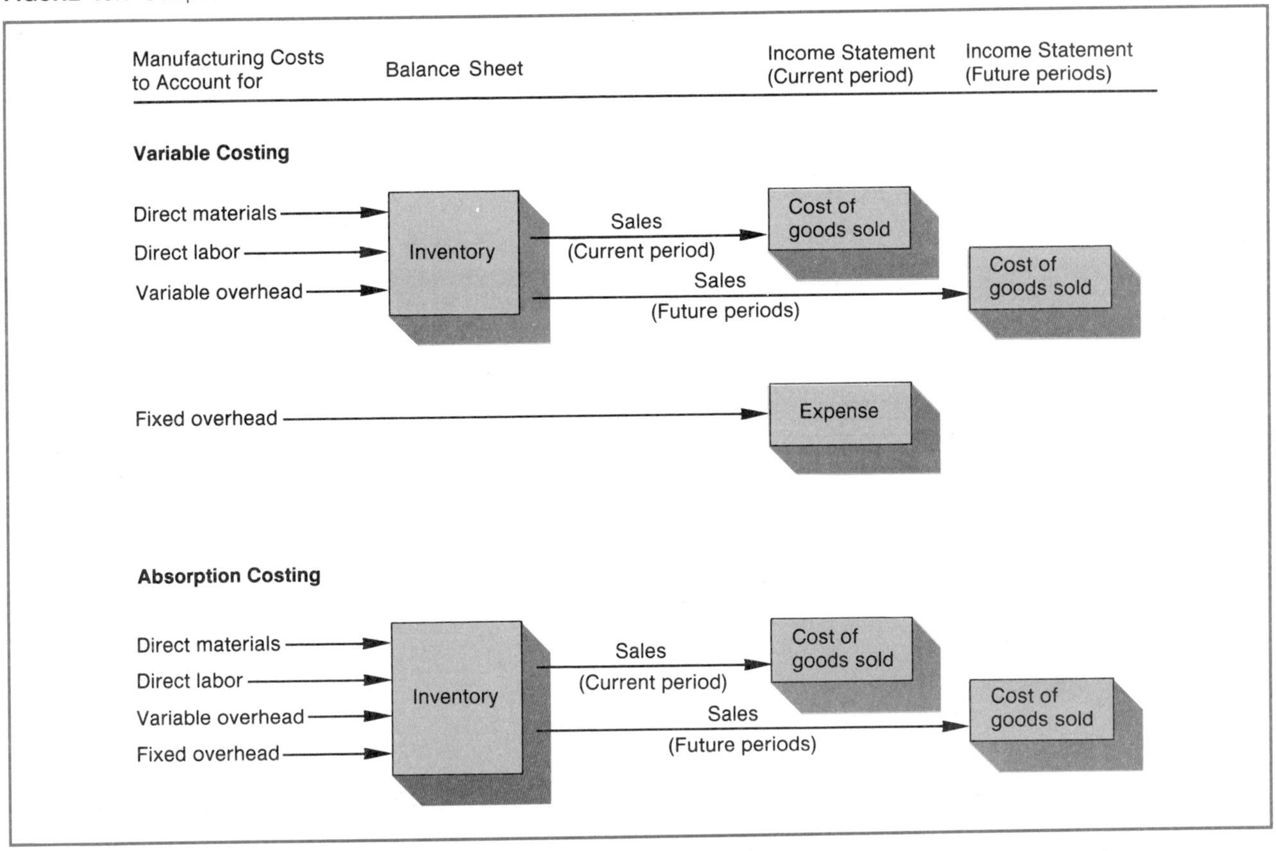

Variable Costing

Direct materials, Direct labor, Variable overhead → Inventory (Balance Sheet) → Sales (Current period) → Cost of goods sold (Income Statement Current period); Sales (Future periods) → Cost of goods sold (Income Statement Future periods)

Fixed overhead → Expense (Income Statement Current period)

Absorption Costing

Direct materials, Direct labor, Variable overhead, Fixed overhead → Inventory (Balance Sheet) → Sales (Current period) → Cost of goods sold (Income Statement Current period); Sales (Future periods) → Cost of goods sold (Income Statement Future periods)

subtle but important impact on product costing and income determination that accountants and managers should fully understand. Figure 19.2 shows a comparison of variable cost and absorption cost income statements for a manufacturing company during its first four years of operation. Assume that the company uses a standard cost system and that the following production and sales statistics are identical to budgeted amounts, except for the volume of production. Fixed manufacturing overhead is applied to work in process based on a long-run average production level of 2,200 units per year.

Standard Manufacturing Costs

	Unit Cost
Direct materials	$ 5.00
Direct labor	4.00
Variable manufacturing overhead	3.00
Total variable manufacturing costs	12.00
Fixed manufacturing overhead	2.00
Total manufacturing costs	$14.00

Manufacturing, Sales, and Inventory Quantity Statistics

Units	Year 1	Year 2	Year 3	Year 4
Beginning inventory	0	200	600	100
Manufactured	2,200	2,500	1,700	2,900
Available for sale	2,200	2,700	2,300	3,000
Sold	2,000	2,100	2,200	2,150
Ending inventory	200	600	100	850

FIGURE 19.2 Comparison of Variable and Absorption Costing Income Statements

Variable Costing

	Year 1	Year 2	Year 3	Year 4
Sales @ $20	$40,000	$42,000	$44,000	$43,000
Variable manufacturing cost of goods sold:				
Direct materials @ $5	$11,000	$12,500	$ 8,500	$14,500
Direct labor @ $4	8,800	10,000	6,800	11,600
Variable manufacturing overhead @ $3	6,600	7,500	5,100	8,700
Total variable manufacturing costs	$26,400	$30,000	$20,400	$34,800
Plus: Beginning inventory	0	2,400	7,200	1,200
Variable manufacturing cost of goods available for sale	$26,400	$32,400	$27,600	$36,000
Less: Ending inventory	2,400	7,200	1,200	10,200
Variable manufacturing cost of goods sold	$24,000	$25,200	$26,400	$25,800
Variable selling and administrative expenses @ $1	2,200	2,500	1,700	2,900
Total variable costs	$26,200	$27,700	$28,100	$28,700
Contribution margin	$13,800	$14,300	$15,900	$14,300
Less: Fixed costs:				
Fixed manufacturing costs	$ 4,400	$ 4,400	$ 4,400	$ 4,400
Fixed selling and administrative costs	1,000	1,000	1,000	1,000
Total fixed costs	$ 5,400	$ 5,400	$ 5,400	$ 5,400
Operating income	$ 8,400	$ 8,900	$10,500	$ 8,900

Absorption Costing

	Year 1	Year 2	Year 3	Year 4
Sales @ $20	$40,000	$42,000	$44,000	$43,000
Cost of goods sold:				
Cost of goods manufactured:				
Direct materials @ $5	$11,000	$12,500	$ 8,500	$14,500
Direct labor @ $4	8,800	10,000	6,800	11,600
Variable manufacturing overhead @ $3	6,600	7,500	5,100	8,700
Fixed manufacturing overhead @ 2	4,400	5,000	3,400	5,800
Total cost of goods manufactured	$30,800	$35,000	$23,800	$40,600
Beginning inventory	0	2,800	8,400	1,400
Cost of goods available for sale	$30,800	$37,800	$32,200	$42,000
Less: Ending inventory	2,800	8,400	1,400	11,900
Cost of goods sold	$28,000	$29,400	$30,800	$30,100
Gross margin	$12,000	$12,600	$13,200	$12,900
Selling and administrative expenses:				
Variable @ $1	$ 2,200	$ 2,500	$ 1,700	$ 2,900
Fixed	1,000	1,000	1,000	1,000
Total selling and administrative expenses	$ 3,200	$ 3,500	$ 2,700	$ 3,900
Operating income before volume variance	$ 8,800	$ 9,100	$10,500	$ 9,000
Volume variance	0	$ 600	$ (1,000)	$ 1,400
Operating income	$ 8,800	$ 9,700	$ 9,500	$10,400

Volume variance:
  Formula: (Actual volume − Budgeted volume) × Fixed overhead per unit
    Year 1: (2,200 − 2,200) × $2.00 = 0
    Year 2: (2,500 − 2,200) × $2.00 = $600 Favorable
    Year 3: (1,700 − 2,200) × $2.00 = $1,000 Unfavorable
    Year 4: (2,900 − 2,200) × $2.00 = $1,400 Favorable

Comparing the results for these two methods for the first year of operations indicates a difference of $400 ($8,800 − $8,400 = $400 in operating income when using variable costing versus absorption costing. This difference is because fixed costs of $400 (200 units @ $2.00 = $400) are carried in inventory at the end of the period when using absorption costing rather than being charged off as an expense when using variable costing.

This can be verified by observing that ending inventories differ by $400 ($2,800 − $2,400 = $400) when these two methods are used. It is important to recognize that if all units produced had been sold in the first year of operations, there would be no difference between the methods in either ending inventory or operating income. Differences arise between these methods only when inventories are maintained from one period to the next.

The significance of all this for income determination can be further illustrated by comparing the results of operations for the subsequent three years, as shown in figure 19.2. Inventory amounts that affect both the balance sheet and income statement are different for each year.

Inventory Amounts

	Year 1	Year 2	Year 3	Year 4
Absorption costing	$2,800	$8,400	$1,400	$11,900
Variable costing	2,400	7,200	1,200	10,200
Difference	$ 400	$1,200	$ 200	$ 1,700

These differences are the result of excluding fixed manufacturing overhead from inventories when using variable costing. This is why inventory values are always lower with variable costing than with absorption costing. When absorption costing is used, fixed costs are applied to inventory as part of the predetermined overhead application rate; when variable costing is used, the only component of the predetermined overhead application rate is variable overhead. Although these inventory differences relate only to the finished-goods inventory, the results would be the same if work-in-process inventories had been included.

Work-in-process inventories have not been included in this chapter's examples to keep the illustrations as uncluttered as possible. These examples also contain no materials, labor, or variable overhead variances. The presence of any such variances would not affect the results when the two methods are compared. The volume variance is included to illustrate how standard cost variances are handled in this type of situation. Note that there is no volume variance with variable costing because fixed costs are treated as a lump sum cost in the period incurred. Also note that variable costing is not dependent on standard costs or budgetary methods. A standard cost environment is used to illustrate variable costing, because it represents a comprehensive and highly probable situation.

The contribution margin, which is computed when using variable costing, is consistently greater than the gross margin, which is computed when using absorption costing (as shown in figure 19.2). Some people argue that a greater contribution margin may lead to different and probably inappropriate management decisions than when gross margin is the reference number. For example, marketing management may lower prices or ask for higher bonuses when using the contribution margin rather than the lower gross margin. Of course, it is to be hoped that managers will have a thorough understanding of the costs that are included and excluded when using either contribution or gross margin information. The effect of variable costing on management decisions will be discussed later in this chapter.

The difference between variable costing and absorption costing is simply a timing difference; that is, fixed manufacturing overhead will ultimately be charged as an expense using both accounting methods, and the differences that are apparent in the short run will not be differences in the long run.

Another observation concerns the difference in the operating income obtained with each method. This difference is simply caused by charging fixed manufacturing costs to inventory when using absorption costing in contrast to not charging any fixed costs to inventory when using variable costing. Therefore, it is relatively easy to reconcile the operating incomes calculated with each method. Figure 19.3 shows two ways to perform this reconciliation.

The operating income fluctuates directly with sales when using variable costing. However, when using absorption costing, operating income does not necessarily fluctuate directly with sales but depends on the relationship of sales to production. For example, in a period when inventories increase, as is the case when production exceeds sales, absorption costing will typically result in higher operating income than the variable costing method. In a period when sales exceed production, variable costing will typically result in higher operating income.

This can be verified by inspecting the comparison of income from operations in figure 19.3. Production volume exceeds sales, and operating income is higher under absorption costing in years 1, 2, and 4 as expected. Also as expected, operating income using variable costing is higher in year 3, when sales exceed production. These relationships hold when using standard costing and LIFO inventory costing methods. When FIFO and average costing inventory valuation methods are used, care should be exercised in generalizing about the preceding relationships.

FIGURE 19.3
Reconciliation of Income from Operations

Calculation of Differences in Income from Operations

	Year 1	Year 2	Year 3	Year 4
Absorption costing	$ 8,800	$ 9,700	$ 9,500	$10,400
Variable costing	8,400	8,900	10,500	8,900
Difference	$ 400	$ 800	(1,000)	$ 1,500

Reconciliation of Differences
(Inventory Change—Dollar Method)

	Year 1	Year 2	Year 3	Year 4
Absorption costing:				
Ending inventory	$ 2,800	$ 8,400	$ 1,400	$11,900
Less: Beginning inventory	0	2,800	8,400	1,400
Change	$ 2,800	$ 5,600	$ (7,000)	$10,500
Variable costing:				
Ending inventory	$ 2,400	$ 7,200	$ 1,200	$10,200
Less: Beginning inventory	0	2,400	7,200	1,200
Change	$ 2,400	$ 4,800	$ (6,000)	$ 9,000
Difference in operating income	$ 400	$ 800	$ (1,000)	$ 1,500

(Inventory Change—Units Method)

	Year 1	Year 2	Year 3	Year 4
Ending inventory	200	600	100	850
Less: Beginning inventory	0	200	600	100
Change—Increase (decrease)	200	400	(500)	750
Fixed costs per unit	× $2	× $2	× $2	× $2
Difference in operating income	$400	$800	$(1,000)	$1,500

The reason the relationship among sales, production, and operating income illustrated in figure 19.3 holds true can be further explained as follows. If there is a difference between the volume of sales and the volume of production during an accounting period, there will be a change in the number of units carried in inventory. Remember that fixed costs are carried in inventory with absorption costing but are not carried in inventory with variable costing. Therefore, the *amount of change* in the cost of ending inventory *will differ* between these two methods.

To illustrate, consider an inventory of 1,200 units with a full cost per unit of $8 and a variable cost per unit of $7. The difference of $1 represents the amount of fixed cost per unit inventoried when using absorption costing. If sales exceed production by 200 units during the next accounting period, there will be a decrease in inventory by 200 units to 1,000 units (1,200 units − 200 units). Therefore, the cost of ending inventory when using absorption costing will decline from $9,600 (1,200 units × $8 per unit) to $8,000 (1,000 units × $8 per unit)—a change of $1,600. When using variable costing, however, the cost of ending inventory will decline from $8,400 (1,200 units × $7 per unit) to $7,000 (1,000 units × $7)—a change of $1,400. The amount of inventory cost change is different by $200 ($1,600 − $1,400) between the two methods. This change can also be found by multiplying the fixed cost component, which is inventoried under absorption costing but not inventoried under variable costing, by the number of units of inventory change ($1 × 200 units = $200).

Finally, the value of ending inventory shown on the balance sheet will differ between methods. A lower inventory cost will be shown for variable costing than for absorption costing because of the fixed cost element.

Variable Costing as a Management Tool

Executives and managers generally agree that variable costing represents a powerful analytical tool. This is true primarily because in a variable costing system, the per-unit direct costs and the contribution margin remain constant for various levels of production and sales. With absorption costing, the relationship among costs, volume, and prices may be obscured because of the way fixed costs are handled. Fixed costs are applied to production in an absorption costing system on a per-unit basis as though they were a function of volume, when, in reality, they are not (as discussed in chapters 13 and 14).

A prerequisite to the installation and use of a variable costing system is the identification and classification of costs into their fixed and variable components (see chapter 3). Once costs are properly classified and the system is in operation, there are a number of ways in which variable costing is particularly advantageous and useful as a management tool.

Variable costs are typically the only costs relevant to short-run, routine decisions. Because variable costs are reliable in forecasting as well as in reporting results of operations, variable costing systems are used to develop budgets and profit plans.

Another practical advantage of variable costing is that net income tends to fluctuate directly with sales volume. This feature enables management to identify changes in sales with their effect on net income.

Nonroutine management decisions are also facilitated by variable costing. Whether or not to expand into new markets, engage in special promotional activities, or produce new product lines are examples of such decisions. The concept of variable costing goes hand-in-hand with the techniques related to nonroutine decision making (see chapters 4 and 21) and facilitates the use of cost-volume-profit analysis (as discussed in chapter 7).

The format of a variable costing income statement enhances management decision making. The contribution margin helps to project changes in net income that accompany changes in sales. Also, fixed costs are reported as a definable group on the variable costing income statement rather than as a component in a number of other cost categories reported on an absorption costing statement. This makes the effect of fixed costs on profits more readily understood.

Results of operations are also more clearly defined under variable costing than under absorption costing. Top management is typically responsible for the level of manufacturing operations relating to both long-run capacity and short-run production volumes. Thus, any variances that arise relating to fixed costs, which are essentially the responsibility of top management, should not be treated as though they are the responsibility of lower-level managers. Variable costing implicitly recognizes this principle by charging fixed costs against revenue in the accounting period when incurred rather than charging them to inventory. Many think that this makes it possible for management reports to be more representative of controllable cost flows than if fixed costs are included in inventory. Production managers should receive reports showing responsibility for only those cost factors that are controllable in production departments. For example, reports for production managers should exclude lump-sum fixed costs and fixed cost variances over which the managers have no control. However, it should be noted that department managers may be responsible for some fixed costs, and when this is so, controllable fixed costs should be included on management reports. The main point is that variable does not mean controllable, and fixed does not mean uncontrollable.

External Reporting Considerations

For internal management, distinguishing between fixed and variable costs and using variable costing in connection with the contribution approach have widespread acceptance. However, neither the Internal Revenue Service, the Securities and Exchange Commission, nor generally accepted accounting principles approve of variable costing for *external* reporting. Therefore, many firms maintain information about fixed and variable costs within their cost accounting systems in sufficient detail to enable the generation of either variable cost or absorption cost financial statements as needed.

The typical procedure is to expand the chart of accounts so that both fixed and variable cost classifications are accommodated. Overhead control accounts are also expanded so that there is a "manufacturing overhead control—variable account" as well as a "manufacturing overhead control—fixed account." This makes it possible to exclude fixed overhead from being inventoried. When overhead is applied to work in process, it is only the variable portion that is applied by means of a "variable manufacturing overhead applied account." Differences between actual and applied variable overhead are calculated and reported as discussed in chapters 15 and 16. The "manufacturing overhead control—fixed account" is closed to income summary as any other period expense account.

When a company sets up its cost accounting system using the variable costing concept, it is necessary for external reporting purposes to convert the financial statements to absorption costing at the end of each reporting period. This requires a few calculations that are neither expensive nor time consuming. The conversion procedure involves adjusting the inventory values and operating income for the period by the amount of fixed costs that were excluded from the determination of inventory values when a variable costing system is used. The information items necessary to make the conversion calculations for each accounting period under a FIFO inventory system are as follows:

1. The number of units manufactured and sold
2. The standard (budgeted or denominator) level of activity
3. The quantities carried in beginning and ending inventories

4. The amount of budgeted fixed costs
5. The changes, if any, in other cost elements

The steps in the actual conversion process are as follows:

1. Calculate the predetermined fixed manufacturing overhead application rate that would have been used under the absorption costing concept.
2. Convert the inventory values under variable costing to absorption costing by adding an amount equal to the number of units in each inventory multiplied by the fixed overhead application rate.
3. Calculate the volume variance by multiplying the difference between budgeted and actual production volumes by the fixed overhead application rate.
4. Construct the absorption costing financial statements using information available in the variable costing statements plus the converted inventory values and the volume variance.

The conversion process's validity can be verified by performing the following:

1. Calculate the increase or decrease in units of inventory.
2. Multiply the increase or decrease in inventory units by the predetermined fixed manufacturing overhead application rate to get the difference in operating income between the variable costing and absorption costing methods.

Assuming that there have been no other changes in costs, this difference in operating income can be used to verify the validity of the conversion process. For example, the following operation traces the conversion and validation process using data contained in figures 19.2 and 19.3 for the second year of operations.

1. The predetermined fixed manufacturing overhead application rate is given as $2.00 per unit.
2. Beginning inventory—converted: $2,400 + (200 × $2) = $2,800.
   Ending inventory—converted: $7,200 + (600 × $2) = $8,400.
3. The volume variance is a favorable $600, as calculated in figure 19.2.
4. Figure 19.2 contains the actual construction of the absorption costing income statement using the preceding data.

A balance sheet is not shown because all relevant information for the conversion is contained in the income statement. Figure 19.3 contains the validation calculations for this procedure. You should now refer to years 3 and 4 in figures 19.2 and 19.3 and perform the conversion and validation calculations.

Conversion of financial statements from absorption costing to variable costing is essentially the opposite of the preceding operation except that there is no need to consider the volume variance, because fixed costs are subtracted as period expenses on the variable cost income statement.

Conversion from variable costing to absorption costing is necessary because of the position taken by the American Institute of Certified Public Accountants (AICPA), the Securities and Exchange Commission (SEC), and the Internal Revenue Service (IRS). Although companies seem to be using variable costing in ever-increasing numbers for internal management purposes, the AICPA, SEC, and IRS believe that variable costing is inappropriate for reporting results of operations externally.

The basis for the AICPA's position is its Accounting Research Bulletin no. 43, which states that "as applied to inventories, cost means in principle the sum of the applicable expenditures and charges directly or *indirectly* incurred in bringing an article to its existing condition and location" (emphasis added). In other words, inventory costs should contain both variable and fixed cost elements. The AICPA does recognize that some overhead items, such as excessive spoilage and rehandling costs, may be charged as period expenses rather than being inventoried. However, the basic position on variable or direct costing remains as stated in Bulletin no. 43. The Financial Accounting Standards Board (FASB), the current standard-setting body, has not yet taken a position contrary to the AICPA position.

The SEC does not accept financial reports based on the variable costing approach unless inventories and income numbers are adjusted to reflect an absorption costing basis. This position is based primarily on the attitude that variable costing is not a generally accepted accounting procedure. The SEC also has a policy to encourage consistency in reporting among regulated companies, and acceptance of variable costing would probably lead to more inconsistency in reporting.

The IRS specifically states that variable or direct costing is "not in accordance with the regulations." The regulations define inventory costs to include "indirect expenses incident to and necessary for production of the particular article, including in such indirect production costs an appropriate portion of management expenses."

CONTRIBUTION MARGIN ANALYSIS

Contribution margin analysis is a technique for performing a detailed analysis of changes in contribution margin between budgeted and actual results or between actual contribution margins of succeeding years. Contribution margin analysis provides information helpful for answering questions such as, Why did contribution margin for the period decrease? Was the decrease caused by reduced sales, increased costs, or a combination of factors?

Contribution margin analysis is especially useful when a company markets several products, because it provides information about how changes in the relative mix of different products sold affect deviations in contribution margin. The affect on contribution margin of changes in the sales volume for different products can also be analyzed.

Management should understand why actual contribution margin deviates from the budget when a standard cost system is being used. When a standard cost system is not being used, management should understand why the contribution margin of one period differs from the contribution margin of the prior period. However, it often is not a simple task to identify specific causal relationships because contribution margin is a composite of a number of sales and cost elements. Without the proper analytical tools, management must guess whether a given change in contribution margin is the result of changes in the volume of sales, changes in one or more cost elements, or changes in the selling prices of one or more products.

Isolating the Components of Variance

The procedures used to analyze changes in contribution margin parallel the procedures used to analyze variances in a standard cost system. However, contribution margin analysis is not dependent on either the use of a standard cost system or a budget. When a cost accounting system other than a standard cost system is used, the results of operations for the previous accounting period are used as the standard in contribution margin analysis. A standard cost system is assumed for the illustration in this chapter because it is the most commonly used. The self-study problem at the end of this chapter illustrates contribution margin analysis when a standard cost system is not in use.

Contribution margin analysis begins by identifying the difference between actual contribution margin and budgeted contribution margin, which is called the **contribution margin variance.** The contribution margin variance is then further analyzed into its component parts—*(a)* a sales price variance, *(b)* a sales mix variance, *(c)* a sales volume variance, and *(d)* a cost price variance. By studying each of these variances, management is provided with the information to effectively investigate and correct undesirable results or to promote desirable outcomes.

The **sales price variance** represents the effect on contribution margin of differences in sales prices between budgeted and actual results. For example, if actual sales prices are not equal to budgeted prices, the amount of the total difference in contribution margin that is attributable to the difference in prices must be determined.

The **sales mix variance** represents the effect on contribution margin of differences in sales mix between budgeted and actual results. The sales mix of a company relates to the relative proportion of each product sold. For example, a company that plans to sell a total of 100,000 units, or 50,000, 40,000, and 10,000 units of products *A, B,* and *C,* respectively, has a sales mix, or relative sales proportion, of 50:40:10. If actual sales result in a total of 100,000 units sold out at a mix of 55,000, 30,000, and 15,000 units of products *A, B,* and *C,* respectively, the actual sales mix of 55:30:15 differs from the planned sales mix. The amount of the total difference in contribution margin that is attributable to the change in relative sales volume must be determined.

The **sales volume variance** represents the effect on contribution margin of differences in the quantities of units sold between budgeted and actual results. For example, if the volume of actual sales is not equal to the budgeted sales volume, the amount of the total difference in contribution margin that is attributable to the difference in volume must be determined.

The **cost price variance** represents the effect on contribution margin of differences in manufacturing costs between budgeted and actual results. When using a standard cost system, the cost price variance can be further analyzed into variances for materials, labor, and manufacturing overhead (as explained in chapters 15 and 16).

Calculating the Variances

The computational procedures of contribution margin analysis are illustrated in figure 19.4. A multiproduct company is assumed for this illustration, because this is the environment in which contribution margin analysis is most beneficial.

In figure 19.4, the difference in the contribution margin of $20,100 between budgeted and actual results represents the contribution margin variance. The challenge is to analyze the variance to determine what portions are the result of *(a)* differences in selling price, *(b)* differences in sales mix, *(c)* differences in sales volume, or *(d)* differences in the costs of production.

A fundamental principle in such an analysis is that in order to isolate the effect of one factor, all other factors must be held constant. To facilitate the application of this principle relative to the sales mix and volume variances, it is necessary to calculate the budgeted average contribution margin per unit. Figure 19.4 shows this computation. Note that the computation of the "budgeted average contribution margin per unit" relates to the *total* expected results. In contrast, the "budgeted contribution margin per unit" relates to the expected results for *each individual product*.

The final procedure is to calculate the effect of price and cost changes by holding the volume factor constant. The effect of sales mix and volume changes is then calculated by holding the price and cost factors constant. Formulas for calculating the variances are given in figure 19.5.

FIGURE 19.4 Income Statement

	Budgeted			**Actual**			**Difference**
	Units	Price/Cost	Amount	Units	Price/Cost	Amount	Amount
Sales:							
Product M	12,000	$30.00	$360,000	10,200	$32.00	$326,400	$(33,600)
Product N	7,000	25.00	175,000	8,400	25.00	210,000	35,000
Product Z	2,000	20.15	40,300	3,000	19.50	58,500	18,200
Total	21,000		$575,300	21,600	(1)	$594,900	$ 19,600
Variable costs:							
Product M	12,000	$24.00	$288,000	10,200	$24.50	$249,900	$(38,100)
Product N	7,000	20.00	140,000	8,400	19.00	159,600	19,600
Product Z	2,000	18.00	36,000	3,000	18.00	54,000	18,000
Total	21,000		$464,000	21,600	(2)	$463,500	$ (500)
Contribution margin		(3)	$111,300			$131,400	$ 20,100

(1) Actual average price per unit = ($594,900 ÷ 21,600) = $27.5416.
(2) Actual average cost per unit = ($463,500 ÷ 21,600) = $21.4583.
(3) Budgeted average contribution margin per unit = ($111,300 ÷ 21,000) = $5.30.
Budgeted contribution margin per unit:
   Product M: ($30.00 − $24.00) = $6.00
   Product N: ($25.00 − $20.00) = $5.00
   Product Z: ($20.15 − $18.00) = $2.15

FIGURE 19.5

Formulas for Contribution Margin Analysis

For Standard Cost Systems

$$\text{Contribution margin variance} = \text{Budgeted contribution margin} - \text{Actual contribution margin}$$

$$\text{Sales price variance} = [\text{Actual prices} - \text{Budgeted prices}] \times \text{Actual sales}$$

$$\text{Sales mix variance} = \left[\begin{array}{c}\text{Budgeted contribution} \\ \text{margin per unit}\end{array} - \begin{array}{c}\text{Budgeted weighted} \\ \text{average contribution margin}\end{array}\right] \times \text{Actual sales}$$

$$\text{Budgeted sales mix variance}^a = \left[\begin{array}{c}\text{Budgeted contribution} \\ \text{margin per unit}\end{array} - \begin{array}{c}\text{Budgeted weighted} \\ \text{average contribution margin}\end{array}\right] \times \text{Budgeted sales}$$

$$\text{Sales volume variance} = \left[\begin{array}{c}\text{Actual} \\ \text{sales}\end{array} - \begin{array}{c}\text{Budgeted} \\ \text{sales}\end{array}\right] \times \text{Budgeted weighted average contribution margin}$$

$$\text{Cost price variance} = [\text{Budgeted costs} - \text{Actual costs}] \times \text{Actual sales}$$

For Other Cost Accounting Systems

The preceding formulas can be adjusted for use with actual or nonstandard types of cost accounting systems by substituting "current year" for "actual" items and "prior year" for "budgeted" items in the formulas.

Note: All prices and costs in these formulas are per-unit amounts. Sales are in units.

[a]This variance and formula are used in the detailed analysis of the sales mix variance.

The computations necessary to analyze the contribution margin variance of $20,100 shown in figure 19.4 are as follows. Unless otherwise noted, all prices, costs, and quantities relate to the units of production and sales.

Sales Price Variance

	Actual Prices	−	Budgeted Prices	×	Actual Sales	=	Sales Price Variance
Product M:	$32.00	−	$30.00 = $2.00	×	10,200	=	$20,400 F
Product N:	25.00	−	25.00 = 0	×	8,400	=	0
Product Z:	19.50	−	20.15 = −0.65	×	3,000	=	1,950 U
Total sales price variance							$18,450 F

The favorable sales price variance of $18,450 indicates that the bulk of the contribution margin variance is due to differences in sales prices for the various products sold by the firm. The preceding product analysis indicates that the price change for product M had a significant positive effect on the increase in contribution margin. Product N did not affect the increase because there was no price change. There was a small negative effect from the decline in the price of product Z.

Sales Mix Variance

	Budgeted Contribution Margin	−	Budgeted Average Contribution Margin	×	Actual Sales	=	Sales Mix Variance
Product M:	$6.00	−	$5.30 = $0.70	×	10,200	=	$7,140 F
Product N:	5.00	−	5.30 = −0.30	×	8,400	=	2,520 U
Product Z:	2.15	−	5.30 = −3.15	×	3,000	=	9,450 U
Total actual sales mix variance							$4,830 U

The total unfavorable sales mix variance indicates that the relative proportion of product sales shifted toward those products with lower contribution margins per unit. For example, because there was a large increase in the relative sales of product Z and because product Z has the lowest contribution margin per unit, the result is a large unfavorable variance.

The sales mix variance should be interpreted carefully to avoid unwarranted conclusions. Confusion can arise because the *total* sales mix variance and the individual product variances should be interpreted separately. For example, the total sales mix variance of $4,830 in the preceding illustration is a valid indicator of the total effect on the contribution margin of the shift in sales mix. However, examination of this impact by individual product should be made relative to budgeted or anticipated variances, which are actually part of the budget. The following is a calculation of the sales mix variance using budgeted results:

Budgeted Sales Mix Variance

	Budgeted Contribution Margin	−	Budgeted Average Contribution Margin	×	Budgeted Sales	=	Budgeted Sales Mix Variance
Product M:	$6.00	−	$5.30 = $0.70	×	12,000	=	$8,400 F
Product N:	5.00	−	5.30 = −0.30	×	7,000	=	2,100 U
Product Z:	2.15	−	5.30 = −3.15	×	2,000	=	6,300 U
Total budgeted sales mix variance							$ 0

As anticipated, the total sales mix variance is zero on a budgeted basis. Because there is a budgeted sales mix variance for each product, it is necessary to compare actual individual product variances with budgeted results to obtain a clearer picture of each product's effect on the change in total mix. Such a comparison might be as follows:

Final Sales Mix Variance

	Actual Sales Mix Variance	Budgeted Sales Mix Variance	Difference
Product M:	$7,140 F	$8,400 F	$1,260 U
Product N:	2,520 U	2,100 U	420 U
Product Z:	9,450 U	6,300 U	3,150 U
Total	$4,830 U	$ 0	$4,830 U

Note that an increase in an unfavorable variance when comparing budgeted with actual results represents an unfavorable outcome. Comparing budgeted and actual variances, as above, gives a clearer indication of the actual effect, by product, of the change in the relative sales mix.

Sales Volume Variance

	Actual Sales	−	Budgeted Sales	×	Budgeted Average Contribution Margin	=	Sales Volume Variance
Product M:	$10,200	−	12,000 = −1,800	×	$5.30	=	$9,540 U
Product N:	8,400	−	7,000 = 1,400	×	5.30	=	7,420 F
Product Z:	3,000	−	2,000 = 1,000	×	5.30	=	5,300 F
Total sales volume variance							$3,180 F

The sales volume variance isolates the effect on contribution margin of changes in sales volume. It is quite clear how much the decreased sales volume of product M and the increased sales volume of products N and Z affected contribution margin.

It is also worthwhile to compare the sales volume variances with the sales mix variances relative to other factors, such as price changes, that occurred during the period. For example, if products M and N are substitute goods for product Z, product Z's price decline from $20.00 to $19.50 per unit may have contributed to the change in sales mix as well as to the increased sales of product Z. If such cause-and-effect relationships can be identified, contribution margin analysis can be helpful in making many production and marketing decisions.

Cost Price Variance

	Budgeted Costs	−	Actual Costs	×	Actual Sales	=	Cost Price Variance
Product M:	$24.00	−	$24.50 = $−0.50	×	10,200	=	$5,100 U
Product N:	20.00	−	19.00 = 1.00	×	8,400	=	8,400 F
Product Z:	18.00	−	18.00 = 0	×	3,000	=	0
Total cost price variance							$3,300 F

The favorable cost price variance of $3,300 would be further analyzed in a standard cost system by calculating the materials, labor, and manufacturing overhead variances to gauge the relative effect of and responsibility for each cost element.

The results of contribution margin analysis can be summarized in a management report that shows each variance component by product and in total. This report can also be used to verify the results of the variance calculations by comparing the grand total of variances with the original contribution margin variance analyzed. Figure 19.6 shows such a report.

As a final note, an aggregate approach to contribution margin analysis can be used to calculate total variances directly without the detail of individual product variances. When individual product detail is not required, the aggregate approach provides a shortcut to contribution margin analysis.

The first step in the aggregate approach is to calculate an income statement using the

FIGURE 19.6

Report of Contribution Margin Analysis

	Product M	Product N	Product Z	Total
Sales price variance	$20,400 F	$ 0	$1,950 U	$18,450 F
Sales mix variance	1,260 U	420 U	3,150 U	4,830 U
Sales volume variance	9,540 U	7,420 F	5,300 F	3,180 F
Cost price variance	5,100 U	8,400 F	0	3,300 F
	$ 4,500 F	$15,400 F	$ 200 F	$20,100 F

actual sales volume at budgeted prices and costs. Such an income statement is presented in figure 19.7 using the data from figure 19.4.

Taking the data from figures 19.4 and 19.7, the contribution margin analysis is repeated below on an aggregate basis. Variances can be verified with those previously calculated.

Sales Price Variance

Average price using actual sales at budgeted prices (figure 19.7)	$26.6875
Actual average price (figure 19.4)	−27.5416
	$ 0.8541
Actual quantity sold	× 21,600
Sales price variance	$ 18,450 F

Sales Mix Variance

Budgeted average contribution margin (figure 19.4)	$ 5.3000
Average contribution margin using actual sales at budgeted prices and costs	− 5.0764
	$ 0.2236
Actual quantity sold	× 21,600
Sales mix variance	$ 4,830 U

Sales Volume Variance

Budgeted total sales	$ 21,000
Actual total sales	− 21,600
	$ 600
Budgeted average contribution margin (figure 19.4)	× 5.30
Sales volume variance	$ 3,180 F

Cost Variance

Actual average cost (figure 19.4)	$21.4583
Average cost using actual sales at budgeted costs (figure 19.7)	−21.6111
	$ 0.1528
Actual total sales	×21,600
Cost variance	$ 3,300 F

Gross Margin Analysis

Changes in gross margin can be analyzed in the same way that changes in contribution margin are analyzed. The procedures are similar, and the same types of questions are answered. However, remember that contribution margin analysis is a tool used to analyze changes in contribution margin when a variable costing system is used, but gross margin analysis is a tool used to analyze changes in gross margin when an absorption costing system is used.

FIGURE 19.7

Income Statement Using Actual Sales and Budgeted Prices and Costs

Income Statement

	Units	Price/Cost	Amount
Sales:			
Product M	10,200	$30.00	$306,000
Product N	8,400	25.00	210,000
Product Z	3,000	20.15	60,450
Total	21,600	(1)	$576,450
Variable cost:			
Product M	10,200	24.00	$244,800
Product N	8,400	20.00	168,000
Product Z	3,000	18.00	54,000
Total	21,600	(2)	$466,800
Contribution margin		(3)	$109,650

(1) Average price per unit using actual sales at budgeted prices = ($576,450 ÷ 21,600) = $26.6875.
(2) Average cost per unit using actual sales at budgeted costs = ($466,800 ÷ 21,600) = $21.6111.
(3) Average contribution margin per unit using actual sales at budgeted prices and costs = ($109,650 ÷ 21,600) = $5.0764.

The variances used to perform gross margin analysis will be briefly explained here and an example analysis presented. Figure 19.8 contains budgeted and actual absorption cost income statements.

Only an aggregate analysis of gross margin is illustrated in this section. A detailed product analysis can be performed by adjusting the formulas in figure 19.5 to reflect the change from contribution margin to gross margin. Figure 19.9 contains an absorption cost

FIGURE 19.8 Income Statement

	Budgeted			Actual			Difference
	Units	Price/Cost	Amount	Units	Price/Cost	Amount	Amount
Sales:							
Product X	20	$20.00	$ 400	40	$30.00	$1,200	$ 800
Product Y	20	40.00	800	40	40.00	1,600	800
Product Z	20	1 60.00	1,200	20	60.00	1,200	0
Total	60		$2,400	100	(1)	$4,000	$1,600
Cost of goods sold:							
Product X	20	$10.00	$ 200	40	$20.00	$ 800	$ 600
Product Y	20	20.00	400	40	20.00	800	400
Product Z	20	30.00	600	20	40.00	800	200
Total	60		$1,200	100	(2)	$2,400	$1,200
Gross margin		(3)	$1,200			$1,600	$ 400

(1) Actual average price per unit = ($4,000 ÷ 100) = $40.
(2) Actual average cost per unit = ($2,400 ÷ 100) = $24.
(3) Budgeted average gross margin per unit = ($1,200 ÷ 60) = $20.

FIGURE 19.9

Income Statement Using Actual Sales and Budgeted Prices and Costs

Income Statement

	Units	Price/Cost	Amount
Sales:			
Product X	40	$20.00	$ 800
Product Y	40	40.00	1,600
Product Z	20	60.00	1,200
Total	100	(1)	$3,600
Cost of goods sold:			
Product X	40	$10.00	$ 400
Product Y	40	20.00	800
Product Z	20	30.00	600
Total	100	(2)	$1,800
Gross margin		(3)	$1,800

(1) Average price per unit using actual sales at budgeted prices = ($3,600 ÷ 100) = $36.
(2) Average cost per unit using actual sales at budgeted costs = ($1,800 ÷ 100) = $18.
(3) Average gross margin per unit using actual sales at budgeted prices and costs = ($1,800 ÷ 100) = $18.

income statement with the actual sales volume at budgeted prices and costs. This information is necessary when performing an analysis on an aggregate basis.

Gross Margin Variance The gross margin variance is the difference between actual gross margin and the budgeted margin. The objective of the gross margin analysis is to separate the gross margin variance into its component parts: (a) sales price variance, (b) sales mix variance, (c) sales volume variance, and (d) cost price variance.

Budgeted gross margin	$ 1,200
Actual gross margin	−1,600
Gross margin variance	$ 400 F

Sales Price Variance The sales price variance shows the effect on gross margin of having the actual selling price be more or less than the budgeted amount.

Average price using actual sales at budgeted prices (figure 19.9)	$ 36
Actual average price (figure 19.8)	− 40
	$ 4
Actual quantity sold	× 100
Sales price variance	$ 400 F

Sales Mix Variance The sales mix variance shows the effect on gross margin of selling more or less high-profit items than the proportions indicated in the original budget.

Budgeted average gross margin (figure 19.8)	$ 20
Average gross margin using actual sales at budgeted prices and costs	− 18
	$ 2
Actual quantity sold	× 100
Sales mix variance	$ 200 U

Sales Volume Variance The sales volume variance, also called the quantity variance, shows the effect on gross margin of the difference between the actual total unit sales and the budgeted total unit sales computed under the assumption that actual sales are in the same unit proportions as budgeted sales.

Budgeted total sales	$ 60
Actual total sales	− 100
	$ 40
Budgeted average gross margin (figure 19.8)	× 20
Sales volume variance	$ 800 F

Cost Price Variance The cost price variance shows the effect on gross margin of actual cost of goods sold being more or less than the level budgeted.

Actual average cost (figure 19.8)	$ 24
Average cost using actual sales at budgeted costs (figure 19.9)	− 18
	$ 6
Actual total sales	× 100
Cost variance	$ 600 F

Summary of variances

Sales price variance	$400 F
Sales mix variance	200 U
Sales volume variance	800 F
Cost price variance	600 U
Gross margin variance	$400 F

SUMMARY

There is almost universal agreement that variable or direct costing is a desirable alternative to the traditional absorption costing system. The separation of variable and fixed costs and the treatment of fixed overhead costs as period costs rather than as inventoriable costs have definite advantages for management use. Variable costing systems are better adapted to management decisions ranging from profit planning to the analysis of departmental operations. However, variable costing is not acceptable for external reporting. Therefore, as a practical matter, a variable costing system is maintained, and adjustments are made to financial statements at the end of accounting periods to reflect results on an absorption costing basis.

Contribution margin analysis provides a way to isolate the reasons actual contribution margin deviated from budgeted contribution margin. If a standard cost system is not in use, contribution margin analysis helps to determine why contribution margin changed between two accounting periods. The difference between actual and budgeted contribution margin can be analyzed into the following component parts:

1. A sales price variance, representing the effect of differences in sales prices
2. A sales mix variance, representing the effect of shifts in relative sales volumes
3. A sales volume variance, representing the effect of differences in actual sales volume
4. A cost price variance, representing the effect of differences in production costs

Contribution margin analysis is especially useful in multiproduct environments because results can be expressed in total or by product class. Information from contribution margin analysis can also be correlated with other operating results to provide information that is useful in a variety of management decisions.

CHAPTER 19: VARIABLE COSTING AND CONTRIBUTION MARGIN ANALYSIS

SELF-STUDY PROBLEMS

Variable Costing

The following information concerns the first two years of operation for a newly created division of a manufacturing company.

Standard Manufacturing Costs

	Unit Cost
Direct materials	$ 4.00
Direct labor	4.00
Variable manufacturing overhead	2.00
Total variable manufacturing costs	$10.00
Fixed manufacturing costs	4.00
Total manufacturing costs	$14.00

Standard capacity—200,000 units
Selling price—$25.00 per unit
Selling and administrative expenses: Variable—$2.00 per unit of sales
Fixed—$300,000

Production and Sales Statistics

	Year 1	Year 2
Units produced	220,000	170,000
Units sold	180,000	200,000
Inventory change	+40,000	−30,000

Required

Prepare partial comparative income statements for the first two years of operations using both absorption costing and variable costing methods. Also, prepare a schedule reconciling the differences in net income, if any, between the two methods.

Solution to the Self-Study Problem
Comparative Income Statements

Variable Costing (in thousands)

	Year 1	Year 2
Sales @ $25	$4,500	$5,000
Variable manufacturing cost of goods sold:		
Direct materials @ $4	$ 880	$ 680
Direct labor @ $4	880	680
Variable manufacturing overhead @ $2	440	340
Total variable manufacturing costs	$2,200	$1,700
Plus: Beginning Inventory	0	400
Variable manufacturing costs of goods available for sale	$2,200	$2,100
Less: Ending inventory	400	100
Variable manufacturing cost of goods sold	$1,800	$2,000
Variable selling and administrative expenses @ $2	360	400
Total variable costs	$2,160	$2,400
Contribution margin	$2,340	$2,600
Less: Fixed costs:		
Fixed manufacturing costs	$ 800	$ 800
Fixed selling and administrative costs	300	300
Total fixed costs	$1,100	$1,100
Operating income	$1,240	$1,500

Absorption Costing (in thousands)

	Year 1	Year 2
Sales @ $25	$4,500	$5,000
Cost of goods sold:		
Cost of goods manufactured		
Direct materials @ $4	$ 880	$ 680
Direct labor @ $4	880	680
Variable manufacturing overhead @ $2	440	340
Fixed manufacturing overhead @ $4	880	680
Total cost of goods manufactured	$3,080	$2,380
Beginning inventory	0	560
Cost of goods available for sale	$3,080	$2,940
Less: Ending inventory	560	140
Cost of goods sold	$2,520	$2,800
Gross margin	$1,980	$2,200
Selling and administrative expenses:		
Variable @ $2	$ 360	$ 400
Fixed	300	300
Total selling and administrative expenses	$ 660	$ 700
Operating income before volume variance	$1,320	$1,500
Volume variance	80	$ (120)
Operating income	$1,400	$1,380

Volume Variance

Formula: (Actual volume − Budgeted volume) × Fixed overhead per unit
Year 1: (220,000 − 200,000) × $4.00 = $ 80,000 Favorable
Year 2: (170,000 − 200,000) × $4.00 = $120,000 Unfavorable

Reconciliation of Differences in Income from Operations
(in thousands)

	Year 1	Year 2
Absorption costing	$1,400	$1,380
Variable costing	1,240	1,500
Difference	$ 160	$ (120)

Reconciliation

	Year 1	Year 2
Change in inventory	$ 40	$ (30)
Fixed costs per unit	× 4	× 4
Difference	$160	$ (120)

Contribution Margin Analysis

The following information concerns two years of operations of a company that does not use a standard cost system. Its management wants to analyze why contribution margin increased so dramatically in the second year of operations. Data from company records concerning sales, cost of goods sold, and contribution margin is as follows:

CHAPTER 19: VARIABLE COSTING AND CONTRIBUTION MARGIN ANALYSIS

Income Statement

	Year 1			Year 2		
	Units	Price/Cost	Amount	Units	Price/Cost	Amount
Sales						
Product A	40,000	$5.23	$209,200	40,000	$6.00	$240,000
Product B	16,000	10.00	160,000	20,000	13.20	264,000
Product C	14,000	8.00	112,000	8,000	7.00	56,000
Total	70,000		$481,200	68,000		$560,000
Variable costs:						
Product A	40,000	4.35	$174,000	40,000	$5.60	$224,000
Product B	16,000	8.00	128,000	20,000	8.00	160,000
Product C	14,000	7.00	98,000	8,000	7.00	56,000
Total	70,000		$400,000	68,000		$440,000
Contribution margin			$81,200			$120,000

Budgeted Weighted Average Contribution Margin per Unit (year 1)

($81,200/70,000) = $1.16

Budgeted Contribution Margin per Unit (year 1)

Product A: ($5.23 − $4.35) = $0.88
Product B: ($10.00 − $8.00) = $2.00
Product C: ($8.00 − $7.00) = $1.00

Required

Analyze the contribution margin increase of $38,800 ($120,000 − $81,200) by calculating sales price, cost price, sales mix, and sales volume variances. Also prepare a report for management detailing your contribution margin analysis.

Solution to the Self-Study Problem

The computation of the variances related to contribution margin analysis using the preceding data is as follows:

Sales Price Variance

	Year 2 Prices	−	Year 1 Prices		×	Year 2 Sales	=	Sales Price Variances
Product A:	$6.00	−	$5.23 =	$0.77	×	40,000	=	$30,800 F
Product B:	13.20	−	10.00 =	3.20	×	20,000	=	64,000 F
Product C:	7.00	−	8.00 =	1.00	×	8,000	=	8,000 U
Total sales price variance								$86,800 F

Actual Sales Mix Variance

	Year 1 Contribution Margin	−	Year 1 Weighted Average Contribution Margin		×	Year 2 Sales	=	Actual Sales Mix Variance
Product A:	$0.88	−	$1.16 =	$−0.28	×	40,000	=	$11,200 U
Product B:	2.00	−	1.16 =	0.84	×	20,000	=	16,800 F
Product C:	1.00	−	1.16 =	−0.16	×	8,000	=	1,280 U
Total sales mix variance								$4,320 U

Budgeted Sales Mix Variance

	Year 1 Contribution Margin	−	Year 1 Weighted Average Contribution Margin	×	Year 1 Sales	=	Budgeted Sales Mix Variance
Product A:	$0.88	−	$1.16 = $−0.28	×	40,000	=	$11,200 U
Product B:	2.00	−	1.16 = 0.84	×	16,000	=	13,440 F
Product C:	1.00	−	1.16 = −0.16	×	14,000	=	2,240 U
Total sales mix variance							$ 0

Comparison of Actual and Budgeted Sales Mix Variance

	Actual Sales Mix Variance	Budgeted Sales Mix Variance	Difference
Product A:	$11,200 U	$11,200 U	$ 0
Product B:	16,800 F	13,440 F	3,360 F
Product C:	1,280 U	2,240 U	960 F
Total	$ 4,320 F	0	$4,320 F

Sales Volume Variance

	Year 2 Sales	−	Year 1 Sales	×	Year 1 Weighted Average Contribution Margin	=	Sales Volume Variance
Product A:	40,000	−	40,000 = 0	×	$1.16	=	$ 0
Product B:	20,000	−	16,000 = 4,000	×	1.16	=	4,640 F
Product C:	8,000	−	14,000 = −6,000	×	1.16	=	6,960 U
Total sales volume variance							$2,320 U

Cost Price Variance

	Year 1 costs	−	Year 2 costs	×	Year 2 Sales	=	Cost Price Variance
Product A	$4.35	−	$5.60 = $−1.25	×	40,000	=	$50,000 U
Product B	8.00	−	8.00 = 0	×	20,000	=	0
Product C	7.00	−	7.00 = 0	×	8,000	=	0
Total cost price variance							$50,000 U

Report of Contribution Margin Analysis

	Product A	Product B	Product C	Total
Sales price variance	$30,800 F	$64,000 F	$ 8,000 U	$86,800 F
Sales mix variance	0	3,360 F	960 F	4,320 F
Sales volume variance	0	4,640 F	6,960 U	2,320 U
Cost price variance	50,000 U	0	0	50,000 U
	$19,200 U	$72,000 F	$14,000 U	$38,800 F

SUGGESTED READINGS

Ajinkya, Bipin; Atiase, Rowland; and Bamber, Linda S. "Absorption versus Direct Costing: Income Reconciliation and Cost-Volume-Profit Analysis." American Accounting Association, *Issues in Accounting Education* 1 (Fall 1986): 268–281.

Baiman, Stanley, and Demski, Joel S. "Variance Analysis Procedures as Motivational Devices." *Management Scence* 26 (August 1980): 840–848.

Carmen-Stone, Marie S. "Unabsorbed Overhead: When Contracts Are Cancelled." *Management Accounting* 68 (April 1987): 55–57.

Chen, Joyce T. "Full and Direct Costing in Profit Variance Analysis." American Accounting Association, *Issues in Accounting Education* 1 (Fall 1986): 282–292.

LaTour, Stephen A. "Variance Explained: It Measures neither Importance nor Effect Size." *Decision Sciences* 12 (January 1981): 150–160.

Schiff, Michael. "A Closer Look at Variable Costing." *Management Accounting* 68 (February 1987): 36–29.

DISCUSSION QUESTIONS

Q19–1. What is the principal difference between variable costing and absorption costing?

Q19–2. Why is variable costing considered unacceptable for external reporting?

Q19–3. What costing system is acceptable for external reporting? Why?

Q19–4. Why does management often keep both variable costing and absorption costing systems?

Q19–5. What are three advantages to management of having an income statement in the variable costing format?

Q19–6. Why is the chart of accounts expanded when direct costing is used?

Q19–7. When will operating income computed using variable costing exceed operating income computed using absorption costing?

Q19–8. Even though variable costing has many merits, explain any hidden dangers that are present in its use.

Q19–9. Define *contribution margin* and explain why its use is important to management.

Q19–10. What causes changes in contribution margin?

Q19–11. Define *mix* and explain how it relates to contribution margin analysis.

Q19–12. Name four variances that can be computed to help explain differences in contribution margin. Explain what information each variance supplies to management about sales or costs.

Q19–13. What are the formulas for calculating each of the contribution margin analysis variances?

Q19–14. Explain how the analysis and interpretation differs between the total sales mix variance and the individual product sales mix variances.

Q19–15. What are the differences in contribution margin analysis between a standard cost system as compared to an actual cost system?

Q19–16. Explain the aggregate procedure for calculating contribution margin variances when detailed product information is not required.

Q19–17. "Analysis of gross margin differences between budget and actual requires a different approach than the one used for contribution margin analysis." Do you agree? Explain.

EXERCISES

E19–1. Absorption and Variable Costing Procedures
Current manufacturing and sales information for the Joplin Juice Company follows:

Units produced	20,000
Units sold	18,000
Units in beginning inventory	0
Direct materials used	$40,000
Direct labor	$44,000
Selling and administrative expenses:	
Variable	$24,000
Fixed	46,000
Factory overhead:	
Variable	$35,000
Fixed	52,000

Required

1. Under the absorption costing method, give the value of the finished-goods ending inventory.
2. Under the variable costing approach, give the value of the finished-goods ending inventory.
3. Which method would show a higher net income for Joplin in the current year? How much higher?

E19–2. Identification of Income Reporting Method
Well Water Incorporated began production of a product called Suvi Sunshine in 19X1. Operating information relating to production of Suvi Sunshine in 19X1 is given here:

Variable costs per unit:	
Direct materials	$ 8
Direct labor	3
Factory overhead	1
Selling and administrative expenses	2
Fixed costs for the year:	
Factory overhead	$140,000
Selling and administrative expenses	180,000

During 19X1, Well Water produced 80,000 units and sold 72,000 units. The finished-goods ending inventory was valued at $96,000 for the unsold units.

Required

1. Is Well Water using absorption costing or variable costing to value the finished-goods ending inventory? Show calculations.
2. Assume that Well Water will be preparing financial statements for its stockholders.
   a. Is $96,000 the correct value for the finished-goods ending inventory on the statements?
   b. If $96,000 is incorrect, what figure should be assigned to the finished-goods ending inventory?

E19–3. Basic Absorption and Variable Costing Procedures
Martino Company produces and sells one product line. Costs recorded in the first year of production are as follows:

Variable costs per unit:		
Direct materials	$10	
Direct labor	4	
Factory overhead	5	
Selling and administrative expenses	3	
Fixed costs per year:		
Factory overhead	$42,000	
Selling and administrative expenses	30,000	

During the first year, Martino manufactured 10,000 units but sold only 6,000. The selling price is $39 per unit.

Required

1. Compute the cost per unit of product under the absorption costing method.
2. Compute the cost per unit of product under the variable costing method.
3. Prepare a simple absorption costing income statement for the current year.
4. Prepare a simple variable costing income statement for the current year.

E19–4. Converting from an Absorption to a Variable Costing Income Report

The Bird Company began operations during the past year. The financial results of this first year are as follows (absorption costing method):

Bird Company
Income Statement

Sales		$825,000
Less: Cost of goods sold:		
Opening inventory	0	
Cost of goods produced (36,000 × $17)	$612,000	
Goods available for sale	$612,000	
Less ending inventory (3,000 × $17)	51,000	561,000
Gross margin		$264,000
Less: Selling and administrative expenses		99,000
Net income		$165,000

The selling and administrative expenses for the year were all fixed. The product's $17 unit cost is made up of the following:

Direct materials	$ 6	
Direct labor	4	
Variable factory overhead	3	
Fixed factory overhead (144,000 ÷ 36,000)	4	
Total unit cost	$17	

Required

1. Prepare an income statement for the Bird Company, using the variable costing method.
2. Explain any differences in net income between your variable costing results and the absorption costing results presented previously.

E19–5. Absorption Costing Income Statement

Hanson's Hoses Incorporated began production of a terrific new product in 19X5. Selected operating results are as follows:

Production:	
Units produced	25,000
Units sold	22,000
Variable costs:	
Direct materials	$62,500
Direct labor	45,000
Factory overhead	30,000
Sales and administrative expenses	22,000
Fixed costs:	
Factory overhead	$50,000
Sales and administrative expenses	35,000
Sales price per unit	$11

Required

1. Prepare, in good form, an income statement for Hanson's Hoses during 19X5 using the absorption costing method.
2. Prepare, in good form, an income statement for the year 19X5 using the variable costing method.

E19–6. Variable Costing Income Statements for Multiple Years Sandberg Mills began production on January 1, 19X3. Using the absorption costing method, Sandberg has reported income as follows for the first two years:

	19X3	19X4
Sales	$798,000	$945,000
Less: Cost of goods sold:		
Beginning inventory	0	56,000
Cost of goods manufactured	588,000	588,000
Goods available for sale	$588,000	$644,000
Less: Ending inventory	56,000	14,000
Cost of goods sold	$532,000	$630,000
Gross margin	266,000	315,000
Less: Selling and administrative expenses (fixed $114,000)	190,000	204,000
Net income	$ 76,000	$111,000

Production took place as follows:

	19X3	19X4
Units produced	42,000	42,000
Units sold	38,000	45,000

No work in process inventories existed at the end of either year.

Variable cost per unit:

Direct materials	$ 3.50
Direct labor	6.00
Factory overhead	2.00
Fixed factory overhead (105,000 ÷ 42,000)	2.50
Total cost per unit	$14.00

Required

1. Prepare, in good form, an income statement for years 19X3 and 19X4 under the variable costing method.
2. Reconcile the net income for each year from the variable costing income statement to the net income of the absorption costing method.

E19–7. Absorption and Variable Costing Comparative Statements (CMA) The vice president for sales of Huber Corporation has received the following income statement for November 19X5. The statement has been prepared on a direct-cost basis and is reproduced below. The firm has just adopted a direct costing system for internal reporting.

Huber Corporation
Income Statement
For the Month of November 19X5
(000s omitted)

Sales		$2,400
Less: Variable standard cost of goods sold		1,200
Manufacturing margin		$1,200
Less: Fixed manufacturing costs at budget	$600	
Fixed manufacturing cost spending variance	0	600
Gross margin		$ 600
Less: Fixed selling and administrative costs		400
Net income before taxes		$ 200

The controller attached the following notes to the statement:

1. The unit sales price for November averaged $24.
2. The standard unit manufacturing costs for the month were:

Variable cost	$12
Fixed cost	4
Total cost	$16

The unit rate for fixed manufacturing costs is a predetermined rate based on a normal monthly production of 150,000 units.

3. Production for November was 45,000 units in excess of sales.
4. The inventory at November 30 consisted of 80,000 units.

Required

1. The vice president for sales is not comfortable with the direct-cost basis and wonders what the net income would have been with the absorption-cost basis.
   a. Present the November income statement on an absorption-cost basis.
   b. Reconcile and explain the difference between the direct costing and the absorption costing net income figures.
2. Explain the features associated with a direct-cost income measurement that should be attractive to the vice president for sales.

E19–8. Absorption Costing Statement and Procedures

Cooper's Hoops 'n Barrels manufactures a barrel that has become popular recently. The operating results for Cooper's first month of production are as follows:

Units produced	1,000
Units sold	850
Selling price per unit	$45

Production costs:
Variable per unit

Direct materials	$10
Direct labor	$15
Overhead	$2
Fixed overhead	$7,200

Selling and administrative costs:

Variable	10% of sales
Fixed	$4,200

Required

1. Prepare, in good form, an income statement under the absorption costing method. Calculate the cost to produce a single barrel.
2. Prepare, in good form, an income statement under the variable costing method. Calculate the cost to produce a single barrel.
3. Which income statement would you be most likely to use in a presentation made to Cooper's creditors? Assume you are in Cooper's management.
4. Reconcile the difference between the net income figures computed in requirements 1 and 2.

E19–9. Analysis of Contribution Margin—Actual versus Budget

The Artell Company shows the following budgeted and actual data for sales and variable costs of each of its three products for the period ended December 31:

	Unit Sales		Unit Sales Price		Unit Variable Costs	
Product	Budgeted	Actual	Budgeted	Actual	Budgeted	Actual
K	20,000	22,000	$10.00	$11.50	$6.00	$6.25
L	8,000	8,000	12.00	10.00	7.00	6.75
M	7,000	4,000	6.00	8.00	2.50	2.75

Required

1. Set up two income statements; one showing budgeted sales, variable costs, and contribution margin, and a second showing actual sales, variable costs and contribution margin.
2. Analyze the difference between budgeted and actual contribution margin determined in requirement 1 into sales price, sales mix, sales volume, and cost price components.
3. Summarize the variances computed in requirement 2 in the form of a report for management.

E19–10. Analysis of Contribution Margin—Actual versus Budget

Budgeted and actual sales and variable cost data for the Stoker Manufacturing Co. for the most recent operating period is summarized below. The company produces and sells three products used as components by firms that produce major parts for the space shuttle.

	Budgeted			Actual		
Product	Units	Sales Price	Variable Cost	Units	Sales Price	Variable Cost
Ring	10	$100	$50	15	$98	$46
Seal	20	60	40	30	54	36
Tap pin	40	30	20	60	35	26

Required

1. Determine the budgeted and actual contribution margin for Stoker Co. Present results with adequate support, and identify the difference in contribution margin for each product and in total.
2. Do a detailed analysis of the contribution margin difference by computing the sales price, sales mix, sales volume, and cost price variances. Show each type of variance for each product and in total. Prepare a report in summary form for management on the variance in contribution margin between budget and actual.

E19–11. Absorption and Variable Costing Income Statement

Randy's Ranges, Inc. started manufacturing and selling a new product in 19X8. Selected operating results are as follows:

Production:	
Units produced	16,000
Units sold	14,500
Variable costs:	
Direct materials	$42,000
Direct labor	36,000
Factory overhead	15,000
Sales and administrative expenses	13,000
Fixed costs:	
Factory overhead	$40,000
Sales and administrative expenses	22,000
Sales price per unit	$12

Required

1. Using the preceding information and Lotus, prepare, in good form, an income statement for Randy's Ranges for the year ended December 31, 19X8, under the absorption costing method.
2. Using the preceding information, prepare (and include on your worksheet from requirement 1) an income statement for Randy's Ranges for the year ended December 31, 19X8, under the variable costing method. Print a copy of your entire worksheet.

PROBLEMS

P19–1. Absorption and Variable Costing Concepts and Procedures

Just Frames began production in 19X5, and it is now the beginning of 19X8. The president of the company, who knows about both the absorption and variable costing methods, would like a summary of the first three years of operations.

Just Frames uses a FIFO inventory method. The yearly operations information is as follows:

Production costs	
Direct materials per unit	$2.00
Direct labor per unit	$1.50
Factory overhead	
Variable per unit	$0.50
Fixed	$144,000
Selling and administrative costs	
Variable	30% of sales
Fixed	$32,000
Sales price (per unit)	$12.50
Sales and production units	

	19X5	19X6	19X7
Sales	45,000	36,000	45,000
Production	45,000	54,000	36,000

Required

1. Prepare a three-year comparative income statement using the absorption costing approach.

2. Prepare a three-year comparative income statement using the variable costing approach.
3. Reconcile the absorption costing and variable costing net income figures for each year.
4. Using the absorption method income statements prepared in requirement 1, prepare a chart comparing sales volume to absorption net income. Explain to the president of Just Frames why the absorption net income does not vary in direct proportion to the sales figures. Compare 19X5 to 19X6 and then 19X5 to 19X7.

P19-2 Absorption and Variable Costing and Their Tie to Standard Costing

Rogers Company uses a standard absorption costing approach, which shows the following account balances as of December 31, 19X5.

Total costs using standard unit prices:	
Raw materials	$ 87,500
Work in process	50,000
Finished goods	150,000
Cost of goods sold	300,000
Total	$587,500

Variances (unfavorable)	
Direct-material quantity	$ 25,000
Direct-material price	30,000
Direct-labor rate	8,000
Direct-labor efficiency	25,000
Underapplied overhead	12,000
Total	$100,000
Sales	$800,000

There are no beginning inventories.

Assume that all variances not prorated are considered to be adjustments to cost of goods sold. Assume that the data given are all that is available and that prorations are therefore made directly to raw materials, work in process, finished goods, and cost of goods sold.

Required

1. Compute the gross margin using the absorption costing method in each of the following specific situations.
    a. A standard costing system is used without any variance proration.
    b. A standard costing system is used with proration of all variances.
    c. A normal absorption costing system is used without proration of underapplied overhead.[1]
    d. A normal absorption costing system is used with proration of underapplied overhead.
    e. A system of historical rather than predetermined costs is used.
2. Analyze the gross margin results found in requirement 1. Does one system write off costs to expense quicker than the others? What other observations can you make in comparing the five systems? Would you say that the current standards are reasonable? Why or why not?
3. Assume more data are available to you now. How would you prorate the variances to make the system more accurate?

P19–3. Alternative Income Results Using Absorption and Variable Costing with Variances from Standard Costs

Hannaphase Incorporated is in its first year of production. It uses the standard absorption costing approach, which shows the following unadjusted account balances at year end:

Raw materials ending inventory	$ 20,000
Work-in-process ending inventory	15,000
Finished-goods ending inventory	25,000
Cost of goods sold	60,000
Direct-materials price variance	8,000
Direct-materials quantity variance	2,000
Direct-labor rate variance	600
Direct-labor efficiency variance	2,000
Factory overhead actually incurred (fixed = 8,000)	20,000
Factory overhead applied at standard rate	16,000
Underapplied factory overhead	4,000
Selling and administrative expenses	24,000
Sales	100,000

All variances are unfavorable for the period described. The materials price variances are measured at purchase and not when materials are used. Assume that the proportion of direct materials, direct labor, and factory overhead remains constant in work in process, finished goods, and cost of goods sold. The direct-materials component represents 60 percent of the ending inventory of work in process, finished goods, and cost of goods sold.

Required

1. Prepare comparative income statements using absorption costing and variable costing methods for each of the following situations:
    a. A standard costing system is used without any variance allocation.
    b. A standard costing system is used with allocation of all variances.
    c. A normal (historical) costing system is used without allocation of underapplied overhead.[2]
    d. A normal costing system is used with allocation of underapplied overhead.
    e. A system of historical rather than predetermined costs is used.
2. Analyze your findings in requirement 1. What differences do you see and why do they exist?

P19–4. Absorption Costing Review of Variance Allocations (CMA)

Packless Incorporated has a standard process-costing system for all products. All inventories are carried at standard during the year. The inventories *and* cost of goods sold are adjusted at fiscal year end for the financial statement. All products are considered to flow through the manufacturing process to finished goods and ultimate sales in a first-in, first-out fashion.

The standard cost of one of Packless's products manufactured in the Mason plant, unchanged from the previous year, is as follows:

Raw materials	$2.00
Direct labor (0.25 hour @ $16.00)	4.00
Manufacturing overhead	3.00
Total standard cost	$9.00

---

1. Normal absorption costing refers to the system in which actual materials and labor and normal or applied factory overhead are charged to inventory.
2. See note in problem 19.2.

There is no work-in-process inventory of this product because of the nature of the manufacturing process. The following schedule reports the manufacturing and sales activity measured at standard cost for the current fiscal year:

	Units	Dollars
Product manufactured	95,000	$855,000
Finished-goods beginning inventory	15,000	135,000
Goods available for sale	110,000	$990,000
Finished-goods ending inventory	19,000	171,000
Cost of goods sold	91,000	$819,000

The manufacturing performance relative to standard costs both this year and last year was not good. The balance of the finished-goods inventory ($140,800) reported on the balance sheet at the beginning of the year included a $5,800 adjustment for variances from standard cost. The unfavorable standard cost variances for labor for the current fiscal year consisted of a wage-price variance of $32,000 and a labor-efficiency variance of $20,000 (1,250 hours @ $16.00). There were no other variances from standard cost for this year.

Required

Assume that the unfavorable labor variances totaling $52,000 are considered material in amount by management and are to be prorated to finished-goods inventory and to cost of goods sold. Determine the amount that will be shown on the year-end balance sheet for finished-goods inventory, as well as the amount that will be shown for cost of goods sold on the income statement prepared for the fiscal year.

P19–5. Multiple Year Comparison Absorption and Variable Costing

The sales department at Jaeger Mix Company is in a tizzy. Kate Michaels, the sales director, just received the comparative income statements for the last three months, and she thinks something is afoul with the projections. In spite of steady increases in sales, the income has been dropping just as steadily. Mrs. Michaels has approached you and your colleagues in the accounting department and voiced her concerns: "If sales increases hurt us this badly, we might as well cut back." The following is the report Mrs. Michaels just received:

Jaeger Mix Company
Monthly Income Statements

	January	February	March
Sales	$250,000	$275,000	$300,000
Less: Cost of goods sold:			
Opening inventory	12,500	50,000	62,500
Cost of current production			
Variable costs	65,000	60,000	40,000
Fixed costs	97,500	90,000	60,000
Goods available for sale	$175,000	$200,000	$162,500
Less: Ending inventory	50,000	62,500	12,500
Cost of goods sold	$125,000	$137,500	$150,000
Underapplied or (overapplied) fixed overhead costs	(7,500)	—	30,000
Cost of goods sold at actual	$117,500	$137,500	$180,000
Gross margin	$132,500	$137,500	$120,000
Less: Selling and administrative expenses	122,500	132,500	142,500
Net income	$10,000	$5,000	$(22,500)

The March loss has Mrs. Michaels especially confused. She is sure there is a better way of reporting income so that she can encourage her sales force.

Operations data for the first quarter are as follows:

	January	February	March
Sales in units	25,000	27,500	30,000
Production in units	32,500	30,000	20,000

The January opening inventory consisted of 2,500 units. Your department uses a budgeted production volume of 30,000 units for applying fixed overhead.

Required

1. Prepare an income statement for the same three months, using the variable costing approach.
2. Compute the breakeven points under absorption costing and variable costing.
3. Reconcile the variable costing income statements to the absorption costing income statements month by month.
4. Explain to Mrs. Michaels the incongruities she expressed to you and why there seems to be no correlation of profit to sales.

P19-6. Analysis of Variances in Contribution Margin (CMA) The Markley Division of Rosette Industries manufactures and sells patio chairs. The chairs are manufactured in two versions—a metal model and a plastic model of a lesser quality. The company uses its own sales force to sell the chairs to retail stores and to catalog outlets. Generally, customers purchase both metal and plastic versions.

The chairs are manufactured on two different assembly lines located in adjoining buildings. The division management and the sales department occupy the third building on the property. The division management includes a division controller, who is responsible for the divisional financial activities and the preparation of reports explaining the differences between actual and budgeted performance. The controller structures these reports with the sales activities distinguished from cost factors so that each can be analyzed separately.

The operating results for the first three months of the fiscal year as compared to the budget are presented in the third column. The budget for the current year was based on the assumption that Markley Division would maintain its present market share of the estimated total patio chair market (plastic and metal combined). A status report had been sent to corporate management toward the end of the second month indicating that divisional operating income for the first quarter would probably be about 45 percent below budget; this estimate was just about on target. The division's operating income was below budget even though industry volume for patio chairs increased by 10 percent more than was expected at the time the budget was developed.

Markley Division
Operating Results for the First Quarter

	Actual	Budget	Favorable (unfavorable) relative to the budget
Sale in units			
Plastic model	60,000	50,000	10,000
Metal model	20,000	25,000	(5,000)
Sales revenue			
Plastic model	$630,000	$500,000	$130,000
Metal model	300,000	375,000	(75,000)
Total sales	$930,000	$875,000	$ 55,000
Less: Variable costs			
Manufacturing (at standard)			
Plastic model	$480,000	$400,000	$(80,000)
Metal model	200,000	250,000	50,000
Selling			
Commissions	46,500	43,750	(2,750)
Bad debt allowance	9,300	8,750	(550)
Total variable costs (except variable manufacturing variances)	$735,800	$702,500	$(33,300)
Contribution margin (except variable manufacturing variances)	$194,200	$172,500	$ 21,700
Less: Other costs			
Variable manufacturing costs variances from standards	$ 49,600	—	$(49,600)
Fixed manufacturing costs	49,200	$ 48,000	(1,200)
Fixed selling and administrative costs	38,500	36,000	(2,500)
Corporation offices allocation	18,500	17,500	(1,000)
Total other costs	$155,800	$101,500	$(54,300)
Divisional operating income	$ 38,400	$ 71,000	$(32,600)

The manufacturing activities for the quarter resulted in the production of 55,000 plastic chairs and 22,500 metal chairs. The costs incurred by each manufacturing unit are as follows:

Raw materials (stated in equivalent finished chairs)			Plastic Model	Metal Model
	Quantity	Price		
Purchases				
Plastic	60,000	$5.65	$339,000	
Metal	30,000	$6.00		$180,000
Usage				
Plastic	56,000	$5.00	280,000	
Metal	23,000	$6.00		138,000
Direct labor				
9,300 hours @ $6.00 per hour			55,800	
5,600 hours @ $8.00 per hour				44,800
Manufacturing overhead				
Variable				
Supplies			43,000	18,000
Power			50,000	15,000
Employee benefits			19,000	12,000
Fixed				
Supervision			14,000	11,000
Depreciation			12,000	9,000
Property taxes and other items			1,900	1,300

The standard variable manufacturing costs per unit and the budgeted monthly fixed manufacturing costs established for the current year are as follows:

	Plastic Model	Metal Model
Raw materials	$ 5.00	$ 6.00
Direct labor		
1/6 hour @ $6.00 per direct-labor hour (DLH)	1.00	
1/4 hour @ $8.00 per DLH		2.00
Variable overhead		
1/6 hour @ $12.00 per DLH	2.00	
1/4 hour @ $8.00 per DLH		2.00
Standard variable manufacturing cost per unit	$ 8.00	$10.00
Budgeted fixed costs per month		
Supervision	$4,500	$3,500
Depreciation	4,000	3,000
Property taxes and other items	600	400
Total budgeted fixed costs for month	$9,100	$6,900

Required

1. Explain the variance in Markely Division's contribution margin attributable to sales activities by calculating the following:
    a. Sales price variance
    b. Sales mix variance
    c. Sales volume variance
2. What portion of the sales volume variance, if any, can be attributed to a change in Markley Division's market share?
3. Analyze the variance in Markley Division's variable manufacturing costs ($49,600) in as much detail as the data permit.
4. Based on your analysis prepared for requirements 1, 2, and 3, answer the following:
    a. Identify the major cause of Markley Division's unfavorable profit performance.
    b. Did Markley's management attempt to correct this problem? Explain your answer.
    c. What other steps, if any, could Markley's management have taken to improve the division's operating income? Explain your answer.

P19–7. Absorption and Variable Costing and the Analysis of Comparative Results (CMA)

CLK Company is a manufacturer of electrical components. The company maintains a substantial inventory of a broad range of finished goods because it has built its business on prompt shipments of any stock item.

CLK manufactured all items it sold until recently, when it discontinued the manufacture of five items. The items were dropped from the manufacturing process because the unit costs computed by CLK's full cost system did not provide a sufficient margin to cover shipping and selling costs. The five items are now purchased from other manufacturers at a price that allows CLK to make a very small profit after shipping and selling costs. CLK keeps these items in its product line in order to offer a complete line of electrical components.

The president is disappointed at recent profitability performance. He thought that the switch from manufacture to purchase of the five items would improve profit performance. However, the reverse has occurred. All other factors affecting profits—sales volume, sales prices, and incurred selling and manufacturing costs—were as expected, so the profit problem can be traced to this decision. The president has asked the controller's department to reevaluate the financial effects of the decision.

The task was assigned to a recently hired assistant controller. She has reviewed the data that were used to reach the decision to purchase rather than to manufacture. Her conclusion is that the company should have continued to manufacture the items. In her opinion the incorrect decision was made because full (absorption) cost data rather than direct (variable) cost data were used to make the decision.

Required

1. List the features of direct (variable) costing as compared to full (absorption) costing that make it possible for her conclusion to be correct.
2. For internal measurement, compare the income, return on investment, and inventory values under full (absorption) costing and direct (variable) costing for periods in which
   a. inventory quantities are rising.
   b. inventory quantities are declining.
   c. inventory quantities are stable.
3. What advantages are said to accrue to decision making if direct (variable) costing is used?

P19–8. Analysis of Variance between Budget and Actual Results JK Enterprises sold 550,000 units during the first quarter ending March 31, 19X1. These sales represented a 10 percent increase over the number of units budgeted for the quarter. In spite of the sales increase, profits were below budget, as shown in the following condensed income statement:

JK Enterprises
Income Statement
For the First Quarter Ending March 31, 19X1
(000s omitted)

	Budget	Actual
Sales	$2,500	$2,530
Variable expenses		
Cost of goods sold	$1,475	$1,540
Selling	400	440
Total variable expenses	$1,875	$1,980
Contribution margin	$ 625	$ 550
Fixed expenses		
Selling	$ 125	$ 150
Administration	275	300
Total fixed expenses	$ 400	$ 450
Income before taxes	$ 225	$ 100
Income taxes (40%)	90	40
Net income	$ 135	$ 60

The accounting department always prepares a brief analysis explaining the difference between the budgeted net income and the actual net income. This analysis, which has not been completed for the first quarter, is submitted to top management with the income statement.

Required

Prepare an explanation of the $125,000 unfavorable variance between the first quarter budgeted and actual before-tax income for JK Enterprises by calculating a single amount for each of the following variations:

1. Sales price difference
2. Variable unit cost difference
3. Volume difference
4. Fixed cost difference

P19–9. Analysis of Actual versus Budget Operating Results (CPA) The income statement of Duo Incorporated is presented below. These data relate to the calculation of variances that explain the differences between the actual profit and budgeted profit in terms of sales price, cost, sales mix, and sales volume.

Duo Inc.
Income Statement for the Year
Ending December 31, 19X7
(000s omitted)

	Product AR-10 Budget	Product AR-10 Actual	Product ZR-7 Budget	Product ZR-7 Actual	Total Budget	Total Actual
Unit sales	2,000	2,800	6,000	5,600	8,000	8,400
Sales	$6,000	$7,560	$12,000	$11,760	$18,000	$19,320
Cost of goods sold	$2,400	$2,800	$ 6,000	$ 5,880	$ 8,400	$ 8,680
Fixed costs	1,800	1,900	2,400	2,400	4,200	4,300
Total costs	$4,200	$4,700	$ 8,400	$ 8,280	$12,600	$12,980
Net profit	$1,800	$2,860	$ 3,600	$ 3,480	$ 5,400	$ 6,340

Required

1. Determine the net effect on profit of the unit sales volume variance for product AR-10.
2. Determine the net effect on profit of the sales price variance for product ZR-7.
3. Determine the net effect on profit from the change in the unit cost of goods sold of product ZR-7.
4. If products AR-10 and ZR-7 are substitutes for each other, a sales mix and sales volume variation for the combined products can be calculated. If this combination is calculated, determine the net effect on profit of the change in the unit sales mix.
5. Determine the sales volume variation calculation that would complement the variance calculated in requirement 4.

P19–10. Absorption and Variable Costing and Gross Margin Analysis (CMA)

Part 1

Indiana Corporation began its operations on January 1. It produces a single product that sells for $9 per unit. Indiana uses an actual (historical) cost system. In the first year, 100,000 units were produced and 90,000 units were sold. There was no work-in-process inventory at December 31.

Manufacturing costs and selling and administrative expenses for the year were as follows:

	Fixed Costs	Variable Costs
Raw materials	—	$1.75 per unit produced
Direct labor	—	1.25 per unit produced
Factory overhead	$100,000	0.50 per unit produced
Selling and administrative	70,000	0.60 per unit sold

Required

1. Determine Indiana's operating income for the year, using the direct costing method.
2. Describe the information that must be known about a production process in order to institute a direct costing system.

Part 2

During January, Gable Incorporated produced 10,000 units of product F with costs as follows:

Direct materials	$40,000
Direct labor	22,000
Variable overhead	13,000
Fixed overhead	10,000
	$85,000

Required

1. Determine Gable's unit cost of product F for January 19X1, calculated on the direct costing basis.
2. Describe and discuss the major factor, related to manufacturing costs, that causes the difference in net earnings computed with absorption costing and net earnings computed with direct costing.

Part 3

Garfield Company, which sells a single product, provided the following data from its income statements for the calendar years 19X1 and 19X0.

	19X1
Sales (150,000 units)	$750,000
Cost of goods sold	525,000
Gross profit	$225,000

	19X0 (Base Year)
Sales (180,000 units)	$720,000
Cost of goods sold	575,000
Gross profit	$145,000

Required

Prepare an analysis of the variation in gross profit between the two years to determine the effects of changes in sales price and sales volume.

CASE

C19–1. Integrative Variable Costing, Absorption Costing, and Factory Overhead

The Pleasant Walnut Grove Co. makes high-quality walnut wood products that are sold in exclusive gift departments in high-priced retail stores. A completely self-contained plant in Santaquin produces and sells a fancy candy dish. The company sells the candy dish for $55 to the retail stores, which then sell the dish at retail for $109.95.

Production of the dishes requires four labor operations: cutting, carving, finishing, and assembly. Standard costs have been set for production of the candy dishes as follows:

	Cost per Unit
Materials	$ 5.850000
Labor	10.500000
Variable factory overhead	9.331013
Fixed factory overhead	2.923170

Production time standards for labor include the following:

Operation	Standard Time
Cutting	1 hour
Carving	¼ hour
Finishing	½ hour
Assembly	½ hour

Flexible overhead budgets are used by the company. The fixed costs and the normal hours included in these budgets for the most recent operating period are as follows:

Operation	Fixed Costs	Normal Hours
Cutting	$1,100	875
Carving	400	250
Finishing	550	600
Assembly	730	452

Variable selling expenses include sales commissions of 6 percent of sales revenue and packing supplies of $0.50 per unit sold. Fixed selling and administrative expenses are $1,575 per period.

During the period just ended, 750 units were sold. Finished goods of 250 units were in the beginning inventory, and 300 units were on hand at the end of the period. Production statistics were as follows for the period:

Operation	Beginning Work in Process Units	% Complete	Ending Work in Process Units	% Complete	New Units Started
Cutting	450	20	150	40	600
Carving	150	60	100	20	900
Finishing	400	10	300	80	950
Assembly	150	40	400	30	1,050

Jim, a manager in the accounting department, has just returned from an intensive Professional Education Program (PEP) on contribution reporting conducted by the NAA. Filled with enthusiasm to apply the concepts learned in the program, Jim prepares and presents to Frank, the Santaquin plant director, the following report of operating results:

Santaquin Plant
Pleasant Walnut Grove Co.
Statement of Income
(Contribution Basis)
For the Period Just Ended

Sales (750 units @ $55)		$41,250.00
Less: Variable costs:		
Standard variable cost of goods sold		
(750 @ $25.681013)	$19,260.76	
Selling expenses ($41,250 × 0.06		
plus 750 × $0.50)	2,850.00	22,110.76
Contribution margin		$19,139.24
Fixed costs:		
Production	$ 2,780.00	
Selling and administrative	1,575.00	4,355.00
Net income		$14,784.24

Frank examines the report after Jim leaves his office and then remembers that, while Jim was attending the PEP course, the traditional end-of-period reports were completed and sent to the company headquarters. Frank hasn't had a chance to go over these reports yet. He pulls a copy from the file and compares the income statement sent to headquarters with Jim's statement. He notices that the one sent to headquarters showed income of $15,305. He is puzzling over the difference when the phone rings. His daughter reminds him of a promise to attend a school play, which begins in five minutes. As he rushes to his car, he mumbles to himself, "These accountants really are just a bunch of bean counters. I wonder if they actually know what they are doing."

Are accountants only good for counting beans? (*Hint:* Make sure your answer contains proof, or refutation, of the $15,305 of traditional income; evidence of detailed factory overhead rates for each operation; and a reconciliation of the two net income amounts.)

Chapter 20

Segment Performance

Outline

CENTRALIZATION AND
    DECENTRALIZATION
RESPONSIBILITY CENTERS
APPROACHES FOR EVALUATING
    PERFORMANCE
Return on Investment
Residual Income
Segment Margin Analysis
CONSIDERATIONS FOR
    IMPLEMENTATION
The Role of Budgets
The Investment Base

Composition
Valuation
    Alternative Depreciation Methods
SUMMARY
APPENDIX 20.1: COMPOUND INTEREST
    METHOD OF DEPRECIATION
SELF-STUDY PROBLEM
SUGGESTED READINGS
DISCUSSION QUESTIONS
EXERCISES
PROBLEMS
CASES

The natural growth and development of business organizations usually results in the delegation of authority to an expanding group of management personnel and the development of well-defined management subdivisions such as departments and branches. These subunits can be specified by product line, geographical area, customer class, or any other criteria appropriate for management reporting and control. In a generic sense, the term *segment* could be used to refer to any type of business subdivision. However, the term *segment* in accounting literature generally refers to a business subdivision that is given responsibility for the profitable utilization of the invested capital in its domain.

This chapter explains how a cost accounting system can be designed to help top management evaluate the performance of business segments. After you have completed this chapter, you should be able to:

1. explain the concepts of centralization and decentralization and describe their implications for the evaluation of segment performance.
2. explain the role of a responsibility center and the difference between cost centers, profit centers, and investment centers.
3. use return on investment, residual income, and contribution margin analysis to evaluate segment performance.
4. handle difficulties that might be encountered in implementing the various approaches to evaluating segment performance.

CENTRALIZATION AND DECENTRALIZATION

Centralization and decentralization are the terms used to describe the degree of management delegation within an organization. These are end points forming a continuum of delegated responsibility. **Decentralization** implies that many job activities and the related decision-making functions are delegated to subordinates. Top management passes to subordinates a large amount of authority to control operational activities and make decisions that affect the outcome. **Centralization** implies that little responsibility for decision making has been delegated to lower levels of management. Top management controls and makes most of the critical decisions that affect the organization. Typically, business organizations are neither completely centralized nor completely decentralized. Most businesses have some degree of decentralization or delegation of authority.

The extent to which authority is delegated depends on a number of factors, including management philosophy and the general business environment. The question is not should an organization be centralized or decentralized, but rather, to what degree is decentralization or delegation appropriate to maintain management control and how should the activities and responsibilities within the firm be divided, coordinated, and controlled?

Firms that exhibit a high degree of decentralization possess some or all of the following characteristics:

1. An organizational structure that is *large, complex,* or *geographically dispersed*
2. A mix of *diversified products*
3. A number of *dispersed customers or suppliers*
4. A need for *timely decisions* in remote parts of the organization
5. A desire for *freedom to make decisions* at lower levels of the organization

The extent to which an organization is decentralized depends on the costs and benefits involved. Some of the claimed benefits of decentralization include the following:

1. *Better decisions* because segment management is more familiar with local conditions
2. *More freedom for top management* to pursue strategic planning, since many decisions are made at lower levels in the organization
3. *Increased incentive for segment managers* to perform well because of greater responsibility for operations
4. *More on-the-job training* for lower level management
5. *Potential for greater job satisfaction* because more people are involved in the management process

Potential costs of decentralization should be considered when making decisions to delegate authority. Some of the costs of decentralization include the following:

1. *Inferior decisions* because of a lack of similar goals between individual segment managers and top management
2. *Duplication of administrative talent and services* in segments
3. *More costly* management reporting and feedback systems because of more levels of administration and more detail
4. *More difficulty in coordinating* interdependent operations

Decentralization usually does not occur instantly; it evolves through growth, experience, trial, and error. The role of an accountant during this process is that of information system designer and manager. The accounting system must be sensitive to organizational changes to provide an effective reporting and feedback system for management control.

The primary accounting challenge in decentralized organizations is finding the best way to measure and evaluate individual segment performance and each segment manager's performance. *Both* the segment and its manager need to be evaluated; however, the decisions that need to be made will be different. Likewise, the corresponding basis for evaluation and the information to be used will also differ. The primary decisions for the segment include whether to expand, contract, maintain, or sell the segment. Decisions for the manager concern whether or not the resources available to the manager have been effectively used as they were intended.

Responsibility accounting, introduced in chapters 4 and 6, provides the basic concepts underlying segment reporting and performance evaluation. All company units need to have their performance evaluated, whether in centralized or decentralized organizations. However, the degree of decentralization affects the scope of management responsibility, which in turn affects the manner in which segments are evaluated. This chapter augments the basic concepts of responsibility accounting with an emphasis on decentralized organizations.

RESPONSIBILITY CENTERS

Decentralization results in an organization being divided into a number of distinct responsibility centers. A **responsibility center** is a subdivision of a business over which control of operations is found. Responsibility centers may include the entire company, a division, a department, an operation, or even an individual employee. As businesses become more decentralized, several distinct types of responsibility centers evolve with unique accounting and control requirements. These different types of responsibility centers include cost centers, profit centers, revenue centers, and investment centers.

Cost centers are subdivisions of a business assigned responsibility only for the incurrence and proper utilization of costs. Cost centers may be further divided into standard cost centers and discretionary cost centers.

Standard cost centers have a well-defined relationship between inputs and outputs. Manufacturing departments that produce goods under a standard cost system are often standard cost centers. A product may require processing in several different departments. Each department attempts to perform its required function while minimizing production costs. A standard cost center's performance is measured by the quality of the product relative to the amount of cost incurred. Budgeted or standard costs provide the basis for comparison.

Discretionary cost centers lack a well-defined relationship between inputs and outputs. An advertising department or a research and development department is an example of a discretionary cost center. Positive results are expected from advertising or research and development expenditures, yet there is not a well-defined relationship between a given amount of expenditure and the amount of anticipated results. The objective is not to minimize the expenditure but to use the budgeted funds as effectively as possible. The funds budgeted to the segment represent the maximum available. Effectiveness is measured by accomplishments, such as new products patented, relative to the available funds.

Profit centers are subdivisions of a business assigned responsibility for both costs and revenues. For example, a producer of instant cake mixes may consider each type of cake mix to be a profit center, because segment management may be assigned responsibility for costs to manufacture and sell the mix as well as for the revenue generated from each mix.

A subset of a profit center is a **revenue center,** which is primarily responsible for the generation of revenue. Sales or marketing segments are the best examples of revenue centers. The objective here is to maximize revenues subject to some cost constraints associated with the segment's operation.

Profit centers are typically evaluated in terms of the relationship of sales and costs to budgeted amounts. In addition, contribution margin, ratio measures, and other indicators of profitable performance may be applied to profit center evaluation. Most profit centers share common facilities, such as buildings, equipment, utilities, and some administrative functions. Care must be exercised in allocating the cost of these common facilities and in evaluating the performance of each segment.

Finally, **investment centers** are assigned responsibility for costs, revenues, and the profitable utilization of invested capital. For example, an appliance division of a large company may be considered an investment center if its management is assigned responsibility for costs incurred, revenues generated, and the profitable utilization of capital invested in the division. The important distinction between profit and investment centers is that profit centers are responsible for profits, but investment centers are responsible for both generating profits *and* efficiently using the capital created by those profits.

Investment centers are usually evaluated with measures that relate profits to invested capital in terms of the rate of return earned by invested funds. The remainder of this chapter focuses on approaches that can be used to measure and evaluate the performance of investment centers as segments of a business. The terms *segment* and *investment center* are considered interchangeable throughout the rest of this chapter.

APPROACHES FOR EVALUATING PERFORMANCE

The accounting approaches for evaluating segment performance that are examined in this section are return on investment, residual income, and segment margin analysis. These methods are used when managers are delegated almost complete authority over their own segments. Where such autonomy exists, managers have almost as much control over operations as if they were running their own business.

One advantage of investment centers is that they are virtually independent operations with little ambiguity about who is responsible for their success or failure. Accordingly, management compensation packages, bonus plans, and funds for expansion of operations are often allocated to segments based on an analysis of how well each segment is doing with currently invested funds. As a result, there may be keen competition among segment managers to do well in these measures. To properly use performance measures as effective management tools, it is important to recognize the power inherent in them. A brief analysis of the questions that arise when considering the desired behavioral outcomes of segment evaluation indicates the importance of an appropriate accounting system being implemented to evaluate segment performance.

First, consider the implications associated with maintaining segment independence. The accounting system should promote autonomy yet insure that segments are behaving in a way that also promotes overall company goals. Even though a segment is independent, some questions arise. Should segment managers be allowed to engage in transactions that enhance segment performance measures but that are detrimental to company profits taken as a whole? Is there some way to preserve the independence of segment managers and yet insure that their decisions will be congruent with overall company goals?

Second, the accounting system should provide an equitable and comparable measure of performance for its managers. This is not always easy in complex organizations. Consider the situation in which a manager with an excellent record of success is asked by top management to take over an ailing segment. To nurse the segment back to good health may take years or may not even be possible. In such situations, questions arise about what performance measures should be used to evaluate a manager who accepts such a task. What compensation scheme should be used? Is it possible for a manager to be equitably treated in such a situation?

Finally, the accounting system should provide information that identifies the most economically profitable segments in the firm. It should identify which segments are using the funds already entrusted to them most profitably. It should also provide information for analyzing potential investment opportunities and giving management a reasonable assurance of investing in the most profitable activities.

These items give rise to analytical and behavioral requirements that make the choice of an appropriate accounting system vital to the profitable operation of decentralized organizations. The methods discussed in this section have gained widespread acceptance largely because they help answer these questions. Generally, these methods foster segment independence, provide an equitable basis for evaluating segment managers, and supply an equitable criterion for channeling investment funds into the most profitable alternatives.

Return on Investment

A widely used measure of business profitability, **return on investment (ROI)** focuses attention on the optimal use of invested capital. The basic components of the ROI equation are net income from the income statement and invested capital from the balance sheet.

$$\text{Return on investment} = \frac{\text{Net income}}{\text{Invested capital}}$$

To illustrate the calculation of ROI, consider a business segment with net income of $50,000 and invested capital of $275,000. The ROI for this segment is 18 percent.

$$18\% = \frac{\$50,000}{\$275,000}$$

ROI has gained widespread use as a measure of business performance for several reasons. First, ROI is easy to calculate from data that are readily available in a traditional accounting system, and it can be applied equally well to individual segments or to a company as a whole. Second, ROI incorporates into one measure a number of important factors that contribute to profitability. Further expansion would show that virtually all elements of the income statement and balance sheet are synthesized in the ROI statistic.

Another reason for the widespread use of ROI is that it focuses management's attention on how well assets are employed in the process of earning profits. Evaluating segment performance on a measure such as net income or sales without regard to the amount of invested capital may be misleading. For example, consider a situation in which two segments of a business have equal net income; however, one segment has a larger asset base with which to generate the same level of income. If management considers only the absolute amount of net income, a more efficient use of assets by one of the segments may be overlooked. The most critical test of profitability is not the absolute amount of sales or profits, but the relationship of profits to the amount of invested capital used to generate them.

A final reason for the popularity of ROI is that it may be used to compare investment opportunities. Projected ROI statistics can be used to guide initial investment dollars. Actual ROI calculations can provide management with an indicator of how well invested capital is currently being employed and whether funds should be shifted from one segment to another. Actual ROI statistics can also be used to verify expected ROI numbers in validating the budgetary process. Finally, comparative ROI statistics for segments can play a key role by simply drawing management's attention to areas where help might be needed or to areas where additional investment might be warranted.

The ROI formula can be expanded using the following relationships:

$$\text{Profit margin} = \frac{\text{Net income}}{\text{Sales}}$$

$$\text{Capital turnover} = \frac{\text{Sales}}{\text{Invested capital}}$$

Combining these relationships, we obtain the following ROI formula:

$$\text{Return on investment} = \frac{\text{Net income}}{\text{Sales}} \times \frac{\text{Sales}}{\text{Invested capital}}$$

or

$$\text{Return on Investment} = \text{Profit margin} \times \text{Capital turnover}$$

To illustrate, a company with a net income of $50,000, sales of $625,000, and invested capital of $312,500 has a profit margin of 8 percent, capital turnover of 2 times, and ROI of 16 percent.

The basic ROI formula and its expanded version recognize the basic ingredients of profit making—sales, costs, and invested capital. Generally, ROI is increased by increasing sales, by decreasing costs, or by reducing the amount of invested capital if funds can be used more profitably elsewhere. The expanded ROI equation also recognizes the importance and interrelationship of profit margin and capital turnover ratios.

Capital turnover is the ratio of sales to invested capital. It is a rough approximation of the number of times assets circulate through the business from cash to inventory, through sales to accounts receivable, and back to cash again.

Profit margin is the ratio of net income to sales and represents the additional amount customers are willing to pay above the cost of goods sold and all other expenses. Overall profitability depends on the interaction of capital turnover and profit margin; that is, each time a dollar of invested capital circulates through the company it is increased by the amount of the profit margin, with total profits being dependent on how many times each investment dollar circulates through the system in an accounting period.

Because the number of times investment dollars circulate through the system is indicated by the capital turnover ratio, increasing either the profit margin or the capital turnover ratio will increase ROI. For example, a company with a profit margin of 10 percent earns 10 cents on each dollar as it circulates through the company. With a capital turnover ratio of 6 times, the company's total return on investment is 60 cents for each dollar of invested capital. Increasing either the 10 percent profit margin or the capital turnover ratio of 6 times will increase ROI.

When one examines the components and interrelationships in the calculation of ROI, it becomes clear that there are a number of alternative ways to improve performance. However, remember that even though ROI is simple to calculate and points to seemingly easy ways to improve ROI performance, the basic economic theory underlying the operation of a firm cannot be ignored. Decision makers and accountants should guard against a naive approach to using ROI. For example, increasing prices in anticipation of increasing sales, net income, and ROI may be a poor decision if the demand curve for the product is elastic. If demand is elastic, increasing prices may actually result in fewer sales, lower net income, and reduced ROI.

Another favorite target for increasing net income and ROI is cutting operating costs. In some business situations, cutting costs may increase net income without adversely affecting other components of ROI. However, in other situations, cutting costs may produce short-run increases in net income but may have detrimental long-run effects. For example, reduced repair and maintenance activities may reduce costs in the short run but may adversely affect the ability of the firm to produce efficiently in the long run.

Traditionally, the management of net income has been the focus for improving profitability. As indicated before, the ROI equation also emphasizes the importance of proper asset management. ROI can be increased by keeping cash, inventory, accounts receivable, and other assets at a minimum. This means that idle cash should be invested, inventories should be kept at proper levels, credit should be judiciously managed, and acquisition of plant assets should be based on an expected level of economic benefit.

The management of invested capital is just as important as the management of net income. However, because the components of net income can be affected more dramatically in the short run than the components of invested capital, net income typically receives the most attention in the ROI equation. This indicates the importance of long range and strategic planning so that invested capital can receive the same degree of control as net income. Attention to all parts of the equation increases the prospect of optimizing the profitability of business operations.

Figure 20.1 gives a few examples from the wide array of possible management options regarding the management of ROI and shows the effect of various business decisions on ROI. Each example in figure 20.1 is independent of the others.

Residual Income

Another measure of business profitability that focuses attention on the optimal use of invested capital is **residual income (RI)**. RI is the amount of net income that is earned during a period beyond that which is needed to provide a minimum desired rate of return on invested capital. The first step in calculating RI is to multiply the amount of invested

FIGURE 20.1

Effects on Return on Investment of Various Management Decisions

	$\dfrac{\text{Net income}}{\text{Sales}}$ × $\dfrac{\text{Sales}}{\text{Invested capital}}$ = ROI
	or
	Profit margin × Capital turnover = ROI
Present situation (in thousands of dollars):	$\dfrac{80}{1{,}600}$ × $\dfrac{1{,}600}{400}$ = 20%
Management decision and result:	
A. Reducing operating expenses by $5,000 results in increased net income, a larger profit margin, and higher ROI.	$\dfrac{85}{1{,}600}$ × $\dfrac{1{,}600}{400}$ = 21%
B. Reducing assets by $40,000 with no change in net income results in more frequent capital turnover and higher ROI.	$\dfrac{80}{1{,}600}$ × $\dfrac{1{,}600}{360}$ = 22%
C. Reduced prices result in a $50,000 increase in sales and a $5,000 increase in net income. The combined effect is a larger profit margin, more frequent capital turnover, and higher ROI.	$\dfrac{85}{1{,}650}$ × $\dfrac{1{,}650}{400}$ = 21%
D. Increased advertising expenditures result in a $100,000 increase in sales but no change in net income. The combined effect is a smaller profit margin, a more frequent capital turnover, but no change in ROI.	$\dfrac{80}{1{,}700}$ × $\dfrac{1{,}700}{400}$ = 20%

capital in a segment by the segment's minimum desired rate of return. This calculation results in **imputed interest** on invested capital. Imputed interest represents a hypothetical or opportunity cost of using the capital invested in the segment.

RI is then calculated by subtracting the amount of imputed interest on invested capital from the segment's after-tax net income. A positive RI indicates that the segment is earning net income in excess of that which is required to provide a minimum desired rate of return. If RI is zero, the segment's net income is exactly equal to the amount required to earn the desired minimum rate of return. If RI is negative, the segment is earning less net income than is necessary to earn a minimum rate of return. The dollar amount of a negative RI indicates the increase in net income that is needed to earn the minimum desired rate of return.

Since RI is a dollar measure rather than a percentage measure, it is most widely used when management wants to emphasize the maximization of the *number of dollars* of income rather than *a percentage* return on investment. Figure 20.2 contains the ROI and RI calculations for a segment with invested capital of $400,000 and a minimum desired rate of return of 20 percent.

Accountants and managers should realize that even though ROI and RI seem to be related measures with similar results, using or emphasizing one over the other may lead to different segment evaluations. For example, consider a company with an overall ROI objective of 20 percent that has a very profitable segment earning a ROI of 25 percent. This very profitable segment accepts an investment opportunity requiring invested capital of $100,000, which is predicted to earn $21,000 in net income—a ROI of 21 percent. From

FIGURE 20.2

Calculation of Residual Income and Return on Investment

Residual Income

Net income (after taxes)	$100,000
Imputed interest (0.2 × $400,000)	80,000
Residual income	$ 20,000

Return on Investment

$$\text{Return on investment} = \frac{\$100,000}{\$400,000} = 25\%$$

a top management point of view, the acceptance of this opportunity is appropriate because it is expected to earn a ROI in excess of the company's objective. However, the use of ROI for evaluation in this case will make it appear that accepting the investment opportunity is a poor decision because the segment's ROI will decline as a result. Its ROI will decline because the expected ROI of the project is less than the segment's current ROI.

If the situation is not understood by top management, the decrease could result in a lower segment evaluation than might be justified. This could also lead to reduced pay or a smaller bonus for the segment manager when compensation is based on segment performance. However, if RI is used for segment evaluation, segment performance will show an improvement consistent with economic reality. This situation is illustrated in figure 20.3.

The situation shown in figure 20.3 makes several important points. First, situations could arise in which segment managers may be inclined to behave in a way that is not preferred from a top management viewpoint. Therefore, segment performance measures should be designed to discourage such suboptimal decisions caused by a lack of goal congruence between individual segment managers and top management.

Second, figure 20.3 shows a subtle but important difference between the objectives of ROI and RI. When using ROI, the objective is to maximize ROI; when using RI, the objective is to maximize the amount of net income in excess of a minimum desired ROI. The choice of methods depends on many factors, including management's philosophy about a compensation scheme for segment managers and about whether emphasis should be placed on percentages or dollars. Since the calculations are not difficult, the presentation of both ROI and RI numbers as shown in figure 20.3 would provide a clear picture of segment performance.

FIGURE 20.3

Comparison of Return on Investment (ROI) and Residual Income (RI)

	Investment Opportunity	Current Situation	Projected Total
Invested capital	$100,000	$400,000	$500,000
Net income (after tax)	$ 21,000	$100,000	$121,000
Imputed interest at 20%			
(0.2 × $100,000)	(20,000)		(20,000)
(0.2 × $400,000)		(80,000)	(80,000)
Residual income	$ 1,000	$ 20,000	$ 21,000
Return on investment:	21%[a]	25%[b]	24%[c]

[a]($21,000 ÷ $100,000)
[b]($100,000 ÷ $400,000)
[c]($121,000 ÷ $500,000)

FIGURE 20.4

Calculation of Weighted Average Cost of Capital

	Percent of Total Equity	Current Cost	Weighted Cost
Debt	0.30	20%	6.0%
Equity	0.70	15%	10.5
			16.5%

The calculation of RI is subject to a number of other top management objectives or preferences. First, instead of using the minimum desired rate of return, the company's average cost of capital might be used to calculate the amount of imputed interest. The average cost of capital incorporates the costs of equity capital and debt capital, weighted by their respective proportions in the total capital structure. Figure 20.4 shows the computation of an average cost of capital using the percentage of debt and equity capital as weights.

The weighted average cost of capital of 16.5 percent can be used in the RI calculation to compute the amount of imputed interest. The management philosophy inherent in using the average cost of capital is that as long as a segment earns a rate of return in excess of the average cost of capital, the segment should expand. (See chapter 24 for additional discussion of cost of capital.)

Another management consideration is the rate of return to be used in calculating imputed interest when various segments are experiencing different rates of return. Generally, each segment should use a different rate of return that is selected by top management in consultation with each segment manager. This makes it possible for top management to recognize the unique identity and role of each segment in the overall company plan. Segments that do not achieve ROI objectives may be considered for sale, and segments that exceed ROI objectives may be expanded. Such factors as the maturity of the segment, its market position, or other situational factors can be more clearly evaluated when individual segment rates of return are used rather than when all segments are tied to a common rate of return.

A final management preference involves the use of segment contribution margin instead of after-tax net income, and the use of controllable investment instead of invested capital. It can be argued that in the short run, segment managers cannot control expenses related to fixed costs. Therefore, it may be believed that segments should be evaluated on variable costs and revenues as incorporated in a segment's contribution margin rather than on numbers that include fixed costs. In addition, investment in working capital may be thought to constitute the controllable portion, in the short run, of invested capital. Thus some believe that the measure of residual income may be made more sensitive for evaluating segment performance by using segment contribution margin and investment in working capital as alternative measures.

Segment Margin Analysis

Another common method of measuring segment performance is segment margin analysis. The *segment margin* is the contribution margin of a segment minus all other direct fixed costs of the segment. Contribution margin analysis differentiates between fixed and variable costs (as discussed in chapter 4) in the calculation of net income. However, when segments are involved, it is advisable to differentiate not only between fixed and variable costs but also between **avoidable fixed costs,** those fixed costs that would be avoided if the segment was discontinued, and **unavoidable fixed costs,** those fixed costs that would

FIGURE 20.5

Segment Margin Analysis for Divisions

	(000s omitted) Company Total	Division A	Division B
Sales	$550,000	$250,000	$300,000
Less: Variable expenses	300,000	100,000	200,000
Contribution margin	$250,000	$150,000	$100,000
Less: Direct fixed costs	25,000	10,000	15,000
Segment margin	$225,000	$140,000	$ 85,000
Less: Indirect fixed costs	20,000		
Net income	$205,000		

continue even though a segment was discontinued. Segment margin analysis is simply contribution margin analysis with the additional differentiation between avoidable and unavoidable fixed costs.

As an example, consider a company that uses segment margin analysis to evaluate the performance of its two divisions. Figure 20.5 shows the numeric components of such an evaluation. The figure shows how segment margin represents income after all costs that are directly attributable to segment operations are subtracted from segment revenue. Segment margin represents the amount that a segment contributes toward net income as well as toward covering those fixed costs that are incurred for the benefit of the company as a whole.

Depending on the detail of segment analysis desired by top management, figure 20.5 may represent only the first level of analysis. For example, suppose that division B handles two important product lines, each of which is in turn considered a segment by top management. Segment margin analysis can be used to evaluate these product lines, as shown in figure 20.6.

The information in figure 20.6 indicates that $14,000 of direct fixed costs can be avoided, depending on the elimination or continuance of either one or both of the product lines—$8,000 related to product 1 and $6,000 related to product 2. However, $1,000 of fixed costs are shared by both products and cannot be eliminated unless the whole division is eliminated. If division B is discontinued, a total of $15,000 of fixed costs will be avoided. The individual product segment margins calculated in figure 20.6 represent the amount of the company's total net income that would change if that particular product line was discontinued. Remember that avoidable fixed costs are those that would be eliminated if a segment was discontinued.

FIGURE 20.6

Segment Margin Analysis for Products

	(000s omitted) Division B	Product 1	Product 2
Sales	$300,000	$250,000	$50,000
Less: Variable expenses	200,000	155,000	45,000
Contribution margin	$100,000	$ 95,000	$ 5,000
Less: Avoidable fixed costs (products)	14,000	8,000	6,000
Segment margin (products)	$ 86,000	$ 87,000	$ (1,000)
Less: Unavoidable fixed costs (division)	1,000		
Segment margin (division)	$ 85,000		

The comparison of product segment margins in figure 20.6 provides some additional insights into segment margin analysis. Product 1 contributes the most per dollar of sales, and it also contributes the most to divisional net income. Any efforts to increase sales will be most profitably spent on product 1. For each dollar of sales of product 1, $0.38 ($95,000/$250,000) of contribution margin is available to cover fixed costs and provide a profit to the company. Product 2 provides only $0.10 ($5,000/$50,000) of contribution margin for each dollar of sales.

Product 2 not only contributes less per dollar of sales, but a negative segment margin raises questions about the viability of the product line. This points out that segment analysis not only provides information for relative performance evaluation but also provides information for decisions that concern whether or not operations should be continued.

A positive segment margin justifies continuing segment operations; a negative segment margin indicates that there may not be justification for continuing the segment. An analysis of segment contribution margin may be helpful in making a final decision. Continuation of a segment with a negative segment margin and a negative contribution margin should be seriously questioned. However, when considering discontinuance, other factors need to be considered. For example, is the situation expected to continue for a short or long period of time? Also, what effect will discontinuance have on other products of the firm?

In situations in which the segment margin is negative and the contribution margin is positive, management may also consider discontinuing segment operations. A positive contribution margin indicates that variable costs are being covered, and a negative segment margin indicates that avoidable fixed costs are not being covered. Not only is the viability of the segment in serious question, but because some fixed costs can be avoided, net income will increase if the segment is discontinued. However, because fixed costs are involved, how soon discontinuance can occur may depend on the time frame within which the firm's commitments to the segment's direct fixed costs can be ended. When direct fixed costs are considered avoidable, the time required for avoidance must be a criterion for classification.

CONSIDERATIONS FOR IMPLEMENTATION

Return on investment, residual income, and segment margin analysis are all flexible and easily adapted to evaluating segment performance in various types of business situations. As a result, the basic approaches to segment evaluation are implemented in many ways. A number of management options have already been mentioned. Other important concepts that relate specifically to the implementation of ROI and RI are examined in this section.

There are important relations between the budgetary process and the effectiveness of ROI or RI as management tools. What is included as invested capital and how invested capital is valued may affect management decisions when using ROI or RI. Therefore, this section focuses on considerations for implementing ROI and RI that are helpful for their effective use in particular business and management environments. Limitations inherent in ROI and RI are also discussed, and suggestions are made on how to overcome them.

The Role of Budgets

Because major differences exist between decisions that concern managers of segments and decisions that concern the segments themselves, it is important to differentiate between the performance of a segment as a business activity and the performance of a segment manager

$$\frac{\text{Index of current prices}}{\text{Index of prices prevailing when asset was acquired}}$$

To illustrate the translation process, consider an asset that cost $1,000 last year when the price index was 80. To restate the value of the asset in terms of current prices when the index is 120, the following calculation is made:

$$\frac{120}{80} = 1.50 \times \$1,000 = \$1,500$$

To further illustrate the usefulness of price-level adjustments to the investment base, consider again the example of divisions A and B with identical net incomes and productive capacities. As long as the specific prices of the assets in the investment base change at the same rate as the general price index, the adjustment to constant dollar accounting will result in the same ROI for both divisions. Figure 20.8 verifies this intuitive reasoning.

Note that in periods of rising prices, as shown in figure 20.8, ROI calculations also become inflated in real economic terms when using historical cost accounting. This happens because the current productive capacity is replaced with more costly plant assets.

Constant dollar accounting has advantages—it is simple to compute, easy to understand, and objective in nature. However, the major disadvantage is that by using general price indexes, the adjustment of the investment base may only approximate actual current values. An approach that may give a more accurate value to the investment base is called current value accounting.

Current value accounting abandons historical costs as a basis for valuation and turns to other methods of obtaining current asset values. When using current value accounting, management is primarily interested in what the investment base is currently worth independent of what costs were incurred to obtain the asset. What is desired is a measure of the true economic value of an asset. From economic theory, this measure is the present value of the future net cash flows from the assets in the investment base.

As a practical matter, however, replacement cost is often used as a measure of the current value of an asset. *Replacement cost* represents what it would cost to obtain similar assets to replace the productive capacity of the current investment base in terms of future net cash flows. The key to measuring replacement cost is expected net cash flows, not technological or physical features of the assets in question.

Determining the replacement cost of some types of assets for which active markets exist may not be very difficult. For example, determining the replacement cost of a delivery truck should be relatively easy because of existing markets for such assets. However,

	Division A	Division B
(1) Investment base in historical dollars	$1,048,951	$1,442,300
(2) Index of current prices	140	140
(3) Index of prices at date of acquisition	98	135
(4) Translation factor (Row 2 ÷ Row 3)	1.43	1.04
(5) Cost of assets in terms of current dollars (Row 4 × Row 1)	$1,500,000	$1,500,000
(6) Net income	$ 150,000	$ 150,000
(7) ROI before constant dollar adjustment (Row 6 ÷ Row 1)	14.3%	10.4%
(8) ROI after constant dollar adjustment (Row 6 ÷ Row 5)	10.0%	10.0%

as a planner, organizer, and controller. Evaluating managers based on only controllable elements of a segment's performance is an important principle in manager evaluation.

The budget is one of the most effective tools for differentiating between manager performance and segment performance. Actual results compared against separate budgeted criteria for both manager and segment performance avoid any unfortunate evaluations of managers based on uncontrollable items. In addition, it may be more appropriate to judge manager performance against budgeted goals than against the performance of other managers or other segments. Also, the budgetary process makes it possible to treat each segment in its unique business environment and avoids inappropriate comparisons among segments for which situational factors make such comparisons invalid.

Use of a budget typically contributes to goal congruence between top management and segment management. The communication channels that open and the dialogue that accompanies a constructive budgetary process foster goal congruence. In situations in which top management simply compiles budgets generated at lower levels or in which budgets are used as punitive tools, the communication necessary to establish goal congruence is usually lacking. When preparation of the budget provides an opportunity for several levels of management to communicate about strategic planning as well as operational matters, there usually emerges a commonality of purpose and commitment to specific goals that is unattainable without such communication.

The use of budgets to attain goal congruence guards against segment managers making decisions that improve segment evaluation measures but that are detrimental to the company as a whole.

The Investment Base

Segment evaluation focuses on the efficiency with which invested capital is utilized. The assets that are actually included as invested capital (the investment base) may differ among companies, because there is no theoretically correct investment base. The selection of an investment base depends on individual situational factors and management philosophy. For example, one segment may include all assets in the investment base whereas another segment may include only working capital.

Another dimension of the investment base concerns the method used to determine the value of assets included in the investment base. For example, historical cost may be used by one company whereas another company may use replacement cost to value its assets. Both the composition and the valuation of the investment base have important implications for proper segment evaluation.

Composition There are various alternative criteria that can be used to determine what should be included in the investment base. For example, total assets available, total assets employed, and total assets employed minus current liabilities are all possible ways to define invested capital. They are not the only ways to define the composition of the investment base, but they are representative of those in popular usage and provide points of departure for the development of other bases more appropriate for a given business situation.

The *total assets available* to the segment manager is probably the most widely used investment base, because it assumes that the segment manager is responsible for the most profitable use of all assets included in the segment. However, some situations may dictate that top management give oversight or custodial responsibility to a segment manager for currently unproductive assets. For example, when construction in process or idle land is involved, only *total assets employed* may be included in the investment base. The manager's stewardship over unemployed assets is typically evaluated on some nonfinancial basis.

The composition of the investment base may be determined by the degree of control that can be exercised over the assets in question. For example, when the segment manager has control over the amount of short-term credit that is used by the segment, there may be an opportunity for manipulation of the amount of assets employed. In such instances, it may be appropriate to exclude from the investment base the amount of assets that are supplied by short-term creditors. In such instances, the investment base could be defined as *total assets employed minus current liabilities*.

In some instances, it may be appropriate to include company assets in the segment's investment base even though they are not explicitly part of the segment. Just as costs of service facilities and home office functions are allocated to benefiting departments, as discussed in chapter 14, it may be appropriate to include *allocated assets* in the investment base for purposes of segment evaluation. For example, if accounts receivable are handled at corporate headquarters and if segment managers are considered to be responsible for all assets resulting from business conducted by the segment, it may be appropriate to allocate accounts receivable to segments. On the other hand, if there is a question about the controllability of centralized accounts receivable by segment managers, it may not be appropriate to allocate the accounts receivable to segments.

An investment base with some appeal for stockholders but one that should be used with caution in segment evaluation is *stockholders' equity*. The rate of return on stockholders' equity is very useful in assessing the outcome of financing decisions from the stockholders' viewpoint. However, return on stockholders' equity has limited usefulness in assessing individual segment performance from a manager's viewpoint. For example, consider division A of a company that has $2 million of employed assets financed with $1,750,000 of common stock. The net income of division A is $400,000. Division A's ROI, using total assets employed and stockholders' equity as investment bases, are 20 percent and 22 percent, respectively. However, consider division B of a company that also has $2 million of employed assets but has financed its assets with $1,000,000 of common stock and $750,000 of long-term debt at 15 percent interest. In terms of ROI comparison, division B presents an entirely different picture. Division B also earns $400,000 of net income before interest on the long-term debt, but net income after deducting interest expense is $287,500 [$400,000 − (0.15 × $750,000) = $287,500]. Figure 20.7 presents

FIGURE 20.7

Stockholders' Equity as an Investment Base

	Division A	Division B
(1) Total assets	$2,000,000	$2,000,000
Current liabilities	$ 250,000	$ 250,000
Long-term debt @ 15%		750,000
(2) Common stockholders' equity	1,750,000	1,000,000
Total liabilities and equity	$2,000,000	$2,000,000
(3) Income before interest expense	$ 400,000	$ 400,000
Interest on long-term debt		112,500
(4) Net income (ignoring taxes)	$ 400,000	$ 287,500
ROI based on total assets and:		
Income before interest on long-term debt (Row 3 ÷ Row 1)	20.0%	20.0%
Income after interest on long-term debt (Row 4 ÷ Row 1)	20.0%	14.4%
ROI based on stockholders' equity and:		
Income before interest on long-term debt (Row 3 ÷ Row 2)	22.9%	40.0%
Income after interest on long-term debt (Row 4 ÷ Row 2)	22.9%	28.8%

FIGURE 20.9

Depreciation and Return on Investment (ROI)

	Year			
	1	2	3	4
Operating income	$10,000	$10,000	$10,000	$10,000
Depreciation expense[a]	7,500	7,500	7,500	7,500
Net income	$ 2,500	$ 2,500	$ 2,500	$ 2,500
Investment base (Cost less accumulated depreciation at beginning of the year)	$30,000	$22,500	$15,000	$ 7,500
Return on investment	8.3%	11.1%	16.7%	33.3%

[a] Assuming assets that cost $30,000 with no residual value are depreciated over four years using the straight-line method.

as assets become more specialized or where no active markets exist, determining the replacement cost becomes more difficult and more subjective. A special-purpose computer may not have a counterpart for which replacement costs are available. In such instances, appraisals may be used to approximate current values. However, appraisals are inherently subjective and should be used with caution.

Specific price indexes for particular categories of assets may also be used to obtain better approximations of current values than would otherwise be available when general price indexes are used. For example, if a specific price index for data-processing equipment is available, it might be used to approximate the current value of a special-purpose computer.

Alternative Depreciation Methods Still another dilemma that concerns the valuation of assets in the investment base is whether depreciable assets should be included at their undepreciated cost or at net book value. The advantage of using net book value is that net income on the income statement and total assets on the balance sheet can be used without adjustment when calculating RI or ROI. However, a difficulty in using net book value is that a decreasing net book value because of depreciation will result in an increasing rate of return on the same assets as they grow older. Figure 20.9 shows this phenomenon.

The results in figure 20.9 would have been even more dramatic if an accelerated method of depreciation had been used. To overcome this difficulty, the use of undepreciated cost in the investment base will provide stable rates of return through time and will facilitate comparisons among segments. However, using undepreciated cost ignores the reality of an asset's declining value with use.

SUMMARY

Return on investment (ROI), residual income (RI), and segment margin analysis are methods used by top management to evaluate the performance of relatively autonomous business subdivisions known as segments. These methods can be used to evaluate both the performance of segments as economic entities and the performance of segment managers as planners, organizers, and controllers. The primary focus of segment evaluation is the profitable utilization of invested capital.

Segment evaluation methods are deceptively simple to apply because they are easy to calculate. However, a number of economic and behavioral considerations should be factored into their use to avoid unexpected results or incongruent management behavior. The use of budgets as a communicative tool is especially important. Other considerations involve determining what rates of return are appropriate, what should be included as invested capital, and how invested capital should be valued.

A primary objective of segment evaluation is to provide an equitable basis for comparisons. Therefore, it is usually desirable to compare actual results with budgeted amounts rather than to evaluate one segment against another. Also, there should be a clear differentiation between segment and manager performance in both budgeted and actual results.

Minimum desired rates of return should be tailored to the specific economic and business circumstances of each segment. The weighted average cost of capital is an interest rate commonly used in segment evaluation. However, judgment should be exercised so that rates are set at levels that promote goal congruence between top management and segment management.

There are a number of ways to determine what constitutes a segment's invested capital. Total assets, assets employed, total assets minus current liabilities, and stockholders' equity represent possible measures of invested capital. The measure that represents controllable assets, as viewed by the segment manager, is usually the most appropriate measure of invested capital for segment evaluation.

Invested capital can be valued by using historical costs, as found in traditional financial records, or by using some form of current value accounting. The use of current values provides a more realistic measure of the actual economic state of affairs. However, current values are less objective than historical costs and should be used with caution.

APPENDIX 20.1 *Compound Interest Method of Depreciation*

To provide a stable rate of return as assets grow older and at the same time to incorporate depreciation changes in the investment base, the compound interest method of depreciation can be used. This depreciation method views depreciation as though it represents cost recovery on investments. The rate of cost recovery is found by using compound interest techniques. For example, consider assets that were purchased for $30,000 and that have an estimated useful life of four years and no salvage value. Budget estimates indicate that the assets are predicted to generate net cash operating income of $10,508 each year for four years. This can be viewed as receiving an ordinary annuity of four rents in the amount of $10,508 whose present value is $30,000—the purchase price of the assets.

The interest rate (in this case, the internal rate of return for these assets) that equates the rents and present value must be calculated or be found by referring to a present value table. The table for the present value of an ordinary annuity indicates that the internal rate of return for this piece of equipment is 15 percent. This rate of return is used to calculate the amount of depreciation (investment recovery) with the compound interest method, as shown in figure 20.10.

In figure 20.10, the use of compound interest depreciation results in a stable rate of return through time. This can also be very useful in evaluating investment performance in comparison with specific ROI target percentages. Any other type of evaluation will be flawed because it does not provide for a constant rate of return over time.

Although the compound interest method of depreciation is useful for segment evaluation, it is not acceptable for external financial reporting because of the subjective considerations in determining the appropriate internal rate of return.

FIGURE 20.10

Depreciation and Return on Investment (ROI)

Calculation of Depreciation Expense Using Compound Interest Method

Year	Investment Base, Beginning of Year	Predicted Net Cash Operating Income	Return on Investment @ 15% per Year	Depreciation Expense	Investment Base, End of Year
1	$30,000	$10,508	$4,500	$6,008	$23,992
2	23,992	10,508	3,599	6,909	17,083
3	17,083	10,508	2,562	7,946	9,137
4	9,137	10,508	1,371	9,137	0

Return of investment @ 15% = 0.15 × Investment base, beginning of year
Depreciation = Predicted net cash operating income − Return of investment @ 15% per year
Investment base end of year (Investment base beginning of next year) = Investment base, beginning of year − Depreciation

Calculation of Return on Investment

	Year 1	Year 2	Year 3	Year 4
Operating income	$10,508	$10,508	$10,508	$10,508
Depreciation expense	6,008	6,909	7,946	9,137
Net income	$ 4,500	$ 3,599	$ 2,562	$ 1,371
Investment base (Cost minus accumulated depreciation at beginning of the year)	$30,000	$23,992	$17,083	$ 9,137
Return on investment	15%	15%	15%	15%

SELF-STUDY PROBLEM

The following are selected financial and operating statistics for the toy products division of a major corporation that routinely evaluates segment performance using methods discussed in this chapter.

Invested capital	$2,000,000
Sales	$3,000,000
Variable cost of sales	1,300,000
Contribution margin	$1,700,000
Fixed costs	800,000
Net income	$ 900,000

Required

1. What is the division's capital turnover ratio?
2. What is the division's profit margin?
3. What is the division's ROI?
4. Assuming that the division imputes interest at 25 percent, what is the division's RI?
5. Assuming that $200,000 of fixed costs are avoidable, what is the division's segment margin?

6. Presented with an investment opportunity that is expected to earn a return of 35 percent what manager behavior can be expected if the firm uses ROI for segment evaluation? RI?

7. What alternative measures are available to define the investment base other than total assets?

8. What alternative ways are available to value the investment base other than historical cost?

Solution to the Self-Study Problem

1. Capital turnover ratio = $\dfrac{\$3{,}000{,}000}{\$2{,}000{,}000}$ = 1.5 times

2. Profit margin = $\dfrac{\$900{,}000}{\$3{,}000{,}000}$ = 30%

3. ROI = $\dfrac{\$900{,}000}{\$2{,}000{,}000}$ = 45%   or   ROI = 1.5 × 0.30 = 45%

4. RI:

Net income	$900,000
Imputed interest ($2,000,000 × 0.25)	500,000
Residual income	$400,000

5. Segment margin:

Sales	$3,000,000
Variable cost of sales	1,300,000
Contribution margin	$1,700,000
Avoidable fixed costs	200,000
Segment margin	$1,500,000

6. If ROI is used to evaluate segment performance, an investment opportunity with an expected ROI of less than 45 percent will be rejected because segment ROI will decline if it is accepted. If RI is used, the opportunities with an expected ROI equal to or greater than a minimum desired rate of return will be accepted. Assuming a minimum desired rate of return of 25 percent, the opportunity will be accepted because it will add to RI.

7. Alternative measures available to define invested capital include total assets available, total assets employed, total assets employed minus current liabilities, and stockholders' equity. The choice of the measure depends on the control that is exercised over the investment base by the segment manager.

8. Alternative ways to value the investment base in addition to historical cost include constant dollar accounting using price level adjustments and current value accounting using such indicators of current value as replacement cost.

SUGGESTED READINGS

Brown, Russell S. "Measuring Manufacturing Performance: A Targeting Approach." *Management Accounting* 61 (June 1980): 25–29.

Chow, Chee W., and Waller, William S. "Management Accounting and Organizational Control." *Management Accounting* 63 (April 1982): 36–41.

Largay, James A., III, and Levy, Ferdinand K. "Using Segment Reporting and Input-Output Analysis for Management Planning." *Management Accounting* 60 (November 1978): 46–50.

Louderback, Joseph G., and Manners, George E., Jr. "Integrating ROI and CVP." *Management Accounting* 62 (April 1981): 33–39.

Mays, Robert L., Jr. "Divisional Performance Measurement and Transfer Prices." *Management Accounting* 63 (April 1982): 20–28.

DISCUSSION QUESTIONS

Q20–1. Define *centralization* and *decentralization*. Why are these management concepts important for cost accounting?

Q20–2. Name some characteristics of firms that are relatively decentralized.

Q20–3. What are some of the claimed benefits and potential costs of decentralization?

Q20–4. Explain the concept of *responsibility center* and describe the differences between cost, profit, and investment centers.

Q20–5. What is the generic meaning of the term *segment* in terms of business organizations? Define *segment* as it is used in cost accounting literature with regard to responsibility centers.

Q20–6. Describe several behavioral implications for evaluating the segments of a business.

Q20–7. What is the general equation for calculating return on investment (ROI)?

Q20–8. How does ROI relate to profit margin and capital turnover ratios?

Q10–9. What are some of the reasons ROI has gained such widespread usage?

Q20–10. "ROI is a broad, long-run measure, whereas net income is a narrow, short-run measure." Explain.

Q20–11. How is residual income (RI) measured?

Q20–12. Define *imputed cost* and describe what role imputed interest has in the calculation of RI.

Q20–13. What is the basic difference between ROI and RI in terms of management philosophy and use?

Q20–14. Describe a circumstance in which a management decision may differ depending on whether ROI or RI is used, as an evaluation method.

Q20–15. What management preferences are available for the calculation of RI?

Q20–16. Describe how segment margin analysis is an extension of contribution margin analysis.

Q20–17. Describe the role budgets play in segment evaluation.

Q20–18. What are several alternative ways of defining invested capital for segment evaluation purposes?

Q20–19. Describe two alternative methods (other than historical cost) that could be employed to value assets used to measure invested capital.

EXERCISES

E20-1. Segment Performance Measures (CPA) Select the best answer for each of the following questions. Items 1 through 5 are based on the following data:

Oslo Company's industrial photo-finishing division, Rho, incurred the following costs and expenses in 19X5:

	Variable	Fixed
Direct materials	$200,000	
Direct labor	150,000	
Factory overhead	70,000	$42,000
General, selling, and administrative expenses	30,000	48,000
Totals	$450,000	$90,000

During 19X5, Rho produced 300,000 units of industrial photo prints, which were sold for $2.00 each. Oslo's investment in Rho was $500,000 at January 1, 19X5, and $700,000 at December 31, 19X5. Oslo normally imputes interest on investment at 15 percent of average invested capital.

1. For the year ended December 31, 19X5, Rho's return on average investment was
   a. 15.0%.
   b. 10.0%.
   c. 8.6%.
   d. (5.0%).

2. For the year ended December 31, 19X5, Rho's residual income (loss) was
   a. $150,000.
   b. $60,000.
   c. ($45,000).
   d. ($30,000).

3. How many industrial photo-print units did Rho have to sell in 19X5 to break even?
   a. 180,000
   b. 120,000
   c. 90,000
   d. 60,000

4. For the year ended December 31, 19X5, Rho's contribution margin was
   a. $250,000.
   b. $180,000.
   c. $150,000.
   d. $60,000.

5. Based on Rho's 19X5 financial data and an estimated 19X6 production of 350,000 units of industrial photo prints, Rho's estimated 19X6 total costs and expenses would be
   a. $525,000.
   b. $540,000.
   c. $615,000.
   d. $630,000.

6. Costs are accumulated by responsibility center for control purposes when using

	Job-Order Costing	Process Costing
a.	Yes	Yes
b.	Yes	No
c.	No	No
d.	No	Yes

7. The capital turnover rate would include
   a. sales in the denominator.
   b. net income in the numerator.
   c. invested capital in the denominator.
   d. invested capital in the numerator.
8. Assuming that sales and net income remain the same, a company's return on investment will
   a. increase if invested capital increases.
   b. decrease if invested capital decreases.
   c. decrease if the capital turnover rate decreases.
   d. decrease if the capital turnover rate increases.

E20–2. Basic Procedures of Segment Analysis

The following information is for the period just ending for the Maximum Company:

	Total	%	X	%	Y	%
Sales	$700,000	100	$	100	$	100
Less: Variable expenses			260,000	65		
Contribution margin	$350,000		$		$	70
Less: Direct fixed expenses				20		
Segment margin	$	20	$ 60,000		$	
Less: Common fixed expenses	105,000					
Net income	$					

Required

Reconstruct the income statement by filling in the blanks.

E20–3. Segment Analysis—ROI and RI

A division has assets of $400,000 and net income of $90,000.

Required

1. What is the division's ROI?
2. If interest is imputed at 16 percent what is the residual income?
3. What effect on management behavior can be expected if ROI is used to guage performance?
4. What effects on management behavior can be expected if RI is used to guage performance?

E20–4. Segment Performance and Contribution Analysis

Mike Lacey, president of Bintub Company, made the following statement. "We're slowly doing better. The latest monthly income statement loss of $21,250 is the smallest yet. If we can just build up segments A and C. . . ." The following is the latest monthly income statement:

	Total	Segment A	Segment B	Segment C
Sales	$500,000	$200,000	$125,000	$175,000
Cost of goods sold	371,250	150,000	90,000	131,250
Gross margin	$128,750	$ 50,000	$ 35,000	$ 43,750
Less: Operating expenses:				
Selling	$ 75,000	$ 30,000	$ 11,250	$ 33,750
Administrative	75,000	30,000	18,750	26,250
Total	$150,000	$ 60,000	$ 30,000	$ 60,000
Net income (loss)	$ (21,250)	$ (10,000)	$ 5,000	$ (16,250)

Leigh Buff, Lacey's new financial consultant, had recommended that he isolate direct and common costs and has come up with the following:

	Segment A	Segment B	Segment C
Variable costs (as a % of sales):			
Production (materials, labor, variable overhead)	20%	30%	25%
Selling	5%	5%	5%
Direct fixed costs:			
Production	$50,000	$15,000	$35,000
Selling (salaries and advertising)	$20,000	$ 5,000	$25,000

In addition:

1. All administrative costs are common to the three segments.
2. All fixed production costs over the $50,000, $15,000, and $35,000 amounts shown in the preceding table should be considered common to the three segments.
3. Work-in-process and finished-goods inventories can be ignored.

However, Lacey was not totally confident in Buff's recommendations and did nothing about them. Later that week, Lacey was informed that because of supply shortages out of Bintub's control, production in either segment A or segment B would have to be cut back. Lacey took a look at the segmented income statement previously presented and declared, "From this income statement, our course of action is obvious. Cut back on segment A!"

Required

1. Prepare a new segmented monthly income statement using the contribution approach. Show both amount and percentage columns for each segment.
2. Do you agree with Lacey's decision to cut back on segment A? Why?
3. Assume that Lacey is also considering elimination of segment C because of its $16,250 loss. What points should Buff raise for or against elimination?

E20–5. Segment Reporting and Analysis Eric Smith is the president of DJ Company, which manufactures products P, Q, and R in two different areas, A and B. For the year ending December 31, the following information was presented to Smith:

	Total Company	Area A	Area B
Sales	$180,000	$105,000	$75,000
Cost of goods sold	130,000	75,000	55,000
Gross margin	$ 50,000	$ 30,000	$20,000
Selling and administrative expenses	30,000	21,500	8,500
Net income	$ 20,000	$ 8,500	$11,500
Ratio of net income to sales	11.1%	8.1%	15.3%

Smith was not satisfied after looking at these results and requested additional information on area A because of the lower ratio of net income to sales. He has even suggested recently that DJ Company may terminate activity in area A. The additional information per Smith's request is as follows:

	Product P	Product Q	Product R
Sales[a]	$ 50,000	$50,000	$80,000
Variable manufacturing expenses as a % of sales	40%	70%	50%
Variable selling expenses	$ 1,000	$ 1,500	$ 1,600
Variable selling expenses as a % of sales	2%	3%	2%

Product Sales	Area A	Area B	Total
P[b]	$ 35,000	$15,000	$ 50,000
Q	40,000	10,000	50,000
R	30,000	50,000	80,000
	$105,000	$75,000	$180,000

[a]Fixed administrative expenses total $8,700 per year. These expenses are common to the two sales areas but were allocated in the income statement to the two sales areas on a basis of sales dollars. This allocation resulted in $5,075 being allocated to area A and $3,625 being allocated to Area B.
[b]Fixed selling expenses total $17,200 per year. $10,000 of this amount is a result of sales activity in area A, and the remainder is incurred in area B.

Fixed manufacturing overhead is common to the two areas.

Required

1. Prepare a contribution-type income statement by area and in total for DJ Company for the year (detail sales, variable manufacturing expenses, and variable selling expenses by product.)
2. Based on the available data, would you recommend elimination of area A? Why?

E20–6. Segment Reporting Cooper Incorporated sells footballs and basketballs. During the past year, Cooper's income statement was as follows:

	Total Sales	Footballs	%	Basketballs	%
Sales	$10,000	$4,000	100	$6,000	100
Less: Variable expenses	4,800	2,200	55	2,600	43⅓
Contribution margin	$ 5,200	$1,800	45	$3,400	56⅔
Less: Direct fixed expenses	3,000	600		2,400	
Segment margin	$ 2,200	$1,200		$1,000	
Less: Common fixed expenses	1,800				
Net income	$ 400				

The prices of both balls are the same in Canada as they are in the United States. They are sold in an American market and a Canadian market as follows:

	American	Canadian
Football sales	$2,400	$1,600
Basketball sales	3,800	2,200
Total sales	$6,200	$3,800

The common fixed expenses are partly traceable to the American market, Canadian market, and general administration as follows:

American market fixed expenses	$ 500
Canadian market fixed expenses	700
General administration fixed expenses	600
Total common fixed expenses	$1,800

Required

Prepare a segmented income statement as above, but this time have the segments defined as the American and Canadian markets. (It is *not* necessary to state segment sales or variable expenses in percentages.) The direct fixed expenses of the product lines should not be allocated to the markets; treat these as common fixed expenses on this segmented statement.

E20–7. ROI and RI Computations and Analysis (CMA)

Lawton Industries has manufactured prefabricated houses for over twenty years. The houses are constructed in sections to be assembled on customers' lots.

Lawton expanded into the pre-cut housing market in 19X0 when it acquired Presser Company, one of its suppliers. In this market, various types of lumber are pre-cut into the appropriate lengths, banded into packages, and shipped to customers' lots for assembly. Lawton decided to maintain Presser's separate identity and, thus, established the Presser Division as an investment center of Lawton.

Lawton uses return on average investment (ROI) as a performance measure, with investment defined as operating assets employed. Management bonuses are based in part on ROI. All investments in operating assets are expected to earn a minimum return of 15 percent before income taxes.

Presser's ROI has ranged from 19.3 to 22.1 percent since it was acquired in 19X0. Presser had an investment opportunity in 19X5 that had an estimated ROI of 18 percent. The division's management decided against the investment because it believed the investment would decrease its overall ROI.

The 19X5 operating statement for Presser Division follows. The division's operating assets employed were $12,600,000 at the end of 19X5, a 5 percent increase over the 19X4 year-end balance.

Presser Division
Operating Statement
For The Year Ended December 31, 19X5
(000's omitted)

Sales revenue		$24,000
Cost of goods sold		15,800
Gross profit		$ 8,200
Operating expenses:		
Administrative	$2,140	
Selling	3,600	5,740
Income from operations before income taxes		$ 2,460

Required

1. Calculate the following performance measures for 19X5 for the Presser Division of Lawton Industries:
   a. Return on average investment in operating assets employed (ROI).
   b. Residual income calculated on the basis of average operating assets employed.

2. Would the management of Presser Division have been more likely to accept the investment opportunity it had in 19X5 if residual income had been used as a performance measure instead of ROI? Explain your answer.
3. The Presser Division is a separate investment center within Lawton Industries. Identify the items Presser must control if it is to obtain a positive evaluation by either the ROI or residual income performance measures.

E20–8. Segment Reporting and Analysis   Texland Company has just published its financial statement. Its income statement appeared as follows:

Texland Company
Income Statement

Sales	$260,000
Less: Variable expenses	140,000
Contribution margin	$120,000
Less: Fixed expenses	115,000
Net income	$ 5,000

Jo Ann Landers, president of Texland, is concerned about the low income figure and is determined to improve it. The following additional information is also available:

> Texland is divided into two sales regions, Alpha and Beta. Reports show that 40 percent of sales came from Alpha and $51,000 of variable expenses are traceable to Alpha. This region is also responsible for $35,000 of fixed expenses, compared to $37,000 for Beta.

Required

Landers has determined that a segmented financial statement would be helpful, as well as a recommendation about what to do. She has asked you to do both.

E20–9. Segment Analysis with a Product Line Emphasis   Anderson Gold Club Company sells two different sets of golf clubs—set A and set B. The following is the income statement for the quarter just ended:

	Total Company	Set A	Set B
Sales	$140,000	$95,000	$45,000
Less: Variable expenses	80,000	60,000	20,000
Contribution margin	$ 60,000	$35,000	$25,000
Less: Direct fixed expenses	45,000	22,000	23,000
Product line segment margin	$ 15,000	$13,000	$ 2,000
Less: Common fixed expenses	11,000		
Net income	$ 4,000		

Anderson will allocate $2,500 to direct advertising, which it plans to use for promoting either set A or set B. If spent on set A, sales of this set will increase by $12,000. If spent on set B, sales of this set will increase by $7,500.

Required

1. Using Lotus or some other electronic spreadsheet, prepare a performance report as shown above. Key in the variable costs as a percentage of sales, but show fixed costs as a constant amount. Make total company sales a total of the dollar amounts entered for the departments. Print out a copy of the results.

2. Change the template developed in requirement 1 for the change in sales and advertising expense and see the change in total company profit. On which set should Anderson Golf Club Company spend the advertising funds? Why?

E20–10. Segment Reporting on Departmental Performance Bogart Company makes overcoats that are sold by two different departments—A and B. The following are operating data for the last year:

	Total Company	Department A	Department B
Sales	$420,000	$180,000	$240,000
Less: Variable expenses	315,000	120,000	195,000
Contribution margin	$105,000	$ 60,000	$ 45,000
Less: Direct fixed expenses	80,000	50,000	30,000
Department segment margin	$ 25,000	$ 10,000	$ 15,000
Less: Common fixed expenses	18,000		
Net income	$ 7,000		

Required

1. Using Lotus or some other electronic spreadsheet, prepare a performance report as shown above. Key in the variable costs as a percentage of sales, but show fixed costs as a constant amount. Make total company sales a total of the dollar amounts entered for the departments. Print out a copy of the results.
2. Change the template developed in requirement 1 for the following items. Print out a copy of each result. Consider each item to be independent of the others, and make each change from the basic data developed in requirement 1.
    a. How much would total net income increase if sales in department A increased by $42,000?
    b. How much would net income increase if sales in department B increased by $42,000?
    c. As president of Bogart Company, in which department would you be most interested in increasing sales? Why?

E20–11. Electronic Spreadsheet to Compute ROI and RI The controller of the company has several divisions for which she frequently needs to know the return on investment (ROI) and residual income (RI). She has asked you to prepare a template using Lotus (or some other electronic spreadsheet) that will include the following inputs to compute both ROI and RI.

Inputs:

- Net income
- Invested capital
- Sales
- Desired rate of return

Required

Prepare a template as desired by the controller. For ROI, show both profit margin and capital turnover, in addition to the final return on investment. Use the following numbers to check your answer:

Net income	$15,000
Invested capital	$78,000
Sales	$275,000
Desired rate of return	20%

Print a copy of your results.

PROBLEMS

P20–1. Segment Analysis—A Review of Concepts (CMA)

1. The basic objective of the RI approach of performance measurement and evaluation is to have a division maximize its
   a. ROI rate.
   b. imputed interest rate charge.
   c. cash flows.
   d. cash flows in excess of a desired minimum amount.
   e. income in excess of a desired minimum return.

2. The imputed interest rate used in the RI approach for performance measurement and evaluation can best be characterized as the
   a. historical weighted average cost of capital for the company.
   b. marginal after-tax cost of new equity capital.
   c. average return on investment that has been earned by the company over a particular time period.
   d. target ROI set by management.
   e. average prime lending rate for the year being evaluated.

3. Which of the following items would most likely *not* be incorporated into the calculation of a division's investment base when using the RI approach for performance measurement and evaluation?
   a. Fixed assets employed in divisional operations
   b. Vacant land being held by the division as a potential site for a new plant
   c. Divisional inventories when division management exercises control over the inventory levels
   d. Divisional accounts payable when division management exercises control over the amount of short-term credit utilized
   e. Divisional accounts receivable when division management exercises control over credit policy and credit terms

4. A segment of an organization is referred to as a profit center if it has the
   a. authority to make decisions affecting the major determinants of profit, including the power to choose its markets and sources of supply.
   b. authority to make decisions affecting the major determinants of profit, including the power to choose its market and sources of supply and significant control over the amount of invested capital.
   c. authority to make decisions over the most important costs of operations, including the power to choose the sources of supply.
   d. authority to provide specialized support to other units within the organization.
   e. responsibility for combining the raw materials, direct labor, and other factors of production into a final output.

5. A segment of an organization is referred to as an investment center if it has the
   a. authority to make decisions affecting the major determinants of profit, including the power to choose its markets and sources of supply.

b. authority to make decisions affecting the major determinants of profit, including the power to choose its market and sources of supply and significant control over the amount of invested capital.
c. authority to make decisions over the most important costs of operations, including the power to choose the sources of supply.
d. authority to provide specialized support to other units within the organization.
e. responsibility for developing markets for and selling the output of the organization.

6. A segment of an organization is referred to as a cost center if it has the
a. responsibility for developing markets for and selling the output of the organization.
b. authority to make decisions affecting the major determinants of profit, including the power to choose its markets and sources of supply.
c. authority to make decisions over the most important costs of operations, including the power to choose the sources of supply.
d. authority to provide specialized support to other units within the organization.
e. responsibility for combining the raw materials, direct labor, and other factors of production into a final output.

P20–2. Segment Analysis—A Division Emphasis
Bodine Corporation began operations on January 1. Operating data for its first year of operations is as follows for the two divisions—Y and Z.

	Total Company	Division Y	Division Z
Sales	$40,000	$26,000	$14,000
Less: Variable expenses	28,000	19,000	9,000
Contribution margin	$12,000	$ 7,000	$ 5,000
Less: Direct fixed expenses	6,000	3,500	2,500
Division segment margin	$ 6,000	$ 3,500	$ 2,500
Less: Common fixed expenses	4,000		
Net income	$ 2,000		

Required

1. How much will division Y's segment margin increase if sales increase by $6,000?
2. How much will division Z's segment margin increase if sales increase by $6,000?
3. If, as sales manager, your salary was based on Bodine's net income, in which division would you be most interested in increasing sales? Why?

P20–3. Segment Analysis—A Division Emphasis
CUTCO has two different divisions—a brick division and a door division. The following information is available about operations for the year ending December 31.

	Total Company	Brick Division	Door Division
Sales	$90,000	$55,000	$35,000
Less: Variable expenses	60,000	38,000	22,000
Contribution margin	$30,000	$17,000	$13,000
Less: Direct fixed expenses	20,000	15,000	5,000
Divisional segment margin	$10,000	$ 2,000	$ 8,000
Less: Common fixed expenses	4,000		
Net income	$ 6,000		

Required

1. How much would the brick division's margin increase if sales increased by $8,000?
2. How much would the door division's margin increase if sales increased by $8,000?
3. What would be the brick division's segment margin if sales increased by $8,000 because of a $1,000 direct advertising expense spent exclusively on the brick division?
4. What would be the door division's margin if sales increased by $12,000 because of a $1,000 direct advertising expense spent exclusively on the door division?

P20–4. Segment Performance by ROI Analysis

The following data are for Dee Company's division A:

Average Available Assets

Receivables	$ 600,000
Inventories	400,000
Fixed assets, net	1,000,000
	$2,000,000
Fixed costs	$500,000
Variable costs	$10 per unit
Desired rate of return on average available assets	25%
Expected volume	400,000 units

Required

1. What average unit sales price does division A need to obtain the desired rate of return on average available assets?
2. What would be the expected turnover of assets?
3. What would be the net income percentage of dollar sales?
4. What rate of return would be earned on available assets if sales volume was 500,000 units, assuming no changes in price or variable costs per unit?

P20–5. Segment Performance Analysis (CMA)

The Jackson Corporation is a large, divisionalized manufacturer. Each division is viewed as an investment center and has virtually complete autonomy for product development, marketing, and production.

Performance of division managers is evaluated periodically by senior corporate management. Divisional ROI is the sole criterion used in performance evaluation under current corporate policy. Corporate management believes ROI is an adequate measure because it incorporates quantitative information from the divisional income statement and balance sheet in the analysis.

Some division managers have complained that a single criterion for performance evaluation is insufficient and ineffective. These managers have compiled a list of criteria they believe should be used in evaluating division managers' performance. The criteria include profitability, market position, productivity, product leadership, personnel development, employee attitudes, public responsibility, and balance between short-range and long-range goals.

Required

1. Jackson's management believes that ROI is an adequate criterion to evaluate division management performance. Discuss the shortcomings or possible inconsistencies of using ROI as the sole criterion to evaluate divisional management performance.
2. Discuss the advantages of using multiple criteria versus a single criterion to evaluate divisional management performance.

3. Describe the problems or disadvantages that can be associated with the implementation of the multiple performance criteria measurement system suggested to Jackson Corporation by its division managers.

P20-6. Performance Analysis Alternatives (CMA) Divisional managers of SIU Incorporated have been expressing growing dissatisfaction with the current methods used to measure divisional performance. Divisional operations are evaluated every quarter by comparison with the static budget prepared during the previous year. Divisional managers claim that many factors are completely out of their control but are included in this comparison. This results in an unfair and misleading performance evaluation.

The managers have been particularly critical of the process used to establish standards and budgets. The annual budget, stated by quarters, is prepared six months before the beginning of the operating year. Pressure by top management to reflect increased earnings has often caused divisional managers to overstate revenues or understate expenses. In addition, once the budget has been established, divisions were required to "live with the budget." Frequently, external factors such as the state of the economy, changes in consumer preferences, and actions of competitors have not been adequately recognized in the budget parameters that top management supplied to the divisions. The credibility of the performance review is curtailed when the budget cannot be adjusted to incorporate these changes. Top management, recognizing the current problems has agreed to establish a committee to review the situation and to make recommendations for a new performance evaluation system. The committee consists of each division manager, the corporate controller, and the executive vice president who chairs the committee. At the first meeting, one division manager outlined an Achievement of Objectives System (AOS). In this performance evaluation system, divisional managers would be evaluated according to three criteria:

1. Doing better than last year. Various measures would be compared to the same measures of the previous year.
2. Planning realistically. Actual performance for the current year would be compared to realistic plans or goals.
3. Managing current assets. Various measures would be used to evaluate the divisional management's achievements and reactions to changing business and economic conditions.

One division manager believed this system would overcome many inconsistencies of the current system because divisions could be evaluated from three different viewpoints. In addition, divisional managers would be able to show how they react and account for changes in uncontrollable external factors.

A second division manager was also in favor of the proposed AOS. However, she cautioned that the success of a new performance evaluation system would be limited unless it has the complete support of top management. Further, this support should be visible within all divisions. She believed that the committee should recommend some procedures that would enhance the motivational and competitive spirit of the divisions.

Required

1. Explain whether or not the proposed AOS would be an improvement over the measure of divisional performance now used by SIU Incorporated.
2. Develop specific performance measures for each of the three criteria in the proposed AOS that could be used to evaluate divisional managers.

3. Discuss the motivational and behavioral aspects of the proposed performance system. Also, recommend specific programs that could be instituted to promote morale and give incentives to divisional management.

P20-7. ROI Analysis (CMA) The Notewon Corporation is a highly diversified company that grants its divisional executives a considerable amount of authority in operating the divisions. Each division is responsible for its own sales, pricing, production, costs of operations, and the management of accounts receivable, inventories, accounts payable, and use of existing facilities. Cash is managed by corporate headquarters; all cash in excess of normal operating needs of the divisions is transferred periodically to corporate headquarters for redistribution or investment.

The divisional executives are responsible for presenting requests to corporate management for investment projects. The proposals are analyzed and documented at corporate headquarters, and the final decision to commit funds to acquire equipment, to expand existing facilities, or to invest rests with corporate management. This procedure for investment projects is necessitated by Notewon's capital allocation policy.

The corporation evaluates the performance of division executives by the ROI measure. The asset base is composed of the fixed assets employed plus working capital exclusive of cash.

The ROI performance of a divisional executive is the most important appraisal factor for salary changes. In addition, the annual performance bonus is based on the ROI results, with increases in ROI having a substantial effect on the amount of the bonus.

The Notewon Corporation adopted the ROI performance measure and related compensation procedures about ten years ago. Notewon did this to increase divisional management's awareness of the importance of the profit-asset relationship and to provide additional incentive to the divisional excutives to seek investment opportunities.

Notewon seems to have benefited from the program. The ROI for the corporation as a whole increases during the first years of the program. Although the ROI has continued to grow in each division, the corporate ROI has declined in recent years. The corporation has accumulated a sizable amount of cash and short-term marketable securities in the past three years.

Notewon's management is concerned about the increase in the short-term marketable securities. A recent article in a financial publication suggested that the use of ROI was overemphasized by some companies, with results similar to those experienced by Notewon.

Required

1. Describe the specific actions division managers might have taken to cause the ROI to grow in each division but decline for the corporation. Illustrate your explanation with appropriate examples.
2. Explain, using the concepts of goal congruence and motivation of divisional executives, how Notewon Corporation's overemphasis on the use of the ROI measure might result in the recent decline in the corporation's ROI and the increase in cash and short-term marketable securities.
3. What changes could be made in Notewon Corporation's compensation policy to avoid this problem? Explain your answer.

P20-8. ROI Analysis (CMA) The Riverside Corporation is a major regional retailer. The chief executive officer (CEO) is concerned with the slow growth of both sales and net income, as well as the subsequent effect on the trading price of the common stock. Selected financial data for the past three years are presented.

Riverside Corporation (in millions of dollars)

	19X1	19X2	19X3
1. Sales	$187.0	$192.5	$200.0
2. Net income	5.6	5.8	6.0
3. Dividends declared and paid	2.5	2.5	2.5
December 31 balances:			
4. Owners' equity	63.2	66.5	70.0
5. Debt	30.3	29.8	30.0
Selected year-end financial ratios:			
Net income to sales	3.0%	3.0%	3.0%
Investment turnover	2×	2×	2×
6. Return on equity	8.9%	8.7%	8.6%
7. Debt to total capital	32.4%	30.9%	30.0%

The CEO believes that the price of the stock has been adversely affected by the downward trend of the return on equity, the relatively low dividend payout ratio, and the lack of dividend increases. To improve the price of the stock, he wants to improve the return on equity and dividends. He believes that Riverside should be able to meet these objectives by:

1. Increasing sales and net income at an annual rate of 10 percent a year.
2. Establishing a new dividend policy calling for a dividend payout of 50 percent of earnings or $3,000,000, whichever is greater.

The 10 percent annual sales increase will be accomplished through a new promotional program. The CEO believes the present net income to sales ratio of 3 percent will be unchanged by the cost of this new program and any interest paid on new debt. He expects that Riverside can accomplish this sales and income growth while maintaining the current relationship of total investment to sales. Any capital needed to maintain this relationship that is not generated internally would be acquired through long-term debt financing. The CEO hopes that debt would not exceed 35 percent of total capital.

Required

1. Using the CEO's program, prepare a schedule showing the appropriate data for the years 19X4, 19X5, and 19X6 for the items numbered 1 through 7 on the preceding schedule.
2. Can the CEO meet all his requirements if a growth in income and sales of 10 percent per year is achieved? Explain your answer.
3. What alternative actions should the CEO consider in order to improve the return on equity and support increased dividend payments?
4. Explain the reasons the CEO might have for wanting to limit debt to 35 percent of total capital.

P20–9. ROI and Residual Income Bio-grade Products is a multi-product company manufacturing animal feeds and feed supplements. The need for a widely based manufacturing and distribution system has led to a highly decentralized management structure. Each divisional manager is responsible for production and distribution of corporate products in one of eight geographical areas of the country.

Residual income is used to evaluate divisional managers' performance. The residual income for each division equals each division's contribution to corporate profits before taxes minus a 20 percent investment charge on a division's investment base. The investment base for each division is the sum of its year-end balances of accounts receivable, inventories, and net plant fixed assets (cost minus accumulated depreciation). Corporate policies dictate that divisions minimize their investments in receivables and inventories. Investments in plant fixed assets are a joint division-corporate decision based on proposals made by divisional plant managers, available corporate funds, and general corporate policy.

Alex Williams, divisional manager for the southeastern sector, prepared the 19X1 and preliminary 19X2 budgets in late 19X0 for his division. Final approval of the 19X2 budget took place in late 19X1 after adjustments for trends and other information developed during 19X1. Preliminary work on the 19X3 budget also took place at that time. In early October of 19X2, Williams asked the divisional controller to prepare a report presenting performance for the first nine months of 19X2. The report is shown on p. 000.

Required

1. Evaluate the performance of Alex Williams for the nine months ending September 19X2. Support your evaluation with pertinent facts from the problem.
2. Identify the features of Bio-grade Products divisional performance measurement reporting and evaluating system that need to be revised if it is to reflect effectively the responsibilities of the divisional managers.

Bio-grade Products—Southeastern Sector
(000s omitted)

	19X2 Annual Budget	19X2 Nine-Month Budget[a]	19X2 Nine-Month Actual	19X1 Annual Budget	19X1 Actual Results
Sales	$2,800	$2,100	$2,200	$2,500	$2,430
Divisional costs and expenses					
Direct materials and labor	$1,064	$ 798	$ 995	$ 900	$ 890
Supplies	44	33	35	35	43
Maintenance and repairs	200	150	60	175	160
Plant depreciation	120	90	90	110	110
Administration	120	90	90	90	100
Total divisional costs and expenses	$1,548	$1,161	$1,270	$1,310	$1,303
Divisional margin	$1,252	$ 939	$ 930	$1,190	$1,127
Allocated corporate fixed costs	360	270	240	340	320
Divisional contribution to corporate profits	$ 892	$ 669	$ 690	$ 850	$ 807
Imputed interest on divisional investment (20%)	420	321[b]	300[b]	370	365
Divisional residual income	$ 472	$ 348	$ 390	$ 480	$ 442

	Budgeted Balance 12/31/X2	Budgeted Balance 9/30/X2	Actual Balance 9/30/X2	Budgeted Balance 12/31/X1	Actual Balance 12/31/X1
Division investment:					
Accounts receivable	$ 280	$ 290	$ 250	$ 250	$ 250
Inventories	500	500	650	450	475
Plant fixed assets (net)	1,320	1,350	1,100	1,150	1,100
Total	$2,100	$2,140	$2,000	$1,850	$1,825
Imputed interest (20%)	$ 420	$ 321[b]	$ 300[b]	$ 370	$ 365

[a] Bio-grade's sales occur uniformly throughout the year.
[b] Imputed interest is calculated at only 15% to reflect that only nine months or three-fourths of the fiscal year has passed.

P20-10. Segment Reporting CMA Music Teachers, Inc. is an educational association for music teachers that had 20,000 members during 19X5. The association operates from a central headquarters but has local membership chapters throughout the United States. Monthly meetings are held by the local chapters to discuss recent developments on topics of interest to music teachers. The association's journal, *Teachers' Forum,* is issued monthly and includes features about recent developments in the field. The association publishes books and reports and sponsors professional courses that qualify for continuing professional education credit. The statement of revenues and expenses for the current year is as follows:

Music Teachers Inc.
Statement of Revenues and Expenses
For the Year Ending November 30, 19X5
(000s omitted)

Revenues	$3,275
Expenses:	
Salaries	$ 920
Personnel costs	230
Occupancy costs	280
Reimbursement to local chapters	600
Other membership services	500
Printing and paper	320
Postage and shipping	176
Instructors fees	80
General and administrative expenses	38
Total expenses	$3,144
Excess of revenues over expenses	$ 131

The board of directors of Music Teachers, Inc. has requested that a segmented statement of operations be prepared showing the contribution of each revenue center (i.e., Membership, Magazine Subscriptions, Books and Reports, Continuing Education). Michelle Doyle has been assigned this responsibility and has gathered the following data prior to statement preparation.

- Membership dues are $100 per year, of which $20 is considered to cover a one-year subscription to the association's journal. Other benefits include membership in the association and chapter affiliation. The portion of the dues covering the magazine subscription ($20) should be assigned to the Magazine Subscriptions revenue center.
- One-year subscriptions to *Teachers' Forum* were sold to nonmembers and libraries at $30 each. A total of 2,500 of these subscriptions were sold. In addition to subscriptions, the magazine generated $100,000 in advertising revenue. The costs per magazine subscription were $7 for printing and paper and $4 for postage and shipping.
- A total of 28,000 technical reports and professional texts were sold by the Books and Reports department at an average unit selling price of $25. Average costs per publication were as follows.

Printing and paper	$4
Postage and shipping	$2

- The association offers a variety of continuing education courses to both members and nonmembers. The one-day courses cost $75 each and were attended by 2,400 students in 19X5. A total of 1,760 students took two-day courses at a cost of $125 for each course. Outside instructors were paid to teach some courses.

- Salary and occupancy data are as follows.

	Salaries	Square Footage
Membership	$210,000	2,000
Magazine Subscriptions	150,000	2,000
Books and Reports	300,000	3,000
Continuing Education	180,000	2,000
Corporate staff	80,000	1,000
	$920,000	10,000

The Books and Reports department also rents warehouse space at an annual cost of $50,000. Personnel costs are 25 percent of salaries.
- Printing and paper costs other than for magazine subscriptions and books and reports relate to the Continuing Education department.
- General and administrative expenses include all other costs incurred by the corporate staff to operate the association.

Doyle has decided she will assign all revenues and expenses to the revenue centers that can be:

- traced directly to a revenue center.
- allocated on a reasonable and logical basis to a revenue center.

The expenses that can be traced or assigned to corporate staff, as well as any other expenses that cannot be assigned to revenue centers, will be grouped with the general and administrative expenses and will not be allocated to the revenue centers. Doyle believes that allocations often tend to be arbitrary and are not useful for management reporting and analysis. She believes that any further allocation of the general and administrative expenses associated with the operation and administration of the association would be arbitrary.

Required

1. Prepare a segmented statement of revenues and expenses that presents the contribution of each revenue center and includes the common costs of the organization that are not allocated to the revenue centers.
2. If segmented reporting is adopted by the association for continuing usage, discuss the ways in which the information provided by the report can be utilized by the association.
3. Michelle Doyle decided not to allocate some indirect or nontraceable expenses to revenue centers because she believes that allocations tend to be arbitrary.
    a. Aside from the arbitrary argument, what reasons are often presented for not allocating indirect or nontraceable expenses to revenue centers?
    b. Under what circumstances might the allocation of indirect or nontraceable expenses to revenue centers be acceptable?

CASES

C20–1. Segment and Employee Evaluations (CMA)
Caprice Company manufactures and sells two products—a small portable office file cabinet that it has made for over fifteen years and a home and travel file introduced in 19X1. The files are made in Caprice's only manufacturing plant. Budgeted variable production costs per unit of product are as follows.

	Office File	Home & Travel File
Sheet metal	$ 3.50	—
Plastic	—	$3.75
Direct labor (@ $8 per direct-labor hour)	4.00	2.00
Variable manufacturing overhead (@ $9 per direct-labor hour)	4.50	2.25
	$12.00	$8.00

Variable manufacturing overhead costs vary with direct-labor hours. The annual fixed manufacturing overhead costs are budgeted at $120,000. A total of 50 percent of these costs are directly traceable to the Office File department, and 22 percent of the costs are traceable to the Home and Travel File department. The remaining 28 percent of the costs are not traceable to either department.

Caprice employs two full-time salespersons—Pam Price and Robert Flint. Each salesperson receives an annual salary of $14,000 plus a sales commission of 10 percent of her or his total gross sales. Travel and entertainment expense is budgeted at $22,000 annually for each salesperson. Price is expected to sell 60 percent of the budgeted unit sales for each file and Flint the remaining 40 percent. Caprice's remaining selling and administrative expenses include fixed administrative costs of $80,000 that cannot be traced to either file plus the following traceable selling expenses:

	Office File	Home & Travel File
Packaging expenses per unit	$2.00	$1.50
Promotion	$30,000	$40,000

Data regarding Caprice's budgeted and actual sales for the fiscal year ended May 31, 19X4, are presented in the following schedule. There were no changes in the beginning and ending balances of either finished-goods or work-in-process inventories.

	Office File	Home & Travel File
Budgeted sales volume in units	15,000	15,000
Budgeted and actual unit sales price	$29.50	$19.50
Actual unit sales		
Pam Price	10,000	9,500
Robert Flint	5,000	10,500
Total units	15,000	20,000

Data regarding Caprice's operating expenses for the year ended May 31, 19X4, follow.

- There were no increases or decreases in raw materials inventory for either sheet metal or plastic, and there were no usage variances. However, sheet metal prices were 6 percent above budget, and plastic prices were 4 percent below budget.
- The actual direct-labor hours worked and costs incurred were as follows.

	Hours	Amount
Office file	7,500	$ 57,000
Home & travel file	6,000	45,600
	13,500	$102,600

- Fixed manufacturing overhead costs attributable to the office file department were $8,000 above the budget. All other fixed manufacturing overhead costs were incurred at the same amounts as budgeted, and all variable manufacturing overhead costs were incurred at the budgeted hourly rates.
- All selling and administrative expenses were incurred at budgeted rates or amounts except the following items.

Non-traceable administrative expenses		$ 34,000
Promotion:		
Office files	$32,000	
Home & Travel files	58,000	90,000
Travel and entertainment:		
Pam Price	$24,000	
Robert Flint	28,000	52,000
		$176,000

Required

1. Prepare a segmented income statement of Caprice Company's actual operations for the fiscal year ended May 31, 19X4. The report should be prepared in a contribution margin format by product and should reflect total income (loss) for the company before income taxes.
2. Identify and discuss any additional analyses that could be made of the presented data that would be of value to Caprice Company.
3. Prepare a performance report for the year ended May 31, 19X4, that would be useful in evaluating the performance of Robert Flint.
4. Discuss the effects of Robert Flint's sales mix on Caprice Company's
   a. manufacturing operations.
   b. profits.

C20-2. Division Performance Evaluation—Cash Flow Approach Lee Parker is pleased that there has been increasing emphasis on liquidity and cash flow in business periodicals. He knows that earnings are significant, but he also believes that cash flows are important, especially in measuring performance of segments within a company. Parker believes that creation of a cash flow is a basic objective of business. A firm holds various types of assets that contribute to the cash flow objective (in other words, that generate more cash than is invested in the assets).

Parker is the manager of the construction division of KY Corporation. He assumed this position five years ago at the urging and request of Bruce Baird, the president of KY. There was a proposal at that time to dispose of the construction division because of its financial problems. Baird was against eliminating the division because it had been the foundation upon which the company had been built. Therefore, he chose Parker, one of his ablest and most trusted executives, to revitalize the division.

When Parker took over as the manager of the construction division, the construction industry and this division were in deep trouble because of recession and rising interest rates. Demand for working capital was heavy due to the division's short-term loan commitments as well as the seasonal nature of the industry. Customary practice in the construction industry is to preserve cash generated during late spring and the summer months to cover working capital needs during the winter and early spring, when construction is slow and the crews are just making repairs and preparing for the busy season. Although other firms in the industry lay off a part of their work force, KY Corporation does not believe in this approach. To aid Parker as he assumed responsibility for the division, working capital was provided by the corporate office.

In the ensuing years Parker was able to turn the division into a profitable operation. Particularly remarkable was the improved liquidity that substantially reduced its dependence on short-term, high interest-bearing loans. The division even generated excess cash for use by the corporate office.

In spite of this success, the division return on investment is still below the cut-off rate required of each division to justify continued commitment of corporate resources. Parker believes that, because of the nature of the construction business, his division would be better evaluated in terms of its ability to generate cash. He is convinced that some type of performance evaluation based on cash flow is highly desirable.

Required

1. Explain the difference between earnings and net cash flow.
2. Lee Parker would like to have his division's performance evaluation made on a cash flow basis. Discuss the advantages and disadvantages of cash flow as a basis for evaluation.
3. Would the statement of changes in financial position prepared for a division, using the all-financial-resources approach, be an appropriate statement to be used in a cash-flow basis evaluation for a division? Explain your answer.

C20-3. Polymer Products Company[1]

Background

In 19X4, the Polymer Products Company was a multinational company engaged in the manufacture of a widely diverse line of products, including chemical and agricultural products, synthetic fibers, electronic materials, health care, process controls, fabricated products, and oil and gas. Sales in 19X4 of $6.7 billion had the following breakdown as to operating units and major markets:

Operating Unit	Percent	Major Markets	Percent
Agricultural products	18	Agriculture	20
Biological sciences	3	Construction and home furnishing	19
Fibers & intermediates	18		
Industrial chemicals	14	Capital equipment	13
Polymer products	28	Pharmaceuticals & personal products	13
Electronic materials & fabricated products	8	Motor vehicles	9
Baker controls	8	Apparel	7
Oil & gas	3	Chemicals and hydrocarbons	7
		Other markets	12

For the past five years the firm had been restructuring its core businesses (industrial chemicals, fibers and intermediates, and polymer products) by withdrawing from those product lines that did not fit with the firm's long-term strategy or that were not expected to produce adequate long-term results.

Polymer's management carefully examined each of the various business units and was prepared to fully support those that have the potential to compete successfully in selected markets. Businesses that could not produce returns that exceed the company's cost of capital were, or will be, disposed of or shut down.

---

1. Edited by Dr. Shane R. Moriarity for the National Association of Accountants. Presented at the NAA symposium at the American Accounting Association Meetings, 1986.

As 19X5 ended, the company revised its financial reporting of operating unit segments to more closely align it with the restructuring and to better reflect the company's operations. These new operating unit segments were as follows:

Agricultural products:
  Crop chemicals
  Animal sciences
Chemicals
Electronic materials
Baker controls
Pharmaceuticals
Sweeteners
Oil and gas (This business was sold during the fourth quarter of 19X5.)

Fibers and intermediates, industrial chemicals, polymer products, and a portion of fabricated products were combined to form a new segment—chemicals. Two new segments, pharmaceuticals and sweeteners, included the acquired operations of a pharmaceutical company. The electronics business was made a separate segment, and the separations business, previously part of fabricated products, was transferred to and combined with baker controls, serving similar process control equipment markets. The former biological sciences segment was eliminated and its animal nutrition products were made part of animal sciences. The health care division was merged with the acquired company and was included in the pharmaceuticals segment.

Company Performance Measurement Philosophy

Up until the start of the decade, Polymer focused on a performance income measure of an operating unit's performance. It assigned only the directly controllable elements of sales, cost of goods sold, marketing, administrative expenses, technical expenses, inventory, and receivables to the operating units for internal reporting purposes. Elements that were not directly controllable, such as corporate staff support groups, interest expense and income, and foreign currency gains and losses were pooled corporately, and various formulas were used to assign these corporate charges to operating units for determining a pro forma net income, return on capital, and cash flow. Such overall bottom-line indicators of performance were thus only directionally representative at the operating unit level.

As some of the company's core businesses matured and declined, an awareness began to emerge of the need to shift business strategies, thus requiring tougher decisions as to divestment-investment-acquisition activities. Top management recognized the need for more accurate measurement and understanding of worldwide operating unit results.

For example, foreign currency gains and losses were treated as a component of corporate charges. Thus, if a U.S.-produced product was sold to a French customer on 180-day terms, the selling business unit reflected the full sales value at the then current exchange rate, leaving the company exposed to devaluation of the French franc. If devaluation occurred, performance of the operating unit was not affected but the overall company results were.

As another example, all operating units applied an average worldwide tax rate to compute pro forma net income, return on capital, and cash flow. When an operating unit had a choice to source the same product from Belgium or the U.K., a dilemma was created. Although costs were nominally higher in the U.K., lowering a unit's performance income, the company was in a nontax position there, which dramatically improved real net income. However, by reporting results using an average worldwide tax rate, all product sourcing from the U.K. appeared disadvantageous. Also, the company was not taking advantage of an entity's tax loss carry-forward situation in various pricing and sourcing decisions.

Top management wanted a reporting and performance measurement system that would bring to operating unit managements' attention *all* of the financial effects of a business decision. To accomplish this, it was decided in 19Y2 that as many of the income statement and balance sheet items as possible would be identified with each operating unit and charged out accordingly. Each operating unit's performance would then be measured by the achievement against goals established for return on capital and cash flow, defined as follows:

$$\text{Cash flow} = \text{Net income} + \text{Depreciation and obsolescence} - \text{Capital expenditures} + \text{or} - (\text{Changes in receivables, inventories, payables, net capitalized interest, deferred taxes, other assets, and other liabilities})$$

$$\text{Return on capital} = \frac{\text{Net income} + \text{After-tax interest expense}}{\text{Average capital employed*}}$$

$$\text{*Capital} = \text{Net fixed investment, Working capital, and Deferred taxes}$$

The incentive compensation system employed for upper management positions essentially was based on the relative success in achieving annual budgets established for the preceding measures. The total corporate annual incentive award was determined somewhat rigidly, based on where bottom-line earnings fell within a budget range determined at the beginning of each year. The award was apportioned to cascade down the organization. Thus a similar quantitative assessment of bottom-line results was made to reward or penalize managers for their ultimate contribution to results. The incentive awards were then presented ⅔ in cash and ⅓ in restricted stock that was accessible only after three years and only if stock prices met certain appreciation tests. This latter feature was recently employed to add a long-term dimension to the program in addition to near-term annual income and cash flow results.

Before this new reporting and measurement scheme (called asset management), the amount of corporately pooled costs allocated as a corporate charge was over 3 percent of worldwide sales. After the asset management program was instituted, along with selected decentralization of certain corporate staff groups, these corporately pooled costs were less than 2 percent of worldwide sales.

Required

Discuss the relative merits of the performance income measure and the asset management program as bases for the evaluation of managers' performance.

Part Five

DECISION ANALYSIS

Techniques for identifying and evaluating relevant costs in decision analysis are outlined in chapters 21 through 26. Cost data is a major input into the decision-making process and it is imperative that the costs be relevant to the decision. Product pricing is another major input into the decision. Establishing product prices for both intercompany sales as well as external sales is an important decision in itself.

    The decision to buy capital equipment is very important because of the size of the investment and because of the length of the investment's life. Capital budgeting assists in making this type of decision.

    An important decision that you must make is which, if any, professional certification to achieve. Cost and managerial accounting topics are a significant part of the examinations that must be passed in order to be a certified public accountant (CPA) or to receive a Certificate in Management Accounting (CMA).

PART FIVE: DECISION ANALYSIS

Let us use the sale of newspapers by a street vendor as an example. Assume the following facts:

Cost per paper	$0.30
Sales price per paper	$0.50

Sales statistics for a typical 200-day period:

Number Sold per Day	Number of Days	% of Total Days
97 or fewer	0	0%
98	20	10
99	40	20
100	60	30
101	50	25
102	30	15
103 or more	0	0
Totals	200	100%

How many papers should the vendor buy to maximize his or her contribution margin?

A *payoff table*, as shown in figure 21.1, can be constructed to help answer the vendor's question. Figure 21.1 shows that if the newspaper vendor purchases 100 papers, the maximum margin will be generated. Purchase of fewer than 100 or more than 100 will result in suboptimal results.

Examining the pattern of analysis and computation used in constructing this table, the following can be observed:

1. The possible margins for each day equal the number of possible papers sold multiplied by the sales price of $0.50 minus the number of possible papers purchased multiplied by the purchase price of $0.30.
2. The number sold cannot exceed the number purchased. Notice that in the first column in figure 21.1, the number purchased was 98; therefore, sales can only be 98.

FIGURE 21.1 Payoff Table—Newspaper Purchase

Possible Sales Events	Probability of Sales Events' Occurrence	Alternative Purchase Quantities (events)				
		98	99	100	101	102
98	.10	.10(98 × .20) = 1.96	.10(98 × .50 − 99 × .30) = 1.93	.10(98 × .50 − 100 × .30) = 1.90	.10(98 × .50 − 101 × .30) = 1.87	.10(98 × .50 − 102 × .30) = 1.84
99	.20	.20(98 × .20) = 3.92	.20(99 × .20) = 3.96	.20(99 × .50 − 100 × .30) = 3.90	.20(99 × .50 − 101 × .30) = 3.84	.20(99 × .50 − 102 × .30) = 3.78
100	.30	.30(98 × .20) = 5.88	.30(99 × .20) = 5.94	.30(100 × .20) = 6.00	.30(100 × .50 − 101 × .30) = 5.91	.30(100 × .50 − 102 × .30) = 5.82
101	.25	.25(98 × .20) = 4.90	.25(99 × .20) = 4.95	.25(100 × .20) = 5.00	.25(101 × .20) = 5.05	.25(101 × .50 − 102 × .30) = 4.98
102	.15	.15(98 × .20) = 2.94	.15(99 × .20) = 2.97	.15(100 × .20) = 3.00	.15(101 × .20) = 3.03	.15(102 × .20) = 3.06
Totals		19.60	19.75	19.80	19.70	19.48

Chapter 21

Decision Analysis:
Specialized Applications

Outline

UNCERTAINTY AND RISK
DECISIONS UNDER UNCERTAIN
    CONDITIONS
PROBABILITY ANALYSIS
Illustration of Probability Analysis
Expected Values and Standard Deviation
Expected Value of Perfect Information
LINEAR PROGRAMMING

Computer Solution and Sensitivity Analysis
SUMMARY
SUGGESTED READINGS
DISCUSSION QUESTIONS
EXERCISES
PROBLEMS
CASES

The basic concepts and procedures of relevant cost analysis in decision making were discussed in chapter 4. This chapter will focus on concepts and techniques for analyzing more complex decisions.

After you have completed this chapter, you should be able to:

1. explain uncertainty and risk.
2. identify situations that contain uncertainty and resource constraints.
3. demonstrate the ability to identify and apply the probability and expected value models for analyzing uncertain decisions.
4. show an understanding of linear programming and apply linear programming to decision situations.
5. perform sensitivity analysis.

UNCERTAINTY AND RISK

Decision making always involves consideration of future events, which in turn often involves *uncertainty* about results. Consider a bank loan as an example. The loan specifies an exact amount of payment for principal and interest. The amounts to be paid are certain; the main uncertainty is whether or not payments will be made by the borrower.

Many business decisions are not as certain as a bank loan. When a manager in a firm considers a future project, she or he may be uncertain about the revenue the project will generate, the costs that will be incurred, and the profit that will be earned. The levels of revenue, cost, and profit are not likely to be predictable exactly. The expected results are more likely to occur within a *range* of possibilities rather than as single precise figures.

Risk refers to the degree of exposure a decision maker bears in connection with a past or current decision. For example, the uncertainty that a banker faces in receiving payment from the borrower is the risk factor. The borrower could become unemployed and would not be able to make timely payments, or, worse still, the borrower could go bankrupt and then would not be able to make payments at all. Even though the amount of the monthly payment is fixed by contract, the risk associated with the contract is whether or not the borrower will be able to make the required payments.

This chapter focuses mainly on the processes available for dealing with uncertainty. Consideration of risk is usually covered in financial management courses.

DECISIONS UNDER UNCERTAIN CONDITIONS

When a firm makes a credit sale to a customer, the transaction price is fixed; there is no uncertainty about the amount that *should be* collected by the seller. Management of the same firm, however, faces operating areas in which there is uncertainty about the amounts to be received or paid. For example, suppose a firm is considering expansion into a new product line. Uncertainty exists about whether or not the product will sell; if it does sell, how much sales revenue can be expected; and what costs will be incurred for materials, labor, and overhead in producing and marketing the product.

Few firms have only a single product. Handling the complexity of multiple products may require special analysis to determine the best or optimal product mix. A firm also may face constraints on resource availability. There may be available only a certain quantity of material or skilled labor, allowing production of a limited number of units. Special analysis may also be needed to decide on the appropriate course of action under such conditions.

CHAPTER 21: DECISION ANALYSIS: SPECIALIZED APPLICATIONS

In the sections that follow, we will describe a model for managing uncertainty in the decision-making process. Special emphasis will be placed on probability analysis. Also, linear programming will be presented as a useful tool to assist in making various types of optimizing decisions.

PROBABILITY ANALYSIS

You will recall that the basic framework for decision analysis was introduced in chapter 4. Although complexity and uncertainty do not change the basic considerations involved in decision analysis, some special models and tools are needed to arrive at the estimates used in the basic analysis.

Probability analysis provides a method for deriving the estimates used in various types of decision problems. This method is based on the following decision-model characteristics:

1. A *quantifiable objective*. Although the objective may be expressed in many forms, the form most often used is contribution margin. The quantified objective is usually designated the *objective function*, and the various courses of action are evaluated by using the objective function, which also provides a basis for selecting the best alternative.
2. A set of specifically considered alternative *courses of action*.
3. A set of all *relevant events* that can occur (often called *states of nature*).
4. A set of *probabilities* that express the likely occurrence of each event.
5. A set of *outcomes* (referred to as *payoffs*) that measure the predicted results of the various possible combinations of actions and events. The outcomes are expressed in terms of the objective function.

Various estimates must be made in applying these characteristics. The determination of an event's probability of occurrence can be particularly troublesome. In some situations the probabilities can be fairly *objective*. For example, in a business firm, past experience with a product's manufacturing process can enable the analyst to identify a reliable predictable percentage of lost units. In other situations mathematical proofs indicate probability of each event's occurrence. The classic example is the probability of getting heads or tails in a coin toss.

Subjective probabilities must be determined in those situations in which past experience or mathematical proofs are absent. An analyst or manager may be able to estimate range of probabilities for possible events. Several analysts' estimates may differ so within the range of events.

Illustration of Probability Analysis

The objective in using probability analysis is to identify the *most likely* outcome range of possible outcomes. Some accountants and analysts get nervous about jective probabilities, but they should remember that decisions have to be made best tools available rather than by default or by the use of naive methods.

A simple example of probability analysis can be drawn from an inventor situation in which an order must be placed for a specified number of product u a sales cycle. At the end of the cycle, any unsold units are discarded or so The purchase of newspapers or Christmas trees is an example of such a situat

3. The *probabilities* of sales at the various levels are weights drawn from the sales experience from the past 200 days. Experience shows that some day's sales will be 98, some days 100, and some days as high as 102. On the average, 10 percent of the time sales will be 98 papers, 20 percent of the time sales will be 99 papers, 30 percent of the time sales will be 100, and so on.
4. Computation efficiency could be obtained by recognizing that the number sold cannot exceed the number purchased. Therefore, probabilities can be added together to save computations. In the first column, if 98 papers are purchased, only 98 can be sold. The margin produced is 98 × $0.20 (the $0.50 price minus the $0.30 cost) = $19.60. Because there is a 100-percent cumulative probability of this event occurring, the detailed breakdown of computations is unnecessary.

In the center column, if 100 papers are purchased, the sale of only 98 will generate a margin of $19 (98 × $0.50 − 100 × $0.30). With a 10-percent probability of occurrence, the *weighted* payoff is $1.90. Sale of 99 and purchase of 100 yields a weighted payoff of $3.90. From that point, because 100 are purchased, only 100 can be sold; the margin cannot exceed $20, and the remaining probabilities can be summed. The sum of .7 (i.e., .30 + .25 + .15) times the $20 possible margin gives a weighted payoff of $14. Thus the total expected payoff is $19.80 ($1.90 + $3.90 + $14).

Note that in the previous example, the probabilities used in the analysis were drawn from the vendor's *actual* experience for a 100-day period. In many decision situations, the manager and accountant will need to make the best subjective estimate of the event's probability of occurrence.

Examples of possible applications of the probability technique might include (but are not limited to) the following:

1. Cost estimates in the special order cases discussed in chapter 4.
2. Estimates of the cost of separate processing of a joint product after the split-off point (discussed in chapter 11).
3. Estimates of revenues and costs in deciding to launch a new product or to enter a new market or sales territory.
4. Estimates of the cash flows in capital expenditure decisions (discussed in chapters 23 and 24).

Expected Values and Standard Deviation

The newspaper vendor example involved a single product to be sold in a defined sales cycle. Let us consider another situation in which the decision maker needs to choose between two projects. Each project has a life cycle of one year, each is expected to cost the same, and the projects are mutually exclusive; that is, if either project is chosen, the other is excluded. The various estimated cash returns and their probability of occurrence are summarized as follows:

Project X		Project Y	
Probability	Cash Return	Probability	Cash Return
.10	$3,000	.10	$4,500
.20	4,500	.25	5,250
.40	6,000	.30	6,000
.20	7,500	.25	6,750
.10	9,000	.10	7,500

An *expected value* can be computed for each of these probability distributions. The expected value is a weighted average that uses the probabilities as weights. You will recognize the expected value as an arithmetic mean. Using the standard symbol $\overline{A}$ for the mean, the expected value of the cash returns for project X is:

$$\overline{A} = .1(3,000) + .2(4,500) + .4(6,000) + .2(7,500) + .1(9,000)$$
$$= \$6,000.$$

For project Y, the expected value is:

$$\overline{A} = .1(4,500) + .25(5,250) + .3(6,000) + .25(6,750) + .1(7,500)$$
$$= \$6,000.$$

Figure 21.2 shows a bar graph of the two projects' probability distributions.

It is evident from an examination of the graphs in figure 21.2 that the *dispersion* from the mean or expected value for the two projects is quite different, even though the expected value is the same. To assist the decision maker further, a measure of the dispersion can be supplied. You will recall that the typical measure of dispersion is the *standard deviation*. The formula for computing the standard deviation is as follows:

$$\sigma = \sqrt{\sum_{x=1}^{n} (A_x - \overline{A})^2 P_x}$$

where A_x = each respective individual value for a given project
$\overline{A}$ = expected value (i.e., the mean)
P_x = the probability of occurrence of each individual value

For project X:

$$\sigma = [0.1(3,000 - 6,000)^2 + 0.2(4,500 - 6,000)^2 + 0.4(6,000 - 6,000)^2 + 0.2(7,500 - 6,000)^2 + 0.1(9,000 - 6,000)^2]^{1/2}$$
$$= \sqrt{2,700,000}$$
$$= \$1,643.$$

For project Y:

$$\sigma = [.1(4,500 - 6,000)^2 + .25(5,250 - 6,000)^2 + .3(6,000 - 6,000)^2 + .25(6,750 - 6,000)^2 + .1(7,500 - 6,000)^2]^{1/2}$$
$$= \sqrt{731,250}$$
$$= \$855.$$

The amount of dispersion is much greater for project X than it is for project Y. It seems that, other things being equal, the decision maker will choose project Y because the risk exposure is less.

The *coefficient of variation* is another measure that frequently is computed to reflect relative dispersion. The standard deviation is divided by the mean, or expected value, to

FIGURE 21.2 Probability Distributions Projects X and Y

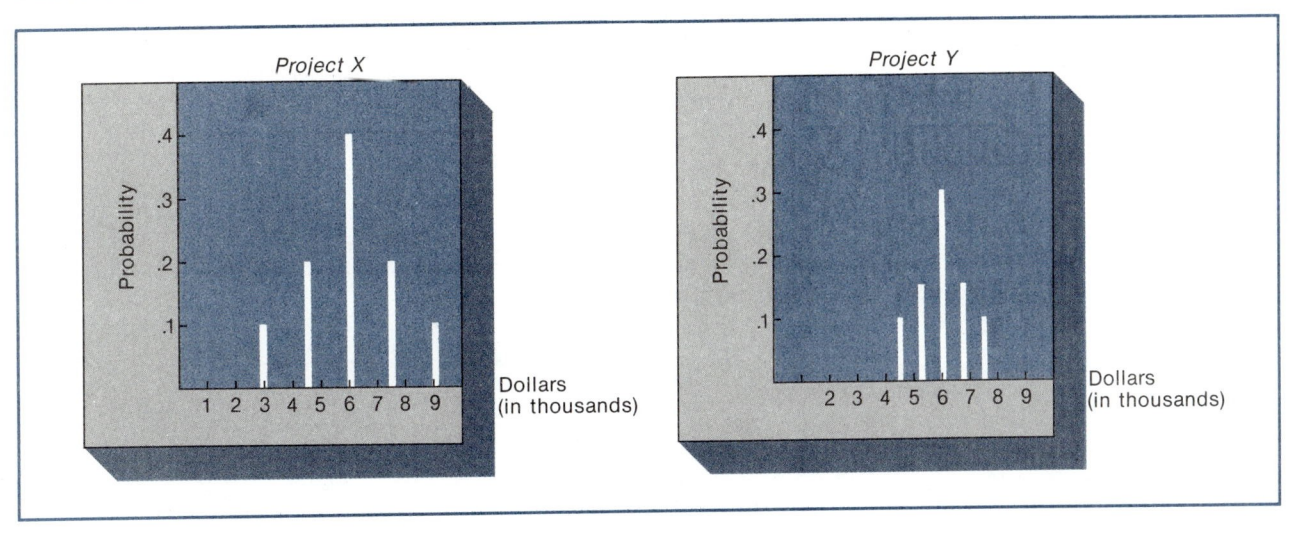

obtain this measure. For project X, the coefficient of variation is 0.27 (1,643 ÷ 6,000). For project Y, the coefficient of variation is 0.14 (855 ÷ 6,000).

We can see from these two measures that project X carries a greater risk, because the relative dispersion of values is greater than for project Y. A higher standard deviation or a higher coefficient of variation is associated with greater risk; a lower standard deviation or coefficient of variation indicates lower risk associated with the project.

Expected Value of Perfect Information

Information is viewed as a scarce resource. Because resources have both values and costs, consideration should be given to cost-benefit relationships of acquiring information. As was indicated in chapter 17, additional information should be provided as long as the marginal value of the new information exceeds its marginal cost. The value of additional information is often difficult to measure. Conceptually it is described as the improvement in management's decision that results from the new information. The cost of information is the amount paid to capture, store, process, and report it to management.

$$\text{Value of information} = \text{Benefit from improved decisions} - \text{Cost of providing information}$$

Following is a brief discussion of a process for determining the value of information.

Suppose that the Magic Toy Company is considering the manufacture of a less expensive laser target toy than the highly successful top-of-the-line model sold last season. This new model, if featured, will be offered for one season only because of expected market saturation by competitors. New equipment, which is available in two models, must be purchased to produce the new model. Such equipment will be used for the one model season only.

The new model toy can be offered in a market niche at a unit price of $20. If type M equipment is acquired for $6,000, the variable production costs are expected to be $14 per unit. Type N equipment will cost $80,000, and the variable production costs are estimated to be $6 per unit.

Demand for the new toy is uncertain. However, considering economic conditions and predictions of expected sales for the coming toy sales season, the following anticipated unit sales and probabilities have been assembled:

Sales Volume	Probability
7,000	.2
10,000	.4
13,000	.3
18,000	.1

Using procedures discussed previously, we can compute the estimated profit from the various sales demand expectations and expected values.

	Estimated Profit[a]	
Demand (units)	Purchase Type M	Purchase Type N
7,000	$ 36,000	$ 18,000
10,000	54,000	60,000
13,000	72,000	102,000
18,000	102,000	172,000

Expected values:

Type M = (36,000) (.2) + (54,000) (.4) + (72,000) (.3) + (102,000) (.1)
    = $60,600.
Type N = (18,000) (.2) + (60,000) (.4) + (102,000) (.3) + (172,000) (.1)
    = $75,400.

Now suppose it is possible to acquire information from a source that is always perfectly reliable. In other words, this source is able to accurately predict every outcome. What is the value of the information from this reliable source?

We can determine the expected value of perfect information and, in turn, how much the decision maker would be willing to pay for such information. First, compute the expected value of the course of action the decision maker would take *after* the information is obtained. In this example, if demand is 7,000 units, type M equipment would be purchased. If demand is 10,000, type N is preferred, and so on. A summary of expected values, given perfect information, is as follows:

Demand	Optimal Action	Profit	Probability	Expected Value
7,000	Type M	$ 36,000	.2	$ 7,200
10,000	Type N	60,000	.4	24,000
13,000	Type N	102,000	.3	30,600
18,000	Type N	172,000	.1	17,200
			Total	$79,000

The decision maker should view the probabilities of various demand levels and the probabilities of obtaining perfect information as being the same; that is, if the decision maker views the probability of a 10,000 unit demand as being 40 percent, the chance of receiving information to that effect should also be 40 percent.

When the expected value of $79,000 obtained with *perfect information* is compared with the $75,400 expected value of the best course of action with *existing information* we

---

[a]Unit sales × Unit price − [(Unit sales × Variable cost) + Cost of equipment]; that is, for type M and demand of 7,000 units, estimated profit = 7,000 × $20 − [(7,000 × $14) + 6,000] = $36,000.

see that the expected return increased by $3,600. This increase is the *expected value* of perfect information.

The purpose of the preceding example and discussion has been to establish a framework for assessing the value of information. Accountants and decision makers cannot assume that all information generated will produce more benefit than the cost of obtaining it. One critical consideration is deciding whether gathering the information will have any effect at all on the decision. Assessing the value of information is a challenging problem. First, one must consider whether information will make a difference in the decision process. Then, if there will be a difference, the information's value must be carefully assessed against the cost of obtaining it.

LINEAR PROGRAMMING

Linear programming is a mathematical tool used for making decisions in situations in which constraining or limiting factors are present. For example, a scarcity of raw materials, limited machine hours, or a shortage of skilled labor may be constraining factors in a production environment. Linear programming is one of the most effective tools for deciding what mix of products to produce under constrained circumstances.

Accountants and managers should know enough about linear programming to be able to *(a)* identify problem areas that could be solved with linear programming, *(b)* help formulate the objective, variables, and constraints in a particular problem situation, and *(c)* understand the solution process sufficiently well to facilitate communication with technical personnel or the computer to obtain a solution. This section provides an introduction to linear programming. Practical applications of linear programming include product mix, production scheduling, and shipping schedules.

Cost-volume-profit analysis was discussed in chapter 7. In that chapter the consideration centered on single products or simple combinations of products for which no resource or market constraints applied. In chapter 4 we discussed a simple case of product contribution margin with a time constraint. In that situation the relevant consideration was not the contribution margin per unit of product but, rather, the contribution per unit of the constraining factor, such as labor hours or machine hours. In many practical situations several constraints may apply. The problem becomes one of obtaining maximum total contribution while giving consideration to several constraints.

In using the linear programming model, the focus remains on contribution margin. In this way we avoid allocations of fixed costs, which are irrelevant in most short-run decisions.[1]

One who is familiar with the basics of mathematics understands simple linear equations. The formula for a straight line cost function, $y = a + bx$, is an example. As more complex situations are encountered, simultaneous equations are needed to solve problems. When the number of unknowns and equations increases, further solutions "by hand" become more difficult. Structuring a problem in a linear programming format and using the computer can be very helpful in these complex situations.

The challenge presented in linear programming situations lies in structuring, or modeling, the problem. The mechanics of the solution, although rigorous, are simpler with the aid of the computer. The approach we suggest is that you (as well as accountants and

---

1. A more complex model is required for situations in which fixed costs can be traced to the object under consideration. See Robert Kaplan, *Advanced Management Accounting* (Englewood Cliffs, N.J.: Prentice-Hall, 1982), Chapter 5.

managers) strive to master the modeling aspect. Leave the technicalities of the solution process to mathematicians, computer specialists, and other quantitative experts.

Consider the following situation in which linear programming can be applied. A firm produces two products, identified as X and Y. The contribution margin of product X is \$26 per unit and the contribution of product Y is \$30 per unit. It takes 6 hours of skilled labor to produce a unit of X and 9 hours of skilled labor to produce a unit of Y. The firm has only 54 hours of skilled labor available each day. It also is faced with a limited supply of an essential material used in the production of both products. Each unit of product X needs 8 pounds of this material, and each unit of Y requires 4 pounds. The daily supply of this raw material is 32 pounds.

Marketing management estimates average daily sales of 3 units of X and as many units of Y as can be produced. All other productive inputs needed for both products are in adequate supply.

The firm wants to maximize contribution margin. Management wants to know how production of the two products should be scheduled to accomplish this objective. The following steps using linear programming can be applied to answer management's questions. Note the systematic process involved in modeling the problem.

1. Determine the objective function, which is a mathematical expression that describes what the firm wants to accomplish.
2. Determine the basic relationships or constraints that specify the available feasible alternatives.
3. Determine which of the feasible alternatives provides the optimal solution.

Each of these steps is applied to the preceding data as follows:

1. *Determine the objective function.* A profit objective may be expressed in terms of minimizing costs or maximizing profits. In this situation the objective is to maximize the total contribution margin. This can be expressed mathematically as:

   Total contribution margin = \$26X + \$30Y,

   where X equals the number of X units sold per day and Y equals the number of Y units sold per day. Each is multiplied by its respective contribution margin per unit. The goal is to determine the number of X and Y units that should be produced and sold to yield the maximum total contribution margin.

2. *Determine the basic relationships or constraints that specify the available feasible alternatives.* From the data in this example, one finds that there are three types of relationships that represent constraints on the production of X and Y. First, a *labor constraint* requires 6 hours of skilled labor for each unit of X and 9 hours for each unit of Y. Because only 54 total hours are available in a day, this constraint can be expressed in mathematical form as follows:

   $6X + 9Y \leq 54$.

The inequality sign ($\leq$) indicates that total production cannot exceed 54 hours. It may be that the optimal level requires less than 54 hours, but it may not exceed 54 hours.

A *material constraint* indicates that the requirement for a particular raw material is 8 pounds per unit of X and 4 pounds per unit of Y. Because there are only 32 pounds of this particular raw material available per day, this constraint is expressed as:

$8X + 4Y \leq 32$.

Finally, a *demand constraint* indicates that an average of only 3 units of X can be sold per day. This constraint is expressed as:

X ≤ 3.

These constraints, taken together, define the feasible alternative solutions from which the optimal solution is selected. The preceding constraints can be combined graphically to obtain an area of feasible production output (see figure 21.3).

The area of feasible productive output is defined by the lines representing each constraint. For example, the labor constraint indicates that if all labor is used to produce Y (X = 0), 6 units of Y can be produced per day. On the other hand, if all labor is used to produce X (Y = 0), 9 units of X can be produced per day.

Combining all of the constraints, the optimal solution falls somewhere on the line that defines the extreme boundary of the area of feasible production output. Actually, because of the mathematical properties involved, the optimal solution is at one of the corners of the boundary of the area of feasible production output.

3. *Determine which of the feasible alternative solutions provides the optimal solution.*

   To determine which alternative provides the optimal solution, the objective function is calculated using the product mix found at each corner of the boundary of feasible production output. The product mix is found by reading values for X and Y from the graph. There are five corners in the feasible area in figure 21.3:

	Product Mix (units)	
Corner	X	Y
1	0	0
2	0	6
3	1.5	5
4	3	2
5	3	0

FIGURE 21.3

Linear Programming—Graphic Solution

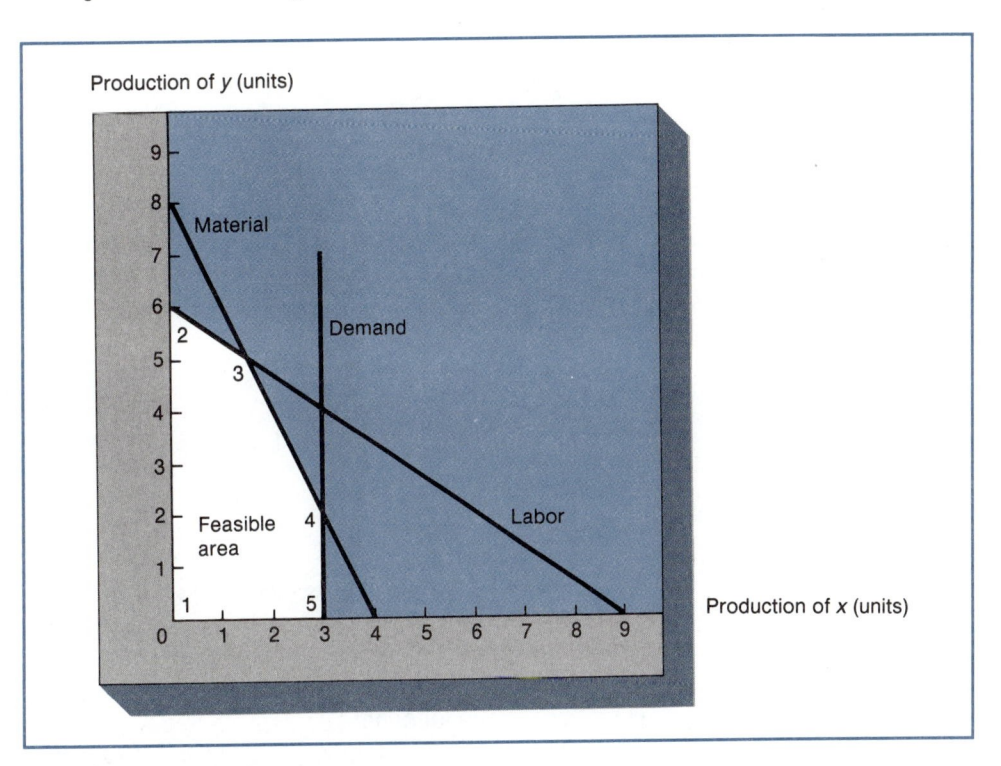

Using these values for X and Y in the objective function results in the following total contribution margins.

X	Y	Total Contribution Margin
26(0) +	30(0)	= 0
26(0) +	30(6)	= 180
26(1.5) +	30(5)	= 189
26(3) +	30(2)	= 138
26(3) +	30(0)	= 78

The firm should produce an average of 1.5 units of X and 5 units of Y each day to obtain a maximum contribution margin of \$189 per day.

Computer Solution and Sensitivity Analysis

The graphic solution approach presented previously has the advantage of enabling the decision maker to visually relate to the solution process. The approach's disadvantages are that it is time consuming and may become impractical in a complex situation with many variables. Fortunately, there is a mathematical technique, known as the *simplex method*, that provides for quick and efficient solution of any linear programming problem.

The simplex method is a step-by-step iterative process that involves solutions with sets of simultaneous equations. Although the method can be applied manually, solution by computer, which uses the simplex process, can be done very rapidly.

To illustrate the power of the mainframe computer, the basic power problem illustrated graphically in the previous section was processed on a Vax computer at a university. A program called LINDO (Linear, Interactive and Discrete Optimizer) was applied, and a solution was obtained in less than one minute.

The solution process involved the following simple steps after logging on:

1. $RUN SHR:LINDO
2. Enter the objective function and the constraints as specified in the graphic solution:
   a. Maximize $26X + 30Y$
   b. Subject to:
      1) $6X + 9Y \leq 54$
      2) $8X + 4Y \leq 32$
      3) $X \leq 3$
3. Obtain the solution. A solution print-out follows:

```
MAX     26 x + 30 y
SUBJECT TO
   2)       6 X + 9 Y <=    54
   3)       8 X + 4 Y <=    32
   4)       X <=    3
END

   LP OPTIMUM FOUND  AT STEP     2

        OBJECTIVE FUNCTION VALUE

  1)         189.000000
```

CHAPTER 21: DECISION ANALYSIS: SPECIALIZED APPLICATIONS

VARIABLE	VALUE	REDUCED COST
X	1.500000	0.000000
Y	5.000000	0.000000

The computer solution, in agreement with a graphic solution, showed that the optimal mix is 1.5 units of X and 5 units of Y. This combination produces $189 of contribution margin and is identical to the graphic solution previously shown.

The computer program output also provides *shadow prices* (shown as dual prices in the output) as follows:

ROW	SLACK	DUAL PRICES
2)	0.000000	2.833333
3)	0.000000	1.125000
4)	1.500000	0.000000

Shadow prices are measures of the contribution forgone by the firm for not having one more unit of each scarce resource available. In this illustration, another $2.83 contribution could be obtained by each increase of one hour of labor time above the present 54 hours available each day. Also, an additional $1.125 contribution would be possible for each additional pound of the scarce raw material that could be made available above the present 32 pounds. Obviously, the 54 labor hours and the 32 pounds of materials may be absolute limits. However, the computer solution gives information about obtaining additional margins if more of these scarce resources could be obtained.

The computer solution may be extended to provide information about the results of faulty estimates or the impact on the results of changes in the variables' values. We have discussed *sensitivity analysis* in previous chapters. Sensitivity analysis involves "what if" questions: for example, what if the prices of resources change?; what if sales prices change?; what if material availability changes?; or what if our estimates of the various coefficients are in error? Testing sensitivity in this illustration by the computer yields the following results:

RANGES IN WHICH THE BASIS IS UNCHANGED

COST COEFFICIENT RANGES

VARIABLE	CURRENT COEF	ALLOWABLE INCREASE	ALLOWABLE DECREASE
X	26.000000	33.999996	6.000000
Y	30.000000	9.000000	16.999998

RIGHTHAND SIDE RANGES

ROW	CURRENT RHS	ALLOWABLE INCREASE	ALLOWABLE DECREASE
2	54.000000	18.000002	18.000002
3	32.000000	8.000000	8.000000
4	3.000000	INFINITY	1.500000

The computer test for sensitivity involves an evaluation of each equation in the original data for the situation being tested. The test is accomplished by examining a given variable to identify the range of possible increases and decreases that can occur in that variable, without changing the optimal results, while the values of other variables are held constant.

The computer-generated sensitivity output indicates that, holding other coefficients constant, the $26 per-unit contribution of product X could increase by $33.99 per unit or could decrease by $6 per unit without changing the optimal solution. The $30 contribution of Y could increase by $9 per unit or decrease by $16.99 per unit without resulting in a change in the optimum.

The 54 currently available labor hours could increase or decrease by 18 hours without causing results to change. Available raw materials of 32 pounds could increase or decrease by 8 pounds before the optimal outcome would change. Finally, the number of units of product X sold, now at 3 per day, could increase by an infinite number or decrease by 1.5 units without causing a change in the optimal results.

Using the computer to solve linear programming problems provides for great efficiency, and it enables the analyst to perform tests that furnish the decision maker with additional information. The example provided here is relatively straight forward, yet the computer enhanced the solution process greatly. Use of the computer can be of even greater value as problems of increased complexity are encountered.

SUMMARY

In this chapter some of the quantitative techniques that may assist in the decision process were discussed. Probability analysis can be a valuable aid in estimating information when uncertainty exists about results. Often uncertain situations require the determination of the best or most likely outcome from a range of possible results.

Linear programming is another tool used for decision making when limiting factors are present. Many decision situations are complex, involving numerous variables and constraints that apply to several of the situation components. Linear programming techniques provide a means of analyzing such complexities to identify an optimal solution.

SUGGESTED READINGS

Chow, Chee W., and Toole, Howard R. "Make Better Decisions: Divide and Conquer." *Management Accounting* 68 (August 1986): 41.

Fasci, Martha A.; Weiss, Timothy J.; and Worrall, Robert L. "Everyone Can Use This Cost/Benefit Analysis System." *Management Accounting* 68 (January 1987): 44–47.

Hale, Jack A., and Ryan, Lanny J. "Decision Science and the Management Accountant." *Management Accounting* 60 (January 1979): 42–45.

Jablonsky, Stephen F., and Dirsmith, Mark W. "Is Financial Reporting Influencing Internal Decision Making?" *Management Accounting* 61 (July 1979): 40–45.

Kim, Suk H. "Making the Long-Term Investment Decision." *Management Accounting* 60 (March 1979): 41–49.

Smith, G. Stevenson, and Tseng, M. S. "Benefit-Cost Analysis as a Performance Indicator." *Management Accounting* 68 (June 1986): 44–49.

DISCUSSION QUESTIONS

Q21-1. Define *uncertainty*.

Q21-2. Define *risk* and contrast your definition with your definition of uncertainty in question 1.

Q21-3. Why is an understanding of uncertainty and of methods to evaluate uncertainty important to a decision maker? to an accountant?

Q21-4. List and briefly discuss some examples of decisions for which uncertainty is likely to be an important consideration.

Q21-5. Describe a decision model.

Q21-6. Identify and briefly discuss the basic characteristics of a decision model.

Q21-7. What is probability analysis?

Q21-8. Discuss the meaning of subjective probability.

Q21-9. Should probability analysis be understood by accountants, or should it be considered the exclusive domain of mathematicians and statisticians? Explain.

Q21-10. Describe and illustrate a payoff table.

Q21-11. Define *standard deviation*, *expected value*, and *coefficient of variation*, and describe the possible value of these measures to a decision maker.

Q21-12. What is the expected value of perfect information? Briefly describe how this value is determined and comment on the usefulness of such information.

Q21-13. Explain what linear programming is and identify the kinds of situations in which linear programming may be a useful tool.

Q21-14. List and briefly describe the basic steps required to formulate a problem for linear programming solution.

Q21-15. Describe the process used in the graphic solution to a linear programming problem.

Q21-16. What is sensitivity analysis in a linear programming situation? Describe how sensitivity analysis may assist a decision maker.

EXERCISES

E21-1. Probability Exercise As the accounting consultant for Leslie Company, you have compiled data on the day-to-day demand rate for product *A* and the lead time to receive product *A* from its supplier. The data are summarized in the following probability tables:

Demand for Product A

Unit Demand per day	Probability of Occurrence
0	.45
1	.15
2	.30
3	.10
	1.00

Lead Time for Product A

Lead Time in Days	Probability of Occurrence
1	.40
2	.35
3	.25
	1.00

Leslie is able to deliver product A to its customers the same day that product A is received from its supplier. All units of product A demanded but not available because of a stock-out are back-ordered and are filled immediately when a new shipment arrives.

Required

1. If Leslie reorders 10 units of product A when its inventory level is 10 units, the number of days during a 360-day year that Leslie will experience a stock-out of Product A is
    a. 0.75 days.
    b. 36 days.
    c. 10 days.
    d. 0 days.
2. The probability of a three-day lead time and of the demand for product A being nine units during that time is
    a. .00025.
    b. .10.
    c. .025.
    d. .25.

E21-2. Probability Analysis of an Investment. (CPA)

You are an investment advisor in a major bank. One of your clients wants your advice on which of two alternatives she should choose. One alternative is to sell an investment now for $10,000. Another alternative is to hold the investment three days, after which it may be sold for a certain selling price based on the following probabilities:

Selling Price	Probability
$ 5,000	.4
8,000	.2
12,000	.3
30,000	.1

Required

1. Determine the expected value of holding the investment.
2. What advice would you give the client and why?

E21-3. Probability Analysis, Expected Value, Standard Deviation, Coefficient of Variation. (CPA)

Olex Company is considering a proposal to introduce a new product, Vee. An outside marketing consultant prepared the following probability distribution describing the relative likelihood of monthly sales volume levels and related income (loss) for Vee:

Monthly Sales Volume	Probability	Income (Loss)
6,000	0.10	$ (30,000)
12,000	0.20	10,000
18,000	0.40	60,000
24,000	0.20	100,000
30,000	0.10	140,000

Required

1. Determine the expected value of additional monthly income from the introduction of the new product, Vee.

2. Determine the standard deviation of expected additional income.
3. Compute the coefficient of variation related to the introduction of Vee.
4. Explain the results of the analysis to management.

E21–4. Linear Programming Formulation
A distributor of toys is analyzing his strategy for assembling Creative Toy sets for the upcoming holiday season. He assembles two kinds of sets. The Big set is composed of 60 sticks and 30 connectors, whereas the Tot set is composed of 30 sticks and 20 connectors. An important factor for this season is that the distributor has a supply of only 60,000 connectors and 93,000 sticks. He will be able to sell all that he assembles of either set. The profit contributions are $5.5 and $3.5 per set for Big and Tot, respectively. How much should he sell of each set to maximize profit?

The formula developed by the distributor is as follows:

B = number of Big sets to assemble
T = number of Tot sets to assemble
S = number of sticks actually used
C = number of connectors actually used

Max $5.5B + 3.5T$
st
$B = 30C + 60S$
$T = 20C + 30S$
$C \leq 60,000$
$S \leq 93,000$

Required

Analyze the model for possible errors and revise it as required so that the proper solution can be derived.

E21–5. Linear Programming
DoGood Electronics produces two types of video cassette recorders (VCRs), the Alpha and the Omega. There are two production lines, one for each machine. The capacity of the Alpha production line is 60 VCRs per day. Whereas the capacity of the Omega line is 50 VCRs per day. The Alpha machine requires one hour of labor, whereas the Omega requires two labor hours. Presently there is a maximum of 120 labor hours per day that can be assigned to production of the two types of VCRs. If the profit contributions are $20 and $30, respectively, for each Alpha and Omega machine, what should be the daily production?

Required

1. Formulate the problem graphically and solve it.
2. Assume that the machines require special computer chips, of which the supply is limited to 630 per day. Alpha requires nine chips whereas Omega requires seven. Add this new constraint to your model and resolve.

PROBLEMS

P21–1. Probability Analysis, Expected Value of Perfect Information
There is a farmer who has the option of planting asparagus, beans, or corn (A, B, or C). Experience has shown that in his region, the weather for the growing season will be either cool

(20% of the time), moderate (30% of the time), or warm (50% of the time). Under each weather condition there is a profit or loss (i.e., payoff) associated with planting each crop. Assume that the farmer must select only one crop to plant and that one of the three weather conditions will prevail.

This situation can be shown by the following payoff matrix:

	Cool 20%	Moderate 30%	Warm 50%
Asparagus	40	40	10
Beans	20	30	30
Corn	5	20	40

The number in each box represents the payoff (profit).

Required

1. With only this much information on weather history, what should the farmer do?
2. Suppose a weather forecaster with a reliable reputation of 100-percent accuracy came to see the farmer and said, "For a price, I will tell you exactly which weather condition will prevail this season." How much should the farmer be willing to pay (i.e., what is the maximum amount he would rationally pay for this information)?

P21–2. Probability Analysis, Expected Value, and Perfect Information

DoGood Electronics makes VCRs. Demand is difficult to predict, but industry averages are helpful in predicting probable ranges of sales volumes. The vice president of operations must decide on whether or not to manufacture a new bottom-of-the-line VCR that will compete with the Korean models. It will sell for $200 a unit. If the VCR is produced it will be made for one season only, as new technology makes the units quickly obsolete. New equipment, which is available in two models (A or B), must be bought to produce the units, and it will be scrapped when production is halted at the end of the year.

	A	B
Cost of equipment	$50,000	$1,000,000
Variable production costs per unit	$139	$90

No matter which equipment is chosen, batches of production can be closely geared to demand so that no unsold units will be left after the season is over. The industry guides predict the following probabilities for the range of anticipated sales volume.

Sales Volume in Units	Probability
5,000	.3
10,000	.4
15,000	.2
20,000	.1

Required

1. Which equipment should be purchased if the objective is to maximize profit?
2. What sales volume would show identical profits regardless of the choice of equipment?
3. How much should DoGood be willing to pay for perfect information?

P21–3. Decision Analysis with Probability Considerations (CMA)

Jackston Incorporated manufactures and distributes a line of Christmas toys. Jackston has neglected to keep its dollhouse line current. As a result, sales have decreased to approximately 10,000 units per year from a previous high of 50,000 units. The dollhouse has been redesigned recently and is considered by company officials to be comparable to its competitors' models. Jackston plans to redesign the dollhouse each year in order to compete efficiently. Joan Blocke, the sales manager, is not sure how many units can be sold during the next year, but she is willing to place probabilities on her estimates. Blocke's estimates on the number of units that can be sold during the next year and the related probabilities are as follows:

Estimated Sales in Units	Probability
20,000	.10
30,000	.40
40,000	.30
50,000	.20

The units would be sold for $20 each.

The inability to estimate sales more precisely is a problem for Jackston. The number of units of this product is small enough that the company can schedule the entire year's sales in one production run. If the demand is greater than the number of units manufactured, sales will be lost. If demand is below supply, the extra units cannot be carried over to the next season and will be given away to various charitable organizations. The production and distribution cost estimates are as follows:

	Units Manufactured			
	20,000	30,000	40,000	50,000
Variable costs	$180,000	$270,000	$360,000	$450,000
Fixed costs	140,000	140,000	160,000	160,000
Total costs	$320,000	$410,000	$520,000	$610,000

Jackston intends to analyze the data to facilitate making a decision about the proper size of the production run.

Required

1. Prepare a payoff table for the different sizes of production runs required to meet the four sales estimates prepared by Joan Blocke for Jackston. If Jackston relied solely on the expected monetary value approach to make decisions, what size of production run would be selected?
2. Identify the basic steps that are taken in any decision process. Explain each step by reference to the situation presented in this problem and to your answer for each requirement.

P21-4. Linear Programming Analysis Universal Aviation currently is investigating the possibility of branching out from its passenger service into the small-lane airfreight business. Universal has $4,000,000 available to invest in the purchase of new twin-engined cargo aircraft. The company is considering three types of planes. Aircraft A, costing $80,000, has a 10-ton payload and is expected to cruise at 350 knots. Aircraft B can haul 20 tons of goods at an average speed of 300 knots and will cost $130,000. The third aircraft, C, is a modified form of B with provisions for a 300-knot cruising speed, a reduced capacity of 18 tons, and a cost of $150,000.

Plane A requires one pilot and, if flown for three shifts, could average 18 hours a day in the air, as could aircraft B. Although transports B and C both require a crew of two, C could average 21 hours of flying per day on a three-shift basis because of superior loading equipment. Universal's operations department currently estimates that 150 pilot-shifts will be available for each day's cargo operations.

The contributions of planes A, B, and C per ton-mile are $10, $20, and $25, respectively. Each day 3,500,000 ton-miles of shipping must be completed, but deliveries not completed by the in-house fleet can still be subcontracted to outside air carriers at a contribution of $0.20 per ton-mile. What mix of aircraft should be purchased if the company wants to maximize its contribution per day?

Notes:

- Consider a knot = 1 mile per hour.
- Ton-miles per day for the three planes are as follows:
  A. $10 \times 18 \times 350 = 63,000$ ton-miles per day
  B. $20 \times 18 \times 300 = 108,000$ ton-miles per day
  C. $18 \times 21 \times 300 = 113,400$ ton-miles per day

Required

A computer output for this model follows, but with some values scaled. Answer the following questions with reference to the output. Be sure to specify units in all of your answers.

1. Describe the optimal purchase plan and interpret the objective function value.
2. Where is the bottleneck in the system?
3. How much are 10 additional pilot-shifts worth? 20?
4. The dual (shadow) price for row 3 is $0.20 and the allowable increase is infinity. Explain.
5. How much would the contribution per ton-mile have to increase on type B planes before they should be bought?
6. Suppose the contribution for subcontracting changes from +$0.20 ton-mile to −$0.20 ton-mile. What effect would this have on your purchase decision?

P21-4. Computer Solution

```
MAX     630 A + 2160 B + 2835 C + 0.2 S
SUBJECT TO
    2)    80 A +  130 B +  150 C       <=  4000
    3)    63 A +  108 B + 113.4 C + S   =  3500
    4)     3 A +    6 B +    6 C       <=   150
END
```

```
           LP OPTIMUM FOUND   AT STEP      2

               OBJECTIVE FUNCTION VALUE

    1)          71008.0000

   VARIABLE           VALUE              REDUCED COST
       A            0.000000              788.760010
       B            0.000000              673.920166
       C           25.000000                0.000000
       S          664.999939                0.000000

    ROW              SLACK               DUAL PRICES
     2)          250.000000                0.000000
     3)            0.000000                0.200000
     4)            0.000000              468.720001

   NO. ITERATIONS =     2

       RANGES IN WHICH THE BASIS IS UNCHANGED

                   COST COEFFICIENT RANGES

   VARIABLE         CURRENT          ALLOWABLE          ALLOWABLE
                     COEF            INCREASE           DECREASE
       A          630.000000         788.760010         INFINITY
       B         2160.000000         673.920166         INFINITY
       C         2835.000000         INFINITY           673.920166
       S            0.200000          24.800001         125.200020

                    RIGHTHAND SIDE RANGES
     ROW           CURRENT           ALLOWABLE          ALLOWABLE
                     RHS             INCREASE           DECREASE
      2          4000.000000         INFINITY           250.000000
      3          3500.000000         INFINITY           664.999939
      4           150.000000          10.000000         150.000000
```

P21–5. Linear Programming Max-it Company produces products O and P. The contribution margin from O is $6 per unit; P produces $8 per unit contribution. Max-it wants to know the number of units of O and P that it should produce and sell to maximize profits.

Careful analyses by the production and marketing staffs have revealed the following characteristics of operations. Product O requires two hours to produce *and* two hours to package. P requires three hours of production time and one hour of packaging time. In each production cycle, twelve hours are available. The packaging operation has eight total hours of time available to package products O and P.

Required

1. Determine the optimal mix of products O and P that will produce the greatest contribution margin.
2. Suppose that the marketing department has just relayed information about the

maximum share of the market that Max-it can expect from Product *P*. This information indicates maximum sales of *P* to be 4 units each period. What effect, if any, will this additional information have on your answer to requirement 1?

CASES

C21–1. Linear Programming—Testing the Reliability of Inputs In November, 19X0, the Bayview Manufacturing Company was in the process of preparing its budget for 19X1. As the first step, it prepared a pro forma income statement for 19X0 based on the first ten months' operations and revised plans for the last two months. This income statement, in condensed form, was as follows:

Sales		$3,000,000
Materials	$1,182,000	
Labor	310,000	
Factory overhead	775,000	
Selling and administrative expenses	450,000	2,717,000
Net income before taxes		$ 283,000

These results were better than were expected and operations were close to capacity, but Bayview's management was not convinced that demand would remain at present levels and hence had not planned any increase in plant capacity. Its equipment was specialized and made to order; more than a year's lead-time was necessary on all plant additions.

Bayview produces three products. Sales, broken down by product, were as follows:

100,000 units of product A @ $20.00	$2,000,000
40,000 units of product B @ 10.00	400,000
20,000 units of product C @ 30.00	600,000
	$3,000,000

Management ordered a profit analysis for each product and had available the following information:

	A	B	C
Materials	$ 7.00	$ 3.75	$16.60
Labor	2.00	1.00	3.50
Factory overhead	5.00	2.50	8.75
Selling and administrative expenses	3.00	1.50	4.50
Total costs	$17.00	$ 8.75	$33.35
Selling price	20.00	10.00	30.00
Profit	$ 3.00	$ 1.25	($ 3.35)

Factory overhead has been applied on the basis of direct-labor costs at a rate of 250 percent. Management asserts that approximately 20 percent of the overhead is variable and does vary with labor costs. Selling and administrative costs have been allocated on the basis of sales at the rate of 15 percent; approximately one-half of this is variable and does vary with sales in dollars. All of the labor expense is considered to be variable.

As the first step in the planning process, the sales department was asked to make estimates of what it could sell; these estimates were reviewed by the firm's consulting economist and by top management. They were as follows:

Product A	130,000 units
Product B	50,000 units
Product C	50,000 units

Production of these quantities was immediately recognized as being impossible. Estimated cost data for the three products, each of which requires activity by both departments, were based on the following production rates:

	Product A	Product B	Product C
Department 1	2 per hour	4 per hour	3 per hour
Department 2	4 per hour	8 per hour	4/3 per hour

Practical capacity in department 1 was 67,000 hours and in department 2 was 63,000 hours. The industrial engineering department concluded that this could not be increased without the purchase of additional equipment. Thus, although last year department 1 operated at 99 percent of its capacity and department 2 at 71 percent of capacity, anticipated sales would require operating both departments 1 and 2 at more than 100 percent capacity.

The following solutions to the limited production problem were rejected: (1) subcontracting the production out to other firms was considered to be unprofitable because of problems of maintaining quality; (2) operating a second shift was impossible because of a shortage of labor; (3) operating overtime would create problems because a large number of employees are moonlighting and would therefore refuse to work more than the normal 40-hour week; and (4) price increases also were rejected. Although they would result in higher profits this year, the long-run competitive position of the firm would be weakened, resulting in lower profits in the future.

The treasurer then suggested that product C had been carried at a loss for too long and that it was the time to eliminate it from the product line. If all facilities were used to produce A and B, profits would increase.

The sales manager objected to this solution because of the need to carry a full line. In addition, she maintained that there was a group of customers who provided and would continue to provide a solid base for the firm's activities and that these customers' needs had to be met. The sales manager provided a list of these customers and their estimated purchases (in units), which were as follows:

Product A	80,000 units
Product B	32,000 units
Product C	12,000 units

Although it was impossible to verify these contentions, they appeared to be reasonable, and because they served to narrow the bounds of the problem, the president concurred.

The treasurer reluctantly acquiesced but maintained that the remaining capacity should be used to produce A and B. Because A produced 2.4 times as much profit as B, he suggested that the production of A (in excess of the 80,000 unit minimum set by the sales manager) should be 2.4 times that of B (in excess of the 32,000 unit minimum set by the sales manager).

The production manager made some quick calculations and said that this would result in budgeted production and sales as follows:

Product A	104,828 units
Product B	42,344 units
Product C	12,000 units

The treasurer then made a calculation of what profits would be. It was as follows:

Product A	104,828 @ $3.00	$314,484
Product B	42,344 @ $1.25	52,930
Product C	12,000 @ ($−3.35)	(−40,200)
		$327,214

As this would represent an increase of almost 15 percent over the current year, there was a general feeling of self-satisfaction. Before final approval was given, however, the president said that she would like to have her new assistant check over the figures. The treasurer agreed, and at that point the group adjourned.

The next day the preceding information was submitted to you as your first assignment on your new job as the president's assistant. Prepare an analysis showing the president what she should do.

Figures 21.4 and 21.5 contain information that you were able to obtain from the accounting system.

FIGURE 21.4

Bayview Manufacturing Co. Direct-Labor and Overhead Expense

	Direct-Labor Expense (000s omitted)			Overhead Expense (000s omitted)		
Year	Dept. 1	Dept. 2	Total	Dept. 1	Dept. 2	Total
19X0	$140	$170	$310	$341	$434	$775
19W9	135	150	285	340	421	762[a]
19W8	140	160	300	342	428	770
19W7	130	150	280	339	422	761
19W6	130	155	285	338	425	763
19W5	125	140	265	337	414	751
19W4	120	150	270	335	420	755
19W3	115	140	255	334	413	747
19W2	120	140	260	336	414	750
19W1	115	135	250	335	410	745

[a]Rounding error

FIGURE 21.5

Bayview Manufacturing Co. Sales (000s omitted)

Year	Product A	Product B	Product C	Total	Selling and Administrative Expenses
19X0	$2,000	$400	$600	$3,000	$450
19W9	1,940	430	610	2,980	445
19W8	1,950	380	630	2,960	445
19W7	1,860	460	620	2,940	438
19W6	1,820	390	640	2,850	433
19W5	1,860	440	580	2,880	437
19W4	1,880	420	570	2,870	438
19W3	1,850	380	580	2,810	434
19W2	1,810	390	580	2,780	430
19W1	1,770	290	610	2,670	425

C21-2. Probability Analysis—Selection of Decision Rule Management of Ace Computer Company is trying to decide whether to open a retail computer store on the corner of 500 South Main Street, or on the corner of 300 West Center Street, or not to open another store at all. Thinking that it needed to have additional information, management formulated a task force, which studied traffic flow and interviewed people in each area to assess their propensity to buy computer hardware and or software. The task force studied competitors and other market conditions in the general vicinity. Its report contained the following:

1. Alternative decisions:
   a. 500 South Main—Open store at this location.
   b. 300 West Center—Open store at this location.
   c. No new store—Do not open another computer store.
2. Environment or likely state of nature: The task force identified three possible business environments and the probabilities associated with each:
   a. As is—No new competitor computer stores will open in the area and no change will occur in traffic flow (50 percent probability).
   b. New competitor store—A competitor may open a computer store in the same area (30 percent probability).
   c. Street improvement—The city may make major repairs on Main Street, which will substantially increase traffic flow (20 percent probability).
3. Summary of the monthly profit (loss) associated with each combination of alternatives and states of nature, as follows:

Alternatives	As Is (50%)	New Competitor Store (30%)	Street Improvement (20%)
500 South Main	4,000	(8,000)	12,000
300 West Center	9,000	(10,000)	5,000
No new store	0	(3,000)	(1,000)

Notice that if management opens a retail outlet on the corner of 500 South Main Street and the environment remains constant, it expects an increase in profit of $4,000 per month. If management does not open a new store and a competitor opens a new store, it expects to lose $3,000 per month from the loss of business.

Required

1. On the basis of the information gathered by the task force, what decision would you recommend to management, and why? (Consider only the information gathered by the task force as presented here.)
2. What additional analysis might be made with the information available? What recommendation would you make to management on the basis of the results of additional analysis?

Chapter 22

Transfer and Product Pricing

Outline

DEFINITION AND COMPARISON OF TRANSFER AND PRODUCT PRICING
PRICING FOR INTRACOMPANY TRANSFERS
Alternative Approaches to Establishing Transfer Prices
  Market Price
  Full Cost
  Variable Cost
  Variable Cost plus Opportunity Cost
  Dual Transfer Prices
  Negotiation
Accounting Entries for Intracompany Transfers
Other Objectives to Transfer Pricing
PRICING FOR PRODUCT SALES
Alternative Cost-Based Approaches to Product Pricing
  Rate of Markup or Gross Margin
  Markup on Variable Cost
  Markup on Conversion Cost
  Cost-Plus Pricing
  Rate of Return on Assets Employed
Considerations for Modification of Cost-Based Prices
  Past versus Future Orientation
  Standard Costs
  Volume Changes
SUMMARY
SELF-STUDY PROBLEMS
  Transfer Pricing
  Product Pricing
SUGGESTED READINGS
DISCUSSION QUESTIONS
EXERCISES
PROBLEMS
CASES

Pricing, in any of its forms, is a complex subject that requires consideration of a number of interrelated factors. Economic theory, statistical analysis, market research, engineering estimates, accounting information, and management judgment are all part of the pricing decision. Cost accounting information is especially important in pricing decisions, because a firm's profitability and long-run viability depend on an appropriate relationship between revenues and costs. Because cost accounting information can range from objective historical costs to estimates of future costs that defy objective measurement, accountants and managers should understand how various types of cost accounting information relate to the pricing decision.

This chapter explains two general areas of pricing—pricing for intracompany transfers and pricing for product sales. After you have completed this chapter, you should be able to:

1. define the role of cost accounting information in pricing goods and services for intracompany transfers and external sales.
2. implement various approaches to establishing transfer prices.
3. account for intracompany transfers.
4. implement various approaches to setting prices for sales to external parties.
5. apply certain principles that might lead to modifications in cost-based prices.

DEFINITION AND COMPARISON OF TRANSFER AND PRODUCT PRICING

There are two general categories of pricing decisions—pricing for intracompany transfers, which is called transfer pricing, and pricing for sales to parties outside the company, which is called product pricing. **Transfer pricing** refers to the assignment of monetary values to goods and services exchanged among subdivisions of an organization. Transfer pricing becomes a relevant consideration when a company is decentralized and divided into relatively autonomous subunits that are usually free to transact business outside as well as inside the company. For example, consider a company that is made up of a number of product divisions, two of which are the refrigeration and electronics divisions. The refrigeration division may acquire needed components either from the electronics division of the company or from outside suppliers. If acquired from the electronics division, the monetary values assigned to the components in such intracompany transfers are termed transfer prices.

On the other hand, **product pricing** refers to the assignment of monetary values to goods and services exchanged with parties external to an organization. For example, if the electronics division in the preceding situation also sells components to others outside the company, the monetary values assigned to components in such transactions are called product prices.

The reason for differentiating between transfer and product pricing is that different management, economic, and cost accounting principles apply in each situation. For example, transfer pricing is only relevant when goods and services are transferred from one subunit of a company to another. However, product pricing is relevant whenever goods and services are sold to external parties.

PRICING FOR INTRACOMPANY TRANSFERS

Transfer pricing is important when relatively independent operating units of a company engage in intracompany transfers of goods and services. However, it is especially important when a company uses segment performance measures, as discussed in chapter 20, to evaluate the functions of the operating units engaging in intracompany transfers. Transfer pricing is important because when intracompany transfers occur, the finished output of one or more subunits becomes the input or raw material of one or more other subunits. This means that the *revenue* of one subunit becomes a *cost* of another subunit. Therefore, the prices used to value intracompany transfers influence the income and costs reported by each subunit. Because there is such a direct linkage between segment performance measures and transfer prices, it is important that transfer prices are set at values that provide appropriate incentives to division managers, encourage goal congruence in management decisions, and foster the desired level of autonomy among segments.

A primary consideration for determining what may be an appropriate transfer price is the degree to which authority and responsibility are delegated to subunit managers. In cost center situations, in which subunit managers are responsible only for costs and not for revenues, transfers of goods and services from one cost center to another may be made at a transfer price equal to the total costs accumulated to date. However, in profit center and investment center environments, in which subunit managers are given responsibility for revenues as well as costs, a cost-based transfer price may not be satisfactory.

This is especially true in situations in which subunit managers have the freedom to buy and sell goods and services to parties external as well as internal to the firm. In such situations, a cost-based transfer price may provide a poor guide to performance evaluation and may even result in suboptimization of company operations. For example, consider a large computer manufacturer that operates a number of component divisions and several assembly divisions. The component divisions make various subassemblies that can either be sold to other computer manufacturers or transferred to one of the company's assembly divisions. Assume that the company is not operating at full capacity.

The assembly divisions acquire needed subassemblies either from outside suppliers or from one or more of the company's component divisions. The following information relates to one subassembly made by a component division that is used in at least one of the company's assembly divisions.

	Cost per Subassembly
Materials	$ 400
Labor	100
Overhead (70% variable)	1,000
Total	$1,500

Management of the component division may think that an appropriate transfer price would be one that at least covers the full cost of production of subassemblies. Accordingly, the component division may set its transfer price at $1,500 per unit. However, the outside purchase price available to the assembly division for an identical subassembly is $1,400—$100 less than it would cost if acquired from the company's component division. Given a transfer price of $1,500, the assembly division manager would be inclined to purchase from the outside supplier because of the apparent cost saving. From a total company viewpoint, the subassembly should be acquired from the component division, because the purchase price is greater than the variable or differential costs incurred in the component division, as illustrated here:

Total cost to the company to purchase externally		$1,400
Costs to the company to transfer internally:		
Materials	$400	
Labor	100	
Variable overhead	700	
Total		1,200
Difference (extra cost to purchase externally)		$ 200

If the assembly division purchases these particular subassemblies from an outside supplier, the entire company's net income will be $200 less for each unit purchased. This situation illustrates a typical dilemma in decentralized organizations and also points out the importance of appropriate transfer pricing policies. Should the assembly division be allowed to purchase the subassemblies from outside suppliers? On the one hand, top management may want to preserve the autonomy of division managers by not interfering in such situations. On the other hand, completely decentralized decision making when such suboptimization could occur is usually not acceptable to top management.

What is needed is a transfer pricing policy that simultaneously accomplishes a number of objectives. First, a transfer pricing policy should motivate subunit managers to fulfill overall company goals and objectives. Second, transfer prices should provide a fair, equitable, and objective basis for evaluation when profit performance is involved. Finally, transfer pricing policies should foster a desired level of autonomy among subunits of the business.

With intracompany transfers, the interests of both the buyer and the seller as well as top management should be considered. An advantage given to any one of these parties may result in a disadvantage to another. The behavioral aspects of this problem become even more apparent when one considers the position of a division manager who is paid a bonus based on the division's profit performance or return on investment. Under such circumstances, division managers are motivated to keep prices high for what is transferred out and to pay the lowest price for what is transferred in. As illustrated in the previous example, division managers motivated in this way may make decisions that are good for the division but detrimental to the company as a whole. The assembly division manager is motivated to purchase the component from an outside supplier, because it will increase the division's net income and, in turn, will increase any bonus based on profitability. However, suboptimization will occur if this course of action is allowed. Perhaps a transfer price based on something other than the full cost of production would be more appropriate in this situation.

For example, a transfer price of $1,400, the outside purchase price, may solve the dilemma. First, a transfer price of $1,400 makes the assembly division management indifferent about the price for the subassemblies. Therefore, the likelihood of keeping the subassembly business within the company accomplishes the first objective of goal congruence. Second, the component division is unlikely to sell any subassemblies to external buyers at a price higher than $1,400 because of the external competition. Therefore, the second objective of transfer pricing is accomplished. To recognize the interdependence of the two divisions, however, the $200 contribution to fixed costs earned by the component division with a transfer price of $1,400 might be allocated between the component and assembly divisions. This procedure would result in an ultimate transfer price of $1,300, calculated as follows:

Transfer Price as Viewed by the Assembly Division

Transfer price based on external market price	$1,400
Less: Shared portion of contribution to fixed costs (one-half of $200)	(100)
Transfer price to internal divisions	$1,300

Transfer Price as Viewed by the Component Division

Total variable costs to internal divisions	$1,200
Plus: Shared portion of contribution to fixed costs (one-half of $200)	100
Transfer price to internal divisions	$1,300

The third objective of autonomy is accomplished through top management formulating a transfer pricing policy that allows division managers to exercise their own decision prerogative and, at the same time to foster overall company goals.

The transfer pricing policies implicit in the previous example illustrate a possible solution in one situation for one firm. However, there are diverse types of situations and a number of alternative approaches to establishing appropriate transfer prices. Several commonly used approaches are discussed in the following section to provide you with a basis for formulating transfer pricing policies in various situations.

Alternative Approaches to Establishing Transfer Prices

There is no all-pervasive rule for establishing appropriate transfer prices. Accounting policies, objectives of transfer pricing, and the diverse nature of business operations make it unlikely that a single approach will satisfy all prerequisites in every situation. Therefore, a number of possible approaches to setting transfer prices have been developed and are used in various business situations. Armed with this background and a repertoire of possible transfer pricing methods, accountants should be well equipped to advise top management on transfer pricing policies.

Market Price The **market price** approach to setting transfer prices uses the prevailing price in external markets at the time the transfer is made. A discount from the market price is usually given to recognize any economies that result from making intracompany transfers. When a number of alternative transfer prices are being considered, the market price establishes a ceiling for all possible transfer prices. Although lower prices may be justified, prices higher than those available in a competitive market rarely are justified. The following are the advantages of using market prices:

1. Arm's-length transactions in the open market are approximated.
2. Subunit autonomy is fostered.
3. Equity is promoted in the evaluation of profit performance.
4. Better control is provided for the source of supply and the quality of products.

The following are the disadvantages of using market prices:

1. Quoted prices may not apply because of differences in quality, quantity, credit, and delivery terms.
2. Dumping or distress prices may cause artificially low market prices.
3. Accounting for transfers is more complex because a profit or loss element is introduced into the system.
4. The actual cost of finished goods is more difficult to determine.

When there is a perfectly competitive external market for the goods or services being transferred, most decentralized companies that use profit performance as an evaluation criterion find that market prices provide an optimal transfer price. Under conditions of perfect competition and profit performance evaluation, all transfer pricing objectives are met when market prices are used. First, the autonomy of subunits is fostered, because market prices approximate an arm's-length transaction as if external parties are dealing with both subunits. Second, because there is usually a profit component in market prices, they provide an appropriate measure when subunits are either profit or investment centers. Finally, overall company goals are usually met when using market prices because there is little chance of suboptimization. This is so because when suboptimization occurs, someone in the external market is selling at a price below differential manufacturing costs. In perfectly competitive markets there is no incentive for a firm to engage in such a pricing activity, because it can sell all of its product at a price that usually covers differential manufacturing costs plus a profit component.

Full Cost Full cost transfer pricing is probably the oldest method and the most widely used when organizations are relatively centralized. **Full cost** transfer pricing includes actual fixed and variable manufacturing costs. A portion of selling and administrative costs may also be added to manufacturing costs for transfer pricing purposes. The following are the advantages of using full cost transfer prices:

1. Data are readily available in existing accounting records.
2. The method is easy to understand and apply, because there are no intracompany profits involved.
3. The costing of finished goods is simplified.
4. Transferred costs may be used to measure production efficiency when compared with budgeted costs.

The following are the disadvantages of using full cost transfer pricing:

1. Measuring profit performance of relatively autonomous subunits is not possible because profits are not included as part of intracompany transfers.
2. The producing subunit may not be motivated to control costs that are to be transferred to other subunits.
3. The objectivity required in segment performance evaluation is lacking because there is no attempt to simulate an arm's-length transaction.
4. Suboptimization may occur if the transferring subunit is not operating at full capacity.

In relatively centralized organizations, full cost transfer pricing may promote management objectives. However, the disadvantages of the full cost approach are such that full cost is not an appropriate transfer pricing method in decentralized organizations. Full costs do not offer a sound basis for management to delegate authority to relatively autonomous subunits of a business and do not provide an accurate guide for decision making under conditions of decentralization. Although the use of cost accounting information as the only basis for setting transfer prices may provide an acceptable short-run measure, it does not incorporate a firm's long-range profitability objectives.

To overcome some of these difficulties, *standard full cost* and *full cost plus a markup* are possible alternative transfer pricing methods. If appropriate care is exercised in setting standards, standard full costs will eliminate the problem of production inefficiencies being passed on by transferring subunits. Standard full cost pricing also promotes planning and timely decision making, because it removes any uncertainty about the prices of goods or services transferred during the budgetary period.

Full cost plus a markup used as a transfer price is intended to provide an artificial market price for making transfers. When it is believed that incorporating actual market prices is too costly or when prevailing market prices are perceived as being unrealistic, full cost plus a markup may provide a good practical substitute for using market prices. However, this approach not only passes on inefficiencies associated with the manufacturing process, but it also encourages inefficiencies. The higher the cost, the higher the profit because of the automatic markup added to cost. Thus employees are rewarded for their inefficiencies.

Variable Cost A variable cost approach to transfer pricing uses actual variable manufacturing costs as the transfer price. In some situations a portion of variable selling and administrative costs may also be included in the transfer price. When considering a range of possible transfer prices, variable cost usually provides the floor or lowest price at which intracompany transfers should be made.

Variable cost transfer pricing has the major advantage of promoting the best utilization of facilities in the short run because contribution margin becomes the focus of attention. As was discussed more fully in chapter 4, contribution margin is especially useful for making management decisions because total fixed costs remain the same in the short run. Fixed costs cannot be ignored in the long run, however, because all costs must be covered to yield a profit. Therefore, transfer prices based on variable costs should be used with caution if there is danger that they may indicate a profitable situation in the short run but encourage unprofitable operations in the long run.

The major disadvantage of variable cost transfer pricing is that it is a cost-based approach that inherits many of the same weaknesses as full cost transfer pricing. To help overcome some of these weaknesses, several refinements to the basic approach might be considered. For example, *standard variable costs* may deal with the problem of cost inefficiencies being passed on to receiving subunits. Also, *variable cost plus a lump sum* based on monthly or annual activity may be used to approximate covering full costs plus a profit. Other objections concerning the lack of a profitability measure may be overcome by allocating the profit received by the selling subunit back to transferring subunits based on some equitable measure of subunit activity. Remember that all allocation methods are arbitrary, however. A variety of methods could be used, each having a different effect on the performance of the segment and segment management, and each method could be equally justified. Decisions made from arbitrarily allocated numbers can always be questioned.

Variable Cost plus Opportunity Cost A transfer price based on the selling unit's variable cost per unit and the opportunity cost associated with outside sales provides the correct incentive for managers, and it results in optimum profitability for the company as a whole. **Opportunity cost** is defined as the cost or value of an opportunity forgone when one course of action is chosen over another. It is not an out-of-pocket cost, or even a future cost associated with the selected alternative, but represents the lost opportunity associated with each of the alternatives that are rejected. *When a product is transferred internally, the opportunity cost is the lost contribution margin per unit on outside sales*. The formula can be expressed as follows:

Transfer price = Variable cost per unit + Lost contribution margin per unit on outside sales

The following examples illustrate this formula and compare the results to cost-based and market-based transfer prices.

Richfield, Inc. has two divisions, a parts division and an assembly division. The assembly division has developed a new Datamonitor that requires a special storage unit. The parts division currently manufactures a storage unit with the following costs and revenues:

Variable cost per unit	$16
Units per year	70,000 units
Sale price per unit (externally)	$30
Fixed costs per year	$420,000

Expected cost and revenue data for the Datamonitor manufactured and sold by the assembly division follow:

Variable costs per unit (in addition to the storage unit)	$27
Units per year	70,000 units
Sale price per unit	$70
Fixed costs per year	$630,000

Let's make several different assumptions about capacity, availability of market prices, and similarity between the storage units currently manufactured and those desired by the assembly division to see their effects on the best transfer price.

Assumption #1 The storage unit currently manufactured meets the specifications for the Datamonitor to be produced by the assembly division. There is also a well-established market for storage units with a market price of $30 each.

The correct transfer price in this situation is obviously $30. This is the price the assembly division would have to pay an outside supplier, and it is the price the parts division can obtain by selling to outside customers. This is also the price established using the variable cost plus opportunity cost transfer price formula:

$$\begin{aligned}\text{Transfer price} &= \$16 + (\$30 - \$16) \\ &= \$16 + \$14 \\ &= \underline{\$30}\end{aligned}$$

The lost contribution margin is the contribution margin per unit lost to the parts division as a result of giving up outside sales: $30 sale price minus $16 variable cost equals a $14 contribution margin.

When there is a well-established market and the units are compatible (homogeneous), the market price provides the optimal transfer price. The buying division should purchase internally as long as the selling division sells at the market price. Otherwise, the buying division should be allowed to purchase externally. The selling division should be free to sell to outside customers, particularly at a price equal to or above the established market.

Assumption #2 Although the storage unit currently manufactured meets the specifications for the Datamonitor to be produced by the assembly division, there is *not a well-established market* for storage units. The parts division can sell them for $30 because of a well-established customer list and long-term contracts, but the assembly division can purchase them for $25 from a new vendor who is cutting prices to establish new customer relations. Let's also assume that the parts division is at *full capacity* of 70,000 units per year.

The central issue under this assumption is whether or not the parts division should sell its output to the assembly division and match the pricing offer received from the outside vendor. The deciding point is the fact that the parts division is at maximum capacity. With the selling division at maximum capacity, the transfer price should be based on its variable cost and opportunity cost. Otherwise, profitability of the selling division and of the company as a whole will be suboptimal.

The results of selling the units internally, versus having the parts division sell externally for $30 and the assembly division acquire externally for $25, are as follows. Notice that the company is $350,000 better off by selling and buying externally.

well as the company's as a whole. The exact transfer price will largely be determined by the negotiating ability of the department supervisors.

The following chart compares the outcome of a negotiated transfer price of $20 with the outcome that would occur if the assembly division acquired the parts externally for $25. A hard line approach by the parts department supervisor requiring $30 per unit for internal transfers, and thereby forcing the assembly department to acquire externally, leaves the company $630,000 worse off.

Parts Division	Internal Sale (000s omitted)	External Sale (000s omitted)
Sales (70,000 @ $30)	$2,100	$2,100
(70,000 @ $20)	1,400	
Variable costs (140,000 @ $16)	2,240	
(70,000 @ $16)		1,120
Fixed costs	420	420
Division profit	$ 840	$ 560

Assembly Division	Acquire Internally (000s omitted)	Acquire Externally (000s omitted)
Sales (70,000 @ $70)	$4,900	$4,900
Storage units (70,000 @ $20)	1,400	
(70,000 @ $25)		1,750
Variable costs (70,000 @ $27)	1,890	1,890
Fixed costs	630	630
Division profit	$ 980	$ 630
Total company profit	$1,820	$1,190

Assumption #4 The storage units currently manufactured by the parts division *do not meet the specifications* for the Datamonitor. The assembly division can buy a storage unit externally for $20 per unit that meets the specifications. The parts division is at full capacity, but it could convert its production process by discontinuing production of the old storage unit and produce the 70,000 storage units to the Datamonitor's specifications. The variable cost for the new storage unit would be $12, a $4 reduction from the $16 variable cost on the current storage unit.

At issue here is whether the parts division should discontinue production for external sales and produce the storage units required by the assembly division. Analysis of the cost data make the switch seem desirable. The variable costs to the parts division for the new storage unit are only $12 per unit, compared to $16 for the old storage unit. Also, the assembly division would have to pay $20 per unit to acquire them externally. However, this type of cost-based analysis omits the opportunity cost associated with the internal transfer.

The statements that follow show both division and company profit and compare internal sale and acquisition with external acquisition and sale. The internal sale and acquisition assumes that the parts division converts the production process and sells 70,000 units to the assembly division for $18, the full cost of production ($12 variable cost + $6 fixed cost per unit). The external sale and acquisition assumes that the parts division continues to produce and sell the old storage unit for $30 each, and the assembly division acquires the new storage units for $20 each from the outside vendor. Notice that total company profit is $420,000 less if the storage units are manufactured and sold internally. Notice also that the cost-based approach to analyze the desirability of the transfer and to establish the transfer price resulted in a bad decision. The cost-based approach has no built-in mechanism to determine when an internal transfer should or should not take place.

Parts Division	Internal Sale (000s omitted)	External Sale (000s omitted)
Sales (70,000 @ $25)	$1,750	
(70,000 @ $30)		$2,100
Variable costs (70,000 @ $16)	1,120	1,120
Fixed costs	420	420
Division profit	$ 210	$ 560

Assembly Division	Acquire Internally (000s omitted)	Acquire Externally (000s omitted)
Sales (70,000 @ $70)	$4,900	$4,900
Storage units (70,000 @ $25)	1,750	1,750
Variable costs (70,000 @ $27)	1,890	1,890
Fixed costs	630	630
Division profit	$ 630	$ 630
Total company profit	$ 840	$1,190

The variable cost plus opportunity cost transfer price formula provides the correct incentive to managers of both divisions. Because the parts division is at full capacity, whatever it manufactures and sells to the assembly division takes away $14 of contribution margin from outside sales. The price established using the transfer price formula is $30:

Transfer price = $16 + ($30 − $16)
= $30

The parts division should use this formula to set a $30 price for internal transfers to the assembly division. Because the assembly division can acquire the units externally for $25, its segment profit, as well as firm profit, will be maximized by doing so. Therefore, the buying division should be allowed to purchase externally. The selling division should also be allowed to sell externally because of the higher price it can obtain.

Assumption #3 The storage unit currently manufactured meets the specifications for the Datamonitors to be produced by the assembly division. A *well-established market does not exist;* the parts division is selling all the storage units it can for $30, but the assembly division can buy them for $25 as described previously in assumption 2. Now let's assume that the parts division is at *50 percent of capacity,* so it could continue to service its outside customers as well as meet the demand for storage units required by the assembly division.

The key here is that the parts department has underutilized capacity. The opportunity cost to the parts division for producing an additional 70,000 units and selling them to the assembly division is zero. There is no lost contribution margin on outside sales for the units sold internally. Because of this, the price established by the variable cost plus opportunity cost transfer price formula is $16:

Transfer price = $16 + 0
= $16

This is the minimum price the parts division should accept for internal transfers. It covers the incremental manufacturing costs and leaves its existing sales and profit margins intact.

The maximum price the assembly division is willing to pay is $25—the price from the external supplier; however, it will be happy to pay less. Therefore, there is a range between $16 and $25 that will improve the profitability of both divisions individually as

Parts Division	Internal Sale (000s omitted)	External Sale (000s omitted)
Sales (70,000 @ $18)	$1,260	
(70,000 @ $30)		$2,100
Variable costs (70,000 @ $12)	840	
(70,000 @ $16)		1,120
Fixed costs	420	420
Division profit	$ 0	$ 560

Assembly Division	Acquire Internally (000s omitted)	Acquire Externally (000s omitted)
Sales (70,000 @ $70)	$4,900	$4,900
Storage units (70,000 @ $18)	1,260	
(70,000 @ $20)		1,400
Variable costs (70,000 @ $27)	1,890	1,890
Fixed costs	630	630
Division profit	$1,120	$ 980
Total company profit	$1,120	$1,540

The variable cost plus opportunity cost transfer price formula is helpful in such situations because it includes the total opportunity cost to the parts division. Its total opportunity cost is $980,000 [($30 − $16) × 70,000 units], and the opportunity cost per unit is $14 ($980,000 ÷ 70,000 units). This, along with the $12 variable cost per unit for the new storage unit, suggests a transfer price of $26 per unit.

Transfer price = $12 + $14
= $26

By comparing the $26 internal transfer price with the $20 external price, management will correctly decide to acquire the units externally.

In most business situations, the theoretical minimum transfer price can be found by adding the variable cost incurred up to the point of transfer to the opportunity cost to the firm as a whole that results from the internal transfer. This is sometimes referred to as the *variable cost plus opportunity cost method* of transfer pricing. This method, along with others discussed previously, helps identify theoretical minimum and maximum transfer prices, but it does not resolve the conflict between managers of the buying and selling divisions.

The use of opportunity cost also has some practical weaknesses. First, opportunity costs are not ordinarily recorded in accounting records, because they are usually difficult and costly to measure on a routine basis. Also, a reliable indication of actual opportunity costs depends on the availability of a perfectly competitive market for the transferred good or service. More often than not, markets for intermediate products are either nonexistent or imperfect, which means that one buyer or one seller, acting alone, can influence the market price for goods or services. This results in intricate cost and price interdependencies that make the determination of opportunity cost and an appropriate transfer price very difficult.

The absence of a perfectly competitive market in such situations presents a complicated analytical environment for decision makers, which leads us to make several important general observations about transfer prices. First, in many business situations there is not *one* correct transfer price but rather a schedule of possible transfer prices based on the various parameters of company operations. In some situations, various transfer prices may depend on the quantities of the intermediate product or finished goods bought or sold in the marketplace. Second, the capacity level at which transferring subunits are operating may have an effect on what is an appropriate transfer price. For example, if the transferring division is operating at full capacity, it would not need to lower its price below the external market price because of the opportunity cost involved. Finally, transfer pricing policies in organizations in which many interdependencies exist should be established and monitored on a firmwide basis.

These observations lead to the consideration of two additional approaches to setting transfer prices—dual transfer prices and negotiation.

Dual Transfer Prices

There may be business situations in which one transfer price does not fulfill all of management's needs. It may be that one method results in transfer prices that are more useful for evaluating performance and another method gives prices that are more appropriate for making economic decisions. For example, market prices may be more useful for evaluating segment performance, whereas variable costs may be more useful for determining if a transfer should be made. In such situations, management may find it beneficial to use **dual transfer prices**—one price for the transferring division and another price for the receiving division.

Dual transfer prices typically enhance the reported results of each subunit and generally encourage appropriate economic decisions from the viewpoint of the organization as a whole. For example, consider the situation in which a chemical company with a mining division produces material that can be sold externally or transferred to a milling division for additional processing and subsequent sale. Business and economic conditions are such that it is advantageous to have the mining and milling divisions cooperate by making internal transfers. On the one hand, the mining division manager may be unwilling to transfer internally at a price less than that available for similar material in the marketplace. On the other hand, the milling division manager may believe that such a transfer price is unfair because it allows the mining division to make a profit at the expense of the milling division. One solution in such a situation would be for top management to determine that the transfer should be made and then to allocate total contribution to the firm between the two cooperating divisions. Such an approach may be equitable from the viewpoint of top management, but it can be damaging in decentralized organizations where subunits are intended to have a great deal of autonomy.

When profit or investment centers are involved, it may be more appropriate to use a dual transfer pricing approach; that is, the mining division may be allowed to use a market-based transfer price to encourage it to make the internal transfer, and the milling division may be allowed to use a variable cost transfer price to overcome the milling division manager's objections. The results of such an arrangement are illustrated below. Assume the transfer of 10,000 tons of material with a variable cost to the mining division of $40 per ton. The external market price for the intermediate product is assumed to be $96 per ton.

Mining Division	
Sales to milling division @ $96	$960,000
Variable costs @ $40	400,000
Contribution	$560,000
Milling Division	
Sales of finished product @ $220	$2,200,000
Variable costs:	
From mining division @ $40	$ 400,000
Milling division @ $120	1,200,000
	$1,600,000
Contribution	$ 600,000

Dual transfer pricing seems to be an acceptable approach in this situation because the mining division manager is receiving the market price and the milling division manager is paying only variable costs. This encourages the division managers to act in accordance with overall company goals.

There is a major weakness in such an approach, however, because situations may arise in which each division manager may appear to benefit but the company as a whole may lose. This could happen for two reasons. First, the relative looseness inherent in dual pricing methods tends to reduce the incentive on the part of subunit managers to control costs. This is particularly true in subsequent processing divisions where raw materials are priced artificially low. Second, if dual pricing methods are adopted without an analysis of their effect on the total company's operations, transfers with an overall effect of reducing the total company's contribution may be made.

To illustrate, if the milling division in the previous example had received $200 per ton rather than $220 per ton for its finished product, making the transfer would not be appropriate. The difference in price alters the overall company contribution, which would decline by $160,000, as follows:

Mining Division

Sales to milling division @ $96	$960,000	
Variable costs @ $40	400,000	
Contribution if sold externally		$560,000

Milling Division

Sales of finished product @ $200	$2,000,000	
Variable costs:		
From mining division @ $40	$ 400,000	
Milling division @ $120	1,200,000	
	$1,600,000	
Contribution if transferred internally		400,000
Lost contribution from transferring internally		$160,000

The loss is apparent when one compares the reduction in contribution provided by each ton of material. The contribution margin is $56 ($96 − $40) to the company if the mining division sells externally. If the material is passed to the milling division for processing and sale, the company's contribution margin drops to $40 ($200 − $40 − $120). The $16 ($56 − $40) decrease in contribution margin on the 10,000 tons makes up the $160,000 loss. This shows the consequences of using dual transfer prices and making the transfer when the mining division should have sold the material in the external market.

Extra care should be exercised under a dual pricing scheme because the performance of each division is enhanced, which may mask detrimental effects to the company as a whole. Also, additional bookkeeping is involved when dual transfer prices are used because profit in transferring subunits needs to be eliminated when company-wide financial statements are prepared for the use of external parties. Even though dual pricing seems to be a viable alternative, it has not achieved widespread usage.

Negotiation Because there are difficulties inherent in other approaches, top management may resort to setting transfer prices by **negotiation.** The objective is to give a fair return to the supplying subunit and a fair cost to the receiving subunit. A negotiated transfer price is an attempt at simulating conditions under which arm's-length or market prices are set. The philosophy when using negotiation is that relatively autonomous subunit managers, bargaining in good faith, will arrive at prices equivalent to those based on actual marketplace negotiations between independent buyers and sellers.

Negotiation may be especially appropriate in situations in which there are large volumes of transferred goods or services. Whereas quoted market prices usually apply to normal order sizes, prices for larger volumes are typically set by negotiation in the marketplace. Therefore, market prices probably are not that much more objective than those set by relatively independent division managers negotiating a mutually agreeable price.

When negotiation is used to set transfer prices, situations may arise in which a reference market for similar goods and services does not exist and subunit managers cannot reach an agreement. Then top management may be required to intervene and arbitrate a transfer price. Although there needs to be sufficient top management review of purchasing and transfer price decisions to avoid suboptimization, frequent intervention by top management may nullify the purposes of decentralization. There must be a balance between taking full control and allowing full autonomy over purchase decisions.

Negotiation is usually quite time consuming and costly to the firm. It typically involves the participation of more management personnel than if market prices are used. Frequent management involvement is also required to reexamine and update transfer prices as business conditions change.

Factors in the business environment determine which of several possible approaches is most appropriate in a specific business situation. Management must recognize the trade-offs of each approach in fulfilling overall company objectives, fostering a desired level of autonomy among subunits, and providing a fair, equitable, and objective basis for evaluating performance.

Accounting Entries for Intracompany Transfers

Transfer prices are usually governed by managerial objectives and not by generally accepted accounting principles for external reporting. Therefore, intracompany transfers are typically made at prices other than at inventoriable cost. This means that when financial statements are prepared for external reporting, inventory balances usually must be adjusted to reflect appropriate cost values, and related intracompany sales and profit must be eliminated. To accomplish this, the accounting system should be designed so that there is a clear distinction between external and internal transactions. At the same time the system should provide management with summary information about the relative importance of intracompany transfers.

To illustrate, assume that division A, the supplying division, transfers goods to division B, the purchasing division, at a negotiated transfer price of cost plus a 25 percent markup on cost. Summary entries to record transfers made between the two divisions are as follows:

Supplying Division's Books

Accounts receivable—division B	20,000	
Sales—intracompany		20,000
Cost of goods sold—intracompany	16,000	
Inventory		16,000

Purchasing Division's Books

Inventory (purchases)—intracompany	20,000	
Accounts payable—division A		20,000

Assume that inventoriable costs of $6,000 are added by division B to the materials transferred from division A. The total inventory value for division B is $26,000. Division B then sells three-fourths of the inventory, $19,500, to external purchasers for $27,500. Entries summarizing this latter event are as follows:

Supplying Division's Books

No entries required

Purchasing Division's Books

Accounts receivable—trade	27,500	
Sales		27,500
Cost of goods sold—trade	19,500	
Inventory—intracompany		19,500

This procedure indicates that the two divisions operate as if they were two different companies when handling intracompany transfers. When the financial statements of all divisions are consolidated for external reporting, however, entries are necessary to adjust the value of ending inventory in the purchasing division and to eliminate intracompany sales, receivables, and profit. The following entries are typically made by the company controller:

Company's Books

Accounts payable—division A	20,000	
Accounts receivable—division B		20,000
Sales—intracompany	20,000	
Cost of goods sold—intracompany		16,000
Cost of goods sold—trade (0.75 × 4,000)		3,000
Inventory—intracompany (0.25 × 4,000)		1,000

The preceding journal entry shows how the intracompany profit of $4,000 ($20,000 − $16,000 = $4,000) "earned" by division A in making intracompany transfers is eliminated from company records. Intracompany profit is passed on to receiving subunits (division B in this example) in the form of increased inventory cost. Because transferred inventory is either sold or still on hand at the end of the period, intracompany profit is eliminated in two steps. First, three-fourths of the transferred inventory was sold to external parties, so three-fourths of the intracompany profit associated with the inventory sold is eliminated from the "cost of goods sold—trade" account. The remaining one-fourth of intracompany profit still resides in division B's ending inventory and is eliminated by reducing the "inventory—intracompany" account balance.

Other Objectives to Transfer Pricing

Thus far we have attempted to develop a transfer price that is fair and that accurately measures the performance of a segment and its management. Sometimes there are incentives for the company as a whole to use transfer prices to accomplish other organizational objectives. This is particularly true when the organization operates in several different states or countries throughout the world. The following are some reasons for manipulating transfer prices.

1. To move cash from one country to another. Some nations have restrictions on taking profits out of the country. However, the restrictions generally do not apply to the payment of goods and services associated with organizational expenses. Transfer prices may be manipulated, within limits, to accomplish the desired flow of funds.
2. To improve the competitive position of a business segment. A new segment's ability to become established and build market share is enhanced by having low costs and hence low prices. A new segment can be partially subsidized by other established segments by having lower transfer prices for materials transferred into the new segment.

3. To move income into segments where taxes are lower. This is becoming more difficult as more states and countries tax the entire income of the company and allow credits for taxes paid to other states and countries.

Many countries have developed, or are in the process of developing, laws that control the creation of acceptable transfer prices. The cost accountant is advised to become familiar with these laws and regulations.

PRICING FOR PRODUCT SALES

Cost accounting information is a vital component in pricing goods and services for sales to external customers. A firm's profitability and long-run viability depend on an appropriate relationship between costs and revenues. Even though this essential relationship exists between costs and revenues, costs are only one of myriad considerations in the pricing decision. Because of this, it is important that accountants have a balanced view of how costs are used in pricing decisions.

The pricing decision is affected by many factors both inside and outside the company, including the expected or actual reaction of customers and competitors to particular pricing decisions. Customers usually have the option of turning to competitors' products, substituting other similar products, or even manufacturing the needed products themselves. Competitors may influence a pricing decision because they usually have the option of either meeting or undercutting prices.

Influences inside the company that affect pricing policies include management's philosophy about a fair return or charging "what the market will bear." The relationship between costs and the volume of production is also an important pricing consideration. Finally, the selection of a long-run or a short-run view affects how management approaches the pricing decision.

Even without an exhaustive discussion on all of the influences on prices, it can be seen that cost accounting information is just one of many considerations in setting prices. However, costs generally provide a starting point for the pricing decision, even if the price ultimately chosen has little or no relationship to underlying costs. Also, cost information provides the vehicle for examining the expected effect on profitability of specific price decisions.

Several approaches to using cost information in establishing pricing policies are explained in the following section. Some complicating factors that may necessitate modifications to these basic approaches also are explored.

Alternative Cost-Based Approaches to Product Pricing

The major advantages of cost-based pricing are that it is understandable, predictable, explainable, and justifiable on objective criteria. Experience has shown that it is generally profitable and seems to be more socially acceptable than other pricing techniques. As a result, cost-based pricing methods are in widespread use. The major shortcomings of cost-based pricing formulas are that they do not take into account such factors as market conditions, product life cycles, or general economic conditions.

Management's challenge is to benefit from the advantages of cost-based pricing approaches and yet to develop pricing policies that are responsive to these other important considerations. The following are ways cost accounting information can be incorporated in pricing policies *in combination with other factors*.

Rate of Markup or Gross Margin One of the most common ways to use costs as a basis for pricing is to apply a target rate of markup or gross margin. A **rate of markup** is a target rate applied against the cost of a product or service to establish a selling price in external markets. This target rate is usually applied to either the purchase cost of a product or to total manufacturing costs. A firm that wants to receive a particular target markup on cost would use the following formula:

$$\text{Selling price} = \text{Cost} + (\text{Target markup} \times \text{Cost})$$

For example, if the cost of a particular product is $0.80 per unit and the company's target markup on cost is 20 percent, the selling price would be $0.96 per unit.

$$\text{Selling price} = 0.80 + (0.20 \times 0.80) = 0.96$$

If a company wants to receive a desired gross margin on sales, the pricing formula is:

$$\text{Selling price} = \text{Cost} \times \frac{1}{1 - \text{Target gross margin}}.$$

Thus, if the cost of a particular product is $0.80 per unit and the company's pricing formula is based on a desired gross margin of 20 percent, the selling price would be $1.00 per unit.

$$\text{Selling price} = 0.80 \times \frac{1}{1 - 0.20} = 1.00$$

This price, based on the desired gross margin, can be verified with the following calculation:

	Dollars	Percent
Sales	$1.00	100%
Cost of goods sold	0.80	80
Gross profit (margin)	$0.20	20%

The target rates used in such formulas are often traditional industry rates that have withstood the test of time. Even though these pricing methods are simple to apply and easy to understand, their weakness is that they explicitly incorporate few of the many factors affecting the pricing decision. Such pricing formulas are not inherently sensitive to market conditions and may result in prices that lose business in weak markets or that fail to take advantage of strong markets. For example, being out of stock on an item or having to hold clearance sales may result from using target rates insensitive to the marketplace. Perhaps a better approach would be to correlate target rates with market indicators. One indicator of market strength is thought to be the percent of plant capacity being utilized in the industry. Excess capacity in an industry usually brings downward pressure on prices, and lower target rates would be more appropriate under such conditions.

A historical relationship between plant capacity (operating rate) and target markups, derived with regression analysis, may provide a basis for systematically adjusting target rates. Other market factors, such as the product life cycle and market growth rate, may also provide useful criteria for adjusting target rates. For example, in the growth phase of a product, higher margins are typically needed to finance new facilities. However, later in the life cycle, lower margins may be appropriate to meet competitive pressures.

Markup on Variable Cost One variation on the rate of markup method is markup on variable cost, which emphasizes the contribution approach to pricing. Sales minus variable costs indicate the amount of contribution made to recovering fixed costs and to providing for a profit on operations. One advantage of paying attention to the contribution margin is that in doing so, variable and fixed costs are identified. Thus cost-volume-profit relationships are more easily discernible and the evaluation of a range of possible prices and their consequences is made possible.

The next major advantage of emphasizing the contribution approach is that it offers more insight into the long-run versus short-run effects of various prices. For example, to preserve a skilled labor force, prices may be allowed to drop in the short run to levels that cannot be sustained in the long run. The proposition facing management in such a situation is whether the expected long-run benefits of preserving a skilled labor force equal or exceed the short-run sacrifice of lost contribution. Information is immediately available to answer such questions if variable costs are routinely made part of the pricing decision.

Some companies fear that if they use a variable cost approach, prices will be consistently under the price necessary to cover *all* costs, both variable and fixed. This could happen, but survey results indicate that a variable cost approach to pricing generally does not result in unprofitable operations (NAA Research Report no. 37). One reason this is true is because a target pricing formula can be developed using variable costs that will result in a selling price similar to one that will be arrived at if markup on full cost is used. To illustrate, consider a product with total per-unit costs amounting to $60, of which $50 of the total is variable. In this situation, a 20 percent markup on the full cost of $60 per unit results in a selling price of $72, which is essentially the same result as using a 44 percent markup on variable cost.

Markup on full cost:	[$60 + (0.20 × $60)] = $72
Markup on variable cost:	[$50 + (0.44 × $50)] = $72

The purpose of this illustration is not to indicate that markup on variable cost is the same as markup on full cost; rather, the point is that markup on variable cost is not inherently unprofitable. Decision makers should realize that to obtain equivalent profitability levels, rates of markup based on variable cost usually must be set higher than rates of markup on full cost. It is generally believed that when the emphasis is on contribution margin rather than on the underlying costs, better pricing decisions will result.

Markup on Conversion Cost Markup on conversion cost is another alternative. It is appropriate when direct-labor and factory overhead costs are the primary cost elements of a good or service, such as when factory capacity is limited by labor constraints or when a customer furnishes materials for the manufacture of a product. For example, consider a production situation in which the amount of available labor is a constraining factor and in which several products require about the same amount of materials but varying amounts of labor and overhead. To generate the same amount of profit per unit of scarce labor resource, management may decide to set selling prices that are based on a percentage markup of conversion cost, as follows:

		Example Product
Materials		$34.00
Conversion costs:		
Labor	$16.00	
Overhead	12.00	
Total		$28.00
Full cost		$62.00
Markup on conversion cost (30% of $28.00)		8.40
Selling price		$70.40

A valid concern when using any of the markup-on-cost methods is that all costs may not be considered in the pricing decision. For example, when prices are set to yield a specific rate of gross margin, selling and administrative expenses are not an explicit part of the computation of gross margin. However, the overall cost situation should be considered in the pricing decision. A distinct advantage of differentiating between variable and fixed costs when the contribution approach is used is that *total* variable costs, including variable selling and administrative expenses, are explicitly incorporated in the markup formula. Also, total fixed costs can be incorporated in the decision when using the contribution approach by using cost-volume-profit analysis.

Cost-plus Pricing Related to a target rate of markup on cost is a pricing method known as *cost-plus pricing*. This method prevails in situations in which it is difficult or impossible to predict the total cost of producing a product or service. For example, the government may want to contract for the production of a new weapons system. Because of the probable lack of experience in producing this product and the attendant risk involved in such situations, rather than set a specific price before proceeding to let a contract, a contract is let on a cost-plus basis. The price in such situations is usually the full cost of production plus a percentage markup on the cost, which constitutes profit.

Cost-plus pricing focuses attention on the proper determination of costs. If a company devotes all of its resources to one product or to one service, there is little difficulty with cost-plus pricing. However, a more typical situation is one in which a cost-plus contract is just one of many activities in a given company. Determining which costs apply to which activities can be quite confusing and even subject to manipulation. The Cost Accounting Standards Board (CASB) was created by Congress for this and other reasons. CASB standards are intended to provide guidance about which costs may be applicable to a particular contract so that misunderstandings and inequities are avoided when the cost-plus pricing approach is used.

Rate of Return on Assets Employed Another common way to incorporate cost information into the pricing decision is to base selling prices on a desired rate of return on assets employed. A **rate of return on assets employed** is a target rate of return applied against total assets employed. There are a number of techniques for implementing this approach, two of which are illustrated here. A per-unit selling price can be directly calculated by using the following formula:

$$\text{Selling price} = \frac{\text{Total cost} + (\text{Desired rate of return} \times \text{Assets employed})}{\text{Unit sales volume}}$$

For example, a firm that has a desired rate of return on assets employed of 22 percent, total assets of $6,000,000, total annual costs of $2,400,000, and an anticipated sales volume of 100,000 units would use a selling price of $37.20 per unit.

$$\text{Selling price} = \frac{\$2,400,000 + (0.22 \times \$6,000,000)}{100,000} = \$37.20$$

This pricing method is appropriate when only one product or a number of very similar products are sold by a company. When a company has a diversified product mix, a pricing method that can be applied on an individual product basis is needed. One way to accomplish this is to calculate a percentage markup on cost that is subsequently applied to individual products. This percentage markup on cost can be derived by using the following formula:

$$\text{Markup on cost} = \text{Desired rate of return} \times \frac{\text{Assets employed}}{\text{Annual costs}}$$

For example, a firm that has a desired return on assets employed of 22 percent, total assets of $6,000,000, and total annual costs of $2,400,000 would use a percentage markup on cost of 55 percent.

$$\text{Markup on cost} = 0.22 \times \frac{\$6,000,000}{\$2,400,000} = 0.55$$

EXAMPLE

If the company expected to produce 100,000 units at $24 each, the sale price would be $37.20 ($24 × 1.55). This would result in the desired 22 percent return on assets employed.

Sales (100,000 units × $37.20)	$3,720,000
Costs (100,000 units × $24.00)	2,400,000
Profit	$1,320,000
Return on assets ($1,320,000 ÷ $6,000,000)	22%

This method is especially useful in firms that sell many types of products with varying costs and selling prices. However, this general method fails to incorporate a number of influences on the pricing decision from sources both inside and outside the firm. For example, the amount of assets employed is an internal factor that influences prices when this method is used. The amount of assets employed typically varies in proportion to sales, because more assets in the form of cash, accounts receivable, and inventories are needed to support increased sales volume. The previous formula that directly calculated a selling price could be adjusted in the following way to incorporate such factors:

$$\text{Selling price} = \frac{\dfrac{\text{Total cost} + (\text{Desired rate of return} \times \text{Fixed assets})}{\text{Unit sales volume}}}{1 - \left(\text{Desired rate of return} \times \dfrac{\text{Current assets}}{\text{Sales}}\right)}$$

EXAMPLE

Continuing with the previous example, suppose current assets need to increase by $200,000 to sustain the $3,720,000 current sales. The price would need to be adjusted slightly to provide an adequate return on the working capital.

$$\frac{[\$2,400,000 + (0.22 \times \$6,000,000)] \div 100,000}{1 - [0.22 \times (\$200,000 \div \$3,720,000)]} = \$37.65$$

Influences on the pricing decision from sources outside the firm can also be incorporated into the preceding formulas in several ways. For example, the target rate of return on employed capital can be based on the current cost of capital after adjustment for such external factors as the risk that the product may not pay off. Or the total cost number may be adjusted to reflect the estimated costs that a competitor (or would-be competitor) would most likely incur to enter the market. In this way, a ceiling below which prices should be set can be established so that surplus capacity is not attracted into the industry.

Considerations for Modification of Cost-Based Prices

Having developed the general numeric techniques for rate of markup on gross margin and rate of return on assets employed, it is important to discuss a number of considerations that could lead decision makers to modify the prices obtained using these basic techniques.

This information will help to reinforce the notion that pricing in any of its forms is a complex matter and should be approached with much judgment. Lack of understanding on the part of the decision maker of all aspects of the decision environment may lead to improper pricing, regardless of the quality and availability of cost accounting information.

Past versus Future Orientation The relevant costs to consider when making pricing decisions are anticipated future costs, not past costs. Historical cost information may provide a valuable basis for predicting future costs, but this should not be confused with anticipated future costs, which are the only relevant costs in the pricing decision. Often the availability, precision, or objectivity of historical costs may entice management to assume that they are relevant costs for pricing decisions.

Many factors, both inside and outside the company, can make historical costs useless even as predictors of future costs. More efficient methods of production, changes in plant facilities, changes in product specifications, labor unrest, and inflation are just a few examples of factors that affect the predictive usefulness of historical costs. Therefore, historical costs must be adjusted for changes in the business environment to make product prices sensitive to actual market conditions.

Another future-oriented consideration concerns the almost inevitable fact that once put on the market, a product will receive almost continuous price revisions. Therefore, it is important that the same degree of attention given to establishing an optimal price at the outset also is given to any subsequent changes in prices. Management should constantly monitor the changing market environment and analyze potential price changes in terms of their profitability due to anticipated changes in costs and revenues.

Standard Costs The use of standard costs in product pricing decisions has several advantages. First, standard costs are quickly available with little added clerical cost. Second, standard costs are usually based on the best estimate of future costs that will be incurred in an efficiently operating plant at actual capacity.

If prices are based on standard costs, it is essential that the standards are current and attainable. If standards are based on theoretical conditions, the standards used for pricing should be adjusted by the ratio of standard costs to actual costs as indicated by normal balances in variance accounts. This type of adjustment converts theoretical standards to currently attainable standards. It is also important that standards are closely monitored and that they receive timely revisions as manufacturing conditions change. Finally, significant deviations between standard and actual costs should be promptly reported to determine if price adjustments should be made.

One way to make standard costs more responsive to current market conditions is to use current market prices for materials and labor. Current costs for these items, combined with standard costs for other elements, provide cost information that is very sensitive to current market conditions yet attuned to the prevailing conditions in the firm.

Volume Changes One of the most perplexing questions facing decision makers is how a price change may affect volume, which in turn affects costs and profits. Basic microeconomic theory is useful in this situation, and some rather fundamental measures can also be helpful in correlating volume and price changes. Many firms find it useful to consider relative price rather than absolute price. This means expressing the company's price as a ratio of the average industry price or as a ratio of the price leader in the industry. It is also useful to express the volume of production in terms of the company's market share of the total volume in the marketplace. This tends to remove the influences of general economic changes when volume measures are used in pricing decisions. With these two measures, it may be possible to discover a correlation between market share and relative prices that has prevailed in the past. If there is such a correlation in the pattern of change, it could be used to predict what may happen in the future. However, care should be taken to screen out of such correlation data price and volume changes arising from abnormal conditions. For example, volume increases from a surge of hedge buying immediately after the announcement of a price increase should be excluded from correlation calculations.

SUMMARY

Pricing includes so many interacting factors that there are usually no easy answers. Pricing decisions require a great deal of judgment, information, and skill. Cost accounting information is one key consideration in both pricing for intracompany transfers and pricing for product sales.

Transfer prices are used in companies that exchange goods and services among operating subunits. When company subdivisions are relatively autonomous, transfer prices become especially important, because the revenue of one division becomes a cost of another division. In such situations, the interests of both the receiving and the transferring subunits should be considered. Top management's interests should also be considered to avoid suboptimization.

There is no all-pervasive rule for establishing appropriate transfer prices. Common bases for establishing transfer prices include using the prevailing price in the marketplace, actual production costs, standard costs, and opportunity costs. Transfer prices should be chosen on the basis of how well they accomplish overall company objectives, foster division autonomy, and provide an incentive for division management. Because of the complexity of the problem, it may be necessary to resort to using negotiated transfer prices or even to setting dual transfer prices, which entail one price for the transferring subunit and another price for the receiving subunit.

Pricing for product sales is even more complex than transfer pricing because of the many external market considerations. Cost accounting information generally provides a starting point for the product pricing decision. Other considerations, such as market conditions or the anticipated response of competitors, are factors that may influence or modify cost-based prices. There are a number of cost-based approaches to product pricing that fall into two general categories—rate of markup or gross margin and rate of return on assets employed.

Decision makers must remember that historical costs are relevant in decisions only to the extent that they are valid predictors of future costs. Predictions based on historical costs should be modified appropriately for anticipated economic and business conditions so that appropriate pricing decisions can be made.

SELF-STUDY PROBLEMS

Transfer Pricing

The Northern Refrigeration Company is a multidivisional company that has delegated full profit responsibility to division managers. The compressor division produces a major subassembly that can be incorporated in the final product of other divisions or can be sold to

CHAPTER 22: TRANSFER AND PRODUCT PRICING

other companies in a competitive market. This subassembly is currently used by the refrigerator division in one of its product lines. Division managers have complete autonomy to accept or reject transfers of goods or services from other divisions.

The following information is available to each division manager about expected costs and selling prices of subassemblies:

Compressor Division

Variable manufacturing costs	$240
Fixed manufacturing costs	120
Total	$360
Expected selling price	$400

Refrigerator Division

Variable costs for completion	$300
Expected selling price	$800

Requirements

1. Prepare an analysis of the effect of using the market price, full cost, variable cost, and variable cost plus opportunity cost approaches to establishing transfer prices.
2. What transfer price do you recommend in this situation? Why?
3. What is your recommendation if the market price for the final product declines to $600?

Solution to the Self-Study Problem

1. Analysis of various approaches to setting transfer prices:

Market Price

	Compressor Division	Refrigerator Division	Northern Company
Prices:			
Transfer price—subassembly	$400		
Selling price—final product		$800	$800
Costs:			
Variable costs—compressor division	$240		$240
Transferred costs—subassembly		$400	
Variable costs—refrigerator division	—	300	300
Total	$240	$700	$540
Contribution margin	$160	$100	$260

Full Cost

	Compressor Division	Refrigerator Division	Northern Company
Prices:			
Transfer price—subassembly	$360		
Selling price—final product		$800	$800
Costs:			
Variable costs—compressor division	$240		$240
Transferred costs—subassembly		$360	
Variable costs—refrigerator division	—	300	300
Total	$240	$660	$540
Contribution margin	$120	$140	$260

Variable Cost

	Compressor Division	Refrigerator Division	Northern Company
Prices:			
Transfer price—subassembly	$240		
Selling price—final product		$800	$800
Costs:			
Variable costs—compressor division	$240		$240
Transferred costs—subassembly		$240	
Variable costs—refrigerator division		300	300
Total	$240	$540	$540
Contribution margin	$ 0	$260	$260

Variable Cost Plus Opportunity Cost

Variable cost		$240
Opportunity cost:		
Market price	$400	
Less: Variable cost	240	
Opportunity cost		160
Total		$400

2. The market price of $400, which is also the transfer price that results when using the variable cost plus opportunity cost approach, is the appropriate transfer price in this situation. When competitive markets are available, the market price usually represents the maximum transfer price that should be considered. In this situation it is also the theoretical minimum transfer price. The compressor division's manager is indifferent about whether subassemblies are sold internally or externally at a transfer price of $400. He or she will be unwilling to transfer subassemblies at a price below $400 because of the ready market for subassemblies at $400. Any price below $400 will reduce the division's contribution margin. The refrigerator division manager should be satisfied with a transfer price of $400 because it is the best price available from any supplier of subassemblies.

3. If the market price for the final product is $600 rather than $800, the refrigerator division either needs to reduce costs or look for some other final product(s) to produce. Otherwise every subassembly used in the refrigerator division of Northern Company will lose $100 in contribution. Compare the contribution margins in the following analysis with those in the previous analyses.

	Compressor Division	Refrigerator Division	Northern Company
Prices:			
Transfer price—subassembly	$400		
Selling price—final product		$600	$600
Costs:			
Variable costs—compressor division	$240		$240
Transferred costs—subassembly		$400	
Variable costs—refrigerator division		300	300
Total	$240	$700	$540
Contribution margin	$160	$(100)	$ 60

Product Pricing

Toyland Products, a newly created toy division of a major conglomerate, will soon begin marketing its first product. The following information is available about the division and its new product:

	New Product (per unit)
Variable costs	$6.00
Fixed costs	2.00
Total	$8.00

Assets employed in the division = $1,500,000
Desired rate of return on assets employed = 24%
Expected level of production and sales = 100,000 units
Average industry markup on cost = 45%

Requirements

1. What would be the selling price for the new product if the average industry markup on cost is used as the pricing method?
2. What rate of gross profit will result if the price derived in requirement 1 is actually used?
3. Calculate the selling price of the new product if the desired rate of return on assets employed is used as the pricing method.
4. What percentage markup on variable cost will yield the same selling price as a 45 percent markup on full cost?

Solution to the Self-Study Problem

1. The selling price based on 45 percent markup on cost:

   Selling price = $8.00 + (0.45 × $8.00) = 1.45 × $8.00 = $11.60

2. The rate of gross profit with a selling price of $11.60:

	Dollars	Percent
Sales	$11.60	100%
Cost of goods sold	8.00	79
Gross profit	$ 3.60	21%

3. The selling price based on 24 percent return on assets employed:

   $$\text{Selling price} = \frac{\$800{,}000 + (0.24 \times 1{,}500{,}000)}{100{,}000} = \$11.60$$

4. The markup rate on variable cost to yield approximately the same price as a 45 percent markup on total cost:

   Basic formula:

   Selling price = Variable cost + (Markup rate × Variable cost)

Basic formula rewritten to solve for the markup rate:

$$\text{Markup rate} = \frac{\text{Selling price}}{\text{Variable cost}} - 1$$

$$\text{Markup rate} = \frac{\$11.60}{\$6.00} - 1 = 93\%$$

SUGGESTED READINGS

Bailey, Earl L., ed. *Pricing Practices and Strategies*. Conference Board Report no. 751. New York: The Conference Board, 1978.

Benke, Ralph L., Jr., and Edwards, James Don. "Transfer Pricing: Techniques and Uses." *Management Accounting* 61 (June 1980):44–47.

Berry, Leonard Eugene. "Advising Clients on Pricing." *Journal of Accountancy* 149 (March 1980): 34–38.

Eccles, R. "Control with Fairness in Transfer Pricing." *Harvard Business Review* 61 (November–December 1983): 149–161.

Gordon, Lawrence A.; Cooper, Robert; Falk, Haim; and Miller, Danny. "The Pricing Decision." *Management Accounting* 62 (March 1981): 59–60.

Hernandez, William H. "Pricing Policies under Inflation." *Management Accounting* 63 (January 1982): 51–55.

Lococo, L. "Selecting the Right Transfer Pricing Model." *Management Accounting* 64 (March 1983): 42–45.

Lucien, K. "Transfer Pricing for the Cost of Funds in a Commercial Bank." *Management Accounting* 60 (January 1979): 23–36.

Merville, L., and Petty, J. W. "Transfer Pricing for the Multinational Firm." *The Accounting Review* 61 (October 1979): 935–939.

Onsi, M. "A Transfer Pricing System Based on Opportunity Cost." *The Accounting Review* 45 (July 1970): 535–543.

Stern, Roy D. "Accounting for Intracompany Inventory Transfers." *Management Accounting* 62 (September 1980): 41–44.

DISCUSSION QUESTIONS

Q22–1. Why is cost accounting information important in pricing decisions?

Q22–2. What are *transfer pricing* and *product pricing?*

Q22–3. Why is transfer pricing so important in relatively decentralized organizations?

Q22–4. What are the objectives of transfer pricing?

Q22–5. What are the advantages and disadvantages of using market prices for intracompany transfers?

Q22–6. What are the advantages and disadvantages of using cost-related transfer prices?

Q22–7. What transfer pricing methods establish the ceiling and theoretical minimum transfer prices?

Q22–8. What is "opportunity cost" in the variable cost plus opportunity cost method of transfer pricing?

Q22–9. When would it be appropriate to use dual transfer prices?

Q22-10. What is the basic philosophy underlying the use of negotiation to set transfer prices?

Q22-11. Describe the series of journal entries that are necessary to account for intracompany transfers.

Q22-12. Explain the role of cost accounting information in setting prices for product sales.

Q22-13. What are the major advantages of a cost-based product pricing method?

Q22-14. Give the basic pricing formulas for using rate of markup, gross margin, and rate of return on assets employed.

Q22-15. Describe two common variations on the rate of markup method for setting product prices.

Q22-16. Explain how the reactions of customers and competitors can affect product prices.

Q22-17. Why is a future versus a past orientation important when setting product prices?

Q22-18. Explain how the effect of volume changes can be incorporated into the pricing decision.

Q22-19. Under what conditions are standard costs useful when making pricing decisions?

EXERCISES

E22-1. Transfer Pricing Mar Company has two decentralized divisions, X and Y. Division X has always purchased certain units from division Y at $75 per unit. Because division Y plans to raise the price to $100 per unit, division X wants to purchase these units from outside suppliers for $75 per unit. Division Y's costs follow:

Y's variable costs per unit	$70
Y's annual fixed costs	$15,000
Y's annual production of these units for X	1,000 units

If division X buys from an outside supplier, the facilities division Y uses to manufacture the units will remain idle. Division X incurs a $50 variable cost on finishing the units and sells them for $200 per unit.

Required

1. What is division Y's opportunity cost?
2. What will be the effect on total company profitability if Mar Company enforces a transfer price of $100 per unit between divisions X and Y?

E22-2. Transfer Pricing Alternatives Julie Bee, Inc. is a multidivision company. It has delegated full profit responsibility to division managers, who have complete autonomy to accept or reject both transfers of goods or services from other divisions and the price to be paid for the goods and services.

The component division makes several subassemblies that are used by other divisions. One of the major subassemblies is used by the pick division; however, it can also be sold externally in a fairly competitive market.

The following information is available to develop an appropriate transfer price and to evaluate the effect of various transfer prices on segment profitability.

Component Division:

Variable manufacturing costs	$145 per subassembly
Fixed manufacturing costs	$85,000 total
Expected selling price (externally)	$500 per subassembly
Normal production volume	10,000 units

Pick Division:

Variable costs for completion	$420 per subassembly
Expected selling price	$800 per subassembly
Expected annual usage	1,000 units

Required

1. Prepare an analysis that shows the contribution margin per unit, per division as well as for the company as a whole, using market, full cost, variable cost, and variable cost plus opportunity cost methods for transfer pricing.
2. Which method would you recommend. Why?
3. Suppose a supplier on the outside made the exact subassembly available to Julie Bee at a price of $300. How would you advise the company?

E22–3. Choosing a Transfer Price

The Timeworks Division of Electrosond Company makes a timer device used in the production of a variety of appliances. The timing device is sold on the open market at $18 per unit. Electrosond has recently acquired a promising microwave oven company that now operates as the Heatwave Division. The oven manufacturer requires a timing device similar to that produced by the Timeworks Division and has been purchasing these from an external source at $18 minus a 5 percent quantity discount. The Timeworks Division has capacity to produce 15,000 timing devices per month and currently sells only 12,000. Electrosond management would like the new Heatwave Division to purchase its required 2,000 timers internally.

Timeworks' per unit cost is calculated as follows:

Materials	$ 6
Labor	5
Overhead: Variable	3
Fixed (based on 12,000 production)	1
	$15

Required

1. Assuming that each division is a profit center, choose a transfer price that you would recommend. Explain the advantages of this price.
2. Assume now that the Timeworks Division is selling all 15,000 units externally at the time of the Heatwave acquisition. What do you recommend under these circumstances?

E22–4. Markup Pricing—Full and Variable Costing

Consider the following per-unit costs of Wilson Company's new product line.

Variable costs:	
Materials	$12.00
Labor	7.00
Manufacturing overhead	3.00
Fixed costs:	
Manufacturing overhead	
(based on expected production	
and sales of 20,000 units)	5.00
Total	$27.00

The average rate of markup on full costs in the industry is 21 percent.

Required

1. Calculate the outside selling price Wilson should set if the markup on full cost method is applied using the industry average rate.
2. What markup percentage would be required to arrive at the same price using the markup on variable cost method?
3. Using the price you found in requirements 1 and 2, find the gross profit percentage (round to the nearest tenth of a percent).
4. Rather than setting the price according to the industry average markup on cost, Wilson wants to achieve a gross margin of 21 percent. Calculate the selling price Wilson will use to reach its goal of 21 percent gross margin on the new product line.
5. Suppose plant capacity and labor restrict the total output of all product lines. Management has therefore adopted a policy of setting the selling price on a 30 percent markup on conversion costs. Calculate the selling price Wilson will use under its conversion cost policy.

E22-5. Alternative Transfer Prices

No standard has been pronounced defining the proper method of setting intracompany transfer prices. An accountant must therefore be prepared to suggest an appropriate pricing technique for each circumstance. The following transfer pricing policies are frequently used:

1. Market price
2. Full cost
3. Variable cost
4. Variable cost plus opportunity cost
5. Dual transfer price
6. Negotiated price

Required

1. Describe the composition of each of the preceding transfer prices; that is, describe the individual components of the final transfer price.
2. Describe a set of circumstances for which each transfer price would be appropriate.

E22-6. Product Pricing—Sensitivity Analysis

Adly Corp. wants to evaluate the effects of a change in price, a change in the units produced and sold, and a change in variable manufacturing cost on the return on investment (ROI) and residual income (RI). The controller has asked you to prepare an electronic spreadsheet that can be used to perform a sensitivity analysis to evaluate the effect of various changes.

Adly wants to earn a 30 percent return on the $100,000 of invested capital used to produce product X. Based on estimated sales of 10,000 units of product X next year, the costs per unit would be as follows:

Variable manufacturing costs	$5
Fixed selling and administrative costs	2
Fixed manufacturing costs	1

Required

Prepare an electronic spreadsheet that will compute ROI and RI for each of the following combinations. Print out the results for each combination.

Combination	Price	Units	Variable Manufacturing Costs
1	$11	10,000	$5.00
2	12	11,000	5.25
3	13	9,000	5.40

E22–7. Pricing and Return on Investment Oden Freezers is new in a competitive industry. Its production of a top-of-the-line freezer employs assets of $45,600,000. Oden hopes to achieve a return on assets employed of 24 percent. Manufacturing and sales cost information is as follows:

	Oden Freezer (per unit)
Total variable costs	$265
Total fixed costs	115
Total cost per unit	$380
Unit sales and production volume	60,000 units

Required

1. Calculate the minimum sales price Oden should use to achieve the desired rate of return on assets employed at the given sales volume.
2. Suppose that sales decreased from 60,000 units to 50,000 units. Calculate the minimum sales price that Oden should use to achieve the same desired rate of return on assets employed.
3. Assume that the freezers produced by Oden Freezers are just one of many product lines. Oden still desires a 24 percent rate of return on assets employed, and the 60,000 unit initial projection is believed to be accurate.
   a. With the given facts, calculate the markup percentage on cost.
   b. What price will Oden set for the freezer if the markup on cost calculated in requirement 3a is used?

E22–8. Product Pricing—Effect on Sales (CPA) Management of Freedom, Inc., has performed cost studies and projected the following annual costs based on 40,000 units of production and sales:

	Total Annual Costs	Percent of Variable Portion of Total Annual Costs
Direct material	$400,000	100%
Direct labor	360,000	75
Manufacturing overhead	300,000	40
Selling, general and administrative expenses	200,000	25

Required

1. Compute Freedom's unit selling price that will yield a projected 10-percent profit if sales are 40,000 units.
2. Assume that management selects a selling price of $30 per unit (40,000 units). Compute Freedom's dollar sales that will yield a projected 10-percent profit on sales, assuming that the preceding variable-fixed cost relationships are valid.

E22–9. Contribution Approach to Pricing Adams Incorporated produces and sells small motors. Recently Adams was asked to submit a bid on the sale of 100 units for a local manufacturer. Per-unit costs were accumulated, and the following estimates are based on 100 additional units produced.

	Per Unit
Direct materials	$ 37
Shipping materials	3
Direct labor	45
Receiving and handling (60% fixed)	6
Factory overhead	
Fixed	12
Variable	19
General and administrative costs	15
Total	$137

Just as the president was about to submit the bid, it was learned that a bid of $120 already had been submitted as the lowest bid.

Required

Can Adams bid lower than the $120 already submitted? What price could Adams submit? Show your computations.

E22-10. Markup Pricing

MacAlbert Products has begun production of a new sprinkler unit. Management is concerned about setting an appropriate selling price for the new unit. The following unit costs are to be assigned:

Variable Costs

Materials	$3.50
Labor	2.00
Manufacturing overhead	0.50

Fixed Costs

Manufacturing overhead (based on 100,000 unit expected production and sales)	1.50
Total cost per unit	$7.50

The industry has recorded near full capacity output in the last two years. Because of the market strength of sprinkler products, the price has risen steadily. The rise has settled recently with the industry average markup being 55 percent of full costs.

Required

1. If MacAlbert chooses to set prices by the markup on full cost approach, what will be the unit sales price of the new product (use the industry average rate)?
2. What will be the gross profit percentage if the price determined in requirement 1 is used?
3. If MacAlbert sets prices using 100 percent markup of conversion costs, what selling price would it use?
4. What would you expect to happen to prices if the firms in the industry began reporting excess capacity?
5. Explain the problems that can arise from using strictly a markup on cost method in pricing.

E22-11. Selling Price

Using Lotus or some other electronic spreadsheet, develop a program, or template, to compute the suggested selling price for any product. Use the rate of return on assets employed and the following input amounts:

- Total cost
- Desired rate of return
- Assets employed
- Expected unit sales volume

Required

Prepare the template as requested. Key in the following data to check your answer, and print out a copy of the results.

Total cost	$400,000
Desired rate of return	25%
Assets employed	$6,000,000
Expected unit sales volume	1,000,000 units

E22–12. Product Pricing—Sensitivity Analysis Omar Companies, Inc. wants to evaluate the effects of a change in price, a change in the units produced and sold, and a change in variable manufacturing cost on the return on investment (ROI) and residual income (RI). The controller has asked you to prepare an electronic spreadsheet that can be used to perform a sensitivity analysis to evaluate the effect of various changes.

Omar wants to earn a 20 percent return on the $250,000 of invested capital used to produce product Z. Based on estimated sales of 13,500 units of product Z next year, the costs per unit would be as follows:

Variable manufacturing costs	$6.50
Fixed selling and administrative costs	2.50
Fixed manufacturing costs	1.25

Required

Prepare an electronic spreadsheet that will compute ROI and RI for each of the following combinations. Print out the results for each combination.

Combination	Price	Units	Variable Manufacturing Costs
1	$14	13,500	$6.50
2	15	12,000	6.80
3	13	15,000	6.40

PROBLEMS

P22–1. Transfer Pricing (CMA) DePaolo Industries manufactures carpets, furniture, and foam in three separate divisions. DePaolo's operating statement for 19X3 is reproduced on page 000. Additional information about DePaolo's operations is as follows:

- Included in the foam division's sales revenue is $500,000 in revenue that represents sales made to the furniture division that were transferred at manufacturing cost.
- The cost of goods sold comprises the following costs.

	Carpet	Furniture	Foam
Direct materials	$ 500,000	$1,000,000	$1,000,000
Direct labor	500,000	200,000	1,000,000
Variable overhead	750,000	50,000	1,000,000
Fixed overhead	250,000	50,000	0
Total cost of goods sold	$2,000,000	$1,300,000	$3,000,000

- Administrative expenses include the following costs.

	Carpet	Furniture	Foam
Segment expenses			
Variable	$ 85,000	$140,000	$ 40,000
Fixed	85,000	210,000	120,000
Home office expenses (all fixed)			
Directly traceable	100,000	120,000	200,000
General (allocated on sales dollars)	30,000	30,000	40,000
Total	$300,000	$500,000	$400,000

- Selling expense is all incurred at the segment level and is 80 percent variable for all segments.

John Sprint, manager of the foam division, is not pleased with DePaolo's presentation of operating performance. Sprint claimed, "The foam division makes a greater contribution to the company's profits than what is shown. I sell foam to the furniture division at cost, and it gets our share of the profit. I can sell that foam on the outside at my regular markup, but I sell to furniture for the well-being of the company. I think my division should get credit for those internal sales at market. I think we should also revise our operating statements for internal purposes. Why don't we consider preparing these internal statements on a contribution approach reporting format, showing internal transfers at market?"

DePaolo Industries
Operating Statement
For the Year Ended December 31, 19X3

	Carpet Division	Furniture Division	Foam Division	Total
Sales revenue	$3,000,000	$3,000,000	$4,000,000	$10,000,000
Cost of goods sold	2,000,000	1,300,000	3,000,000	6,300,000
Gross profit	$1,000,000	$1,700,000	$1,000,000	$ 3,700,000
Operating expenses				
Administrative	$ 300,000	$ 500,000	$ 400,000	$ 1,200,000
Selling	600,000	600,000	500,000	1,700,000
Total operating expenses	$ 900,000	$1,100,000	$ 900,000	$ 2,900,000
Income from operations before taxes	$ 100,000	$ 600,000	$ 100,000	$ 800,000

Required

1. John Sprint believes that the intracompany transfers from the foam division to the furniture division should be at market rather than at manufacturing cost for divisional performance measurement.
   a. Explain why Sprint is correct.
   b. Identify and describe two approaches used for setting transfer prices other than manufacturing cost, as used by DePaolo Industries, and market price, as recommended by Sprint.
2. Using the contribution approach and market-based transfer prices, prepare a revised operating statement by division for DePaolo Industries for 19X3 that will promote the evaluation of divisional performance.
3. Discuss the advantages of the contribution reporting approach for internal reporting purposes.

P22-2. The Contribution Approach on the Pricing Decision The Newhouse Company has established a pricing formula for its single product by using the following absorption cost estimates:

Sales	$200,000
Cost of goods sold	120,000[a]
Gross margin	$ 80,000
Selling and administrative expenses	60,000[b]
Estimated net income	$ 20,000

[a]Including $40,000 of fixed costs.
[b]Including $40,000 of fixed costs.

The sales price would be determined by adding two-thirds (80,000 ÷ 120,000) of the cost of production to the cost of production.

Required

1. Prepare an estimated income statement based on the contribution margin concept.
2. Determine the markup percentage based on variable costs that would be used in pricing if the contribution approach were used.
3. Compare and contrast the absorption costing and contribution approaches to pricing. Indicate the advantages and disadvantages of each.

P22-3. Product Pricing (CMA) The Fiore Company manufactures office equipment for sale to retail stores. Meg Lucas, vice president of marketing, has proposed that Fiore introduce two new products to its line—an electric stapler and an electric pencil sharpener.

Lucas has requested that Fiore's profit planning department develop preliminary selling prices for the two new products for her review. Profit planning is to follow the company's standard policy for developing potential selling prices, using as much data as available for each product. Data accumulated by profit planning about these two new products are as follows:

	Electric Stapler	Electric Pencil Sharpener
Estimated annual demand in units	12,000	10,000
Estimated unit manufacturing costs	$10.00	$12.00
Estimated unit selling and administrative expenses	$4.00	Not available
Assets employed in manufacturing	$180,000	Not available

Fiore plans to employ an average of $2,400,000 of assets to support its operations in the current year. The condensed pro forma operating income statement that follows represents Fiore's planned goals with respect to cost relationships and return-on-assets employed for the entire company for all of its products.

Fiore Company
Pro Forma Operating Income Statement
For the Year Ending May 31, 19X5
(000s omitted)

Revenue	$4,800
Cost of goods sold (manufacturing costs)	2,880
Gross profit	$1,920
Selling and administrative expenses	1,440
Operating profit	$ 480

Required

1. Calculate a potential selling price for the:
   a. electric stapler, using return-on-assets pricing.
   b. electric pencil sharpener, using gross margin pricing.
2. Could a selling price for the electric pencil sharpener be calculated using return-on-assets pricing? Explain your answer.
3. Which of the two pricing methods—return-on-assets pricing or gross margin pricing—is more appropriate for decision analysis? Explain your answer.
4. Discuss the additional steps Meg Lucas is likely to take after she receives the potential selling prices for the two new products (as calculated in requirement 1) to set an actual selling price for each of the two products.

P22–4. Pricing Methods
Merriweather Patio Division will soon be marketing its first line of patio umbrellas. The outside selling price is now being sought. The following information has been collected about this division:

	Umbrellas (per unit)
Variable costs	$12.50
Fixed costs	4.50
Total per unit	$17.00

Assets employed in the division	$890,000
Desired rate of return on assets employed	21%
Expected level of first-year sales and production	180,000 units
Average industry markup on cost	55%

Required

1. Give the outside selling price Merriweather will set if the average industry markup on full cost is used as the pricing method.
2. What rate of gross profit will result if Merriweather uses the price calculated in requirement 1? (Round to three decimals.)
3. What markup percentage on variable costs would be used to calculate the same price as a 55 percent markup on full cost?
4. What would be the selling price of the umbrella if the desired rate of return on assets employed method was used for pricing?

P22–5. Pricing and Rate of Return on Assets Employed
Hollis Hampers is a new manufacturing firm that is gearing up for production of clothes hampers. Assets used for these clothes hampers have a value of $350,000. Hollis has a desired rate of return of 20 percent on assets employed. The following total costs of manufacturing and sales have been estimated:

	Hollis Hampers (per unit)
Variable costs	$7.50
Fixed costs (based on production and sales of 20,000 units)	2.30
Total costs	$9.80

Required

1. Calculate the minimum sales price Hollis Hampers must use to reach its desired rate of return on assets employed.

2. Assume that Hollis sells numerous products of which the hamper is just one. Assume also that the assets employed have not changed and that the per-unit costs given now represent all units of production. Calculate the percentage markup on cost Hollis might use to calculate sales prices if the desired rate of return on assets employed is raised to 22 percent. (Round to three figures.)

P22–6. Product Pricing Strategies (CMA) Hall Company specializes in packaging bulk drugs in standard dosages for local hospitals. The company has been in business since 19X8 and has been profitable since its second year of operation. Beth Greenway, director of cost accounting, installed a standard cost system after joining the company in 19Y2.

Wyant Memorial Hospital has asked Hall Company to bid on the packaging of one million doses of medication at full cost plus a return on full cost of no more than 9 percent after income taxes. Wyant defines cost as including all variable costs of performing the service, a reasonable amount of nonvariable overhead, and reasonable administrative costs. The hospital will supply all packaging materials and ingredients. Wyant has indicated that any bid over $0.015 per dose will be rejected.

Greenway accumulated the following information before the preparation of the bid:

Direct labor	$4.00/direct-labor hour
Variable overhead	$3.00/direct-labor hour
Fixed overhead	$5.00/direct-labor hour
Administrative costs	$1,000 for the order
Production rate	1,000 doses/direct-labor hour

Hall Company is subject to an effective income tax rate of 40 percent.

Required

1. Calculate the minimum price per dose that Hall Company would bid for the Wyant Memorial Hospital job that would not reduce Hall's net income.
2. Calculate the bid price per dose using the full cost criterion and the maximum allowable return specified by Wyant Memorial Hospital.
3. Without prejudicing your answer to requirement 2, assume that the price per dose that Hall Company calculated using the cost-plus criterion specified by Wyant Memorial Hospital is greater than the maximum bid of $0.015 per dose that Wyant allows. Discuss the factors that Hall Company would consider before deciding whether or not to submit a bid at the maximum price of $0.015 per dose.
4. Discuss the factors that Wyant Memorial Hospital should have considered before deciding whether or not to employ cost-plus pricing.

P22–7. Contribution Approach to Pricing (CMA) E. Berg and Sons build custom-made pleasure boats that range in price from $10,000 to $250,000. For the past thirty years, Ed Berg, Sr., has determined the selling price of each boat by estimating the costs of material, labor, and a prorated portion of the overhead, and adding 20 percent to these estimated costs.

For example, a recent price quotation was determined as follows:

Direct materials	$ 5,000
Direct labor	8,000
Overhead	2,000
	$15,000
Plus 20%	3,000
Selling price	$18,000

The overhead figure was determined by estimating total overhead costs for the year and allocating them at 25 percent of direct labor.

If a customer rejected the price and business was slack, Mr. Berg, Sr., would often be willing to reduce his markup to as little as 5 percent over estimated costs. Thus, average markup for the year is estimated to be 15 percent.

Ed Berg, Jr., has just completed a course on pricing and believes the firm could use some of the techniques discussed in the course. The course emphasized the contribution approach to pricing, and Mr. Berg, Jr., thinks that such an approach would be helpful in determining the selling prices of the custom-made pleasure boats.

Total overhead, which includes selling and administrative expenses for the year, has been estimated to be $150,000, of which $90,000 is fixed and the remainder is variable in direct proportion to direct labor.

Required

1. Assume that the customer in the example rejected the $18,000 quotation and also rejected a $15,750 quotation (5 percent markup) during a slack period. The customer countered with a $15,000 offer.
    a. What is the difference in net income for the year between accepting or rejecting the customer's offer?
    b. What is the minimum selling price Mr. Berg, Jr., could have quoted without reducing or increasing the company's net income?
2. What advantages does the contribution approach to pricing have over the approach used by Mr. Berg, Sr.?
3. What possible dangers are there, if any, to the contribution approach in pricing?

P22–8. Transfer Pricing For several years the Yardbird Company has operated a washing machine division. The division uses 40,000 pumps annually in its production. It has been purchasing the pumps from an independent supplier for $20.

This year Yardbird acquired a pump division, which produces a pump that fits the specifications of the washing machine division. In the past these pumps have been sold on the market for $22 apiece. The costs of producing the pump are as follows:

Direct materials	$ 7
Direct labor	6
Variable overhead	3
Fixed overhead[a]	2
Total cost per unit	$18

[a]Based on total capacity of 120,000 units.

The pump division is presently selling 80,000 units per year. Sales discussions have begun between the two divisions, which are treated as separate profit centers.

Required

1. If you were the manager of the pump division, would you be willing to meet the washing machine division's price of $20 per unit? What would be the minimum price that you would accept to supply the washing machine division's need and not hurt your division's results?
2. Should the pump division be required to accept the $20 per-unit price from the washing machine division for the good of Yardbird as a whole? Explain.
3. Suppose the pump division agrees to supply all the internal pump needs, but it

requires a price to be set at $22 apiece. How will accepting this price affect the following?

    a. The pump division
    b. The washing machine division
    c. Yardbird Company as a whole

4. Suggest a transfer pricing policy other than those described in requirements 2 and 3 that would be equitable for both divisions. Show your computations.

5. Assume now that the pump division is already selling 120,000 units externally. If the pump division is required by Yardbird's management to sell 40,000 units to the washing machine division, how would the operating income of Yardbird Company be affected?

P22–9. Transfer Pricing Consider the following independent situations:

1. Division S manufactures product D. Cost and revenue data for product D are as follows:

External sales price per unit	$50
Variable costs per unit	$38
Fixed costs per unit (based on capacity)	$6
Division S capacity	30,000 units

Division S is currently producing and selling all 30,000 units of product D annually. The home office has approached the division S manager and has requested that S supply division T with 5,000 units of product E. To make room for production of product E, division S must cut production of D back by a third, to 20,000 units. Division S has estimated the following costs of product E:

Variable costs per unit	$66
Fixed costs per unit	22

Division S will use the same equipment and personnel for both products. What transfer price should division S charge division T for each unit of product E?

2. Division M has only one product. Its cost and revenue data are as follows:

External sales price per unit	$60
Variable costs per unit	$40
Fixed costs per unit (based on capacity)	$10
Capacity	18,000 units

At present, division M produces and sells at capacity to outside customers. If it sells instead to division O, $3 can be trimmed off the variable unit cost. Division O currently is supplied by an outside producer at a unit cost of $56. From an overall company point of view, what price should be used for any sales to division O of M's product?

3. Refer to part 2. Would you expect the proposed transaction to take place? Explain your reasoning. What circumstances would reverse your expectations?

P22–10. Transfer Pricing The yellow division of Laboratory Products Incorporated completes the final steps in the company's process. The yellow division has as its sole supplier of an intermediate product the red division of Laboratory Products. Because of the highly technical nature of the product, red division's costs are essentially fixed. Production and costs are as follows:

Units per Day	Total Costs per Day
1,000	$250
2,000	300
3,000	350
4,000	400

(The minimum cost per day is $250, and each increment of 1,000 units beyond the first 1,000 units costs an additional $50.)

The red division has set its price at $0.20 per unit. This price is found to be the optimal price.

The yellow division adds its own costs in completing production. Its divisional costs are as follows:

Units of Output	Total Cost of Output
1,000	$ 625
2,000	750
3,000	875
4,000	1,000

(Any output up to 1,000 units costs $625 in the yellow division. For each additional 1,000 units output, the cost increases by $125.)

The final product is sold by the yellow division to external customers. Because sales volume increases only if price is decreased or more is spent on sales promotion, the marginal revenue decreases as sales increase. Estimates of sales show the following:

Sales in Units	Net Revenue at Sales Level
1,000	$ 875
2,000	1,325
3,000	1,650
4,000	1,850
5,000	2,000
6,000	2,000

Required

1. Prepare a schedule of revenues, costs (including transfer costs), and net income at varying levels of output for the yellow division.
2. From your answer to requirement 1, locate yellow division's maximum net income. What are red division's and Laboratory Products' net incomes at this level?
3. If you were to combine the two divisions into one investment and profit center, the results may differ. Repeat requirement 1 after combining the red and yellow divisions into one profit center. What is the maximum net income now?
4. Compare the overall net income results for Laboratory Products found in requirements 2 and 3. Why do they differ? Which transfer pricing policy would assist in maximizing overall company profits when red and yellow are maintained as separate investment and profit centers?

CASES

C22-1. Negotiated Transfer Pricing (CMA) National Industries is a diversified corporation with separate and distinct operating divisions. Each division's performance is evaluated on the basis of total dollar profits and return on division investment.

The Windair Division manufactures and sells air-conditioner units. The coming year's budgeted income statement, based on a sales volume of 15,000 units, follows:

Windair Division
Budgeted Income Statement
For the Coming Fiscal Year

	Per Unit	Total (000s omitted)
Sales revenue	$400	$6,000
Manufacturing costs:		
Compressor	$ 70	$1,050
Other raw materials	37	555
Direct labor	30	450
Variable overhead	45	675
Fixed overhead	32	480
Total manufacturing costs	$214	$3,210
Gross margin	$186	$2,790
Operating expenses:		
Variable selling	$ 18	$ 270
Fixed selling	19	285
Fixed administrative	38	570
Total operating expenses	$ 75	$1,125
Net income before taxes	$111	$1,665

Windair Division's manager believes that sales can be increased if the unit selling price of the air conditioners is reduced. A market research study conducted by an independent firm at the request of the manager indicates that a 5 percent reduction in the selling price ($20) would increase sales volume by 16 percent or 2,400 units. Windair has sufficient production capacity to manage this increased volume with no increase in fixed costs.

At present, Windair uses a compressor in its units, which it purchases from an outside supplier at a cost of $70 per compressor. The division manager of Windair has approached the manager of the Compressor Division about the sale of compressor units to Windair. The Compressor Division currently manufactures and sells a unit exclusively to outside firms that is similar to the unit used by Windair. The specifications of the Windair compressor, which are slightly different, would reduce the Compressor Division's raw materials cost by $1.50 per unit. In addition, the Compressor Division would not incur any variable selling costs for the units sold to Windair. The manager wants all of the compressors it uses to come from one supplier and has offered to pay $50 for each compressor unit.

The Compressor Division has the capacity to produce 75,000 units. The following budgeted income statement for the Compressor Division is based on a sales volume of 64,000 units without considering Windair's proposal.

native solutions may be appropriate in these situations, particularly in attempting to evaluate these organizations based on their profitability.

The Problem

This case concerns the component division's semiconductor plant, which produces random access memories (RAMs) for ultimate consumption by several product division profit centers in the manufacture of finished equipment ranging across the entire product line. Figure 22.1 depicts the flow of these shipments to the various product divisions. Approximately 75 to 80 percent of the plant's total annual output is functionally substitutable for products manufactured by outside vendors in the U.S. and abroad. The remainder of the plant's annual output (20 to 25 percent) is composed of unique, proprietary logic modules and chips for use in selected products.

Until five years ago, the component division plant supplied all of the company's domestic requirements for RAMs. In fact, volume rose continuously during that period.

FIGURE 22.1

Typical Shipment Flow of Memory Units

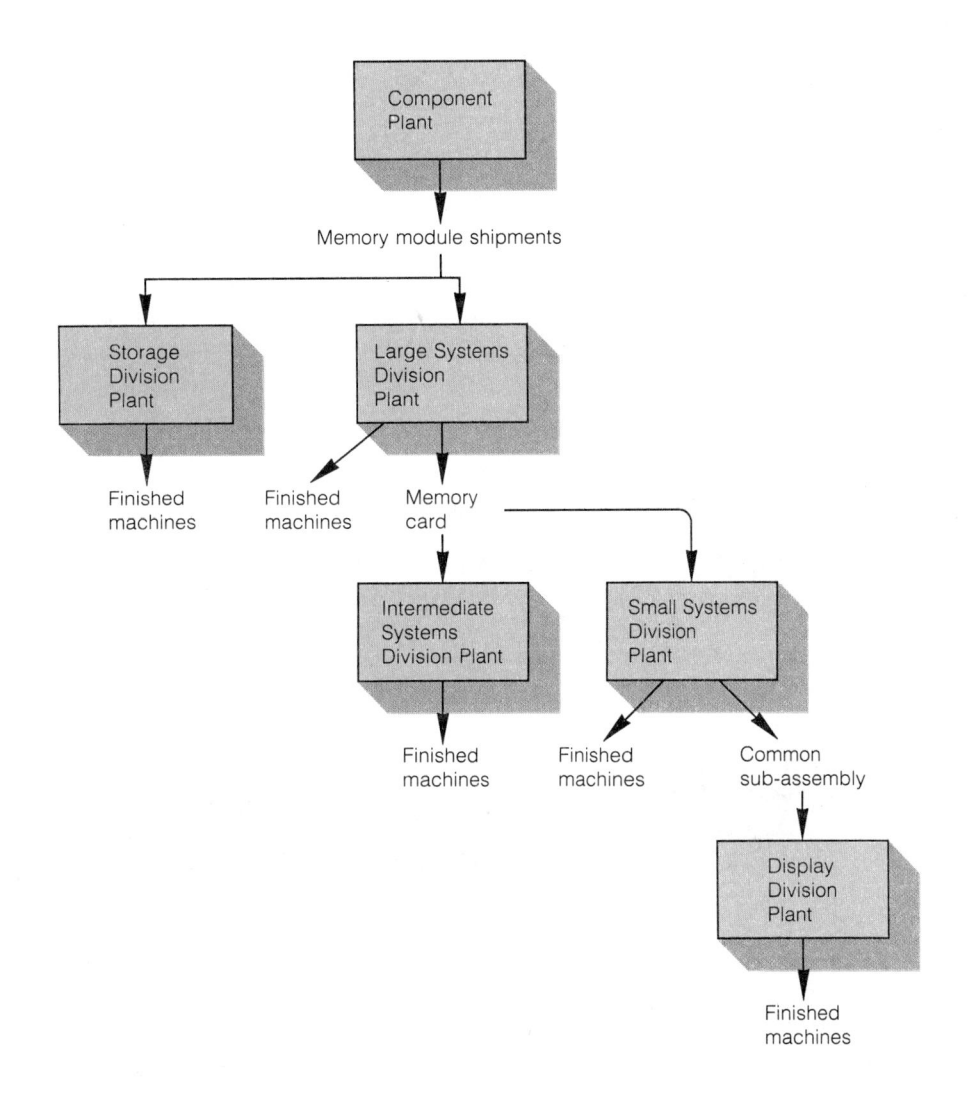

Compressor Division
Budgeted Income Statement
For the Coming Fiscal Year

	Per Unit	Total (000s omitted)
Sales revenue	$100	$6,400
Manufacturing costs:		
Raw materials	$ 12	$ 768
Direct labor	8	512
Variable overhead	10	640
Fixed overhead	11	704
Total manufacturing costs	$ 41	$2,624
Gross margin	$ 59	$3,776
Operating expenses:		
Variable selling	$ 6	$ 384
Fixed selling	4	256
Fixed administrative	7	448
Total operating expenses	$ 17	$1,088
Net income before taxes	$ 42	$2,688

Required

1. Should Windair Division institute the 5 percent price reduction on its air-conditioner units even if it cannot acquire the compressors internally for $50 each? Support your conclusion with appropriate calculations.

2. Without prejudicing your answer to requirement 1, assume that Windair needs 17,400 units. Should the Compressor Division be willing to supply the compressor units for $50 each? Support your conclusion with appropriate calculations.

3. As the manager of the Compressor Division, what is the minimum transfer price you could charge for the new compressor? Show computations.

4. Without prejudicing your answer to requirement 1, assume that Windair needs 17,400 units. Would it be in the best interest of National Industries for the Compressor Division to supply the compressor units at $50 each to the Windair Division? Support your conclusion with appropriate calculations.

C22–2. Information Systems Corporation[1] The Information Systems Corporation is a vertically integrated organization with heavy interdependence among profit centers. The existing practice within the corporation has been to make all interdivisional transfers at cost within the United States. Past corporate studies have confirmed the wisdom of this practice; the key reasons cited have been the following:

1. The difficulty of eliminating profits from published profit and loss statements and plant inventories
2. The problems created when the sum of the divisional income statements does not reflect the true corporate profit
3. The potential for unit executives to suboptimize, to maximize their own profit instead of optimizing for the company as a whole

Nevertheless, application of the ground rule may create the appearance of inequities or may not provide adequate incentives for the management of specific functions. Alter-

---

1. Edited by Dr. Shane R. Morarity for the National Association of Accountants. Presented at the NAA symposium at the American Accounting Association Meetings, 1986.

But five years ago it was necessary, despite continued plant expansion, to turn to outside vendors to respond to rising demand and to meet schedules. Foreign competition, recognizing this growing demand, entered the U.S. market with a series of high-quality products and aggressive price actions.

The domestic industry, faced with this competitive pressure and potential overcapacity, initiated a series of deepening price reductions to maintain market share. The U.S. reductions were immediately countered by foreign competition. In a short time, prices for comparable products purchased from outside vendors began to meet the semiconductor plant's costs and, in many instances, began even to undercut those costs.

The corporation's product managers within each division for the various segments of the industry have responsibility for product revenue and costs. A key component of the performance evaluation for these managers is annual profitability. In pursuing their annual profitability targets, they are given considerable autonomy in choosing the source of the components they use in their products. Not surprisingly, these managers began to use outside vendors rather than continue to be penalized with what they saw as excessive costs of RAMs produced internally by the component division.

Management's Dilemma

As a consequence, the component division site suffered from idle capacity. Because manufacturing costs are primarily fixed, remaining production had to bear additional costs, which in turn caused a further competitive deterioration. In response, more product managers sought alternative suppliers, and so it went.

The first reaction by the component division's site management was to focus on its cost structure to make certain that it remained cost competitive. Addressing the cost structure enabled the plant to increase its productivity considerably, tighten spending controls, and reduce indirect manpower, with resulting cost improvements. The plant's costs were improved noticeably over the costs estimated in previous plans. Figure 22.2 depicts this cost comparison.

Nonetheless, the continued erosion in volumes made it difficult to make these savings visible to the product managers. Many of these savings were not immediate but would be

FIGURE 22.2

Average Cost Comparison—Memory

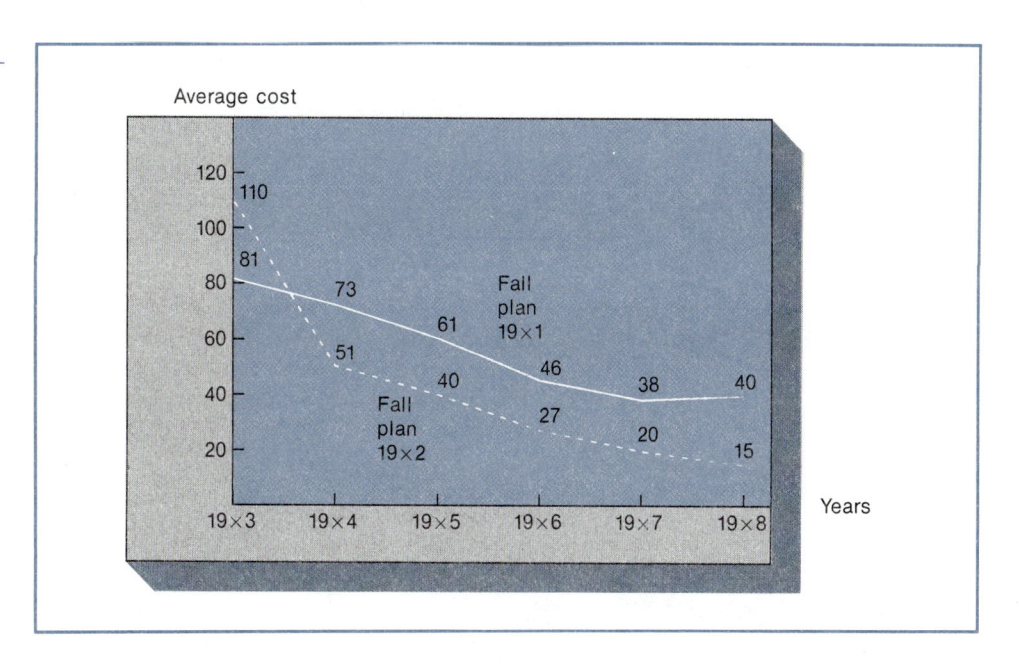

realized in future years. Although the plans were likely to be achieved, failure would mean increased costs in the future, which would be passed along to the ultimate users when the products were transferred at actual cost. In deciding to take the risk that the plant would meet its plan, a product manager did not have any commitment from the plant and could suffer the consequences if planned volumes did not materialize or if the plant was unable to meet its cost objectives.

The site general manager, recognizing this dilemma, asked the financial staff to recommend a different system for interdivisional transfers. This new system, at a minimum, should convey to its internal customers the direction the site was taking on cost control and productivity. The system should also provide a sense of commitment that these objectives would be met. Furthermore, product managers who used the site as a source of components would need some assurance that they would not feel the impact of future penalties and that they would enjoy future benefits as early as possible.

With these instructions, the plant controller's staff initiated a study of the plant, comparing it to the semiconductor industry. The results of the study are summarized in figure 22.3.

Required

1. What alternatives would you have the controller recommend to the general manager for interdivisional transfers?
2. What would you recommend as an appropriate pricing strategy for these interdivisional transfers?
3. What recommendations would you have for some of the major accounting elimination issues, including:
    a. an approach to duplicate profit?
    b. inventory valuation?

FIGURE 22.3

Comparison of Semiconductor Industry versus Site

Industry Practices	Site
Forward pricing	Full cost recovery by year
Total price includes all charges	Additional allocations of other costs & expenses

Price independent of other customers
  -Price is function of total volume and insensitive to volume shifts
	Cost dependent on other customers' stability
	  -Dramatic unit cost changes with shifts in volume

Variable markups
  -Standard product—low
  -Unique product—high
	None; costs are costs

Terms & conditions explicit	Difficult to make terms & conditions explicit

Measured as a business
  -Revenue
  -Profit/margin
  -Return on assets
  -Cash flow
	Plan/commitment measurements
	  -Cost versus plan
	  -Schedules versus plan

Chapter 23

Capital Budgeting: Part I

Outline

INTRODUCTION TO CAPITAL BUDGETING
Cash Flow Orientation
Charting Cash Inflows and Outflows
CAPITAL BUDGETING TECHNIQUES
Net Present Value
   Analysis of a Single Investment Alternative
   Analysis of Multiple Investment Alternatives
   Incremental Versus Total Cost Approach for Comparing Investment Alternatives
   Strengths and Weaknesses of Net Present Value
Internal Rate of Return
   Single Investment Alternative with Equal Annual Cash Flows
   Single Investment Alternative with Unequal Annual Cash Flows
   Multiple Investment Alternatives
   Strengths and Weaknesses of Internal Rate of Return
Payback
   Payback Period
   Decision Analysis Using Payback Period
   Evaluation of the Payback Period
   Modifications of Payback
   Present Value Payback

Accounting Rate of Return
   Decision Making Using Accounting Rate of Return
   Strengths and Weaknesses of the Accounting Rate of Return
Disinvestment Decisions
SELECTING THE EVALUATION TECHNIQUE
Selection Criteria
   Unequal Investment Lives
   Unequal Initial Investments
Planning and Control Over Capital Expenditures
   Control of Capital Budgeting Expenditures
   Post-Operational Evaluation
Complications to Capital Budgeting
SUMMARY
APPENDIX 23.1: TIME VALUE OF MONEY
SELF-STUDY PROBLEM
SUGGESTED READINGS
DISCUSSION QUESTIONS
EXERCISES
PROBLEMS
CASE

Acquisitions of property, plant, and equipment are among the most important decisions made by management because of their long-term effect on the company. Equipment may last as long as fifteen to twenty years and buildings commonly last thirty to fifty years. An error in the acquisition of one of these assets affects not only the current year but the ensuing years as well. Occasionally, a company is not able to recover from a bad decision in acquiring one of these capital assets. Buildings and equipment are often specialized, and the only way the original investment can be recovered is through normal use in business operations.

The analytical techniques and tools available to help make these capital investment decisions is the topic of this chapter. This chapter also identifies what capital budgeting is and explains the alternative capital budgeting procedures commonly used, with greater emphasis on those techniques that help management choose the best alternative. After you have completed this chapter, you should be able to:

1. define capital budgeting.
2. use each of the following techniques in making capital budgeting decisions:
   a. Net present value
   b. Internal rate of return
   c. Payback
   d. Accounting rate of return
3. describe the strengths and weaknesses of each of the preceding methods.

INTRODUCTION TO CAPITAL BUDGETING

Capital budgeting is the process used to identify whether a capital investment will be profitable or to select from a variety of capital investment alternatives those that will be the most profitable. **Capital assets,** more commonly referred to as fixed assets, are the entity's larger or more prominent assets. They are long-term, relatively durable assets, such as buildings, machinery, or a tract of land, that can be used repeatedly in the production of goods and services. Budgeting, you will recall, is a plan of operations based on estimates of the future. The master budget includes an itemized allotment of funds for the future period, including an allocation for capital assets. Therefore, **capital budgeting** *refers to the allocation of money for the acquisition or maintenance of a company's fixed assets.*

There are many types of capital budgeting decisions. Among the most common are the following:

1. Acquisition of new equipment to reduce operating costs through increased mechanization
2. Construction of a new factory or warehouse to increase capacity or reduce dependence on an outside supplier
3. Replacement of an old machine with a new machine to do the same job (which is complicated somewhat by the fact that the new machine may have more capacity, cost less to operate, and improve quality)

Cash Flow Orientation

The philosophy behind investments in capital assets is no different than that for any other investment. For example, a primary objective of an investment in stock is to increase wealth. An investment is considered to be a good investment when the cash received through dividends and final sale of the stock returns the original investment *and* provides a return on the investment.

The objective of investing in capital assets is to obtain cash by providing goods and services to customers or by saving cash that is currently being paid to provide those same goods and services. A good investment is made when the cash earned or saved is enough to return the original investment and provide a competitive return on the investment. Figure 23.1 shows a comparison of the cash flows associated with investments in stock and capital assets.

The same type of analysis is relevant for all investment proposals. The important assumptions and criteria of the analysis include the following:

1. Each investment alternative is considered to be a separate project.
2. The cash that is paid for the investment is compared with the cash that it returns to evaluate its desirability.
3. The entire life of the investment must be considered.
4. Each investment alternative should be able to return its original investment in cash and provide an adequate return on the money invested.

Note that the cash flow orientation of capital budgeting differs from the accrual concept followed in financial accounting. The concept of revenue recognition under the accrual basis of accounting requires concentration on the earning process rather than on the timing

FIGURE 23.1

Investment Characteristics of Capital Assets

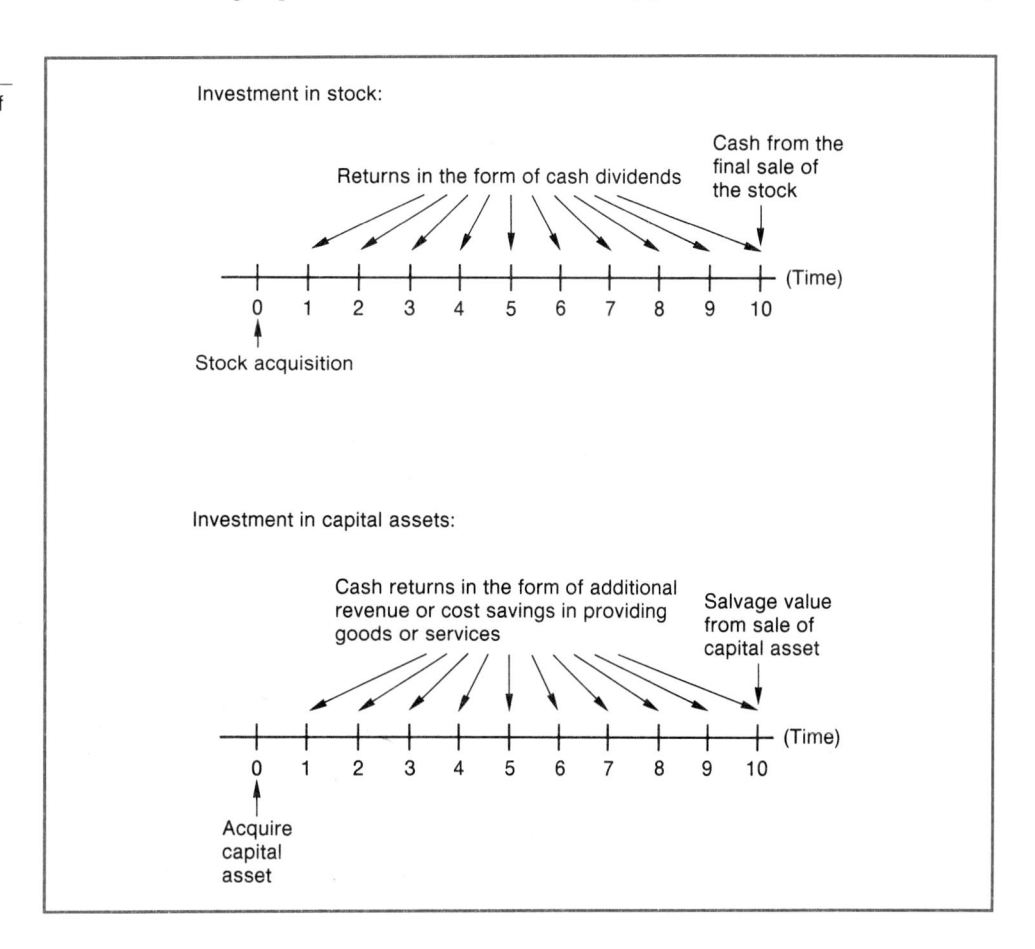

of cash receipts. Revenue is recognized when it is earned, and expenses, including depreciation, are matched with the revenues they generate. Capital budgeting ignores revenue recognition and matching concepts and considers the cash receipts and cash disbursements associated with a project. *The entire focus of capital budgeting is on the amounts and timing of cash flows.*

The differences between capital budgeting and the accrual concepts of financial accounting are presented in figure 23.2, which shows the life of an organization and the assets that the organization uses. The life of each asset is represented on the horizontal axis. Suppose that the organization is in the fifth year of its life. For financial reporting, net income is measured by identifying the revenues that each asset provides during the year and by matching expenses incurred in generating those revenues. Because the fixed assets are used to generate revenues, a portion of the original cost is charged to expense through an acceptable depreciation method. The relevant time period and data for this analysis are identified by the shaded portion of figure 23.2, which represents the annual accounting period for year 5.

Notice that equipment *E* was acquired during year 5. The decision to acquire it was a capital budgeting decision. The shaded portion of equipment *E* shows the relevant time period and data for the capital budgeting decision to consider the desirability of purchasing that piece of equipment. The purchase price of the equipment was compared to the cash flows equipment *E* is expected to provide over its useful life (which may be twenty to thirty years long) to see if there was an adequate return on the investment. The difference between the relevant information for a capital budgeting decision and annual reporting can be seen by comparing the two shaded areas in figure 23.2. The procedures used to determine the adequacy of the return will be explained later, but first we need to review the concept of cash flows.

Charting Cash Inflows and Outflows

Cash that a company receives or saves as a result of a capital investment is called *cash inflow*, whereas the money that is spent to acquire, maintain, or operate the asset is a *cash outflow*. Cash inflows and outflows are generally identified as one of the three following types.

FIGURE 23.2
Capital Budgeting Versus Accrual Accounting

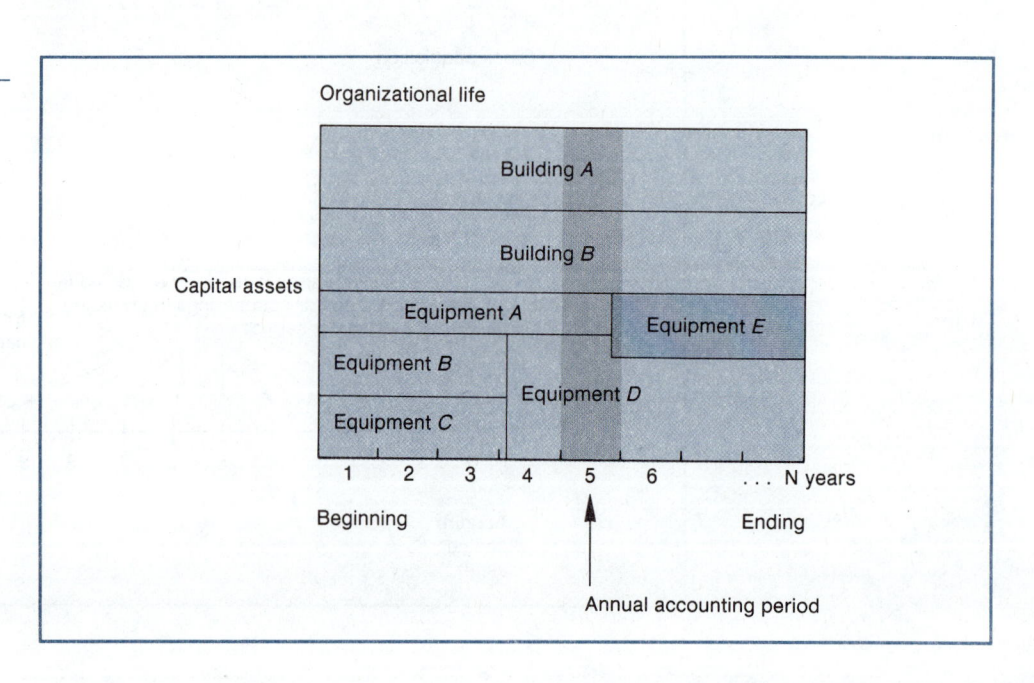

1. *Cash outflow associated with the initial investment.* The initial investment is made at the start of the project's life. If the life of an investment is depicted on a time line, time period zero represents the beginning of the capital investment project. Suppose that equipment E in the previous example costs $100,000. The cash outflow associated with the initial investment can be charted on a time line as follows:

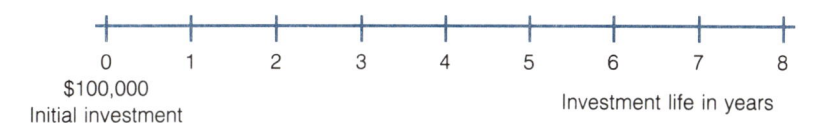

```
  +----+----+----+----+----+----+----+----+
  0    1    2    3    4    5    6    7    8
$100,000                      Investment life in years
Initial investment
```

2. *Net cash flows from operating the asset over its useful life.* The operation of a capital asset generally results in both cash inflows and outflows. The term *cash inflows* is used in a broad sense to include both *cash revenues* and *cash savings*. Cash outflows refer to the actual costs of operating and maintaining the asset. The cash inflows and outflows from operating the asset are netted together to provide an annual net cash inflow or outflow from operating a project.

EXAMPLE

Equipment E will be used to produce an existing product and a new product. The new product will provide $16,000 of additional sales each year, and direct materials and labor for the product will cost $10,000 annually. In addition, there will be one less direct laborer working on the existing product, thus saving $8,500 in cash that would have to be paid to the worker if the equipment is not acquired. The cash outlay for electricity, repairs, maintenance, and other overhead is expected to be $2,000 per year. The net cash flows resulting from the operation of equipment E are $12,500.

Revenue	$16,000
Direct costs	(10,000)
Direct labor	8,500
Overhead	(2,000)
Net cash inflow	$12,500

These are added to the time line as follows:

```
              Net annual cash flows

     $12,500 $12,500 $12,500 $12,500 $12,500 $12,500 $12,500 $12,500
  +----+----+----+----+----+----+----+----+
  0    1    2    3    4    5    6    7    8
$100,000
Investment
```

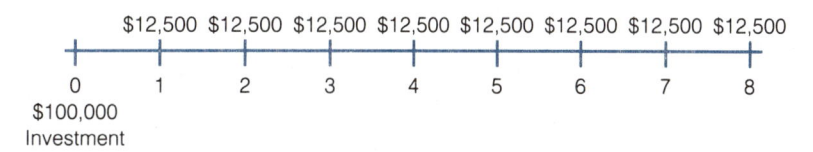

Notice that in this example depreciation is not included. Recall that depreciation is the allocation of the original investment over its useful life in an attempt to correctly match expenses with revenues. Because capital budgeting is cash-flow oriented, the entire initial investment is considered to be an outflow at time period zero. Ignoring income taxes, there is no cash flow associated with depreciation, so it is excluded from the analysis. Chapter 24 explains the effect income tax has on capital budgeting decisions and how depreciation affects the payment of income taxes.

Technically, it could be argued that because the cash flows are expected to occur evenly throughout the year, they should be shown on the time line at a midyear point rather than at a year-end point. However, this would complicate the analysis, because present and future value tables explained later in this chapter commonly assume that the cash flow occurs at the beginning or end of the period. Using a mid-year point would require using a different set of present value tables for capital budgeting techniques that consider the time value of money. Also, the additional precision provided by using a mid-year timing of cash flow is not thought to be justified given the lack of precision involved in estimating cash flows. Therefore, all capital budgeting techniques assume that cash flows occur at the end of each year.

3. *Salvage value of the capital asset at the end of its useful life*. Most capital assets can be sold for a nominal amount at the end of their useful life. The cash provided is an inflow and should be considered in the analysis.

Suppose that equipment E can be sold for $1,000 at the end of eight years. The time line and the related cash flows from equipment E will be shown as follows:

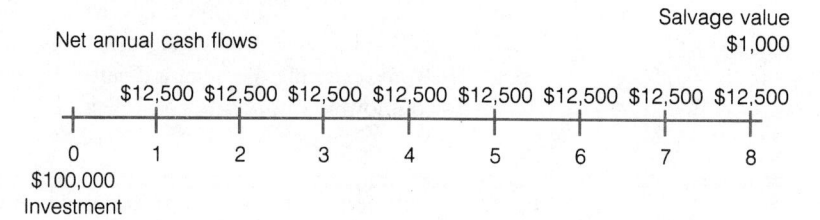

```
                                                                    Salvage value
Net annual cash flows                                                      $1,000

      $12,500  $12,500  $12,500  $12,500  $12,500  $12,500  $12,500  $12,500
  +------+-------+-------+-------+-------+-------+-------+-------+
  0      1       2       3       4       5       6       7       8
$100,000
Investment
```

Charting the cash flows for equipment E can be useful in setting up the relevant information for a capital budgeting decision. It is customary to put cash outflows *below* the line representing the investment's useful life. The annual net cash inflows from operations are recorded *above* the time line, along with any salvage value. This type of cash flow analysis is most useful because it shows not only the amounts but also the *timing* of cash flows, which is very important in several of the approaches to capital budgeting.

A tabular format is an alternative to the time line approach and is more convenient for making many of the computations associated with the capital budgeting techniques. The amounts, timing, and identity of the cash flows for the equipment E proposal are listed in columns as follows:

Cash Flow for Equipment E Proposal

Type	Timing	Amount
Initial investment	Now	$100,000
Net cash inflows	Years 1–8	12,500 per year
Salvage value	Year 8	1,000

The tabular approach will be used throughout this chapter.

CAPITAL BUDGETING TECHNIQUES

There are many techniques used in making capital budgeting decisions. The various techniques can be broadly classified into the four following categories:

1. Net present value
2. Internal rate of return
3. Payback period
4. Accounting rate of return

Capital budgeting decisions usually take one of two forms—**screening decisions,** in which one investment alternative is being considered and the objective is to know if it is a desirable investment, or **preference decisions,** in which several alternatives are being considered and the objective is to select from the competing alternatives the ones that are most profitable.

Some projects compete directly with other projects so that if one project is selected, the others must be rejected. These are sometimes called *competing investment alternatives* or *mutually exclusive investments*. Consider, for example, a company that needs only one piece of equipment to perform a specialized function. Two machines are under consideration, each requiring a different mix of raw material and direct-labor inputs. If machine *A* is selected as the most profitable proposal, machine *B* must be rejected. The benefits of owning it completely disappear by the adoption of machine *A*.

Net Present Value

The **net present value** method is generally considered to be the most accurate technique for capital budgeting decisions; it considers the time value of money, allows for an adjustment for risk, and provides a measure of the investment's profitability. Both the amount and timing of cash flows are important because of the time value of money. Money received today is more valuable than money that will be received several years in the future, because money on hand today can be invested to earn a return that compounds with time. Hence, *an investment opportunity that promises early returns is more desirable than one that provides late returns*.[1]

The information that must be collected to use the net present value method includes *(a)* the cash outflow associated with the acquisition, *(b)* the net cash inflows associated with annual operations, and *(c)* the estimated salvage value. In addition, a minimum desired rate of return or **cut-off rate** (also called *cost of capital* or *hurdle rate*) must be selected. This rate of return is generally specified by management and identifies a *minimum level of profitability* that must be achieved by the investment. The processes by which it is selected and computed are discussed in chapter 24.

Analysis of a Single Investment Alternative
The net present value of a proposed investment is computed by subtracting the present value of the cash outflows from the present value of the cash inflows. The investment proposal is desirable at the specified rate of return when the net present value is greater than or equal to zero. A positive net present value means that the investment's rate of return is greater than the minimum desired rate of return. A net present value of zero means that the investment rate of return equals the minimum desired rate of return. A negative net present value indicates that the rate of return on the capital investment is less than management's cut-off rate. Therefore, it is an undesirable investment at the specified rate of return.

Another way to think of net present value is as the additional amount that could be paid for the investment (if the net present value is positive) and still earn the minimum desired rate of return. Or, if the net present value is negative, it is the reduction required in the cost of the investment to earn the minimum desired rate of return.

---

1. It is assumed that you have had experience in working with present and future value concepts. You should understand the difference between present value and future value and should be able to compute the present value or future value of a dollar amount or an annuity from present and future value tables. Appendix 23.1 at the end of this chapter reviews each of these concepts. A quick review may be helpful at this point.

EXAMPLE

Problem

Chapman Incorporated is considering an expansion of its product line that will require the acquisition of new and rather expensive equipment, called TR1. The equipment costs $250,000 and will have a useful life of seven years with $20,000 salvage value. It is expected that the annual net cash inflows from operations will be $70,000. Will the proposed expansion be profitable if Chapman has a minimum desired rate of return of 20 percent for this type of capital investment?

Solution

The cash flows are as follows:

Type	Timing	Amount
Investment	Now	$250,000
Net cash inflows	Years 1–7	70,000 per year
Salvage value	Year 7	20,000
Desired rate of return		20 %

The net present value is computed as follows:

Present Value of Cash inflows

Net cash from operations
  ($70,000 × 3.605) $252,350
Salvage value
  ($20,000 × 0.279)   5,580
  Total $257,930

Present Value of Cash Outflows

Initial investment
  ($250,000 × 1.0)   250,000
Net present value $ 7,930

Decision

The investment proposal is desirable at a 20 percent minimum rate of return.

Notice that in the preceding solution the present values of the cash inflows and outflows are computed by multiplying the dollar amounts by the present value factors obtained from the present value tables in appendix 23.1 at the end of this chapter. Calculators that have built-in present and future value functions offer a convenient way to compute present values. As an alternative, the time value formulas can be used and the analysis performed on any calculator. The formulas for each of the present and future value computations are shown at the top of each table in the appendix. The present value of the cash outflows is subtracted from the present value of the cash inflows to obtain the project's net present value.

The positive net present value of $7,930 in this example indicates that the rate of return exceeds 20 percent and that it is a desirable investment. In other words, the investment could cost $257,930 ($250,000 + $7,930) and the company would still be able to earn the 20-percent minimum rate of return.

The minimum desired rate of return is important in determining the investment's desirability. A slightly different rate of return may change the results.

EXAMPLE

Problem

Suppose that Chapman Incorporated in the preceding example specified a 22-percent desired minimum rate of return. Is the investment desirable at this rate?

Solution

The net present value is computed using a 22-percent interest rate.

Present Value of Cash Inflows

Net cash from operations ($70,000 × 3.416)	$239,120	
Salvage value ($20,000 × 0.249)	4,980	
Total		$244,100

Present Value of Cash Outflows

Initial investment ($250,000 × 1.0)	250,000	
Net present value		($ 5,900)

Decision

Reject the proposal at a 22-percent cut-off rate.

This analysis has considered only one investment alternative, and the investment is considered to be desirable if the net present value is positive at the desired minimum rate of return.

Analysis of Multiple Investment Alternatives

When two or more investment alternatives are being considered, it is a preference decision. The net present value of each investment is computed using the minimum rate of return. As long as the cost and life of the investment alternatives are equal, the one with the highest net present value is most profitable. When the alternatives' costs are not equal, a *profitability index* is computed by dividing the present value of the cash flows by the initial investment.

$$\text{Profitability index} = \frac{\text{Present value of cash flows}}{\text{Initial investment}}$$

The alternative with the highest profitability index is generally the most desirable, because it provides the *highest return per dollar of investment*. The profitability index does not identify profitability in an absolute sense but profitability relative to the amount invested.

EXAMPLE

Problem

Assume that Chapman Incorporated, referred to in the previous example, is content with a 20-percent minimum rate of return and that it has two other alternatives—equipment TR2 and TR3—for producing the new product. TR2 also costs $250,000, is slightly cheaper to operate, but has no salvage value. Annual net cash flows from operations are expected to be $71,000 per year. Cash flows for TR2 are as follows:

Cash Flows for TR2

Type	Timing	Amount
Investment	Now	$250,000
Net cash inflows	Years 1–7	71,000 per year
Desired rate of return		20%

TR3 costs only $221,500 and has no salvage value, but repair and maintenance costs are expected to increase each year over the life of the asset. Its expected net cash flows are as follows:

Cash Flows for TR3

Type	Timing	Amount
Investment	Now	$221,500
Net cash inflows	Year 1	75,000
	Year 2	70,000
	Year 3	65,000
	Year 4	60,000
	Year 5	55,000
	Year 6	50,000
	Year 7	45,000
Desired rate of return		20%

Which of the three equipment proposals is most profitable?

Solution

The computation of the net present values is shown in figure 23.3. The net present value and profitability index for each alternative are as follows:

Equipment	Net Present Value	Profitability Index	
TR1	$7,930	1.032	($257,930 ÷ $250,000)
TR2	5,955	1.024	($255,955 ÷ $250,000)
TR3	7,525	1.034	($229,025 ÷ $221,500)

The net present value can be used to compare TR1 and TR2 because they both require the same initial investment and have the same useful life. The higher net present

FIGURE 23.3

Computation of Net Present Values for Investment Alternatives of Chapman, Inc.

TR2: Present value of cash inflows:		
Net cash from operations		
($71,000 × 3.605)		$255,955
Present value of cash outflows:		
Initial investment		
($250,000 × 1.0)		250,000
Net present value		$ 5,955
TR3: Present value of cash inflows:		
Net cash from operations		
Year 1 ($75,000 × 0.833)	$62,475	
Year 2 ($70,000 × 0.694)	48,580	
Year 3 ($65,000 × 0.579)	37,635	
Year 4 ($60,000 × 0.482)	28,920	
Year 5 ($55,000 × 0.402)	22,110	
Year 6 ($50,000 × 0.335)	16,750	
Year 7 ($45,000 × 0.279)	12,555	
Total		$229,025
Present value of cash outflows:		
Initial investment		
($221,500 × 1.0)		221,500
Net present value		$ 7,525

value for TR1 indicates that it is more profitable than TR2. However, it is not valid to compare the net present values of TR1 and TR3, because their initial investments are different. As the profitability index shows, TR3 is a better investment than TR1; even though the net present value is lower, it provides a greater return on the dollars invested than TR1.

Incremental versus Total Cost Approach for Comparing Investment Alternatives

An incremental approach or a total cost approach can be used to chart cash flows when only two competing proposals are being considered. The *total cost approach* has been used in the previous examples. It considers each proposal separately and charts the relevant cash flows for each. The net present value is computed using the cut-off rate.

Under the *incremental approach,* the added cost of investing in the most expensive proposal is charted as the initial investment, and the additional revenues and salvage value that it provides are charted as the annual net cash inflow. The net present value of these cash flows should equal the difference between the net present value of the competing alternatives under the total cost approach.

To illustrate the two approaches, assume that Midway Company is trying to decide between purchasing or leasing a warehouse. Either way it will have use of the warehouse for its entire remaining life of five years. The relevant cash flows on a total cost approach are as follows:

Cash Flows for Purchase and Lease

Type	Timing	Purchase Amounts	Lease Amounts
Initial investment	Now	$60,000	$11,000
Net cash inflows	Years 1–5	23,000 per year	5,000 per year
Salvage value	5	10,000	0
Desired rate of return		20%	20%

The net present value for each proposal is computed, and the difference between them is $8,858.

Present Value of Cash Inflows

	Lease	Purchase
($5,000 × 2.991)	$14,955	
($23,000 × 2.991)		$68,793
($10,000 × 0.402)		4,020
Total	$14,955	$72,813
Initial investment	11,000	60,000
Net present value	$ 3,955	$12,813
Difference		$8,858

For an incremental approach, the cash flows for the lease option are subtracted from the purchase option. The initial investment is $49,000 ($60,000 − $11,000), the annual cash flow is $18,000 ($23,000 − $5,000), and salvage value is $10,000 ($10,000 − $0).

Incremental Cash Flows for Purchase rather than Lease

Type	Timing	Amount
Initial investment	Now	$49,000
Net cash inflows	Years 1–5	18,000 per year
Salvage value	Year 5	10,000
Desired rate of return		20%

The net present value is computed using the same cut-off rate with the same $8,858 difference.

Present Value of Cash Inflows

($18,000 × 2.991)	$53,838
($10,000 × 0.402)	4,020
Total	$57,858
Initial investment	49,000
Net present value	$ 8,858

The difficulty in using the incremental approach is in knowing whether the additional net present value is worth the additional investment. In this case Midway Company is investing an additional $49,000 for an increased net present value of $8,858. Because the net present value is positive, we can conclude that the return on the additional investment is greater than the 20-percent cut-off rate, but we need to go back to the total cost approach to identify which proposal is most profitable. The profitability index shows that the lease option is most profitable.

	Profitability Index
Purchase	
($72,813 ÷ $60,000)	1.21
Lease	
($14,955 ÷ $11,000)	1.36

The incremental approach is most useful when comparing two investment proposals with equal investments but unequal and uneven cash flows over their useful lives.

Figure 23.4 summarizes the objective, informational requirements, computation format, and decision rules for the net present value method.

Strengths and Weaknesses of Net Present Value

The major strength of the net present value method is that it considers both the amount and timing of all cash flows in measuring an investment's rate of return against the minimum rate of return specified by

FIGURE 23.4

Net Present Value

Objective: Determine whether the present value of future cash flows at a desired rate of return will be greater than or less than the cost of the proposed investment.

Informational requirements:
1. Initial investment
2. Annual net cash inflows
3. Minimum desired rate of return

Computation format:
  Present value of net cash inflows:
    (Cash flow) × (Present value factor) $ _____
  Present value of cash outflows:
    (Initial investment) $ _____
  Net present value $ _____

Decision rules:
  Single investment alternative: Accept the investment proposal when the net present value is greater than or equal to zero.

  Multiple investment alternatives: The alternative with the highest profitability index is the most profitable.

$$\text{Profitability index} = \frac{\text{Present value of cash inflows}}{\text{Initial investment}}$$

management. A positive net present value indicates that the investment is profitable. Even though it does not identify an exact rate of profitability, it does measure profitability as compared to the cut-off rate.

Another advantage of the net present value method is the minimum amount of computation required to identify investment profitability. Given a desired cut-off rate, only one series of calculations is required to compute the net present value or the profitability index. This is much more efficient than the trial-and-error method often required under the internal rate of return method.

For a person unfamiliar with present value concepts, this method may be difficult to work with, and the concept of positive versus negative net present values may not make much sense. Instruction in present value and future value computations is relatively recent in formal business education. People who have not had a college education or who received their education several years ago may be unfamiliar with present value concepts. Even those managers who have had some education in present value concepts seem to have difficulty understanding net present values and interpreting their meaning in capital investment decisions. An internal rate of return seems to be more meaningful to them.

Internal Rate of Return

Several names are used to describe this technique, including internal rate of return, discount yield, time adjusted rate of return, and compound return on investment. We will use the title *internal rate of return* because it is fairly descriptive of the results and because it is a common title.

The items of information required for this method are the initial cash investment and the estimated net cash inflows, including salvage value, over the life of the investment. The **internal rate of return** is the interest rate that equates the present value of future cash inflows with the initial cash investment. Under this method, the net present value is specified as zero and the *objective* of the computation *is to identify the interest rate that results in a zero net present value*. A minimum desired rate of return is not required for the computation; nevertheless, management must have some minimum rate in mind to compare with the internal rate to determine the desirability of the investment. The project is desirable as long as the internal rate of return equals or exceeds the cut-off rate. From a profitability standpoint, any project whose internal rate of return is below the desired minimum should be rejected. The internal rate of return may be thought of as the maximum rate of interest a company could pay for borrowed funds to finance the acquisition and be no worse off than if the investment had not been pursued.

Single Investment Alternative with Equal Annual Cash Flows The internal rate of return method is easiest to apply when the investment alternative has equal annual cash flows and no salvage value. An equal annual cash flow is an annuity, the present value of which can be computed by multiplying the amount of the annuity by the present value factor. When the net present value is specified as zero, the relationship between the present value of the cash flows and the initial investment can be manipulated as follows:

$$\underbrace{(\text{Annual net cash flow}) \times (\text{Annuity factor})}_{\text{Present value of annual cash flows}} - \text{Initial investment} = \underset{\underset{\text{specified as zero}}{\text{Net present value}}}{0}$$

$$(\text{Annual cash flow}) \times (\text{Annuity factor}) = \text{Initial investment}$$

$$\text{Annuity factor} = \frac{\text{Initial investment}}{\text{Annual cash flows}}$$

Given the initial investment and annual cash flows, the annuity factor can be computed using the preceding equation. If the annuity factor and the years of useful life are known, the internal rate of return can be determined from the table of present values of an annuity.

EXAMPLE

Problem

Dean Incorporated is considering the acquisition of equipment that will cost $100,000 and have a useful life of five years with zero salvage value. The equipment will be used to manufacture a subassembly that has been purchased from an outside supplier. Annual net cash inflows (savings) from manufacturing this part internally are expected to be $33,400. Management believes that investment proposals of this type should provide at least a 23-percent rate of return to enhance the overall profitability of the company. What is the internal rate of return on this project, and should the equipment be acquired?

Solution

The annuity factor that will equate the present value of the cash inflows with the investment is 2.994.

$$\text{Annuity factor} = \frac{\$100,000}{\$33,400} = \underline{2.994}$$

The interest rate associated with this factor is obtained from the table of present values of an annuity by locating the row of annuity factors corresponding with the useful life of the project. Because the equipment has a useful life of five years, go down the column of periods to 5 and across the table until an annuity factor is located that is equal to 2.994. The desired factor of 2.994 lies between 3.127 at 18 percent and 2.991 at 20 percent. Because the annuity factor of 2.991 is so close to the desired factor, we can say that the internal rate of return is slightly under 20 percent. Management should therefore reject the equipment proposal because it does not meet its minimum expectation of 23 percent.

Present and future value tables can be purchased that have periods from 1 to 10,000 and interest rates that vary by each 1/8 percent from 1/8 percent to 99 7/8 percent. The internal rate of return can always be obtained from these tables without any interpolation. However, interpolation may be required when using summary tables as presented in appendix 23.1 and when the annuity factors in the table are not close to the specified annuity factor. Even then, the answer may be obvious and interpolation may not be necessary. For example, if the cut-off rate is 16 percent and the internal rate of return is between 20 percent and 22 percent, interpolation will not improve the decision-making process.

Interpolation is a process of estimating an intermediate interest rate between those listed in the table. The relative position of the desired annuity factor to those listed in the table is used to estimate the interest rate.

EXAMPLE

Problem

Suppose that Dean Incorporated in the previous example estimates that annual cash flows will be $26,000. What is the internal rate of return associated with this investment proposal?

Solution

The desired annuity factor of 3.846 ($100,000 ÷ $26,000) lies between 3.993 at 8 percent and 3.791 at 10 percent. The following computation illustrates the interpolation process.

Interest Rates	Annuity Factor	Difference
8%	3.993 ⎫	0.147
?	3.846 ⎬	
10%	3.791 ⎭	0.055
Total 2%		0.202

The interpolated interest rate is:

8% + [(0.147 ÷ 0.202) × 2%] = 8% + 1.46% = 9.46%.

Notice that the desired annuity factor of 3.846 is 72.7 percent (0.147 ÷ 0.202) of the way between 3.993 and 3.791. Therefore, 72.7 percent of the difference between 8 percent and 10 percent is added to the 8-percent rate to estimate the internal rate of return.

Single Investment Alternative with Unequal Annual Cash Flows A trial-and-error approach must be used to determine the internal rate of return when the annual cash flows are not equal. The process involves selecting an estimated internal rate of return and using it to compute the net present value. If the net present value is *positive,* a higher rate is selected. When the net present value is *negative,* a lower rate is selected. The net present value is again computed under the newly selected interest rate, and the process continues until the net present value is (approaches) zero. Interpolation may be required when the actual internal rate of return is not equal to one of the interest rates for which present value factors are listed in the table.

EXAMPLE

Problem

Dean Incorporated is also considering the acquisition of a truck and semitrailer to be used to haul its raw materials from the supplier and its finished product to the retail outlets. The combined cost of the rig is $90,000, and the expected cash inflows (savings) over its useful life along with the salvage value are shown below:

Cash Flows for Truck and Semitrailer

Type	Timing	Amount
Initial investment	Now	$90,000
Net annual savings	Year 1	40,000
	Year 2	30,000
	Year 3	30,000
	Year 4	20,000
	Year 5	15,000
Salvage value	Year 5	15,000

What is the internal rate of return on this proposal, and is it a desirable investment alternative?

Solution

First pick an estimated internal rate of return and compute the net present value. Suppose we first pick 24 percent. We compute the net present value of −$3,850, as shown in figure 23.5. A negative net present value indicates that the rate selected is too high, so a lower rate is selected, say 20 percent. At this rate a positive net present value of $3,210 is computed, so we know that the actual rate lies between 20 and 24 percent. A third rate of 22 percent is used and the net present value is −$390. The negative amount indicates

FIGURE 23.5

Trial-and-Error Calculation for Internal Rate of Return

Present value of cash inflows:

Year	Amount	Present Value at 24%		Present Value at 20%		Present Value at 22%	
1	$40,000	(0.806)	$32,240	(0.833)	$33,320	(0.820)	$32,800
2	30,000	(0.650)	19,500	(0.694)	20,820	(0.672)	20,160
3	30,000	(0.524)	15,720	(0.579)	17,370	(0.551)	16,530
4	20,000	(0.423)	8,460	(0.482)	9,640	(0.451)	9,020
5	30,000	(0.341)	10,230	(0.402)	12,060	(0.370)	11,100
Total			$86,150		$93,210		$89,610

Present value of cash outflows:
($90,000 × 1.0) $90,000 $90,000 $90,000
Net present value   ($ 3,850) $ 3,210   ($ 390)

	Interest Rate	Net Present Value	Difference
Interpolation:	20%	$3,210	$3,210
	?	0	
	22%	($ 390)	390
Difference	2%		$3,600

Internal rate of return = 20% + [(3,210 ÷ 3,600) × 2%] = **21.78%**

---

that the internal rate of return lies between 20 and 22 percent. Without interpolation we would say that it is slightly below 22 percent. Interpolation indicates that it is 21.78 percent.

Multiple Investment Alternatives The internal rate of return is a measure of profitability, and it can be used to select from among alternative investment proposals. Other things being equal, an investment alternative with the highest internal rate of return will be the most profitable and should be selected. Let's continue to use Dean Incorporated as an example. Suppose that management believes that any investment alternatives yielding over 18 percent will enhance company profitability.

Assume that the two proposals outlined previously are the only ones being considered. The relevant data are summarized below. If Dean Incorporated only has enough cash to finance one project, which should it be?

Proposal	Cost	Internal Rate of Return
Manufacturing equipment	$100,000	20.0%
Truck and trailer	90,000	21.8%

The truck and trailer will probably be selected. The $90,000 invested in the truck and trailer will yield 21.78 percent, which is higher than the 20 percent return on the manufacturing equipment.

Figure 23.6 summarizes the objective, informational requirements, computation format, and decision rules for the internal rate of return method.

Strengths and Weaknesses of Internal Rate of Return The internal rate of return method, like the net present value method, considers both the amount and timing of all cash flows over the life of the investment and adjusts them for the time value of money.

FIGURE 23.6

Internal Rate of Return

> Objective: Compute an interest rate that equates the present value of the projected future net cash flows with the initial investment.
>
> Informational requirements:
>
> 1. Initial investment
> 2. Annual net cash flows
>
> Computation format:
>
> 1. Equal annual cash flows: Compute the annuity factor by dividing the initial investment by the annual cash flows and locate the internal rate of return from the present value tables that corresponds with the computed annuity factor and the years of useful life of the proposal.
> 2. Unequal annual cash flows: Through trial and error, using various interest rates, identify the interest rate that provides a net present value of zero.
>
>   Present value of cash flows:
>   (Cash flow) × (Present value factor) $_____
>   Initial investment $_____
>   Net present value $ 0
>
> 3. Use interpolation when necessary.
>
> Decision rules:
>
> Single investment alternative: Accept the investment proposal if the internal rate of return exceeds a minimum rate specified by management.
>
> Multiple investment alternatives: Select the investment alternative(s) with the highest internal rate of return as long as it (they) exceeds the minimum rate specified by management.

A benefit of this method over the net present value method is that it computes the exact rate of the investment's profitability in the form of a percentage rate of return. Some people find that interest rates are more meaningful to work with than net present values. This seems to be particularly true for users who have not been trained in the use of positive and negative net present values.

A weakness of the internal rate of return method is that no consideration is given to the relative dollar size of alternative investments. Also, additional computations are required when using the trial-and-error approach, which can be tedious and time consuming when one has only a small calculator and an old set of present value tables. The advent of the computer with package software has eliminated much of the tedious computation. Mini- and microcomputers have made computer processing available to even the medium- and smaller-sized organizations.

Payback

The payback method computes a **payback period,** which is the length of time required to recover the initial investment. This method continues to be one of the most widely used yardsticks for appraising capital investment proposals. It is often used in connection with the net present value method or the internal rate of return method because it provides a different type of information.

The information required to compute payback is the initial investment and the annual cash flows from earnings or savings. Management must also have a desired payback period in mind that it can use to determine the acceptability of the proposal. However, that is part of the decision analysis and not part of the computation.

Payback stresses risk reduction by identifying projects that have the shortest length of time during which the initial investment is outstanding. The emphasis is on cost recovery rather than profitability.

Payback Period Payback period is the length of time required for the initial investment to be recovered from earnings or savings. Generally, the time value of money is not considered.

For investments with equal annual cash flows, the payback period is computed by dividing the initial investment by the annual net cash inflow.

$$\text{Payback period} = \frac{\text{Initial investment}}{\text{Annual cash inflows}}$$

EXAMPLE

Problem
MOC Incorporated is considering the construction of a new warehouse at a cost of $300,000. The warehouse is expected to have a useful life of twenty years and $60,000 salvage value. The new facility will provide storage space for finished products that are currently being stored at a leased facility. In addition, MOC will be able to produce the finished product at a more even rate throughout the year rather than having to constantly adjust the production level to meet short-term fluctuations in demand. The expected annual cost savings from these benefits are $50,000 per year. Compute the payback period.

Solution
The initial investment will be recovered in six years, computed as follows:

$$\text{Payback period} = \frac{\$300,000}{\$50,000} = \underline{6 \text{ years}}$$

If the annual cash flows are not equal, they are accumulated until the cumulative amount of cash flows equals the initial investment. Just remember that the payback period is the length of time required to recover the initial investment. Interpolation may be required to determine the portion of the payback year required to recover the initial investment. When making the interpolation, it is assumed that cash flows occur evenly throughout the year.

EXAMPLE

Problem
MOC Incorporated is also considering the purchase of a $40,000 computer with an estimated useful life of five years and no salvage value. The computer will be used for internal accounting, and any excess time will be sold on a time-share basis. The annual cash flows are as follows:

Year 1	$ 9,000
Year 2	12,000
Year 3	15,000
Year 4	12,000
Year 5	5,000

What is the payback period?

Solution

The cash flows are accumulated until the initial investment is recovered. Notice that only part of the cash flows in year 4 are required for the cumulative cash flows to equal $40,000. The column "years of payback" shows the portion of the year included in the payback period. The payback period is 3.33 years.

Year	Annual Cash Flows	Cumulative Cash Flows	Years of Payback
1	$ 9,000	$ 9,000	1.00
2	12,000	21,000	1.00
3	15,000	36,000	1.00
4	12,000	40,000	0.33[a]
Payback period			3.33 years

[a] Straight-line interpolation indicates that one third of year 4 is required to recover the last $4,000 ($40,000 − $36,000) of the initial investment.

$$\frac{\$4,000}{\$12,000} \times 1 \text{ year} = 0.33 \text{ year}$$

Decision Analysis Using Payback Period When only one investment proposal is being considered, management must identify an acceptable payback period to be used as a benchmark for accepting or rejecting the proposal. The proposal is rejected unless its payback period is within the desired length of time specified by management.

EXAMPLE

Problem
Assuming MOC Incorporated is considering only the warehouse construction project previously described and that it has a maximum payback period of six years for capital investment projects, should the warehouse be constructed?

Solution
The warehouse construction project would be accepted because the expected payback period of six years is within the maximum allowable.

When several investment proposals are being considered, the payback periods are ranked from low to high. The proposals with the *shortest* payback periods are the most desirable, but only as long as they are within management's desired payback period.

EXAMPLE

Problem
Assume that MOC Incorporated is considering both the warehouse and the computer projects but it has only the resources to do one of them this year. Which should it select?

Solution
Comparing the payback periods indicates that the initial investment in the computer is recovered more than two years faster than the investment in the warehouse. Under the payback method, the computer probably would be accepted.

Project	Payback Period
Warehouse	6 years
Computer	3⅓ years

Evaluation of the Payback Period The objective of the payback method is not to measure profitability but to measure the amount of time necessary to generate an amount of cash inflow equal to the original cost of the asset. There is always some risk associated with future cash flows, but the payback method seeks to reduce this risk as much as possible by selecting projects that return the initial investment in the shortest period of time.

This type of analysis can be useful for companies that have a poor cash position. Timely cash flows are often more critical than profit maximization for newly established or developing companies. Therefore, a project that returns the initial investment quickly may be more desirable than a more profitable project that ties up money for an extended period of time.

A major weakness of the payback method is that it does not measure profitability. Remember that measuring profitability is not one of the objectives of this method. Nevertheless, decisions based on the payback period often result in minimizing profits. This can be shown using the warehouse and computer proposals for MOC Incorporated.

The cash flows for both proposals are summarized here:

Type	Timing	Warehouse Amount	Computer Amount
Initial investment	Now	$300,000	$40,000
Net cash flows	Years 1–20	50,000	
	Year 1		9,000
	Year 2		12,000
	Year 3		15,000
	Year 4		12,000
	Year 5		5,000
Salvage value	Year 20	60,000	
	Year 5		0

For an investment to be profitable, it must return an amount greater than the initial investment. The more an investment returns after investment recovery and the quicker it is received, the more profitable the investment. However, the payback period does not consider any cash flows after recovery of the initial investment. For example, it ignores the fact that the warehouse will continue in operation 14 years after investment recovery and also ignores the $60,000 salvage value. In comparing the projects, it does not recognize that the computer provides only 1⅔ years of service after investment recovery and that it has no salvage value.

The net present value method or the internal rate of return method can be used to compare the profitability of the two investments. The detail of these computations is shown in figure 23.7, and the final answers are as follows:

Net Present Value Method @ 16%

Project	Net Present Value	Profitability Index	Internal Rate of Return
Warehouse	($490)	0.998	15.97%
Computer	($4,707)	0.882	10.73%

As shown by the profitability index and the internal rate of return, the warehouse is a more profitable investment than the computer, even though its payback period is almost twice as long.

Another major weakness of the payback method is that it does not consider the time value of money. This can be illustrated by assuming two investment alternatives that cost $12,000 each and provide the following cash flows.

FIGURE 23.7

Computation of Net Present Value and Internal Rate of Return for MOC Incorporated Investment Alternatives

Warehouse

Present value of cash flows at 16%:		Present value of cash flows at 14%:	
Annual ($50,000 × 5.929)	$296,450	Annual ($50,000 × 6.623)	$331,150
Salvage ($60,000 × 0.051)	3,060	Salvage ($60,000 × 0.073)	4,380
Total	$299,510	Total	$335,530
Initial investment	300,000	Initial investment	300,000
Net present value	($ 490)	Net present value	$ 35,530
Profitability index	0.998	Internal rate of return	15.97%
($299,510 ÷ $300,000)		[14% + ($35,530 ÷ $36,020 × 2%)]	

Computer

Present value of cash flows at 16%:

Year		
1	($ 9,000 × 0.862)	$ 7,758
2	($12,000 × 0.743)	8,916
3	($15,000 × 0.641)	9,615
4	($12,000 × 0.552)	6,624
5	($ 5,000 × 0.476)	2,380
Total		$ 35,293
Initial investment		40,000
Net present value		($ 4,707)
Profitability index		0.882
($35,293 ÷ $40,000)		

Present value of cash flows at 10%:

Year		
1	($ 9,000 × 0.909)	$ 8,181
2	($12,000 × 0.826)	9,912
3	($15,000 × 0.751)	11,265
4	($12,000 × 0.683)	8,196
5	($ 5,000 × 0.621)	3,105
Total		$ 40,659
Initial investment		40,000
Net present value		$ 659
Internal rate of return		10.73%
[10% + ($659 ÷ $5,366 × 6%)]		

Cash Flows for Proposals A and B

Type	Timing	Proposal A Amount	Proposal B Amount
Initial investment	Now	$12,000	$12,000
Net cash flows	Year 1	0	4,000
	Year 2	0	4,000
	Year 3	12,000	4,000
	Year 4	4,000	12,000
	Year 5	4,000	0
	Year 6	4,000	0
Desired rate of return		10%	10%

Notice that both proposals have a payback period of three years, which would indicate an indifference about their relative desirability. If, however, the time value of money is considered, it is obvious that proposal B is more desirable. Using the net present value method and a 10 percent interest rate, figure 23.8 shows that the present value of the return on proposal B is worth $4,392 ($8,876 − $4,484) more than for proposal A.

Modifications of Payback Modifications of the payback method have been developed in an attempt to minimize its deficiencies. The modifications include payback reciprocal and present value payback methods.

The **payback reciprocal** method is intended to provide a measure of an investment's profitability. It is computed by dividing the annual cash flows by the initial investment.

$$\text{Payback reciprocal} = \frac{\text{Annual cash flows}}{\text{Initial investment}}$$

FIGURE 23.8

Comparison of Proposals with Equal Payback Periods using Net Present Value Method

	Proposal A	
Present value of cash flows at 10%:		
Year		
3	($12,000 × 0.751)	$ 9,012
4–6	[$ 4,000 × (4.355 − 2.487)]	7,472
	Total	$16,484
Initial investment		12,000
	Net present value	$ 4,484

	Proposal B	
Present value of cash flows at 10%:		
Year		
1–3	($ 4,000 × 3.170)	$12,680
4	($12,000 × 0.683)	8,196
	Total	$20,876
Initial investment		12,000
	Net present value	$ 8,876

As long as the useful life of the project is *at least twice as long* as the payback period, the payback reciprocal will provide a reasonable estimate of the internal rate of return. However, the payback reciprocal method can only be used to evaluate investment proposals that have equal annual cash flows.

Let's continue to use the example of the warehouse proposal for MOC Incorporated. It has equal annual cash flows of $50,000 per year, and the useful life of twenty years is more than twice the payback period of six years. The payback reciprocal is 16.6 percent.

$$\text{Payback reciprocal} = \frac{\$ 50,000}{\$300,000} = 16.6\%$$

Notice that this is a reasonable approximation of the internal rate of return of 15.97 percent that was computed earlier (see figure 23.7).

The constraints under which the payback reciprocal method will provide valid results can be summarized as follows:

1. Annual cash flows must be equal in amount.
2. The useful life of the project must be at least twice as long as the payback period for the payback reciprocal to provide a reasonable approximation of the internal rate of return.

These constraints limit its usefulness considerably. This method simply cannot be used to evaluate many proposals because they do not satisfy one or both of these constraints. Also, the payback reciprocal only approximates the internal rate of return. Because the internal rate of return can be easily computed when the annual cash flows are equal, most people who understand the time value of money and know how to use the present value tables compute the internal rate of return directly rather than approximate it by the payback reciprocal method.

Present Value Payback The **present value payback** method utilizes the time value of money concepts to compute the payback period. The present value payback period is the length of time required for the present value of the cash flows to equal the initial investment. In addition to knowing the initial investment and annual cash flows, a minimum desired rate of return must be identified. The present value of the annual cash flows is computed and accumulated until the cumulative amount is equal to the initial investment.

The present value payback period for MOC Incorporated's warehouse proposal is computed in figure 23.9, using a minimum desired rate of return of 10 percent. The present value payback period is 9.63 years.

The procedure shown in figure 23.9 must be used when the annual cash flows are not equal. However, if the annual cash flows are equal, the present value payback period can be obtained from the present value of an annuity table. We want to determine the number of periods that will equate the present value of the annuity to the original investment. This can be represented in the following equation form:

$$\text{Initial investment} = (\text{Annual cash flows}) \times (\text{Present value factor})$$

Manipulating it, we get the following:

$$\text{Present value factor} = \frac{\text{Initial investment}}{\text{Annual cash flows}}$$

The present value factor can be computed and used with the minimum desired rate of return to locate in the table the years required to recover the initial investment. The number of years associated with the specified interest rate and computed annuity factor is the present value payback period.

The present value factor for the warehouse proposal is 6.0 ($300,000 ÷ $50,000). Using the present value of an annuity table, go down the minimum desired rate of return column, which is specified by MOC Incorporated as 10%, until you come to an annuity factor of 6.0. It lies between 5.759 at 9 years and 6.145 at 10 years. Interpolation would be used to compute 9.63 years as the present value payback period.

FIGURE 23.9

Warehouse Proposal—MOC Inc.

Year	Annual Cash Flow	Present Value Factor	Present Value Amount	Cumulative Present Value	Years of Payback
1	$50,000	0.909	$45,450	$ 45,450	1.00
2	50,000	0.826	41,300	86,750	1.00
3	50,000	0.751	37,550	124,300	1.00
4	50,000	0.683	34,150	158,450	1.00
5	50,000	0.621	31,050	189,500	1.00
6	50,000	0.564	28,200	217,700	1.00
7	50,000	0.513	25,650	243,350	1.00
8	50,000	0.467	23,350	266,700	1.00
9	50,000	0.424	21,200	287,900	1.00
10	50,000	0.386	19,300	300,000	0.63[a]

Present value payback   9.63 years

[a] (12,100 ÷ 19,300) × 1 year = 0.63 or 63 percent of year 10 to recover the balance of the $300,000 investment.

FIGURE 23.10

Payback

> Objective: Identify the period of time required for cash flows from earnings or savings to recover the initial investment.
>
> Informational requirements:
>
> 1. Initial investment
> 2. Annual net cash flows from earnings or savings
>
> Computation format:
>
> 1. When annual cash flows are equal:
>
> $$\text{Payback period} = \frac{\text{Investment}}{\text{Annual cash flows}}$$
>
> 2. When annual cash flows are not equal:
>   Accumulate the annual cash flows until the cumulative amount equals the initial investment.
>
> Decision rules:
>
> Single investment alternative: Accept an investment proposal if the payback period is within a limit specified by management.
>
> Multiple investment alternatives: Rank the payback periods from low to high and accept the proposals with the shortest payback periods, as long as they are within the limit specified by management.
>
> Modifications of payback:
>
> 1. $\text{Payback reciprocal} = \dfrac{\text{Annual cash flows}}{\text{Initial investment}}$
>
> 2. Present value payback: The length of time for the present value of cash flows at the desired rate of return to recover the initial investment.

The present value payback method utilizes present value techniques to compute the minimum life necessary for the proposal to recover the initial investment and still earn the minimum rate of return specified by management. It is related to the net present value method in that the cash flows are discounted at the desired rate of return. If the present value of all cash flows does not recover the initial investment, it is similar to a negative net present value, and the project should be rejected. A present value payback period indicates a positive net present value and a profitable investment. However, this method falls short because it does not consider the amount or timing of cash flows after the present value payback period.

Figure 23.10 summarizes the objectives, computations, and major decision rules for the payback method and related modifications.

Accounting Rate of Return

The **accounting rate of return method** is also called the unadjusted rate of return, approximate rate of return, book-value rate of return, and financial statement method. Each of these titles has some merit. For example, this method does not adjust for the time value of money and is occasionally used to estimate the internal rate of return. Thus the titles "unadjusted" and "approximate" are descriptive of these characteristics. Also, this method is designed to provide a rate of return that is consistent with the rate of return on total assets that would be computed under the accrual basis of accounting. Hence, the titles "book value," "financial statement," and simply "accounting" provide descriptions of these characteristics.

The objective of the accounting rate of return is to compute a rate of return on the proposed capital investment that is consistent with the rate of return on total assets computed under the accrual basis of accounting. The rate of return on total assets is generally computed by dividing the total assets into the net income. Under the accrual basis of accounting, the net income is net of the depreciation expense and the total assets include the book values of depreciable fixed assets.

The formula for the accounting rate of return divides the average annual net income by either the initial investment or the average investment.

$$\text{Accounting rate of return} = \frac{\text{Average annual net income}}{\text{Initial investment}}$$

or

$$\text{Accounting rate of return} = \frac{\text{Average annual net income}}{\text{Average investment}}$$

where   Average annual net income is the average annual cash flow minus depreciation expense.
Average investment (also called average book value) is the initial investment plus salvage value divided by two.

To be consistent with the accrual concept of net income, the annual cash flows are adjusted for depreciation expense. When annual cash flows are not equal, an annual average is computed. Straight-line depreciation is used because it gives an annual average of depreciation expense for any of the depreciation methods.

No consensus has been reached among accountants about the correct denominator value for the equation. The initial investment is perhaps the most commonly used and is justified because it provides a rate of return on the incremental dollars invested in the project. The average investment method, however, is more consistent with the rate of return on total assets computed under the accrual basis of accounting. The book values of fixed assets decrease each year by the depreciation expense. An on-going business will have assets at all stages—some new, some ready for salvage, and some at mid-life. Therefore, an average investment is more consistent with the average book values of all fixed assets within an organization. Unless specified otherwise, we will use the initial investment to compute the accounting rate of return.

For capital budgeting, the denominator amount will not make any difference in the relative ranking of investment alternatives under the accounting rate of return method as long as the salvage value is zero on all projects. The rate of return on average investment will be twice the rate on the initial investment, but the relative ranking should be the same. However, if there is a salvage value on some projects, their rate of return will not double. The result may be a different ranking of investment alternatives.

EXAMPLE

Problem

Kelly's Flour Mill is considering the two following investment proposals.

Mill *X*—This new mill utilizes the latest technology in mill design to cool the grinding stones. Cooling the stones keeps the flour cool and allows continuous production at a higher rate of output. The new mill will cost $60,000, will provide increased cash flows of $10,000 per year, and will last for fifteen years with zero salvage value. The existing mill will be kept for back-up purposes.

Bagger—The flour is currently weighed and packaged by hand. The new bagger has the capability of weighing the flour, bagging it, and sealing the bag. It will cost $30,000 and is expected to last ten years with $5,000 salvage value. Annual cash flows are expected to be as follows:

Years	Amount
1–3	$4,000 per year
4–6	5,000 per year
7–10	6,000 per year

The cash flows for this investment will increase over time as production increases. The new bagger will be able to handle the increase, thus avoiding the need to hire additional manual labor.

Compute the accounting rate of return for each proposal, using both (a) initial investment and (b) average investment as the denominator amount.

Solution

Using the initial investment as the denominator for the equation, the following rates are computed:

Mill X

$$\text{Rate} = \frac{\$10,000 - \$4,000^a}{\$60,000} = \underline{10\%}$$

^{a}Depreciation expense: $\frac{\$60,000}{15 \text{ years}} = \$4,000$ per year

Bagger

$$\text{Rate} = \frac{\$5,600^b - \$2,500^c}{\$30,000} = \underline{10.3\%}$$

^{b}Average annual cash flows:

Years		
1–3	(3 × $4,000)	$12,000
4–6	(3 × $5,000)	15,000
7–10	(4 × $6,000)	24,000
Salvage value		5,000
Total		$56,000
Divide by years of useful life		÷ 10
Average annual cash flow		$ 5,600 per year

^{c}Depreciation expense: $\frac{\$30,000 - \$5,000}{10 \text{ years}} = \$2,500$ per year

Using the average investment as the denominator for the equation, the following rates are computed:

Mill X

$$\text{Rate} = \frac{\$10,000 - \$4,000}{\$30,000^d} = \underline{20\%}$$

^{d}Average investment: $\frac{\$60,000 + 0}{2} = \$30,000$

Bagger

$$\text{Rate} = \frac{\$5,600 - \$2,500}{\$17,500^e} = \underline{17.7\%}$$

^{e}Average investment: $\frac{\$30,000 + \$5,000}{2} = \$17,500$

Decision Making Using Accounting Rate of Return Management must identify a *minimum acceptable rate of return* that can be used as a benchmark to determine the desirability of an investment proposal. One argument in favor of using an accounting rate of return is that management can look to existing financial statements to compute a rate of return that is being earned on existing assets. If the proposed investments provide a rate of return higher than the existing rate, the company's profitability would be enhanced by the new investment.

When one investment alternative is being considered, it is a desirable investment if the accounting rate of return equals or exceeds the minimum rate specified by management. When several alternatives are being considered, their accounting rates of return are ranked from high to low. Those with the highest rates are most desirable as long as they equal or exceed the minimum rate specified by management.

Management of Kelly's Flour Mill has specified a 10 percent minimum rate of return on capital investment decisions using the initial investment as the denominator amount. Assuming that mill X is the only proposal being considered, it would be acceptable because its rate of return equals the minimum rate specified by management.

If both the bagger and mill X proposals are being considered and only one proposal can be funded, the bagger proposal will be considered more desirable because of its slightly higher rate of return. Notice, however, that mill X is more desirable when an average investment is used as the denominator amount.

| | Accounting Rate of Return ||
Project	Initial Investment	Average Investment
Mill X	10%	20%
Bagger	10.3%	17.7%

Strengths and Weaknesses of the Accounting Rate of Return The accounting rate of return is a measure of profitability that is consistent with profitability measures normally computed from accrual-based financial statements. Not only does it provide a measure that can be used to evaluate investment proposals, but similar computations can be made on the actual results of operations over the life of the asset using the accounting numbers generated by normal accounting procedures so that actual results can be compared with the planned results. Thus it is useful for both decision analysis and for subsequent evaluation and follow-up.

The primary weakness of the accounting rate of return is that it is an averaging technique that does not consider the time value of money. Many people view this weakness as being so important that it completely negates the usefulness of this method. The problems are most significant for proposals with uneven cash flows. Kelly's Flour Mill can be used to illustrate the danger of basing investment decisions on the accounting rate of return. When both the mill and the bagger were being considered and the initial investment was used as the denominator amount, the bagger was identified as the most profitable investment. Considering the time value of money by either the net present value or the internal rate of return (as shown in figure 23.11) methods, the bagger was found to be far less profitable than the mill.

Project	Profitability Index at 14% Rate	Internal Rate of Return
Mill X	1.024	14.5%
Bagger	0.881	11.6%

Notice also that the accounting rate of return was not a very good predictor of the internal rate of return.

Figure 23.12 summarizes the objectives, computation, and major decision rules for the accounting rate of return method.

FIGURE 23.11

Computation of Net Present Value and Internal Rate of Return for Kelly's Flour Mill Investment Proposals

---

Mill X

Present value of cash flows at 14%:		Present value of cash flows at 16%:	
($10,000 × 6.142)	$61,420	($10,000 × 5.575)	$55,750
Initial investment	60,000	Initial investment	60,000
Net present value	$ 1,420	Net present value	($ 4,250)
Profitability index	1.024	Internal rate of return	14.5%
($61,420 ÷ $60,000)		[14% + ($1,420 ÷ $5,670 × 2%)]	

Bagger

Present value of cash flows at 14%:
Years

1–3 ($4,000 × 2.322)	$ 9,288
4–6 ($5,000 × 3.889 − 2.322)	7,835
7–10 ($6,000 × 5.216 − 3.889)	7,962
Salvage value ($5,000 × 0.270)	1,350
Total	$26,435
Initial investment	30,000
Net present value	($ 3,565)
Profitability index	0.881
($26,435 ÷ $30,000)	

Present value of cash flows at 8%:
Years

1–3 ($4,000 × 2.577)	$10,308
4–6 ($5,000 × 4.623 − 2.577)	10,230
7–10 ($6,000 × 6.710 − 4.623)	12,522
Salvage value ($5,000 × 0.463)	2,315
Total	$35,375
Initial investment	30,000
Net present value	$ 5,375
Internal rate of return	11.6%
[8% + ($5,375 ÷ $8,940 × 6%)]	

Disinvestment Decisions

Throughout the chapter we have used various capital budgeting techniques to identify desirable investment alternatives. The same procedures can be used to evaluate disinvestment decisions.

A disinvestment decision is one in which the company owns and operates a capital

---

FIGURE 23.12

Accounting Rate of Return

Objective: Compute a rate of return that is consistent with the rate normally computed under the accrual basis of accounting.

Informational requirements:

1. Initial investment
2. Annual net cash flows
3. Annual depreciation (straight-line method)

Computation format:

$$\text{Rate} = \frac{\text{Annual cash flow} - \text{Depreciation}}{\text{Initial investment}}$$

Decision rule:

Single investment proposal: Accept an investment proposal if the accounting rate of return exceeds a minimum rate specified by management.

Multiple investment proposals: Rank the investments from high to low according to their rate of return. Those exceeding the minimum specified by management are desirable.

Modification:

Use average investment as the denominator in the preceding equation with an adjustment in the minimum acceptable rate specified by management.

CHAPTER 23: CAPITAL BUDGETING: PART I

asset and, although the asset may be providing a positive return to the company, an opportunity has come to sell the asset. The question is whether the company would be better off to sell the asset or to continue normal operations.

The opportunity cost associated with asset disposition is used as the investment cost in the disinvestment decision, and the cash flow from normal operations is the cash inflow for the analysis. The methods for evaluating capital budgeting decisions are applied normally to the investment and projected cash flows.

EXAMPLE

Problem

Suppose DRG Corporation has a machine that originally cost $75,000 and that has a book value of $45,000 and a current market price of $30,000. The machine generates $4,000 of cash flows annually, has an estimated remaining life of nine years, and has zero expected salvage value. If the company requires 12 percent as a minimum rate of return, should the company sell the machine?

Solution

The original acquisition cost and current book value are irrelevant to the decision. The $30,000 current market price is used as the investment cost. Net present value can be used as follows to make the decision.

Present value of cash flows ($4,000 × 5.3283)	$21,313
Initial investment (Opportunity cost/Market value)	30,000
Net present value	($ 8,687)

The negative net present value indicates that the company would be better off selling the equipment. The cash flow associated with the internal use does not provide the minimum desired rate of return on the investment (opportunity cost) that is required for continued ownership.

SELECTING THE EVALUATION TECHNIQUE

There are many techniques available for capital budgeting. The computation and analysis of the strengths and weaknesses of each technique provide useful information for selecting a technique that is best for the analysis. Our objective here is to summarize the selection criteria and to compare the net present value method with the internal rate of return method to identify their differences and the additional factors that should be considered when selecting one of them.

Selection Criteria

The technique selected for capital budgeting decision analysis should satisfy the following criteria:

1. It should accurately summarize the merits of the investment proposal, preferably into a single number.
2. It should be understandable to those who use it.

3. It should facilitate comparisons between projects.
4. It should provide an accurate measure that is consistent with the long-term objectives of the company in terms of liquidity or profitability.

The last criterion is probably the most important for selecting one technique over another. The evaluation technique selected for a capital budgeting decision should be consistent with the objective to be achieved. If the primary objective is cash flow and liquidity, the payback method is appropriate. It indicates how long money is at risk and how soon it will be recovered. This may be most important when stability, uncertainty, and technological change make it difficult to predict cash flows beyond the first few years of investment life. If profitability is the primary objective of the investment, the net present value or internal rate of return methods should be used. Both of these methods are superior to payback reciprocal, present value payback, and accounting rate of return methods, because they consider the time value of money and all cash flows over the entire life of the investment. In this section we compare the net present value method with the internal rate of return method to identify their differences and the factors that should be considered when selecting one of them.

The net present value method and the internal rate of return method will give the same answer in capital budgeting decisions that compare investment alternatives of equal lives and equal dollar investments. This can be illustrated with proposals Y and Z. Each proposal costs $40,000 and has a useful life of ten years. The annual cash flows and salvage values are as follows:

Proposal	**Y**	**Z**
Cost	$40,000	$40,000
Annual cash flow	6,000	8,000
Salvage value	20,000	0
Useful life	10 years	10 years
Analysis		
Net present value at 14%	($3,304)	$1,728
Internal rate of return	12.2%	15.1%

The net present values are −$3,304 and $1,728 for proposal Y and Z, respectively, using a 14%-percent cut-off rate. Because of the negative net present value at this rate, proposal Y would be considered unprofitable and would be rejected. Proposal Z's positive net present value means that it is profitable and probably would be accepted.

The same results are obtained using the internal rate of return. Because the 12.2-percent return on proposal X is less than 14 percent, it would be rejected. The 15.1-percent return on proposal Y is over the cut-off rate and is, therefore, a profitable project.

The net present value method and the internal rate of return method may not give the same results when the lives of the investment alternatives are not equal or when they require a different initial investment. Also, the two methods are not equally easy to work with when allocating limited money to competing investment alternatives. The investment proposals for TLC Incorporated, shown in figure 23.13, will be used as examples to investigate these differences.

TLC Incorporated has $12,000 available for investment in capital equipment. Any money not invested in equipment will be put into a savings certificate at 14 percent, which is also the company's minimum desired rate of return. Three investment proposals, labeled A, B, and C, have been developed. The net present value and internal rate of return have also been developed for each proposal. Which proposal or set of proposals would you recommend to TLC Incorporated? No doubt your decision will be confused by the differences in useful lives and initial investments. Let's consider each separately.

FIGURE 23.13

Investment Alternatives with Unequal Lives and Unequal Investments

| | Capital Equipment Proposals ||| Savings Certificate |
	A	B	C	
Cost	$10,000	$10,000	$12,000	$2,000
Useful life	2 years	5 years	5 years	Variable
Cash flows:				
Year 1	$6,545	$3,200	$3,795	$ 280
2	6,545	3,200	3,795	280
3	—	3,200	3,795	280
4	—	3,200	3,795	280
5	—	3,200	3,795	280
Salvage	0	0	0	2,000
Analysis:				
Net present value at 14%	$780	$986	$1,029	0
Internal rate of return	20%	18%	17.5%	14%

Unequal Investment Lives Proposals A and B each cost $10,000, but proposal A has a useful life of only two years and proposal B lasts for five years. If the internal rate of return is used as the decision criterion, proposal A seems to be the most profitable at 20 percent. If the net present value is used, proposal B at $986 seems more profitable than proposal A at only $780.

The difference between these results is caused by the difference in the rate at which dollars are assumed to be reinvested during the remaining life of the shortest project. Notice that there are no cash flows shown for proposal A for years 3 through 5. The internal rate of return method assumes that proposal A will be repeated or that another project will be available that will provide a rate of return equal to the 20 percent earned on proposal A. Therefore, it assumes that money will be reinvested at the internal rate of return of the project under consideration.

The net present value method assumes that money will be reinvested at the discount rate. Because the net present value of money invested at the discount rate is zero, the $780 net present value for proposal A is based entirely on year 1 and year 2 cash flows. This accounts for a lower net present value for proposal A than for proposal B.

The problem of unequal lives can best be resolved by making an assumption about the reinvestment of money from the project with the shortest life. If money will be reinvested at the minimum desired rate of return, the net present value most accurately reflects investment profitability. If the project can be repeated or if equally profitable projects will be available, the internal rate of return accurately reflects investment profitability. The net present value method can still be used under the second assumption, but the cash flows from the reinvestment need to be charted, discounted, and included in the net present value. When this is done, the two methods will give the same answer.

Assume that any money TLC Incorporated receives from proposal A will be reinvested at the cut-off rate and that proposal B is determined to be more profitable than proposal A. Proposals B and C must now be evaluated because of the difference in initial investment.

Unequal Initial Investments Proposals B and C each have a useful life of five years, but B costs only $10,000 and C costs $12,000. Once again, the results from the net present value method seem to contradict those of the internal rate of return method. Proposal B has the highest internal rate of return (18 percent versus 17.5 percent), and proposal C has the highest net present value ($1,029 versus $986).

A further complication is the amount of money available for investment. TLC

Incorporated has $12,000 available for investment. If proposal B is adopted, the remaining $2,000 would be invested in a savings certificate at 14 percent, which would provide a zero net present value and an internal rate of return of 14 percent. The investment choice is between proposal C or a combination of proposal B and the savings certificate.

In situations such as this, the net present value method provides the easiest answer. The most profitable combination of projects will be that with the highest combined net present values. Proposal B and the savings certificate have a combined net present value of $986 ($986 + 0), which is less than the $1,029 from proposal C. Therefore, proposal C is more profitable.

If we try to use internal rates of return, we can't combine 18 percent and 14 percent to compare with the 17.5 percent without additional computation. Proposal C costs $2,000 more than B but yields $595 ($3,795 − $3,200) more cash flow per year. The internal rate of return on the additional money invested in proposal C must be computed to compare with the 14-percent alternative provided by the savings certificate.

$$\text{Annuity factor} = \frac{\$2,000}{\$595} = 3.3613$$

Percent	Annuity Factor	Difference
14%	3.433	0.072
?	3.361	
16%	3.274	0.087
Total		0.159
Internal rate of return		14.91%

[14% + (0.072 ÷ 0.159 × 2%)]

A 14.91 percent return on the additional money invested in proposal C is more than the savings certificate provides and is the most profitable project.

In summary, the net present value method is generally easier to work with than the internal rate of return method. It requires only one set of computations. Net present values can be combined when allocating money to competing investment alternatives to identify the most profitable combination of projects. When dealing with projects of unequal lives, some assumption must be made about reinvestment of money from the shorter-lived project. The net present value method is consistent with the assumption that money is reinvested at the minimum desired rate of return.

Planning and Control Over Capital Expenditures

Development of the capital budget is part of the normal budgeting process, described in detail in chapter 6. One section of the master budget is called the capital budget. It identifies the capital assets to be acquired or constructed and the amount of money to be allocated to each. The procedures discussed in this chapter deal with identifying the projects that are most profitable and allocating money to them.

The capital budget can only be as good as the projects included in it. Every attempt must be made to identify the most profitable projects available to the company. This requires input from all segments of the organization and a fairly exhaustive search of alternatives to existing processes. Too often organizations become used to the status quo and stop looking for alternatives or reject some desirable alternatives without adequate consideration.

The accountant's role in developing the capital budget primarily involves data gathering and quantifying the effect of a proposed change on revenues and operating costs. Assistance is also provided to management in quantifying and selecting a cut-off rate and in evaluating the profitability of alternative proposals. Many people at the top management level are involved in the final decision, but the computations, analysis, and manner of presentation provided by the accountant have a strong influence on the outcome.

Control of Capital Budgeting Expenditures Each capital investment is handled as a separate project or job, as in a job-order cost system. The estimated cost of the investment used in the capital budgeting process becomes the budgeted cost for the project. Actual costs should be accumulated in categories that are consistent with the budgeted costs. Frequent comparisons need to be made between budgeted and actual costs, and significant variances should be investigated.

The cause or responsibility for an unfavorable variance is often difficult to determine. Each project is unique, and the problem could have resulted from a poor estimate, inefficient workers or management, changes in prices or quality of materials, or similar items. Also, if the project requires construction over an extended period of time, it may be difficult to accurately determine the percentage of completion. Despite these problems, it is extremely important to track the expenditure of funds, identify responsibility for the expenditures, and hold individuals accountable for activities under their control.

Post-Operational Evaluation A proposal that identifies the projected costs, benefits, and risks associated with a project is usually developed to request an expenditure of capital investment funds. Based on the proposed estimates, the project is either approved or rejected. If it is approved, an evaluation ought to be performed after the project has been implemented to see if actual costs and benefits are in line with those projected and to determine whether or not the organization is obtaining the estimated rate of return. This is sometimes called a *post-operational evaluation,* a *reappraisal,* or a *post-audit of operating results.*

The objective of the post-operational audit is to reconcile actual results with anticipated results. It is important that the follow-up evaluation is consistent with the technique used to evaluate the desirability of the proposal in the first place. For example, an accounting rate of return on the actual results is not comparable to an internal rate of return on expected results. An accurately performed post-implementation review may reveal one of several things, including the following:

1. The expected benefits are being achieved and the capital investment project is profitable as anticipated.
2. The expected benefits are not being achieved because conversion to the new process or equipment has not been completed. Some people continue to use the old methods, which result in duplicate processing costs.
3. The project is not as profitable as anticipated, because the estimates of projected benefits were overstated or estimated costs were understated. This information can be very helpful in refining the estimation techniques used for future capital budgeting decisions.

Once again the accountant plays an important role in this post-implementation review. For the analysis to be meaningful, accrual accounting numbers must be adjusted and special reports must be prepared.

Complications to Capital Budgeting

Capital budgeting is complicated somewhat by three factors.

1. *Income tax considerations:* Almost every cash flow has a related effect on income taxes that must be paid to the state and federal governments. Some items, such as

depreciation, do not by themselves affect cash flows, but, when income taxes are considered, there is a related cash flow.
2. *Selecting a minimum desired rate of return:* The two most useful capital budgeting techniques both require a cut-off rate. The net present value method uses it as part of the computation, and the internal rate of return method uses it as a benchmark to accept or reject a proposal. The development of an acceptable cut-off rate for a particular organization is a complex and controversial problem.
3. *Projecting future cash flows:* Future cash flows have been provided in the examples in this chapter as if we had a crystal ball that could predict the future with 100-percent certainty. This is rarely the case, and small errors in predicting cash flows may have a notable effect on the outcome of a decision. Sensitivity analysis is useful in evaluating the effect of estimation errors on the outcome of the decision.

Chapter 24 covers each of these complications in some detail.

SUMMARY

Capital budgeting is a process used to determine investment profitability or to select from a variety of investment alternatives those that will be most profitable. The results of this analysis constitute the capital budget section of the master budget.

The profitability of a proposed investment is based on expected net cash flows over the life of the project. Cash flows may be analyzed using *(a)* net present value, *(b)* internal rate of return, *(c)* payback period, or *(d)* accounting rate of return methods. The net present value or the internal rate of return are considered superior to the other methods because they consider both the amount and timing of cash flows over the entire life of the investment. The net present value method is generally easier to work with than the internal rate of return method because it requires less computation. The payback period method measures liquidity rather than profitability. Its use is often justified in situations in which cash flow is more critical than maximizing profits.

Care must be exercised in selecting and using a capital budgeting technique. The objective of the analysis should first be identified, and a technique should be selected that meets the objective. Also, the assumptions on which the technique operates should be kept in mind when the results are used in a decision-making process.

APPENDIX 23.1 Time Value of Money

The value of money at different points in time is not comparable, because inflation and the opportunity cost associated with idle cash make comparisons inaccurate. This complicates capital budgeting decisions, because they have a relatively long life. Present value or future value computations are made to adjust for time and interest so that all cash flows are at a common point in time.

Future Value of $1 Sum

A sum of money *(P)* invested today at a given interest rate *(i)* will increase in value over time *(n)*. The future value can be computed as:

$$F = P(1 + i)^n.$$

CHAPTER 23: CAPITAL BUDGETING: PART I

Factors have been computed for various combinations of i and n $[F_{in} = (1 + i)^n]$ and are shown in the future value tables. A portion of a future value table follows. The equation $F = P(F_{in})$ is relevant when using a factor from the table. The sum of money (P) is multiplied by the factor obtained from the table for the given interest rate and number of periods to obtain the future value (F).

The Future Amount of $1: $F_{in} = (1 + i)^n$

Period	8%	10%	12%
1	1.0800	1.1000	1.1200
2	1.1664	1.2100	1.2544
3	1.2597	1.3310	1.4049
4	1.3605	1.4641	1.5735
5	1.4693	1.6105	1.7623

A more complete table of future amounts of $1 is shown as table 1 on page 881.

EXAMPLE

How much will $10,000 be worth in four years if money is worth 10 percent?

Formula Solution:

$F = \$10{,}000\,(1 + 0.10)^4$
$= 10{,}000\,(1.4641)$
$= \underline{\$14{,}641}$

Table Solution:

$F = \$10{,}000\,(1.4641)$
$= \underline{\$14{,}641}$

Notice that the factor of 1.4641 is obtained from the preceding table using 4 as the number of periods and 10 percent as the interest rate. You should be familiar with the equations presented here and be able to use the table factors to compute the future value of a sum of money when the number of periods and interest rate are given.

Present Value of $1 Sum The present value or discounted value of a $1 sum is just the opposite of a future value. The questions is, What amount (P) must be invested today at a given interest rage (i) to be worth a specified amount (F) in a given number of years (n)? The future value equation can be solved for P to obtain the following:

$$P = F \frac{1}{(1 + i)^n}.$$

The interest factor can be specified as follows. Notice that this is the reciprocal of F_{in} computed previously.

$$P_{in} = \left(\frac{1}{(1 + i)^n}\right)$$

Various combinations of i and n have been computed and are included in the following present value table.

The Present Amount of $1: $P_{i,n} = \left[\dfrac{1}{(1+i)^n}\right]$

Period	8%	10%	12%
1	0.9259	0.9091	0.8929
2	0.8573	0.8264	0.7972
3	0.7938	0.7513	0.7118
4	0.7350	0.6830	0.6355
5	0.6806	0.6209	0.5674

A more complete table of present values of $1 is shown as table 2 on page 882.

The present value amount is computed by multiplying the present value factor obtained from the table by the future dollar amount.

EXAMPLE

An investment will pay $14,641 in four years. What is the present value of the payout if money is worth 10 percent?

Table solution: P = $14,641 (0.6830)
          = $10,000

The present value factor of 0.6830 is obtained from the present value table using 4 as the number of periods and 10 percent as the interest rate.

Annuity An *ordinary annuity* is a series of equal cash flows at the end of equal intervals of time. An *annuity due* is a series of equal cash flows at the *beginning* of equal intervals of time.

Example of a 3-year Ordinary Annuity of $100

```
         $100    $100    $100
  ─────────────────────────────── Time in years
  0       1       2       3
```

Example of a 3-Year Annuity Due of $100

```
 $100    $100    $100
  ─────────────────────────────── Time in years
  0       1       2       3
```

Future Value of an Annuity The future value of an annuity can be computed by moving each of the annuity amounts to the end of the annuity's life using the factors from table 1 on page 881.

EXAMPLE

What is the future value of a $100 *ordinary annuity* for three years when money is worth 10 percent?

F = $100(1.2100) + $100(1.100) + 100(1.000)
  = $100(3.3100)
  = $331

The direct formula for computing the future value of an ordinary annuity is:

$$F = A \dfrac{(1+i)^n - 1}{i}.$$

CHAPTER 23: CAPITAL BUDGETING: PART I   879

Values of the interest factor have been computed and are shown in the following table.

Amount of Ordinary Annuity of $1: $FA_{i|n} = \left[\dfrac{(1 + i)^n - 1}{i}\right]$

Period	8%	10%	12%
1	1.0000	1.0000	1.0000
2	2.0800	2.1000	2.1200
3	3.2464	3.3100	3.3744
4	4.5061	4.6410	4.7793
5	5.8666	6.1051	6.3528

A more complete table of future values of ordinary annuities is shown as table 3 on page 882.

Notice that the factor for 10 percent and three periods in the preceding table is 3.3100, which is the same as the factor computed in the previous example when the annual factors obtained from table 1 were totaled. The computation in the preceding example is simplified by obtaining the annuity factor directly from the annuity table. The future value of the annuity is then computed by multiplying the annuity factor by the annuity amount.

Ordinary annuity factors in the preceding table can be converted to annuity due factors by adding 1 to the number of periods and subtracting 1.0000 from the factor.

EXAMPLE

What is the future value of a $100 *annuity due* for three years when money is worth 10 percent?

$F = \$100\ (3.641)$
$ = \underline{\$364.10}$

The factor 3.641 is computed by obtaining the table factor for four periods (3 + 1) at 10 percent (4.641) and subtracting 1.0000 from the factor.

Present Value of an Annuity The present value of an annuity can be computed by moving each of the annuity amounts to the present time period using the factors from table 2 on page 882. However, it is more efficient to compute the present value using the annuity formula or by using a factor from the table of present values of an annuity of $1.

The formula for computing the present value of an ordinary annuity is as follows:

$$P = A\dfrac{1 - (1 + i)^{-n}}{i}$$

Interest factors have been computed and are included in the table entitled "present value of an ordinary annuity of $1". A portion of this table follows, and a more complete table is shown as table 4 on page 883.

Present Value of an Ordinary Annuity of $1: $PA_{i|n} = \left[\dfrac{1 - (1 + i)^{-n}}{i}\right]$

Period	8%	10%	12%
1	0.9259	0.9091	0.8929
2	1.7833	1.7355	1.6901
3	2.5771	2.4869	2.4018
4	3.3121	3.1699	3.0373
5	3.9927	3.7908	3.6048

To find the present value of an ordinary annuity, multiply the annuity amount by the annuity factor obtained from the table for the given number of periods and interest rate.

EXAMPLE

What is the present value of an *ordinary annuity* of $100 for three years when interest is 10 percent?

P = $100 (2.4869)
  = $248.69

The ordinary annuity factors in the preceding table can be changed to annuity due factors by subtracting 1 from the number of periods and adding 1.0000 to that factor.

EXAMPLE

What is the present value of a $100 *annuity due* for three years where there is a 10-percent interest rate?

P = $100 (2.7355)
  = $273.55

The factor 2.7355 used in the preceding equation is computed by obtaining the factor from the table for two periods (1.7355) and adding 1.0000 to it.

Compound Interest   Unless stated otherwise, it is assumed that interest is compounded anually. Frequently, however, interest will be stated as an annual amount but is compounded semiannually, quarterly, or even monthly. In these cases you must adjust the interest rate and number of periods. The following rules are useful when making these adjustments.

1. Adjust the interest rate according to the compounding period. If, for example, the interest rate is 16 percent compounded semiannually, you would use an 8-percent (16% ÷ 2) interest rate per period.
2. Adjust n from the number of years to the number of compounding periods. For example, if a note is for five years with interest compounded semiannually, you would use 10 (5 × 2) periods.

The revised interest rate and number of periods would then be used in any of the preceding formulas or tables.

TABLE 1 Future Amount of $1 in n Periods $F = P(1 + i)^n$

n	2%	8%	10%	12%	14%	16%	18%	20%	22%	24%	30%
1	1.0200	1.0800	1.100	1.120	1.140	1.160	1.180	1.200	1.22	1.24	1.30
2	1.0404	1.1664	1.210	1.254	1.300	1.346	1.392	1.440	1.49	1.54	1.69
3	1.0612	1.2597	1.331	1.405	1.482	1.561	1.643	1.728	1.82	1.91	2.20
4	1.0824	1.3605	1.464	1.574	1.689	1.811	1.939	2.074	2.22	2.36	2.86
5	1.1041	1.4693	1.611	1.762	1.925	2.100	2.288	2.488	2.70	2.93	3.71
6	1.1262	1.5869	1.772	1.974	2.195	2.436	2.700	2.986	3.30	3.64	4.83
7	1.1487	1.7138	1.949	2.211	2.502	2.826	3.185	3.583	4.02	4.51	6.27
8	1.1717	1.8509	2.144	2.476	2.853	3.278	3.759	4.300	4.91	5.59	8.16
9	1.1951	1.9990	2.358	2.773	3.252	3.803	4.435	5.160	5.99	6.93	10.60
10	1.2190	2.1589	2.594	3.106	3.707	4.411	5.234	6.192	7.30	8.59	13.79
11	1.2434	2.3316	2.853	3.479	4.226	5.117	6.176	7.430	8.91	10.66	17.92
12	1.2682	2.5182	3.138	3.896	4.818	5.936	7.288	8.916	10.87	13.21	23.30
13	1.2936	2.7196	3.452	4.363	5.492	6.886	8.599	10.699	13.26	16.39	30.29
14	1.3195	2.9372	3.797	4.887	6.261	7.988	10.147	12.839	16.18	20.32	39.37
15	1.3459	3.1722	4.177	5.474	7.138	9.266	11.974	15.407	19.74	25.20	51.19
16	1.3728	3.4259	4.595	6.130	8.137	10.748	14.129	18.488	24.09	31.24	66.54
17	1.4002	3.7000	5.054	6.866	9.276	12.468	16.672	22.186	29.38	38.74	86.50
18	1.4282	3.9960	5.560	7.690	10.575	14.463	19.673	26.623	35.85	48.04	112.46
19	1.4568	4.3157	6.116	8.613	12.056	16.777	23.214	31.948	43.74	59.57	146.19
20	1.4859	4.6610	6.728	9.646	13.743	19.461	27.393	38.338	53.36	73.86	190.05
21	1.5157	5.0338	7.400	10.804	15.668	22.574	32.324	46.005	65.10	91.59	247.06
22	1.5460	5.4365	8.140	12.100	17.861	27.186	38.142	55.206	79.42	113.57	321.18
23	1.5769	5.8715	8.954	13.552	20.362	30.376	45.008	66.247	96.89	140.83	417.54
24	1.6084	6.3412	9.850	15.179	23.212	35.236	53.109	79.497	118.21	174.63	542.80
25	1.6406	6.8485	10.835	17.000	26.462	40.874	62.669	95.396	144.21	216.54	705.64

TABLE 2 Present Value of $1 in n Periods $\quad P = F\left[\dfrac{1}{(1 + i)^n}\right]$

n	2%	8%	10%	12%	14%	16%	18%	20%	22%	24%	30%
1	0.9804	0.9259	0.9091	0.8929	0.8772	0.8621	0.8475	0.8333	0.8197	0.8065	0.7692
2	0.9612	0.8573	0.8264	0.7972	0.7695	0.7432	0.7182	0.6944	0.6719	0.6504	0.5917
3	0.9423	0.7938	0.7513	0.7118	0.6750	0.6407	0.6086	0.5787	0.5507	0.5245	0.4552
4	0.9238	0.7350	0.6830	0.6355	0.5921	0.5523	0.5158	0.4823	0.4514	0.4230	0.3501
5	0.9057	0.6806	0.6209	0.5674	0.5194	0.4761	0.4371	0.4019	0.3700	0.3411	0.2693
6	0.8880	0.6302	0.5645	0.5066	0.4556	0.4104	0.3704	0.3349	0.3033	0.2751	0.2072
7	0.8706	0.5835	0.5132	0.4523	0.3996	0.3538	0.3139	0.2791	0.2486	0.2218	0.1594
8	0.8535	0.5403	0.4665	0.4039	0.3506	0.3050	0.2660	0.2326	0.2038	0.1789	0.1226
9	0.8368	0.5002	0.4241	0.3606	0.3075	0.2630	0.2255	0.1938	0.1670	0.1443	0.0943
10	0.8203	0.4632	0.3855	0.3220	0.2697	0.2267	0.1911	0.1615	0.1369	0.1164	0.0725
11	0.8043	0.4289	0.3505	0.2875	0.2366	0.1954	0.1619	0.1346	0.1122	0.0938	0.0558
12	0.7885	0.3971	0.3186	0.2567	0.2076	0.1685	0.1372	0.1122	0.0920	0.0757	0.0429
13	0.7730	0.3677	0.2897	0.2292	0.1821	0.1452	0.1163	0.0935	0.0754	0.0610	0.0330
14	0.7579	0.3405	0.2633	0.2046	0.1597	0.1252	0.0985	0.0779	0.0618	0.0492	0.0254
15	0.7430	0.3152	0.2394	0.1827	0.1401	0.1079	0.0835	0.0649	0.0507	0.0397	0.0195
16	0.7284	0.2919	0.2176	0.1631	0.1229	0.0930	0.0708	0.0541	0.0415	0.0320	0.0150
17	0.7142	0.2703	0.1978	0.1456	0.1078	0.0802	0.0600	0.0451	0.0340	0.0258	0.0116
18	0.7002	0.2502	0.1799	0.1300	0.0946	0.0691	0.0508	0.0376	0.0279	0.0208	0.0089
19	0.6864	0.2317	0.1635	0.1161	0.0829	0.0596	0.0431	0.0313	0.0229	0.0168	0.0068
20	0.6730	0.2145	0.1486	0.1037	0.0728	0.0514	0.0365	0.0261	0.0187	0.0135	0.0053
21	0.6598	0.1987	0.1351	0.0926	0.0638	0.0443	0.0309	0.0217	0.0154	0.0109	0.0040
22	0.6468	0.1839	0.1228	0.0826	0.0560	0.0382	0.0262	0.0181	0.0126	0.0088	0.0031
23	0.6342	0.1703	0.1117	0.0738	0.0491	0.0329	0.0222	0.0151	0.0103	0.0071	0.0024
24	0.6217	0.1577	0.1015	0.0659	0.0431	0.0284	0.0188	0.0126	0.0085	0.0057	0.0018
25	0.6095	0.1460	0.0923	0.0588	0.0378	0.0245	0.0160	0.0105	0.0069	0.0046	0.0014

TABLE 3 Future Amount of an Annuity of $1 per Period $\quad F = A\left[\dfrac{(1 + i)^n - 1}{i}\right]$

n	2%	8%	10%	12%	14%	16%	18%	20%	22%	24%	30%
1	1.000	1.000	1.000	1.00	1.00	1.00	1.00	1.00	1.00	1.00	1.0
2	2.020	2.080	2.100	2.12	2.14	2.16	2.18	2.20	2.22	2.24	2.3
3	3.060	3.246	3.310	3.37	3.44	3.51	3.57	3.64	3.71	3.78	4.0
4	4.122	4.506	4.641	4.78	4.92	5.07	5.22	5.37	5.52	5.68	6.2
5	5.204	5.867	6.105	6.35	6.61	6.88	7.15	7.44	7.74	8.05	9.0
6	6.308	7.336	7.716	8.12	8.54	8.98	9.44	9.93	10.44	10.98	12.8
7	7.434	8.923	9.487	10.09	10.73	11.41	12.14	12.92	13.74	14.62	17.6
8	8.583	10.637	11.436	12.30	13.23	14.24	15.33	16.50	17.76	19.12	23.9
9	9.755	12.488	13.579	14.78	16.09	17.52	19.09	20.80	22.67	24.71	32.0
10	10.950	14.487	15.937	17.55	19.34	21.32	23.52	25.96	28.66	31.64	42.6
11	12.169	16.645	18.531	20.65	23.04	25.73	28.76	32.15	35.96	40.24	56.4
12	13.412	18.977	21.384	24.13	27.27	30.85	34.93	39.58	44.87	50.89	74.3
13	14.680	21.495	24.523	28.03	32.09	36.79	42.22	48.50	55.75	64.11	97.6
14	15.974	24.215	27.975	32.39	37.58	43.67	50.82	59.20	69.01	80.50	127.9
15	17.293	27.152	31.772	37.28	43.84	51.66	60.97	72.04	85.19	100.82	167.3
16	18.639	30.324	35.950	42.75	50.98	60.92	72.94	87.44	104.93	126.01	218.5
17	20.012	33.750	40.545	48.88	59.12	71.67	87.07	105.93	129.02	157.25	285.0
18	21.412	37.450	45.599	55.75	68.39	84.14	103.74	128.12	158.40	195.99	371.5
19	22.840	41.446	51.159	63.44	78.97	98.60	123.41	154.74	194.25	244.03	484.0
20	24.297	45.762	57.275	72.05	91.02	115.38	146.63	186.69	237.99	303.60	630.2
21	25.783	50.423	64.003	81.70	104.77	134.84	174.02	225.03	291.35	377.46	820.2
22	27.299	55.457	71.403	92.50	120.44	157.41	206.35	271.03	356.44	469.06	1067.3
23	28.845	60.893	79.543	104.60	138.30	183.60	244.49	326.24	435.86	582.63	1388.5
24	30.422	66.765	88.497	118.16	158.66	213.99	289.49	392.48	532.75	723.46	1806.0
25	32.030	73.106	98.347	133.33	181.87	249.21	342.60	471.98	650.96	898.09	2348.8

CHAPTER 23: CAPITAL BUDGETING: PART I

TABLE 4 Present Value of an Annuity of $1 per Period $\quad P = A\left[\dfrac{1 - (1 + i)^{-n}}{i}\right]$

n	2%	8%	10%	12%	14%	16%	18%	20%	22%	24%	30%
1	0.980	0.926	0.909	0.8929	0.8772	0.8621	0.8475	0.8333	0.8197	0.8065	0.7692
2	1.942	1.783	1.736	1.6901	1.6467	1.6052	1.5656	1.5278	1.4915	1.4568	1.3609
3	2.884	2.577	2.487	2.4018	2.3216	2.2459	2.1743	2.1065	2.0422	1.9813	1.8161
4	3.808	3.312	3.170	3.0373	2.9137	2.7982	2.6901	2.5887	2.4936	2.4043	2.1662
5	4.713	3.993	3.791	3.6048	3.4331	3.2743	3.1272	2.9906	2.8636	2.7454	2.4356
6	5.601	4.623	4.355	4.1114	3.8887	3.6847	3.4976	3.3255	3.1669	3.0205	2.6427
7	6.472	5.206	4.868	4.5638	4.2883	4.0386	3.8115	3.6046	3.4155	3.2423	2.8021
8	7.325	5.747	5.335	4.9676	4.6389	4.3436	4.0776	3.8372	3.6193	3.4212	2.9247
9	8.162	6.247	5.759	5.3283	4.9464	4.6065	4.3030	4.0310	3.7863	3.5655	3.0190
10	8.983	6.710	6.145	5.6502	5.2161	4.8332	4.4941	4.1925	3.9232	3.6819	3.0915
11	9.787	7.139	6.495	5.9377	5.4527	5.0286	4.6560	4.3271	4.0354	3.7757	3.1473
12	10.575	7.536	6.814	6.1944	5.6603	5.1971	4.7932	4.4392	4.1274	3.8514	3.1903
13	11.348	7.904	7.103	6.4235	5.8424	5.3423	4.9095	4.5327	4.2028	3.9124	3.2233
14	12.106	8.244	7.367	6.6282	6.0021	5.4675	5.0081	4.6106	4.2646	3.9616	3.2487
15	12.849	8.559	7.606	6.8109	6.1422	5.5755	5.0916	4.6755	4.3152	4.0013	3.2682
16	13.578	8.851	7.824	6.9740	6.2651	5.6685	5.1624	4.7296	4.3567	4.0333	3.2832
17	14.292	9.122	8.022	7.1196	6.3729	5.7487	5.2223	4.7746	4.3908	4.0591	3.2948
18	14.992	9.372	8.201	7.2497	6.4674	5.8178	5.2732	4.8122	4.4187	4.0799	3.3037
19	15.678	9.604	8.365	7.3658	6.5504	5.8775	5.3162	4.8435	4.4415	4.0967	3.3105
20	16.351	9.818	8.514	7.4694	6.6231	5.9288	5.3527	4.8696	4.4603	4.1103	3.3158
21	17.011	10.017	8.649	7.5620	6.6870	5.9731	5.3837	4.8913	4.4756	4.1212	3.3198
22	17.658	10.201	8.772	7.6446	6.7429	6.0113	5.4099	4.9094	4.4882	4.1300	3.3230
23	18.292	10.371	8.883	7.7184	6.7921	6.0442	5.4321	4.9245	4.4985	4.1371	3.3253
24	18.914	10.529	8.985	7.7843	6.8351	6.0726	5.4509	4.9371	4.5070	4.1428	3.3272
25	19.523	10.675	9.077	7.8431	6.8729	6.0971	5.4669	4.9476	4.5139	4.1474	3.3286

SELF-STUDY PROBLEM

The Elder Company is planning to purchase a new machine at a cost of $300,000. It will be depreciated by the straight-line method over a ten-year useful life with no salvage value, and a full year's depreciation will be taken in the year of acquisition. The new machine is expected to produce a cash flow from operations of $66,000 a year in each of the next ten years. A 16-percent rate of return and a four-year payback are desired on all capital investments.

Required

1. Compute the net present value.
2. Compute the internal rate of return.
3. Compute the payback period.
4. Compute the accounting rate of return.
5. How would you advise management on the proposed acquisition?

Solution to the Self-Study Problem

Requirement 1

The net present value is computed by subtracting the initial investment from the present value of the cash flows at a 16 percent interest rate.

Present Value of Cash Flows

($66,000 × 4.8332)	$318,991.20
Initial investment	300,000.00
Net present value	$ 18,991.20

Requirement 2

The internal rate of return is the interest rate that equates the present value of the cash flows with the initial investment. The present value factor that equates these is computed by dividing the initial investment by the annual cash flows. (This can only be done when annual cash flows are equal.) The interest rate is then obtained from the present value table.

Present Value Factor

($300,000 ÷ $66,000)   4.5455

From the present value table we can see that the interest rate is between 16 and 20 percent. Through interpolation, the interest rate is found to be approximately 17.8 percent.

Interest Rates	Annuity Factor	Difference
16%	4.8332	0.2877
?	4.5455	
20%	4.1925	0.3530
4%		0.6407

16% + [(0.2877 ÷ 0.6407) × 4%] =   17.8%

Requirement 3

When annual cash flows are equal, the payback period can be computed by dividing the initial investment by the annual cash flows.

Payback Period

($300,000 ÷ $66,000)   4.5 years

Requirement 4

The accounting rate of return is computed by dividing the average net income (annual cash flow less depreciation expense) by the initial investment or average book value. Using the initial investment as the denominator, the accounting rate of return is 12 percent.

Accounting Rate of Return

$$\frac{\$66,000 - \$30,000^a}{\$300,000} = 12\%$$

[a]Depreciation expense
($300,000 ÷ 10 years) = $30,000

Requirement 5

The proposed investment satisfies the 16-percent minimum desired rate of return but falls slightly short of a four-year payback. Management must decide whether cash flow or profitability is most important. With the major emphasis on profitability, the proposal should be accepted.

SUGGESTED READINGS

Bierman, H., and Smidt, S. *The Capital Budgeting Decision,* 6th ed. New York: Macmillan, 1984.

Brealey, R., and Myers, S. *Principles of Corporate Finance.* New York: McGraw-Hill, 1984.

Hertz, David B. "Incorporating Risk in Capital Expenditure Analysis." In *Controller's Handbook,* edited by Sam R. Goodman and James S. Reece. Homewood, Ill.: Dow Jones-Irwin, 1978.

Hillier, F. S. "The Derivation of Probabilistic Information for the Evaluation of Risky Investments." *Management Science* 9 (April 1963): 443–457.

House, William C., Jr. "Sensitivity Analysis in Making Capital Investment Decisions." *NAA Research Monograph #3.* New York: National Association of Accountants, 1968.

Kempster, John H. "Financial Analysis to Guide Capital Expenditure Decisions." *NAA Research Report #43.* New York: National Association of Accountants, 1967.

Murdy, J. L. "Analyzing Capital Expenditure Proposals." In *Controller's Handbook,* edited by Sam R. Goodman and James S. Reece. Homewood, Ill.: Dow Jones-Irwin, 1978.

National Association of Accountants. "Financial Analysis Techniques for Equipment Replacement Decisions." *NAA Research Monograph #1.* New York: National Association of Accountants, 1965.

DISCUSSION QUESTIONS

Q23–1. What are capital assets? Why is capital budgeting analysis required when purchasing capital assets?

Q23–2. Depreciation expenses must be treated separately from other revenues and expenses in capital budgeting decisions. Why is this so and how should they be treated?

Q23–3. Distinguish between a screening decision and a preference decision in capital budgeting.

Q23–4. Describe how to compute a net present value. If the net present value is a negative number, should the proposal be rejected? Explain.

Q23–5. Explain what the controller meant by the following: "We are rejecting many capital investment proposals in today's economy that would have been acceptable only a few years ago." How could this be true when the cost of the investments and their net cash flows have not changed?

Q23–6. Why is the minimum desired rate of return so important in capital budgeting decisions?

Q23–7. How is the profitability index computed and what does it mean?

Q23–8. Describe how to compute an internal rate of return. Given an internal rate of return of 12 percent, should the proposal be accepted or rejected?

Q23–9. Describe how to compute the payback period. Given a payback period of five years, should the proposal be accepted or rejected?

Q23–10. Why is present value payback an improvement over the regular payback analysis? What does it mean when the present value payback period is longer than the life of the capital asset?

Q23–11. Does the net present value method stress profitability or cash flow? Explain.

Q23–12. Comparing net present value, internal rate of return, payback, and accounting rate of return, which method(s) is (are) the best? Explain.

Q23–13. Describe how to compute the accounting rate of return.

Q23–14. Net present value and internal rate of return may not provide the same answer when two investment proposals with *different investment lives* are compared. Why is this so and which method provides the best answer?

Q23–15. Net present value and internal rate of return may not provide the same answer when two investment proposals with *different initial investments are compared*. Why is this so and which method provides the best answer?

EXERCISES

23–1. Basic Capital Budgeting Analysis for Disinvestment Decision Clark Company has equipment that is expected to produce $48,000 in operating cash inflows during each of the next five years. It has also been estimated that the equipment can be sold for $176,000 today, but it will be worthless in five years. The equipment cost $420,000 and has a book value of $140,000.

Required

Should Clark Company dispose of the equipment now or continue to use it for the next five years, assuming the cost of capital is 10 percent?

E23–2. Internal Rate of Return Analysis G & A Corporation has just acquired a three-year contract with a government agency to produce 1,000 computer chips per year for use with a new computer hardware system. The sales price will be $130 per chip. Total variable costs, including overhead but exclusive of the machinery required, are estimated to be $50 per chip. The president of the corporation is evaluating several alternatives to meet this demand.

One alternative is the purchase of a new chip assembler machine at a cost of $160,000. Maintenance requirements would be about $800 per year. This new machine is expected to have a negligible salvage value at the end of three years because of the product's obsolescence.

Depreciation of all equipment is done on a straight-line basis, and 20 percent is the minimum desired rate of return on new investments.

Required

Compute the internal rate of return on the initial investment and give your recommendations to the president of G & A Corporation.

E23–3. Investment Analysis Consider each of the following situations independently.

A. Clark Company can obtain additional equipment at a cost of $90,000. This equipment will produce an expected annual operating cash flow of $23,500 for the next five years.

Required

Assuming a 10-percent cost of capital, should the equipment acquisition be made?

B. Tracy Corporation is planning to invest $80,000 in a three-year project. Tracy's expected rate of return is 10 percent. The present value of $1 at 10 percent for one year is 0.909, for two years is 0.826, and for three years is 0.751. The expected cash flow will be $30,000 for the first year (present value of $27,270) and $36,000 for the second year (present value of $29,736).

Required

Assuming the rate of return is exactly 10 percent, determine the cash flow for the third year.

C. Hamilton Company has invested in a two-year project that has an internal rate of return of 12 percent. The project is expected to produce cash flows from operations of $60,000 in the first year and $70,000 in the second year. The present value of $1 for one period at 12 percent is 0.893 and for two periods at 12 percent is 0.797.

Required

How much will the project cost?

E23–4. Capital Budgeting Concepts

Choose the best answer for each of the following questions.

1. In capital budgeting analysis, the payback reciprocal may provide a quick and useful estimate of the internal rate of return only when
   a. cash inflows do not extend beyond the length of the payback period.
   b. cash inflow amounts vary erratically during the life of the investment.
   c. most of the cash inflows from an investment precede the investment outlay.
   d. cash inflows are uniform throughout the life of an investment that is long relative to its payback period.
   e. the investment outlays are made uniformly throughout the life of the investment.

2. The net present value capital budgeting technique can be used when cash flows from period to period are

	Uniform	Uneven
a.	No	Yes
b.	No	No
c.	Yes	No
d.	Yes	Yes

3. Making the common assumption in capital budgeting analysis that cash inflows occur in lump sums at the end of individual time periods during the life of an investment project, when in fact they flow more or less continuously through that life,
   a. results in increasingly overstated estimates of net present value as the life of the investment project increases.
   b. results in understated estimates of net present value.
   c. results in a higher estimate for the internal rate of return of the investment.

d. will result in inconsistent errors being made in estimating net present values so that projects cannot be evaluated reliably.
e. is done because present value tables for continuous flows cannot be constructed.

4. The net present value of a proposed project represents the
   a. cash flow minus the present value of the cash flows.
   b. cash flows minus the original investment.
   c. present value of the cash flows plus the present value of the original investment minus the original investment.
   d. present value of the cash flows minus the original investment.

5. Which of the following is necessary to calculate the payback period for a project?
   a. Useful life
   b. Minimum desired rate of return
   c. Net present value
   d. Annual cash flow

6. On May 1, 19X5, a company purchased a new machine that it does not have to pay for until May 1, 19X7. The total payment on May 1, 19X7, will include both principal and interest. Assuming interest at a 10-percent rate, the cost of the machine would be the total payment multiplied by what time value of money concept?
   a. Future amount of annuity of 1.
   b. Future amount of 1.
   c. Present value of annuity of 1.
   d. Present value of 1.

7. Budcon Incorporated has a small capital budget. When faced with indivisible projects, each of which is estimated to generate a return that exceeds the company's cost of capital, Budcon should select the combination of projects that will fully utilize the budget and
   a. maximize the sum of the net present values.
   b. maximize the sum of the internal rates of return.
   c. minimize the sum of the payback periods.
   d. have the highest present value indexes.
   e. that are ranked the highest by their net present values.

8. Future Incorporated is in the enviable situation of having unlimited capital funds. The best decision rule, in an economic sense, would be for the company to invest in all projects in which
   a. the payback was less than four years.
   b. the accounting rate of return is greater than the earnings as a percent of sales.
   c. the payback reciprocal is greater than the internal rate of return.
   d. the internal rate of return is greater than zero.
   e. the net present value is greater than zero.

E23–5. Capital Budgeting—A Potpourri of Concepts (CPA) Choose the best answer for each of the following questions.

1. Which of the following capital budgeting techniques consider(s) cash flow over the entire life of the project?

	Internal Rate of Return	*Payback*
a.	Yes	Yes
b.	Yes	No
c.	No	Yes
d.	No	No

CHAPTER 23: CAPITAL BUDGETING: PART I

2. The payback capital budgeting technique considers

	Income over Entire Life of Project	*Time Value of Money*
a.	No	No
b.	No	Yes
c.	Yes	Yes
d.	Yes	No

3. The net present value and time-adjusted rate of return methods of decision making in capital budgeting are superior to the payback method because they
    a. are easier to implement.
    b. consider the time value of money.
    c. require less input.
    d. reflect the effects of depreciation and income taxes.

4. What capital budgeting method assumes that funds are reinvested at the company's cost of capital?
    a. Payback
    b. Accounting rate of return
    c. Net present value
    d. Time-adjusted rate of return

5. A proposed project has an expected economic life of eight years. In the calculation of the net present value of the proposed project, salvage value would be
    a. excluded from the calculation of the net present value.
    b. included as a cash inflow at the estimated salvage value.
    c. included as a cash inflow at the present value of the estimated salvage value.
    d. included as a cash inflow at the future amount of the estimated salvage value.

6. It is assumed that cash flows are reinvested at the rate earned by the investment in which of the following capital budgeting techniques?

	Internal Rate of Return	*Net Present Value*
a.	Yes	Yes
b.	Yes	No
c.	No	No
d.	No	Yes

7. The accountant from Ronier Incorporated has prepared an analysis of a proposed capital project using discounted cash flow techniques. One manager has questioned the accuracy of the results because the discount factors employed in the analysis assumed that the cash flows occurred at the end of the year when actually the cash flows occurred uniformly throughout each year. The net present value calculated by the accountant
    a. will not be in error.
    b. will be slightly overstated.
    c. will be unusable for actual decision making.
    d. will be slightly understated but usable.
    e. will produce an error the direction of which is undeterminable.

E23-6. Basic Procedures of Capital Budgeting

As the new manager of division X of the Stinger Corporation, you have just been given the following information. For $60,000, you can buy a newly developed machine that will save $12,000 in cash operating costs for the next eight years, after which the machine will have no value. Stinger has recently set its minimum desired rate of return at 12 percent.

Required

Calculate the following:

1. Payback period
2. Net present value
3. Internal rate of return
4. Net present value or profitability index

E23–7. Budgeting Analysis You are a recent graduate from State U, and have just been handed the following information concerning two options available to Jamrock Corporation:

	Required	Net Cash Inflows			
Option	Investment	Year 1	Year 2	Year 3	Year 4
1	$105,000	$45,000	$40,000	$30,000	$20,000
2	$160,000	$60,000	$50,000	$50,000	$50,000

You know that Jamrock previously has been able to earn 8 percent on similar options.

Required

Advise the management of Jamrock Corporation about which option should be selected by submitting computations of net present values. Your job depends on it! Compute a profitability index for each option.

E23–8. Capital Budgeting Methods (CPA) Allo Foundation, a tax-exempt organization, invested $200,000 in a five-year project at the beginning of 19X5. Allo estimated that the annual cash savings from this project would amount to $65,000. The $200,000 of assets will be depreciated over their five-year life on the straight-line basis. On investments of this type, Allo's desired rate of return is 12 percent.

Required

Compute each of the following:

1. The net present value of the project.
2. Allo's internal rate of return on this project.
3. For the project's first year, Allo's accounting rate of return, based on the project's average book value for 19X5.

E23–9. Practice Problems on Capital Budgeting (CPA) Choose the best answer for each of the following questions.

1. Womark Company purchased a new machine on January 1, 19X1, for $90,000. The machine has an estimated useful life of five years and a salvage value of $10,000. The machine is expected to produce cash flows from operations of $36,000 a year for each of the next five years. The payback period would be
    a. 2.2 years.
    b. 2.5 years.
    c. 4.0 years.
    d. 4.5 years.

Questions 2 and 3 are based on the following data:

Amaro Hospital, a nonprofit institution not subject to income taxes, is considering the purchase of new equipment costing $20,000 in order to achieve cash savings of $5,000 per year in operating costs. The equipment's estimated useful life is ten years, with no net residual value. Amaro's cost of capital is 14 percent. For ten periods at 14 percent, the present value of $1 is 0.270, whereas the present value of an ordinary annuity of $1 is 5.216.

2. What factor contained in or developed from the preceding information should be used in computing the internal rate of return for Amaro's proposed investment in the new equipment?
   a. 5.216
   b. 4.000
   c. 1.400
   d. 0.270

3. How much is the accounting rate of return based on Amaro's initial investment in the new equipment?
   a. 27%
   b. 25%
   c. 15%
   d. 14%

4. Heller Company has purchased a machine for $500,000 that has a useful life of five years and no salvage value. The machine is being depreciated using the straight-line method, and it is expected to produce annual cash flows from operations, net of income taxes, of $150,000. The present value of an ordinary annuity of $1 for five periods at 14 percent is 3.43. The present value of $1 for five periods at 14 percent is 0.52. Assuming that Heller uses a time-adjusted rate of return of 14 percent, what is the net present value?
   a. $280,000
   b. $250,000
   c. $180,000
   d. $14,500

5. Garwood Company has purchased a machine that will be depreciated on the straight-line basis over an estimated useful life of seven years and that has no salvage value. The machine is expected to generate cash flows from operations net of income taxes of $80,000 in each of the seven years. Garwood's expected rate of return is 12 percent. Information on present value factors is as follows:

Present value of $1 at 12 percent for seven periods	0.452
Present value of an ordinary annuity of $1 at 12 percent for seven periods	4.564

Assuming a positive net present value of $12,720, what is the cost of the machine?
   a. $240,400
   b. $253,120
   c. $352,400
   d. $377,840

6. Oran Company has the opportunity to invest in a two-year project that is expected to produce cash flows from operations of $100,000 in the first year and $200,000 in the second year. Oran requires an internal rate of return of 20 percent. The present value of $1 for one period at 20 percent is 0.833 and for two periods at 20 percent is 0.694. For this project, Oran should be willing to invest immediately a maximum of

a. $283,300.
b. $249,900.
c. $222,100.
d. $208,200.

E23–10. Present Value Procedures of Capital Budgeting Consider each of the following situations independently.

A. Gene Incorporated invested in a machine with a useful life of six years and no salvage value. The machine was expected to produce annual cash inflows of $2,000. The present value of an ordinary annuity of $1 for six periods at 10 percent is 4.355. The present value of $1 for six periods at 10 percent is 0.564.

Required

Assuming that Gene used a time-adjusted rate of return of 10 percent, what was the amount of the original investment?

B. Cooper plans to invest $2,000 at the end of each of the next ten years. Assume that Cooper will earn interest at an annual rate of 6 percent compounded annually. The future value of an ordinary annuity of $1 for ten periods at 6 percent is 13.181. The present value of $1 for ten periods at 6 percent is 0.558. The present value of an ordinary annuity of $1 for ten periods at 6 percent is 7.360.

Required

Determine the amount of the investment after the end of ten years.

C. Jill Horn, management consultant for a successful corporation in west Texas, has been asked to evaluate three different projects, each of which will produce a yearly cash flow of $35,000. Initial investment in each of the three projects is $140,000. Project 1 has a useful life of four years, project 2 has a useful life of six years, and project 3 has a useful life of five years. The company requires a minimum return of 12 percent on capital projects.

Required

1. Assuming that payback time is the sole criterion for her decision, which project should Jill Horn select? Why?
2. Which project will yield the highest rate of return? Compute the actual rate of return on each of the projects.

E23–11. Budgeting Cash Receipts and Capital Budgeting—Spreadsheet Application Provo City has an olympic-size swimming pool, but because of the potential legal liability should an accident or death occur, the city has decided not to operate it. It has offered to let you operate the pool for five years for $50,000 plus 10 percent of the annual swimming revenue collected. The initial payment is due on signing the agreement, and the annual rental payment is due at the end of each year. At the end of the five years, the pool will revert back to the city, which will have the option to operate it or enter into another lease agreement.

The revenues and costs for the first year of operation, along with the projected increases for the next four years, are as follows:

Revenues & Costs	1st Year	Projected Increase
Revenues	$90,000	10% per year
Labor	22,000	7% per year
Insurance	12,000	0% per year
Utilities	18,000	4% per year
Repairs	6,000	1% per year
Rental	10% of revenue	0% per year

Assume that your minimum desired rate of return is 15 percent. Also assume that because this is for the city, you will qualify for tax-exempt status at both the federal and state levels.

Required

1. Set up an electronic spreadsheet to determine the desirability of accepting the offer from Provo City. Project the annual cash flows and use the net present value and internal rate of return functions. Print out a copy of your results.
2. Suppose that the preceding estimates of costs and the projected increases in both costs and revenues are accurate, but that the projected revenues for the first year of operations are not known with much accuracy. How much would revenues need to be during the first year, with everything else remaining the same, to provide a 20-percent return on the investment?

E23–12. Net Present Value and Internal Rate of Return Methods (CPA)
The net present value method and the internal rate of return method are both sophisticated capital budgeting techniques.

Required

1. State the advantages that both the net present value method and the internal rate of return method have over the payback method.
2. State the limitations of the net present value method.
3. State the limitations of the internal rate of return method.
4. How does each method (net present value and internal rate of return) handle depreciation? Discuss the rationale for your answer. Ignore income tax considerations in your answer.

PROBLEMS

P23–1. Capital Budgeting Analysis—Electronic Spreadsheet
The manager of division B is considering two different projects, each of which will require the same initial investment of $25,000. The following schedule shows prospective operating income for both projects 1 and 2.

	Cash Inflows	
Year	Project 1	Project 2
1	$20,000	$10,000
2	5,000	10,000
3	5,000	10,000
4	10,000	10,000
Total	$40,000	$40,000

Assume that the company considers 10 percent to be a minimum rate of return.

Required

1. Use an electronic spreadsheet to determine which project the manager should select. Compute net present value, internal rate of return, and accounting rate of return. Print your results.
2. Does the relative desirability of the two projects change if the minimum rate of return is reduced to 2 percent? Print your results.
3. How does the relative desirability of the two projects change when the minimum rate of return is increased to 20 percent? Print out your results.

P23-2. Net Present Value and Accounting Rate of Return (CPA)

Leif Company is faced with the necessity of making the two following unrelated decisions involving its Sigma Division:

A. *Discontinuance of a currently produced product and acquisition of a new machine.* Sigma's manager, Baum, has recommended that an unprofitable product, called Sago, be discontinued, which would decrease Sigma's current sales volume by 10 percent. In addition, Baum wants to improve efficiency by investing $100,000 in a new machine. Baum believes that implementation of his two recommendations would increase the pretax income rate on sales to 12 percent.

Sigma's current rate of pretax income is 10 percent on annual sales of $2,000,000. Financing of this current level of annual sales requires an investment of $600,000. Leif measures Sigma's performance by the pretax accounting rate of return based on the initial investment.

B. *Financing of a distributor.* Cote Corporation, which is one of Sigma's distributors, wants to borrow $200,000 from Leif and to repay this loan within three years. As an inducement, Cote is offering Leif a participation in Cote's income for three years. Payments by Cote at the end of each of the three years would include principal plus 5 percent of Cote's net income for each of these years. The estimated amounts to be remitted by Cote to Leif under this arrangement would be as follows:

At the End of Year	Amount
1	$ 50,000
2	90,000
3	110,000
Total estimated remittances	$250,000

Leif would be willing to grant Cote's loan request if the annual pretax internal rate of return on this loan exceeds Leif's hurdle (discount) rate of 20 percent on investment. Present value factors yielding 20 percent are approximately as follows:

Year	Factor
1	0.8
2	0.7
3	0.6

Required

1. a. Compute Leif Company's current pretax accounting rate of return on its investment in Sigma Division.

b. Compute Leif Company's expected pretax accounting rate of return on its proposed investment in Sigma Division if Baum's two recommendations are implemented.

2. Regarding the possible financing of Cote Corporation by Leif Company, compute the net present value of Leif Company's investment opportunity on the proposed loan to Cote Corporation, and state whether the investment would earn Leif a minimum internal rate of return of 20 percent.

P23-3. Basic Analysis of Capital Budgeting

Disco Dippo Incorporated is faced with the decision of continuing to use its old equipment or purchasing new equipment at a cost of $23,000. This new equipment is expected to have a useful life of nine years and is expected to save the company $5,000 for each of the first three years, $4,000 for the next three years, and $2,000 for the final three years. Disco's minimum rate of return is 10 percent.

Required

Compute the following:

1. Payback period
2. Internal rate of return
3. Net present value
4. Profitability index

P23-4. Net Present Value Analysis

You have recently been approached by a friend about a go-cart racetrack investment that would cost $80,000 in cash. This price would allow you to use an existing track, subject to an annual lease payment of $16,700 (these payments are made at the end of each year), for the remaining life of the lease. The price also includes go-carts that have an expected salvage value of $9,000 at the end of eight years, which is when the lease will expire. The leased property originally cost $45,000. Yearly income is expected to be $70,000, and yearly operating costs will be $38,000.

Required

Using the net present value criterion, would the go-cart racetrack be a wise investment? Assume a 12-percent interest rate. Compute the net present value.

P23-5. Various Procedures of Capital Budgeting

Stallcab Incorporated has been in the manufacturing business for ten years. Although its machinery is still functioning satisfactorily, it has been suggested that new, more efficient machinery would be cost-beneficial.

Last week, a sales representative stopped by and displayed a new equipment line that would reduce cash operating costs by $11,000 per year. The cost of the machinery is $96,000, and it has an estimated useful life of eighteen years, with zero salvage value.

Required

Assuming that the salesperson's estimations are correct, compute the following:

1. Payback period
2. Internal rate of return

You are unsure of the salesperson's integrity. Therefore, compute the internal rate of return if the following are true:

1. The useful life is ten years instead of eighteen.
2. The useful life is twenty-five years instead of eighteen.
3. The cash operating costs' reduction is $7,000 per year instead of $11,000 (eighteen-year useful life).

P23-6. Various Procedures of Capital Budgeting

The Criddle Company has been operating a small food counter for the convenience of its employees. The counter, which uses space not feasibly used for any other purpose, has been managed by a senior citizen whose annual salary is $3,000. Yearly operations have consistently shown a loss as follows:

Sales		$20,000
Food and supplies cash expenses	$19,000	
Salary	3,000	22,000
Net loss		$ (2,000)

An equipment company has offered to sell Criddle automatic vending machines for a total cost of $13,000 cash. Old equipment not used in the food counter operation is carried at zero book value; it could be sold now for $1,000. Sales terms are COD (cash on delivery). The old equipment will be worth nothing ten years from now.

The predicted useful life of the equipment is ten years, with zero scrap value. The new vending machines will easily serve the same volume that the food counter handled. A catering company will completely service and supply the machines. Prices and variety of food and drink will be the same as those that prevailed at the food counter. The catering company will pay 5 percent of gross receipts to the Criddle Company and will pay all costs of foods and repairs. The senior citizen will be discharged, but other opportunities will be available to him. Criddle's only cost will be the initial outlay for the new machines. Assume Criddle Company feels an obligation to its employees to provide some kind of food service and these two options are the best options available.

Required

1. Prepare a prospective annual income statement under the new plan. What is the annual income difference between the alternatives? (Assume straight-line depreciation.)
2. Compute the payback period.
3. Compute the following:
   a. The present value under the discounted cash flow method if relevant cost of the company's capital is 20 percent. Compute the profitability index.
   b. The rate of return under the discounted cash flow method.
4. Compute the payback reciprocal.
5. Management is unsure of the prospective revenue from the vending equipment. Suppose that the gross receipts amounted to $14,000 instead of $20,000. Repeat the computation in requirement 3a.
6. What would be the minimum amount of annual gross receipts from the vending equipment that would justify making the investment? Show your computations.
7. Suppose Criddle Company increases its cost of capital to 30 percent and the catering company is willing to increase the revenue sharing from 5 percent to 15 percent. Compute the net present value and profitability index under this new assumption.

P23-7. Evaluation of the Procedures for Capital Budgeting (CMA)

Peterdonn Corporation made a capital investment of $100,000 in new equipment two years ago. The analysis made at that time indicated that the equipment would save $36,400 in operating expenses per year over a five-year period, or a 24-percent return on capital before taxes per year based on the internal rate of return analysis.

The department manager believed that the equipment had lived up to its expectations. However, the departmental report showing the overall return on investment (ROI) rate for the first year in which this equipment was used did not reflect as much improvement as had been expected. The department manager asked the accounting section to break out the figures related to this investment to find out why it did not contribute more to the department's ROI.

The accounting section was able to identify the equipment and its contribution to the department's operations. The report presented to the department manager at the end of the first year is shown below.

Reduced operating expenses due to new equipment	$ 36,400
Less: Depreciation—20% of cost	20,000
Contribution before taxes	$ 16,400
Investment—beginning of year	$100,000
Investment—end of year	$ 80,000
Average investment for the year	$ 90,000

$$\text{ROI} = \frac{16,400}{90,000} = 18.2\%$$

The department manager was surprised that the ROI was less than 24 percent because the new equipment had performed as expected. The staff analyst in the accounting section replied that the company ROI for performance evaluation differed from that used for capital investment analysis. The analyst commented that the discrepancy could be solved if the company used a different method of depreciation for its performance evaluation reports.

Required

1. Explain why the return on investment of 18.2 percent for the new equipment as calculated in the department's report by the accounting section differs from the 24-percent internal rate of return calculated at the time the machine was approved for purchase.
2. Will the use of a different method of depreciation solve the discrepancy, as the analyst claims? Explain your answer.
3. Explain how Peterdonn Corporation might restructure the data from the discounted cash flow analysis so that the expected performance of the new equipment is consistent with the operating reports received by the department manager.

P23-8. Capital Budgeting—Post Audit (CMA) Dickson Incorporated has formal policies and procedures to screen and ultimately approve capital projects. Proposed capital projects are classified as one of the following types:

1. Expansion requiring new plant and equipment
2. Expansion by replacement of present equipment with more productive equipment
3. Replacement of old equipment with new equipment of similar quality

All expansion projects and replacement projects costing more than $50,000 must be submitted to the top management capital investment committee for approval. The investment committee evaluates proposed projects, considering the costs and benefits outlined in the supporting proposal and the long-range effects on the company. The projected revenue and expense effects of the projects, once operational, are included in the proposal. Once a project is accepted, the committee approves an expenditure budget for the project from its inception until it becomes operational. The expenditures required each year for the expansions or replacements are also incorporated into Dickson's annual budget procedure. The budgeted revenue and cost effects of the projects, for the period in which they become operational, are incorporated into the five-year forecast.

Dickson Incorporated does not have a procedure for evaluating projects once they have been implemented and become operational. The vice president of finance has recommended that Dickson establish a post-completion audit program to evaluate its capital expenditure projects.

Required

1. What are the benefits a company could derive from a post-completion audit program for capital expenditure projects?
2. What are the practical difficulties in collecting and accumulating information that would be used to evaluate a capital project once it becomes operational?

P23-9. Various Methods of Capital Budgeting for Uneven Cash Flows

The Meiga Drilling Company is considering the purchase of a new hydralift machine. The cost of the machine is $56,000. Useful economic life is estimated to be seven years, and disposal costs are expected to equal salvage value. Assume a straight-line depreciation method is used by Meiga Drilling Company on all assets. Estimates of cash-operating cost savings have been made by the special projects group as shown below. Assume conventional straight line depreciation is used on all assets.

Year	Amount
1	$20,000
2	16,000
3	12,000
4	8,000
5	7,000
6	6,000
7	5,000
	$74,000

Required

1. Determine the payback period.
2. Determine the net present value. Assume a minimum required return of 14 percent. Compute the profitability index.
3. Determine the internal rate of return.
4. Determine the accounting rate of return.

P23-10. Capital Budgeting and Sensitivity Analysis

Salem Community Hospital is considering replacing some hospital kitchen equipment with new more efficient items. The new equipment will cost $40,000 and is estimated to save $10,000 in cash-operating costs per year.

The old equipment was purchased twelve years ago at a cost of $15,000 and is fully depreciated. There is no evident salvage or trade-in value for the old equipment. It could be used indefinitely.

The new equipment is expected to have a useful life of ten years and will have no salvage value at the end of the ten years.

Required

1. Determine the payback period.
2. Determine the net present value. Assume a cut-off rate of return of 12 percent.
3. The project analysis team is uncertain about the reliability of the life estimate and the amount of the operating savings. You have been asked to compute the net present value under each of the following *changes* in the original conditions:

- a. Useful life of eight years instead of ten years
- b. Useful life of twelve years instead of ten years
- c. Operating savings of $7,000 instead of $10,000
- d. Operating savings of $14,000 instead of $10,000
- e. Operating savings of $8,000 instead of $10,000 and a useful life of six years instead of ten years

CASE

C23-1. Lyons, Inc.—Developing a Financial Analysis and Capital Budgeting

Lyons, Inc. manufactures and sells ringlets. Al Lyons, president and CEO of the company, has been concerned for some time now about problems in the data processing area. Mr. Lyons has decided to investigate possible changes in the data processing area. The following information has been collected on the company and its data processing centers.

Background

Al Lyons inherited the business four years ago from his rich uncle Harry Lyons. Harry Lyons began Lyons, Inc. shortly after returning home from active duty in World War II. Business was somewhat slow during the remainder of the 1940s and the early part of the 1950s. However, business boomed during the late 1950s and 1960s as ringlet popularity caught on with the youth. Everybody had to have at least one ringlet, and two or three automatically qualified a person for the "in group."

During this period of prosperity, Lyons, Inc. became a national organization. The country was divided into six regions: Northeast, Southeast, Midwest, Southwest, Utah, and Northwest. Each region developed its own production facility. Several sales offices were established and continue to operate in each region. Accounting and data processing were organized into two data-processing centers: the East center supports the Northeast, Southeast, and Midwest regions, and the West center supports the Southwest, Utah, and Northwest regions.

Each of the data processing centers have been free to develop the applications they thought were needed most for the operation and management of the business. Harry Lyons never felt the need to learn much about accounting or computer data processing. It all seemed so complex. Besides, he frequently said, "I know every salesperson, every sales territory, and exactly how production is doing in every one of my plants. What can your ledgers or computers tell me that I don't already know?"

Accounting and data processing personnel have always had to work overtime at year-end to consolidate the annual financial statements. The file structures and intercompany pricing systems set by each center are slightly different and always changing. Harry frequently said that they were wasting their time. "I can tell you within $10,000 what our net income is going to be for the year," he would say. When he and the business were in their prime, the estimates were right on. That wasn't bad for a company turning a net income of $250,000 per year.

Business declined during the late 1960s and throughout the 1970s. Harrys health deteriorated from what the doctor said was overwork and too little exercise. Upon his death the court awarded the business to Al Lyons, Harry's only known survivor.

Recent Developments

When Al took over the business, it was in a sharp decline. Morale was low. Sales were down, and competition was increasing. Selling the business and living on the cash reserves was a big temptation to Al. But because he needed something to do and wanted a challenge to make life exciting, he decided to keep the business and try to turn it around.

His first efforts were to redesign the ringlet and update the marketing approach. These efforts have been very successful. Production and sales have turned around and both are at their all time high.

Growth in production and sales have magnified the problems in data processing. Al is bright, but regardless of how much time he spends, he can never seem to get on top of the numbers. Neither can anyone else in the company.

Request for Information

In an attempt to obtain useful data on accounting and data processing, Al asked each center to provide him with operating cost data. The data were to be organized in a tabular format. Data on production and sales were to be summarized, but data on accounting and data processing were to be provided by each major cost category.

Figures 23.14 and 23.15 contain the actual cost data for 19X5 for the East Processing Center and the West Processing Center, respectively.

The data provided by the centers were transferred across communication lines (appropriately encrypted). Lyons, Inc. has several IBM PCs and Lotus software that can be used to prepare projected operating statements for data processing for the next several years.

Al asked Kelly, a college intern with the company, to review the history of cost increases in each major cost category and to develop percentages that could be used to project future costs. Kelly provided the following summary of projected cost increases for the next eight- or nine-year period.

1. Manager, analyst, and programmer salaries will increase 9 percent per year for the East and 11 percent for the West.
2. Operator and data entry costs will increase 5 percent per year in the East and 4 percent in the West.

FIGURE 23.14

East Processing Center Summary Cost Data 19X5

Personnel	Amount	
Manager	$ 50,250	
Analyst	127,500	
Programmer	149,150	
Operator	118,500	
Data entry	129,500	
Subtotal		$574,900
Direct Materials		
Supplies	$ 10,375	
Subtotal		10,375
Overhead		
Power	$ 78,170	
Support	100,740	
Occupancy	34,750	
Depreciation	87,500	
Other	11,498	
Subtotal		312,658
Total		$897,933

Dallas Burnett, Controller. Dallas Burnett had been the controller for only six years, but he seemed to have a clear understanding of the data processing problems.

"Bryce Young seemed more than willing to move to New York," said Mark. "He would probably be here next week if we decided to go ahead with it. However, Nina Wilcox couldn't be more negative!"

"That is too bad," responded Dallas. "Nina is by far the best DP manager of the two individuals. She is very competent technically, gets along well with people, and is quite aggressive. She would do a super job in heading up a new data processing facility."

"What has been the problem between the two processing centers?" asked Mark. "Nina said they hadn't worked well together and that the East Processing Center is the cause of the late reports."

"That's true," said Dallas. "Nina has tried a couple of times to develop common systems with Bryce, but Bryce likes to do his own thing. As for the lateness of the reports, Bryce is an easy-going guy. If someone is not pushing him, he does things when he feels like doing them."

"Both of the DP managers said most of their employees would seek other employment before they would accept a transfer to New York. Do you think that is accurate?" asked Mark.

"I think that is an overstatement. The company would have to increase salaries to offset the higher cost of living in New York. They would also have to pay a moving allowance. But I think about half of the operators, analysts, programmers, and managers would be willing to make the change," said Dallas.

Data Processing Facility Costs

Mark Owen spent a good deal of time with an IBM sales representative and a couple of systems analysts to try to organize some cost data and identify the activities that would be required to open a new data processing center.

The analysts were particularly helpful in developing software specifications and evaluating the software currently used by Lyons, Inc. Mark noted the following as some of their more important conclusions:

1. The software developed and used by the West Processing Center is better than that used by the East Processing Center. It is more complete, better integrated, more user-friendly, and better documented.

2. Software currently used by the company would be processable by any of the new computers that Lyons, Inc. may acquire. Although there are some good software packages available for purchase, none of them are exactly what the company would like. The cost to acquire the software and modify it to fit the company's needs seems to be more than the cost of modifying the existing software for processing on the new equipment.

3. Some consideration was given to moving the hardware from one or both of the existing facilities. However, that idea was discarded quickly when the moving cost, age, capacity, and speed of processing were considered.

4. One analyst commented, "I don't know how the production and sales managers are going to respond to the consolidated data processing center. They are just like Al; they want fast numbers and quality information to manage and control their own areas. Al will get his reports quickly, but these other people will have to wait for their reports. I don't think they will like that!"

5. The analysts, Mark, and the IBM sales representative struggled with the data entry problem. The sales representative suggested that they investigate some source data

FIGURE 23.15

West Processing Center Summary Cost Data 19X5

Personnel	Amount	
Manager	$ 49,980	
Analyst	121,525	
Programmer	150,646	
Operator	119,955	
Data entry	112,333	
Subtotal		$554,439
Direct Materials		
Supplies	$ 9,540	
Subtotal		9,540
Overhead		
Power	$ 71,496	
Support	46,068	
Occupancy	27,125	
Depreciation	92,500	
Other	11,089	
Subtotal		248,278
Total		$812,257

3. Supply costs are expected to stay constant in the East for two years and then to increase at 4 percent per year during the next six years. For the West they are expected to decline by 2 percent per year for the first two years and then to increase by 5 percent per year thereafter.

4. Power costs in both the East and West centers will probably increase 7 percent per year.

5. Support and occupancy costs are made up of several different items that change at different rates. An average increase per year of 10 percent for the East and 8 percent for the West is expected.

6. Depreciation relates entirely to the computers used at the two processing centers. A straight-line method has been used. However, because both computers are now (12/31/X5) fully depreciated, depreciation will be zero for subsequent years.

7. Other costs are variable at 2 percent of total personnel costs. This relationship is expected to continue for the next eight years.

A seven- or eight-year planning period is standard for Lyons, Inc. Anything beyond eight years is so far in the future, especially when dealing with data processing, that projections are not too accurate. Al thought it might be helpful to have the three following reports, but no one has been assigned to prepare them:

1. Projected accounting and data processing costs for the East Center for the next eight years.
2. Projected accounting and data processing costs for the West Center for the next eight years.
3. Projected accounting and data processing costs for the East and West Centers combined for the next eight years.

Al Lyons was impressed by the promptness with which the cost data were prepared for the individual processing centers. They were the first fast numbers he had received since taking charge of the business four years ago. Having some control of the numbers and the ability to generate useful information quickly gave Al an idea. "Why don't we consolidate all data processing into one central processing facility near corporate headquarters?"

One quick telephone call from Al turned into several days' work to collect the relevant information. Al's specific charge was to investigate the cost, feasibility, and desirability of moving all data processing to Westchester County, N.Y.

Current Data Processing

Data processing (DP) for the eastern regions has been performed in Atlanta, Georgia. This was the location of corporate headquarters until Al took over four years ago. Not wanting to move his family out of its dream home in Tarrytown, N.Y., Al decided to relocate corporate headquarters in Westchester County, N.Y.

To date, most of Al's time has been devoted to product redesign and marketing. Data processing and reporting have been so low on his list of priorities that it didn't seem to matter much that corporate reports were developed out of the Atlanta office. However, the recent desire to have more control over data processing and faster access to the numbers prompted his idea of consolidating the DP centers.

The data processing for the western regions has been performed in San Jose, California. Both the East and West processing centers have a qualified group of people, and most of them have been with Lyons, Inc. for several years. Feeling a need to know more about each data processing center and the attitude of its employees, Mark Owen, an assistant, was asked to make telephone calls to each of the DP managers and to the controller of the company. He was also asked to collect relevant cost data on a centralized data processing facility in Westchester County, N.Y. The following summarizes his data collection activities.

Bryce Young, DP Manager East. Bryce Young, the DP manager at the East Processing Center, did not seem at all surprised by the telephone call. "When Al took over the business and decided to locate corporate headquarters in New York, I figured it was only a matter of time until data processing would follow. I'm a little surprised it has taken four years to finally be considered," he said.

When asked about the employees' attitudes toward such a move, Bryce responded, "Some of us are from upstate New York and would jump at a chance to move back. I, and a couple of my key people—Robert Joy and Evelyn Zundel, would be willing to move with only a few weeks' notice. But then, some of my people are from the south and would probably seek new employment before they would move to New York. That would be too bad, because these are good workers who have been with the company for many years. It would be a shame to lose them."

The conversation then turned to some of the detailed data processing concerns. The following notes were made from the telephone conversation.

1. The East Processing Center uses all IBM equipment. Employees have been trained on it and seemed biased toward its use. If new equipment is acquired, they would like it to be IBM.
2. All the equipment is fairly old and fully depreciated. It has been well maintained, so it could be used for another six to eight years if needed. But Bryce complained about the lack of speed and high-power usage.
3. There is some excess capacity on the existing equipment. However, if the company continues to grow at the rate experienced during the last two years, the excess capacity will last only another four to six years. At that time some system upgrades will be

CHAPTER 23: CAPITAL BUDGETING: PART I

required to meet further growth. Bryce had no idea about the specific hardware changes that would be required or about the cost of the system upgrades.

4. Bryce questioned the data entry process. He indicated that data are currently sent from the production facilities in each region and from each of the sales offices on original (hard copy) documents. A key-to-tape system is used by data entry personnel at the data processing center to convert the data to machine readable form. Bryce specifically asked which activities were to be moved: data entry, data processing, or report preparation.

Bryce seemed more than willing to do research and provide additional information. He promised to send a resumé on himself, Robert Joy, and Evelyn Zundel. It almost seemed as if he was ready to pack his disk packs and come to New York.

Nina Wilcox, DP Manager West. Nina could not have been more surprised at the possibility of moving the data processing center. "I specifically talked with Harry Lyons about this ten years ago when I accepted the job of DP manager. Harry assured me that there would always be a DP manager's job for me here on the west coast. Harry liked the western lifestyle and frequently visited our processing center. I've only seen Al at our center twice during the last four years. I don't think he appreciates the qualified people we have or the amount of work we do for the company. Data processing problems are not caused by us; they are caused by the East Processing Center. They are very slow. We have all of our reports complete within a few days after the end of a period. Sometimes it takes them a month or two to finish their reports and then a month or two to consolidate our reports with their reports. If Al wants fast response time, he ought to make us the head processing center."

When asked about the attitude of other employees to such a move, Nina responded, "I only have one analyst, Gerold Smith, who might be willing to move to New York. Gerold worked there for a few years. He even met his wife while living there. I know she would like to go back and I think Gerold would take her if the price was right. The rest of my people would be willing to move to any other western location, but please, not New York."

Nina indicated that her data processing equipment was almost identical in age, capacity, and future usability to that which Bryce had at the East Processing Center. The West purchased identical equipment the same year as the East. Therefore, their equipment is also fully depreciated.

Nina had several complaints that she specifically wanted noted:

1. The East and the West processing centers have not been able to work well together in the past. "It is absurd for us to develop and maintain the same software packages as the East. Our operations are not so much different that we (or they) need to always develop and maintain our own software."

2. Much of the data processing cost is tied up in data entry. "Key-to-tape data entry was the best that was available when we acquired our hardware several years ago," she said. "But there are much more efficient ways available on the market today to enter our data."

The things that Nina said made a lot of sense. However, much of what she said about the attitudes of her people did not fit in with the concept of centralized data processing, at least in the New York area. She seemed more than willing to provide information, so a copy of Gerold Smith's data sheet was requested.

automation devices to capture data in machine-readable form in the factories and sales offices. However, the analysts thought that was too much change too fast. Therefore, the equipment configuration and data processing costs used to make the analysis are based on key-to-disk entry at the DP center using original documents sent by the factories and sales offices.

Figure 23.16 summarizes the costs required to establish and operate a centralized data processing center in Westchester County, N.Y. In developing these numbers, it is assumed that it would take one year to perform all activities to make the center completely operational. One year was simply an estimate and did not represent a detailed analysis of the amount of time involved in individual implementation activities.

Mark's Summary

Mark delivered his information this morning. He apologized for taking two days to obtain it but indicated that matching schedules with everyone was sometimes difficult.

In reviewing the material, Mark indicated that he could provide a list of names and salaries of each manager, analyst, operator, and programmer at the existing processing facilities. "At some point you will probably have to identify who will participate in this project and what responsibilities they will have," said Mark. "Such a list, however, will take a couple of days to prepare."

General Company Information

Lyons, Inc. is not subject to federal or state income tax. Its minimum desired rate of return for capital budgeting decisions is 15 percent.

Although the computers used by the existing processing centers are both functional, they are not worth very much. Assume that they can be sold for their salvage value ($92,500) on January 1, 19X7 when the new systems becomes operational.

Required

After providing you with the preceding information, Al said, "I need to know the desirability of combining the data processing centers and locating them in New York. Here is a list of the analyses that I would like as soon as possible." Al then handed you the following list:

1. Projected operating costs of the East Processing Center.
2. Projected operating costs of the West Processing Center.
3. Combined projected operating costs for continuing the East and West processing centers as they currently operate.
4. Projected costs of opening a new processing center in New York that combines the two processing centers.
5. Comparison of the results of items 3 and 4 and a capital budgeting analysis performed to determine if the cost savings for the new processing center in New York is desirable at the company's minimum rate of return.

An eight-year planning period is desired for all projections. Assume that it will take one year to make the New York center operational. Project the operating costs for seven years after the development year and use that period for the comparison.

FIGURE 23.16

Estimated Costs to Establish and Operate New Data Processing Center

Start-up Costs (to be incurred during 19X6):

New computer and related hardware	$1,200,000
Building remodeling and installation	150,000
Systems analysis and design costs:	
1 manager for 12 months at $6,500 per month	78,000
1 analyst for 12 months at $6,000 per month	72,000
2 programmers for 6 months at $5,600 per month	67,200
Conversion costs	300,000
Support rate charge for 8 months at $2,500 per month	20,000
Moving expense allowance for employees	260,000
Building rental during start-up period,	
$32,000 per month for 10 months	320,000

Note: All equipment prices are based on the estimated cost to the company and include any sales and use taxes. Salary rates for personnel are fully burdened.

Operating Costs:

Type	Expected 19X7	Expected Increase (decrease) per Year for Seven Years
Personnel:		
Manager	$ 60,000	12% per year increase
Analysts	200,000	14% per year increase
Programmers	240,000	10% per year increase
Operators	150,000	6% per year increase
Data entry	260,000	5% per year increase
Subtotal	$ 910,000	
Direct Materials:		
Supplies	30,000	4% per year increase
Subtotal	$ 30,000	
Overhead:		
Power	80,000	7% per year increase
Support	80,000	10% per year increase
Occupancy	40,000	10% per year increase
Depreciation	240,000	(See note below)
Other	18,200	Variable at 2% of total personnel cost
Subtotal	$ 458,200	
Total cost	$1,398,200	

Start-up Costs and Depreciation Expense:

All start-up costs will be incurred in 19X6 except the hardware acquisition. All costs except the cost of hardware will be expensed in 19X6. The hardware will be acquired on January 1, 19X7, and will be depreciated using 5-year ACRS. However, because the company is not subject to income tax, the depreciation is a noncash expense.

ACRS percentages and depreciation are:

Year	%	Depreciation
1	20.0%	$240,000
2	32.0%	384,000
3	19.2%	230,400
4	11.5%	138,000
5	11.5%	138,000
6	5.8%	69,600
Total		$1,200,000

    To keep the analysis as simple as possible, assume that all start-up costs will be paid on December 31, 19X6. The proposed equipment will have enough capacity to meet current and expected processing needs for the next seven to ten years.

Chapter 24

Capital Budgeting: Part II

Outline

INCOME TAX EFFECTS ON CAPITAL BUDGETING
Income Tax Effect on Normal Cash Flows
Accelerated Cost Recovery System—Depreciation
The Impact of Accelerated Cost Recovery on Capital Investment
Salvage Value
Comprehensive Illustration
  Net Present Value
  Internal Rate of Return
  Payback Period
  Accounting Rate of Return
COST OF CAPITAL
Cost of Capital Defined
Marginal Cost of Capital (MCC)
Cost of Debt
Cost of Preferred Stock
Cost of Common Stock and Retained Earnings
Comprehensive Illustration
SENSITIVITY ANALYSIS IN CAPITAL BUDGETING
Selecting a Minimum Desired Rate of Return

Errors in Estimating the Component Cost of Capital Stock
Rate Adjustment for Nonproductive Projects
Variable Rate Among Projects
Variable Rate Per Year for an Individual Project
Predicting and Evaluating Cash Flows
  Expected Value
  Multiple Computations of Net Present Value
SUMMARY
APPENDIX 24.1: INVESTMENT TAX CREDIT (ITC)
SELF-STUDY PROBLEM
SUGGESTED READINGS
DISCUSSION QUESTIONS
EXERCISES
PROBLEMS
CASES

Capital budgeting is the process of allocating money for the purchase or construction of capital assets. Chapter 23 outlined four techniques that are commonly used in capital budgeting decisions. The application of these techniques is complicated somewhat by income taxes, which we have ignored, and by the determination of a minimum desired rate of return, which we assumed has been given. In addition, one of the questions often asked in capital budgeting is how the decision would change if actual operating results were slightly different from the estimates. Sensitivity analysis can be used to evaluate the effect of changes in the input values.

This chapter investigates these complications to the capital budgeting process. After completing the chapter, you should be able to:

1. explain the impact of income taxes on capital budgeting decisions and adjust cash flows for the effects of income taxes.
2. define *cost of capital* and explain its relationship to the minimum desired rate of return for capital budgeting decisions.
3. compute cost of capital using a weighted average of both debt and equity capital.
4. apply sensitivity analysis to determine the potential effect on the decision for variations in the input data.

INCOME TAX EFFECTS ON CAPITAL BUDGETING

Chapter 23 introduced capital budgeting but ignored the effect of income taxes on cash flows resulting from a capital investment project. Many organizations, such as universities and governmental units, do not pay any income taxes, so the cash flows require no tax adjustment. The analysis presented in chapter 23 is applicable to these entities.

Most profit-oriented entities are subject to income taxes, and the expected cash flows must be adjusted for income tax effects. The major effects of income taxes can be broadly classified into two areas: effects on normal cash flows, and depreciation. Each of these areas will be explored in detail and then integrated with a comprehensive illustration.[1]

Since the late 1960s, the investment tax credit (ITC) has been adopted and abolished three times. The 1986 Tax Reform Act repealed the ITC for property acquired after December 31, 1985. However, many tax experts believe that the ITC will be reestablished within a very short time. Therefore, appendix 24.1 contains a brief discussion of the investment tax credit and its effects on capital budgeting decisions.

Income Tax Effect on Normal Cash Flows

Cash flows have been classified as (a) net cash flows from operations, (b) initial investments, and (c) salvage (terminal) values. Let's first consider the net cash flows from operations and the related income taxes.

Net cash flows from operations result from cash inflows in the form of additional revenues and from cash savings in the form of expense reductions. Either way, the organization is not able to retain the entire benefit. A cash inflow in the form of revenue increases net income and income taxes payable to the government. Cash savings in the

---

1. Our objective here is not to provide a comprehensive review of the effects of income taxes on capital budgeting. Only the highlights will be reviewed in an attempt to illustrate the process that must be followed to compute the net of tax cash flows and how they are used in each capital budgeting technique. You are referred to the income tax code and regulations for a more comprehensive review of income taxes.

form of an expense reduction take away from deductible items on the tax return. This also increases both taxable income and taxes payable.

The following example will be used to show the net of tax computation for normal cash flows from operations. Brown, Incorporated is a consulting organization owned and operated by Ed Brown. Mr. Brown is a consultant for top management of several large corporations around the country. Brown, Incorporated is considering the acquisition of a private plane that can be used for traveling from one company to another. It is expected to result in additional revenue of $13,000 per year by eliminating the travel delays commonly experienced on commercial flights. Additional operating costs associated with the plane, excluding depreciation, will be $6,000 per year. Brown, Incorporated is subject to a 40-percent marginal income tax rate.

The comparative income statements that follow show the income tax effect on the annual cash flows from operations.

Brown, Inc.
Projected Income Statements
(excluding depreciation)

	Without Proposed Airplane	With Proposed Airplane	Difference
Revenue	$80,000	$93,000	$13,000
Less: Expenses			
Wages	20,000	20,000	0
Travel	40,000	46,000	6,000
Net taxable income	$20,000	$27,000	$ 7,000
Tax payable (40%)	8,000	10,800	2,800
Net income	$12,000	$16,200	$ 4,200

The difference in net income can be summarized as follows:

Additional revenue	$13,000	
Less: Increase in tax payable (40%)	5,200	
Net of tax		$7,800
Additional expense	$ 6,000	
Less: Decrease in tax payable (40%)	2,400	
Net of tax		3,600
Combined net of tax increase in cash flows		$4,200

Notice that in the preceding example the net of tax cash flow for both taxable cash receipts and tax-deductible cash expenditures can be computed by multiplying one minus the tax rate by the before-tax cash flow amount [$13,000 × (1 − 0.40) = $7,800].

Two formulas can be developed from this to compute the net of tax cash flows from operations:

Taxable Cash Receipts in the Form of Additional Revenue

(1 − Tax rate) × Cash receipt = Net of tax cash inflow

Tax Deductible Cash Expenditure

(1 − Tax rate) × Cash expenditure = Net of tax cash outflow

As long as both cash inflows and outflows are subject to income taxes, they can be offset against each other before adjusting for the income tax effect.

No adjustment is required for cash flows not subject to income taxes. For example, a cash flow associated with an increase in working capital is not deductible for tax purposes. The amount of the increase in working capital is the cash flow included in the investment analysis.

Accelerated Cost Recovery System—Depreciation

Depreciation is the allocation of the cost of an asset to accounting periods over its useful life. For financial reporting, the objective of depreciation is to match the cost of the asset to the benefits it provides. A depreciation method that is systematic and rational and that relates costs to benefits should be selected for financial reports.

Capital budgeting is cash-flow oriented, and the cost of an asset is a cash outflow when payment is made. The entry to record depreciation has been ignored until now because, by itself, it does not affect cash flow (a debit to depreciation expense and a credit to accumulated depreciation). However, depreciation has an effect on cash flows for companies that are required to pay income taxes. Because depreciation is a deductible item on the income tax return, it reduces taxable income and taxes payable. The reduction in taxes payable is a cash saving that must be included in the investment analysis.

The Economic Recovery Tax Act of 1981 made notable changes in the income tax deduction allowed for depreciation. Congress was convinced that the asset lives allowed for existing depreciation methods were not providing the stimuli essential for economic expansion; thus the Accelerated Cost Recovery System (ACRS) was developed. *Depreciable property* is called "recovery property," and depreciation is referred to as **cost recovery.** Under ACRS, the cost of recovery property is *recovered* (expensed), using accelerated methods of recovery, over periods of time that are much *shorter* than their useful lives.

Modifications in the tax laws since 1981 have changed the classifications of property and adjusted their recovery periods, generally extending the recovery periods so that they are closer to the useful lives of the assets. The procedures outlined in the 1986 Tax Reform Act will be used in this chapter.

Recovery property is divided into one of eight groups, depending on the type of asset and its use. The following summarizes each group and the types of assets that are included.

1. 3-year ACRS class property
    a. Special tools and handling devices used in light manufacturing that have useful lives of four years or less under the class life asset depreciation range (ADR) system
    b. Hogs, race horses more than two years old, and other horses more than twelve years old
2. 5-year ACRS class property
    a. Automobiles, light and heavy general purpose trucks, airplanes, and buses
    b. Computers, data handling equipment, and qualified technological equipment
    c. Renewable energy and biomass properties that include small power production facilities, research and experimentation property, and semiconductor manufacturing equipment
    d. Equipment with an ADR midpoint of more than four years and less than ten years
3. 7-year ACRS class property
    a. Equipment used in the manufacture of tobacco, fabric, wood, paper, rubber, leather, glass, metals, motor vehicles, and similar products
    b. Equipment with an ADR midpoint over ten years but less than sixteen years

        c. Single-purpose agricultural or horticultural structures and property not classified under the ADR system
4. 10-year ACRS class property
    a. Equipment used in the manufacture of grain, sugar, and vegetable oils
    b. Manufactured homes, railroad tank cars, and other property with an ADR midpoint of sixteen years and more and less than twenty years
5. 15-year ACRS class property
    a. Equipment used to manufacture cement and sewage treatment plants, and equipment used in two-way exchange of voice and data communications
    b. Land improvements, pipeline transportation, and property with an ADR midpoint of twenty years and more and less than twenty-five years
6. 20-year ACRS class property
    a. Public utility property and sewer pipes
    b. Property with an ADR midpoint of 25 years or more, and real estate with an ADR midpoint of less than 27.5 years
7. 27.5-year real estate
    a. Residential rental property
8. 31.5-year real estate
    a. Nonresidential real property
    b. Real property that is not residential rental property and that does not have an ADR midpoint of less than 27.5 years

The amount of cost recovery to be taken in any year is determined by multiplying the cost or adjusted basis of the asset by the applicable percentage from the table shown in figure 24.1. Various columns of the table used different depreciation methods. For example:

- The 3-year, 5-year, 7-year, and 10-year classes use 200-percent declining balance depreciation with a switch-over to a straight-line rate.

FIGURE 24.1

Cost Recovery Percentages

Year	3-Year	5-Year	7-Year	10-Year	15-Year	20-Year
1	0.33	0.200	0.143	0.100	0.050	0.038
2	0.45	0.320	0.245	0.180	0.095	0.072
3	0.15	0.192	0.175	0.144	0.086	0.067
4	0.07	0.115	0.125	0.115	0.077	0.062
5		0.115	0.089	0.092	0.069	0.057
6		0.058	0.089	0.074	0.062	0.053
7			0.089	0.066	0.059	0.049
8			0.045	0.066	0.059	0.045
9				0.065	0.059	0.045
10				0.065	0.059	0.045
11				0.033	0.059	0.045
12					0.059	0.045
13					0.059	0.045
14					0.059	0.045
15					0.059	0.045
16					0.030	0.045
17						0.045
18						0.045
19						0.045
20						0.045
21						0.017

- The 15-year and 20-year classes use 150-percent declining balance depreciation with a switch-over to a straight-line rate.
- The 27.5-year and 31.5-year real estate classes both use a straight-line method.

Also built into the table is a **half-year convention**—a half year of depreciation is taken in the year of purchase regardless of when the asset was purchased. Salvage value under ACRS is ignored in computing the annual cost recovery.

The airplane purchase that Brown, Incorporated is considering can be used to illustrate the computation of cost recovery and its effect on income taxes. The airplane will be purchased in 19X4 for $40,000. It is expected to have a useful life of twelve years with $5,000 salvage value. The airplane is eligible for a 5-year cost recovery even though the useful life is more than twice that long. The following computations are used for annual cost recovery and the net of tax cash flows. Notice that salvage value is excluded from the computations.

Year	Computation	Recovery Amount	Tax Rate	Net of Tax Cash Flow
1	20.0% × $40,000	$ 8,000	40%	$3,200
2	32.0% × $40,000	$12,800	40%	$5,120
3	19.2% × $40,000	$ 7,680	40%	$3,072
4	11.5% × $40,000	$ 4,600	40%	$1,840
5	11.5% × $40,000	$ 4,600	40%	$1,840
6	5.8% × $40,000	$ 2,320	40%	$ 928

By allowing additional depreciation expense on the tax return, income taxes payable are reduced by the income tax rate times the additional depreciation expense. The cash flow associated with depreciation is computed as follows:

(Depreciation) × (Tax rate) = Net of tax cash inflow

The following financial statements with and without the aircraft depreciation in the first year of operations illustrate the net-of-tax cash inflow (savings) associated with the depreciation.

Brown, Inc.
Projected Income Statement—First Year

	Without Aircraft Depreciation	With Aircraft Depreciation
Revenue	$93,000	$93,000
Less: Expenses		
Wages	20,000	20,000
Travel	46,000	46,000
Depreciation	0	8,000
Net taxable income	$27,000	$19,000
Taxes payable (40%)	10,800	7,600
Net income	$16,200	$11,400

Note that the reduction in taxes payable of $3,200 ($10,800 − $7,600) is equal to the first year depreciation multiplied by the tax rate ($8,000 × 40% = $3,200).

The Impact of Accelerated Cost Recovery on Capital Investment

The Economic Recovery Tax Act of 1981 and subsequent revisions in the Tax Code allow a taxpayer to elect not to use the accelerated write-off method described previously. For one or more classes of property placed in service during the year, the straight-line depreciation method may be used. However, the half-year convention must still be used in the year of purchase, and salvage value is ignored. Figure 24.2 contains the percentages to be used when electing the straight-line method.

When is it rational for a taxpayer to select the straight-line method over the same period of recovery? The proposed airplane purchase by Brown, Incorporated illustrates the effect of the new cost recovery method on a capital investment. The net of tax cash inflows associated with cost recovery are shown in figure 24.3 using (a) 5-year cost recovery and the accelerated method and (b) 5-year cost recovery and the straight-line method. The present value of the tax savings obtained by using the accelerated method is $891 ($11,809 − $10,918). In present value dollars, Brown Incorporated is $891 better off by using the faster cost recovery.

As long as the taxpayer has taxable income that depreciation can be offset against, the taxpayer will be better off to use the accelerated cost recovery method. This includes current-year income as well as prior-years' income that a net operating loss could be carried back and offset against to receive an immediate income tax refund.[2] Money received now or in the immediate future is worth more than money received over an extended period of time because of the time value of money. As a general rule, the accelerated cost recovery method over the shortest possible time period should be selected as long as the company is operating at a profit.

This example also shows why ACRS stimulates capital investment. The ACRS allows greater depreciation in the early years of the asset that results in less income taxes. By paying less income tax during the early years of the project, the company has more money for operations or other investments. Thus projects that are only marginally profitable when depreciated over their useful life became very profitable when depreciated over the lives specified by ACRS.

FIGURE 24.2

Straight-Line Depreciation for Property other than Real Estate

ACRS Class	First Recovery Year	Other Recovery Years — Years	Other Recovery Years — %	Last Recovery Year — Years	Last Recovery Year — %	Percentage Total
3-year	0.167	2–3	0.333	4	0.167	1.000
5-year	0.100	2–5	0.200	6	0.100	1.000
7-year	0.071	2–7	0.143	8	0.071	1.000
10-year	0.050	2–10	0.100	11	0.050	1.000
15-year	0.033	2–15	0.067	16	0.029	1.000
20-year	0.025	2–20	0.050	21	0.025	1.000

---

2. Income tax laws require a net operating loss to be carried back against income of the previous three years. If income tax has been paid during those years, an immediate refund may be received. When the loss is greater than the income for the previous three years, the remaining loss is carried forward to be offset against income of subsequent years.

FIGURE 24.3

Effect of Accelerated Cost Recovery on Capital Investment

Accelerated, 5-Year Cost Recovery

Cash flows

Type	Timing	Amount
Reduction in taxes payable	Year 1	$3,200
	Year 2	5,120
	Year 3	3,072
	Year 4	1,840
	Year 5	1,840
	Year 6	928

Desired rate of return   12%

Net of tax cash inflows and present value computation:

Year	Cost Recovery	Tax Rate	Net of Tax Cash Flow	Present Value Factor @ 12%	Present Value
1	$ 8,000	40%	$3,200	0.893	$ 2,858
2	12,800	40	5,120	0.797	4,081
3	7,680	40	3,072	0.712	2,187
4	4,600	40	1,840	0.636	1,170
5	4,600	40	1,840	0.567	1,043
6	2,320	40	928	0.507	470
Total					$11,809

Straight-line, 5-Year Cost Recovery

Type	Timing	Amount
Reduction in taxes payable	Year 1	$1,600
	Years 2–5	3,200
	Year 6	1,600

Desired rate of return   12%

Net of tax cash inflows and present value computation:

Year	Cost Recovery	Tax Rate	Net of Tax Cash flow	Present Value Factor @ 12%	Present Value
1	$4,000	40%	$1,600	0.893	$ 1,429
2–5	8,000	40	3,200	2.712[a]	8,678
6	4,000	40	1,600	0.507	811
Total					$10,918

[a](3.605 − 0.893 = 2.712)

Salvage Value

Salvage value is not considered in computing annual cost recovery under ACRS. Therefore, the entire cost of the asset will be written off during the recovery period, which in most cases will be much shorter than the useful life of the asset.

When the asset is sold or retired, there is a potential gain or loss based on the difference between the sale price and book value. As a general rule, the gain (loss) is taxed as ordinary income (loss).

The cash flow associated with salvage value must be computed net of tax. The following equation can be used to compute the net-of-tax cash flow for an asset sold at a gain or loss, with or without salvage value.

$$\text{Cash proceeds from sale} - \left[\left(\text{Cash proceeds from sale} - \text{Book value}\right) \times (\text{Tax rate})\right] = \text{Net of tax cash flow}$$

The center portion of the equation computes the gain or loss by subtracting the book value from the sale price. The income tax effect is computed by multiplying the gain (loss) by the tax rate. In the case of a gain, this amount is then subtracted from the cash proceeds from the sale; a loss is added to the cash proceeds for the net-of-tax cash flow.

The expected salvage value from the airplane that Brown Incorporated is considering is $5,000. Because the airplane will be fully depreciated at the end of year 5, a book value of zero is used in the computation. The after-tax cash flow expected in year 12 from the sale of the airplane is $3,000.

$$\$5,000 - [(\$5,000 - 0) \times 40\%] = \underline{\$3,000}$$

In capital budgeting proposals, the asset generally is expected to be held beyond the recovery period so that the asset will be fully depreciated at the time the salvage value is received. In this case the entire proceeds will be ordinary income, and the net-of-tax cash flow can be computed as other revenue. Be sure to note that this is applicable only to *fully depreciated* assets.

$$\text{Cash proceeds from sale of fully depreciated asset} \times (1 - \text{Tax rate}) = \text{Net of tax cash flow}$$

For Brown, Incorporated, the computation is:

$$(\$5,000) \times (1 - 0.40) = \$3,000.$$

Comprehensive Illustration

The proposed airplane acquisition by Brown, Incorporated will be used to illustrate the various capital budgeting techniques when income tax is included. The relevant facts are summarized as follows:

Proposal: Brown, Incorporated is considering the acquisition of an airplane at a cost of $40,000. It is expected to have a useful life of twelve years with $5,000 salvage value. As a result of having the airplane, revenues are expected to increase by $13,000, and annual cash outlays for operating the airplane are expected to be $6,000 more than current travel costs. Management has elected to use the ACRS over five years, has identified a 12-percent minimum desired rate of return, and is subject to a 40% marginal tax rate.

Compute the *(a)* net present value, *(b)* internal rate of return, *(c)* payback period, and *(d)* accounting rate of return.

The procedures followed in analyzing the investment proposal are the same as those discussed in chapter 23. The cash flows associated with the investment, annual operations, and salvage value are charted and applied to one or more of the capital budgeting techniques. The only difference is that each of the cash flows (initial investment, operations, and salvage value) must be taken net of any related income tax. The computations for each of these items have been illustrated previously. The resulting cash flows are shown in figure 24.4.

FIGURE 24.4

Brown, Inc.—Expected Cash Flows for Airplane Acquisition

Type	Timing	Amount
Initial investment	Now	$40,000
Tax savings from cost recovery	Year 1	3,200
	Year 2	5,120
	Year 3	3,072
	Years 4–5	1,840 per year
	Year 6	928
Annual inflow from other operations	Years 1–12	$ 4,200 per year
Salvage value	Year 12	3,000

Net Present Value The net present value is computed by subtracting the initial investment from the present value of expected cash flows at the minimum desired rate of return. If the net present value is positive, the investment is desirable at the cut-off rate.

Present value of cash flows at a 12-percent cut-off rate is found as follows:

Cost Recovery

Year		
1	($3,200 × 0.893)	$2,858
2	($5,120 × 0.797)	4,081
3	($3,072 × 0.712)	2,187
4–5	($1,840 × 1.203)	2,213
6	($ 928 × 0.507)	470
		$11,809

Other Annual Inflows from Operations

1–12	($4,200 × 6.194)	26,015

Salvage Value

12	($3,000 × 0.257)	771
Total		38,595
Initial investment		40,000
Net present value		($1,405)

The negative net present value of $1,405 means that the investment is not desirable at a 12-percent cut-off rate.

Internal Rate of Return The internal rate of return is the interest rate that equates the present value of future cash flows with the initial investment. The investment is desirable when the interest rate exceeds a minimum rate specified by management.

Because the net present value is negative with a 12-percent rate, a slightly lower rate, say 10 percent, is used and the net present value is computed again.

Present value of cash flows at 10 percent is found as follows:

Cost Recovery

Year		
1	($3,200 × 0.909)	$2,909
2	($5,120 × 0.826)	4,229
3	($3,072 × 0.751)	2,307
4–5	($1,840 × 1.304)	2,399
6	($ 928 × 0.565)	524
		$12,368

CHAPTER 24: CAPITAL BUDGETING: PART II

Other Annual Inflows from Operations

1–12	($4,200 × 6.814)	28,619

Salvage Value

12	($3,000 × 0.317)	951
Total		$41,938
Initial investment		40,000
Net present value		$ 1,938

The net present values for 12 percent and 10 percent can be used to interpolate the internal rate of return.

Rate	Net Present Value
10%	$1,938
12%	1,405
Total	$3,343
Internal rate of return	11.2%

10% + [$1,938 ÷ $3,343) × 2%]

Payback Period Payback period is the length of time required to accumulate cash flows equal to the initial investment. The proposal is desirable if the period of time is less than a maximum time specified by management. The payback period for Brown, Incorporated is 5.77 years.

Year	Annual Cash Flows	Cumulative Cash Flows	Payback Years
1	$7,400	$ 7,400	1.00
2	$9,320	$16,720	1.00
3	$7,272	$23,992	1.00
4	$6,040	$30,032	1.00
5	$6,040	$36,072	1.00
6	$5,128	$40,000	0.77[a]
Total			5.77 Years

[a]($3,928 ÷ $5,128 × 1.0)

Accounting Rate of Return The accounting rate of return is computed by dividing the average cash flows net of tax minus annual depreciation by the initial investment.

$$\frac{\text{Annual cash flow} - \text{Depreciation}}{\text{Initial investment}} = \text{Accounting rate of return}$$

The investment is desirable if the rate of return exceeds the minimum rate specified by management.

The average annual cash flows are computed by adding the cash flows net of tax ($69,400) and dividing by the life of the asset (twelve years.) The average annual cash flow for Brown, Incorporated is $5,783 ($69,400 ÷ 12 years). For financial reporting purposes, Brown, Incorporated has elected to use straight-line depreciation with a useful life of twelve years and zero salvage value. Annual depreciation is $3,333 ($40,000 ÷ 12 years). The accounting rate of return is 6.1 percent.

$$\frac{\$5,783 - \$3,333}{\$40,000} = 6.1\%$$

In summary, income tax is an important item in capital budgeting decisions. Almost every item must be adjusted for the effect it has on income taxes paid to the government. The capital budgeting techniques do not change, only the computation of the cash flows used in the analysis. Depreciation, with the option to use ACRS, has a substantial effect on cash flows when income taxes are considered.

COST OF CAPITAL

In applying the capital budgeting techniques, we have given a cut-off rate. The cost of capital is generally used as a basis for developing the minimum desired rate of return. The computation of cost of capital is a controversial issue with divergent points of view, and a detailed study of the cost of capital is reserved for a finance course. Our objective here is to identify what the cost of capital is, to explain how it relates to cost accounting and capital budgeting, and to review some of the basic concepts involved in its computation.

Cost of Capital Defined

The **cost of capital** is the rate of return that must be earned on invested capital in order to leave the market price of the firm's common stock unchanged. It identifies the breakeven point for the organization. If the firm earns more than (less than) this rate, the value of the firm and the market price of the common stock will increase (decrease). Therefore, it is an appropriate rate to use as the minimum desired rate of return for investment decisions.

Capital (financial) **components** include liabilities, preferred stock, and common stock. All assets, including the acquisition of property, plant, and equipment, must be financed by one or more of these capital components.

Each capital component has a cost that is called the **component cost.** For example, the cost of a bond is the after-tax cost of interest. For preferred stock it is the annual dividend that is expected to be paid. The cost of common stock is based on expected dividends plus appreciation in the value of the stock. All of these component costs must be combined in a meaningful way into an average cost of capital that can be used in investment decisions. A weighted average is commonly used.

To illustrate the computation of the weighted average, assume that Capital Corporation is begun by selling 100 shares of common stock at $40 per share ($4,000). In pricing the common stock, management evaluated the expected business activity and the risk associated with it. It also looked at the alternative uses of the money. After careful consideration, a 15-percent rate of return was considered to be a fair return on the firm's money. Bonds are also issued for $2,000. The bonds carry a 10-percent interest rate and are sold at their face value. The balance sheet of the newly organized Capital Corporation is as follows:

Capital Corporation
Balance Sheet

Assets		Liabilities & Owners' Equity	
Cash	$6,000	Bonds payable	$2,000
		Common stock	$4,000
		Total	$6,000

The critical question is, How much must Capital Corporation earn during its first year of operations to leave the price of its common stock at $40 per share? Assuming that the corporate tax rate is 40-percent and that the 15-percent estimate of the return required by the common stockholders is accurate and remains constant during the year, the weighted average cost of capital can be computed. The after-tax cost of each capital component is weighted by the proportion of the total capital that it provides.

Capital Component	Proportion of Total Capital	×	Component Cost	=	Weighted Average Cost of Capital
Bonds	1/3	×	0.06[a]	=	0.02
Common stock	2/3	×	0.15	=	0.10
Total					0.12

[a]The after-tax cost is obtained by multiplying the interest rate by one minus the tax rate [0.10 × (1 − 0.40)].

Capital Corporation must earn 12-percent after tax on its investments or 20-percent [12% ÷ (1 − 40%)] before interest and taxes in order to satisfy the expectations of the common stockholders. This can be illustrated by a simplified version of the income statement.

Capital Corporation
Income Statement
Year 1

Earnings before interest and taxes (20% × $6,000)	$1,200
Interest (10% × $2,000)	200
Net income before taxes	$1,000
Income taxes (40% × $1,000)	400
Net income	$ 600
Return required by common stockholders	15%
Total market value ($600 ÷ 15%)	$4,000
Market price per share ($4,000 ÷ 100 shares)	$ 40

By earning $1,200 (20% × $6,000) before interest and taxes, Capital Corporation is able to pay the interest on the bonds and the taxes to the government and still have $600 for the common stockholders. This is equal to 15-percent of its investment, which satisfies the stockholders' expected return. Thus, the value of their common stock will remain at $40 per share.

Had the earnings been more, the return would have exceeded the stockholders' expectations. If the higher rate of return was expected to continue, potential investors would be attracted and the price of the stock would be bid up. On the other hand, if net income had been lower, say $400, common shareholders would have been disappointed. Because they could invest their money in other corporations of less risk and earn 10-percent, or in corporations of equal risk and earn 15-percent, they would want to sell their stock in Capital Corporation, and the price of the stock would be driven down. Only by earning a rate of return that was equal to the weighted average cost of capital would the value of the firm remain the same.

Marginal Cost of Capital (MCC)

The **marginal cost of capital** (MCC) is the rate of return that must be earned on *additional* capital in order to leave the market value of the common stock unchanged. Many capital budgeting projects are financed out of capital that is new to the organization. The marginal cost of capital should be used as a cut-off rate in evaluating these proposals.

To illustrate, assume that Capital Corporation invested the $6,000 at the beginning of year 1 in a long-term project that yields 12-percent after tax. Also assume that the net income of $600 was paid to the common shareholders in the form of a dividend at the end of year 1. At the beginning of year 2, Capital Corporation is considering another investment proposal that will cost $2,000. Management has decided to raise the needed capital by issuing additional bonds carrying a 10-percent interest charge. However, this additional debt financing will increase the debt to equity ratio to 50:50. The threat of bankruptcy and the costs associated with it increases substantially as the amount of debt increases to 50-percent or more of total capital. As a result of the increased risk, common shareholders will require a 20-percent rate of return on their investment in Capital Corporation. What is the new weighted average cost of capital? What is the marginal cost of capital associated with the new debt financing? How much must Capital Corporation earn on the new investment to leave the price of the common stock unchanged?

The weighted average cost of capital is changed by two factors. First, a higher proportion of total capital is now being financed by debt with a lower after-tax cost of capital. Second, the component cost for common stock has increased because of higher risk associated with the debt financing. The new weighted average cost of capital is computed as follows:

Capital Component	Proportion of Total Capital	×	Component Cost	=	Weighted Average Cost of Capital
Bonds	1/2	×	0.06	=	0.03
Common stock	1/2	×	0.20	=	0.10
Total					0.13

Capital Corporation must now earn 13-percent after taxes or 21.67-percent [13% ÷ (1 − 40%)] before interest and taxes for the price of common stock to remain the same. Notice on the partial income statement and the analysis that follow that the price of the common stock stays at $40 per share as long as the new expectations are met.

Capital Corporation
Income Statement
Year 2

Earnings before interest and taxes (21.67% × $8,000)	$1,734
Interest (10% × $4,000)	400
Net income before taxes	$1,334
Income taxes (40% × $1,334)	534
Net income	$ 800
Return required by common stockholders	20%
Total market value ($800 ÷ 20%)	$4,000
Market price per share ($4,000 ÷ 100 shares)	$ 40

The key concept from this analysis is that the marginal cost of the new capital ($2,000 of new debt) may not be equal to the cost of that capital component (10-percent before tax or 6-percent after tax). This can be seen by comparing the income statements for years 1 and 2. For the value of the firm to remain the same, earnings before interest and taxes must increase $534 ($1,734 − $1,200). However, the $6,000 of original capital was invested on a long-term basis to yield only $1,200 before interest and taxes. The $534 of additional earnings must come entirely from the new investment. Thus the before-interest-and-income-tax rate of return must be 26.7-percent ($534 ÷ $2,000), and the after-tax rate of return must be 16-percent [26.7% × (1 − 40%)].

A standard equation can be used to compute the marginal cost of capital. To apply the equation, first compute the weighted average cost of capital under the old and new capital structures, and then compute the increase (decrease) in the weighted average cost of capital. The equation is:

$$MCC = \text{New weighted average cost of capital} \pm \left[\text{Increase (decrease) in weighted average cost of capital} \times \left(\frac{\text{Capital before the increase}}{\text{Increase in capital}} \right) \right]$$

Applying the equation to Capital Corporation, we have the following:

$$\text{MCC} = 13\% + 1\% \left[\left(\frac{\$6,000}{\$2,000} \right) \right] = \underline{\underline{16\%}}$$

A 16-percent minimum desired rate of return should be used in evaluating Capital Corporation's new investment proposal. If the investment provides anything less than this amount, the expectations of the common shareholders will not be met and the price of the common stock will be driven down. Of course, a return greater than 16-percent will exceed their expectation and the value of the firm will increase.

In summary, a project financed by new debt should not be evaluated with the interest cost of the debt; the interest rate charged is only the explicit cost of the debt. The total cost of the new debt is equal to the explicit cost of the debt plus the effect that the use of additional debt financing has on the cost and availability of existing debt and equity capital. *The marginal cost of capital is the rate that must be earned on additional capital to leave the value of the firm unchanged, and it is the rate that should be used as the cut-off rate for capital investment decisions.*

Up to this point in the analysis, we have assumed that the after-tax cost of capital for each capital component is known. We will now consider how each of these is computed.

Cost of Debt

A debt that has no interest charge, such as accounts payable, has no explicit cost associated with it. When we talk about the cost of debt, we are generally talking about notes payable, mortgages, or bonds, all of which bear interest.

Without any income taxes, the cost of debt would be equal to the *effective interest rate* paid on the debt. The effective interest rate, also called the yield to maturity, is the interest rate that equates the present value of future interest and principal payments to the amount of money received from investors. It should not be confused with the face rate or coupon rate of the bond, which identifies the amount of interest to be paid. If the effective interest rate is more than (less than) expected by potential investors, the amount they will be willing to pay for the bond will be more than (less than) the face value of the bond.

Because interest expense is deductible when computing taxable income, companies subject to income taxes must adjust the effective interest rate for the income tax savings that the interest provides. The after-tax cost of debt can be computed as follows:

After-tax cost of debt = Effective interest rate × (1 − Tax rate)

To illustrate the after-tax cost of debt, assume that Super Sales Incorporated issues $5,000 of 11-percent face-value bonds to yield 10-percent. They are ten-year bonds that pay interest of $275 semiannually. The amount of cash received on issuance is $5,312 (the present value of twenty annuity payments of $275 and $5,000 in twenty periods at 5-percent). With an income tax rate of 45-percent, the after-tax cost of the debt is:

After-tax cost of debt = 10% (1 − 45%) = <u>5.5%</u>.

Notice that the yield rate, not the face interest rate, is used to compute the cost of debt. The yield rate is an accurate before-tax cost of debt because it is based on the amount that must be paid for principal and interest over the life of the bond, relative to the sale price of the bond.

Cost of Preferred Stock

The cost of preferred stock is based on the dividend that must be paid annually. Preferred stock may have a variety of dividend policies, including noncumulative or participating, but the most common dividend policy is a cumulative dividend specified as a percentage of the stock's par value. A 9-percent cumulative preferred stock with a $100 par value will pay an annual dividend of $9.

Income taxes are not relevant when computing the cost of preferred stock because preferred dividends are not deductible. Also, there is no maturity date for preferred stock;[3] it is assumed that the annual dividend will be paid forever. The present value of an annuity that lasts forever is computed as follows:

$$\text{Present value of a perpetual annuity} = \frac{\text{Annuity amount}}{\text{Interest rate}}$$

The present value of the perpetual dividend is the amount an investor will be willing to pay for the preferred stock. The price of the stock is determined in the market as an average of the yield rates acceptable to potential investors. The actual price may be higher or lower than the par value, depending on the market rate as compared to the dividend rate. Potential investors will use a market rate that reflects their attitude toward the risk of the investment as well as the opportunity cost of their money. The price they pay is known, but the interest rate they use is unknown, which is the item of information that is needed to compute the weighted average cost of capital. The preceding equation can be manipulated as follows to compute the interest rate, given the price of the preferred stock and the annual dividend:

$$\frac{\text{Interest rate}}{\text{(cost of preferred stock)}} = \frac{\text{Annuity (dividend) amount}}{\text{Purchase price of the stock}}$$

EXAMPLE

Problem

What is the component cost of capital for a $100 par-value, 9-percent cumulative preferred stock that is sold for $90?

Solution

$$\frac{\text{Interest rate}}{\text{(cost of preferred stock)}} = \frac{\$9}{\$90} = \underline{10\%}$$

The component cost of capital in this example is 10-percent. This is the yield rate used by investors to compute the purchase price of the stock. It is also the component cost that should be used in computing the weighted average cost of capital.

Cost of Common Stock and Retained Earnings

The capital provided by common shareholders is contained in several accounts, including common stock, paid-in capital in excess of par, and retained earnings. The amounts in each of these accounts must be combined to compute the proportion of total capital provided by common shareholders.

---

3. Convertible preferred stock provides an added complexity that will not be considered here.

CHAPTER 24: CAPITAL BUDGETING: PART II

Common shareholders have the right to receive dividends declared by the board of directors and to share in the growth of the firm from earnings retained and reinvested in the business. They generally share in growth by *(a)* selling their stock at an appreciated value at some time in the future or by *(b)* receiving larger dividends with the passage of time.

The procedures for computing the cost of common stock and retained earnings can be viewed as extensions of those used in computing the cost of preferred stock. In addition to the expected dividend and price of the stock, a growth factor must be added to the equation. The following equation is generally used to compute the cost of common stock and retained earnings.

$$\text{Cost of common stock[4] and retained earnings} = \frac{D}{MPPS} + G$$

Where: D = Cash dividend at the end of the first year
$MPPS$ = Current market price per share
G = Constant growth rate

The market price per share is the only factor in the preceding equation that is known with any degree of certainty. The dividend expected to be paid at the end of the year can be estimated by management with some degree of accuracy, but it is clearly not as precise as the interest rate on bonds or the dividends on preferred stock. The expected growth rate is the most difficult to predict. Techniques for estimating the expected growth rate are based on dividend policy and appreciation in the market value of the stock.

Growth in the annual dividend can be used for companies that have a stable dividend history and that pay out most of their earnings as dividends.

EXAMPLE

Company X has common stock outstanding that has a current market price of $20 per share. Its dividend record over the past four years has been as follows:

19X3	$2.00
19X4	2.20
19X5	2.42
19X6	2.66

Analysis of the dividend record shows a compound annual rate of increase of 10-percent. However, changes in the economic environment cause management to question its ability to maintain this growth rate. An 8-percent rate seems more likely, and the dividend for 19X7 is projected to be $2.87. Cost of common stock and retained earnings is computed at 22.35 percent.

$$\text{Cost} = \frac{\$2.87}{\$20.00} + 8\% = \underline{22.35\%}$$

Some companies either do not pay dividends or have an erratic dividend history. For these companies, it is more useful to look at the appreciation in the value of their common stock.

---

4. If it is a new issue of common stock, the full market price is generally not received. A portion of the sale price is usually paid as an underwriter's fee. For such issues, the net amount received per share should be substituted in the equation for the market price per share.

EXAMPLE

Company Y has paid $3 per share annually on its common stock outstanding and has reinvested all additional earnings within the business. As a result, the company has grown and the market price has increased. Year-end market prices and the annual growth percentages are as follows:

	Year-end Market Price	Annual Growth Percentage
19X1	$33.25	
19X2	36.50	9.8%[a]
19X3	39.12	7.2
19X4	42.75	9.3

[a] [($36.50 − $33.25) ÷ $33.25]

An average of the annual growth percentages indicate that company Y will probably grow at 8.8 percent [(9.8% + 7.2% + 9.3%) ÷ 3] during the year. Its cost of common stock and retained earnings is computed to be 15.8%.

$$\text{Cost} = \frac{\$3.00}{\$42.75} + 8.8\% = \underline{15.8\%}$$

Comprehensive Illustration

The capital structure of Blaylock, Incorporated will be used to illustrate the computation of each component cost and the weighted average cost of capital. Figure 24.5 summarizes the capital components of Blaylock, Incorporated. To keep the example as simple as possible, it is assumed that the book values and market values of the debt and stock are equal. Therefore, the weighting would not change if market values rather than book values were used. The notes to the financial statement contain important information for the computations that follow.

FIGURE 24.5

Blaylock, Inc.—Capital Structure

Liabilities

Current liabilities		$ 26,300	12.5%
Bonds payable	$50,000		
Less: Discount	1,550	48,450	23.0%

Owners' Equity

Preferred stock (400 shares of 8%, $100 par value)	$38,400		18.3%
Common stock ($1 par)	25,000	}	46.2%
Retained earnings	71,850		
Total		135,250	
Total liabilities and owners' equity		$210,000	100.0%

Notes to the financial statement:
1. The bonds that carry a 13.5% interest rate and mature in 15 years were sold to yield 14%.
2. Preferred stock is 8% cumulative on a par value of $100. It was sold for $96 per share.
3. Annual dividend on common stock is expected to be $2.50 per share, based on an annual growth rate of 8%. The current market price per share is $15.
4. Blaylock Incorporated is subject to a 40% income tax rate.

The component cost of each capital component must first be computed as follows:

Current liabilities: The current liabilities are non–interest bearing, so their component cost is zero.[5]

Bonds payable: The yield rate is used, not the bond interest rate.

$$\text{Component cost} = 14\% \times (1 - 40\%) = \underline{8.4\%}$$

Preferred stock: The yield rate is computed as follows:

$$\text{Component cost} = \frac{\$8}{\$96} = \underline{8.33\%}$$

Common stock and retained earnings:

$$\text{Component cost} = \frac{\$2.50}{\$15.00} + 8\% = \underline{24.67\%}$$

Each component cost is combined to compute the weighted average cost of capital.

Capital Component	Proportion of Total Capital	×	Component Cost	=	Weighted Average Cost of Capital
Current liabilities	12.5%	×	0.00%	=	0.00
Bonds payable	23.0	×	8.40	=	1.93
Preferred stock	18.3	×	8.33	=	1.52
Common stock	46.2	×	24.67	=	11.40
					14.85%

The weighted average cost of capital for Blaylock, Incorporated is 14.85 percent. Blaylock's operations and investments must earn 14.85 percent after tax for the common stock to continue to sell for $15 per share. A 14.85-percent cut-off rate is appropriate for capital budgeting decisions using money that is reinvested in the company. Projects that earn exactly 14.85 percent will leave the value of the firm unchanged. Those that earn more than 14.85 percent will enhance the value of the firm and will have a positive effect on the market price of its common stock.

SENSITIVITY ANALYSIS IN CAPITAL BUDGETING

Sensitivity analysis can be used to measure the effect of a change in one or more of the input values in a capital budgeting decision. Sensitivity analysis cannot eliminate estimation errors or the risks associated with the selection of any given project. It provides a means for evaluating the effect of errors on the outcome to show where the greatest risks lie. Based on this information, management can elect to investigate certain estimates more

---

5. There is no common agreement on how to handle current liabilities. Even though there is no explicit cost associated with accounts payable, there may be an implicit cost due to loss of cash discounts, higher prices for goods purchased on account by slow paying customers, and similar items. Some people recommend estimating these costs and associating them with current liabilities. Other people suggest that cost of capital should be based only on long-term financing, so they exclude any current liabilities in the computation. To keep our example both simple and complete, we will include current liabilities but will assume that their component cost is zero.

thoroughly before making a final decision, accept the proposal as it is, or reject the proposal without further analysis. A decision to investigate certain areas more intensively may lead to improved estimates and thereby reduce the risk of making a wrong choice.

This discussion of sensitivity analysis will use the net present value technique. The technique is easy to use and provides a good measure of investment profitability. A similar analysis could be performed with other investment analysis techniques.

The basic inputs to a capital budgeting decision using net present value are (a) minimum desired rate of return, (b) initial investment, (c) net cash flows from operations, and (d) salvage value. Sensitivity analysis can be used to measure the effect on net present value when one or more of these input values are changed. Small changes in input values that have a large impact on net present value are of most interest. These are the areas in which further analysis will be most useful.

Selecting a Minimum Desired Rate of Return

Cost of capital has been recommended as the most appropriate cut-off rate for capital investment decisions because it is the rate of return that must be earned on invested capital in order to leave the market price of the firm's common stock unchanged. The value of the firm and the market value of the common stock will increase if the firm is able to earn more than this rate. Because this rate is so important in sensitivity analysis, we should evaluate the basis on which it is developed and compute the effect of changes in those basic assumptions. Also, there may be some cases in which the discount rate should be different than the cost of capital because of the risk associated with the investment being analyzed. Let's consider several possibilities.

Errors in Estimating the Component Cost of Capital Stock

Recall from the discussion on cost of capital the importance of the component cost of each capital component in computing the weighted average cost of capital. The information used in computing the component cost of long-term debt and preferred stock is fairly accurate, but subjective estimates are often required with common stock. The expected dividend and growth rate are quite tentative. Sensitivity analysis can be used to measure the effect of an error in these estimates on the cut-off rate.

To illustrate, assume that Cutt-off, Incorporated is a fairly new company without an established dividend history or stock-price pattern. Its capital structure consists of non-

FIGURE 24.6 Cutt-Off Inc.—Weighted Average Cost of Capital

Capital Component	Proportion of Total Capital	×	After-Tax Cost L	O	P	=	Weighted Average Cost of Capital L	O	P
Current debt	10%	×	0%			=	0%	0%	0%
Long-term debt	30	×	6			=	1.8	1.8	1.8
Common stock	60	×	20			=	12.0		
				24.5%				14.7	
					9%				5.4
Total	100%						13.8%	16.5%	7.2%

L—Most likely estimate
O—Optimistic estimate
P—Pessimistic estimate

interest-bearing current liabilities, bonds with a 6 percent after-tax cost, and common stock. The proportion of total capital provided by each is shown in figure 24.6. Common stock currently sells for $10 per share. In estimating the component cost of common stock, a dividend of $1.00 is most likely, although it could be as high as $1.25 or as low as $0.30 per share. Also, although a growth rate of 10 percent is thought to be most likely, it could be as high as 12 percent or as low as 6 percent. The component cost of common stock is first computed using these most likely, optimistic, and pessimistic estimates. The results are then used in computing the weighted average cost of capital. Figure 24.6 shows the computation of the weighted average cost of capital.

Most Likely (L)

$$\text{Cost} = \frac{\$1.00}{\$10.00} + 10\% = \underline{20\%}$$

Optimistic (O)

$$\text{Cost} = \frac{\$1.25}{\$10.00} + 12\% = \underline{24.5\%}$$

Pessimistic (P)

$$\text{Cost} = \frac{\$.30}{\$10.00} + 6\% = \underline{9\%}$$

The weighted average cost of capital for Cutt-off, Incorporated may be as high as 16.5 percent or as low as 7.2 percent, but the most likely estimate is 13.8 percent. This is a rather wide range; perhaps some additional analysis should be required.

Rate Adjustment for Nonproductive Projects

By using the weighted average or marginal cost of capital as the cut-off rate in capital budgeting decisions, we are assuming that all capital investment projects have a productive rate of return. Projects for pollution control, OSHA, or sanitation may be required by government regulation or by a sense of moral obligation to employees or the community, but they do not generally provide a direct cash flow. Therefore, the rate of return on productive projects must be set higher than the cost of capital for the average return on all projects to equal or exceed the breakeven point.

To illustrate, assume that Cutt-off, Incorporated has determined that its after-tax cost of capital is 14 percent. If the balance between productive and nonproductive projects is 75:25, the productive projects must earn 18.67 percent after tax for the average rate of return to be 14 percent. This can be illustrated as follows:

Type	Proportion	Amount Invested	Rate of Return	After-Tax Return
Productive	75%	$ 75,000	18.67%	$14,000
Nonproductive	25	25,000	0.00	0
Total	100%	$100,000		$14,000

$$\text{Average return} = \frac{\$14,000}{\$100,000} = \underline{14\%}$$

The rate of return required on productive projects can be computed by dividing the desired average return by the percentage of productive projects (14% ÷ 75% = 18.67%).

Variable Rate Among Projects

The weighted average cost of capital represents the average risk associated with investments in a company's capital securities. Investors in each security assess both the risk and opportunity cost associated with the investment when determining the price they are willing to pay. The weighted average cost of capital is computed from the price of the various securities.

Each individual capital investment project has some risk associated with the amount and time of cash flows. If the project's risk is higher than the firm's average risk and the project is adopted, the firm's average risk and the cost of capital will increase. To adjust for this, **a higher cut-off rate may be selected for higher risk projects.** Likewise, **a lower cut-off rate can be selected for projects that are less risky than the firm's average.**

Cutt-off, Incorporated uses its weighted average cost of capital of 14 percent on projects with an average amount of risk. The rate may be adjusted upward (or downward) in proportion to the increased (decreased) risk associated with the project. The following rates have been selected for the current proposals.

Proposal	Amount	Risk Rating	Cut-off Rate
ZOL-1	$50,000	Average	14%
ZOL-2	25,000	Risky	16%
BL-10	25,000	Very risky	20%

Variable Rate per Year for an Individual Project

Cash flows in the immediate future can be predicted with more accuracy and are less risky than cash flows in the distant future. One benefit of the net present value method is that a variable rate can be used for different cash flows each year to reflect the difference in risk associated with each.

To illustrate, assume that a service bureau is considering the acquisition of a computer that costs $52,000. Contracts for work during the first five years will provide $12,000 annual cash flows net of tax. Cash flows in the following five years are expected to be $6,000 annually, but they are heavily dependent on technological advances. Salvage value is expected to be $5,000, but only if there are no notable changes in technology. The firm's 14 percent cost of capital is used to discount the cash flows for the first five years, but an 18 percent discount rate is thought to more accurately assess the risk associated with cash flows, including salvage value, during the last five years. The net present value is computed as follows:

Present Value of Cash Flows

Years	Rate		
1–5	14%	($12,000 × 3.433)	$41,196
6–10	18%	($ 6,000 × 1.367)	8,202
Salvage	18%	($ 5,000 × 0.191)	955
		Total	$50,353
Investment			52,000
Net present value			($1,647)

Had the 14 percent cost of capital been used on all cash flows, the project would have had a positive net present value of $1,244 ($53,244 − $52,000). At that rate it appears to be a desirable investment. However, when the discount rate is adjusted to more accurately reflect the risk associated with the individual cash flows, it is not as desirable. The $1,647 negative net present value indicates that the proposal should not be accepted.

Predicting and Evaluating Cash Flows

Of the cash flows associated with capital budgeting, only the initial investment can be known with any degree of accuracy. Even that may not be fixed when it involves the construction or development of an asset with a risk of budget overruns that the company must absorb. Cash inflows from operations are among the most difficult to predict, yet they are the most important in determining the desirability of the project. Salvage value is generally not too critical because it is a one-time receipt and because it is received so far in the future that its present value is generally not significant.

Expected Value Expected value is a technique for estimating the expected cash flow when there is a range of possible cash flows and probabilities associated with various points within that range. The probabilities are multiplied by the dollar amounts and totaled to compute the expected value.

To illustrate, the purchase of a new kidney machine is being considered by Cache Valley Hospital. The annual range of possible cash flows varies from a high of $46,000 to a low of $13,000. Estimated probabilities for those points and various points in between are as follows. The expected value is $27,800.

Possible Annual Cash Flows	×	Probability	=	Expected Value
$13,000	×	20%	=	$ 2,600
26,000	×	50	=	13,000
38,000	×	20	=	7,600
46,000	×	10	=	4,600
Total		100%	=	$27,800

The actual cash flows will vary from year to year based on machine usage. However, the expected value is the best estimate of the annual cash flows. If the range and probabilities are accurate and if the machine is operated for several years, the average cash flow over time will be $27,800. Expected value is useful in reducing the range of possible values to an average value that can be used with one of the capital budgeting techniques.

Multiple Computations of Net Present Value Net present value can be computed several times using different assumptions about possible cash flows to measure the effect on the outcome on the decision. The results may be charted on a graph to show how the net present value or profitability index changes with the different cash flows.

Cache Valley Hospital frequently has overcrowding in the emergency room because of a bottleneck around the X-ray machine. Patients are frequently sent to the Children's Hospital for X rays and returned to Cache Valley Hospital for treatment. A new X-ray machine will cost $200,000 installed and will have a useful life of fifteen years with a zero salvage value. A 10-percent cut-off rate is used for investment decisions. The new X-ray machine will generate $60 of revenue per hour when it is being used. Is it a desirable investment if it is used for 600 hours per year? Will it be profitable at only 500 or 400 hours per year?

The net present value and profitability index is computed for each level of output. Figure 24.7 summarizes the results.

The indifference point for Cache Valley Hospital lies between 400 and 500 hours of usage per year. If management believes that the usage will exceed this amount, the investment should be pursued. Management might commission a study to log the number of patients that are sent to Children's Hospital and the type of X ray needed. These results could be used to estimate more precisely how much usage the new machine will have and would put management in a better position to make an informed decision.

FIGURE 24.7

X-ray Machine of Cache Valley Hospital

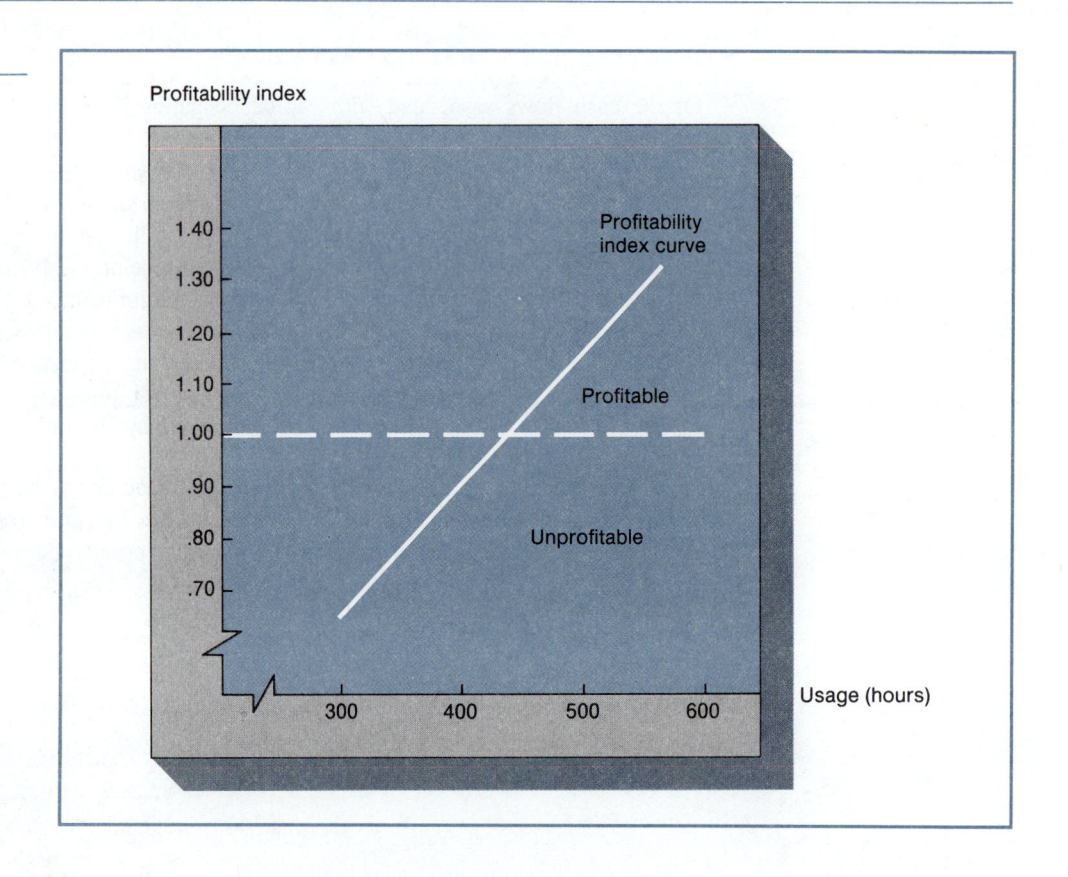

Figure: Profitability index curve plotted against Usage (hours). Horizontal dashed line at 1.00 separates "Profitable" (above) from "Unprofitable" (below). The profitability index curve rises from about 0.70 at 300 hours to about 1.35 at 600 hours, crossing 1.00 near 450 hours.

Present Value of Cash Flows

	600 hours	500 hours	400 hours
Revenue:			
[($60 × 600) × 7.606]	$273,816		
[($60 × 500) × 7.606]		$228,180	
[($60 × 400) × 7.606]			$182,544
Initial investment	$200,000	$200,000	$200,000
Net present value	$ 73,816	$ 28,180	($ 17,456)
Profitability index	1.37	1.14	0.91

SUMMARY

Capital budgeting is the process of allocating money for the purchase or construction of fixed assets. The process involves estimating the cash flows associated with each project and comparing them with the initial investment to see whether or not the project is desirable.

Income tax laws have a substantial effect on estimated cash flows for profit-oriented businesses. Cash inflows in the form of revenue cannot be fully realized because of the additional income tax that must be paid, whereas cash outflows in the form of operating expenses don't really cost the full amount because of the reduction in taxes payable. Depreciation (cost recovery) also has a related cash flow when income taxes are included in the analysis. Finally, the salvage value must be adjusted for the tax on the gain (loss). In general, almost every cash flow has a related income tax effect. All items must be computed net of the related income tax effects before one of the capital budgeting techniques can be applied.

Cost of capital is the rate of return that must be earned on invested capital for the market price of the firm's common stock to remain unchanged. A weighted average cost of capital can be computed using the after-tax cost of each capital component and the proportion of total capital that each component provides. When internally generated funds are used, the weighted average cost of capital is the minimum desired rate of return for capital investment decisions. When new funds are being raised to finance investment projects, the marginal cost of capital should be used.

Sensitivity analysis helps to measure the effect of small changes in one or more of the input values on the results of a capital investment decision. The cut-off rate may be adjusted for potential errors in computing the weighted average cost of capital. The rates also may be adjusted for unproductive projects or for projects having a risk factor that differs from the average risk associated with the firm. Different rates can even be applied each year to cash flows within the same project to reflect the different risks associated with each cash flow.

Expected value is useful in developing the estimated cash flows when the potential cash flows are within a range and probabilities are associated with points throughout the range. As an alternative, the net present value can be computed several times with different cash flow estimates to test the effects on the decision.

APPENDIX 24.1: *Investment Tax Credit (ITC)*

The 1986 tax act repealed the investment tax credit (ITC) on equipment purchases made after December 31, 1985. A short discussion of the ITC is included here because many tax experts believe that it will soon be reinstituted. This discussion is based on the procedures that were in existence before the repeal.

The investment tax credit was a credit against income taxes for depreciable personal property (excluding buildings and their structural components) purchased and placed in service during the year. Unlike depreciation, which is a deduction in computing taxable income, the investment tax credit was subtracted from income taxes that were computed on taxable income. Thus there was a dollar-for-dollar cash flow associated with the ITC. The investment credit could only be taken in the year of purchase; the immediacy of the return made the ITC very valuable.

The amount of investment tax credit was based on the recovery period of the property used in determining the deduction for cost recovery. The ITC was 10 percent of the cost of the asset. For eligible property with a recovery period of five years or over, 100 percent of the cost qualified for the 10-percent credit. For eligible 3-year property, only 60 percent of the cost of the property qualified, which was equivalent to a 6-percent credit.

EXAMPLE

Streuling Company purchased a car for $12,000 and some manufacturing equipment for $30,000 at various times during 19X3. The investment credit would have been computed as follows:

Asset	Recovery Period	Cost	Applicable Credit	Investment Credit
Car	3-years	$12,000	6%	$ 720
Manufacturing equipment	5-years	$30,000	10%	$3,000
Total				$3,720

The taxpayer had two options in accounting for the investment tax credit and cost recovery.

1. Use the normal investment credit percentages as outlined previously and reduce the basis of the property by one half of the investment credit. Cost recovery percentages were applied to the adjusted basis of the property.
2. Reduce the investment credit by 2-percent and use the full cost of the property in computing annual cost recovery.

EXAMPLE

Let's assume a delivery truck (heavy-duty) was purchased on January 1, 19X3, for $16,000. This qualified as 5-year recovery property. The ITC and ACR under the options outlined before are computed as follows:

Option 1

ITC: 10% × $16,000 = $1,600

ACR:
Cost	$16,000
Half of ITC (1/2 × $1,600)	800
Adjusted basis	$15,200

Year	Adjusted Basis	× ACR %	= ACR
1	$15,200	20.0%	$3,040
2	15,200	32.0%	4,864
3	15,200	19.2%	2,918
4	15,200	11.5%	1,748
5	15,200	11.5%	1,748
6	15,200	5.8%	882

Option 2

ITC: 8% × $16,000 = $1,280

ACR:

Year	Basis	× ACR %	= ACR
1	$16,000	20.0%	$3,200
2	16,000	32.0%	5,120
3	16,000	19.2%	3,072
4	16,000	11.5%	1,840
5	16,000	11.5%	1,840
6	16,000	5.8%	928

The option that was most profitable depended on the marginal tax rate and cost of capital for each individual taxpayer.

Any available investment tax credit was generally deducted from the cost of the investment to compute the net cash outflow required for the acquisition. An immediate deduction was justified because of the quarterly tax deposits required for the payment of estimated income taxes. The purchase of a qualifying asset with its related investment credit provided an immediate reduction in the current quarter's federal income tax deposits.

EXAMPLE

The airplane that Brown, Incorporated was considering earlier in the chapter is personal depreciable property with a cost recovery period of five years. Assuming that the full $40,000 cost qualified for the 10-percent investment credit, the cash outflow associated with the acquisition would have been $36,000, computed as follows:

Acquisition price	$40,000
Less: Investment credit ($40,000 × 10%)	4,000
Net of tax cash outflow	$36,000

SELF-STUDY PROBLEM

Josephinski, Incorporated has had a problem with stock-outs of major inventory items for several years. Preliminary analysis indicates that this occurs because poor information is provided on quantities in inventory, which is the result of slow processing of data on sales and purchases of items with high turnover. A special study was just completed showing that an average of thirty days' sales were lost (based on current sales and a 360-day year) as a result of stock-outs. Total sales during the preceding year were $720,000, with a gross profit margin of 40 percent. It is estimated that 80 percent of the lost sales could have been avoided with a computerized information system.

A proposal has been made to buy a small computer facility at a total cost of $200,000. A net reduction of three bookkeeping employees at an average salary of $10,800 per year is expected. Annual operating costs of the computer facility, other than employee wages, are expected to be $5,000 per year. The expected useful life of the facility is ten years, with an estimated salvage value of zero. The effective tax rate is 40-percent, and the Accelerated Cost Recovery System (ACRS) using a 5-year life is employed for both book and tax purposes.

Analyze the desirability of this proposal using the net present value method. Assume that money is worth 10-percent and that all cash flows are at the end of the year, except the investment, which will occur at the beginning of year 1.

Solution to the Self-Study Problem

The net-of-tax cash flows must first be computed for each item. Present value factors are then applied to these amounts.

Reduction in Bookkeeping Employees

Annual cash savings	
(3 employees at $10,800 per year)	$ 32,400
Net of tax [$32,400 × (1 − 0.40)]	19,440
Present value of savings ($19,440 × 6.1446)	$119,451

Increase in Gross Profits by Reducing Lost Sales

Annual loss in sales per year	
($720,000 ÷ 360 days = $2,000/day × 30 days)	$ 60,000
Reduction by new computer ($60,000 × 80%)	48,000
Increased gross profit ($48,000 × 40%)	19,200
Net of tax [$19,200 × (1 − 0.40)]	11,520
Present value of increase ($11,520 × 6.1446)	$ 70,786

Reduction in Income Tax for Cost Recovery (Depreciation)

Cost $200,000

Year	ACR Computation	ACR	Tax Rate	=	Cash Flow	×	Present Value Factor	=	Present Value
1	($200,000 × 20%)	$40,000	40%		$16,000		0.9091		$14,546
2	($200,000 × 32%)	64,000	40%		25,600		0.8264		21,156
3	($200,000 × 19.2%)	38,400	40%		15,360		0.7513		11,540
4	($200,000 × 11.5%)	23,000	40%		9,200		0.6830		6,284
5	($200,000 × 11.5 %)	23,000	40%		9,200		0.6209		5,712
6	($200,000 × 5.8%)	11,600	40%		4,640		0.5645		2,619
								Total	$61,857

Computer Operating Costs

Annual cash outflow	$ 5,000
Net of tax [$5,000 × (1 − .40)]	3,000
Present value of cost ($3,000 × 6.1445)	$18,434

Net Cost of Investment

Investment cost $200,000

All of the preceding items are combined as follows to compute the net present value.

Present Value of Cash Inflows

Bookkeeping	$119,451
Gross profit	70,786
Cost recovery	61,857
Operating costs	(18,434)
Total	233,660
Initial investment	200,000
Net present value	$ 33,660

SUGGESTED READINGS

Bierman, H., and Smidt, S. *The Capital Budgeting Decision,* 6th ed. New York: Macmillan, 1984.

Edwards, James W. "Effects of Federal Income Taxes on Capital Budgeting." *NAA Research Monograph #5*. New York: National Association of Accountants, 1969.

Hertz, David B. "Incorporating Risk in Capital Expenditure Analysis." In *Controller's Handbook,* edited by Sam R. Goodman and James S. Reece. Homewood, Ill.: Dow Jones-Irwin, 1978.

House, William C., Jr. "Sensitivity Analysis in Making Capital Investment Decisions." *NAA Research Monograph #3*. New York: National Association of Accountants, 1968.

Kaplan, R. *Advanced Managerial Accounting*. Englewood Cliffs, N.J.: Prentice-Hall, 1982.

Kempster, John H. "Financial Analysis to Guide Capital Expenditure Decisions." *NAA Research Report #43*. New York: National Association of Accountants, 1967.

Magee, R. *Advanced Managerial Accounting*. New York: Harper & Row, 1986.

Murdy, J. L. "Analyzing Capital Expenditure Proposals." In *Controller's Handbook,* edited by Sam R. Goodman and James S. Reece. Homewood, Ill.: Dow Jones-Irwin, 1978.

National Association of Accountants. "Financial Analysis Techniques for Equipment Replacement Decisions." *NAA Research Monograph #1*. New York: National Association of Accountants, 1965.

2. Carco Incorporated wants to use discounted cash flow techniques when analyzing its capital investment projects. Carco is aware of the uncertainty involved in estimating future cash flows. A simple method some companies employ to adjust for the uncertainty inherent in their estimates is
   a. to prepare a direct analysis of the probability of outcomes.
   b. to use accelerated depreciation.
   c. to adjust the minimum desired rate of return.
   d. to increase the estimates of the cash flows.
   e. to ignore salvage values.

3. The accountants for OEM Incorporated have proposed that sensitivity analysis be incorporated into the company's capital budgeting program. This proposal is based on the fact that the major contribution of sensitivity analysis will be the determination of
   a. a measure of the probability distribution of cash outflows.
   b. a financial measure of the new investment from alternative values for the input parameters.
   c. a financial measure of the value of the new investment.
   d. a measure of the probability of the calculated outcome.
   e. a measure of the probable maximum rate of return.

4. Depreciation is incorporated explicitly in the discounted cash flow analysis of an investment proposal because it
   a. is a cost of operations that cannot be avoided.
   b. results in an annual cash outflow.
   c. is a cash outlay for income taxes.
   d. reduces the cash outlay for income taxes.
   e. represents the initial cash outflow spread over the life of the investment.

5. The minimum return that a project must earn for a company in order to leave the value of the company unchanged is the
   a. current borrowing rate.
   b. discount rate.
   c. capitalization rate.
   d. cost of capital.

6. How are the following used in the calculation of the net present value of a proposed project? Ignore income tax considerations.

	Depreciation Expense	*Salvage Value*
a.	Include	Include
b.	Include	Exclude
c.	Exclude	Include
d.	Exclude	Exclude

7. If income tax considerations are ignored, how is depreciation expense used in the following capital budgeting techniques?

	Internal Rate of Return	*Payback*
a.	Excluded	Excluded
b.	Excluded	Included
c.	Included	Excluded
d.	Included	Included

CHAPTER 24: CAPITAL BUDGETING: PART II

DISCUSSION QUESTIONS

Q24–1. When computing the net-of-tax cash flows associated with cost recovery (depreciation), do you take the reduction in taxes payable or the increase (decrease) in net income associated with the cost recovery? Explain.

Q24–2. Why must both cash revenues and cash expenditures be adjusted for income taxes when making capital budgeting decisions?

Q24–3. What is the formula to compute the net-of-tax cash flows from taxable receipts? What is the formula to compute the net-of-tax cash flows for cost recovery? Why are the formulas different?

Q24–4. Why does one generally deduct any investment credit from the cost of the initial investment rather than include it as a cash flow at the end of year 1?

Q24–5. Why should enterprises that are operating at a profit always use ACRS over the shortest period of time?

Q24–6. How does the computation of the internal rate of return differ when income taxes are included in the analysis?

Q24–7. Explain how salvage value is adjusted for income taxes for a net cash flow.

Q24–8. Define *cost of capital*.

Q24–9. Why is cost of capital an appropriate measure for the minimum desired rate of return?

Q24–10. Differentiate between weighted average cost of capital and component cost of capital.

Q24–11. Differentiate between weighted average cost of capital and marginal cost of capital.

Q24–12. Explain how to compute the component cost of capital for a bond payable.

Q24–13. Explain how to compute the component cost of capital for preferred stock. Why is income tax ignored in this computation?

Q24–14. Explain how to compute the component cost of capital for common shareholders.

Q24–15. Describe expected value and identify where it is most effectively used in capital budgeting decisions.

EXERCISES

E24–1. Capital Budgeting Tax Effects (CMA) Choose the best answer for each of the following questions.

1. Ander Company can invest $4,980 in a piece of equipment with a three-year life. If the minimum desired rate of return is 10-percent after taxes and the annual expected cash savings net of taxes is $2,500, the amount (rounded to the nearest dollar) by which the annual cash flows could change before the company would be indifferent to acquiring the equipment is a
    - a. decrease of $415.
    - b. decrease of $2,480.
    - c. decrease of $1,245.
    - d. decrease of $500.
    - e. decrease of $2,000.

E24–2. Capital Budgeting—Adjusting for Income Taxes

On January 1, Jenkins, Incorporated purchased for $520,000 a new machine with a useful life of ten years and no salvage value. The machine will be depreciated for tax purposes by the straight-line method using the 7-year ACRS percentages. It is expected to produce an annual cash flow from operations, before taxes, of $130,000. Jenkins is subject to a 40-percent marginal tax rate and has set 14 percent as a cut-off rate. For book purposes, the machine will be depreciated over a ten-year useful life by the traditional straight-line method.

Required

Compute each of the following on an after tax basis:

1. The net present value.
2. The internal rate of return.
3. The accounting rate of return.
4. The payback period.

E24–3. Capital Budgeting and Cash Flow from Operations

Jarvis, Incorporated, a calendar-year company, purchased a new machine for $28,000 on January 1. The machine, which has an estimated useful life of eight years and no salvage value, is being depreciated on a straight-line basis using the 7-year ACRS percentages. The accounting (book value) rate of return is expected to be 15 percent after tax on the initial increase in required investment. Jarvis has a 40-percent marginal tax rate.

Required

1. Compute the average annual cash savings associated with the depreciation on the machine.
2. Compute the average annual cash flow from operation before income taxes.

E24–4. Capital Budgeting and Alternative Analyses using an Electronic Spreadsheet

Roberts, Incorporated is contemplating the purchase of a machine for $240,000. The machine has a useful life of eight years and a $20,000 salvage value. The company will use the 5-year ACRS to maximize the present value of its cash flows. The machine is expected to generate $80,000 of cash flow from operations before income taxes in each of the eight years. Roberts' expected rate of return is 14 percent after tax. The firm is subject to a 40-percent tax rate. Roberts uses straight-line depreciation for financial reporting.

Required

Using an electronic spreadsheet, compute the net present value, internal rate of return, and accounting rate of return on the initial investment. Set up the spreadsheet so that you can vary the annual cash flows from operations before taxes and the initial investment. After you have computed and printed the results using the preceding data, substitute the following amounts and print out a copy of each of the results.

1. $100,000 before-tax cash flow and $280,000 purchase price.
2. $60,000 before-tax cash flow and $270,000 purchase price.

E24–5. Component Cost of Capital

Davis Corporation has its assets financed from several different sources.

a. Current payables for accounts, salaries, and wages average $35,000. Most of these are paid within twenty-five to forty days. When payment extends beyond this time, it is because of a disagreement in the amount due.

b. Current notes payable are $40,000. These notes are due in six months and carry a 16-percent interest rate. Both principal and interest are due at maturity.

c. Long-term notes total $98,000 and carry an average interest rate of 12-percent. The maturity value is $100,000, and they were sold to yield 11.5 percent.

d. There are 10,000 shares of 8.25-percent, $50 par value, preferred stock outstanding that were sold for $58.93 per share.

e. There are 20,000 shares of common stock outstanding with a par value of $1 per share. The company has paid $2 per share in dividends since the first year of operations, but it has reinvested excess earnings within the business. The year-end market price of the stock for the past four years has been $20, $23, $27, and $32, respectively.

Required

Compute the component cost of capital for each of the preceding items for Davis Corporation, assuming a 35-percent tax rate.

E24–6. Weighted Average Cost of Capital The liability and owners' equity sections of R. D. Sales' balance sheet follow. Notes at the bottom of the statement summarize important information about some of the items.

R. D. Sales
Partial Balance Sheet

Liabilities		
Accounts payable	$ 25,000	
Wages payable	5,000	
Product warranty	12,500	
Notes payable (18%)	40,000	
Mortgage payable (12%)	100,000	
Bonds payable	47,000	
Total liabilities		$229,500
Owners' Equity		
Preferred stock (500 shares, 8%, $60 par)	$ 30,000	
Additional paid-in capital—preferred	2,500	
Common stock (1$ par)	50,000	
Additional paid-in capital—common	150,000	
Retained earnings	200,000	
Total owners' equity		432,500
Total liabilities and owners' equity		$662,000

Notes:

1. The notes payable and mortgage have a yield rate that is the same as the face rate. However, the bonds were sold to yield 10 percent when their face rate is 11 percent.
2. All 500 shares of preferred stock were sold at the same price.
3. Common stock dividend has averaged $1.50 per share, and the annual growth rate has averaged 10 percent. The year-end market price on common stock is $18.
4. The applicable tax rate is 40 percent.

Required

Compute the weighted average cost of capital.

E24–7. Marginal Cost of Capital
Lund Tissue has been very conservative in its use of debt, borrowing only for short-term needs. Its total capital is currently $800,000. The capital structure and the after-tax component cost of each item are as follows:

Capital Component	Percentage of Total	Component Cost—After Tax
Current payables	20%	0
Notes payable	20	11%
Common stock	60	15

Lund Tissue is considering the acquisition of another company at a cost of $200,000. Management believes that it has two options:

1. Issue at par preferred stock with $100 par value per share and a 10-percent annual dividend requirement. If preferred stock is issued, the component cost of common stock is expected to increase to 16 percent. Other capital components should remain about constant in amount and cost.
2. Issue bonds that will have a face and yield rate of 13 percent. If bonds are issued, the component cost of common stock is expected to increase to 18-percent. Once again, other capital components should remain about constant in amount and cost.

The applicable tax rate is 40 percent.

Required

Compute the marginal cost of capital for each of the two options. Which option would you advise management to adopt and why?

E24–8. Capital Budgeting Using Net Present Value and Payback Period
Energy Company is planning to spend $84,000 for a new machine with a twelve-year useful life that will be depreciated using the accelerated cost recovery system over five years. The related cash flow from operations, before income taxes, is expected to be $10,000 a year for each of the first five years and $12,000 for each of the next seven years. Salvage value is expected to be $4,000. The company is subject to a 40-percent tax rate.

Required

1. Compute the net present value using a 12-percent cut-off rate.
2. Determine the payback period.

E24–9. Capital Budgeting (including tax effect), ITC, and Net Present Value Analysis
Juan Carlos, president of Beto's Tortilla Company, is presently considering an investment of $69,000 to purchase a tortilla-making machine that will last twelve years, at which point the machine will have no residual value. Cash operating savings of $12,000 before income tax will result annually if the new machine is purchased. The tortilla company's minimum desired rate of return is 12 percent after taxes.

1. Compute the net present value of the new machine, disregarding income tax effects.
2. Compute the net present value of the new machine, assuming a 40-percent tax rate and use of accelerated cost recovery depreciation, with the equipment qualifying for 5-year recovery.
3. Compute the net present value of the new machine, assuming the same facts in requirement 2 and, in addition, an investment tax credit of 10 percent. Assume that the company elects to adjust the amount of investment credit and recover the full cost of the machine.

E24–10. Capital Budgeting (including tax effect), ITC, and Various Evaluation Methods
If June Corporation acquires the new equipment currently being considered, cash savings of $6,000 a year before income tax for the next nine years will result. The new equipment will cost $27,000 and will have a $1,000 residual value at the end of its nine-year useful life. June Corporation's minimum desired after-tax rate of return is 10 percent. The tax rate is estimated to be 45 percent of taxable income.

Required
Assume that June Corporation will elect to use 5-year accelerated cost recovery for depreciation and take full investment credit with an adjusted basis.

1. Compute the payback period.
2. Compute the internal rate of return.
3. Compute the net present value.
4. Compute the profitability index.

E24–11. Consolidation of Capital Budgeting Concepts
Choose the best answer for each of the following questions.

1. For a project to be acceptable to a company using the present value method of analysis, the return on invested capital must
   a. at least equal the amount of cash to cover interest and principal payments for any debt obtained to finance the project.
   b. generate sufficient capital to pay for itself within the economic life of the assets committed to the project.
   c. at least equal the return on invested capital currently being generated by the company.
   d. generate sufficient capital resources to justify any additional capital expenditures and reduce idle capacity within the company.
2. What technique is used to deal with a range of possibilities in a capital budgeting model?
   a. Present value concepts
   b. Sensitivity analysis
   c. Markov analysis
   d. Discounted cash flow
3. Nelson Company is planning to purchase a new machine for $500,000. The new machine is expected to produce cash flow from operations, before income taxes, of $135,000 a year in each of the next five years. Depreciation of $100,000 a year will be charged to income for each of the next five years. Assume that the income tax rate is 40-percent. The payback period would be approximately
   a. 2.2 years.
   b. 3.4 years.
   c. 3.7 years.
   d. 4.1 years.
4. On January 1, 19X1, Studley Company purchased a new machine for $100,000 that has an estimated useful life of five years and no salvage value. For book and tax purposes, the machine will be depreciated using the conventional straight-line method, and it is expected to produce annual cash flows from operations, before income taxes of $40,000. Assume that Studley uses a time-adjusted rate of 12 percent and that its income tax rate will be 40% for all years. The present value of $1 at 12 percent for five periods

is 0.57, and the present value of an ordinary annuity of $1 at 12 percent for five periods is 3.61. The net present value of the machine should be
- a. $15,520 positive.
- b. $15,520 negative.
- c. $14,000 positive.
- d. $13,680 negative.

Questions 5 through 7 are based on the following data:

Logg Company is planning to buy a coin-operated machine costing $40,000. For tax purposes, this machine will be depreciated over a five-year period using the conventional straight-line method; it has no salvage value. Assume that the investment tax credit is *not* applicable to this purchase. Logg estimates that this machine will yield an annual cash inflow, net of depreciation and income taxes, of $12,000. The discount rates and the net present values of the investment in this machine are as follows:

Discount Rate	Net Present Value
12%	+$3,258
14%	+ 1,197
16%	− 708
18%	− 2,474

Logg's desired rate of return on its investments is 12-percent.

5. Logg's accounting rate of return on its initial investment in this machine is expected to be
   - a. 30%.
   - b. 15%.
   - c. 12%.
   - d. 10%.
6. Logg's expected payback period for its investment in this machine is
   - a. 2.0 years.
   - b. 3.0 years.
   - c. 3.3 years.
   - d. 5.0 years.
7. Logg's expected internal rate of return on its investment in this machine is
   - a. 3.3%.
   - b. 10.0%.
   - c. 12.0%.
   - d. 15.3%.
8. How are the following used in calculating a proposed project's internal rate of return, including any income tax considerations?

	Depreciation Expense	Salvage Value
a.	Included	Included
b.	Included	Excluded
c.	Excluded	Included
d.	Excluded	Excluded

PROBLEMS

P24–1. Net Present Value and Internal Rate of Return Bailie, Incorporated has had a problem with a high reject rate on machine Y-120 for several months. Efforts to replace and correct the tolerance mechanism have not been successful. A special study was just completed showing that an average of $40,000 per year is lost because of bad units that cannot be reworked. It is estimated that 80 percent of the lost units could be avoided if computerized manufacturing equipment is acquired.

A proposal has been made to buy a new computerized machine at a total cost of $250,000. A net reduction of three employees at an average salary of $26,000 per year is expected if the new machine is acquired. Annual operating costs of the new machine, other than employee wages, are expected to be $15,000 per year higher than was required for the old machine. The expected useful life of the machine is seven years, with an estimated salvage value of zero. The effective tax rate is 45 percent, and the Accelerated Cost Recovery System (ACRS) using a 5-year life is employed for both book and tax purposes.

Required

Analyze the desirability of the preceding proposal on an electronic spreadsheet using the net present value and internal rate of return methods. Assume that money is worth 12 percent and that all cash flows occur at the end of the year.

P24–2. Capital Budgeting (including tax effect) and Project Analysis A small manufacturing company is contemplating the purchase of a small computer in order to reduce the cost of its data processing operations.

Presently the manual bookkeeping system involves the following direct-cash expenses *per month:*

Salaries	$7,500
Payroll taxes	1,700
Supplies	600
	$9,800

Existing furniture and equipment are fully depreciated in the accounts and have no salvage value. The cost of the computer, including installation and accessory equipment, is $100,000. This entire amount is depreciable for income tax purposes using the accelerated cost recovery system over five years.

Estimated *annual* costs of computerized data processing are as follows:

Supervisory salaries	$15,000
Other salaries	24,000
Payroll taxes	7,400
Supplies	7,200
	$53,600

The computer is expected to be obsolete in six years, at which time its salvage value is expected to be $20,000. The company follows the practice of treating salvage value as an inflow at the time that is likely to be received.

Required

1. Compute the savings in annual cash outflow after taxes. Assume a 50-percent tax rate.

2. Decide whether or not to purchase the computer, using the present value method of discounted cash flow analysis. Assume a minimum rate of return of 20 percent after taxes.

P24–3. Various Methods of Capital Budgeting and After-Tax Analysis (CMA)

Hazman Company plans to replace an old piece of equipment that is obsolete and is expected to be unreliable under the stress of daily operations. The equipment is fully depreciated, and no salvage value can be realized upon its disposal.

One piece of equipment being considered would provide annual cash savings of $7,000 before income taxes. The equipment would cost $18,000 and have an estimated useful life of five years. No salvage value would be used for depreciation because the equipment is expected to have no value at the end of five years.

Hazman will use the accelerated cost recovery system for 5-year property on all equipment for both book and tax purposes. Hazman is subject to a 40 percent tax rate and has an after-tax cost of capital of 14 percent.

Required

Assume all operating revenues and expenses occur at the end of the year.

1. Calculate for Hazman Company's proposed investment in new equipment the after-tax
   a. payback period.
   b. accounting rate of return.
   c. net present value.
   d. profitability (present value) index.
   e. internal rate of return.

2. Identify and discuss the issues Hazman Company should consider when deciding which of the five decision models identified in requirement 1 it should employ to compare and evaluate alternative capital investment projects.

P24–4. Capital Budgeting and After-Tax Effects—Selective Analysis (CMA)

Rockyford Company must replace some machinery. This machinery has zero book value, but its current market value is $1,800. One possible alternative is to invest in new machinery that has a cost of $40,000 and that would produce estimated annual pretax operating cash savings of $12,500. The estimated useful life of the machinery is five years. Rockyford uses straight-line depreciation with half-year depreciation in the year of purchase. The new machinery would have an estimated salvage value of $2,000 at the end of five years. The investment in this machinery would require an additional investment in working capital of $3,000.

If Rockyford accepts this investment proposal, the disposal of the old machinery and the investment in the new equipment will take place on December 31, 19X1. The cash flows from the investment will occur during the calendar years 19X1 through 19X6.

Rockyford is subject to a 40-percent income tax rate for all income and has a 10-percent after-tax cost of capital. All operating and tax cash flows are assumed to occur at year end.

Required

1. Determine the present value of the after-tax cash flow arising from the disposal of the old machinery in 19X1.
2. Determine the present value of the after-tax cash flows for all five years attributable to the operating cash savings.
3. Determine the present value of the tax shield effect of remaining depreciation at the end of year 1, December 31, 19X2.
4. Determine the present value of the after-tax cash flows arising from the disposal of the new machinery at its salvage value at the end of year 5, December 31, 19X6.
5. Determine the present value of the net effect on the income tax payments related to the project in year 2.
6. Describe how Rockyford's additional investment in working capital of $3,000 required in year 1 should be handled when evaluating the replacement project.

P24-5. Capital Budgeting and the Cost of Capital (CMA) The following income statement and bar graph were among the financial information presented at the November meeting of the board of directors of the Martin Company. The meeting was to be devoted to an analysis of the past year's results (a record year for sales and earnings) as well as to the consideration of major asset acquisitions.

The bar graph was intended to display the relationship of various expense categories to revenues. The interest, preferred stock dividends, and earnings available to common stockholders were combined into one figure entitled "cost of capital" because an estimate of the cost of capital would be an important part of the discussions about the asset acquisitions.

Martin Company
Income Statement
For the Year ended September 30, 19X1
(in millions)

	Amount	Percent
Revenues:		
Sales	$225	90%
Other	25	10
Total revenue	$250	100%
Expenses:		
Wages and salaries	$ 50	20%
Merchandise and supplies	105	42
Depreciation	20	8
Interest	25	10
Income taxes	25	10
Total expense	$225	90%
Net income	$ 25	10%
Less: Cash dividends to preferred stockholders	5	2
Earnings available to common stockholders	$ 20	8%

Required

1. Evaluate the cost of capital percentage (20 percent) displayed in the bar graph. Is this cost of capital suitable for use in the asset acquisition? Why or why not?
2. If you reject the use of the 20 percent cost of capital, describe how Martin Company should develop a cost of capital figure for the board meeting that is suitable for use in asset acquisition analysis.

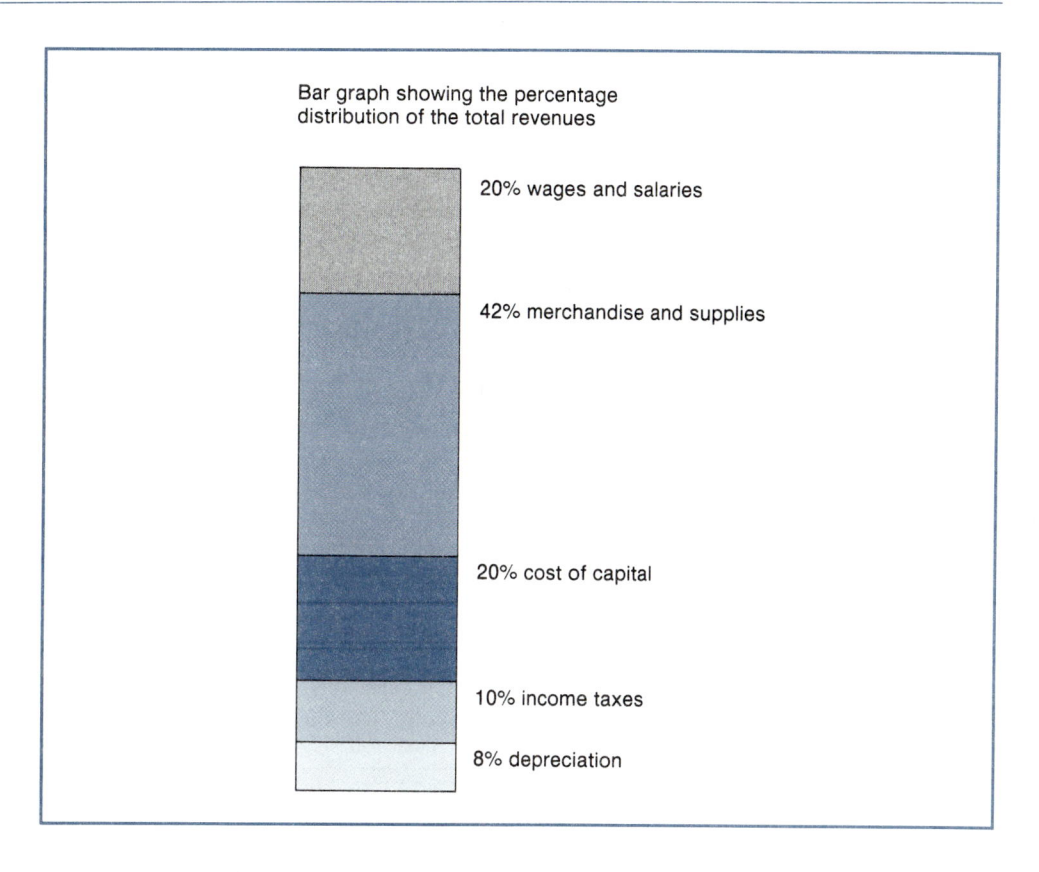

Bar graph showing the percentage distribution of the total revenues

- 20% wages and salaries
- 42% merchandise and supplies
- 20% cost of capital
- 10% income taxes
- 8% depreciation

P24-6. Net Present Value Analysis Wyle Company is considering a proposal to acquire new manufacturing equipment. The new equipment has the same capacity as the current equipment but will provide operating efficiencies in direct and indirect labor, direct-materials usage, indirect supplies, and power. Consequently, the savings in operating costs are estimated to be $150,000 annually.

The new equipment will cost $300,000 and will be purchased at the beginning of the year when the project is started. The equipment dealer is certain that the equipment will be operational during the second quarter of the year in which it is installed. Therefore, 60 percent of the estimated annual savings can be obtained in the first year. Wyle will incur a one-time expense of $30,000 to transfer the production activities from the old equipment to the new equipment. No loss of sales will occur, however, because the plant is large enough to install the new equipment without interfering with the operations of the current equipment. The equipment dealer states that most companies use a 3-year life when depreciating this equipment under the accelerated cost recovery system.

The current equipment has been fully depreciated and is carried in the accounts at zero book value. Management has reviewed the condition of the current equipment and has concluded that it can be used an additional five years. Wyle Company would receive $5,000 net of removal costs if it elected to buy the new equipment and dispose of its current equipment at this time.

Wyle currently leases its manufacturing plant. The annual lease payments are $60,000. The lease, which will have four years remaining when the equipment installation would begin, is not renewable. Wyle Company would be required to remove any equipment in the plant at the end of the lease. The cost of equipment removal is expected to equal the salvage value of either the old or new equipment at the time of removal.

Wyle Company is subject to a 40-percent income tax rate and requires an after-tax return of at least 12 percent on any investment.

Required

1. Calculate the annual incremental after-tax cash flows for Wyle Company's proposal to acquire the new manufacturing equipment.
2. Calculate the net present value of Wyle Company's proposal to acquire the new manufacturing equipment using the cash flows calculated in requirement 1, and indicate what action its management should take. For ease in calculation, assume all recurring cash flows take place at the end of the year.

P24–7. Capital Budgeting Analysis (CMA)
Wisconsin Products Company manufactures several different products. One of the firm's principal products sells for $20 per unit. The sales manager thinks she could sell more units of this product if they were available. A market research study, conducted last year at a cost of $44,000 to determine potential demand, indicated that Wisconsin Products could sell 18,000 units of this product annually for the next six years.

The equipment currently in use has the capacity to produce 11,000 units annually. The variable production costs are $9 per unit. The equipment has a book value of $60,000 and a remaining useful life of six years with straight-line depreciation in use. The salvage value of the equipment is negligible now and will be zero in six years.

A maximum of 20,000 units could be produced annually on the new machinery that can be purchased. The new equipment costs $300,000 and has an estimated useful life of six years with no salvage value at the end of six years. Wisconsin Product's production manager has estimated that the new equipment would provide increased production efficiencies that would reduce the variable production costs to $7 per unit.

Wisconsin Products Company would use the accelerated cost recovery system for 5-year property for tax purposes. The firm is subject to a 40-percent tax rate, and its after-tax cost of capital is 16 percent.

The sales manager believed so strongly in the need for additional capacity that she attempted to prepare an economic justification for the equipment, although this was not one of her responsibilities. Her analysis, presented below, disappointed her because it did not justify acquiring the equipment.

Required Investment

Purchase price of new equipment		$300,000
Disposal of existing equipment:		
Loss on disposal	$60,000	
Less: Tax benefit (40%)	24,000	36,000
Cost of market research study		44,000
Total investment		$380,000

Annual Returns

Contribution margin from product:	
Using the new equipment [18,000 × ($20 − $7)]	$234,000
Using the existing equipment [11,000 × ($20 − $9)]	121,000
Increase in contribution margin	$113,000
Less: Depreciation	60,000
Increase in before-tax income	$ 53,000
Income tax (40%)	21,200
Increase in income	$ 31,800
Less: 16% cost of capital on the additional investment required	
(0.16 × $380,000)	60,800
Net annual return of proposed investment in new equipment	$(29,000)

Required

1. The controller of Wisconsin Products Company plans to prepare a discounted cash flow analysis for this investment proposal. The controller has asked you to prepare corrected calculations of the required investment in the new equipment and the recurring annual cash flows. Explain the treatment of each item of your corrected calculations that is treated differently from the original analysis prepared by the sales manager.
2. Calculate the net present value of the proposed investment in the new equipment.

P24–8. Net Present Value Analysis (CMA) The WRL Company makes cookies for its chain of snack food stores. On January 2, 19X1, WRL Company purchased a special cookie cutting machine; this machine has been utilized for three years. WRL Company is considering the purchase of a newer, more efficient machine. If purchased, the new machine would be acquired on January 2, 19X4. WRL Company expects to sell 300,000 dozen cookies in each of the next four years. The selling price of the cookies is expected to average $0.50 per dozen.

WRL Company has two options—to continue to operate the old machine or to sell the old machine and purchase the new machine. No trade-in was offered by the seller of the new machine. The following information has been assembled to help management decide which option is more desirable.

	Old Machine	New Machine
Original cost of machine at acquisition	$80,000	$120,000
Salvage value at the end of useful life for depreciation purposes	$10,000	$20,000
Useful life from date of acquisition	7 years	4 years
Expected annual cash operating expenses:		
Variable cost per dozen	$0.20	$0.14
Total fixed costs	$15,000	$14,000
Depreciation method used for tax purposes	Straight-line	Accelerated cost recovery, 3-year
Estimated cash value of machines:		
January 2, 19X4	$40,000	$120,000
December 31, 19X7	$ 7,000	$ 20,000

WRL Company is subject to an overall income tax rate of 40 percent. Assume that all operating revenues and expenses occur at the end of the year. Also assume that any gain or loss on the sale of machinery is treated as an ordinary tax item.

Required

1. Use the net present value method to determine whether WRL Company should retain the old machine or acquire the new machine. WRL requires an after-tax return of 16 percent.
2. Without prejudice to your answer to requirement 1, assume that the quantitative differences are so slight between the two alternatives that WRL Company is indifferent to the two proposals. Identify and discuss the nonquantitative factors important to this decision that WRL Company should consider.
3. Identify and discuss the advantages and disadvantages of using discounted cash flow techniques (for example, the net present value method) for capital investment decisions.

P24–9. Capital Budgeting—Net Present Value Analysis and Inflation Considerations (CMA) Catix Corporation is a divisionalized company. Each division has the authority to make capital expenditures up to $200,000 without approval from the corporate headquarters. The corporate controller has determined that the cost of capital for Catix Corporation is 12 percent. This rate does not include an allowance for inflation, which is expected to occur at an average rate of 8 percent over the next five years. Catix pays income taxes at a rate of 40 percent.

The Electronics Division of Catix is considering the purchase of an automated assembly and soldering machine for use in the manufacture of its printed circuit boards. The machine would be placed in service in early 19X1. The divisional controller estimates that if the machine is purchased, two workers' positions will be eliminated, yielding a cost savings for wages and employee benefits. However, the machine would require additional supplies and more power to operate the machine. The cost savings and additional costs in current 19X1 prices are as follows:

Wages and employee benefits of the two positions eliminated ($25,000 each)	$50,000
Cost of additional supplies	$ 3,000
Cost of additional power	$10,000

The new machine would be purchased and installed at the end of 19X0 at a net cost of $80,000. If purchased, the machine would be depreciated on a straight-line basis for both book and tax purposes using 3-year ACRS class percentages. The machine will become technologically obsolete in four years and will have no salvage value at that time.

The Electronics Division compensates for inflation in capital expenditure analyses by adjusting the expected cash flows by an estimated price level index. The adjusted after-tax cash flows are then discounted using the appropriate discount rate. The estimated year-end index values for each of the next five years are as follows:

Year	Year-End Price Index
19X0	1.00
19X1	1.08
19X2	1.17
19X3	1.26
19X4	1.36
19X5	1.47

The Plastics Division of Catix compensates for inflation in capital expenditure analyses by adding the anticipated inflation rate to the cost of capital and then using the inflation-adjusted cost of capital to discount the project cash flows. The Plastics Division recently rejected a project with cash flows and economic life similar to those associated with the machine under consideration by the Electronics Division. The Plastics Division's analysis of the rejected project was as follows:

Net pretax cost savings	$37,000
Less: Incremental depreciation expenses	20,000
Increase in taxable income	$17,000
Increase in income taxes (40%)	6,800
Increase in after-tax income	$10,200
Add back non-cash expense (depreciation)	20,000
Net after-tax annual cash inflow (unadjusted for inflation)	$30,200
Present value of net cash inflows using the sum of the cost of capital (12%) and the inflation rate (8%) or a minimum required return of 20%	$77,916
Investment required	(80,000)
Net present value	$(2,084)

All operating revenues and expenditures occur at the end of the year.

Required

1. Using the price index provided, prepare a schedule showing the net after-tax annual cash flows adjusted for inflation for the automated assembly and soldering machine under consideration by the Electronics Division.
2. Without prejudice to your answer to requirement 1, assume that the net after-tax annual cash flows adjusted for inflation for the project being considered by the Electronics Division are as follows:

	19X1	19X2	19X3	19X4
Net after-tax annual cash flow adjusted for inflation	$30,000	$35,000	$37,000	$40,000

Calculate the net present value for the Electronics Division's project that will be meaningful to management.

3. Evaluate the methods used by the Plastics Division and the Electronics Division to compensate for expected inflation in capital expenditure analyses.

P24–10. Capital Budgeting—Lease versus Purchase (CMA)

LeToy Company produces a wide variety of children's toys, most of which are manufactured from stamped parts. The production department recommended that a new stamping machine be acquired and further recommended that the company consider using the new stamping machine for only five years. Top management has concurred with the recommendation and has assigned Ann Mitchum of the budget and planning department to supervise the acquisition and to analyze the alternative financing available.

After careful analysis and review, Mitchum has narrowed the financing of the project to two alternatives. The first alternative is a lease agreement with the manufacturer of the stamping machine. The manufacturer is willing to lease the equipment to LeToy for five years, even though it has an economic useful life of ten years. The lease agreement requires LeToy to make annual payments of $62,000 at the beginning of each year. The manufacturer (lessor) retains the title to the machine, and there is no purchase option at the end of five years. This agreement would be considered a lease by the Internal Revenue Service.

The second alternative would be for LeToy to purchase the equipment outright from the manufacturer for $240,000. Preliminary discussions with LeToy's bank indicate that the firm would be able to finance the asset acquisition with a 15-percent term loan.

LeToy would depreciate the equipment over five years using the accelerated cost recovery method. The market value of the equipment at the end of five years would be $45,000.

All maintenance, taxes, and insurance are the same under both alternatives and are paid by LeToy. LeToy requires an after-tax cut-off return of 18 percent for investment decisions and is subject to a 40-percent corporate income tax rate.

Required

1. Calculate the relevant present value cost of the leasing alternative for LeToy Company.
2. Calculate the relevant present value cost of the purchase alternative for LeToy Company.

CASES

C24–1. Lease or Buy Decision for Personal Automobile The decision to lease or buy a new automobile for personal use is very important to many people. Buying the car has the fewest strings attached: you control the automobile, enjoy any appreciation in value, and bear all risks of ownership. Some of the terms of a lease include the following:

1. If you turn in a car with a dented fender, noisy muffler, or other problems at the end of the lease term, you pay for the repair cost.
2. You pay a penalty, generally $0.08 to $0.10 per mile, for mileage over the specified maximum, generally 15,000 miles per year.
3. Getting out of a contract early requires a termination fee, which usually runs $1,000 or more.
4. The amount of your monthly payments is dependent on the estimated market value of the automobile at the end of the lease. If the car does not have the specified market value, you may be required to make up the difference.

In analyzing the options, the following schedule was developed to summarize the four-year cost of a $15,000 car.

If You Lease			*If You Buy*	
Security deposit	$ 300		Down payment	$ 2,250
Payments ($285 per month)	13,680		Payments ($320 per month)	15,360[a]
Interest forgone[b]	96		Interest forgone	720
Tax savings[c]	None		Tax savings	785
Resale proceeds	None		Resale proceeds	6,000
Net cost	$13,776		Net cost	$12,043

[a]Assuming a 9.5% loan rate.
[b]Income from investing security deposit or down payment at 8% tax-free.
[c]Assuming phase-out of interest deduction: 35% tax bracket in 19X7, and 28% in future years ($460 in 19X7; $235 in 19X8; $75 in 19X9; and $15 in 19Y0).

Required

Do you agree or disagree with the preceding analysis? Prepare a schedule to summarize your analysis.

C24–2. Lyons, Inc. - Adjusting for Income Taxes In case 23.1, Lyons, Inc. was not subject to either federal or state income tax. Recent tax rulings and an IRS audit have revoked the company's nontaxable status.

Revise the analysis in case 23.1, assuming Lyons, Inc. is subject to a combined federal and state marginal tax rate of 45 percent for all years under consideration. The investment tax credit was eliminated by recent tax-law changes and is not relevant to the decision. Lyons' minimum desired rate of return for capital budgeting decisions remains at 15 percent.

The hardware that is expected to be acquired on January 1, 19X7, will be depreciated for tax purposes by the 5-year ACRS percentages as follows:

19X7	20%
19X8	32%
19X9	19.2%
19X0	11.5%
19X1	11.5%
19X2	5.8%

Required

Adjust the capital budgeting analysis for the imposition of the new tax requirements. Are the cost savings provided by the new data processing center in New York enough to make it desirable at the company's minimum desired rate of return?

C24-3. Lake City Plant: Building a "Business Case" for Internal Equipment[6]

Dick Johnson, the data processing manager at the Lake City plant of CBI Inc., arrived at work early this Wednesday morning to get a jump on his major project of the day. Phil Lee, the plant manager, had asked Dick to make a presentation at 2:00 P.M. concerning *(a)* alternatives for solving some of the data processing problems and *(b)* recommendations as to the most attractive alternative. The future growth of the plant seemed to rest on the data processing center's ability to provide relevant and timely information to production, purchasing, and inventory control so that they can perform their jobs more efficiently.

Background

As Dick sat down at his desk and the mountain of information he had collected on the problem, he paused to reflect on the events that put them in this situation. Until two years ago the Lake City plant manufactured and assembled card readers and tape drives for large mainframe computers. Production, however, had dropped steadily in prior years, and the future of the plant was not very bright. As a result, few changes had been made in the data processing facility for at least six years.

Changes in technology that made mini- and micro-computers available to medium- and smaller-sized organizations at an attractive price essentially saved the Lake City plant. When CBI Inc. decided to enter the personal computer market, the Lake City plant was a natural spot to assemble the finished product.

The change in the production process two years ago went very smoothly. There was considerable cooperation among the functional areas. Each group made a successful transition to the new product.

Nobody knew quite how the new product would turn out. However, no one in his wildest dreams thought it would be so successful. Demand consistently exceeded the plant's ability to supply the finished product. Everything happened so quickly over the past two years that many things were done just to "get through the month" without taking time to plan, analyze, and build systems that were needed for long-term growth. The data processing and accounting areas had been so involved with meeting the needs of the current applications that they did not have time to create new applications that would help the plant run more efficiently.

When the plant was converted to the new product, the only modifications to the financial information system were those required to meet short-term needs. Future requirements were not addressed. The only system that required substantial change was the cost accounting system. Once again, however, the analysts and programmers worked quickly and were able to perform the final test of the new programs before the first production run of the new product.

The one area in which the data processing facility had been grossly inadequate was in integrating raw materials purchasing and inventory control with the production control system. Under the old manufacturing process, these areas were small enough that they were never computerized. The production needs were well defined and their suppliers could provide whatever was needed within a short period of time. Accounting and data

---

6. Copyright by IBM Corporation 1984. Reprinted with permission from IBM.

processing had originally planned to develop these applications, but to date they have had neither the time nor the computer capacity to do the development. Things are so tight now that even if they were able to acquire existing applications, they would not have capacity to process them on the existing computer.

The lack of relevant information on inventory needs and stock levels has created problems for personnel in purchasing, warehousing, and production. At first the problem was handled by buying large quantities of parts and subassemblies from each supplier and storing them next to the assembly areas. By having such large quantities of these raw materials on hand, the assembly lines could run as fast as possible and not worry about running out of necessary parts.

All but a few components are purchased from non-CBI Inc. manufacturers. The keyboard is manufactured by the CBI Inc. plant in Pine Rapids, and the cathode-ray tube (CRT) display units are assembled by the CBI Inc. plant in New Dallas. There are about twenty other non-CBI Inc. suppliers that are important in providing parts and subassemblies for the Lake City plant.

Personnel in inventory control order new parts and subassemblies by using a "red line" method. They have a red line on the floor or wall, and whenever the quantity in stock gets below the red line, they order a standard quantity from the established supplier. Their system helps them take advantage of all quantity discounts, and it generally assures an adequate supply of raw components for the assembly lines.

To meet the growing demand for personal computers, the assembly lines have expanded their production area and have taken over part of the space that had been used for storing parts and subassemblies. This has created more problems for warehousing, purchasing, and production personnel. The warehouse is constantly in a state of change, and the wrong red lines have been used for purchasing some components. Other components have not been purchased at all, and the assembly line has occasionally been temporarily shut down while parts and subassemblies were rush-ordered.

Some consideration has been given to the possibility of constructing a new building adjoining the existing facility to provide additional space for warehouse or production. However, the land that is needed for such a building is in an estate that is tied up in a court battle among the heirs of the estate. The law suit is not expected to be resolved any time in the near future.

About three weeks ago, Phil Lee gave Dick Johnson an assignment to prepare a presentation that identifies alternatives to solve the data processing problems and to make a recommendation "based on solid facts." Dick immediately appointed a task force to identify alternatives and collect relevant data for the analysis and the presentation. Its report was given to Dick just yesterday. Although the task force did not have a lot of time for its analysis, Dick thought it had done an excellent job.

Task Force Report

The task force consisted of a representative from I/S, accounting, production, purchasing, and warehousing. The task force identified five alternatives. The following information was extracted from the report.

1. *Continue business as usual.*

The Lake City plant could continue to operate in its present mode for at least a year or two. There are several significant "costs" associated with this alternative. *(a)* Inventory of parts and subassemblies are much larger than they need to be to run smoothly. It is estimated that inventory could be reduced by $1.5 million if the purchasing and inventory departments had good information with which to manage inventory. *(b)* The number of people in inventory and purchasing is larger than would be needed if better information was available. It is estimated that three people who currently earn $35,000 per year could be reassigned to the expanding production area. *(c)* The temporary shutdowns on the production line because of part and subassembly shortages would be entirely eliminated. They have been averaging about one shutdown per month during recent months, and each shutdown costs the plant about $12,000. These costs are summarized in figure 24.8.

2. *Replace the existing computer with a new model computer.*

Some of the major problems with the current computer are lack of capacity and slow processing speed. A new-model computer could be purchased to handle all the existing software and to provide the needed capacity to implement the proposed integrated production control, purchasing, and inventory control system. In fact, the new-model computer is so much faster and more efficient that it is expected to save $3,000 per month in power cost and about $12,000 per year in other overhead costs. A production, purchasing, and inventory software package is available on the market at a cost of $30,000 that will require only minimal programming to integrate it with existing software. There would be some building remodeling required to install the new computer and some cost to convert existing programs and files and to test them on the new computer. Also, the support rate charge for the new computer would be about $2,500 per month more than on the existing computer. The occupancy cost would remain unchanged. These costs are summarized in figure 24.9.

FIGURE 24.8

Business As Usual

Excess inventory (opportunity cost 15%)		$1,500,000
Excess personnel	(3 @ $35,000 ea. per year)	
Plant shutdowns	(1 per month @ $12,000 ea.)	

Note: All the cost data provided in the case are incremental; that is, all the costs and savings for each alternative are additional to the business-as-usual option. Therefore, the costs of staying with the business-as-usual option are the costs that could be avoided or the revenue that could be generated by switching to another option. The costs of operating the existing facility are irrelevant except as they change for the different alternatives. The changes or incremental costs are those that are provided throughout the case.

FIGURE 24.9

System Replacement

Computer—new		$1,200,000
Building remodeling and installation		$150,000
System analysis and design costs:		
Analyst	1 for 1 month at $6,200 per month	
Programmers	2 for 1 month at $6,000 each per month	
Conversion costs		$300,000
Software acquisition		$30,000
Support rate charge	$2,500 per month	

Note: All equipment prices in the case are based on expected cost to the company and include any sales and use taxes. Salary rates for personnel throughout the case are fully burdened. The "other overhead costs" include such items as property taxes.

One of the advantages the task force saw in this proposal was a useful life of seven years. Based on the number of transactions being currently processed and the projected increase in transaction processing, along with the processing capacity of the new computer in millions of instructions per second (MIPS), there will be excess capacity throughout the useful life. This surplus capacity is expected to put the Lake City plant in "good shape" for the next seven years.

The task force did not anticipate any salvage value from the existing computer. The computer is fully depreciated (net book value of zero), and it is not one of the new products currently sold on the market.

3. *Expand the existing computer system to handle the additional data processing required by the proposed integrated production control, purchasing, and inventory control system.*

The present hardware could handle the proposed software if several modifications were made. An additional printer and disk drive could be added to provide the needed capacity, and the central processing unit could be modified to provide some increased processing speed. However, the operating hours of the computer facility would need to be extended from two shifts to three, and additional employees would need to be hired.

The task force struggled with the problem of software for this alternative. No software could be found that was compatible with the existing hardware and software without significant modifications. Therefore, the task force recommended that the new application be developed internally. Figure 24.10 summarizes the costs associated with this alternative

This alternative was described by the task force as a "get-by" approach. It will provide the capacity needed to implement the new system but no surplus. The Lake City plant will face a similar crisis in about two more years because of a lack of computing capacity.

4. *Buy a used computer system (including central processing unit and peripherals) that is the same configuration as the computer currently used and use it to supplement the existing computer.*

This alternative would provide excess productive capacity, and much of the data processing that is currently being performed during the evening shift could be performed during regular working hours. The second computer could act as a backup for the current computer. This would essentially eliminate downtime when the plant is left without any computing power.

FIGURE 24.10

Cost of Expanding the Existing Computer System

Additional printer	1 at $33,000	
Additional disk-pack	1 at $32,000	
Upgrade to central processing unit		$70,000
Additional employees	5 at $35,000 each per year	
Operating costs:		
Power—additional shift		$6,300 per month
Support rate charge		$1,000 per month
Other		$4,500 per month
System analysis and design costs:		
1 analyst for 6 months at $6,200 per month.		
2 programmers for 6 months at $6,000 each per month.		

CHAPTER 24: CAPITAL BUDGETING: PART II

All of the existing systems could be immediately processed on the second computer. However, because no software for the production control, purchasing, and inventory control system could be found that is compatible with these computers, this would still have to be developed internally. Figure 24.11 summarizes the costs associated with this alternative.

The capacity provided by the additional computer would put the plant in good shape for the next seven years. It would not meet the data processing manager's dream of a model computer center, but it would be both functional and adequate.

5. *Buy new-model minicomputers with on-line terminal access by purchasing, inventory control, and production control personnel.*

One of the things that the production control, purchasing, and inventory control personnel on the task force want most is to have a system that gives them on-line access to the status of items in inventory and on order and the status of the production process. To date, everything has been processed in a batch mode, and all information must be obtained by thumbing through thick reports. This alternative would require more user training than the alternatives identified previously. However, software of the type needed is available on this model and could be made operable with minimal programming. All that would be required is a program to transfer data from the existing computer to the new computers. Figure 24.12 summarizes the costs associated with this alternative.

FIGURE 24.11

Buy a Used Computer of Same Model

Same model computer—used		$700,000
Additional employees	4 at $45,000 each per year	
Building remodeling and installation costs		$200,000
Operating costs:		
Power	$6,500 per month	
Support rate	$3,000 per month	
Occupancy	$2,500 per month	
Other overhead	$1,500 per month	
System analysis and design costs:		
1 analyst for 6 months at $6,200 per month.		
2 programmers for 6 months at $6,000 each per month.		

FIGURE 24.12

Buy New Mini-Computers with On-Line Access by Internal Personnel

Minicomputers (3 new)		$500,000
Operating costs of new computer:		
Power	$2,000 per month	
Support charge	$ 900 per month	
Occupancy cost	$2,000 per month	
Overhead	$5,000 per month	
Additional employee 1 @ $45,000 per year		
Building remodeling and installation costs		$75,000
In-house communication cables		$50,000
Terminals (18 @ $1,800 each)		
System analysis and design costs:		
1 analyst for 2 months at $6,200 per month.		
4 programmers for 2 months at $6,000 each per month.		
Training cost associated with new on-line users		$200,000
Software acquisition		$50,000

This alternative is expected to have a useful life of seven years. The excess computing capacity on the new machines can relieve the existing computer of some of its work load. However, some reprogramming of existing applications will be needed to achieve this benefit. The reprogramming is not thought to be all that bad because the modifications and updates will need to be completed some time in the future, and having a current-model computer in-house will make the update process more gradual.

6. *Buy a new computer and develop a network to tie the Lake City plant with the Pine Rapids and New Dallas plants. The three plants would access the same computer and share an integrated purchasing, inventory control, and production control system.*

The illustration in figure 24.13 shows a proposed network structure for this alternative. A new-model computer, larger than the one proposed for the on-line, in-house system described before, would be needed to handle the communication network. A front-end processor, modems, microprocessors, and terminals would also be needed for this alternative.

Much of the benefit from the network would accrue to the Pine Rapids and New Dallas plants. Because they do not know the production schedule for the Lake City plant, both the Pine Rapids and New Dallas plants carry large quantities of finished-goods inventory in order to meet the large orders of keyboards and display units from the Lake City plant. By having current information on the needs of the Lake City plant, the Pine Rapids plant and the New Dallas plant could each cut $1.5 million of their finished-goods inventory and eliminate two people earning $35,000 each from their staff of warehouse personnel. These are in addition to the benefits the Lake City plant will enjoy from the new system.

The cost data collected by the task force on the proposed network system is summarized in figure 24.14. This system alternative is expected to have a useful life of seven years. The task force thought that the Lake City plant was the best place for the central computer facility. It was not sure if it was unbiased in the recommendation, however, because Bob Green, the data processing manager at the Pine Rapids plant, had expressed an interest in having it at the Pine Rapids plant. Also, the task force thought that the cost should be equally shared among the three plants. Bob Green, however, thought that the Lake City plant should pay more of the cost if it were located there. "You people will be able to use it much easier," he said, "if it is located at your facility."

Current Situation

Dick put down the report from the task force and tried to think what to do next. One of the things he did not think he had a very good feel for was the attitude of the data processing managers at the Pine Rapids and New Dallas plants. He immediately picked up the telephone and dialed Bob Green, the data processing manager at the Pine Rapids plant. Bob has been in this position less than a year now, but he has made significant changes in the data processing center. He is bright, dynamic, and a very aggressive individual.

When Dick asked about Pine Rapids' integrated production, purchasing, and inventory control system, Bob said, "We don't have anything like that! We're still back in the 1960s when it comes to integrated systems. Our plant really needs something like that. In fact, what we need is some way to integrate our production plans with your assembly schedule. You have become our biggest customer, and if we knew what you were planning to produce, we could plan our production accordingly. The way it is now, we have to carry large quantities of finished keyboards in stock so that we can meet those large orders from your purchasing department.

FIGURE 24.13

Proposed Network Configuration

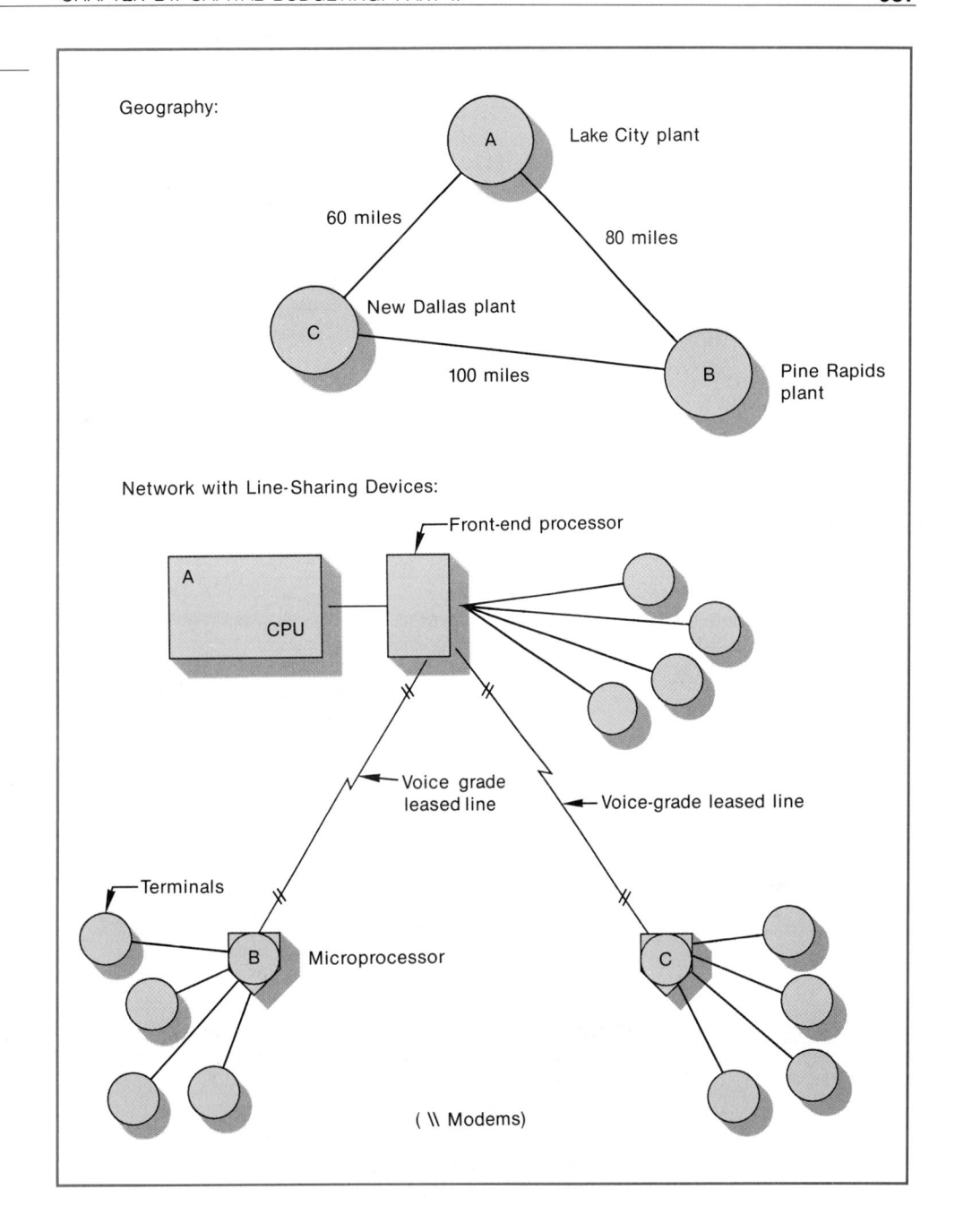

Geography:
- A — Lake City plant
- B — Pine Rapids plant
- C — New Dallas plant
- A to C: 60 miles
- A to B: 80 miles
- C to B: 100 miles

Network with Line-Sharing Devices:
- A CPU connected to Front-end processor
- Voice grade leased line to B (Microprocessor) with Terminals
- Voice-grade leased line to C with Terminals
- (\\ Modems)

"I would really like to see a common computer system that both plants could share. We could each do our production planning, purchasing, and inventory control, but you could share your production schedule with us so that we could be more effective. We're short on computer capacity ourselves, so the new computer would provide us with needed capacity."

As Dick hung up the telephone, he noticed that his heart was beating fast and his blood pressure was up. Putting his feet on his desk, he thought back on the high school state track meet where Bob and he both competed in the mile run. Dick represented Jordan

FIGURE 24.14

Cost Data for Proposed Network Configuration

Computer—new		$1,200,000
Front-end processor		$45,000
Additional employees (operate new computer):		
4 at $45,000 each per year		
Other operating costs: Power		$3,200 per month
Support rate		$5,500 per month
Occupancy		$500 per month
Overhead		$3,250 per month
Building remodeling and installation cost		$200,000
In-house communication cables:		
Lake City plant	$50,000	
Pine Rapids plant	$40,000	
New Dallas plant	$40,000	
Terminals (30 @ $1,800 each)		
Microprocessors (2 @ $2,000 each)		
Voice-grade leased line costs per line (full duplex):		

Miles	$/month/mile	
1–25	$3.30	Note: This is an incremental price structure.
26–75	2.50	The first 25 miles of each line cost $3.30/
75+	1.75	mi., etc.

Modems (4 @ $1,900 each)
System analysis and design costs:
  3 analysts for 2 months at $6,200 each per month
  12 programmers for 2 months at $6,000 each per month
Training costs associated with new on-line users $400,000
Software acquisition $40,000

High and Bob represented South High. It was a very close race all the way, but Dick was ruled the winner in a disputed finish.

Dick's next encounter with Bob came only a few years later. Dick was attending State University and Bob was attending Island University, and both were MBA students with an emphasis in information systems. Island University sponsored a competitive computer programming contest and, as luck would have it, both Dick and Bob were selected to represent their universities. The final round of competition found Dick and Bob competing for the championship trophy. This time it was Dick's turn to feel bad. Bob was awarded the trophy in another disputed finish. Once again there was a heated discussion between the members of both teams following the competition, and some hard feelings were created.

In an attempt to get his mind off old times, Dick walked out of his office to get a drink. As he reached the drinking fountain, he noticed some empty office space at the end of the hall. "That would be a great spot to house a new computer," he said to himself as he turned on the drinking fountain. "We would have to do some remodeling to convert it to a computer room, but it would surely be handy. It's too bad the production area doesn't have some of our extra office space," he thought. As he bent down to get his drink, he noticed his tie had been hanging in the water fountain and was completely soaked. Quickly he wrung out the excess water and headed back to his office to change his tie. He hung the wet blue tie on the coat rack to dry, pulled out his "junk" drawer, and dumped it on his desk to find the brown tie that he had saved from the last time the drinking fountain attacked him.

Picking up the telephone once more, he called Barbara Elwood, the data processing manager at the New Dallas plant. She was also interested in a network-type computer system. Barbara is an outstanding person in general and one of the best people around at designing integrated systems and setting up network structures. "I helped your task force set up the proposed network structure," said Barbara. "I think it will work very well and will provide us with substantial savings. We would like to work with you on it."

Dick hung up the phone as Phil Lee charged into his office, threw his suit coat on the chair beneath the coat rack, and asked Dick, "Well, what are we going to do about our data processing problems?" Dick said he had collected some good information and had identified several options, but he had not yet finished his analysis.

Lee said, "I really don't have time to discuss them now. I just wanted to make sure you remembered about our meeting today and that you are prepared to lead the discussion. By the way, I think it would be very helpful if you have the internal rate of return and the payback period computed for each alternative. Joe (the financial director) thinks a 15-percent rate of return is good to use for both investing excess funds and as a cut-off rate for potential capital investments. A tax rate of 45 percent is appropriate for your analysis. (Investment credit has been eliminated by recent tax law changes.) Joe might also like to see a net present value and a profitability index computed on each option. He graduated in finance, you know, and he really likes to get into this type of analysis."

"Okay," Dick reluctantly replied.

Lee grabbed his suit coat and left Dick's office wondering why his desk was so messy, if blue suits and brown ties were coming into fashion, and how his suit coat had become moist.

Chapter 25

Cost Accounting in an Information Age

Outline

COMPUTER SOFTWARE
Operating System
Program Language Translators
Utility Routines
Application Programs
Special-Purpose Programs
DECISION SUPPORT SYSTEMS
Decision Support Systems Defined
Decision Support Software (DSS)
APPLICATION PROGRAMS FOR
    TRANSACTION PROCESSING
DATA-BASE MANAGEMENT SYSTEMS
Data Base
  General Definition
  Specific Definition
Data-Base Administrator
Data-Base Management System
How a Data-Base Management System
    Works

SPREADSHEETS
Spreadsheets As Decision Support
    Systems
MODELING SOFTWARE
Entering the Model
Compiling the Model
Viewing the Base Model
Analyzing the Model ("What If . . ."
    Analysis)
Comparing Spreadsheets and Modeling
    Software
EXPERT SYSTEMS
General Concepts
Applications
SOFTWARE EVALUATION
SELF-STUDY PROBLEM
SUGGESTED READINGS
DISCUSSION QUESTIONS
CASES

Cost and managerial accountants today face a more complex environment because of the increased volume of information and the many processing alternatives. The sheer immensity of the amount of information can be mind boggling. Never before have companies been so large and transactions so complex as in recent years. Nevertheless, the success of a company depends on the ability to organize, process, and report the information generated by it to keep management abreast of changes affecting the business.

Cost accountants have had to turn to the computer to meet the growing demands placed on them. The computer, when used properly, can be a valuable assistant, providing a means of handling large volumes of data efficiently and accurately. In recent years the computer has evolved from a luxury affordable only to large firms to its present status as a necessity to most medium- and small-sized companies. An effective cost accountant, therefore, must possess an adequate understanding of the potential usefulness of the computer in an information age.

This chapter presents a review of computer software and some of the software packages available to assist in the decision support function performed by management accountants. After you have completed this chapter, you should be able to:

1. identify the various levels of software used by a computer system.
2. define a decision support system.
3. describe the different types of decision support software available today.
4. evaluate the effectiveness of a cost accounting system in meeting its objectives.

COMPUTER SOFTWARE

Knowledge of program language levels is a prerequisite to understanding how the computer works and how it can be used effectively. The National Association of Accountants (NAA), in its *Common Body of Knowledge for Management Accountants,* emphasized this as part of the technological literacy of information systems:

> Management accountants should be conversant with the principles and levels of programming languages, without which they cannot communicate effectively with computer analysts or professional programmers.[1]

Software refers to the programs that make the computer work. It is the collection of programs and routines that facilitate the programming and operation of the computer. All of the operations of the computer, as well as the data representations within the computer, are in an on/off state; there is either the presence or absence of an electrical impulse. This is much more limited than written human communication, which uses numerals from 0 to 9, letters of the alphabet, and numerous special characters such as dollar signs, periods, and commas. Various programs are required to convert conventional data and instructions into a format that is processable by the computer.

There are many different categories of software. Some of the more common ones include operating systems, program language translators, utility routines, application programs, and special-purpose programs. Each of these will be considered separately.

---

1. "NAA Issues SMA 1D: The Common Body of Knowledge for Management Accountants." *Management Accounting* 68 (August 1986): 61.

Operating System

The operating system is a set of routines that directs the operation of the computer. It handles the communication with the operator, performs administrative functions such as job scheduling and allocation of primary memory for programs and data, coordinates input and output operations, and maintains an operating log and statistics on each job. Every computer must have an operating system, which generally is provided with the hardware.

When operating a microcomputer, such as an IBM-PC, you will frequently interact with the operating system called DOS, which stands for Disk Operating System. With a DOS disk (containing a file named COMMAND.COM) in drive A, the computer will automatically load the operating system into memory when the computer is turned on. The operating system will ask for the current date and time and, after providing some copyright information, it will display "A>". This means that the default drive is A and that it is your turn to tell the operating system what to do. If, for example, you type in a program's name, the operating system will go to drive A and attempt to run the program. If it cannot locate the named program, it will respond with, "Bad command or file name" and display another "A>". Once again, it means that it is your turn to communicate.

Program Language Translators

The computer itself is merely a piece of machinery that will do what it is told. You can program the computer to do almost anything you want; all that is required is a detailed set of instructions that tells the computer step by step what to do. However, the computer understands *machine language,* which consists only of 1s and 0s that represent the presence or absence of an electrical impulse. In the early days of computers, the programs were written in machine language, which is very difficult and time consuming. Errors are easy to make and quite hard to identify.

To make programming easier, symbolic and procedure-oriented languages were developed. A *symbolic language* has a one-to-one correspondence with a machine-level language instruction. A program called an *assembler* converts a program written in symbolic language to machine language. Examples of symbolic languages include SPS, BAI, and AUTO-CODER.

A *procedure-oriented language* generally has a one-to-many correspondence with machine-level language instructions; that is, one command in procedure-oriented language converts to many commands at the machine language level. There are two types of programs, *compilers* and *interpreters,* that convert procedure-oriented languages to machine language.

- *Compiler*—A compiler attempts to convert the entire program from procedure-oriented language to machine language before the program is executed (or run) by the computer. The procedure-oriented level program is called *source code* and the machine-level program is called *object code*. Once the errors have been removed from the program (it has been debugged), the object code can be saved and run by the computer in all subsequent program runs. Thus the compilation process must be performed only once. COBOL is an example of a procedure-oriented language that uses a compiler.
- *Interpreter*—An interpreter converts a procedure-oriented language line by line as the program is being run by the computer. The program is saved as a procedure-level language, but the machine-level language usually is not saved. Therefore, each time the program is run by the computer, it must be converted to machine language by the interpreter. BASIC generally is a procedure-oriented language that uses an interpreter.

In summary, there are three types of program language translators: assemblers, compilers, and interpreters. These programs convert programs written in symbolic or procedure-oriented languages for processing by the computer. If you intend to write your own customized programs, you will need to know a programming language and have a program language translator for the computer to be able to run your program.

Utility Routines

Utility routines are programs that perform common data processing functions. Many of the programs on the DOS disk for the IBM-PC would be classified as utility routines. The following are some examples with a short description of what each will do:

FORMAT	Analyzes the disk for defective tracks and marks and addresses the sectors so that data can be stored on it.
DISKCOPY	Copies the complete contents of one disk onto another disk.
PRINT	Prints a list of data files on the printer.
COPY	Copies a specified file from one disk to another.
TYPE	Displays the contents of the specified file on the screen.

Application Programs

Application programs are those that have been written to perform a specific function for the user. Because the function often involves the processing of business transactions, these are sometimes called data processing or transaction processing applications. All of the programs written to perform accounting functions would be classified as application programs. Some of the more common ones include the following:

- *General ledger program*—updates the general ledger.
- *Payroll program*—maintains the payroll records and prepares the payroll checks.
- *Accounts receivable package*—records all sales and payments by customers on account, prepares customer statements, and performs an aging and analysis of accounts receivable.
- *Job-order cost system*—maintains the subsidiary ledger of work in process for a job-order manufacturing firm.

The list could go on and on. The application programs an organization requires depends on the type of business it is in, the type of decisions that are made, and its reporting requirements.

Special-Purpose Programs

There are many other programs, some generalized and some specific, that have been written to perform various activities. These include word processing, spreadsheet analysis, financial modeling, statistical analysis, graphics, and data-base management. Some of these special-purpose programs will be discussed in more detail later in the chapter.

DECISION SUPPORT SYSTEMS

Managerial and cost accounting was defined in chapter 1 as the process of identifying, measuring, accumulating, analyzing, preparing, interpreting, and communicating financial information to management to assist in planning and controlling an organization. The importance of the computer in carrying out this process was recognized by the NAA in *The Common Body of Knowledge for Management Accountants* when it wrote:

> Rapid technological change has expanded the ways in which computers can be employed in the accounting function. Software can be used to speed up routine aspects of planning, budgeting, and forecasting. Other software is designed to enhance management accountants' analytical, interpretive, and communication skills. Familiarity with generalized software such as spreadsheets, graphics, and statistical packages is an important part of a management accountant's knowledge. Specialized application packages, such as linear programming and materials resource planning, are important decision-support tools for a management accountant.[2]

Decision Support Systems (DSS) Defined

Broadly defined, a decision support system is any system, application, or program that provides information to help a user make an informed decision. However, as the term normally is used today, it refers to a computer-based information system that provides support to a decision-making process. Decision support systems usually have the following characteristics:

1. They are oriented toward decision making rather than information processing.
2. They support the decision maker rather than automate the decision-making function.
3. They respond quickly to the changing needs of the decision maker and have interactive capability; that is, they have the ability to provide "what if . . . ?" analysis to simulate the effects of alternative choices.
4. They are continually evolving as additional experience is gained with their use. Good DSS are easy to modify and update for newly acquired knowledge.
5. They are used most frequently with semi-structured to unstructured decisions. The amount of structure associated with any decision is a function of the problem solvers knowledge and experience with it.
6. They frequently combine the knowledge of several disciplines (e.g., computer science, accounting, operations research, finance, and management) from several different departments or functional areas within an organization (e.g., production, accounting, finance, personnel, and marketing).

Decision Support Software

A wide variety of software is available to the cost accountant. This can range from the simple programs that fit into very little memory space to complex applications that require vast amounts of computer memory. Because of the swiftness of change in the industry, it is difficult to keep abreast of all the advances in computer technology and software applications. Nevertheless, software developments can be categorized into five areas.

- application programs for transaction processing
- data-base management systems
- spreadsheets
- modeling software
- expert systems

All of these categories of software provide information that is used by management in a decision-making function. However, not all of them fall under the title of decision support

---

2. Ibid., 61.

systems as it is more narrowly defined. Each of these categories of software will be reviewed and its characteristics compared to those of a decision support system.

APPLICATION PROGRAMS FOR TRANSACTION PROCESSING

Application programs for transaction processing are used extensively in the accounting profession. A transaction processing application gathers, updates, and posts business transactions according to a predefined procedure. The predefined procedure may be referred to as an algorithm or set of algorithms.

An *algorithm* is defined as any particular procedure for solving a certain type of problem. It is a systematic procedure that, if followed, guarantees a correct outcome.

EXAMPLE The algorithm for computing net pay of an employee of a particular company is: compute gross pay by multiplying hours worked by the wage rate; compute and subtract required withholding for FICA, federal income tax, and state income tax; and compute and subtract voluntary withholdings for union dues, health insurance, and retirement saving.

EXAMPLE A program that computes the economic order quantity (EOQ) for inventory uses the EOQ algorithm to determine the amount of inventory that should be purchased with each order. If the user knows the demand, the ordering or set-up cost, and the carrying cost and correctly applies the formula, the economic order quantity can always be computed.

An algorithm may be simple or complex, but it is teachable and is usable without much thought once the user understands the the algorithm's objective and any underlying assumptions.

Application programs were the first programs written for the computer. The first computers that were designed to tally the U.S. Census results used simple rules of mathematics, which were nothing more than an algorithm for accumulating the numbers. The computer has evolved from its humble beginnings, but most applications run on computers have continued to use algorithms to solve problems. The algorithm was placed on the computer because of the speed with which the computer could solve problems, not because the problems proved too difficult for the majority of people. Even though almost everyone can add, subtract, multiply, and divide, the computer can do these operations (or algorithms of numbers) faster.

Application programs provide much useful data for management in planning and controlling the business, but they would not be classified as decision support systems. In general, application programs are oriented more toward information processing than toward decision making. Data from an application program frequently must be processed further to be useful in a decision-making activity.

EXAMPLE A payroll program is not very useful for making a decision about a pay raise. The payroll program accurately computes the payroll, but it does not provide useful data to evaluate the effect of the pay increase on the profitability of the business.

Usually the decision maker cannot interact with the application program to obtain any "what if . . ." analyses. Application programs often are designed to be run in a batch mode during off hours to minimize the processing cost.

DATA-BASE MANAGEMENT SYSTEMS

Data-base management systems are among the most powerful decision support systems available today. They are available on both mainframe computers and microcomputers, although most microcomputer versions are rather crude data-base management systems.

In this section we identify what a data base is, what a data-base management system consists of, and some of the software frequently used with a data base as a decision support system.

Data Base

General Definition When *data base* is used in its broadest sense, it refers to all the data relating to a particular firm, whether in desk drawers, in file cabinets, or stored in the computer.

Computer data processing uses the term *data base* to refer to the subset of logically arranged data that is stored on media accessible by the computer. Figure 25.1 illustrates the computer data base under this definition. Notice that the data base consists of several files for accounting, as well as other functional areas of the organization, and that each application or set of applications has its own file. Each file is structured to meet the specific needs of the application programs that it serves.

A great deal of computer data processing is based on a generalized definition of a data base. However, this approach is nothing more than the application processing system we discussed earlier, which did not qualify as a decision support system.

Specific Definition The term *data base* has a more precise definition to the sophisticated computer user. It is more than a mere collection of the existing files in an organization. To qualify as a data base, it must contain a collection of data designed to be used by different programs. This implies that redundant data elements are almost nonexistent. The collection of interrelated data is stored together to control redundancy and to serve more than one application in an optimal fashion. Data must be stored so that they are independent of the programs that use the data. Also, a common and controlled approach is used in adding new data and modifying and retrieving existing data within the data base. The data base is company-wide rather than application-wide, and it cuts across functions as well as levels in the organization.

If a company has a true data base, the data base should be able to support a variety of application programs from all functional areas of the organization. This requires a change in focus from application processing to data identification, organization, and storage. The first things that are established are the items about which information is to be stored in the data base (called "entities"), characteristics about the entities that are important to a decision maker (called "attributes"), possible values that the attributes may have (called "attribute values"), and the relationships that exist among them. These are organized so that they remain valid regardless of the type of processing. The processing applications are then developed to meet individual user needs.

A more complex system of hardware, software, and people are required to manage the company-wide data base. Hardware generally requires communication networks to access this centralized resource. Communication lines, modems, multiplexors, and a variety

FIGURE 25.1

Concept of Data base Under General Definition

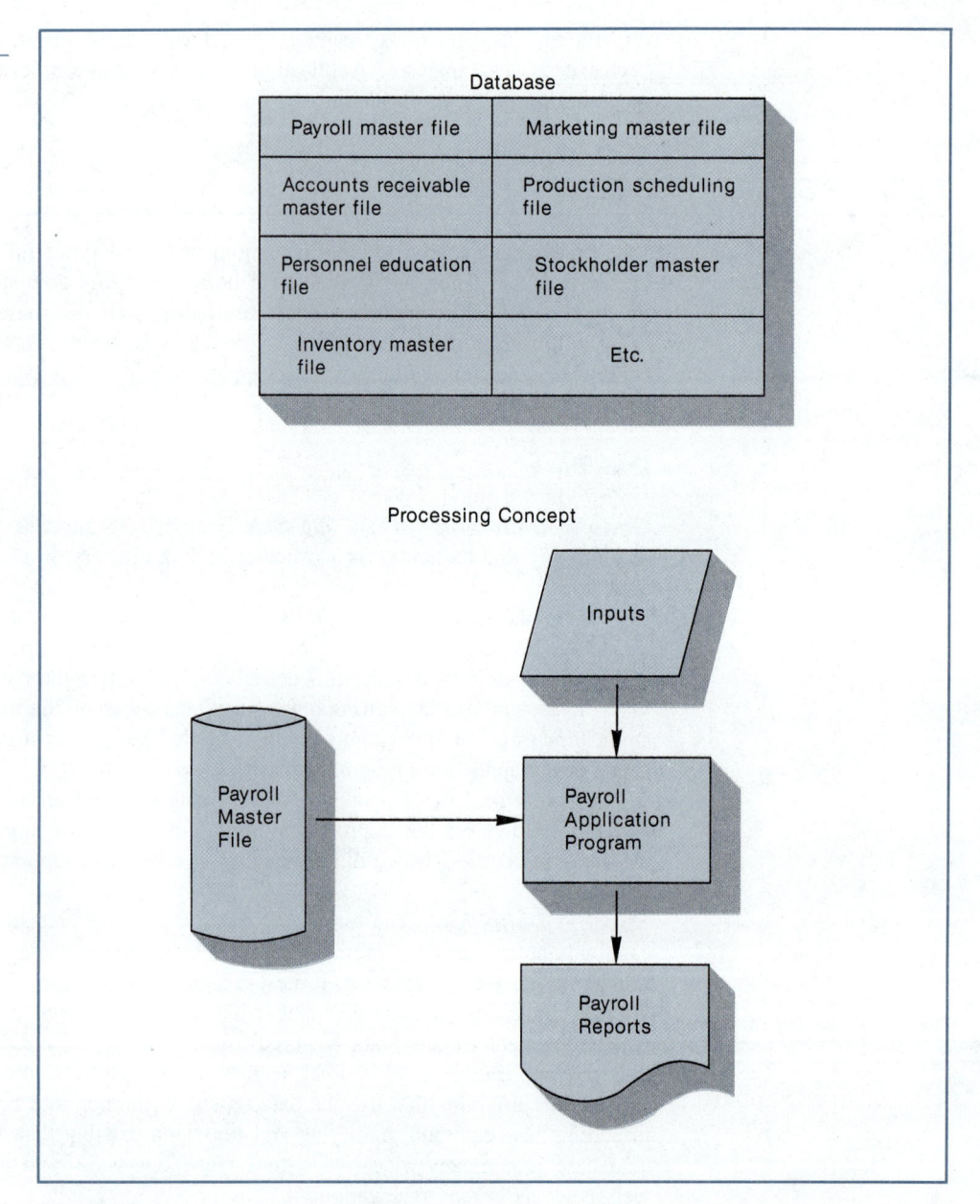

Database

Payroll master file	Marketing master file
Accounts receivable master file	Production scheduling file
Personnel education file	Stockholder master file
Inventory master file	Etc.

Processing Concept

Inputs → Payroll Application Program

Payroll Master File → Payroll Application Program

Payroll Application Program → Payroll Reports

of other hardware, as well as communication software, are important elements of the database system.

Data-Base Administrator

A *data-base administrator* is generally assigned to organize, monitor, and maintain the data base. During the organization phase, the data-base administrator will identify the data structure, assign file and field names, select search strategies, assign priorities and privacy keys, and load data into the data base. The data-base administrator regularly monitors the data base for usage, response time, privacy breach, and necessary modifications. As a result of the information collected, the data-base administrator will initiate changes to maintain the data base. An important part of data-base maintenance is removing "dead" records and compacting space.

Data-Base Management System

A *data-base management system* (DBMS) is the computer software that manages the data and handles the interface between the data in the data base and the application programs.

The combination of the data-base administrator and the data-base management system provides the controlled approach to developing and maintaining the data base. It ensures that data redundancy is minimized or eliminated; that data are independent of individual application programs; that a common and controlled approach is taken to add new data and modify or retrieve existing data; and that the data base serves the entire company.

Figure 25.2 illustrates this type of data base. Notice how all application programs access the data through the data-base management system. The application programs merely identify the data to be added, accessed, or modified, and the data-base management system handles those requests.

The data-base management system was conceived as a solution to the problems of duplicate information. As one department collects data, it often has data that are useful to other departments within the organization. For example, both the credit department and the collections department need information about customers, such as the customers' addresses, telephone numbers, and payment status. With the data-base management system, the information would be entered once and then shared between the collections and credit departments.

The combined storage, or **integrated data base,** is useful in many ways. Because the information is collected and written only once, the company can save on computer processing–related costs. The information is more timely, accurate, and consistent across functional areas. Also, the company reduces the chance for errors that result from recording and updating duplicate information.

How a Data-Base Management System Works

Data are stored in a **relational structure** in the data base. A *relation* in a relational data base is simply a two-dimensional table that has a specific number of columns and a number of unordered rows. Each row represents an entry in the relation, or table. Each row contains either a value or a null (empty) entry in each column. Thus, when you hear the terms *relation* or *relational data base,* you ought to think in terms of data stored in tables.

Figure 25.3 shows how data may be stored in a relational structure for a hospital. There are three relations, or tables, titled Patient, Services, and Payments. The Patient table contains basic information about each individual that is admitted to the hospital. As services are provided to the individual, they are recorded in the Services table. Payments that are received from the patient are recorded in the Payments table.

Let's focus on the Services table. Notice that it has four columns and ten rows. The columns represent attributes about the services provided and are titled NUMBER, SERVICE, AMOUNT, and DATE. Each row contains information about services provided to one entity, a patient. The services are identified with an individual by the patient NUMBER. The elements of the rows of a table are called *fields*. A row has a value in each field or column of the table. For example, the first row of the Services table has field values of 2811, EKG—Reading, 14.50, and 12/2/x6.

FIGURE 25.2 Sophisticated Data Base

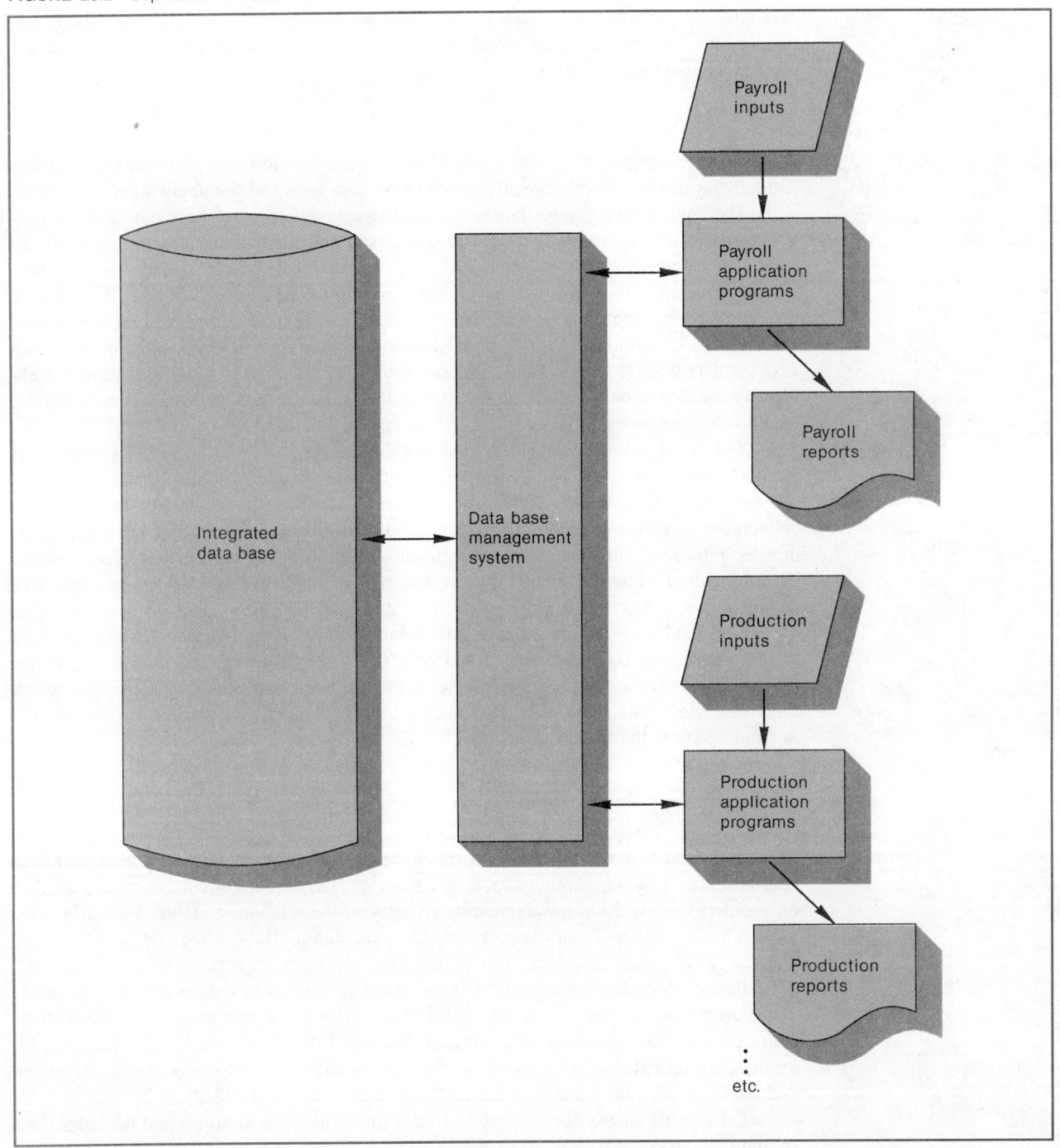

A variety of operations can be performed on a table, including the following:

- Creating or deleting a table
- Retrieving data from a table through a query
- Updating, inserting, or deleting data

FIGURE 25.3

Relational Data Base—Example

Patient

NAME	ADDRESS	CITY	STATE	NUMB
Anderson, A	1224 Slick St.	Tarrytown	NY	4585
Brubaker, G	456 High St.	Plainview	NY	8537
Garbo, R.	45 W. 58 N.	Orem	UT	2811

Services

NUMBER	SERVICE	AMOUNT	DATE
2811	EKG—Reading	14.50	12/2/x6
8537	Blood work	18.24	12/2/x6
2811	EKG—Analysis	25.88	12/2/x6
5555	Operating room	450.00	12/2/x6
2811	Operating room	550.00	12/2/x6
8537	Pharmacy	8.50	12/2/x6
3922	Pharmacy	9.25	12/2/x6
2811	Pharmacy	12.85	12/2/x6
4585	X-ray	125.00	12/2/x6
4585	Anaesthetic	285.50	12/2/x6

Payments

NUMB	DATE	AMT
5555	12/5/x6	1,255.25
3922	12/5/x6	500.00

- Adding new columns to a table
- Copying data from one table to another

A query is an operation that is used in a decision-making capacity, and there are several software packages that support the query function. Query Management Facility (QMF) is a data-base management system developed and marketed by IBM for mainframe computers that allows interactive query and report writing. QMF uses Structured Query Language (SQL), which is an English-like language that requires the use of a few key words. It is relatively free form, which means that spacing and word placement on the screen are not critical to successful processing. Because the format and syntax of SQL is similar to most data-base management systems, it will be used as an example to illustrate their use.

Data is accessed from the data base by developing a *query,* which describes the *data* wanted and the *action* to be taken. Actions include retrieving, updating, and inserting data. If the user wants to create a report, the query is first run to retrieve the desired data and the results are then formatted into a *report* using a *form.* Thus a form describes how retrieved data should be tailored into a report.

A query in SQL is structured as follows:

```
SELECT ____, ____, ____
FROM ____
WHERE ____
ORDER BY ____
```

The SELECT statement tells the computer to obtain data from the data base. The names that follow SELECT identify the columns from which data are to be taken.

The FROM statement tells the computer the table or tables from which the columns specified in the SELECT statement are to be taken.

The WHERE statement indicates the conditions for retrieval—in other words, what type of data is to be taken from the column(s). The characteristics that the data must satisfy are listed in this place and only those data will be extracted.

The ORDER BY statement specifies sort procedures. The order may be in ascending or descending order of the group and by subgroups within the group.

A short example will illustrate the query process and how it can be used as a decision support function. Suppose that R. Garbo, patient number 2811, took a turn for the worse and the doctor wants to review the services the patient has received during the last twenty-four hours. The query and the report presented in figure 25.4 would provide the desired information. Notice how little the doctor must enter to receive the report.

The tables would generally be much larger and would provide more information on each patient. More information facilitates a greater variety of decisions. Nevertheless, the

FIGURE 25.4

SQL Query for Doctor's Decision

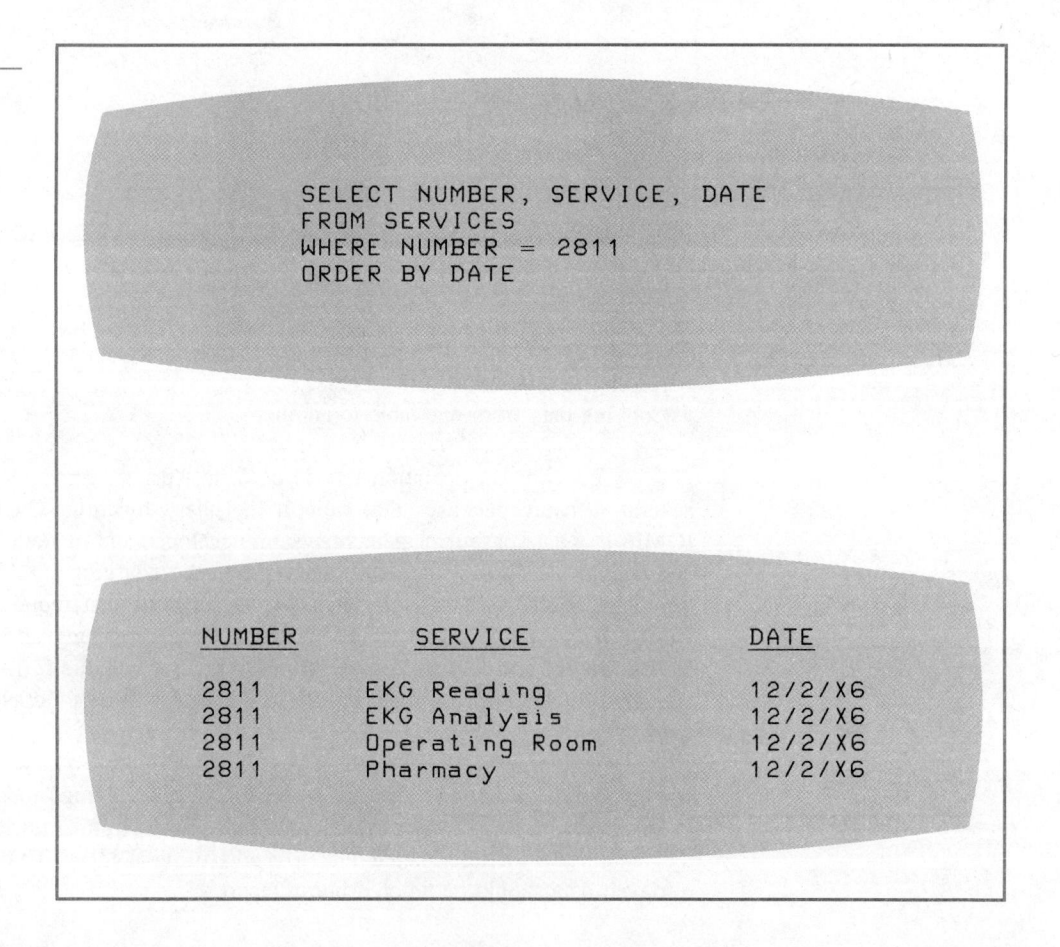

```
SELECT NUMBER, SERVICE, DATE
FROM SERVICES
WHERE NUMBER = 2811
ORDER BY DATE
```

NUMBER	SERVICE	DATE
2811	EKG Reading	12/2/X6
2811	EKG Analysis	12/2/X6
2811	Operating Room	12/2/X6
2811	Pharmacy	12/2/X6

CHAPTER 25: COST ACCOUNTING IN AN INFORMATION AGE   973

limited data-base information that supported the doctor's query can be used for various other uses. For example, information from the three tables could be used to bill the patient. The Patient table could be used to evaluate the geographic area serviced by the hospital. Information from the Services table could also be used to evaluate the volume of services being provided by various departments of the hospital.

SPREADSHEETS

A **spreadsheet** is a "blank slate" similar to a worksheet that consists of horizontal rows and vertical columns. Some worksheets have as many as 8,192 rows and 256 columns. Each intersection of a row and a column forms a cell in which data can be stored. There could be as many as 2,097,152 cells available for use in one spreadsheet. Each cell can contain either a label or numeric data (i.e., a formula or a number).

The spreadsheet does not require a program. The user enters data and formulas on a spreadsheet in a way that is similar to the way they would be entered on a paper worksheet. This makes it easy to use and very versatile.

The power of the spreadsheet comes from its ability to reference data in one cell for computation in a formula in another cell. By tying together cells using formulas and relationships and by changing the input in key cells, the user can determine the implications of various possibilities on the final outcome. This "what if . . . " capability makes a spreadsheet extremely attractive and useful as a decision support system.

There are various spreadsheet packages on the market today, including Lotus 1-2-3, SuperCalc, Multiplan, and VisiCalc. The fact that Lotus 1-2-3, a microcomputer spreadsheet, currently sells better than any other microcomputer software application demonstrates the usability of spreadsheets.

Spreadsheets as Decision Support Systems

The power of the "what if . . . " capability provided by a spreadsheet can be illustrated with the following example using Lotus 1-2-3.

EXAMPLE

Broadbow, Inc. is a cement manufacturing company. It has received a request from the government to bid on the cement cost associated with the construction of a new air base in Arizona. To service the contract, a new cement plant will need to be constructed at a cost of $100,000 (paid at the beginning of year 1). The contract would specify a minimum quantity of concrete: 20,000, 30,000, 25,000, 10,000, and 7,500 cubic yards for years 1 through 5, respectively. However, the amounts could be as high as 30,000 cubic yards in year 1 and 40,000 cubic yards in year 2. Cost of goods sold is consistently 70 percent of sales. The only other expenses are: administration costs, which are expected to be $85,000, $90,000, $95,000, $50,000, and $30,000 for years 1 through 5, respectively; and income taxes, which are at 40 percent of before-tax net income. The company desires a 20-percent return on its investment. Because there is no alternative use for the cement plant in the area after the completion of the contract, it will be sold for scrap value at the end of year 5.

Figure 25.5 illustrates a Lotus 1-2-3 approach to solving the problem. The top part of the figure shows a pro forma statement under the assumption that the contract specified

FIGURE 25.5 Broadbow, Inc. Cement Price for Government Contract Spreadsheet Approach

```
                         Broadbow, Inc.
                Cement price for government contract
                      Spreadsheet approach I

                   Year 0    Year 1    Year 2    Year 3    Year 4    Year 5

Government demand            20,000    30,000    25,000    10,000     7,500
Investment        $100,000        0         0         0         0         0
Price                         $20.00    $20.00    $20.00    $20.00    $20.00

Sales                       $400,000  $600,000  $500,000  $200,000  $150,000
Cost of goods sold           280,000   420,000   350,000   140,000   105,000

Gross margin                 120,000   180,000   150,000    60,000    45,000
Other expenses:
Administrative expenses       85,000    90,000    95,000    50,000    30,000

Before-tax net income         35,000    90,000    55,000    10,000    15,000
Income tax                    14,000    36,000    22,000     4,000     6,000

Net income       ($100,000)  $21,000   $54,000   $33,000    $6,000    $9,000


Internal rate of return (year 5)      9.14%
Net present value (year 5)         ($19,392)
```

a price of $20 per cubic yard of cement. Notice that at this price, Broadbow obtains only a 9.14-percent internal rate of return.

Figure 26.6 shows the values and formulas contained in the individual cells of the worksheet. By studying these, you will see that many of the formulas tie back to the entry in cell D-10, which is the contract price in year 1. By changing this one number, the rest of the values in the worksheet are automatically updated.

To identify the contract price that yields the desired 20-percent return on investment, the price in year 1 can be changed by small increments, gradually focusing in on 20-percent internal rate of return. A table showing internal rates of return with different contract prices per cubic yard is presented in figure 25.7. Notice that a price of $21.81 would need to be charged to obtain the desired minimum rate of return. However, this is accurate only if the government purchases the minimum amount in years 1 and 2.

To see what happens if the government purchases the maximum amount during the first two years, we can change the quantity in cell D-8 to 30,000 and in cell E-8 to 40,000. Going back to the original price of $20 per cubic yard, the internal rate of return is 41.47 percent, as illustrated in figure 25.8. Once again a sensitivity analysis similar to that illustrated in figure 25.9 is needed to find the price that yields a 20-percent return.

The spreadsheet has given the decision maker a low price of $17.37 for the maximum quantity to be purchased and a high price of $21.81 for the minimum quantity to be purchased. This is all that the spreadsheet can do. The user must evaluate the most likely quantity purchased by the government, the alternative bids likely to be submitted, and similar factors that are relevant to the bid amount.

FIGURE 25.6 Broadbow, Inc. Cement Price for Government ContractSpreadsheet Values and Formulas

	A	B	C	D	E	F	G	H
1				Broadbow, Inc.				
2				Cement price for government contract				
3				Spreadsheet values and formulas				
4								
5			Year 0	Year 1	Year 2	Year 3	Year 4	Year 5
6								
7								
8	Government demand			20000	30000	25000	10000	7500
9	Investment		1000000	0	0	0	0	0
10	Price			20	+D10*1	+E10*1	+F10*1	+G10*1
11								
12	Sales			+D8*D10	+E8*E10	+F8*F10	+G8*G10	+H8*H10
13	Cost of goods sold			+D12*0.7	+E12*0.7	+F12*0.7	+G12*0.7	+H12*0.7
14								
15	Gross margin			+D12-D13	+E12-E13	+F12-F13	+G12-G13	+H12-H13
16	Other expenses:							
17	Administrative expenses			85000	90000	95000	50000	30000
18								
19	Before-tax net income			+D15-D17	+E15-E17	+F15-F17	+G15-G17	+H15-H17
20	Income tax			+D19*0.4	+E19*0.4	+F19*0.4	+G19*0.4	+H19*0.4
21								
22	Net income		-C9	+D19-D20	+E19-E20	+F19-F20	+G19-G20	+H19-H20
23								
24								
25								
26	Internal rate of return (year 5)			@IRR(0.2,C22..J22)				
27	Net present value (year 5)			+C22+@NPV(0.2,D22..H22)				

FIGURE 25.7

Broadbow, Inc. Contract Price and Internal Rate of Return Assuming *Minimum* Quantity Purchased by Government in Years 1 and 2

Contract Price	Internal Rate of Return
$21.00	15.29%
22.00	21.14
21.50	18.25
21.75	19.70
21.82	20.11
21.80	19.99
21.81	20.05

MODELING SOFTWARE

Modeling software possesses many of the same features as a spreadsheet. Most models use a matrix format consisting of columns and rows. Each row of the matrix represents a variable and its corresponding values. Each column usually represents an increment of time (i.e., a quarter or a year) and contains the values that apply in that time period.

Modeling consists of identifying the variables that affect the result that is important in a decision-making process. The relationship between these variables is then defined in mathematical terms. The model is a collection of the mathematical statements that describe a certain situation. Because the results of the models are generally stated in financial terms, these models are often called financial models. There are several financial modeling packages available on the market, including IFPS/Personal, ENCORE, and PLAN80.

FIGURE 25.8 Broadbow, Inc. Cement Price for Government Contract Spreadsheet Analysis of Change in Demand

```
                         Broadbow, Inc.
                Cement price for government contract
                 Spreadsheet analysis of change in demand

                       Year 0     Year 1    Year 2    Year 3    Year 4    Year 5

Government demand                 30,000    40,000    25,000    10,000     7,500
Investment            $100,000        $0        $0        $0        $0        $0
Price                                $20       $20       $20       $20       $20

Sales                           $600,000  $800,000  $500,000  $200,000  $150,000
Cost of goods sold               420,000   560,000   350,000   140,000   105,000

Gross margin                     180,000   240,000   150,000    60,000    45,000
Other expenses:
Administrative expenses           85,000    90,000    95,000    50,000    30,000

Before-tax net income             95,000   150,000    55,000    10,000    15,000
Income tax                        38,000    60,000    22,000     4,000     6,000

Net income          ($100,000)   $57,000   $90,000   $33,000    $6,000    $9,000

Internal rate of return (year 5)    41.47%
Net present value (year 5)         $35,608
```

One of the most useful features of financial models is their ability to perform "what if . . . "-type sensitivity analysis. However, most financial models go beyond that which is offered by other decision support software discussed in this chapter by including probability distributions that can be used to test the sensitivity of the result to random changes in the input values.

IFPS/Personal will be used here to illustrate the structure and power of financial modeling software and to compare them to spreadsheet applications. IFPS stands for Interactive Financial Planning System. It is not a programming language; rather, it provides natural language syntax for model formulation. There are four phases to modeling in IFPS/Personal. Each of these will be illustrated using the Broadbow, Inc. example presented in the previous section.

FIGURE 25.9

Broadbow, Inc. Contract Price and Internal Rate of Return Assuming *Maximum* Quantity Purchased by Government in Years 1 and 2

Contract Price	Internal Rate of Return
$17.00	16.47%
18.50	29.62
17.75	23.34
17.35	19.87
17.40	20.31
17.36	19.95
17.37	20.04

FIGURE 25.10 IFPS Model for Broadbow, Inc.

```
 1 COLUMNS 1 THRU 5
 2 GOVERNMENT = 20000,30000,25000,10000,7500
 3 INVESTMENT = 100000,0,0,0,0
 4 PRICE = 20
 5 SALES = (PRICE * GOVERNMENT)
 6 COST OF GOODS SOLD = SALES * .7
 7 GROSS MARGIN = SALES - COST OF GOODS SOLD
 8 ADMIN EXPENSES = 85000, 90000, 95000, 50000, 30000
 9 BTNI = GROSS MARGIN - ADMIN EXPENSES
10 TAX = BTNI * .4
11 INCOME = BTNI - TAX
12 INTERNAL R OF R = IRR(INCOME,INVESTMENT)
-→ NET PRESENT VALUE = NPVC (INCOME, .20, INVESTMENT)

Menu                    Modified        EDIT MODE     Model: BOW.MOD
Edit:   Append  Copy  Delete  Get      Include
        Locate  Move  Name    Replace  Save    Undo   Visual
```

Entering the Model

Entering the model consists of developing the conceptual design, keying the model into the computer, and editing any obvious errors. IFPS/Personal provides a clear screen with a cursor and a pointer for entering the model. The software automatically numbers the lines as they are entered.

The first line of the model is a columns definition statement that tells the computer how many columns wide the model will be. It is followed by statements that tell the computer, row by row, what is to be included in the model.

Figure 25.10 shows the model constructed for Broadbow, Inc. Notice that it is designed to have five columns of data, numbered 1 through 5. The first row of the solution will be titled Government and the values will represent annual government demand for each of the five years. The second row will be Investment and the third row Price. Because the $20 price is shown only once, the model knows to repeat that amount in each of the following columns. The fourth row will be Sales, and the amount in each column is computed by multiplying price in row 3 by the government demand in row 1. Each of the rows that follow are either mathematically computed from prior rows or are constant values. BTNI stands for before-tax net income. Internal rate of return and net present value shown near the bottom are computed using functions built into IFPS/Personal.

This model follows essentially the same logic used in developing a pro forma income statement. We have added the investment, internal rate of return, and net present value to facilitate the decision-making process for this example.

Compiling the Model

Before the model can be viewed, it must be compiled into a machine-level language for processing by the computer. The computer does the compilation process on its own, and the user is able to view the results immediately, provided that there are no errors in the model. The computer is good at identifying syntax errors, which are inconsistencies in the use of variable names or a failure to follow prescribed structure in entering a model statement. However, the computer is not good at identifying logic errors. The model may be compiled and run by the computer, but it may not be correct because of an error in the model logic. If there are errors identified during compilation, they must be corrected before the computer will process the solution.

Figure 25.11 shows the computer response to a typing error that occurred while the model was being entered. Notice that the equal sign (=) was omitted from the second line of the model. Although this seems like a small error, the computer cannot process the result because it is not able to interpret this line.

Viewing the Base Model

The solution, or as much of it as can be shown, is displayed on the top portion of the screen. IFPS/Personal uses default values for column width, decimal places, negative values, etc. The middle portion of the screen contains the first several lines of the model. At the bottom of the screen is a menu that allows the user to do several things while viewing the model.

Using the cursor, the user can scroll through the solution or the model to view portions that are not initially visible on the screen. Also, the size of any of the windows can

FIGURE 25.11 IFPS Compilation Error Messages

```
  2     GOVERNMENT     20000,30000,25000,10000,7500
-------------------------^-****
 Syntax error here. Please correct.
Undefined variable: GOVERNMENT.
      5    Columns            13   Variables         0   Simultaneous groups
      1    Errors              1   Undefined variables
 Compilation found errors. Please correct them before proceeding.
 Compiled model cannot be solved

   Ready for command                                     Model BOW.MOD
IFPS:  Model      Edit         Files      Profile   Interface  Log
       eXecute    Consolidate  Datafile   Quit      Help
```

be changed to view more of the solution and less of the model, or vice versa. Figure 25.12 shows a screen printout of the initial view with the size of the windows modified to show the entire result.

Analyzing the Model ("What if . . ." Analysis)

The "What_if" menu option allows the user to manipulate the base model. Using it, one can change the price or government demand to see their effect on internal rate of return and net present value.

When the "What_if" option is selected, a third window titled Case is opened on the screen, replacing the bottom portion of the model. This allows the user to enter or edit changes in any of the variables in the base model and to view the effect of the change on the solution. For the first case in this example, we can enter "Price = 22" and solve; the result is illustrated in figure 25.13. (Part of the solution has been omitted from this and subsequent figures to focus attention on the relevant parts of the information provided. Also, the results are shown as presented by the computer during the "what if . . ." interactive session. Print options allow output to be edited for final reporting.) Notice that the internal rate of return is 21 percent and the net present value is $2,137.15. We could continue to make additional changes in the price, as we did with the spreadsheet, to find the price that yields a 20-percent internal rate of return and zero net present value. However, IFPS/Personal provides a "gOal_seek" option that finds the solution automatically.

The "gOal_seek" option allows the user to identify a goal value for some variable, identify the variable to be changed, and let IFPS/Personal calculate a new value that sat-

FIGURE 25.12 Broadbow, Inc. IFPS Screen Printout of Initial View

```
                              1          2          3          4          5
GOVERNMENT              20000.00   30000.00   25000.00   10000.00    7500.00
INVESTMENT             100000.00       0.00       0.00       0.00       0.00
PRICE                      20.00      20.00      20.00      20.00      20.00
SALES                  400000.00  600000.00  500000.00  200000.00  150000.00
COST OF GOODS SOLD     280000.00  420000.00  350000.00  140000.00  105000.00
GROSS MARGIN           120000.00  180000.00  150000.00   60000.00   45000.00
ADMIN EXPENSES          85000.00   90000.00   95000.00   50000.00   30000.00
BTNI                    35000.00   90000.00   55000.00   10000.00   15000.00
TAX                     14000.00   36000.00   22000.00    4000.00    6000.00
INCOME                  21000.00   54000.00   33000.00    6000.00    9000.00
INTERNAL R OF R                                    0.04       0.06       0.09
NET PRESENT VALUE      -82500.00  -45000.00  -25902.78  -23009.26  -19392.26

GOVERNMENT = 20000,30000,25000,10000,7500
INVESTMENT = 100000,0,0,0,0
PRICE = 20
SALES = (PRICE * GOVERNMENT)
COST OF GOODS SOLD = SALES * .7
GROSS MARGIN = SALES - COST OF GOODS SOLD
ADMIN EXPENSES = 85000, 90000, 95000, 50000, 30000
    Base Solution                       VIEW MODE          Model BOW.MOD
    View:  What_if     wIndows     Variables    Columns
           Set         Format      Analyze
```

FIGURE 25.13 Broadbow, Inc. IFPS Case 1 Solution

```
                          1          2          3          4          5
GOVERNMENT          20000.00   30000.00   25000.00   10000.00    7500.00
INVESTMENT         100000.00       0.00       0.00       0.00       0.00
PRICE                  22.00      22.00      22.00      22.00      22.00
    .
    .
INTERNAL R OF R                                 0.16       0.19       0.21
NET PRESENT VALUE  -76500.00  -31500.00   -7194.44   -2564.81    2137.15

GOVERNMENT  = 20000,30000,25000,10000,7500
INVESTMENT  = 100000,0,0,0,0
PRICE = 20
  Case
PRICE = 22

   What If Solution                     VIEW MODE            Model BOW.MOD
What_if:  Base     Get          Name          Save
          solVe    gOal_seek    Edit_case     Update
```

isfies the goal for this adjustment variable. Broadbow's goal is a 20-percent internal rate of return on the project—that is, a 20-percent IRR or a net present value of zero at the end of year 5. The variable to be changed is Price. However, we want the price to be the same for the entire life of the contract. To make the price constant, we edit the case as illustrated in figure 25.14, entering the goal as NET PRESENT VALUE [5] = 0 and the adjustment variable as PRICE [1]. Solving this gives a price of $21.80. The "gOal_seek" option saves time by avoiding the trial-and-error method.

To compute the price required for a 20-percent rate of return assuming the government purchases the maximum amount, we merely change the case by inserting the higher government demand and solve the same "gOal_seek" criteria. Figure 25.15 shows the modified case and the result.

Comparing Spreadsheets and Modeling Software

Both electronic spreadsheets and financial modeling software are useful as decision support systems. In many cases they can be used interchangeably; whether one uses a spreadsheet or a financial model is largely a matter of personal choice. Yet there are differences between them. Some of the more important ones include the following:

1. Modeling software generally requires more initial learning before the user can build a model and get it to run. The user must understand the logic of the model, be able to key it into IFPS/Personal or other software, and debug it before she or he can see what the model looks like. With a spreadsheet the user can see the solution develop as the logic and the model are created.

FIGURE 25.14 Broadbow, Inc. IFPS Goal Seeking Solution at *Minimum* Demand

```
                          1           2           3           4           5
GOVERNMENT         20000.00    30000.00    25000.00    10000.00     7500.00
INVESTMENT        100000.00        0.00        0.00        0.00        0.00
PRICE                 21.80       21.80       21.80       21.80       21.80
   .
   .
   .
INTERNAL R OF R                                  0.14        0.17        0.20
NET PRESENT VALUE -77095.60   -32840.09    -9051.55    -4594.26        0.00
─────────────────────────────────────────────────────────────────────────────
GOVERNMENT = 20000,30000,25000,10000,7500
INVESTMENT = 100000,0,0,0,0
PRICE = 20
 Case
PRICE = 20, PREVIOUS * 1

   Goal Seek Solution              VIEW MODE         Model BOW.MOD
Goal:   NET PRESENT VALUE [5] = 0
Adjust: PRICE [1]
```

FIGURE 25.15 Broadbow, Inc. IFPS Goal Seeking Solution at *Maximum* Demand

```
                          1           2           3           4           5
GOVERNMENT         30000.00    40000.00    25000.00    10000.00     7500.00
INVESTMENT        100000.00        0.00        0.00        0.00        0.00
PRICE                 17.37       17.37       17.37       17.37       17.37
   .
   .
   .
INTERNAL R OF R                                  0.08        0.18        0.19        0.20
NET PRESENT VALUE -64356.25   -15029.87    -2793.90    -2187.47       -0.00
─────────────────────────────────────────────────────────────────────────────
GOVERNMENT = 20000,30000,25000,10000,7500
INVESTMENT = 100000,0,0,0,0
PRICE = 20
 Case
PRICE = 20, PREVIOUS * 1
GOVERNMENT = 30000,40000,25000,10000,7500

   Goal Seek Solution              VIEW MODE         Model BOW.MOD
Goal:   NET PRESENT VALUE [5] = 0
Adjust: PRICE [1]
```

2. Spreadsheets provide immediate feedback that is often useful in identifying logic and keying errors. When using a financial model, these errors are frequently not detected until the compilation process.
3. Goal optimization options available with the modeling software are very powerful. They cut down on or eliminate the trial and error that is so often associated with a goal optimization solution on a spreadsheet.
4. Models can be modified more easily using a financial model than using a spreadsheet. Modeling software presents the entire model in English-like words in one section, whereas the formulas for a spreadsheet are hidden in the cells and are spread out over the entire worksheet. When modifying a spreadsheet, it is difficult to know when all the cells have been updated.
5. Modeling software, such as IFPS/Personal, allows the user to explicitly include uncertainty in the definition of any variable. Risk analysis does not predict the future, but it is helpful in understanding and dealing with uncertainty. Either deterministic solutions or probabilistic (Monte Carlo) solutions may be obtained on IFPS. This type of analysis is not available on spreadsheets.
6. The macro feature built into many spreadsheets allows them to be used in a program mode. A macro is a pseudo-program that can control input, processing, output, and other interactions with the user. This is one of the most powerful features of spreadsheet software and one that is not available with modeling software.

EXPERT SYSTEMS

General Concepts

An expert system is a computer program that utilizes knowledge generally possessed by an expert to solve problems in a specific domain. It is designed to emulate the knowledge and problem-solving techniques of the human expert. Unlike traditional programing techniques, the expert system has the ability to solve problems involving uncertainties. It can store many decision rules and draw conclusions from the manipulation of these rules.

Expert systems are useful only in selected and well-defined problem areas. The defined subject area for any expert system is called its *problem domain*. Problems adaptable to expert systems should contain the following characteristics:

1. The problem requires a solution that cannot be solved using algorithms or well-structured techniques.
2. The problem requires the decision maker to use judgment, rules, and experience to solve the problem.
3. The problem is in a narrowly defined area that has practical applications.
4. Expertise in the subject area is difficult to acquire by the general public, and the area contains a small number of experts that are recognized as such.
5. The experts are significantly better at making correct decisions than the general public or others that might be faced with the problem.

An expert system consists of two parts: a knowledge base and an inference engine. The **knowledge base** stores the knowledge accumulated to solve the problem domain. It is composed of rules, truths, and common relationships that help solve the problem. The **inference engine** is the motor of the system. It is a shell that requests data from the user, manipulates the knowledge base, and provides a recommendation back to the user to solve a specific problem. Figure 25.16 illustrates these parts and their relationship to the user.

Knowledge engineers, who are trained to encode the decision rules of an expert, develop the knowledge base. The knowledge engineer is responsible for adequately "capturing the mind" of the expert to create a useful expert system. This task proves to be difficult and time consuming. The complexity of capturing and encoding expertise is a major factor behind the enormous expense of developing the expert system.

Once the knowledge base is completed, the knowledge engineer tests the expert system for accuracy. Typically, the expert system is given actual problems, and its performance and recommendations are compared to those of the human expert.

An expert system may be used for consultation or training. For either purpose it works the same way. The inference engine asks questions of the user to gather data on the current problem. To determine which decision rule applies, the inference engine traces through the rules and asks the user various questions to verify facts. The inference engine then uses the user's responses to determine which rules are satisfied and evaluates the effect of the decision rules on possible recommendations.

An important feature of the expert system is its ability to explain the reasons for recommending a solution or for asking a particular question. The expert system can duplicate the logic path it followed when reaching its conclusion or asking a question. This teaches the user the rules incorporated in the decision process, and it allows the knowledge engineer to trace the logic path when debugging the system during the development phase.

Applications

The expert system is a powerful tool with a promising future in business. It represents a new approach to problem solving that is still largely unexplored. Of notable absence in the expert systems field are expert systems that examine functions related to cost or management accounting. Currently, no expert systems exist in development or practice within the cost accounting area.

FIGURE 25.16

Expert System Concepts

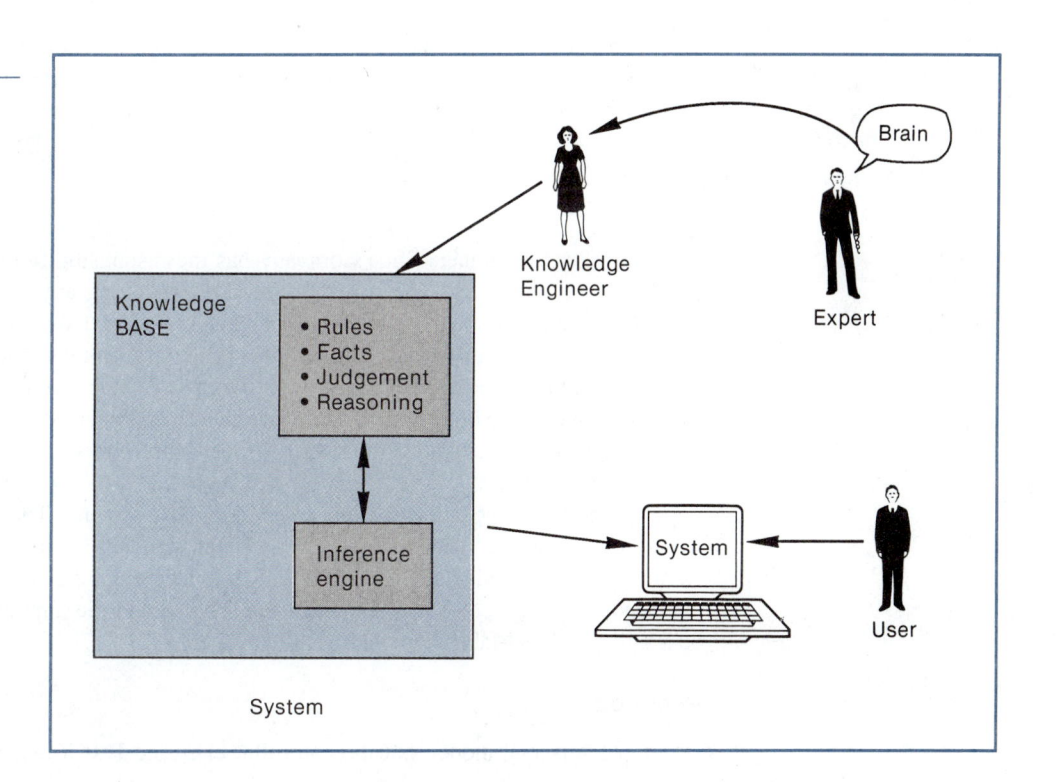

Several reasons explain the lack of expert systems in the cost accounting area. First, cost accounting is a field in which most of the problems can be solved using algorithms. There are only a limited number of problems related to cost accounting (i.e., planning and forecasting) that require expert knowledge. Second, until recently most expert systems were unavailable to most businesses and accountants. Because the science is new, the technology has been difficult to acquire and adapt to a variety of applications. As the technology becomes available and as theories of problem solving become refined, more and more applications will be developed. Finally, the development costs of expert systems are extremely high and may prevent use of these systems to any great extent. The majority of the current applications were funded and developed by university research centers. Nevertheless, new generalized expert system packages for microcomputers are now being marketed. As costs drop, cost accounting expert systems may be developed.

SOFTWARE EVALUATION

From a cost accountant's perspective, the most important criteria in evaluating computer software are its ease of use and the relevance of the information it provides. How easy a software package is to use can easily be determined by working with it for a short period of time. Weaknesses and problems show up quite quickly. Relevant information is determined by the decision or decisions to which the output information relates. The analysis proceeds as follows:

1. Identify the type of decisions that the user must make.
2. Identify the information that will make a difference to the decision.
3. Compare the information that the system provides with the information that is needed. Any differences require a change, update, or modification in the system.

From a systems perspective, there are many other factors that are relevant in evaluating software, such as speed of processing, memory requirements, and ease of maintenance. Cost accountants generally rely on systems personnel to consider these factors.

SELF STUDY PROBLEM

The controller for Runners Shoe Company has the responsibility to set the overhead application rate each year. He also is responsible for explaining any overhead variances.

The controller would like to have a financial model that will compute a two-way, three-way, and four-way analysis of over- or underapplied overhead. The items that should be entered into the model are actual fixed overhead, actual total variable overhead, budgeted fixed overhead, budgeted variable overhead per direct-labor hour, overhead application rate per direct-labor hour, number of direct-labor hours worked, and number of shoes manufactured.

Runners Shoe Company uses a standard cost system. The standard is currently 2 direct-labor hours per shoe. However, a tighter standard is under consideration. For the coming year, the budgeted fixed overhead is expected to be $50,000, budgeted variable overhead is expected to be $5 per direct-labor hour, and the application rate is expected to be $5.40 per direct-labor hour.

Required

Develop a financial model that the controller can use. Test it using the following assumptions:

1. Assume that the company continues to use the existing standard and projections outlined previously. Also assume the following:

- Actual fixed overhead, $47,640
- Actual variable overhead, $619,000
- Direct-labor hours worked, 131,000
- Shoes manufactured, 63,000

2. Assume all of the preceding data except that the standard is changed to 1.9 direct-labor hours per shoe. How do the variances change under the new standard?

Solution to the Self-Study Problem, Assumption 1

```
                RUNNERS SHOE COMPANY
              VARIANCE ANALYSIS, ASSUMPTION 1

Enter the data requested in the unprotected cells and press F9.

Actual fixed overhead:                                    $47,640
Actual total variable overhead:                          $619,000
Budgeted fixed overhead:                                 $ 50,000
Budgeted variable overhead per direct-labor hour:           $5.00
Overhead application rate per direct-labor hour:            $5.40
Direct-labor hours worked:                                131,000
Shoes manufactured:                                        63,000

VARIANCE ANALYSIS:
    Favorable (Unfavorable)

                    Two-Way:
            Controllable        $ 13,360
            Volume                   400

            Total               $ 13,760

                   Three-Way:
            Spending            $ 38,360
            Efficiency           (25,000)
            Volume                   400

            Total               $ 13,760

                    Four-Way:
            Fixed spending       $2,360
            Variable spending    36,000
            Efficiency          (25,000)
            Volume                  400

            Total               $ 13,760
```

Formulas for Self-Study Problem, Assumption 1

```
         A           B           C           D           E           F

 1                              RUNNERS SHOE COMPANY
 2                              VARIANCE ANALYSIS
 3
 4  Enter the data requested in the unprotected cells and press F9.
 5
 6  Actual fixed overhead:                                    $47,640
 7  Actual total variable overhead:                          $619,000
 8  Budgeted fixed overhead:                                  $50,000
 9  Budgeted variable overhead per direct-labor hour:           $5.00
10  Overhead application rate per direct-labor hour:            $5.40
11  Direct-labor hours worked:                                131,000
12  Shoes manufactured:                                        63,000
13
14  VARIANCE ANALYSIS:
15     Favorable (Unfavorable)

                              Two-Way:
          Controllable        +F8+(F9*(F12*2))-(F6+F7)
          Volume              +F10*(F12*2)-(F8+(F9*(F12*2)))

          Total               @SUM(F18..F20)

                              Three-Way:
          Spending            (F8+(F9*F11))-(F6+F7)
          Efficiency          +F8+(F9*(F12*2))-(F8+(F9*F11))
          Volume              +F10*(F12*2)-(F8+(F9*(F12*2)))

          Total               @SUM(F24..F27)

                              Four-Way
          Fixed Spending      +F8-F6
          Variable Spending   (+F9*F11)-F7
          Efficiency          +F8+(F9*(F12*2))-(F8+(F9*F11))
          Volume              +F10*(F12*2)-(F8+(F9*(F12*2)))

          Total               @SUM(F31..F35)
```

Solution to the Self-Study Problem, Assumption 2

```
              RUNNERS SHOE COMPANY
            VARIANCE ANALYSIS, ASSUMPTION 2

Enter the data requested in the unprotected cells and press F9.

Actual fixed overhead:                                $47,640
Actual total variable overhead:                      $619,000
Budgeted fixed overhead:                              $50,000
Budgeted variable overhead per direct-labor hour:       $5.00
Overhead application rate per direct-labor hour:        $5.40
Direct-labor hours worked:                            131,000
Shoes manufactured:                                    63,000

VARIANCE ANALYSIS:
    Favorable (Unfavorable)

                    Two-Way:
        Controllable            ($18,140)
        Volume                    (2,120)

            Total               ($20,260)

                   Three-Way:
        Spending                 $38,360
        Efficiency               (56,500)
        Volume                    (2,120)

            Total               ($20,260)

                    Four-Way:
        Fixed Spending            $2,360
        Variable Spending         36,000
        Efficiency               (56,500)
        Volume                    (2,120)

            Total               ($20,260)
```

SUGGESTED READINGS

Clifford, Jim; Jarke, Matthias; and Vassiliou, Yannis. "A Short Introduction to Expert Systems." *IEEE Database Engineering Bulletin* 8 (December 1983): 3–16.

Holsapple, Clyde W., and Whinston, Andrew B. *Business Expert Systems*. Homewood, Ill.: Dow-Jones Irwin, 1987.

Leigh, William E., and Doherty, Michael E. *Decision Support and Expert Systems* Cincinnatti, OH.: South-Western Publishing Company, 1986.

Michaelsen, Robert, and Michie, Donald. "Expert Systems in Business." *Datamation* 29 (November 1983): 240–246.

"NAA Issues SMA 1D: The Common Body of Knowledge for Management Accountants." *Management Accounting* 68 (August 1986): 56–61.

Shurkin, Joel N. "Expert Systems: The Practical Face of Artificial Intelligence." 86 *Technology Review* (November–December 1983): 72–78.

DISCUSSION QUESTIONS

Q25–1. What is the difference between a compiler and an interpreter?

Q25–2. What are the identifying characteristics of a decision support system?

Q25–3. Why are application programs not considered to be decision support systems?

Q25–4. What is the difference between the general definition of a data base used by most people and the definition used when discussing a data-base management system?

Q25–5. What are the responsibilities of a data-base administrator?

Q25–6. What is a data-base management system?

Q25–7. Describe a relational data base.

Q25–8. How do electronic spreadsheets differ from modeling software?

Q25–9. Is an electronic spreadsheet a decision support system? Explain.

Q25–10. Is financial modeling software a decision support system? Explain.

Q25–11. What is an expert system?

Q25–12. What type of problems are adaptable to expert systems?

Q25–13. Identify and distinguish between the knowledge base and the inference engine of an expert system.

Q25–14. What part does a knowledge engineer play in the development of an expert system?

Q25–15. Why are there not more expert systems in the cost accounting area?

CASES

C25–1. Analyzing the Impact of Inventory Turnover on Short Term Cash Needs Holly, Inc. has been in business for only three years. Summarized financial statements for 19x1 follow. This past year has been Holly's best year yet, as marketing, production, and management finally seem to be working together.

During a recent budget session for 19X2, the financial vice president indicated that the company was going to have serious cash flow problems. She said it would either have to increase its short-term notes payable or considerably improve inventory turnover.

Sales are expected to increase 60 percent over 19X1 levels. Gross margin percentage and income tax rates are expected to remain constant. Other operating expenses are expected to increase by 10 percent over 19X1 costs.

Holly, Inc. makes all sales on account, with payment due in thirty days. Inventory is manufactured internally. A just-in-time inventory system is used for raw materials. Essentially, all production costs are due within thirty days. Holly, Inc. has just adopted a policy of maintaining a cash balance equal to twice the expected balance in accounts payable.

Property, plant, and equipment originally cost $100,000 and are being depreciated using the straight-line method over ten years. Bonds are not due for twelve more years.

Holly, Incorporated
Income Statement
December 31, 19X1

Sales	$500,000
Cost of goods sold (76%)	380,000
Gross margin	120,000
Other expenses	70,000
Before-tax net income	50,000
Taxes (40%)	20,000
Net income	$ 30,000

Balance Sheet
December 31, 19X1

Assets

Cash	$ 50,000
Accounts receivable	41,670
Inventory	95,000
Property, plant, and equipment (net)	70,000
Total assets	$256,670

Liabilities

Accounts payable	31,500
Notes payable	47,000
Bonds payable	50,000
Total liabilities	128,500

Owners' Equity

Common stock	$60,000	
Retained earnings	68,170	
Total owners' equity		128,170
Total liabilities and owners' equity		$256,670

Assume a 360 day year and that sales and expenses occur uniformly throughout the year.

Required

Develop a financial model of the company's financial statements and use it to answer the following questions. Assume a 360 day year and that sales and expenses occur evenly throughout the year.

1. Assuming Holly, Inc. maintains the same inventory turnover (four times per year), how much will notes payable have to increase?

2. Assuming Holly, Inc. is not able to borrow any additional money, how many times will inventory have to turn over in the coming year?
3. Suppose the company is able to borrow $20,000. What inventory turnover is required in 19X2 to meet projected demands?

C25–2. Price and Cost Changes—Their Impact on Monthly Cash Flow Racer Bikes, Inc. manufactures racing bikes. Sales fluctuate during the year, with peak demand occurring in the fall, when retail stores buy for Christmas, and in the spring in preparation for the summer season. January 1, 19X5, balances in key accounts are:

Cash	$16,000
Accounts receivable	14,700
Raw material inventory	9,000 (150 units @ $60)
Accounts payable	27,000
Finished-goods inventory	24,000 (120 bicycles)

The standard cost to manufacture one racing bike is $200. All manufacturing costs require a cash flow expenditure because the company occupies a rented building and each employee is required to provide his or her own tools. Therefore, Racer Bikes, Inc. has no depreciation of property, plant, or equipment.

Direct materials	$ 60.00
Direct labor	100.00
Factory overhead	40.00
Total	$200.00

The company wants to have in raw materials and finished-goods inventories at the end of each month 150 percent of the following month's expected demand. Other relevant information include the following:

1. Sales price per unit is expected to be $350 per unit.

Racer Bikes, Inc.
Projected Unit Sales—19X5

January	80
February	90
March	120
April	150
May	160
June	100
July	60
August	80
September	140
October	120
November	70
December	60
Total	1,230

2. Payment for 30 percent of sales is received in the month of sale. The remainder is received the following month.
3. Cash is paid for all raw materials at the time of purchase. Half of the conversion costs are paid in the month incurred and half the following month.
4. Variable selling and administrative expenses are 6 percent of sales and are paid as incurred. Fixed selling and administrative expenses are $2,500 per month.
5. No taxes will need to be paid because of an operating loss carryforward.
6. A $40,000 one-year note with interest at 18 percent is due on June 15, 19X5.

7. Projections for January 19X6 include sales of 80 bicycles and production of 95 bicycles

8. Assume the standard costs projected for 19X5 are accurate projections of actual costs incurred.

Required

Racer Bikes, Inc. wants to know month-by-month the expected cash flows and the month-end cash balance (shortage). It would also like to evaluate *(a)* the effect of a 10-percent increase in its sales price, *(b)* the effect of a 15-percent increase in direct-labor costs, and *(c)* the effect of both *(a)* and *(b)* combined on cash flows. Develop a financial model that will provide the information requested.

C25–3. Selecting Optimum Pricing and Advertising Strategies

Lo-Babe, Inc. is considering the acquisition of a new product patent at the cost of $100,000. The patent is expected to have a five-year useful life. The cost would be amortized using straight-line depreciation over five years, and the patent has zero residual value.

The product to be developed would be called Baby-Lo. Expected annual sales in units at various prices as well as at various levels of advertising are as follows:

Expected Unit Sales Per Year

Price	Probability Estimate	Advertising Expenditure $20,000	$50,000	$100,000
$10/unit	20%	5,000 units	7,000 units	11,000 units
	50%	10,000 units	16,000 units	23,000 units
	30%	13,000 units	19,000 units	28,000 units
$7.50/unit	25%	12,000 units	15,000 units	27,000 units
	50%	17,000 units	23,000 units	31,000 units
	25%	21,000 units	27,000 units	38,000 units
$4.00/unit	40%	35,000 units	55,000 units	87,000 units
	50%	51,000 units	69,000 units	103,000 units
	10%	64,000 units	81,000 units	130,000 units

Annual fixed costs associated with the manufacture and sale of the product are $20,000 per year. Variable manufacturing costs are $2.00 per unit and variable selling costs are 10 percent of the sales price. All costs associated with the product, except the initial patent, require out-of-pocket expenditures in the year of sale.

Required

Assuming Lo-babe, Inc. wants a 20-percent internal rate of return, what is the optimal strategy it should follow? Develop a financial model and perform the requested analysis.

C25–4. Pricing to Yield a Desired Internal Rate of Return

Billie Joe has always wanted to be a truck driver. His father owns and operates four trucks and trailers. As a high school graduation present Mr. Joe plans to sell one of the truck and trailer sets to Billie Joe.

Mr. Joe thinks that if Billie pays for the truck and trailer set he will take better care of it and that Billie will become more independent and self-reliant. However, he wants to set the price so that it will return Billie Joe 30 percent after tax.

Currently, each truck and trailer set generates $45,000 of revenue per year. This is expected to increase 5 percent each year with inflation. Variable operating expenses other than repairs are expected to be 45 percent of revenues. Fixed expenses (requiring a cash expenditure) are projected at $5,000 per year. Repairs are expected to be 15 percent of revenue in the first year and 16 percent in the second year, and will continue to increase by 1 percent each year for the five years of remaining life.

Because this is a related-party transaction, Billie Joe must use his father's basis for tax purposes. For the truck and trailer set, the father's records show a book value of $60,000, with five years remaining and the straight-line depreciation method used. Billie Joe's expected marginal tax rate is 20 percent.

Required

Develop a financial model to answer the following questions.

1. What price should Mr. Joe charge Billie for the truck and trailer set?
2. Revenue generated by the truck and trailer is one of the key variables in determining a fair price. Suppose that the revenues are only $40,000 in the first year but that they increase with inflation over the useful life. What would be a fair price for the truck and trailer?
3. Repairs are another key variable. Suppose that revenues are as originally projected, but repairs increase by 3 percent rather than 1 percent each year. What would be a fair price for the truck and trailer?

C25-5. Sensitivity Analysis Using Economic Order Quantity

Warehouse, Inc. wants to develop an economic order quantity (EOQ) model that it can use on any product in inventory. Any input value should be able to be changed to perform sensitivity analysis on the results.

The output of the model should include economic order quantity, safety stock, and reorder point.

Input values should include annual demand, working days per year, maximum lead time, normal lead time, unit cost, inventory carrying cost as a percent of unit cost, and order cost. Use the following data for the input values:

Annual demand	20,000 units
Working days per year	250 days
Maximum lead time	15 days
Normal lead time	10 days
Unit cost	$5
Carrying cost percentage	12%
Order cost	$1,000

Required

1. Prepare the inventory model and the base solution for the data given.
2. How does the economic order quantity change when demand increases to 25,000 units and order cost to $1,300?
3. How does safety stock change when maximum lead time goes to 20 days and normal lead time to 12 days, assuming 25,000 unit demand per year?

C25-6. Projecting and Analyzing Cash Flow Projections

B&B Associates owns and manages apartment buildings. The owners are concerned about future cash flows and profitability under different assumptions about increases in rent revenue and operating expenses.

A current balance sheet and an income statement for the most recent year are provided below. Additional information is provided as follows:

1. The note receivable and accrued interest from Brown is due in the first month of 19X1. This is the balance on an installment sale of a previously owned apartment

building. The portion of the unrealized gain associated with the Brown note is also recognized in year 1.

2. The Skankey note pays $2,400 annually as an interest-only payment. The principal and accrued interest reported on the balance sheet are due in January 19X4. This also is the balance of an installment sale on a previously owned apartment building. The portion of the unrealized gain associated with the Skankey note is recognized in year 4.

3. The buildings are being depreciated over a 15-year life using ACRS. Depreciation for years 1 through 4 is $11,670, for years 5 through 10 is $9,725, and the balance is deductible in year 11.

4. There are four mortgages. The annual payment, interest rate, remaining life, and balance due are shown in the supporting schedules.

5. The notes and interest payable are all due in January 19X1.

6. Deposits are expected to remain constant.

B&B Associates
Balance Sheet
December 31, 19X0

ASSETS

Cash		$ 3,157
Notes receivable		23,841
Total current assets		26,998
Buildings	$194,490	
Less: Accumulated depreciation	(87,520)	
Net book value		106,970
Land		30,000
Total assets		$163,968

LIABILITIES

Unrealized gain	$ 21,694	
Mortgages	155,272	
Notes and interest payable	5,270	
Deposits	1,400	
Total liabilities		183,636

OWNERS' EQUITY

Owner capital		(19,668)
Total liabilities & owners' equity		$163,968

B&B Associates
Income Statement
Year Ending December 31, 19X0

REVENUES

Rental		$25,670
Interest		3,869
Realized gain—Installment sales		5,068
Total revenues		34,607

EXPENSES

Interest	$18,233	
Depreciation	13,614	
Utilities	1,231	
Repairs/Supplies	853	
Insurance/Taxes	2,685	
Management/Professional fees	1,500	
Miscellaneous	88	
Total expenses		38,204
Net income (Loss)		$ (3,597)

**B&B Associates
Supporting Schedules
December 31, 19X0**

Notes Receivable:		
Brown	—Principal	$ 5,792
	—Accrued interest	140
Skankey	—Principal	16,362
	—Accrued interest	1,547
	Total	$ 23,841
Deposits:		
8 apts. @ $175 ea.		$ 1,400

Mortgages:

	Interest Rate	Annual Payment	Remaining Years	Balance
Herbert & Loan	(10¼%)	4,980	9.7	$29,709
Herbert & Loan	(10¼%)	4,620	9.3	26,835
Deseret Federal	(10½%)	6,420	14.7	47,159
American Savings	(8½%)	6,210	15.0	51,569
Total				$155,272

Notes Payable:	
Mark Brinkerhoff	5,156
Accrued interest	114
Total	$ 5,270
Unrealized Gain:	
($5,792 @ 100%) Brown	5,792
($16,362 @ 97.19%) Skankey	15,902
Total	$21,694

Required

Prepare a twelve-year financial model that the owners can use to determine annual cash flow and the year-end cash balance under the following assumptions:

1. Rental revenues and operating expenses, other than interest and depreciation, remain constant.
2. Rental revenues increase by 5 percent per year beginning in 19X1, and operating expenses, other than interest and depreciation, remain constant.
3. Rental revenues remain constant, and operating expenses, other than interest and depreciation, increase by 5 percent per year beginning in 19X1.

C25–7. Projecting and Analyzing Profit Projections Refer to the data provided in case 25.6 for B&B Associates.

Required

Prepare a twelve-year financial model that the owners can use to determine *annual profit* under each of the following assumptions:

1. Rental revenues and operating expenses, other than interest and depreciation, remain constant.
2. Rental revenues increase by 5 percent per year beginning in 19X1, and operating expenses, other than interest and depreciation, remain constant.

3. Rental revenues remain constant, and operating expenses, other than interest and depreciation, increase by 5 percent per year beginning in 19X1.

C25-8. Sensitivity Analysis on Product Profitability Soft Drink, Inc. manufactures and sells a lemonade-type drink in bottles. Sales during the most recent year were 600,000 bottles at $1.70 per bottle. Production capacity is 750,000 bottles per year.

Analysis of the cost data yielded the following:

Fixed costs:	Production	$127,000
	Administration	80,000
	Advertising	35,000
	Interest	30,000
Variable costs:	Labor	$0.36 per bottle
	Liquid materials	0.60 per bottle
	Bottle materials	0.15 per bottle

Mrs. Crawford, the president, thinks that profits are too low. She believes that the return on sales (ROS = profit before tax divided by sales) should be at least 10 percent.

Required

Assume that all items remain constant except for the one item under consideration. How much would that item need to be in order to provide the president's minimum 10-percent return on sales?

1. What sales price would be required to provide the 10-percent ROS?
2. What fixed administrative cost is required to yield the 10-percent ROS?
3. What *total* variable cost per unit will provide the 10-percent ROS?

C25-9. Decision Making using Spreadsheet Macros The manager of Stewart & James, an investment broker, is frequently asked to perform financial statement analysis. As he complained about the amount of computation required, you suggested he develop a spreadsheet macro that would prompt him on entering the relevant data and perform the required calculations. He liked the idea, but said he did not know anything about spreadsheets and had never heard of a spreadsheet macro.

To give him a sample of how it might work, you agreed to develop a "mini" version that will compute the following two ratios:

1. Current ratio (current assets / current liabilities)
2. Price earnings ratio (market price / earnings per share)

Required

Develop a program on an electronic spreadsheet using macros to do the financial analysis summarized above. Use a menu option and allow for looping so that the manager can perform several calculations without having to execute the program each time.

Use the following data to test your program:

Current assets	$25,000
Current liabilities	18,000
Market price per share	$100.00
Earnings per share	12.50

C25-10. Sensitivity Analysis Using a Learning Curve Prepare a financial model that can be used to evaluate the effect on the average cumulative unit production time (or cost) for varying amounts of *(a)* input quantity required to produce the first unit of output, *(b)* cumulative number of units produced, and *(c)* learning curve percentage.

The relevant formula is as follows:

$$y = ax^b$$

where: y = average cumulative unit production time (or cost)
a = production time (or cost) to produce the first unit
x = cumulative number of units produced
b = exponent reflecting the rate of learning, which is computed as

$$\frac{\log r}{\log 2}$$

where r is the learning rate as a percentage.

Required

1. Use the following data to check your model:

    Production cost is $50
    Cumulative units produced equal 7
    Learning curve is 80 percent

    What is the average cumulative unit production cost after the seventh unit?

2. Use the preceding data but change the learning curve percentage to 85 percent. Now what is the average cumulative unit production cost after the seventh unit?

Chapter 26

The Management Accounting Profession

Outline

DEFINITION AND OBJECTIVES OF MANAGEMENT ACCOUNTING
CHARACTERISTICS OF A PROFESSION
PROFESSIONAL EXAMINATIONS
Certificate in Management Accounting
  Content of the CMA Examination
  Examination Questions
Certified Public Accountant
  Content of the Uniform CPA Examination
  Examination Questions
CODE OF ETHICS
On-the-Job Experience
Continuing Education
SUMMARY
SUGGESTED READINGS
DISCUSSION QUESTIONS
CASES

By studying the previous chapters, you have covered the major concepts and procedures of cost accounting. The various chapters have emphasized cost finding for use in external financial reports and cost analysis for aiding management in planning, controlling, and decision making.

In this chapter a summary of the professional field of management accounting is presented. After you have completed this chapter, you should be able to:

1. define *management accounting* and state the major objectives of management accounting.
2. outline and describe the general characteristics of a profession.
3. delineate the key areas of the *Common Body of Knowledge for Management Accountants*.
4. distinguish between the CMA and CPA examinations and describe the content, role, and purpose of each.
5. explain the importance of codes of ethics and demonstrate an understanding of the *Standards of Ethical Conduct for Management Accountants*.
6. assess ethical situations and resolve ethical dilemmas.

DEFINITION AND OBJECTIVES OF MANAGEMENT ACCOUNTING

A review and reemphasis of the definition and objectives of management accounting is important to keep cost accounting in perspective. *Statement on Management Accounting (SMA) 1A* issued by the National Association of Accountants (NAA) sets forth the following definition of management accounting, as well as a brief explanation of the key terms in the definition:

Definition

Management accounting is the process of identification, measurement, accumulation, analysis, preparation, interpretation, and communication of financial information used by management to plan, evaluate, and control within an organization and to assure appropriate use of and accountability for its resources. Management accounting also comprises the preparation of financial reports for non-management groups such as shareholders, creditors, regulatory agencies, and tax authorities.

To facilitate comprehension, the most significant terms used in the definition are defined as follows:

Management accounting is the process of:

Identification—the recognition and evaluation of business transactions and other economic events for appropriate accounting action.

Measurement—the quantification, including estimates, of business transactions or other economic events that have occurred or may occur.

Accumulation—the disciplined and consistent approach to recording and classifying appropriate business transactions and other economic events.

Analysis—the determination of the reasons for, and the relationships of, the reported activity with other economic events and circumstances.

Preparation and Interpretation—the meaningful coordination of accounting and/or planning data to satisfy a need for information, presented in a logical format, and, if appropriate, including the conclusions drawn from those data.

Communication—the reporting of pertinent information to management and others for internal and external uses.

Management accounting is used by management to:

Plan—to gain an understanding of expected business transactions and other economic events and their impact on the organization.

Evaluate—to judge the implications of various past and/or future events.

Control—to ensure the integrity of financial information concerning an organization's activities or its resources.

Assure accountability—to implement the system of reporting that is closely aligned to organizational responsibilities and that contributes to the effective measurement of management performance

Many of the activities constituting the field of management accounting are interrelated and thus must be coordinated, ranked, and implemented by the management accountant in such a fashion as to meet the objectives of the organization as perceived by him or her. A major function of the management accountant is that of tailoring the application of the process to the organization so that the organization's objectives are achieved effectively.

The definition of management accounting in SMA 1A was further amplified by the NAA in a Statement of Objectives—SMA 1B. These objectives are illustrated in figure 26.1.

The statements of definition and objectives clearly indicate a broad spectrum of knowledge and responsibility for management accountants. Competent performance in the various areas of responsibility requires considerable training, education, and practical application. The knowledge that a practicing professional in management accounting must possess is extensive. The requirements that must be met to achieve recognition as a management accounting professional are being codified and refined at this time.

The remaining sections of this chapter will focus on the characteristics of a profession, and the present status of the management accounting profession as related to each characteristic will then be discussed.

CHARACTERISTICS OF A PROFESSION

Webster's dictionary defines a profession as "a calling requiring specialized knowledge and often long and intensive academic preparation." The "learned" professions, which include medicine, law, and, to an increasing extent, accounting generally involve the following characteristics:

1. *A common body of knowledge,* the acquisition of which usually involves years of intensive, formal education
2. *A rigorous examination* designed to determine whether a participant has the required level of understanding of the common body of knowledge

FIGURE 26.1 Objectives of Management Accounting

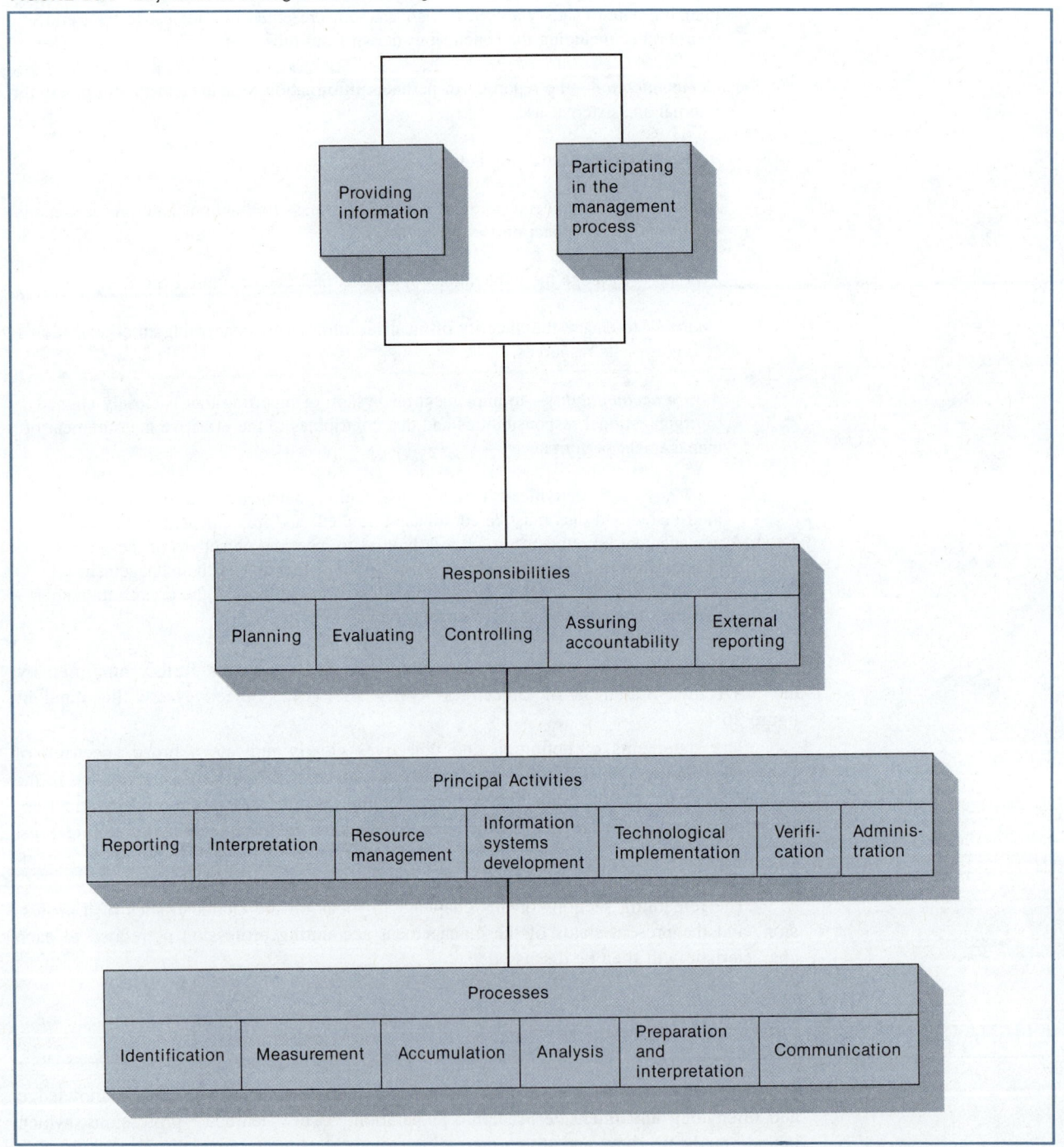

```
                    ┌─────────────┬──────────────┐
                    │ Providing   │ Participating│
                    │ information │ in the       │
                    │             │ management   │
                    │             │ process      │
                    └─────────────┴──────────────┘
                              │
          ┌───────────────────────────────────────┐
          │            Responsibilities           │
          ├────────┬─────────┬─────────┬──────────┬──────────┤
          │Planning│Evaluating│Controlling│Assuring│External │
          │        │          │           │account-│reporting│
          │        │          │           │ability │         │
          └────────┴─────────┴─────────┴──────────┴──────────┘
                              │
     ┌──────────────────────────────────────────────────────┐
     │              Principal Activities                    │
     ├─────────┬────────────┬─────────┬────────┬──────────┬─────┬──────┤
     │Reporting│Interpretation│Resource│Info.   │Techno-  │Verif│Admin.│
     │         │              │mgmt    │systems │logical  │ica- │      │
     │         │              │        │dev.    │impl.    │tion │      │
     └─────────┴────────────┴─────────┴────────┴──────────┴─────┴──────┘
                              │
     ┌──────────────────────────────────────────────────────┐
     │                   Processes                          │
     ├──────────────┬───────────┬────────────┬────────┬──────────────┬─────────────┤
     │Identification│Measurement│Accumulation│Analysis│Preparation   │Communication│
     │              │           │            │        │and           │             │
     │              │           │            │        │interpretation│             │
     └──────────────┴───────────┴────────────┴────────┴──────────────┴─────────────┘
```

3. *Adherence to a defined code of ethical behavior*
4. *On-the-job experience,* or apprenticeship, before formal recognition of full professional status
5. *Continued education* to retain professional status

The Common Body of Knowledge has been codified recently by the NAA in SMA 1D. We have referred to selected sections of this statement in several topic areas covered in previous chapters. SMA 1D categorized three core-of-knowledge areas, with detailed subcategories within each of the three core areas. These knowledge areas are presented in outline form in figure 26.2. A more thorough explanation can be obtained by reference to SMA 1D.

The knowledge areas identified in the *Common Body of Knowledge for Management Accountants* clearly indicate that a professional in the field must be trained and educated in the breadth and depth of accounting. In addition, the professional must be well grounded

FIGURE 26.2

Statement of Management Accounting 1D

I. Information and Decision Processes
   A. Management decision processes
      1. Repetitive
      2. Nonprogrammed
      3. Strategic
   B. Internal reporting
      1. Generating data
      2. Organizing and analyzing information
      3. Presenting and communicating information
   C. Financial planning and performance evaluation
      1. Forecasting and budgeting
      2. Analysis and evaluation

II. Accounting Principles and Functions
   A. Organization structure and management
      1. Structure and management of the accounting function
      2. Internal control
      3. Internal audit
   B. Accounting concepts and principles
      1. Nature and objectives of accounting
      2. Accounting practices

III. Entity Operations
   A. Principal entity operations
      1. Finance and investments
      2. Engineering and research and development
      3. Production and operations
      4. Sales and marketing
      5. Human resources
   B. Operating environment
      1. Legal environment
      2. Economic environment
      3. Ethical and social environment
   C. Taxation
      1. Taxation policies
      2. Structure and types of taxes
      3. Tax planning
   D. External reporting
      1. Reporting standards
      2. Information needs of user groups
   E. Information systems
      1. Systems analysis and design
      2. Data-base management
      3. Software applications
      4. Technological literacy
      5. Systems evaluation

in the functional areas of entity operations as well as in the environmental areas that affect the firm and individuals within the firm.

PROFESSIONAL EXAMINATIONS

There are several comprehensive examinations that relate to the various fields of accounting. The Certified Public Accountant (CPA) examination is most widely known and has been in existence for many years. Recently several additional examinations (and certificate programs) have been established. These examinations include the Certificate in Management Accounting (CMA), the Certified Internal Auditor (CIA), and Certified Data Processor (CDP). The following discussion will center on the CMA and CPA programs.

Certificate in Management Accounting

The Certificate in Management Accounting provides the professional designation for persons who follow careers in management accounting and financial management. Although there is no legal requirement to have a CMA in order to perform services as a management or cost accountant, employers prefer and some are beginning to require a CMA for those employed as management accountants. Academic institutions also recognize it as a professional designation.

The CMA examination is academically oriented; that is, the material tested on the CMA examination is best learned in an academic program, and performance on the exam does not improve with an extended period of time in practice. Therefore, an individual would be well advised to take the CMA examination as soon as possible after completing college. Many people fail to take it at that time because they intend to pursue a career in public accounting; that is a very short-term approach to developing a career, however. A majority of the people who begin their careers in public accounting eventually find themselves working in management, management accounting, or financial management. Passing the CMA examination early in one's career provides increased flexibility in selecting a career path.

To obtain a Certificate in Management Accounting, an individual must (a) pass all five parts of the examination within a consecutive three-year period and (b) complete two years of professional experience in management accounting within seven years after passing the examination. Full-time continuous experience at a level where judgments that employ the principles of management accounting are regularly made satisfies the professional experience requirement.

Content of the CMA Examination The National Association of Accountants (NAA) organized the Institute of Management Accounting (IMA) in 1972. It was recently redesignated as the Institute of Certified Management Accountants (ICMA). The institute's major function is to administer the CMA designation, which includes the preparation and grading of the CMA examination. An individual must be a member of the ICMA to sit for the CMA examination and to hold a Certificate in Management Accounting. Admission as a member of the institute requires the applicant to have a good moral character, to be employed or expect to be employed in management accounting, and to satisfy one of the following conditions:

1. Hold a baccalaureate degree from an accredited college or university. Application for membership can be made in the last term or semester, and permission will be granted to sit for the CMA examination pending receipt of the degree.

2. Obtain a satisfactory score on the Graduate Record Examination (GRE) or the Graduate Management Admissions Test (GMAT). The credentials committee of the institute makes the determination of what constitutes a satisfactory score.
3. Be a Certified Public Accountant or hold a comparable professional certification in a foreign country.

The examination is given semiannually in June and December in several major cities throughout the United States. An individual may select from among the announced locations the city in which he or she wants to sit for the examination.

The examination consists of the five following parts:

1. Economics and business finance
2. Organization and behavior, including ethical considerations
3. Public reporting standards, auditing, and taxes
4. Periodic reporting for internal and external purposes
5. Decision analysis, including modeling and information systems

The exam parts are scheduled consecutively over a 2½ day period, and each part is 3½ hours in length. Figure 26.3 lists some subtitles for each part of the exam to provide an idea of the concepts tested.

FIGURE 26.3

Content of Individual Parts of the CMA Examination

Part 1: Economics and Business Finance
  A. Enterprise economics—Microeconomics
  B. Institutional environment of business
  C. National and international economics
  D. Working and capital management
  E. Long-term finance and capital structure

Part 2: Organization and Behavior, including Ethical Considerations
  A. Organization theory and decision making
  B. Motivation and perception.
  C. Communication
  D. Behavioral science application in accounting
  E. Ethical consideration

Part 3: Public Reporting Standards, Auditing, and Taxes
  A. Reporting requirements
  B. Audit protection
  C. Tax accounting

Part 4: Periodic Reporting for Internal and External Purposes
  A. Concepts of information
  B. Basic financial statements
  C. Profit planning and budgetary controls
  D. Standard costs for manufacturing
  E. Analysis of accounts and statements

Part 5: Decision Analysis, including Modeling and Information Systems
  A. Fundamentals of the decision process
  B. Decision analysis, including Modeling and Information Systems
  C. Nature and techniques of model building
  D. Information systems and data processing

Parts may be taken in any combination and in any order as long as at least two parts are taken each time an individual sits for the examination until only one part remains. However, all parts must be passed within a consecutive three-year period. A minimum successful passing grade is 70 percent.

Examination Questions The types of questions included on the exam are objective questions, essay questions, and accounting problems. Between 10 to 15 percent of the questions for each part are multiple choice, except for part II, which is all essay. One difference between CMA exam questions and CPA exam questions is that the CMA questions are more analysis oriented. Essay questions and accounting problems are generally combined. As a result the questions frequently require mathematical computations, but they almost always require an analysis and interpretation of results as well.

An analysis of previous examinations can provide a good indication of topics covered and the amount of time allocated to them. Individual parts of the exam will be reviewed with respect to the cost accounting topics covered in each.

- *Part I—Economics and Business Finance:* Between 25 and 35 percent of this part of the exam is devoted to cost accounting. Topics that are most frequently tested include budgeting, cost-volume-profit analysis, differential cost analysis, cost of capital, and capital budgeting. Individual problems typically require thirty minutes to complete and focus on the effect of an event or decision alternative on a business organization.
- *Part II—Organization and Behavior:* The cost accounting topics in this section of the examination include performance analysis and behavioral considerations associated with budgeting, standard costing, cost allocation, and report content. These topics constitute about 30 to 35 percent of this part of the examination. Most are essay questions, with an estimated time of thirty minutes allotted for each.
- *Part III—Public Reporting Standards:* Usually there are no cost accounting topics covered on this part of the examination.
- *Part IV—Periodic Reporting for Internal and External Purposes:* Approximately 50 percent of this portion of the exam is on cost accounting topics. Recent examinations have had a set of multiple-choice questions as the first problem. The time allotted to this problem varies (as does the number of multiple-choice questions), but it ranges between twenty to forty minutes.

The remainder of the questions are accounting problems and essay questions. They vary in length and require between twenty to sixty minutes to finish. Frequently tested topics include budgeting, standard costing and variance analysis, performance analysis, and overhead allocation. Other topics in this part in recent years have included transfer pricing, direct costing versus absorption costing, process costing, capital budgeting, gross-profit analysis, and accounting for by-products and scrap.
- *Part V—Decision Analysis:* Depending on one's definition of cost accounting, this part of the exam may contain either a rather high or a low percentage of cost accounting topics. If cost accounting is defined broadly to include most quantitative techniques as well as the analysis and design of cost accounting systems, 70 to 80 percent of the exam relates to cost accounting. If the systems and quantitative techniques are excluded, only 30 to 40 percent is cost accounting.

Most of the questions are problem oriented and require some essay analysis of the results. The first problem is often a set of multiple-choice questions. Estimated time for all problems generally varies between twenty and forty minutes.

Cost accounting topics that are most frequently tested include capital budgeting, differential cost analysis, and product pricing. Each exam usually has one and sometimes two problems on systems analysis and design or computer data processing. Quantitative techniques that have been tested recently include linear programming, learning curves, economic order quantity, PERT/cost, probability analysis, simulation analysis, and regression analysis.

As you will notice from the preceding discussion, there are a few cost accounting topics that are tested in more than one part of the examination. Within the individual parts there are some topics that are tested so frequently that even though they appear in only one part of the exam, they should constitute a major part of the candidate's preparation time. These more important topics are the following:

1. Budgeting, including behavioral problems associated with budgets
2. Differential cost analysis
3. Standard costing and variance analysis
4. Performance analysis
5. Capital budgeting
6. Quantitative techniques
7. Systems design and report content

Certified Public Accountant

To be licensed as a certified public accountant (CPA), an individual must pass the Uniform CPA Examination and satisfy other state requirements with respect to residency, continuing education, and experience in the practice of public accounting under the direction of a licensed CPA. The license allows a person to perform accounting services for others. In most states it is a class B misdemeanor to offer accounting services to others without a license to practice. A common penalty for each offense is six months in the county jail, a $299 fine, or both.

Many states have recently adopted the policy of providing a CPA Certificate upon successful completion of the Uniform CPA Examination. Holders of a CPA Certificate can identify themselves as CPAs but are not allowed to offer accounting services by themselves. They must work under the direction of someone else who has a license to practice.

Passing the Uniform CPA Examination and being able to identify oneself as a CPA is a major accomplishment. In the next section we identify the content of the Uniform CPA examination with special emphasis on the cost and managerial accounting concepts that are frequently tested.

Content of the Uniform CPA Examination The Uniform CPA Examination is prepared by the board of examiners of the American Institute of Certified Public Accountants (AICPA). All states use the same examination and offer it at the same time. It is given twice each year, in early November and early May.

Questions for the examination come from several sources. A substantial portion of the examination is prepared by the staff of the AICPA examination division. Consultants, who are usually educators, are frequently asked to develop questions in specified areas or on designated topics. However, anyone can submit questions for use in the examination, and many people do. Contributions not used in the current examination are stockpiled for use in future examinations.

The examination is divided into five parts. The title of each part, the day on which it is offered, and the time allocation is shown in figure 26.4. Notice that the entire exam is given in 2½ days, for a total of 19½ hours. In addition, most states have an ethics examination that takes 2 to 2½ hours on Wednesday morning. Thus it is a long and grueling examination.

FIGURE 26.4

Parts of the Uniform CPA Examination

Part	Day	Time	Total Hours
Accounting Practice, Part I	Wednesday	1:30 P.M.–6:00 P.M.	4½
Auditing	Thursday	8:30 A.M.–12:00 noon	3½
Accounting Practice, Part II	Thursday	1:30 P.M.–6:00 P.M.	4½
Business Law	Friday	8:30 A.M.–12:00 noon	3½
Accounting Theory	Friday	1:30 P.M.–5:00 P.M.	3½
			19½

The accounting practice portion of the examination has two parts that are combined for grading and reporting purposes, making a total of four parts on the uniform examination. Each part is worth 100 points, and 75 points are required for a passing score. Cost accounting is covered in the accounting practice and theory sections of the examination; both parts I and II of accounting practice have a substantial portion devoted to cost accounting.

On September 25, 1984, the board of examiners of the AICPA adopted "Revised Content Specification Outlines for the Uniform Certified Public Accountant Examination," to be effective May 1986. Figures 26.5 and 26.6 show the content specifications for the practice and theory portions of the examination. Included in each outline is a percentage breakdown by topic area of the 100 points available for each part. Notice that 10 percent of each part is devoted to the cost accounting topics "Cost Accumulation, Planning, and Control."

Figure 26.7 shows the topics listed under the "Cost Accumulation, Planning, and Control" section in detail. The topics are the same for both the accounting practice and theory sections of the examination. In fact, most topics under accounting practice and

FIGURE 26.5

Content Specification Outline for the Uniform CPA Examination

Accounting Practice

I. Presentation of financial statements or worksheets (15%)

II. Measurement, valuation, realization, and presentation of assets in conformity with generally accepted accounting principles (10%)

III. Valuation, recognition, and presentation of liabilities in conformity with generally accepted accounting principles (10%)

IV. Ownership structure, presentation, and valuation of equity accounts in conformity with generally accepted accounting principles (5%)

V. Measurement and presentation of income and expense items, their relationship to matching and periodicity, and their relationship to generally accepted accounting principles (15%)

VI. Other financial topics (5%)

VII. Cost accumulation, planning, and control (10%)

VIII. Not-for-profit and governmental accounting (10%)

IX. Federal taxation—individuals, estates, and trusts (10%)

X. Federal taxation—corporations, partnerships, and exempt organizations (10%)

FIGURE 26.6

Content Specification Outline for the Uniform CPA Examination

Accounting Theory

I. General concepts, principles, terminology, environment, and other professional standards (15%)

II. Measurement, valuation, realization, and presentation of assets in conformity with generally accepted accounting principles (15%)

III. Valuation, recognition, and presentation of liabilities in conformity with generally accepted accounting principles (10%)

IV. Ownership structure, presentation, and valuation of equity accounts in conformity with generally accepted accounting principles (5%)

V. Measurement and presentation of income and expense items, their relationship to matching and periodicity, and their relationship to generally accepted accounting principles (20%)

VI. Other financial topics (15%)

VII. Cost accumulation, planning, and control (10%)

VIII. Not-for-profit and governmental accounting (10%)

theory are the same except for federal income taxes, which is omitted from the accounting theory section. Therefore, study for the theory and practice sections should be done simultaneously. An adequate study of the theory behind a concept as well as its application to accounting problems should prepare an individual for both sections of the examination.

FIGURE 26.7

Detailed Content of Cost Accumulation, Planning, and Control Topics on the Uniform CPA Examination

A. Nature of cost elements
   1. Direct materials
   2. Direct labor
   3. Overhead
B. Process costing and job-order costing
C. Standard costing
D. Joint and by-product costing, spoilage, waste, and scrap
E. Absorption and variance costing
F. Budgeting and flexible budgeting
G. Breakeven and cost-volume-profit analysis
H. Capital budgeting techniques
   1. Net present value
   2. Internal rate of return
   3. Payback period
   4. Accounting rate of return
I. Performance analysis
   1. Return on investment
   2. Residual income
   3. Controllable revenue and costs
J. Other
   1. Regression and correlation analysis
   2. Economic order quantity
   3. Probability analysis
   4. Variance analysis
   5. Gross profit analysis
   6. Differential cost analysis
   7. Product pricing

PART FIVE: DECISION ANALYSIS

Examination Questions There are various types of questions on the CPA examination, including accounting problems, multiple-choice questions, and essay questions. Accounting practice parts I and II contain problems and multiple-choice questions; the theory portion has multiple-choice questions and essay problems. Usually each section of the examination is composed of approximately 40 percent objective questions and 60 percent problems or essay questions.

By studying previous examinations, a candidate can get a fairly good idea of the type of questions that will be asked and the topics that are most frequently tested. Cost accounting topics are generally as follows:

- *Accounting Practice I*—A set of twenty objective questions covering both managerial accounting and quantitative methods. The estimated time is between forty-five and fifty-five minutes, or
- *Accounting Practice II*—A major problem on a cost accounting topic. The estimated time is between forty-five and fifty-five minutes, and
- *Accounting Theory*—Several objective questions that may be grouped separately as a small problem or combined with other topics to form a large problem. Regardless of the way the section is presented, about thirty to forty minutes is allocated to objective questions on managerial accounting and quantitative methods. In addition, there may be one essay question on a cost accounting topic. Historically, one such question has been included about half the time, and fifteen to thirty minutes have been allocated for it.

Figure 26.8 shows the topic frequency within the cost accounting portions of the examination. As you can see, some topics are given rather heavy emphasis. Process costing, standard costing, and variance analysis are tested most often—a combined total of approximately 41 percent of the questions are in these areas. The nature of cost elements,

FIGURE 26.8

Cost Accounting—Topic Frequency on CPA Examination

Cost Accumulation, Planning, and Control Topic Areas	Percentage of Cost Accounting Time Allocated to Each Exam Topic Area[a]
Nature of cost elements	15%
Job-order costing	5
Process costing	10
Standard costing and variance analysis	11
Joint costing, by-product costing, spoilage, and scrap	7
Absorption and direct costing	7
Transfer pricing and product pricing	6
Budgeting and flexible budgeting	7
Breakeven and cost-volume-profit analysis	7
Decision analysis and quantitative techniques	10
Capital budgeting techniques	11
Performance analysis	4
Total	100%

[a] These percentages are based on examinations for the period May 1982 through November 1986. Accounting practice parts I and II and accounting theory were combined for the computation. The amount of time devoted to individual topics was determined by counting the number of multiple-choice questions, problems, and essay questions on each topic and the estimated time allocated for them.

joint costing, budgeting, cost-volume-profit analysis, capital budgeting, and quantitative techniques also receive heavy emphasis, with a combined total of 43 percent in these areas. Candidates would be well advised to spend a significant amount of the cost accounting study time on these topics.

One final note about the CMA and CPA examinations. There is a substantial element of similarity in the topics included on many sections of the two examinations. This overlap is understandable when one considers the importance of sound reporting standards. Because both examinations are academic in orientation, a candidate planning to sit for the exams should consider doing the following: *(a)* preparing for both experiences simultaneously; and *(b)* sitting for both exams during the same time period; that is, sitting for the CPA exam in May or November and the CMA exam in June or December). Following this strategy will make the most efficient use of a candidate's time and money.

CODE OF ETHICS

Ethical behavior (or lack of it) constitutes one of the most important issues in our day. There seems to be a constant stream of reports describing misconduct on the part of some person or persons. The expansion of business operations and trade to a global scale increases not only the complexity of reporting operating results but also the possibility of conflict in the area of ethical conduct.

It is not appropriate or even possible to establish detailed codes of behavior that guide individuals in every conceivable situation. At the same time, professional organizations believe there is a need to promulgate some broad guidelines to govern behavior. The NAA issued SMA 1C in June 1983, titled *Standards of Ethical Conduct for Management Accountants*. Because the statement provides standards that are brief in content but broad in implication, it is presented here in its entirety.

STANDARDS OF ETHICAL CONDUCT FOR MANAGEMENT ACCOUNTANTS

Management accountants have an obligation to the organizations they serve, their profession, the public, and themselves to maintain the highest standards of ethical conduct. In recognition of this obligation, the National Association of Accountants has promulgated the following standards of ethical conduct for management accountants. Adherence to these standards is integral to achieving the *Objectives of Management Accounting*.[1] Management accountants shall not commit acts contrary to these standards nor shall they condone the commission of such acts by others within their organizations.

Competence

Management accountants have a responsibility to:
- Maintain an appropriate level of professional competence by ongoing development of their knowledge and skills.
- Perform their professional duties in accordance with relevant laws, regulations, and technical standards.
- Prepare complete and clear reports and recommendations after appropriate analyses of relevant and reliable information.

---

1. National Association of Accountants, *Statements on Management Accounting: Objectives of Management Accounting*, Statement No. 1B, (New York: NAA, June 17, 1982).

Confidentiality

Management accountants have a responsibility to:
- Refrain from disclosing confidential information acquired in the course of their work except when authorized, unless legally obligated to do so.
- Inform subordinates as appropriate regarding the confidentiality of information acquired in the course of their work and monitor their activities to assure the maintenance of that confidentiality.
- Refrain from using or appearing to use confidential information acquired in the course of their work for unethical or illegal advantage either personally or through third parties.

Integrity

Management accountants have a responsibility to:
- Avoid actual or apparent conflicts of interest and advise all appropriate parties of any potential conflict.
- Refrain from engaging in any activity that would prejudice their ability to carry out their duties ethically.
- Refuse any gift, favor, or hospitality that would influence or would appear to influence their actions.
- Refrain from either actively or passively subverting the attainment of the organization's legitimate and ethical objectives.
- Recognize and communicate professional limitations or other constraints that would preclude responsible judgment or successful performance of an activity.
- Communicate unfavorable as well as favorable information and professional judgments or opinions.
- Refrain from engaging in or supporting any activity that would discredit the profession.

Objectivity

Management accountants have a responsibility to:
- Communicate information fairly and objectively.
- Disclose fully all relevant information that could reasonably be expected to influence an intended user's understanding of the reports, comments, and recommendations presented.

Resolution of Ethical Conflict

In applying the standards of ethical conduct, management accountants may encounter problems in identifying unethical behavior or in resolving an ethical conflict. When faced with significant ethical issues, management accountants should follow the established policies of the organization bearing on the resolution of such conflict. If these policies do not resolve the ethical conflict, management accountants should consider the following courses of action:

- Discuss such problems with the immediate superior except when it appears that the superior is involved, in which case the problem should be presented initially to the next higher managerial level. If satisfactory resolution cannot be achieved when the problem is initially presented, submit the issues to the next higher managerial level.

  If the immediate superior is the chief executive officer, or equivalent, the acceptable reviewing authority may be a group such as the audit committee, executive committee, board of directors, board of trustees, or owners. Contact with levels above the immediate superior should be initiated only with the superior's knowledge, assuming the superior is not involved.
- Clarify relevant concepts by confidential discussion with an objective advisor to obtain an understanding of possible courses of action.
- If the ethical conflict still exists after exhausting all levels of internal review, the management accountant may have no other recourse on significant matters than to

resign from the organization and to submit an informative memorandum to an appropriate representative of the organization.

Except where legally prescribed, communication of such problems to authorities or individuals not employed or engaged by the organization is not considered appropriate.

The October 1986 NAA newsletter, *Association Leader,* reported the following, which provides just one example of a current situation that involves ethical considerations.

The process of negotiating mergers and acquisitions can be a true test of one's business ethics, reveals a survey of members of the Business Planning Board of the National Association of Accountants.
Board members . . . voted two to one that the benefits of mergers and acquisitions outweigh the harm. *However the majority (70%) said it is too easy to bend the truth, break promises and in general forget or set aside one's ethical principles in the high stakes world of negotiating mergers and acquisitions* (emphasis provided).

Many accountants and business executives face situations that will test their ethics. As one prepares to enter the profession, serious consideration should be given to the formulation of a sound process of evaluating situations for their ethical implications. The individual must also establish a firm resolve to behave with integrity, even in the face of pressure to compromise.

On-the-Job Experience

As indicated in a previous section, two years of management accounting experience are required for a person to receive the CMA Certificate. This experience is referred to as "related professional experience," which is defined as full-time continuous employment at a level where judgments that employ the principles of management accounting are regularly made.

Continuing Education

Keeping abreast of current developments, particularly in one's chosen profession, is very important if an individual is to maintain the ability to provide quality service. Most professional fields require continuing education and development of the professional in the field. The CMA, as a professional designation, has a continuing education requirement; ninety hours of continuing education are required of CMAs in every three-year period subsequent to passing the CMA examination. These hours must be earned to remain in good standing as a CMA.

SUMMARY

In this chapter, the definition and objectives of management accounting were reviewed and the characteristics of a profession were summarized. The management accounting profession is characterized by the following: (1) the common body of knowledge for management accountants; (2) the certifying examinations (CMA and CPA); (3) the standards of ethical conduct for management accountants; (4) on-the-job experience required for the certificate; and (5) continuing education to remain in good standing.

As a student of cost and managerial accounting, you would be well advised to carefully consider the career path you wish to pursue. Make your education count in terms of mastery of the common body of knowledge. As you select the certifying examinations you wish to take, determine to make your preparation thorough. Consider, in this regard, the desirability of attempting more than one exam and certification if that fits your career plan.

Give careful and thoughtful consideration to your beliefs and your foundation of ethical conduct. Resolve to behave honorably, even in the face of pressure from others. Finally, determine to pursue a life-long process of involvement in professional activities and continued learning.

SUGGESTED READINGS

American Institute of Certified Public Accountants. *Information for CPA Candidates*. New York, N.Y.: AICPA, 1975.

Gleim, Irvin N. *CMA Examination Review*. Gainesville, Fla.: Accounting Publications, 1981.

Gleim, Irvin N., and Delaney, Patrick R. *CPA Examination Review*. Somerset, N.J.: John Wiley & Sons, annually.

Institute of Management Accountants. *CMA: A Professional Designation for Management Accountants and Financial Managers*. Ann Arbor, Mich.: Institute of Management Accountants, 1982.

Krause, Paul, and Adams, Steven J. "Are Management Accountants Professionals?" *Management Accounting* 68 (April 1987): 36, 62.

Needles, Belverd E., Jr., and Williams, Doyle Z. *The CPA Examination: A Complete Review*. Boston, Mass.: Houghton Mifflin, annually.

DISCUSSION QUESTIONS

Q26–1. List and briefly discuss the key elements of the definition of management accounting.

Q26–2. Identify and briefly discuss the objectives of management accounting.

Q26–3. Identify and discuss the major characteristics of a profession.

Q26–4. What is meant by a common body of knowledge?

Q26–5. Discuss the importance of the common body of knowledge in a professional field, with specific reference to management accounting.

Q26–6. Is a professional certification important to you? Why?

Q26–7. What does one need to do to qualify for a CMA?

Q26–8. What does one need to do to become a CPA?

Q26–9. Why may one want to consider becoming both a CMA and a CPA?

Q26–10. Identify the main subject areas included on the CMA examination; the CPA examination.

Q26–11. What are the common topic areas on both the CMA and CPA examinations?

Q26–12. Discuss the importance of codes of ethics in professional fields.

Q26–13. Identify the key elements in the *Standards of Ethical Conduct for Management Accountants*.

Q26–14. Write an essay about your own personal code of conduct.

Q26–15. What is meant by an ethical dilemma?

Q26–16. What differences, if any, do you perceive may exist between the ethical situations faced by a practicing CMA (one in management accounting) and a practicing CPA (one in public accounting)? How might the individuals practicing in the two respective areas resolve ethical dilemmas?

Q26–17. Do you believe that a commitment to life-long learning is important? Why?

CASES

Note: The following cases involve ethical considerations and are included to give the reader exposure to the resolution of difficult ethical dilemmas that arise in organizations.

The reader is referred to numerous problems included in the end of chapter materials, for examples of CMA and CPA problems. There are, of course, many sources of examination materials from past CMA and CPA examinations.

C26–1. Kazunas Industries (CMA) Kazunas Industries is a manufacturer of auto parts with 70 percent of its sales to the large domestic auto companies and 30 percent to auto part retailers. Kazunas' sales to retailers are increasing at a 20-percent annual rate, largely because of the increasing average age of U.S. automobiles. However, sales to domestic auto companies are decreasing because many of the parts are not compatible with new auto technology.

Domestic auto companies currently are decreasing the number of their suppliers as they seek better inventory management and quality control, and Kazunas Industries is a prime candidate for deletion. Also, the sales to retailers have a built-in decline as old technology automobiles reach the end of their life cycles.

Kazunas has decided to build new production facilities and has applied for a $20 million loan from Commerce Bank to finance the modernization. Loan conditions were agreed to in a meeting between Peter Lisko, Kazunas' vice president of finance, and David Pearson, a loan officer for the bank. The loan conditions limit Kazunas' cash dividend payments to 50 percent of net income and provide for Commerce Bank's approval of several types of transactions should the current ratio fall below 1.5 to 1. The terms of the agreement were approved by Commerce Bank's loan committee, and Kazunas Industries received the cash on August 15, 19X3.

Joan Miraldi, Kazunas' controller, received instructions from Peter Lisko about the preparation of financial statements for the year ended May 31, 19X4. After reviewing the preliminary statements, Lisko instructed Miraldi to capitalize some ordinary repairs and to charge some unrelated maintenance labor cost to the installation of new equipment. Lisko also directed Miraldi not to record a May 30 purchase and to omit it from the inventory.

Miraldi met with Lisko to tell him that she believes these actions are contrary to proper accounting practice and may materially misstate the financial statements. Lisko told Miraldi that he did not think these actions violated generally accepted accounting principles and that these principles were just guidelines anyway. He explained the loan conditions to her and said, "The loan conditions were sweeteners suggested by the bank's loan committee. We are bound by the loan conditions but not by generally accepted accounting principles. Therefore, I want you to do as I told you so that these loan conditions are met!"

Required

1. Discuss the ethical considerations that Joan Miraldi should recognize in this situation.
2. Identify possible courses of action that are available to Joan Miraldi in this situation.

3. Recommend the course of action you would follow:
    a. explaining the reasons for recommending this course of action.
    b. discussing the consequences, if any, of this course of action.

C26-2. Brockman Company (CMA) The Brockman Company became a subsidiary of Planto Industries in early 19X9 when Sid Brockman, founder and president, sold it to Planto. At Planto's request, Brockman, along with his controller, sales manager, and plant manager, continued to manage the subsidiary. The three members of this team report to the appropriate corporate officer for their function as well as to Brockman. This management team has been together for many years and had made Brockman Company very successful. Planto looks for solid management in its acquisitions, establishes minimum controls, and gives subsidiary managements extensive freedom.

The Brockman management has gotten along well with Planto management. The only area of friction between the Brockman team and Planto is Planto's insistence that the subsidiary develop stable as well as growing earnings. Historically, Brockman Company had experienced short-term earnings swings, but over its life there had been substantial growth in sales and earnings.

Brockman has called a meeting of his team for the purpose of developing a strategy that could be used to moderate the variations in earnings. The strategy should not cause major changes in the nature of the business and should not have a detrimental economic effect (i.e., not affect net cash flows over a two-year period). In addition, any actions considered should not strain the subsidiary's relationship with Planto management. The following recommendations were made during the meeting:

1. Vary the useful lives on new asset acquisitions within appropriate limits, depending on need for earnings.
2. Adjust percentage estimates for accounts receivable bad debts to the extent possible.
3. Review inventory stocks and idle machinery in periods of high earnings to establish obsolesence write-offs.
4. Change to weighted-average inventory methods to reduce the effect of production variations on cost.
5. Sell or inventory scrap materials as needed to change revenues.
6. Arrange short-term leases for assets, with the option to purchase in years of high earnings.
7. Delay or accelerate manufacture and delivery of product to those customers who are flexible about delivery dates.
8. Vary the customer credit policy as needed to increase or decrease revenues.

Required

1. Is the requirement for stable as well as growing earnings an appropriate objective for Planto Industries to ask of the Brockman management? Explain your answer.
2. For each of the eight recommended actions, explain whether the act described will have a detrimental economic effect (i.e., affect net cash flows in a two-year period) on Brockman Company. Disregard income tax considerations.
3. For each of the eight recommended actions, explain whether the act described would be considered an acceptable subsidiary response by Planto's management to its desire to achieve stable but growing earnings.

C26-3. Nova Company (CMA) The Nova Company is currently undergoing the annual audit of its financial statements by an external audit firm. In connection with the audit, Nova's chief executive officer (CEO) and chief financial officer (CFO) will be asked to sign a representation letter confirming the continued appropriateness of the information obtained in discussions with management. The letter drafted by the external auditor will contain the words, "we confirm, to the best of our knowledge and belief," and will include the following among the representations in the letter:

- Provision, when material, has been made to reduce excess or obsolete inventories to their estimated net realizable value.
- Provision has been made for any material loss to be sustained as a result of purchase commitments for inventory quantities in excess of normal requirements or at prices in excess of the prevailing market prices.

Nova manufactures a line of home game players and video games. The major and most profitable product within the line is the Nova 223 game player. This particular unit has been largely responsible for the company's growth in recent years. During 19X3 Nova's competitors introduced more versatile game players, and Nova 223 sales have slowed dramatically. Nova stopped manufacturing Nova 223 and will shortly replace it with a more modern version. Management believes this new model will restore sales performance to that of earlier years.

The principal difference between the models is a newly designed circuit board. A three-month supply of circuit boards used in the manufacture of the old model remains in inventory and cannot be used in any other products. Circuit boards are the most expensive part of the game players.

Nova signed a four-year purchase commitment for a contact switch, another expensive component, used in the Nova 223. The long-term purchase commitment was considered necessary to hold down costs during a period of double-digit inflation. Changing manufacturing techniques and moderating inflation have reduced the current cost of the switches below the commitment price. Fortunately for Nova, the switch is an integral part of the new model, so the quantities contained in the purchase commitment can be used.

Curt Simmers, vice president of operations, has the major responsibility for sales, manufacturing, and design of Nova's products. His annual bonus and standing within the company are influenced by Nova's financial results. Simmers told both the CEO and CFO, in response to direct questions, that there was no obsolete inventory nor any inventory or commitment for inventory for which current prices were significantly below acquisition or commitment price. These answers were given even though Jane Grala, chief operations accountant, had previously informed him of the obsolete inventory and the considerable loss associated with the four-year purchase commitment.

Grala is part of the operations staff and reports directly to Simmers. She also reports to an assistant controller on the CFO's staff on an indirect basis. Nova maintains a functional reporting relationship between operating accounting personnel and the corporate accounting staff. Grala has worked closely with the audit manager from the external audit firm, and people in her department have provided information and assistance to the external auditors during the course of the audit. In a recent discussion, Grala learned that the external audit manager was unaware of the inventory and purchase commitment problems and that Simmers had stated that there were no problems in this area. She is concerned about this situation and is not sure what to do about it.

Required

1. Identify possible courses of action that Jane Grala, chief operations accountant, should consider as she decides what to do about this situation.
2. Identify the alternative in requirement 1 that you would recommend, and explain the reasons for recommending this course of action.

C26-4. FulRange, Inc, (CMA) FulRange, Inc. produces complex printed circuits for stereo amplifiers. The circuits are sold primarily to major component manufacturers, and any production overruns are sold to small manufacturers at a substantial discount. The small manufacturer market segment appears to be very profitable because the basic operating budget assigns all fixed expenses to production for the major manufacturers, the only predictable market.

A common product defect that occurs in production is a "drift" that is caused by failure to maintain precise heat levels during the production process. Rejects from the 100 percent testing program can be reworked to acceptable levels if the defect is drift. However, in a recent analysis of customer complaints, George Wilson, the cost accountant, and the quality control engineer have ascertained that normal rework does not bring the circuits up to standard. Sampling shows that about one-half of the reworked circuits will fail after extended, high-volume amplifier operation. The incidence of failure in the reworked circuits is projected to be about 10 percent over one to five years' operation.

Unfortunately, there is no way to determine which reworked circuits will fail, because testing will not detect this problem. The rework process could be changed to correct the problem, but the cost-benefit analysis for the suggested change in the rework process indicates that it is not feasible. FulRange's marketing analyst has indicated that this problem will have a substantial effect on the company's reputation and customer satisfaction if the problem is not corrected. Consequently, the board of directors would interpret this problem as having serious negative implications on the company's profitability.

Wilson has included the circuit failure and rework problem in his report that has been prepared for the upcoming quarterly meeting of the board of directors. Because of the potential adverse economic effect, Wilson has followed a long-standing practice of highlighting this information.

After reviewing the reports to be presented, the plant manager and his staff were upset and indicated to the controller that he should control his people better. "We can't upset the board with this kind of material. Tell Wilson to tone that down. Maybe we can get it by this meeting and have some time to work on it. People that buy those cheap systems and play them that loud shouldn't expect them to last forever."

The controller called Wilson into his office and said, "George, you'll have to bury this one. The probable failure of reworks can be referred to briefly in the oral presentation, but it should not be mentioned or highlighted in the advance material mailed to the board."

Wilson feels strongly that the board will be misinformed on a potentially serious loss of income if he follows the controller's orders. Wilson discussed the problem with the quality control engineer, who simply remarked, "That's your problem, George."

Required

1. Discuss the ethical considerations that George Wilson should recognize in deciding how to proceed in this matter.
2. Explain what ethical responsibilities should be accepted in this situation by the:
    a. Controller.
    b. Quality control engineer.
    c. Plant manager and his staff.
3. What should George Wilson do in this situation? Explain your answer.

C26-5. Farbell Company (CMA) Farbell Company is a manufacturer of automotive components, with annual sales of $85 million. An internal audit department was established four years ago, and it is supervised by the manager of audits who reports directly to the controller. There is no audit committee, but five of the six members of the board of directors are outside directors.

Farbell's business had declined sharply over the past two years. The controller, looking for ways to reduce costs, asked the company auditors, Cross & Gill Company, for suggestions to reduce the audit fees. They indicated that the audit fee could be reduced if a member of Farbell's internal audit staff could be assigned to assist Cross and Gill in some of the audit steps that need to be conducted. Cross and Gill would design and supervise the audit procedures, but the Farbell employee would actually do the work. The areas Cross & Gill suggested were to:

- verify vendors' balances in accounts payable at year-end.
- value year-end inventory of productive materials.
- review the adequacy of allowance accounts and all expense accruals at year-end.

John Wallace, who has worked in the internal audit department for the past six months, was given the assignment. Wallace is a young, career-oriented employee who has developed a reputation as a meticulous worker since joining Farbell two years ago upon graduation from college. Both the controller and manager of audits assured Wallace that working with Cross & Gill while still a member of the internal audit department would provide substantial near-term benefits and would not cause any serious problems. They further assured him that any possible conflict of interest or the issues of responsibility and objectivity were inconsequential because nothing significant would be discovered in the areas in which he was to audit.

Reassured by his superiors, Wallace conducted the prescribed audit procedures, but he had minimal direction and very little supervision by Cross & Gill. In fact, much to his disappointment, he was left on his own for most of the work. The following problems were discovered during the audit.

1. Farbell's account with D. J. Smith Metals Co. revealed that several small invoices for shipments of specialty metals had been outstanding for several months. The amount of these unpaid invoices totaled just over $12,000, which is not a significant amount with respect to all of the invoices from Smith Metals or the total vendors' balances in accounts payable. Invoices for purchases of standard metals, ranging from $25,000 to $100,000, had all been paid on time, even though some had been received after the invoices for the specialty metals. Wallace's investigation revealed that the accounts payable manager, Dan Smith, had intercepted the checks issued to "D. J. Smith" for payment of the small shipments and had cashed them for his personal use.
2. Upon review of the year-end productive materials inventory, Wallace discovered a substantial amount of obsolete items that were valued at incurred historical cost. These items would have little, if any, salvage value upon disposal.
3. Both the year-end allowance adjustments and expense accruals had been understated, enabling Farbell to come closer to its forecasted profit for the year.

Wallace took the following action with respect to the three preceding problems:

- Wallace confronted Smith, telling him that he intended to report the embezzlement to the manager of audits and the controller. Several days after Wallace reported the embezzlement, the controller told Wallace that he had reviewed the case with the manager of audits. They had concluded after their review that no further action would be necessary because the amount was not material and Smith had repaid the embezzled funds in full. Furthermore, Cross & Gill would not need to be informed because this was an internal matter that had been resolved.
- Wallace met with the controller to discuss the obsolete inventory and the understated

allowance adjustments and expense accruals. Wallace believed that neither problem was significant alone, but the combination of the two did have a notable effect on earnings. The controller stated that he did not want to recognize the inventory loss until the exact amount could be determined upon disposal next year. The controller admitted that the allowance accounts and expense accruals were understated. He stated, "These actions won't affect the well-being of the company. The accruals will return to realistic levels in the next accounting period. These items are judgment items that should be left to the discretion of internal management. There is no need to make special note of them in the audit papers prepared for Cross & Gill."

Upon completion of the audit work, Wallace submitted his work papers to Cross & Gill without any mention of the three problems he had discovered. Cross & Gill has completed its audit field work in Farbell's offices. Cross & Gill has not met with Farbell's management to discuss its audit findings, and there has been no mention of the three problems in their conversations to date. The management letter and opinion on the financial statements are expected to be issued in the next thirty days. Farbell has issued a press release giving an estimate of the company's earnings for the current year.

Required

1. Were John Wallace's concerns about conflict of interest, objectivity, and the responsibility issue valid? Explain your answer.
2. Explain whether John Wallace acted ethically with respect to his handling of the problems he discovered during the audit when he:
    a. presented his findings to his superiors at Farbell Company.
    b. failed to mention the problems in the work papers he submitted to Cross & Gill Company.
3. Was it ethical for Farbell Company's management to agree to the arrangement it made with its external auditor Cross & Gill Company? Explain your answer.

Glossary

Abnormal rate of loss The rate of loss that is not expected to occur under efficient operating conditions.

Abnormal spoilage Spoilage that is caused by unusual or unexpected factors occurring in production.

Absorption costing An approach to product costing and income determination that charges all manufacturing costs to inventory. Manufacturing costs become an expense in the period in which inventory is sold. Absorption costing is also known as full costing or traditional costing.

Accounting The process of recording, classifying, summarizing, and reporting the economic activities of an organization.

Accounting rate of return A measure of investment profitability computed by dividing the average annual cash inflows less depreciation by the initial investment. Average book value of the investment is frequently used in the denominator in place of the initial investment.

Activity base A measure of volume of business activity that is highly correlated with the amount of cost incurred.

Administrative controls Controls concerned with getting the right people into the right jobs initially and with managing them effectively during their employment with the firm.

Administrative cost Expenses incurred in carrying out the administrative or general management functions of a firm. Expenses are charged to the period; that is, they are matched against revenue in the period in which they are incurred.

Average cost method An inventory cost flow assumption that uses the average cost of materials purchased to determine the cost of materials issued.

Avoidable fixed costs Costs that can be reduced or eliminated by reducing the level of operations or by discontinuing some element of operations.

Breakeven analysis A study of the relationships between costs, revenues, and profits to identify a breakeven point.

Breakeven chart A graph that contains a total revenue curve and a total cost curve. The point of their intersection identifies the breakeven point.

Breakeven point The level of sales volume, specified in either units of output or sales dollars, at which total revenues equal total costs and the business has neither earnings nor losses.

Budget An itemized estimate of the operating results of an enterprise for a future time period. A formal quantitative expression of an enterprise's plans.

Budgeted costs Costs that are expected to be incurred in a future period.

By-product A joint product with a relatively minor sales value when compared with other joint products.

Capital asset Larger, more prominent assets of an entity that are relatively durable and can be used repeatedly in the production of goods and services.

Capital budgeting Determining the desirability of investing in fixed assets.

Capital components Items on the right-hand side of the balance sheet, including liabilities, preferred stock, and common stock. These items provide money for the purchase of assets.

Capital cost A term used to describe the cost of plant and equipment.

Capitalized cost (*See* unexpired cost.)

Centralization A management term which implies that little responsibility for decision making has been delegated to lower levels of management. (*See* decentralization.)

1019

Chart of accounts A listing of all accounts used by a company in its accounting system.

Clearing account An account used to facilitate the accounting process; holds cost data until it can be transferred or distributed to other accounts.

Coefficient of correlation A value (r) that measures the association or correlation between two variables. In flexible budgeting, the variables are manufacturing costs and an activity base.

Coefficient of determination A value (r^2) that measures the amount of variation of the dependent variable y that is explained by the independent variable x.

Committed cost A cost that is the inevitable consequence of a previous commitment.

Common fixed costs Those fixed costs that are common to segments.

Component cost The after-tax cost associated with each capital component.

Continuous budgeting A method that requires the budget for the next fiscal year (four quarters) to be revised and updated at the end of each quarter.

Contribution margin The sale price per unit minus variable cost per unit, or the amount that each unit contributes to cover fixed costs and provide a profit.

Contribution margin ratio The sales price less variable costs divided by sales price, or the ratio of contribution margin to sales.

Contribution report An income statement format that focuses first on cost behavior and then on management function. The report follows a format of revenue less variable costs equals contribution margin less fixed costs equals net income.

Control The ongoing process of implementing management's plans and providing feedback of actual results so managers can evaluate performance and make any needed adjustments to keep operations in line with plans and objectives.

Control account A summary account in the general ledger that is supported in detail by individual accounts in a subsidiary ledger.

Controllable cost A cost that is subject to significant influence by a particular manager within the time period under consideration.

Controllable variance The sum of the spending and variable overhead efficiency variance.

Controller The person responsible for all accounting activities within the organization.

Conversion costs Costs that are required to convert raw materials into a finished product.

Cost A measurement, in monetary terms, of the amount of resources used to acquire goods or services. As related to standards, it is the outlay or sacrifice that is incurred for each unit of output.

Cost accounting The process of accumulating the costs of a manufacturing process and identifying them with the units produced.

Cost center A subdivision of a business assigned responsibility for only the incurrence and proper utilization of costs.

Cost cycle The steps taken in tracing the flow of manufacturing costs through the accounts.

Costing The accumulation and assignment of costs to cost objectives such as units of production, departments, or other activities for which management desires a separate measurement or evaluation.

Cost objective The purpose for which a cost is measured, assigned, or classified.

Cost of capital The rate of return that must be earned on invested capital in order to leave the market price of the firm's common stock unchanged.

Cost price variance The effect on gross margin of differences in manufacturing costs between budgeted and actual results.

Cost recovery Terminology used in the Economic Recovery Tax Act of 1981 to describe depreciation.

Cost-volume-profit analysis A study of the relationships between costs and volume and their impact on profit.

Currently attainable standards A level of standard that allows for ordinary equipment failure, normal lost time, and normal spoilage.

Cut-off rate An interest rate that identifies the minimum rate of return acceptable to management. Also called a hurdle-rate.

Data bank A data base that contains all information relating to a particular organization.

Data base A common source of information.

Decentralization A management term that implies that many job activities and related decision-making functions have been delegated to subordinates by higher levels of management. (*See* centralization.)

Defective units Goods that do not meet quality control standards and are either sold "as is" as second-quality goods or reworked and sold as first-quality goods.

Department A subunit of a manufacturing firm created to facilitate product costing and cost control.

Dependent variable The variable y that is under investigation and is described by another variable.

Differential costs The increase in total company costs incurred as a result of an alternate decision. (*See* relevant costs.)

Direct cost A cost that can be economically traced to a single cost object.

Direct fixed costs Those fixed costs that can be directly identified with a segment.

Direct labor The cost of employees who work directly on the product and whose efforts can be economically traced to a particular unit of finished product.

Direct material Raw material components that can be physically identified with or traced to the finished product.

Direct method A method for allocating service department costs directly to production departments with no allocation of service department costs to any other service department.

Direct product cost (*See* separable cost.)

Discretionary cost A cost for which the size or the time of incurrence is a matter of choice.

Dual transfer prices One transfer price for the transferring subunit and another transfer price for the receiving subunit.

Economic order quantity (EOQ) The order size for purchases that minimizes the total cost of ordering plus the cost of carrying inventory.

Equivalent units As used in process costing, a measure of the work effort of a department, process, or operation.

Expected capacity The level of productive activity for the accounting period that is expected to meet consumer demand for the upcoming year; a short-run measure.

Expected realizable value The ultimate predicted selling price of a joint product less anticipated costs of completion and sales.

Expired cost A cost with an immediate benefit that is recorded as an expense.

Factory overhead (*See* indirect manufacturing costs.)

Factory overhead applied account The account used to record the amount of overhead applied to work in process by using the predetermined overhead application rate.

Factory overhead control account The account used to accumulate actual overhead costs incurred.

Final cost objective An object of final cost accumulation such as a job, a unit of production, or a government contract. A term used by the Cost Accounting Standards Board.

Financial accounting Accounting that specializes in satisfying the information needs of external users, such as stockholders, potential investors, creditors, and governmental agencies.

First-in, first-out (FIFO) method An inventory cost flow assumption that differentiates between costs of the previous period that are contained in a work-in-process beginning inventory, and costs incurred during the current period.

Fixed costs Costs that remain constant in dollar amount as the volume of production or sales changes.

Fixed overhead Manufacturing costs that remain constant or fixed as the volume of manufacturing activity changes.

Fixed overhead budget variance The difference between actual fixed overhead incurred and budgeted fixed overhead.

Flexible budget A formula used to adjust budgeted cost at various levels of business activity.

Flexible budgeting A technique used to adjust the budget for various levels of business activity.

Flowcharting An approach used to summarize the flow of documents and information through the use of symbols which depict the system's characteristics.

Full cost Actual fixed and variable costs of producing a good or service. For pricing purposes, the full cost may also include an allocated portion of selling and administrative expenses.

Gross margin The margin obtained from subtracting the cost of goods sold from sales revenue.

Gross margin analysis A technique for performing a detailed analysis of changes in gross margin between budgeted and actual results or between actual gross margin of succeeding years. Also known as gross profit analysis.

Gross margin variance The difference between actual gross margin and budgeted gross margin.

Half-year convention A half year of depreciation is taken in the year of purchase regardless of when the asset was purchased.

High-low method A method of developing a cost equation by analyzing the change in cost that corresponds to the change in volume between the high and low points of activity.

Historical costs Costs that were incurred in a past period.

Home office A function or office that is responsible for managing or directing other parts of the business. A term used by the Cost Accounting Standards Board.

Homogeneity of overhead costs Costs that are similar so they can be grouped for accounting and allocation without compromising the accuracy of final product costs.

Ideal standards These standards are sometimes referred to as perfect or theoretical standards. Standards under this philosophy relate to the least possible costs that can be expected under the best conceivable manufacturing conditions.

Imputed interest A hypothetical or opportunity cost of using the capital invested in the segment. A cost that is not entered into the accounting records but is useful for cost analysis.

Incremental costs (*See* marginal costs.)

Independent variable The variable x that is used to describe another dependent variable.

Indirect cost A cost that is not directly traceable to the manufactured product, is associated with the manufacture of two or more units of finished product, or is an immaterial cost that cannot be economically traced to a single unit of finished product.

Indirect manufacturing costs All manufacturing costs other than direct materials and direct labor. Also referred to as overhead.

Inference engine Computer program that requests data from the user, manipulates the knowledge base, and provides a recommendation back to the user.

Input controls Controls designed to verify that the input into the computer process is complete and accurate.

Integrated data base A common data base that serves multiple application programs, functional areas, and levels of management.

Internal rate of return The interest rate that equates the present value of future cash inflows with the initial investment.

Interpolation A process of selecting an intermediate point based on the relative distance of the desired point to those that are listed.

Investment center A subdivision of a business assigned responsibility for costs, revenues, and the profitable utilization of invested capital.

Irrelevant costs Costs that do not relate to any of the decision alternatives, are historical in nature, or are the same under all decision alternatives.

Job-order costing A method for costing inventories in industries characterized by dissimilar jobs or orders that receive varying amounts of work effort.

Job-order cost system A system of accounting used for manufacturing processes that produce products in batches or by unique divisible orders.

Joint product Products produced whenever a single resource or input results in more than one useful output.

Joint product cost Those manufacturing costs incurred during the processing of original inputs before the point where joint products become individually identifiable.

Knowledge One's understanding of reality or the true state of nature. Knowledge concerns what is, what was, and what may be.

Knowledge base Storage area consisting of rules, truths, and common relationships that an expert uses to solve a problem in the problem domain.

Last-in, first-out (LIFO) method An inventory cost flow assumption by which the cost of the last materials received is assumed to be the cost of the first materials issued.

Lead time The time between placing an order and having the materials delivered.

Learning curve A graphical (mathematical) representation of the relationship between labor time and production quantity when learning exists in a repetitive production environment.

Least-squares method A method of developing a cost equation for an observed set of data by mathematically computing a regression line that minimizes the sum of the squares of the lengths of the vertical-line segments from the observed data points to the regression line.

Level of aspiration A goal that, when barely achieved, has associated with it subjective feelings of success, and when not achieved, subjective feelings of failure.

Managed cost (*See* discretionary cost.)

Management by exception The philosophy that managers should focus their attention on areas of the business in which current operations are significantly different from previous operations or from the budget.

Management information system A computer-based information-processing system that supports the operation, management, and decision-making functions of the organization.

Managerial accounting An internal accounting process designed to provide management with the necessary information to operate a business successfully.

Manufacturer A type of firm that performs the manufacturing function, and that converts raw materials into units of finished product.

Manufacturing costs All costs from the acquisition of raw materials, through production, until the product can be turned over to the marketing division to be sold.

Marginal cost of capital The rate of return that must be earned on additional capital in order to leave the market value of common stock unchanged.

Marginal costs The costs associated with the next unit or the next project.

Margin of safety Actual or budgeted sales over sales at the breakeven point; the amount of reduction in sales that could occur without sustaining a loss.

Market basket An assumed basket containing the average sales mix of an entity.

Market price The prevailing monetary value of goods and services in markets external to an organization.

Master budget A budget that contains a complete set of pro forma financial statements with detailed supporting schedules. Also called comprehensive budgeting.

Master plan A plan that contains a summary of current capabilities of the information system as well as a projection of future requirements for labor, hardware, software, and financial resources.

Matching concept The criterion used to determine when a cost (asset) becomes an expense.

Mixed costs (*See* semivariable costs.)

Mixed overhead Indirect manufacturing costs that have both a fixed cost component and a variable cost component.

Negotiation The process of setting transfer prices by discussion or bargaining between subunit managers.

Net present value The present value of future cash inflows less the present value of future cash outflows, discounted at a minimum desired rate of return.

Network flow The manufacture and movement of products through various processes or departments as needed.

Nonroutine decisions All management decisions not directly related to the ordinary, repetitive production cycle of the business.

Normal capacity The level of productive activity that is expected to meet consumer demand for three to five years; a long-run measure.

Normal rate of loss The rate of loss that is expected to occur under efficient operating conditions.

Opportunity cost In a transfer pricing context, the maximum contribution to profits that are lost by the firm as a whole if goods and services are transferred internally rather than being sold externally. The cost or value of an opportunity foregone when one course of action is chosen over another.

Outlay cost Cash outflows incurred to the point of transfer as a result of producing transferred goods and services.

Out-of-pocket costs Costs that must be met with a current expenditure.

Output controls Controls designed to assure that the output is complete, that no errors were identified by the computer during processing, and that the output is safeguarded and used by those who are authorized to examine it.

Overapplied overhead The amount by which applied overhead exceeds actual overhead.

Overhead A brief expression for indirect manufacturing costs.

Overhead application The assignment of overhead costs to units of production.

Parallel flow The simultaneous manufacture of component parts that are subsequently assembled to form a finished product.

Payback period The number of years required for the cumulative cash flows to equal the initial investment.

Payback reciprocal An estimate of the internal rate of return that is computed by dividing annual cash flows by the initial investment.

Performance reporting Technique used to report the results of operations. Operating results are organized and presented according to an individual's ability to control an item and in such a way as to compare budgeted results with actual results.

Period costs Costs assigned to a time period or the costs matched against revenue in the period of incurrence.

Practical capacity The level of expected production at which machine breakdowns, machine maintenance, and other idle time events are considered to be a normal part of operations.

Predetermined overhead application rate A rate per unit of activity base used to apply overhead costs to work in process. The predetermined overhead application rate is calculated by dividing total budgeted overhead by the total budgeted units of the chosen activity base.

Preference decision Analysis involving several investment proposals where the objective is to identify the proposals that are most profitable.

Present value payback The number of years required for the present value of future cash flows, discounted at a minimum desired rate of return, to equal the initial investment.

Price index A measure of relative prices used to adjust historical costs for changes in the general price level.

Prime costs The most important or significant costs traceable to units of finished product.

Process costing A method used for costing inventories in industries characterized by the continuous mass production of similar finished units.

Process cost system A system of accounting used for manufacturing processes that produce a single product continuously for an extended period of time.

Processing controls All controls connected with data processing by the computer, including hardware controls, program controls, operating system controls, and file reconstruction capability.

Product costs Cost assigned or charged to a product. These costs "flow" through the stages of initial recognition of costs and subsequent regroupings of costs where they are recorded in inventory accounts. These costs are matched against revenue or become period costs when a unit of product is sold.

Production department A department that is directly engaged in a manufacturing activity and contributes directly to the content and form of the finished product.

Product pricing Assigning monetary values to goods and services exchanged with parties external to an organization.

Profit center A subdivision of a business assigned responsibility for both costs and revenues.

Profit-volume graph A graph that contains a profit line showing the amount of profit (loss) at different levels of volume.

Pro forma statement Budgeted financial statement.

Programmed cost (*See* discretionary cost.)

Purchase discounts A percentage the buyer may deduct from the total invoice price if payment is made within the discount period. Also referred to as cash discounts.

Pyramid reporting A reporting structure used in responsibility accounting that shows detailed information on individual items that are controllable at that level of management and summary information on items that are controllable at lower levels of management.

Qualitative considerations Those aspects of a decision situation that are difficult to express in terms of numbers or other types of mathematical expressions.

Quantitative considerations Those aspects of a decision situation that may be expressed in terms of numbers.

Rate of markup A target rate applied against the cost of a product or service to establish a selling price in external markets.

Rate of return on assets employed A target rate applied against total assets employed to establish a selling price for goods and services in external markets.

Reciprocal method A method of allocating service department costs when service departments render services to one another in a mutual or complementary relationship.

Relational structure The way data are stored in the data base; a two-dimensional table that has a specified number of columns and a number of unordered rows.

Relative sales value A product's estimated selling price less estimated costs of completion and sale.

Relevant costs Future costs that are different under one decision alternative than under another decision alternative.

Relevant range of production A range of operating volume within which the cost relationships will be reliable.

Reorder point The point at which a purchase requisition is triggered when the number of units on hand declines.

Residual income (RI) A measure of business profitability that focuses attention on the optimum use of invested capital. RI is the amount of net income that is earned during a period beyond that needed to provide a minimum desired rate of return on invested capital. RI is a dollar measure.

Responsibility accounting A form of internal reporting

that is based on the ability to control. Each individual's report contains the items they have the ability to control.
Responsibility center A subdivision of business over which control of operations is found.
Return on investment (ROI) A widely used measure of business profitability that focuses attention on the optimum use of invested capital. ROI is calculated by dividing net income by invested capital. ROI is a ratio measure.
Routine decisions Decisions relating to the accumulation and reporting of information for everyday control of operations and for ordinary product-costing purposes.

Safety stock Inventory supply that protects against stockouts.
Sales mix The ratio or relative combination of each product's sales to total sales. The composition of total sales broken down by products, product mix, or product lines.
Sales mix variance The effect on gross margin of differences in sales mix between budgeted and actual results.
Sales price variance The effect on gross margin of differences in sales prices between budgeted and actual results.
Sales volume variance The effect on gross margin of differences in the quantities of units sold between budgeted and actual results.
Scatter diagram A graph with the values of observed data plotted on it.
Scattergraph method A method of developing a cost equation by visually fitting a regression line to observed data points plotted on a graph.
Screening decision Analysis involving only one investment proposal. The objective of this analysis is to determine if it meets minimum standards for acceptance.
Segment A segment is a separable part or activity of a company about which cost data may be prepared for analysis. A subdivision of a business that typically has a service or reporting relationship to a home office. A term used by the Cost Accounting Standards Board.
Segment margin Contribution margin of a segment less direct fixed costs.
Segment reporting The process of breaking an enterprise into reportable segments and preparing financial information by segments.
Selling costs All costs associated with the marketing and selling of a product.
Semivariable costs Costs that have both a fixed and a variable cost element.

Sensitivity analysis A "what if" analysis that examines the effect on the outcome for changes in one or more input values.
Separable costs Costs that are incurred after the split-off point and can be identified with individual joint products. Also referred to as direct product costs.
Sequential flow The manufacture and movement of products from one process or department to the next in a serial fashion.
Service department A department that provides services or assistance to production departments.
Shrinkage Lost units resulting from a reduction in volume of output due to such things as evaporation, temperature variations, or chemical reaction.
Shut-down point The minimum volume of production and sales that is necessary to justify operation of a product line or a segment of a business.
Slope The amount of change in y for each unit change in x.
Spending variance This variance is an indicator of how well actual overhead expenditures are kept within the budget independent of the efficiency with which the activity base was utilized.
Split ledger An accounting system in which the administrative office maintains the general ledger and the factory maintains a factory ledger.
Split-off point The point in the manufacturing process where joint products become individually identifiable.
Spoilage Production that does not meet quality control standards and as a result is junked or sold for a relatively low disposal value.
Spreadsheet An electronic worksheet consisting of horizontal rows and vertical columns with each intersection being a cell. Each cell can contain a label or numeric data such as a formula or number.
Standard A criterion for measurement. Standards in cost accounting refer to a norm or normal amount of quantities or prices to be paid for the materials and labor required to make a product or provide some service.
Standard activity level The expected level or volume of production for the coming accounting period.
Standard cost The expected cost of production under normal operating conditions. A standard cost is typically a unit cost concept.
Static budget A budget that is relevant to only one level of business activity and is not easily adjustable for changes in the level of operation.
Step method A method of allocating service department costs to production departments when service departments render services to each other.
Step-variable cost A variable cost that increases or de-

creases in "chunks" of cost with small changes in volume.

Subsidiary ledger A ledger that provides a detailed breakdown of the contents of the control account to which it relates.

Sunk costs Past costs that have already been incurred.

Theoretical capacity The upper limit of production capabilities.

Total cost All costs associated with a particular activity or limited to a specific category.

Total manufacturing cost The combined cost of direct material, direct labor, and factory overhead.

Transfer pricing Assigning monetary values to goods and services exchanged among subunits of an organization.

Transferred-in costs The accumulated cost of materials, labor, and overhead applied in all previous processes or departments.

Translation factor The ratio of a current price index to a historical price index used to adjust historical costs for changes in the general price level.

Treasurer The financial executive responsible for all functions classified under money management.

Unavoidable fixed costs Costs that cannot be reduced or eliminated by reducing the level of operations or by discontinuing some element of operations.

Uncontrollable costs Costs over which a given manager does not have a significant influence.

Underapplied overhead The amount by which actual overhead exceeds applied overhead.

Unexpired cost A cost with a future benefit that is recorded as an asset.

Unit cost The cost associated with a single unit of product or limited to a specific category.

Variable costing An alternative approach to product costing and income determination that charges fixed manufacturing overhead as an expense in the period incurred rather than fixed manufacturing overhead becoming a cost of inventory and charged to expense in the period in which the inventory is sold. Variable costing is also known as direct costing.

Variable costs Costs that vary in total as the volume of production or sales changes.

Variable overhead Manufacturing costs that vary in proportion to the level of manufacturing activity.

Variable overhead efficiency variance This variance evaluates the efficiency with which the activity base is utilized.

Variable overhead spending variance The difference between actual expenditures due to differences in prices.

Volume variance The difference between budgeted fixed factory overhead and applied fixed factory overhead.

Waste and scrap Terms for residue such as smoke, dust, or shavings that result from a manufacturing process.

Weighted average method An inventory cost flow assumption that averages costs of the previous period, that are contained in a work-in-process beginning inventory, and costs incurred during the current period.

Y intercept Identifies the amount of y when x is zero.

Index

ABC method, 424
Abnormal rate of loss, 353
Abnormal spoilage, 418–421
Absorption costing, 690
   versus variable costing, 690–695
Accelerated Cost Recovery System (ACRS), 910–914
Account
   clearing, 273
   control, 271, 273
   factory overhead applied, 466
   factory overhead control, 466
Accounting, 4
   accrual, 846
   constant dollar, 743
   cost, 4, 5–6
   current value, 744
   financial, 4–5
   fixed overhead, 578–580
   general, as controller's responsibility, 13
   general ledger, 466–470
   income tax, 5
   for lost units, 351–353
   managerial, 4, 5
   for overhead, 466–470
   responsibility, 200–206
   specialized areas of, 4–6
Accounting entries for intracompany transfers, 812–813
Accounting principles and procedures, 6–9
Accounting rate of return, 866–870, 917–918
   defined, 866
Accounting Research Bulletin (AICPA), 697, 698
Accounts
   chart of, 271–274
   clearing, 273
   control, 271

   multiple work-in-process, 285
   payroll summary, 273–274
   overhead, 286–287
Accounts receivable package (program), 946
Accrual accounting, 846
ACRS. *See* Accelerated Cost Recovery System
Activity bases, 192, 460–461, 462–464
Actual overhead, versus budgeted overhead, 467–468
Adams, Steven J., 1012
Additional information, value of, 646–649
Administrative controls, 662–663
Administrative cost, 21
   flexible budgeting for, 199–200
Administrative-expense budget, 152, 153
After-tax profit, 242
Aggarwal, Sumer C., 598
Ajinkya, Bipin, 710
Algorithm, 966
Allocation
   methods, 498–503
   of costs, by behavior, 506
Allocations, reciprocal, using matrix algebra, 511–514
American Institute of Certified Public Accountants (AICPA), 6, 697, 698, 1005, 1006
Amey, Lloyd R., 399
Amortization, 20
Annuity, 878–880
Application programs, 964, 966–967
   expert systems, 983–984
   special purpose, 964
Applied account, factory overhead, 466
Aspiration, level of, 206
Assemblers, 963
Assets employed, rate of return on, 717–718
Association Leader (NAA), 1011

AT&T, 71
Atiase, Rowland, 710
Auditing, 4–5
AUTO-CODER, 963
Available feasible alternatives, 782, 783
Average cost method, 417
Averaging costs, 314
Avoidable fixed costs, 738

Backes, Robert W., 444
BAI, 963
Bailey, Earl L., 824
Baiman, Stanley, 710
Balance sheet, budgeted, 157
Bamber, Linda S., 710
Bartenstein, Edwin, 120
Barton, M. Frank, 399
Bases, activity. *See* Activity bases
Basic cash concepts. *See* Cash concepts
Behavior
   and allocation of costs, 506
   analysis of, 62–64
   cost, 23, 54–73, 95
   patterns, 54–55
   quantifying, 64–73
Behavioral considerations
   of budgeting, 163–165
   in reporting, 205–206
   in standard cost system, 625–626
   of systems analysis, 656–657
Benke, Ralph L., Jr., 824
Beresford, Dennis R., 37, 476
Berry, Leonard Eugene, 824
Biddle, Gary C., 399
Bierman, H., 211, 885, 934
Blanchard, Garth, 167, 517
Blecki, Thomas R., 167
Breakeven analysis, 230–239
   for multiple products, 235–239
   in sales dollars, 233–235, 236–237

in units, 231–233, 235–236
Breakeven charts, 232, 238
  in sales dollars, 235
Breakeven point, 230, 231–232
Brealey R., 885
Brown, Russell S., 748
Brownell, Peter, 167
Budget
  administrative-expense, 152, 153
  analysis of, 157–158
  cash, 152–156
  defined, 140
  developing, 144–145
  flexible, 189
  intermediate, 141–142
  line-item, 159–160
  long-range, 141–142
  master, 143–144
  overhead, 575–576
  performance evaluation and, 740–741
  production, 148–150
  program, 160
  purpose of, 140–141
  raw materials purchases, 151
  selling-expense, 152, 153
  short-term, 141–142
  static, 188
  variances, 202–205
Budgetary goals and benchmarks, standards as, 538–540
Budget committee, 144–145
Budgeted balance sheet, 157
Budgeted income statement, 156
Budgeted overhead, versus actual overhead, 467–468
Budgeting, 140–165
  behavioral considerations of, 163–165
  capital. *See* Capital budgeting
  complications to, 875–876
  continuous, 142, 143
  as controller's responsibility, 13
  coordinated, 140
  flexible, 144, 188–200
  in general, 140–144
  and income tax, 875–876, 908–918
  in not-for-profit sector, 158–163
  in profit sector, 158–159
  sensitivity analysis in, 925–930
  techniques, 848–876
  time and, 141–142
Budget variances, 202–205
Bulloch, James, 598
Bullock, R. J., 556
Burch, John G., 670
Buy, or make, decision, 108–109
By-products, 382–384
  accounting for, 390–394
  defined, 382, 383

Calvasina, Eugene J., 555
Calvasina, Richard V., 555

Capacity concepts, 465–466
Capital
  acquiring, 12
  components, 918
  cost, 22
  cost of, 908, 918–925
  expenditures, 874–875
  investment, and accelerated cost recovery, 913–914
  marginal cost of, 919–921
  provision of, 14
  stock, 926–927
  turnover, 734
Capital assets, 844, 845
Capital budgeting, 844–876, 908–930
  complications to, 875–876
  defined, 844
  and income tax, 875–876, 908–918
  introduction to, 844–848
  sensitivity analysis in, 925–930
  techniques, 848–876
Carbone, Frank J., 293
Carmen-Stone, Marie S., 711
Carmichael, D. R., 335
CASB. *See* Cost Accounting Standards Board
Cash
  balance, 156
  budget, 152–156
  disbursements, 154–156
  flow. *See* Cash flow
  forecast, 152–156
  inflows, charting, 846–848
  outflows, charting, 846–848
  receipts, 152–154, 155
Cash Flow, 844–846
  future, 876
  and income tax, 908–910
  predicting and evaluating, 928–930
Cats-Baril, William L., 399
Centralization, 730–731
Certificate in Management Accounting (CMA), 663, 771, 998, 1002, 1004
  examination for, 1002–1005, 1009, 1011
Certified Internal Auditor (CIA), 1002
Certified Public Accountant (CPA), 663, 771, 998, 1002, 1003, 1004, 1011
  examination for, 1005–1009
Chart of accounts, 271–274
Chen, Joyce T., 711
Chenhall, Robert H., 167
Cherrington, David J., 167, 211
Cherrington, J. Owen, 211
Chow, Chee W., 167, 517, 748, 786
Clearing account, 273
Clifford, Jim, 986
Clock card, 440
Clough, Richard H., 293
CMA. *See* Certificate in Management Accounting
Coefficient of correlation, 196

alternate computations for, 207–208
Coefficient of determination, 197
  alternate computations for, 207–208
Coefficient of variation, 778–779
Collection procedures, 14
Collins, Frank, 167
Committed cost, 24
Common body of knowledge for management accounts, The, 7, 8, 640, 641, 643, 650, 962, 965, 998, 1001
Common stock, cost of, 922–924
Compilers, 963
Component cost, 918, 926–927
Components, capital, 918
Compound interest, 880–883
  method of depreciation, 746–747
Computer. *See also* Computer software for cost acounting
  analysis, 71–73
  hardware, 71
  software, 71–72, 984
  solutions, and sensitivity analysis, 784–786
Computer software for cost accounting, 962–985
  evaluation of, 984
  modelling, 975–982
Constraining factor, 106
Constraints, 782–783
Contribution approach, 106–107
Contribution margin, 96–101
  analysis, 698–706
  versus gross margin, 97–98, 234
  ratio, 97, 234
  variance, 699
Contribution report, 95–96
Contribution reporting, 94–116
  example of, 98–99
  relevant cost objectives and terminology for, 94–96
Control
  budgeting and, 141
  complete and partial, 205
  defined, 412
  input, 665–666
  labor, 435–437, 440–441
  limits, 622
  materials, 422–432, 438–440
  output, 667–668
  and overhead, 470–473
  processing, 666–667
  systems, cost, 536
Control account, 273, 273
  factory overhead, 466
Control report, 660
Controllable cost, 23
  versus uncontrollable cost, 204–205
Controllable variance, 581
Controller, role of, 11–14
  versus treasurer, 13–14
Conversion cost, 29, 816–817

Cooper, Robert, 824
Coordinated budgeting, 140
Cost, Costs
  administrative, 21
  allocation of, by behavior, 506
  averaging, 314
  avoidable fixed, 738
  budgeted, 20
  and by-products, 391–393
  capital, 22
  capitalized, 19
  committed, 24
  of common stock and retain earnings, 922–924
  component, 918, 926, 927
  concepts, basic, 18–26
  controllable, 23, 204–205
  conversion, 29, 816–817
  of debt, 921
  decreasing, 59
  defined, 18
  differential, 494
  direct, 22, 63, 193–194
  direct product, 383
  discretionary, 24, 158
  engineered, 158
  expected future, 103
  expired, 19–20
  factory overhead, 28, 30–31, 63–64, 194–198, 458
  fixed, 23, 56, 245–246, 506
  fixed overhead, 420
  flow of, 29–32, 274–277, 279–284
  full, 102, 493, 804–805
  future, 395
  historical, 20
  increasing, 58
  incremental, 24–25, 395
  indirect, 22
  indirect manufacturing, 28–29, 458
  inventoriable, 590–593
  irrelevant, 23
  joint, 394–397
  joint product, 383
  managed, 24
  manufacturing, 21
  marginal, 24–25
  material-related, 414–416
  mixed, 57
  mixed overhead, 459
  nonlinear, 58–59
  opportunity, 25, 109, 805–810
  out-of-pocket, 25
  past, 395
  period, 21
  of preferred stock, 922
  prime, 29
  product, 21, 28–32, 59–61, 158
  programmed, 24
  relevant, 23, 94–96
  replacement, 744
  responsibility, 493–494
  role of, in decision, 101–107
  sales, 21, 111
  semivariable, 57–58
  separable product, 383
  standard, 537–538, 819
  step-variable, 58
  sunk, 25
  total, 55, 105–106
  total manufacturing, 55–56
  traceability of, 495
  transferred in, 286–323
  unavoidable fixed, 738–739
  uncontrollable, 23, 204–205
  unexpired, 19–20
  unit, 55–56
  variable, 23, 56–57, 111, 245–246, 506, 805–810, 816
Cost accounting, 5–6
Cost accounting and computers
  applications programs for transaction processing, 966–967
  data-base management systems, 967–973
  decision support systems, 964–966
  expert systems, 982–984
  software and, 962–964, 975–982, 984
  spreadsheets, 973–975
Cost accounting standards, 7
  application of, overhead accounting, 507–511
Cost Accounting Standards Board (CASB), 89, 390, 507–511, 817
Cost accounting systems. *See also* Cost accounting and computers
  additional information, cost-benefit analysis of, 646–649
  data versus information in, 657–661
  development of, 649–657
  internal controls, 661–668
  requirement information, 645–646
Cost allocation methods for joint products, 384–389
Cost analysis, 18
  historical, 62, 63–64
Cost approach, total, 853–854
  to nonroutine decisions, 105–106
Cost-based pricing, 814–820
Cost behavior, 23, 54–73, 95
  quantifying, 64–73
Cost behavior analysis, 54–56, 62–64
  computers and, 71–73
  historical cost approach, 63–64
  industrial engineering approach, 62–63
  in a production process, 192
  terminology of, 54–56
Cost behavior patterns, 54–55
Cost-benefit analysis, 646–649
  of variance investigation, 624–625
Cost centers, 731–732
Cost classifications, 20–26, 27
Cost concepts, 18–26
Cost control systems, 536
Cost curve, total, 60, 61
Cost cycle, 274
Cost determination, 270
Cost equations, 65
Cost expenditure, 24
Cost finding, 18, 26, 270
Cost flows, 353–365
Cost groupings, 96
Cost information
  analysis of, for nonroutine decisions, 103–107
  role of, in decisions, 101–102
Costing
  absorption, 690–695
  defined, 412
  labor, 432–435
  materials, 412–422
  operation, 329–330
  process. *See* Process costing
  production, overhead for, 459–465
  variable, 690–698
Cost object, 19, 26
Cost objectives, 18–19, 26, 94–96
  final, 509–510
Cost of capital, 908, 918–925
  defined, 918
  marginal, 919–921
Cost of debt, 921
Cost of goods sold, 20
  budget, 151–152
  statement, 27
Cost patterns, 56–59
  application of, 73
  product, 59–61
Cost-plus pricing, 817
Cost price variance, 699, 706
Cost sheet, job order, 279, 280
Cost-volume-profit analysis, 230–249
  applications of, 241–249
  assumptions underlying, 239–241
  sources of data for, 240–241
Courses of actions, 775
Cox, Jeff, 628
CPA. *See* Certified Public Accountant
Credit and collection procedures, 14
Critical activity, 145
Cummins, Peter, 334
Currently attainable standards, 548–549
Current value accounting, 744
Cushing, Barry E., 670
Cut-off rate, 849
  defined, 657
  inaccurate, 621
  versus information, 657–661

Data
  define, 657
Data bank, 94, 95
Data base, 642
  administrator, 968–969
  defined, 967–968

management system, 967–973
    relation, 969
Data processing, 13
Dean, Joel, 78
Debt, cost of, 921
Decentralization, 730–731
Decisions
    disinvestment, 870–871
    management, 394–397, 643–645
    nonroutine, 101, 108–116
    preference, 849
    product-line, 112–114
    role of cost in, 101–107
    routine, 101
    screening, 849
Decision significance, 23, 95–96
Decision support systems (DSS), 964–966
    defined, 965
    software, 965–966
Decreasing cost, 59
Defective units, 417
Dellinger, Roy E., 293
Demand constraint, 783
Deming, W. Edwards, 444, 628
Demski, Joel S., 37, 710
Departmentalization
    advantages of, 503
    of overhead costs, 492–503
Departmental overhead accounts and rates, 286–287
Departments, 314
    accumulation of overhead costs by, 495–496
    defined, 492
    multiple, 285–286
    number and configuration of, 503–505
Dependent variable, 64
Depletion, 20
Depreciable property, 910
Depreciation, 20
    alternative methods of, 745
    compound interest method of, 746–747
Differential cost, 494
Digital, 71
Direct cost, 22, 63, 193–194
Direct labor, 28, 29–30, 62–63, 193–194
    cost (activity base), 463
    hours (activity base), 463
    mix and yield variances, 616–618
Direct materials, 28, 29–30, 63, 193–194
    mix and yield variances, 613–616
Direct method, 498–499
Direct overhead, 495–496
Direct product costs, 383
Dirsmith, Mark W., 786
Disbursements, 153, 154–156
Discontinue point, 113–114
Discounts, purchase, 413
Discretionary cost, 24
    centers, 732
Disinvestment decisions, 870–871

Disk operating system (DOS), 71, 963, 964
Doherty, Michael E., 986
Dorward, Neil, 555
Dowis, Robert H., 293
Dual transfer prices, 810–811
Dyckman, T. R., 211

Eccles, R., 824
Economic analysis, of cost, volume, and profit, 239–240
Economic order quantity (EOQ) models, 424–428, 429, 441–442, 966
Economic Recovery Tax Act, 910
Edwards, James Don, 824
Edwards, James W., 885
Efficient operations, and favorable variances, 621–622
Electronic spreadsheets, 72
ENCORE, 975
Ending inventory levels, 148–149
EOQ. See Economic order quantity models
Equations
    for breakeven point in sales dollars, 233–235
    for breakeven point in units, 231–232
    cost, 65
    developing, 66–73
    semivariable, 66
    variable, 66
Equivalent units, 319–320
Estimating revenues, 159
Ethics, Code of, for accountants, 1009–1011
Evaluation of segment performance, 732–740
Evaluation technique, selecting, 871–876
Examinations, professional, 1002–1009
Expected capacity, 465
Expected future costs, 103
Expected value, 777–779, 929
    of perfect information, 779, 781
Expenditures, capital, 874–875
Expenses,
    depreciation, 746–747. See also Depreciation
    factory overhead. See Overhead costs
    home office, 508–509
    period, 587–590
Expert systems, 982–984

Factory burden, 458
Factory overhead, 28, 30–31, 63–64, 194–198, 283, 574
    applied account, 466
    control account, 466
    cost concpets, 458–459
    costing and control, 458–473, 492–507

costs, 458
flexible budget for, 575
standard costs for, 574–575
subsidiary ledger
Falk, Haim, 824
Farmer, David, 120
FASB. See Financial Accounting Standards Board
Fasci, Martha, 786
Federal Trade Commission (FTC), 390
FEI. See Financial Executives Institute
FICA, 433, 966
FIFO. See First-in, first-out
Final cost objectives, 509–510
Finance division, functions of, 11–13
Financial accounting, 4–5
Financial Accounting Standards Board (FASB), 6, 9, 390, 698
Financial controls, establishing, 13
Financial Executives Institute (FEI), 7
Financial goals, setting, 12
Financial reporting, 5
Financial statements, 277
    basic, 26–34
    illustration of, 32
Financial vice president, 11
Financing, short-term, 14
Finished goods, 32, 283–284
Finished product, 26
Finn, Don W., 167
First-in, first-out (FIFO), 325–329, 350, 353, 359, 361, 416, 545, 595, 694, 696
Fixed cost, 23, 56, 245–246, 506
    avoidable, 738
    equation, 65
    unavoidable, 738–739
Fixed overhead
    accounting, 578–580
    costs, 459
    reporting, 471–473
    spending variance, 584
Flexible budget
    defined, 189
    example, 189–191
Flexible budget formula, 191
    developing, 192–200
Flexible budgeting, 188–200
    defined, 189–191
Flow
    network, 315
    parallel, 315
    sequential, 315
Flowcharting, 652
Flow of costs, 29–32, 274–277, 279–284
Ford, Jerry L., 120
Forecasting, 13
Foreign Corrupt Practices Act, 645
Four-way analysis of overhead variances, 583–585
Fox, Robert F., 444

INDEX

Franks, Davis D., 211
Fremgen, James M., 37
FTC. *See* Federal Trade Commission
Full cost, 102, 493, 804–805
    fallacy of, 102
Fully integrated management information system, 642–645
Fultz, Jack F., 517
Future cash flows, 876
Future costs, 395
Future value. *See* Time value of money

GAAP. *See* Generally accepted accounting principles
Gambino, Anthony J., 120
Garrett, L., 293
GASB. *See* Government Accounting Standards Board
Gatti, James F., 399
General administration, 21
General ledger, 283
    program, 964
General ledger accounting, 466–470
    overhead application and, 576
Generally accepted accounting principles (GAAP), 6–7, 96
Gillespie, Jackson F., 444
Gleim, Irvin N., 1012
GMAT. *See* Graduate Management Admission Test
Goals, financial, 12
Goldratt, Eliyahu M., 444, 628
Goodman Sam R., 15, 37, 78, 120, 211, 252, 293
Goods, finished, 32, 283–284
Gordon, Lawrence A., 824
Gordon, Paul N., 368
Goulet, Peter G., 252
Gourley, Keith C., 167
Government Accounting Standards Boards (GASB), 7
Graduate Management Admission Test (GMAT), 1003
Graduate Record Examination (GRE), 1003
GRE. *See* Graduate Record Examination
Grinell, D. Jacque, 399, 476
Grossman, Steven D., 252
Gross margin, 34, 97–98, 815
    analysis, 690, 703–706
    versus contribution margin, 97–98
Grudnitski, Gary, 670

Hakala, Gregory, 476
Hale, Jack A., 786
Half-year convention, 912
Hardware, 71
Hall, Robert W., 556
Hartl, Robert J., 252

Hays, William L., 211
Hernandez, William H., 824
Hertz, David B., 885, 934
High-low methods, 67–68, 73, 194–195
Hillier, F. S., 885
Historical cost, 20
    analysis, 62, 63–64
Holsapple, Clyde W., 986
Home office expenses, 508–509
Homogeneity of overhead costs, 504, 505
House, William C., Jr., 885, 934
Howell, Robert, 15, 37, 476
Hunt, R., 293

IBM, 71
Ideal standards, 548
IFPS. *See* Interactive Financial Planning System
IMA. *See* Institute of Management Accounting
Implementation, 11, 140, 655–656, 740–745
Imputed interest, 736
Income residual. *See* Residual income
Inaccurate data, 621
Inappropriate standards, 621
Income statement, budgeted, 156
Income tax, 242
    and capital budgeting, 875–876, 908–918
Income tax accounting, 5
Increasing cost, 58–59
Incremental approach, 853–854
Incremental cost, 24–25, 395
Independent variable, 64
Indexes, 743
Indicators, social, 161
Indirect cost, 22
    pools, 510–511
Indirect manufacturing cost, 28–29, 458
Indirect overhead, 495–496
Industrial-engineering analysis, 62–63
Information
    versus data, 657–661
    defined, 657
    existing, 780
    expected value of perfect, 779–781
Inman, Mark Lee, 598
Input controls, 665–666
Input value errors, 243–245
Institute of Management Accounting (IMA), 1002
Institute of Certified Management Accountants (ICMA), 1002
Interactive Financial Planning System (IFPS), 975, 976–982
Interest
    compound, 746–747, 880–883
    imputed, 736
Interference engine, 982

Intermediate budget, 141–142
Internal controls, 661–668
Internal rate of return, 855–859, 916–917
Internal Revenue Code, 646
Internal Revenue Service (IRS), 6, 390, 646, 696, 697, 698
Interpolation, 856
Interpreters, 963
Intracompany transfers
    accounting entries for, 812–813
    pricing for, 800–814
Inventoriable cost, 590–593
Inventory levels, ending, 148, 149
Investment base, and implementation, 741–745
Investment centers, 732
Investment tax credit (ITC), 931–933
Investor relations, 14
IRS *See* Internal Revenue Service
ITC. *See* Investment tax credit

Jablonsky, Stephen F., 786
Jarke, Matthias, 986
Jayson, Susan, 15
Job cost system. *See* Job order cost system
Job order cost accounting system. *See* Job order cost system
Job order cost sheet, 279, 280
Job order cost system, 279–291
    defined, 277
    flow of costs in, 279–284
    for manufacturing firms, 279–284
    process cost system versus, 277–279
    program, 964
    for service organizations, 284
Jobs, partially completed, 289–291
Job ticket, 440
Johnson, H. Thomas, 15
Joint costs, 394–397
Joint product cost allocation methods, 384–389
    alternatives to, 390
Joint product costs, 383
Joint products, 382–384
Just-in-time (JIT) inventory-control philosophy, 430–432

Kaplan, R., 934
Kaplan, Robert S., 15, 211, 293, 368, 628
Kefalas, Asterios G., 670
Kempster, John H., 885, 934
Kim, Suk H., 786
Kleinbaum, David G., 78
Knowledge, 101
    base, 982
Krause, Paul, 1012
Kupper, Lawrence L., 78

Labor
  constraint, 782
  control, 435–437, 440–441
  costing, 432–434
  direct, 28, 29–30, 62–63, 193–194
  efficiency (usage) variance, 540
  mix, 613
  mix variance, 613
  rate variance, 540
  recording, 281–283
  variances, 540–548
Lambert, Richard H., 628
Language translators, 963–964
Largay, James A., III, 749
Last-in, first-out (LIFO), 416–417, 545, 694
LaTour, Stephen A., 711
Lead time, 426
Learning curve, 442
Least-squares method, 69–71, 73
Least-squares regression analysis, 69–71, 72, 196–198
  alternative approch to, 74–75
Ledger
  general, 283
  split-, system, 287–289
  subsidiary, 271, 273, 283
Legal compliance reports, 660
Leigh, Wiliam E., 986
Lere, John C., 556
Lesser, Frederic E., 78
Level of aspiration, 206
Level of volume, and breakeven point, 241–242
Levy, Ferdinand K., 749
Lewin, Arie Y., 167
LIFO. *See* Last-in, first-out
LINDO. *See* Linear, Interactive and Discrete Optimizer
Linear, Interactive and Discrete Optimizer, 784
Linear programming, 781–786
Line-item budget, 159–160
Lococo, L., 824
Long-range budget, 141–142
Long-run considerations, versus short-run, considerations, 115
Loss
  abnormal rate of, 353
  normal rate of, 352–353
Lost units, accounting for, 351–353, 355–362
Lotus, 644, 973
Louderback, Joseph G., 749
Lucien, K., 824
Luoma, Gary A., 120

McCormick, Edmund J., 120
McElroy, Elam E., 78
McInnes, Robert, 167

Machine hours (activity base), 463
Machine language, 963
Mackey, Jim, 37
Magee, R., 934
Maintenance, of cost accounting system, 656
Make, or buy, decision, 108–109
Managed cost, 24
Management accountants, common body of knowledge for, 640–649
Management accounting, definitions and objectives of, 998–999
Management Accounting Practices Committee, 7, 640
Managment by exception, 202–205
Management cycle, 642
Management decisions, 643–645
  and joint costs, 394–397
  process, 641
  and reporting of overhead, 470–473
Management function, 21, 95
Management information system, 641–649
  components of a, 643
  cost accounting as subsystem of, 641–642
  data-base, 967–973
  definition, 641
  fully integrated, 642–645
  management decision process and, 641
Management planning and control, accounting systems for, 640–668
Management process, 9–11
  decision, 641
Managerial accounting, 4, 5
Managerial influence, 23–24
Manners, George E., Jr., 749
Manufacturing, 21
  accounting system, 270–277, 285–291
  expense, 458
  firms, job order cost systems for, 279–284
Manufacturing cost, 21
  behavior analysis, terminology of, 54–56
  relationship of, 29
  total, 59–62
Manufacturing resource planning (MRP II), 428–430
Margin
  contribution, 96–101, 234, 698–706
  gross, 34, 97–98, 815
  segment, 99
Marginal cost, 24–25
Marginal cost of capital (MCC), 919–921
Margin of safety, 242–243
  ratio, 243
Market basket, 235, 743
Marketing, 21
Market measures, 386–389
Market price, 803

Markup, rate of, 815–817
Mason, Robert D., 78
Master budget, 143–144
  developing, 144–145
  example, 146–158
Master plan, 650–656
Matching concept, 20
Matching of expenses, 20
Material constraint, 782
Material-related costs, 414–416
Material requirements planning (MRP), 428–430
Materials
  control, 422–432
  costing, 412–422, 438–440
  costs (activity base), 464
  direct, 28, 29–30, 63, 193–194
  issued, 416–417
  issuing, 440
  maintaining, 440
  mix, 613
  mix variance, 613
  price variance, 540, 551–552
  purchasing, 438–440
  quantity (usage) variance, 540
  raw, 62, 280–281
  received, 412–413
  requisition, 440
  variances, 540–548
  yield, 613
  yield variance, 613
Matrix algebra, 511–514
Mays, Robert L., Jr., 749
MCC. *See* Marginal cost of capital
Measures
  market, 386–389
  physical, 385–386
  process, 161
  results, 161
Merville, L., 824
Merz, C. M., 193
Method of neglect, 357
Michaelsen, Robert, 987
Michie, Donald, 987
Miller, Jeffrey G., 598
Miller, Danny, 824
Mills, John R., 476
Minimum desire rate of return, 876, 926–928
Mister, William G., 598
Mix, 612–618
  defined, 612
  labor, 613
  materials, 613
  production, 612
  sales, 612
Mixed cost, 57
Mixed overhead costs, 459
Modeling software, 975–982
  compared to spreadsheets, 980–982
Money, time value of, 115–116, 876–883

Mong, Han Kang, 334
Moscove, Stephen A., 670
Motivation, and budgeting, 140
Multimate, 644
Multiplan, 973
Multiple departments, 285–286
Multiple products, breakeven analysis for, 235–239
Multiple work-in-process accounts, 285
Munter, Paul, 167
Murdy, J. L., 885, 934
Myers, S., 885

NAA. *See* National Association of Accountants
National Association of Accountants (NAA), 7, 8, 640, 641, 643, 650, 661, 962, 965, 998, 999, 1001, 1009, 1011
  Common Body of Knowledge for Management Accountants, 7, 8
  Statements on Management Accounting, 7, 640, 998, 999
Neary, Robert D., 37, 444
Needles, Belverd E., Jr., 1012
Neglect, method of, 357
Negotiation, 811–812
Net present value, 849, 849–855, 916, 929–930
Net realizable value, 388–389
Network flow, 315
Niles, Timothy J., 293
Nonlinear cost, 58–59
  graphical representation of, 59
Nonproductive projects, 927
Nonprogrammed decisions, 644
Nonroutine decisions, 101, 114–116
  analysis of cost information for, 103–107
  examples of, 108–114
Noreen, Eric, 167
Normal capacity, 465
Normal random fluctuations, 620–621
Normal rate of loss, 352–353
Normal spoilage, 418–421
Not-for-profit sector, budgeting in, 158–163
  compared to for-profit sector, 158–159

Objective function, 775, 782
Objective probability, 775
Objectives
  cost, 18–19, 26, 94–96
  final cost, 509–510
  organizational, 10
  quantifiable, 775
Objectives of Management Accounting (NAA), 1009
Obligations, corporate social, 13

Onsi, M., 824
Operating plan, 10
Operating system, 963
Operation costing, 329–330
Operational report, 659
Operations
  efficient, and favorable variances, 621–622
  out-of-control, 622
Opportunity cost, 25, 109, 805–810
Optimized production technology (OPT), 429
Orders, special, 109–112
Organizational objectives, 10
Outcomes, 775
Out-of-control operations, 622
Out-of-pocket cost, 25
Output controls, 667–668
Overapplied overhead, 467–470
Overhead
  accounts, 286–287
  application of cost accounting standards to, 507–511
  applied account, 287
  budget, 575–576
  budgeted versus actual, 467–468
  defined, 458
  departmental, 286–287
  direct, 495–496
  factory. *See* Factory overhead
  fixed, 471–473, 578–580
  indirect, 495–496
  management reporting of, 470–473
  overapplied, 31, 467–470
  for production costing, 459–465
  underapplied, 31, 467–470
  variable, 470–471
  variances, analysis of, 580–585
Overhead application, 459–465
  defined, 460
  and general ledger accounting, 576–578
  process, concepts underlying, 462–465
  rate, predetermined, 461
Overhead costs
  allocation of, by behavior, 506
  departmentalization of, 492–505
  fixed, 459
  homogeneity of, 503–505
  mixed, 459

Parallel flow, 315
Past costs, 395
Payback, 859–864
  period, 859, 860–864
  present value, 865–866
Payback reciprocal, 863
  program, 863
Payoffs, 775
Payoff table, 776
Payroll summary account, 273–274

Performance, evaluation of, 732–740
Performance report, 660
Performance reporting, 13, 144
Period cost, 21
Period expense, 587–590
Petty, J. W., 824
Physical measures, 385–386
Physical standards, 549–550
PLAN80, 975
Planning and overhead, 470–473
Planning-Programming-Budgeting Systems (PBS), 161
Planning report, 660
Plum, Charles, 252
Possett, R. W., 293
Practical capacity, 465
Predetermined factory overhead rate, 30
Predetermined overhead application rate, 461
Preference decisions, 849
Preferred stock, cost of, 922
Present value. *See* Time value of money
Present value payback, 865–866
Price, market, 803–804
Price index, 743
Prices, dual transfer, 810–811
Pricing
  cost-based, 814–820
  cost-plus, 817
  for intracompany transfer, 800–814
  product, 246–247, 800–820
  for product sales, 814
  transfer, 800
Prime costs, 29
Probabilities, 775
Probability analysis, 775–781
  illustration of, 775–777
Procedure-oriented language, 963
Process cost accounting system. *See* Process cost system
Process costing, 314–330, 347–365. *See also* Process cost system
  accounting for lost units, 351–353
  addition of materials in subsequent processes, 348–351
  characteristics of, 314–317
  defined, 314
  standard costs and, 593–595
Process costing procedures, 317–330
  cost flows and, 353–365
Process cost system, 270. *See also* Process costing
  defined, 278
  versus job-order cost system, 277–279
Processes, 314
Processing controls, 666–667
Process measures, 161
Product, finished, 26
Product cost, 21, 28–29
  direct, 383
  flow of, 29–32

patterns, 59–61
separable, 383
Product costing, overhead for, 459–465
Production, units of (activity base), 464
Production budget, 148–150
Production departments, 492–493, 535
Production mix
  defined, 612
  and yield, 612–618
Production process, cost behavior in, 192
Product-line decisions, 112–114
Product mix, changes in, 247–249
Product pricing, 246–247, 800
  alternative cost-based approaches to, 814–820
Products
  joint. See Joint products
  multiple, 235–239
Profession, characteristics of a, 999–1002
Professional examinations, 1002–1005
Profit, 241–242
  margin, 735
  sector, budgeting in, 159–160
Profitability index, 851
Profit-volume graph, 232–233
Pro-forma statements, 140
Program budget, 160
Program effectiveness, techniques for evaluating, 161–163
Program language translators, 963–964
Programmed cost, 24
Programming, linear, 781–786
Programs, application, 964, 966–967
  special purpose, 964
Projects, nonproductive, 927
Proposal, request for, 654
Proposal for application development, 650
Public Law Number 95-213, 645
Purchase discounts, 413
Purchase order, 438
Purchase price variance, 545, 551–552
Purchase requisition, 438
Purchasing, materials, 438–440
P/V graph. See Profit-volume graph
Pyramid reporting, 200–201

Qualitative considerations, 116
Quality
  defined, 417
  spoilage and, 417–418
Quantitative considerations, 116
Query, 971
Query Management Facility (QMF), 971

Ramsay, Lewis P., 628
Random fluctuations, normal, 620–621
Range of probabilities, 775
Rate, variable, 927–928
Rate of loss, 352–353

Rate of markup, 815–817
Rate of return
  accounting, 866–870, 917–918
  on assets employed, 817–818
  internal, 855–859, 916–917
  minimum acceptable, 868
  minimum desired, 876, 926–928
Rates, departmental overhead, 286–287
Raw materials, 62, 280–281
  purchases budget, 151
Receipts, 152–154, 155
Receiving report, 439
Reciprocal allocations, using matrix algebra, 511–514
Reciprocal method, 498, 500–503
Recording, of variances, 544–546
Reece, James S., 15, 37, 78, 120, 211, 252, 293
Relation, 969
Relational data base, 969
Relational structure, 969
Relations,
  corporate social, 13
  investor, 14
Relative sales value, 387
Relevant cost, 23
  objectives, 94–96
  role of, in decisions, 102–103
Relevant events, 775
Relevant range of production, 61–62
Reorder point, 426
Repetitive decisions, 644–645
Replacement cost, 744
Reporting
  external, and variable costing, 696–698
  financial, 4
  for partially completed jobs, 289–290
  performance, 13, 144
  pyramid, 200–201
  SEC, 5
  segmented, 200
  variances, 585
Reports
  contribution, 95–96
  design output, 661
  preparatoin of, 658
  receiving, 439
  types of, 659–660
  variance, 618–620
Request for proposal (RFP), 654
Residual income (RI), 735–738
Resources
  allocation of, 159–161
  scarce, 106–107
Responsibility, for variances, 542–544
Responsibility accounting, 200–206
Responsibility centers, 731–732
Responsibility costs, 493–494
Results measures, 161
Retained earnings, cost of, 922–924
Return, rate of. See Rate of return

Return on investment (ROI), 431, 733–735, 746, 747
Revenue center, 732
Revenues, estimating, 159
RI. See Residual income
Richards, Jim E., 368
Risk, 774
ROI. See Return on investment
Romney, Marshall B., 670
Ross, Timothy, 556
Routine decisions, 101
Rubin, Mathew S., 556
Rules of thumb, 623
Ryan, Lanny J., 786

Safety, margin of, 242–243
Safety stock, 426
Sales costs, 111
Sales dollars, 230
  breakeven analysis in, 233–235, 236–237
  breakeven charts in, 235
  level of volume in, 241
Sales forecast, 147–148
Sales mix, 235, 247–249
  variance, 699, 705
Sales volume variance, 659, 705–706
Salvage value, 848, 914–915
Sandretto, Michael J., 334
Scarce resources, 106–107
Scatter diagram, 68
Scattergraph, 68
Scattergraph method, 68–69, 73, 195–196
Schiff, Michael, 167, 711
Schoderbek, Charles G., 670
Schoderbek, Peter P., 670
Schwarzbach, Henry R., 476
Scrap, 417, 421–422
Screening decisions, 849
SEC. See Securities and Exchange Commission
SEC reporting. See Securities and Exchange Commission
Securities Act of 1934, 645, 661
Securities and Exchange Commission (SEC), 6–7, 390, 660, 690, 696, 697, 698
Securities and exchange commissions, 5
Seed, Allen H., III, 335
Segment, 99, 508, 730
  margin analysis, 99–101, 738–740
  performance, 730–746
  reporting, 200
Seidler, Lee J., 335
Selling cost, 21, 199–200
Selling-expense budget, 152, 153
Semivariable cost, 57–58
  equation, 66
Sensitivity analysis, 243–249
  in capital budgeting, 925–930

computer solutions and, 784–786
Separable product costs, 383
Sequential flow, 315
Service departments, 492–495, 505
Service organizatoins, job order cost systems for, 284
Shaw, Robert J., 368
Short-run, versus long-run, considerations, 115
Short-term budget, 141–142
Short-term financing, 14
Shurkin, Joel N., 987
Siegel, Joel G., 556
Simkin, Mark G., 670
Sinclair, Kenneth P., 252
Singhvi, Surendra S., 517
Skinner, Wickham, 476
Slope, 64
Smidt, S., 885, 934
Smith, G. Stevenson, 786
Social indicators, 161
Software. See Computer software
Sorenson, James E., 211
Soucy, Stephen R., 15, 37, 476
Special orders, 109–112
Special-purpose programs, 964
Spending variance, 583
Split-ledger system, 287–289
Split-off point, 383
Spoilage, 417
  normal and abnormal, 418–421
  quality and, 417–418
Spreadsheets, 72, 973
  compared to modeling software, 980–982
SPS, 963
Standard activity level, 576, 578
Standard cost, 819
  centers, 732
  defined, 537–538, 574
  for factory overhead, 574–575
  variances, 546–547, 585–592
Standard costs, process costing and, 593–595
Standard deviation, 777–779
Standards
  budgets and relationship between, 142–143
  of CASB, 507–511
  cost account, 7
  currently attainable, 548–549
  development, 548–550
  as goals and benchmarks, 538–540
  ideal, 548
  inappropriate, 621
  physical, 549–550
Standard-setting philosophies, 548–549
Standards of Ethical Conduct for Management Accounts, 998, 1009–1011
Statement of Objectives, 999

Statements
  basic financial, 26–34
  budgeted income, 156
  financial, 277
  pro-forma, 140
Statements on Management Accounting, 7, 640, 998, 999
Static budget, 188
Statistical analysis, 203–204
Statistical techniques, 623–624
Steinwurtzel, Samuel L., 399
Step method, 498, 499–500, 501
Step-variable cost, 58
Stern, Roy D., 824
Stock
  capital, 926–927
  common, 922–924
  preferred, 922
  safety, 426
Stockholders' equity, 742
Straight line, mathematical properties of, 64–66
Strategic decisions, 644
Structured Query Language (SQL), 971
Subjective probability, 775
Subsidiary ledger, 271, 273, 283
  factory overhead, 466–467
Sunk cost, 25
SuperCalc, 973
Symbolic language, 963
Systems, two-bin, 423–424
Systems analysis, 652–656
Systems analysis and design life cycle, 649

Talbott, James A., Jr., 252
Taxes
  and capital budgeting, 875–876, 908–918
  investment tax credit, 931–933
  and time value of money, 115–116
Tax on income, 242
Tax planning and reporting, 13
Theoretical capacity, 465
Three-way analysis of overhead variances, 583
Time card, 440
Time periods, 20–21
  classification, 21
  considerations in overhead applications, 464
Time value of money, 876–883
Toole, Howard R., 786
Total cost, 55
  curve, 60, 61
Total cost approach, 853–854
  to nonroutine decisions, 105–106
Total expected volume, 461
Total manufacturing cost, 55, 59–62
  curve, 60

Total quality control (TQC), 431, 432
Traceability of costs, 495
Transaction processing, application programs for, 966–967
Transfers, intracompany. *See* Intracompany transfers
Transfer prices
  dual, 810–811
  establishing alternative approaches to, 803–812
Transfer pricing, 800, 813–814
Transferred-in costs, 286, 323
Translation factor, 743
Treasurer, 11
  role of, versus controller, 13–14
Tseng, M. S., 786
Two-bin system, 423–424
Two-way analysis of overhead variances, 581–583

Umapathy, Srinivasan, 167
Unavoidable fixed costs, 738–739
Uncertain conditions, decisions under, 774–775
Uncertainty, 774
Uncontrollable cost, 23
  versus controllable cost, 204–205
Underapplied overhead, 467–470
Unequal initial investments, 873–874
Uniform CPA Examination, 1005–1009
Unit cost, 55–56
Units
  breakeven analysis in, 231–233, 235–236
  defective, 417
  equivalent, 319–320
  increasing, 349–351
  level of volume in, 241–242
  lost, 351–353, 355–362
  no change in, 348–349
  of production (activity base), 464
Units of output, 230
Usage price variance, 545, 551–552
Utility routines, 964

Variable, dependent and independent, 64
Variable cost, 23, 56–57, 245–246, 506, 805–810, 816
  equation, 690
Variable costing, 690
  compared to absorption costing, 690–695
  and external reporting, 696–698
  as management tool, 695–606
Variable manufacturing costs, 111
Variable overhead
  efficiency variance, 583
  reporting, 470–471
  spending variance, 584

Variable rate, 927–928
Variance. *See also* Variances
  calculating, 699–703
  components of, 698–699
  contribution margin, 699
  controllable, 581
  cost price, 699, 706
  fixed overhead spending, 584
  gross margin, 705
  labor mix, 613
  labor yield, 613
  materials mix, 613
  materials yield, 613
  sales mix, 699, 705
  sales price, 699, 705
  sales volume, 699, 705–706
  spending, 583
  variable overhead efficiency, 583
  variable overhead spending, 584
  volume, 472, 473
Variance reports, 618–620
Variances. *See also* Variance
  budget, 202–205
  direct labor mix and yield, 616–618
  direct materials mix and yield, 613–616
  disposition of, 546–547
  investigation of, 547–548, 620–625
  materials and labor, 540–548, 551–552
  overhead, analysis of, 580–585
  recording of, 544–546
  reporting, 585
  responsibility for, 542–544
  standard cost, 546–547, 585–592
Vassiliou, Yannis, 986
Visacalc, 644, 973
Vollmann, Thomas W., 598
Volume
  changes, 819–820
  level of, and breakeven point, 241–242
  measures, 192
  total expected, 461
  variance, 472, 473

Waller, William S., 748
Wang, 71
Waste, 417, 422
Weighted average method, 318–325, 350, 353, 359
Weiss, Allen, 211
Weiss, Timothy J., 786
Welker, Robert B., 252
Whinston, Andrew B., 986
Wight, Oliver W., 444
Wilkinson, Joseph, 670
Williams, Doyle Z., 1012
Work in process, 32, 280–284
  accounts, multiple, 285
Worrall, Robert L., 786

Yield
  defined, 612
  labor, 613
  materials, 613
  and production mix, 612–618
Y-intercept, 64

Zero base budgeting (ABB), 161, 162, 163
Zimmerman, Jerold L., 399, 517